Black American
Military Leaders

Black American Military Leaders

A Biographical Dictionary

WALTER L. HAWKINS

McFarland & Company, Inc., Publishers

Jefferson, North Carolina, and London

LIBRARY OF CONGRESS CATALOGUING-IN-PUBLICATION DATA

Hawkins, Walter L., 1949–
Black American military leaders : a biographical dictionary / Walter L. Hawkins.
p.   cm.

ISBN-13: 978-0-7864-2486-3
(illustrated case binding : 50# alkaline paper) ∞

1. African American generals — Biography — Dictionaries.   2. African
American admirals — Biography — Dictionaries.   3. United States —
Armed Forces — Biography — Dictionaries.   4. United States —
Armed Forced — African Americans — Biography — Dictionaries.
5. African American soldiers — Biography — Dictionaries.   6. Medal of
Honor — Biography — Dictionaries.   7. United States — History,
Military — Dictionaries.   I. Title.
E181.H382   2007   355.0092'396073 — dc22   2006039251

British Library cataloguing data are available

On the cover, from the top: John L. Estrada, Sergeant Major, Marine Corps;
Bettye Hill Simmons, Brigadier General, Army; Jesse A. Wilson,
Commander, Navy; Gloria J. Harden, Sergeant Major, Marine Corps;
Louis T. Cannon, Jr., Commander, Navy; Mary L. Saunders, Major General,
Air Force; flag background ©2007 Comstock Images

Manufactured in the United States of America

*McFarland & Company, Inc., Publishers
Box 611, Jefferson, North Carolina 28640
www.mcfarlandpub.com*

To my daughter,
Staff Sergeant Winter L. Hawkins,
United States Air Force Reserves

ACKNOWLEDGMENTS

I should like to express my thanks to all the officers and enlisted personnel of the United States military for their assistance. I am grateful to the many people in the Department of Defense who performed valuable services in the preparation of this book.

I wish to express my appreciation to the Department of the Army, the United States Air Force, Marine Corps, Navy, Coast Guard, and the Commanding General of the United States Army Reserves, Lieutenant General James Hemly.

CONTENTS

PREFACE

The military heritage of black Americans dates from the first black presence in North America. Beginning with the first recorded visits of a black person to what is now the United States in 1528, blacks — both the enslaved and the free — have participated in military or quasimilitary action.

During the Revolutionary War one-sixth of those who fought for freedom were black. And in every conflict since, black Americans have worn the uniform of the United States as proudly and courageously as all other Americans. In every conflict we have had our heroes and leaders.

This book does not attempt to chronicle the full range of black contributions to America's military. Rather, it presents 295 black generals and admirals; 260 other black officers, and 550 senior enlisted personnel who changed the image of the United States military organizations. This is the only book to include all black officers who have attained the rank of general or its naval equivalent.

Blacks occupy more leadership positions in the military than in any other sector of American society. The purpose of this book is to inform the public of the significant impact these black individuals have had on the United States military.

While American military history is filled with many important milestones and achievements, until the publication of this book the contributions of black American leaders remained obscure. This is the only book that lists the many contributions of black officers and enlisted leaders in all branches of America's military.

Recognition of black American military leaders' contributions to America's defenses is especially fitting at a time when the nation faces so many challenges associated with its global leadership, particularly regarding the war on terrorism.

All information and comments can be mailed to:

Walter L. Hawkins
CSM, USAR (Ret.)
P.O. Box 1883
Fayetteville, GA 30214-1364

Or

CSMHawkins@aol.com

BLACK AMERICAN MILITARY LEADERS

Aarons, Clifton G.
COMMAND SERGEANT MAJOR—ARMY

A native of Saint Mary, Jamaica, he enlisted in the United States Army in December 1977. Aarons completed Basic Combat Training at Fort Knox, Kentucky, and Advanced Individual Training at Fort Rucker, Alabama.

His military education includes all Noncommissioned Officer Education System Courses; the Army Logistics Management Course; Aviation Life Support Equipment Course; Instructor Training Course; Small Group Leader Course; UH-60 Tactical Transport Helicopter Course; Battle Staff Course; First Sergeant Course; and the United States Army Sergeants Major Academy (Class 51).

Aarons has held numerous leadership positions including Squad Leader; Section Sergeant; Senior Instructor and Writer; Small Group Leader; Platoon Sergeant; Airfield NCOIC; Detachment NCOIC; First Sergeant; Battalion Operations Sergeant and Command Sergeant Major. He has recently served on deployed assignments to Afghanistan and Iraq in support of the Global War on Terrorism.

Abernathy, Karl, II
COMMAND CHIEF MASTER SERGEANT—AIR FORCE

Abernathy was born in January 1954, and grew up in Philadelphia, Pennsylvania, graduating from West Catholic High School in 1971.

He enlisted into the United States Air Force in 1973, and after completion of Basic Military Training, began his career on a fast track. Abernathy demonstrated technical expertise in Aircraft Maintenance in Technical School, graduating as an Honor Student, and was selected to remain as a pipeline Instructor. While at Chanute Air Force Base in Illinois, he was the youngest and lowest ranking individual to ever garner the prestigious Air Training Command Master Instructor rating. He was also the base's first below-the-zone promotion recipient.

His military education includes all Noncommissioned Officer Education System Courses; the First Sergeant Academy at Keesler Air Force Base; Academic Instructor School at Maxwell Air Force Base; Technical Instructor Course at Chanute Air Force Base; and Senior Noncommissioned Officer Academy at Maxwell Air Force Base. Abernathy holds an associate's degree in Applied Science, Aircraft Maintenance Technology and an associate's degree in Applied Science, Instructor Technology, both from the Community College of the Air Force; and also earned a Bachelor of Science Degree in Workforce Development and Education from Southern Illinois University.

Abernathy's distinguished career includes a vast array of diverse assignments and accomplishments. His key leadership assignments include serving as First Sergeant for the 51st Maintenance Squadron at Osan Air Base; First Sergeant for the 78th Mission Support Squadron at Robins Air Force Base; First Sergeant for the 35th Operations Support Squadron at Misawa Air Base; First Sergeant for the 306th Air Refueling Squadron at Altus Air Force Base; First Sergeant for the 340th Maintenance Support Squadron at Altus Air Force Base; Maintenance Flight Chief/Superintendent for the 340th Organizational Maintenance Squadron at Altus Air Force Base; First Sergeant for the 4th Combat Communications Squadron at Kwang Ju Air Base, Korea; First Sergeant for the 2002nd Communications Squadron at Altus Air Force Base; Master Instructor for the Field Training Detachment 524th at Travis Air Force Base in California; Master Crew Chief (SAC) for the 307th Consolidated Aircraft Maintenance Squadron at Chanute Air Force Base; Aircraft Maintenance Instructor for the Instructor and Tech School Squadron at Chanute Air Force Base; and Command Chief Master Sergeant of the Warner Robins Air Logistics Center at Robins Air Force Base.

Abernethy, R. Sydney, III
CAPTAIN—NAVY

Born in Baltimore and raised in Annapolis, Maryland, Abernethy is a 1981 graduate of the United States Naval Academy, where he was recognized as a two-time All-American lacrosse player. After commissioning, he reported to Naval Flight Officer training at VT-10, Naval Air Station Pensacola. He completed advanced Naval Flight Officer training at Mather Air Force Base and received his wings in March 1983.

Abernethy was assigned to Antarctic Devron Six (VXE-6), Naval Air Station Point Mugu in 1983. Flying the LC-130 in support of scientific research, he made three six-month deployments to Antarctica in the three years he was assigned to the command. In 1986, Abernethy requested and was favorably granted a transition to the VQ community. After electronic warfare training at Cory Station, Pensacola, he reported to Fleet Air Reconnaissance Squadron One (VQ-1), Naval Air Station Agana Guam, flying the EP-3E aircraft. Abernethy qualified as a Senior Electronic Tactical Evaluator and Mission Commander, flying reconnaissance

squadron missions in support of national and Seventh Fleet tasking.

In 1989, he was transferred to the Joint Chiefs of Staff, where he was assigned to the Unified Command Support Element of the Intelligence Directorate (J-2). During his tour, Abernethy provided operational intelligence support to the United States Marine Corps and deployed to Jubayl, Saudi Arabia for the duration of Operation Desert Shield/Storm. He was specially chosen to return to Saudi Arabia in October 1991 for support during re-strike planning when Iraq failed to comply with United Nations sanctions. He returned to VQ-1 for his Department Head tour in November 1992 and served as the squadron's Administrative and Operations Officer. Abernethy's next assignment was to the Bureau of Naval Personnel as the Aviation Minority Affairs Officer and the VQ Aviation Assignment Detailer until June of 1996.

He then served as VQ-2's Commanding Officer in Rota, Spain. After assignment to and graduation from the Naval War College in June of 1999, Abernethy was assigned to Commander, Carrier Group Seven (COMCARGRU 7) onboard USS *John C. Stennis* (CVN 74) during its Persian Gulf deployment. He was assigned as the Operations Officer for the Center for Career Development in Millington, Tennessee. In March 2005, Abernethy was serving as the Special Assistant for Minority Affairs to the Chief of Naval Personnel. He has accumulated over 3,400 flight hours.

Abney, J.C.
COLONEL—ARMY

J.C. Abney was born in Greenwood, South Carolina and was commissioned through the Reserve Officer

Training Corps in 1981. He is a graduate of the Military Police Officer Basic and Advanced Courses, the Combined Arms Service Staff School, the United States Army Command and General Staff College, the Industrial College of the Armed Forces and the FBI National Academy. Abney holds a Bachelor of Arts degree from Furman University and a Master of Science degree from the National Defense University.

His key military assignments include the 10th Military Police Battalion, as Training Officer, Battalion Operations Officer, and Assistant Brigade S-4; Administrative Branch Chief, Division Chief, Central America Joint Intelligence Team in the Defense Intelligence Agency at the Pentagon; Military Police Captain's Assignment Officer for PERSCOM at Alexandria, Virginia; Brigade S-3 for the 1st Military Police Brigade, and Executive Officer for the 504th Military Police Battalion at Fort Lewis, Washington; Discipline, Law and Order Officer for the Human Resources Directorate, DCSPER, G-1, Department of the Army at the Pentagon; Commander of the 759th Military Police Battalion and Installation Provost Marshal at Fort Carson, Colorado; Military Police Investigations Officer, Provost Marshal, Operations Officer, Commander, Headquarters and Headquarters Company, Law Enforcement Command in the Republic of Panama; and Deputy Director of the Joint Security Directorate (FWD) USCENTCOM, Kingdom of Saudi Arabia. Colonel Abney served in Haiti during the United Nations mission and in Afghanistan during Operation Enduring Freedom. He is currently Garrison Commander at Fort Leonard Wood, Missouri.

Abrams, Courtney O.
COMMAND MASTER CHIEF—NAVY

Courtney Abrams entered the United States Navy on February 8, 1982. Following Recruit Training Command in Orlando, Florida, he attended Hospital "A" School in San Diego, California. After completing school, he was transferred to the Naval Regional Medical Center in Orlando.

In May 1988, Abrams was accepted to Preventive Medicine Technician's School (HM-8432). Upon graduation for Preventive Medicine Technician School, he transferred to the WESTPAC deployed on board USS *Acadia* (AD-42), where he served as a Preventive Medicine Technician. While on board he earned his Enlisted Surface Warfare Specialist qualification. Abrams would complete two WESTPAC deployments to the Persian Gulf in support of Operation Desert Shield/Desert Storm.

In 1999, he completed the Senior Enlisted Academy, Naval Station, in Newport, Rhode Island, and transferred to the Navy Environmental Health Center, where he filled a Command Master Chief billet as a Senior Chief providing oversight for 10 Field Activities and a staff of over 600 military and civilian personnel worldwide. In June 2002, Abrams reported to the Naval Hospital, Roosevelt Roads, Puerto Rico as the Command Master Chief, and served there until its de-

commissioning in March 2004. In February 2005, he was serving as the Command Master Chief at the Naval Hospital in Yokosuka, Japan.

Adams, Charity
LIEUTENANT COLONEL—ARMY

Adams was born in Columbia, South Carolina, where she graduated as valedictorian of Booker T. Washington High School. She received her bachelor's degree from Wilberforce University in Ohio, and attended graduate school at Ohio State University.

In July 1942, she was sworn into the Women's Auxiliary Corps, which later became the Women's Army Corps. Adams was one of the women who would be part of the first officer candidate class for the WAAC, stationed at Fort Des Moines, Iowa. She was assigned to the Third Platoon consisting of thirty-nine black women who had been selected for the program. At that time the Army had a quota of ten percent black females, making it the only service organization accepting black women.

In August of 1942, Adams became the first black woman to be commissioned an Officer in the WAAC. Alphabetically, she should have been the first woman of either race sworn in, but for this graduation, the Army broke with tradition and each class was sworn in by platoon.

In mid–1943, Adams was assigned as a training supervisor to Fort Des Moines Headquarters. Her next assignment was in Washington, D.C. In early 1944, she was assigned as Training Center control officer with the new Women's Army Corps, and was the only black woman assigned to the Training Center Headquarters. In December 1944, Adams received orders to proceed to London and Scotland. In March 1945, she assumed Command of the 6888th Central Postal Directory Battalion, responsible for delivering mail to approximately seven million American troops stationed in Europe. In late 1945, the 6888th was moved to Paris. Her last assignment was at WAC Headquarters in the Pentagon. She was promoted to Lieutenant Colonel, making her the highest ranking black female and the first to obtain that rank in the WACs. She left the service in March 1946.

Adams, Cheryl D.

COMMAND CHIEF MASTER SERGEANT—AIR FORCE

Adams was born in St. Louis, Missouri, and enlisted in the Air Force on October 15, 1977. She earned an Associate Degree in Personnel Administration from the Community College of the Air Force. Her military education includes the United States Air Force Non-Commissioned Officer Academy; United States Air Forces Senior Non-Commissioned Officer Academy; Senior Non-Commissioned Officer Leadership Development; and Medical Service Specialist School at Lackland Air Force Base, Texas.

She graduated from Basic Training at Lackland AFB and attended Medical Service Specialist School at Sheppard AFB, Texas. Following an active duty training tour, Adams returned to fulfill her Reserve commitment with the former 52nd Medical Services Squadron, now the 932nd Aeromedical Staging Squadron (ASTS), in August 1978.

Her career progression included assignments as Staff Technician; Section Supervisor; and Superintendent of Nursing Services. In 1991, during Operation Desert Shield/Desert Storm, Adams served as facility nursing superintendent at Al Jubail, Saudi Arabia. In May 1995, she became the Senior Enlisted Advisor, subsequently Command Chief Master Sergeant, for the 932nd Airlift Wing at Scott Air Force Base, Illinois. In February 2001, Adams was selected to serve as the Command Chief Master Sergeant for the Air Force Reserve Command at Robins Air Force Base, Georgia. As the Com-

mand Chief Master Sergeant for Air Force Reserve Command, she advises the Commander on matters influencing the health, morale, welfare and effective utilization of more than 70,000 active duty and reserve members within the command and serves as the commander's representative to numerous committees, councils, boards and military and civilian functions. Adams is the first African American female in the history of the Air Force Reserves to be selective for this position.

Adams, Daniel S., Jr.

COLONEL—AIR FORCE

Colonel Daniel S. Adams, Jr. was commissioned through the United States Air Force Academy in May of 1980. He received a Bachelor of Science degree in Aeronautics and a commission to second lieutenant from the Air Force Academy in Colorado Springs, Colorado. In 1985, he earned a Master of Science degree in Management Information System, from Lesley College in Cambridge, Massachusetts. Adams earned a second Master of Science degree in Aeronautics in 1986 from Stanford University. His military education includes Squadron Officer School at the Air University, Maxwell Air Force Base, Alabama; Air Command and Staff College (distinguished graduate) at the Air University; Armed Forces Staff College at the National Defense University, Norfolk, Virginia; and the Air War College at the Air University. Adams is a senior space and missile officer and has served in several assignments as an Aeronautical Engineer. His most recent assignments include serving from June 1994 to June 1996 as Senior Military Analyst in Headquarters United States European Command, at Stuttgart-Vaihinger, Germany; from 1996 to June 1997, as Operations Officer with the

704th Missile Squadron at Minot Air Force Base, North Dakota; from June 1999 to June 2002, as Deputy Chief, later Chief, of the Weapon Systems Liaison Division in the Secretary of the Air Force's Office of Legislative Liaison at the Pentagon. In June 2002, Adams was selected to serve as the commander of the 367th Recruiting Group at Warner Robins Air Logistics Center, Robins Air Force Base, in Georgia.

Adams, Richard, Jr.
COMMAND SERGEANT MAJOR—ARMY

A native of St. Louis, Missouri, Adams entered the United States Army in 1982, and completed Basic Combat Training and Advanced Individual Training at Fort Dix, New Jersey as a Motor Transport Operator (64C). His military education includes all Noncommissioned Officer Education System Courses; Drill Sergeant School (Commandant's List); Airborne School; First Sergeants Course; and the United States Army Sergeants Major Academy. He holds an Associate of Arts degree and a Bachelor of Science degree in Management Studies, both from the University of Maryland, and also earned an Applied Science Degree in Transportation (with Honors) from City Colleges of Chicago.

Adams' key leadership assignments include serving as Drill Sergeant of A Company, 2/39th Infantry; Drill Sergeant Instructor at the United States Army Drill Sergeant School; Senior Instructor in D Company, 36th Transportation Battalion, at Fort Dix, New Jersey; Platoon Sergeant/Truck Master for the 76th Transportation Company (Top of the Rock), at Pirmasens, Germany; Senior Transportation Supervisor, HHC, 37th TRANSCOM; First Sergeant for the 66th Transportation Company at Kaiserslautern, Germany; and Division Transportation Sergeant Major for the 1st Cavalry Division at Fort Hood, Texas. In August 2004, he was serving as the Command Sergeant Major for the 180th Transportation Battalion at Fort Hood, Texas.

Adams, Robert B.
MAJOR GENERAL—ARMY

Adams was born in Buffalo, New York, and married Karen S. Nagel. Upon completion of the Reserve Officers Training Corps curriculum and the course of study at Canisius College, he was commissioned a second lieutenant and awarded a Bachelor of Business Administration in Accounting Auditing. Adams also holds bachelor's and master's degrees in Automatic Data Processing from George Washington University. His military education includes completion of the Air Defense Artillery School; the Finance School; the United States Army Command and General Staff College; and the United States Army War College.

Adams has held a wide variety of important command and staff positions, culminating in Deputy Chief of Staff for Resource Management at the United States Army Materiel Command in Alexandria, Virginia. Other key assignments include: Assistant Comptroller for resource Policy and Financial Planning at the Office of the comptroller of the Army in Washington, D.C.; and Deputy Commanding General, Deputy Chief of Staff, Comptroller, United States Army, Vietnam Finance and Accounting, United States Army at Fort Benjamin Harrison, Indiana. He returned to Fort Belvoir, Virginia, as a special Projects Officer at the United States Army Computer Systems Command. After attending the United States Army War College at Carlisle Barracks, Pennsylvania, Adams became Chief of the Financial Management and Accounting Division; later Director of the Nonappropriated Funds Directorate, then Comptroller of the Adjutant General

Adams-Ender, Clara L.
BRIGADIER GENERAL—ARMY

The daughter of a sharecropper in Wake County, North Carolina, and the fourth of ten children, Adams-Ender received her Bachelor's degree in Nursing from North Carolina Agricultural and Technical State University at Greensboro, North Carolina. She earned her Master of Science in Nursing from the University of Minnesota, and a Master of Military Art and Science from the United States Army Command General Staff College at Fort Leavenworth, Kansas. Her military education includes graduation from the United States Army War College and the United States Army Medical Office Advanced Course. While attending North Carolina A&T State University in Greensboro, Adams-Ender worked as a domestic and beautician to earn extra money.

She joined the Army because she wanted to finish her education, and needed money to do it. A veteran of over 30 years in the Army, General Adams-Ender has held such diverse assignments as chief nurse of two medical centers, assistant professor of nursing, inspector general, and Chief Army nurse recruiter. During the Vietnam War, Adams-Ender served as a staff nurse with the 121st Evacuation Hospital. She was promoted to Brigadier General on September 1, 1987.

General Adams-Ender served as Chief, Army Nurse Corps/Director of Personnel in the Office of the Surgeon General at Falls Church, Virginia. From August 1991 to August 1993, she served at Fort Belvoir, Virginia, as the Commanding General, United States Army Fort Belvoir/Deputy Command General, United States Army Military District of Washington.

Alcendor, Ralph
COMMAND SERGEANT MAJOR—ARMY

Ralph Alcendor was born in Grand Bay, Dominica, and enlisted in the United States Army in 1978 in St. Thomas, U.S. Virgin Islands. He completed Basic Combat Training at Fort Dix, New Jersey.

Alcendor's education includes all levels of the Noncommissioned Officer Education System Courses; the First Sergeant Course; Airborne School; and the United States Army Sergeants Major Academy at Fort Bliss, Texas. He holds a First Class FCC License in Electronics.

Alcendor's key military assignments include serving in Operation Desert Shield/Desert Storm (1991); Operation Restore Hope in Somalia (1994); Operations Provide Comfort in Haiti (1994); and Operation Enduring Freedom, in Kandahar, Afghanistan (2004). He has also served as the Installation Sergeant Major, 20th Support Group in Camp Hialeah at Pusan, Korea. In 2004, he was assigned as United States Army Aviation Taskforce Command Sergeant Major with the "Screaming Eagles" of the 9th Battalion, 101st Airborne Division at Fort Campbell, Kentucky.

Alexander, Alfred
COMMAND SERGEANT MAJOR—ARMY

CSM Alexander entered the army on June 30, 1977, and attended Basic Combat Training at Fort Knox, Kentucky and Advanced Individual Training (AIT) at Fort Rucker, Alabama, graduating as a Helicopter Repairer in December 1977.

CSM Alexander's military education includes the Jump-Master Course; Aviation Safety Course; Technical Inspector Course; Aviation Life Support Course; Airborne Course; Master Fitness Course; Air Assault

Course; Equal Opportunity Course; Light Fighter Course; Battle Staff Course; Army Family Team Building Course and Army Family Team Building Instructor Course; and the United States Army Sergeants Major Academy.

He holds an associate's degree in Management from Hawaii Pacific University; a Bachelor of Science degree in Public Management from Austin Peay State University; and a Master of Science degree in Management and Technology from Murray State University.

CSM Alexander has risen from Crew to Command Sergeant Major in Aviation Units. Additionally, he has served as a Mechanic, Crew Chief, Technical Inspector, Platoon Sergeant, Production Control NCO and First Sergeant in a variety of duty stations and units. CSM Alexander has been serving as the Fort Campbell Garrison Sergeant Major since August 2001.

Alexander, Clifford L., Jr.
SECRETARY OF THE ARMY

Clifford Alexander was born in New York City, the only child of Clifford Leopold Alexander, Sr., and Edith McAllister Alexander. He received a Bachelor of Arts Degree in American Government from Harvard University, graduating cum laude in 1955 and earned an LL.B. Degree from Yale Law School in 1958. Alexander then enlisted in the 369th Field Artillery Battalion of the New York National Guard, and afterwards completed a six-month tour of active duty as a private at Fort Dix, New Jersey. President Jimmy Carter announced his appointment of Alexander as Secretary of the Army on January 19, 1977. As Secretary of the Army, Alexander was under the direct authority of the President and the Secretary of Defense. The main responsibility of the Department of the Army is to organize, train, and equip active duty and reserve land forces for the national defense in cooperation with the other branches of the national military team. Some of its other duties include protecting the environment in certain areas of

the country; providing emergency aid to state and local authorities; providing civil administration in some foreign territories, operating the Panama Canal; and administering public works programs. At the time Alexander took office, the department's budget amounted to $28.8 billion and its personnel included 370,000 civilian employees in addition to the 1,300,000 Army regulars, reservists and National Guardsmen. Some of the issues that confronted Alexander were whether to grant pardons or amnesty to Vietnam war resisters, and under what circumstances less than honorable discharges given to Vietnam veterans should be upgraded. Other issues involved the effects of a cheating scandal at West Point, the diminishing number of Army reservists, and the debate over unionization of the armed forces. Of particular concern to the Secretary of the Army was the future status of the controversial four-year experiment with all-volunteer armed forces, which had replaced the draft after the Vietnam War. He took issue with critics who charged that the all-volunteer army was uneconomical, that the quality of its recruits was inferior, or that its large proportion of blacks (22.2 percent, as compared with 11 percent of the general population) detracted from its effectiveness. While noting that many young blacks see opportunities in a military career that are lacking in civilian life, Alexander believed that large numbers were motivated by patriotism when they volunteer.

Alexander, George A.
MAJOR GENERAL—ARMY

Major General Alexander completed premedical studies at Columbia University. He earned an M.D. degree from the College of Medicine at Howard University and received Advanced Biostatistics training at the Johns Hopkins University School of Public Health.

Alexander was commissioned as a first lieutenant in the Medical Corps in the District of Columbia Army National Guard, and was initially assigned as a General Medical Officer with the 115th Combat Support Hospital, District of Columbia Army National Guard, and the 117th Combat Support Hospital, Texas Army National Guard. After volunteering for airborne duty, he served as a Medical Officer with the 20th Special Forces Group (Airborne) of the Maryland Army National Guard. Later key assignments included Flight Surgeon for the 28th Aviation Battalion, 28th Infantry Division, Pennsylvania Army National Guard; Brigade Surgeon for the 28th Combat Aviation Brigade, 28th Infantry Division, Pennsylvania Army National Guard; Commander of the 116th Mobile Army Surgical Hospital, Delaware Army National Guard; Staff Surgeon for the Headquarters 261st Signal Command, Delaware Army National Guard; Commander of the 135th Combat Support Hospital, Maryland; Commander of Detachment 3 (Medical Det.), Headquarters, State Area Command, Maryland Army National Guard; and Assistant Surgeon General for Mobilization, Readiness and National Guard Affairs at the Office of the Army Surgeon General. In October 2002, Brigadier General Alexander was selected as the Deputy Surgeon General for the Army National Guard, Office of the Army Surgeon General.

Alexander, Richard C.
MAJOR GENERAL—ARMY

General Alexander was born in Cleveland, Ohio, and he and his wife, LaVera, have two sons, Jeff and Ronald, and a daughter, Gail. He is a 1954 graduate of East Technical High School in Cleveland, and attended Franklin University in Columbus. His military education includes Aviation Radar Repair (1956); Basic Elec-

tronics (1956); FCS Maintenance Course (1964); Air Defense Basic Officer Course (1966); Missile Site Security (1969); Air Defense Advance Officer Course (1970); Air Defense Missile Staff Officer Course (1971); Defense Race Relations Institute (1972); Internal Review Analysis Course (1972); the Reserve Components National Security Course (1987); and United States Army War College, Corresponding Studies Course (1983).

Alexander entered the military service on October 20, 1954, when he enlisted in the United States Marine Corps. He was honorably discharged from the Marine Corps on December 18, 1958, as a sergeant but continued to serve in the Marine Corps Reserve through June 29, 1960. On June 30, 1960, he enlisted in Battery C, 1st Missile Battalion (Nike-Hercules), 137th Artillery of the Ohio Army National Guard, where he began full-time career as an Army National Guard technician. On May 6, 1965, he was appointed a second lieutenant in the Artillery Branch, Ohio National Guard.

Alexander, Willie Abner
MAJOR GENERAL—ARMY

General Alexander was born in China Grove, North Carolina. He graduated from Landis High School in 1959, and received a Bachelor of Science Degree in Business Administration from Alabama State University. His military education includes the Field Artillery Officer Basic Course; Ordnance and Quartermaster Officer Advance Courses; SAILS Management Course; Quartermaster Supply Course; Command and General Staff College; and the National Security Management Course.

Alexander began his military career on active duty as a Military Policeman from 1959 to 1962, at Fort Bragg, North Carolina, and in Germany. He was commissioned a second lieutenant on August 16, 1966, and was

assigned to Fort McClellan, Alabama, where he served as training officer, XO, S-2, and Leadership School commander. Alexander then spent a year with the 4th Missile Command in Korea before leaving active duty.

In October 1972, he joined the Alabama Army Guard's 1167th Stock Control Company as Ammunition Surveillance officer, and later as Chief of the Surveillance Section. On June 24, 1992, he was promoted to Colonel, and assigned as Assistant Adjutant General for Army, Alabama National Guard. On June 22, 1995, he was appointed Brigadier General (Line), and became Deputy Commander, 167th Support Command (Corps), in January 1997. Alexander was appointed Adjutant General of Alabama on January 18, 1999, and became the First African American to serve this position.

Alford, Gregory H.
COMMAND SERGEANT MAJOR—ARMY

Command Sergeant Major Gregory H. Alford was born in Greenville, South Carolina, on February 20, 1956. He entered the Army as an 11B (Infantryman) in 1976. In 1980, he reenlisted as a 24E and entered the Air Defense Artillery. His military education includes completion of the First Sergeants Course and the United States Army Sergeants Major Academy.

Alford has held a variety of leadership positions including Team Leader, Squad Leader, and Rifles Platoon Sergeant in the Infantry; HAWK Firing Section Mechanic, Chief Firing Section Mechanic, Electronic Missile Maintenance Inspector, and First Sergeant in the Air Defense Arena; and Senior ROTC Instruction, as the Command Sergeant Major of the 3rd Squadron (Air Combat), 6th Cavalry Brigade at Camp Humphreys in Korea. His most recent assignment was as Command Sergeant Major of 1st Battalion, 56th Air Defense Artillery Regiment. He currently serves as the Command Sergeant Major of the 6th Air Defense Artillery Brigade.

Allen, Doris
CHIEF WARRANT OFFICER—ARMY

Doris Allen enlisted in the Army in 1950. In 1967, she volunteered to serve in Vietnam as an enlisted intelligence officer for three years. Allen predicted the Tet Offensive shortly after arriving in country, but her prediction was ignored. Allen worked as a special agent with both Military Intelligence and the Defense Investigative Service until her retirement. She retired as a Chief Warrant Officer with 30 years of dedicated service.

Allen, Joseph R.
COMMAND SERGEANT MAJOR—ARMY

Joseph Allen entered active military service in July 1975, and completed Basic Combat Training and Advanced Individual Training at Fort Jackson, South Carolina. His first duty assignment was as a Light Wheel Vehicle Mechanic in the 5th Signal Command at Worms, Germany. After returning from Germany, he attended Basic Airborne School and Infantry Advanced Individual Training at Fort Benning, Georgia.

In December 1978, Allen was assigned to Combat Support Company (GSC) 1st Battalion, 505th Airborne Infantry as a Rifleman. In July 1983, he was assigned to Foxtrot Company, 82nd Aviation as an Attack Helicopter Repairman and Squad Leader. In December 1985, he returned to Germany as a TAC Sergeant Instructor and later as the First Sergeant of Golf Troop, 2nd Squadron, 2nd Armored Cavalry Regiment in Bamberg, Germany.

In August 1988, he was assigned to 5/16 Infantry, Fort Riley, Kansas as an Anti-Armor Maintenance Supervisor. In January 1990, Allen returned to Germany

where he was assigned to the 2nd Brigade, 3rd Armored Division in Geluhausen as the First Sergeant, deploying to Saudi Arabia for operation Desert Shield/Storm. He was then assigned to the 414th Base Support Battalion as the First Sergeant and later as the Battalion Command Sergeant Major. In October 1995, he was assigned to the 82nd Forward Support Battalion as the Battalion Command Sergeant Major. In June 2002, he was assigned as the Command Sergeant Major for the 1st Corps Support Command.

Allen, Reginald E.
LIEUTENANT COLONEL—ARMY

Lieutenant Colonel Reginald E. Allen graduated from North Carolina A&T State University in 1985, and was commissioned as a Second Lieutenant in Armor and Cavalry. His civilian and military education includes a Bachelor of Science in Business Administration, with a master's degree in Training Management from the University of Louisville; Armor Officer Basic Course; Mortar Platoon Leader's Course; Cavalry Leader's Course; Armor Officer Advance Course; Joint Firepower Control Course; Combined Arms Services and Staff School; and Command and General Staff College.

His military assignments include service with the 2nd Armored Cavalry Regiment during Operation Desert Shield/Storm; as a Troop Commander in the 3rd Squadron, 2nd Armored Cavalry in Amberg, Germany; later as the Commander of a Tank Company, 3rd Battalion, 77th Armor Regiment in Mannheim, Germany; as the Aide-de-Camp and later as Special Assistant to the Commanding General for Force XXI;

as the Director for Strategic Planning at Fort Knox; as Operations Officer and Battalion Executive Officer for the 3rd Battalion, 69th Armor Regiment at Fort Stewart, Georgia; as Assistant Deputy Director for Operations, National Military Command Center at the Pentagon. In June 2003, Lieutenant Colonel Allen was assigned to command the 1st Squadron of the 10th United States Cavalry (Buffalo Soldiers) on the Iran/Iraq border, where the Squadron served from March 2003 to March 2004 in support of Operation Iraqi Freedom.

Allen, Ulysses
CHIEF WARRANT OFFICER 5—ARMY

Ulysses Allen was born and grew up in rural southern Georgia and spent much of his childhood in the 1940s and 1950s working on the family farm. In 1964, he enlisted in the United States Army in the Intelligence field. Over the next few years of his service Allen served in an Armor Unit in West Germany; as a Drill Instructor at Fort Campbell, Kentucky; and finally as an infantryman with the 3rd Battalion, 7th Infantry in Vietnam.

After six months his enlistment ended, and Allen returned to civilian life and in 1969, moved to South Florida. In 1977, he joined the Florida National Guard and a few years later became a Warrant Officer in the Maintenance Field. In 2003, Ulysses Allen was promoted to Chief Warrant Officer 5, becoming the First African American to receive the CW5 rank in the Florida National Guard. He serves with the 53rd Infantry Brigade in Tampa, Florida.

Allensworth, Allen
LIEUTENANT COLONEL—ARMY

Allen Allensworth was born into slavery in Louisville, Kentucky in 1842. His mother, Phyliss Allensworth, told her son she couldn't send him to school, but that

after school, he must have their owner's little boy "play school every day" with him. He did, and in this manner learned to read and write.

In 1863, he escaped, posing as a servant with the Union Army marching south from Louisville. His former owner's son, unknown to him, joined the Union Army and remained in the service after the war.

After the war Allensworth and his brother operated two highly successful restaurants in St. Louis, while Allen also managed to continue his formal education. In 1871, he became a minister, and in 1877 met and married Josephine Leavel. In 1886, he accepted a commission in the Army as a chaplain, with the rank of captain, to serve in the all-black 24th Infantry. He was surprised to meet his former owner's son in the Army with a lower rank than himself. When he retired in 1906, he held the rank of lieutenant colonel and was not only the highest ranking chaplain in the Army, but the highest ranking black officer at that time.

Alston, Patrick Z.
COMMAND SERGEANT MAJOR—ARMY

Patrick Alston began his military career as a medical specialist at Fort Belvoir, Virginia. His next assignment was as a medical specialist in the 3rd Battalion, 325th Infantry Regiment, 82nd Airborne Division, where he took part in Operation Urgent Fury (in Grenada) and earned his Combat Medical Badge.

His military education includes all Noncommissioned Officer Education System Courses; Drill Sergeant School on the Commander's List; Air Assault School as a Distinguished Honor Graduate; Technical Escort Course; First Sergeant Course on the Commander's List; and the United States Army Sergeants Major Academy.

Alston has served as a Platoon Sergeant with the 34th Support Group in Korea; as the First Sergeant of Head-

quarters and Headquarters Company, Soldier and Biological Chemical Command, Technical Escort Battalion; as a Master Sergeant acting as the First Technical Escort Battalion Command Sergeant Major; as Division Chemical Sergeant Major in Korea; as Command Sergeant Major, 23rd Chemical Battalion; and as Chemical Bridge Command Sergeant Major for the 23rd Area Support Group. In January 2005, Alston was Command Sergeant Major for the 10th Regiment.

Anbiya, Tracey
COMMAND SERGEANT MAJOR—ARMY

A native of Chesapeake, Virginia, Anbiya entered the Army on August 28, 1984, as a Personnel Administration Specialist. After completing Basic Combat Training and Advanced Individual Training, she was assigned to the 522nd Military Intelligence Battalion, where she served as the Battalion SIDPERS Clerk.

Her civilian and military education includes an Associate of Arts and a Bachelor of Science Degree from the University of Maryland; and a master's degree from Oklahoma University. She has completed all Noncommissioned Officer Education System Courses; Drill Sergeant Course; the Army's Master Fitness Course; NBC Officer Course; Instructor Training Course; the United States Army First Sergeants Course; and the United States Army Sergeants Major Course (class 54).

Her other assignments include serving as Company Clerk, C Company, 498th Medical Battalion, in Garlstedt, Germany; as Drill Sergeant, A Company, 2/13th Infantry Battalion, at Fort Jackson, South Carolina; as Personnel Non-Commissioned Officer, Berlin Brigade, Germany; as Personnel Sergeant 2/1 Aviation Battalion at Katterbach, Germany; as Chief Non-Commissioned Officer in Charge and Brigade Adjutant for the 26th Area Support Group in Heidelberg, Germany; as the

Commandant for the Secretary of the General Staff; as First Sergeant for Headquarters Company, United States Army Europe and Seventh Army. In June 2005, Anbiya was serving as the Command Sergeant Major for the Headquarters Battalion at Fort Belvoir.

Anderson, Cassandra L.
MASTER SERGEANT—AIR FORCE

Anderson is a native of Fort Wayne, Indiana, and originally entered the Air Force in 1986, specializing in career fields that included Air Transportation, Passenger Service, Data Records, and Aircraft Load Planning.

Her past assignments included Ramstein Air Base in Germany; Eielson Air Force Base in Alaska; and Travis Air Force Base in California. She studied piano and music theory at Solano College in California, and voice at Sacramento University. She studied with David Stroud at The Voice Studio in San Francisco. Prior to joining the band career field, Anderson performed two consecutive tours with "Tops in Blue," and was a featured artist on the "Jackson Singers" gospel CD, in Frankfurt, Germany. While stationed at Travis Air Force Base, California, she sang the Anthem for professional baseball games that included the Oakland A's and the San Francisco Giants. She also wrote and performed an original song that was featured as background music on the soap opera *All My Children*. Anderson joined the United States Air Force Academy Band in February 2002.

Anderson, Charles Alfred "Chief"
AEROSPACE PIONEER

Anderson was born February 9, 1907, in Bridgeport, Pennsylvania, and became known as the "Father of Black Aviation." He organized the Civilian Pilot training program at Howard University in 1939. In 1940, after gaining additional acrobatic training at the Chi-

cago School of Aviation, Anderson went to the Tuskegee Institute, where he became the first black pilot employed by the school.

He instructed the first advanced course under the Civilian Pilot Training program at Tuskegee, and later became the Chief Civilian Flight Instructor for the Army Primary Training for Aviation Cadets under the United States Army Air Corps (now Air Force) at Tuskegee. During World War II Anderson trained members of the Tuskegee Airmen 99th Pursuit Squadron.

After the War, he continued to teach as a flight and ground instructor at Tuskegee's Motion Field under the G.I. Bill and ROTC.

Anderson, Curtis
LIEUTENANT COLONEL—ARMY

Anderson is a graduate of Northeast Missouri State University where he received a Bachelor of Science degree in Business Administration in 1986. He was commissioned a Second Lieutenant in the Armor Corps after completion of the Reserved Officers Training Corps, and holds a Master of Arts degree in Administration from Central Michigan University.

His military education includes the Armor Officer Basic Course; Airborne School; Ordnance Officer Advance Course; Logistics Management Development Course; Combined Arms and Service Staff School; Command and General Staff College; and the Joint Forces Staff College.

His key military assignments include serving as Tank Platoon Leader, Tank Company Executive Officer, Headquarters and Headquarters Company Executive Officer and Battalion Maintenance Officer for the 1st Battalion, 34th Armor, 1st Infantry Division at Fort Riley, Kansas; as Commander of the 539th Maintenance Company; Commander of the 546th Maintenance Company; as Support Operations Maintenance Officer for the 142nd Corps Support Battalion at Fort Polk, Louisiana; as Captain Assignments Officer for the Ordnance Branch of Total Army Personnel Command at Alexandria, Virginia; as Support Operations Officer with the 227th Maintenance Battalion, 501st Corps Support Group in South Korea; Aide de Camp to Commanding General, Eighth United States Army and Chief of Staff, United States Forces Korea; Battalion Executive Officer of the 702nd Main Support Battalion, 2nd Infantry Division in South Korea; as Observer/Trainer with Joint Forces Command, J3/4, at Norfolk, Virginia; and as Commander of the 501st Forward Support Battalion at Friedberg, Germany.

Anderson, Curtis
SERGEANT MAJOR—MARINES

He was born in Little Rock, Arkansas in December 1957. Upon graduating from high school in 1976, he enlisted into the Marine Corps in August of that year. Upon graduating from Charlie Company, 1st Recruit Training Battalion, Marine Corps Depot, San Diego, California, he completed Infantry Training School at Camp Pendleton, California.

In September 1994, Anderson was assigned to the 1st Marine Division, 2nd Battalion as a Weapon Company Operation Chief and Company Gunnery Sergeant; in October 1997, he was assigned as Chief Drill Instructor at Marine Recruit Depot in San Diego, California, and Company First Sergeant with Charlie Company, 1st Recruit Training Battalion. He also served as First Sergeant in the 3rd Marine Aircraft Wing at Camp Pendleton and as First Sergeant of the 3rd Low Attitude Air Defense Battalion, Headquarters and Service Battalion. In February 2003, Anderson was deployed to the Middle East where he participated with Coalition Forces in Operation Iraqi Freedom; in May 2003, he was promoted to Sergeant Major, and assigned as Squadron Sergeant Major with Marine Fighter Attack Squadron 225.

Anderson, Dorian T.
MAJOR GENERAL—ARMY

Major General Anderson serves as Commanding General of United States Total Army Personnel Command. He graduated from the United States Military Academy in 1975, and was commissioned a second lieutenant on June 4, 1975. He was promoted to brigadier general on July 1, 2000, and later promoted to Major General.

He holds a master's Degree in Management from Webster University, and attended Infantry Officer Basic and Advanced Courses, United States Army Command and General Staff College, and the United States Army War College.

Major General Anderson has held a wide variety of important command and staff positions including Executive Officer of 3rd Battalion, 75th Ranger Regiment at Fort Benning, Georgia; Chief of the Operations Division, Office of the Deputy Chief of Staff for Operations, United States Army Pacific at Fort Shafter,

Hawaii; Chief of the Tactics Division (later Director, Combined Arms Tactics Division), United States Army Infantry School at Fort Benning, Georgia; Command of Ranger Training Brigade at Fort Benning, Georgia; and Director of the Officer Personnel Management Directorate, United States Total Army Personnel Command at Alexandria, Virginia. He is currently Commanding General of Joint Task Force 6 at Fort Bliss, Texas.

Anderson, Frank J., Jr.
BRIGADIER GENERAL—AIR FORCE

Brigadier General Anderson is married to the former Bonnie Washington of Houston, Texas, and they have two children, Trina and Jim. He received a Bachelor of Arts degree in Business Management and Economics from Chapman College in Orange, California. He earned a master's degree in Management from Central Michigan University. His military education includes the Air Force Squadron Officer School; Air Command and Staff College at Maxwell Air Force Base, Alabama; Defense Systems Management College at Fort Belvoir, Virginia; and the Industrial College of the Armed Forces at Fort Lesley J. McNair in Washington, D.C.

From August 1994 to July 1995, Anderson was Director of the Weapons, Air Base and Range Product Support Office at the Aeronautical Systems Center at Eglin Air Force Base, Florida. In August 1995, he was assigned as Manager of the Armament Product Group at the Aeronautical Systems Center at Eglin Air Force Base. In July 1996, he was selected the Director of Contracting at the Aeronautical Systems Center at Wright-Patterson Air Force Base, Ohio. In August 1997, he was selected as Deputy Assistant Secretary for Contracting

in the Office of the Assistant Secretary for Acquisition, and Air Force Competition Advocate General, at United States Air Force Headquarters in the Pentagon. He was appointed Brigadier General on September 1, 1997.

In July 1999, Anderson was selected to serve as Commandant of the Defense Systems Management College at Fort Belvoir, Virginia.

Anderson, Michael P.

LIEUTENANT COLONEL—AIR FORCE

Anderson was born in Plattsburgh, New York, but considered Spokane, Washington, to be his hometown. He graduated from Cheney High School in Cheney,

Washington, in 1977, and received a Bachelor of Science degree in Physics/Astronomy from the University of Washington in 1981. He also earned a Master of Science degree in Physics from Creighton University in 1990.

After graduating from the University of Washington, Anderson was commissioned as a second lieutenant in the United States Air Force. After completing a year of technical training at Keesler Air Force Base in Mississippi, he was assigned to Randolph Air Force Base in Texas. At Randolph he served as Chief of Communication Maintenance for the 2015 Communication Squadron and later as Director of Information System Maintenance for the 1920 Information System Group. In 1986, he was selected to attend Undergraduate Pilot Training at Vance Air Force Base, Oklahoma. Upon graduation he was assigned to the 2nd Airborne Command and Control Squadron, at Offutt Air Force Base, in Nebraska as an EC-135 pilot, flying Strategic Air Command's Airborne Command Post code-named "Looking Glass." From January 1991 to September 1992, he served as an Aircraft Commander and Instructor Pilot in the 920th Air Refueling Squadron, at Wurtsmith Air Force Base in Michigan. From September 1992 to February 1995, he was assigned as an Instructor Pilot and Tactics Officer to the 380th Air Refueling Wing at Plattsburgh Air Force Base in New York. He has logged over 3000 hours in various models of the KC-135 and the T-38A aircraft.

Anderson was selected by NASA as an astronaut in December 1994, and reported to the Johnson Space Center in March 1995. He completed a year of training and evaluation, and was qualified for flight crew assignment as a mission specialist. He was initially assigned technical duties in the Fight Support Branch of the Astronaut Office. Most recently, he flew on the crew of STS-89. In completing his first space flight Anderson had logged over 211 hours in space over 8 days and traveled 3.6 million miles in 138 orbits of the Earth. He was assigned to the crew of STS-107, which launched on January 16, 2003, and returned on February 1, 2003. Lieutenant Colonel Anderson was killed when the Space Shuttle *Columbia* broke apart above north-central Texas at an altitude of about 203,000 feet during its re-entry into Earth's atmosphere.

Anderson, Rodney O.

BRIGADIER GENERAL—ARMY

Anderson was commissioned into the United States Army as a Second Lieutenant on June 6, 1979, and holds a Bachelor of Science degree in Economics from Wofford College; and a Master of Arts degree in National Security and Strategic Studies from the United States Naval War College. His military education also includes the Field Artillery Officer Basic and Advanced Course; and the United States Army Command and General Staff College.

His key military assignments include serving as Aide-de-Camp to the Deputy Commander-in-Chief, United States Central Command (Forward) during Operations Desert Shield/Storm in Saudi Arabia from July 1989 to

Her leadership assignments include: serving from October 1982 to June 1984, as Chief of the Cargo Division at McGuire Air Force Base, New Jersey; from June 1984 to October 1985, as Chief of Systems, Reports, and Analysis at McGuire Air Force Base; from October 1985 to October 1988, as Squadron Operations Officer for the 6th Aerial Port Squadron at Howard Air Force Base, Panama; from October 1988 to August 1991, as Chief of the Channel Requirements Division at Headquarters Military Airlift Command at Scott Air Force Base, Illinois; from August 1991 to August 1992, as Squadron Operations Officer of the 438th Aerial Port Squadron at McGuire Air Force Base; from August 1992 to August 1994, as Commander of the 438th Aerial Port Squadron at McGuire Air Force Base; from July 1994 to July 1995, as Transportation Coordinator for the United States Atlantic Command at Norfolk, Virginia; from July 1995 to July 1997, as Deputy Chief of Training Simulation and Analysis for Logistics at United States Atlantic Command at Norfolk, Virginia; from July 1997 to July 1998, as Commander of the 86th Logistics Support Squadron at Ramstein Air Base, Germany; from July 1998 to June 2000, as Deputy Commander of the 86th Logistics Group at Ramstein Air Base, Germany; from June 2000 to August 2001, as Assistant for Air Transportation Policy in the Office of the Secretary of Defense at the Pentagon; and from June 2002 to June 2003, as the Deputy Chief of Staff for Passenger and Personnel Property at Headquarters Military Traffic Management Command, in Alexandria, Virginia.

Since June 2003, Anderson has served as Commander of the 78th Mission Support Group at Robins Air Force Base, Georgia. As Commander, she manages and leads 1,800 military and civilian personnel, and operates

June 1991; as Deputy Fire Support Coordinator for the 82nd Airborne Division, at Fort Bragg, North Carolina, as Commander of the 3rd Battalion, 319th Airborne Field Artillery Regiment, at Fort Bragg as Deputy Fire Support Coordinator for the 82nd Airborne Division at Fort Bragg as Deputy Chief of the War Plans Division at the Strategy, Plans and Policy Directorate in the Office of the Deputy Chief of Staff for Operations and Plans, United States Army, Washington, D.C.; as Commander of Division Artillery for the 25th Infantry Division (Light) at Schofield Barracks, Hawaii; and as Chief of the Operations Division in the Information Operations Directorate, J-3, at the Joint Staff, Washington, D.C. In October 2003, Anderson was assigned as the Executive Assistant to the Chairman of the Joint Chiefs of Staff at the Pentagon. On March 28, 2005, he became the Assistant Division Commander of the 82nd Airborne Division at Fort Bragg.

Anderson, Silvia Signars

COLONEL—AIR FORCE

Colonel Anderson received her commission through the Reserve Officer Training Corps at Indiana University and has served in a variety of support, major command, education, and joint duty assignments throughout her career.

Her civilian and military education includes a bachelor's degree in Business Administration and Management from Indiana University, in Bloomington, Indiana; a master's degree in Logistics Systems at the Air Force Institute of Technology at Wright-Patterson Air Force Base, Ohio; and a master's in National Resource Strategy, from the Industrial College of the Armed Forces at Fort McNair, Washington, D.C. At Maxwell Air Force Base in Alabama, she also attended Squadron Officer School, Air War College, and Air Command and Staff College.

all support functions required to maintain the combat readiness and effectiveness of the Warner Robins Air Logistics Center, 78th Air Base Wing, and more than 60 tenant units. She also oversees a $45M annual budget for the operation of communications, mission support, security forces, logistics readiness, civilian personnel, and services (including the commissary and base exchange).

Andrews, Annie B.
CAPTAIN—NAVY

Andrews is a native of Midway, Georgia, and received a Bachelor of Science degree in Criminal Justice from Savannah State University in 1983, and earned a Master of Science degree in Management from Troy State University in 1986.

In 1999, Andrews received a master's degree in National Security and Strategic Studies from the College of Naval Command and Staff at the Naval War College. She has also attended the Joint Forces Staff College, fulfilling the requirements for Joint Professional Military Education (JPME) Phases I and II. In April 2000, she was designated a Joint Specialty Officer (JSO).

Andrews was commissioned as an Ensign in August 1983, and reported to Naval Air Station Whiting Field at Milton, Florida, where she was assigned as Billeting Officer and subsequently served as Assistant Administrative Officer for Training Air Wing Five, and Assistant Flight Support Coordinator of Helicopter Training Squadron Eight. In December 1986, she was assigned to the Joint Intelligence Center Pacific (JIC-PAC) in Honolulu as an Intelligence Analyst. During this tour she was selected as the Executive Assistant to Commander, Joint Intelligence Center Pacific. In April 1990, she served overseas as Director of the Counseling and Assistance Center at Naval Air Station Keflavik, Iceland. In November 1991, she assumed the duties as

Officer-in-Charge, Navy Personnel Support Activity Detachments Subic Bay and Cubi Point and served as Area Commander of United States Forces Philippines. In December 1992, she was assigned to the Bureau of Naval Personnel in Washington, D.C., where she served as Branch Head, Deserter Branch/Deserter Apprehension Program (PERS-842). In June 1995, she served as the Commander of Boston Military Entrance Processing Station. In September 1999, Andrews was assigned to the Pentagon where she served as Chief of the Requirements Branch and Joint Manpower Planner, Manpower and Personnel Directorate J-1, the Joint Staff, Washington, D.C. From October 2001 to March 2002, she served on the OPNAV (N13) Staff in Washington, D.C. as the Assistant Human Resources Community Manager, assisting in the transformation of the Fleet Support Community. Captain Andrews reported to Navy Recruiting District San Francisco in June 2002 as Executive Officer and assumed the duties of Commanding Officer of Navy Recruit Depot San Francisco in December 2003. During her tenure, Team San Francisco earned both the Officer and Enlisted Recruiting "R" Excellence Awards for three consecutive years. She assumed her duties as Executive Officer for Recruit Training Command in April 2005.

Captain Andrews is an accomplished vocalist. Throughout her career, she has performed as a soloist for numerous professional and community ventures. She is the recipient of the 2002 W.C. Shipman "Trail Blazer" Award, recognizing her contributions to the community, the Navy and the nation. In March 2002, she received the Army Chief of Chaplains' "Scroll of Honor" Award for her contributions to the Pentagon Chapel Music Program. Most significantly, Captain Andrews arranged all of the music and performed at the President's National Day of Prayer Service at the Pentagon following the 11 September attacks.

Archer, Fred
CHIEF MASTER SERGEANT—AIR FORCE

Archer was born in New York in 1921, and was 17 years old when he joined the New York National Guard in 1939, serving two years in the Infantry before going on active duty with the Army Air Corps in 1941.

Congress created the 99th Pursuit Squadron in 1941 to see if blacks were capable of operating and maintaining aircraft. Archer, along with 13 other blacks, left New York for Chanute Field, Illinois, where they received their technical training. These airmen were then sent to Tuskegee Airfield and became the support crew for the famous Tuskegee Airmen, the First African Americans to train as Army Air Corps pilots. He served with the 99th during World War II in the Mediterranean and in Europe, where they were joined by the 332nd Fighter Group.

After World War II, he was assigned to Davis-Monthan Air Force base in Tucson, where he was in charge of the Armament Shop. During his 33-year career in the Air Force, Archer served as Non-Commissioned Officer in Charge of Munitions Mainte-

nance, Armament and Electronics at Davis-Monthan.

Chief Archer was the first black in the United States Air Force to earn the rank of Chief Master Sergeant, and was nominated three times for the position of Chief Master Sergeant of the Air Force.

Armstead, Michael A.
LIEUTENANT COLONEL—ARMY

Armstead is a 1985 Distinguished Military Graduate (DMG) from Rust Springs, Mississippi, where he was commissioned a Second Lieutenant. He attended the Armor Officer Basic Course at Fort Knox, Kentucky. Following graduation from the Basic Course he was a Platoon Leader for Charlie Company, 1/40 Armor Battalion, 5th Infantry Division (Mechanized) at Fort Polk, Louisiana. In 1988, he was assigned as a Truck Platoon Leader for Bravo Company, 705th Main Support Battalion, Division Support Command, 5th Infantry Division (M) at Fort Polk, Louisiana.

He served as the Motor Transportation Officer, Eight Army, Special Troops, Yongson Korea. In addition, he served as Company Commander, 21st Transportation Company, 34th Area Support Group. He returned to the United States and was assigned as Assistant S3, Commander (Baton Rouge) and S3 for the New Orleans Recruiting Battalion. He went to Saudi Arabia where he served as the Transportation Management Officer, United States Mission to Saudi Arabia. He returned to the United States and was assigned to the Military Traffic Management Command Eastern Area at Bayonne, New Jersey, where he served as the Chief of Plans and Mobility.

In 1996, Armstead served as the Support Operation Officer for Division Support Command, 3rd Infantry Division (Mechanized), at Fort Stewart, Georgia. In 1997, he deployed in support of Operation Joint Guard and served as Brigade S3 Plans and Operation (Forward) for the 1st Transportation Movement Control Brigade in Taszar, Hungary; Slovonski Brod, Croatia; and Tuzla, Bosnia-Herzegovina. Upon redeployment, he became the S3 for the 26th Support Battalion, Division Support Command, 3rd Infantry Division (Mechanized) at Fort Stewart, Georgia.

He served as the Executive Officer for the 180th Transportation Battalion, 64th Corps Support Group (CSG) and as the S3 for the 64th CSG, 13th Corps Support Command at Fort Hood, Texas, from 1999 to 2001. He served in J-4 International Division Headquarters United States European Command at Stuttgart, Germany, where he was the Chief of the Black Sea Caucasus Group in the Joint Contact Team Program. In addition, he served as the Chief of Movement

Force, North in Incirlik, Turkey, in support of Operation Iraqi Freedom.

Armstead is a graduate of the Army Command and General Staff College and he also holds a Master of Science Degree in Administration from Central Michigan University.

Armstrong, Ernest W., Sr.
COLONEL—ARMY

Colonel Armstrong was born in Soper, Oklahoma, the son of Giles H. Armstrong and Vinnie Armstrong. He received his high school diploma from Booker T. Washington High School in Tulsa and received a bachelor's degree in Religion and Philosophy from Dillard University in New Orleans. He served as an Army Chaplain from 1949 to 1969, and retired as a Colonel. His military awards include the Army Chaplain School Award; the Army Defense Medal; the Bronze Star (v) for military combat; the Far East Operations Medal; the Japanese Occupation Medal; the United States State Department Foreign Service Institute Award; the European Theater of Operations Award; and the German Occupation Award.

Armstrong, Larona
SERGEANT MAJOR—MARINES

Larona Armstrong enlisted the Marine Corps on the Delayed Entry Program on 12 December 1978 and reported to Recruit Training at Parris Island, South Carolina. His military assignments include serving as Guns Platoon Sergeant for Delta Battery of the 2nd Battalion, 11th Marines at Camp Pendleton, California; as an Instructor in the Fleet Assistance Program in Officer School at Camp Pendleton; as the Field Artillery Chief/Battery Gunnery Sergeant for the 5th Battalion, 14th Marines at El Paso, Texas; First Sergeant for Kilo

Battery, 2nd Battalion, 12th Marines at Camp Pendleton; and as the Inspector Instructor First Sergeant for the 2nd Battalion, 23rd Marines at Port Hueneme, California; and as Sergeant Major for Combat Service Support Battalion-10, 1st FSSG.

Arnold, Wallace C.
MAJOR GENERAL—ARMY

He was born in Washington, D.C. He received a Bachelor of Science degree in Industrial Education from the Hampton Institute and a Master of Arts in Personnel Management and Administration from George Washington University. He received an ROTC commission to Second Lieutenant in May 1961. He was promoted to Lieutenant Colonel on June 1, 1974. From August 1976 to July 1977, Arnold was a student at the Naval War College at Newport, Rhode Island. From July 1977 to June 1979, he served as a Computer Systems Software and Analysis Officer in the Functional Systems Division at the Office of the Assistant Chief of Staff for Automation and Communications, United States Army, Washington, D.C. From June 1979 to June 1981, he served as Military Assistant in the Office of the Under Secretary of the Army in Washington, D.C.

He was promoted to Brigadier General on August 1, 1985. From June 1987 to May 1990, he was the Commanding General of the First Reserve Officer Training Corps Region at Fort Bragg, North Carolina. He was promoted to Major General on October 18, 1989. In May 1990, he was assigned as Commanding General of the United States Army Reserve Officer Training Corps Cadet Command at Fort Monroe, Virginia. Major General Arnold retired on June 30, 1995.

Ash, Willie
COMMAND SERGEANT MAJOR—ARMY

He entered into the United States Army in June 1978 at Fort Jackson, South Carolina. His military education includes the United States Army Airborne School, Master Fitness Course, Master Gunner Course, Drill Sergeant Course, Primary Noncommissioned Officer Course, Basic Noncommissioned Officer Course, Advanced Noncommissioned Officer Course, and the First Sergeant Course. He is also a graduate of the United States Army Sergeants Major Academy (class 47). He has an associate's degree from the University of Maryland, and is presently working toward a bachelor's degree in Business at Western Illinois University.

He has served in numerous leadership positions including Team Leader; Command Sergeant Major for the 1/38th Infantry; Command Sergeant Major for the 1/15th Infantry Battalion; Command Sergeant Major 98th ASG, Brigade. In 2004 he was serving as Command Sergeant Major for 2nd Brigade of the 1st Armored Division.

Atkinson, William Earl
COLONEL—ARMY

Colonel William Earl Atkinson was commissioned an Infantry Officer upon graduation from Infantry Officer Candidate School in 1972. His first duty assignment was as Detachment Executive Officer for the 2nd Battalion, 5th Special Forces Group (SFG) (Airborne), at Fort Bragg, North Carolina.

His subsequent duty assignments include Company Executive Officer, Service Company, with the 5th Special Forces Group, Fort Bragg, North Carolina; Heavy Mortar Platoon Leader and Company Commander, Company B, 1st Infantry Battalion, at Camp Casey, Korea; Battalion S-3 (Operations), 2nd Battalion, 31st Infantry, at Fort Ord, California; Assistant Brigade S-3 (Operations), with the 1st Brigade, 7th Division, Fort Ord, California; Troop Commander, with the Special Operations Detachment (SFOD), Delta Force (Airborne), at Fort Bragg; S-3 (Operations), for 1st Battalion, 75th Ranger Regiment, at Hunter Army Air Field,

Georgia; Special Operations Staff Officer, United States Army Special Operations Agency, at Headquarters, Department of the Army (HQDA) at Washington, D.C.; Assistant Executive Officer, Deputy Chief of Staff for Operations and Plans, at the Headquarters of the Department of the Army at Washington, D.C.; Commander of the 3rd Battalion, 7th Special Forces Group (Airborne), at Fort Bragg; G-3 (Operations), for the United States Army Special Operations Integration Command, at Fort Bragg; Assistant Executive Officer to the Under Secretary of the Army in Washington, D.C.; and Operations Officer at the Joint Operations Division (PACIFIC), United States Army Element, J-3/Joint at the Pentagon.

On August 3, 2000, Atkinson was assigned as the Deputy Director for Antiterrorism, in the Office of the Assistant Secretary of Defense for Special Operations and Low-Intensity Conflict, in Washington, D.C.

Aubain, Anthony
COMMAND SERGEANT MAJOR—ARMY

Aubain is a native of St. Thomas, Virgin Islands and attended Basic Combat Training at Fort Dix, New Jersey.

His military education includes all Noncommissioned Officer Education System Courses; the First Sergeant Course; the United States Army Sergeants Major Academy; Survival, Evasion, Resistance and Escape Instructor Course; Airborne Course; Dynamics of International Terrorism Course; Antiterrorist Driving and Surveillance Detection Course; Institute of Advance Weapon Craft; Jungle Operation Course; Special Forces High Altitude Low Opening Parachute Curse; United States Infantry Ranger School; USAIMA Special Force Qualification Course; and the Canadian Parachute School.

His assignments include serving with the 4th Infantry Division at Fort Carson, Colorado; the 10th Special Forces Group (1st Special Forces) at Fort Devens,

Massachusetts; the Joint Special Operation Command (JCU) at Fort Bragg, North Carolina; 782nd MSB, 82nd Airborne Division, 203FSB 3rd Brigade, 3rd Infantry Division, at Fort Benning, Georgia; 101st CSD at Fort Campbell, Kentucky; and 3rd Corps Support Command in Wiesbaden, Germany. In June 2005, Aubain was serving as Regimental Command Sergeant Major of the Ordnance Corps.

Augustine, Carla J.
CAPTAIN—ARMY

Carla Augustine is a native of New Orleans, and began her military career as a private in the Judge Advocate General's Corps in 1993. Upon her completion of Advanced Individual Training she was assigned as a legal specialist to the United States Army Ordnance Center and School at Aberdeen Proving Ground, Maryland. While serving a short tour in South Korea, she was awarded an Army ROTC scholarship and re-entered Loyola University of New Orleans. She was awarded a Bachelor of Arts Degree in Political Science and was commissioned as a Second Lieutenant in the Adjutant General's Corps in 1997.

Her first assignment after receiving her commission took her back to South Korea, where she was assigned to the United States Army Troop Command — Korea. There she served as the Battalion Adjutant and S1 in support of army personnel assigned to the Eighth United States Army, United States Forces Korea, Combined Forces Command, and the United Nations Command. Upon completion of this tour, she was assigned to the Phoenix Military Entrance Processing Station in Phoenix, Arizona, and served as the Test Control Officer from March 1999 to March 2001. During her time there she earned a master's degree in Business Ad-

ministration/Global Management from the University of Phoenix. In April 2001, she was reassigned to Fort Jackson, South Carolina for the Captain's Career Course. Her previous assignment was with the United States Central Forces Command — Kuwait, where she served as the Personnel Service Support Chief/S1.

In January 2005, Augustine was serving as the Commander, Joint Sub-Regional Command South Central, United States Army, with NATO.

Austin, Lloyd J., III
MAJOR GENERAL—ARMY

Major General Austin received a Bachelor of Science Degree from the United States Military Academy in June 1975. He earned a master's degree in Education Administration from Auburn University and a Master of Arts in Management from Webster University. His military education includes Infantry Officer Basic and Advanced course, United States Army Command, and General Staff College and the United States Army War College. He received his commission as a Second Lieutenant from the United States Military Academy at West Point on June 2, 1975.

From June 1999 to July 2001, he was assigned as Chief of Joint Operations Division of J-3, the Joint Staff, in Washington, D.C. In July 2001, he was selected Assistant Division Commander (Maneuver) of the 3rd Infantry Division (Mechanized) at Fort Stewart, Georgia. He was promoted to Brigadier General on January 1, 2002.

From July 2003 to September 2003, he served as Commanding General of the 10th Mountain Division (Light) at Fort Drum, New York. From September 2003 to April 2004, he served as the Commanding General of the 10th Mountain Division (Light)/Commander, Combined Joint Task Force 180 and Operation

Enduring Freedom, Afghanistan. He was promoted to Major General on January 1, 2005.

His military awards and decorations include the Legion of Merit; the Meritorious Service Medal (with 4 Oak Leaf Clusters); the Army Commendation Medal (with Oak Leaf Cluster); the Expert Infantryman Badge; and the Master Parachutist Badge and Ranger Tab.

Bagby, Byron S.
MAJOR GENERAL—ARMY

General Bagby received his commission as a Second Lieutenant on July 2, 1978, after graduating from ROTC. He also received a Bachelor of Arts degree in Business Economics from Westminster College. He earned a Master of Arts degree in Education Administration from the University of North Carolina. His military education includes completion of the Basic and Advanced Courses for Field Artillery Officers. In June 1991, he graduated from the United States Army Command and General Staff College. In June 1997, Bagby completed the United States Army War College.

From June 1997 to July 1999, Bagby served as Commander of Division Artillery for the 101st Airborne Division (Air Assault) at Fort Campbell, Kentucky. From July 1999 to July 2000, he served as the Chief of the Middle East Division, J-5, for the Joint Staff, in Washington, DC. In July 2000, he was assigned as the Assistant Deputy Director for Politico-Military Affairs (Asia/Pacific), J-5, for the Joint Staff, Washington, DC. From July 2001 to July 2002, he was assigned as the Executive Officer to the G-8, United States Army, in Washington, DC. In July 2002, he was selected as the Assistant Division Command (Support), later Assistant Division Commander (Operations), for the 10th

Mountain Division at Fort Drum, New York. He was promoted to Brigadier General on January 1, 2003.

In August 2004, Bagby was selected to serve as Chief of the Office of Military Cooperation at the American Embassy in Egypt. In May 2005, he was promoted to the rank of Major General.

Bailem, Lester
COMMAND SERGEANT MAJOR—ARMY

Command Sergeant Major Lester Bailem was born in Mobile, Alabama, and entered the Army in 1977. He attended Basic and Advanced Individual Training at Fort Bliss, Texas, graduating with honors as a Nike Hercules Missile Crew member (16B).

He is currently pursuing a bachelor's degree in Re-source Management. His military education includes the First Sergeants Course and the United States Army Sergeants Major Academy.

Bailem's military assignments includes serving as a Launcher Platoon Sergeant in the 2nd Battalion, 43rd Air Defense Artillery, at Hanau, West Germany; Platoon Sergeant and First Sergeant with the 4th Battalion, 7th Air Defense Artillery, at Fort Lewis, Washington; Noncommissioned Officer in Charge of the Inspector Generals Office at the United States Air Defense Center at Fort Bliss, Texas; First Sergeant of the 1st Battalion, 4th Air Defense Artillery, in Wackerheim, West Germany; Operations Sergeant Major of the 1st Battalion, 62nd Armored Corps, at Schofield Barracks, Hawaii; and Operations Sergeant Major of the 69th Air Defense Artillery Brigade, in Giebstadt, Germany. Bailem's most recent assignment was as Battalion Command Sergeant Major in the 6th Battalion, 52nd Air Defense Artillery, at Ansbach, Germany. He is currently serving as the Command Sergeant Major of the 1st Space Battalion, Army Space Command.

Bailey, Margaret E.
COLONEL—ARMY

Colonel Bailey was born in Selma, Alabama, and graduated from Dunbar High School in Mobile. She attended the Fraternal Hospital School of Nursing in Montgomery, Alabama, before receiving a Bachelor of Science degree in Nursing from San Francisco State College.

She entered the United States Army in June 1944. She has held a wide variety of important command and staff positions, including assignments at Fort Huachuca, Arizona; Station Hospital at Florence, Arizona; United States Army Hospital at Camp Beale, California; Halloron General Hospital at Staten Island, New York; Tilton General Hospital at Fort Dix, New Jersey; Percy Jones General Hospital at Battle Creek, Michigan; Madigan General Hospital in Tacoma, Washington; Letterman General Hospital in San Francisco, California; and Fitzsimmons General Hospital at Denver, Colorado.

Her overseas assignments include assignments at the Ninety-Eighth General Hospital in Munich, Germany; the Second General Hospital in Landstuhl, Germany; the United States Army Hospital in Zama, Japan; the 130th General Hospital in Chinon, France; and the United States Army Element in the Job Corps Health Office at the Department of Labor in Washington, D.C.

At Fitzsimmons Hospital, Colonel Bailey was in charge of the Nightingale program which entailed visiting schools of nursing in the Denver area. She was also active in the Colorado Nursing Association and the Colorado League of Nursing.

In 1964, she became the first black Nurse in the United States Army to attain the rank of Lieutenant Colonel. While assigned as Chief Nurse at the 130th General Hospital, in France, she was promoted to Colonel. She became the first black female Nurse to be promoted to full Colonel in the history of the United States Army Nurse Corps.

Baker, Mark
COMMAND MASTER CHIEF—NAVY

Mark Baker is a native of Ann Arbor, Michigan. He enlisted in the Navy on 12 June 1978 and attended recruit training at Recruit Training Command in Illinois. At sea, he served on board USS *Albany* (CG10), USS *Truxtun* (CGN 35), USS *Sacramento* (AOE 1), USS *Nimitz* (CVN 68), USS *John C. Stennis* (CVN 74). Ashore, he served at Security Force Detachment at Naval Air Station Detachment Gaeta, Italy, COMNAVSURFGRUMED/GTG 63, in Naples, Italy. He served as an Instructor/Training Liaison Officer with Afloat Training Group Middle Pacific at Pearl Harbor, Hawaii; and as RDC/Fleet LCPO with Recruit Training Command, Great Lakes. In October 2004, Baker was serving as the Command Master Chief on the USS *Momse* DDG 92.

Baker, Tony L.
COMMAND SERGEANT MAJOR—ARMY

A native of High Point, North Carolina, Baker entered the Army in August 1982, and attended Basic Combat Training at Fort Jackson, South Carolina. He received his Advanced Individual Training for MOS 88k (Watercraft Operator) at Fort Eustis, Virginia.

His civilian and military education includes an associate's degree in Management from Excelsior College; all Noncommissioned Officer Education System Courses; the United States Army Basic Recruiting Course; Drill Sergeant School; NBC Course; and the Unit Equal Opportunity Leaders Course.

His military leadership assignments include serving as Command Sergeant Major of the 37th TRANS-COM; Command Sergeant Major of the 10th Trans-

portation Battalion (Terminal), 7th Transportation Group, at Fort Eustis, Virginia; Task Force 10 Command Sergeant Major for Operation Iraqi Freedom; First Sergeant for Headquarters and Headquarters Company, 24th Transportation Company, 24th Transportation Battalion, at Fort Eustis, Virginia; First Sergeant for E Company, 71st Transportation Battalion, 8th Transportation Brigade, at Fort Eustis, Virginia; First Sergeant for 66th Transportation Company, 28th Transportation Battalion, 37th TRANSCOM in Germany. He has three combat tours: Operation Desert Shield/Storm, Operation Uphold Democracy, and Operation Iraqi Freedom.

Bakker, Esmond
COMMAND SERGEANT MAJOR—ARMY

Command Sergeant Major Esmond Bakker enlisted in the Army on October 30, 1979, and completed Basic and Advanced Individual Training at Fort Jackson, South Carolina. He also attended Advanced and Individual Training and Basic Airborne Training at Fort Benning, Georgia. He has an associate's degree in Management from Regents University and an associate's degree in Information Management from Campbell University; he has earned a Bachelor of Science degree in Information Management from Park College.

His military education includes Pre-Commissioned Officer Course; Battle Staff NCO; Battalion Training Management System; Equal Opportunity NCO; Master Fitness Trainer Course; Operating Room Specialist; Medical Aidman; Personnel Management Specialist; First Sergeant Course at USAREUR; and the United States Army Sergeants Major Academy.

CSM Bakker's most recent assignments include serving as the G-1 Sergeant Major in the 1st COSCOM at Fort Bragg, North Carolina. He is presently serving as the Command Sergeant Major of the United States Army Garrison at Fort Hamilton, New York.

Ballard, Anthony L.
SERGEANT MAJOR—ARMY

Sergeant Major Ballard was born and raised in Atlanta, Georgia. He enlisted in the Army in 1978, and completed his Basic Combat Training and Advanced Individual Training at Fort Benning, Georgia. His military education includes all the Noncommissioned Officers Education System Courses; Senior Leader Course; Equal Opportunity Course; NBC Defense Course; Master Fitness School; United States Army First Sergeants Course; the United States Army Sergeants Major Academy; Drill Sergeant School; Airborne School; and Air Assault Schools.

He has served as Tow Gunner; Squad Leader; Section Sergeant; Senior Drill Sergeant; Platoon Sergeant; Platoon Leader; Company First Sergeant; Noncommissioned Officer in Charge, G3 Plans Section; Battalion Operation Sergeant; Noncommissioned Officer, Force Integration/Force; Operation Sergeant Major; and Chief Enlisted Adviser. In August 2004, Ballard was serving as Sergeant Major with the 3rd Battalion, 196th Infantry Brigade.

Ballard, Joe Nathan
LIEUTENANT GENERAL—ARMY

Ballard was born in Meeker, Louisiana, and grew up in Oakdale, Louisiana. He married the former Tessie LaRose, and they are the parents of three daughters. He received a Bachelor of Science degree in Electrical Engineering from Southern University in Baton Rouge in 1965. He received a Master of Science degree in Engineering Management from the University of Missouri in 1972. He attended the Engineer Officers Basic and Advance Courses, United States Army Command and General Staff College, and the United State Army War College.

He began his career at Fort Dix as a Platoon Leader in the 86th Engineer Battalion, and served his first tour in Vietnam as a Platoon Leader in the 84th Engineer Battalion. He returned to the United States to command Company C, 2nd Training Brigade, at Fort Polk. After attending the Engineer Officer Advanced Course, General Ballard began his second tour in Vietnam where he was commander of Company C, 864th Engineer Battalion, then chief of Lines of Communications Section Operations of the 18th Engineer Brigade.

From August 1990 to January 1991, he served as the Assistant Deputy Chief of Staff, Engineers, United States Army, Europe. In January 1991, he became the Assistant Commandant of the United States Army Engineer School and Deputy Commanding General of Fort Leonard Wood. He was promoted to Brigadier General on October 1, 1991.

From July 1992 to July 1993, Ballard was assigned as Special Assistant to the Director of Management for the Total Army Basing Study in the Office of the Chief of Staff of the United States Army in Washington, D.C. From July 1993 to June 1995, he served as Commanding General of the United States Army Engineer Center at Fort Leonard Wood, Missouri. He was promoted to Major General on August 1, 1994.

From July 1995 to September 1996, he served as Chief of Staff for the United States Army Training and Doctrine Command at Fort Monroe, Virginia. In September 1996, he was selected to serve as the Chief of Engineers and Commanding General of the United States Army Corps of Engineers in Washington, D.C. On October 1, 1996, Ballard was promoted to Lieutenant General. He retired on August 31, 2000.

Ballard, John R.
SERGEANT MAJOR—MARINES

Ballard enlisted into the United States Marine Corps in January of 1978 under the delayed entry program. He reported to Parris Island, South Carolina on May 16, 1978, at Company I, 3rd Recruit Training Battalion.

Upon completion of Recruit Training in July of 1978, he reported to Marine Corps Service Support Schools at Camp Johnson, Camp Lejeune, North Carolina for training as a Basic Automotive Mechanic.

He has held a variety of key leadership positions including serving as a Drill Instructor and Senior Drill Instructor; as Motor Transport Maintenance Chief at Camp Hansen in Okinawa, Japan; as Maintenance/Mimms Chief for the MWSG 27th at New River Air Station in Jacksonville, North Carolina; as Maintenance Chief with the MWSS-273 in Saudi Arabia during Desert Shield/Desert Storm; as Motor Transport Maintenance Chief with H&S Company, 3rd Surveillance Reconnaissance Intelligence Group in Okinawa, Japan; as Maintenance Chief and Company First Sergeant for H&S Company, 8th Comm. Battalion, 2nd Surveillance Reconnaissance Intelligence Group, Camp Lejeune; and as First Sergeant for "Alpha" and "Bravo" Companies of the 2nd Radio Battalion, where he received his Airborne Training and Gold Jump wings. In August 1996, Ballard was assigned to Company "A," Headquarters Battalion, at Henderson Hall, Headquarters of the Marine Corps, where he served as Company First Sergeant until his promotion to Sergeant Major in 1999; he was assigned as the Battalion Major for the 3rd Battalion, 2nd Marine Division, where he served as the Battalion Sergeant Major until August 2003. During that assignment, he participated in two unit deployments, three Combined Arms Exercises, and Salmon Challis Idaho, to fight the Western Wildfires of 2000. He also participated in Combat Operations during Operation Iraqi Freedom from January 2003 to June 2003. In November 2004, he was Sergeant Major for Marine Wing Support Group 27, Second Marine Aircraft Wing, at Cherry Point, North Carolina.

Ballard, Tina
DEPUTY ASSISTANT SECRETARY OF THE ARMY

Tina Ballard holds a Bachelor of Arts degree in English, and has also earned a Master of Science degree in Management and a Master of Science degree in National Resource Strategy. She has completed the Industrial College of the Armed Forces Senior Acquisition Course and Leadership for a Democratic Society Federal Executive Institute.

Prior to her current appointment as the Deputy Assistant Secretary of the Army, Ballard served as the Director of Combat Support Operations and the Deputy Executive Director of Contract Management Operations in the Defense Contract Management Agency. In these positions her responsibilities included contingency contract administration services in multiple theatres of military operations, supplier risk management, quality assurance and engineering support, delivery management, pricing/modification actions, business and financial systems, payment and financial management, contract closeout and industrial base analysis.

As Deputy Assistant Secretary of the Army (Policy and Procurement), she directly supports the Army Acquisition Executive and the Assistant Secretary of the Army (Acquisition, Logistics and Technology), serving as the Army's principal authority for all Army acquisition and procurement programs. In addition, she is responsible for the management and execution of Army contracts.

Banks, Barbaralien

SERGEANT MAJOR—ARMY

A native of New Orleans, Louisiana, where she graduated from Alfred Lawless high School, Banks enlisted in the United States Army in 1988.

She deployed with the 25th Infantry Division to Afghanistan in June 2004, and was promoted to Sergeant Major. Through online correspondence courses, she earned two college degrees in Business Management and Computer Science. Banks planned to return to Schofield Barracks (home of the 25th Infantry Division) in June 2005 and then attend the United States Army Sergeants Major Academy.

She was killed on April 6, 2005, when a CH-47 Chinook helicopter went down in bad weather near Ghazni, about 100 miles southwest of Kabul, Afghanistan's capital, killing 15 U.S. service members and three civilian contractors in the largest single loss of U.S. life in Afghanistan since 2001.

Sergeant Major Banks was the mother of two grown children and a grandmother of three. Her sister, Sergeant First Class Cassandra Jeanpierre, was serving in Kuwait with the 377th Theater Support Command at the time of Banks' death.

Banks, Evelyn P.

COMMAND MASTER CHIEF—NAVY

Command Master Chief Evelyn P. Banks is a native of Memphis, Tennessee, and graduated with honors from Byhalia High School. She enlisted in the United States Navy on January 28, 1984, and completed recruit training in Orlando, Florida.

During her first tour of duty, onboard USS *Samuel Gompers* (AD 37), she attended Mess Management Specialist "A" School, and graduated with honors. Her following tours included the Navy Recruiting District in Memphis, Tennessee, and the Naval Air Station in Adak, Ark. While in Adak, she advanced to Chief Petty Officer and qualified as an Enlisted Aviation Warfare Specialist. Following this assignment, Master Chief Banks served on USS *Acadia* (ad 42). Before the decommissioning of *Acadia* and her transfer to the Navy Recruiting District in Jacksonville, Florida, she advanced to Senior Chief Petty Officer.

Banks attended the Air Force Senior Non-Commissioned Officer Academy at Montgomery, Alabama, prior to arriving to the Pre-commissioning Unit *Decatur* (PCU). At PCU *Decatur*, she advanced to Master Chief Petty Officer. Her first Command Master Chief billet was at Navy Support Facility Diego Garcia, where she accomplished unprecedented milestones

in leadership for the command and the 27 tenant commands under her cognizance.

In addition, Banks is a graduate of the United States Navy Senior Enlisted Academy and served on the Academy Staff as a Faculty Advisor prior to assuming her current position as the Command Master Chief of Carrier Air Wing 14 in Lemoor, Louisiana. She is the First African American female to serve as the Command Master Chief of a Carrier Air Wing. In this capacity she completed a historic 10-month deployment in support of Operation Iraqi Freedom, during which her unit won the coveted Ramage Award for the best CVN team. In February 2005, Banks was serving as CNO Directed Command Master Chief (Aviation/Surface Warfare) for the Commander of Navy Recruiting Command.

Banton, William C., II

BRIGADIER GENERAL—AIR FORCE

William Banton was born in Washington, D.C., and earned a Bachelor of Science degree in Liberal Arts and Science from Howard University. He also received a Doctorate of Medicine from Howard University College of Medicine, and a Master of Public Health from the Johns Hopkins School of Hygiene and Public Health.

Banton was commissioned a Second Lieutenant in the United States Air Force during World War II. He went on to serve in the Korean War, the Cuban Missile Crisis, and the Vietnam War. While serving in the United States Air Force Reserve as General Officer Mobilization Augmentee to the Strategic Air Command, he established a medical management system for SAC's Medical Reserves whereby reserve active duty time was utilized to support United States active force manpower

shortages at SAC bases on a worldwide, year-round basis. This system was subsequently adopted at other United States Major Air Commands. He retired from the United States Air Force Reserve as a Brigadier General, to which rank he had been promoted on April 6, 1973.

His military awards and decorations include the World War II Victory Medal; American Campaign Medal; the Armed Forces Longevity Service Award; the Armed Forces Reserve Medal; the South Vietnam Campaign Medal; the National Defense Service Medal; and the Expert Marksman Medal.

Barfield, Edward

CAPTAIN—NAVY

Barfield began his Navy career in 1980 at Officer Candidate School (OCS) in Newport, Rhode Island. He holds a Bachelor of Arts Degree from Ramapo College of New Jersey and a Master of Arts Degree in National Security and Strategic Studies from the Naval War College.

After commissioning in September 1980, he was assigned to USS *Worden* (CG-18) at Pearl Harbor, where he served as Machinery Division Officer, Boilers Division Officer and Assistant Operation Officer.

In April 1984, he was assigned to COMNAVSUR-FGRU WESTPAC, CTF 7375 at Subic Bay in the Philippines where he served as Cruiser, Destroyer and Frigate Type Desk Officer for the Seventh Fleet. Following completion of Department Head School in February 1987, Barfield was deployed to Sasebo, Japan and served two Department Head tours as Chief Engineer in USS *San Bernardino* (LST 1189) and USS *St Louis* (LKA 116). From August 1991 to June 1992, he attended the College of Naval Command and Staff at the Naval War College at Newport, Rhode Island. In December 1992, Barfield returned to sea duty in Japan onboard USS *San Bernardino* (LST 1189) where he served as Executive Officer until April 1994. From May 1994 to March 1996, he served as Amphibious and TYCOM Placement Officer at the Bureau of Naval Personnel, duties as Naval Branch Head, Current Operations (US-CENTCOM) in Tampa, Florida. In September 1998, he assumed duties as Commanding Officer of USS *Comstock* (LSD 45) the flagship for the Commander of Squadron One during the Cooperation Afloat Readiness and Training (CARAT) deployment to Southeast Asia in 1999. During his tour, *Comstock* was awarded the CNO Afloat Safety award, the CINCPACFLT Golden Anchor and the Battle Efficiency "E" award.

Following command, he was assigned to the staff of Commander Seventh Fleet as Fleet Operations Officer aboard USS *Blue Ridge* (LCC19) in Yokosuka, Japan. In August 2002, Barfield reported to the Pentagon as Special Assistant to the Chief of Operations for Equal Opportunity and Diversity.

Barnes, Thomas N.

COMMAND CHIEF MASTER SERGEANT—
AIR FORCE

Chief Barnes was born in Chester, Pennsylvania, where he attended elementary and secondary schools. He is a graduate of the 8th Air Force Noncommissioned Officer Academy and the United States Air Force Senior NCO Academy pilot class. In 1949, he entered the United States Air Force, and received his basic training at Lackland Air Force Base in Texas. He later attended Aircraft and Engine School and Hydraulic Specialist School at Chanute Technical Training Center in Illinois. He was promoted to Chief Master Sergeant on December 1, 1969, and was transferred to Headquarters Air Training Command in October 1971 to assume duties as Command Senior Enlisted Adviser.

On October 1, 1973, Barnes became Chief Master Sergeant of the Air Force. At the expiration of the position's initial two-year tenure, his term was extended for an additional year by the Chief of Staff. In February 1979, he was selected by the Chief of Staff to serve an unprecedented second year extension. He served as Advisor to Secretaries of the Air Force John L. McLucas and Thomas C. Reed and also Chief of Staffs of the Air Force General George S. Brown and General David C. Jones on matters concerning the welfare, effective utilization, and progress of the enlisted members of the Air Force. He was the Fourth Chief Master Sergeant appointed to this position, the highest a noncommissioned officer can reach in the Air Force, and the first African American to be so selected.

Barr, Caleb, III

SERGEANT MAJOR—ARMY

Sergeant Major Barr is a native of Denver, Colorado, and enlisted in the United States Army in November 1974. He attended Basic Combat Training at Fort Leonard Wood, Missouri and Advanced Individual Training for Armor Crewmen at Fort Knox, Kentucky.

His military education includes all Noncommissioned Officer Education System Courses; Civilian Personnel Management Course; Joint Readiness Training Center Observer Controller Course; School of Cadet Command Training Course; and the United States Army Sergeants Major Academy.

Barr's key leadership assignments include serving three tours in West Germany; a tour in the Middle East during Operation Desert Storm; and a tour in South Korea. He has served as a Combat Brigade and Battalion Operations Sergeant Major; a Tank Company First Sergeant; a Tank Platoon and Section Sergeant; a Tank Commander; a Radar Team Leader; a and Cavalry Scout Squad Leader.

Bartelle, Michael
COMMAND SERGEANT MAJOR—ARMY

A native of the Bronx, New York City, Bartelle entered the Army on June 29, 1979, and attended One Station Unit Training at Fort Gordon, Georgia. His military and civilian education includes all Noncommissioned Officer Courses, NBC Officer Defense Course, Air Assault School, Communication-Electronics Course, and the United States Army Sergeants Major Academy (class of 49).

Since entering the Army, he has served five tours overseas. He served as Command Sergeant Major for the 125th Signal Battalion, 25th Infantry Division (Lt); as First Sergeant on two tours with the 1st Signal Brigade in South Korea; as Platoon Sergeant with the 32nd Army Air Defense Command and with V (US) Corps. In August 2004, Bartelle was serving as the Command Sergeant Major for the United States Army with NATO.

Battle, Reginald C.
COMMAND SERGEANT MAJOR—ARMY

Born in Valdosta, Georgia, Battle entered the United States Army on July 10, 1979, and attended Basic Training at Fort McClellan, Alabama and Advanced Individual Training at Redstone Arsenal, Alabama where he was designated MOS 55B-Ammunition Storage Specialist.

His military and civilian education include all Noncommissioned Officer Education System Courses; the Air Assault and Rappel Master Course at Fort Campbell, Kentucky; the United States Army Recruiter Course at Fort Benjamin Harrison, Indiana; the First Sergeant Course at Vilseek, Germany; the First Sergeant Course at Fort Bliss, Texas; Cadre Training Course at Fort Jackson, South Carolina; and the United States Army Sergeants Major Academy (class 51). He also earned an associate's degree from Excelsior College.

Battle has held numerous leadership positions, including serving as Squad Leader; Advanced Individual Training Instructor; Storage Noncommissioned Officer; Section Sergeant; Platoon Sergeant; Operations Sergeant; First Sergeant; Brigade S-3 Sergeant Major; and Support Operations Sergeant Major. In September 2004, he was serving as Command Sergeant Major for the 6th Ordnance Battalion, 19th Theater Support Command.

Battle, Timothy
COMMAND SERGEANT MAJOR—ARMY

Timothy Battle was born in Georgia and entered the Army in November 1977. He attended Basic and Advanced Individual Training at Fort Gordon, Georgia, qualifying as a Radio Teletype Operator (O5F). His military education includes all Noncommissioned Officer Courses, Airborne School, Air Assault Course, and Sergeants Major Academy. He has also completed two years of college in pursuit of a degree in Military Science.

During his twenty-five years of service, Battle served in leadership positions ranging from Radio Teletype Team Chief to Interim Command Sergeant Major. He served as Operation Sergeant Major with the Headquarters and Headquarters Company, 7th Signal Brigade. In August 2004, he was serving as Command Sergeant Major for the 10th Signal Battalion, 10th Mountain Division (LT).

His awards include the Bronze Star, Meritorious Service Medal (first oak leaf cluster), Army Achievement Medal (four oak leaf clusters), Good Conduct Medal, Southwest Asia Medal (with 3 campaign stars), Kuwait Liberation Medal (Kuwait and Saudi Arabia), Air Assault Badge, and Airborne Badge.

Bayless, Harvey
MAJOR—AIR FORCE

Harvey Bayless was inducted into the armed services in May 1943. Serving in the 96th Service Group in support of the 332nd Fighter Group in Italy in 1944, he received a field promotion to Second Lieutenant and served as a Communications Maintenance Officer. He was honorably discharged in 1946.

The Air Force recalled Bayless to active duty during the Korean War. Serving in several capacities during the conflict, he was honorably discharged from the Air Force in 1953 and reassigned to the Air Force Reserves. He retired from the Reserves in 1984.

Beason, Stanley H.
COMMAND MASTER CHIEF—NAVY

Command Master Chief Stanley H. Beason enlisted in the Navy in September 1974 in Milwaukee, Wisconsin. After attending Recruit Training at Naval Station Great Lakes in Illinois, he reported aboard the USS *Denver* (LPD-9) in January 1975. In March of 1975, he made his first deployment to the Western Pacific, participating in the evacuation of Saigon. In November 1978, he reported to USS *Sperry* (AS-12) at Ballast Point in San Diego, California. In March 1981, Beason reported aboard USS *Alamo* (LSD-33) in San Diego, California. He was screened for recruiting duty in March 1983, and was assigned to Navy Recruiting District Albuquerque, New Mexico. After a successful tour as a recruiter he served again on USS *Alamo* (LSD-33) from June 1986. While stationed aboard the *Alamo*, he was promoted to Chief Petty Officer.

In January 1990, Beason received orders to Naval Air Station Corpus Christi, Texas where he served as Airfield Facilities Officer. In February 1994, he reported aboard USS *Fort Fisher* (LSD-40), where he qualified as Officer of the Deck (Underway), and was promoted to Senior Chief Petty Officer. In February 1998, he received orders to Navy Region Southwest Transient Personnel Unit in San Diego, California, serving as Discipline Department Head and Command Master Chief. He attended the Senior Enlisted Academy in 2001, and after graduation became Command Master Chief Helicopter Anti-Submarine Squadron Six at North Island, California.

Beckles, Benita J. Harris
COLONEL—AIR FORCE

Colonel Beckles was born in Chicago, Illinois, to Felicia and Benjamin Harris, and she attended elementary and high school in Chicago. She married Lionel Beckles and they have two sons. Beckles received a Bachelor of Arts degree in Sociology from Hampton University in 1971 and a Master of Arts degree in Education from George Washington University in 1977. She was commissioned a Second Lieutenant in the Air Force on October 19, 1973 after completing Officer Training School at Medina Annex, Lackland Air Force Base, Texas. From October 1973 to November 1975, she was assigned as a personnel officer with the 4500 Air Base Wing at Langley Air Force Base, Virginia. She was promoted to First Lieutenant on October 19, 1975. From December 1975 and June 1979, Beckles was a Test Control Officer and Joint Processing Officer at the Chicago Military Enlistment Processing Station. She was promoted to Captain on October 19, 1977.

In 1979, she attended Squadron Officer School at Maxwell Air Force Base, Alabama. Her next assignment was that of Personnel Officer with the 56th Combat Support Group at MacDill Air Force Base, Florida, from July 1979 to July 1980. From February 1981 to November 1988, she was Personnel Officer with the 403rd Combat Support Squadron at the 927th Airlift Group at Selfridge Air National Guard Base, Michigan. She was promoted to Major on October 19, 1987. From June 1991 to October 1993, she served as Chief of Personnel with the 927th Mission Support Squadron at Selfridge Air National Guard Base. In October 1993, she was selected as Commander of the 927th Mission Support Squadron and part of the 27th Air Refueling Wing, at Selfridge Air National Guard Base. In this

position, she is responsible for providing the management and overall direction of a full range of support programs, including Military Personnel, Information Management, Morale, Welfare and Recreation, Food Services, and Family Readiness. She was still serving in this position in 1997. She was promoted to Lieutenant Colonel on October 19, 1994, and has also served as an Air Force Academy Liaison Officer.

Beckles' military awards and decorations include the Air Force Meritorious Service Medal; the Joint Service Commendation Medal; and the National Defense Service Medal. She was also a 1995 Regional Finalist in the White House Fellowship Program.

Becton, Julius W.
LIEUTENANT GENERAL—ARMY

Born in Bryn Mawr, Pennsylvania, Becton married the former Louise Thornton, and they have five children, Shirley, Karen, Joyce, Renee, and Wesley. They also have six grandchildren. General Becton's public service career includes two key federal positions after nearly 40 years of active commissioned service in the United States Army, rising to the rank of Lieutenant General. He is the first graduate of Prairie View A&M University to be unanimously elected president by the Board of Regents.

He enlisted in the United States Army in July 1944 and graduated from Officer Candidate School in 1945. A veteran of World War II and the Korean and Vietnam conflicts, he served in various positions at scores of posts in this country. Overseas duties carried him to Germany, the Philippines, France, the Southwest Pacific, Korea and Japan. Prior to his acceptance of the position of president of Prairie View A&M University, he served

as Chief Operating Officer for American Coastal Industries. In 1996, became superintendent of the Washington, D.C. schools.

Beldo, April D.
COMMAND MASTER CHIEF—NAVY

Beldo's military assignments include serving at Naval Hospital ARD in Corpus Christi, Texas; on the USS *Abraham Lincoln* (CVN 72); and USS *Kitty Hawk* (CV 63) at HS-6 Naval Air Station at North Island, California; at the Recruit Training Command in Great Lakes, Illinois; Commander, Naval Force, United States Atlantic Fleet, AMMT, at Norfolk, Virginia; and on the USS *George Washington* (CVN 73) at Norfolk, Virginia.

She was selected into the Command Master Chief Program in November 2002, and is a graduate of the Senior Enlisted Academy (class 100 Gold) in Newport, Rhode Island. In February 2005, she was serving as the Command Master Chief of the USS *Bulkeley* (DDG-84).

Bell, Leroy Crawford
BRIGADIER GENERAL—ARMY

Born in Tampa, Florida, Bell studied at Florida A&M University, Shippensburg State College, Air Defense Artillery School, Airborne School, Field Artillery School, Command and General Staff College, and the United States Army War College.

His military career began in 1955, when he was commissioned as a second lieutenant in the Field Artillery through the ROTC program at Florida A&M University. His early assignments included duty with the 32nd Air Defense Brigade in Langekoph, Germany, and command of A Battery, 2nd Battalion, 42nd Field Artillery at Fort Benning, Georgia, from 1964 to 1965. From 1965 to 1966, he served in Vietnam where he

commanded A Battalion, 19th Field Artillery, with the 1st Air Cavalry Division.

He graduated from the United States Army War College in 1976 and was assigned as Chief of the Manpower Survey Team in the Inspections and Surveys Division in the Department of the Army's Inspector General Agency in Washington, D.C., from September 1976 to January 1979. In 1979, Leroy Crawford Bell was promoted to the rank of Brigadier General, and assigned as the adjutant general for the District of Columbia Army National Guard.

Bell, Wayne R.
SERGEANT MAJOR—MARINES

He was born in Washington, D.C., and enlisted in the Marine Corps on February 26, 1977, in Boston, Massachusetts. Upon completion of recruit training at Parris Island, South Carolina, he was assigned to AAV School at the 2nd Assault Amphibian Battalion at Camp Lejeune, North Carolina. Upon completion of the school he reported to Company D for duty as an AAV Crewman.

His military leadership assignments include serving as Crew Chief and Classroom Instructor at School's Battalion at the Assault Amphibian School, MCB at Camp Pendleton, California; Section Leader; Company Gunnery Sergeant; Guard Chief; Training Staff Noncommissioned Officer in Charge; First Sergeant; and Sergeant Major, 1st Marine Division.

Bellamy, Jefferson
SERGEANT MAJOR—MARINES

Bellamy entered into the United States Marine Corps in 1980, and attended Recruit Training at the Marine

Corps Recruit Depot at Parris Island, South Carolina. In October 1986, he attended Nuclear Ordnance Training School at Marie Barracks at Naval Air Station North Island San Diego, California. In February 1990, he attended Aviation Life Support System School in MATSG, NATTC, at Lakehourst, New Jersey. Upon completion of Parachute Rigger School, he was assigned to HMLA 269, MAAG 29, MCAS New River at Jacksonville, North Carolina. Shortly after reporting to New River, he assumed the duty of Senior Noncommissioned Officer in Charge of Flight Equipment. In September 1993, he attended Drill Instructor School at Marine Corps Recruit Depot, Parris Island, South Carolina. Upon completion of Drill Instructor School he was assigned to Alpha Company, 1st Recruit Training Battalion as Drill Instructor, Senior Drill Instructor and Series Chief Instructor. In October 1995, Bellamy was assigned as Squad Instructor at the Drill Instructor School at Parris Island. In May 1998, he served as First Sergeant at the 1st Stinger Battery MACG-18. In October 2004, he was serving as the Sergeant Major of Marine Air Control Squadron 2, Marine Air Control Group 21, 2nd Marine Aircraft Wing.

Bennett, Kevin S.
SERGEANT MAJOR—MARINE

Sergeant Major Kevin S. Bennett enlisted in the Marine Corps in June 1971 and underwent training at 3rd Recruit Training Battalion at Parris Island, South Carolina. Upon completion of Recruit and Infantry Training Schools at Camp Geiger, North Carolina and San Onofre, Camp Pendleton, California, he was assigned to Charlie Company, 1st Battalion, 7th Marines and later to Lima Company, 3rd Battalion, 1st Marines, from which he was honorably discharged from active service in August 1973.

He returned to active duty in 1976 as a Lance Corporal and was assigned to Echo Company, 2nd Battal-

ion, 1st Marines. In August 1978, he was transferred to Okinawa, Japan where he served with Fox Company, 2nd Battalion, 4th Marines.

In December 1998, Bennett was transferred to Headquarters Marine Corps for duty as the Inspector General Sergeant Major for the Marine Corps. In November 1999, he was transferred to Quantico, Virginia, where he assumed his present duties as the Sergeant Major of the Marine Corps Combat Development Command.

Bentley, Lynn, Jr.
CHIEF MASTER SERGEANT—AIR FORCE

Bentley was born in September 1937 in Thomson, Georgia. A graduate of McDuffie High School, he enlisted in the United States Air Force on March 18, 1955. He served his first two years in a Refueling Unit at Turner Air Force Base in Albany, Georgia. From August 1959 to July 1968, Bentley served as a fuels warehouse attendant, with a Refueling Unit, Hydrant Fuels, and Oils Warehouse attendant, at first Hunter Air Force Base, in Georgia and later at Goose Air Base, in Labrador.

In August 1968, he was assigned as a Distribution Supervisor Non-Commissioned Officer in Charge/Attendant of the Fuels Storage Section at Ubon Airfield in Thailand, and later at Richard Gebaur Air Force Base in Missouri.

In January 1973, he became the Non-Commissioned Officer in Charge of Base Fuels Quality Control at Luke Air Force Base in Arizona. In July 1974, as a Master Sergeant, Bentley was assigned as the Distribution Non-Commissioned Officer in Charge and Fuels Manager at Eielson Air Force Base in Arkansas.

In June 1977, he assumed duties of Logistics Fuels Manager at Tyndall Air Force Base in Florida. In Au-

gust 1982, he became Fuels Manager for 15 MAC Base Fuels Branches at Scott Air Force Base in Illinois. He was promoted to Chief Master Sergeant in October 1982, and retired from the Air Force on April 1, 1985.

Benton, Valerie D.
COMMAND CHIEF MASTER SERGEANT—
AIR FORCE

Chief Master Sergeant Valerie D. Benton is the eighth Command Chief Master Sergeant for the Director of the Air National Guard at the National Guard Bureau in Washington, D.C. She is responsible for all affairs concerning the enlisted personnel of the Air

National Guard, and was promoted to Chief Master Sergeant on October 1, 2000.

She was an active duty Air Force enlisted member for twelve years, and then served as an Active Guard/Reserve member of the Kansas Air National Guard. She then served as the Air National Guard First Sergeant Functional Manager, United States Air Force First Sergeant Academy, at Maxwell Air Force Base, in Alabama, until her current assignment.

In August 2004, she received the eagle statue during a ceremony.

Bernard, Victor E.
COMMAND MASTER CHIEF—NAVY

He is a native of Brooklyn, New York, where he joined the Navy in January 1977. He completed Basic Training and Fire Controlman "A" and "C" School at Naval Training Center Great Lakes Illinois, graduating as an FTG3.

From June 1990 to July 2003, he served sea tours onboard USS *Arleigh Burke* (DDG 51) and USS *Mitscher* (DDG 57) as the Combat Systems Maintenance Manager (CSMM). He served on the commissioning crew of USS *Oscar Autin* (DDG 79) and USS *Cole* (DDG 67), post blast crew as department Leading Chief Petty Officer and CSMM. Upon completion of his tour onboard USS *Mitscher*, he advanced to Senior Chief Petty Officer. Upon completion of his tour onboard USS *Oscar Austin* he qualified as Command Duty Officer. While serving onboard USS *Cole*, he was advanced to Master Chief Petty Officer in March 2002. Upon completion of his tour onboard USS *Cole* he attended the Navy Senior Enlisted Academy and became Command Master Chief onboard the USS *Nitze* (DDG 94).

Berthoud, Kenneth M., Jr.
LIEUTENANT COLONEL—MARINES

Berthoud was born on December 28, 1928, in New York, New York, and attended high school grammar and high schools there. He attended Lincoln University in Pennsylvania for two years and graduated with a Bachelor of Arts degree from Long Island University

in 1952. He was commissioned in the Marine Corps Reserve as a second lieutenant after completing a course at the Basic School at Quantico, Virginia, on December 13, 1952. He accepted a Regular appointment on July 13, 1953, and was the second black officer to receive a Regular Marine Corps commission.

He served as a group and Battalion Operations Officer in Viet-

nam until his return to the United States in 1967. From 1967 to 1970, he was assigned as a Special Advisor in the G-1 (Personnel) Division of the Headquarters of the Marine Corps to develop plans for increasing the number of black officers in the Marine Corps. He married the former Joyce Elsie Hunt and they have three children.

Billups, Rufus L.
MAJOR GENERAL—AIR FORCE

Billups was born in Birmingham, Alabama, and married the former Margaret C. Talton of New Orleans. They have three children Eric, Geraldine and Robert. He graduated for Parker High School in Birmingham, Alabama, and earned a Bachelor of Science from the Tuskegee Institute in Alabama in 1949. He received a Master of Science in Business from the University of Colorado in 1957, and has an honorary Doctorate from Guadalupe College of Texas.

During the Korean War, he was assigned as an Air Force Liaison Officer at the Army Ports of Pusan and Inchon. In August 1968, he was assigned to Tan Son Nhut Air Base in Vietnam as Director of Aerial Port Operations for the 2nd Aerial Port Group. During this one-year tour of duty, he flew 56 combat missions. He was appointed Commander of the Defense General Supply Center at the Defense Supply Agency in Richmond, Virginia, in September 1975. He became the Director of Logistics Plans, Programs, and Transportation in the Office of the Deputy Chief of Staff, Logistics, and Engineering at the Headquarters of the United States Air Force in Washington, D.C., in August 1978.

He was appointed Major General on July 1, 1978, with date of rank September 1, 1974.

Bishop, Robert
COMMAND SERGEANT MAJOR—ARMY

A native of Starkville, Mississippi, Bishop enlisted in the United States Army in September 1974, and attended Basic and Advanced Individual Training at Fort Polk, Louisiana.

His military and civilian education includes all Noncommissioned Master Fitness Courses; Instructor Training Course; the First Sergeant Course; and the United States Army Sergeant Major Academy (class 42). He is also pursuing a degree in Aviation Maintenance.

Bishop has served in every leadership position in the Aviation Field, including duty with the 58th Infantry Brigade at Fort Benning, Georgia; 82nd Airborne Division at Fort Bragg, North Carolina; Aviation School at Fort Eustis, Virginia; 24th Infantry Division at Fort Stewart, Georgia; and the elite Task Force 160th Special Operations Regiment at Fort Campbell, Kentucky.

Bivens, Nolen V.
BRIGADIER GENERAL—ARMY

Bivens received an ROTC commission as Second Lieutenant on June 2, 1976. His military and civilian education includes Infantry Officer Basic and Advanced Courses; the United States Army Command and General Staff College; and the National War College. He earned a Bachelor of Science in Chemistry from South Carolina State University; a Master of Science in Management from Naval Postgraduate School; and a Master of Science in National Security and Strategic Studies from the National Defense University.

He has held a wide variety of command and staff assignments including Commander of the 3rd Battalion, 7th Infantry, 24th Infantry Division (Mechanized) at Fort Stewart, Georgia; Chief of the Combat Analysis Division (Later Chief of War Gaming, Simulations, and Analysis Division, J-5/J-7) of United States Special Operations Command at MacDill Air Force Base, Florida; Commander of the Basic Combat Training

Brigade at Fort Benning, Georgia; Chief of the Support Agency at Reform and Assessment Division, Joint Warfighting Capability Assessment Directorate, later Chief of Staff of the Office of the Director for Force Structure, Resources and Assessment, J-8, at the Joint Staff, Washington, D.C.; Deputy Director for Requirements at the Office of the Deputy Chief of Staff, G-3, United States Army, Washington, D.C. On July 1, 2004, he was promoted to Brigadier General and assigned as Assistant Division Commander (Maneuver) of the 4th Infantry Division (Mechanized) at Fort Hood, Texas. On April 12, 2005, he was assigned as Assistant Chief of Staff, C-3, Coalition Forces Land Component Command, at Camp Arifjan, Kuwait.

His awards and decorations include the Defense Superior Service Medal; the Legion of Merit; the Defense Meritorious Service Medal; Meritorious Service Medal (with 5 Oak Leaf Clusters); Army Commendation Medal (with Oak Leaf Cluster); Army Achievement Medal; Expert Infantryman Badge; Parachutist Badge; Joint Chiefs of Staff Identification Badge; and the Army Staff Identification Badge.

Black, Berry
REAR ADMIRAL—NAVY

Rear Admiral Black is a native of Baltimore, Maryland, and an alumnus of Oakwood College, Andrews University, North Carolina Central University, Eastern Baptist Seminary, Salve Regina College, and United States International University. He earned Master of Arts degrees in Divinity, Counseling, and Management, as well as a doctorate's degree in Ministry and Psychology.

Commissioned as a Navy Chaplain in 1976, Rear Admiral Black's first duty station was the Fleet Religious Support Activity in Norfolk, Virginia. Subsequent assignments included Naval Support Activity in Philadelphia, Pennsylvania; U.S. Naval Academy at

Annapolis, Maryland; First Marine Aircraft Wing at Okinawa, Japan; Naval Training Center at San Diego, California; USS *Belleau Wood* (LHA 3) at Long Beach, California; Naval Chaplains School Advanced Course at Newport, Rhode Island; Marine Aircraft Group Thirty-One at Beaufort, South Carolina; Assistant Staff Chaplain, Chief of Naval Education and Training at Pensacola, Florida; and Fleet Chaplain for the U.S. Atlantic Fleet in Norfolk, Virginia.

In 2000, he was promoted to Rear Admiral (upper half) Chief of Navy Chaplains. He is the first African American to serve in this position.

Black, Carl E.

CHIEF WARRANT OFFICER—ARMY

He entered the United States Army in September 1953 in Wilmington, North Carolina. After completing Basic Training at Fort Jackson, South Carolina, and AIT at Fort Sill, Oklahoma, he remained at Fort Sill through 1955. He completed Basic Airborne School at Fort Bragg, North Carolina in 1956 and was assigned to the 101st Airborne Division at Fort Campbell, Kentucky, where he completed Jumpmaster School and served as Senior Message Clerk until September 1957. He was assigned to the 7th Infantry Division in South Korea as Communications Team Chief from September 1957 to September 1958, returning to the 101st Airborne Division as Operations and Intelligence Sergeant until January 1965. He trained as Apprentice Criminal Investigator at Fort Campbell in Detachment C of the 3rd Military Police Group until 1966, then continued this training with the 1st Brigade, 101st Airborne Division in Vietnam. He returned to the United States in 1967 and completed the Criminal Investigator Course at Fort Gordon, Georgia.

He was promoted to Warrant Officer in 1969 at Fort

Bragg where he served as a Criminal Investigator and commanded the 125th Military Police Detachment (Criminal Investigation) until October 1970. After formal schooling, he became a Legal Administrative Technician (MIS 713A) serving at XVIII Airborne Corps and subsequently at the 82nd Airborne Division SJA Offices from October 1972 until 1977.

After a tour at U.S. Army Forces Command at Fort McPherson, Georgia, CW4 Black returned to the 82nd Airborne Division until he retired in October 1984. Mr. Black returned home to Wilmington, North Carolina, where he taught Junior Reserve Officer Training Corps cadets for five years; opened a branch campus for Campbell University at Camp Lejeune, North Carolina; and became the Executive Director of non-profit Family Resource Center in Wilmington. He also teaches "Welfare to Work" and high school classes.

CW4 (R) Black was made the Honorary Regimental Warrant Officer of the Judge Advocate General's Corps in 1999.

Blackwell, William S.

COMMAND SERGEANT MAJOR—ARMY

He enlisted in the United States Army in January 1980, and attended One Station Unit Training at Fort Knox, Kentucky. His military education includes all the Noncommissioned Officer Education System Courses; Drill Sergeant School; Air Assault Course; Battle Staff Course; First Sergeant Course; United States Army Sergeants Major Academy (class 51); and the Command Sergeant Major (D) Course.

His military leadership assignments include serving as a Platoon Sergeant with the 3-35 Army in Bamberg, Germany; as a Drill Sergeant at Fort Knox; as First Sergeant for E-Company, 2-1 46th Infantry; and as Senior ROTC Instructor at Central State University in Wilberforce, Ohio. He served as Command Sergeant Major for the 1st Battalion, 37th Armor Regiment at Friedberg, Germany; Command Sergeant Major of the 1st Squadron, 1st US Cavalry; and Command Sergeant Major of the 279th Base Support Battalion in Bamberg, Germany.

Blair, Jimmie A.

SERGEANT MAJOR—MARINES

Blair enlisted into the United States Marine Corps in July 1977. His military education includes Drill Instructor School; Platoon Sergeants Course; and Staff Noncommissioned Officers Academy.

His key leadership positions include serving as Platoon Sergeant at Marine Barracks Yorktown, Virginia; Dragons Platoon Section Leader; and Platoon Sergeant for the 2nd Battalion, 5th Marine Regiment, 1st Marine Division. In June 1992 he reported to Marine Barracks 8th and I, Washington, D.C., where he served as Platoon Sergeant for the Marine Corps Silent Drill Platoon. He also served at Headquarters and Support Battalion, Marine Corps Base where he was the First Sergeant of the Military Police Company. In October 2004, he became Sergeant Major of Marine Medium

Helicopter Squadron 261, Group 26, 2nd Marine Aircraft Wing.

Blakely, Shirley A.
CAPTAIN—NAVY

Blakely became a registered dietitian following completion of a dietetic internship at Fitzsimons General

Hospital in Denver, Colorado, and worked as a dietitian in the United States Army. She later obtained her Master of Science and Ph.D. degrees in nutritional sciences.

She was selected as the Chief Professional Officer for the dietitian category effective September 1, 2000. As Chief Dietitian Officer, she is responsible for providing leadership and coordination of Public Health Service (PHS) dietitian professional affairs for the Office of the Surgeon General and the Dietitian Professional Advisory Committee on matters such as recruitment, retention, and career development of PHS dietitians.

Blanks, Charles O'Neal
COMMAND MASTER CHIEF—NAVY

Blanks began his naval career in September 1978, attending Basic Training at Naval Technical Training Center Orlando, Florida. He attended and graduated from AD "A" School in Memphis, Tennessee. In October 2004, he was serving as Command Master Chief for Strike Fighter Squadron One Two Five (VFA 125, Rough Raider).

Blount, Harold
COMMAND SERGEANT MAJOR—ARMY

Blount was born in Bradley, Georgia and joined the Army in November 1976. He received his Basic Combat Training at Fort Dix, New Jersey and was an Honor Graduate of his Advanced Individual Training at Fort Lee, Virginia. He holds an associate's degree from Georgia Military College, in Milledgeville, Georgia, and a bachelor's degree (cum laude) from Excelsior College in Albany, New York.

His military education includes all the Noncommissioned Officer Education System Courses; Recruiter Trainer Course; Master Fitness Trainer Course; Station Commander Course; Recruiter Trainer Course; First Sergeant Course; Command Sergeant Major Course; and the United States Army Sergeants Major Academy.

In 1982, Blount began his career with the United States Army Recruiting Command. His assignments include serving as a Field Recruiter; on-Production Station Commander; Limited-Production Station Commander; Recruiter Trainer; Instructor at the Recruiting and Retention School (1989 Instructor of the Year); First Sergeant (United States Army Recruiting East Command First Sergeant of the Year 1992–1993); Sergeant Major of the Columbus Recruiting Battalion; Sergeant Major of the New York Recruiting Battalion; Recruiting and Retention School Command Sergeant Major from August 1999 to August 2001; and 5th Recruiting Brigade Command Sergeant Major from September 2001 to May 2003. In October 2004, Blount was serving as the Command Sergeant Major for the United States Army Recruiting Command at Fort Knox, Kentucky.

Bluford, Guion Stewart
COLONEL—AIR FORCE

worked with the Space Shuttle's Remote Manipulator System (RMS), Spacelab-3 experiments, Shuttle Avionics Integration Laboratory (SAIL), and the Flight Systems Laboratory (FSL). Bluford first served as a mission specialist on STS-8, which was launched from Kennedy Space Center, Florida, on August 30, 1983. This was the third flight for the shuttle *Challenger* and the first mission with a night launch and night landing. During the mission, the STS-8 crew deployed the Indian National Satellite (INSAT-1B), operated the Canadian-built Remote Manipulator System (RMS) with the Payload Flight Test Article (PFTA), operated the Continuous Flow Electrophoresis System (CFES) with live cell samples, conducted medical measurements to understand biophysiological effects of space flight and activated various earth resources and space science experiments, along with four Getaway Special canisters. STS-8 completed 98 orbits of the Earth in 145 hours before landing at Edwards Air Force Base, California, on September 5, 1983. Bluford was next a mission specialist on STS 61-A, the German D-1 Space lab mission, which was launched from Kennedy Space Center, on October 30, 1985, aboard the *Challenger.* This was the largest crew to fly to date, and was the first dedicated Spacelab mission under the direction of the German Aerospace Research Establishment (DFVLR) and the first U.S. mission in which payload was transferred to a foreign country (German Space Operations Center in Oberpfaffenhofen, Germany). After completing 111 orbits of the Earth in 169 hours the *Challenger* landed at Edwards Air Force Base, California, on November 6, 1985. With the completion of this flight Bluford had logged a total of 314 hours in space. In 1987, he served as astronaut office point of contact for generic Space lab issues and external tank issues, including payload development, hazard analysis, crew interface issues and design certification.

Born in Philadelphia, Pennsylvania, Colonel Bluford married the former Linda Tull of Philadelphia, and they have two sons, Guion Stewart III and James Trevor. He graduated from Overbrook Senior High School in Philadelphia in 1960. He received a Bachelor of Science in Aerospace Engineering from Pennsylvania State University in 1964; an Master of Science with distinction in Aerospace Engineering from the Air Force Institute of Technology in 1974; a Ph.D. in Aerospace Engineering with a minor in Laser Physics from the Air Force Institute of Technology in 1978; and an M.B.A. from the University of Houston at Clear Lake in 1987. Bluford attended pilot training at Williams Air Force Base, Arizona, and received his wings in January 1965. He then underwent F-4C combat crew training in Arizona and Florida and was assigned to the 557th Tactical Fighter Squadron at Cam Ranh Bay, Vietnam. He flew 144 combat missions, 65 of which were over North Vietnam. In July 1967, he was assigned to the 3530th Flying Training Wing at Sheppard Air Force Base, Texas, as a T-38A instructor pilot, serving as a standardization/evaluation officer and as an assistant flight commander. In early 1971, he attended Squadron Officers School and returned as an executive support officer to the deputy commander of operations and as school secretary for the wing. In 1974, he was assigned to the Air Force Flight Dynamics Laboratory at Wright-Patterson Air Force Base, Ohio, as a staff development engineer. He served as deputy for advanced concepts for the Aeromechanics Division and as branch chief of the Aerodynamics and Airframe Branch in the laboratory. Bluford has written and presented several scientific papers in the area of computational fluid dynamics. He has logged over 4,800 hours jet flight time in the T-33, T-37, T-38, T-4C, U-2/TR-1, and F-5A/B, including 1,300 hours as a T-38 instructor pilot. He also has an FAA commercial pilot's license. Bluford became a NASA astronaut in August 1979, and has

Blunt, Roger Reckling

MAJOR GENERAL—ARMY

Born in Providence, Rhode Island, Blunt married the former DeRosette Y. Hendricks, and they have four children, Roger, Jr., Jennifer Mari, Jonathan Hendricks, and Amy Elizabeth. He was graduated from the United States Military Academy in 1956 with a Bachelor of Science degree, and was the only black in his class. He also received a Master of Science from the Massachusetts Institute of Technology in 1962. He entered the United States Army Corps of Engineers as an engineer officer in

1956 and served in numerous assignments until 1969, when he transferred to the United States Army Reserves. He was appointed Major General in the United States Army Reserves in 1983. He was awarded the Distinguished Service Medal in 1986.

He has served as CEO and Chairman of the Tyroc Construction Company, and Chairman of the Board and President of Blunt Enterprises, Inc.

Bly, William H., Jr.
SERGEANT MAJOR—MARINE

Bly enlisted in the United States Marine Corps in June 1977 and attended Recruit Training at the Marine Corps Recruit Depot in San Diego, California. He attended training for Armored Assault Vehicles at Camp Pendleton, California. Upon graduation from Military Occupational Specialty, he was transferred to Inspector and Instruction at Little Creek, Virginia.

His key military assignments include serving as Drill Instructor; Platoon Commander; Senior Drill Instructor; Series Chief Drill Instructor; and First Sergeant. In January 2000, he was assigned to the 26th Marine Expeditionary Unit where he served as Sergeant Major for Marine Expeditionary Unit Service Support 26 Group. In June 2002, he was assigned to II Marine Expeditionary Force, 2nd Force Reconnaissance Company where he served as the very first First Sergeant Major of that Unit. In April 2004, he was assigned as the Sergeant Major of the 2nd Marine Aircraft Wing, MAG29, at New River, North Carolina.

Boddie, James T., Jr.
BRIGADIER GENERAL—AIR FORCE

Born on October 18, 1931 in Baltimore, Maryland, Boddie married the former Mattye Dwiggins of Tuske-

gee, Alabama, and they have five sons. Known by his friends and associates as "Tim," he graduated from Frederick Douglass High School in Baltimore in 1949. He received a bachelor's degree from Howard University in Washington, D.C., in 1954, and graduated from the Academic Instructors School and Squadron Officer School, both located at Maxwell Air Force Base, Alabama. He is also a graduate of the Industrial College of the Armed Forces at Fort Lesley J. McNair, Washington, D.C., and the Air War College at Maxwell AFB. He earned a Master of Public Administration degree from Auburn University in Alabama.

He received his commission through the Air Force Reserve Officers Training Corps program, and was awarded the Convair Aviation Association Award for his outstanding accomplishments as a cadet. Boddie entered primary pilot training in March 1955 at Bartow Air Force Base, Florida, where he flew PA-18s and T-6Gs. From there he went to single-engine basic pilot training at Laredo Air Force Base, Texas, flying T-28s and T-33s and earning his wings in March 1956. His first operational assignment was with the 560th Strategic Fighter Squadron at Bergstrom Air Force Base, Texas, which was equipped with F-84F Thunderstreaks. In May 1957, he was assigned to Nellis Air Force Base, Nevada, for gunnery weapons delivery training in the F-100 Super Sabre. Upon completion in September 1957, he was assigned to the United States Air Forces in Europe Weapons Center at Wheelus Air Base in Tripoli, Libya. For the next 45 months he performed instructor pilot, flight-test, and standardization duties, requiring that he be simultaneously qualified in T-33s, F-86s, F-100s and B-57s.

He returned to the Air Force Reserve Officers Training Corps program in February 1961 as Commandant

of Cadets at the Tuskegee Institute in Alabama. He also taught Military Aspects of World Political Geography and International Relations to senior cadets. In June 1965, he joined the 4453rd Combat Crew Training Wing at Davis-Monthan Air Force Base, Arizona, where he flew and instructed in F-4s.

The following year he volunteered for combat duty in Southeast Asia and was assigned to the 559th Tactical Fighter Squadron at Cam Ranh Bay Air Base in Vietnam in October 1966. In addition to his duties as Operations and Scheduling Officer, he flew 201 F-4 combat missions, including 57 missions over North Vietnam. Boddie returned to the 4453rd at Davis-Monthan Air Force Base in August 1967, and commanded the F-4 replacement training unit weapons school of the 4457th Tactical Training Squadron until July 1971. During this tour of duty, he was also appointed provisional Squadron Commander of the 40th Tactical Fighter Squadron, which was beginning to receive A-7D's.

His next assignment took him to the Headquarters of the Air Force Military Personnel Center at Randolph Air Force Base, Texas, as Chief of the Flying Status Branch in the Directorate of Personnel Program Actions until August 1974, when he entered the Air War College. Following his studies at the Air War College, in July 1975 he was assigned to the Headquarters of Tactical Air Command at Langley Air Force Base, Virginia, as Chief of the Maintenance Standardization and Evaluation Division of the Directorate of Maintenance Engineering. He led a 27-member team that evaluated the aircraft maintenance effectiveness of all the command's units.

In August 1976, he moved to Moody Air Force Base, Georgia, where he served as Deputy Commander for Operations of the 347th Tactical Fighter Wing. The next year he became Vice Commander of the Wing. In June 1978, he became 51st Composite Wing (Tactical) Vice Commander at Osan Air Base in South Korea and took command in June 1979. In June 1980, he was assigned as Deputy Director for Operations, J-3, National Military Command Center, and Organization of the Joint Chiefs of Staff, Washington, D.C. He was appointed Brigadier General August 1, 1980, with date of rank July 25, 1980. He retired July 1, 1983.

General Boddie was a Command Pilot with more than 4,000 hours in jet fighter aircraft. His military awards and decorations include the Legion of Merit; the Distinguished Flying Cross; the Meritorious Service Medal (with two oak leaf clusters); the Air Medal (13 oak leaf clusters); the Air Force Commendation Medal; the Air Force Outstanding Unit Award ribbon (three oak leaf clusters and "V" device); the Combat Readiness Medal; the National Defense Medal (with service star); the Armed Forces Expeditionary Medal; the Vietnam Service Medal (with three service stars); the Republic of Vietnam Gallantry Cross (with palm) and Vietnam Campaign Medal; and the Joint Chiefs of Staff badge.

Bolden, Charles F.
MAJOR GENERAL—MARINES

He was born in Columbia, South Carolina to Mrs. Ethel M. Bolden, and married the former Alexis (Jackie) Walker of Columbia, with whom he has two children, Anthony C. and Kelly M. Bolden graduated from C.A. Johnson High School in 1964; received a Bachelor of Science in Electrical Science from the United States Naval Academy in 1968; and a Master of Science in Systems Management from the University of Southern California in 1978. Bolden accepted a commission as a second lieutenant in the United States Marine Corps following graduation from the United States Naval Academy in 1968. He underwent flight training at Pensacola, Florida, Meridian, Mississippi, and Kingsville, Texas, before being designated a naval aviator in May 1970. He flew more than 100 sorties into North and South Vietnam, Laos and Cambodia in the A-6A Intruder, while assigned to VMA (AW)-533 at Nam Phong, Thailand, from June 1972 to June 1973. Upon returning to the United States, Bolden began a two-year tour as a Marine Corps officer selection officer and recruiting officer in Los Angeles, California, followed by three years in various assignments at the Marine Corps Air Station at El Toro, California.

In June 1979, he graduated from the United States Naval Test Pilot School at Patuxent River, Maryland, and was assigned to the Naval Air Test Center's Systems Engineering and Strike Aircraft Test directorates. While there, he served as an ordnance test pilot and flew numerous test projects in the 6-E, EA-6B, and A-7C/E airplanes. He has logged more than 5,000 hours of flying time; Selected by NASA in May 1980, Bolden

became an astronaut in August 1981, qualified for assignment as a Pilot of Future Space Shuttle Flight Crews. His technical assignments to date include Astronaut Office Safety Officer, Technical Assistant to the Director of the Johnson Space Center, Astronaut Office Liaison to the Safety, Reliability and Quality Assurance Directorates of the Marshall Space Flight Center, and the Kennedy Space Center, Chief of the Safety Division At JSC, and lead Astronaut for Vehicle Test and Checkout at the Kennedy Space Center.

On his first mission Bolden was pilot of STS-61C, which launched from the Kennedy Space Center, Florida, on January 12, 1986. During the six-day flight on *Columbia* the crew deployed the SATCOM KU satellite and conducted experiments in astrophysics and materials processing. STS-61C made a successful night landing at Edwards Air Force Base, California, on January 18, 1986. With the completion of his first space flight Bolden logged 146 hours in space. More recently, Bolden was pilot of STS-31, which was launched aboard space shuttle *Discovery,* on April 24, 1990, from the Kennedy Space Center. During this five-day mission, crewmembers deployed the Hubble Space Telescope and conducted a variety of mid-deck experiments. They also utilized a variety of cameras, including both the IMAX in-cabin and cargo bay cameras, for earth observations from their record-setting altitude of 380 miles. Following 75 orbits of the earth in 121 hours, STS-31 *Discovery* landed at Edwards Air Force Base on April 29, 1990. With the completion of his second mission, Bolden had logged a total of 267 hours in space.

On his third mission in 1992, he commanded the Space Shuttle *Atlantis* on the first Space Laboratory (SPACELAB) mission dedicated to NASA's "Mission to Planet Earth." During this nine-day mission, the crew operated the ATLAS-1 (Atmospheric Laboratory for Applications and Science), a system composed of twelve experiments which succeeded in making a vast amount of detailed measurements of the chemical and physical properties of Earth's atmosphere. Immediately following this mission, he was appointed Assistant Deputy Administrator for the National Aeronautics and Space Administration.

He held this Washington, D.C. post until assigned as the commander of STS-60, the 1994 flight of a six member crew on the Space Shuttle *Discovery*. This landmark eight day mission was the first joint United States/Russian Space Shuttle Mission. The crew conducted a series of joint United States/Russian science activities and carried the Space Habitation Module-2 and the Wake Shield Facility–01 into space. Upon completion of this fourth mission, Major General Bolden left the space program, having logged more than 680 hours in space.

After leaving the space program, he was assigned as the Assistant Commandant of Midshipmen at the United States Naval Academy. President Clinton nominated him for promotion to Brigadier General in January 1995. He was confirmed by the United States Senate, and he joined Major General Stanley as the only

other black general in the United States Marine Corps on active duty at that time.

Bolden was next assigned as the Assistant Wing Commander of the 3rd Marine Aircraft Wing in Miramar, California. In July 1997, he was assigned as the Deputy Commanding General, I MEF, Marine Forces, Pacific. From February 1998, he served as Command General, I MEF (FWD) in support of Operation Desert Thunder in Kuwait. In July 1998, he was promoted to Major General and assigned as the Deputy Commander of United States Forces in Japan. On August 9, 2000, he became the Commanding General of the 3rd Marine Aircraft Wing.

Bolden is a member of the Marine Corps Association, the Montford Point Marine Association and the United States Naval Institute. His military awards and decorations include the Defense Superior Service Medal; the Air Medal; the Strike Flight Medal (8th award); and the NASA Exceptional Service Medal (1988). He has received Honorary Doctorates from several distinguished universities.

Bolton, Claude M., Jr.
MAJOR GENERAL—AIR FORCE

Bolton married the former Linda Roll of Alma, New Mexico, and they have two daughters, Cynthia and Jennifer. He received a Bachelor of Science in Electrical Engineering from the University of Nebraska, Lincoln, and earned a master's degree in management from Troy State University in Alabama. His military education includes Squadron Officer School at Maxwell Air Force Base, Alabama; Air Command and Staff College; Program Management Course at the Defense Systems Management College; and the Naval War College at Newport, Rhode Island.

He entered the Air Force in 1969 as a student pilot

and received his wings in 1970. He has served in a variety of positions during his career, including Squadron and Wing Safety Officer, Instructor Pilot, Wing Standardization and Evaluation Flight Examiner, Scheduler, Test Pilot and Acquisition Professional. He is a command pilot with more than 2,700 flying hours in 27 different aircraft. During the Vietnam War he flew 232 combat missions, 40 of them over North Vietnam. He was a test pilot for the F-4, F-111 and F-16 and the first Program Manager for the Advanced Tactical Fighter Technologies Program which evolved into the F-22 System Program Office. During his tour at the Pentagon, he was the F-16 Program Element Monitor and also saw duty in the Office of Special Programs. He was the Deputy Program Director for the B-2 System Program Office and Program Director for the Advanced Cruise Missile System Program Office. Prior to assignment at DSMC, he was the Inspector General for Air Force Materiel Command at Wright-Patterson Air Force Base. In March 1993, he was selected Commandant of the Defense Systems Management College (DSMC) at Fort Belvoir, Virginia. The college is a graduate level institute which promotes and supports the adoption and practice of sound systems management principles by the acquisition work force through education, research, consulting and information dissemination. Bolton was promoted to Brigadier General on August 1, 1993.

He has served as the Director of Requirements at Air Force Materiel Command Headquarters. He served as the Program Executive Officer for Air Force Fighter and Bomber Programs with the Office of the Assistant Secretary of the Air Force for Acquisition. Major General Bolton was selected to serve as the Commander of the Air Force Security Assistant Center, at Air Force Materiel Command, and Assistant to the Commander for International Affairs at Headquarters Air Force Materiel Command at Wright-Patterson Air Force Base in Ohio.

His military awards and decorations include the Legion of Merit; the Distinguished Flying Cross with oak leaf cluster; the Meritorious Service Medal (with two oak leaf clusters); the Air Medal (with 17 oak leaf clusters); the Vietnam Service Medal (with three service stars); the Republic of Vietnam Gallantry Cross; the Republic of Vietnam Campaign Medal.

Bolton, Larry S.

COLONEL—ARMY

Bolton received an undergraduate degree in Health Services Administration from California State University at Sacramento and he holds a master's degree in Health Services Administration from Webster University. His military education includes completion of Command and General Staff College and a Masters of Science in National Resource Strategy awarded by the Industrial College of the Armed Forces (ICAF) of the National Defense University in Washington, D.C.

Bolton has served in numerous key assignments including the S-3 in the 25th Medical Battalion, which

later became the 225th Forward Support Battalion (FSB). He then served as the Support Operations Officer in the 225th Forward Support Battalion. He became the Battalion Executive Officer for the 725th Main Support Battalion. He was selected to serve as the 25th DISCOM S-3/Plans and Operation Officer. He returned to the Washington, D.C. area to an assignment on the Headquarters Department of the Army (HQDA) Staff as the Personnel Systems Staff Officer (PERSSO) at the Pentagon. He was selected to serve as a Special Staff Officer to the Director of the Army Staff, serving the Chief of Staff of the Army. He assumed Command of the 210th Forward Support Battalion, 10th Mountain Division at Fort Drum, New York. He was assigned to the Office of the Surgeon General, as the Chief of Personnel Policy, Plans and Operations, and then the Deputy Director of Personnel. He served as Commander of the Walter Reed Army Medical Center Brigade, and was most recently assigned as Chief of Medical Service Corps Branch at PERSCOM.

Boney-Harris, Gwendolyn

COLONEL—ARMY

A native of Georgia, Colonel Boney-Harris grew up in Miami, Florida, where she graduated from high school. She entered Saint Augustine's College in Raleigh, North Carolina to study Criminal Justice and Political Science. While in there she joined the Reserve Officers Training Corps (ROTC).

She was commissioned in the United States Army in May 1980, following graduation from Saint Augustine's College with a bachelor's degree in Criminal Justice and a graduate degree in National Strategic Studies from the United States Army War College. Her military education includes completion of the Quartermaster

Officer Basic and Advanced Courses at Fort Lee, Virginia; United States Army Command and General Staff College at Fort Leavenworth, Kansas; and the United States Army War College at Carlisle Barracks, Pennsylvania.

She has held key leadership and staff positions to include serving as the Technical Supply Officer for the 597th Maintenance Company, 68th Transportation Battalion at Fort Carson, Colorado; Deputy Division Property Officer of the 24th Infantry Division, Support Command at Fort Stewart, Georgia; Commander of the Supply Company, 299th Support Battalion, 1st Infantry Division (Forward), United States Army Europe, Germany; Support Operations Officer for the 224th Forward Support Battalion at Fort Stewart, Georgia; Commander of the Logistic Task Force for 1-64 Armor Battalion in Somalia; Assistant Division G-4 of the 24th Infantry Division at Fort Stewart, Georgia; Logistic Officer, G-4 in the United States Army Europe, Germany; Commander of the 47th Forward Support Battalion, 1st Armored Division in United States Army Europe; and as the Special Assistant to the Army Chief of Staff at the Pentagon. In 2005, Colonel Boney-Harris was Garrison Commander of the Installation Management Agency, European Region, at Army Garrison Stuttgart.

Booker, Robert L.
COMMAND SERGEANT MAJOR—ARMY

Booker entered the United States Army in August 1979. He attended OSUT Armor Training at Fort Knox, Kentucky. His military and civilian and education includes; all the Noncommissioned Officer Education System Courses; Drill Sergeant School; and the United States Army Sergeant Major Academy. He also holds an associate's degree and a Bachelor of Arts.

He began his military career in the position of Loader. He then moved into the leadership positions of

Gunner, Tank Commander, Platoon Sergeant, 1st Sergeant and Operations Sergeant Major. He has also served in the teaching positions of Drill Sergeant and ROTC Instructor. In August 2004, he was serving as the Command Sergeant Major of the 2/12 Cavalry Battalion, with the 1st Cavalry Division.

Bookert, Reubin B.
REAR ADMIRAL—NAVY

Bookert is a native of Columbia, South Carolina, and graduated from North Carolina A&T State University. He entered the Navy through Officer Candidate School and was commissioned in February 1975. He

earned a Master of Arts degree in National Security and Strategic Studies from the Naval War College and a Master's of Science in Management from Salve Regina College, Newport, Rhode Island.

He reported to his first fleet assignment in March 1976 as Communications Officer in USS *Truett* (FF 1095). Subsequent sea tours include the staff of Commander Destroyer Squadron Twenty-Four as Communications Officer, Weapons Officer in USS *Joseph Hewes* (FF 1078), Operations Officer in USS *Lamoure County* (LST 1194) and Executive Officer on USS *Blakely* (FF 1072). His command at sea tours include USS *Lamoure County* (LST 1194) and the amphibious assault ship USS *Kearsarge* (LHD 3).

Ashore, he served at Navy Recruiting District, Atlanta, Georgia, and United States Special Operations Command at MacDill AFB, Florida. In July 1995, Bookert assumed duties as Special Assistant to the Chief of Naval Personnel and Director of the Professional Relationship Division (PERS-61) in the Bureau of Naval Personnel. Other shore assignments include Special Assistant to the Chief of Naval Operations, Head of the Amphibious Warfare Branch (OPNAV N753), and Deputy Director of the Expeditionary Warfare Division (OPNAV N75). He reported to his assignment as Commander of Amphibious Group Two in August 2003.

Boone, Antonio Frenail

FIRST SERGEANT—ARMY

Boone was born in Ashburn, Georgia, and graduated from Turner County High School in May 1988. He enlisted into the United States Army in July 1988, and completed his Basic Combat Training and Advanced Individual Training at Fort Sill, Oklahoma.

His military education includes all levels of the Noncommissioned Officer Education System Courses; Master Fitness Trainer Course; Drill Sergeant Candidate Course; Equal Opportunity Leaders Course; Instructors Training Course; Fast Rope Master Course; Rappel Master Course; Air Assault Course; Combat Lifesaver Course; Environmental Compliance Officer Course; Field Artillery Weapon (U6) Course; NBC School; Drivers Training Course; and Drill Sergeant School. He holds an associate's degree in General Studies from Central Texas College.

Boone's key military assignments include serving as a Gunnery Sergeant; Senior Drill Sergeant; Drill Sergeant; Howitzer Section Chief; Air Assault Instructor; Ammunition Team Chief; Gunner; NBC Noncommissioned Officer; and Cannoneer. In March 2005, he was serving as the First Sergeant for Alpha Battery, 11th Field Artillery, at Fort Wainwright, Alaska.

Boone, Layne R.

COMMANDER—NAVY

Commander Boone was commissioned through Officer Candidate School in 1983 in Newport, Rhode Island. She received a bachelor's degree in Math from Fisk University in Nashville, Tennessee, in 1970. She also earned a master's degree in Education from the University of Virginia in Charlottesville, Virginia. She holds a masters degree in Operations Research from the Naval Postgraduate School in Monterey, California.

Her professional military education includes the Ocean Systems Watch Officer Course, Division Officer Training Course, and the Coordinated Anti-Submarine Warfare Operations Course.

She has held a variety of key military assignments to include serving as Oceanographic Watch Officer at the

Oceanographic Processing Facility at Dam Neck, Virginia; as the Main Evaluation Center Watch Officer/Training Officer for Oceanographic Systems Pacific at Ford Island, Hawaii; as the Officer-In-Charge of Personnel Support Detachment at Holy Loch, Scotland; as Operations Analyst for the Commander of Navy Recruiting Command at Arlington, Virginia; as the Detailer and Placement Officer at the Bureau of Naval Personnel in Washington, D.C.; as Commander of Tampa Military Entrance Processing Station at Tampa, Florida; and as Head of Chaplain Corps and Religion Program Specialist Manpower Branch for the Chief of Chaplains in Washington, D.C. In July, 2003, Boone became the Commander of the New York Military Entrance Processing Station in New York City.

Bostick, Thomas P.

MAJOR GENERAL—ARMY

Brigadier General Bostick graduated from the United States Military Academy in 1978 with a Bachelor of Science degree. He also holds a master's degree in both Civil Engineering and Mechanical Engineering from Stanford University. His military education includes the Engineer Officer Advanced Course, the United States Army Command and General Staff College, and the Army War College.

Since his commissioning, Brigadier General Bostick has served in a variety of command and staff assignments both in the continental United States and overseas. He served as a Platoon Leader, Battalion Maintenance Officer; Executive Officer; and Commander of Company B while assigned to the 54th Engineer Battalion in Germany. After attending Stanford University, he was assigned as an instructor in the Department of Mechanics at the United States Military Academy. In 1989, Brigadier General Bostick was se-

lected as a White House Fellow and served with the Department of Veterans Affairs. He returned to United States Army Europe where he served as S-3 (operations) in the 40th Engineer Battalion, 1st Armored Division and S-3 for the 1st Armored Division Engineer Brigade. He returned to the National Capital Region and was Executive Officer to the Chief of Engineers. In 1994, Brigadier General Bostick assumed command of the 1st Engineer Battalion, 1st Infantry Division. After attending the Army War College in 1997, he assumed command of the Engineer Brigade of the 1st Armored Division while deployed in support of the NATO Stabilization Force in Bosnia-Herzegovina. Brigadier General Bostick was Executive Officer to the Chief of Staff, United States Army from June 1999 through May 2001. In May 2001, he was assigned as the Deputy Director of Operations for the National Military Command Center, J-3, with the Joint Staff. He was next selected to serve as the Assistant Division Commander for Maneuvers for the 1st Cavalry Division at Fort Hood, Texas and Operation Iraqi Freedom in Kuwait. He was promoted to Brigadier General on May 1, 2002.

In June 2004, he was assigned as the Director of Military Programs, United States Army Corps of Engineers with duty as Commander of the Gulf Region Division during Operation Iraqi Freedom. On March 28, 2005, he was assigned as Deputy Chief of Engineers/Deputy Commanding General of the United States Army Corps of Engineers in Washington, D.C. He was promoted to Major General in May 2005.

His military awards and decorations include the Defense Superior Service Medal; Legion of Merit (with Oak Leaf Cluster); Defense Meritorious Service Medal; Meritorious Service Medal (with 4 Oak Leaf Clusters); Joint Service Commendation Medal; Army Commendation Medal (with Oak Leaf Cluster); Parachutist Badge; Ranger Tab; and the Army Staff Identification Badge.

Bowen, Clotilde Dent

COLONEL—ARMY

Bowen was born in Chicago, Illinois, and earned her Bachelor of Arts and Medical Degrees from Ohio State University. She completed her internship at the Harlem Hospital in New York in 1948.

She was commissioned in the United States Army Reserves in 1959. She entered active duty in 1967, becoming the first black Female Medical Doctor in the U.S. Army. Her military assignments include serving from 1967 to 1968 at the United States Army Tripler Hospital as Chief of Psychiatric Services; and from 1968 to 1970 as Chief of the Review Branch of the Army's Medicine Insurance Program (CHAMPUS).

Her other assignments include Fitzsimmons Army Medical Center in Aurora, Colorado; as Commander of the United States Army Hawley Army Medical Center at Fort Benjamin Harrison, Indiana; and as Chief of the Department of Primary Care at Fitzsimmons Army Medical Center. She also served in Vietnam.

Colonel Bowen was the first black female in the

United States Army to be promoted to the rank of full Colonel, and was the first black female to graduate from Ohio State University Medical School.

Her military awards and decorations include the Bronze Star; the Legion of Merit; the Meritorious Service Medal; and the Vietnam Service Medal.

Bowers, Timothy O.

COMMAND SERGEANT MAJOR—ARMY

Command Sergeant Major Timothy O. Bowers

earned a Bachelor of Science degree from Paine College in August, Georgia. His military education includes Noncommissioned Officer Logistics Course; Personnel and Logistics Course; Inspector General Course; Contractor Officers Representative Course; First Sergeants Course and the United States Army Sergeants Major Academy.

Bowers entered the United States Army in 1973 at Fort Knox, Kentucky, where he completed his Basic Training. He attended Advanced Individual training at Fort Ord, California.

He currently serves as the Command Sergeant Major of Fort Hood, Texas.

Bowman, George Fletcher

MAJOR GENERAL—ARMY

Major General Bowman is married to the former Marcianna C. Jenkins of Chicago, Illinois, and they have seven children, Captain George Bowman, Jr., James Bowman, Danielle Bowman Jordan, Marc Anthony Bowman, Yeshelle Jenkins, Paul Jenkins, and Malcom Jenkins.

His military education includes the Signal Officer Basic Course; Air Ground Operations; Battle Staff Course; Command and General Staff College; Reserve Components National Security Course; and the Army War College. He holds a bachelor's degree in History from South Carolina State College, and earned a Masters in Public Administration from Shippensburg University in Pennsylvania.

He has held a variety of command and staff positions that have included Signal Support Division Chief and Chief of Plans Divisions for the 335th Signal Command at East Point, Georgia. He served as Operations and Plans Officer with the Third Army at Fort McPherson, Georgia. He was assigned as a Personnel Manage-

ment Officer and Branch Chief of Signal Branch, next as Chief of the Retired Activities Division at the Army Reserves Personnel Center. He was selected as United States Army Reserve Advisor, Joint Plans/MOB Officer, for FORSCOM, Fort McPherson, Georgia. Other assignment include serving in Germany with the 7th Signal Brigade and South Korea in the 2nd Infantry Division. He served as Deputy Commander of the Army Reserve Personnel Center (ARPERCEN) at St. Louis, Missouri.

General Bowman assumed the position of Deputy Commanding General of the 311th Theater Signal Command at Fort George G. Meade, Maryland, on May 9, 1997. He was promoted to Brigadier General on April 9, 1998. In October 1999, he was selected as the Commanding General of the 311th Signal Command. He was promoted to Major General on October 6, 2000.

Boykin, Louis
COMMAND CHIEF MASTER SERGEANT—
    AIR FORCE
Boykin is the Command Chief Master Sergeant at the Headquarters of the Pennsylvania Air National Guard. In this position, he serves as the Senior Enlisted Advisor for the Adjutant General and the Commander and

Staff of the Pennsylvania Air National Guard. At the controls of the nation's fourth largest Air Guard, he helps chart the course for the 3,800 member enlisted force.

Braddock, Terry L.
COMMAND SERGEANT MAJOR—ARMY
A native of Chicago, Illinois, Braddock enlisted in the United States Army in April 1974, attending Basic Combat Training at Fort Polk, Louisiana, and Advanced Individual Training at Fort Knox, Kentucky.

His military and civilian education includes all the Non-Commissioned Officer Education System Courses; First Sergeant School; and the United States Army

Sergeants Major Academy (class 47). He received an associate's degree in General Studies from Central Texas College; and a Bachelor of Arts in Public Administration from Century University.

His military assignments include serving in tactical and strategic leadership positions from squad leader leading to his present position.

He has served as Command Sergeant Major of the 57th Signal Battalion, 3rd Signal Brigade, at Fort Hood, Texas; Command Sergeant Major of the 3rd Signal Brigade at Fort Hood; and Command Sergeant Major of the 2nd Signal Brigade. In March 2005, he assumed his current position as Command Sergeant Major of the Northwest Region of the Installation Management Agency where he serves as the principle advisor to the Director on all issues impacting the well-being of soldiers and their families.

Bradley, R.
SERGEANT MAJOR—MARINES
Bradley is a native of Daytona Beach, Florida and entered the United States Marine Corps in February 1977. He attended recruit training at the Marine Corps Recruit Depot at Parris Island, South Carolina.

His key military assignments include serving as Personnel Chief; Noncommissioned Officer in Charge of the Recruit Administration

Center; and First Sergeant at Camp Pendleton, California, and Annette Island, Alaska. He was promoted to Sergeant Major in May 1999, and in August 2004, he was serving as Sergeant Major of Marine Aircraft Group 16.

Brailsford, Marvin D.
LIEUTENANT GENERAL—ARMY

General Brailsford was born in Burkeville, Texas, and received a Bachelor of Science degree in Biology from Prairie View A&M University and a Master of Science degree in Bacteriology from Iowa State University. His military education includes the Armor School Basic Course; the Chemical School Advance Course; United States Command and General Staff College; and the United States Army War College.

In August 1959, Brailsford entered the United States Army via ROTC as a Second Lieutenant and student in the Armor Officer Basic Course at the United States Army Armor School at Fort Knox, Kentucky. From October 1959 to July 1961, he served as a Platoon Leader of the 3rd Armored Cavalry Regiment at Fort Meade, Maryland. He was promoted to First Lieutenant on December 15, 1960. From August 1961 to May 1962, he was a student in the Chemical Officer Advanced Course at the United States Army Chemical School at Fort McClellan, Alabama. From May 1962 to November 1962, he served as a Platoon Leader for the 12th Chemical Company of the 100th Chemical Group at Fort McClellan. From November 1962 to December 1963, he was a Chemical Adviser for the 22nd Infantry Division of the United States Military Assistance Group in Vietnam.

He was promoted to Captain on June 17, 1963. From March 1964 to February 1966, he was a student at Iowa

State University in Ames, Iowa. From February 1966 to July 1969, he served as the deputy chief of the Special Operations Division, later the Executive Officer, and later the Deputy Commander of the United States Army Biological Laboratories at Fort Detrick, Maryland.

Brailsford was promoted to Major on August 1, 1967. From August 1969 to June 1970, he was a student at the United States Army Command and General Staff College at Fort Leavenworth, Kansas. From June 1970 to June 1972, he served as Chief of the Academic Operations Division, (later Deputy Director of Instruction) at the United States Army Chemical Center and School at Fort McClellan. From June 1972 to January 1973, he served as a staff officer in the Chemical Division of the Chemical and Nuclear Operation Directorate at the Office of the Assistant Chief of Staff for Force Development, United States Army, in Washington, D.C. From January 1973 to December 1974, he served as a Logistics Staff Officer in the Operations Division, where he worked on Logistics Plans, Operations, and Systems in the Office of the Deputy Chief of Staff for Logistics, United States Army, Washington, D.C.

Brailsford was promoted to Lieutenant Colonel on May 30, 1973. From December 1974 to August 1976, he was the Commander of the 101st Ordnance Battalion, 60th Ordnance Group, VII Corps, United States Army in Europe. From August 1976 to May 1977, he served as Deputy Commander of Kaiserslautern Army Depot in West Germany. From August 1977 to June 1978, he was a student at the United States Army War College at Carlisle Barracks, Pennsylvania. From June 1978 to May 1982, he served first as Assistant Project Manager for Logistics, later Assistant Development Project Officer for Select Ammunition, the Chief of Systems Evaluation, then Deputy chairman for Operations for the Division Air Defense Gun Source Selection Board, and later as Chief of the Program Management Office in the United States Army Armament Research and Development Command at Dover, New Jersey.

He was promoted to the rank of Colonel on January 1, 1980. From June 1982 to October 1984, he was the Commander of the 60th Ordnance Group, 21st Support Command, United States Army in Europe. From October 1984 to June 1987, Brailsford was the Commanding General of the 59th Ordnance Brigade, United States Army in Europe. He was promoted to Brigadier General on August 1, 1985. From June 1987 to October 1987, he served as the Deputy Commanding General for Armaments and Munitions, United States Army Armament, Munitions, and Chemical Command Commanding General, United States Army Armament Research and Development Center at Picatinny Arsenal in Dover, New Jersey. From October 1987 to June 1990, he was the Commanding General of the United States Army Armament, Munitions, and Chemical Command at Rock Island, Illinois.

He was promoted to Major General on August 1,

1988. On June 11, 1990, he was promoted to Lieutenant General and selected as the Deputy Commanding General of Materiel Readiness, Executive Director for Conventional Ammunition, United States Army Materiel Command in Alexandria, Virginia. He retired on February 29, 1992.

General Brailsford received numerous awards and decorations including the Distinguished Service Medal; the Legion of Merit; the Bronze Star; the Meritorious Service Medal (with four oak leaf clusters); the Army Commendation Medal; the Parachutist Badge; and the Army Staff Identification Badge.

Brame, Sherwood A.

COMMAND SERGEANT MAJOR—ARMY

A native of Kittrell, North Carolina, Brame entered the United States Army in August 1977 and attended Basic Combat Training at Fort Dix, New Jersey. After completing basic training, he reported to Fort Devens, Massachusetts, in the MOS O5G Signal Specialist.

After completion of Advanced Individual Training, he reported to the 15th Military Intelligence Company of the 5th Infantry Division at Fort Polk, Louisiana.

His military and civilian education includes all the Noncommissioned Officer Education System Courses; the First Sergeant Course; Master Fitness Course; Vision Net Controller Course; NBC Course; the United States Army Sergeants Major Academy (class 50); and the Command Sergeant Major Course. He also holds an associate's degree in General Studies from Barton Community College; and earned a Bachelor of Science from Excelsior College.

His military leadership assignments include serving as Team Leader; Section Sergeant; Platoon Sergeant;

Detachment Noncommissioned Officer in Charge; First Sergeant; Operation Sergeant; and Battalion Operation Sergeant Major. He was assigned to the 205th Military Intelligence Brigade in Darmstadt, Germany, and deployed with the unit to Operation Iraqi Freedom. In January 2005, he was serving as the Command Sergeant Major for 205th Military Intelligence Brigade, V Corps, in Wiesbaden, Germany.

Branch, Carlton J.

COMMAND SERGEANT MAJOR—ARMY

A native of Murfreesboro, North Carolina, Branch enlisted into the United States Army in September 1978. He attended Basic Combat Training and Advanced Individual Training at Fort Dix, New Jersey.

His key military assignments include serving as Platoon Sergeant, Dining Facility Manager, Battalion Food Service Sergeant, Installation Food Service Supervisor, Chief Training Developer/Evaluator; First Sergeant of Headquarters and Headquarters Company, 266th Quartermaster Battalion at Fort Lee, Virginia; First Sergeant, Basic Noncommissioned Officer Course at NCO Academy at Fort Lee; First Sergeant of Headquarters and Headquarters Company, Garrison/CASOM at Fort Lee; Sergeant Major of A Company, United States Army Sergeants Major Academy at Fort Bliss, Texas; and Command Sergeant Major of the 701st Main Support Battalion at Kitzingen, Germany.

Branch, Fred C.

CAPTAIN—MARINE

In 1943, a young man from Hamlet, North Carolina, entered the United States Marine Corps. He had considered the Army's Officer Program while he was attending Temple University in Philadelphia in 1943, and took a test to become an Army officer but was drafted into the Marine Corps before he received the results. He

served at Montford Point, at Camp Lejeune, North Carolina, along with men like Sergeant Major "Hashmark" Johnson and Sergeant Major Edgar Huff.

After graduating boot camp, he learned that he had successfully passed the Army Officer's test. He still wanted to become an officer more than ever at Montford Point, where white officers and noncommissioned officers were in charge.

Upon his graduation from boot camp at Montford Point as a corporal, he was assigned to the 51st Defense Battalion and deployed to Ellis Island in the Pacific Ocean during World War II. The 51st Composite Defense Battalion was trained and equipped as a combat unit, and so was the 52nd which followed it. They were the only two black combat units created during the Second World War.

He was selected to attend the Navy's V-12 program (a college-level preparatory program for future military officers) at Purdue University, where he made the dean's list. Branch was then sent to Quantico to attend the Commander's Class, Officer Candidates School. In a class of 250 students, Branch was the only black Officer Candidate, and he succeeded in earning a commission.

He was the First black Officer in the United States Marine Corps, and his first assignment was as Commanding Officer of a black volunteer training unit in Philadelphia after completing officer training.

As a first lieutenant, Branch was assigned to Quantico and later moved to Camp Pendleton, California, where he was a Platoon Commander, Battery Executive Officer and Battery Commander in the First Anti-

Aircraft Artillery Automatic Weapons Battalion. He served on active duty until May 1952. He remained in the Marine Corps Reserves, was promoted to Captain in February 1954, and resigned his commission in 1955.

Brashear, Carl Maxie
COMMAND MASTER CHIEF—NAVY

Master Chief Carl Maxie Brashear was born on January 19, 1931, the son of a sharecropper in Tonieville, Larue County, Kentucky. He is father of four children, Shazanta, DaWayne, Phillip M, and Patrick S.

He enlisted in the United States Navy on February 25, 1948, the same year President Harry S. Truman ordered racial integration of the military. He entered the Naval Training Center at Great Lakes, Illinois—Recruit Training. In May 1948, he was assigned to the Officer's Mess of Squadron VX-1, PBM Beachmasters Unit, at Key West, Florida. From November 1951 to March 1955, he was as USS *Tripoli* (CVE 64), as a second Division Petty Officer, Master-at-Arms, with Temporary Additional Duty at Salvage Diving School. In March 1955, he was assigned as a Salvage Diver; Section Leader; and Repair Party Leader, aboard USS *Opportune* (ARS-64). In June 1964, he graduated from Deep-Sea Diving School in Washington, D.C., as a First Class Diver. In June 1970, he earned a Master Diver evaluation from Deep-Sea Diving School, in Washington, D.C. His last assignments included serving as a Master Diver; and in Port Officer of the Deck; a Minority Affairs Officer; Repair Party Leader; Enlisted Watch Officer; Work Center Supervisor.

Brashear retired from the United States Navy as a Master Chief Petty Officer and Master Diver on April

1, 1979. He was the first African American Diver and Master Diver in the history of the United States Navy, overcoming race, poverty and, later, the loss of a leg, to become a Master Diver. The movie *Men of Honor*, in which Cuba Gooding Jr. starred as Brashear, was released to theaters in October 2000. It accurately portrays his courage, determination and perseverance.

Brault, Laurell A.
COMMANDER—NAVY

Commander Brault is originally from Nassau in the Bahamas, and enlisted in the United States Navy in December 1974, serving as a Hospital Corpsman for ten years. She graduated from Officer Candidate School in Newport, Rhode Island in February 1985 as an Ensign in the General Unrestricted Line (1100) community. Her enlisted duty stations included Naval Hospital Great Lakes, Illinois; Portsmouth, Virginia; Subic Bay, the Philippines; and Marine Corps Officer Selection Office, New York City.

Following her commission, she was assigned to the Comptroller's Office on the Staff of the Commander of the United States Atlantic Fleet in Norfolk, Virginia. In 1988, she graduated from Oceanographic Watch Officer School and was later designated as an Integrated Undersea Surveillance Officer. Subsequent duty assignments included Current Operations Officer at Naval Facility Bermuda; Commander of Area ASW Forces Sixth Fleet at Naples, Italy; and Officer-in-Charge of the Operations Research Detachment at Okinawa, Japan. In 1994, she returned to Naples as the Operations Officer for the Commander of Military Sealift Command Mediterranean.

In September 1996, she became the Navy Element Commander at Headquarters, Allied Forces Southern Europe, for United States Navy personnel assigned to NATO in the Mediterranean theater. Following her Executive Officer assignment, she transferred to the Office of the Chief of Naval Operations, Shore Installation Management, and was subsequently selected as a Legislative Fellow. From January to December 1999, she served as a Defense Fellow on the staff of Senator Olympia Snowe (R-Maine), where she was responsible for providing staff support on national security and foreign affairs issues. Brault was then assigned as a

Congressional Liaison Officer for Appropriation Matters on the staff of the Assistant Secretary of the Navy (Financial Management and Budget). She reported to the Navy Personnel Command in April 2000, where she served initially as the Director of Staff Support and Strategic Communications; and later as the Fleet Support Officer Community Manager and Head Detailer. In October 2004, she was serving as the Commander of the Naval Ocean Processing Facility at Naval Air Station Whidbey Island.

Brewer, David Lawrence, III
VICE ADMIRAL—NAVY

Vice Admiral Brewer was born in Farmville, Virginia. He married the former Richardene Ruth Brown of Winnsboro, South Carolina, and they have one daughter, Stacey McAlister Brewer. He received a Bachelor of Science degree in Pre-Medicine from Prairie View Agricultural and Mechanical College of Texas. His military education includes Fleet Anti-Air Warfare Training; Naval Guided Missiles School; Naval Amphibious School; Surface Warfare Officers School; and the Naval War College at Newport, Rhode Island.

He enlisted in the United States Navy on September 18, 1968, and served as an enlisted member until honorably discharged on May 16, 1970. On June 3, 1970, he was commissioned an ensign in the United States Naval Reserve and assigned to USS *Little Rock* (CLG4) as an Electronics Warfare Officer. From March 1972 until June 1972, he served as Minority Recruiting Officer at Naval Recruiting District, Memphis, Tennessee. In June 1975, he returned to sea as the Combat Information Center Officer aboard the guided missile cruiser USS *California* (CGN36).

In 1977, Vice Admiral Brewer attended the Surface

Warfare Officer's Department Head School in Newport, Rhode Island. From August 1978 to October 1980, he served as the Weapons Officer aboard the guided missile cruiser USS *William H. Standley* (CG32). In 1981, he reported as the Engineering Officer aboard the amphibious helicopter carrier USS *Okinawa* (LPH3). From March 1983 to December 1984, he served as the Executive Officer aboard the Tank Landing Ship USS *Fresno* (LST1182).

In January 1985, Vice Admiral Brewer returned ashore and served as the Enlisted Community Manager for Combat Systems' ratings in the Office of Naval Operations (OP13), Washington, D.C. From June 1986 to September 1988, he commanded the tank landing ship USS *Bristol County* (LST1198). During his command tour, *Bristol County* earned several awards, including in Battle Efficiency "E."

In 1988, Brewer was selected by Admiral Trost, Chief of Naval Operations, as Special Assistant for Equal Opportunity. In this capacity, Vice Admiral Brewer was the advisor to the Navy's top leadership and the Chief of Naval Operations' personal representative at equal opportunity forums nationwide. From April 1991 to December 1992, he commanded USS *Mount Whitney* (LCC20), the Second Fleet's flagship.

In March 1993, he attended the Senior Officer's Course at the Naval War College. In December 1993; he was nominated for promotion to the rank of Rear Admiral (lower half).

From August 1994 to December 1996, Brewer served as Commander of U.S. Naval Forces Marianas/Commander in Chief U.S. Pacific Command Representative Guam/Commonwealth of the Northern Marianas Islands/Federated States of Micronesia/Republic of Palau. In March 1999, he was assigned as Vice Chief of Naval Education and Training in Pensacola, Florida. On August 27, 2002, he took the helm as the commander of Military Sealift Command. In this capacity, Vice Admiral Brewer is daily responsible for a fleet of more than 110 ships around the world. Military Sealift Command (MSC) ships provide critical food, fuel and supplies to Navy ships underway, keeping the fleet at sea and mission ready. MSC ships also perform myriad special missions for the Department of Defense, from surveying the world's oceans to supporting counter-drug operations to pre-positioning military equipment at sea near potential hotspots around the globe. Finally, MSC ships provide fast sealift of equipment and supplies for the Department of Defense both in peacetime and in war. Brewer was promoted to Vice Admiral in October 2002.

His military awards and decorations include the Legion of Merit; Meritorious Service Medal (with Gold Star); Navy Achievement Medal; Navy "E" Ribbon; Navy Expeditionary Medal; National Defense Medal (with one Bronze Star); and Sea Service Deployment Ribbon (with Gold Star).

Brewer, Herbert L.

COLONEL—MARINES

Born in San Antonio, Texas, Brewer married the former Nellie M. Middleton of Philadelphia and they have five daughters. He graduated from Phillis Wheatley High School in San Antonio, Texas, in 1941.

He enlisted in the Marine Corps in July 1942, serving with the Fifty-First Defense Battalion at Camp Lejeune, North Carolina until January 1944, when the unit deployed to the Pacific Theater of Operations. He attained the rank of sergeant as a fire control equipment technician and returned to the United States in August 1944 to attend Purdue University under the Navy's V-12 program. He received a Bachelor of Science degree in Civil Engineering from Purdue and was commissioned a Marine second lieutenant in June 1946.

He completed work on a master's degree in 1950, and in November of that year he was recalled to active duty, and ordered to Quantico, Virginia. Later he was assigned to Camp Pendleton, California, where he served as Battery Officer of the First Anti-Aircraft Artillery Automatic Weapons Battalion until March 1952, when he was released from active duty. In June 1952, he was promoted to the rank of captain, and in 1957 he became a major.

As a member of the Marine Corps Reserves he was promoted to lieutenant colonel on July 1, 1963. He was the first black promoted to full colonel in the United States Marine Corps Reserves in July 1968.

Bridges, Timothy K.

COLONEL—AIR FORCE

Bridges is a 1979 graduate of the Virginia Military Institute in Lexington, Virginia, with a Bachelor of Science degree in Civil Engineering. He was as a distinguished Air Force ROTC graduate and was commissioned in the United States Air Force in May 1979. He has earned a Master of Science degree in Business Management and Supervision from Central Michigan

Monitor and Integrated Process Team Chief in the Office of the Civil Engineer, Deputy Chief of Staff for Installations and Logistics in the Headquarters of the United States Air Force at the Pentagon. From June 1998 to June 1999, he served as the Commander of the 11th Civil Engineer Squadron, at Bolling Air Force Base in Washington, D.C. From July 2000 to July 2002, he served as the Chief of the Environmental Quality Division with the Headquarters Pacific Air Forces Civil Engineer Directorate at Hickam Air Force Base in Hawaii. Bridges was promoted to Colonel on October 1, 2001. In August 2002, he was selected to serve as Commander of Detachment 1 of 15th Air Base Wing at Johnston Atoll, located approximately 800 miles southwest of Oahu. Colonel Bridges is responsible for Air Force control and host management responsibilities on Johnston Atoll, mainly in support of the Johnston Atoll Chemical Agent Disposal System and for carrying out installation closure activities.

Bridgewater, Tony
COMMAND SERGEANT MAJOR—ARMY

Bridgewater enlisted in the United States Army in 1974, attending Basic Training at Fort Knox, Kentucky and Advanced Individual Training at Fort Belvoir, Virginia. His military and civilian education includes all the Noncommissioned Officer Education System Courses; the First Sergeant Course; the Motor Sergeant Course; Master Fitness Course; the Drill Sergeant School and the United States Army Sergeants Major Academy. He holds a Bachelor of Science degree in Liberal Arts from Regents College. He also earned an associate's degree in Liberal Arts from Harold Washington College.

He has held numerous leadership positions, including serving as Squad Leader in the 5th Signal Battalion

University. His military education includes Squadron Officer School at Maxwell Air Force Base in Alabama; Air Command and Staff College at Maxwell Air Force Base; and Air War College at Maxwell Air Force Base. From June 1979 to June 1982, he was assigned as Mechanical Engineering Section Chief and then Chief of Planning, Operations and Maintenance Branch of the 436th Civil Engineering Squadron at Dover Air Force Base in Delaware. From July 1982 to July 1983, he was assigned as Chief of Engineering for Detachment 1, 554th RED HORSE Squadron, at Kunsan Air Base in South Korea. Bridges was promoted to Captain on June 4, 1983. From August 1983 to June 1986, he served as Chief of Engineering Contract Management and Chief of Operations for the 48th Civil Engineering Squadron at Royal Air Force Lakenheath in the United Kingdom. From June 1986 to July 1989, he served as Assistant Professor of Aerospace Studies for Air Force ROTC Detachment 805 at Texas A&M University in College Station, Texas. From August 1989 to July 1990, he was assigned as Readiness Planning Staff Officer with Headquarters Tactical Air Command Readiness Directorate at Langley Air Force Base in Virginia. From August 1990 to March 1991, he served as an Air Force Engineering Liaison with the United States Central Command at Riyadh, Saudi, Arabia. He was promoted to Major on August 1, 1990. From March 1991 to June 1997, he was assigned as Chief of Policy and Oversight Division with Headquarters Tactical Air Command Environmental Directorate at Langley Air Force Base. From July 1993 to December 1995, he was assigned as Chief of Operations, and later as Commander, of the 24th Civil Engineer Squadron at Howard Air Force Base, Panama. He was promoted to Lieutenant Colonel on January 1, 1996. From June 1997 to June 1998, he was assigned with the Operations Division as Real Property Maintenance Activities Program Element at Landstuhl, Germany; Section Sergeant USAIC in Augsburg, Germany; Platoon Sergeant in the 226th Maintenance Company at Fort Sill, Oklahoma; Senior Instructor for VII Corp Noncommissioned Officers Academy in Augsburg; Senior Drill Sergeant in the 16th Ordnance Battalion at Aberdeen Proving Grounds, Maryland; Senior Instructor in the 8th Army Noncommissioned Officers Academy at Baumholder, Germany; First Sergeant for the 47th Forward Support Battalion at Baumholder; Command Sergeant Major with the 2nd Forward Support Battalion, Camp Hovey, South Korea; Command Sergeant Major of the 703rd Main Support Battalion at Fort Stewart, Georgia. In August 2004, he was serving as the DISCOM, Command Sergeant Major with the 3rd Infantry Division (Mechanized) at Fort Stewart/Hunter Army Airfield.

Brinkley, Ronald W.

CAPTAIN—NAVY

Captain Ronald W. Brinkley was born in Norfolk, Virginia and raised in Virginia Beach. He finished First Colonial High School in 1973, and graduated from the United States Naval Academy in June 1977 with a degree in International Security Affairs. After completing Surface Warfare Officer School, he was assigned to USS *Coontz* (DDG 40), where he served as a first lieutenant, Electronic Warfare Officer, and Combat Information Center Officer. During his tenure, *Coontz* deployed to the Mediterranean and the North Atlantic.

After attending the Command, Control, and Communications Course at the Armed Forces Staff College in December 1990. Captain Brinkley reported to the Joint Staff in the Operations Directorate, where he was assigned as a Branch Chief in the Command Systems Operations Division. Subsequent, he commanded USS *Gunston Hall* (LSD 44) from April 1994 to October 1995. During that tour, his ship received its second

consecutive Battle Efficiency "E." In November 1995, he reported to the United States Naval Academy as the Third Battalion Officer and served there until May 1998. From June 1998 to July 1999, he served as Assistant Chief of Staff for Operations for the Commander of Amphibious Group Two. In December 1999, he served as the Commander of USS *Cleveland* (LPD 7). During his tenure, *Cleveland* won the Battle Efficiency "E" for the 4th and 5th consecutive years. In July 2001, he was assigned as the Commander of the Surface Warfare Officers School Command.

Brinson, Sammy J., Jr.

COMMAND SERGEANT MAJOR—ARMY

Brinson is a native of Leesburg, Florida. He entered the United States Army in November 1977, and completed Basic Combat Training and Advanced Individual Training for Tracked Vehicle Mechanics at Fort Knox, Kentucky.

His military education includes all the Noncommissioned Officer Education System Courses; the First Sergeant Course; the Nuclear, Biological, and Chemical School; the Equal Opportunity School; the Instructor's Training Course; the Master Diagnostician Course; the United States Army Drill Sergeant School; and the United States Army Sergeants Major Academy.

His leadership assignments include serving as Squad Leader, Platoon Sergeant, Senior Drill Sergeant, First Sergeant, Company Motor Sergeant, Battalion Motor Sergeant, Brigade Motor Sergeant, and Senior Instructor/Writer for MOS 63 B/63 H), In November 2004, he was serving as the Command Sergeant Major for 71st Corps Support Battalion in Bamberg, Germany.

Briscoe, Carl E.

BRIGADIER GENERAL—ARMY

Born in Atlantic City, New Jersey, Briscoe was drafted into the United States Army Air Corps on August 28, 1943. He served as Chief Clerk at Headquarters, McClellan Field, California, and on February 5, 1946, he was discharged as a sergeant.

He joined the New Jersey Army National Guard on March 1, 1948, as a sergeant and was later promoted to sergeant major of the 122nd A W Battalion. In January 1951 he accepted an appointment as warrant officer, junior grade. After completion of the 10 Series, he was commissioned a second lieutenant on June 29, 1953, and assigned as adjutant of the 122nd AAA Gun Battalion. He served in that capacity until April 1955, at which time he was transferred to the 116th AAA Gun Battalion (On-Site) in the Camden area as the battalion adjutant. The unit was reorganized as a Nike-Ajax on-site unit, and on June 29, 1956, he was promoted to first lieutenant. Briscoe completed the 20 and 30 series air defense and on May 22, 1958, he was promoted to captain, and attended the Nike-Ajax Officer Orientation Course at Fort Bliss, Texas. On May 2, 1962, Briscoe was reassigned to the 5th Battalion, 112th Field Artillery, in Atlantic City, New Jersey, as adjutant and completed the Officer Familiarization Field Artillery

extension course. On January 24, 1966, he was promoted to major, field artillery and assigned as S-3. He was reassigned as battalion executive officer on July 1, 1970, and on December 7, 1974, he completed Command and General Staff College.

On February 1, 1976, he was appointed Commanding Officer of the 50th Armored Division Artillery and was promoted to Colonel on February 7, 1976. On September 1, 1977, he was transferred to the Headquarters of the New Jersey Army National Guard as Executive Officer, and on May 1, 1979, he was appointed Director of the State Area Command. He was promoted and federally recognized as Brigadier General on August 23, 1979. General Briscoe was appointed Adjutant General of the United States Virgin Islands at St. Croix, USVI, in December 1982. He exercised the supervision and direct command of the National Guard of the Virgin Islands, promulgating in the name of the Governor orders, directives and regulation to maintain the National Guard of the Virgin Islands trained, disciplined, uniformed, and equipped at all times. He was responsible for 132 federal technicians and 10 territory employees, and retired from the National Guard on July 15, 1983.

His military awards and decorations include the Meritorious Service Medal; Army Commendation Medal; National Defense Service Medal; American Campaign; World War II Victory; Armed Forces Reserve Medal; Army Reserve Components Achievement Medal; New Jersey Medal of Merit; New Jersey Medal of Honor; and New Jersey Recruiting Award.

Bristol, James A.
SERGEANT MAJOR—MARINE

Bristol enlisted in the Marine Corps in June 1978 and attended Recruit Training at Marine Corps Recruit Depot Parris Island, South Carolina. Upon graduating from Recruit Training, he attended Shore Partyman School at Camp Lejeune, North Carolina.

His key military assignments include serving as Operations and Logistics Chief with the 4th Force Service Support Group; Company Gunnery Sergeant and First Sergeant for Charlie Company, 3rd Force Service Support Group in Okinawa, Japan; First Sergeant in Bravo Company, 2nd Tank Battalion, 2nd Marine Division at Camp Lejeune; First Sergeant at Marine Corps Engineer School at Camp Lejeune; Sergeant Major, 12th Marine Corps District as the Recruiting Station; Sergeant Major of the 4th Maintenance Battalion at Charlotte, North Carolina; and Sergeant Major for the 6th Marine Corps District.

Brock, Donna A.
COMMAND SERGEANT MAJOR—ARMY

A native of Los Angeles, California, Brock entered the Army in December 1979 and completed Basic Combat Training at Fort Leonard Wood, Missouri. She completed her Advanced Individual Training as a Combat Medic at Fort Sam Houston, Texas.

Her military and civilian education includes all the Noncommissioned Officer Education System Courses; Air Assault School; Medical Noncommissioned Officer Course; Drill Sergeant School; Battle Staff Noncommissioned Course; First Sergeant Course; Master Fitness Course; the United States Army Sergeants Major Academy (class 50); and the Command Sergeants Major Course. She earned her Associates Degree from Hawaii Pacific University and is currently pursuing her Bachelor's Degree through Thomas Edison State College.

She has served in a variety of leadership positions including Emergency Room Noncommissioned Officer; Clinical Noncommissioned Officer in Charge; Training Noncommissioned Officer; Operations Noncommissioned Officer; Squad Leader; Platoon Sergeant; First Sergeant; and Command Sergeant Major.

Bronson, Gary J.
COMMAND SERGEANT MAJOR—ARMY

Bronson is a native of Columbus, Georgia, and entered the Army on June 1978. He attended Basic Combat Training and Advanced Individual Training at Fort Sill, Oklahoma. His military and civilian education includes the Noncommissioned Officer Course Leadership Courses; the Drill Sergeants School; the Air Assault School; Master Fitness Course; First Sergeants Course; and the United States Army Sergeants Major Academy (class #50). He holds an Associate of Arts degree in Science at MC Community College and a Bachelor of Arts in Liberal Arts from Regents College.

He has served in a variety of leadership positions including Howitzer Section Chief: Platoon Sergeant; Drill Sergeant; Senior Drill Sergeant; Operations Sergeant; First Sergeant; Operations Sergeant Major; Senior Observer Controller Fire Support Division (JRTC); and Senior Army Enlisted Advisor for the 1st United States Army. In August 2004, he was serving as the Command Sergeant Major for the 75th Field Artillery Brigade.

Brooks, Denise
COMMAND SERGEANT MAJOR—ARMY

A native of New Orleans, Louisiana, Brooks entered on active military duty in the United States Army in February 1980 as a Motor Vehicle Operator and attended Basic and Advanced Individual Training at Fort Dix, New Jersey.

Her military education includes all the Non-Commissioned Officers Education System Courses; the Drill Sergeant School; Equal Opportunity Leaders Course; the First Sergeant Course; the United States Army Ser-

geants Major Academy (class 50); and the Command Sergeant Major Course.

Her military assignments include serving as a Heavy Vehicle Operator; Squad Leader; Driver's Training Instructor; Platoon Sergeant; Truck Master; Transportation Section Non-Commissioned Officer in Charge; First Sergeant; and Command Sergeant Major.

Her assignments include the 501st Transportation Company, 53rd Transportation Battalion, in Kaiserslautern, Germany; the 628th Transportation Company at Fort Hood, Texas; 51st Transportation Company, and Headquarters and Headquarters Company of the 181st Transportation Battalion in Mannheim, Germany; Charlie Company, 4th Battalion, 25th Infantry and 36th Transportation Battalion at Fort Dix, New Jersey; the 396th Transportation Company in Stuggart, Germany, where she deployed in support of Operation Desert Shield/Desert Storm; the 360th Transportation Company at Fort Carson, Colorado, where she deployed to Somalia in support of Operation Restore Hope; Headquarters and Headquarters Company, 13th COSCOM, and 418th Transportation Company at Fort Hood, Texas; Headquarters and Headquarters Detachment of the 39th Transportation Battalion in Kaiserslautern; and USAMC at Fort Bliss, Texas.

In July 2005, Sergeant Major Brooks was serving as the Command Sergeant Major of the 11th Transportation Battalion (Terminal) at Fort Story, Virginia.

Brooks, Elmer T.
BRIGADIER GENERAL—AIR FORCE

Brooks was born in Washington, D.C., and married the former Kathryn M. Casselberry of Dayton, Ohio. They have one daughter, Karen, and three sons, Victor,

Eric, and Mark. He received a Bachelor of Arts degree in Zoology from Miami University at Oxford, Ohio, in 1954. He was commissioned through the Air Force Reserve Officer Training Corps program. In 1973, he received a Master of Science degree from George Washington University in Washington, D.C., and was graduated from the Industrial College of the Armed Forces at Fort Lesley J. McNair in Washington, D.C. In 1978, he completed the Executive Program of the Colgate Darden Graduate School of Business Administration at the University of Virginia, under the Air Force's Advanced Management Program.

Brooks entered the United States Air Force in April 1955 and was assigned to a Continental Air Command Air Reserve Flying Center at Greater Pittsburgh, Pennsylvania, Airport as Unit Adjutant, then as Base Director of Personnel. He then went to the Philippines as a Radar Station Commander and later as a Personnel Division Chief at the Headquarters of the 13th Air Force at Clark Air Base. In July 1961, he returned to the United States and was assigned as a Missile Combat Crew Commander and Instructor Missile Crew Commander with the Atlas Intercontinental Ballistic Missile System at Lincoln Air Force Base, Nebraska. From November 1965 to May 1968, he served in Houston, Texas, as a Flight Control Technologist for Gemini and Apollo Space Missions at the National Aeronautics and Space Administration's Manned Spacecraft Center. He then became a Resource Manager and Section Chief at the Force Military Personnel Center at Randolph Air Force Base, Texas, until August 1972. After completing the Industrial College of the Armed Forces, he was assigned to the Office of the Secretary of the Air Force, Space Systems Office, as Executive Officer. He became the Military Assistant to the Special Assistant to the Secretary and Deputy Secretary of Defense in June 1975. He

later served as Military Assistant to Secretaries of Defense.

General Brooks became Vice Commander of the 381st Strategic Missile Wing, a Titan II Intercontinental Ballistic Missile Unit at McConnell Air Force Base, Kansas, in July 1978 and Commander of the Wing from January 1979 until October 1981. He then returned to Washington, D.C., as Assistant Deputy Director of International Negotiations at the Organization of the Joint Chiefs of Staff, and was appointed by the President as Deputy Commissioner of the U.S.-USSR Standing Consultative Commission. In September 1982 he became Deputy Director of International Negotiations, and Organization of the Joint Chiefs of Staff. He was assigned as Assistant Deputy, Under Secretary of Defense for Strategic and Theater Nuclear Forces, in Washington, D.C., in August 1983. He was appointed Brigadier General on September 1, 1981, with the same date of rank.

The general's military awards and decorations include the Defense Superior Service Medal (with oak leaf clusters); the Legion of Merit; Meritorious Service Medal (with oak leaf cluster); Joint Service Commendation Medal; Air Force Commendation Medal; Air Force Outstanding Unit Award Ribbon (with two oak leaf clusters); Readiness Medal; Master Missile Badge; and the Space Badge.

Brooks, Harry W.

MAJOR GENERAL—ARMY

He was born in Indianapolis, Indiana. He is the son of Harry W. Brooks, Sr., and Nora E. Brooks. He married the former June Hezekiah, and they have three children, Harry W. III, Wayne L., and Craig E. He received a Bachelor of Science degree in Business Administration from the University of Omaha, earned a Master Arts from the University of Oklahoma. His military education includes: the Quartermaster School, Basic

Course; the Artillery and Guided Missile School, Basic and Advanced Courses; United States Army Command and General Staff College; United States Army War College.

General Brooks' military career began as a private in 1947, and on July 1, 1949, he was commissioned a second lieutenant in the United States Army. From February 1962 to October 1963, he served as an Adviser to United States Army Reserve units in the northern New York Sector, II United States Army Corps, in Syracuse, New York. He was the Commanding Officer of the United States Army Reserve Center, northern New York Sector, II United States Army Corps, also in Syracuse from October 1963 to August 1965. From August 1965 to June 1966, he was a student at the United States Command and General Staff College at Fort Leavenworth, Kansas. From June 1966 to November 1967, he was assigned first as Commanding Officer of the 2nd Battalion, 40th Artillery, 199th Infantry Brigade, then as a Special Assistant to the Deputy Commanding Officer of the 199th Infantry Brigade in Vietnam. From December 1967 to July 1969, he served as a staff officer in the Doctrine Branch of the Doctrine and Concepts Division at the Doctrine and Systems Directorate under the Assistant Chief of Staff for Force Development, United States Army, in Washington, D.C. From August 1969 to July 1970, Brook was a student at the United States Army War College at Carlisle Barracks, Pennsylvania. From July 1970 to January 1972, he served as Commanding Officer of the 72nd Field Artillery Group in Europe. From January 1972 to January 1973, he served as Director of Equal Opportunity Programs in the Office of the Deputy Chief of Staff for Personnel, United States Army, in Washington, D.C. From January 1973 to June 1974, he was the Assistant Division Commander for the 2nd Infantry Division in South Korea.

In June 1974, he was appointed Major General and assigned as the Commanding General of the 25th Infantry Division in South Korea. He retired on August 31, 1976.

General Brook's military awards and decorations include the Legion of Merit (with oak leaf cluster); Bronze Star Medal (with oak leaf cluster); Meritorious Service Medal; Air Medal (seven Awards); and the Army Commendation Medal.

Brooks, Janice M.
MASTER SERGEANT—MARINE

Born in Baltimore, Maryland, in 1951, Brooks attended College at Frostburg State University in Maryland where she earned a Bachelor of Science degree in Health and Physical Education. After teaching high school in the Baltimore City Public School System, she enlisted in the United States Marine Corps in December 1974. She attended Boot Camp at Marine Corps Recruit Depot at Parris Island, South Carolina.

She served on active duty from June 1975 to April 1997. Taking advantage of off-duty educational opportunities, she earned a Master of Arts from Webster University while stationed at Marine Corps Recruit Depot at Parris Island.

During her 22 year Marine Corps career, Brooks' primary Military Occupational Specialty (MOS) was that of Contract Specialist. She also held two secondary occupational specialties as Health and Fitness Instructor and Drill Instructor. She has been assigned to Marine Air Ground Task Force Training Center at Twenty-nine Palms, California; Marine Corps Logistics Base at Barstow, California; Marine Corps Base Smedley D. Butler at Okinawa, Japan; Marine Barracks "8th & I" in Washington, D.C.; Marine Corps Recruit Depot at Parris Island; and Marine Corps Base Camp Lejeune, North Carolina. Her final duty station was Camp Butler at Okinawa where she served two In-Place Consecutive Overseas Tours for a total of 7 years.

After retirement from the military, she served as Naval Science Instructor for Naval JROTC at Curtis High School in the state of Washington.

She is married to Sergeant Major Carl M. Brooks, the Sergeant Major of Marine Corps Security Force Company at the Naval Submarine Base in Bangor, Washington.

Brooks, Leo Austin
BRIGADIER GENERAL—ARMY

Born in Washington, D.C., he is the son of Rev. and Mrs. Houston G. Brooks, Sr., of Alexandria, Virginia. His father is the pastor of Mt. Calvary Baptist Church in Rockville, MD. He has three brothers, Dr. Houston G. Brooks, Jr., a chemist with American Cyanamid Somerset, N.J.; Dr. Henry C. Brooks, head of the Department of Psychology at Andover Theological Seminary in Newton Center, Massachusetts; and Francis K. Brooks, a high school Chemistry teacher in Montpelier, Vermont; and a sister, Mrs. Nellie B. Quander, Assistant to the Superintendent of Fairfax County Public Schools. He married the former Naomi Ethel Lewis, also a native of Alexandria, and they have two sons, Brigadier General Leo A. Jr., and Brigadier General Vincent Keith, both graduates of the United States Military Academy at West Point. They have one daughter, Marquita Karen, a graduate of James Madison University at Harrisonburg, Virginia.

He graduated from Parker-Gray High School in 1950, and received a Bachelor of Science degree in Instrumental Music Education from Virginia State University at Petersburg, Virginia. He was designated a distinguished military graduate from the Army Reserve Officers Training Corps, where he received a commission as second lieutenant in 1954. In 1966, he received a master's degree in Financial Management from George Washington University in Washington, D.C. He also is a graduate of the United States Army Command and General Staff College and the National War College.

General Brooks has held a wide variety of important command and staff positions, culminating in his most recent assignments, which include Congressional Coordinator with the Department of the Army in Washington, D.C., from 1967 to 1970. He was assigned as the Cambodian Desk Officer for the Joint Chiefs of Staff in Washington, D.C., from 1972 to 1974. In 1974, he was assigned as the Commanding Officer of the Sacramento Army Depot. From 1976 to 1978, he served as Commanding Officer of the 13th Corps Support Command at Fort Hood, Texas. In 1978, he was appointed Commanding General of the United States Army Troop Support Agency at Fort Lee, Virginia. He was promoted to Brigadier General on July 1, 1978.

His military awards and decorations include the Legion of Merit (with two oak leaf clusters); the Bronze Star; the Meritorious Service Medal; and the Army Commendation Medal.

Brooks, Leo Austin, Jr.
BRIGADIER GENERAL—ARMY

General Brooks is a native of Alexandria, Virginia. He is the son of Brigadier General Leo A. Brooks, Sr. and Naomi E. Brooks, and is the brother of Brigadier General Vincent K. Brooks. He graduated from the United States Military Academy in 1979 and began his career as a rifle and anti-tank platoon leader with the 1-503rd Infantry, 101st Airborne Division (Air Assault). Subsequent to these assignments, he served as the Aide-de-Camp to the Assistant Division Commander for Operations and then commanded C Company, 3d Battalion, 327th Infantry (Air Assault) from July 1982 to December 1983.

General Brooks spent the next four years assigned to the 1st Battalion, 75th Infantry Ranger Regiment where he was the Battalion S-4 and Commander of A Company from June 1986 to February 1988. He served the next three years, from 1988 to 1991, in South Korea as a Ground Operations Officer in the Joint Staff of the Combined Forces Command. In 1992, he was assigned

to the 82nd Airborne Division, where he was the Executive Officer for the 1st Battalion, 504th Parachute Infantry Regiment and the Deputy G-3 of the Division.

Upon departing the 82nd Airborne in January 1994, General Brooks was assigned as the Aide-de-Camp to the Chief of Staff of the United States Army where he served until June 1995. On October 19, 1995, he took command of the 1st Battalion, 504th Parachute Infantry Regiment, with the 82nd Airborne Division. Upon completion of Battalion Command, he was assigned as the Chief of Operations for the XVIII Airborne Corps G-3. After 10 months as the Chief of Operations for the XVIII Airborne Corps, he attended the Army War College in Carlisle, Pennsylvania. On June 22, 1999, he assumed command of the 1st Brigade, 504th Parachute Infantry Regiment, with the 82nd Airborne Division as the 31st Colonel of the Regiment. He commanded the 504th Parachute Infantry Regiment for the following two years until May 31, 2001. In August 2004, he was assigned as Vice Director of the Army Staff, United States Army, at the Pentagon.

He was promoted to Brigadier General that same month in May 2001 and was next assigned as the Assistant Division Commander for Maneuver of the 1st Armored Division, with duty in Baumholder, Germany as the Senior Tactical Commander for that military community from July 2001 until June 2002. On June 28, 2002, General Brooks assumed command of the United States Corps of Cadets at West Point as its 68th Commandant. In July 2005, he was serving as the Vice Director of the Army Staff, at the Pentagon.

His awards and decorations include the Legion of Merit (with two oak leaf clusters); the Defense Meritorious Service Medal (with oak leaf cluster); the Meritorious Service Medal (with four oak leaf clusters), the Army Commendation Medal, the Army Achievement Medal (with two oak leaf clusters), and the Multinational Force and Observer's Medal. He is authorized to wear the Expert Infantryman's Badge, the Ranger Tab, the Master Parachutist Badge, the Pathfinder Badge, the Air Assault Badge, and the German and French Parachutist Badges; and the Army Staff Identification Badge.

Brooks, Vincent K.
MAJOR GENERAL—ARMY

General Brooks is part of an Army family that shares a piece of history. His father, Leo Sr., is a retired Brigadier General. His brother, Leo Jr., serves as the 68th commandant of the United States Corps of Cadets at West Point.

Brigadier General Vincent Brooks graduated from West Point in 1980, and on January 1, 2003 became the first in his class to receive a promotion to Brigadier General.

His military education includes attending Infantry Officer Basic and Advanced Course; United States Army Command and General Staff College; the School of Advanced Military Studies; Senior Service College Fellowship at Harvard University; and the United States Army Command and General Staff College.

From October 1980 to December 1983, he was Weapons Platoon Leader with B Company (later Heavy Mortar Platoon Leader/Executive Officer and Scout Platoon Leader) 1st Battalion (Airborne), 504th Infantry, 82nd Airborne Division at Fort Bragg, North Carolina. In January 1984 he attended Infantry Officer Advanced Course at the United States Army Infantry School at Fort Benning, Georgia. In July 1984 he was assigned as the S-1 (Adjutant), later Commander, B Company, later Commander, Headquarters and Headquarters Company, 4th Battalion (Mechanized), 16th Infantry, 1st Infantry Division (Forward), United States Army Europe and Seventh Army, Germany. From November 1987 to June 1990, he was Personnel Assignment Officer, Infantry Branch, later Professional Development Officer, Combined Arms Division, Officer Personnel Management Directorate, United States Total Army Personnel Command at Alexandria, Virginia.

In August 1990, he was a student at Command and General Staff Officer Course at Command and General Staff College in Fort Leavenworth, Kansas. Later in June 1991, he was a student in the School of Advanced Military Studies Program at United States Army Command and General Staff College in Fort Leavenworth, Kansas. From May 1992 to May 1993 he served as Plans and Exercises Officer, G-3, 1st Cavalry Division, later as S-3 (Operations), 2nd Battalion, 5th Cavalry, 1st Cavalry Division, at Fort Hood, Texas. From January 1995 to June 1995, he was selected to serve as Infantry Systems Integrator in the Combat Maneuver Division at Force Development Directorate of the Office of the Deputy Chief of Staff for Operations and Plans, United States Army, Washington, D.C.

In June 1995, he served as Aide-de-Camp to the Vice Chief of Staff for the Army in Washington, D.C. From April 1996 to May 1998, he served as the Commander, 2nd Battalion, 9th Infantry, 2nd Infantry Division,

Eighth United States Army, in South Korea. In July 1998, he was a Senior Service College Fellow at the John F. Kennedy School of Government, Harvard University, in Cambridge, Massachusetts. From June 1999 to June 2000, he served as Chief of the Plans and Programs Division, G-3, Third United States Army/Army Forces Central Command at Fort McPherson, Georgia and C-5/J-5 (Plans and Policy), Coalition/Joint Task Force, Kuwait. From June 2000 to June 2002, he served as the Commander of 1st Brigade, 3rd Infantry Division (Mechanized) at Fort Stewart, Georgia and during Operation Joint Guardian in Kosovo.

In June 2002, Brooks was selected to a General Officer assignment as Deputy Director for Global/Multilateral Issues/International-American Affairs, J-5, The Joint Staff, in Washington, D.C. From June 2002 to May 2003, he served as Deputy Director for Political Military Affairs, J-5, The Joint Staff, Washington, D.C., later Deputy J-3, Chief Operations Spokesman for United States Central Command at Camp As Sayliyah, Qatar and Operation Enduring Freedom, Qatar. From May 2003 to July 2004, he served as Deputy Director for War on Terrorism, J-5, The Joint Staff, Washington, D.C. From July 2004 to December 2004, he served as the Deputy Chief for Army Public Affairs at the Office of the Secretary of the Army, in Washington, D.C. In December 2004, he was selected to serve as the Chief of Army Public Affairs at the Office of the Secretary of the Army, at the Pentagon.

His decorations and badges include the Defense Superior Service Medal; the Legion of Merit (with oak leaf cluster); the Defense Meritorious Service Medal; Meritorious Service Medal (with seven oak leaf clusters); Joint Service Commendation Medal; Army Commendation Medal (with oak leaf cluster); Army Achievement Medal (with two oak leaf clusters); Expert Infantryman Badge; Senior Parachutist Badge; Ranger Tab; Joint Chiefs of Staff Identification Badge; and the Army Staff Identification Badge.

Brown, Bruce

COMMAND SERGEANT MAJOR—ARMY

Brown is a native of Lockport, New York, and entered the United States Army in April 1975. He attended Basic Combat Training at Fort Dix, New Jersey and received his Advanced Individual Training at Fort Huachuca, Arizona, where he was trained as a 17K Ground Surveillance Radar Crewman.

His military education includes all the Noncommissioned Officer Education System Courses; Battle Staff Course; Security Manager Course; the Air Assault Course; First Sergeant Course; and the United States Army Sergeants Major Academy.

He has held numerous key leadership positions including the CMF Training Manager for Headquarters INSCOM in January 1990; First Sergeant for A Company, 532nd Military Intelligence Battalion, in South Korea in January 1996; Instructor at the First Sergeant Course in January 1997; and as the Command Sergeant Major for the 104th Military Intelligence Battalion at

vices; and Superintendent of the Medical Operations Squadron all at Keesler Air Force Base, Mississippi. From 1998 to 2001, he was assigned as the Superintendent of the 48th Medical Operations Squadron, and later Superintendent of the 48th Medical Group at RAF Lakenheath, United Kingdom. In February 2001, he was selected to serve as the Command Chief Master

Sergeant of the 48th Fighter Wing at RAF Lakenheath.

Brown, Dallas C., Jr.
BRIGADIER GENERAL—ARMY

General Brown was born in New Orleans, Louisiana, the son of Dallas C. Brown and Sydney Taylor Brown. He and his wife, Dr. Elizabeth T. Brown, have five children, Dallas C. III, Leonard G., Jan B., Karen L., and Barbara A. He received a Bachelor of Arts degree in History from West Virginia State College; and earned a Master of Arts degree in government from Indiana University. His military education includes Infantry School, Basic Course; Artillery School, Battery Officer and Advanced Course; Defense Language Institute, Russian; United States Army Command and General Staff College; and the United States Naval War College.

Fort Hood, Texas. In October 2004, Brown was serving as the Command Sergeant Major at the 205th Military Intelligence Brigade.

Brown, Carl L.
COMMAND CHIEF MASTER SERGEANT—
    AIR FORCE

Command Chief Master Sergeant Carl L. Brown entered the United States Air Force in 1977 and received Technical Training as an Inventory Management Specialist at Lowery Air Force Base, Colorado. He cross-trained in 1982, and became a Medical Services Technician.

His civilian and military education includes an associate's degree in Science; an associate's degree in Emergency Medical Technology; a bachelor's degree in Psychology from the University of Southern Mississippi in Hattiesburg, Mississippi; and a master's degree in Business Administration from William Carey College in Hattiesburg. He graduated from the Inventory Management Technical Training School at Lowry Air Force Base, Colorado; Medical Service Technical Training School at Sheppard Air Force Base, Texas; TAC NCO Academy at Tyndall Air Force Base, Florida; and Senior NCO Academy at Maxwell Air Force Base, Alabama.

From 1987 to 1991, Brown was assigned as Superintendent of Clinical Services and Superintendent of the Obstetrics Unit at Torrejon Air Base in Spain; while in this assignment he was deployed during Operation Desert Shield/Storm, and served as Superintendent of the Air Transportable Hospital. From 1991 to 1998, he was assigned as Superintendent of the Aeromedical Staging Facility. He was later Superintendent of the Department of Medicine; Superintendent Nursing Ser-

He began his 30-year career in the Regular Army as an Infantry Platoon Leader in the 82nd Airborne Division. Subsequently, he served in various units in Korea, Germany, and the United States. In Vietnam he commanded the 519th Military Intelligence Battalion, which received a Meritorious Unit Commendation for General Brown's period of command. He later commanded the United States Army Field Station in Berlin. After being designated a Foreign Area Officer (Russian) in 1970, he served as a specialist on Soviet affairs in various positions in the Defense Intelligence Agency, including Deputy Vice Director for Foreign Intelligence. General Brown also served as a United States Delegate and Chief Delegate at five NATO intelligence conferences involving all of Europe and the Middle East. His final assignment was Deputy Commandant of the United States Army War College. He has written and lectured extensively throughout the United States on Soviet, communist, and military affairs. He was appointed Brigadier General on September 1, 1978.

His military awards and decorations include the Defense Superior Service Medal; Master Parachutist Badge; Army Commendation Medal; Joint Service Commendation Medal; Meritorious Service Medal; and Aircraft Crewman Badge. He retired from active duty in 1984 and served as an associate professor of history at West Virginia State College.

Brown, Dwight J.
COMMAND SERGEANT MAJOR—ARMY

Command Sergeant Major Dwight J. Brown, a na-

tive of Lexington, Kentucky, enlisted in the Army in January 1973. He is a graduate of the United States Army Sergeants Major Academy; First Sergeants Course; the Drill Sergeant School; Operations and Intelligence (Battle Staff) Course; and Joint Fire Power Air Ground Operations Course.

Brown was assigned in July 1997 as the Command Sergeant Major of the 1st Armored Division in Bad Kreuznach, Germany; from January 2000 to October 2000, he served as the Command Sergeant Major for the Third United States Army/United States Forces Central Command.

Brown, Edward L., Jr.
COMMAND SERGEANT MAJOR—ARMY

Sergeant Major Edward L. Brown, Jr. is a native of Baltimore, Maryland. He enlisted in the United States Army on July 7, 1976, and completed Basic Combat Training and Advanced Individual Training at Fort Knox, Kentucky. He is a graduate of the Instructors Course; the First Sergeants Course; and the United States Army Sergeants Major Academy.

His most recent assignments include serving as First Sergeant for B Company, 1st Signal Battalion, 11th Signal Brigade; as the First Sergeant with the 385th Signal Company, 86th Signal Battalion; as the First Sergeant at Headquarters and Headquarters Detachment with the 86th Signal Battalion, 11th Signal Brigade; and as the S-4 Sergeant Major with the 172nd SIB Brigade. Brown is currently serving as the Sergeant Major for Letterkenny Army Depot.

Brown, Emma
LIEUTENANT COMMANDER—NAVY

A native of Georgia, Brown graduated from Savannah State College in 1993, where she earned a Bachelor of Science in Mathematics and her commission via the NROTC scholarship program. She was designated a General Unrestricted Line Officer.

Her first permanent duty assignment was at Naval Computer and Telecommunications Station, Pensacola, Florida. She served as the Naval Telecommunications Center Division Officer. During this tour, her designation changed to Fleet Support Officer.

In January 1995, she reported to the Joint Maritime Facility at St. Maugan in the United Kingdom. She served as a Tactical Watch Officer and was later promoted to the Communication Officer.

In September 1998, she reported to Naval Postgraduate School at Monterey, California in the Information Warfare curriculum. She completed her Master of Science degree in Systems Engineering in 2000 and transferred to Pers-3 of the Naval Personnel Command at Millington, Tennessee as the Electronic Military Personnel Record Systems (EMPRS) Operations Officer. She was re-designated an Information Professional in October 2001. During this tour, she volunteered to support Operation Enduring Freedom and later, Operation Iraqi Freedom and was forward deployed on the ground in Kuwait from January to July 2003 as the CJTF-4 Knowledge Manager.

Commander Brown reported in August 2003 to Naval Computer and Telecommunications Station, Jacksonville, Florida as the Communications Officer. In September 2004, she was promoted to the Executive Officer of Naval Computer and Telecommunications Station, Jacksonville.

Brown, Eric

CHIEF WARRANT OFFICER 5—NAVY

After graduating from high school in Beaufort, South Carolina, Brown found himself faced with the decision in which branch of the armed forces to enlist: Army or Navy? He felt that the Navy was a better option for him at the time, so he enlisted into the United States Navy.

Since that time, he has been stationed aboard four aircraft carriers; USS *John F. Kennedy* (CV 67), USS *Carl Vinson* (CVN 70), USS *Theodore Roosevelt* (CVN 71), USS *Coral Sea* (CV43), and the amphibious assault ship USS *Kearsarge* (LHD 3). He also spent several years of shore duty at Navy Auxiliary Landing Field Fentress in Chesapeake, Virginia, where he was in charge of the crash crew that handled emergency situations.

In September 1988, with nearly 14 years of his naval career completed, he became a Chief Warrant Officer aboard USS *Theodore Roosevelt*. Chief Brown reported to Naval Air Systems Command at Patuxent River, Maryland in May 2002 as the head of the station's Airfield Facilities Division.

Eric Brown was promoted to Chief Warrant Officer 5 during a ceremony March 1, 2004. Brown became the first Navy Chief Warrant Officer 5 in Pax River history, and only the fifth since the Navy implemented the grade in 2002.

Chief Warrant Officer Brown, the first Navy Chief Warrant Officer 5 at Patuxent River, was joined at his promotion by a former shipmate. The first Chief in the Navy to receive the new CWO5 rank, CWO5 Leon Cole, was there to see Chief Brown receive his CWO5.

CWO5 Brown is now serving at the Naval Aviation Technical Training Center in Pensacola, Florida.

Brown, Erroll M.

REAR ADMIRAL—US COAST GUARD

Rear Admiral Brown is married to the former Monica Hayes of Groton, CT., and they have two children, Monica and Elise-Estee. He received a commission from the United States Coast Guard Academy in 1972, and a bachelor's degree in Marine Engineering. He earned a master's degree in Naval Architecture and Marine Engineering and a second master's in Industrial

and Operations Engineering, both from the University of Michigan. He received a Master of Business Administration degree from Rensselaer Polytechnic Institute in 1986. In 1994, he graduated from the Naval War College with a master's degree in National Security and Strategic Studies.

Brown has held a variety of both career building and command staff assignments. As Damage Control Assistant and Assistant Engineer Officer aboard the Coast Guard Icebreaker *Burton Island* (WAGB-283), and Maintenance Type Deck Officer for the Eleventh Coast Guard District, Naval Engineering Branch. While assigned at Coast Guard Headquarters, he served in the Small Boat Branch as the Supervisor for two resident Inspection Officers, overseeing their small boat construction projects. He served as the Engineer Officer aboard the Coast Guard Cutter *Jarvis* (WHEC-725), as an Instructor in the Marine Engineering Department at the United States Coast Guard Academy, and as Executive Officer aboard Coast Guard Cutter *Rush* (WHEC-723). A Program Reviewer in the Office of the Chief of Staff, Programs Division in Coast Guard Headquarters, he has also served as the Military Assistant to the Secretary of Transportation. Rear Admiral Brown was assigned as Chief of the Budget Division in the Office of the Chief of Staff in Coast Guard Headquarters. Most recently, he was Commanding Officer of United States Coast Guard Integrated Support Command at Portsmouth, Virginia. In January 2003, he was serving as Commander of Maintenance and Logistics Command Atlantic at Norfolk, Virginia.

His awards and decorations include the Legion of Merit; Meritorious Service Medal; Secretary's Award for Meritorious Achievement; United States Coast Guard Commendation Medal (2 awards); Unit Commendation; Meritorious Unit Commendation; National Defense Service Medal; Special Operations Ribbon (3 awards); Bicentennial Unit Commendation Ribbon; Antarctica Service Medal; Sea Service Deployment Ribbon; Expert Rifleman Medal; and the Expert Pistol Shot Medal.

Brown, Fredrick
LIEUTENANT COLONEL—ARMY

Brown is a native of Natchez, Mississippi, and 1980 enlisted in the 95th Infantry Army Reserve Corp, in Monroe, Louisiana. Upon completion of ROTC as a Distinguished Military Graduate in 1985, he was commissioned a Second Lieutenant in the Ordnance Corps and received a Bachelor of Arts degree in Sociology from Northeast Louisiana University at Monroe. He also holds a Master of Arts degree in Business Administration from Central Michigan University at Mt. Pleasant. His military education includes the Ordnance Officer Basic and Advanced Courses, CAS3, Logistic Management Course, Air Assault Course, Support Operations Course, and the Army Command and General Staff College.

His assignments include serving as Branch Chief for Logistics Support Operations at United States Euro-

pean Command J-4; as the Executive Officer of the Division Material Management Center, 25th Infantry Division, at Schofield Barracks, Hawaii; as Executive Officer of the 725th Main Support Battalion, 25th Infantry Division (Light); Support Operations Officer for the 225th Forward Support Battalion, 25th Infantry Division (Light); Assistant Professor of Military Science at Jackson State University in Jackson, Mississippi; as aide de camp to the Chief of Ordnance at Aberdeen Proving Ground, Maryland; the Battalion S-3 Operations Officer, Headquarters and Headquarters Company, 725th Main Support Battalion, 25th Infantry Division (Light), at Schofield Barracks, Hawaii; as the Company Commander of Charlie Company, Light Maintenance, 24th Infantry Division (Heavy), at Fort Stewart, Georgia during Operation Desert Shield/Storm; the Class IX Supply Officer, Shop Officer and Maintenance Platoon Leader, Delta Company, 724th Main Support Battalion, at Fort Stewart, Georgia; and as the Commander of Special Troops Battalion, 3rd Corps Support Command.

Brown, George J.
BRIGADIER GENERAL—ARMY

Born in the Bronx, New York, Brown married the former Lynn Marie Meaney, and they have three children, George, Joseph, and Lisa. He received a Bachelor of Arts degree in Biology from Hampton Institute at Hampton, Virginia, and a Doctorate of Medicine from Boston University in Boston, Massachusetts. General Brown entered the Army in 1972. He completed his internship and residency at Fitzsimons Army Medical Center in Denver, Colorado, and a gastroenterology fellowship at Walter Reed Medical Center. His military education includes United States Army Medical Officer Basic and Advanced Courses; United States Army Command and General Staff College; and the United States Army War College. He was promoted to

Captain on May 20, 1973. From May 1973 to May 1976, Brown was a resident of internal medicine at Fitzsimmons Army Medical Center, Aurora, Colorado. He was promoted to Major on May 20, 1976, and served as the Chief of the Gastroenterology Section in the Department of Medicine, United States Army Medical Department Activity, at Fort Carson, Colorado.

He was promoted to Lieutenant Colonel on September 30, 1980, and served as Instructor in Medicine and Assistant Clinical Professor at the Uniformed Services University of the Health Sciences at Bethesda, Maryland; Chief of Gastroenterology Service and Chief of the Department of Medicine at William Beaumont Army Medical Center in El Paso, Texas.

He was promoted to Colonel on September 30, 1986, and served as Internal Medicine Consultant at the Headquarters of the 7th Medical Command in Heidelberg, Germany; Commander of United States Army Hospital, Berlin; Commander of the Letterman Army Institute of Research in San Francisco, California; Commander of Blanchfield Army Community Hospital at Fort Campbell, Kentucky; Deputy Commander for Clinical Services at Walter Reed Health Army Medical Center, Washington, D.C.; and Commander of Walter Reed Health Care System at Walter Reed Army Medical Center, Washington, D.C.

Brown was promoted to Brigadier General on January 1, 1996. He assumed duties as Commanding General at Madigan Army Medical Center, Lead Agent Region 11, and Commander of Northwest Health Service Support Area at Fort Lewis, Washington, on 30 January 1996. He retired from the military on January 31, 1999.

General Brown is certified by the National Board of Medical Examiners, the American Board of Internal Medicine and Gastroenterology, and the American Board of Medical Management. He is a member of the American College of Physician Executives, American College of Physicians, and the American Gastroenterological Association.

His numerous military awards include the Legion of Merit (with three oak leaf clusters); Meritorious Service Medal (with oak leaf cluster); Army Commendation Medal (with oak leaf cluster); the Order of Military Medical Merit; and the Order of Saint Barbara.

Brown, Jerry P.
COLONEL—ARMY

Colonel Jerry P. Brown is a 1978 graduated of Clemson University, where he received a bachelor's degree in History. He also holds a master's degree in Administration from Central Michigan University at Mt. Pleasant, Michigan. His military education includes the Air Defense Artillery Basic and Advanced Courses; Combined Arms; Services Staff School; the United States Army Command and General Staff College; and the Army War College.

Colonel Brown entered the Army as a second lieutenant in 1978. He served as Platoon Leader, Maintenance Officer, and Executive Officer with the 3rd Battalion, 61st Air Defense Artillery (ADA), 11th ADA Brigade (Sep), at Fort Bliss, Texas; as Brigade Maintenance Officer and Commander, Headquarters Company, 7th Signal Brigade (Sep), in Mannheim, Germany; as the S-3 (Operations), with the 1st Battalion, 2nd Air Defense Artillery, 11th Air Defense Artillery (Sep), at Fort Stewart, Georgia; and as Commander, 5th Battalion, 2nd Air Defense Artillery, 69th Air Defense Artillery Brigade, in Bamberg, Germany.

Colonel Brown was selected to serve with the United States Army Kwajalein Atoll/Reagan Test Site, after serving the last three years as Chief of War Plans at the

Headquarters of the Department of the Army at the Pentagon.

Brown, Jesse LeRoy
ENSIGN—NAVY

Brown was born in Hattiesburg, Mississippi, on October 13, 1926. He enlisted in the Naval Reserve in 1946 and was appointed a Midshipman in the United States Navy the following year. After attending Navy pre-flight school and flight training, he was designated a Naval Aviator in October 1948, becoming the first black aviator to achieve this status.

He was assigned to Fighter Squadron 32, and received his commission as Ensign in April 1949.

During the Korean War, his squadron operated from USS *Leyte* (CV-32), flying in support of the United Nations forces. On December 4, 1950, while on a close air support mission near the Chosin Reservoir, Ensign Brown's plane was hit by enemy fire and crashed. Despite heroic efforts by other aviators, he could not be rescued and died in his aircraft. He was awarded the Distinguished Flying Cross for his Korean War combat service.

The United States Navy named a ship after this pioneering African American Naval Aviator, USS *Jesse L. Brown* (FF-1089).

Brown, Jimmie
SERGEANT MAJOR—MARINES

Brown was born in Dooly County, Georgia, and moved to Philadelphia, Pennsylvania as a child, graduating from Simon Gratz High School in 1976. He entered the Marine Corps Recruit Depot at Parris Island, South Carolina, in July 1976, and completed Infantry Training at Camp Pendleton, California. He was transferred to Sea School at Marine Corps Recruit Depot at San Diego, California. Upon graduating from Sea School he transferred to Marine Detachment USS *Kitty Hawk* (CV-36).

He was assigned to the 2nd Battalion, 8th Marines Dragon Platoon Sergeant for one float and a (UDP) unit deployment program with 2nd Platoon Golf Company, 2nd Battalion, 8th Marines from December 1984 to April 1987. Brown was then assigned to Drill Instructor School. Upon graduation, he was assigned to D Company, 2nd Recruit Training Battalion in May 1987. In July 1989, he was assigned as Assistant Marine Officer Instructor University of Notre Dame, and was then assigned to 3rd Battalion, 8th Marines Regiment as Company Gunnery Sergeant for Headquarters & Service and Kilo Company. He was promoted to First Sergeant in August 1995, and was assigned as Company First Sergeant of India Company, 3rd Battalion, 8th Marines until February 1996. He was assigned to Inspector Instructor Staff in Harrisburg, Pennsylvania, Echo Company, 2nd Battalion, 25th Marines Regiment from March 1996 to August 1998, and in October 2001 became Sergeant Major of Marine Corps Air Facility at Quantico, Virginia.

Brown, John M., Sr.
MAJOR GENERAL—ARMY

Born in Vicksburg, Mississippi, Brown is the son of Joeddie Fred Brown and Ernestine Helen Foster Brown. He married the former Louise (Lou) Yvonne Dorsey. They have four children, Ronald Quinton, Jan Michelle, John Mitchell, and Jay Michael.

He was commissioned a second lieutenant and awarded a Bachelor of Science degree in Engineering by the United States Military Academy. He also holds a Master's degree in Comptrollership and has completed the Advanced Management Program at the University of Houston. His military education includes completion of the Basic and Advanced Courses of the Infantry School, the United States Army Command and General Staff College, and the Industrial College of the Armed Forces.

Brown has held a wide variety of important command and staff positions, culminating in his assignment as Deputy Commanding General of III Corps at Fort Hood, Texas. Other key assignments held recently include Assistant Division Commander of the 2nd Infantry Division in South Korea; Deputy Director of Materiel Plans and Programs at the Office of the Deputy Chief of Staff for Research, Development, and Acquisition in Washington, D.C.; and from February 1983 to July 1985, as the Deputy Chief of Staff, Comptroller, United States Army Forces Command, at Fort McPherson, Georgia.

He served in a variety of important career-building assignments preparatory to his most recent duties. He was Operations Research Analyst (later Chief) of the Cost Methodology Branch, Cost Research Division, and later Executive Officer of the Directorate of Cost Analysis in the Office of the Comptroller of the Army in Washington, D.C. He was then assigned as Assistant Secretary of the General Staff (Staff Action Council) in the Office of the Chief of Staff, United States

Army, Washington, D.C. He then departed for Europe where he commanded the 1st Battalion, 87th Infantry, 8th Infantry Division, in Europe. After completion of the Industrial College of the Armed Forces at Fort Lesley J. McNair, in Washington, D.C., he served as Executive to the Comptroller of the Army in Washington, D.C. He then departed for South Korea, where he commanded the 3rd Brigade, 2nd Infantry Division, and subsequently became the Assistant Chief of Staff Comptroller, United Nations Command, United States Forces in Korea, Eighth United States Army. He was promoted to Major General on July 1, 1984, and he retired in 1988. General Brown's military awards and decorations include the Legion of Merit; Bronze Star; Meritorious Service Medal; Army Commendation Medal (with two oak leaf clusters); Combat Infantry Badge; Parachutist Badge; Ranger Tab; and Army General Staff Identification Badge. He received a city of Atlanta proclamation designating June 19, 1985, as "John M. Brown Day" in the state of Georgia.

Brown, Raymond C.

LIEUTENANT COMMANDER—COAST GUARD

A native of Charleston, South Carolina, Lieutenant Commander Brown graduated from North Carolina Agricultural and Technical State University in Greensboro, North Carolina in 1984 with a Bachelor of Science degree in Mechanical Engineering. He is an honor graduate of Southeastern University in the District of Columbia, where he received a Masters in Business Administration (Management) in 1987. He began his military career in the United States Army, as a Reserve Direct Commission Officer in the Adjutant General Corps. His initial assignment was with the 277th Ribbon Bridge Unit at Fort Belvoir, Virginia from 1987 to 1991. He was commissioned in the United States Coast Guard as a Direct Commission Officer (Engineer) in September 1991 and first served at United States Coast Guard Headquarters in the District of Columbia in the Naval Engineering Branch as the Assistant 210th and Mature Class Cutter–type desk manager from 1991 to 1993. There he coordinated the maintenance, conversion and repair for Coast Guard Cutter Eagle, 230th, 213th, 210th, 205th and 180th Medium Endurance Cutters and was the 210th Major Maintenance Availability Assistant Project Officer.

His subsequent assignments included Reserve Quota Manager from 1993 to 1994 and Reserve Officer Evaluations Manager from 1994 to 1997, both in the Reserve Personnel Management Division of the Coast Guard Personnel Command at the United States Coast Guard Headquarters. In 1997, he was assigned to Port Security Unit 305th, at Fort Eustis, Virginia, as the Logistics Officer from 1997 to 2000, preparing a composite Active and Reserve contingency unit for worldwide deployments. At Integrated Support Command New Orleans, he was responsible for coordinating the management and training of more than 900 Reserve personnel in the coastal region of the 8th Coast Guard District. He was responsible for managing the largest mobilization of Coast Guard Reservists since World War II for Operation Liberty Shield, which significantly increased Maritime Security at strategic ports throughout the United States. He served as the Chief of the Force Optimization and Training Branch of Integrated Support Command in New Orleans. In November 2004, Brown was serving as the Commander of the Miami Military Entrance Processing Station in Miami, Florida.

Brown, William E., Jr.
LIEUTENANT GENERAL—AIR FORCE

Lieutenant General Brown was born in Bronx, New York, and married the former Gloria Henry of Plainfield, New Jersey. They have three children, Nancy, Louis, and Bill. He graduated from Dwight Morrow High School in Englewood, New Jersey, in 1945 and received a Bachelor of Science degree from Pennsylvania State University in 1949. He has done graduate work in systems management at the University of Southern California and attended the Harvard Business School's advanced management program. The general graduated from Squadron Officer School at Maxwell Air Force Base in Alabama in 1956; Armed Forces Staff College in Norfolk, Virginia, in 1966; and the Industrial College of the Armed Forces at Fort Lesley J. McNair, Washington, D.C., in 1973.

He was commissioned in December 1951 at Craig Air Force Base, Alabama. After completing pilot training as a distinguished graduate, his first assignment was at Williams Air Force Base, Arizona, as a student in the F-80 Shooting Star jet transition program. From 1952 to 1970, Brown served principally in fighter aircraft in various squadron, wing, and numbered Air Force positions. He flew 125 combat missions in F-86 Sabres with the 4th Fighter-Interceptor Wing in South Korea and another 100 combat missions in F-4 Phantoms during tours of duty in Thailand at Ubon Royal Thai Air Force Base in 1966 and Udorn Royal Thai Air Force base in 1969. He also served overseas in Spain and Germany.

In January 1971, he was assigned to the Department of Defense Manpower and Reserve Affairs Office at the Pentagon, serving as Special Assistant for domestic actions to the Assistant Secretary of Defense. From June 1973 to April 1974, he served as Deputy Commander of Operations for the 64th Flying Training Wing. In February 1975, he took Command of the 1st Composite Wing, Military Airlift Command, at Andrews Air Force Base in Maryland. From June 1977 to October 1978, he served as Chief of Air Force Security Police at the Headquarters of the United States Air Force in Washington, D.C. From October 1978 to August 1980, he served as Commander of the 17th Air Force at Sembach Air Base, West Germany. In September 1982, he was the Commander of the Allied Air Forces, Southern Europe, and Deputy Commander in Chief of United States Air Forces in Europe, Southern Area in Naples, Italy.

He was appointed Brigadier General on August 1,

1975; Major General on April 1, 1979; and Lieutenant General on September 15, 1982. Lt. Gen. William E. Brown, Jr., is a command pilot whose decorations include the Distinguished Service Medal; the Legion of Merit (with two oak leaf clusters); Distinguished Flying Cross (with one oak leaf cluster); Air Medal (with four oak leaf clusters); Air Force Commendation Medal (with one oak leaf cluster); and the Purple Heart. He received a Distinguished Alumni award from Pennsylvania State University in 1981.

Brundidge, Gregory L.
COLONEL—AIR FORCE

Colonel Gregory L. Brundidge graduated from the Air Force Academy in 1979 with a Bachelor of Science degree in Biological Science. He earned a Master of Science degree in Information Systems from the Air Force Institute of Technology at Wright-Patterson Air Force Base in Ohio, as well as a Master of Science degree in National Security Studies from the National War College at Fort Lesley J. McNair in Washington, D.C. His military education includes Squadron Officer School at Maxwell Air Force Base, Alabama; Armed Forces Staff College in Norfolk, Virginia; and Air Command and Staff College.

He has worked as a Staff Officer at Air Force Headquarters, developing mission concepts to be used for future programs. He has also led software maintenance and development teams, commanded communications squadrons, and led Air Combat Command's network division.

In July 1996, Brundidge was assigned as Commander of the 86th Communications Squadron at Ramstein Air Base in Germany; in November 1998, he was assigned as the Chief of the Networks Division at the Communications Directorate, Headquarters Air Combat Command, Langley Air Force Base, Virginia. In

July 2001, he was selected to serve as the Commander of the 3rd Combat Communications Group at Tinker Air Force Base in Oklahoma.

Bryant, Albert

BRIGADIER GENERAL—ARMY

Born in Glen Allen, Mississippi, Bryant is a graduate of Xavier University, where he received a Bachelor of Science degree. He earned a Master of Art degree from Central Michigan University. His military service includes serving as Executive Officer of the 253rd

General Hospital; Deputy Commander of the 220th Military Police; Commander of the 220th Military Police Brigade; and Deputy Director of Pharmacy Service at the Veteran's Administration in Washington, D.C. He was promoted to the rank of Brigadier General in the United States Army Reserves.

Bryant, Albert, Jr.

BRIGADIER GENERAL—ARMY

He was commissioned a Second Lieutenant and received a Bachelor of Science on June 5, 1974, after graduating from the United States Military Academy at West Point. His military and civilian education includes completion of the Armor Officer Basic and Advance Courses; United States Army Command and General Staff Course; the School of Advanced Military Studies. He is also an Advanced Operational Studies Fellow, and holds a Master of Science in Operations Analysis from Stanford University.

He has held a wide variety of command and staff assignments, including Chief of Plans and Exercises, G-3 (Operations), for the 5th Infantry Division (Mechanized) at Fort Polk, Louisiana; Commander of the 4th Battalion, 67th Armor, 1st Armored Division, United

States Army Europe and Seventh Army, Germany; Chief of Plans Division, G-3 (Operations), V Corps, United States Army Europe and Seventh Army in Germany and Operation Joint Endeavor in Kaposvar, Hungary; Commander of the 3rd Brigade, 1st Armored Division, at Fort Riley, Kansas; Chief of Western Hemisphere Division, J-3 (Operations), at the Joint Staff, Washington, D.C.; Director of the Center for Army Tactics at United States Army Command and General Staff College at Fort Leavenworth, Kansas; and Assistant Division Commander (Support) for the 4th Infantry Division (Mechanized) at Fort Hood, Texas and in Operation Iraqi Freedom, Iraq. On June 1, 2004, Bryant was promoted to Brigadier General and assigned as Deputy Commanding General/Assistant Commandant of the United States Army Armor Center and Fort Knox, Kentucky.

His military awards and decorations include the Defense Superior Service Medal; the Legion of Merit; Defense Meritorious Service Medal; Meritorious Service Medal (with six oak leaf clusters); Army Commendation Medal (with two oak leaf clusters); Army Achievement Medal (with oak leaf cluster); Parachutist Badge; Joint Chiefs of Staff Identification Badge; and Army Staff Identifications Badge.

Bryant, Alvin

MAJOR GENERAL—ARMY

He was born in Miami, Florida, and earned a bachelor's degree in Biology from Florida A&M University in 1959. Bryant's next academic degree was a master's degree in Zoology from Purdue University in 1966, which he attended on a National Science Foundation scholarship that allowed him to study for several summers.

His degrees gave Bryant a broad science background

from which to draw when he enrolled in medical school at Howard University in Washington, D.C. After earning his medical degree in 1977 and completing his residency in General Surgery at Newport News General Hospital (then Whittaker Hospital) recruited him to practice in the predominantly black east end of Newport News, Virginia. His military education includes Infantry Officer Basic Course; Airborne Course; Ordnance Officer Advanced Course; Army Command and General Staff College; Army War College; Tactical Nuclear Awareness; and the Combat Service Support Command Refresher. After he received an ROTC Commission to second lieutenant on June 1, 1959, he served as an infantry officer, and then an ordnance officer. "I knew I was going into the Army and spend two years on active duty when I finished college," General Bryant commented, remembering how well ROTC helped him develop leadership and discipline skills.

General Bryant has 33 years of service as a commissioned officer, and with the exception of a few weeks work with a National Guard unit, he has never used his medical skills in the Reserve. He has served as a research member of the 3372nd Research and Development (REINF). At the 300th Inventory Control Center, he has been Chief of Installations and Construction and Chief of the Repair Parts Management Materiel Division. He also has been Chief of Missile and Munitions Division at the 55th Materiel Management Center. At 310th TAACOM, he served as Chief of Training Plans and Programming at the Logistics Readiness Office; Assistant Chief of Staff of the Service Division; Commander of the 300th Support Group (Area); and Deputy Commander. General Bryant had wanted to use his medical skills in the Army Reserve. While a Lieutenant Colonel, he asked to switch to the Medical Corps. The Army gave approval on con-

dition that he drop back in rank to Major, and Bryant declined. Later, Bryant asked for a second skills specialty listing and again was told he could have it if he dropped back to Major. He refused again.

With the exception of his first two years of medical school, General Bryant has been in the Army Reserve since completing two years of active duty in 1961.

His military decorations and awards include the Meritorious Service Medal, the Army Commendation Medal (with oak leaf cluster), Army Reserve Components Achievement Medal (with three oak leaf clusters), the National Defense Service Medal, the Army Service Ribbon, Army Reserve Components Overseas Training Ribbon with eight numerals, and the Parachutist Badge. He was appointed major general on May 15, 1991.

Bryant, Thomas Milton
COLONEL—ARMY

Colonel Bryant was born in Baltimore, Maryland in November 1941, and graduated from Dunbar High School in Baltimore, Maryland. He then attended Morgan State University where he received a Bachelor of Science degree in Mathematics in 1963. He also earned a master's degree in Computer Science from Kansas State University in 1976, and is a graduate of the Command and General Staff College and the Army War College.

During his 30 years with the United States Army, he served in a variety of command and staff positions, including as a Company Commander in Vietnam; Assistant Professor of Military Science at Michigan State University; Staff Officer for the Joint Chiefs of Staff; Battalion Commander; Group Commander in Germany; and the Inspector General at the Pentagon. He retired from the Army in July 1993.

He died on November 18, 2003, in Fairfax, Virginia, at the age of 62.

Burch, Harold E.

BRIGADIER GENERAL—ARMY

He was born in Lake Wales, Florida. He married the former Jewelle Cheek, and they have two children, Karla and Daryl. He was graduated from Tuskegee University with a Bachelor of Science degree in 1964 and a Master of Science degree in Agronomy in 1966.

After completing the Infantry Officer Basic Course, he served as Executive Officer for Company C, 3rd Battalion, 199th Infantry Brigade (Light) at Fort Benning, Georgia. Assigned to Vietnam from December 1966 through December 1967, he held positions as Executive Officer, Company C, later Assistant S2 (Intelligence) 3rd Battalion, 7th Infantry, 199th Infantry Brigade, United States Army in Vietnam; from July 1967 to December 1967, he was assigned as the S-1/Detachment Commander, 7th Support Battalion (DISCOM), 199th Infantry Brigade, United States Army, in Vietnam; in October 1968, after graduating from the Quartermaster Officer Advanced Course, he was assigned as the Commander of A Company, 24th Supply and Transportation Battalion, 24th Infantry Division, at Fort Riley, Kansas; from May 1970 to May 1971, he served as a Senior Advisor for the 90th Parachute Maintenance and Aerial Delivery Base Depot, Military Assistance Command, Vietnam.

From May 1971 to May 1974, he was assigned to V Corps, United States Army, Europe, West Germany, as Assistant G-4 (Logistics). Returning from overseas, he taught at the United States Army Armor School at Fort Knox, Kentucky, from May 1974 through June 1977. After graduation from the United States Army Command and General Staff College, he was assigned as the Division Parachute Officer, Company E, and later as Executive Officer, 407th Support and Supply Battalion (Airborne), 82nd Airborne Division, at Fort Bragg,

North Carolina, from July 1978 through October 1980.

Reassigned to Japan, he served as Chief of the Maintenance and Services Division in the Directorate of Industrial Operations at Honshu Sagami Depot from October 1980 through May 1983. He commanded the 75th Support Battalion, 194th Armored Brigade, in Fort Knox, Kentucky, from May 1983 through May 1985. Assigned to Korea, he served as the Assistant Chief of Staff, F-4 (Logistics), 2nd Infantry Division, Eighth United States Army, from May 1985 through May 1986.

After attending the Industrial College of the Armed Forces at Fort McNair, Washington, D.C., he was appointed as the Deputy Executive Director of the Technical Services and Logistics Directorate in Defense Logistics Agency at Cameron Station, Virginia, from June 1987 through June 1988. From August 1988 through November 1990, he served as the Commander of the Division Support Command, 1st Cavalry Division, in Fort Hood, Texas. He was reassigned to the 21st Theater Army Area Command, West Germany, on January 11, 1991, as Deputy Commander. He was promoted to the rank of Brigadier General on October 1, 1991.

From July 1992 to September 1994, he served as Commander of United States Army and Air Force Exchange in Europe. From September 1994 to October 1995, he served as Executive Director for Distribution at the Defense Logistics Agency at Cameron Station, in Alexander, Virginia. He retired on October 31, 1995.

His decorations and awards include the Legion of Merit (with oak leaf cluster), Bronze Star medal (with oak leaf cluster), Meritorious Service Medal (with three oak leaf clusters), Army Commendation Medal (with oak leaf cluster), Army Achievement Medal, National Defense Service Medal, Senior Parachutist Badge, Ranger Badge, and Combat Badge.

Burke, Rossatte Y.

MAJOR GENERAL—ARMY

Major General Burke was born in Pittsburgh, Pennsylvania, and has one son, Tirlon Burke. She graduated from high school in Pittsburgh, then completed Harlem Hospital School of Nursing in New York City. She received a Bachelor of Science degree in Nursing from Aldelphi University in Garden City, New York. She earned a Master of Science degree in Health Care Administration from C.W. Post College, Long Island University, New York. Her military schools attended include Academy of Health Science, Army Medical Department Officer Basic Course; Academy of Health Sciences, Army Medical Department; Reserve Component General Staff College; Academy of Health Sciences, Chief Nurse Orientation Course; National Defense University, Reserve Component National Security Course; and Army War College. She was appointed a First Lieutenant in the United States Army Reserves on February 12, 1962.

From April 1962 to December 1966, Burke was assigned as General Duty Nurse, later as Supervisor and

Instructor with the 808th Station Hospital. In February 1967, she was assigned Supervisor and Instructor at the 912th Surgical Hospital. From February 1972 to February 1975, she was assigned as Medical Surgical Nurse, at the 912th Surgical Hospital. In February 1975, she was selected as Chief Nurse of the 74th Field Hospital. On September 15, 1978 she became a Lieutenant Colonel in the United States Army Reserves.

From December 1980 to May 1983, she served as Chief Nurse of the 815th Station Hospital. In May 1983, she was selected as Deputy Chief Nurse of the 364th General Hospital. On September 14, 1983, she was promoted to Colonel in the United States Army Reserves. In May 1985, she was assigned as the Chief Nurse of the 364th General Hospital, later as Chief of Nursing Service at the 364th General Hospital. From February 1993 to April 1994, she was assigned as Chief Nurse at Headquarters, State Area Command, and New York Army National Guard. On February 12, 1993, she became a Colonel in the New York National Guard.

In April 1994, she became Adjutant General, Headquarters and Headquarters Detachment, State Area Command, New York Army National Guard. She was promoted to Brigadier General on July 28, 1995, the first woman general in the 220-year history of the New York Army National Guard. She is also the first female Assistant Adjutant General in New York State and of the Army National Guard.

Burke was the first female to receive the brevet promotion to Major General in the history of the New York Army National Guard and in the Army National Guard. She retired from the New York Army National Guard in February 1997.

Her military awards and decorations include the Army Commendation Medal (with oak leak cluster); Army Reserve Components Achievement Medal (with

silver oak leaf cluster); National Defense Service Medal; Armed Forces Reserve Medal (with two hourglass devices); and the Army Service Ribbon. She received the Medgar Evers Courage Award (Capital District NAACP 1996).

Burs, Daniel
SERGEANT MAJOR—MARINES

He entered the United States Marine Corps in July 1979, and attended Recruit Training at Parris Island, South Carolina with Alpha Company, 1st Recruit Training Battalion. Upon completion of Recruit Training Combat Engineer School, he was promoted to Private First Class and assigned to 8th Engineer Support Battalion, 2nd FSSG.

In November 1983, he was assigned to 7th Engineer Support Battalion, for duty as a Platoon Sergeant and later Platoon Commander. He received orders in June of 1984 to Drill Instructor School and upon completion, he was assigned to Echo Company, 2nd Recruit Training Battalion where he served as Drill Instructor and was meritoriously promoted to Staff Sergeant.

After a successful tour on the drill field, he received orders to 3rd Combat Engineer Battalion, 3rd Marine Division in October of 1987, where he served as Platoon Sergeant and Company Gunnery Sergeant until November of 1988. He was then transferred to 1st Combat Engineer Battalion, 1st Marine Division, for duty where he served as Platoon Sergeant and Company Gunnery Sergeant deploring to the Western Pacific and Middle East Regions with Battalion Landing Team 1/3. In December 1990, he received orders to Marine Barracks Annapolis where he was promoted to the rank of Gunnery Sergeant and was assigned as Guard Chief and Operations Chief.

He was transferred in July of 1993 to 1st Combat

Engineer Battalion, 1st Marine Division where he served as a Platoon Sergeant, Company Gunnery Sergeant, and Company First Sergeant. While assigned to 1st Combat Engineer Battalion, he deployed with Battalion Landing Team 1/4 and was subsequently promoted to the rank of First Sergeant.

Upon promotion to First Sergeant in May 1996, he was transferred to Truck Company, Headquarters Battalion, 1st Marine Division where he served until October 1996, when he was transferred to Battalion landing team 2/4, 31st Marine Expeditionary Unit. Upon return from deployment, he was transferred in October 1997 to Communication Company and Headquarters and Service Company, Headquarters Battalion, 2nd Marine Division for duty as Company First Sergeant.

SGM Burs was selected to the grade of Sergeant Major in 1999 and transferred for duty with 1st Battalion, 8th Marines where he served from October 1999 and December 2001. He transferred in December 2001 for duty as the Battalion Sergeant Major for 9th Engineer Support Battalion. In July 2002, he was transferred to Headquarters and Service Battalions Camp Sergeant Major. In January 2004, he was again transferred to III Marine Expeditionary Force Headquarters Group, Camp Hansen and III Marine Expeditionary Battalion, for duty as the Sergeant Major. In December 2004, he received orders to Marine Corps Mobilization Command, for duty as the Command Sergeant Major.

Burton, William

SERGEANT MAJOR—MARINE

He enlisted into the United States Marine Corps in October 1983, and attended Recruit Training at Marine Corps Recruit Depot at Parris Island, South Carolina. Upon completion of Recruit Training, he was transferred to Lakeland Air Force Base at San Antonio, Texas where he attended Military Police Basic School.

His key military assignments include serving as a Drill Instructor and Senior Drill Instructor, 1st Recruit Training Battalion, at Parris Island, South Carolina; as Watch Commander, Customs Senior Non-Commissioned Officer in Charge, Fiscal Chief, and Supply Senior Non-Commissioned Officer in Charge while serving at Marine Corps Air Station Futenma in Okinawa, Japan; and as the Senior Drill Instructor, Series Gunnery Sergeant, Battalion Drill Master and Headquarters Company First Sergeant at Marine Recruit Depot, 1st Recruit Training Battalion, at Parris Island. In February 1999, he was selected as the Regimental Drill Master for the Recruit Depot; in May 2000, he was transferred to the Third Marine Division in Okinawa, where he served as District Senior Non-Commissioned Officer in Charge for Military Police Department aboard Camp Courtney; in May 2001, he was transferred to Marine Corps Detachment, at Fort Sill, Oklahoma, for duty as the First Sergeant of Marine Battery 2/80th; in November 2003, he was assigned as First Sergeant for India Company, Marine Corps Re-

cruit Depot, Parris Island, South Carolina; in February 2004, he was assigned as First Sergeant for Headquarters Company, Headquarters and Service Battalion, Marine Corps Recruit Depot; and in January 2005, he was assigned as the Sergeant Major, VMFA Marine All Weather Fighter Attack Squadron 224.

Burton, William W., Jr.

COMMAND MASTER CHIEF—NAVY

He enlisted in the United States Navy in December 1975. He attended Basic Recruit Training at the Recruit Training Center in San Diego, California, and also attended MS "A" School at the Naval Training Center in San Diego. He is a graduate of the United

States Navy Senior Enlisted Academy (class 108). He received an Associate of Arts degree in Applied Science from National University in 1982, and holds a Bachelor of Science degree in Business Administration from Chapman University in December 1985. He also earned a Masters Certificate in Human Resources from Chapman University in December 2002; and a Master of Arts degree in Organization Leadership from Chapman University in September 2003.

His military assignments include serving at Naval Air Station Whidbey Island, Washington; as Leading Petty Officer of Supply Department at Naval Station San Diego; and as Senior Enlisted Advisor of Supply Department for Naval Air Station Whidbey Island. In October 2004, he was serving as Command Master Chief for Surface Warfare/Aviation Warfare.

Bush, Kenneth D.

SERGEANT MAJOR—MARINES

Born in Washington, D.C., Bush enlisted in the United States Marine Corps and reported to Marine Corps Recruit Depot at Parris Island, South Carolina in December 1978 for Recruit Training. Upon completion of Recruit Training in March 1979, he reported to MATSG, NATTC, at Lakehurst, New Jersey to undergo training for Aircrew Survival Equipment "A" Course, for his primary MOS.

Bush served as the 800 Division Senior Noncommissioned Officer in Charge of Aviation Life Support Systems at Cherry Point, North Carolina. In April 1998, he received orders to report to Inspector-Instructor Staff Phoenix, Arizona, for duty. In February 2003, he was promoted to Sergeant Major and received orders to report for duty with Marine Medium Helicopter Squadron 165, MAG-16, 3DMAW, Miramar, California, as the "White Knights" Squadron Sergeant Major.

His Squadron was forward deployed aboard USS *Boxer* (LHA-4) in support of Operation Enduring Freedom. His unit then was deployed to a forward operating base located in Southern Iraq, in support of Operation Iraqi Freedom.

Bussey, Charles D.

MAJOR GENERAL—ARMY

Bussey was born in Edgefield, South Carolina, and raised in Washington, D.C. He is the son of Alex William Bussey, Sr., and Mattie Lou Bussey, and married the former Eva Lois Gray. They have three children, Terry Lyn, Tonia Marie, and Charles Frederick. He received a Bachelor of Science degree in English and a commission as a second lieutenant of Infantry from the Agricultural and Technical College of North Carolina in June 1955. He also has a Master of Arts in Journalism from Indiana University and a Master of Science in Communication Science, from Shippensburg State College. His military schooling includes completion of the Infantry Officer Basic; and Advanced Course; Army Information School; Armed Forces Staff College and War College.

General Bussey has held varied command and staff posts, including troop assignments with eight combat divisions and a separate brigade. In Washington, D.C., he was Chief of Personnel Actions in Legislative Liaison and Chief of the Policy and Plans Division in the Office of the Chief of Public Affairs. He also was Professor of Military Science for the Indianapolis public schools Junior ROTC program.

He commanded a rifle company in the 1st Cavalry Division in Korea, an Infantry Battalion in the 82nd Airborne Division, and an Infantry Brigade in the 2nd Infantry Division in Korea. For two years, he was Deputy Commander and chief of staff of the 172nd Infantry Brigade in Alaska. His overseas service includes two tours in Korea and one each in Vietnam, Germany, and Alaska.

In July 1982 he was reassigned to Washington, D.C., as the Deputy Chief of Public Affairs. General Bussey became the Chief of Public Affairs in the Office of the Secretary of the Army on August 13, 1984. In 1987 he was assigned as Chief of Staff for Personnel. He retired on May 31, 1989. His military awards and decorations include two Legions of Merit, two Bronze Stars, three Meritorious Service Medals, three Army Commendation Medals, the Air Medal, the Combat Infantryman Badge, the Parachutist Badge, and the Army General Staff Identification Badge.

Butler, George

COMMAND SERGEANT MAJOR—ARMY

Command Sergeant Major George Butler graduated from Roberts High School in Holly Hill, South Carolina. He and his wife Patricia, have a daughter Ariel.

He attended Basic and Advanced Individual Training at Fort Gordon, Georgia, and has earned an associate's degree from Georgia Military College. He is a graduate of the Frequency Manager Course; the First

Sergeant Course; and the United States Army Sergeants Major 121st Signal Battalion.

His most recent assignments include serving as a Drill Sergeant at Fort Jackson, South Carolina for two years in Basic Training; and one at the United States Army Drill Sergeant Academy as an Instructor; as a Project Officer with the Director of Training and Doctrine at Fort Gordon, Georgia; he was assigned as an Operations Sergeant with the 307th Signal Battalion at Camp Carol, South Korea; as First Sergeant and also worked in the 1st Cavalry Division G-6 shop as the Frequency Manager, Plans NCOIC and Operations NCOIC; as the First Sergeant in Charlie Company 13th Signal Battalion in which he deployed for a tour in Bosnia-Herzegovina. After Butler finished his tour as the First Sergeant in Headquarters and Headquarters Company, 13th Signal Battalion, he was assigned to the S-3 (Operations) with the 121st Signal Battalion. He is currently serving as the Command Sergeant Major of the 121st Signal Battalion.

Butler, Remo

BRIGADIER GENERAL—ARMY

Born in Egypt, Mississippi, Butler was commissioned as a second lieutenant in the United States Army in 1974, after graduating from Austin Peay State University. He holds a Bachelor of Science degree in Political Science and a Master of Science degree from Troy State University in Personnel Management.

His military education includes the Field Artillery Officer Basic Course, Airborne School, and the Infantry Officer Advanced Course. He is a graduate of the Armed Force Staff College, United States Marine Command and General Staff College, and the United States Army War College.

His initial tour of duty was with the 2/17th Field Artillery at Camp Pelham, South Korea. Returning to the United States, he was assigned from March 1976 to April 1977 as a Platoon Leader and then as a Company Executive Officer with the 1st Cavalry Division at Fort Hood, Texas. After completing the Special Forces Qualification Course in July 1977, he was assigned as a detachment Commander in Company C, and later as Executive Officer of Company A, 3rd Battalion, 7th Special Forces Group in February 1984, and served as Company Executive Officer and Battalion S-3 respectively, until assuming Command of Company C, 2/7th Special Forces Group (Airborne). After completing the Armed Forces Staff College, General Butler was assigned in 1988 to Special Operations Command South, Panama, as Director J-3 and as a Special Operations Plans Officer. He was also a participant in Operation Just Cause. He departed Panama in July 1991 to become an instructor at the Armed Forces Staff College until December 1992, when he returned to Fort Bragg to Command 1st Battalion, 7th Special Forces Group (Airborne) from December 1992 to January 1995. He was then assigned as Deputy Chief of Staff to United States Army Special Forces Command until his departure to the United States Army War College. After the War College, he was assigned as Chief of the Special Operations Coordination Element, XVII Airborne Corps. General Butler commanded the 1st Special Warfare Training Group (Airborne), United States Army Special Warfare Center and School, from May 1997 through May 1999. In June 1999, he was assigned as Deputy Commanding General of the United States Army Special Operations Command at Fort Bragg, North Carolina. In June 2000, he was made Commanding General of Special Operations Command South. Butler was promoted to Brigadier General on January 1, 2001.

His awards and decorations include the Legion of Merit, Defense Meritorious Service Medal (with one oak leaf cluster); Meritorious Service Medal (with four oak leaf clusters); Joint Service Achievement Medal; Army Commendation Medal (with three oak leaf clusters); Combat Infantryman Badge; Master Parachutist Badge; Military Freefall Parachutist Badge; Venezuelan Parachutist Badge; Honduran Parachutist Badge; Special Forces Tab; and Ranger Tab.

Butts, Robert J.

SERGEANT MAJOR—MARINE

Butts graduated from Marine Corps Recruit Training Depot at Parris Island, South Carolina in August 1974. After graduation he transferred to WERS-27 2nd MAW MCAS at Cherry Point, North Carolina for duty as a Bulk Fuel Specialist.

He was promoted to First Sergeant in 1991, and transferred to SOI MCB Camp Lejeune, North Carolina in March 1992. During this tour he served as the First Sergeant of "H" Company MCT, "C" Company ITB, AITC, and Headquarters Service Company. On May 14, 1996, he transferred to MCRD Parris Island and served as Sergeant Major of 3rd Recruit Training Battalion until June 1997. From June 1997 to June 1999, he served as the Weapons and Field Training Battalion Sergeant Major. In January 2005, he was serving as Headquarters Battalion Sergeant Major of the 3rd Marine Division.

Byrd, Melvin Leon

BRIGADIER GENERAL—ARMY

Born in Suffolk, Virginia, Byrd received a Bachelor of Arts degree in Accounting from Howard University and a Master of Business Administration from Babson College. From February 1959 to March 1959, he was a student at the Infantry Officer Basic Course at the United States Army Infantry School at Fort Benning, Georgia.

From March 1959 to September 1959, he was an Administration Officer for the United States Army Garrison at Camp Drum, New York. From September 1959 to November 1961, he served as a Platoon Leader for the 5th Ordnance Company at Aberdeen Proving Ground, Maryland, with duty station at Camp Drum, New York. He was promoted to First Lieutenant on November 26, 1960. From December 1961 to May 1963, he was the Supply Officer for Company B, 801st Maintenance Battalion, 101st Airborne Division at Fort Campbell, Kentucky. On May 27, 1963, he was promoted to Captain. From June 1963 to October 1964, he served as an Ordnance Adviser with the Military Advisor Group of the United States Army Element in Iran.

From October 1964 to March 1965, he was a student at the Ordnance Officer Advanced Course at the United States Army Ordnance Center and School at Aberdeen Proving Ground, Maryland. From March 1965 to May 1966, he was an Ordnance Adviser with the United States Military Assistance Command, Vietnam. From May 1966 to November 1967, he was Chief

of Welding, Metal Body Division, and Maintenance Officer at the United States Army Ordnance Center and School at Aberdeen Proving Ground. One June 20, 1967, he was promoted to Major. From November 1967 to September 1968, he served as a Civilian Affairs Officer with the 199th Infantry Brigade, United States Army, in Vietnam. From September 1968 to June 1969, he was the Executive Officer of the 7th Combat Support Battalion, 199th Infantry Bridge, United States Army, Vietnam. From June 1969 to July 1972, he was Chief of the Maintenance Management Branch at the United States Army Quartermaster School at Fort Lee, Virginia. From July 1972 to June 1973, he was a student at the Marine Corps Command and Staff College at Quantico, Virginia. From June 1973 to December 1974, he was a student at Babson College, Babson Park, Massachusetts. From December 1974 to July 1976, he served as a Logistics Staff Officer in the Materiel Management Division in the Office of the Deputy Chief of Staff for Logistics, United States Army, Washington, D.C. From September 1976 to September 1977, he was Commander of the 702nd Maintenance Battalion, 2nd Infantry Division, United States Army, South Korea. From September 1977 to July 1979, he served as an Inspector General in the Assistance Division, United States Army Inspector General Agency, Washington, D.C.

On September 30, 1979, Byrd was promoted to Lieutenant Colonel. From July 1979 to June 1980, he was a student at the United States Army War College at Carlisle Barracks, Pennsylvania. From June 1980 to January 1981, he served as the Deputy Director for Joint Actions, Plans, Force Structure and Systems Directorate in the Office of the Deputy Chief of Staff for Logistics, United States Army, Washington, D.C. He was promoted to Colonel on July 1, 1980. From March 1981 to June 1983, he was the Commander of Division

Support Command, 82nd Airborne Division, at Fort Bragg, North Carolina. From June 1983 to July 1986, he was the Commander of the United States Army Electronics Materiel Readiness Activity at Vint Hill Farms Station at Warrenton, Virginia. From July 1986 to July 1988, he was the Commanding General of the United Army Materiel Command in Europe. He was promoted to Brigadier General on October 1, 1986. He has received numerous decorations, badges and awards including the Legion of Merit; Bronze Star (with two oak leaf clusters); Meritorious Service Medal (with two oak leaf clusters); the Air Medal; the Army Commendation Medal (with oak leaf cluster); Combat Infantryman Badge; Senior Parachutist Badge; and the Staff Identification Badge.

Byrd, Willie
COMMAND SERGEANT MAJOR—ARMY

Command Sergeant Major Byrd was born in Troy, Alabama. He entered the United States Army in 1977, and completed his Basic Combat Training and Advanced Individual Training at Fort Sill, Oklahoma. He is also a graduate of the Pershing Noncommissioned Officers Course; the First Sergeants Course; and the United States Army Sergeants Major Academy at Fort Bliss, Texas.

His most recent assignments includes serving as the Senior Noncommissioned Officer with the 29th Infantry Division (Light) Artillery; as the Command Sergeant Major with the 3rd Battalion, 18th Field Artillery; and most recently as the Command Sergeant Major for the 111th Armored Corps Artillery.

Cabey, Jihad
FIRST SERGEANT—ARMY

He entered the Army in September 1978. In 1988, he was assigned to the VII Corps Band in Stuttgart, West Germany. While assigned to the VII Corps Band, he was deployed to the Middle East in support of Operation Desert Storm in November 1990. Upon his return from the Middle East, he completed his bachelor's degree in Business Management with the University of Maryland and was assigned to the 3rd Infantry Division Band in Wurzburg, Germany.

This assignment lasted until 1995, when he moved to the 24th Infantry Division Band at Fort Stewart, Georgia. In January 1999, he was assigned as First Sergeant of the I Corps Band at Ft. Lewis, Washington. In September 2002, Cabey became the First Sergeant of the Signal Corps Band.

Cade, Alfred Jackal
BRIGADIER GENERAL—ARMY

Brigadier General Cade was born in Fayetteville, North Carolina. He received a Bachelor of Science degree in General Psychology from Virginia State College, then a Master of Business Administration in Comptrollership from Syracuse University. His military schooling includes Field Artillery Officer Basic Course; United States Army Command and General Staff College; and the Industrial College of the Armed Forces at Fort Lesley J. McNair in Washington, D.C.

Cade was commissioned a second lieutenant in 1954. From 1966 through 1967, he served as an Assistance Sector Advisor and Sector Advisor with the United States Military Command, Phu Yen Province, South Vietnam. He served as Commander of the 1st Battalion, 92nd Artillery, United States Army, Vietnam, from 1967 to 1968. He returned to the United States in 1968 serving as first Budget Operations Officer until 1970 with the Director of Army Budget in Washington, D.C., then as Executive Officer with the Army's Materiel Command and Assistant Comptroller for Budget, Washington, D.C., until 1973 through 1974, he served as Commander of the 210th Field Artillery Group in Europe. He was appointed Brigadier General on April 1, 1975, and retired December 31, 1978.

Brigadier General Cade's decorations include the Legion of Merit (with two oak leaf clusters); Bronze Star (with three oak leaf clusters); Meritorious Service Medal; Air Medal; Army Commendation Medal; and the Parachutist Badge.

Cadet, Eusebius P.
COMMAND SERGEANT MAJOR—ARMY

He was born in St. Lucia in the West Indies. After graduating from high school, he moved to the Virgin Islands where he enlisted in the United States Army in June 1973. He has served as Command Sergeant Major for the 528th Special Operations Support Command at Fort Bragg, North Carolina; Command Sergeant Major for the 46th Corps Support Group at Fort Bragg; Command Sergeant Major for the 1st Corps Support

Command at Fort Bragg; and currently as the Garrison Command Sergeant Major at Camp Zama, Japan.

Cadoria, Sherian G.
BRIGADIER GENERAL—ARMY

Brigadier General Cadoria was born in Marksville, Louisiana. She received a Bachelor of Science in Business Education from Southern University A&M College and a Master's from the University of Oklahoma.

She received a commission by direct appointment, and from January 1962 to May 1963 she was a Platoon Officer for Company B, Women's Army Corps Training Battalion, at Fort McClellan, Alabama. From June 1963 to May 1965, she served as Executive Officer, of the Women's Army Corps Company, and Assistant Adjutant for the United States Army Communications Zone, Europe. From June 1965 to July 1966, she served as Adjutant of Special Troops at the United States Army Quartermaster Center at Fort Lee, Virginia.

She was promoted to Captain on May 1, 1965. From July 1966 to December 1966, she was a student at the Adjutant General School at Fort Benjamin Harrison, Indiana. From January 1967 to December 1967, she was the Administrative Officer in the Provost Marshal's Office, United States Army, Vietnam. From January 1968 to October 1969, she served as the Protocol Officer in Qui Nhon Support Command, Vietnam. She was promoted to Major on August 1, 1968. From November 1969 to July 1970, she served as Chief of the Personnel Division/Adjutant at the United States Army Ordnance Center and School at Aberdeen Proving Ground, Maryland.

From July 1970 to June 1971, she was a student at the United States Army Command and General Staff College at Fort Leavenworth, Kansas. From June 1971 to June 1973, she was an Instructor at the Officer Education and Training Branch, United States Army Women's Army Corps Center and School at Fort McClellan, Alabama. From June 1973 to June 1975, she served as a Personnel Management Officer, later Executive Officer, Women's Army Corps Branch, Officer Personnel Directorate, United States Army Military Personnel Center in Alexandria, Virginia. From June 1975 to December 1976, she served as a Personnel Staff Officer with the Law Enforcement Division of the Human Resources Development Directorate at the Office of the Deputy Chief of Staff for Personnel, United States Army, Washington, D.C.

On July 1, 1976, Cadoria was promoted to Lieutenant Colonel. From December 1976 to July 1978, she was Commander of the Student Battalion of the Training Brigade at the United States Army Military Police School, Fort McClellan, Alabama. From July 1978 to June 1979, she was a student at the United States Army War College at Carlisle Barracks, in Pennsylvania. From June 1979 to May 1982, she served as a Special Assistant to the Provost Marshal, later Chief of the Physical Security Division, the Office of the Provost Marshal, United States Army, Europe, and Seventh Army.

On September 1, 1980, she was promoted to Colonel. From May 1982 to July 1984, she was the Commander of the First Region, United States Army Criminal Investigation Command at Fort George G. Meade, Maryland. From July 1984 to July 1985, she served as Chief of the Law Enforcement Division in the Human Resource Development Directorate, Office of the Deputy Chief of Staff for Personnel, United States Army, in Washington, D.C. From August 1985 to September 1987, she served as Director of Manpower and Personnel, J1, Organization of the Joint Chiefs of Staff, Washington, D.C. On October 1, 1985, she was promoted to Brigadier General. In September 1987, she was assigned as Deputy Commanding General of Total Army Personnel Command in Alexandria, Virginia. She has received numerous decorations and badges, including the Defense Superior Service Medal; the Legion of Merit; the Bronze Star (with two oak leaf clusters), Meritorious Service Medal (with oak leaf cluster); Air Medal, Army Commendation Medal (with three oak leaf clusters); and the Joint Chiefs of Staff Identification Badge.

Caffie, Leon
COMMAND SERGEANT MAJOR—U.S. ARMY RESERVES

Caffie entered the United States Army on April 2, 1970. He served in the Vietnam War from August 1970 to June 1971, and joined the United States Army Reserve on March 31, 1972. His military education includes the Drill Sergeant Course, First Sergeant Course and the Sergeants Major Academy. He earned an Associate of Arts degree in General Education from Santa Fe Community College in Gainesville, Florida and his Bachelor of Science in Communications from Regents College in Albany, New York. He has completed numerous civilian law enforcement courses and certifications. He has a diploma in Criminal Justice Education from the University of Virginia in Charlottesville and he grad-

uated with distinction from the FBI National Academy at Quantico in June 1991.

Command Sergeant Major Caffie serves as the Command Sergeant Major for the 377th Theater Support Command. During Operation Enduring Freedom he served as the Camp Arifjan Command Sergeant Major.

His civilian position is with the Alachua County Sheriff's Office, Florida, as Division commander of the Criminal Investigations Division.

Cagle, Yvonne Darlene
COLONEL—UNITED STATES AIR FORCE

Colonel Cagle was born in West Point, New York, but considers Novato, California, to be her hometown. She graduated from Novato High School in 1977; received a Bachelor of Arts degree in Biochemistry from San Francisco State University in 1981, and received a Doctorate in Medicine from the University of Washington in 1985. She underwent transitional internship at Highland General Hospital in Oakland, California, in 1985; received Certification in Aerospace Medicine from the School of Aerospace Medicine at Brooks Air Force Base, Texas, in 1988; completed residency in family practice and Ghent FP at Eastern Virginia Medical School in 1992; and received certification as a Senior Aviation Medical Examiner from the Federal Aviation Administration in 1995. She is a certified FAA Aviation Medical Examiner, is ACLS Instructor qualified and has taught fitness courses. She is a Clinical Assistant Professor at UTMB, Galveston. While a United States Air Force Reservist, she was assigned to the Pentagon Flight Medicine/Special Mission Clinic.

Her medical training was sponsored by the Health Professions Scholarship Program, through which she received her commission as an officer with the United States Air Force, and subsequently was awarded her board certification in family practice. During her initial active duty tour at Royal Air Force Lakenheath, United Kingdom, she was selected to attend the School of Aerospace Medicine at Brooks Air Force Base, Texas. In April 1988, she became certified as a flight surgeon logging numerous hours in diverse types of aircraft. She was actively involved in mission support of aircraft providing medical support and rescue in a variety of aeromedical missions.

From 1994 to 1996, she served as the Deputy Project Manager for Kelsey-Seybold Clinics, practicing as an occupational physician at the NASA-JSC Occupational Health Clinic. In addition to conducting job-related exams, routine health screenings, and providing acute care for on-site injuries and illness, she designed the medical protocols and conducted the screenings for selected NASA remote duty operations. In May 1989, while a flight surgeon assigned to the 48th Tactical Hospital in the United Kingdom, she volunteered to serve as the Air Force Medical Liaison Officer for the STS-30 *Atlantis* Shuttle Mission to test the Magellan Spacecraft. She was assigned to the Trans Atlantic (TAL) Landing site at Banjul, West Africa, to provide emergency rescue and evacuation of the shuttle crew should it have been required. She has contributed ongoing data to the Longitudinal Study on Astronaut Health, and served as a consultant for space telemedicine. She was a member of the NASA Working Group and traveled to Russia to establish international medical standards and procedures for astronauts. She also conducted health screenings of Mir-18 consultants from the Russian Federation.

Selected by NASA as an astronaut in April 1996, she reported to the Johnson Space Center in August 1996. Having completed two years of training and evaluation, she is qualified for flight assignment as a mission specialist. Currently, she is assigned technical duties in the Astronaut Office Operations Planning Branch, supporting Shuttle and Space Station operations.

Cain, Eddie
BRIGADIER GENERAL—ARMY

He was born in Steen, Mississippi. He received a Bachelor of Science degree in Chemistry, from Jackson State University in Jackson, Mississippi. His military education includes completion of the Chemical Officer Basic and Advanced Courses; the United States Army Command and General Staff College; and the United States Army War College.

He entered active military service in August 1971 as a second lieutenant. In December 1971, he was assigned as the Commander of Headquarters and Headquarters Company for the Rocky Mountain Arsenal in Denver, Colorado. On April 22, 1973, he was promoted to First Lieutenant. He was assigned as Chief of Human Relations Division for the Sixth Region, United States Army Air Defense Command, at Fort Baker, California, in November 1973. From June 1974 to February 1975, he served as Assistance Operations Officer with the Directorate of Plans, Training and Security at the Presidio of San Francisco, California. In March 1975, he served first as Equipment Maintenance Platoon Leader, next as Commander of the 588th Maintenance Company, United States Army Europe and Seventh Army, Germany. In August 1975, he was promoted to Captain.

In March 1977, he served as Chemical Officer, 2nd Brigade, 8th Infantry Division (Mechanized), United States Army Europe and Seventh Army, Germany. From March 1978 to October 1978, he was a student at the Chemical Officer Advanced Course, Aberdeen Proving Ground, Maryland.

From October 1978 to May 1980, he was assigned as Chemical Officer, 2nd Brigade, 1st Cavalry Division, Fort Hood, Texas.

In May 1980, General Cain was assigned as Chief of the Human Resources Division, G-1 (Personnel), 1st Cavalry Division, Fort Hood, Texas. In June 1981, he served as Aide-de-Camp to the Deputy Commanding General of the Fifth United States Army at Fort Sam Houston, Texas. In January 1982, he was assigned as the Chemical Branch Advisor at the United States Army Readiness and Mobilization Region VII, Fifth United States Army, Fort Sill, Oklahoma. He was promoted to Major on April 1, 1983.

From June 1984 to June 1985, he was a student at the United States Army Command and General Staff College at Fort Leavenworth, Kansas. In June 1985, he was assigned as Executive Officer of the 2nd Chemical Battalion, III Corps, at Fort Hood. Next he was assigned in October 1986, as Operations Officer, 13th Corps Support Command, III Corps, Fort Hood. In November 1987, he was assigned as Chemical Officer, 1st Cavalry Division, at Fort Hood. In December 1988, he became Political-Military Affairs Officer at the Office of the Secretary of State, Washington, DC. He was promoted to Lieutenant Colonel on May 1, 1989.

In July 1990, he was selected as Commander of the 23rd Chemical Battalion, Eighth United States Army, South Korea. From June 1992 to July 1993, he was a student at the United States Army War College, at Carlisle Barracks, Pennsylvania. In August 1993, he was assigned as the Deputy Commander of the United States Army Chemical Materiel Destruction Agency at Aberdeen Proving Ground. On June 1, 1994, he was promoted to Colonel. In July 1994, he was assigned as Commander of United States Army Chemical Activity Pacific, United States Army Pacific, at Johnston Island. In August 1995, he was assigned as the Chemical Officer for III Corps at Fort Hood. In June 1998, he was assigned as the Joint Program Manager with the Biological Defense, in Falls Church, Virginia. He was promoted to Brigadier General on October 1, 1998, and retired in June 2000.

His military decorations and badges include the Legion of Merit; Defense Meritorious Service Medal; Meritorious Service Medal (with four oak leaf clusters); Army Commendation Medal; Army Achievement Medal; Air Assault Badge; and Office of the Secretary of Defense Identification Badge.

Caldwell, John R.

COMMAND SERGEANT MAJOR—ARMY

Caldwell enlisted in the United States Army in June 1979 as an Armor Crewman. He attended Basic Training and Advanced Individual Training at Fort Knox, Kentucky. He is a graduate of Elba High School in Elba, Alabama, and earned an associate's degree from Regents College in Applied Science and is currently pursuing a bachelor's degree in Physical Education.

His military education includes all the Non-Commissioned Officer Education System Courses; Drill Sergeant School; Master Fitness Trainer's Course; Instructor Trainer's School; and First Sergeants School.

His military assignments include serving as Tank Commander; Drill Sergeant; Platoon Sergeant; First Sergeant; Instructor at the United States Army Sergeants Major Academy (First Sergeants Course); Command Sergeant Major for the 2nd Squadron, 3rd Armored Cavalry Regiment; and the Regimental Command Sergeant Major, 3rd Armored Cavalry Regiment.

Campbell, James F.

COMMAND SERGEANT MAJOR—ARMY

Campbell is a native of Marion, South Carolina, and entered the military on May 27, 1976. He received his Basic Combat and Advanced Individual Training at Fort Sill, Oklahoma, where he received his initial training as a Fire Direction Specialist. Upon completion of initial entry training, his first duty position was as a Horizontal Chart Operator in the Battalion Fire Direction Center for the 1st Battalion, 78th Field Artillery at Fort Hood, Texas.

His military and civilian education includes all the Noncommissioned Officer Education System Courses; the First Sergeant Course; and United States Army

Sergeant Major Academy (class 49). He holds an associate's degree in Business from Mount Wachusett Community College and bachelor's degree in Business Management from the University of Maryland.

His military assignments include serving as Chief Computer, A Battery, 1st Battalion, 7th Field Artillery at Fort Riley, Kansas; Battalion TACFIRE NCO, 2nd Battalion, 5th Field Artillery at Fort Riley; DIVARTY TACFIRE NCO/Platoon Sergeant, HHB, 8th Infantry Division Artillery at Baumholder, West Germany; Chief Readiness NCO, Readiness Group Devens at Fort Devens, Massachusetts; First Sergeant, 2nd Battalion, 80th Field Artillery at Fort Sill; Operations Sergeant Major, United States Army Field Artillery Training Center at Fort Sill, and 1st Infantry Division Artillery at Bamberg, Germany; and Battalion Command Sergeant Major for 1st Battalion, 33rd Field Artillery at Bamberg. In August 2004, he was serving as the Commandant for the 7th Army NCO Academy in Grafenwoehr, Germany.

Campbell, Michael B.
SERGEANT MAJOR—MARINES

Sergeant Major Campbell enlisted in the Marine Corps in January 1975 as a K-3 reservist upon completion of recruit training at Marine Corps Recruit Depot at Parris Island; he was transferred to Charlie Company, 1st Battalion, 8th Marines and subsequent Field Skills Training Unit at Camp Geiger, North Carolina. In July 1975, he was transferred to Picatinny Arsenal at Dover, New Jersey, to fulfill his reserve obligation as a 0351MOS anti-tank assaultman.

Six months later, he requested to join the active duty forces, at which time he was transferred to Headquar-

ters and Service Company, 1st Battalion, 1st Marine Division, MCB, at Camp Pendleton, California, for duty as an anti-tank assaultman.

In 1987, he was assigned to the Staff Noncommissioned Officer Academy at Quantico, Virginia, where he served as a Career Course Instructor and Course Coordinator/Chief Instructor until promoted to First Sergeant in 1991. Campbell was transferred to Headquarters and Service Battery, 1st Low Altitude Air Defense Battalion and then 1st Stinger Battery, both with Marine Air Control Group 18, 1st Aircraft Wing, in Okinawa, Japan. During July 1996, Sergeant Major Campbell was transferred to the 2nd Marine Division at Camp Lejeune, North Carolina, to duties as Battalion Sergeant Major for the 2nd Light Armored Reconnaissance Battalion. During March 2000, he was assigned as the Sergeant Major Headquarters Battalion, 2nd Marine Division, Camp Lejeune. On January 12, 2001, he was assigned as the Sergeant Major for the Officer Candidates School at Marine Corps University.

Campbell, Phyllis C.
SENIOR EXECUTIVE SERVICE

Campbell is a native of Steelton, Pennsylvania, and entered the Federal Service in the Transportation Division at the Defense Distribution Depot at Ogden, Utah in 1973 with selection into the Depot's Management Intern Program. In 1979, she became a Supply Systems Analyst in the newly formed Defense System Automation Center, which later became the DLA System Design Center. In 1982, she returned to the Ogden installation, becoming Chief with responsibility for all

operations and administrative systems and procedures. In 1985, she was promoted to Division Chief, assuming additional responsibility for a $30 million depot modernization program, In 1989, she reached a career benchmark with her selection as Deputy Director Office of Technology and Information Services.

In 1990, Campbell was selected by the Office of Secretary of Defense to be the Deputy for the Corporate Information Management Distribution Prototype Group. This group was chartered to develop a standard distribution system for use throughout the Department of Defense. In 1991, she was reassigned to DLA's Defense Distribution Systems Center as its Business Manager. In 1993, she returned to the Office of the Secretary of Defense Comptroller's Officer of Financial Review and Analysis. Until her appointment to Deputy Commander, in 1995, she served as Director of Distribution Operations with the Defense Distribution Center. In January 2005, she was serving as Deputy Commander of the Defense Distribution Center.

Cannon, Louis T., Jr.
COMMANDER—NAVY

He is a native of Washington, D.C., and a 1986 graduate of Florida A&M University with a Bachelor of Science in Accounting. He was commissioned in December 1986 through the Naval Reserve Officers' Training Corps (NROTC) at FAMU. He earned his Navy "Wings of Gold" and was designated a Naval Flight Officer in October 1988 at Naval Air Station Pensacola, Florida.

He reported to Fighter Squadron ONE TWO FOUR (VF-124, Naval Air Station Miramar, California) for initial F-14 Tomcat training as a Radar Intercept Officer (RIO) in November 1988 and was assigned to the "Bounty Hunters" of VF-2 in March 1990. During this

tour, he completed two deployments aboard USS *Ranger* (CV-61), including flight operations in support of Operation Desert Shield and Desert Storm, together with Southern Watch and Restore Hope. He served as AE Branch Officer, AV/ARM Division Officer, Schedules Officer, and Quality Assurance Officer (QAO).

In May 1993, "Loose" retuned to VF-124 as an Instructor RIO. During his tour with the Gunslingers, he served as Schedule Officer and ADFAS Phase Leader. Upon the decommissioning of VF-124, he remained at Miramar with the newly established VE-101 DET Miramar as an F-14D instructor. He served as ADFAS Phase Leader and Assistant Officer-in-Charge (AOIC). In November 1995, he was assigned to Carrier Air Wing 14 (CVW-14) as the Air Warfare Officer, Wing Safety Officer and Wing ADP Officer aboard USS *Abraham Lincoln* (CVN-72).

After refresher training at VF-101 in the F-14A, Commander Cannon reported to the Black Aces of VF 41 in September 1998 for his Department Head tour. He deployed onboard USS *Theodore Roosevelt* (CVN-71), including flight operations in support of Operations Allied Force and Southern Watch. He served as Safety Officer, Assistant Aircraft Maintenance Officer (ASMC) and Aircraft Maintenance Officer (AMO).

Commander Cannon reported to the Naval War College in Newport, Rhode Island, in November 2000. While there, he earned a master's degree in National Security and Strategic Studies. In November 2001, he reported to the staff of the Joint Chiefs of Staff in Washington, D.C., where he served in the Current Operations Division of the Directorate for Command, Control, Communications, and Computer Systems (J-6). He reported to Navy Recruiting District Seattle in

February 2005 where he is currently serving as the Executive Officer.

He has logged over 2600 flight hours and accumulated over 420 carrier-arrested landings.

Carr, Gary
COMMAND SERGEANT MAJOR—ARMY

Carr is a native of Wallace, North Carolina, and entered the United States Army in July 1977. He attended Basic Combat Training at Fort Leonard Wood, Missouri, and Advance Infantry Training at Fort Benning, Georgia.

His military and civilian education includes all the Noncommissioned Officer Education System Courses; First Sergeant Course; Battle Staff Course; and the United States Army Sergeant Major Academy. He holds a Bachelor of Science in Organization Management from Summit University, as well as a Bachelor of Science in Human Resources. He also earned a master's degree in Business Administration from Almeda College and University.

His military assignments include serving as Team Leader; Squad Leader; Platoon Sergeant; First Sergeant; Command Sergeant Major of the 1st Battalion, 28th Infantry Regiment Basic Combat Training, at Fort Jackson, South Carolina; in August 2004, he was serving as the Command Sergeant Major for Fort A.P. Hill.

Carson, Larry J.
SERGEANT MAJOR—MARINES

Carson was born in Natchez, Mississippi. He graduated from Presley High School in 1971 and began his Marine Corps career in February 1972. He received Recruit Training at Marine Corps Recruit Depot at San

Diego, California, and Infantry Training at Camp Pendleton, California. He was promoted to his present rank in February 1992.

Carter, Clinton
SERGEANT MAJOR—MARINES

Carter entered the United States Marine Corps in October 1981. He underwent Recruit Training at Parris Island, South Carolina, and upon completion of

Recruit Training he was promoted to PFC and reported to Naval Base in Norfolk, Virginia for MOS Embarkation Specialist. He was promoted to the rank of Lance Corporal after MOS School.

In February 1987, he attended Recruiter School and upon successful completion, was assigned the billet of Canvassing Recruiter at Recruiting Substation Saint Joseph, Missouri; during this tour his performance earned him the Recruiter of the Year Award in 1988. In 1989, he earned the Noncommissioned Officer of the Year award; in 1996, he was assigned as First Sergeant, Alpha Company at Headquarters Battalion at 29 Palms, California; and in December 1998 he was transferred to Headquarters and Service Battalion Company at MCB Butler on Okinawa, Japan. Upon being selected for Sergeant Major in March 2000, he was transferred to the 1st Marine Aircraft Wing, where he assumed duties as Squadron Sergeant Major for Marine Wing Support Squadron 172. In July 2003, Carter assumed duties as Sergeant Major of Marine Attack Training Squadron 203, Second Marine Aircraft Wing.

Carter, Normia E.
CHIEF MASTER SERGEANT—AIR FORCE

Carter entered the United States Air Force in 1974, beginning her successful career as an Administration Specialist at Plattsburgh Air Force Base in New York.

During her first tour she completed in the Air Force "Tops in Blue" Competition, winning Best Female Vocalist and Best of the Show in 1976. In 1977 she cross-trained to the Social Actions career field as a Drug Abuse Counselor. After another "Tops in Blue" competition and another Best Female Vocalist Award, she auditioned for the Band Career Field.

Her assignments include the 590th Air Force Band at McGuire Air Force Base, New Jersey. She served with the United States Air Force Europe Band at Einsiedlerhof Air Station in Germany, and was assigned to Scott Air Force Base, Illinois with the Headquarters Air Mobility Command Band.

She returned the United States Air Force Europe Band in 1991 to serve as the First Sergeant and Vocalist. In 1997 she spear-headed the move of the United States Air Force Europe Band from Einsiedlerhof Air Station to its present duty station at Sembach Air Base, Germany. During her extended tour she also served as Regional Band Superintendent Resource Advisory, and interim Band Manager. In August 1998 she became the Band Director of the Band of the Pacific—Hawaii.

Carter, Randall
SERGEANT MAJOR—MARINE

He was born and raised in Brooklyn, New York. He enlisted in the Marine Corps August 1978. He reported to Parris Island, South Carolina in July 1979 for training with 2nd Recruit Training Battalion. He reported to Infantry Training School at Camp Geiger, North Carolina for training as a 0311.

His military education includes Drill Sergeant School; Air Defense Course; Audio Visual Support Course; and the Field Radio Course.

His military assignments include serving with the 3D Low Altitude Air Maintenance Battalion, 2D Marine Air Wing at Marine Corps Air Station, Cherry Point, North Carolina where he served as a Section Chief; as a Drill Sergeant with the Delta Company, 1st Battalion, Recruit Training Regiment; as SNCOIC for the ITV Section for Training and Audio Visual Support Center at Marine Corps Air Station El Toro, California; as First Sergeant for Engineer Company B, 6th Engineer Support Battalion, at South Bend, Indiana; as Sergeant Major for "The Professionals," 2nd Battalion, 1st Marines. Carter was promoted to Sergeant Major in November 2001.

Carter, Reginald
LIEUTENANT COLONEL—ARMY

Reginald Carter received a Bachelor of Arts degree from Morris Brown College in June 1960. He attended the Interdenominational Theological Center in Atlanta in 1967. His military education includes the United States Army Officers Branch Course (Advanced Studies) at Fort Hamilton, New York (1971); Introduction to Hospital Ministry at Walter Reed Army Medical Center, completed May 8, 1987; and United States Army Command and General Staff College, completed 1983. He was commissioned a 1st Lieutenant in the United States Army National Guard on June 10, 1970, becoming the first black commissioned officer appointed to the Georgia Army National Guard. From 1970 to 1975, he was assigned as Battalion Chaplain for the 360th Engineer Battalion in Columbus, Georgia. He was promoted to Captain in 1973. From 1975 to 1978, he was assigned as Chaplain for the 519th

Military Police Battalion at Fort Meade, Maryland, assigned to the parish ministry and ministry to the post stockade. From 1978 to 1980, he was assigned as Chaplain with the 526th Maintenance Battalion in Macon, Georgia. He was promoted to Major in 1980. From 1980 to 1987, he served as a Staff Chaplain with the Third United States Army as a Reserve Soldier at Fort McPherson, Georgia. In 1987, he was assigned to his last posting before retirement as Staff Chaplain for the 3297th United States Army Hospital (1000B) in Chamblee, Georgia, where he was promoted to Lieutenant Colonel. His military awards and decorations include: the Armed Forces Meritorious Service Medal Army Commendation Medal (with two oak leaf clusters); the National Defense Medal; Armed Service Ribbon; and the Armed Forces Reserves Medal. Lieutenant Colonel Carter also wrote, produced and directed a one-act play entitled *Peace*, for the Army post-wide Black History program. The play received acclaim post wide for its content, dramatization, message, and direction. He was nominated and received notoriety to appear in the publication, "YOUNG MEN OF AMERICA," in 1972. LTC Carter became the first black appointed as Chaplain for the City of Atlanta Marta Police Department.

Carter, Ronald L.
COMMAND MASTER CHIEF—NAVY

Carter is a native of New Orleans, Louisiana, and he enlisted into the United States Navy in November 1961. His military assignments included serving as acting Command Master Chief for the Nucleus crew, Precommissioning Unit for *Abraham Lincoln* (CVN 72); as Command Master Chief for Helicopter Sea Control Wing One; and as Command Master for the Com-

mander of Naval Air Force, United States Fleet. He was the First African American to serve in this position in the United States Navy. In this position, he was responsible for the personnel issues, health and welfare for more than 60,000 enlisted men and women assigned to 156 subordinate commands, including 14 shore stations, over 100 squadrons and 10 aircraft carriers.

Cartwright, Roscoe Conklin
BRIGADIER GENERAL—ARMY

Born in Kansas City, Kansas, Cartwright received a B.A. degree in social science from San Francisco College, and earned an M.B.A. in business administration from the University of Missouri. His military education includes completion of the Artillery School, Advanced Course; United States Army Command and General Staff College; and Industrial College of the Armed Forces.

He has held a wide variety of important command and staff positions, culminating in the following major permanent duty assignments in the last 10 years of his 31-year career. He was Comptroller of the United States Army Garrison at Fort Leavenworth, Kansas, from November 1963 to August 1966. From August 1966 to July 1968, he served as Management Analyst (later Chief), Research and Development Division, Office of the Director of Management, Office of the Comptroller of the Army, Washington, D.C. From August 1968 to June 1969, he was a student at the Industrial College of the Armed Forces, Fort Lesley J. McNair, Washington, D.C. After completion of the Industrial College, he was assigned as Commanding Officer of the 108th Artillery Group, then as Deputy Commanding Officer of the United States Army Support Command at Cam Ranh Bay, Pacific-Vietnam, from August 1969 to July 1970.

In August 1970 he returned to the United States and was assigned as Chief of Budget and Five-Year Defense

Program, Coordination Division, Manpower and Forces Directorate, Office of the Assistant Chief of Staff for Force Development, United States Army, in Washington, D.C. From July 1971 to November 1971, he served as Special Assistant, Assistant Chief of Staff for Force Development, United States Army, in Washington, D.C. From February 1972 to July 1973, he served as Assistant Division Commander of the 3rd Infantry Division, United States Army in Europe. In August 1973 he was assigned as Deputy Chief of Staff in the Office of the Comptroller, United States Army, Europe, and Seventh Army. He was promoted to Brigadier General on August 1, 1971.

Cartright retired on August 31, 1974. His military awards and decorations include the Legion of Merit (with oak leaf cluster), Bronze Star (with two oak leaf clusters), Meritorious Service Medal, Air Medal (three awards), and Army Commendation Medal (with two oak leaf clusters).

Caulk, Charles Colton
CHIEF WARRANT OFFICER 5—ARMY

Caulk is a native of Philadelphia, Pennsylvania and enlisted in the United States Army in 1959. After serving 13 years as an enlisted soldier and obtaining the rank of Sergeant First Class, he was appointed Warrant Officer One in December 1972.

After his appointment to Warrant Officer One, he processed though the ranks and was promoted to Chief Warrant Officer Five in October 1994. Over a career of 43 years, he has served in France, Germany, Panama, Korea, Japan, Vietnam, Thailand and numerous locations in the United States. He served as Chief for the COMSEC Management Office, 1st Signal Brigade, in Yongsan, South Korea.

CWO Caulk has served in the Vietnam War; Operation Desert Shield/Desert Storm; Operation Joint Endeavor; and Operation Iraqi Freedom. He has trained countless young soldiers, and still serves as a role model as an Army Civilian working as a leader/development specialist at the Center for Army Leadership.

Ceaser, Deritha M.
SENIOR MASTER SERGEANT—AIR FORCE

Ceaser is a native of New Orleans, Louisiana, and holds a Bachelor of Arts degree in Sociology from the University of Texas at Arlington.

Her military assignments include Wing's Human Resources Office (HRO) remote designee with primary responsibility for all the wing's full-time manning issues. From December 1983 to 2004, she served in various fulltime roles within the Military Personnel Flight including Retention Office Manager (ROM), Base Education and Training Manager, NCOIC Customer Support, and Noncommissioned Officer in Charge of Career Enhancement. In 2004, she was serving as the Senior Noncommissioned Officer in the Personnel Career Field, and Representative on the Air National (ANG) Advisory Council to the Air Force Association. She has over 22 years of experience in the Personnel Field, and serves as an AGR assigned as the Personnel Superintendent for the 136th Airlift Wing at Fort Worth, Texas.

Chambers, Andrew P.
LIEUTENANT GENERAL—ARMY

Born in Bedford, Virginia, Chambers married the former Norita E. (Rita) Garner. They have four children, Kathy, Linda, Steven, and David. Upon completion of the Reserve Officers Training Corps curriculum and the educational course of study at Howard University in 1954, he was commissioned a second lieutenant and awarded a Bachelor of Science degree in physical education. He also holds a Master of Science in Communications from Shippensburg State College. His military education includes the Basic and Advanced Officer Courses at the Infantry School, the United States Army Command and General Staff College, and the United States Army War College.

He has held a wide variety of important command and staff positions, culminating in his current assignment as Commanding General of VII Corps, United States Army in Europe. Other key assignments include Assistant Deputy Chief of Staff for Personnel, United States Army, Washington, D.C.; Commanding General of Readiness and Mobilization Region VII; Deputy Commanding General of the Fifth Army at Fort Sam Houston, Texas; and Commanding General of the 1st Cavalry Division at Fort Hood, Texas. General Chambers served in a variety of important career-building assignments preparatory to his most recent duties. He served as an Instructor/Author at the United States Army Command and General Staff College at Fort Leavenworth, Kansas, followed by assignment to Europe in the Office of the Deputy Chief of Staff for Personnel. While in Europe, he served as a Deputy Infantry Brigade Commander and an Infantry Battalion Commander.

General Chambers assumed duty as Chief of Force Programs Analysis for the Chief of Staff, United States Army, in Washington, D.C. While in Washington, he also served as Deputy, later Director, of the Army Equal Employment Opportunity Program. Upon reassignment, he was Commander of the 9th Infantry Division Support Command at Fort Lewis, Washington, and Director of Personnel, J1, for the Inspector General of Pacific Command, Hawaii. He then served as Assistant Division Commander of the 1st Cavalry Division at Fort Hood, Texas.

From May 1981 to July 1982, he served as the Commanding General of United States Army Readiness and Mobilization Region VII and Deputy Commanding General of the Fifth United States Army at Fort Sam Houston. In July 1987, he served as the Deputy Commanding General of the United States Army Forces Command and Commanding General of the Third United States Army, with the United States Army Forces Command at Fort McPherson, Georgia.

He retired on March 31, 1989. His awards and decorations include the Bronze Star (with "V" device), Distinguished Service Medal, Soldier's Medal, Defense Superior Service Medal, Legion of Merit, Meritorious Service Medal (with oak leaf cluster), Air Medal, Army Commendation Medal (with two oak leaf clusters), Combat Infantryman Badge, and Senior Parachutist Badge.

Chambers, Lawrence C.
REAR ADMIRAL—NAVY

Admiral Chambers was born in Bedford, Virginia, and married the former Phyllis D. Richter of Reno, Nevada. They have two daughters, Lori C. and Leila C. He entered the United States Naval Academy as a Midshipman on June 30, 1948.

On June 6, 1952, he was appointed an Ensign, and from June 1952 to November 1952 he was assigned to the USS *Columbus* (CA 74). From November 1952 to October 1953, he was a student at NABTC at NAS Pensacola, Florida. From October 1953 to March 1954, he was a student at NAAS in Kingsville, Texas. He was designated a Naval Aviator (HTA) on June 9, 1954. From March 1954 to June 1954, he was a student at NABTC at NAS Pensacola. From June 1954 to June 1955, he served in Air Anti-Submarine Squadron 37. From June 1955 to April 1957, he was assigned to Attack Squadron 215.

On July 1, 1956, he was promoted to Lieutenant. From April 1957 to August 1959, he was a student at the Naval Postgraduate School, Monterey. From August 1959 to September 1960, he was a student at the NROTC Unit, Stanford University in Stanford, California. From September 1960 to July 1961, he was assigned to Attack Squadron 125. From July 1961 to December 1963, he was assigned to Attack Squadron 22 (OIC).

On September 1, 1961, Chambers was promoted to Lieutenant Commander. From December 1963 to January 1967, he served as Assistant Curriculums Officer in the Aeronautical Engineering Programs at the Naval Postgraduate School in Monterey. He was promoted to Commander on July 1, 1966. From January 1967 to August 1968, he served on the USS *Ranger* (CVA 34).

From August 1968 to November 1971, he served as a PCO, Attack Squadron 67, later Commander, Attack Squadron 67, then Commander, Attack Squadron 15, and USS *Oriskany* (CVA 34)

From November 1971 to June 1973, he served as the Deputy Project Manager at A-7E Project Office at Naval Air Systems Command. He was promoted to Captain on July 1, 1972. From June 1973 to January 1975, he was the Commander of the USS *White Plains* (AFS 4). From January 1975 to December 1976, he was the Commander of the USS *Midway* (CVA 41).

From December 1976 to November 1978, he was Assistant Chief of Naval Personnel for Enlisted Personnel Development and Distribution at the Bureau of Naval Personnel. On August 1, 1977, he was promoted to Rear Admiral. From November 1978 to April 1979, he served as Chief of Naval Personnel at Naval Military Personnel Command. From April 1979 to August 1979, he was a student in the Senior Officers Ships Material Readiness Course at Idaho Falls, Idaho. From August 1979 to May 1981, he served as Commander of Carrier Group 3; and from May 1981 to March 1, 1984 as Deputy Commander of ASW for the Naval Air System Command.

He has received numerous medals and awards including the Bronze Star; Meritorious Service Medal; Navy Unit Commendation awarded the USS *Oriskany* (CVA 34); China Service Medal; the National Defense Service Medal (with one bronze star); the Armed Forces Expeditionary Medal (Korea); Vietnam Service Medal (with three bronze stars); and the Republic of Vietnam Campaign Medal with Device.

Chance, Lennox A.

CHIEF WARRANT OFFICER—ARMY

A native of Georgetown, Guyana, Chance emigrated to the United States of America in May 1970. He was drafted into the United States Army in December 1972 and completed his Basic Combat Training at Fort Jackson, South Carolina. He completed his Advanced Individual Training at Fort Ord, California, where he attained "71B" Company Clerk MOS, and the second at Fort Benjamin Harrison, Indiana, where he was awarded "71D" Legal Clerk MOS.

His education includes a Bachelor of Arts in Economics from Queens College in New York as well as the 1st Warrant Officer Advanced Course at TJAGLCS in February 2000.

He was an Assistant Instructor for three consecutive years at the Naval Justice School from 1979 through 1982, where he taught Court Reporting to reservists. The highest enlisted rank attained by Chief Chance was Master Sergeant prior to his appointment as the Warrant Officer.

In 1996, he was serving as a member of the Army Reserves, when he was called to active duty in support of Operation Joint Endeavor. He served with the V Corps, OSJA, in Heidelberg, Germany. He returned to active duty a second time in November 1997, with duty assignment at Fort McNair, Washington, D.C.,

and got involved immediately in a high-profile court martial case.

He served a second tour in Germany from July 2000 through May 2002 with the 1st Armored Division in Wiesbaden. After completion of this tour, he was assigned at TJAGLCS as the Executive Officer, Student Detachment.

Chandler, Allen E.

MAJOR GENERAL—ARMY

Born in Hagertown, Maryland, Major General Chandler married the former Barbara Hardiman, and they are the parents of three children.

Chandler was graduated from North Street High

School in Hagerstown in 1953. He began his military career as a private on May 18, 1955, in the United States Army Reserve. He continued his enlisted service until he was commissioned on June 3, 1957. He was a Distinguished Military Graduate of the ROTC program and graduated summa cum laude with a Bachelor of Science degree in Chemistry from Morgan State College in Baltimore, Maryland. Chandler served as a Supervisory Nurse with the 30th General Hospital from October 15, 1957, to June 13, 1959, while attending Jefferson Medical College in Philadelphia. He was promoted to First Lieutenant, Medical Service Corps, on June 5, 1959, while serving with the 361st General Hospital.

Chandler received his doctorate in medicine in 1961, graduating with honors from Jefferson Medical College. Chandler served a rotating internship at the Fitzgerald Mercy Hospital in Darby, Pennsylvania, during 1961 and 1962 and completed a pediatric residency at Jefferson Medical College from June 1962 through May 1964.

He served on active duty as Chief of the Pediatric Department at General Leonard Wood Army Hospital at Fort Leonard Wood, Missouri, from 1964 to 1966. He performed this duty as a Captain in the Medical Corps. He was certified by the American Board of Pediatrics in 1966. He joined the Pennsylvania Army National Guard on September 14, 1976, as the Chief of Medical services for the 108th Combat Support Hospital.

He was promoted to Lieutenant Colonel on March 10, 1977, and assumed Command of the 108th Combat Support Hospital on October 1, 1977. He took a reorganized unit that had formerly been a Field Artillery Battalion and developed it into a high-priority hospital. Chandler completed the Army Medical Department Command and General Staff College on April 4, 1980, continuing his service as commander of the 108th Combat Hospital.

Until his selection as State Surgeon for Headquarters State Area Command, Pennsylvania, Chandler was responsible for the development of medical plans, policies, and training, utilizing all medical assets of the state, both military and domestic. He also served as the FUSA advisor to the National Guard Bureau Surgeon from 1984 to 1988.

He was assigned as the Assistant Adjutant General in July 1987 and promoted to Brigadier General on March 24, 1988. In this capacity, his duties include supervision of personnel, logistics, maintenance, medical, chaplain, judge advocate, provost marshal, safety, and selective service activities.

He is a pediatrician in private practice in Philadelphia, Pennsylvania. He is also the senior pediatrician in the Philadelphia Health Department and serves responsibilities relative to the overall wellness of the youth of Philadelphia. Chandler is also the Medical Director of the Childhood Lead Poisoning Program of Philadelphia and has years of experience in the area of heavy-metal intoxication. He develops, manages, and monitors all programs that affect the health of all children in Philadelphia from birth to age 18. He directly supervises 45 board-certified pediatricians and four senior pediatric consultants, with a budget of $7.5 million, and has over 300,000 patient visits per year.

Academically, Chandler has served on the professorial staff of Thomas Jefferson University since 1964. He served as a member of the Admissions Committee there from 1971 to 1979. From 1972 to 1978, he was the director of Minority Admissions at Jefferson Medical College. On March 24, 1988, Allen E. Chandler's promotion to Brigadier General made him the first black American to hold that position in the Pennsylvania Army National Guard at Fort Indiantown Gap, Pennsylvania. Brig. Gen. Allen E. Chandler serves as assistant adjutant general, Headquarters, State Area Command.

In 1992, General Chandler was promoted to Major General. He was nominated by President Bush and confirmed by the Senate to serve as the Department of the Army deputy surgeon general for National Guard Affairs and Mobilization.

Chandler, Cleveland, Jr.
MASTER SERGEANT—AIR FORCE

Chandler is a native of Baltimore, Maryland, and career in the United States Air Force began in 1997. He graduated from the Baltimore School of Arts in 1989, and earned a Bachelor of Music Degree of Music from the Peabody Conservatory of Johns Hopkins University. In 1995, he earned a Master of Music Degree in Violin Performance from the Cleveland Institute of Music. He received a professional studies degree from the same institution in 1997.

Before joining the Air Force, he participated in The Festival of Two Worlds in Spoleto, Italy and the Moscow Conservatory International Summer School. Additionally, he performed with the Youngstown Symphony, Erie Philharmonic, Akron Symphony Orchestra and National Orchestral Institute. While in Moscow, he studied with Sergei Kravchenko and Victor Melnikov. He also studied at the Aspen Music Festival and the Johannesen International School of the Arts in Victoria, Canada.

He serves as a violinist with The United States Air Force Band Strings, at Bolling Air Force Base, Washington, D.C.

Cheatham, James Arthur
MAJOR GENERAL—ARMY

Major General Cheatham received Bachelor of Science in Civil Engineering, from Prairie View A&M University and a Master Degree in Civil Engineering from Purdue University. He was commissioned into the United States Army Reserves in August 1971 as a Second Lieutenant.

In June 1988, Cheatham serving as the Commander of Company A of the 972nd Engineer Battalion at Fort Snelling, St. Paul, Minnesota; in October 1990, he became Assistant Deputy Chief of Staff for Operations in the 88th United States Army Reserve Command at

Fort Snelling; in December 1992, as Deputy Chief of Staff, Personnel, 88th United States Army Reserve Command, Fort Snelling, St. Paul, Minnesota; in November 1995, he served as Commander of the 372nd Engineer Group in Des Moines, Iowa; and was later Assistant Chief of Staff Comptroller for the 416th Engineer Command in Chicago, Illinois. In August 1999, he was assigned as the Commander of the 411th Engineer Brigade in Newburgh, New York, and was promoted to Brigadier General in October 2000.

In April 2002, Cheatham was selected to serve as the Deputy Chief of Engineers, Reserve Components, in the United States Army Corps of Engineers, in Washington, D.C. He was promoted to Major General on May 23, 2002. In March 2005, he was the Deputy Chief of Engineers (IMA), United States Army Corps of Engineers, in Washington, D.C.

Cherry, Fred
COLONEL—AIR
FORCE

Colonel Cherry was a noted Korean War fighter ace. During the Vietnam War, his F-105 was hit while flying a mission. He completed his mission in his crippled aircraft, but was forced to eject over North Vietnam. For the next 7½ years, he was a prisoner of war in the infamous "Hanoi Hilton."

During his time as a POW, the North Viet-

namese placed him with Commander Porter Halyburton, a white officer hoping to create stress by the racial tensions prevalent at the time. Instead a lifelong bond was created as each helped the other to survive.

Chestnut, Melvin O'Neal
SERGEANT MAJOR—MARINES

Chestnut was born in Sumter, South Carolina, and entered the Marine Corps in June 1978. Upon completion of Recruit Training, he attended Infantry Training School (ITS) at Camp Pendleton, California.

His key military assignments include serving as Drill Instructor for Golf Company, 2nd Battalion in San Diego, California; Platoon Sergeant, Platoon Commander, Assistant Operations Chief and Company Gunner Sergeant, while with the 1st Battalion, 8th Marines, during which time he also participated in Operation Desert Shield/Desert Storm; as a Drill Instructor, Senior Drill Instructor and Series Gunnery Sergeant with Charlie Company, 1st Battalion, Drill Instructor School, at San Diego; in September 1994, he was assigned to Drill Instructor School Staff as Standard Operation Procedure (SOP) Instructor and Squad Instructor; in July 1995, he was assigned to the Recruit Training Regimental Staff as the Regimental Training and Special Projects Chief; in October 1996, as First Sergeant and Gunnery Sergeant with the 3rd Battalion, 4th Marines; as First Sergeant of Alpha Company, 1st Battalion, Marine Corps Recruit Depot at San Diego and, in September 2000, as First Sergeant of Headquarters Battery, 11th Marine Regiment, at Camp Pendleton, where he deployed in support of Operation Enduring Freedom/Operation Iraqi Freedom in June 2003. In July 2003, Chestnut assumed duties as Sergeant Major of Marine Tactical Air Command Squadron 38, Marine Wing Communications Squadron.

Chiles, Farrell J.
CHIEF WARRANT OFFICER—ARMY

Chiles began his federal government career in 1992 as a Military Personnel Specialist with the United States Army Reserve's 300th Military Police Command at Inkster, Michigan. In 1993, he accepted a Management Analyst position with the West Los Angeles Veterans Administration Hospital. In 1996, he became the Chief of the Special Actions Branch at the 63rd Regional Readiness Command until he was promoted to his current position.

His education includes a Bachelor of Science degree in Political Science from the University of the State of New York. He is a graduate of the Greater Los Angeles Federal Executive Board's Leadership Associates Program; and has completed the Organizational Leadership for Executive Board's Leadership Associates Program; as well as the Organizational Leadership for Executive Program and the Personnel Management for Executive Course.

Chiles is a Vietnam Veteran and a Chief Warrant Officer in the United States Army Reserve with over

33 years of service to his country. He was elected President of the Los Angeles/Long Beach Area Chapter of blacks in Government in January 2000. As President, he increased the Chapter's membership from thirteen members to 125 within eight months. In January 2001, he joined blacks in Government's National Board of Directors representing Region IX. He was elected Chairman of the Board in January 2002 and re-elected as Chairman in 2003 and 2004.

Christopher, Dale A.
COMMAND SERGEANT MAJOR—ARMY

Christopher is a native of St. Thomas, United States Virgin Islands. He enlisted in the United States Army in September 1978, attended Basic Combat Training at Fort Jackson, South Carolina and Advanced Individual Training for Medical Specialist at Fort Sam Houston, Texas.

He earned an Associate in Arts degree from Regency College in May 2001. His military education includes all the Noncommissioned Officer Education System Courses; First Sergeant Course; the United States Army Sergeants Major Academy; and the Command Sergeant Major Course.

He has held numerous leadership positions including serving as Command Sergeant Major of the 28th Combat Support Hospital at Fort Bragg, North Carolina; as Command Sergeant Major for the 261st Area Support Medical Battalion at Fort Bragg; as Senior Enlisted Advisor at the Defense Medical Readiness Training Institute at Fort Sam Houston, Texas; as First Sergeant of Charlie Company, 302nd Forward Support Battalion, at Camp Casey, South Korea; as First Sergeant of the 57th Medical Company (AA) at Fort Bragg; as First Sergeant of the 5th Mobile Army Surgical Hospital at Fort Bragg; as Detachment Sergeant in the 214th Medical Detachment (AA) at Albrook, Panama; and as Operation Sergeant of the 142nd Medical Battalion Forward at Fort Clayton, Panama. In January 2005, Christopher was serving as the Command Sergeant Major of the 30th Medical Brigade.

Clark, David M.
COMMAND SERGEANT MAJOR—ARMY

Clark enlisted in the United States Army in November 1984, and completed Basic Combat Training and Advanced Individual Training at Fort Leonard Wood, Missouri. His leadership positions as a Combat Engineer include DDS Chief and Drill Sergeant Leader. He also served as a Squad Leader; Platoon Sergeant; First Sergeant; and Battalion Command Sergeant Major.

His military and civilian education includes all the Noncommissioned Officer Education System Courses; the United States Army Sergeants Major Academy (class 54); Battle Staff Course; Drill Sergeant School, Sapper Leader Course; and the First Sergeant Course. He holds an associate's degree in Management from Central Texas College.

In March 2005, he was serving as Command Sergeant Major for the 65th Engineer Battalion, 25th Infantry Division (Light), in Hawaii.

Clark, Jeffrey R., Sr.
COMMAND MASTER CHIEF—NAVY

Born in Washington, D.C., Clark enlisted in the United States Navy through the Delayed Entry Program in 1981.

He is a graduated of the Senior Enlisted Academy

and received the Peter Tomich Distinguished Graduate Award from the Commissioned Officers' Association.

He completed recruit and apprenticeship training at Great Lakes, Illinois. His first duty station was with Fleet Air Logistics Support Squadron Forty (VRC 40) at Norfolk, Virginia.

Other shore duty assignments have included Naval Air Test and Evaluation Squadron One (VX 1) at Patuxent River, Maryland; Naval Aviation Depot Operations Center Detachment at Naples, Italy; and Naval Aviation Pacific Repair Activity at Atsugi, Japan.

Various sea duty assignments have included two tours with Patrol Squadron Five Six (VP 56) at Jacksonville, Florida; Fleet Air Reconnaissance Squadron Six (VQ 6) at Cecil Field, Florida; and USS *Independence* (CV 62) and USS *Kitty Hawk* (CV 63) both homeported in Yokosuka, Japan. In December 2004, he was serving as the Command Master Chief onboard the USS *Reuben James* (FFG57).

Clark, Patrina

REGIONAL EXECUTIVE DIRECTOR—NAVY

Clark assumed the position of Regional Executive Director for Naval District Washington on June 28, 2004. As Regional Executive Director, she serves as one of two principal deputies to the Commandant of Naval District Washington, and is Naval District Washington's Senior Civilian.

She attended the University of Texas, where she began her undergraduate studies as a National Merit Scholar and University of Texas Presidential Scholar majoring in Electrical Engineering. She completed her undergraduate studies at Thomas Edison State College with an emphasis in Communications and Human Resources Management. She has undertaken graduate studies at Cornell University in Ithaca, New York, and George Washington University in the District of Co-

lumbia. She has a graduate certificate from Cornell's School of Industrial Labor Relations in Human Resources Management and a master's certificate in Project Management from George Washington University.

She began her federal career with the Internal Revenue Service in 1986. With the exception of a one-year assignment with the Veteran's Administration, her entire federal career has been with the Internal Revenue Service. She has held leadership positions in both tax administration and human resources/support, with an emphasis in training and labor/employee relations.

Clark, William, Jr.

COMMAND SERGEANT MAJOR—ARMY

Clark began his military career in 1974 when he enlisted into the United States Army in Combat Construction, assigned to the 14th Engineer Battalion at Fort Ord, California.

His military and civilian education includes all the Noncommissioned Officer Education System Courses; the United States Army Sergeants Major Academy; and the First Sergeant Course. He also holds an associate's degree in the Administration of Justice from Monterey Peninsula College.

After three years on active duty, he joined the California National Guard. He served as Tank Commander, Platoon Sergeant, and First Sergeant for Company A, 1-149th Armor. He was later assigned to Headquarters and Headquarters Company, 1-149th Armor as the First Sergeant and later as First Sergeant, Intelligence Sergeant and later as the Operations Sergeant Major for Company A, 1-149th Armor. In 1998, he was promoted to Command Sergeant Major and assigned to the 1-149th Armor. He was selected to serve as the Command Sergeant Major for the 3rd Brigade, 40th Infantry Division (Mechanized) in 2001.

Clarke, Jerry
COMMAND SERGEANT MAJOR—ARMY

A native of Smithfield, Virginia, Clarke entered the United States Army on 28 July 1977. He attended Basic Training at Fort Knox, Kentucky, and attended his Advanced Individual Training, 67V10 Observation Helicopter Repairman Course, at Fort Rucker, Alabama. His military and civilian education includes all the Noncommissioned Officer Education System Courses and the Sergeants Major Academy Class 50. He holds an associate's degree in Applied Science from Regents University. Some other courses he has attended during his 26 years of military service include the Aerial Observer Course; Aircraft Technical Inspector Course; Strategic Mobility Course; Aviation Life Support Equipment Course; Aviation Safety Course; Hazardous Cargo Certification Course; Master Fitness Course; and the Army's Pre-Commissioned Officer Course.

He has held every leadership position from First Line Supervisor to Brigade Command Sergeant Major. He served as Battalion Command Sergeant Major for 2nd Battalion, 2nd Aviation Regiment CP at Camp Stanley, South Korea. In August 2004, he was serving as the Command Sergeant Major for the 2nd Aviation Brigade, 2nd Infantry Division, South Korea.

Claxton, Vincent
SERGEANT MAJOR—MARINES

Sergeant Major Claxton enlisted into the Marine Corps in June 1980. After graduating from Basic Training at Parris Island, South Carolina, he was assigned to the School of Infantry aboard Camp Geiger, North Carolina, and graduated with a Military Occupational Specialty (MOS) of 0311 (Infantry Rifleman).

His leadership assignments include serving as a Primary Marksmanship Instructor, training over 1500 recruits; as a Squad Leader with India Company, 3rd Bat-

talion, 2nd Marines, Second Marine Division, at Camp Lejeune, North Carolina; as both a Drill Instructor and Senior Drill Instructor with First Recruit Training Battalion; as Chief Instructor with the Marine Security Forces Training Company in Chesapeake, Virginia in January 1991; as a Rifle Platoon Sergeant with the 1st Battalion, 6th Marines, Second Marine Division at Camp Lejeune, North Carolina in January 1994; as a Detachment Commander at American Embassy in Seoul Korea and American Embassy Dhaka Bangladesh; and as the Company Gunnery Sergeant for Lima Company, 3rd Battalion, 6th Marines, Second Marine Division in August 2000. In May 2000, Claxton was frocked as First Sergeant, 2nd Radio Battalion, II Marine Expeditionary Force; in July 2003, he was assigned as Company First Sergeant, Golf Company, 2nd Battalion, 2nd Marines, 2nd Marines Division. He was attached to the 1st Marine Division, Task Force 2/2 and deployed to Iraq in support of Operation Iraqi Freedom II. In January 2005, he was promoted to Sergeant Major and assigned to Marine Wing Support Squadron 274, Marine Wing Support Group 27, 2nd Marine Aircraft Wing for duty as the Squadron Sergeant Major.

Clay, Aaron
GUNNERY SERGEANT—MARINES

He holds a Bachelor of Science in Performance from West Virginia Wesleyan College in Buckhannon, West

Virginia. He joined the United States Marine Corps Band in July 1994. His past professional experience before the band include the United States Navy Band and a top 40 band in college.

Clay, Patricia
COLONEL—ARMY

Colonel Clay holds a Bachelor of Science degree in Nursing, from Tuskegee Institute, Tuskegee, Alabama, and earned a Master of Science in Nursing, from the Medical College of Virginia, in Richmond, Virginia. She is a graduate of the Army Command and General Staff College. She has attended numerous military Medical Courses; such as the Executive Skills Course; the Intensive Care Nursing Course; Clinical Head Nurse Course; and the Combat Casualty Care Course.

She has held a variety of positions including two ICU Head Nurse Positions, one at Kenner Army Community Hospital at Fort Lee, Virginia, and the other one as FORSCOM Nurse assigned to the 85th Evacuation Hospital at Fort Lee. She has been a critical Care and Cardiac Clinical Nurse Specialist/Case Manager at Dwight David Eisenhower Army Medical Center at Fort Gordon, Georgia. She was the Chief of Nursing Administration Days at Keller Community Hospital, West Point, New York, before being assigned to Fort Benning, Georgia, in August 1998. Prior to her current position, she served as the Chief of Inpatient Nursing Section/Chief of Nursing Administration Days. On June 2, 2000, she was assigned as the Deputy Commander for Nursing at Martin Army Community Hospital at Fort Benning.

Cleckley, Julia J.
BRIGADIER GENERAL—ARMY

Cleckley was raised in Aliquippa, Pennsylvania, and is the mother of two daughters, Helene and Ellen. She holds a bachelor's degree in Psychology and Education from Hunter College in New York City, New York. She earned a master's degree in Human Resource Management from Golden Gate University in San Francisco.

She was selected to attend the United States War College in 1992 and studied at the Fletcher School of Law and Diplomacy at Tufts University in Boston.

She enlisted in the Women's Army Corps after finishing high school. She then joined the New York National Guard and received her commission in the Adjutant General Corps with the 42nd Infantry Division in 1976, while she was a schoolteacher. She has served full-time with the National Guard Bureau in northern Virginia since 1987.

After serving in the military for 26 years, on July 1, 2002, she was promoted to Brigadier General. Lieutenant General Roger Schultz, the Army Guard's director, promoted the pioneering career officer from New York during the National Guard's Year of Diversity. She became the first woman to be assigned as Special Assistant to the Chief of the National Guard for Human Resources Readiness (G-1), in the history of the Army National Guard.

General Cleckley's became the third Brigadier General among the 42,000 women serving in the Army Guard. Her accomplishments include being the first minority woman to become a Branch Chief at the National Guard Bureau; the first African American woman to be promoted to Colonel in the Active Guard; and the first woman or minority member to serve on the Army Guard Director's special staff as Chief of Human Resources. She has also served a professor of military science at the ROTC program at Hampton University in Virginia.

Clemmons, Reginal G.
MAJOR GENERAL—ARMY

Clemmons was born in Wilmington, North Carolina, and he and his wife Sylvia have two daughters,

Regina and Adrienne. He received a Bachelor of Science degree in Mathematics from North Carolina Agricultural & Technological State University. He also earned a Master of Education degree from South Carolina State College. His military education includes Field Artillery Officer Basic and Advanced Courses; Armed Forces Staff College; and the United States Army War College.

He was commissioned a second lieutenant on June 5, 1968. From December 1968 to December 1969, he was assigned as a Forward Observer, later Liaison Officer, with the 7th Battalion, 13th Field Artillery, in the United States Army, Vietnam. From December 1969 to July 1970, he served as Commander, of the Headquarters Battery, 5th Battalion, 80th Field Artillery, 4th Infantry Division (Mechanized), at Fort Carson, Colorado. In July 1970, he served as Commander of Battery B, 1st Battalion, 27th Field Artillery, 4th Infantry Division (Mechanized), at Fort Carson. He was promoted to first lieutenant on June 5, 1971.

In May 1971, Clemmons was a student in the Field Artillery Officers Advanced Course at the United States Army Field Artillery School at Fort Sill, Oklahoma. From March 1972 to November 1972, he was assigned as Assistant S-3 (Operations), next from November 1972 to February 1974; he was assigned as Commander of Company B, later as Assistant S-3 (Operations), while assigned with the 3rd Battalion, 21st Field Artillery, United States Army Europe and Seventh Army, Germany. In September 1974, he was assigned as Liaison Officer for the 1st Battalion, 80th Field Artillery, United States Army Europe and Seventh Army, Germany. He was promoted to captain on June 5, 1975.

In August 1975, he returned to the United States to serve as Assistant Professor of Military Science, United States Army Reserve Officers Training Corps Instructor Group, at South Carolina State University in Orangeburg, South Carolina. He was promoted to major on March 3, 1979.

In September 1979, Clemmons was assigned as Assistant Fire Support Coordinator of Division Artillery, later Executive Officer of the 1st Battalion, 38th Field Artillery, 2nd Infantry Division, Eighth United States Army, South Korea. In September 1980, he returned to the United States to serve as Operations Research Analyst in the Concepts and Doctrine Directorate, later Logistics Assessment Officer, Logistics Assessment Task Group, United States Army Logistics Center at Fort Lee, Virginia. From January 1984 to June 1984, he was a student in the Armed Forces Staff College, Norfolk, Virginia. On December 1, 1984, he was promoted to lieutenant colonel.

In June 1984, he was assigned Deputy Assistant Fire Support Coordinator/Operations Officer, later Executive Officer, with the XVIII Airborne Corps Artillery, XVIII Airborne Corps, at Fort Bragg, North Carolina. In May 1987, he was assigned as Commander of the 2nd Battalion, 319th Field Artillery, 82nd Airborne Division, at Fort Bragg, North Carolina. From June 1989 to July 1990, he was assigned as Senior Observer/Controller with the United States Army Joint Readiness Training Center, at Little Rock Air Force Base, Arkansas. On December 1, 1990, he was promoted to colonel.

From August 1990 to June 1991, he was a student at the United States Army War College at Carlisle Barracks, Pennsylvania. In July 1991, he was assigned as Commander of the 1st Battlefield Coordination Detachment, XVIII Airborne Corps, at Fort Bragg. In July 1992, he was assigned as Commander of Division Artillery, 25th Infantry Division (Light), Schofield Barracks, Hawaii. From July 1994 to August 1995, he served as Director of the Fire Support and Combined Operations Directorate at the United States Army Field Artillery Center at Fort Sill. In August 1995, he was selected Assistant Chief of Staff for Operations, Headquarters, Land Forces Central Europe. He was promoted to Brigadier General on September 1, 1995.

He was the Assistant Division Commander of the 1st Infantry Division in Germany from October 1996 to November 1997. He served as the Deputy Commander for Allied Land Forces in Southeastern Europe and Turkey from November 1997 to August 1999. He was promoted to Major General on September 1, 1998.

In August 1999, he was assigned as the Deputy Commanding General of the Army's V Corps in Germany. On August 31, 2000, the General became the 23rd Commandant of the National War College, one of the National Defense University's senior colleges.

His military awards and decorations include the Legion of Merit, Bronze Star; the Meritorious Service Medal (with four oak leaf clusters); Army Commendation Medal (with two oak leaf clusters); and the Master Parachutist Badge.

Cleveland, Martha D.
COLONEL—ARMY

She received her Bachelor of Science degree from Hampton Institute in Virginia, and graduated from St. Phillips's Hospital School of Nursing at the Medical College of Virginia. She was commissioned into the United States Army Nurse Corps in April 1945. During the Korean conflict, she served in Korea with the 11th Evacuation Hospital. She received the Legion of Merit and the Korean Service Medal.

Clifford, Thomas E.
MAJOR GENERAL—AIR FORCE

Major General Clifford was born in Washington, D.C., and he and his wife, Edith, have four children, Maria, Edwin, Larry, and Mark. He attended school in Washington, D.C., graduating from Paul Lawrence Dunbar High School in June 1945. He then entered Howard University where he majored in Accounting and was a cadet in the Air Force Reserve Officer Training Corps program.

In June 1949 he graduated cum laude with a Bachelor of Arts degree in Business Administration. He also completed the Reserve Officer Training Corps program as a distinguished military graduate and was commissioned a second lieutenant in the United States Air Force. He entered active military service in September 1949 as a supply officer in the 225th Overseas Replacement Depot, Camp Kilmer, New Jersey. In August 1950 he completed the Air Tactical School (forerunner of Squadron Officer School) at Tyndall Air Force Base, Florida. In November 1950 he entered pilot training at Connally Air Force Base in Waco, Texas. He earned his wings in December 1951, and then received combat crew training in fighter-interceptor operations at Moody Air Force Base, Georgia, and Tyndall Air Force Base, Florida.

In April 1952 General Clifford was assigned as an F-94 Pilot in the 5th Fighter-Interceptor Squadron at McGuire Air Force Base, New Jersey. In June 1953 he went to the 449th Fighter-Interceptor Squadron at Ladd Air Force Base in Fairbanks, Alaska, where he was elevated to the position of Flight Commander and flew F-94 and F-89 aircraft. In January 1956 he moved to the 437th Fighter-Interceptor Squadron at Oxnard Air Force Base, California, and was again assigned as a Flight Commander in F-89 aircraft. A year later he was selected as the first Chief of the 27th Air Division Jet Instrument School, which he organized at Oxnard Air Force Base and Commanded for two years.

In May 1959 he was assigned to the 329th Fighter-Interceptor Squadron at George Air Force Base, California, where he served successively as Flight Commander, Weapons Training Officer, and Assistant Operations Officer while flying F-102 and F-106 aircraft. He left the squadron in June 1962 to commence in-residence graduate study at George Washington University, Washington, D.C. Upon graduation in June 1963 with a Master of Business Administration in Management, he was assigned to Headquarters, United States Air Forces, Europe (USAFE), at Lindsey Air Station in Wiesbaden, West Germany, Directorate of Management Analysis.

During this tour he became Chief of the Progress Analysis Division, which tracked the status of all major programs being implemented throughout the USAFE.

In July 1966 General Clifford went to the Pentagon, where he served for 18 months in the Directorate of Aerospace Programs under the Deputy Chief of Staff for Programs and Resources. In December 1967 he was selected to be a Military Assistant in the Directorate of Organizational and Management Planning in the Office of the Assistant Secretary of Defense for Administration. He completed his Pentagon tour in July 1969 and entered the Industrial College of the Armed Forces at Fort McNair, Washington, D.C. Upon graduation (with honors) in June 1970, he proceeded to George Air Force Base for F-4 training.

Upon completion, he went to Vietnam, where he served from March to November 1971 in the 366th Tactical Fighter Wing at Da Nang Air Base, first as Deputy Commander for Operations, then as Wing Vice Commander, flying in more than 90 combat missions. He was then sent directly from Vietnam to Germany to become the first Commander of the 52nd Tactical Fighter Wing at Spangdalem Air Base. General Clifford commanded the wing from December 1971 until July 1973 when he was transferred to Sembach Air Base, Germany, to become Vice Commander of the 17th Air Force.

In July 1974 he returned to the United States for duty as the United States Air Force Director of Inspection at Norton Air Force Base, in California. This was followed in April 1976 by his assignment as Commander of the 26th North American Air Defense Command, Region/Air Division, with Headquarters at Luke Air Force Base, Arizona. In September 1978, he was assigned as Deputy Assistant Secretary of Defense for Public Affairs, with offices in the Pentagon. He assisted in the formulation of policies and directives covering public affairs and community relations throughout the Department of Defense (DOD).

His military decorations and awards include the Legion of Merit (with two oak leaf cluster), Distinguished Flying Cross, Air Medal (with four oak leaf clusters), Air Force Commendation Medal (with one oak leaf cluster), Air Force Outstanding Unit Award, and Republic of Vietnam Gallantry Cross (with palm).

He was appointed Major General on January 18, 1977, with date of rank November 1, 1973.

Coaxum, Velva D.
SERGEANT MAJOR—MARINES

Coaxum enlisted into the Marine Corps in November 1979 and completed recruit training in January 1980. Upon completion of recruit training she returned to St. Louis, Missouri, where she worked as a recruiter assistant. She reported to MATSG NTTC Naval Air Station Meridian, Mississippi for the basic Aviation Supply course in March 1980. Upon completion of Aviation Supply School as a supply clerk, she reported to her first duty station at the 3rd Marine Aircraft Wing, Marine Corps Air Station, El Toro, California, where

she was joined for duty with H&S —13, MAG-13, transferred to VMA (AW) 242 for a 6-month oversees deployment to 1st MAW, MAG-12, in Iwakuni, Japan.

In January 1984, she was transferred to 2nd Marine Aircraft Wing H&S-31, Marine Aircraft Group 31, Marine Corps Air Station at Beaufort, South Carolina; she was then transferred to 1st Marine Aircraft Wing H&MS-36, Marine Aircraft Group-36, in Okinawa, Japan assigned as the Consumables Material Chief. In September 1989, she was transferred to the 2nd Marine Aircraft Wing, MALS-31, MAG-31, Marine Corps Air Station Beaufort for duty as the Repairable Management Chief until January 1991 when she was transferred to Drill Instructor School. Upon completion of Drill Instructor School, she was assigned to the 4th Recruit Training Battalion.

In March 1993, upon completion of Drill Instructor Duty, she was transferred to the 3rd Marine Aircraft Wing MALS-39, MAG-39, Marine Corps Air Station, at Camp Pendleton, California, where she served as the Consumables Management Chief. Upon return, she was transferred to Reserve Unit, 4th MAW MAG-46, DETA Marine Corps Air Station at Camp Pendleton as the Supply/Fiscal Chief. In July 1999, Sergeant Major Coaxum was transferred to III MEF 7th Communication Battalion, where she was assigned to Headquarters Company. During this tour she transferred to Alpha Company and served in operations Ulchi Focus Lens '00 Pohang, Korea; Tandem Thrust 2001 in Rock Hampton, Australia; and the Kingdom of Thailand, in support of Freedom Banner #5 and Cobra Gold 2002.

In August 2002, she was assigned as the Sergeant Major of the 2nd Medical Battalion. During this tour she deployed to Kuwait in support of Operation Enduring Freedom. Upon her return, in June 2004, she was reassigned to 2nd Transportation Support Battalion.

Sergeant Major Coaxum holds an Associate of Sci-

ence degree in Business and a Bachelor of Science with Distinction in Management Finance.

Coaxum, Victor J.
SERGEANT MAJOR—MARINES

Coaxum enlisted in the Marine Corps on October 8, 1980. Upon completion of recruit training at Marine Corps Recruit Depot at Parris Island, South Carolina, he attended Aviation Supply School at Naval Air Station Meridian, Mississippi. After completion of Aviation Supply School he was assigned to Marine Corps Air Station El Toro, California, where he was attached to Marine Aircraft Group 13, Headquarters and Maintenance Squadron 13 as a supply clerk. He was transferred to Marine Corps Air Station Iwakuni, Japan, to Marine Aircraft Group 15, Headquarters and Maintenance Squadron 15 where he served as Aviation Supply Repairable Division Clerk.

In December of 1982, he was transferred to Marine Corps Air Station Beaufort, South Carolina, Marine Aircraft Group 31, Headquarters and Maintenance Squadron 31 where he served as Aviation Supply Accounting Clerk and Operations Clerk until April of 1984. He was then transferred to Naval Air Station Belle Chase, Louisiana, as Supply Expeditor for Marine Aircraft Group 46 until September 1985. When he was reassigned to Marine Recruit Depot Parris Island, South Carolina, he served a successful tour as Drill Instructor until July of 1988. He then transferred to Marine Corps Air Station Okinawa, Japan, Marine Aircraft Group 36, Marine Aviation and Logistics Squadron 36, where he was assigned as Non-Commissioned Officer of Supply Response Division until his transfer in July of 1989.

He was then transferred back to Marine Corps Air Station, Beaufort, South Carolina, at the Naval Air

Maintenance Training Group and assigned as the Group Supply Chief until his transfer to Marine Corps Air Station Camp Pendleton, California, Marine Aircraft Group 39. He was assigned as Marne Aircraft Group 39 Fiscal Chief until his promotion to Gunnery Sergeant. In April 1997, he returned to Marine Corps Recruit Depot, Parris Island, South Carolina, for a second tour of Drill Instructor Duty, serving as Senior Drill Instructor, Series Chief Drill Instructor, and Leadership Instructor at Drill Instructor School until December of 1999.

Sergeant Major Coaxum was transferred to Marine Corps Air Station, Okinawa, Japan, with Marine Aircraft Group 36, where he was assigned as a fiscal officer until his promotion to First Sergeant. His first assignment as First Sergeant was at Engineer Support Battalion, 3rd Force Service Support Group in Okinawa in April 2001.

He was next transferred to the 8th Engineer Support Battalion, 2nd Force Service Support Group, at Camp Lejeune, North Carolina, in 2002, where he deployed with the Bulk Fuel Company to Kuwait in support of Operation Iraqi Freedom and also served as Sergeant Major of Marine Logistics Command Detachment Alpha during this tour of duty.

In August 2003, Sergeant Major Coaxum was assigned as MEU Service Support Group 24 Sergeant Major.

Cochran, Donnie

CAPTAIN—NAVY

Captain Cochran and his wife Emarvanay have five children, Chris, Tobi, Donnie Jr., Destiny and Alyshia. He was raised in Pelham, Georgia, and graduated from Pelham High School in 1972. He graduated from Sa-

vannah State College in 1976 with a Bachelor of Science degree in Civil Engineering Technology, simultaneously earning his commission as an ensign from the Naval Reserve Officer Training Corps (NROTC) program. Donnie completed basic and advanced jet training at Naval Air Station (NAS) Kingsville, Texas, earning his wings of gold in June 1978. He reported to Light Photographic Squadron 63 (VFP-63) at NAS Miramar, California in August 1978. There he completed the RF-8G Crusader Replacement Pilot Training Program and was assigned to VFP-63, deploying to the Mediterranean Sea and Indian Ocean aboard the aircraft carrier USS *Nimitz* (CVN-68). In November 1980, he joined the "Gunfighters" of Fighter Squadron 124 (VF-124) for transition training to the F-14A Tomcat. One year later he reported to the "Blacklions" of VF-213 where he completed two deployments to the Western Pacific Ocean aboard the aircraft carrier USS *Enterprise* (CVN-65). He reported back to VF-124 in February 1985 as an instructor pilot. In August of that year he was selected to the Navy Flight Demonstration Squadron (the Blue Angels). He flew one year in the A-4F Skyhawk at left wing (#3) and two years in the F/A-18, one as left wing and one as slot pilot. During his three years with the Blue Angels, he flew over 1,600 hours in 240 air shows before an estimated 22 million spectators throughout the United States and Canada. He returned to VF-124 for F-14 refresher training in January 1989. In April 1989, he joined the "Bounty Hunters" of VF-2 while that squadron was deployed aboard the aircraft carrier USS *Ranger* (CV-61) in the Western Pacific and Indian Oceans. He served VF-2 as both maintenance and safety officer. Commander Cochran was then selected to attend the Air War College at Maxwell Air Force Base in Montgomery, Alabama. While there he also earned a masters degree in human resource management from Troy State University. Having completed his studies, he reported to VF-1 in March 1992 as executive officer. He assumed command of VF-1 in July 1993 and served in that capacity until the squadron was disestablished in September 1993. He then reported to the "Sun Downers" of VF-111 in October 1993 as executive officer, assuming command on October 29. He turned over command of VF-111 on September 1, 1994. Commander Cochran rejoined the Blue Angels in October 1994, becoming the first African American commanding officer and flight leader of the United States Navy's Flight Demonstration Squadron. He took command of the Blue Angels in a ceremony held at the National Museum of Naval Aviation at Naval Air Station, Pensacola, Florida. He has accumulated over 4,630 flight hours in seven different naval aircraft and 888 carrier landings. His military awards and decorations include the Meritorious Service Medal; Air Medal; and the Navy Commendation Medal as well as numerous unit and campaign awards.

Cofer, Jonathan H.

BRIGADIER GENERAL—ARMY

General Cofer was born in Philadelphia, Pennsylvania.

He received a Bachelor of Science degree in Psychology from La Salle University, and earned a Master of Arts degree in Personnel Management and Administration from Central Michigan University. His military education includes Armor Officer Basic Course; Military Police Officer Advanced Course; United States Army Command and General Staff College; and the United States Army War College.

He was commissioned a second lieutenant on June 5, 1972. From November 1972 to January 1974, he was assigned a Platoon Leader with Company C, 2nd Battalion, 77th Armor, 9th Infantry Division, at Fort Lewis, Washington. In January 1974, he was assigned as Security Platoon Leader with the 9th Military Police Company, 9th Infantry Division, at Fort Lewis. In September 1974, he was assigned as Platoon Leader, later Executive Officer, of the 534th Military Police Company, 193rd Infantry Brigade, at Fort Clayton, Panama. He was promoted to 1st lieutenant on June 7, 1974. In May 1976, he was made Commander of the 534th Military Police Company, 193rd Infantry Brigade, at Fort Clayton. He was promoted to Captain on June 7, 1976.

In August 1977, he was assigned as Investigation Officer, 227th Military Police Detachment, 193rd Infantry Brigade, at Fort Clayton.

From December 1977 to July 1978, Cofer was a student in the Military Police Officer Advanced Course at Fort McClellan, Alabama. In August 1978, he became an Assistant Professor of Military Science in the United States Reserve Officer Training Corps at Valley Forge Military Academy at Wayne, Pennsylvania. In July 1981, he was assigned as Commander of the 980th Military Police Company at Sierra Army Depot at Herlong, California. From August 1983 to June 1984, he was a student at the United States Army Command and General Staff College at Fort Leavenworth, Kansas. He was promoted to Major on October 1, 1983.

In July 1984, he became an Automated Data Processing Officer, later Chief of Plans, Requirements and Policy Division, in United States Information Systems Engineering Command at Fort Belvoir, Virginia. In June 1987, he was assigned as Executive Officer of the 716th Military Police Battalion at Fort Riley, Kansas. He was promoted to Lieutenant Colonel on November 1, 1989.

In December 1989, he was assigned as Project Officer of the Combat Development Directorate at the United States Army Military Police School at Fort McClellan, Alabama. In July 1990, he served as Commander of the 787th Military Police Battalion at Fort McClellan, Alabama. From June 1992 to June 1993, he was a student at the United States Army War College at Carlisle Barracks, Pennsylvania. In June 1993, he was assigned as Chief of Combating Terrorism Branch, United States Army Special Operations and Plans, United States Army, Washington, DC. From July 1994 to June 1996, he served as Commander of the United States Army Military Police Command, United States Army South at Fort Clayton. He was promoted to Colonel on February 1, 1995. In September 1996, he was selected

Provost Marshal of United States Central Command at MacDill Air Force Base in Tampa, Florida. From July 1998 to July 2000, he served as the Commander of the Joint Rear Area Coordinator with the United States Central Command at MacDill Air Force Base. He was promoted to Brigadier General on December 1, 1998.

He was selected to serve with the Joint Staff in the Office of the Deputy Director of Operations (Combating Terrorism), J-34, at the Pentagon.

General Cofer's military awards and decorations include the Legion of Merit; Meritorious Service Medal (with four oak leaf Clusters); Army Commendation Medal (with three oak leaf clusters); the Army Achievement Medal; the Parachutist Badge; and the Air Assault Badge.

Coffey, Vernon C.
LIEUTENANT COLONEL—ARMY

Vernon Coffey became the second black to serve as an army aide to the President of the United States when, in December 1970, he was appointed United States Army Aide to President Richard M. Nixon. He is a graduate of St. Benedict's College in Atchison, Kansas and the United States Army Command and General Staff College.

He served as a Battalion Commander in Vietnam and was awarded the Silver Star while serving there with the First Infantry Division. He was responsible for coordinating all army supervised logistics required to support the president.

As the President's Aide he was concerned with the planning of specific official functions, including Medal of Honor presentations and wreath-laying ceremonies, briefing the president in times of emergency, assisting him at honor ceremonies and being available to the president at official functions and journeys.

Cole, Carmen E.
CHIEF WARRANT OFFICER—MARINE

On February 1, 1993, CWO Carmen E. Cole was promoted to Warrant Officer, making her the first African American Warrant Officer in the United States Marine Corps, Motor Transport Maintenance Field (3510). Her promotions to Chief Warrant Officer Two and Three were also first in the U.S. Marine Corps, Motor Transport Maintenance Field. She retired a Chief Warrant Officer Three on May 1, 2001.

Cole, Eddie L.
COLONEL—ARMY

Colonel Eddie L. Cole was born in Bells, Tennessee and received a Bachelor of Science degree and a Master of Science degree from the University of Tennessee at Martin, Tennessee. His military education includes the Air Assault Course; the Basic Airborne Course; the Engineer Officer Advance Course; the Naval Command and Staff College, and the United States Army War College. He served as a Noncommissioned Officer in South Vietnam from April 1967 until March 1968.

Colonel Cole was commissioned in the Engineers upon graduation from Officer Candidate School at Fort Benning, Georgia, in 1979. He subsequently served with the 230th Engineer Battalion as Detachment Commander, Executive Officer, and Company Commander from 1979 to 1986; following those assignments, he served as an Assistant Professor of Military Science at the University of Central Florida in Orlando from 1988 to 1989. He was assigned from 1989 to 1992 as Senior Instructor at the professional Education Center at Camp Robinson, Arkansas. From 1993 to 1995, he was assigned as the G-3 (Operations) and Deployment Team Chief with the 101st Airborne Division (Air Assault) at Fort Campbell, Kentucky. From 1995 to 1997, he was assigned as the G-3 (Operations) Exer-

cise Coordinator with the United States Army Forces Command at Fort McPherson, Georgia. In 1997, he was assigned as the Mobilization Division Chief for the First United States Army at Fort Gillem, Georgia. In 1999, he was ordered to serve as Senior Army National Guard Advisor with the XVIII Airborne Corps at Fort Bragg, North Carolina. On March 7, 2001, he was selected to serve as the Assistant Chief of Staff for the Army National Guard (ARNG) at the United States Army Forces Command at Fort McPherson.

Cole, Leon A.
CHIEF WARRANT OFFICER 5—NAVY

Aboard USS *Ronald Reagan*, Chief Warrant Officer Leon A. Cole made history as the first officer in the Navy to be promoted to the rank of Chief Warrant Officer Five (CWO5) since its reintroduction in October 2002 to ensure the Navy attracts and retains the very best technical leadership for a full 30-year career. His son Ensign Christopher Cole administered the reaffirmation of the Oath of Office to his father during a ceremony held aboard the ship on October 1, 2003.

Cole was the first of 17 to be advanced from a field of 222 candidates to the rank of CWO5.

Chief of Naval Personnel Vice Admiral Gerald L. Hoewing embarked on the USS *Ronald Reagan* to help promote Cole.

The Antigua, West Indies, native joined the Navy in 1974 at the age of 24. In his career, Cole was assigned to 13 various commands, and his hard-work ethics and strong leadership always attracted the attention of his co-workers.

Coleman, Gary G.
COMMAND CHIEF MASTER SERGEANT—AIR FORCE

Command Chief Master Sergeant Gary G. Coleman serves as the Command Chief Master Sergeant for the 12th Air Force and United States Southern Command Air Forces at Davis-Monthan Air Force Base, in Arizona.

Chief Coleman entered the Air Force in 1977. After completion of basic training, he was assigned to Barks-

served as the S-4A, S-4, Supply Officer, Candidate Platoon Commander and as Director of the Marine Corps Development and Education Command Non-Commissioned Officer School.

General Coleman attended Amphibious Warfare School during the 1981—1982 academic years and, upon graduation, was assigned to Headquarters Marine Corps Officer Assignments where he served as a Company Grade Monitor and Administrative Assistant to the Director of the Personnel Management Division. In August 1985, following his promotion to Major, he was assigned as an Instructor at the Amphibious Warfare School at Quantico, Virginia. In 1987, he was selected to attend the Marine Corps Command and Staff College.

He was again transferred to the 3rd Force Service Support Group in 1988, serving as the Operations Officer of the 3rd Landing Support Battalion; Executive Officer of the 3rd Maintenance Battalion; and Commanding Officer of Combat Service Support Detachment 35, Contingency Marine Air Group Task Force 4-90. Returning to the United States in June 1991, he reported to Headquarters Marine Corps and served as the Logistics Project Officer and Head of the Maintenance Policy Section, Installations and Logistics Branch. He was promoted to Lieutenant Colonel in the spring of 1992 and transferred to Camp Lejeune the following summer.

General Coleman assumed duty as Commanding Officer of the 2nd Maintenance Battalion, 2nd Force Service Support Group in June 1993, and in December 1994 was reassigned as the Group's Deputy Operations Officer. He reported to the Industrial College of Armed Forces at the National Defense University in August 1995. Following graduation in 1996, he reported to the Pentagon, serving in the Logistics Directorate J-4, Mobility Division as an Action Officer and Deputy Division Chief at the Logistic Readiness Center.

He was promoted to Colonel in July 1997 and a year later returned to Camp Lejeune for duty with the 2nd Marine Division as the Assistant Chief of Staff, G-4. In April 1999, he deployed to the Balkans where he served as the J-4 and Chief of Staff for Joint Task Force Shining Hope. He assumed command of the 2nd Supply Battalion on July 27, 1999, and was selected for promotion to Brigadier General in March 2001. He reported to the Headquarters of the United States Marine Corps in June 2001, as the Assistant Deputy Commandant for Installations and Logistics. He was nominated by the President to Lieutenant General on September 7, 2006.

General Coleman holds a master's degree in National Strategic Resources. His awards and decorations include the Defense Meritorious Service Medal; Meritorious Service Medal (with gold star); the Joint Service Commendation Medal; and the Combat Action Ribbon.

dale Air Force Base, Louisiana, as a dental technician. In 1984, he became a Professional Military Education Instructor at the Eighth Air Force NCO Leadership School. In September 1988, he was selected as Chief of the Enlisted Evaluations Division for the Ira C. Eaker Center for Professional Development at Maxwell Air Force Base, Alabama. In January 1992, he developed the first standardized NCO Academy curriculum outline which is now taught at every NCO Academy. During this assignment he helped lay the groundwork for the establishment of the College of Enlisted Professional Military Education. In September 1992, he became a First Sergeant and served in that capacity for three consecutive assignments. In August 1998, he was selected as Vice-President of Student Relations at the Community College of the Air Force at Maxwell Air Force Base.

Coleman, Ronald S.
LIEUTENANT GENERAL—MARINES

Coleman enlisted in the United States Navy in April 1968 and was discharged upon his return from Danang, South Vietnam in June 1970. He enrolled in Cheyney State College and graduated with a Bachelor of Science degree in Education in 1973. A high school teacher and football coach in Darby, Pennsylvania, he was commissioned a Marine Second Lieutenant in December 1974, following graduation from Officer Candidate School.

Following completion of Basic School and Ground Officer Supply School, Second Lieutenant Coleman reported for duty with the 2nd Marine Regiment at Camp Lejeune where he served as Battalion Supply Officer, Platoon Commander, Regimental Supply Officer and S-4A. In November 1977, he transferred to the 3rd Force Service Support Group in Okinawa, Japan, as the Operations Officer for Landing Support Unit Foxtrot. In November of 1978, he transferred to Officer Candidate School, at Quantico, Virginia, where he

Coley, Lloyd
COMMAND SERGEANT MAJOR—ARMY

Command Sergeant Major Lloyd Coley was born in Richmond, Virginia, on June 19, 1954. Following previous service, he reentered the military in October 1981, after his April 1980 ETS. His military education includes the United States Army Sergeants Major Academy; Advanced Noncommissioned Officers Course; and the Primary Leadership Development.

He has served in a variety of leadership positions including Brigade S-3 (Operations NCO); Sergeant Major of the 35th Air Defense Artillery Brigade at Fort Bliss, Texas; First Sergeant, HHB, in the 1-44 Air Defense Artillery at Fort Hood, Texas; First Sergeant of D Battery in the 5-5 Air Defense Artillery at Camp Stanley, South Korea; First Sergeant, HHB, in the 31st Brigade at Fort Hood; and First Sergeant B Battery, 2-2 Air Defense Artillery (later First Sergeant A Battery, 2-5 Air Defense Artillery) at Fort Hood. He is currently serving as the Command Sergeant Major of the 1-44th Air Defense Artillery at Fort Hood.

Collins, August L.
BRIGADIER GENERAL—ARMY

August L. Collins is the first black General in the Mississippi National Guard. He was born in Okolona, Mississippi, graduating from Booneville High School in 1975 and from Northeast Mississippi Junior College with an Associate of Arts degree in Business. He continued his education at the University of Mississippi with a Bachelor of Arts degree in Business, and from Jackson State University with a Master of Business Administration. His military education includes the Armor Officer Basic and Advanced Course; the United States Army Command and General Staff Course; and the United States Army War College.

He began his military career when he enlisted in the 1st Battalion, 198th Armor in 1977, and was commissioned as a Second Lieutenant of Armor in 1980 through the Mississippi Military Department's Officer Candidate School (OCS). He has served in command and staff positions in units at every level including Company, Battalion, Brigade and Major Subordinate Commands. A full-time technician for the Mississippi Army National Guard since 1988, he has held a variety of senior staff positions including Deputy Inspector General, Assistant Chief of Staff, and Deputy Director of Logistics and Military Personnel for the State Area Command of the Mississippi Army National Guard. He was appointed Deputy Chief of Staff for Personnel of the Mississippi Army National Guard in June 1999. In May 2005, he was promoted to Brigadier General while serving in Iraq.

Collins, Harry L.
COMMAND SERGEANT MAJOR—ARMY

A native of Scooba, Mississippi, Collins enlisted in the United States Army in August 1976. He attended Basic Combat Training and Advanced Individual Training at Fort Leonard Wood, Missouri.

His military education includes all the Noncommissioned Officer Education System Courses; Instructor Training Course; First Sergeant Course; and the United States Army Sergeants Major Academy.

His key leadership assignments include serving as Platoon Sergeant/Operation Sergeant for the 293rd Engineer Battalion in Baulmholder, Germany; Regional Trainer in St. Louis, Missouri; Quality Assurance Representative with the Army Corps of Engineers in Teague, South Korea; Directorate of Logistics and Engineer Sergeant Major at Fort Jackson, South Carolina; Command Sergeant Major of the 92nd Engineer Battalion at Fort Stewart, Georgia; Command Sergeant

Major for the 29th Engineer Battalion (T) at Fort Shafter, Hawaii; and Command Sergeant Major of the 45th Corps Support Group, 25th Infantry Division.

Collins, Joseph

COMMAND SERGEANT MAJOR—ARMY

Collins is a native of West Point, Mississippi, and entered the Army in November 1975. He completed Basic Combat Training at Fort Leonard Wood, Missouri, and Advanced Individual Training at Fort Sill, Oklahoma.

His military and civilian education includes all the Noncommissioned Officer Education System Courses; the Officer Pre-Commissioning Course; First Sergeant Course; and the United States Army Sergeants Major Academy (class 47). He holds an associate's degree from Central Texas College.

He his leadership positions include serving as Howitzer Section Chief at Fort Benning, Georgia and Camp Pelham, South Korea; Gunnery Sergeant, Chief of Firing Battery and Platoon Sergeant at Kitzingen, Germany; Senior Instructor of the 13B Track, Career Management Field 13 Chief, and First Sergeant of the Basic Noncommissioned Officers Course, III Corps NCO Academy, at Fort Hood, Texas; First Sergeant of A-Battery, 6-37th Field Artillery, at Camp Essayons, South Korea, and HHB 4-41st and 1-10th Field Artillery, 3rd Infantry Brigade, at Fort Benning; and Command Sergeant Major of 1-15th Field Artillery at Camp Casey, South Korea and 2-5th Field Artillery at Fort Sill, Oklahoma. In August 2004, he was serving as Command Sergeant Major of the 214th Field Artillery Brigade.

Combs, Osie V., Jr.

REAR ADMIRAL—NAVY

Born in Longview, Texas, Combs married the former Iris Parks of Bay City, Texas, and father of Melany and Natalie. He graduated from Prairie View A&M University in June 1971, with a degree in Electrical Engineering. Upon graduating from Prairie View A&M University, he was the school's outstanding Senior Engineering Student. Additionally, he was selected as the Outstanding Student Engineer of the Year by the Texas Society of Professional Engineers. This excellence in engineering led to his selection to the Navy's Elite Engineering Duty Officer Community as an Ensign.

Following his tenure as Assistant Boilers Officer in USS *Coral Sea* (CVA 43), he attended Post Graduate School at the Massachusetts Institute of Technology. There he was awarded two advanced Engineering degrees. He completed his Masters of Science in Mechanical Engineering and Post Masters degree in Ocean Engineering (Naval Architecture) in 1977. In addition to formal education, he is a graduate of the Program Manager's Course from the Defense Systems Management College and Executive Training for Professionals from Carnegie Mellon University.

He was a Midshipman in the U.S. Naval Reserve, Naval Reserve Officers Training Corps. He was commissioned an Ensign on June 9, 1971, and entered on active duty on July 3, 1971.

The Norfolk Naval Shipyard was his assignment for the next four years. He served in several key positions, including Surface and Submarine, Surface and Submarine Ship Type Desk Office and Backup Docking Officer. During this tour Combs completed his qualifications in Submarines (Engineering Duty). As part of the qualification program he served in USS *Woodrow Wilson*, SSBN 624 (Gold). He was promoted to Lieutenant (junior grade) on December 9, 1972, and promoted to Lieutenant on July 1, 1975.

Prior to his affiliation with the *Seawolf* Program, he functioned as the Assistant Project Officer for the construction of *Los Angeles* (SSN 688) class submarines as the Supervisor of Shipbuilding, Conversion and Repair in Newport News, Virginia, and was the Submarine Tender Repair Officer for the USS *Proteus* (AS 19). He was promoted to Lieutenant Commander on March 1, 1980.

Rear Admiral Combs reported to the Naval Sea Systems Command (PMS 350—*Seawolf* Program Office) in 1985. At command headquarters, he was Program Manager for and responsible for the delivery of *Seawolf*'s Large Scale Vehicle (LSV), and autonomous submarine. He then served as the Assistant Program Manager for Design and Construction of the *Seawolf* class submarine program. In 1990, he transferred to the Supervisor of Shipbuilding, Conversion and Repair in Groton, Connecticut, where he served as the Project Officer for construction of the *Seawolf* as well as the Program Manager's representative. He was promoted to Commander on May 1, 1986.

In 1992, he returned to Washington as *Seawolf* Program Manager, part of the Program Executive Officer, Submarines (PEO SUB), organization. He was promoted to Captain on March 1, 1992.

He is currently the Program Director for C41 Systems at Space and Naval Warfare Systems Command. He was promoted to Rear Admiral (lower half) on September 1, 1996.

From November 1997 to July 1998, he served as the Vice Commander of the Space and Naval Warfare Systems Command (SPAWARSYSCOM) in San Diego. In July 1998, he was selected to serve as the Deputy Commander for Submarines, SEA 92, at the Naval Sea Systems Command.

His military awards and decorations include the Legion of Merit; Meritorious Service Medal (with one gold star); the Navy Commendation Medal; the Navy Unit Commendation (with two bronze stars); the Navy "E" Ribbon (with second Battle "E"); the National Defense Service Medal (with one bronze star); the Sea Service Ribbon; the Vietnam Service Medal (with one bronze star); and the Republic of Vietnam Campaign Medal.

Cook, Odie "J"
COMMAND MASTER CHIEF—NAVY

He enlisted into the United States Navy in February 1978, and attended Boot Camp at Recruit Training Command in San Diego, California, followed by Signalman "A" School in Orlando, Florida.

He reported to Naval Air Station Corpus Christi, Texas in 1998 where he served as Deputy Director of the Family Service Center and was advance to Master Chief Signalman, eventually serving as the Command Master Chief for the entire Air Station. He requested and was accepted into the Command Master Chief Program and reported to the Senior Enlisted Academy in August of 1999. Following the Academy, he then joined the Aviation community by serving as the Command

Master Chief of Electronic Attack Squadron One Three Five (VAQ-135) "The Black Ravens." He next served as Command Master Chief for Carrier Air Wing Eleven and cruised aboard the USS *Carl Vinson* (CVN-70) and USS *Nimitz* (CVN-68). In March 2005, he was serving as the Command Master Chief (VFA-122) LEMOORE.

Cooper, Billy Roy
BRIGADIER GENERAL—ARMY

Brigadier General Cooper was born in Dallas, Texas. He received a Bachelor of Science degree in Education Administration from Cameron University. He also earned a master's in Education Administration. His military education includes the Field Artillery School Basic and Advanced Courses; United States Army Command and General Staff College; and the National War College. He was commissioned a Second Lieutenant on December 20, 1968.

From December 1968 to September 1969, he was assigned as Training Officer for Company C, 2nd Battalion, 1st Basic Training Brigade at the United States Army Training Center at Fort Lewis, Washington. In October 1969, he was assigned as Forward Observer, later Executive Officer for Battery A, 1st Battalion, 21st Artillery, 1st Cavalry Division in Vietnam. He was promoted to First Lieutenant on December 20, 1969.

In October 1970, he was assigned as Artillery Tactics Instructor on the Staff and Faculty Battalion at the United States Army Field Artillery School at Fort Sill, Oklahoma. He was promoted to Captain on December 20, 1970.

In June 1972, he was made Adjutant, later Commander, at Battery C, 1st Battalion, 22nd Artillery, 1st

Armored Division, United States Army Europe and Seventh Army, Germany.

In July 1974, he was assigned as Deputy Installation Coordinator for the 1st Armored Division, United States Army Europe and Seventh Army, Germany. From October 1975 to June 1976, he was a student at Cameron University in Lawton, Oklahoma. In July 1977, he became Assistant Professor of Military Science at Fort Valley State College in Fort Valley, Georgia with duty at Albany State College at Albany, Georgia. He was promoted to Major on November 9, 1979.

In August 1980, he was assigned as Field Artillery Staff Officer on the Staff and Faculty Battery at the United States Army Field Artillery School at Fort Sill. In June 1982, he was assigned as an Operations Officer in the S-3 section, 214th Field Artillery Brigade, Fort Sill, Oklahoma. He has also served as Research and Development Coordinator, United States Army Material Systems Analysis Activity, Aberdeen Proving Ground, Maryland. He was promoted to Lieutenant Colonel on November 1, 1985.

From June 1987 to August 1989, he served as Commander of the 2nd Battalion, 1st Field Artillery, 1st Armored Division, United States Army Europe and Seventh Army, Germany. From August 1989 to June 1990, he was a student at the National War College at Fort McNair, Washington, D.C.

From June 1990 to October 1991, he was assigned as Senior Operations Officer J-3, (National Military Command Center), Joint Staff, Washington, DC. He was promoted to Colonel on September 1, 1991.

From October 1991 to July 1993, he served as TRADOC System Manager, Fire Support Command, Control and Communications Systems at the United States Army Field Artillery School at Fort Sill, Oklahoma. From July 1993 to August 1995, he served as Commander of the 214th Field Artillery Brigade, III Corps Artillery, at Fort Sill, Oklahoma. In September 1995, he was selected Chief of the Fire Support Division in the Office of the Deputy Chief of Staff for Operations and Plans, Washington, DC. He was promoted to Brigadier General on November 1, 1996.

From May 1997 to July 1998, he served as Joint Rear Area Coordinator for United States Central Command at MacDill Air Force Base, Florida. From July 1998 to July 2000, he was assigned as the Deputy Commanding General of United States Army Recruiting Command (East), at Fort Knox, Kentucky. In July 2000, he was selected as the Deputy Commanding General, United States Army Recruiting Command (West), at Fort Knox, Kentucky. He retired on July 31, 2001.

His military awards and decorations include the Legion of Merit; the Bronze Star; Defense Meritorious Service Medal; Meritorious Service Medal (with three oak leaf clusters); Joint Staff Commendation Medal; the Air Medal; Army Commendation Medal (with three oak leaf clusters); Army Achievement Medal; and the Joint Chiefs of Staff Identification Badge.

Cooper, Irma H.
LIEUTENANT COLONEL—ARMY

Cooper was born in Natchez, Mississippi in 1953, and earned a master's degree from the University of California in San Francisco in 1986. She began her military career in March 1983, after she was commissioned as a Second Lieutenant into the United States Army's Nurse Corps.

Her military education includes the AMEDD Officer Basic and Advanced Courses; the 124th Army Reserve Command Equal Opportunity Representative Course; the Defense Equal Opportunity Management Institute (DEOMI); the United States Army Reserve Component Combined Arms and Services Staff School (CAS3); United States Army Reserve Component Command and General Staff College; AMEDD Head Nurse Course; AMEDD Medical Management of Chemical Casualty Course; AMEDD Medical Management Biological Casualty Course; Combat Casualty Care Course Phase I and Phase II; Team Leader Development Course; and the FORCOM United States Army Reserve Command/Detachment PRE-COMMAND Course.

She has held numerous leadership assignments, including serving as Equal Opportunity Advisor for the 63rd RSC in Los Alamitos, California; as Special Project Officer with the 349th General Hospital in Los Angeles, California; as Head Nurse in ICU, DEPMEDS Field Policy Special Project at the 349th General Hospital; as Head Nurse ICU, Training Officer at the VA Hospital in Los Angeles, California; as Head Nurse ICU, Quality Assurance Officer at the 349th General Hospital; Head Nurse ICU, Special Projects Officer, Personnel Records Audit Team, with the 349th General Hospital, in Los Angeles, California; as Head Nurse ICU Sanitation Officer, 352nd Evac Hospital, OARB; and as Head Nurse ICU at the 352nd Evac Hospital at Oakland, California. She was selected to serve as the Commander of the 113th Medical Company, supporting Operation Iraqi Freedom, between April 2003 and March 2004. Her responsibility as the Commander of the 113th Medical Company was to oversee 85 unit members and provide the prevention and treatment of

combat stress, and to treat and help soldiers and civilians affected by attacks including the bombing of the Al Rasheed Hotel, the United Nations Building and other sites. She was awarded the Bronze Star for her leadership.

Cooper, James S.
COLONEL—ARMY

Colonel Cooper was born in Millhaven in Screven County, Georgia. He is married to the former Mirriam Roberts and they have three children, Lenton Douglas, James Simon II, and Annette Evelyn. He received a Bachelor of Arts degree from Morris Brown College (1970) in Atlanta, Georgia, majoring in Psychology and Pastoral Care. He earned a Master of Arts degree from Princeton Theological Seminary (June 1983) in Princeton, New Jersey. He earned a Doctor of Ministry in 1980 from San Francisco Theological Seminary in San Anselmo, California. His military education includes United States Chaplain School Basic Course (1973); United States Chaplain School Advance Course (1979) and Command & General Staff College (1986). He has held a wide variety of important chaplain and staff positions, including HHC, 2nd Brigade Air Mobile, Fort Campbell, Ky., in 1973; HHC, DISCOM, 2nd ID, Camp Casey, South Korea, in 1974; HQ Det., US-AADABCT, at Fort Bliss, Texas, in 1975; HHB, 1st AD Battalion (Hawk), Fort Bliss, Texas, in 1976; HHB, 1st AD BN, Schofield Barracks, Hawaii, in 1979. In 1983 he was a member of the staff and faculty of the United States Army Chaplain School at Fort Monmouth, New Jersey, and in 1986, became HHC, 2nd Brigade, 24th ID, at Fort Stewart, Georgia, during which time he served in Operation Desert Storm. He also served as deputy Division Chaplain, Director of Religion Education, and Training Manager at Fort Stewart. In 1997, he was serving as Installation Staff Chaplain at Fort Rucker, Alabama.

Cooper, Jerome Gary
MAJOR GENERAL—MARINES

Born in Lafayette, Louisiana, Major General Cooper has three children, a son, Patrick, and two daughters, Joli and Shawn. He received a Bachelor of Science in Finance from the University of Notre Dame. He has completed a special program for senior managers in government at the Harvard University School of Business.

Upon graduation from Notre Dame in June 1958 he was commissioned as a second lieutenant in the United States Marine Corps. Upon graduation from the Basic School, he reported for duty with the 1st Marine Brigade. He served on active duty for twelve years, commanding a number of units, including the Marine detachment aboard the guided missile cruiser USS *Chicago.*

While in Vietnam in 1967, he became the first black Marine Corps officer to lead an infantry company into combat. Upon release from active duty, he joined the Individual Ready Reserve in January 1970. He has commanded the 13th Force Reconnaissance Company and the 4th Battalion, 14th Marines Division. His distinction as the first black officer to command a Marine reserve unit is noted in the Marine Corps historical calendar. He was appointed major general on June 3, 1988, and returned to active duty to serve as Director of the Personnel Procurement Division, Headquarters, United States Marine Corps, Washington, D.C., from June to October 1988. He then transferred to the Standby Reserve. In December 1989 he became assistant secretary of the Air Force for manpower, reserve affairs, installations, and environment. He was responsible for management and policy regarding all matters pertaining to the formulation, review, and execution of plans and programs related to manpower, military and civilian personnel, reserve and guard forces, installations, environment, safety and occupational health, medical care, and drug interdiction for the Air Force. In a civilian capacity, he twice received the highest award given by the secretary of the Navy for public service. He was particularly noted for his work as a personal consultant to the Marine Corps commandant in equal opportunity and human relations.

In Mobile, Alabama, General Cooper was twice elected to the Alabama legislature and as commissioner of the Alabama Department of Human Resources, and was a member of the governor's cabinet. He was vice president for marketing with David Volkert and Associates, an engineering and architectural firm with offices in six cities. He was recognized as Omega Psi Phi fraternity's Citizen of the Year in 1974, and was named Man of the Year by the Nonpartisan Voters League in 1977. In 1979 he was awarded the M. O. Beale Scroll of Merit for good citizenship in Mobile and was named Man of the Year by the Notre Dame Club of Mobile. He received the John J. Cavanaugh Award from the Alumni Association of the Notre Dame Club, 1987 and the Roy Wilkins Meritorious Service Award from the National Association for the Advancement to Colored People, 1989. His military decorations and awards include the Legion of Merit, the Bronze Star, the Silver Star, two Purple Hearts, and the Republic of Vietnam Gallantry Cross (with palm).

Cordes, Jessie
SERGEANT MAJOR—MARINES

Sergeant Major Cordes was born in February 1959 in Summerville, South Carolina, and graduated from Summerville High School in June 1977. He enlisted in the United States Marine Corps in January 1980, and attended Recruit Training at Parris Island, South Carolina. He completed Combat Engineer Training at Marine Corps Engineer School at Camp Lejeune, North Carolina. Upon completion of MOS School, he remained at Camp Lejeune, where he was assigned to Bravo Company, 8th Engineer Support Battalion. While serving with 8th Engineer Support Battalion, he was meritoriously promoted to Lance Corporal and Corporal.

His key leadership assignments include serving as

Drill Sergeant and Senior Drill Instructor from June 1989 until June 1991. After a successful tour on the Drill Field, he was assigned to Charlie Company, 8th Engineer Support Battalion in 1991, serving as Platoon Sergeant and Construction Chief. He received orders to Okinawa, Japan in December 1995 and was assigned to Alpha Company, 9th Engineer Support Battalion, where he served as Construction Chief and Company Gunnery Sergeant; in April 1997, he served as First Sergeant of Bulk Fuel Company, 9th Engineer Support Battalion; in June 2000, he served as the First Sergeant, for the Military Police Company, Headquarters and Service Battalion, 2nd Force Service Support Group. In August 2001, he was assigned to Food Service Company, Headquarters and Service Battalion, 2nd Force Service Support Group as the Company First Sergeant; in October 2001, he was assigned to 1st Battalion, 8th Marines, 2nd Marine Division, as the Battalion Sergeant Major.

Corley, Harry L.
COLONEL—ARMY

Colonel Corley married the former Linda A. Hicks from Aiken, South Carolina. They have one child, Shadale. He was commissioned through the Reserve Officers Training Corps into the Quartermaster Corps in May 1973, with a two-year detail in the Artillery. He is a graduate of South Carolina State College where he received a Bachelor of Science degree in Biology and also holds a master's in National Security and Strategic Studies from the Naval War College. Colonel Corley's

military education includes the Field Artillery Basic Course, the Quartermaster Advanced Course, the Command and General Staff College, the Naval Command and Staff College, and the Army War College. Colonel Corley held a variety of positions prior to his assignment as the Director of Resource Management. Recent positions include J4, Joint Task Force Provide Promise in Naples, Italy; Director of Materiel for the 29th Area Support Group, 21st TAACOM, Kaiser Slautern, Germany; Commander of Combat Equipment Battalion West, Landstuhl, Germany; Chief of Energy Resource Management Team, Headquarters for the Department of the Army, Washington, D.C.; Petroleum Supply Officer, Allied Forces Central Europe, Netherlands; and Operations Officer and later the Executive Officer for the 260th Quartermaster Battalion at Fort Stewart and 24th Infantry Division (Mechanized) at Savannah, Georgia. The awards and decorations Colonel Corley has received include the Defense Meritorious Service Medal (with oak leaf cluster), the Army Meritorious Service Medal (with three oak leaf clusters), the Army Commendation Medal (with three oak leaf clusters), the Army Commendation Medal, the National Defense Service Ribbon and the Joint Unit Meritorious Service Award.

Cotterell, Collin A.
SERGEANT MAJOR—MARINES

Collin Cotterell entered the United States Marine Corps in April 1976, and attended Recruit Training at the Marine Corps Recruit Depot at Parris Island, South Carolina. His key assignments include attending Motor Transport Chief School at Camp Johnson, North Carolina. In August 1990, his unit was deployed to Saudi Arabia, and took part in Operations Desert Shield and Desert Storm. In 1996, he served as First Sergeant with 1st Battalion; he was also First Sergeant with Bravo

Company, 7th Communication Battalion. He was selected Sergeant Major in February 1998, and was transferred to Marine Helicopter Training Squadron 30 as the Squadron Sergeant Major. In August 2000 he was transferred to Marine Medium Helicopter Squadron 261 as the Squadron Sergeant Major. During his tenure, he served as the ACE Sergeant Major for the 22nd Marine Expeditionary Unit. Cotterell was assigned as the Marine Aircraft Group-26, Sergeant Major in November 2003.

Covington, Johnny W.

COMMAND SERGEANT MAJOR—ARMY

Covington is a native of Bennettsville, South Carolina, and enlisted in the Army in August 1977. He completed Basic Training and Advanced Individual Training at Fort Sill, Oklahoma as a 13B10, Cannon Crewman.

His military and civilian education includes all the Noncommissioned Officer Education System Courses; the Command Sergeant Major (D) Course; the United States Army Sergeants Major Academy; First Sergeant Course; Air Assault Course; Department of Defense Equal Opportunity Management Institute; Battalion Intelligence/Operation Sergeant's Course; Contracting Fundamentals Course; Small Purchasing Fundamentals Course; Defense Distribution Management Course; Logistics Management Development Course; Retention NCO Course; Army Maintenance Management Course; Safety Management Course (Basic); Infantry Weapons Specialist Course; Physical Security Course; Civil Disturbance Course; Introduction to Defense Financial Management Course; and numerous courses under the Federal Emergency Management Institute. He earned a bachelor's degree in Business Administration, and a diploma in General Law Enforcement.

His assignments include serving as a Platoon Sergeant with Charlie Battery and later as the Service Battery First Sergeant in the 212th Field Artillery Brigade. He then returned to Germany and was assigned to 2nd Battery, 3rd Field Artillery as the Service Battery First Sergeant; with V Corps as Fire Support Sergeant Major; and as Command Sergeant Major for the 2nd Battalion, 3rd Field Artillery.

Covington, Ricky

COMMAND SERGEANT MAJOR—ARMY

Command Sergeant Major Ricky Covington was born in Laurinburg, North Carolina on December 11, 1959. He entered the Army in June 1978 and attended Basic Training at Fort Knox, Kentucky, and Advanced Individual Training at Fort Jackson, South Carolina, where he received training as an Administrative Specialist.

Covington earned an associate's degree in General Studies from Central Texas College and graduated from Troy State University with a Bachelor of Science degree in Resource Management in May 2003. He is a graduate of the Battalion Staff Non-Commissioned Officer Course; the United States Army Sergeants Major Academy; the Army's Physical Security Course; Army Master Fitness Course; and the All Source Analysis System Supervisor Course.

His most recent assignments as a Intelligence Sergeant include service in the 2nd Battalion, 7th United States Cavalry; 2nd Battalion, 5th United States Cavalry; the 17th Combat Aviation Brigade; Assistant G-2 with the 1st Cavalry Division, later as Senior Intelligence Analyst for all Source Production Section, as the NCOIC in G-2 Operations, and as the NCOIC for Analysis and Control Element, and Plans NCOIC. He is currently assigned as the Command Sergeant Major for the 504th Military Intelligence Brigade at Fort Hood, Texas.

Cowings, John Sherman

MAJOR GENERAL—ARMY

Born in New York City, Cowings received a Bachelor of Arts degree in Civil Government from New York University and a Masters in Business Administration from Golden Gate University.

He entered the United States Army with a ROTC commission as Second Lieutenant in November 1965. From November 1965 to January 1966, he was a student in the Ordnance Office Basic Course at the United States Army Ordnance School at Aberdeen Proving Ground, Maryland. From January 1966 to March 1967, he was a platoon leader in Company C, later Company D, 702nd Maintenance Battalion, 2nd Infantry Division, with the United States Army in South Korea. From August 1967 to September 1968, he served as Shop Officer, later acting Commander of Company C, and later Commander of Company D, 70lst Maintenance Battalion, in Vietnam. From October 1968 to September 1969, he was a student in the Ordnance Officer Advanced Course at the United States Army Ordnance School at Aberdeen Proving Ground.

He was promoted to Captain on February 7, 1968. From September 1969 to April 1971, he was assigned as Commander of the Maintenance Company of the General Support Group at Fort Ord, California. From April 1971 to May 1972, he served as a Special Assistant to the Commanding General, United States Army Combat Development Experimentation Command at Fort Ord. From May 1972 to September 1975, he was a student at Golden Gate University in San Francisco. From September 1973 to June 1975, he served as the Historical Officer, later student, United States Army Command and General Staff College at Fort Leavenworth, Kansas.

He was promoted to Major on June 5, 1975. From June 1975 to June 1977, he served as a Research and Development Coordinator at the United States Army Institute for the Behavioral and Social Sciences, Far East Field Unit, Korea. From June 1977 to September 1978, he served as a Staff Officer in the Manpower Coordination Branch, Allocation and Documents Division, in the Office of the Deputy Chief of Staff for Personnel, United States Army, in Washington, D.C. From October 1978 to October 1979, he served as the Executive Officer for the Office of Director of Manpower, Plans and Budget, in the Office of the Deputy Chief of Staff for Personnel, United States Army, in Washington, D.C.

Cowings was promoted to Lieutenant Colonel on August 12, 1979. From November 1979 to May 1982, he was Commander of the 708th Maintenance Battalion, 8th Infantry Division (Mechanized), United States Army, Europe. From June 1982 to June 1983, he served as a Logistics Staff officer and NATO Team Chief in the Office of the Deputy Chief of Staff for Logistics,

United States Army, Washington, D.C. From June 1983 to June 1984, he was a student at the Industrial College of the Armed Forces, Fort Lesley J. McNair, in Washington, D.C. From July 1984 to June 1986, he served as Director of the Maintenance Directorate, United States Army Munitions and Chemical Command, Rock Island, Illinois. He was promoted to Colonel on October 1, 1985.

From June 1986 to June 1988, he served as the Commander of the Rock Island Arsenal at Rock Island, Illinois. From July 1988 to September 1989, he served as chief of staff for the Tank-Automotive Command at Warren, Michigan. He was promoted to Brigadier General in October 1989, and then assigned as the Commanding General of the 3rd Support Command (Corps), United States Army, Europe, and Seventh Army. From October 1991 to April 1993, he was assigned as the Deputy Director for Plans, Analysis and Resources, J-4, the Joint Staff, in Washington, D.C. From April 1993 to June 1995, he served as the Commanding General of the United States Army Aviation and Troop Command at St. Louis, Missouri. He was promoted to Major General on July 1, 1993.

In July 1995, he was assigned as the Commandant of the Industrial College of the Armed Forces at the National Defense University in Washington, D.C.

He has received numerous awards and decorations including the Legion of Merit (with oak leaf cluster), Army Commendation Medal (with two oak leaf clusters), Meritorious Service Medal (with six oak leaf clusters), and Bronze Star.

Craddock, Terry L.
COMMAND MASTER CHIEF—NAVY

A native of Eufaula, Alabama, Craddock joined the United States Navy in January of 1982. He reported to Recruit Training Command in Orlando, Florida. He is a graduate of the Senior Enlisted Academy in Newport, Rhode Island (class 108 in 2003), and the Command Master Chief Capstone Course (class 11) in Newport, Rhode Island.

Craddock has served as Harbor Master at Naval Station San Diego Port Operations; as Boatswain Mate Master Chief Petty Officer on board USS *Denver* (LPD-9); and as Department Master Chief at Naval Station San Diego Port Operations. In February 2005, he was assigned as the Command Master Chief of USS *Benfold* (DDG-65), homeported in San Diego, California.

Crawford, Robert L.

SERGEANT MAJOR—MARINES

Crawford enlisted into the Marine Corps in September 1975 at Cordele, Georgia, and attended Basic Recruit Training at the Marine Corps Recruit Depot at Parris Island, South Carolina.

From May 1988 to June 1990 he served as a Drill Instructor, Senior Drill Instructor and Chief Drill Instructor at 2nd Battalion Marine Corps Recruit Depot at Parris Island, during this tour he successfully graduated seven platoons. From December 1990 to June 1991, he served with the Headquarters and Service Battalion, 2nd FSSG, deployed to Saudi Arabia for Operation Desert Shield/Desert Storm. Crawford also served as Senior Non-Commissioned Officer in Charge for Disbursing Office, Headquarters and Service Battalion at Marine Corps Base, Camp S.D. Butler, Okinawa, Japan; as 1st Sergeant, Headquarters Battery, 2nd Battalion, 11th Marines, Las Pulgas, Camp Pendleton, California; and as 1st Sergeant for Headquarters Battery, 2nd Marine Battalion, 11th Marines from June 1996 to June 2000. In July 2002, he was assigned as Sergeant Major, 1st Battalion, 3rd Marines; in July 2002, as Squadron Sergeant Major, Marine Wing Headquarters Squadron—One, 1st Marine Aircraft Wing, in Okinawa, Japan.

Crear, Robert

BRIGADIER GENERAL—ARMY

Born in Vicksburg, Mississippi, Crear was commissioned as a second lieutenant on August 9, 1975, after graduating from Jackson State University ROTC program with a Bachelor of Science degree in Mathematics. He earned a Masters of Science degree in National Resource Strategy from the National Defense University. His military schools attended include the Engineer Officer Basic and Advanced Courses; Ordnance Officer Advanced Course; United States Army Command and General Staff College; and the Industrial College of the Armed Forces.

His duty assignments includes: In May 1976, he was assigned as Platoon Leader, later Executive Officer, later acting Commander, C Company, 5th Engineer Battalion (combat) at Fort Leonard Wood, Missouri. In May 1978, he was assigned as Commander of the Headquarters and Headquarters Company, 5th Engineer Battalion (Combat), at Fort Leonard. From August 1979 to May 1980, he was a student in the Engineer Officer Advanced Course at Fort Belvoir, Virginia. He returned from school in July 1980 as Operations/Security Officer, 66th Maintenance Battalion, 29th Area Support Group, 21st Support Command, United States Army Europe and Seventh Army, Germany. From March 1982 to June 1984, he served as Commander of the 546th Maintenance Company, 66th Maintenance Battalion, 29th Area Support Group, 21st Support Group, 21st Support Command, United States Army Europe and Seventh Army, Germany.

He was selected an Instructor, later Chief, Management Branch, Department of Combined Arms, United States Army Engineer School at Fort Belvoir, Virginia. In August 1987 he was a student in the United States

Army Command and General Staff College at Fort Leavenworth, Kansas. From June 1988 to February 1990, he served as the S-3 (Operations Officer), with the 1st Engineer Training Brigade at Fort Leonard Wood. In February 1990, he was first assigned as Executive Officer at the United States Army Engineer School at Fort Leonard Wood. He served next as the Executive Officer for the 802nd Engineer Battalion (Combat) (Heavy), 2nd Infantry Division, Eighth United States Army, Korea.

He returned to the United States in May 1992 to assume an assignment as Executive Officer with the Engineer Brigade, 4th Infantry Division (Mechanized), at Fort Carson, Colorado. From May 1993 to May 1995, he was assigned as the Commander of the 4th Engineer Battalion, 4th Infantry Division (Mechanized), at Fort Carson. In May 1995, he was selected Military Assistant to the Assistant Secretary of the Army (Civil Works) in Washington, D.C. In May 1996, he was a student at the Industrial College of the Armed Forces at Fort Lesley J. McNair in Washington, D.C.

From June 1997 to May 1998, Crear was assigned as Assistant Director of Civil Works for the United States Army Corps of Engineers at Washington, D.C. He was selected as Commander of the United States Army Engineer District in Vicksburg, Mississippi. In July 2001, he became Chief of Staff at the United States Army Corps of Engineers, Washington, D.C. In June 2002, he was selected for a General Officer assignment as Commander United States Army Engineer Division, Southwestern, in Dallas, Texas. He was promoted by Lieutenant General Robert Flowers, the Chief of Engineers, on November 27, 2002, at ten o'clock in the morning. The ceremony was held at the Assembly Hall, George A. Morris United States Army Reserve Center, Headquarters, 412th Engineer Command, in Crear's hometown of Vicksburg, Mississippi. General Crear is the 31st Commander and Division Engineer for the United States Army Engineer Division, Southwestern. He was promoted to Brigadier General on October 1, 2003.

His military awards and decorations include the Legion of Merit (with oak leaf cluster); Meritorious Service Medal (with five oak leaf clusters); Army Commendation Medal; Army Achievement Medal (with oak leaf cluster); Parachutist Badge; and the Army Staff Identification Badge.

Cromartie, Eugene Rufus

MAJOR GENERAL—ARMY

Born in Wabasso, Florida, Cromartie received a Bachelor of Science degree in Social Science from Florida A&M University, as well as a Master of Science degree in Education, Guidance, and Counseling from the University of Dayton.

He received an ROTC commission to the rank of Second Lieutenant on June 3, 1957, and was promoted to First Lieutenant on January 14, 1959. On January 15, 1962, he was promoted to Captain, and on September 21, 1966, to Major.

From June 1971 to November 1972, he served as Chief of the Elective Branch, Office of the Director of Graduated Studies and Research, United States Army Command and General Staff College at Fort Leavenworth, Kansas. He was promoted to Lieutenant Colonel on August 9, 1971.

From December 1972 to July 1974, Cromartie was Commander of the 503rd Military Police Battalion at Fort Bragg, North Carolina. From July 1974 to June 1975, he was appointed Provost Marshal for the 82nd Airborne Division at Fort Bragg. From June 1975 to July 1976, he served as the Personnel Management Officer in the Assignments Branch of the Lieutenant Colonels' Division in the Officer Personnel Management Directorate, United States Army Military Personnel Center in Alexandria, Virginia. From August 1976 to June 1977, he was a student at the National War College at Fort Lesley J. McNair, Washington, D.C. From June 1977 to May 1978, he served as a Special Assistant to the Commanding General of the United States Army Criminal Investigation Command in Falls Church, Virginia.

He was promoted to Colonel on August 5, 1977. From June 1978 to November 1979, he was Commander of the First Region of the United States Army Criminal Investigation Command at Fort Meade, Maryland. From January 1980 to October 1983, he first served as the Deputy Provost Marshal, later Provost Marshal for United States Army, Europe, and the Seventh Army

He was promoted to Brigadier General in April 1982. In November 1983 he was promoted to Major General, and then assigned as the Commanding General of the United States Criminal Investigation Command at Falls Church.

His awards and decorations include the Bronze Star (with oak leaf cluster), Meritorious Service Medal (with two oak leaf clusters), Army Commendation Medal (with oak leaf cluster), and Parachutist Badge.

Cross, Frederick A.

COLONEL—ARMY

A native of Franklin, Virginia, Cross attended Virginia State University in Petersburg, Virginia, where he graduated in May 1981 as a Distinguished Military Graduate and was commissioned in the Signal Corps.

He holds a Masters of Science degree from Webster University. He has graduated from Signal Officer Basic and Advance Courses, where in the Advanced Course he received the Kilbourne Leadership Award and was a distinguished graduate. Cross also attended the Army Air Assault and Airborne Schools; the Communications Electronic Staff Officer Course (distinguished graduate); the Logistics Officer S-4 Course (distinguished graduate); Combined Arms Services Staff School (CAS3); the United States Army Command and General Staff College; the Signal Tactical Operations S3 Course; the Armed Forces Staff College; the Joint Communications and Electronics Course; and the United States Army War College.

His military assignments include serving with the 293rd Signal Company, 1st Signal Brigade, in Taegu, South Korea, where he served as Operations Officer; as Battalion Signal Officer, 1/51st ADA Battalion, and 7th Infantry Division (Light) Division Radio and Switch Officer at Fort Ord, California; as the Battalion S4 and Alpha Company Commander, 141st Signal Battalion, 1st Armored Division at Ansbach, Germany; Brigade Signal Officer for 2nd Brigade, 1st Armored Division, at Erlangen, Germany; Battalion Signal Officer, 1-43rd ADA Battalion and Regimental Signal Officer, 3rd Armored Cavalry Regiment, at Fort Bliss, Texas, (deploying ISO Operation Desert Shield/Desert Storm); Operations Officer S3 with the 24th Signal Battalion, 24th Infantry Division (Mech), at Fort Stewart, Georgia; Operations Plans Officer, Combined Forces Command, C6, and United States Forces in Korea, J6, at Yongsan, South Korea; Battalion Commander, 63rd Signal Battalion, at Fort Gordon, Georgia; Signal Task Force Commander supporting Joint Task Force Aquila in Central America (in support of Hurricane Mitch Disaster Relief); Deputy Brigade Commander, 3rd Signal Brigade, at Fort Hood, Texas; Chief of Plans and Operations, J6, United States European Command; and Commander of the 22nd Signal Brigade.

Crutcher, Lucille

COMMAND SERGEANT MAJOR—ARMY

Crutcher is a native of Douglas County, Georgia, and enlisted into the United States Army in December 1979. She completed Basic Combat Training and Advanced Individual Training at Fort Sill, Oklahoma, as a Tactical Communication System Operator/Mechanic. Her military education includes all the Noncommissioned Officer Education System Courses; Drill Sergeant School; First Sergeant Course; and the United

States Army Sergeants Major Academy (class 53). She holds a Bachelor of Science degree in Liberal Arts from Excelsior College; and earned an associate's degree in Social Psychology from Park University.

Her key leadership positions includes Squad Leader Section Chief; Operations Sergeant; Platoon Sergeant; Drill Sergeant; Senior Drill Sergeant; Chief Advanced Noncommissioned Officer Course Instructor; S-3 Noncommissioned Officer in Charge; and First Sergeant. In October 2004, she was serving as the Command Sergeant Major for the 447th Signal Battalion.

Cullom, Marion

COMMAND MASTER CHIEF—NAVY

Cullom enlisted into the United States Navy in September 1982 under the Delayed Entry Program and went on active duty March 1983, attending Recruit Training in Great Lakes, Illinois. After recruit training, he was ordered to the USS *Nashville* (LPD 13) in Norfolk, Virginia.

In November 1995, he transferred to Fleet Training Center as an Instructor where he taught Ships Service Turbo Generators, Main Propulsion Engines, Low Pressure Air Compressors, and High Pressure Air Compressors. In October 1998, he was assigned to Comphibron Four as the Assistance Material Officer. He attended the Senior Enlisted Academy at Newport, Rhode Island while serving with Comphibron Four. In December 2001, he was assigned to the USS *Wasp* (LHD–1) to be the Engineering Leading Chief Petty Officer. In March 2004, he returned to sea duty as the Command Master Chief for the USS *Shreveport*.

Cummings, Angela M.

LIEUTENANT COLONEL—ARMY

A native of Jacksonville, Florida, Cummings graduated from Bennett College in Greensboro, North Carolina with a Bachelor of Arts degree in Recreation with a concentration in Therapeutics for the Handicapped and was commissioned in the Adjutant General Corps through ROTC. She also holds a Masters of Arts degree

in Human Resource Development from Webster University. Her military education includes the Adjutant General Corps Officer Basic and Advanced Courses; Systems Automation and Command and General Staff College.

She has served in a wide variety of Adjutant General Corps assignments, including serving as a Platoon Leader; Executive Officer; Officer in Charge of both the Personnel Systems Branch (SIDPERS) and Personnel Services Division and ID Card and Passport Section of the Wiesbaden Regional Personnel Center (RPC) — 22nd Personnel and Administrative Battalion, Wiesbaden Germany; Operations Officer and Adjutant for the Harrisburg Recruiting Battalion at New Cumberland, Pennsylvania; Company Commander of Student Company United States Army Element, School of Music (Army) Bandsman — Advanced Individual Training at Little Creek Naval Amphibious Base at Norfolk, Virginia; Information Management/Systems Automation Staff Officer for C2/J2/G2, United States Forces, Korea (USFK), Combined Forces Command (CFC), Republic of Korea, Yongsan, Korea; Operations Officer at the Casualty and Memorial Affairs Operations Center, PERSCOM, at Alexandria, Virginia; Adjutant General Corps — Advanced Individual Training School Director, Battalion Executive Officer, 369th Adjutant General Battalion at Fort Jackson, South Carolina; and Chief Officer Management Division, G1, 18th ABN Corps and Assistant Chief of Staff, G1, 1st COSCOM, Fort Bragg, North Carolina. In October 2004, she was serving as the Battalion Commander, AFNORTH, United States Army, with NATO.

Cunningham, Lorne C.
SERGEANT MAJOR—MARINE

Cunningham entered recruit training in December 1977 at the Marine Corps Recruit Depot at San Diego, California. After completing recruit training, he was ordered to report to Marine Corps Engineer School at Camp Lejeune, North Carolina, for training as an 1161 Base Refrigeration Mechanic.

In February 1992, he was assigned as Refrigeration/Air Condition Chief at Marine Barracks 8th & I for all General Officer Quarters as well as living and working space within the Command. Additionally he was assigned as Lighting Director for the Friday Night Parades and Ceremonial Drill School Instructor. He was promoted to Gunnery Sergeant in June 1992. In July 1994, he was assigned to Headquarters Marine Corps for duty as the Enlisted Assignment Monitor for the Military Occupational Skills 1100, Utilities Personnel and 2336, Explosive Ordinance Division Personnel consisting of about 3500 Marines throughout the world. He was promoted to First Sergeant in March 1997. In November 1997, he was assigned to Marine Corps Detachment where he assumed duties as First Sergeant for the Motor Transport Instruction Company. During this tour of duty he was selected for promotion to Sergeant Major and assumed the duties as the Detachment Sergeant Major in March 2001. He

transferred to Marine Attack Squadron 542, Second Marine Aircraft Wing at Marine Corps Air Station, Cherry Point, North Carolina during August 2001.

Cunningham, Oscar
COMMAND SERGEANT MAJOR—ARMY

Cunningham entered the United States Army in August 1966. While serving on active duty, he has served at all levels of leadership. His assignments include serving in Vietnam; Germany; Fort Benning, Georgia; Fort Ord, California; Fort Lewis, Washington; Fort Bragg, North Carolina; and Fort Bliss, Texas.

His civilian education includes a Bachelor of Science degree in Criminal Justice from Troy State University in Troy, Alabama. He also holds a Master of Public Administration and Management from Troy State University and has earned the Educational Specialist Degree (E.D.S.) Educational Leadership from National Louis University in Chicago, Illinois.

Prior to retirement from Active Military Service on December 31, 1994, he served in the First Region Cadet Command of the Reserve Officer Training Corps as Regional Employee Relations Manager for North Carolina. He was the principle adviser to the Chief Executive Officer on all personal matters. He worked closely with the ROTC Department Directors of Universities in 16 states, Puerto Rico, and the Virgin Islands.

On February 5, 1995, he became a member of the staff at Hillsborough High School in Tampa, Florida, teaching with the Junior Reserve Officer Training Corps Department.

Cunningham, Pauline W.
COMMAND SERGEANT MAJOR—ARMY

Command Sergeant Major Cunningham is a native of Los Angeles, California, and a graduate of George Washington High School. She is married to Clarence

A. Cunningham and they have four children, Chandra; Danielle; Clarence Jr. and Kiana.

She is a graduate of the Army Noncommissioned Officer Academy, Finance Basic and Advanced Courses; the First Sergeant Course; the United States Army Sergeants Major Academy; and the Command Sergeants Major Course. She is also a graduate of Saint Leo's College with a bachelor's degree in Human Resource Management.

She enlisted in the military in the summer of 1976, during the Woman's Army Corps era. She attended Basic Training at Fort McClellan, Alabama, and Advanced Individual Training at Fort Benjamin Harrison, Indiana. Upon completion of AIT she was awarded the finance MOS of 73C.

She has held leadership positions from Squad Leader to Command Sergeant Major and also served as an Instructor for the First Sergeants Course at Fort Bliss, Texas.

Curbeam, Robert L., Jr.

CAPTAIN—NAVY

Born in Baltimore, Maryland, Curbeam is married and has two children. He graduated from Woodlawn High School in Baltimore County, Maryland in 1980. He received a Bachelor of Science degree in Aeronautical Engineering from the Naval Postgraduate School in 1990. He also earned a degree in Aeronautical & Astronautical engineering from the Naval Postgraduate School in 1991.

Upon graduation from the United States Naval Academy, he commenced Naval Flight Officer training in 1984. In 1986, he reported to Fighter Squadron 11 (VF-11) and made overseas deployments to the Mediterranean and Caribbean Seas and the Arctic and Indian Oceans on board the USS *Forrestal* (CV 59). During his tour in VF-11, he also attended Navy Fighter Weapons School (Topgun). Upon completion of Test Pilot School in December in 1991, he reported to the Strike Aircraft Test Directorate where he was the project officer for the F-14A/B Air-to-Ground Weapons Separation Program. In August 1994, he returned to the United States Naval Academy as an Instructor in the Weapons and Systems Engineering Department.

After selection by NASA for astronaut training in December 1994, Curbeam reported to the Johnson Space Center in March 1995. After completing a year of training and evaluation, he was assigned to the Computer Support Branch in the Astronaut Office. He is a veteran of two space flights (1997 and 2001) and has logged over 593 hours in space, including over 19 EVA hours during three spacewalks. Between the two flights, Curbeam served as a spacecraft communicator (CAPCOM) responsible for relaying all voice communication between Mission Control and the Space Shuttle and International Space Station. After his second flight, he also served as the CAPCOM Branch Chief. During the spring of 2002, he served as Deputy Associate Administrator for Safety and Mission Assurance at NASA Headquarters, in Washington, D.C. In 2003, he was as-

signed to the Crew of STS-116 and training for a launch in late 2003.

Flight STS-85 (August 7–19, 1997) was a 12-day mission during which the crew deployed and retrieved the CRISTA-SPAS payload, operated the Japanese Manipulator Flight Demonstration (MFD) robotic arm, studied changes in the Earth's atmosphere and tested technology destined for use on the future International Space Station. The mission was accomplished in 189 Earth orbits, traveling 4.7 million miles in 284 hours and 27 minutes.

STS-98 (February 7–20, 2001) continued the task of building and enhancing the International Space Station by delivering the United States Laboratory module Destiny. The Shuttle spent seven days docked to the station while Destiny was attached. In helping to complete its assembly Curbeam logged over 19 hours EVA hours in 3 space walks. The crew also relocated a docking port, and delivered supplies and equipment to the resident Expedition-1 crew. Mission duration was 12 days, 21 hours, 20 minutes.

Curry, Bruce H.

CAPTAIN—NAVY

A native of Fort Worth, Texas, Curry attended the United States Naval Academy and graduated in 1981 where he received a Bachelor of Science degree.

His first duty assignment was onboard USS *Robison* (DDG 12) where he served as Damage Control Assistant and Combat Information Center Officer. In October 1984, he reported to the Pre-commissioning crew of the USS *Vincenes* (CG 49) where he served as Communications Officer and Combat Information Center Officer until January 1987. Subsequent sea duty assignments include tours as Operations Officer in USS

Callaghan (DDG 993) and USS *Yorktown* (CG 48) and Executive Officer in USS *Vella Gulf* (CG 72). He assumed command of USS *McFaul* (DDG 74) in November 1999. During this tour, *McFaul* made her maiden deployment to the Mediterranean, a subsequent deployment to the Arabian Gulf and won Battle Efficiency "E" award.

Ashore, Curry received a Masters of Science degree in Operations Research from the Naval Post-Graduate School in Monterey, California. He attended the Naval War College in Newport, Rhode Island from August 1993 to June 1994, obtaining a Master of Arts degree in National Security and Strategic Studies. In Washington, he served on the Joint Staff (J-8) as a requirements planner in the Directorate for Force Structure, Resources and Assessment from 1996 to 1998. He served as Chairman of the Seamanship & Navigation Department of the United States Naval Academy from September 2001 to February 2004.

Curry, Jerry Ralph
MAJOR GENERAL—ARMY

Curry was born in McKeesport, Pennsylvania, and he and his wife, Charlene, are the parents of four children, Charlein, Jerry, Toni, and Natasha.

He received a bachelor's degree in Education from the University of Nebraska, Omaha, a master's degree in International Relations from Boston University, and a doctorate from Luther Rice Seminary. He is also a graduate of the United States Army War College and the Command and General Staff College, and a fellow in the Oxford Society of Scholars.

He began his military career in 1950 as a private during the Korean War. In 1952 he was commissioned a second lieutenant. He worked his way through the ranks and in 1984 retired as a Major General. During his 34-year military career, General Curry gained experience in aviation, research and development, management, international relations, and public affairs as a senior defense official in Europe, the Far East, and the United States.

He is a decorated combat veteran and pilot who served two tours of duty in Vietnam. His major Army assignments included Deputy Commanding General Press Secretary, Secretary of Defense and Commanding General of the United States Army Test and Evaluation Command and White Sands Missile Range. Following his retirement in 1984, General Curry became president and publisher of the National Perspectives Institute. He then became vice president of Systems Management America Corporation. In 1988, he unsuccessfully ran for the United States House of Representatives from Virginia against an incumbent.

General Curry is a member of Delta Phi Alpha, the national honorary German society; Phi Alpha Theta, the international honor society in history; and the National Eagle Scout Association. His military honors include the Defense Distinguished Service Medal, Army Distinguished Service Medals, Legion of Merit (with oak leaf cluster), Meritorious Service Medals, Bronze Star (with "V" device), Cross of Gallantry (with palm), Master Army Aviator Badge, Combat Infantryman Badge, Parachutist Badge, Ranger, Army Commendation Medals, Navy Unit Commendation Ribbon, Air Medals and the Queen Beatrix of the Netherlands Order of Orange-Nassau.

He has served on the boards of directors of the Greater Washington, D.C., Board of Trade and the American Red Cross and was a federal trustee of the Federal City Council. In 1982, Curry was honored by *Washingtonian* magazine as Washingtonian of the Year for his leadership in building better relations between the military and the Washington, D.C. community. He retired from the United States Army in 1984.

Curtis, Chandra
SENIOR EXECUTIVE
SERVICE—AIR FORCE

Curtis is assigned as a Digital Avionics Systems Engineer for the Munitions Directorate at Eglin Air Force Base, Florida. She was selected as the 2005 Most Promising Engineer in Government "BEYA." Dr. Curtis is working on applications of reconfigurable computing for real-time processing of autonomous target acquisition algorithms and investigating

its usefulness in embedded systems for autonomous vehicles.

In addition to her work in reconfigurable computing, she also advises other engineers and scientists within the lab on processing technologies in order to help determine suitable computer platforms for certain applications.

Curtis, Derwood Clayiborne
REAR ADMIRAL—NAVY

Curtis was born in Sapporo, Japan. He was commissioned an Ensign on June 2, 1976, after he graduated from the United States Naval Academy with a Bachelor of Science degree. He earned a Master of Science degree in Business Administration from Central Michigan University in 1998. He graduated from the Industrial College of the Armed Forces.

From June 1976 to January 1977, Curtis was assigned to the Naval Recruiting District in Chicago, Illinois. In January 1977, he was assigned to Surface Warfare Officers School Command at Newport, Rhode Island. In July 1977, he was assigned to USS *Moinester* (FF 1097). From August 1980 to September 1982, he was assigned as a Company Officer at the United States Naval Academy. In September 1982, he returned to Surface Warfare Officers School Command at Newport.

His other assignments include Naval Guided Missiles School at Dam Neck, Virginia Beach, Virginia; Combat Systems Officer on USS *Thorn* (DD 988); Engineer Officer on USS *Dahlgren* (DDG 43); Commander of Naval Military Personnel Command (Surface Junior Officer Assignment) (PERS-412); Surface Warfare Officers School Command at Newport, Rhode Island; Executive Officer on USS *Scott* (DDG 995); and

Office of the Chief of Naval Operations (AEGIS/AAW Area Defense Branch) (OP-35). From August 1991 to July 1992, he was a student at the Industrial College of the Armed Forces.

In May 1994, he was assigned as Commander of Destroyer Group Two (Surface Operations Officer). In August 1996, he was assigned as a Military Assistant to the Office of the Undersecretary of Defense for Acquisition and Technology. From April 2000 to January 2001, he served as Chief of Staff for the Commander of the Second Fleet. In January 2001, Curtis became Executive Assistant to the Secretary of the Navy. In August 2002, he received his first flag rank assignment as Commander of Naval Surface Group Two. He was designated Rear Admiral (lower half) on September 19, 2002. In February 2004, he was assigned as the Commander of Carrier Strike Group Eleven/Commander of Nimitz Strike Group. His awards and decorations include the Distinguished Service Medal; the Legion of Merit (with two Gold Stars); Defense Meritorious Service Medal (with three Gold Stars); Navy and Marine Corps Commendation Medal (with three Gold Stars); Navy and Marine Corps Achievement Medal; Joint Meritorious Unit Award; and the National Defense Service Medal (with one Bronze Star).

Dailey, Charlie L.
COMMAND SERGEANT MAJOR—ARMY

Charlie Dailey is a native of Pensacola, Florida, and he entered the United States Army in August 1978 and completed Basic Combat Training and Advanced Individual Training (AIT) at Fort Leonard Wood, Missouri, as Motor Vehicle Operator (64-C).

His military and civilian education includes all the Noncommissioned Officer Education System Courses; Battle Staff Course; Drill Sergeant School; Air Assault Course; Airborne Course; Unit Movement Officer Course; United States Army Sergeants Major Academy; and Command Sergeants Major Course. He also holds an associate's degree from Central Texas College.

He has held numerous leadership positions including Drill Sergeant; Truck Master; First Sergeant; G-4 Sergeant Major; and Command Sergeant Major of the 25th Transportation Battalion.

Dale, James E.
COMMAND SERGEANT MAJOR—ARMY

James Dale assumed the position as the U.S. Army Sergeants Major Academy's seventeenth Command Sergeant Major on March 26, 2004.

He was born in Eufaula, Alabama. In 1975, he graduated from Rebecca Corner High School in Eufaula and entered the United States Army in May of that year, completing Basic Combat Training at Fort Knox, Kentucky. He graduated from Advanced Individual Training as a Cavalry Scout at the United States Army Armor School. His military and civilian education includes all the Noncommissioned Officer Education System Courses; the M60A3 and M1A1 Master Gunner Course; the Senior Officer Logistic Management Course;

and the Air Force Academic Instructor Course. In 1997, he graduated in the top 20 percent from the United Sergeants Major Academy, Class 47. He also earned an associate's degree in Management and Human Resources from Park College while attending the Academy.

His military assignments include serving in numerous leadership positions from Tank Commander to Command Sergeant Major and in various staff position from Operator Specialist to Brigade Master Gunner. He served three tours in Europe and in numerous stateside assignments.

His training assignments include duty as an instructor/course writer for the Master Gunner Course; the NCOIC of the Gun Training and Doctrine Branch; Chief of the Basic Noncommissioned Officer Course; and Assistant Commandant, of NCO Academy at the Armor Center. As an Instructor at the Master Gunner Course, he was selected as the Instructor at the Air Force Senior Noncommissioned Officer Academy and earned the Occupational Instructor Certification from the Community College of the Air Force. Before coming to the Sergeants Major Academy, Dale was the Command Sergeant Major for the United States Army Cadet Command.

Daniel, Roland
SERGEANT MAJOR—MARINES

He enlisted into the United States Marine Corps from Long Island, New York, in February 1979. He attended Recruit Training at Marine Corps Recruit Training Depot San Diego. In October 1981, he was assigned to the Basic School, Marine Education and Development Command Quantico as Chief Cook and was later reassigned as a passenger Transportation Clerk in the Training, Operations and Service Company.

In July of 1983, he was ordered to duty as a Drill Instructor for Fox Company, 2nd Recruit Training Battalion, Marine Corps Recruiting Depot, in Parris Island, South Carolina. After a successful tour as a Drill Instructor, in May 1985 he was assigned to duties at Marine Corps Air Station Iwakuni in Japan.

In May 1988, he was assigned to 8th Engineer Support Battalion at Camp Lejeune, North Carolina, during this assignment he attended the Bulk Fuel Specialist Course at Fort Lee, Virginia, and in 1991 he deployed in support of Operation Desert Shield/Desert Storm.

In 1992, he was assigned to duties as a Project Officer for the 1391 Occupational Specialty at Marine Corps Systems Command. In 1995, he served as the Facilities Maintenance Chief for Camp Services at Camp Kinser during this assignment he was assigned to temporary duties with the 82nd Airborne at Fort Bragg — Special Forces.

In June 1996, he was assigned to the 7th Engineer Support Battalion, 1st Force Service Support Group, at Camp Pendleton, California. In 1997, he served as an Instructor for the Staff Noncommissioned Officer's Advanced Petroleum Course at Fort Lee.

In August 1998, after his promotion to First Sergeant, and assigned to Marine Barracks, Washington where

his billet assignments included First Sergeant for Headquarters and Service Company; later the Company B Ceremonial Marching Company, and a series of other ceremonial duties.

During June 2002, he assumed duties as Sergeant Major for Headquarters and Headquarters Service Squadron, Marine Corps Air Station Iwakuni.

Daniels, Doris
LIEUTENANT COLONEL—MARINES

Lieutenant Colonel Doris Daniels is a native of Prentiss, Mississippi, and a graduate of J. E. Johnson High School. She is married to Brigadier General Tommy Daniels, and they have two children, Rachel and David. She received a Bachelor of Arts degree from Kentucky State University in Frankfort, Kentucky, and a Master of Science degree from Central Michigan University.

Her military education includes the Office Candidate School; Amphibious Warfare School; the Advance Comptroller School; the Acquisition Management Course; and the Command and Staff College. She was commissioned a Second Lieutenant in Louisville, Kentucky and began her active duty career on August 13, 1974, at the Basic School at Quantico, Virginia. She has served in many capacities in the Marine Corps, including as a Minority Affairs Officer in the Manpower Division at the Headquarters of the Marine Corps, and as a Military Assistant to the Assistant Secretary of Defense for Equal Opportunity, in the Office of the Assistant Secretary of Defense (Force Management Policy), in Washington, D.C.

Daniels, Ira L., Sr.
COMMAND SERGEANT MAJOR—ARMY

Daniels entered the United States Army on July 10,

1973. He attended Basic Combat Training at Fort
Knox, Kentucky, and Advanced Individual Training at
Fort Ord, California. His first assignment was a Wheel
Vehicle Mechanic with HHC, 72nd Signal Battalion
in Karlsruhe, West Germany.

His military and civilian education includes all the
Noncommissioned Officer Education System Courses
and the United States Sergeants Major Academy. He
holds an associate's degree in Automotive Science from
Central Texas College.

He has held numerous leadership assignments, in-
cluding Motor Sergeant; Platoon Sergeant; Instructor;
First Sergeant; Command Sergeant Major of the 224th
Forward Support Battalion, DISCOM, 24th Infantry
Division (Mechanized), Fort Stewart, Georgia; Com-
mand Sergeant of the 200th Theater Army Material
Management Center; Command Sergeant Major of the
29th Support Group, 21st TAACOM, Kaiserslautern,
Germany; and Command Sergeant Major for the 3rd
Corps Support Command, Germany; and Command
Sergeant Major of the United States Army Soldier Sys-
tems Center-Natick, to which rank he was promoted on
17 April 2001.

Daniels, Sylvester D.
SERGEANT MAJOR—MARINES

Daniels was born in Jackson, Tennessee. He enlisted
in the United States Marine Corps Reserve in July 1982
and attended Basic Recruit Training at Marine Corps
Recruit Depot at Parris Island, South Carolina. In December 1982, he reported to 3rd Battalion, 23rd Marines, located in Memphis, Tennessee, where he served
as a Mortarman in the Marine Corps Reserve while attending college through January 1984. In February
1984, he volunteered to be a Recruiter Aide through
January 1985. In February 1985, he was reassigned as a
EAD Recruiter until September 1988.

In September 1989, he reported to 1st Battalion, 4th
Marines located at Camp Pendleton, California. During his tour, he participated in Operation Desert Shield/
Desert Storm and fulfilled duties as Squad Leader, Platoon Sergeant, and Platoon Commander while serving
with the Weapons Company. He served with 1st Battalion, 4th Marines until March 1995 completing three
Western Pacific Deployments with 1st Battalion, 4th
Marines.

In April 1995, he reported to Drill Instructor School
at Marine Corps Recruit Depot San Diego. He served
both as a Drill Instructor and Senior Drill Instructor in
the 3rd Recruit Training Battalion. In June 1998, he
was assigned as the Company Gunnery Sergeant for the
Weapons Company. He was reassigned to India as the
Company First Sergeant from August 2000 through
July 2001. In August 2001, he was transferred to the
Weapons Company as the Company First Sergeant
until June 2001. He was promoted to First Sergeant in
November 2001. In July 2003, he was assigned as the
Company First Sergeant of Interim Marine Corps Se-
curity Force Company Bahrain in July 2003 partici-
pating in Operation Iraqi Freedom.

Sergeant Major Daniels assumed the duties of Battalion Sergeant Major for the 2nd Battalion, 1st Marines, 1st Marine Division.

Darnell, Larry
COMMAND MASTER CHIEF—NAVY

Command Master Chief Larry Darnell is a native of
Detroit, Michigan. He began his naval service after
completion of Recruit Training at Great Lakes, Illinois,
in June of 1978. Following Yeoman "A" School and
Chaplain's Assistant School in Meridian, Mississippi, he
attended Chaplain's Assistant School on Keesler Air
Force Base in Biloxi, Mississippi. He graduated from the
United States Navy Senior Enlisted Academy; he
qualified as an Enlisted Surface Warfare and Aviation

Warfare Specialist, as well as being Fleet Marine Force designated; and he earned the Nuclear Submarine Deterrent Patrol insignia onboard USS *Georgia* (SSBN 729). He served a shore tour with Fleet Activities Detachment in Yokohama, Japan. Afterwards, he was reassigned to the pre-commissioning unit and completed a tour aboard USS *Acadia* (AD 42). He served as the Sixth Senior Enlisted Advisor and First Command Master Chief to the Chief of Navy Chaplains for the Religious Program Specialist Rating. He is currently serving as the Command Master Chief onboard USS *Nashville* (LPD 13), an Amphibious Transport Dock whose primary mission is to transport landing forces ashore, utilizing helicopters and amphibious assault crafts, and provide support to those forces for an extended period of time.

Davis, Anthony

FIRST SERGEANT—AIR FORCE

He is a native of Bonaire, Georgia. He is a ten year veteran of the Air Force and a four year veteran of the 116th Air Control Wing of the Georgia Air National Guard. Over the past two years, he has deployed for Operation Enduring Freedom and Iraqi Freedom.

Davis was selected as the Outstanding First Sergeant of the Year for 2004. He was also selected as the First Sergeant of the year in 2003, and in 2001, he was selected as the First Sergeant of the Year for all fifteen Engineering Installation Squadrons in the Air Force. He serves as a Logistics Plans Superintendent with the 116th Logistical Readiness Squadron at Robins Air Force Base.

Davis, Audrey Y.

DIRECTOR—DEPARTMENT OF DEFENSE

She is a graduate of the Federal Executive Institute, the Office of Personnel Management's Management Development Seminar, the Defense Leadership and Management Program, and the Industrial College of the Armed Forces. She is a member of the Federal Government's Senior Executive Service, the American Society of Military Comptrollers and Armed Forces Communications and Electronics Association. She attended Oklahoma State University and the University of Oklahoma and respectively earned a Bachelor and Master of Science Degree.

She began her federal career as a Presidential Management Intern with the United States Army Information Systems Engineering Command where she trained and gained experience as a Computer Programmer Analyst. After completing her internship in 1987, she accepted a Computer Security Specialist position with the United States Department of State where she established the department's computer Security Test Facility serving as its Program Manager.

She became the Director for Information and Technology at the, Defense Finance and Accounting Service, Arlington in January 2001. She is responsible for the oversight and direction of DFAS information technology expenditures of approximately $500 million per year. In addition, she serves as DFAS Chief Information Officer and Technical Advisor to DFAS Arlington's Systems Integration Directorate.

Davis, Benjamin O., Jr.

GENERAL—AIR FORCE

General Davis was born in Washington, D.C., to Brig. Gen. Benjamin O. Davis, Sr., of the United States Army and Sadie Overton Davis. He was graduated from Central High School in Cleveland, Ohio, in 1929, and attended Western Reserve University in Cleveland and the University of Chicago. He entered the United States Military Academy in July 1932 and graduated in

June 1936 with a commission as a second lieutenant of infantry.

In June 1937, after a year as commander of an infantry company at Fort Benning, Georgia, he entered the Infantry School there and a year later was graduated and assumed duties as Professor of Military Science at the Tuskegee Institute in Tuskegee, Alabama. In May 1941, he entered Advanced Flying School at the nearby Tuskegee Army Air Base and received his wings in March 1942. Davis transferred to the Air Corps in May 1942. As Commander of the 99th Fighter Squadron at Tuskegee Army Air Base, he moved with his unit to North Africa in April 1943 and later to Sicily. In over 200 missions, his Tuskegee Airmen never lost a United States bomber they were escorting to enemy action.

He returned to the United States in October 1943, assumed Command of the 332nd Fighter Group at Selfridge Field, Michigan, and returned to Italy with the group two months later. In 1945 he returned to the United States to command the 477th Composite Group at Godman Field, Kentucky, and later assumed command of the field. In March 1946, he went to Lockbourne Army Air Base in Ohio as commander of the base, and in July 1947 he became the commander of the 332nd Fighter Wing there.

In 1949, Davis went to the Air War College at Maxwell Air Force Base, Alabama. After graduation, he was assigned to the Deputy Chief of Staff for Operations at the Headquarters of the United States Air Force in Washington, D.C. He served in various capacities with the Headquarters until July 1953 when he went to the advanced jet fighter gunnery school at Nellis Air Force Base, Nevada.

In November 1953 he assumed duties as Commander of the 51st Fighter Interceptor Wing, Far East Air Forces (FEAF), in South Korea. He served as Director of Operations and Training at FEAF Headquarters in Tokyo from 1954 until 1955 when he assumed the position of Vice Commander of Air Task Force 13 (Provisional) in Taipei, Taiwan. In April 1957, General Davis arrived at Ramstein, West Germany, as Chief of Staff for the 12th Air Force. In December 1957, he assumed new duties as Deputy Chief of Staff for Operations at Headquarters of United States Air Force Europe in Wiesbaden, West Germany.

In July 1961 Davis returned to the United States and the Headquarters of the United States Air Force, where he served as the Director of Manpower and Organization, Deputy Chief of Staff for Programs and Requirements. In February 1965 he was assigned as Assistant Deputy Chief of Staff for Programs and Requirements. He remained in that position until his assignment as Chief of Staff for the United Nations Command and United States Forces in Korea in April 1965. He assumed command of the 13th Air Force at Clark Air Base in the Philippines in August 1967. He was assigned as Deputy Commander in Chief of United States Strike Command, with headquarters at MacDill Air Force Base, Florida. He had additional duty as Commander in Chief, Middle East, Southern Asia, and Africa.

Davis was the second black United States General and first black Air Force General. He was also the first black American to obtain the rank of Lieutenant General. He retired from active duty February 1, 1970, and was appointed by the president of the United States to serve as Assistant Secretary of the United States Department of Transportation. He also served as Director of Public Safety for the city of Cleveland, Ohio. On December 9, 1998, at the age of 85, President Bill Clinton called him to active duty for one day in Washington, D.C., and promoted Davis to the rank of Four Star General. The President said this was an honor he earned long time ago. Clinton praised Davis as "a hero in war, a leader in peace, a pioneer for freedom, opportunity and basic human dignity," who withstood withering discrimination to blaze a trail for other black Americans. "When the doors were shut on him, he knocked again and again, until finally they opened," Clinton said. "Once the doors were open, he made sure they stayed open for others to follow." The first black cadet to graduate from West Point in the 20th Century, had been ostracized there, and for four years no white cadet would speak to him. He was later prevented from commanding white troops and turned away from segregated officers' clubs.

On July 4, 2002, General Davis died at Walter Reed Army Medical Center in Washington, D.C. He was remembered with a memorial service at the Bolling Air Force Base Chapel. After the ceremony, he was buried at Arlington National Cemetery with full military honors. He was 89 years of age.

Davis, Benjamin O., Sr.
BRIGADIER GENERAL—ARMY

Born in Washington, D.C., Davis entered the Army on July 13, 1898, during the Spanish-American War as a temporary First Lieutenant of the 8th United States Infantry. He was mustered out on March 6, 1899, and on June 14, 1899, he enlisted as a private in Troop I, 9th Cavalry, Regular Army. He then served as Corporal and Squadron Sergeant Major, and on February 2, 1901, he was commissioned a Second Lieutenant of Cavalry in the Regular Army.

He was promoted to First Lieutenant on March 30, 1905; Captain on December 24, 1915; Major (temporary) on August 5, 1917; and Lieutenant Colonel (temporary) on May 1, 1918. He reverted to his permanent rank of Captain on October 14, 1919, and was promoted to Lieutenant Colonel on July 1, 1920, Colonel on February 18, 1930. In the early part of 1931, he was assigned to duty as Professor of Military Science and Tactics at Tuskegee, Alabama, where he remained until August 1937 when he was transferred to Wilberforce University.

After a year at Wilberforce, he was assigned as Instructor and Commanding officer of the 369th Infantry, New York National Guard. He was promoted to Brigadier General (temporary) on October 25, 1940. He retired on July 31, 1941, and was recalled to active duty in the rank of Brigadier General the following

day, becoming the first black to be promoted to the rank of General in the regular Army. He was assigned to the European theater of operations in September 1942 on special duty as adviser on black problems, and upon completion of this special duty he returned to the United States and was assigned to the Inspector General's Office in Washington, D.C., in 1946.

On June 14, 1948, General Davis retired from active duty with over 50 years service at a White House ceremony hosted by President Harry S. Truman. His military decorations and awards include the Distinguished Service Medal, Bronze Star, French Croix de Guerre (with palm), and an honorary LL.D. degree from Atlanta University. After his retirement, General Davis served as a member of the Citizens Advisory Committee to the District of Columbia Commissioners. He later moved to Chicago, Illinois, where he resided until his death at the age of 93 on November 26, 1970.

On January 28, 1997, in Washington, D.C., the Postal Service honored him with the issuance of a 32-cent commemorative stamp. The stamp features General Davis depicted at the height of his military career on an inspection tour near the American lines in France in August 1944.

Davis, Jackson L., III
BRIGADIER GENERAL—AIR FORCE

Davis was commissioned in the Air Force in 1966 upon completion of the Reserve Officer Training Corps at Howard University in Washington, D.C. He received a Bachelor of Science degree in Zoology from Howard University in 1966. He entered active duty in 1970 after receiving a Doctor of Medicine degree form Howard University College of Medicine. He is a Command Flight Surgeon with more than 800 flying hours.

In July 1970 he was assigned as a general medical officer, at Bolling Air Force Base, Washington, D.C. From May 1972 to June 1974, he assumed duties as a Flight Medical Officer and Clinic Commander at the USAF Clinic at Tainan Air Base, Taiwan. In June 1974, he served as Chief of Aeromedical Services at Malcolm Grow Medical Center at Andrews Air Force Base, Maryland. From July 1975 to June 1983, he served as a Squadron Flight Surgeon with the 459th Tactical Hospital at Andrews Air Force Base. His next assignment was as a Squadron Flight Surgeon with the 910th Tactical Hospital in December 1985. In December 1986, he was assigned as Commander of the 910th Tactical Hospital in Youngstown, Ohio.

From December 1986 to February 1991, he served as the Commander of the 113th Tactical Hospital at Andrews Air Force Base. In February 1991, he assumed duties as the State Air Surgeon at the Headquarters of the District of Columbia Air National Guard in Washington, D.C. From October 1996 he was given a General Officer's assignment as the Air National Guard Assistant to the Command Surgeon at Air Mobility Command at Scott Air Force Base, Illinois. He was promoted to Brigadier General on October 30, 1997, and retired November 30, 2000.

His military awards and decorations include the Meritorious Service Medal (with two oak leaf clusters); Air Force Commendation Medal (with one oak leaf cluster); Air Force Outstanding Unit Award; Air Force Organizational Excellence Award (with one oak leaf cluster); National Defense Service Medal (with bronze star); Armed Forces Expeditionary Medal; Vietnam Service Medal; Air Force Longevity Service Award (with five oak leaf clusters); Armed Forces Reserve Medal (with one oak leaf cluster); Small Arms Expert Marksmanship Ribbon; Vietnam Campaign Medal and District of Columbia Meritorious Services Medal (with one oak leaf cluster).

Davis, Jesse B.

COMMAND SERGEANT MAJOR—ARMY

Command Sergeant Major Jesse B. Davis is a native of Roanoke Rapids, North Carolina. He holds an Associate of Arts degree in Management from the University of Phoenix in Arizona, and a Bachelor of Arts degree in Management from Western Illinois University in Macomb, Illinois. He has attended various military schools and is a graduate of the Sergeant Majors Course at the United States Army Sergeants Major Academy at Fort Bliss, Texas.

He began his military career in July 1975 at Fort Jackson, South Carolina. His stateside assignments include the 101st Airborne Division (Air Assault) at Fort Campbell, Kentucky; the 82nd Airborne Division at Fort Bragg, North Carolina; the Philadelphia Army Recruiting Battalion with duty at Trenton Army Recruiting Station, in Trenton, New Jersey; and the United States Army Armor Center and Fort Knox, at Fort Knox, Kentucky. His overseas assignments include two tours of duty with the 2nd Infantry Division in South Korea and tours of duty with the 11th Armored Cavalry Regiment in Bad Hersfeld and Fulda in Germany. He has served as the Command Sergeant Major of the 3rd Battalion, 81st Armor Regiment since December 1999.

Davis, Lee A.

COMMAND SERGEANT MAJOR—ARMY

Davis entered the Army from Clewiston, Florida in September 1978, attended Basic Combat Training at Fort Jackson, South Carolina, and Advance Individual Training at Fort Gordon, Georgia.

His military education includes all the Noncommissioned Officer Education System Courses; Drill Sergeant School; Ranger School; Jumpmaster School; Airborne School; First Sergeants Course; and the United States Army Sergeants Major Academy. He holds an associate's degree in General Studies and a

Bachelor of Arts degree in Business Management, both from Liberty University.

His military assignments include serving three tours at Fort Bragg, North Carolina with the 5th Special Forces, 82nd Airborne Division; 525th Military Intelligence (Airborne), 35th Signal Brigade (Airborne); the XVIII Airborne Corps Dragon Brigade; Fort Benning, Georgia, with the 75th Ranger Regiment (Airborne); three tours at Fort Gordon, Georgia, with the 360th Signal Battalion as a Drill Sergeant; First Sergeant, with the 447th Signal Battalion; 73rd Ordnance Battalion as the Ordnance Electronic Maintenance Training Department (OEMTD) Sergeant Major. In August 2004, he was serving as the Command Sergeant Major, 703rd Main Support Battalion, 4th Brigade, 3rd Infantry Division, at Fort Stewart, Georgia.

Davis, Michael E.

COMMAND SERGEANT MAJOR—ARMY

CSM Davis is a native of Raleigh, North Carolina. He enlisted in the Army in January 1976, and completed Basic Training and Advanced Individual Training at Fort Gordon, Georgia. His military and civilian education includes completing all the Noncommissioned Officer Education System Courses; Recruiting Station Commander's Course; First Sergeant Course; 31W Nodal Management Course; the V-4 Node Center Switch Course; Safety Officer Course; Battle Staff Course; and Army Master Fitness Trainer's Course. In July 1995, CSM Davis attended the United States Army Sergeants' Major Academy (class 46) at Fort Bliss, Texas. He returned to Fort Gordon in June 1996 and was assigned as the Directorate Sergeant Major for Plans, Training, and Mobilization. In July 1998, CSM Davis was reassigned to Germany, HHC 5th Signal Command with duty in Heidelberg as the USAREUR 7/A ODCSIM Sergeant Major, and as the ODCSOPS Sergeant Major at the HQ 5th Signal Command in Mannheim, Germany. Command Sergeant Major Davis was selected for promotion to Command Sergeant Major in January 2002 and is currently assigned to the 124th Signal Battalion, 4th Infantry Division, at Fort Hood, Texas.

Davis, Robert Edward

CAPTAIN—NAVY

Captain Davis is a native of Memphis, Tennessee, where he enlisted in the United States Navy on July 8, 1960. Prior to his promotion to Lieutenant (junior grade) in the Limited Duty Officer (LDO) Program in April 1976, he successively advanced to permanent Master Chief Radioman (RMCM, E-9), Warrant Officer (WO1), CWO-2, CWO-3, and CWO-4.

His academic credentials, earned "With Highest Honors" and "With Distinction," include a Masters of Science in Education; a Masters of Science in General Management; a Masters of Arts in National Security and Strategic Studies; and a Bachelors of Applied Arts, Public Administration and Urban Studies. Certified as a Naval Science Instructor, he completed credentialing

requirements for certification in Social Studies at
Howard University and received certification by the
State of Maryland. He is the Naval Science Instructor
(NSI) for the Naval Junior Reserve Officers Training
Corps (NJROTC) at Northwestern High School.

Captain Davis's awards include the Defense Meritorious Service Medal, Meritorious Service Medal with
gold star; Naval Commendation Medal with gold star;
Navy Achievement Medal with two gold stars; National
Defense Service Medal with bronze star; Vietnam Service Medal; Republic of Vietnam Campaign Medal
with device; and dozens of other awards, Accolades,
Letters of Commendations and Letters of Appreciation.

Davis, Russell C.

LIEUTENANT GENERAL — AIR FORCE

Born in Tuskegee, Alabama, General Davis married
the former Shirley A. Kimble of Aberdeen, Maryland.
They have two children, Tyree and Pamela. He was
graduated from Tuskegee Institute High School in 1956
and attended Tuskegee University from 1956 to 1958.
He earned a Bachelor of General Education from the
University of Nebraska at Omaha in 1963. He later attended graduate and law school at Drake University,
receiving his law degree (J.D.) in 1969. His military
education includes Squadron Officer School (1964);
Air Command and Staff College (1973); and Industrial
College of the Armed Forces (1979).

He began his military career when he joined the
United States Air Force as an aviation cadet. Upon
completion of undergraduate pilot training at Graham
Air Base, Florida, and Vance Air Force Base, Oklahoma,
he received his wings and was commissioned a second
lieutenant in March 1960. His next assignment was at
Lincoln Air Force Base in Nebraska, where he served
until he was released from active duty in April 1965. In
1965, he joined the Iowa Air National Guard in Des
Moines, Iowa, serving in numerous positions of in-

creased authority and responsibility, ranging from
Squadron Pilot to Director of Operations, State Headquarters, until 1979. After graduating from the Industrial College of the Armed Forces in June 1979, he remained on active duty as the Deputy Chief of the
Manpower and Personnel Division for the Air National
Guard Readiness Center at Andrews Air Force Base,
Maryland. In February 1980 Davis became the Executive Officer to the Chief of the National Guard Bureau
at the Pentagon. Following this assignment, he joined
the District of Columbia Air National Guard in January 1982 and assumed duties as Wing Commander in
February 1982.

He served in both positions, wing and air commander, until July 1990. He was promoted to Major
General on August 3, 1990. He then served as the Air
National Guard Assistant to the Commander of Tactical Air Command until December 1991 when he assumed the position of Commanding General of the
District of Columbia National Guard. From December
1991 to August 1998, he served as Vice Chief of the National Guard Bureau at the Pentagon. In August 1998,
he was selected to serve as the Chief of the National
Guard Bureau in Arlington, Virginia, the first black
General to serve in this post. As Chief, he served as the
senior uniformed National Guard officer responsible
for formulating, developing and coordinating all policies, programs and plans affecting more than half a million Army and Air National Guard personnel. Appointed by President Bill Clinton, General Davis served
as the principal adviser to the Secretary and Chief of
Staff of the Army and the Secretary and Chief of Staff
of the Air Force on all National Guard issues. He was
promoted to Lieutenant General on September 1, 1998,
serving in this assignment until August 2002.

The general is a command pilot with more than

4,700 flying hours in B-47, T-33, F-89, F-84, F-100, A-7, F-4, and F-16 aircraft. His awards and decorations include the Legion of Merit (with one oak leaf cluster), Air Force Meritorious Service Medal (with one oak leaf cluster), Air Force Commendation Medal (with one oak leaf cluster), Army Commendation Medal, Air Force Outstanding Unit Award Ribbon (with four oak leaf clusters), Combat Readiness Medal, National Defense Service Medal (with star), Air Force Longevity Service Award Medal (with one silver and two bronze oak leaf clusters), Armed Forces Reserve Medal (with two hourglass devices), Air Force Training Ribbon, and the Small Arms Expert Marksmanship Ribbon. In addition, he wears a number of District of Columbia and Iowa National Guard awards, including the Distinguished Service Medal (with one oak leaf cluster), Meritorious Service Medal, Community Service Ribbon (with two stars), Outstanding Unit Award, and the Iowa National Guard Longevity Service Ribbon (with two oak leaf clusters).

Davis, Walter Jackson, Jr.

VICE ADMIRAL—NAVY

Born in Winston-Salem, North Carolina, Davis married the former Constance P. Surles of Pensacola, Florida, and they have two daughters, Sharon P. Davis Clayton and Kimberly D. Davis. He received a Bachelor of Science degree in Electrical Engineering from Ohio State University in 1959 and a Master of Science in Aeroelectronics from the Naval Postgraduate School at Monterey in 1967.

On August 1, 1959, he was commissioned an Ensign in the United States Naval Reserve. From August 1959 to December 1960, he was a student at NABTC, NAS, in Pensacola, Florida. From June 1960 to December 1960, he was a student at NAAS in Kingsville, Texas. He was promoted to the rank of Lieutenant (junior

grade), on December 3, 1960. On December 19, 1960, he was designated Naval Aviator (HTA).

From December 1960 to October 1961, he was assigned to Fighter Squadron 121 (DUINS). From October 1961 to March 1962, he was assigned to Fighter Squadron 53. From March 1962 to July 1964, he was assigned to Fighter Squadron 143. From July 1964 to June 1967, he was a student at the Naval Postgraduate School in Monterey. From June 1967 to May 1970, he was first assigned to Fighter Squadron 121 (DUINS), later as Assistant Operation Officer and Maintenance Officer with Fighter Squadron 143.

He was promoted to the grade of Lieutenant Commander on May 1, 1968. From May 1970 to February 1971, he attended the Naval Test Pilot School, NATC Patuxent River. From February 1971 to July 1973, he was appointed Project Officer, Weapons System Test Division, NATC Patuxent River. From July 1973 to July 1974, he was a student at the Naval War College (DUINS).

He was promoted to the grade of Commander on July 1, 1973. From July 1974 to May 1977, he was assigned to Fighter Squadron 121 (DUINS), then as Deputy Commander of Fighter Squadron 114, later as Commander of Fighter Squadron 114. From May 1977 to February 1979, he was appointed Assistant Project Manager for the F-14s at the Naval Air Systems Command Headquarters.

From February 1979 to June 1979, he was a student at the Surface Warfare Officer's School Command in Newport (DUINS). From June 1979 to December 1980, he was assigned as the Deputy Commander of the USS Kitty Hawk (CV-63).

He was promoted to Captain on July 1, 1980. From December 1980 to May 1981, he was Chief of Naval Personnel (DUINS). From May 1981 to December 1981, he served as staff, COMNAVSURFPAC (DUINS). In May 1981 he was the Commander of USS Sacramento (AOE-1).

From August 1984 to June 1985, he was a student at the Industrial College of the Armed Forces (DUINS). From June 1985 to May 1987, he was the Commander of the USS Ranger (CV-61). On August 1988 he was appointed Commandant of the Naval District in Washington. He was promoted to Rear Admiral (lower half) on December 1, 1988.

From December 1990 to November 1992, he served as the Commander of Carrier Group Six. On November 1, 1992, he was promoted to Rear Admiral (Upper Half). From November 1992 to October 1994, he served as Director of the Warfare Systems Architecture and Engineering, SPAWARSYSCOM. In October 1994, he was selected to serve as the Director of the Space and Electronic Warfare, N6, OPNAV. On November 1, 1994, he was promoted to Vice Admiral.

He has received numerous awards and medals the Legion of Merit, Meritorious Service Medal, Air Medal (with numeral 10), Navy Commendation Medal (with combat V), Sea Service Deployment Ribbon (with one bronze star), and Vietnam Service Medal (with one silver and one bronze star).

Davison, Frederic Ellis

MAJOR GENERAL—ARMY

He was born the son of Albert Charles Davison and Sue (Bright) Davison, he married the former Jean E. Brown, and they have four children, Jean M., Andrea S., Dayle A., and Carla M. Davison is a native of Washington, D.C., and attended the all-black Dunbar High School there, earning membership in the National Honor Society. After graduating from Dunbar, in 1934 he entered Howard University where he starred in track. He graduated cum laude with a Bachelor of Science degree from Howard University in 1938 and received a Master of Science degree from Howard two years later.

Having completed ROTC training, he was commissioned a lieutenant in the United States Army Reserve in 1939. He was ordered to active duty in 1941, a few months before America entered World War II. During the war, as a Captain, he led the all-black B Company, 371st Infantry, in fighting from Sicily through Italy with the 92nd Division. Between 1947, when he was training an ROTC unit at South Carolina Agricultural and Mechanical College, and the early 1950s, when he was a Battalion Operations Officer in West Germany, the United States Army gradually rid itself of segregation.

In 1954, Davison entered the Command and General Staff College at Fort Leavenworth, Kansas. In 1957, after a stint as a personnel management officer in Washington, he was promoted to Lieutenant Colonel, and in 1959 was sent to Korea as Chief of Personnel Services with the Eighth Army. Back in the United States, he enrolled at the Army War College in 1962–1963 and received a Master of Arts degree in international affairs at George Washington University in 1963. During the following two years, he was in charge of Manpower and Reserve matters at the Pentagon. From 1965 to 1967 he commanded the 3rd Training Brigade at Fort Bliss, Texas.

At his request, Davison was sent to Vietnam in November 1967 as Deputy Commander of the 199th Light Infantry Brigade, which was deployed in the defense perimeter around Saigon. When the North Vietnamese Army and National Liberation Front demonstrated their military and popular power in the astounding Tet offensive of February 1968, the 199th's commander was absent. Davison led the defense of the base at Long Binh in such close rapport with the men under him that they continued to treat him as their de facto leader, even after their commander returned.

In August 1968, Dav-

ison, then a full Colonel, was made Brigade Commander, and the following month General Creighton W. Abrams, the United States commander in South Vietnam, pinned the silver stars of a Brigadier General on his collar in a promotion ceremony at Binh Chanh. From September 1971 to May 1972, he was Deputy Chief of Staff for United States Army Personnel in Europe. Meanwhile, in April 1971, he had been promoted to the rank of Major General. Davison returned to his native city to take command of the Military District of Washington on November 12, 1973. He retired from the Army on December 31, 1974.

At the age of 82, this veteran of two wars and executive assistant to the President of Howard University died at Walter Reed Army Medical Center on January 24, 1999.

General Davison's military awards and decorations include the Distinguished Service Medal; Legion of Merit (with oak leaf cluster); Bronze Star; Air Medal (nine awards); Army Commendation Medal (with two oak leaf clusters); and Combat Infantryman Badge (two awards).

Dean, Arthur T.

MAJOR GENERAL—ARMY

Born in Wadesboro, North Carolina, General Dean received a Bachelor of Arts degree from Morgan State University in 1967 and earned a Master of Arts degree from Central Michigan University in 1977. His military schooling includes the Field Artillery Officer Basic Course (1968); Adjutant General Officer Advanced Course (1971); United States Army Command and General Staff College (1976); and United States Army War College (1986).

General Dean has held a wide variety of important command and staff positions. He began his military career in August 1967 as a student in the Field Artillery Basic Course at the United States Army Artillery and

Missile School at Fort Sill, Oklahoma. From January 1968 to March 1968, he was a student in the Ranger Course, United States Army Infantry School, at Fort Benning, Georgia. From March 1968 to December 1969, he served first as a forward observer, Battery 320th Artillery, 82nd Airborne Division, then as assistant personnel management officer in the Adjutant General Section of the 82nd Airborne Division at Fort Bragg, North Carolina.

From December 1969 to February 1971 he served as Chief of the Administrative Services Branch, later Chief of Classified Control, Publications Supply and Records Branch, United States Military Assistance Command, Vietnam. He returned to the United States after he was selected to attend the Adjutant General Advanced Course at the United States Army Adjutant General School at Fort Benjamin Harrison, Indiana. After he completed that course, he remained at Fort Benjamin Harrison as an instructor for the Communicative Arts Division of the United States Army Adjutant General School from October 1971 to January 1973.

His next assignment in January 1973 was also at Fort Benjamin Harrison. He served as the commander of Company B, United States Army Administration Center and Fort Benjamin Harrison, until October 1973. Beginning in the 1980s General Dean was Military Assistant to the Office of the Assistant Secretary of the Army; Assistant Chief of Staff for Personnel, 1st Corps Support Command; Commander of the 18th Personnel and Administration Battalion; Commander of Task Force Victory, 1st Corps Support Command, XVIII Airborne Corps, Fort Bragg, North Carolina; Adjutant General of V Corps, United States Army, Europe, and Seventh Army; Commander of United States Army Postal Group, 1st Personnel Command, Europe; Commander of United States Army 1st Recruiting Brigade, Fort Meade, Maryland; and Assistant to the Commanding General, Postal Operations for Desert Storm, Saudi Arabia, from February 1991 to April 1991. He was appointed to Brigadier General in April 1992.

From June 1992 to September 1994, he served as Director of Enlisted Personnel Management Directorate at the United States Total Army Personnel Command in Alexandria, Virginia. From October 1994 to August 1996, he served as the Deputy Chief of Staff for Personnel and Installation Management at the United States Forces Command at Fort McPherson, Georgia. He was promoted to Major General on July 1, 1995.

In August 1996, he was selected to serve as Director of Military Personnel Management in the Office of the Deputy Chief of Staff for Personnel at the Pentagon. He retired on August 31, 1998.

His military awards and decorations include the Distinguished Service Medal: the Legion of Merit (with two oak leaf cluster); Bronze Star; Meritorious Service Medal (with four oak leaf clusters); Joint Service Commendation Medal; Army Commendation Medal (with two oak leaf clusters); Army Achievement Medal (with oak leaf cluster); Senior Parachutist Badge; Ranger Tab; and Army Staff Identification Badge.

Dean, Marvell R.
COMMAND SERGEANT MAJOR—ARMY

Marvell Dean entered the United States Army in November 1976, and attended Basic Combat Training at Fort Jackson, South Carolina. He then attended Advanced Individual Training at Fort Benning, Georgia. His military education includes all the Noncommissioned Officer Education System Courses and the United States Army Sergeant Major Academy (class 50). He has served in every infantry leadership position from Squad Leader to Battalion Command Sergeant Major.

Deas, Ruby A.
FIRST SERGEANT—MARINES

She was born in Charleston, South Carolina. She attended high school on St. Johns Island, South Carolina. She enlisted into the United States Marine Corps in August 1971.

During her military career, she has held numerous staff, administrative and leadership positions, including service as the Battalion Supply Chief at Headquarters Battalion, Headquarters United States Marine Corps; Supply Chief at the Marine Corps Air Facility at Quantico, Virginia; and Supply Chief for Detachment A, Marine Air Group–41, 4th Marine Air Wing.

DeBerry, Harold L.
CHIEF WARRANT OFFICER 5—ARMY

DeBerry entered the U.S. Army in September 1968 and received a direct appointment to Warrant Officer in September 1981, while assigned to the 782nd Maintenance Battalion, 82nd Airborne Division, at Fort Bragg, North Carolina.

His civilian and military education includes a Bachelor of Science degree (cum laude) in Workforce Education Training and Development with a specialization in Curriculum Development from Southern Illinois University at Carbondale, Illinois; an Associate of Science Degree in Technologies from Pierce College in Tacoma, Washington; the Warrant Officer Senior Staff Course; Warrant Officer Staff Course; Warrant Officer Advanced Course; Warrant Officer Basic Course; Training Army Pre-commission Course; Senior Training Managers Course; Training Developer Middle Manager Course; Jumpmaster Course; and Air Movement Operations Course.

He was recently assigned as Chief Warrant Officer of the Professional Development Division, Command and Staff Department, USAOC&S APG, Maryland. He also served as Brigade Maintenance Technician in the 130th Engineer Brigade during Operation Iraqi Freedom, CENCOM and Hanau Germany. He is currently serving as the 5th Regimental Chief Warrant Officer of the Ordnance Corps.

Delandro, Donald J.

BRIGADIER GENERAL—ARMY

Born in New Orleans, Louisiana, Delandro received a Bachelor of Science degree in Business Administration from Southern University in 1956 and earned an M.B.A. in Business Administration from the University of Chicago in 1966. General Delandro completed the Command and General Staff College in 1971 and the United States Army War College in 1974.

From 1957 to 1958, he served as Platoon Leader, 3rd Brigade, and United States Army Training Center at Fort Ord, California. From 1959 to 1962, he was AG Administrative Officer, G-1, Headquarters, Fifth United States Army, USARAL; and from 1963 to 1967, served as First Administrative Officer, G-1, Headquarters of the

Fifth United States Army, then Action Officer, G-1, at the Headquarters of the Fifth Army in Chicago, Illinois.

From 1967 to 1968, Delandro was assigned as the G-1/Advisor, with the 1st Imperial Iranian Army in Iran. From 1968 to 1970, he was assigned to the Joint Chiefs of Staff in Washington, D.C. From June 1971 to November 1971, he served as the Adjutant General for the 23rd Infantry Division in Vietnam. From November 1971 to April 1972, he was assigned as Chief of the Enlisted Personnel Division, Military Personnel Directorate, Office of the Adjutant General, at the Headquarters of the United States Army in Vietnam. From May 1972 to December 1972, he was assigned as the Executive Officer, Weapons Systems Analysis Directorate, in the Office of the Assistant Vice Chief of Staff of the United States Army in Washington, D.C. From January 1973 to July 1973, he was Administrative Executive in the Office of the Deputy Chief of Staff for Military Operations, United States Army, in Washington, D.C. In August 1974, he was selected to attend the United States Army War College at Carlisle Barracks, Pennsylvania. From June 1975 to June 1978, he served as Chief of Combat Service Support Division, later as Chief of Enlisted Distribution Division, Enlisted Personnel Management Directorate, at the United States Army Military Personnel Center in Alexandria, Virginia. He was appointed Colonel on February 1, 1976.

From June 1978 to July 1980, he served as Chief of Staff at the United States Army Military Personnel Center. From July 1980 to April 1981, he was assigned as Chief of Staff for the United States Army Recruiting Command at Fort Sheridan, Illinois. From April 1981 to September 1984, he was selected to serve as the Deputy Adjutant General for Administrative Systems and General Center with the United States Army in Washington, D.C. He was appointed Brigadier General on June 1, 1981, and promoted on January 22. 1982.

From September 1984 to September 1985, he served as Adjutant General for the United States Army and Commanding General of the Adjutant General Center, with additional duties as Commanding General of the United States Army Reserve Components Personnel and Administration Center and Commanding General of the Physical Disability Agency, in Washington, D.C. He retired from the military on September 30, 1985.

His military awards and decorations include the Distinguished Service Medal; the Legion of Merit; Bronze Star; Air Medal; Joint Service Commendation Medal; Army Commendation Medal (with oak leaf cluster); and the Meritorious Service Medal.

Deloatch, Veneer (Von)

BRIGADIER GENERAL—ARMY

A native of Tarboro, North Carolina, Deloatch and his wife Janie have three children. He was commissioned a second lieutenant in 1964, after he graduated from North Carolina A&T University with a Bachelor of Science degree in History and Social Studies. He was a distinguished graduate of the Reserve Officers Training Corps program. In 1973, he earned a Masters of Science degree in Public Administration at Howard University in Washington, D.C. He also completed course work for a Ph.D. in Public Administration at the University of Southern California.

His current military assignment is Commanding Officer of the 352nd Civil Affairs Command in Riverdale, MD. While serving in this position, stationed in Bosnia and Herzegovina, he was promoted to the rank of Brigadier General by United States Secretary of Defense William J. Perry and the Commander Implementation Forces Admiral Leighton W. Smith, Jr.

His military awards and decorations include the Bronze Star; the Meritorious Service Medal (with three oak leaf clusters); Army Commendation Medal (three oak leaf clusters); the Air Medal; and the National Defense Service Medal.

Deloney, Thurmon L.

COLONEL—AIR FORCE

Colonel Deloney's education includes a Bachelor of Science degree in Electrical Engineering from North Carolina Agricultural and Technical University at Greensboro, North Carolina where he was Valedictorian and AFROTC Distinguished Graduate. He holds a master's degree in Electrical Engineering from the Massachusetts Institute of Technology at Cambridge, Massachusetts. He earned a Ph.D. in Electrical Engineering from Leland Stanford Jr. University at Palo Alto, California.

His military education includes, Squadron Officer School at Maxwell Air Force Base, Alabama (1981); Program Management Course at Defense Systems Management College in Fort Belvoir, Virginia; Air War College at Maxwell Air Force Base (1995); and Academic Instructor School at Maxwell Air Force Base (1999).

In January 2005, he was serving as the Director of Policy and Integration for the Air Force Office of Scientific Research at Ballston, Virginia. As Director of AFOSR's largest directorate, he is responsible for planning, budget formulation, financial management, data and information management, communications/computer systems, protocol, public affairs and marketing, security and policy management, facility and supply management, and historical record maintenance in support of the execution of AFOSR's basic research mission.

Prior to coming to AFOSR, he was the Chief of the Modeling and Simulation Division, Advanced Computational Analysis Directorate, Aeronautical Systems Center, Wright-Patterson Air Force Base, Ohio. He led a 50-man active duty and reserve military, government and contractor organization which performed virtual and distributed simulations of aeronautical systems. This team of engineering and program professionals are also responsible for operating the Simulation and Modeling Facility (SIMAF), maintaining and updating the DOD air-to-air model MILAASPM, and developing the follow-on model EAAGLES.

Denson, Antoine C.

COMMAND SERGEANT MAJOR—ARMY

A native of South Bronx, New York, Denson enlisted into the United States Army in November 1979, and attended Basic Combat Training and Advanced Individual Training at Fort Sill, Oklahoma.

His military and civilian education includes all the Noncommissioned Officer Education System Courses; the Recruiting and Retention Course; Airlift Planners Course; Basic Airborne School, Advance Airborne Recondo School; Air Movement Operation and Transportation for Hazardous Material Course; Drill Sergeant School; 8-Inch Atomic Projectile Supervisor Course; Field Artillery System Mechanic Course (M198); Equal Opportunity Representative Course; Senior Enlisted Equal Opportunity Course; First Sergeant Course; and United States Army Sergeants Major Academy. He holds an Associates Degree in Applied Science and Applied Technology from Central Texas College.

In October 2004, he was serving as the Command Sergeant Major for the 4th Battalion, 27th Field Artillery.

Dent, Kennis J.

COMMAND SERGEANT MAJOR

A native of Huntsville, Alabama, Kennis Dent entered the United States Army in October 1982, and completed Basic Combat Training at Fort Jackson, South Carolina, and Advanced Individual Training at Fort Gordon, Georgia, as a Radio Teletypewriter Operator (O5C).

His military and civilian education includes all of the Noncommissioned Officer Education System Courses; Drill Sergeant School; Radio Operator Course; USAFE AN/GSC-40 Satellite Course; Instructor Training Course; SATCOM Terminal Operation Course; First Sergeant Course; and the United States Army Sergeants Major Academy (class 53). He earned a master's degree in Management from Webster University; a Bachelor of Science degree in Occupational Education from Wayland Baptist University; and a diploma in Electronics and Computer Technology from the Electronic and Computer Institute.

His leadership assignments include serving as a Mechanical System Supervisor with Headquarters Company, Walter Reed Army Medical Center, Washington, D.C.; as Brigade Senior Signal Noncommissioned Officer, 120th Infantry Brigade, at Fort Sam Houston, Texas; Senior Telecom Plans Noncommissioned Officer, 311th TSC, DET 2, Korea; and as the First Sergeant for Charlie Company, 86th Signal Battalion, Fort Huachuca, Arizona. As of January 2004, he has served as the Command Sergeant Major for the 369th Signal Battalion, 15th Signal Brigade, at Fort Gordon, Georgia.

DePriest, Oscar S., IV
BRIGADIER GENERAL—ARMY

General DePriest graduated with a bachelor's degree from Harvard University and received his Doctor of Dental Medicine degree from Boston University. His military education includes the Army Medical Department Basic and Advanced Courses, AMEDD Company Grade Pre-Command Course; Army Command and General Staff College; and the Army War College.

His military career began with his selection to the Army Health Professions Scholarship Program while at Boston University Dental School. Upon graduation, he entered active duty, initially as a general practice res-

ident at William Beaumont Army Medical Center at Fort Bliss, Texas, then as Chief for Removable Prosthetics, United States Army Dental Activity, Fort Devens, Massachusetts.

He has served in a variety of command and staff assignments as a member of the Army Reserve. He previously served as the Commander of the 309th Combat Support Hospital at Bedford, Massachusetts; Readiness Officer with the 804th Medical Brigade at Devens Reserve Forces Training Area, Massachusetts; Commander of the 455th Medical Company at Devens RFTA, Massachusetts; Commander of the 455th Medical Detachment at Hanscom Air Force Base, Massachusetts; and Executive Officer at the 399th Combat Support Hospital in Taunton, Massachusetts.

His military awards include the Meritorious Service Medal (with two oak leaf clusters), Army Commendation Medal (with four oak leaf clusters), Army Achievement Medal (with two oak leaf clusters), National Defense Service Medal (with star), Army Reserve Components Achievement Medal (with four oak leaf clusters), and Armed Forces Reserve Medal (with silver hourglass).

Dickens, Timmothy
CHIEF MASTER SERGEANT—AIR FORCE

Dickens was born into an Air Force family in November 1958 at Donaldson Air Force Base in Greenville, South Carolina. He graduated from Bossier High School in Bossier City, Louisiana, in June 1976. He enlisted in the United States Air Force in July 1976 and completed Basic Military Training as an Honor Graduate.

His military education includes Noncommissioned Officer Orientation Course at Randolph Air Force Base, Texas, and Supervisory Development Course at Bolling Air Force Base in Washington, D.C. He was a Distinguished Graduate and winner of the Speech Award at Military Airlift Command Noncommissioned Officer Academy at McGuire Air Force Base, New Jersey. He was an Honor Graduate at Supply Systems Analyst Technical School at Lowery Air Force Base, Colorado, and also attended Senior Noncommissioned Officer Academy at Gunter Air Force Base, Alabama.

His first duty assignment was Randolph Air Force Base, Texas, working as a Materiel Facilities Specialist in the 12th Supply Squadron. While there, he served as a member of the Base Honor Guard and later went on to become the Noncommissioned Officer in Charge as an Airman First Class. In the summer of 1979 he applied and was selected for an assignment with the United States Air Force Honor Guard and reported for duty in October. During his tenure, he served in various positions and was subsequently selected as Noncommissioned Officer in Charge and Drill Instructor of the United States Air Force Honor Guard's Silent Drill Team. In 1987, he was assigned as Superintendent for Supply Systems, 554th SUPS, at Nellis Air Force Base, Nevada. In 1989, he served as Second Group Sergeant Major, for the United States Air Force Academy at

Colorado Springs, Colorado. From 1991 to 1998, he served as the Superintendent of the United States Air Force Honor Guard at Bolling Air Force Base, in Washington, D.C. In 1998, he was selected to serve as the Command Chief Master Sergeant, 3rd Wing, at Elmendorf Air Force Base, Alaska. In 2001, he was assigned as the Command Chief Master Sergeant, 12th Flying Training Wing, at Randolph Air Force Base.

Dickerson, Ira L.
COMMAND SERGEANT MAJOR—ARMY

A native of Artesia, Mississippi, Ira Dickerson entered the United States Army in February 1977. He attended his Basic Combat Training at Fort Jackson, South Carolina, and completed his Advanced Individual Training at Fort Benning, Georgia.

His military education includes all the Noncommissioned Officer Education System Courses; Battle Staff Course; Air Assault School; First Sergeants Course; Drill Sergeants Course; the United States Army Sergeants Major Academy. He also holds a bachelor's degree.

In November 2004, he was serving as the Command Sergeant Major for the 15th Forward Support Battalion.

Diego-Allard, Victoria H.
COLONEL—ARMY

Colonel DiegoAllard enlisted in the Army in 1979 as a Signal Intelligence Electronic Warfare Analyst. Upon completion of Advanced Individual Training she attended Officers Candidate School at Fort Benning, Georgia, and was commissioned in Ordnance.

His civilian and military education includes a bachelor's degree in Political Science and Economics at Boston University (1981), and a Jurist Doctorate at Hamline University (1993). She also participated in the Army's Training with Industry Program at Honeywell/ Alliant Techsystems (1987–1989); graduated from the Defense Systems Management College Program Management Course (1998); and is a Senior Service College Fellow-University of Texas at Austin (2001–2002).

She has held a variety of important positions, including Shop Officer in the 5th Maintenance Company, 66th Maintenance Battalion; Commander of the Heavy Maintenance Company, 122nd Maintenance Battalion; Division Readiness Officer for the 3rd Armored Division; Chief of Contracts at Defense Contract Management Command in Twin Cities, Minnesota; Proponency Officer, Contracts Management Career field, Office of the Assistant Secretary of the Army, Research Development and Acquisition (OASARDA); and Speechwriter and Military Assistant to the Military Deputy, Office of the Assistant Secretary of the Army, Acquisition, Logistics and Technology, at the Pentagon.

Diggs, Michael
SERGEANT MAJOR—MARINE

Diggs enlisted in the Marine Corps on January 19, 1984, and attended Recruit Training at Marine Corps Recruit Depot at Parris Island, South Carolina on September 11, 1984.

In May 1985, after completing Air Traffic Control School at Naval Air Station Millington, Tennessee, he transferred to Marine Corps Air Station Kaneohe Bay, Hawaii. He was attached to Marine Air Control Squadron Two and served as an Air Traffic Controller. During this tour, he was certified as a Tower Watch Supervisor. Also, on September 2, 1986, he was meritoriously promoted to the rank of Sergeant.

In August 1986, he transferred to Marine Corps Air Station, El Toro, California. He was attached to Marine Air Traffic Control Squadron Thirty Eight. During this tour he served as a Tower Watch Supervisor and Air

Traffic Control Training NCO. In 1990, he deployed to
Saudi Arabia in support of Operation Desert Shield/
Desert Storm.

In April 1992, he transferred to Marine Corps Air
Station Beaufort, South Carolina. He was promoted
to Staff Sergeant on February 1, 1993. He attended the
Staff Non-Commissioned Officers Career Course and
finished as a distinguished graduate. During this tour,
he served as a Tower Watch Supervisor and Crew Chief.

In January 1995, he reported to Drill Instructor
School. He graduated in the top three of his class and
was the Class Leadership Honor Graduate. He was as-
signed to Delta Company, First Recruit Training Bat-
talion, where he served as a Drill Instructor, Senior
Drill Instructor, Series Gunnery Sergeant, and Staff
Noncommissioned Officer in Charge (SNCOIC) of
Academics.

In July 1997, he transferred to Marine Corps Air Sta-
tion Beaufort and was assigned to Maine Air Control
Squadron Two. After his arrival, he deployed to
Twenty-nine Palms, California as the Detachment
SNCOIC in support of a Combined Armed Exercise
(CAX). He was promoted to Gunnery Sergeant in December 1997. During this tour, he served as the Operation and Training Chief. In May 1998, he attended
the Staff Non-Commissioned Officers Advanced
Course, and finished as the Honor Graduate. He also
deployed to Norway in support of Exercise Battle
Griffin 99 and to Taszar, Hungary in support of Op-
eration Joint Task Force Noble Anvil.

In December 2000, Sergeant Major Diggs transferred to Marine Corps Air Station Iwakuni, Japan. He
served as Facility Watch Officer, and Tower Operations
Chief. During this tour, he was selected for promotion
to First Sergeant. In June 2001, he attended and completed the First Sergeants Course.

In November 2001, he transferred to Camp Hansen,
Okinawa, Japan, where he served as the First Sergeant
of Headquarters Battery, 12th Marine Regiment. During this assignment, he also served as the director of
the 12th Marine Regiment Corporals Leadership
Course, and completed the Far East Regional First
Sergeant Master Sergeant Course in July 2002.

In November 2002, he transferred to Marine Corps
Base Camp Lejeune, North Carolina, where he served
as the First Sergeant of Headquarters and Service Company, Marine Corps Engineer School, and the First
Sergeant of Utilities Instruction Company.

He was selected for promotion to Sergeant Major in
November 2004, and transferred to 2nd Marine Aircraft
Wing, Cherry Point, North Carolina, to serve in his
current position as the Sergeant Major of Marine Air
Control Squadron Two.

Dillard, Oliver W.

MAJOR GENERAL—ARMY

General Dillard was born in Margaret, Alabama. He
and his wife, Helen, have four children, Oliver, Jr.,
Stephen, Diane, and Dennis. He received a B.G.E. degree from the University of Omaha, a Master of Science

degree in international affairs from George Washington
University.

He has held a wide variety of important command
and staff positions. From August 1963 to August 1964,
he served as Chief of the Europe, Africa, and Middle
East Section, later Chief of the Foreign Intelligence Assistance Section, Special Warfare and Foreign Assistance Branch, Combat Intelligence Development Division, Assistant Chief of Staff for Intelligence, United
States Army, Washington, D.C. From August 1964 to
June 1965, he was a student at the National War College in Washington, D.C. After completion of the War
College, he was assigned as Operations and Training
Staff Officer in the Special Studies Division, later Op-
eration Training Staff Officer in the Analysis Division,
and later Chief of the Analysis/Coordination Branch,
Study Division 3, Special Studies Directorate, United
States Army Combat Developments Command Insti-
tute of Special Studies at Fort Belvoir, Virginia, from
July 1965 to January 1967.

In January 1967 he was assigned as the Commanding Officer of the 5th Combat Support Training
Brigade at Fort Dix, New Jersey. From December 1968
to July 1969, he was a student at the Vietnam Training
Center in the Foreign Service Institute at the Department of State in Washington, D.C. From July 1969 to
June 1971, he was Senior Military Adviser on Advisory
Team 41, Military Region II, United States Military
Assistance Command in Vietnam. General Dillard returned to the United States in July 1971 and was assigned as the Deputy Assistant Chief of Staff for intelligence, United States Army, in Washington, D.C. He
was appointed Brigadier General on February 1, 1972.

In February 1973 he returned to Vietnam and served
as Director of Intelligence for United States Military
Assistance Command. From May 1973 to June 1973, he
served as Special Assistant to the Commanding General

of Continental Army Command at Fort McPherson, Georgia. In July 1973 he was first assigned as Deputy Chief of Staff for Intelligence to the United States Army Forces Command at Fort McPherson. From April 1974 to July 1975, he served as Assistant Division Commander for the 2nd Armored Division at Fort Hood, Texas. From July 1975 to October 1978, he served as Deputy Chief of Staff for Intelligence, United States Army, in Heidelberg, Germany. He was appointed Major General on August 1, 1975.

In October 1978, he was selected to serve as the Commanding General of United States Army Readiness Region II at Fort Dix, New Jersey.

He retired on January 31, 1980. General Dillard's awards and decorations include the Purple Heart; Distinguished Service Medal; Legion of Merit (with two oak leaf clusters); Bronze Star (with oak leaf cluster); Air Medal; Army Commendation medal (with oak leaf cluster); Combat Infantryman Badge; and the Silver Star.

Dimery, Clark, Sr.

COMMAND SERGEANT MAJOR—ARMY

He was born in November 1956, in Ozona, Texas. He entered the United States Army in September 1975 and attended Basic and Advanced Individual Training at Fort Gordon, Georgia.

Dingle, Generett, Sr.

SERGEANT MAJOR— MARINES

Dingle attended recruit training in August 1977, at Marine Corps Recruit Depot at Parris Island, South Carolina. Upon graduation he was transferred to the 2nd Marine Division, at Camp Lejeune, North Carolina for duty as a Base Motor Transport Operator with the Sixth Marine Regiment. In July 1979, he attended the Noncommissioned Officer School at Camp Geiger, North Carolina. In February 1982, he was assigned to Headquarters and Service Company at Quantico, Virginia as a Motor Transport NCO. In May 1983, he was transferred to Drill Instructor School at Parris Island.

Upon completion of Drill Instructor School in July 1983, he was assigned to "A" Company, 1st Recruit Training Battalion as a Drill Instructor. In April 1986 he attended the Staff NCO Academy in Quantico, Virginia. In June 1988, he was transferred to the 3rd Marine Corps Division in Okinawa, Japan, assigned to the 3rd Armored Assault Battalion as the Motor Transport Operation Chief.

In August 1989, he attended Drill Instructor School

for his second tour as a Drill Instructor. In September 1989, he was reassigned to "A" Company, 1st Recruit Training Battalion as a Drill Instructor. In August 1991, he was transferred to Marine Corps Service Support School (MCSSS), Camp Lejeune, North Carolina, where he served as an Instructor with Motor Transport School.

In August 1993, Dingle was transferred to the 1st Marine Aircraft Wing at Okinawa, Japan, for duty as the Motor Transport Chief. In April 1996 he was transferred to Headquarters Battalion, 3rd Marine Division as the First Sergeant of Truck Company. In December 1997, he was transferred to Naval Air Station, Jacksonville, Florida, where he served as the Inspector-Instructor Staff First Sergeant for Bravo Company, 4th Amphibious Assault Battalion. In June 1999, he was assigned as the 4th Amphibious Assault Battalion's Sergeant Major in Tampa, Florida. In November 1999, he was transferred to the Marine Corps Recruiting Station Atlanta for duty as Sergeant Major. In October 2004, he was serving as the Sergeant Major for Marine Aviation Logistics Squadron 14, Second Marine Aircraft Wing.

Dix, Richard B.

LIEUTENANT COLONEL—ARMY

Richard Dix was born in Atlanta, and raised in Decatur, Georgia. In 1987, he graduated from South Carolina State University Army ROTC Program as a Distinguished Military Graduate. He received a Reserve Commission as an Armor Officer in 1987.

His military education includes the Armor Officer Basic Course; the Quartermaster Officer Advanced Course; the Combined Arms Services and Staff School; and Command and General Staff College at Fort Leavenworth, Kansas. He holds a Bachelor of Science degree in Marketing from South Carolina State University and

a Master of Arts degree in Procurement and Acquisitions Management from Webster University.

He has held numerous key military assignments including serving as the Executive Officer of Headquarters and Headquarters Detachment, 224th Forward Support Battalion, prior to and during Operations Desert Shield/Storm and, from 1994 to 1996, serving at Fort Bragg as Reports Officer in Charge for the 2nd MMC, Support Operations Officer at the 530th Supply, and Service Battalion and Brigade S4 507th Corps Support Group. In December of 1994, he was assigned as the Commander of the 406th General Supply Company, and in September 1996, he was transferred to Fort Gillem, Georgia, where he served as the 1st Army Deputy Chief of Staff for Logistics, Plans and Operations. In 2000, Dix was selected to serve as the Deputy Chief G-3, Plans and Exercises, Deputy Chief Operations, for the 21st Theater Support Command, and then as Brigade S3, 29th Support Group, and Support Operations Officer for the 200th Materiel Management Center at Kaiserslautern, Germany.

Dixon, Althea Green
COMMAND SERGEANT MAJOR—ARMY

Dixon was born in Trinidad and enlisted in the United States Army at St. Croix, United States Virgin Islands, in August 1977. She attended basic training at Fort Jackson, South Carolina, followed by Advanced Individual Training at Fort Sam Houston, Texas.

She has completed numerous military courses, including all the Noncommissioned Officer Education System Courses; the Battle Staff Noncommissioned Officer Course; the Security Managers Course; and the Training Managers Course; the Medical Specialist Course (Honor Graduate); the Joint Deployment Officer Course; the Ear, Nose and Throat Specialist Course (Distinguished Honor Graduate); and the United States Army Sergeant Major Academy (class 47), where she received the General Ralph E. Hanes Award for Outstanding Student Research, as well as a commendation for outstanding performance on the Army Physical Fitness Test. She holds a Master of Science degree in Business from the University of LaVerne in California.

Her leadership assignments include serving as Section Noncommissioned Officer in Charge; Platoon Sergeant; First Sergeant; and Operations Sergeant and Command Sergeant Major. In August 2004, she was assigned to Fort Gordon, Georgia, as the Command Sergeant Major of Dwight David Eisenhower Medical Center and the Southeast Regional Medical Command.

Dixon, McArthur
COMMAND SERGEANT MAJOR—ARMY

Dixon is a native of Davisboro, Georgia, and entered the United States Army in June 1979. He attended Basic Combat Training and Advanced Individual Training at Fort Jackson, South Carolina.

His military education includes all the Noncommissioned Officer Education System Courses; Battle Staff Course; First Sergeants Course; Logistics Management

Development Course; the Army Maintenance Management Course; and the United States Army Sergeants Major Academy (class 52). He holds a Bachelor of Science in Business Management from American Military University and an associate's degree in Law Enforcement from Central Texas College.

He has served in every leadership position from Squad Leader to Sergeant Major. His assignments include serving as Motor Sergeant of Bravo Company, 127th Signal Battalion, Fort Ord, California; First Sergeant of Bravo Company, Aviation Regiment, Hunter Army Airfield, Georgia; Operation Sergeant Major for Division Support Command (DISCOM), Fort Stewart, Georgia; Command Sergeant Major of the 3rd Forward Support Battalion, 3rd Infantry Division (Mechanized), Fort Stewart.

Doctor, Henry, Jr.
LIEUTENANT GENERAL—ARMY

Born in Oakly, South Carolina, Doctor married the former Janie M. Manigault (Jane). They have three children, Lori, Kenneth, and Cheryl. Upon completion of the Reserve Officers Training Corps curriculum and graduation from South Carolina State College, he was commissioned a second lieutenant and awarded a Bachelor of Science degree in Agriculture in 1954. He also earned a Master of Arts degree in Counseling and Psychological services from Georgia State University. His military education includes completion of the Infantry School; the United States Army Command and General Staff College; and the United States Army War College.

General Doctor served in a wide variety of important career-building assignments preparatory to his most recent duties. He was Executive Officer of the 1st Battalion, 4th Infantry Division, and later served as the Assistant G-3 (operations and training), 4th Infantry

Division, in Vietnam. Upon his return to the United States, General Doctor served as the Personnel Management Officer and later Chief, Personnel Actions Section, Infantry Branch, Office of Personnel Operations, Washington, D.C. General Doctor commanded the 1st Battalion, 29th Infantry, with a follow-on assignment as Deputy Brigade Commander, 197th Infantry Brigade, at Fort Benning, Georgia.

He remained at Fort Benning to serve as Chief of the Modern Volunteer Army Control Group at the United States Army Infantry Center. Following his studies at Georgia State University and the United States Army War College, General Doctor served as the Director of Psychometrics at the United States Army War College.

From July 1975 to March 1977, he served as Commander of the 1st Brigade, 25th Infantry Division, at Schofield Barracks, Hawaii. From March 1977 to June 1979, he was assigned as Director of Enlisted Personnel Management at the United States Army Military Personnel Center in Alexandria, Virginia. He was promoted to Brigadier General on August 1, 1977.

From June 1979 to July 1980, he was assigned as the Assistant Division Commander of the 24th Infantry Division at Fort Stewart, Georgia. He was promoted to Major General on July 1, 1980.

From July 1980 to August 1982, Doctor was assigned as the Director of Personnel, Training and Force Development in the United States Army Materiel Development and Readiness Command at Alexandria, Virginia. From August 1982 to July 1983, he was assigned as Chief of Staff at the United States Army Materiel Development and Readiness Command in Alexandria. From July 1983 to August 1985, he served as the Commanding General of the 2nd Infantry Division, Eighth United States Army, in Korea. From September 1985 to June 1986, he was assigned as the Deputy Inspector General for Investigations, Assistance, Training and Information Management for the United States Army in Washington, D.C. He was promoted to Lieutenant General on July 1, 1986. From July 1986 to August 1989, he served as the Inspector General, for the United States Army, in Washington, D.C.

His military awards and decorations include the Distinguished Service Medal (with oak leaf cluster); the Legion of Merit; Bronze Star Meritorious Service Medal; Air Medal; Army Commendation medal (with three oak leaf clusters); and the Combat Infantryman Badge.

Donald, James Edward

MAJOR GENERAL—ARMY

Born in Forest, Mississippi, Donald received Bachelor of Arts degree in Political Science from the University of Mississippi. He also earned a Master of Public Administration degree in Organization Behavior from the University of Missouri. His military training includes the Infantry Officer Basic and Advanced Courses; United States Army Command and General Staff College; and the National War College.

He was commissioned a Second Lieutenant on September 24, 1970. His assignments during his first ten years of service include Tactical Officer with the 52nd Company (later 53rd Company), 5th Student Battalion, The School Brigade, United States Army Infantry School at Fort Benning, Georgia; Executive Officer with the 53rd Company; Rifle Platoon Leader, later Mortar Platoon Leader, later S-4 (Logistics) of the 1st Battalion, 9th Infantry, 2nd Infantry Division, Eighth United States Army, Korea; Instructor at the Leadership Department, United States Army Infantry School at Fort Benning; Company Commander of the 50th Company, 5th Student Battalion, The School Brigade, United States Army Infantry School at Fort Benning; S-1 (Adjutant) of the 1st Battalion, 87th Infantry, 8th Infantry Division, United States Army Europe, in Germany; Commander of Company C, 1st Battalion, 87th Infantry, 8th Infantry Division, United States Army Europe, in Germany; and Infantry Branch Advisor in United States Army Reserve Mobilization Region I at Fort Devens, Massachusetts with duty in Newburgh, New York.

He has held a wide variety of important command and staff positions, including service as Assistant Inspector General of the 101st Airborne Division (Air Assault) at Fort Campbell, Kentucky; Executive Officer for the 2nd Battalion, 502nd Infantry, 101st Airborne Division; S-3 (Operations Officer), with the 2nd Brigade, 101st Airborne; Army Training Battle Simulation System Team Chief and Battle Command Training Program Project Officer of the 101st Airborne Division (Air Assault).

General Donald served in a variety of important career-building assignments preparatory to his most recent duties, including service as the Commander of the 1st Battalion, 502nd Infantry, 101st Airborne Division (Air Assault); Staff Officer in the Office of the Deputy

Chief of Staff for Operations, United States Army, in Washington, DC; and Commander of the 1st Brigade, 101st Airborne Division (Air Assault). He then returned to Washington to serve as Chief of the Military Support Division in the Office of the Deputy Chief of Staff for Operations and Plans, United States Army. In October 1995, he was assigned as Deputy J-3 (Operations), United States Pacific Command at Camp H. M. Smith, Hawaii. In November 1996, he was selected Assistant Division Commander (Maneuvers) for the 25th Infantry Division (Light), at Schofield Barracks, Hawaii. From June 1998 to August 2000, he served as the Deputy Commanding General/Chief of Staff of the United States Army Pacific, at Fort Shafter, Hawaii. In August 2000, he was selected to serve as Deputy Chief of Staff for Personnel and Installation Management at United States Army Forces Command at Fort McPherson, Georgia. He was promoted to Brigadier General on October 1, 1996, and promoted to Major General on February 1, 2000.

His military awards and decorations include the Legion of Merit; the Bronze Star; Meritorious Service Medal (with four oak leaf clusters); Army Commendation Medal (with oak leaf cluster); Combat Infantryman Badge; Expert Infantry Badge; Parachutist Badge; Pathfinder Badge; and Air Assault Badge.

Dorsey, Johnny L., Sr.
COMMAND SERGEANT MAJOR—ARMY

Dorsey entered the United States Army in June 1978. He completed Basic Combat Training and Advanced Individual Training under the One Station Unit Training program at Fort Gordon, Georgia.

His military and civilian education includes all the Noncommissioned Officer Education System Courses; Airborne Course; Telecommunication Course; COM-SEC—Custodian Course; Radio Teletypewriter Team

Chief Course; Communication Chief Course; DGM (Tri-Tac) Course; Communication System Training Course; First Sergeant Course; United States Army Sergeants Major Academy; and United States Army Command Sergeant Major Course. He also holds a bachelor's degree from Regents University.

His leadership positions include serving as Platoon Sergeant; First Sergeant; Group Sergeant Major for Regional Signal Group SHAPE (RSGS); Battalion Command Sergeant Major and Installation Sergeant Major, 304th Signal Battalion at Camp Colbern, South Korea; Battalion Sergeant Major, 369th Signal Battalion, 15th Regimental Signal Brigade at Fort Gordon; and Command Sergeant Major for the 3rd Signal Brigade at Fort Hood, Texas.

Dougherty, Alonzo D.
BRIGADIER GENERAL—ARMY

Dougherty was born in Leavenworth, Kansas. He and his wife, Ellen, are the proud parents of four sons and two daughters. He entered the military service on May 12, 1955, at Leavenworth, Kansas, when he enlisted in Company A, 174th Military Police Battalion, Kansas Army National Guard. By February 1959, he had advanced to the rank of Sergeant when his unit was reorganized as infantry.

On June 18, 1962, he was commissioned a Second Lieutenant in the infantry with Company A, 2nd Battalion, 137th Infantry, at Leavenworth, Kansas. Lieutenant Dougherty continued his career serving as a Platoon Leader and Executive Officer. On February 8, 1968, he was promoted to Captain and assigned as Company Commander of the Headquarters Company, 2nd Battalion, 137th Infantry, 69th Infantry Brigade. In May 1968 Captain Dougherty was ordered to extended active duty and reported with his command to

Fort Carson, Colorado. It was in November of the same year that Captain Dougherty reported as an individual replacement to the South Vietnam. He was assigned to the 3rd Battalion, 7th Infantry, 199th Infantry Brigade, where he commanded Company D and later served as S-3, Air, for the same Battalion.

Following his tour in Vietnam, Captain Dougherty returned to the Kansas Army National Guard and the 69th Infantry Brigade, serving in various assignments, including Company Commander and Battalion and Brigade Staff Officer. He was promoted to Major in May 1973, and in January 1974 he left the 69th Infantry Brigade to serve on the State Headquarters Staff as Equal Employment Opportunity Officer, later as the Assistant G-3.

He was promoted to Lieutenant Colonel in May 1977 while continuing in his assignment as Assistant G-3. In December 1979, Lieutenant Colonel Dougherty became Commander of the 2nd Battalion, 137th Infantry, and served in that assignment until December 1981. Lieutenant Colonel Dougherty was promoted to full Colonel in December 1981 and assigned as the Assistant G-3 in STARC Headquarters until September 19, 1983. On September 19, 1983, Colonel Dougherty assumed the duties of Deputy Brigade Commander for the 69th Infantry Brigade (Mechanized) and assumed Command of the 69th Infantry Brigade on November 19, 1984.

His military awards include the Bronze Star (with two oak leaf clusters), Air Medal (with two oak leaf clusters), Army Commendation Medal, National Defense Service Medal, Vietnamese Campaign Medal, and Combat Infantryman's Badge.

Douglas, André
COMMAND SERGEANT MAJOR—ARMY

Born in Meriden, Connecticut, Douglas joined the Army in July 1981 and attended Basic Training at Fort Knox, Kentucky, and Advanced Individual Training at Fort Benjamin Harrison at Indianapolis, Indiana.

His military education includes all the Noncommissioned Officer Education System Courses; the First Sergeants Course; Battle Staff Course; Air Assault Course; the United States Army Sergeants Major Academy; and the Command Sergeants Major Course.

His civilian education includes an associate's degree in Public Administration from Fayetteville, North Carolina; a Bachelor of Science in Public Administration from Upper Iowa University; and a Masters Degree in Human Resource Development from Webster University.

His key military assignments include serving as Senior Instructor at the United Army NCO Academy, Hawaii; Observer/Controller of the Combat Service Support Joint Readiness Training Center at Fort Polk, Louisiana; Personnel Service Center Noncommissioned Officer in Charge at Fort Ritchie, Maryland; First Sergeant Army World Class Athlete Program at Fort Carson, Colorado; Strength Manager at FORSCOM Headquarters at Fort McPherson, Georgia; Command

Sergeant Major of the 55th Personnel Services Battalion in Germany; and Command Sergeant Major at Fort Belvoir, Virginia.

Douglas, Phillip D.
COMMAND SERGEANT MAJOR—ARMY

A native of Sacramento, California, Douglas entered the United States Army on February 27, 1979, and completed Basic Combat and Advanced Individual Training under the One Station Unit Training as a 36C Wire Systems Installer at Fort Gordon, Georgia in May 1979. He is a graduate of the United States Army Sergeants Major Academy (class 51), and the Command Sergeants Major (D) Course 1-02.

He has served in a multitude of assignments and prior to his current posting he served as an NCOES Evaluator for the Directorate of Evaluations and Standards (DOES); Noncommissioned Officer in Charge for the Deputy Chief of Staff, HQ 5th Signal Command at Mannheim Germany; First Sergeant of HHC, 44th Signal Battalion at Mannheim; First Sergeant of Delta Company, 86th Signal Battalion at Fort Huachuca, Arizona; Detachment Sergeant for HHD, 58th Signal Battalion at Okinawa, Japan; and Drill Sergeant for Delta Company, 369th Signal Battalion, at Fort Gordon.

Drew, Benjamin Alvin
LIEUTENANT COLONEL—AIR FORCE

Drew was born in Washington, D.C., where he graduated from Gonzaga College High School in 1980. He holds a Bachelor of Science in Astronautical Engineering from the United States Air Force Academy; a Bachelor of Science in Physics from the United States Air Force Academy; and a Master of Science in Aerospace Science from Embry Riddle University.

He received his commission as a Second Lieutenant from the United States Air Force Academy in May 1984. He completed Undergraduate Pilot Training, Helicopter at Fort Rucker, Alabama and earned his wings in March 1985. His initial assignment was to the HH-3E flying combat rescue. He transitioned to the MH-60G and was assigned to Operations Just Cause, Desert Shield/Desert Storm and Provide Comfort. He completed the United States Air Force Fixed-Wing Qualification in April 1993 and the United States Naval Test Pilot School in June 1994. He has commanded tow flight test units and served on the Air Combat Command Staff. He is a Command Pilot with 3000 hours flying time in over 30 types of aircraft.

Drew was selected as a mission specialist by NASA in July 2000, and he reported for training in August 2000. Following the completion of two years of training and evaluation, he was assigned technical duties in the Astronaut Office Station Operation Branch.

Driver, Anthony R.
COMMAND MASTER CHIEF—NAVY

Driver was born in Chicago, Illinois, where he graduated from Rich South High School in Chicago. He entered the Navy in March 1984, attending Recruit Training at Recruit Training Center Great Lakes, Illinois.

His key military assignments include serving with the Presidential Honor Guard in Washington, D.C., and as Chief Boatswain's Mate aboard USS *Tempest*; He became an Enlisted Surface Warfare Specialist while

assigned to USS *Anzio*, and served as Leading Chief Petty Officer for Seamanship Training Division at Service School Command at Great Lakes, Illinois and as Command Master Chief for Strike Fighter Squadron 137 at Naval Air Station Lemoore, California. He deployed onboard USS *Constellation* (CV), participating in combat operations during Operation Iraqi Freedom. In August 2004, Drew assumed Command as Chief of Naval Operations Directed Command Master Chief at Naval Service Training Command, Great Lakes.

Dryden, Charles
LIEUTENANT COLONEL—AIR FORCE

Dryden was born in September 1920 in New York City to Jamaican parents. He graduated from Peter Stuyvesant High School and earned a Bachelor of Arts Degree in Political Science from Hofstra University, and a Master of Arts Degree in Public Law and Government from Columbia University.

In August 1941, he was selected for Aviation Cadet Training at the Tuskegee Army Flying School in Alabama. In April 1942, Dryden was commissioned as a Second Lieutenant from Aviation Cadet Training at the segregated training facility in Tuskegee, Alabama. As a Second Lieutenant in a class of only three graduates, he was in the second class of black pilots to graduate in the history of the U.S. Army Air Corps. He was a member of the famed 99th Pursuit Squadron, later the 332nd Fighter Group, which served in North Africa, Sicily, and Italy during World War II.

On June 9, 1943, Lieutenant Charles Dryden, in his P-40 nicknamed "A-Train," led a flight of six pilots engaging enemy fighter aircraft in aerial combat over Pantelleria, Sicily. It was the first time in aviation history that black American pilots of the United States Army Air Corps engaged enemy aircraft in combat.

Colonel Dryden's 21-year military career also included combat missions in Korea and duty assignments in Japan, Germany and ten different bases in the United States. He also served as a Professor of Air Science at Howard University and retired in 1962 as a Command Pilot with 4,000 hours flying time.

Dublin, Marvin D.
COMMAND MASTER CHIEF—NAVY

A native of Raleigh, North Carolina, Dublin graduated from William G. Enloe High School in 1975 and enlisted in the Navy in July 1976. His first duty station was aboard USS *Ranger* (CV 61), where he was assigned to V03 division. In February of 1978, he requested and was approved to attend Aviation Machinist's Mate School in Memphis, Tennessee.

In January 1980, he transferred to Patrol Squadron Thirty-One at Naval Air Station Moffett Field in Mountain View, California. There he was assigned to the Power Plants Branch of the Aircraft Division. After a short time onboard, he was transferred to the Quality Assurance Division of the Maintenance Department.

From March 1983 to July 1987, he was attached to Patrol Squadron Forty (Fighting Marlins), again stationed at Moffett Field. He was assigned as Work Center Supervisor to the Improved Maintenance Program (Phase Crew). There he was awarded a Letter of Commendation for his maintenance contribution to the squadron's maintenance efforts during the search and rescue operations for Korean Airlines Flight 007.

He became a Recruit Company Commander in September 1987, and was selected as Company Commander School's Class Honorman. Because of his unique style and superior leadership ability, he was selected to receive the coveted Distinguished Leadership Award for his duties as Company Commander between February and April 1988.

He then attended the Navy's Senior Enlisted Academy from March through May 1992, at Newport, Rhode Island. Upon completion, he transferred to Carrier Airborne Early Warning Squadron 112 (VAW 112) at Naval Air Station Miramar in San Diego, California. There he supervised Quality Assurance and eventually became the Maintenance Master Chief.

From June 1996 to September 1998, he was assigned as Department Leading Chief of the Aircraft Intermediate Maintenance Department Naval Air Station at North Island in Coronado, California. From AIMD, he was selected to the Command Master Chief program.

Dublin's first assignment was aboard the USS *BlueRidge* (LCC 19), flagship for COMSEVENTHFLT, COPHIBFORSEVENTHFLT, and COMLANDFORSEVENTHFLT Forward Deployed to Yokosuka, Japan. This assignment was normally held by a Command Master Chief on his second tour. He reported to the USS *Kitty Hawk* (CV 63) in January 2001.

Dubose, William, Jr.
SERGEANT MAJOR—MARINES

Dubose enlisted in the United States Marine Corps on May 30, 1975, and reported for recruit training at Marine Corps Recruit Depot, Parris Island, South Carolina on July 2, 1975. He graduated from boot camp on September 29, 1975, and was meritoriously promoted to Private First Class. Following boot camp, he reported to Infantry Training School (ITS) at Camp Pendleton, California, where he received his primary Military Occupational Specialty of 0311, Infantrymen.

In January of 1980, he attended Drill Instructor School at Marine Corps Recruit Depot, Parris Island. Upon graduation from Drill Instructor School, he was assigned to 1st Recruit Training Battalion, where he completed five cycles as a drill instructor, and two as Senior Drill Instructor. In 1985, he served with Echo Company, 2nd Battalion, the 2nd Marine Division, as a Platoon Sergeant, Platoon Commander, and Company Gunnery Sergeant. In 1988, he was assigned to Massachusetts Institute of Technology's (MIT) Naval Reserve Officer Training Corps Unit in Cambridge, Massachusetts, for duty as the Assistant Marine Officer Instructor. In September 1991, he deployed to the Middle East with 1st Battalion, 8th Marines, 22nd Marine Expeditionary Unit. In August 1993, he deployed aboard the USS *America* as part of the Special Multitask Assault Force. During this deployment he participated in Operation Deny Flight as part of CTF 62 and JTF Provide Promise in the Adriatic Sea. He also participated in Operation Continued Hope/UNOSOM II as part of COMMARFORSOMALIA, and JTF

Somalia in the Indian Ocean. In September 1994, he was promoted to 1st Sergeant and reported to 1st Force Service Support Group, and was assigned the Company 1st Sergeant for Engineer Maintenance Company, 1st Maintenance Battalion. In October of 1995, he was reassigned to Headquarters and Service Company. In May 1997, he was promoted to Sergeant Major, and assigned as the Command Sergeant Major for Expeditionary Warfare Training Group Pacific in Coronado, California. In October 2004, he was serving as Sergeant Major at the Basic School.

Duckett, Louis

MAJOR GENERAL—ARMY

A native of Chicago, Illinois, Duckett was graduated from the City College of New York. He entered the New York National Guard on June 23, 1948, as a Private. General Duckett has served in a variety of important career-building assignments preparatory to his last assignment. He served as the executive officer for the Battery C, 879th AAA Gun Battalion.

In November 1967 he was assigned as group operations and training officer for the 187th Artillery Group. Duckett became commander of the 369th Transportation Battalion. He was appointed to the rank of Brigadier General in the New York Army National Guard on March 13, 1979, and was promoted to the rank of Major General on July 16, 1984.

Duncan, Elmer H.

FIRST SERGEANT—ARMY

Born in Detroit, Michigan, Elmer Duncan entered the United States Army in November 1983, and after training was assigned as a Field Artillery Surveyor at Fort Sill, Oklahoma.

His military education includes all levels of the Noncommissioned Officers Education System Courses; the

First Sergeant Course; the Instructor's Training Course; the United States Army Recruiters Course; Cadet Command Leaders Course; and the Air Movement Operations Course.

His key military assignments include positions such as Survey Section Chief; Chief of Survey; UAV Senior Air-Vehicle Operator; Battery First Sergeant; Army Recruiter; Instructor/Writer; Cadet Command Senior Military Instructor and Field Artillery Operations Sergeant. In February 2005, he was serving as the First Sergeant for Headquarters and Service Battery, 1-82nd Field Artillery, at Fort Hood, Texas.

Duncan, Linda A.

DEPUTY GARRISON COMMANDER—ARMY

A native of Springfield, Massachusetts, Duncan attended Howard University in Washington, D.C. where she earned a Bachelor of Arts degree in Sociology in 1973. Following graduation she attended graduate school at Ohio State University in Columbus, Ohio, where she earned a Master of Arts Degree in Guidance and Counseling. Her military education includes the Army Management Staff College and she attended several other professional development courses, including the Community and Family Support Management; Contracting Officers Representative; and the Garrison Pre-command Course. After graduate school Ms. Duncan returned to Springfield, Massachusetts where she began her career as a guidance counselor.

Her civil service career begins with the Department of the Army in September 1977 as a guidance counselor at Pinder Barracks, West Germany. In October 1980, she accepted a position as Education Specialist with the Department of the Navy at Navy Recruiting District, New York. In September 1984, she accepted an assignment as Education Specialist at the Army Education Center, New York Area Command and Fort

Hamilton, Brooklyn, New York. In December 1990, she was selected as the Education Service Officer for the New York Area Command and served until November 1995.

Ms. Duncan currently serves as Civilian Executive Assistant, Base Operations, United States Army Garrison Fort Hamilton, the position she has held since November 1995. In addition, she serves as the Base Transition Coordinator for Fort Totten and Bellmore Logistics Facility, sub-installations of Fort Hamilton.

Durham, Archer L.

MAJOR GENERAL—AIR FORCE

Born in Pasadena, California, Durham married the former Sue M. Harrison of Los Angeles. They have four children, Debra, Beverly, David, and Steven. He graduated from Utah State University with a Bachelor of Science degree in Political Science in 1960 and earned a Master of Science degree in International Affairs from George Washington University in 1975. He completed Squadron Officer School in 1960, Air Command and Staff College in 1961, Industrial College of the Armed Forces in 1973, National War College as a distinguished graduate in 1975, the Advanced Management Program at Columbia University and the program for Senior Executives in National and International Security at the John F. Kennedy School of Government, Harvard University.

Durham began his military career in January 1953 as an Aviation Cadet and in April 1954 received his commission and wings at Laredo Air Force Base, Texas. In August 1954 he was assigned as a Pilot with the 744th Troop Carrier Squadron at Charleston Air Force Base, South Carolina, and in October 1955 he transferred with the Squadron to Kadena Air Base, Okinawa. From June 1956 to June 1958, he was assigned to the 2720th

Maintenance Group, an Air Force Logistics Command Unit, at Clark Air Base in the Philippines as a Flight Test Maintenance Officer.

He then served with the 28th Logistics Support Squadron at Hill Air Force Base, Utah, as an Aircraft Commander and Squadron Plans and Mobility Officer (the squadron was redesignated as the 28th Air Transport Squadron and assigned to the Military Airlift Command in 1962). In August 1963 General Durham transferred to the 1622nd Support Squadron at Paris, where he performed duties as an Airlift Command Post Controller until the Squadron was disbanded in June 1964. From July 1964 through September 1966, he was assigned to the 322nd Air Division at Chateauroux Air Station in France as a Plans Officer in the Directorate of Plans and Programs.

Returning to the United States in October 1966, he served at Headquarters of Military Airlift Command at Scott Air Force Base, Illinois, then Chief of Advanced Programming and Policy Division at the Office of the Deputy Chief of Staff for Plans until December 1968. General Durham was assigned to Headquarters of the United States Air Force in Washington, D.C., in the Directorate of Plans, Office of the Deputy Chief of Staff for Plans and Operations, in January 1969. During this tour of duty, he served as a Plans Action Officer and Assistant Deputy Director for Plans and Policy for Joint Chiefs of Staff matters.

From June 1973 to June 1974, he was assigned to the 314th Air Division at Osan Air Base, South Korea, as Director of Plans and Programs for United States Air Forces, Korea. He then returned to the United States to attend the National War College. General Durham transferred to McGuire Air Force Base, New Jersey, in August 1975, as Deputy Base Commander and became Base Commander in February 1976. He commanded the 1606th Air Base Wing at Kirtland Air Force Base, New Mexico, from July 1977 to February 1979, when he transferred to Dover Air Force Base, Delaware, as Commander of the 436th Military Airlift Wing, the only all–C-5 Wing in the Air Force.

In February 1980 the general assumed command of the 76th Military Airlift Division at Andrews Air Force Base in Maryland. In February 1982 he was assigned as vice commander of Military Traffic Management Command in Washington, D.C. General Durham became the Director of Plans, Programs, and Policy (J-5) and Inspector General of United States Readiness Command at MacDill Air Force Base, Florida, in March 1984. He was assigned as Director of Deployment at the Joint Deployment Agency at MacDill Air Force Base in April 1985. In June 1987 he was assigned as Director of Deployment at United States Transportation Command at MacDill Air Force Base. He was appointed to Major General on June 1, 1984, with a date of rank September 1, 1980.

The general is a command pilot with more than 6,000 flying hours. His military decorations and awards include the Defense Superior Service Medal, Legion of Merit (with two oak leaf clusters), Meritorious Service Medal (with oak leaf cluster), Air Force Commendation Medal (with oak leaf cluster), and Air Force Outstanding Unit Award (with three oak leaf clusters).

Dyer, Michael A.

COLONEL—MARINES

Dyer is a native of Trinidad and Tobago in the West Indies. In June 1978, he graduated from the United States Naval Academy with a Bachelor of Science degree, was commissioned a Second Lieutenant and received orders to the Basic School (TBS) at Quantico, Virginia. He completed flight training at Pensacola, Florida, in December 1980.

His key military assignments include serving as Commander of Marine Wing Headquarters Squadron, 1st Marine Air Wing in June 1998. He was assigned to Marine Air Group 36 as Executive Officer in October 1999; he was transferred to Headquarters NORAD at Peterson Air Force Base in June 2000 and was promoted to Colonel on April 1, 2001. While at HQ NORAD, he served as the Deputy Chief of Readiness Division and Battle Staff Director during Operation Noble Eagle; he was assigned to Okinawa as the Inspector, Marine Corps Bases Japan and Marine Corps Base, Camp Smedley D. Butler in June 2002. In June 2002, Dyer was ordered to Marine Corps Air Station Iwakuni, Japan, as Commanding Officer.

Ebbesen, Samuel Emanuel

LIEUTENANT GENERAL—ARMY

Born in Saint Croix, Virgin Islands, Ebbesen received a Bachelor of Science in Political Science from the City College of New York. He received a master's degree in Public Administration from Auburn University.

Ebbesen enlisted in the Army in September 1961, and, until March 1962, he was a platoon leader in Company D, 1st Training Regiment, Fort Dix, New Jersey. He went on to serve the Army in numerous assignments. In March 1963 he was the Commander of Company F, 1st Training Regiment, Fort Dix, New Jersey; in July 1965, Commander of Headquarters Company, 1st Battalion, 15th Infantry, 3rd Infantry Division, United States Army in Europe.

From July 1966 to November 1967, he was assigned as an Infantry Training Advisor, at the School and Training Detachment, Training Directorate, at the United States Military Assistance Command in Vietnam. In January 1968, he was ordered to attend the Infantry Officer Advanced Course at the United States Army Infantry Center at Fort Benning, Georgia. From September 1968 to July 1969, he served as Chief of the Operations Branch, Plans and Operations Division,

with the Directorate of Operations and Training at the United States Army Infantry Center at Fort Benning.

From July 1969 to November 1969, he served as Headquarters Commandant for the 4th Infantry Division, United States Army in Vietnam. From November 1969 to April 1970, he served as the Battalion S-3 (Operations), for the 1st Battalion, 8th Infantry Brigade, 4th Infantry Division, United States Army in Vietnam. From April 1970 to August 1970, he was assigned as District Senior Advisor, Advisor Team 15, XXIV Corps, United States Military Assistance Command in Vietnam. From August 1970 to May 1971, he was assigned as a Staff Officer in the Office of the Study Coordinator, Office of the Deputy Chief of Staff for Operations and Plans, United States Army Combat Development Command, at Fort Belvoir, Virginia. In August 1971, he was a student at the Command and General Staff College at Fort Leavenworth, Kansas; in July 1977, he served as Commander of the 2nd Battalion, 32nd Infantry, 7th Infantry Division, Fort Ord, California. He was promoted to Colonel on September 1, 1982.

From May 1983 to August 1985, he served as the Commander of the 1st Brigade, 101st Airborne Division (Air Assault), at Fort Campbell, Kentucky. From August 1985 to October, 1986, he served as Chief of Staff for I Corps at Fort Lewis, in Washington. From October 1986 to July 1988, he was assigned as Deputy Chief, Legislative Liaison, Office of the Chief of Legislative Liaison, United States Army, in Washington, D.C. He was promoted to Brigadier General on January 1, 1988.

From July 1988 to April 1990, Ebbesen was assigned as Assistant Division Commander with the 6th Infantry Division at Fort Wainwright, Alaska. From April 1990 to July 1992, he served as the Commanding General for the 6th Infantry Division (Light) at Fort Wainwright. He was promoted to Major General on January 1, 1991.

In July 1992, he was selected to serve as the Commanding General of the Second United States Army at Fort Gillem, Georgia. He was appointed Lieutenant General on August 3, 1992.

He has received numerous medals and badges, including the Distinguished Service Medal; the Legion of Merit (with three oak leaf clusters); Bronze Star (with "V" device and two oak leaf clusters); the Meritorious Service Medal (with oak leaf cluster); the Air Medal; the Army Commendation Medal (with two oak leaf clusters); Combat Infantryman Badge; Parachutist Badge; Air Assault Badge; and the Army Staff Identification Badge.

Edmonds, Albert J.

LIEUTENANT GENERAL—AIR FORCE

Born in Columbus, Georgia, Edmonds married the former Jacquelyn Y. McDaniel of Biloxi, Mississippi. They have three daughters, Gia, Sheri, and Alicia. He was graduated from Spencer High School in Columbus in 1960, earned a Bachelor of Science degree in Chemistry from Morris Brown College in Atlanta in 1964 and received a Master of Arts degree in Counseling Psychology from Hampton Institute in 1969. He was graduated from Air War College as a distinguished graduate in 1980 and completed the National Security program for Senior Officials at Harvard University in 1987.

He entered the Air Force in August 1964 and was commissioned upon graduation from Officer Training School, at Lackland Air Force Base, Texas, in November 1964. After completing the basic communications-electronics course at Keesler Air Force Base, Mississippi, in February 1966, Edmonds was assigned as a

data systems officer to Tactical Communications Area, Langley Air Force Base, Virginia. In February 1969, he was assigned to Pacific Communications Area at Hickam Air Force Base, Hawaii. While there, he served successively as an Inspection Team Chief, Office of the Inspector General, contributing editor, Project Corona Harvest, and director of emergency mission support.

He later served as Chief of Operations of the 2083rd Communications Squadron (Provisional) at Takhli Royal Thai Air Force Base, Thailand. He was assigned to Air Force Headquarters in May 1973 as an action officer in the Directorate of Command, Control, and Communications, responsible for Managing Air Communications Programs in the continental United States, Alaska, Canada, South America, Greenland, and Iceland.

In June 1975 Edmonds was assigned to the Defense Communications Agency and headed the Commercial Communications Policy office, responsible for establishing Department of Defense policies for the acquisition of long-line communications and overseeing the procurement activities of the Defense Commercial Communications Office. Edmonds was assigned to Anderson Air Force Base on Guam in 1977, as Director of Communications-Electronics for Strategic Air Command's 3rd Air Division and as commander of the 27th Communications Squadron. He was promoted to Colonel on February 1, 1980.

After completing Air War College in June 1980, he returned to Air Force Headquarters as Chief of the Joint Matters Group, Directorate of Command, Control and Telecommunications, Office of the Deputy Chief of Staff, Plans and Operations. From June 1, 1983, to June 14, 1983, he served as Director of Plans and Programs for the Assistant Chief of Staff for Information Systems. In June 1983 he was assigned to Headquarters, Tactical Air Command, Langley Air Force Base, as assistant Deputy Chief of Staff Communications and Electronics and Vice Commander, Tactical Communications Division. In January 1985, he was assigned as the Deputy Chief of Staff for Communications and Computer Systems, Tactical Air Command Headquarters, and Commander, Tactical Communications Division, Air Force Communications Command at Langley Air Force Base. He was promoted to Brigadier General on July 1, 1988.

In July 1988, he was assigned as the Director of Command and Control, Communications and Computer Systems Directorate, with the United States Central Command, at MacDill Air Force Base, Florida. From May 1989 to November 1990, he was assigned as the Assistant Chief of Staff of Systems for Command, Control, Communications and Computers, at Air Force Headquarters, Washington, D.C. From November 1990 to August 1991, he served as the Assistant Deputy Chief of Staff for Command, Control, Communications and Computers, at Headquarters of the United States Air Force, in Washington, D.C. He was promoted to Major General on February 1, 1991.

From September 1991 to July 1994, he served as

Director for Command, Control, Communications, and Computer Systems Directorate (J6), the Joint Staff, in Washington, D.C. He was promoted to Lieutenant General on March 26, 1993. In July 1994, he was selected to serve as Director of the Defense Information Systems Agency and Manager at the National Communications System, in Arlington, Virginia.

His military awards and decorations include the Defense Distinguished Service Medal; the Defense Superior Service Medal; the Legion of Merit; Meritorious Service Medal (with three oak leaf clusters); the Air Force Commendation Medal (with three oak leaf clusters); the Joint Staff Identification Badge; and the Air Force Staff Identification Badge.

Edmonds, Ralph
COMMAND SERGEANT MAJOR—ARMY

Command Sergeant Major Ralph Edmonds began his military service on September 9, 1973, and attended Basic Combat Training at For Knox, Kentucky, and Advanced Individual Training at Fort Sill, Oklahoma. His military education includes the First Sergeant Course; the Air Assault Course; Master Physical Fitness School; and the Command Sergeant Major Course.

From 2000 to 2002, he served as the Command Sergeant Major for the 7th Signal Brigade in Mannheim, Germany, and from 1996 to 2000, he was assigned as the Command Sergeant Major for the 72nd Signal Battalion in Linderhofe, Germany.

On April 1, 2002, he was selected to serve as the Command Sergeant of the National Capital Region-DOIM at Fort Belvoir, Virginia.

Edwards, Kirk
CHIEF WARRANT OFFICER—COAST GUARD

Kirk Edwards is a native of Madera, California. Despite his family's financial struggles and the nation's struggle with race, he was able to pursue academics in his chosen vocation through work-study (working as much as 40 hours a week), a small scholarship in high school, grants and loans. He even got some cash by entering and winning a clarinet competition in college. Hard work and perseverance finally paid off when he earned a Bachelor's Degree in Music from California State University–Northridge in 1980, after transferring from Fresno City College.

After college he joined the United States Coast Guard, and in 1997 he was finally accepted in the Coast Guard band. The next year, he completed his Masters Degree in Music at the University of Connecticut.

At the height of his career in the Coast Guard Band, the 6-foot 4-inch Edwards was primarily a clarinetist, but also played the saxophone and the flute. As an arranger and composer, his piece, "Trilogy to Martin L. King," was published by Cimarron Music and Production in Dallas.

In 2000, he was select to serve as Director of the Coast Guard Academy Cadet Bands. Chief Edwards leads the NiteCaps Jazz Band, Concert Band, the Regimental Band, and the Windjammers Drum and Bugle Corps. He is also the Director and Founder of the Academy Gospel Choir. In addition, he is also the Chairman of the Coast Guard Academy Human Relations Council, a position where he does not have to perform musically.

He served in the Coast Guard nineteen years before he decided to become an advisor, and instructor and a role model for cadets. In March 2005, in conjunction with the USO, he took the band on a 10-day whirlwind tour to entertain troops stationed in Italy.

Eichelberger, Claude J.
COLONEL—AIR FORCE

Born in Columbia, South Carolina, Eichelberger graduated from C. A. Johnson Preparatory Academy in 1966, and then enlisted in the United States Army. He served four years with one tour in Germany and one tour in Vietnam. Upon discharge from active duty, he enrolled in the University of South Carolina and graduated in 1974 with a bachelor's degree in Psychology. He has also earned a bachelor's degree in Finance from the University of South Carolina, and received a Master of Arts in Computer Resources and Information Management.

In 1972, he joined the South Carolina Air National Guard as a member of the 240th Combat Communications Squadron. He was selected to attend the Academy of Military Science and was subsequently commissioned as a Second Lieutenant, becoming the first black person to be commissioned in the South Carolina Air National Guard. He is a graduate of the Defense Equal Opportunity Management Institute; Squadron Officer School; Air Command and Staff College; and Air War College.

He has served in a variety of assignments including serving as Commander of the 169th Mission Support Flight; Commander of the 169th Support Group; and as the Director of Support at Headquarters South Carolina Air National Guard, at McEntire Air National Guard Station at Eastover, South Carolina.

Elam, Otis J.
COLONEL—ARMY

Born in Charlotte County, Virginia, Elam is married to the former Shirley Jones of Portsmouth, Virginia, and has two children, Tonya and Jeronica. He entered the Army through the Reserve Officer's Training Corps (ROTC) at Norfolk State University where he was commissioned a second lieutenant. While at

Norfolk State University, he earned a Bachelor of Science degree in Industrial Education. Additionally, he served as president of the Industrial Education Club, commanded the Ranger Detachment, and commanded a ROTC Battalion. He has also earned Master of Science degrees in Counseling and Public Administration, and a doctorate in Administration and Management. After being commissioned he was assigned to the 3rd Brigade (Training) at Fort Ord, California. Subsequently, he served as the Deputy Commandant with the 25th Infantry Division, Vietnam; and Training Officer, Operations Officer (S-3), Executive Officer, and Commander with the 80th Division (Training), at Fort Belvoir, Virginia. Additionally, he served as Recruiting and Retention Officer with the 85th Division in Chicago, Illinois; Chief of Force Structure with the 310th Theater Army Area Command (TAACOM), Fort Belvoir, Virginia; and Chief of a Mobilization Branch with the Department of Army (Pentagon). In 1988, he attended the Army War College at Carlisle, Pennsylvania. In 1989, Colonel Elam returned to the Pentagon and was assigned as the Assistant Director for Mobilization Planning in the Office of the Assistant Secretary of Defense for Force Management and Personnel. In January 1990, he was assigned to the Education Directorate as Associate Director for Education Policy. In November 1990, he was assigned as the Associate Director for Veterans and Service Members Educational Benefits and the Junior ROTC program. In September 1992, Colonel Elam was transferred and assigned as the Director of the Office of Personnel Management Directorate at the Army Reserve Personnel Center at St. Louis, Missouri. In August 1994, he became the Chief of Staff and in July 1995 became Deputy Commander. He is a graduate of the Basic and Advanced Infantry Schools at Fort Benning, Georgia; the Command and General Staff College at Fort Leavenworth, Kansas; and the Army War College at Carlisle, Pennsylvania. His military awards and decorations include the Bronze Star (with oak leaf cluster); Defense Meritorious Service Medal; Meritorious Service Medal (with oak leaf cluster); Army Commendation Medal (with oak leaf cluster); Army Achievement Medal; National Defense Service Medal (with two bronze stars); Vietnam Service Medal; Republic of Vietnam Campaign Medal (with 60 Device); Combat Infantryman's Badge; Office of the Secretary of Defense Staff Badge; and Department of Army Staff Badge.

Elders, M. Jocelyn
VICE ADMIRAL—SURGEON GENERAL

She was born Minnie Lee Jones in Schaal, Arkansas on August 13, 1933, and is the daughter of Curtis L. Jones and Haller Reed Jones. She married Oliver B. Elder, Jr. and they have two children, Eric D. and Kevin M. In college, she changed her name to Minnie Joycelyn Lee (later using just Joycelyn). In 1952, she received her Bachelor of Arts degree in Biology from Philander Smith College in Little Rock, Arkansas. After working as a nurse's aid in a Veterans Administration

hospital in Milwaukee, she joined the Army in May, 1953, and was commissioned a Second Lieutenant. She was assigned to Brooke Army Medical Center, where she was trained as a Physical Therapist. She then attended the University of Arkansas Medical School, where she obtained her Medical Doctor degree in 1960. After completing an internship at the University of Minnesota Hospital and a residency in pediatrics at the University of Arkansas Medical Center, She earned a Masters of Science degree in Biochemistry in 1967. She worked as an as Assistant Professor in Pediatrics at the University of Arkansas Medical Center in 1967. She was promoted to associate professor in 1971 and professor in 1976. In 1987, she was appointed Director of the Arkansas Department of Health by then Governor Bill Clinton. In 1992, she was elected President of the Association of State and Territorial Health Officers. On September 8, 1993, President Bill Clinton appointed her Surgeon General of the United States. She became the first black Surgeon General in history. The Surgeon General carries the Navy rank of Vice Admiral as a member of the Uniformed Public Health Service.

Ellis, Larry Rudell
GENERAL—ARMY

A native of Cambridge, Maryland, Ellis was commissioned a second lieutenant on February 5, 1969,

after graduating from Morgan State University with a Bachelor of Science degree and completing the ROTC program. He earned a Masters of Science degree in Physical Education from Indiana University in 1975. His military education includes the Infantry Officer Basic (1969) and Advanced (1974) courses; Armed Forces Staff College (1979); and the United States Army War College (1986).

His military career began in February 1969 as a student in the Infantry Officer Basic Course at Fort Benning, Georgia, as a second lieutenant. He has held a wide variety of important command and staff positions. He was Assistant Secretary of the General Staff, Command group, United States Army Europe and Seventh Army, Germany; Deputy Chief of Staff for Operations and Plans; Assistant Deputy Chief of Staff for Personnel, Headquarters of the Department of the Army; Assistant Chief of Staff, C3/J3/G3, United Nations Command/Combined Forces Command/United States Forces Korea/Eighth United States Army, Korea; Deputy Director for Strategic Planning and Policy, Headquarters of United States Pacific Command, Hawaii; Deputy Director for Military Personnel Management, Office of the Deputy Chief of Staff for Personnel, Headquarters of the Department of the Army; Force Structure Analyst and Chief, Manpower and Force Structure Division, Program Analysis and Evaluation Directorate, Office of the Chief of Staff, Headquarters of the Department of the Army; Staff Officer, Headquarters, United States Army Europe, Germany; Staff and Faculty, United Military Academy, West Point; Battalion Staff Officer, 101st Airborne Division, Fort Bragg, North Carolina.

With more than 33 years of Army service, General Ellis has served in the United States, Vietnam, Germany, South Korea, and Bosnia and Herzegovina. His command assignments includes: 1st Armored Division,

Germany; Multinational Division (North), Bosnia and Herzegovina; Assistant Division Commander 2nd Infantry Division, South Korea; Brigade Commander 3rd Infantry Division, Germany; Battalion Commander, 5th Infantry Division, Fort Polk, Louisiana; Company Commander, 101st Airborne Division, Vietnam; and 82nd Airborne Division, Fort Bragg, North Carolina.

General Ellis assumed Command of the United States Army Forces Command on November 19, 2001, following his assignment as the Deputy Chief of Staff for Operations and Plans at the Department of the Army. He is only the second black General to serve as the Commander of Forces Command, which directs operations and training for all active and Reserve troop units in the Continental United States as well as all Army National Guard units in the 48 continental states, Alaska, Puerto Rico and the Virgin Islands. General Colin Powell was the first black General to hold this position.

He was promoted to Brigadier General on July 1, 1992; promoted to Major General on August 1, 1995; promoted to Lieutenant General on August 6, 1999; and promoted to General on November 19, 2001. He is the fourth black four star General ever selected in the United States Army. In March 2003, he was the only black four star general in the United States Army, and only one of two black four star generals on active duty in the United States Military. General Lester L. Lyles of the United States Air Force was the other black four star general on active duty at this time. Ellis retired from the military on July 1, 2004.

General Ellis' awards and decorations include the Defense Distinguished Service Medal; the Army Distinguished Service Medal; the Defense Superior Service Medal; the Legion of Merit (with two oak leaf clusters); the Bronze Star; the Meritorious Service Medal (with two oak leaf clusters); the Air Medal; the Army Commendation Medal (with oak leaf cluster); the National Defense Service Medal (with three stars); the Armed Forces Expeditionary Medal; the Vietnam Service Medal (with three stars); the Armed Forces Medal; the Vietnam Cross of Gallantry/Palm; the Korean Cheonsu Medal; the German Armed Forces Honor Cross (Gold); the NATO Medal; the Combat Infantryman Badge; the Senior Parachutist Badge; the Office of Secretary of Defense Staff Identification Badge; the Joint Chiefs of Staff Identification Badge; and the Army General Staff Identification Badge.

Ellis, Ronnie T.
COLONEL—ARMY

Ellis is a native of Montgomery, Alabama and was commissioned into the Regular Army as a ROTC Distinguished Military Graduate from the University of Alabama in 1980, where he received a Bachelor of Science degree in Commercial Transportation. He also earned a Master of Public Administration degree from the University of Oklahoma in 1997.

His military education includes Transportation Officer Basic Course; Transportation Officer Advanced Course; United States Army Command and General Staff College; the Armed Forces Staff College Joint Professional Military Education Phase II, and the United States Army War College.

He has served in a wide variety of command and staff assignments, including Platoon Leader and Transportation Analyst, Company A, 203rd Military Intelligence Battalion, Aberdeen Proving Ground, Maryland; Platoon Leader and Executive Officer, 46th Transportation Company, Camp Carroll, South Korea; Aide-de-Camp to the Commanding General, 19th Support Command, Camp Henry, South Korea; Commander of the 365th Transportation Company, Fort McClellan, Alabama; Training With Industry Program with AMTRAK, Washington, D.C.; Transportation Management Officer, Military Surface Deployment and Distribution Command, Falls Church, Virginia; Operations and Executive Officer in the 28th Transportation Battalion, Mannheim, Germany; Logistics Staff Officer, Office of the Deputy Chief of Staff for Logistics, United States Army Europe, Heidelberg, Germany; Transportation Staff Officer, J3/J4 United States Strategic Command, Offutt Air Force Base, Nebraska; Congressional Affairs Contact Officer to the Deputy Chief of Staff for Logistics, Department of the Army, Washington, D.C.; Commander, 58th Transportation Battalion (AIT), Fort Leonard Wood, Missouri; and Legislative Liaison Officer in the Office of Chief of Legislative Liaison, Department of the Army, Washington, D.C. In January 2005, he was serving as the Garrison Commander of Fort Eustis and the United States Army Transportation Center.

Ellis, Trent O.
COMMAND SERGEANT MAJOR—ARMY

He was born in Fredericksburg, Virginia. After graduating from high school, he enlisted in the Army at

Fort Jackson, South Carolina, and underwent Advanced Individual Training at Fort Lee, Virginia.

His military education includes all the Noncommissioned Officer Education System Courses; the First Sergeants Course; the United States Army Sergeants Major Academy; Battalion Staff NCO Course; Airborne School; Standard Property Book System; and the Support Operations Course.

He earned an Associate of Science degree in Management from Harold Washington College and a Bachelor of Science degree in Liberal Arts from Excelsior College.

His past military assignments include serving as Logistics Sergeant Major for the Armed Forces Inaugural Committee (54th Presidential Inauguration); DMMC Sergeant Major of the 2nd Infantry Division; Logistics NCO of the 3rd United States Infantry Regiment (The Old Guard) Fort Myer, Virginia; and First Sergeant of C Company Support Battalion at Fort Bragg, North Carolina.

English, Mark A.
LIEUTENANT COLONEL—ARMY

English enlisted into the United States Army at the age of 17 and completed Basic Combat Training at Fort Dix, New Jersey, in 1972. He graduated from the United States Military Academy Preparatory School in June 1973. Upon graduation from the United States Military Academy in June 1978, he was commissioned as an Air Defense Artillery Officer for I Corps.

His education includes the Basic and Advanced Air Defense Artillery Courses at Fort Bliss, Texas; the Jordanian Armed Forces Infantry Officer Advanced Course at Amman, Jordan; the United States Army Command and General Staff College; and the National War College. He earned his master's degree in Civil Government from Campbell University and a Ph.D. in Curriculum Instruction and Foreign Language Education at the University of Texas at Austin.

As a Middle East Foreign Area Officer fluent in Arabic, he was selected to return to West Point as an Assistant Professor in the Department of Foreign Languages in 1988. From 1992–1994, he served as the Chief of Army Programs, Office of Military Cooperation, United State Embassy, Oman and was the West Point Visiting Professor at the National War College 1997–1998, where he conducted a seminar on National Security Policy. In 1998, he returned to West Point as an Associate Professor of Arabic and Middle East Studies. In 2002, he was selected as a United States Fulbright Scholar to Jordan were he conducted research on the education of women in Arab societies and served as a visiting Professor of English and Linguistics at the University of Jordan. On June 6, 2003, he became the 24th Commandant of the United States Military Academy Preparatory School.

English, Norman E.
COMMAND SERGEANT MAJOR—ARMY

A native of Sumter, South Carolina, English completed Basic Combat Training and Advanced Individual Training at Fort Knox, Kentucky. His military and civilian education includes all the Noncommissioned Officer Education System Courses; Bradley Master Gunner Course; Air Assault Course; Army Pathfinder Course; First Sergeant Course; and the United States Army Sergeants Major Academy (class 51). He has an associate's degree from Central Texas College and a Bachelor of Science degree from the University of Louisville.

He served in every leadership position including Scout Track Commander, Scout Squad Leader; Scout Section Sergeant; Scout Platoon Sergeant; First Sergeant; Chief Instructor; and Command Sergeant Major, Task Force 1-35th ARMOR.

Epps, Marry A.
BRIGADIER GENERAL—AIR FORCE

Epps' military career begin by enlisting in the Connecticut Air National Guard in June 1976, and she received a commission as a first lieutenant on February 26, 1977. Her education includes: a Bachelor of Science degree in Human Services from Hampshire College in Manchester, New Hampshire in 1994. She also graduated from the Air War College, Maxwell Air Force Base, in Alabama.

From February 1977 to July 1984, she was assigned as a Clinical Nurse with the 103rd Tactical Clinic at East Granby, Connecticut. In July 1984, she was assigned as a Medical Surgical Nurse with the 103rd Tactical Clinic at East Granby. From August 1989 to September 1990, she served as Chief of Nursing Services in the 103rd Tactical Clinic at East Granby. In September 1990, she assumed the duties of Commander of the 103rd Medical Squadron, 103rd Tactical Clinic, again

at East Granby. While in this assignment, she was promoted to Colonel on December 23, 1994. She became the first African American and the first female to achieve this rank in the history of the Connecticut Air National Guard. From September 1997 to March 2001, she served as Advisor to the Defense Equal Opportunity Management Institute at Patrick Air Force Base, Florida.

On March 30, 2001, she was promoted to Brigadier General, and selected to serve as the Assistant Adjutant General-Air, who also serves as the Commander of the Connecticut Air National Guard. She is responsible for formulating, developing, and coordinating all policies, plans, and programs affecting over 1,100 members of the Connecticut Air National Guard and is tasked with ensuring their ability to respond to peacetime contingencies while maintaining readiness to accomplish their war missions.

Her military awards and decorations include the Defense Superior Service Medal; the Air Force Meritorious Service Medal (with device); Air Force Commendation Medal; Air Force Achievement Medal; Air Force Outstanding Unit Award (with two devices); National Defense Service Medal; Air Force Reserve Medal (with two devices); Air Force Longevity Service Award (with four devices); Air Force Training Ribbon; State of Connecticut Medal of Merit; and State of Connecticut Long Service Medal (with twenty year device).

Estrada, John L.

SERGEANT MAJOR OF THE MARINE CORPS—MARINES

He enlisted on September 5, 1973 and attended recruit training at Marine Corps Recruit Depot at Parris Island, South Carolina. After completing F-4 aircraft maintenance schools at Naval Air Station, Memphis, Tennessee and Marine Corps Air Station, Cherry Point,

North Carolina, Private First Class Estrada was assigned to Marine Fighter Attack Squadron 451 at MCAS Beaufort, South Carolina in March 1974.

In December 1974, Lance Corporal Estrada was transferred to Marine Fighter Attack Squadron 232, 1st Marine Aircraft Wing, in Iwakuni, Japan. He was meritoriously promoted to Corporal in March 1975. In February 1976, Sergeant Estrada served with Marine Fighter Attack Training Squadron 101 at MCAS Yuma, Arizona. In September 1977, he transferred to Marine Fighter Attack Squadron 314 at MCAS El Toro, California. Reassigned to Marine Fighter Attack Squadron 323 in December 1978, he deployed with the squadron in November 1979 for 7 months aboard the aircraft carrier USS *Coral Sea* to the Western Pacific and Arabian Gulf. In June 1980, Staff Sergeant Estrada transferred to Marine Reserve Fighter Attack Squadron 321, Marine Aircraft Group 41, Detachment "A" at Andrews AFB, Maryland.

In August 1982, Staff Sergeant Estrada was ordered to Drill Instructor Duty at Marine Corps Recruit Depot, San Diego, California, where he served with Kilo Company, 3rd Recruit Training Battalion. He was meritoriously promoted to Gunnery Sergeant in January 1984. In October, 1984, Gunnery Sergeant Estrada returned to MCAS Beaufort for duty with Marine Fighter Attack Squadron 251 as the Noncommissioned Officer in Charge of the Airframes Division. In November 1985, he was reassigned to Marine Fighter Attack Squadron 451 and deployed to the Western Pacific from January to July 1986 under the Unit Deployment Program. From January to March 1987, Gunnery Sergeant Estrada attended aircraft maintenance schools at Naval Air Stations Cecil Field and Jacksonville, Florida retraining as an FA-18 Hydraulic/Structural Mechanic.

In October 1987, Gunnery Sergeant Estrada returned to Drill Instructor duty, this time at MCRD Parris Island. He served as Series Chief Drill Instructor with India Company, 3rd Recruit Training Battalion and subsequently as Standing Operations Procedures Instructor and Drill Master at Drill Instructor School until his promotion to First Sergeant in October 1990.

From December 1990 to March 1995, First Sergeant Estrada served as First Sergeant for Intelligence Company, 3rd Surveillance Reconnaissance and Intelligence Group, at Camp Hansen, Okinawa, Japan; Marine Security Force Company at Norfolk, Virginia; Electronics Maintenance Company, 1st Maintenance Battalion, 1st Force Service Support Group at Camp Pendleton, California; and Alpha Company, 1st Company, 1st Light Armored Reconnaissance Battalion, 1st Force Service Support Group at Camp Pendleton; and Alpha Company, 1st Light Armored Reconnaissance Battalion, 1st Marine Division at Camp Pendleton.

From March 1995 to May 1998, Sergeant Major Estrada served as Sergeant Major for 2nd Battalion, 1st Marines, BLT 2/1, 1st Marine Division, Camp Pendleton; and deployed with the 11th Marine Expeditionary Unit (SOC) and 15th Marine Expeditionary Unit (SOC) to the Western Pacific and the Arabian Gulf.

In May, 1998, Sergeant Major Estrada assumed the duties as Sergeant Major for Recruiting Station Sacramento, California in the 12th Marine Corps District, Western Recruiting Region. From April 2000 to October 2001, Sergeant Major Estrada was assigned as Sergeant Major, Recruit Training Regiment, MCRD Parris Island, South Carolina.

From December 2001 to May 2003, Sergeant Major Estrada served as the Sergeant Major, 3rd Marine Aircraft Wing. During this assignment, he was forward deployed and participated in Operation Southern Watch and Operation Iraqi Freedom.

Sergeant Major Estrada assumed his current post as the 15th Sergeant Major of the Marine Corps on 26 June 2003.

His personal awards include the Meritorious Service Medal with three gold stars, the Joint Service Achievement Medal, the Navy and Marine Corps Commendation Medal and the Navy and Marine Corps Achievement Medal.

Etienne, Luis

COMMAND SERGEANT MAJOR—ARMY

Etienne was born in Panama City in the Republic of Panama. He enlisted in the United States Army in January 1976. He received his Basic Combat Training at Fort Knox, Kentucky, and Advanced Individual Training as a Medical Specialist at Fort Sam Houston, Texas. He holds an associate's degree in General Studies from the Northwestern States University at Natchitoches, Louisiana. His military education includes the Noncommissioned Officers Leadership Courses; the First Sergeants Course; and the United States Army Sergeants Major Academy.

He has served in a variety of positions to include serving as Medical Corpsman; Senior Medic; Squad Leader; Section Sergeant; NCOIC Health Clinic; NCOIC Primary Care Clinic; Platoon Sergeant; First Sergeant; Senior Medical NCO; Senior Instructor; Troop Command Sergeant Major; and Battalion Command Sergeant Major.

Etienne, R. M.

COMMAND MASTER CHIEF—NAVY

He was born in London, England, and grew up in New York City. After graduating from high school, he enlisted in the United States Navy in September 1979. He completed Recruit Training in Great Lakes, Illinois, subsequently attending Aviation Machinist Mate "A" School in Memphis, Tennessee.

His first command was Naval Weapons Center China Lake, California. He worked and qualified as plane captain on both A-4 and F/A-18 Aircraft. His next assignment was Fleet Air Reconnaissance Squadron One (VQ-1) at Agana, Guam. During this tour he advanced to Third and Second Class Petty Officer. His next tour of duty was as instructor with Tactical Electronic Warfare Squadron Three (VAQ-33) at Key West, Florida.

In September 1991, he reported to Helicopter Anti-Submarine Squadron Light Four Eight, (HSL-48) at Mayport, Florida. He advanced to First Class Petty Officer and was certified as Collateral Duty Inspector on the SH-60B aircraft. In February 1996, he transferred to the Consolidated Brig in Charleston, South Carolina, and advanced to Chief Petty Officer. In March 1999, he transferred to Naval Air Station, Keflavik, Iceland, serving as Air Operations Leading Chief and advanced to Senior Chief Petty Officer. In November 2001, he reported as the Quality Assurance Supervisor to VAQ-136 in Atsugi, Japan. In March 2002, he advanced to Master Chief Petty Officer and was selected into the Command Master Chief Program. Master Chief Etienne attended the United States Navy Senior Enlisted Academy, Class 107, serving as Class President and graduating with military distinction.

Eubanks, Daniel A.

COMMAND SERGEANT MAJOR—ARMY

He is a native of Thomson, Georgia, and entered the United States Army after graduating from high school in 1981. He attended Basic Recruit Training and Advanced Individual Training at Fort Leonard Wood, Missouri.

His military education includes all the Non-Commissioned Officer Education System Courses; Drill Sergeant School; the First Sergeant Course; the United States Army Sergeant Major Academy; and the Command Sergeant Major Course.

His leadership assignments include serving as Motor Sergeant and Platoon Sergeant for the 188th Medical Detachment in Bamberg, Germany; as Drill Sergeant and Senior Drill Sergeant at Fort Knox, Kentucky; Transportation Motor Pool Non-Commissioned Officer

He moved to New York City in 1903 to pursue a musical career. Work as a violinist was scarce, so he turned to the piano and found work in several cabarets. He helped found an African American fraternity known as "the Frogs" and, in 1910, established the Clef Club, the first African American music union and booking agency.

On May 2, 1912, Europe' Clef Club Orchestra became the first African American band and the first jazz band to play in New York City's famous Carnegie Hall. The orchestra's debut there was so well received that it was booked for two more engagements in 1913 and 1914.

He enlisted as a private in the 15th Infantry, a black New York National Guard Unit, on September 18, 1916. Europe became one of the few African Americans of the day to attend officers' training and was commissioned a Second Lieutenant. The 15th Infantry was later redesignated the 369th Infantry, which the French nicknamed "The Harlem Hellfighters" after the black soldiers showed their mettle in combat.

His regimental commander, Colonel William Hayward, asked the new lieutenant to organize "the best damn brass band in the United States Army." Europe recruited musicians from Harlem and reportedly put together one of the finest military bands that ever existed. He even recruited woodwind players from Puerto Rico because there weren't enough in Harlem. He also recruited singers, comedians, dancers and others who could entertain troops. He recruited the best drum major he could find, Harlem dancer Bill "Bojangles" Robinson.

When the 369th and its band arrived in France, they were assigned to the 16th "Le Gallais" Division of the Fourth French Army because white United States Army units refused to fight alongside them. Trained to command a Machine Gun Company, Europe learned to fire French machine guns and became the first american officer and first African American to lead troops in battle during the war.

The Harlem Hellfighters would serve 191 days in combat, longer than any other United States unit, and reputedly never relinquished an inch of ground. The men earned 170 French Croix de Guerres for bravery. Europe earned the Purple Heart Medal, after he was shot during a nighttime raid against the Germans. While recuperating in a French hospital, he penned the song "One Patrol in No Man's Land."

Europe and his musicians were ordered to the rear in August 1918 to entertain thousands of soldiers in camps and hospitals. They also performed for high-ranking military and civilian officials and for French citizens in cities across France. After Germany surrendered, the Hellfighters Band became popular performing throughout Europe. When the Regiment returned home in the spring of 1919, it paraded up New York's 5th Avenue to Harlem led by the band playing its raggedy tunes to the delight of more than a million spectators.

Europe was preparing for a show at Mechanics Hall in Boston when he was killed on May 13, 1919, by one of his band members, a deranged drummer named

in Charge and Transportation Division Non-Commissioned Officer in Charge at Camp Red Cloud, South Korea; Motor Sergeant for 2/1 Air Defense Artillery Battalion at Fort Bliss, Texas; First Sergeant for Headquarters and Headquarters Battery, 11th Air Defense Artillery Brigade, at Fort Bliss; Non-Commissioned Officer in charge in the Inspector General Office, Inspection Branch, at Fort Bliss; Battalion Motor Sergeant for the 304th Signal Battalion in South Korea; Installation First Sergeant for Camp Kyle and 61st Maintenance Company; First Sergeant of the 494th Transportation Company at Fort Campbell, Kentucky; Operation Sergeant Major and Division Rear Sergeant Major for the 1st Armored Division Support Command (DISCOM) in Wiesbaden, Germany; and Command Sergeant Major, 10th Forward Support Battalion, 10th Division Support Command, at Fort Drum, New York. Eubanks deployed to Afghanistan in support of Operation Enduring Freedom and was selected as the Command Sergeant Major for the 10th Support Brigade, 10th Mountain Division (LI), at Fort Drum.

Europe, James Reese
LIEUTENANT—ARMY

The son of a former slave father and a free mother, Europe was born in Mobile, Alabama on February 22, 1881. Lorraine and Henry Europe were both musicians and encouraged their children's talents. When he was about 10, the family moved to Washington and lived a few houses from Marine Corps bandmaster John Philip Sousa. He and his sister, Mary, took violin and piano lessons from the Marine band's assistant director, Enrico Hurlei.

Herbert Wright, who cut Europe's jugular vein with a penknife.

Europe, James R., Jr.
LIEUTENANT—MERCHANT MARINES

He is the only child of Lieutenant James Reese Europe, the famous Band Leader and officer with the 369th Infantry in World War I (The Harlem Hellfighters).

He is a native of North Bellmore, Long Island, New York. During World War II, he joined the United States Merchant Marine, and was commissioned a Lieutenant.

Evans, Darlin
COMMAND CHIEF MASTER SERGEANT—AIR FORCE

Command Chief Master Sergeant Darlin Evans was born in Moscow, Tennessee. He graduated from North Natchez Adams High in Natchez, Mississippi, in June 1972. He enlisted in the United States Air Force in May 1973 and attended Technical Training as an Aircraft Maintenance Specialist at Sheppard Air Force Base, Texas.

He holds an associate's degree in Maintenance Production Management from the Community College of the Air Force; a bachelor's degree in Business Administration from Wayland Baptist University; and a master's degree in Management and Human Resources Development from Webster University. Evans is also a graduate of the Strategic Air Command Noncommissioned Officers Academy at Barksdale Air Force Base, Louisiana; the United States Air Force Senior Noncommissioned Officers Academy at Gunter Air Force base, in Alabama.

Chief Evans has served as primary augmentee to the

Tactical Air Command Maintenance Standardization and Evaluation Team; USAFE Inspector General Team for the Ground Launched Cruise Missile (GLCM); the Headquarters of the Air Education and Training Command Inspector General Team; Operations Group Maintenance Superintendent, Senior Enlisted Advisor; 8th Fighter Wing at Kunsan Air Base, South Korea; Senior Enlisted Advisor, Human Systems Center, at Brooks Air Force Base, in Texas; and Command Chief Master Sergeant, 311th Human Systems Wing at Brooks Air Force Base, Texas.

Evans, Renall L.
COMMAND MASTER CHIEF—NAVY

Evans was born in Los Angeles, California, and after graduating from John C. Freemont High School in 1979, he enlisted in the United States Navy in August 1979. Upon completion of Basic Training in San Diego, California, he attended Aviation Storekeeper "A" School in Meridian, Mississippi.

After a tour on the staff of Commander, Naval Air Forces, United States Pacific Fleet (COMNAVAIRPAC), he reported to the VAW-116 "Sun Kings," completing three deployments, including one in support of Operation Desert Storm with CVW-2 and USS *Ranger* (CV 61). In November 1996, he was selected for the Command Master Chief (CMC) program. Completing the Senior Enlisted Academy Course, he reported to VFA-151 "Vigilantes" at NAS Lemoore as the Command Master Chief, deploying once again with CVW-2 and USS *Constellation*. Next he reported as Command Master Chief to the VS-41 "Shamrocks," the S-3B Viking Fleet Replacement Squadron at NAS North Island, California. In July 2003, he transferred to the VS-29 "Dragonfires," deployed with CVW-11

and USS *Nimitz* Strike Group in support of Operation Iraqi Freedom. In October 2004, he was serving as the Command Master Chief assigned to the mighty USS *Carl Vinson* (CVN-70), the "Gold Eagle."

Evans, Stephen
COMMANDER—NAVY

Evans is the son of a United States Marine, and considers Beaufort, South Carolina, home. He received his Bachelor of Arts in History from The Citadel in May

1986 and is a 1998 graduate of the Naval War College, where he obtained his master's degree in National Security and Strategic Studies.

His first sea duty tour was as First Division Officer and Navigation Division Officer in USS *Theodore Roosevelt* (CVN 71) from October 1986 to September 1989. His next sea duty tours were in USS *Deyo* (DD 989) as Fire Control Officer and USS *Hewitt* (DD 966) as Combat Systems Officer. He then served as Executive Officer in USS *Hue City* (CG 66) from September 2000 to November 2001.

His shore duty assignments include serving as Flag Lieutenant to Commander Operational Test and Evaluation Force, Instructor at the Surface Warfare Officers School, Chief of Special Operations Support then Chief of Southern Command Support at the Joint Warfare Analysis Center, and Lieutenant Commander Detailer then Deputy Director in the Surface Warfare Officer Distribution Directorate at the Navy Personnel Command. He is a designated Joint Specialty Officer. In October 2004, he was serving as the Commander of USS *Mitscher* (DDG 57).

Evans, William T.
SERGEANT MAJOR—ARMY

Evans was born in Wilmington, North Carolina, and enlisted in the United States Army in July 1950. His key military assignments include serving from 1956 to 1960 as Supply Sergeant at the United States Engineer School at Fort Belvoir, Virginia; from 1960 to 1961 as Supply Sergeant with the 25th Artillery Battery in South Korea; he served as the Battalion Supply Officer for the 3rd Howitzer Battalion, 3rd Artillery Battery, at Fort Knox, Kentucky, from 1961 to 1964; in 1964, he served with the 25th Infantry Division in Hawaii and Vietnam, 4th United States Army DSCLOG at Fort Sam Houston, Texas; and next with the 8th United States Army, G4 in South Korea; Upon his promotion to Sergeant Major he became the Noncommissioned Officer in Charge, Logistics Division, with the United States Army General Equipment Test Activity (GETA) at Fort Lee, Virginia from 1970 to 1972. He served three years (1972 to 1975) at TASCOM Headquarters in West Germany, then returned to Fort Lee from 1975 to 1980. His final active duty tour was as Noncommissioned Officer in Charge for the Housing Division at the Directorate of Facilities Engineering.

Evans, Willie
CAPTAIN—NAVY

His military career began in 1979, serving until 1982 onboard the USS *Belleau Wood* (LHA-3) with an 8-month deployment to the Western Pacific and the Indian Ocean during the Iran hostage crisis. He completed a 2½-year tour (1984 to 1986) onboard the USS *Copeland* (FFG-25) serving as the Supply Department Head and the only black officer of 16 officers with a total crew size of 200. During this tour, the USS *Copeland* deployed 3 times to the Western Pacific with the last deployment consisting of six months in the

Persian Gulf performing escort duty for oil tankers. On this deployment, his department was the only one out of the entire squadron to be awarded the Navy's coveted "Supply E" for outstanding performance and superlative supply and logistics support.

His two shore assignments included serving a two-year contracting tour (1982–1984) at the Naval Air Systems Command Headquarters in Washington, D.C.; and a 3½-year tour at the Naval Regional Data Automation Center in Washington, D.C. where he served as the Deputy Director of Contracts.

After 11 years on active duty, in 1990 he joined the Naval Reserves. His assignments in the Naval Reserves include serving at the Navy Regional Contracting Center in Washington, D.C. (1990 to 1993); at Naval Systems Command Headquarters (1993 to 1994); and at the Defense Contract Management Command (1994 to 1996). He was selected to serve in the Office of the Assistant Secretary of the Navy for Research and Development (Acquisition Business Management) serving as Executive Officer (1996 to 1998); as Commander of Fleet Industrial Support Center Norfolk Detachment Washington (1998 to 2000); and as Executive Officer with the Military Sealift Command, European Forces (2000 to 2001). In 2001, he was assigned to Headquarters of the Military Sealift Command, and in October 2004, he was assigned as the Commanding Officer for Reserve Units assigned to the Defense Contract Management Agency Maryland, located in Baltimore.

Evy, Lacy
SERGEANT MAJOR—ARMY

In August 2004, Evy was assigned as the Equal Opportunity Sergeant Major with the United States Army's V Corps in Heidelberg, Germany.

Felder, Robert J.
COMMAND SERGEANT MAJOR—ARMY

A native of Columbia, South Carolina, Felder entered the United States Army in June 1983, and at-

tended Basic Combat Training at Fort Jackson, South Carolina. He completed his Advanced Individual Training at Fort Gordon, Georgia.

His military and civilian education includes all the Noncommissioned Officer Education System Courses; the Drill Sergeant School; Master Fitness Course; Jumpmaster Course; Instructors Training Course; the Army Safety Course; United States Army Sergeants Major Academy; and Command Sergeants Major Course. He holds an associate's degree from Texas College, a Bachelor of Science Degree from Excelsior College, and is pursuing a master's degree in Management and Human Resource Management from Troy State University.

He has served in every enlisted leadership position from Avionic Mechanic to Command Sergeant Major. His assignments include serving as Senior Instructor Writer; MACOM Maintenance Noncommissioned Officer in Charge INSCOM; Scout Helicopter Division Sergeant Major; Task Force Angel Command Sergeant Major; Command Sergeant Major 3rd Battalion of the 229th; and Command Sergeant Major, 2nd Battalion, 25th Aviation Regiment.

Ferguson, Alonzo L.
BRIGADIER GENERAL—AIR FORCE

He was born in Washington, D.C., he married the former Frances Thorne of Washington, D.C. They have four daughters, Theresa, twins Pamela and Cynthia, and Lisa. He was graduated from Dunbar High School in 1947 and from Howard University in June 1952 with a Bachelor of Science degree in Psychology. He was commissioned a second lieutenant in the United States Air Force through the ROTC program and is a graduate of the Armed Forces Staff College at Norfolk, Virginia.

He began active duty in July 1952. After completion of flight and jet fighter training, he served in Korea as a T-6 Mosquito forward air controller from July 1954 to June 1955. He was then assigned to the 4520th Combat Crew Training Wing at Nellis Air Force Base, Nevada, where he instructed in T-33s, F-86s and F-100s. From June 1961 through September 1964, he served at Wheelus Air Base, Libya, as an F-105 weapons instructor. He also acted as liaison officer for the 36th Tactical Fighter Wing at Bitburg Air Base in West Germany, which conducted weapons qualification training at Wheelus.

Following this assignment, he returned to Nellis as an F-105 instructor pilot and operations officer for the 4523rd Combat Crew Training Squadron. In August 1966 Ferguson entered the Armed Forces Staff College. In April 1967 he was assigned to Takhli Royal Thai Air Force Base, Thailand. He flew 103 combat missions with the 355th Tactical Fighter Wing in F-105s over North Vietnam. General Ferguson returned to South Korea in February 1974 and served until February 1975 at Osan Air Base as vice commander of the 1st Air Base Wing and commander, 51st Combat Support Group, 51st Composite Wing (Tactical).

He was named vice commander of the 355 Tactical Fighter Wing at Davis-Monthan Air Force Base, Arizona, in March 1975 and took command of the wing in February 1976. He became Deputy Director, J-3, of the National Military Command Center of the Joint Chiefs of Staff in August 1977. General Ferguson was appointed Deputy Director for Readiness Development in the Directorate of Operations and Readiness, under the Deputy Chief of staff for operations and Plans, Headquarters United States Air Force, in September 1978. In June 1979 he assumed command of the 21st North American Air Defense Command Region at Hancock Field, New York. He also served as commander of the 21st Aerospace Defense Command Region, and commander of the 21st Air Division, the air defense component of the Tactical Air Command.

He was responsible for air defense operations in the northern United States and portions of Canada. A command pilot, General Ferguson's military decorations and awards include the Silver Star (with oak leaf cluster), Legion of Merit, Defense Meritorious Service Medal (with oak leaf cluster) Air Medal (with three oak leaf clusters), and Air Force Commendation Medal (with oak leaf cluster). He is a member of the Daedalians, the Air Force Association, and the Red River Valley Fighter Pilots Association. He was appointed to Brigadier General August 1, 1977, with date of rank July 28, 1977.

Ferguson, Edward A., Jr.
BRIGADIER GENERAL—ARMY

Ferguson received a Bachelor of Business Administration degree (Finance) from Iona College and earned a Masters of Business Administration degree from Saint John's University. His military education includes the Transportation Officer Basic Course; the Academy of

Health Science, Army Medical Department Officer Basic and Advanced Course; Nuclear, Biological, Chemical Defense School, Nuclear, Biological, Chemical Defense Officer Course; Command and General Staff College; Academy of Health Sciences; Army Medical Department Theater Medical Operations (Reserve Component); Army War College; Reserve Component National Security Issues Seminar; Armed Forces Staff College; Reserve Components National Security Seminar; John F. Kennedy Special Warfare Center and School, Terrorism in Low Intensity Conflict Course; National Defense University, Reserve Component National Security Course; Ohio Military Academy, Battle Focused Instructor Training Course; and Logistics Management College, Combat Services Support Pre-Command Course.

He received an OCS commission to second lieutenant on August 16, 1968, with the New York National Guard and assigned as a Platoon Leader with the 1469th Transportation Company in New York City. Next he was assigned as a Highway Regulation Officer with the 669th Transportation Detachment in New York. In June 1971, he was assigned as a Platoon Leader with the 1469th Transportation Company. Later he was assigned as Platoon Leader with the 1569th Transportation Company in New York. In January 1972, he was ordered to report to an assignment as Adjutant/S1 with the 569th Transportation Battalion in New York City. From November 1972 to March 1973, he was assigned as Platoon Leader, 719th Transportation Company, in New York City. In March 1973, he was assigned Commander of the 1569th Transportation Company in New York. He was promoted to Captain on October 12, 1973.

In January 1977 he joined the United States Army Reserves and was assigned as Comptroller at Headquarters Company of the 8th Medical Brigade in Brooklyn,

New York. He was promoted to Major on June 15, 1978. From January 1981 to February 1984, he served as Executive Officer with the 817th Evacuation Hospital at Webster, New York. He was promoted to Lieutenant Colonel on November 15, 1982. In February 1984, he was assigned as Secretary of the 1159th United States Army Reserve School in Webster.

He joined the Ohio State National Guard in March 1985, and assumed the duties as Health Services Manpower Officer, later Plans Officer, with the 112th Medical Brigade in Worthington, Ohio. He was appointed Army National Guard Lieutenant Colonel on March 19, 1985. His next assignment was that of Plans, Operations, Intelligence and Training Officer with the 112th Medical Brigade in Columbus, Ohio. He was promoted to Colonel on January 24, 1990. In August 1993, he assumed duties as Commandant of Detachment 3, Headquarters, State Area Command, in Columbus. From October 1994 to September 1995, he served as the Commander of the 73rd Troop Command, State Area Command in Columbus. In October 1995, he was selected to serve as Assistant Adjutant General for Training, with attachment to Commander, 73rd Troop Command, in Columbus. He was promoted to Brigadier General on September 19, 1996.

His awards and decorations include the Meritorious Service Medal; Army Commendation Medal (with bronze oak leaf cluster); Army Achievement Medal (with bronze oak leaf cluster); Army Reserve Components Achievement Medal (with silver oak leaf cluster); National Defense Service Medal; Armed Forces Reserve Medal (with bronze hourglass device); Army Service Ribbon; and Army Reserve Components Overseas Training Ribbon (with numeral 3).

Fetherson, Parise Y.
SERGEANT MAJOR—MARINE

She entered the United States Marine Corps in 1979. Upon completion of Boot Camp at Marine Corps Recruit Depot at Parris Island, South Carolina, she was assigned the administration School MOS and attended the Basic Personnel Administration School and Unit Diary School at Parris Island.

Upon completion of MOS school, she was assigned as a Unit Diary Clerk at Headquarters and Headquarters Squadron 28, Marine Air Control Group-28, 2nd Marine Aircraft Wing at Cherry Point, North Carolina. During her tour at Cherry Point, She was meritoriously promoted to the rank of Corporal.

In October 1980, she was transferred to her first overseas assignment to Headquarters and Maintenance Squadron 12, Marine Aircraft Group 12, 1st Marine Aircraft Wing at Iwakuni, Japan, where she served as the Unit Diary Chief. During her tour at Iwakuni, she was selected as the Group Noncommissioned Officer of the Month.

She returned to Marine Corps Recruit Depot, Parris Island, South Carolina, in 1981, and served as a Unit Diary Chief with Weapons Training Battalion, 3rd Recruit Training Battalion and Headquarters and Service

Battalion. During this tour she was promoted to the rank of Sergeant in 1982. Also during this tour she served as the Battalion Career Planner for 3rd Recruit Training Battalion. Next she was transferred to Marine Corps Development and Education Command at Quantico, Virginia, in 1984 where she served as a Platoon Sergeant and the Unit Diary Chief at Officer Candidate School. During this tour, she was selected as a member of the 1986 Women's All Marine Basketball Team.

In 1986, she was again assigned to an overseas tour with Marine Wing Headquarters Squadron 1, 1st Marine Aircraft Wing, in Okinawa, Japan, where she served as the unit Diary Chief. During this tour, she deployed to Pohang, South Korea in support of Team Spirit 87. She was promoted to the rank of Staff Sergeant in 1988, and was subsequently reassigned to the Wing Personnel Section as the Administration Chief.

In 1989, she reported to 2nd Force Service Support Group at Camp Lejeune, North Carolina where she served as an Admin Chief with Headquarters Service Battalion and 2nd Landing Support Battalion.

In 1992, she was once again assigned to Marine Corps Recruit Depot at Parris Island. During this tour she served with Headquarters and Service Battalion at the Depot Consolidated Admin Center as an Admin Chief. She was promoted to the rank of Gunnery Sergeant in 1993, and was subsequently reassigned to the Manpower and Human Resources Division where she served as the Admin Chief.

In 1996, she was once again transferred to Okinawa, Japan. During this tour she served with Headquarters and Service Battalion, 3rd Force Service Support Group where she was assigned to the Administrative Assistance Team as an Inspector and the Officer-in-Charge. While with the Team, she was redirected to Marine Corps Expeditionary Camp at Pohang to participate in Ulchi

Focus Lens-96. She was promoted to First Sergeant in 1998 and was assigned as the Company First Sergeant for Headquarters and Support Company, 3rd Support Battalion, 3rd Force Service Support Group. During her tour at 3rd Support Battalion she was assigned as the First Sergeant for the Combat Service Support Detachment of the Air Contingency Marine Air Ground Task Force. She once again deployed to the Marine Expeditionary Camp at Pohang, where she served as the Detachment First Sergeant for Combat Service Support Detachment 39. She was transferred to Headquarters and Service Battalion, Marine Corps Base Camp Lejeune, North Carolina, in 1999, where she served as the Company First Sergeant for Brig Company and B Company.

In 2001, she was transferred to Marine Security Guard Battalion at Quantico, Virginia, where she served as the Company First Sergeant for Headquarters Company. In August 2004, she was serving as Sergeant Major for the MCAF.

Fetherson, Ronald E.
SERGEANT MAJOR—MARINE

On 1 June 2004, Sergeant Major Ron Fetherson, United States Marine Corps (Ret) joined the Marine

Corps Association as the Deputy Director of Professional Development. In his new role, he manages the awards program and serves as the association's enlisted advisor at Marine Corps Base Quantico (MCBQ) and stations in the surrounding area.

Ficklin, Reginald
COMMAND SERGEANT MAJOR—ARMY

Command Sergeant Major Reginald Ficklin was born in Chicago, Illinois, and raised in Tort Valley, Georgia, where he graduated from Henry A. Hunt High School in 1967. He enlisted in the United States

Army on May 17, 1973. He attended Basic Combat Training at Fort Jackson, South Carolina. He attended Advance Individual Training at Fort Bliss, Texas, where he obtained the MOS 16E10, Hawk Fire Control Operator.

His military assignments include two tours in South Korea; two tours in the West Germany; one tour in Key West, Florida; one tour in Fort Hood, Texas; and three tours in Fort Bliss, Texas.

His military education includes the Drill Sergeant School; United States Army First Sergeants Course; the United States Army Sergeants Major Course; and the Command Sergeant Major Course.

He is currently assigned as the Command Sergeant Major at the United States Army Space Command in Colorado Springs, Colorado.

Fields, Arnold
MAJOR GENERAL—MARINES

His military education includes a Bachelor of Science degree in Agriculture and a Master of Arts degree in Management. He is a graduate of the Amphibious Warfare School, the Marine Corps Command and Staff College, and the Army War College.

He was commissioned a second lieutenant in November 1969. Completing the Basic School Course 21 weeks later, he was assigned to the 2nd Marine Division where he held positions as Infantry Platoon Commander and Company Executive Officer. In February 1971, he was assigned to the 3rd Marine Division on Okinawa, Japan, where he served as an 81-mm mortar Platoon Commander and Company Executive Officer with the 2nd Battalion, 4th Marines.

He returned to the United States in February 1972 and was assigned to the Marine Corps Recruit Depot

Fields

158

at Parris Island, South Carolina. His service there in-
cluded assignments as Recruit Series Commander and
Assistant Director of the Drill Instructor School. During July 1974, he was transferred to the Marine Corps
Development and Education Center. He also completed a year of study at the Amphibious Warfare
School at Quantico before being transferred to the 3rd
Marine Division during June 1978. He was an Infantry
Company Commander during this one year tour with
the 3rd Division. He was assigned to the 6th Marine
Corps District in June 1979 and served for three years
as Officer in Charge of the District Contact Team. Following one year at intermediate level school, he returned to the 6th District where for three years he
served as the Commanding Officer of the Marine Corps
Recruiting Station at Orlando, Florida. Following this
tour, he transferred to North Africa and served as the
Commanding Officer of Company B (Middle East),
Marine Security Guard Battalion. He and his Marines
provided security to all American Embassies and Con-
sulates throughout North Africa, the Middle East, and
Southwest Asia. Completing this assignment in July
1988, he was transferred to the Army War College,
where he remained until his assignment to the 2nd Marine Division in June 1989. Initially assigned as the Assistant Deputy Chief of Staff for Readiness, he was later
selected to Command the 3rd Battalion, 6th Marines,
2nd Marine Division. During this tour, he and his Battalion participated in combat operations against Iraqi
forces in Kuwait during Operation Desert Shield and
Desert Storm.

In October 1991, he was assigned duty as the Commanding Officer of the Marine Corps Support Activity at Kansas City, Missouri. He was later selected to
Command Headquarters Battalion at Camp Fuji,
Japan, where he remained until ordered to his next assignment as the Chief Evaluation and Analysis Division, Operational Plans and Interoperability Directorate, J-7, Joint Staff, Washington, D.C. His next
assignment was as the Commander, Forward Headquarters Element/Inspector General, United States
Central Command, MacDill Air Force Base, Florida. He
then served as the Deputy Commanding General, III
Marine Expeditionary Force/Marine Corps Base,
Hawaii. During his most recent assignment he served
as the Director of the Marine Corps Staff, Headquarters United States Marine Corps. He was promoted to
Major General on August 6, 1999.

His awards and decorations include the Defense Su-
perior Service Medal (with oak leaf cluster in lieu of
second award); the Bronze Star with Combat "V"; Mer-
itorious Service Medal; Joint Service Commendation
Medal; Navy and Marine Corps Commendation
Medal; Navy and Marine Corps Achievement Medal;
Combat Action Ribbon; Joint Meritorious Unit Award;
Navy Unit Citation; Meritorious Unit Citation; Viet
Nam Service Medal; Southwest Asia Service Medal;
and the Kuwait Liberation Medal.

Fields, Evelyn J.
REAR ADMIRAL—NATIONAL OCEANIC AND
ATMOSPHERIC ADMINISTRATION

Rear Admiral Field is the Director of the Office of the
National Oceanic and Atmospheric Commissioned
Corps Operations and Commissioned Corps. She was
nominated for this position by President Bill Clinton on
January 19, 1999, confirmed by the Senate on May 6,
1999, and subsequently promoted from Captain to Rear
Admiral, Upper Half. She is the first woman and the
first African American to hold this position.

Her career with the National Oceanic and Atmospheric Administration (NOAA) began in 1972 as a car-
tographer at NOAA's Atlantic Marine Center in Norfolk, Virginia. She was commissioned as an ensign and
served on board the NOAA Ship *Mt. Mitchell* as junior officer. Her later ship tours included the NOAA
ship *Pierce* as Operations Officer, NOAA Ship *Rainier*
as Executive Officer, and the NOAA Ship *McArthur*
as Commanding Officer. Admiral Fields was the first female to serve as Commanding Officer of a NOAA ship
and a United States government oceangoing vessel.

Following her command at sea tour, she was selected
as a fellow to the United States Department of Commerce Science and Technology Fellowship Program.
Her follow-on land assignments included tours as the
Administrative Officer of NOAA's National Geodetic
Survey and Chief of Coast Survey's Hydrographic Surveys Division, followed by her tenure as Director of the
NOAA Corps' Commissioned Personnel Center. Prior
to her confirmation as Director of the NOAA Corps,
she served as Deputy Assistant Administrator for
NOAA's National Ocean Service.

Fields, Shirley L.

SENIOR EXECUTIVE SERVICE—
    DEPARTMENT OF DEFENSE

She serves as the first Chief Information Officer for the Defense Information System Agency. Prior to this appointment, she served as Head of DISA's Defense Information Infrastructure Hardware/Software Department.

She was selected and awarded the NAACP's Roy Wilkins Renown Service Award, for her "unparalleled leadership in human and civil rights opportunity and human resource development" at the Defense Information Systems Agency, in Arlington, Virginia.

The citation citer her unwavering community support and her establishment to annual college scholarship funds through Saint Timothy's Episcopal and Cedar Hill Baptist Churches that help disadvantaged minority students.

Figuerres, John M.

COMMANDER—NAVY

Figuerres is a native of Carmel, California, and a 1985 graduate of the United States Naval Academy. In December 1990 he reported to the Naval Postgraduate School in Monterey, California, to study Space Systems Engineering. He completed Department Head School in April 1994.

He was assigned to USS *Halyburton* (FFG 40) as Operations Officer, completing Operation Southern Watch, Middle East Force deployment, during which time *Halyburton* played a key role in the rescue of survivors from the cruise ship *Achille Lauro*. In June 1996 he reported to the USS *Ticonderoga* (CG 47) as Operations Officer in the Caribbean and Eastern Pacific, and assigned as Auxiliaries Officer on board USS *Carl Vinson* (CVN 70). In June 2000, he reported to the

Navy International Programs Office in Washington, D.C. as the Egyptian Country Program Director. During this period he was responsible for a Foreign Military Sales program that totaled over $2.14 billion. He worked closely with the State Department and the Office of the Secretary of Defense and was called upon numerous times to brief several Senate and House committees and Congressmen on sensitive arms sales programs. In May 2003, Figuerres assumed command of the USS *Reuben James* (FFG 57), based in Pearl Harbor, Hawaii.

Fishburne, Lillian

REAR ADMIRAL—NAVY

Born in Maryland, Fishburne graduated from Lincoln University at Oxford, Pennsylvania, in 1971, with a Bachelor of Arts degree in Sociology. She received a Masters of Arts in Management from Webster College in St. Louis, Missouri, in 1980. Fishburne was awarded a Masters of Science degree in Telecommunications Systems Management from the Naval Postgraduate School in Monterey, California, in 1982. She is also a 1993 graduate of the Industrial College of the Armed Forces at Fort McNair, Washington, D.C. Fishburne was commissioned an Ensign upon completion of Women Officers School at Newport, Rhode Island, in February 1973.

Her first duty assignment was Personnel and Legal Officer at the Naval Air Test Facility at Lakehurst, New Jersey. She was reassigned to Navy Recruiting District at Miami, Florida as an Officer Programs recruiter from August 1974 until November 1977. From November 1977 to August 1980, she was the Officer in Charge of the Naval Telecommunications Center, Great Lakes, Illinois. Next, she spent two years as a student at the Naval Postgraduate School in Monterey, California.

Upon completion of postgraduate school, she reported to the Command, Control, Communications Directorate, Chief of Naval Operations, where she served as the Assistant Head of the Joint Allied Command and Control Matters Branch until December 1984.

Her next assignment was Executive Officer at the Naval Communication Station in Yokosuka, Japan. In February 1987, she was reassigned to the Command, Control, and Communications Directorate, Chief of Naval Operations as a Special Projects Officer. Her next duty assignment was Commanding Officer of the Naval Computer and Telecommunications Station at Key West, Florida, from July 1990 to July 1992. Following this, she was a student at the Industrial College of the Armed Forces until 1993. Upon graduation, she was assigned to the Command, Control, Communications and Computer Systems directorate. While serving at the Joint Staff, Washington, D.C., she assumed the position of Chief of the Command and Control Systems Support division in December 1994.

Admiral Fishburne assumed command of Naval Computer and Telecommunications Area Master Station, Eastern Pacific, at Wahiawa, Hawaii, on August 25, 1995. Next she was assigned to Staff Duty at the Space, Information Warfare, Command and Control Directorate, Chief of Naval Operations, Washington, D.C. She was promoted to her current rank of Rear Admiral on February 1, 1998. She was the first African American female to be selected as Rear Admiral, and as of January 2003, she was still the only African American female Rear Admiral in United States Navy history.

Her awards and decorations include the Defense Superior Service Medal; the Legion of Merit; Meritorious Service Medal (two awards); Navy Commendation Medal (two awards); and the Navy Achievement Medal.

Fleetwood, Christian A.
SERGEANT MAJOR—ARMY

Fleetwood was born on July 21, 1840, in Baltimore, Maryland. He enlisted in the United States Army 4th United States Colored Troops on August 11, 1863.

He graduated in 1860 from Ashmun Institute (later Lincoln University) in Pennsylvania. He enlisted into the Union Army on August 11, 1863, as a Sergeant in Company G, 4th Regiment, United States Colored Volunteer Infantry. On August 19, 1863, he was promoted to Sergeant Major. The regiment was assigned to the 3rd Division, he deployed with the 10th, 18th, and 25th Army Corps in campaigns in North Carolina and Virginia. He was awarded the Congressional Medal of Honor for heroism during the battle of Chaffin's Farm on the outskirts of Richmond (September 29, 1864). Every officer of the regiment sent a petition for Fleetwood to be commissioned an officer, but Secretary of War Edwin Stanton did not recommend his appointment. He was honorably discharged on May 4, 1866.

It was his military career that probably inspired his interest in the Washington Colored National Guard

and the colored high school Cadet Corps. A Washington Cadet Corps, organized and commanded by Captain D. Graham on June 12, 1880, was expanded into the Sixth Battalion of the District of Columbia National Guard on July 18, 1867, with Fleetwood appointed Major and Commanding Officer. After reorganizations, several black battalions were consolidated into the first separate battalion in 1891. Passed over as its commanding officer, Fleetwood resigned in 1892. Meanwhile he and Major Charles B. Fisher, who had commanded the Fifth Battalion, were instrumental in organizing the Black High School Cadet Corps of the District of Columbia in 1888.

Fleming-Makell, Rhonda
LIEUTENANT COMMANDER—COAST GUARD

She was the first African American female Coast Guard officer to earn a 20-Year retirement. Fleming-Makell was a regular commissioned officer in the United States Coast Guard and completed 20 years of military service for her county in 2004. In addition, she is the first African American woman commissioned officer to earn a retirement in the history of the United States Coast Guard, nearly 30 years after women first started serving their country in this capacity in 1976.

Fleming-Makell was born in Morganton, North Carolina, and raised in Greenville, South Carolina. She is a 1985 graduate of South Carolina State University, earning a Bachelor of Science degree in Psychology with a minor in Special Education. In addition, she successfully completed a Masters of Business Administration with a concentration in Technology Management from the University of Phoenix and is a member of Delta Sigma Theta Sorority.

In June of 1984, she enlisted in the United States Coast Guard while still in college. Upon completion

of Coast Guard Recruit Training at Cape May, New Jersey, she returned to school in Orangeburg, South Carolina, to complete her undergraduate degree. She is a 1986 graduate of the Coast Guard Officer Candidate School (OCS) located in Yorktown, Virginia. After graduation from OCS, she was assigned to the Third Coast Guard District as the Human Relations Counselor in New York City and became a qualified trainer and counselor in the areas of Human Relations and Civil Rights.

Upon completion of her tour as Human Relations Counselor, she was assigned to Coast Guard Support Center New York as the Assistant Special Services Officer. Shortly after, Lieutenant Commander Fleming-Makell was stationed at Coast Guard Group New York. As a junior officer, she was assigned to the operations division, successfully qualifying as a Duty Officer responding to Search and Rescue (SAR), Law Enforcement, and Marine Safety emergencies. Other duties included, but were not limited to, Assistant Operations Officer, Classified Material Control Officer, and Communications Officer.

In 1991, her next duty assignment was the Coast Guard Command Center in Washington, D.C. As Operations Officer, she was responsible for the collection, dissemination, and reporting of all oil spills in the United States. Following this tour in 1994, Lieutenant Commander Fleming-Makell was assigned as Assistant Operations Officer at one of the busiest units in the Coast Guard, "Group Miami."

As Assistant Operations Officer, she was directly responsible for all delegated tasks related to collection, evaluation, and dissemination of operational tasking/assignments, and information to four multi-mission Stations, two Aids-to-Navigation Teams, nine patrol boats, and one buoy tender. Duties included Search and Res-

cue, Law Enforcement, Illegal Migration Operations, and Aids-to-Navigation. During her tenure at Group Miami she conducted many joint law enforcement operations with the Customs Service and FBI, successfully seizing millions of dollars worth of cocaine, marijuana and other illegal contraband. Three years late, in September of 1997, she was transferred to the Seventh Coast Guard District.

As the Chief of District Personnel, she managed personnel support programs for all Seventh District units, in an area covering the entire Caribbean basin and points between the North and South Carolina border and the easternmost portions of the Gulf of Mexico, which included but was not limited to, five Group units, five Marine Safety Offices, four Air Stations, 25 patrol boats, 20 Multi-Mission stations, eight cutters, four buoy tenders, 9 Aids-to-Navigation Teams, and one LORAN Station. Upon completion of this tour, she was assigned to Coast Guard Headquarters, Office of Law Enforcement in Washington, D.C., for her final tour in August 2001.

In her final assignment, she was responsible for development of a Coast Guard-wide law enforcement policy, program management for several Department of Homeland Security initiatives, Maritime Law Enforcement Schools, Law Enforcement Councils and maintenance of a $1 million budget. As Program Manager of several Homeland Security initiatives, she successfully implemented the first official Coast Guard Canine Program since World War II. Most recently, on March 8, 2004, her efforts with the Canine Program recently thwarted a potential terrorist situation when the Coast Guard Canine Team, searching with ATF, found Improvised explosive devices such as pipe bombs, electric, and non-electric blasting caps in a house.

Flipper, Henry O.
LIEUTENANT—ARMY

From 1873 until his graduation from West Point in 1877, Cadet Flipper was subjected to every overt and covert type of harassment and racial discrimination imaginable. And even those few cadets who were sympathetic dared not associate with him for fear of reprisal from the majority cadet student body. Of the twenty black candidates admitted to the United States Military Academy in the 19th century, only three would graduate. Henry O. Flipper was to be the first. He was not the first black to attend, however. That honor belongs to James W. Smith of South Carolina, who entered the Academy in 1870. Cadet Smith was so tormented by his fellow white cadets that, finally, unable to bear the hostility any longer, he struck back at his assailants and was expelled. In spite of this hostile, charged atmosphere, Henry O. Flipper graduated 50th in a class of 76, in June 1877. He was commissioned as a Second Lieutenant in the 10th Cavalry. From 1878 to 1882, Lieutenant Flipper received the same kind of social isolation from his fellow white officers that he received at the Academy. Again, he prevailed. Fortunately, officers of the 10th were too busy fighting Indian warriors like

Victorio and Geronimo to have time to fight among themselves. It was while serving at Fort Concho, Texas, that an event was to take place that would have a profound impact on the career of Henry O. Flipper.

He was seen riding with a pretty young white woman. A short while later, in 1882, while serving as Commissary Officer at Fort Davis, Texas, he was framed by his fellow white officers for embezzling Army funds and conduct unbecoming an officer. At his trial, Lt. Flipper pleaded innocent. He was acquitted on the first charge, but was found guilty of the second, and was dismissed from the service. In December 1976, the Army, at the behest of the first black graduate of the U.S. Naval Academy, Commander Wesley A. Brown, and the historian Ray O. MacColl, reviewed the circumstances surrounding Flipper's discharge and issued an Honorable discharge in his name. In 1977, through the efforts of Mr. H. Minton Francis, the Deputy Assistant Secretary of Defense (Equal Opportunity), the U.S. Military Academy dedicated a memorial bust and alcove in the cadet library in honor of Lt. Flipper on the 100th anniversary of his graduation.

Flowers, Alfred K.
BRIGADIER GENERAL—AIR FORCE

He was commissioned following graduation from Officer Training School as a distinguished graduate of the December 1978 class. His education includes a Bachelor of Science Degree from Southern Illinois University and a Master of Arts Degree from Ball State University. He also attended Squadron Officer School at Maxwell Air Force Base, in Alabama; Professional Military Comptroller School at Maxwell Air Force Base; Air Command and Staff College; Armed Forces Staff College at Norfolk, Virginia; and Air War College. He earned a Master of Science Degree from the Industrial College of the Armed Force at Fort Lesley J. McNair, Washington, D.C., and completed the Advanced Management Program at the Federal Executive Institute

in Charlottesville, Virginia; and the Senior Leader Orientation Course in Washington, D.C.

He first served as a budget officer at the squadron, major command and Air Staff levels. In 1990, he was assigned as Chief of the Budget Operations Division for the Air Combat Command at Langley Air Force Base, Virginia, where he would later serve as the Chief of Budget. He served on the Joint Staff as Defense Resource Manager, and in 1999 he was the Director of Budget Programs for the Department of the Air Force. From September 2001 to August 2003, he served as Comptroller at Headquarters Air Education and Training Command at Randolph Air Force Base, Texas. From September 2003 to February 2004, he served as Chief Financial Executive, Center for Force Structure, Resources and Strategic Assessments, Headquarters United States Special Operations Command, at MacDill Air Force Base, Florida. In March 2004, he was assigned as Director of the Center for Force Structure, Requirements, Resources and Strategic Assessments, J8, at Headquarters United States Special Operations Command, at MacDill Air Force Base, in Florida. He was promoted to Brigadier General on September 1, 2004.

Flowers, Michael C.
BRIGADIER GENERAL—ARMY

Flowers received an ROTC commission as Second Lieutenant on August 10. 1977. His military and civilian education includes Armor Officer Basic Course; Infantry Officer Advanced Course; United States Army Officer Rotary Wing Aviator Course; Armed Forces Staff College; and United States Army War College. He holds a Bachelor of Science Degree in History from the University of Kansas, and earned a Master of Public Administration from Shippensburg University.

He has held a wide variety of command and staff assignments including Executive Officer, 1st Squadron, 17th Cavalry, 82nd Airborne Division, Fort Bragg, North Carolina and Operations Desert Shield/Storm, Saudi Arabia; S-3 (Operation), 82nd Aviation Brigade, 82nd Airborne Division, Fort Bragg; Commander, 1st Squadron, 17th Cavalry, 82nd Airborne Division, Fort Bragg and Operation Restore/Uphold Democracy, Haiti; Commander, 18th Aviation Brigade (Corps) (Airborne), XVIII Airborne Corps, Fort Bragg; Chief of the Joint Training and Exercises Division, later Chief, Operations Plans Division, J-3, United States European Command, Germany; Director of the Center for Army Leadership, United States Army Command and General Staff College, Fort Leavenworth, Kansas; and Director of the Human Resources Policy Directorate, Office of the Deputy Chief of Staff, G-1, United States Army, Washington, D.C. On July 1, 2004, he was promoted to Brigadier General and assigned as Chief of Staff, KFOR (Main), Pristina Film City, Camp Bondsteel, APO AE.

His military awards and decorations include the Defense Superior Service Medal; the Legion of Merit (with oak leaf cluster); Bronze Star; Defense Meritorious Service Medal; Meritorious Service Medal (with three oak leaf clusters); Air Medal; Army Commendation Medal (with oak leaf cluster); the Air Medal; Army Commendation Medal (with oak leaf clusters); Army Achievement Medal (with three oak leaf clusters); Senior Army Aviator Badge; Master Parachutist Badge; and the Ranger Tab.

Floyd, Harold F.

FIRST SERGEANT—ARMY

Sergeant Floyd enlisted into the United States Army under the Delayed Entry Program in 1982, and entered Basic Combat Training at Fort Benning, Georgia, in February 1983. Since then, he has served in every leadership position from Team Leader to First Sergeant.

His military and civilian education includes all the Noncommissioned Officer Education System Courses; Winter Operations in Northern Areas Course; Light Fighter Combat Leader Course; Jungle Warfare Training Course; Infantry Leaders Course; Equipment Preparation/Loader Course; Airlift Planners Course; Unit Movement Officer Course; United States Army Marksmanship Trainer's Course; Alcohol and Drug Coordinator's Course; Air Assault School (Distinguished Honor Graduate); and the Airborne School.

His assignments include serving as Track Commander and Team Leader, 7th Battalion, 6th Infantry, 1st Armored Division, in Bamberg, Germany; Squad Leader, 3rd Battalion, 17th Infantry and Training NCO, Headquarters and Headquarters Command, 7th Infantry Division Light, at Fort Ord, California; Platoon Sergeant, 1st and 3rd Battalion, 187th Infantry and Land Manager, 3rd Brigade, 187th Infantry, at Fort Campbell, Kentucky; Platoon Sergeant, 1st Battalion, 506th Infantry, 2nd Infantry Division, in Korea; Battalion Operations Noncommissioned Officer in Charge, Headquarters and Headquarters Company, United States Army Garrison, at Fort Polk, Louisiana. He assumed the position as Deputy Commandant of the JRTC and Fort Polk Noncommissioned Officer Academy on 25 August 2003.

Font, Johnnie M.

COMMAND SERGEANT MAJOR—ARMY

Command Sergeant Major Font enlisted in the Army in 1970. She attended Basic Combat Training at Fort McClellan, Alabama, and was assigned to Fort Jackson, South Carolina, for Advanced Individual Training. She has served in a variety of Noncommissioned Officer Leadership positions throughout her 30 years of service. Some of the positions she held were Detachment First Sergeant, Senior Enlisted Advisor, and Material Management Sergeant Major. She is a graduate of Class

35 of the United States Army Sergeants Major Academy at Fort Bliss, Texas.

Ford, Ralph
COMMAND SERGEANT MAJOR—ARMY

A native of Meridian, Mississippi, Ford enlisted into the United States Army in September 1983, on the Delayed Entry Program. In July 1984, he reported for active duty to Fort Jackson, South Carolina, and attended Basic Combat Training and advanced Individual Training to become a Heavy Wheeled Vehicle Mechanic.

His military and civilian education includes all the Noncommissioned Officer Education System Courses; Drill Sergeant School; the First Sergeant School; the United States Army Sergeants Major Academy; Command Sergeants Major Course; and the Garrison Sergeants Major Course. He holds an Associate's Degree in General Studies from Pikes Peak College and a Bachelor's Degree in Management from American Military University.

He has held numerous leadership positions, including serving as a Squad Leader; Platoon Sergeant; Shop Foreman; Motor Sergeant; Drill Sergeant; Senior Maintenance Supervisor; First Sergeant; and Command Sergeant Major. He served as Drill Sergeant, Charlie Company, 187th Ordnance Battalion, at Fort Jackson, South Carolina; Senior Maintenance Supervisor, Headquarters and Headquarters Company, 7th Infantry Division; First Sergeant, Headquarters and Alpha Company, 64th Forward Support Battalion; acting Command Sergeant Major, 64th Forward Support Battalion, at Fort Carson, Colorado; and Command Sergeant Major 98th ASG.

Ford, Robert L.
CAPTAIN—NAVY

Ford graduated from Southern University in Baton Rouge, Louisiana, in August 1979 with a Bachelor of Science Degree.

Following graduation, he served the USS *Racine* (LST 1191) as Assistant to the DCA. He reported as a student to Surface Warfare Officers School Detachment in Coronado, California, in January 1980. Upon graduation, he served the USS *St. Louis* (LKA 116) as Second Division Officer and Ship's Navigator. He was assigned to the USS *Mount Vernon* (LSD 39) as Operations Officer in May 1982.

In January 1984, he reported to the United States Naval Academy in Annapolis, Maryland, as Minority Admissions Officer. Upon completion of his tour at the Naval Academy, he attended the Surface Warfare Officers School Department Head course in June 1986. His next assignment was a follow-on tour in Operations aboard USS *Fort Fisher* (LSD 40) from January 1987 to November 1987. From December 1987 to July 1988, he served as First Lieutenant.

In July 1988, he was assigned to Commander, Amphibious Group ONE staff as Flag Secretary. In January 1990, he attended the Naval War College junior course at Newport, Rhode Island, and received his Master of Arts Degree in National Security and Strategic Studies. He was awarded the Master of Science Degree in Management from Salve Regina University in May 1991.

Returning to sea, he was ordered to USS *Vancouver* (LPD 2) to assume duties as Executive Officer and served in that capacity until March 1992. Following the decommissioning of *Vancouver*, he was assigned as Executive Officer, USS *White Plains* (AFS 4) in June 1992.

In November 1993, he was assigned to the Armed Forces Staff College, Norfolk, Virginia, as a Joint Command and Control Warfare Staff Officer Instructor. In October 1995, Captain Ford was ordered to San Diego, California, to become the Commanding Officer of USS *Ogden* (LPD 5). He served as Commanding officer of *Ogden* from May 1996 to January 1998. In February 1998, he was assigned to Surface Warfare School Command, Newport, Rhode Island, as a Prospective Commanding Officer Course Instructor.

Captain Ford was next assigned as the Special Assistant for Minority Affairs to the Chief of Naval Personnel, Washington, D.C. After his assignment in Washington, Captain Ford next assumed command of the Savannah State University and Armstrong Atlantic State University Naval Reserve Officer Training Corps Unit in Savannah, Georgia.

Forrest, Delores G.

COLONEL—AIR FORCE

Born in Danville, Illinois, Colonel Forrest was commissioned a Second Lieutenant into the United States Air Force in September 1979.

Her military and civilian education includes a Bachelor of Science in Nursing, Northern Illinois University; a Master's Degree in Human Resource Management and Personnel Administration, Troy State University; United States Air Force Flight School; Nursing Service Management; Air Command and Staff College; and Air War College.

Her key military assignments include serving from June 1993 to June 1996 as Nurse Manager, Multi Service Unit, 1st Medical Group, Langley Air Force Base, Virginia; August 1996 to May 1998, Nurse Manager, Orthopedic—Neurosurgery, Wilford Hall Medical Center, Lackland Air Force Base, Texas; from May 1998

to May 1999, Chief of Health Care Integration, Wilford Hall Medical Center, Lackland Air Force Base, Texas; from May 1999 to July 2001, Deputy Commander, 6th Medical Operations Squadron, and Deputy Chief Nurse Executive, 6th Medical Group, MacDill Air Force Base, Florida; and from July 2001 to July 2003, Commander of the 9th Medical Operations Squadron and Chief Nurse Executive, 9th Medical Group, Beale Air Force Base, California. In July 2003, she was assigned as the Commander, 27th Medical Group, Cannon Air Force Base, New Mexico.

Forster, Diane M.

COMMAND SERGEANT MAJOR—ARMY

Forster entered the military in May 1983 and attended Basic Combat Training at Fort Dix, New Jersey. Afterward, she attended Advanced Individual Training at Fort Eustis, Virginia, where she was awarded the Military Occupation Specialty as a 67Y Cobra Helicopter Mechanic.

Her military and civilian education includes all the Noncommissioned Officer Education System Courses; the First Sergeant Course; and the United States Army Sergeants Major Academy (class 51). She holds an Associate's Degree in Liberal Arts from Central Texas College; a Bachelor of Science Degree in Psychology from University of Maryland; a Master of Science Degree in Human Resource Management; and a Master's Degree in Public Administration with a concentration in Criminology.

Her duty assignments include serving with the 503rd Attack Helicopter Battalion, 4th Aviation Brigade; HHC 3rd Armored Division; 3rd Staff and Faculty Company, USAALS; 1-227th Aviation Battalion; 1st Calvary Division, Fort Hood, Texas; HHC, United States Army Sergeants Major Academy, Fort Bliss, Texas; and 1-13th Aviation Battalion, Fort Rucker, Alabama. She also served in Desert Storm. In August 2004, she was serving as the Command Sergeant Major, 2/52nd Aviation Battalion, 17th Aviation Brigade.

Forte, Johnnie, Jr.

MAJOR GENERAL—ARMY

Born in New Boston, Texas, Major General Forte married Delores B. Bowles Johnson (Dee). They have three children, Denise M., Mitchell C., and Shermaine L. Johnson. Upon completion of the Reserve Officers Training Corps curriculum and the educational course of study at Prairie View A&M University, he was commissioned a second lieutenant and awarded a Bachelor of Science degree in political science. He also holds a Master of Science degree in Public Administration from Auburn University. His military education includes completion of the Field Artillery School, the Air Defense Artillery School, the United States Army Command and General Staff College, and the Air War College.

His key assignments include Deputy Commanding General, 32nd Army Air Defense Command, United

States Army, Europe; Commander, 108th Air Defense Command, United States Army, Europe; Director of Personnel, J-1, Inspector General, United States European Command. He served as Director of Personnel, Plans and Systems, Office of the Deputy Chief of Staff for Personnel, Washington, D.C., and as Assistant Division Commander of the 8th Infantry Division (Mechanized), United States Army, in Europe. General Forte served in a variety of important career-building assignments in preparation for his most recent duties. In Vietnam he commanded the 41st Civil Affairs Company, 1st Field Force, and subsequently became the Assistant Inspector General of the 1st Field Force.

He returned from overseas as Personnel Management Officer in the Air Defense Artillery Branch, Officer Personnel Directorate, Office Personnel Operations, Washington, D.C. He commanded the 4th Battalion, 61st Air Defense Artillery, 4th Infantry Division (Mechanized), Fort Carson, Colorado. After completing the Air War College at Maxwell Air Force Base, Alabama, he returned to the European theatre to serve as the liaison officer to the United States Air Force, Europe, United States Army, Europe, Liaison Group, Germany. His military awards and decorations include the Defense Superior Service Medal, Legion of Merit (with oak leaf cluster), Meritorious Service Medal, Army Commendation Medal (with two oak leaf clusters), Air Force Commendation Medal, Aircraft Crewman Badge, and Army General Staff Identification Badge.

Foster, Mack D.

COLONEL—AIR FORCE

Colonel Foster and his wife, Delores, have two sons, Milton and David. He received his commission through the ROTC program at North Carolina A & T State University in 1970. He has a Master's Degree in Business Administration, University of Tampa, in Tampa, Florida. His military education includes Squadron Officer School; Air Command and Staff College; and Air War College at Maxwell Air Force Base in Alabama.

From September 1970 to June 1972, he was assigned as Base Deputy Accounting and Finance Officer, Air Force Guidance and Meteorology Center, Newark Air Force Station, in Ohio. From June 1972 to August 1973, he served as Fiscal Control Officer, 56th Special Operations Wing, at Nakon Phanom Royal Thai Air Force Base in Thailand. In August 1973, he was assigned as Accounting and Finance Officer, Budget Officer and Director of Management and Budget, with the 56th Tactical Fighter Wing, at MacDill Air Force Base in Florida. He was promoted to Captain on June 12, 1977.

From June 1978 to February 1981, he was assigned as the Budget Officer, 50th Tactical Fighter Wing, Hahn Air Force Base, in Germany. From February 1981 to June 1983, he served as Chief of the Mission Branch and Chief of Mission Support Branch, Deputy Chief of Staff Comptroller, at Headquarters United States Air Forces in Europe, Ramstein Air Base, in Germany. In April 1987, he was assigned as the Commander, 96th

Bomb Wing Comptroller Squadron, at Dyess Air Force Base, in Texas. He was promoted to Major on August 8, 1982.

From October 1989 to June 1992, he was assigned as Commander of the 401st Tactical Fighter Wing Comptroller Squadron, Torrejon Air Base, Spain. From June 1992 to June 1994, he was assigned as Chief, Financial Analysis, at Headquarters Air Education and Training Command at Randolph Air Force Base, Texas. He was promoted to Colonel on July 1, 1992.

In June 1994, he was assigned as the Director of Resources at Headquarters Air University, Maxwell Air Force Base, Alabama. As director, he was responsible for informing the commander and staff on all issues of fiscal programming and budgeting, manpower, personnel, communications and computers, and all Air Force Reserve Personnel Management matters affecting the command.

Fountain, Terry

COMMAND SERGEANT MAJOR—ARMY

Born in Atlanta, Georgia, Terry Fountain enlisted into the United States Army in January 1978 as a Telecommunication Center Specialist. In 1980 he became a Chemical Specialist.

His military and civilian education includes the Telecommunication Center Specialist School; Airborne School; Jump Master School; Recondo School; Jungle Expert School; Ranger School; Air Assault School; NWT Instructor Course; Instructor Trainer; Mountain Training; First Sergeant Course; Battle Intelligence Course; United States Army Sergeants Major Academy; and the Command Sergeant Major Course. He earned an Associate's Degree in General Studies from Central Texas College and is pursuing a Bachelor's Degree from Touro University International.

His key leadership assignments include serving as NBC Noncommissioned Officer, Bravo Company, 82nd Signal Battalion (Airborne); NBC Noncommissioned Officer (NCO), Reenlistment NCO, and Supply Sergeant with Bravo Company, 2nd Battalion, 75th Infantry Regiment; Senior Instructor and NBC NCO, at the NCO Academy, at Camp Jackson, Korea; Brigade NBC NCO, 504th PIR; Platoon Sergeant, 21st Chemical Company, 82nd Airborne Division; Senior Drill Sergeant, Charlie Company, 82nd Chemical Battalion; Operations Sergeant for Headquarters and Headquarters Company, 84th Chemical Battalion, at Fort McClellan, Alabama; Chemical NCO Advisor assigned to CGJ Chemical Section, Joint, 8th Army in Korea; First Sergeant, 34th ASG, 8th Army in Korea; DDE NBC/Plans NCO, 12th Aviation; First Sergeant, 12th Chemical Company; Senior Chemical NCO, Headquarters and Headquarters Company, 1st Infantry Division; G-3 Sergeant Major, 13th Corps Support Command, at Fort Hood, Texas; Command Sergeant Major, 13th Corps Distribution Command, at Fort Hood, Texas.

Francis, Andre

SERGEANT MAJOR—MARINE

Francis was born in White Plains, New York. He enlisted in the Marine Corps on 25 July 1977 and attended recruit training at Marine Corps Recruit Depot, Parris Island, South Carolina.

In May 1992, he was assigned to the University of Cornell, where he served as the Assistant Marine Officer Instructor for the Navy ROTC Program. In June 1993, he served as Platoon Sergeant at Officer Candidates School. In August 1995, he was assigned to Kaneohe Bay, Hawaii, 2nd Battalion, where he served as Company Gunnery Sergeant for Golf Company and later as

the Company First Sergeant. In July 1998, he served as First Sergeant for Aviation Maintenance Squadron Two. In July 2001, he served as Squadron Sergeant Major at Marine Fighter Attack Squadron MAG-11 VMRA (AW) 121.

Francis, Keith E.

COMMAND SERGEANT MAJOR—ARMY

Francis graduated from Suwannee High School in Live Oak, Florida, in June of 1977, and immediately enlisted into the United Stated Army. Six months later he attended Basic Combat Training at Fort Dix, New Jersey, later he attended Advanced Individual Training at Aberdeen Proven Ground in Maryland.

His military education includes all the Noncommissioned Officers Education System Courses; the First Sergeant Course; and the United States Army Sergeants Major Academy. He holds an Associate's Degree in Applied Arts.

He has held numerous key leadership positions, including serving as an Instructor, at Aberdeen Proving Ground; Platoon Sergeant at Camp Stanley, Korea; Maintenance Support Team Chief/First Sergeant, 227th Maintenance Battalion; First Sergeant, CASCOM, at Fort Lee, Virginia; and G-3 Sergeant Major at 13th COSCOM at Fort Hood, Texas. In August 2004, he was serving as the Command Sergeant Major for the 284th Base Support Battalion in Giessen, Germany.

Franklin, Calvin G.

MAJOR GENERAL—ARMY

Franklin was born in DeQueen, Arkansas. He married Betty Marzett of Los Angeles, California. They have three children, Gail, Steven, and Kevin. Franklin

graduated from Sevier County High School in 1947 and received an Associate of Arts Degree in Industrial Electronics from San Diego City College. He was graduated magna cum laude with a Bachelor of Technology degree in Industrial Engineering from National University in 1972. In 1974 he earned a Master of Arts Degree in Human Behavior from the United States International University of San Diego. His military education includes the Transportation Officer Basic Course, 1955; Signal Officers Career Course, 1961; Command and General Staff College, 1970; Industrial College of Armed Forces, 1972; United States Army War College, 1977; and the Harvard University Program for Senior Managers in Government, 1986.

He began his military career on November 30, 1948, by enlisting in the California Army National Guard. Mobilized with the 1402nd Engineer Battalion, he served on active duty from September 1950 to June 1952 at Fort Lewis, Washington, and in West Germany. Upon his release from active duty, he returned to the California National Guard. On September 18, 1954, he was commissioned a Second Lieutenant, Transportation, after graduating from the California National Guard Officer Candidate School. His assignments included Platoon Leader; Company Commander, 118th Signal Battalion and 240th Signal Battalion; Communications Officer, Intelligence Officer (S-2), and Training Officer (S-3), 111th Armor Group.

In November 1971 he assumed command of the 3rd Battalion, 185th Armor. In 1974 he was assigned as the Civil-Military Affairs Officer (G-5), 40th Infantry Division, where he served until November 1975, when he became Commander of the 240th Signal Battalion. In 1976 he entered active duty to attend the Army War College. After his graduation in 1977, he was assigned as Chief, Mobilization Improvement, and Director, Nifty Nugget Mobilization Exercise 78, Headquarters,

United States Army Forces Command. In May 1979 he was assigned to the District of Columbia Army National Guard as the Operations and Training Officer (F-3).

In October 1979 he returned to active duty as director of an Army study group with a charter to determine the minimum requirements needed by reserve components to train for required readiness levels. In May 1980 he was appointed Assistant Adjutant General of the California Army National Guard and was federally recognized as a Brigadier General on August 18, 1980. He also served as the Assistant Division Commander for the 40th Division until assuming his present position as Commanding General of the District of Columbia National Guard on December 4, 1981.

He was appointed Major General, Adjutants General Corps, on March 2, 1982. His military awards and decorations include the Legion of Merit, Meritorious Service Medal (two oak leaf clusters); Army Commendation Medal; Army Achievement Medal; Good Conduct Medal; Army of Occupation Medal; National Defense Service Medal, Humanitarian Service Medal, Armed Forces Reserve Medal (with 10-year device); Reserve Components Achievement Medal (three oak leaf clusters); Army Service Ribbon; and Reserve Components Overseas Service Ribbon. He also received the Selective Service Exceptional Service Award, the District of Columbia Distinguished Service Medal, and the National Guard Association of United States Distinguished Service Medal.

General Franklin is a member of the Greater Washington Board of Trade, Federal City Council, Kiwanis Club of Washington, D.C., Community Foundation of Greater Washington, D.C., and the D.C. Armory Board. He is also a member of the United Negro College Fund Advisory Board and the Air-Space America National Advisory Council. He retired on December 31, 1991.

Franks, Anthony E.
SERGEANT MAJOR—MARINE

Franks enlisted into the United States Marine Corps Reserve in August 1976 and attended recruit training at Marine Corps Recruit Depot at Parris Island. Upon graduation from recruit training he was assigned to Headquarters Battery, 2nd Battery, 10th Marine, 2nd Marine Division, while awaiting his MOS school. After graduation from Field Radio Operators School, he reported to M Battery, 4th Battalion, 14th Marines, 4th Marine Division in Alabama.

In June 1980, he was ordered to Drill Instructor Duty at Marine Corps Recruit Depot at Parris Island, and was assigned to H Company, 3rd Recruit Training Battalion, where he trained seven platoons and served as senior drill instructor. In June 1982, he was assigned to Quantico, Virginia, at the Education Center Company, where he served as an instructor at the Communication Officer Course and as a Platoon Sergeant and Tactics Instructor at the Officer Candidate School during the summer months. In October 1985, he was

ordered to Okinawa, Japan, to serve as the Communication Chief, Radio Platoon, for MWCS 18, 1st Marine Air Wing. He was assigned to Camp Lejeune in October 1986 to serve as the Communications Chief, Multi-channel Platoon, Communications Company, Headquarters Battalion, 2nd Marine Division, and was later reassigned as the Communications Chief for 2nd Battalion, 10th Marines. Sergeant Major Franks was re-designated from Master Sergeant to First Sergeant in November 1989 and was assigned as the Battery First Sergeant for Headquarters, Delta and Golf Batteries, 2nd Battalion, 10th Marines, and participated in combat operations in support of Operations Desert Storm and Desert Shield. In September 1993, he was transferred to 2nd CEB and served as the First Sergeant for H&S Company. He was promoted to Sergeant Major in May 1996 and transferred to Marine Fighter Attack Squadron (Air Wing) 225, Marine Air Group 11, 3rd Marine Air Wing in August 1996 as the Squadron Sergeant Major. In March of 2000, Sergeant Major Franks was transferred to Marine Wing Support Group 37, where he served as the Support Group Sergeant Major and deployed to Kuwait and Iraq, participating in combat operations in support of Operation Iraqi Freedom. In July of 2003, Sergeant Major Franks was transferred to Marine Corps Base Hawaii to assume the post as Base Sergeant Major.

Freeman, Warren L.

Major General—Army

Warren Freeman was born in Jackson, Georgia, on August 20, 1947. He married Barbara Ann Lynch, and they have two sons, Brandon and Kevin. Freeman is a graduate of Eastern High School in Washington, D.C. He has a Bachelor of Business Administration degree

and is a graduate of National-Louis University in Evanston, Illinois, where he received a Master of Science degree in Management.

His military education includes the Infantry and Military Police Basic Courses; Military Police Advanced Course, Command and General Staff College; National Security Management Course; Battalion/Brigade Pre-Command Course, United States Army War College; Senior Reserve Component Officer Course; DEOMI Senior Executive; Equal Opportunity Seminar; and Harvard University, National and International Security Management Seminar.

The general began his military career on September 11, 1966, when he enlisted in the 107th Engineer Company, District of Columbia Army National Guard. He served in several junior enlisted positions, from Bridge Specialist to Military Police. Upon graduation from the District of Columbia National Guard Officer Candidate School as the Distinguished Graduate, he was commissioned a Second Lieutenant in July 1969.

He has served in numerous positions of increased authority and responsibility, including Platoon Leader, Company Commander, Battalion Executive Officer, Battalion Commander, Deputy Brigade Commander, and Chief of Staff at the District of Columbia Army National Guard. His appointment was approved by President Bill Clinton and confirmed by the Senate. He was promoted to Major General on December 18, 1995, and he assumed command as the Commanding General of the District of Columbia National Guard, Washington, D.C. As Commanding General he was responsible for command and control of the District of Columbia Army and Air National Guard. He was responsible for operational readiness, command and control of the D.C. Army and Air National Guard, with an authorized strength of 3,200 soldiers and airmen. He retired on December 31, 2002.

His awards and decorations include the Legion of Merit; Army Meritorious Service Medal (with oak leaf clusters); Army Commendation Medal (with four oak leaf clusters); Air Force Commendation Medal; Army Achievement Medal (with one oak leaf cluster); Army Achievement Medal (with one oak leaf cluster); Army Reserve Component Achievement Medal (with four oak leaf clusters); National Defense Service Medal (with bronze service star); Humanitarian Service Medal; Armed Forces Reserve Medal (with gold hour glass device); Army Service Ribbon and Reserve Component Overseas Ribbon (with numeral three); District of Columbia Distinguished Service Medal; Meritorious Service Medal (with two oak leaf clusters); Emergency Service Ribbon; Community Service Ribbon; Medal for Long and Faithful Service and Outstanding Unit Award.

Friday, Ronald D.

COMMAND SERGEANT MAJOR—ARMY

A native of Timmonsville, South Carolina, Friday entered the United States Army in June 1977 upon graduation from high school. He attended One Station Unit Training at Fort Sill, Oklahoma.

His military and civilian education includes all the Noncommissioned Officer Education System Courses; Drill Sergeant School; Basic Recruiter Course; Station Commanders Course; First Sergeant Course; Battle Staff Course (Honor Graduate); Air Assault School; Garrison Sergeants Major Course; the United States Army Sergeants Major Academy (class 49); and Garrison Command Sergeants Major Course. He holds an Associate's Degree (with honors) from Central Texas College.

He has served in numerous leadership positions, including Section Chief; Drill Sergeant; Station Commander; Platoon Sergeant; Battalion Operations Sergeant; and Battery First Sergeant. He was selected as Vice President of Class 49 of the United States Army Sergeants Major Academy. In August 2004, he was serving as the Command Sergeant Major for the Garrison, Fort Jackson, South Carolina.

Fritz, Dennis L.

CHIEF MASTER SERGEANT—AIR FORCE

Fritz entered the United States Air Force in September 1975 as a Basic Trainee at Lackland Air Force Base, Texas. He earned an Associate's Degree in Information Management, Community College of the Air Force.

He has held a wide variety of important command and staff positions. From September 1989 to January 1992, he was assigned as Assistant Executive Officer, Legislative Liaison, in the Office of the Secretary of the Air Force at the Headquarters of the United States Air Force, in Washington, D.C. From January 1992 to January 1994, he was assigned as Chief of Executive Services for the Deputy Chief of Staff of Logistics at Headquarters United States Air Force in Washington, D.C. From January 1994 to October 1996, he served as the Senior Enlisted Advisor with the 374th Airlift Wing at Yokota Air Base, Japan. From October 1996 to August 1998, he served as Pacific Air Forces Senior Enlisted Advisor with Headquarters Pacific Air Forces, Hickman Air Force Base, Hawaii. From August 1998 to February 2000, he was assigned as the Air Force Space Command, Command Chief Master Sergeant, with Headquarters Space Command at Peterson Air Force Base, Colorado.

In May 2000, he was selected to serve as the Com-

mand Chief Master Sergeant for the 89th Airlift Wing, Andrews Air Force Base, Maryland. As the Command Chief Master Sergeant, he serves as the Wing Commander's Senior Enlisted representative and voice for approximately 7,000 enlisted men and women assigned to Andrews Air Force Base. He was promoted to Chief Master Sergeant on December 1, 1993.

Frye, D. Scott

SERGEANT MAJOR—MARINE

Sergeant Major Frye is a native of New Haven, Connecticut. He enlisted in the Marine Corps on October 2, 1975. Upon completion of recruit training at Parris Island, South Carolina, he was assigned the 5831 MOS and underwent the MOS training for Correctional Specialist at Fort McClellan, Alabama.

On November 1, 1989, he was promoted to First Sergeant and assigned as the First Sergeant of the Marine Corps Security Forces Company at Diego Garcia. In August 1994, he was selected as the Sergeant Major of 1st Battalion, 7th Marines. In February 1997, he served as the Sergeant Major, Marine Barracks, 8th & I, in Washington, D.C. He served as the Sergeant Major, Marine Corps Base, at Quantico, Virginia, before assuming the assignment of Sergeant Major of the United States Marine Corps Forces, Atlantic and South.

Frye, William S.

BRIGADIER GENERAL—ARMY

General Frye was born in Montclair, New Jersey. He graduated from Rutgers University in 1947. General Frye entered active service in March 1943 at Fort Dix,

New Jersey. After serving in the 429th Medical Battalion in Mississippi and California, he was transferred to the 590th Ambulance Company and served with that unit in the European Theatre of Operations from March 1944 through September 1945, during which time he participated in the campaigns of Ardennes-Alsace, central Europe, Normandy, Northern France, and the Rhineland. He was discharged as a staff sergeant in October 1945.

He was appointed as Second Lieutenant, Medical Service Corps, in the 311th AAA Battalion, New Jersey Army National Guard, on February 2, 1948. He changed branches to join the Coast Artillery Corps on December 8, 1949, and was promoted to First Lieutenant, Coast Artillery Corps, on March 9, 1950. He continued to serve in the 311th AAA Battalion, was assigned as Battalion S-2, 109th AAA Gun Battalion, on July 1, 1954, and as Major, Artillery, in June 1957 as S-3 of the 109th (later re-designated as the 1st Missile Battalion, 245th Artillery). He was reassigned to Battalion Commander of that unit on February 10, 1964, and promoted to Lieutenant Colonel on February 24, 1964. He served as Battalion Commander for over five years.

In November 1969 he was assigned as Inspector General, 50th Armored Division, a position he held until April 1972, at which time he was promoted to Colonel and assigned as commander, 44th Area Headquarters. On June 1, 1976, he was reassigned to Headquarters Detachment as Inspector General. He was promoted and federally recognized as Brigadier General on June 30, 1977.

He was assigned as Commander, State Area Command, Headquarters Detachment, New Jersey Army National Guard. His military decorations and awards include the Meritorious Service Medal; Army Commendation Medal; American Campaign Medal; European-African-Middle Eastern Campaign Medal (with five bronze stars); World War II Victory Medal; Army of Occupation Medal Germany; Armed Forces Reserve Medal (with hourglass device); Army Reserve Components Achievement Medal; and the New Jersey Medal of Honor (25 years).

Fuller, Sherman L.
COMMAND SERGEANT MAJOR—ARMY

Born in Torrance, California, Sherman Fuller entered the United States Army in June 1978. He attended Basic Combat and Advanced Individual Training at Fort Leonard Wood, Missouri. His military and civilian education includes completing all Noncommissioned Officer Education System Courses; Anti-Armor and M-60 Leaders Course; Battle Staff Course; the First Sergeant Course; and the United States Army Sergeants Major Academy (class 48). He holds an Associates Degree from Pierce College and Troy State University and is pursuing a Bachelor of Science Degree in Human Recourse Management.

He has held numerous leadership positions, including serving as First Sergeant, C Company and Headquarters and Headquarters Company, 3rd Battalion, 75th Ranger Regiment, Fort Benning, Georgia; Deputy Commandant of the Henry Caro Noncommissioned Officer Academy, Fort Benning, Georgia; Commandant of Cadets at the University of Colorado, Colorado Springs; Command Sergeant Major, 2nd Battalion, 6th Infantry Division; Command Sergeant Major 2nd Brigade, 1st Armored Division Combat Team; and Command Sergeant Major, Task Force Falcon in Kosovo. In August 2004, he was serving as the Command Sergeant Major of JRTC and Fort Polk, Louisiana.

Fullford, Eric W.
SERGEANT MAJOR—ARMY

Fullford entered the United States Army in June of 1975 at Fort Jackson, South Carolina, where he completed basic training. After completing basic training, he attended the Unit Supply Specialist Course for Advanced Individual Training at Ford Lee, Virginia. He is currently pursuing his Bachelor's Degree in Liberal Arts. His military education includes Sergeants Major Academy; Noncommissioned Officer Logistic Course; and ALMC Logistic Management Course.

He is currently serving as the Senior Enlisted Advisor to the Deputy Chief of Staff, G-4 (Logistics NCOIC). He serves as the liaison between the Sergeant Major of the Army and the DCS, G-4 on troop support programs, maintenance, readiness, and logistical matters. He assumed these duties on July 1, 2002.

Fussell, Macea E.
REAR ADMIRAL—NAVY

Commissioned an Ensign in January 1961, Macea Fussell was appointed to the Ensign 1915 program. After completing medical school at Meharry Medical College in Nashville, Tennessee, in 1964, he was called to active duty in 1965 and augmented to regular Navy where he served as a General Medical Officer at United States Naval Hospital at Great Lakes, Illinois, for one year. He then was assigned to Naval Hospital, San Diego, California, as an orthopedic resident until completion of his studies in 1970. He became Board Certified in Orthopedic Surgery in 1972.

From 1970 until 1972, he was Chief of Orthopedics at Naval Hospital, Port Hueneme, California. He resigned his regular commission as a Lieutenant Commander, United States Navy, and became a reservist. He has been Commanding Officer of several reserve

Futrell, James R.

SERGEANT MAJOR—MARINE

Futrell enlisted into the United States Marine Corps in July 1979. He graduated from Marine Corps Recruit Depot, Parris Island, South Carolina.

His key military assignments include serving as a Recruiter/Noncommissioned Officer in Charge, Recruiting Station, Raleigh, North Carolina; as Platoon Sergeant/Platoon Commander, Bravo Battery, 1st LAAD Battalion, 1st Marine Air Wing, Okinawa, Japan; Battery Gunnery Sergeant/Training Chief/Operations Chief, 2nd LAAD Battalion, Marine Corps Air Station, Cherry Point, North Carolina; Gunnery Sergeant, deployed with the 4th Marine Expeditionary Brigade to participate in Operation Desert Shield/Desert Storm; as an Instructor/Senior Noncommissioned Officer in Charge, Stinger School, Marine Corps Detachment, Fort Bliss, Texas; Sergeant Major, Recruiting Station, 6th Marine Corps District, Fort Lauderdale, Florida; Sergeant Major for Inspector Instructor, 4th Maintenance Battalion, 4th Force Service and Supply Group, Charlotte, North Carolina; and Sergeant Major of the 4th Marine Corps District, New Cumberland, Pennsylvania. In January 2005, he was serving as Sergeant Major for Marine Corps Recruiting Command, Quantico, Virginia.

Gabriel, Berhane

COMMAND SERGEANT MAJOR—ARMY

Gabriel enlisted in the Army in March 1983, attending One Station Unit Training (OSUT) at Fort Knox, Kentucky, as a 19D Cavalry Scout. He has served in every position in the Armored Cavalry Field from Dismounted Scout to Command Sergeant Major.

He served as the Command Sergeant Major of the 3rd Squadron with the 7th Cavalry in Iraq in 2003.

He was assigned as a Dismounted Scout, Driver, with Gunner and Squad Leader in C Troop Squadron, 12th Cavalry, 3D Armored Division, Budingen, Germany; Track Commander and Section Sergeant in HHC 4th Battalion, 64th Armor, 24th Infantry Division, Fort Stewart, Georgia; Drill Sergeant and Senior Drill Sergeant with E and B Companies, 4th Battalion, 26th Infantry, 2nd Training Brigade, Fort Dix, New Jersey; Platoon Sergeant in HHC 2nd Battalion, 15th Infantry, in Schweinfurt, Germany; and 3rd Infantry Division Operations Sergeant in HHT 2nd Squadron, 4th Cavalry, 24th infantry, later re-designated 30 Squadron, 7th Cavalry, 3rd Infantry Division, Fort Stewart, Georgia. He assumed the position of Command Sergeant Major of the 3rd Squadron, 7th Cavalry, 3rd Infantry Division (Mech), at Fort Sewart, Georgia, on June 20, 2002.

Gaines, George L.

CAPTAIN—NAVY

George L. Gaines is a native of St. Louis, Missouri. He enlisted into the United States Navy in August 1955, and after advancing to Petty Officer Second Class he separated from active duty in 1958. He then completed

medical units. He has performed active duty training at numerous medical treatment facilities, including Naval Medical Clinic, Pearl Harbor; Naval Hospital, Bremerton, Washington; Naval Hospital, San Diego, California; Naval Hospital, Camp Pendleton, California; and the Marine Mountain Warfare Training Center, Bridgeport, California.

He has participated in several advanced leadership and executive courses and has worked on special projects at the Pentagon, the Bureau of Medicine and Surgery, and the Naval War College at Newport, Rhode Island.

In 1988, he was appointed Director of Health Service REDCOM 19, San Diego, California, the largest REDCOM in the nation. In 1989, he served as Brigade Surgeon for the Marine exercises Cold Winter '89 (Fort McCoy, Wisconsin) and Alpine Warrior '89 (Norway).

In 1990, he was assigned Force Medical Officer for the Reserve Naval Construction Force, Gulfport, Mississippi, where he served until September 1993. He was promoted to the rank of Rear Admiral in November 1992. On October 1, 1993, he was appointed Deputy Fleet Surgeon CINCPACFLT, Honolulu, Hawaii.

In August 1994 he was appointed Commander, Naval Medical Forces, Korea, where he was responsible for all active duty and reserve medical forces deployed to Korea in the event of hostilities.

He was appointed Chief of the Reserve Medical Corps in September 1994. In that position he functioned as the Corps Chief and Coordinator of all reserve matters organic to the Reserve Medical Corps with the office of OOMC.

In January 1995 the Secretary of the Navy appointed Rear Admiral Fussell to the Navy's National Naval Reserve Policy Board (NNRPB).

Officer Training through the Reserve Officer Training Candidate Program (ROTC) in August 1962.

He received a commission as an Ensign and initially served as an Assistant Communications Officer and Assistant Navigation Officer on the USS *Oklahoma City* (CLG 5).

His education includes a Master's Degree from the Naval Postgraduate School; Naval Destroyer School; and Missile and Fire Control School.

He held numerous key assignments, including serving as the Weapons Officer and Executive Officer onboard USS *Providence* (CLG 6); Executive Officer, USS *Turner Joy* (DD 951); Commanding Officer, USS *Parsons* (DDG 33); and Chief of the Naval Advisory Group, Military Assistance Command, Vietnam, in Saigon, RVN. He has served at the United States Naval Academy; the Naval Sea Systems Command (MK 86 Gun Fire Control System Program Manager); Naval Ship Weapon System Engineering Station (TARTAR Department Head); and as the Executive Officer/Senior Combat System Member of the Pacific Fleet Board of Inspection and Survey.

Gaines, John M., Jr.

COMMAND SERGEANT MAJOR—ARMY

John M. Gaines, Jr., was born in Providence, Rhode Island, and entered the United States Army in October 1981. He attended Basic Combat Training at Fort Dix, New Jersey, and Advanced Individual Training at Fort Lee, Virginia. His military education includes all the Noncommissioned Officers Education System Course;

the First Sergeants Course; and the United States Army Sergeants Major Academy. He holds an Associate's Degree in General Studies from City College of Chicago, Harold Washington.

His key leadership assignments include serving as Section Sergeant; Class I Noncommissioned Officer in Charge; Platoon Sergeant; Noncommissioned Officer in Charge of the Supply and Services Division and Administrative NCO to the United States Mission to NATO; First Sergeant for B Company, 710th MSB, and Battalion Operations Sergeant. He served as the Noncommissioned Officer in Charge for Combat Service Support at West Point for the cadets; in 1999, he was reassigned to the 526th Forward Support Battalion (FSB), 101st Airborne Division (Air Assault) where he served as Battalion Operations Sergeant. In August 2004, he was serving as the Command Sergeant Major for the 254th Base Support Battalion.

Gardley, Carl A.

COMMAND MASTER CHIEF—NAVY

Command Master Chief Carl A. Gardley joined the United States Navy in June 1974. After Recruit Training at Great Lakes, Illinois, he served aboard USS *Joseph Strauss* (DDG 16), USS *Sacramento* (AOE 1), and USS *Coral Sea* (CV 43).

His next assignment was Naval District Headquarters at Washington, D.C. Upon completion of his first shore duty, he returned to sea on board USS *Camden* (AOE 2) and USS *Sacramento* (AOE 1). His next assignment was at Naval Station, Everett, Washington, where he was assigned as Harbor Master and Operations Department Leading Chief Petty Officer. In 1997, he was selected into the Command Master Chief Program and assumed his duties as Command Master Chief of USS *Rainier* (AOE 7) in October 1997. In September 2001,

he assumed his present duties as Command Master Chief of Naval Intermediate Maintenance Facility, Pacific Northwest.

Garner, William C.

CHIEF MASTER SERGEANT—AIR FORCE

Garner is a native of Dennison, Ohio, and graduated from Dover High School in Dover, Ohio, in June 1974. He enlisted into the United States Air Force in March 1977. Upon completion of Basic Military Training, he attended technical training in Aerospace Food Service at Lowry Air Force Base, Colorado. He was a Distinguished Graduate of the SAC Noncommissioned Officer Leadership School and also attended the Senior Noncommissioned Officer Academy. He holds an associate's degree in Food Service Management and Instructor of Technology in Military Science as well as a bachelor's degree in Workforce Education and Development.

In May 1989, he was assigned to the 7274th Services Squadron at RAF Chicksands, United Kingdom, as the Dining Facility Manager where he departed as Chief of the Military Support Flight. In March 1993, he was reassigned to the 48th Morale, Welfare, Recreation and Services Squadron at RAF Lakenheath, United Kingdom, as the First Sergeant and Food Service Manager. In May 1995, he was assigned to the 60th Services Squadron at Travis Air Force Base as the Food Services Officer. In June 1998, he was assigned to the 51st Services Squadron at Osan Air Base, South Korea, as the Food Services Officer. He returned to Travis and became Chief Master Sergeant and Services Chief for Air

Training Command, headquartered at Randolph Air Force Base, San Antonio, Texas.

Garrett, Ronnie

COMMAND SERGEANT MAJOR—ARMY

Garrett was born in California, and entered the United States Army in August 1978. He attended Basic Combat Training at Fort Leonard Wood, Missouri, and Advanced Individual Training at Fort Rucker, Alabama. His military and civilian education includes all the United States Army's Noncommissioned Officer Education System Courses; Drill Sergeant School; First

Sergeant Course; Battle Staff Course; and the United States Army Sergeants Major Academy. He has earned an Associate of Arts Degree from the University of Maryland, and holds a Bachelor of Science Degree from Excelsior College.

He has held every key Noncommissioned Officer leadership position in a variety of tactical assignments, ranging from Squad Leader to Command Sergeant Major of the 1st Battalion, 501st Aviation Regiment in Hanau, Germany; Command Sergeant Major of the 2-4th Aviation Regiment at Fort Hood, Texas; Command Sergeant Major of the 6th Cavalry Brigade at Camp Humphreys, South Korea; and the Command Sergeant Major and Commandant of USARAK Noncommissioned Officer Academy, Alaska.

Gaskill, Roberts Clarence

MAJOR GENERAL—ARMY

Born in Yonkers, New York, Gaskill received a Bachelor of Arts degree from Howard University and a Master's of Business Administration from George Washington University.

In 1952 Gaskill was commissioned a second lieutenant in the United States Army after completing with distinction the Army Reserve Officers Training Course (ROTC) at Howard University. Initially he served in various infantry positions. Following assignment to the Quartermaster Center at Fort Lee, Virginia, he has held numerous key Army logistical positions. He served as Deputy Commanding General of the 1st Support Brigade, United States Army, Europe, which he helped organize. He served as Commanding General of the 21st Support Command, United States Army, in Europe. He served as the Commanding General of Letter Kenny Army Depot in Pennsylvania. He has served in

Staff positions with the Military Assistance Command in Vietnam and in the office of the Deputy Chief of Staff for Logistics, Department of the Army, Washington, D.C.

He is a graduate of the United States Army Command and General Staff College, the Army Forces Staff College, the Army Logistics Management Center, the Army Institute for Military Assistance and Navy Postgraduate School. From 1971 to 1972, he was a student at the Army War College and became a faculty member, teaching command management and executive development until 1974. In 1977 he was promoted to major general.

In October 1978 he was assigned as the Deputy Director of the Defense Logistics Agency. As the Deputy Director of the Defense Logistics Agency, his responsibilities encompassed the agency's worldwide activities, which provide all the armed forces with a vast range of supplies and logistic support services.

He has received numerous awards and decorations, including the Distinguished Service Medal, Legion of Merit, Meritorious Service Medal (with oak leaf cluster), and the Honor Medal 1st class from the Republic of Vietnam.

Gaskin, Walter E.

MAJOR GENERAL—MARINES

Gaskin graduated from Savannah State University NROTC Scholarship Program in 1974 with a Bachelor of Science degree. He later earned a master's degree in Public Administration from the University of Oklahoma in 1972.

He was commissioned a second lieutenant on June 2, 1974. After graduation from Basic School, he was assigned to the Second Marine Division where he served

as a Rifle Platoon Commander and Executive Officer of Company K and 106th Recoilless Rifle Platoon Commander in Third Battalion, Second Marines Regiment.

In May 1977, he was ordered to Okinawa where he served as the S-3 for Logistic Support Units (LSU) Echo and Foxtrot, 3rd Force Service Support Group. He also served as the Senior Watch Officer in the 3rd Marine Divisions Command Center.

In May 1978, he reported to Marine Corps Recruit Depot, Parris Island, where he served as a Series Commander and Commanding Officer of Company F, Second Recruit Training Battalion. In 1980, he was assigned as the Marine Officer Instructor (MOI) at the NROTC Unit, Savannah State University until ordered to Amphibious Warfare School, Quantico, Virginia in 1983.

In July 1984, he joined the 1st Battalion, Second Marines, where he served as the Battalion Operations Officer (S-3). He was subsequently selected to attend the United States Army Command and General Staff College at Fort Leavenworth, Kansas, in July 1986.

From 1987 until 1990, he served as an Action Officer Headquarters Marine Corps/MCCDC in charge of Unit Environmental Training Programs (Jungle, Cold Weather, and Combined Arms Exercises). In 1990, he was assigned to the Combined Forces Command, Seoul Korea where he served as Head of Ground Forces Branch, Operations Division, C/J-3. In July 1992, he reported to II MEF where he served as G-3 Current Operations Action Officer and Operations Officer for II MEF (FWD) during the planning and execution of Battle Griffin Exercise in Norway.

In July 1993, he attended the Army War College at Carlisle Barracks, PA. After graduation in June 1994, he was assigned as the Executive Officer of the Sixth Marine Regiment, Second Marine Division.

In April 1995, he assumed command of the Second Battalion, Second Marines (2/2). In January 1996, he deployed to the Mediterranean Sea as the Commanding Officer of Battalion Landing Team 2/2 (BLT 2/2) as part of the 22nd Marine Expeditionary Unit, Special Operations Capable [22nd MEU (SOC)] as the Landing Force Sixth Fleet (LF6F). During the deployment, he participated in Operations Assured Response and Quick Response in defense of American embassies in Liberia and the Central African Republic.

From September 1996 to July 1998, General Gaskin served as the Ground Colonel's Monitor at Headquarters Marine Corps. In August 1998, Colonel Gaskin returned to Camp Lejeune for duty as Head of Expeditionary Operations, G-3, II MEF.

In January 1999, he assumed duty as the Commanding Officer of the 22nd Marine Expeditionary Unit (SOC). In September 1999, he deployed his Marine Expeditionary Unit acting as the Landing Forces for the Sixth Fleet (LF6F) to the Mediterranean Sea. The 22nd MEU (SOC) participated in many training exercises including participation in Exercise Bright Star 99/00 in Egypt. This exercise proved to be the largest military endeavor of its kind since Operation Desert Shield/Desert Storm, including more than 20,000

United States troops and a dozen countries working together. Also during this period the 22nd MEU was the strategic backup for possible operations in Kosovo and Bosnia. General Gaskin then led his MEU through the Suez Canal to participate in Exercise Infinite Moonlight with Jordanian forces. The 22nd MEU (SOC) returned to Camp Lejeune in March 2000.

In March 2000, he was promoted to the rank of Brigadier General and subsequently transferred to MCB Quantico, to assume the duties of Commanding General of Training Command. He was promoted to Brigadier General in October 2001.

He served as the Chief of Staff for Naval Striking and Support Forces Southern Europe and as the Deputy General of Fleet Marine Forces Europe in Naples, Italy. Next he was selected to serve as the Commanding General of Marine Recruiting Command. On February 1, 2005, he was nominated by the President to the rank of Major General.

His awards and decorations include the Legion of Merit (with gold star in lieu of second award); Bronze Star (with combat "V"); Defense Meritorious Service Medal; Meritorious Service Medal; Navy and Marine Corps Commendation Medal (with three gold stars in lieu of fourth award); Navy and Marine Corps Achievement Medal; and the Combat Action Ribbon.

Gaston, Mack Charles

REAR ADMIRAL—NAVY

Born in Dalton, Georgia, Gaston married the former Lillian Bonds of Dalton, and they have a daughter, Sonja. He received a Bachelor of Science in Electrical Engineering from Tuskegee Institute in 1964 and a Master of Science in Business Administration from Marymount College of Virginia in 1984.

On August 20, 1964, he enlisted in the United States Navy. From 1965 to 1967, he served on the USS *Buck* (DD-761). He attended Naval Destroyer School at Newport, Rhode Island, from March 1967 to September 1967. He served on the USS *O'Brien* (DD-725) from September 1967 to May 1969. Then, until May 1971, he served on the staff of the Commander of Destroyer Squadron 5.

From May 1971 to December 1972, he was assigned to the Office of Chief of Naval Operations as Personal Aide to the Director of Research, Development, Test and Evaluation. From December 1972 to June 1974, he was assigned to the Bureau of Naval Personnel as Junior Officer in the Detail Branch. From June 1974 to August 1976, he was assigned to the USS *Conyngham* (DDG 17) as Executive Officer. From August 1976 to July 1977, he was a student in the Naval War College (DUINS). From July 1977 to October 1979, he served as the commander of USS *Cochrane* (DDG 21). From October 1979 to April 1981, he was assigned to the Naval Military Personnel Command as Head of the Junior Officer Assignment Branch. From April 1981 to March 1982, he was assigned as the Commander of the USS *Cone* (DD 866). From March 1982 to July 1982, he was assigned to the Naval Military Personnel Command as Head of Lieutenant Commander Surface Assignment Branch. From July 1982 to June 1983, he was a student at the Industrial College of the Armed Forces (DUINS). From June 1983 to August 1984, he was assigned to the Office of the Chief of Naval Operations (OP 39) as Head of the Surface Warfare Training Branch. From August 1984 to August 1985, he was assigned to the Naval Military Personnel Command as Special Assistant for Minority Affairs. From September to November 1985, he attended the Senior Officer for Ship Material Readiness Course at Idaho Falls, Idaho. In February 1986, he became commander of USS *Josephus Daniels* (CG-27). In July 1988, Gaston was assigned to the Office of the Chief of Naval Operations as Director for Surface Warfare Manpower and Training Requirement. In June 1990 he became Commander of Field Command at the Defense Nuclear Agency.

Mack Charles Gaston was promoted to Rear Admiral (lower half) on March 1, 1991. His military awards and decorations include: the Defense Superior Service Medal, the Meritorious Service Medal (with gold star), Navy "E" Ribbon, Vietnam Campaign Medal (with device), Vietnam Service Medal (with bronze star), and Navy Commendation Medal (with combat "V").

Gathers, John F.
COMMAND SERGEANT MAJOR—ARMY

Gathers is a native of Sumter, South Carolina. After graduating from high school in 1976, he joined the United States Army. He attended Basic Combat Training at Fort Jackson, South Carolina, and Advanced Individual Training at Fort Benning, Georgia. After a reclassification he attended his second Advanced Individual Training at Fort Jackson, South Carolina. His military and civilian education includes all the Non-

commissioned Officer Education System Courses; Drill Sergeant School; First Sergeants Course; Battle Staff Course; Air Assault School; and the United States Army Sergeants Major Academy (class 49). He earned an associate's degree from Regents College.

His military assignments include serving as First Sergeant of B 120th AG Reception Battalion; First Sergeant of Headquarters Company Training Center Command at Fort Jackson, South Carolina; and First Sergeant of the 3rd Infantry Division Replacement Detachment. In August 2004, he was serving as Command Sergeant Major, 1st Personnel Command.

Gay, Earl L.
CAPTAIN—NAVY

Captain Earl L. Gay was born in Atlanta, Georgia, and is a 1980 graduate of the United States Naval Academy. He graduated from the Air War College at Air University in Montgomery, Alabama. He earned a master's degree from Troy State University.

Following designation as a Naval Aviator in November 1981, he flew Search and Rescue missions in the High Sierra Nevada Mountains. In October 1983, he recorded the highest rescue in the contiguous United States, recovering an injured hiker at the 14,000 feet on Mount Whitney, California. In December 1983, Captain Gay reported to Helicopter Anti-Submarine Squadron Light Three One (HSL 31) for SH-2F pilot training and was assigned to the world famous "Magicians" of HSL 35. He embarked onboard USS *Fletcher* (DD 971), USS *Cook* (FF 1083) and USS *Leftwich* (DD 984) completing several deployments to the Eastern/Western Pacific and Indian Oceans serving as Detachment Operations, Maintenance and Officer in Charge (OIC).

In August 1995, he reported to HSL 43 as Executive Officer and assumed command of the "BattleCats" in

October 1996. During his command tour HSL 43 deployed the Navy's first Hellfire Missile/Night Vision Goggle (NVG) detachment and conducted the first fleet warshot firing of AGM-119 Penguin missile. The squadron additionally earned the Meritorious Unit Commendation, COMBNAVAIRPAC Battle Efficiency Award, Lockheed-Martin Superior Maintenance Award and the CNO Safety Award.

He reported to USS *Boxer* (LHD 4) as Air Boss in April 1998 and deployed to the Western Pacific and Arabian Gulf with the embarked 13th Marine Expeditionary Unit (MEU). During this tour *Boxer* earned 2 consecutive COMNAVSURFPAC Battle "E" Awards. Captain Gay's personal awards include the 1993 NAACP Roy Wilkins Award for outstanding community service. He is currently serving as the Executive Officer of the USS *Belleau*.

George, D. R.
SERGEANT MAJOR—MARINES

George enlisted in the Marine Corps in May of 1982. He completed recruit training at Marine Corps Recruit Depot in San Diego, California. Upon completion he was transferred to Camp Pendleton, California, where he completed the Infantry Training School (ITS).

His key military assignments include participating in security operations in Panama and Operation Desert Shield/Desert Storm in the Persian Gulf. In August 1996, he was transferred to 3rd FSSG on Okinawa, Japan, and served as Chief Instructor to Tactics Training and Readiness (TRT). Upon completion of duty with 3rd FSSG, he was assigned to 2nd Battalion, 3rd Marines, Golf Company, in Kaneohe Bay, Hawaii, where he served as Company Gunnery Sergeant and Company First Sergeant. Upon his completion of duty with the 2nd Battalion, 3rd Marines, he was assigned to 1st Marine Division, Division Schools, as chief instructor for heavy machine guns. In August of 2003, he was promoted to the rank of First Sergeant and assumed the position of Battalion First Sergeant for Headquarters Battalion, Marine Corps Logistics Base. In December 2004, he was serving as the Acting Battalion Sergeant Major at Marine Corps Logistics Base, Barstow, California.

Gholson, James L.
COMMAND SERGEANT MAJOR—ARMY

Gholson enlisted in the United States Army on February 19, 1976. Upon completion of Army Initial Training and Military Occupation Skill Training as a Field Radio Computer Repairman, he was assigned to Company A of the 2/60th Air Defense Artillery in Germany as a Radio Computer Repairman.

His military and civilian education includes all the Noncommissioned Officer Leadership Courses; the First Sergeant Course; and the United States Army Sergeants Major Academy. He holds a bachelor's degree in Human Relations from McGuire College and an associate's degree from Georgia Military College.

He has served in various units, such as Headquarters

and Headquarters Detachment, 240th Quartermaster Battalion; 555th MP Company; Headquarters and Headquarters Battery, 2/27th Field Artillery, 267th Quartermaster Company; Company B, 2nd Battalion, 60th Air Defense Artillery; HHS, 532nd Military Intelligence Company; Company A, 369th Signal Battalion; 56th Signal Battalion; 235th Satellite Company, 67th Signal Battalion; and 1st Satellite Control Battalion. In August 2004, he was serving as the Command Sergeant Major for the 54th Signal Battalion.

Gibson, Eddie L.
COMMAND SERGEANT MAJOR—ARMY

Gibson is a native of Saluda, South Carolina, and entered the United States Army in August 1979. He attended Basic Combat Training at Fort Leonard Wood, Missouri, and Advanced Individual Training at Fort Sam Houston, Texas. His military education includes all the Noncommissioned Officers Education System Courses; Drill Sergeants School; Instructor Training Course; First Sergeant Course; the United States Army Sergeants Academy (53); and Command Sergeant Major Course.

He has served in a myriad of positions and assignments such as Emergency Room Technician in the 209th General Dispensary at Hanau, Germany; Line Medic 2/68th Armor at Fort Hood, Texas; Medical NCO in the 1/36th Infantry (M) at Friedberg, Germany; Evacuation NCOIC 1st FSB at Fort Stewart, Georgia; Aid Station NCOIC in the 2/68th Armor at Baumholder, Germany; Section Sergeant HHT, 3rd ACR, Fort Bliss, Texas; Clinical NCOIC and Training NCO at William Beaumont Army Medical Center at Fort Bliss; Platoon Sergeant in the 1/63rd Armor at Vilseck, Germany; First Sergeant and Command Sergeant Major in the 232nd Medical Battalion at Fort Sam Houston; and Command Sergeant Major, Troop Command, Fort Gordon, Georgia. In August 2004, he was serving as the Command Sergeant Major of the 21st Combat Support Hospital.

Gill, Harold L.

COMMAND SERGEANT MAJOR—ARMY

Command Sergeant Major Harold L. Gill was born in Shelby, North Carolina, and graduated from Crest High School in 1975. He entered the Army March 5, 1976, attending Basic Combat Training and Advanced Individual Training at Fort Bliss, Texas. He initially served in Headquarters and Headquarters Battery, 1st Battalion, 3rd Air Defense Artillery, 101st Airborne Division at Fort Campbell, Kentucky. From there, he went to South Korea to serve in Battery A, 2nd Battalion, 61st ADA.

His military education includes the United States Army First Sergeants Course; the United States Army Sergeants Major Course; the Airborne School; Air Assault School; and Jumpmaster School.

His most recent assignments include serving as First Sergeant, B/3-4 ADAR, 82nd Airborne Division at Fort Bragg and the Joint Readiness Training Center (JRTC) Operations Group, at Fort Polk, Louisiana; as Command Sergeant Major for the Corps Air Defense Artillery Element (CADE) at Fort Bragg as well as the Task Force Command Sergeant Major for Task Force 2-1 ADA in Southwest Asia; and as the Command Sergeant Major for 2nd Battalion 1st ADA Battalion PATRIOT (PAC 3). He is currently assigned as Command Sergeant Major for the United States Army Forces Central Command in Kuwait (ARCENT-KUWAIT) in 2002–2003.

Gillespie, Lawrence E., Sr.

BRIGADIER GENERAL—ARMY

Gillespie was born in Hamilton, Ohio, and is a grad-uate of Garfield Senior High School. He received a Bachelor of Science degree in Liberal Studies from New York State University in Albany, New York. He earned a master's degree in Public Administration from Shippensburg University in Shippensburg, Pennsylvania. His military education includes the Infantry Officer Candidate School (1964); Rotary Wing (R/W) Aviation School (1965); Infantry Officer Advance Course (1972); Military Police Advance Course (1980); Command and General Staff College (1980); and the United States Army War College (1989).

He enlisted in the United States Army in 1963, and was commissioned as a second lieutenant in 1964. His various assignments include two tours in Vietnam as Section Commander, Platoon Leader, Armed Rotary Wing Pilot and Liaison Officer of an Infantry Brigade. He was released from active duty in 1972 and transferred to the Ohio National Guard as the S-2 of an Infantry Battalion.

He joined the District of Columbia Army National Guard in 1978. He has serve in various assignments to include Assistant G-2 State Headquarters, 715th PAD Commander, Executive Officer of the 163rd Military Police Battalion, ADP Officer, Director of Security, Commandant of DC Military Academy, Deputy DARC Commander and Commander, Troop Command. He was promoted to Colonel on July 16, 1986, and was appointed as the Commander of the 260th Military Police Command on December 5, 1992. He was promoted to Brigadier General on February 22, 1994, while on this assignment. In January 1998, he was selected Assistant Deputy Commanding General (ARNG) of Army Material Command. He retired on August 1, 2000.

His awards and decorations include the Distinguished Flying Cross; Soldiers Medal; Meritorious Service Medal (with two oak leaf clusters); Air Medal (with four oak leaf clusters and V device); Army Commendation Medal (with two oak leaf clusters); Army Reserve Component Achievement Medal, National Defense Service Medal (second award); Vietnam Service Medal (with two bronze stars and one silver star); Armed Forces Reserve Medal; Army Service Ribbon; Overseas Training Ribbon; Army Reserve Components Overseas Training Ribbon; Republic of Vietnam Campaign Medal; Combat Infantry Badge; Army Aviator Master Wings; and Parachute Badge. In addition he wears a number of District of Columbia Awards including the Meritorious Service Medal; Medal for Faithful Service (with ten year device); Community Service Ribbon (with two stars); and Attendance Ribbon (with 14 year device).

Gilley, Alfonsa
MAJOR GENERAL—ARMY

Gilley was born in Bradenton, Florida. He married the former Ruthie Hubert, and they have one child, Michael. He graduated for the University of Maryland in 1975 with a Bachelor of Arts degree in Psychology and three years later earned a Jurist Doctorate (JD) from the University of Maryland Law School. He has passed the bars in Maryland and Pennsylvania and is licensed to practice law in both states. He completed Infantry Officer Candidate School (OCS) in 1967, the Military Intelligence Officer Advanced Course in 1972, the United States Army Command and General Staff College in 1984, and the Army War College in 1995.

After two years of enlisted service and his OCS commissioning, he was assigned as an Army Security Agency student at Fort Devens, Maryland, in 1967. He served in South Vietnam in 1968 with the 374th Radio Research Company as the Communication Security (COMSEC) Officer for the 4th Infantry Division.

In January 1969, he was assigned as an Instructor at the United States Army Security Agency School in Fort Devens, Maryland. Two years later he became was selected Chief of the school's Signal Security (SIGSEC) Division. He was a student at the Military Intelligence Officer Advanced Course at Fort Huachuca, Arizona, in 1972 and served his last active duty assignment as a COMSEC Analyst for the National Security Agency at Fort Meade, Maryland, in 1973.

He entered the United States Army Reserve in September 1973 as a SIGSEC Officer, Mobilization Designee, United States Army Forces Command, Fort McPherson, Georgia. In 1975, he was reassigned as a Loudspeaker Team Leader, 12th Psychological Operations (PSYOP) Company, in Washington, D.C. Other PSYOP assignments in Washington, D.C., followed, as Audio Visual Team Leader, 12 PSYOP Company; Supply Officer, 7th PSYOP Battalion, Current Intelligence Team Leader, 5th PSYOP Group, and Propaganda Development Team Leader, 5th PSYOP Group.

He was assigned as the Commander of the 12th PSYOP Company in 1984. In 1986, he became a Command and General Staff Office Course Instructor, and later Director of Enlisted Courses for the 207th United States Army Reserve Forces School at Fort Belvoir, Virginia. In January 1989, he served as Chief of the Individual Training Division, Office of the Deputy Chief of Staff for Training, 97th Army Command (ARCOM), at Fort Meade, Maryland. He became the Commander of the 338th Michigan Battalion (CEWI), Affairs, 354th Civil Affairs Brigade, in Riverdale, Maryland.

He commanded the 428th MI Detachment from January 1992 to October 1995, until he was selected as Brigadier General and the Deputy Commanding General of the United States Army Intelligence and Security Command (IMA), INSCOM, on April 27, 1995.

In October 1999, he was selected to serve as the Assistant Deputy Chief of Staff for G2 (IMA), in the Office of the Deputy Chief of Staff, G2, in Washington, D.C. He was promoted to Major General on October 6, 2000.

His military awards and decorations include the Bronze Star; Meritorious Service Medal (with oak leaf cluster); Army Reserve Component Achievement Medal (with four oak leaf clusters); National Defense Service Medal (with one service star); Vietnam Service Medal; Armed Forces Reserve Medal; and the Vietnam Campaign Medal (with six devices).

Gilliam, Haywood S.
BRIGADIER GENERAL—ARMY

He was born in Petersburg, Virginia. He received a Bachelor of Arts degree in Chemistry from Hampton Institute in Hampton, Virginia. He earned a Medical Doctor degree (cum laude) from Creighton University School of Medicine in Omaha, Nebraska. After completing medical school, he began active military duty, where he subsequently completed Internship and Residency at Fitzsimons Army Medical Center in Aurora, Colorado, in Categorical Surgery. He also received a

fellowship in Cardiothoracic Surgery from 1984 to 1986 at Letterman Army Medical Center in the Presidio of San Francisco, California. He was a student at the Chemical School at Fort McClellan in 1970.

From 1982 to 1984, he was Chief of General Surgery Service at Fort Stewart, Georgia; from 1986 to 1989, he served as Assistant Chief of Cardio-thoracic Surgery at Letterman Army Medical Center; and in 1991, he was assigned as Thoracic Surgeon, at the 2nd General Hospital in Landstuhl, Germany, where he was Activated in support of Desert Shield and Desert Storm from January to May 1991). In May 1991, he was assigned as Thoracic Surgeon in the 44th General Hospital at Madison, Wisconsin; from November 1991 to November 1995, he served as the Commander for the 44th General Hospital; and from November 1995 to 1997, he served as the Commander for the 804th Medical Brigade in Deven, Massachusetts. He was promoted to Brigadier General on September 18, 1996.

His military awards and decorations include the Meritorious Service Medal (with oak leaf cluster); Army Commendation Medal; Army Achievement Medal (with oak leaf cluster); Army Reserve Component Achievement Medal; National Defense Service Medal (with bronze star); Armed Forces Reserve Medal (with 10 year device; Army Service Ribbons; Overseas Service Ribbon (with numeral 2); Expert Field Medical Badge.

Gilliam, Michael
SERGEANT MAJOR—ARMY

Gilliam is a native of Columbia, South Carolina, and entered the United States Army in July 1978. His military and civilian education includes all the Non-commissioned Officer Education System Courses; Personnel Logistics Course; Inspector General Course;

Deployment Staff Officers Course; NBC Officer/NCO Defense Course; Basics of Contracting Course; the Air Assault Course; and the United States Army Sergeants Major Academy (class 51). He holds a Bachelor of Science degree in General Studies, with a concentration in Sociology from Regents College.

During his career he has served in a variety of leadership positions to include Squad Leader; Section Sergeant; Platoon Sergeant; Detachment Sergeant; Assistant Inspector General; and Sergeant Major.

Gilmore, Cornell Winston
SERGEANT MAJOR—ARMY

Sergeant Major Gilmore is a native of Baltimore, Maryland. He graduated from the University of Mary-

land in 1980 with a Bachelor of Science degree in Sociology and a minor in Criminal Justice. He enlisted in the United States Army in October 1981. He completed Basic Training at Fort Jackson, South Carolina, and he completed Advanced Individual Training at Fort Benjamin Harrison, Indiana, in March 1982.

His military assignments include serving as NCOIC, Criminal Law, 3rd Infantry Division, Wuerzberg, Germany; Chief Legal NCO, 3rd Infantry Division, Wuerzberg, Germany; Chief Legal NCO, 1st Infantry Division, Wuerzberg, Germany; Chief Legal NCO, 25th Infantry Division, Schofield, Barracks, Hawaii; and Chief Legal NCO, I Corps, Fort Lewis, Washington. In June 2002, he was assigned as the Sergeant Major of the Judge Advocate General's Corps, United States Army.

The Sergeant Major was killed when the Black Hawk helicopter he was flying in was struck by enemy fire and crashed near Tikrit, Iraq, on November 7, 2003.

Godbolt, Enoch L.
SERGEANT MAJOR—ARMY

Godbolt was born in Florence, South Carolina. He enlisted in the United States Army in August 1981. He completed One Station Unit Training (OSUT) for MOS 11C at Fort Benning, Georgia. He began his military career as a mortar man with the completion of OSUT in December 1981.

His military education includes all the Noncommissioned Officer Education System Courses; the First Sergeant Course; Airborne School; Air Assault School; Pathfinder School; Drill Sergeant School; Ranger School; Light Leader's School; Nuclear Biological Chemical School; Observer Course Academy; Combat Lifesaver; Safety Course; Support Operations Course; Supervisor Development Course; the Logistic Management Development Course; and the United States Army Sergeants Major Academy.

He has served in numerous key leadership positions, including as Squad Leader in the 3/22nd Infantry at Schofield Barracks, Hawaii; and as Drill Sergeant assigned to the 4/13th Infantry at Fort Jackson, South Carolina, where he received the award for "Drill Sergeant of the Cycle." He was selected to serve as First Sergeant for D Company, "The Old Guard" at Fort Myer, Virginia, until February 2000, and he was assigned as the Noncommissioned Officer-In-Charge, AOC Pentagon, CCSA, Washington, D.C.

His deployments and special assignments include Cobra Gold '88; North Wind Japan '89; Team Spirit '89; Cobra Gold '92; JTF-6 '93; and NTC '94. He was selected to participate in the 1st interface with the Singapore Army in conjunction with a future Singapore Exchange Program, and in February 1996, he became a member of the Operations Group Tarantula Team at Fort Irwin, California.

In May 2002, he was assigned as the 8th Sergeant Major for the Army Research Laboratory (ARL) in Adelphi, Maryland.

Golder, Steven M.
SERGEANT MAJOR—MARINES

Golder enlisted in the United States Marine Corps in October 1979. He attended recruit training at Marine Corps Recruit Depot, Parris Island, in South Carolina. In September 1980, he completed Construction Surveying School at Fort Belvoir, Virginia. In January 1981, he returned to Fort Belvoir to be trained as a Geodetic Surveyor.

His key military assignments include serving from March 1997 to January 1998 as the Company First Sergeant of Bulk Fuel Company "C" in Wilmington, Delaware. In January 1998, he was ordered to serve as Company First Sergeant of Bulk Fuel Company "C" in Folsom, PA. In September 2001, he was assigned to Headquarters & Service Company, 2nd Battalion, 25th Marines, Garden City, New York, and from January 2002 to March 2003, he was activated and mobilized in support of operation Enduring Freedom with the 2nd Marine Division. In April 2003, he was assigned as Squadron Sergeant Major of Marine Medium Helicopter Squadron 774, 4th Marine Aircraft Wing, in Norfolk, Virginia.

Goodly, Baxter A.
COMMANDER—NAVY

He was born in Orleans, France, the son of a career United States Army Soldier. He graduated from Tulane University in 1985, where he earned a Bachelor of Arts degree in History and received his commission through the Aviation Officer Candidate School in February 1986. He was designated a Naval Aviator in June 1987.

Following SH-3H "Sea King" Fleet Replacement Squadron (FRS) training at Helicopter Anti-Submarine Squadron One (HS-1) in Jacksonville, Florida, he was assigned to Helicopter Anti-Submarine Squadron Fifteen (HS-15) in January 1988. During this tour, the

Goosby, Keith
COMMAND MASTER CHIEF—NAVY

Master Chief Keith Goosby was born in Chicago Heights, Illinois, and graduated from Momence High School in Momence, Illinois. He joined the United States Navy on November 11, 1974, and reported as a recruit to Naval Training Center (NTC) Orlando, Florida. After graduating from NTC, he attended and graduated from Aviation Electrician "A" School in Millington, Tennessee.

His first assignment was as in Helicopter Combat Support Squadron Three (HC 3) San Diego where he deployed on the USS *Niagara Falls* (AFS 3) and USS *White Plains* (AFS 4). He was assigned to Helicopter Anti-Submarine Squadron Six (HS 6) San Diego where he made on Western Pacific/Indian Ocean deployment and one "around the world" cruise on USS *Enterprise* (CVN 65) he then transferred to Naval Aviation Maintenance Training Group Detachment (NAMTRA-GRUDET) at North Island San Diego. During this tour he earned his Master Training Specialist designation while serving as an instructor.

While assigned with Carrier Airborne Early Warning Squadron One One Two (VAW 112) where he served as Quality Assurance and Night Shift Maintenance Control Senior Chief Petty Officer. VAW-112 made two Western Pacific/Arabian Gulf cruises on board the USS *Nimitz* (CVN 68) during his tour. It was there that he was promoted to Master Chief Petty Officer and served his first tour as a Command Master Chief. He then transferred to Helicopter Anti-Submarine Squadron Light Four Five (HSL 45) as Command Master Chief, but after only two months was selected as the Regional Command Master Chief for the Commander of Naval Base San Diego. Before assuming the job, he attended

squadron made deployments to the North Arabian Sea and the Mediterranean while embarked in USS *Forrestal* (CV 59). In November 1990, he reported for duty as Flag Lieutenant/Personal Aide to Commander, United States Naval Forces, Marianas (COMAVMAR), based in Guam.

In September 1996, following SH-60F/H ("Sea Hawk") transition training at HS-1, he reported to Helicopter Anti-Submarine Squadron Eleven (HS-11) where he served as the Administrative Officer and Operations Officer. During this tour while serving in USS *George Washington* (CVN 73), he was deployed to the Mediterranean to participate in Exercise Bright Star and to the Arabian Gulf in support of Operation Southern Watch. He reported to his next assignment at the Bureau of Naval Personnel in Washington, D.C., in December 1998 where he served as the Assistant Aviation Officer Community Manager (N131V). While serving in this capacity, he was selected for the charter class of the Navy D.C. Intern Program. This two-year graduate education program culminated in a 6-month internship at the United States Department of State and conferment of a Masters Degree in Organizational Management from the George Washington University in May 2001.

He reported NAF Atsugi, Japan as Executive Officer of Helicopter Anti-Submarine Squadron Fourteen (HS-14) in February 2002. In early 2003, the squadron embarked in USS *Kitty Hawk* (CV 63), and deployed to the Arabian Gulf in support of Operations Enduring Freedom and Iraqi Freedom. In June 2003, he assumed command of the world famous HS-14 Chargers, the Navy's only permanently forward deployed HS squadron. During his tenure as Commanding Officer, the Chargers were awarded the Thach and Isbell Awards for ASW Excellence as well as the 2003 CNAP Battle E.

the Senior Enlisted Academy at Newport Rhode Island. While a Commander at Naval Base San Diego, Master Chief Goosby applied for and was one of six finalists for the position of Master Chief Petty Officer of the Navy. He next embarked on a successful tour as Regional Master Chief of "America's Flagship," where he served until selected as Force Master Chief for Naval Air Force, United States Pacific Fleet in June 2000.

Gorden, Fred Augustus
MAJOR GENERAL—ARMY

General Gorden was born in Anniston, Alabama. He received a Bachelor of Science degree from the United States Military Academy and a Master of Arts in Foreign Language Literature from Middleburg College. From August 1962 to October 1962, he was a student at the Field Artillery Officer Basic Course at the United States Army Artillery and Missile School in Fort Sill, Oklahoma. From November 1962 to January 1963, he was a student in the Ranger Course at the United States Army Infantry School at Fort Benning, Georgia.

From January 1963 to November 1965, he served as a Forward Observer, later Liaison Officer, later Assistant Executive Officer, and later Executive Officer of Battery B, 22nd Artillery, 193rd Infantry Brigade, at Fort Kobbe in the Panama Canal Zone. He was promoted to 1st Lieutenant on December 6, 1963. From November 1965 to March 1966, he served as Assistant S-3 in the 193rd Infantry Brigade at Fort Kobbe.

He was promoted to Captain on November 9, 1965. From March 1966 to December 1966, he was a student in the Artillery Officer Advanced Course at the United Army Air Defense School at Fort Bliss, Texas. From December 1966 to January 1968, he first served as the Assistant S-3 (Operations), later Liaison Officer, later Commander of Battery C, then an Assistant S-3 of 2nd

Howitzer Battalion, 320th Artillery, 1st Brigade, 101st Airborne Division in the United States Army, Vietnam.

From May 1968 to August 1969, Gorden was a student at Middlebury College at Middlebury, Vermont. He was promoted to Major on December 31, 1968. From August 1969 to June 1972, he was appointed to Instructor of Spanish, later Assistant Professor (Spanish), in the Department of Foreign Language at the United States Military Academy. From June 1972 to January 1973, he was a student in the Armed Forces Staff College at Norfolk, Virginia. From January 1973 to May 1975, he was an Assignment Officer, later Personnel Management Officer in the Field Artillery Branch at the United States Army Military Personnel Center at Alexandria, Virginia.

From May 1975 to July 1976, he was Executive Officer, 1st Battalion, 15th Field Artillery, 2nd Infantry Division, in South Korea. On June 7, 1976, he was promoted to Lieutenant Colonel. From July 1976 to March 1977, he served as Special Assistant to the Commander, later S-3, Division Artillery, 25th Infantry Division, at Schofield Barracks, Hawaii.

From September 1978 to June 1979, he served as Inspector General of the 25th Infantry Division at Schofield Barracks. From August 1979 to June 1980, he was a student at the National War College at Fort McNair in Washington, D.C. From June 1980 to August 1982, he served as Executive Officer in the Office of the Chief of Legislative Liaison, United States Army, Washington, D.C.

Gorden was promoted to Colonel on August 7, 1980. From August 1982 to October 1984, he was Commander of the Division Artillery, 7th Infantry Division, at Fort Ord, California. From October 1984 to October 1986, he served as Director of the Inter-American Region, Office of the Assistant Secretary of Defense (International Security Affairs), Washington, D.C. He was promoted to Brigadier General on October 1, 1985. From October 1986 to August 1987, he served as Assistant Division Commander in the 7th Infantry Division at Fort Ord. From August 1987 to January 1990, he was Commandant of Cadets at the United States Military Academy.

On July 1, 1989, he was promoted to Major General. In January 1990, he was assigned as Commanding General of the 25th Infantry Division (Light) at Schofield Barracks. In March 1992, he was assigned as the Acting Director of the Military Personnel Management Office of the Deputy Chief of Staff for Personnel, United States Army, in Washington, D.C. In May 1993, he was assigned as the Commanding General of the United States Army Military District of Washington, Washington, D.C. From September 1995 to September 1996, he served as the Chief of Public Affairs in the Office of the Secretary of the Army at the Pentagon. He retired on September 30, 1996.

He has received numerous awards and decorations, including the Defense Distinguished Service Medal, Legion of Merit, Bronze Star (with "V" device and oak leaf cluster), Meritorious Service Medal (with oak leaf cluster), Air Medal, Army Commendation Medal (with oak leaf cluster), Parachutist Badge, and Ranger Tab.

Gordon, Robert L., III

COLONEL—ARMY

Gordon is a 1979 graduate of the United States Military Academy at West Point, where he earned a Bachelor of Science degree in Public and National Security. He is also a graduate of the National War College and the Army Command and General Staff College; and earned a master's degree and completed coursework and preliminary examinations toward a doctorate in Public Affairs from Princeton University.

From 1992 to 1993, he served as a White House Fellow as the Director of Special Operations for the Office of National Service. In this position he was a member of the president's staff that founded the AmeriCorps program. Before serving in the White House, he was the Special Assistant to the Secretary of Veterans Affairs. Prior to the White House Fellowship, he was the executive officer of and an assistant professor in the Department of Social Sciences at West Point. He has held a number of field artillery command and staff positions, including two tours in the 4th Infantry Division at Fort Carson, Colorado, and a tour in Germany. He also has taught the interagency process and national security at the National War College in Washington, D.C., and the Federal Executive Management Center in Shepherdstown, West Virginia; and served as a Center for Public Management Fellow at the Brookings Institution. In March 2005, he was serving as the Director of the American Politics Division in the Department of Social Sciences at the United States Military Academy at West Point. He oversees the administration, conduct, and teaching of the core course on American Politics and Policy, and fifteen elective courses taught to over 1,100 cadets. He teaches the advanced course in American Politics and the Public Policymaking Process.

Gosha, Lucius G., Jr.

COMMAND SERGEANT MAJOR—ARMY

Gosha entered the United States Army in June 1982. He attended Basic Combat Training and Advanced Individual Training at Fort Sill, Oklahoma, as a Fire Support Specialist (13F). He was selected as an Honor Trainee of Training Cycle 37-82. His Military Education includes all the Noncommissioned Officer Education System Courses; the Nuclear, Biological and Chemical Course; Military Operations on Urbanized Terrain (MOUT) Course; Light TACFIRE Course; Fire Support MAN Naval School; the Equal Opportunity Representative Course; Initial Fire Support Automation System Course; First Sergeants Course; and the United States Army Sergeants Major Academy.

His military assignments include serving as Fire Support Sergeant and First Sergeant, Headquarters and Headquarters Battalion and B 3/41 with duty at 3/15 Infantry and 3rd Brigade, 24th Infantry Division at Fort Stewart, Georgia; First Sergeant, HHB 2/17 Field Artillery, 2nd Infantry Division at Camp Hovey, South

Korea; and First Sergeant, HHB 1/9 Field Artillery and Senior Fire Support Operations Sergeant Major, 3rd Infantry Division at Fort Stewart, Georgia. In August 2004, he was assigned as the Command Sergeant Major at the 2/4 Field Artillery, 3rd Infantry Division, and served a combat tour in Iraq during Operation Iraq Freedom.

Gourdin, Edward Orval (Ned)

BRIGADIER GENERAL—ARMY

Born in Jacksonville, Florida, General Gourdin is the son of Walter Holmes and Felicia Garvin Gourdin. He married the former Amalia Ponce and they had four children, Elizabeth, Ann Robinson, Amalia Lindal and Edward O., Jr. He attended Stanton and Cambridge Latin High Schools. He received a B.A. degree from Harvard University and earned a L.L.B. degree from Harvard Law School.

He gained fame as an athlete during his college career, winning the silver medal and adding points to the American team victory in the broad jump at the 1924 Olympic Games in Paris. This was accomplished in spite of final law exams, lack of training and leg injuries. He also was a member of the National Championship Rifle Team. After he passed the bar, Gourdin practiced law in Boston, Massachusetts. While at Harvard he joined the Student Army Training Corps to be commissioned a second lieutenant in October 1925. On March 3, 1941, he became commander of the all-black 3rd Battalion of the 372nd Infantry Regiment with the rank of lieutenant colonel. In December 1941, he assumed command of the entire regiment with the rank of colonel.

For several months the regiment was assigned to guard duty in New York City and its metropolitan area. A training battalion was rotated to Fort Dix, N.J., from 1941 to 1944. Some 1200 troops were taught not only basic military training, but also literacy, basic education and citizenship. Gourdin took an active role in these programs. From 1943 to 1944, he participated in post-college workshops and seminars in counseling, law, communications and Negro history.

From April 23, to November 8, 1944, the Chief of Army Ground Forces assigned the regiment to Camp Breckenridge, Kentucky. In November 1944, Colonel Gourdin and the 372nd were assigned to Fort Huachuca, Arizona. In April 1945, the regiment left this staging area, as part of the Fourth Army, from Fort Lawton, Washington, for the Pacific Theater. When the war in Europe officially came to an end on May 8, 1945, there were celebrations aboard transports bound for Honolulu. The Middle Pacific Command reassigned Gourdin's 372nd to the "Jungle Training Combat Command." The regiment was assigned to ground defense of Oahu and other Hawaiian islands from May to September 2, 1945, when the Japanese officially surrendered. This event changed the nature of Gourdin's assignment to one of rehabilitation, education and coordination of the return of eligible personnel to civilian life.

Colonel Gourdin became a member of the Mid-Pacific Sociology and Psychiatry Board. In February 1946, the 372nd reassembled at Schofield Barracks, was deactivated, and returned to National Guard status. Colonel Gourdin returned to the United States on February 11, 1946, and until 1947 served on the Discharge and Review Board under the Secretary of War. When he returned to the Massachusetts National Guard, he served as acting chief of staff, acting judge advocate general, and as plans and training general staff officer for defense of the Boston area as well as aide to the governor of Massachusetts.

When he retired in 1959, he was a brigadier general. He resumed his position as assistant U.S. District Attorney. In 1952, he was appointed to be a special justice of the Roxbury District Court, the third African American to serve on the state bench. In 1958, Governor Fosler Furcolo appointed him to the Massachusetts

Superior Court. Gourdin was elected president of the National Olympic Athletes Association in 1965.

Gourdin died of cancer on July 22, 1966, in City Hospital, Quincy, Massachusetts. In 1969, the Harvard Varsity Club placed in its Hall of Fame a plaque, the Edward O. "Ned" Gourdin Memorial Award, honoring him for his accomplishments as a track jumper, for his exemplary character and for his contributions to the Harvard community. The Colonel Edward O. Gourdin Post 5298, Veterans of Foreign Wars of the United States, was chartered in Springfield Gardens, Queens County, New York in 1968.

Graham, Christopher
LIEUTENANT COMMANDER—NAVY

A native of Gordon, Alabama, Graham graduated from the United States Naval Academy with a Bachelor of Science degree in Political Science and was commissioned an Ensign in 1991. He holds a Master of Arts Degree in National Security and Strategic Studies from the Naval War College.

His initial assignment was to the conventional carrier USS *Ranger* (CV-61). While onboard, he served as Repair Division Officer and completed USS *Ranger*'s last deployment to the Persian Gulf in support of Operations Southern Watch and Restore Hope.

His next assignment was as Navigator onboard USS *Anchorage* (LSD-36). During this tour, he completed his second deployment to Mogadishu, Somalia, in support of Operation Restore Hope. His third sea assignment was as Combat Systems Officer on USS *Paul F. Foster* (DD-964), where he completed his third deployment to the Persian Gulf in support of Operation Southern Watch. His next sea assignment was as Operations Officer at Amphibious Squadron Seven (COMPHIBRON SEVEN). During this tour, he

completed his fourth deployment to the Persian Gulf conducting bilateral operations during Operations Infinite Moonlight, Eager Mace, and Red Reef. In October 2004, he was serving as the Executive Officer onboard USS *Preble* (DDG 88).

Graham, Frank L.
COMMAND SERGEANT MAJOR—ARMY

Graham is from Moncks Corner, South Carolina, and entered the National Guard in September 1978 as a rifleman in the Mechanized Infantry. He entered active duty in January 1980.

His military education includes all the Noncommissioned Officer Education Systems Courses; the First Sergeant Course; and the United States Army Sergeants Major Academy.

His military assignments includes: serving as Team Leader, 6th Battalion, 31st Infantry, Fort Ord, California; Team Leader, 1st Battalion, 32nd Infantry, 7th Infantry Division; RTO/Team Leader, 1st Battalion, 31st Infantry, 2nd Infantry Division, Camp Howze, South Korea; Senior Security Sergeant, D Team, 52nd USAAD, Oedingen, Germany; Section Leader & Squad Leader, 3rd Battalion, 19th Infantry, 24th Infantry Division, Fort Stewart, Georgia; Platoon Sergeant, B Company, 2nd Battalion, 15th Infantry, 3rd Infantry Division, Schweinfurt, Germany; First Sergeant, B Company, 1st Battalion, 26th Infantry, 1st Infantry, Schweinfurt, Germany; S-2 Non-Commissioned Officer-in-Charge, 1st Battalion, 26th Infantry, 1st Infantry Division, Schweinfurt, Germany; First Sergeant, Headquarters and Headquarters Company, 1st Battalion, 26th Infantry 1st Infantry Division, Schweinfurt, Germany; Brigade Operations Sergeant Major, 2nd Brigade, 1st Infantry Division, Schweinfurt, Germany; and Command Sergeant Major, 1st Battalion, 36th Infantry.

Granger, Elder
MAJOR GENERAL—ARMY

General Granger is a native of West Memphis, Arkansas, and began his career with the Army Medical

Department in 1971 as a Combat Medic with the United States Army National Guard. He earned his Bachelor of Science degree from Arkansas State University in 1976. A Distinguished Military Graduate, he was initially commissioned as a Quartermaster Officer through the Reserve Officer Training Corps (ROTC) and was reappointed as a Medical Service Corps Officer upon entry into the Health Professional Scholarship Program. He earned his medical degree from the University of Arkansas College of Medicine in 1980, where he was awarded the Henry Kaiser Medical Fellowship for Medical Excellence and Leadership. He completed a residency in Internal Medicine in 1983 at Fitzsimons Army Medical Center and a fellowship in Hematology-Oncology in 1986. His military schooling includes the Army Medical Department Officer Basic and Advanced Courses, the Combat Casualty Care Course and the United States Army Command and General Staff College and the Army War College.

He has had a broad array of Command and Staff assignments, most recently commanding the Landstuhl Regional Medical Center from August 1999 through July 2001. He also commanded Ireland Army Community Hospital and the United States Army Medical Department Activity at Fort Knox, Kentucky, from July 1997 through July 1999. He served as Staff Hematologist/Oncologist, at Fitzsimons Army Medical Center at Aurora, Colorado; Division Surgeon, 4th Infantry Division, at Fort Carson, Colorado; Deputy Commander for Clinical Services, United States Army Medical Department Activity, Fort Huachuca, Arizona and Chief of the Department of Medicine/Chief of Hematology Service, 2nd General Hospital, Landstuhl, Germany. In July 2001, he served as the Acting Assistant Surgeon General for Force Projection, Office of The Surgeon General, Department of the Army, Falls Church, Virginia. He took command of the United States Army's Europe Regional Medical Command and became the Command Surgeon for United States Army in Europe and 7th Army on June 26, 2002. Headquartered in Heidelberg, Germany, the Europe Regional Medical Command is a major subordinate command of the United States Army Medical Command, headquartered at Fort Sam Houston, Texas, and is responsible for the operation of medical treatment facilities in Germany, Belgium, and Italy. He was promoted to Brigadier General on June 1, 2002.

From August 2004 to November 2004, he served as the Commanding General, 44th Medical Command/Corps Surgeon, XVIII Airborne Corps, at Fort Bragg, North Carolina. In November 2004, he was assigned as the Commanding General, 44th Medical Command/Corps Surgeon, XVIII Airborne Corps, deployed in support of Operation Iraqi Freedom, in Iraq. He was promoted to Major General in August 1, 2005.

Granger is the recipient of numerous awards, decorations and honors, including the Legion of Merit (with one oak leaf cluster); the Meritorious Service Medal (with four oak leaf clusters); the Order of the Military Medical Merit; the Expert Field Medical Badge; the Army Commendation Medal (with oak leaf cluster); and the Army Achievement Medal. He is board certified by the American Board of Internal Medicine and the board of Hematology and Oncology. Additionally, the Army Surgeon General has bestowed upon him the "A" proficiency designator for healthcare professionals.

Grant, Timothy W.
COMMAND SERGEANT MAJOR—ARMY

He is a native of Houston, Texas, and enlisted into the United States Army Reserves in 1981, and attended Basic Combat Training at Fort Sill, Oklahoma. In 1982, he was released from the Army Reserves, and enlisted in the active Army and attended Initial Entry Training at Fort Bliss, Texas.

His military education includes all the Noncommissioned Officer Education System Courses; Air Assault School; Master Fitness School; Jungle Training; the Recruiter Course; the First Sergeants Course; the United States Army Sergeants Major Academy (class 52); and the Command Sergeant Major Course. He holds a Bachelor of Science degree in Management from Excelsior College in Albany, New York.

He has served in numerous leadership positions in Short Range Air Defense Artillery units throughout the Army. He served as an Operations and Intelligence Assistant (16H) in the 4th Battalion 61st Air Defense Artillery, 4th Infantry Division, at Fort Carson, Colorado; and the 1st Air Defense Artillery, 108th ADA Brigade, at Spangdahlem, Germany. He served as a Training Sergeant, Master Gunner and Senior Intelligence Analyst with the 2nd Battalion, 44th Air Defense Artillery, 101st Airborne Division (Airborne Air Assault), at Fort Campbell, Kentucky. In August 2004, he was serving as the Command Sergeant Major for 1-62nd Air Defense Artillery.

Grant, William M.
COMMAND SERGEANT MAJOR—ARMY

Command Sergeant Major William M. Grant is a native of Sumter, South Carolina, and married to the former Loria Ann Brown. They have four daughters, Margaret, Stephanie, Willietta, and Lydia.

He entered military service in June 1978. His military education includes graduating from the First Sergeants Course and the United States Army Sergeants Major Academy.

Throughout his military career, he has served in virtually all leadership positions in the Infantry. His tours include duty as Infantry Team/Squad Leader; Bradley Gunnery Instructor; Platoon Sergeant; First Sergeant; and Operations Sergeant Major. During his most recent assignment he served as the III Corps and Fort Hood

Equal Opportunity Sergeant Major, and is currently serving as the Command Sergeant Major for the 1st Battalion, 5th Cavalry Brigade, 1st Cavalry Division.

Gravely, Samuel Lee, Jr.

VICE ADMIRAL—NAVY

Born in Richmond, Virginia, Admiral Gravely married the former Alma Clark, having three children, Robert, David, and Tracey. He is a graduate of Virginia Union University (A.B., 1948). He enlisted in the U.S. Naval Reserve (1942) and completed Midshipmen School at Columbia University (1944), becoming the first black man to be commissioned an ensign in World War II.

He was assigned to the submarine chaser PC-1264, on which he served successively as communications officer, electronics officer, and personnel officer. Released from active duty in 1946, he completed college in 1948. In August 1949, the Navy recalled him to active duty, and he saw both sea and shore duty during the Korean War. He transferred from the Navy Reserve to the Regular Navy in 1955.

In February 1961, as temporary skipper of the destroyer USS *Chandler,* he became the first black man ever to command a Navy vessel. Rising to lieutenant commander, he was given his own ship, the radar picket destroyer USS *Falgout.* Two other commands followed. He was promoted to captain in 1967 and to rear admiral and Director of Naval Communications in 1971.

In 1973 he was named commander of a flotilla of 30 ships. He distinguished himself as a naval communications expert, ship captain, and eventually commander of the Third Fleet. He was the navy's first black three-star naval officer as well as the first black ever to obtain the rank of admiral. He retired from the Navy in 1980.

Since that time he has served on several corporate boards and as a consultant to defense contractors while living in rural Haymarket, Virginia. Vice Admiral Gravely has been awarded the Legion of Merit, Bronze Star, Meritorious Service Medal, Joint Services Commendation Medal, and Navy Commendation Medal (with bronze star and combat "V"). He is also authorized to wear the World War II Victory Medal, Naval Reserve Medal (for 10 years' service in the U.S. Naval Reserve), American Campaign Medal, Korean Presidential Unit Citation, National Defense Medal (with bronze star), China Service Medal (extended), Korean Service Medal (with two bronze stars), United Nations Service Medal, Armed Forces Expeditionary Medal, Vietnam Service Medal (with six bronze stars), Vietnamese Campaign Medal, Antarctica Service Medal, and Venezuelan Order of Merit Second Class.

Gray, Kenneth Darnell

MAJOR GENERAL—ARMY

General Gary was born in Excelsior, West Virginia, and married the former Carolyn Jane Trice of Glen Jean, West Virginia. They have two sons, Christopher and Michael. He received his Bachelor of Arts degree from West Virginia State College in 1966 and his Law degree from West Virginia University in 1969.

He was commissioned a second lieutenant in 1966 from ROTC and entered active duty with the Judge Advocate General's Corps in June 1969. He has completed the JAGC Basic Course, the Military Judge's Course, the JAGC Graduate Course, Command and General Staff College, and the Industrial College of the Armed Forces.

General Gray has served in extensive assignments in the JAGC. His initial tour of duty was in the Office of the Staff Judge Advocate at Fort Ord, California, where

he served as a Defense Counsel and Legal Assistance Officer. He was then assigned to the Danang Support Command, Vietnam, from June 1970 to August 1971, where he served in various assignments, including part-time Military Judge, Trial and Defense Counsel, Legal Assistance Officer, Deputy Command Judge Advocate, and Command Judge Advocate.

After his tour in Vietnam, from January 1972 to May 1974, he was assigned to the Office of the Judge Advocate General as a Personnel Management Officer in the Personnel, Plans, and Training Office. After graduation from the JAGC Advanced Course, he served from May 1975 to June 1978 as an Instructor and Senior Instructor in the Criminal Law Division of the Judge Advocate General's School at Charlottesville, Virginia. From June 1978 to June 1980 he served as Deputy Staff Judge Advocate of the 1st Armored Division at Ansbach, West Germany. Upon completion of Command and General Staff College, he served as Staff Judge Advocate of the 2nd Armored Division at Fort Hood, Texas, from June 1981 to June 1984. From June 1984 to July 1987, he served as Chief Personnel, Plans, and Training Officer in the Office of the Judge Advocate General in Washington, D.C. Following completion of the Industrial College of the Armed Forces, he was assigned as Staff Judge Advocate for III Corps at Fort Hood in June 1988. From September 1989 to March 1990 he served as special assistant in the Office of Judge Advocate General, United States Army, Washington, D.C. In March 1990 he was assigned as Acting Commander of the United States Army Legal Services Agency, Associate Judge, with the Army Court of Military Review in Falls Church, Virginia. He was promoted to Brigadier General on April 1, 1991.

In October 1993, he was selected to serve as the Assistant Judge Advocate General, in the Office of the Judge Advocate General, for the United States Army in Washington, D.C. He was promoted to Major General on October 1, 1993.

From October 1993 to April 1997, he served as the Assistant Judge Advocate General, Office of the Judge Advocate General, United States Army, in Washington, D.C.

His decorations and awards include the Legion of Merit, Bronze Star, Meritorious Service Medal (with two oak leaf clusters), Army Commendation Medal, Army Achievement Medal, and Army General Staff Identification Badge.

Gray, Kenneth E.
SERGEANT MAJOR—MARINE

Kenneth Gray was born in Augusta, Georgia, where he graduated from Jones County High School. After graduation from High School, he joined the Marine Corps under the Delayed Entry Program in July 1980. In October 1980, he attended Recruit Training at the Marine Corps Recruit Depot at Parris Island, South Carolina. After completing recruit training, he attended Infantry Training School at Camp Lejeune, North Carolina, where he trained for his primary Military Occupational Specialty of 0331, Machine Gunner.

His key military assignments include serving as a Drill Instructor and Senior Drill Instructor with Lima Company, 3rd Recruit Training Battalion, Marine Corps Recruit Depot at San Diego, California; as Squad Leader and Company Operations Chief, while assigned to Enlisted Instructor Company, The Basic School, Marine Corps Combat Development Command, Quantico, Virginia; and as Sergeant Instructor, Physical Training Instructor and Platoon Sergeant, at Officer Candidate School, Quantico, Virginia. In August 1990, he was assigned as Section Leader, Platoon Sergeant and Platoon Commander, Weapons Company, 1st Battalion, 1st Marine Division, and in January 1991, he deployed to South West Asia and participated in Operations Desert Shield/Desert Storm. He has also served as Assistant Marine Officer Instructor at Naval Training Corps, Rice University, Houston, Texas; as Company Gunnery Sergeant, Gulf Company, Marine Combat Training Battalion, School of Infantry, Camp Pendleton, California; as Chief Instructor for the Tactics Section, Marine Combat Training, Camp Pendleton; as First Sergeant, Hotel Company, Marine Combat Training, School of Infantry, Camp Pendleton; and as First Sergeant, Support Company, Headquarters and Support Battalion, Marine Corps Base, Camp Pendleton. In April 2003, he was assigned as Sergeant Major, Marine Wing Support Squadron 372, 3rd Marine Air Wing, United States Marine Corps Forces Europe.

Gray, Robert Earl
LIEUTENANT GENERAL—ARMY

He was born in Algoma, West Virginia. He and his wife, Annie, have three children, Frances, Edith, and Parker. He graduated from Ohio State University with a bachelor's degree in Computer and Information Science. He was also awarded a Master of Military Arts and Sciences from the United States Army Command and General Staff College.

General Gray first enlisted in the United States Army as a private in 1959. He remained in the enlisted ranks until May 1966 when he received his commission as a second lieutenant in the United States Army. He is a graduate of the Signal Officer Advanced Course and the Army War College. From 1966 to 1967, he was a student in the Signal Officer Basic Course at the United States Army Signal School in Fort Monmouth, New Jersey.

From March 1967 to October 1968 he served as a Communications Officer with the 56th Artillery Group, United States Army in Europe. He was promoted to First Lieutenant on May 26, 1967, and promoted to Captain on May 26, 1968. From October 1968 to May 1969, he was the Commander of Company C, 97th Signal Battalion, Seventh United States Army Communications Command, Europe. From May 1969 to June 1970, he served as S-4 (logistics officer) and Commander of Company A, 501st Signal Battalion, 101st Airborne Division (Airmobile), United States Army, Vietnam. From June 1973 to November 1974, he served

General of the United States Army Signal Center, and Assistant Commandant of the United States Army Signal School. In August 1990 he was assigned as the Deputy Director for Plans, Programs, and Systems in the Office of the Director of Information Systems for Command, Control, Communication, and Computers in the Office of the Secretary of the Army, Washington, D.C. From August 1991 to August 1994, he served as the Commanding General of the United States Army Signal Center and Commandant of the United States Army Signal School. He became the first black General to serve in this position. He was promoted to Major General on January 1, 1993. From August 1994 to May 1995, he was assigned as the Chief of Staff for the United States Army Europe and Seventh Army in Germany. He was promoted to Lieutenant General on May 25, 1995.

In May 1995, he served the Deputy Commander in Chief, United States Army Europe and Seventh Army, at Heidelberg, Germany. He retired from the military on July 31, 1997.

He has received numerous awards and decorations, including the Distinguished Service Medal; the Legion of Merit; the Bronze Star; the Air Medal; the Meritorious Service Medal (with two oak leaf clusters); Army Commendation Medal (with oak leaf cluster); Masters Parachutist Badge; and the Army Staff Identification Badge.

Green, Carl R.
SERGEANT MAJOR—MARINE

He is a native of Beaufort, South Carolina. He enlisted in the United States Marine Corps in January 1978. He reported to Marine Corps Recruit Depot (MCRD) at Parris Island, South Carolina in September of 1978.

His key military assignments include serving Naval Gunfire, Artillery Liaison Chief, at Headquarters Battery, 3rd Battalion, 12th Marines; First Sergeant, 2nd

as an Automatic Data Processing Officer in the Computer Security Element, Counter Intelligence and Security Division, Defense Intelligence Agency, Washington, D.C. From November 1974 to July 1976, he was assigned as a Communications-Electronics Staff Officer in the Plans and Policy Branch, Systems Management Division, Information/Systems Directorate, Defense Intelligence Agency, Washington, D.C.

He was promoted to Major on August 19, 1975. From July 1976 to June 1977, he was a student at the United States Army Command and General Staff College at Fort Leavenworth, Kansas. From June 1977 to August 1978, he served as the Executive Officer of the 50th Signal Battalion, 35th Group, XVIII Airborne Corps at Fort Bragg, North Carolina. From August 1978 to April 1980, Gray served as Tactical Plans Officer, G-3 (operations), Contingency Plans Division, XVIII Airborne Corps at Fort Bragg.

He was promoted to Lieutenant Colonel on August 13, 1979. From May 1980 to June 1983, he served as Commander of the 82nd Signal Battalion, 82nd Airborne Division, at Fort Bragg. From June 1983 to June 1984, he was a student at the United States Army War College at Carlisle Barracks, Pennsylvania. From June 1984 to February 1986, he served as Chief, Command, Control, and Communications Division, United States Army Combined Arms Combat Development Activity, Fort Leavenworth, Kansas. From February 1986 to June 1988, he was the Commander of the 35th Signal Brigade, XVIII Airborne Corps, at Fort Bragg. He was promoted to Colonel on November 1, 1984.

From July 1988 to October 1988, he served as Special Assistant to the Commanding General, XVIII Airborne Corps, at Fort Bragg. He was promoted to Brigadier General on April 1, 1990, and was assigned to Fort Gordon, Georgia, as Deputy Commanding

Combat Engineer Battalion, 2nd Marine Division; and First Sergeant, Headquarters and Service Company and Engineer Support Company. In July 1999, he was transferred to 8th Communication Battalion for duty as Battalion Sergeant Major. In June 2001, he was assigned to the 1st Marine Aircraft Wing in Okinawa, Japan, for duty as Sergeant Major of Marine Medium Helicopter Squadron 262. During his tour with Helicopter Marine Medium–262, he also served 18 months as the ACE Sergeant Major with the 31st Marine Expeditionary Unit (SOC). In April 2004, he was reassigned to Marine Wing Service Support Group 17 as the Group Sergeant Major. Sergeant Major Green assumed duties as the Sergeant Major for the 2nd Force Service Support Group in April 2005.

Green, Clement D.
COMMAND SERGEANT MAJOR—ARMY

He was born in Savannah, Georgia, and entered the United States Army in June 1979. He completed Basic and Advanced Individual Training at Fort Benning, Georgia. During his career, he has served as Team Leader, Squad Leader, Platoon Sergeant, First Sergeant, Operations Sergeant, Operations Sergeant Major and Battalion Command Sergeant Major.

He received a associate's degree in Justice Administration from Hawaii Pacific University, and is currently pursuing a bachelor's degree there. He has also completed the Primary Noncommissioned Officer Course; Basic and Advanced Noncommissioned Officer Course; Battle Staff Course; First Sergeant Course; Drill Sergeant Course; NBC Course; Airborne School; and the Sergeant Major Academy.

His assignments include C Company, 2-21st Infantry, at Fort Stewart, Georgia; B Company 2-28th Infantry, Mainz, West Germany; Infantry Training Group at Fort Benning, Georgia; C Company, 4-30th Infantry (Drill Sergeant) Fort Benning, Georgia; B Company 3/75th Ranger Battalion, Fort Benning, Georgia; S2 Section, 75th Ranger Regiment, at Fort Benning, Georgia; E Company, 51st Infantry (LRS), Darmstadt, West Germany; C Company, 1-504th PIR and HHC 1-504th PIR, at Fort Bragg, North Carolina; and 3rd Brigade, 25th Infantry Division (Light), 1/196th Infantry (Senior Advisor), Schofield Barracks and Fort Shafter, Hawaii.

Green, Everett L.
CAPTAIN—NAVY

Green entered the Naval Academy on June 29, 1966, as a Midshipman. He graduated in June 1970 as a Ensign, with a bachelor's degree in Naval Science. He earned a master's degree in Systems Technology from the Naval Postgraduate School, and also graduated from the United States Naval War College.

His assignments include serving as Team One Navy Seal at the Naval Amphibious Base, Coronado, in San Diego, California; as Executive Officer for Naval Special Warfare Unit One at MacDill Air Force Base, Florida; as Naval Operations Officer in the Joint Special Operations Command at Fort Bragg, North Carolina; as Commanding Officer of the Special Boat Unit Twelve at Fort Bragg; as Commander of Special Boat First Squadron with the Pacific Fleet; and as Commander of Boat Squadron One, Special Warfare Unit, Pacific Fleet.

He military awards and decorations include the Legion of Merit; the Defense Meritorious Service Medal; the Meritorious; Service Medal the Navy Commendation Medal with two Gold Stars; the Navy Achievement Medal; the Combat Action Ribbon; the Presidential Unit Citation; the Republic of Vietnam Gallantry Cross Unit Citation; and the Humanitarian Service Medal.

He was selected as Rear Admiral of the Lower Half on July 1, 1994.

Green, Leon J., Jr.
COMMAND SERGEANT MAJOR—ARMY

A native of New Orleans, Louisiana, Green entered the Army in 1982. He attended Basic Combat Training at Fort McClelland, Alabama, and Advanced Individual Training (AIT) at Fort Gordon, Georgia, graduating as a Radio Teletype Operator (O5C).

His military and civilian education includes all the Noncommissioned Officer Education System Courses; First Sergeants Course; Airborne School; Drill Sergeant School; and the United States Army Sergeants Major Academy (class 53). He holds a Bachelor of Science degree in Health Science and Physical Education and a Bachelor of Arts degree in Biblical Counseling.

He has served in numerous leadership positions, including Team Chief; Section Chief; Platoon Sergeant; First Sergeant; and Command Sergeant Major. Additionally, he served as a Senior Radioman onboard the Motor Vessel Sutton and Logistical Support Vessel LSV-4 (US General Bunker), at Fort Eustis, Virginia. He also served as a Battalion Communications Chief, S-3 Operations Sergeant Drill Sergeant, and Student Advisor at the United States Army Sergeants Major Academy.

Sergeant Major Green's other assignments include B Company, 1st Battalion, 39th Infantry, 8th Infantry (Mechanized) Division at Baumholder, Germany; Headquarters and Headquarters Battery, 3rd Battalion, 16th Field Artillery, 8th Infantry at Baumholder, Germany; Headquarters and Headquarters Company, 10th Transportation Battalion, 7th Transportation Group at Fort Eustis, Virginia; Headquarters and Headquarters Battery, 42nd Field Artillery Brigade at Giessen, Ger-

many; Headquarters and Headquarters Company, 2nd Battalion, 16th Infantry, 1st Infantry (Mechanized) Division at Fort Riley, Kansas; Headquarters and Headquarters Company, 37th Transportation Command at Kaiserslautern, Germany; Headquarters and Headquarters Company, 191st Ordnance Battalion at Miesau, Germany; Headquarters and Headquarters Company and A Company. 50th Signal Battalion, Airborne, 35th Signal Brigade at Fort Bragg, North Carolina; C, D, and F Companies, 447th Signal Battalion, 15th Signal Brigade at Fort Gordon, Georgia; Headquarters and Headquarters Company, 57th Signal Battalion, 3rd Signal Brigade at Fort Hood, Texas; and Staff and Faculty, United States Army Sergeants Major Academy at Fort Bliss, Texas.

Green, Phyllis J.
LIEUTENANT COLONEL—AIR FORCE

Green is a native of Gary, Indiana. She earned a bachelor's and master's degree from Ball State University and Louisiana Tech University. During her 22 years of military service, she served in Greece, Guam, and Egypt, along with the West Coast, Southwest and East Coast of the United States.

Now retired from the United States Air Force, she serves as Senior Aerospace Science Instructor at Westfield High School JROTC program.

Greer, Edward
MAJOR GENERAL—ARMY

General Greer was born in Gary, West Virginia, and married the former Jewell Means. They have three children, Gail Lyle, Michael, and Kenneth. He received a B.S. degree (Biological Science) from West Virginia State College in 1948, and a Master of Science degree from George Washington University in Washington, D.C., in 1967.

General Greer's military career began following his eighteenth birthday when he joined the Army Reserve. Called to active duty on May 12, 1943, he attained the grade of Master Sergeant during World War II. Upon receipt of his honorable discharge at the end of the war, he resumed his education at West Virginia State College. As a member of the Reserve Officer Training Corps, he continued his interest in the military while a student.

He was commissioned a Second Lieutenant of Artillery in the Regular Army upon graduation in 1948. On July 12, 1948, he was called to active duty, his first duty station being Fort Riley, Kansas. The outbreak of the Korean War in 1950 found General Greer serving on the front lines during some of the most decisive battles. He acquitted himself with valor and distinction while accomplishing combat missions involving great personal risk. His exemplary and heroic service during this period was recognized by awards of the Silver Star and Bronze Star medals.

A series of important assignments following the Korean War gave every indication that the Army had identified General Greer a rising star in the officer corps. He was rapidly promoted to Captain. After advanced schooling in 1955, he was selected for assignment to the Department of the Army General Staff in Washington, D.C. Three years later, he was selected for accelerated promotion to Major. He is a graduate of the Command and General Staff College at Fort Leavenworth, Kansas. After graduation, a year of service at Fort Lewis, Washington, as second in command of a Combined Rocket and Howitzer Battalion further prepared him for higher-level command. During the next three years, General Greer again served on the Army General Staff in Washington as a Personal Planner and Manager of Assignments for Artillery Officers.

He was promoted to Lieutenant Colonel in January 1963. In 1964 he returned to Korea where he first served as an Artillery Operations Officer in a major headquarters and subsequently was assigned to the most coveted position available for a Lieutenant Colonel, Command of a Battalion. In 1965 he was again assigned to the Command and General Staff College, this time as an Author-Instructor. His normal tour was interrupted, however, by selection for the highest military schooling available in the Army, the National War College. While a student at the National War College, General Greer also earned his Master's degree from George Washington University. He then returned to Washington as an Operations Officer in the Office of the Joint Chiefs of Staff. During his assignment, he was promoted to Colonel. In April of 1970, General Greer was assigned to Vietnam where he served initially as Deputy Commander of Artillery, United States Army XXIV Corps. Further acknowledgement of the special trust and confidence placed in General Greer by the Army came when he was selected to command an entire artillery group. He was honored for his service in the war by awards including the Legion of Merit and the Vietnamese Cross of Gallantry with gold star. Combat service in his third war ended in March 1971 when he was reassigned to the Office of the Assistant Secretary of Defense. During this assignment, he was selected for promotion to Brigadier General on October 1, 1972. He then moved to Fort Leonard Wood, Missouri, where he became the Deputy Commanding General.

In 1974 General Greer was reassigned to the Washington, D.C., area as Deputy Commanding General of the United States Army Military Personnel Center. Less than a year later, his rapid rise continued when he received a second star as Major General. On November 1, 1976, General Greer requested that he be placed on the United States Army retired list. His request was granted, and on November 30, 1976, one of the Army's most distinguished soldiers retired with honor. Besides his many citations for valor on the battlefield and meritorious achievement in peacetime, General Greer was awarded the Distinguished Service Medal, Silver Star, Legion of Merit (with oak leaf cluster), Bronze Star (with oak leaf cluster), Air Medal, Joint Service Commendation Medal, and Army Commendation Medal (with oak leaf cluster).

Gregg, Arthur James
LIEUTENANT GENERAL—ARMY

He was born in Florence, South Carolina, and received a Bachelor of Science degree in Business Administration from Benedict College. His military schooling included completion of the Quartermaster School Basic and Advanced Courses; the United States Army Command and General Staff College; and the United States Army War College.

His military career began on May 19, 1950, and expanded over 31 years of service in a succession of demanding staff and command assignments. From February 1960 to August 1963, he served as Operations

Officer of the 95th Quartermaster Battalion, United States Army in Europe. From August 1963 to July 1964, he was a student in the United States Army Command and General Staff College at Fort Leavenworth, Kansas. In January 1965 he was assigned as Logistics Plans Officer, United States Army Materiel Command, then as Assistant Secretary, General Staff, United States Materiel Command, Washington, D.C., until February 1966.

From February 1966 to July 1967, he served as Commanding Officer of the 96th Quartermaster Battalion (later redesignated 96th Supply and Service Battalion) Fort Riley, Kansas, and later Vietnam. He returned to the United States in July 1967 and was selected a student in the United States Army War College at Carlisle Barracks, Pennsylvania. After graduating from the War College, he was assigned first as Logistics Officer, J-4, United States European Command, then Commanding Officer, Nahbollenbach Army Depot, United States Army in Europe. In March 1972 General Gregg returned to the United States and was assigned as Deputy Director for Troop Support, Office of the Deputy Chief of Staff for Logistics, United States Army, Washington, D.C. In March 1972 he served as Director of Troop Support, Office of Deputy Chief of Staff for Logistics, United States Army, Washington, D.C. From September 1972 to March 1973 he served first as Special Assistant to the Director of Supply and Maintenance Office; Deputy Chief of Staff for Logistics; then Deputy Director, Supply and Maintenance Office, Deputy Chief of Staff for Logistics, United States Army, Washington, D.C.

After this assignment, General Gregg was reassigned to Europe as Commander of the European Exchange System in March 1973. He retired on July 31, 1981. His military awards and decorations include the Legion of

Merit (with oak leaf cluster), Meritorious Service Medal, Joint Service Commendation Medal, and Army Commendation Medal (with two oak leaf clusters).

Gregory, Frederick D.
COLONEL—AIR FORCE

Born in Washington, D.C., Gregory married the former Barbara Archer of Washington. He graduated from Anacostia High School, Washington, in 1958; received a Bachelor of Science degree from the United States Air Force Academy in 1964, and a master's degree in information systems from George Washington University in 1977. After graduating from the United States Air Force Academy in 1964, he entered pilot training and attended helicopter training at Stead AFB, Nevada. He received his wings in 1965 and was assigned as an H-43 helicopter rescue pilot at Vance Air Force Base, Oklahoma, from October 1965 until May 1966. In June 1966, he was assigned as an H-43 combat rescue pilot at Danang Air Base, Vietnam. When he returned to the United States in July 1967, Gregory was assigned as a missile support Helicopter Pilot flying the UH-1F at Whiteman Air Force Base, Missouri. In January 1968, he was retrained as a Fixed-Wing Pilot flying the T-38 at Randolph Air Force Base, Arizona. He attended the United States Naval Test Pilot School at Patuxent River Naval Air Station, Maryland, from September 1970 to June 1971. Following completion of this training, he was assigned to the 4950th Test Wing at Wright-Patterson Air Force Base, Ohio, as an Operational Test Pilot flying fighters and helicopters. In June 1974, he was detailed to the National Aeronautics and Space Administration (NASA), Langley Research Center, Hampton, Virginia. He served as a Research Test Pilot at Langley until selected for the Astronaut Program in January 1978.

Gregory has logged more than 6,500 hours flying time in over 50 types of aircraft, including 550 combat missions in Vietnam. He holds an FAA commercial and instrument certificate for single — and multi-engine qualities and cockpit design. His technical assignments have included Astronaut Office Representative at the Kennedy Space Center during initial Orbiter checkout and launch support for STS-1 and STS-2, Flight Data File Manager, lead Capsule Communication (CAPCOM), Chief of Operation Safety at NASA Headquarters in Washington, Chief of Astronaut Training, and a Member of the Orbiter Configuration Control Board, and the Space Shuttle Program Control Board. He has flown on two Shuttle Missions, STS-51B and STS-33. On his first mission, Gregory was pilot on STS-51B/Spacelab-3 (*Challenger*) which launched from Kennedy Space Center, Florida, on April 29, 1985. After seven days of around the-clock scientific operations, *Challenger* and its laboratory cargo landed on the dry lakebed at Edwards Air Force Base, California, on May 6, 1985. He was the spacecraft commander on STS-33, which launched at night from Kennedy Space Center on November 22, 1989, on board the Orbiter *Discovery.* The mission carried Department of Defense payloads and other secondary payloads. After 79 orbits of the earth, this five-day mission concluded on November 27, 1989, with a hard surface landing on Runway 4 at Edwards AFB. With the completion of his second mission, Gregory has logged over 288 hours in space. In March 1991, he was working on his third mission, the STS-44 that he commanded in the later part of the summer of 1991. The mission deployed a Department of Defense satellite and participated in other military activities.

Grell, Theodore

GUNNERY SERGEANT—MARINES

He is a native of the Bronx, New York, and has served as the Senior Non-Commissioned Officer in Charge of the Recruiting Substation Jamaica, Recruiting Station New York. He was selected to receive the Patriot Award as the Senior Non-Commissioned Officer of the month May, 2005.

A consistent mission maker, Grell's aggressive and relentless leadership style enables him to keep his team as the top performers in the Recruiting Station. As Commander of a five-man station, he firmly holds his Marines accountable for prospecting and selling accepting nothing less.

Griffin, Gregory M.

COMMAND SERGEANT MAJOR—ARMY

Command Sergeant Major Gregory M. Griffin is a native of Mississippi. He entered the Army in September 1976 and graduated from Basic Training at Fort Jackson, South Carolina. He received Advanced Individual Training at Fort Sam Houston, Texas, where he was awarded the Military Occupational Specialty 91B, Combat Medical Specialist.

He is a graduate of Mississippi Valley State University and the United States Army Sergeants Major Academy in June 1992.

His military assignments include two overseas tours to West Germany (1987–1991) and one tour to the South Korea (1995–1996). He was also assigned to Fort Dix, New Jersey; Fort Sam Houston, Texas; Fort Jackson, South Carolina; Fort Benning, Georgia; Fort Campbell and Fort, Knox Kentucky. He currently serves as the Command Sergeant Major and Senior Enlisted Advisor at Blanchfield Army Community Hospital at Fort Campbell, Kentucky.

Grimes, Annie L.

CHIEF WARRANT OFFICER—MARINES

Grimes was born in Arlington, Tennessee. She graduated from high school in Summerville, Tennessee in 1946, and the Ray Vogue Trade School in Chicago. She enlisted in the United States Marine Corps, on February 2, 1950, in Chicago. She was assigned to Parris Island, South Carolina, where she completed recruit training and was promoted to Private First Class. In April 1951, she was promoted to Corporal; in November, 1951, she was promoted to Sergeant; in June, 1952, to Staff Sergeant, and in June 1953 to Gunnery Sergeant. From 1950 to 1953, she served with the

supply branch at the Headquarters of the United States Maine Corps. In January, 1961, she was promoted to Master Sergeant and received a commission to Warrant Officer in July 1966. In August, 1968, she was promoted to Chief Warrant Officer. She is the first black woman to receive an appointment to Warrant Officer in the United States Marine Corps.

Her military assignments include serving as Procurement Chief at the Marine Corps Depot of Supplies in San Francisco, California; at Marine Corps Base Camp Pendleton, California; and at Marine Corps Supply School Camp Lejeune, North Carolina. In 1967 she was assigned as the Project Officer at the Marine Corps Supply Center, Woman Marine Company in Barstow, California. She retired from the Marine Corps in 1971.

Grooms, Bruce E.

REAR ADMIRAL—NAVY

He is a native of Cleveland, Ohio, graduated from the United States Naval Academy in 1980 with a Bachelor of Science degree in Aerospace Engineering. He earned a master's degree in National Security and Strategic Studies (with distinction) from the Naval War College, and attended Stanford University as a National Security Affairs Fellow.

Following completion of nuclear power training, he served in nearly every capacity aboard a variety of submarines including a tour as Executive Officer aboard USS *Pasadena* (SSN 752) where he twice deployed to the Persian Gulf. In 1997 he assumed command of the USS *Asheville* (SSN 758) and completed a Western Pacific deployment. During his tour the ship received the Battle Efficiency "E" award, the Golden Anchor and the Silver Anchor for the highest retention in the submarine force. USS *Asheville* twice earned the Engineering Excellence "E" award, won the Fleet Commodore's Cup as the best all programs, and twice won the Submarine Squadron Three Commodore's Cups as the best all-around submarine in non-battle efficiency, and the Pacific Fleet Ney Memorial Award finalist. Captain Grooms was selected as the Vice Admiral Stockdale Inspirational Leadership Award winner for 1999.

Other shore tours included service as a Company Officer at the United States Naval Academy, as the Senior Member of the Atlantic Fleet Nuclear Propulsion Examining Board and as the Senior Military Aide to the Under Secretary of Defense for Policy.

His last sea assignment included serving as Commander Submarine Squadron Six, responsible for operations and maintenance of five fast attack submarines and a floating dry-dock. Additionally, he provided local oversight for two Guided Missile Submarines (SSGN) undergoing refueling and conversion.

On Thursday June 2, 2005, he relieved Captain Charles J. Leidig Jr. in a small private ceremony to become the 81st Commandant of Midshipmen at the United States Naval Academy. He is the first black Commandant of Midshipmen, a position similar to the Dean of Students at a civilian college or university. The Commandant of Midshipmen is responsible for the training and development of the Academy's 4,200 midshipmen to prepare them to be leaders of character for the Navy and Marine Corps. He was frocked to Rear Admiral on May 26, 2006.

Guerrero, Valentin

SERGEANT MAJOR—MARINES

Guerrero was born in La Romana, Dominican Republic. He enlisted into the United States Marine Corps in March 1975 in New York, New York. He attended Recruit Training at Marine Corps Recruit Training Depot at Parris Island, South Carolina. He completed the Basic Infantry School at Camp Pendleton, California.

He next served as Drill Instructor, Senior Drill Instructor and Chief Drill Instructor, Company M, 3rd Recruit Training Battalion, Marine Corps Recruit Depot, San Diego, California. In May 1986, he was assigned as the S-3 (Operations) Chief, 3rd Recruit Training Battalion, Marine Corps Recruit Depot, San

Diego, California. In April 1987, he was assigned aboard the USS *John F Kennedy* where he served as the Detachment Gunnery Sergeant, and later as the First Sergeant. In July 1991, he was assigned as First Sergeant, Station Operations and Engineering Squadron (SOES), at Marine Corps Station, Cherry Point, North Carolina. He served as Sergeant Major of Marine Medium Helicopter (HMM) Squadron 268 (Red Dragons), Marine Corps Air Station at El Toro, California, and as the Sergeant Major for the Air Command Element (ACE), 11th Marine Expeditionary Unit (11th MEU). On February 6, 1998, HMM-268 deployed for six months to the Persian Gulf with the 11th Marine Expeditionary Unit Special Operations Capable (SOC) and returned on August 6, 1998. In March 1999, he served as Sergeant Major of Marine Fighter Attack Training Squadron 101, Marine Air Group 11, 3rd Marine Air Wing, Marine Forces Pacific; and as Sergeant Major, Marine Air Group–11, 3rd Marine Air Wing, Marine Forces Pacific. In January 2005, Guerrero was serving as the Sergeant Major of Marine Aircraft Group 39, 3rd Marine Air Wing.

Guillory, Victor G.
REAR ADMIRAL—NAVY

Rear Admiral Guillory is a native of New Orleans and he graduated from the United States Naval Academy in 1978, earning a Bachelor of Science degree in Management and Technology. He is a graduate of the National Defense University (Industrial College of the Armed Forces).

He served his early sea assignments in the guided missile destroyer USS *Towers* (DDG 9) in Engineering and Operations departments; the guided missile frigate USS *Lewis B. Puller* (FFG 23) as a ship Control Officer; and the cruiser USS *Vincennes* (CG 49) as Operations Officer. He was the Commissioning Executive Officer

in the cruiser USS *Gettysburg* (CG 64), as well as the Commander of the guided missile frigate USS *Underwood* (FFG 36) and the cruiser USS *Lake Champlain* (CG57).

Ashore, his assignments include a tour in Officer Recruiting in New Orleans and several Washington-area assignments in the Bureau of Naval Personnel, the Officer of the Chief of Naval Operations as the Surface Warfare Division Branch Head for Combat Systems and as Assistant Deputy of Surface Ships. He also served in the Joint Staff as the J-3 Readiness Branch Chief. In October 2004, he was serving as the Commander of Amphibious Force Seventh Fleet, Amphibious Group One, Task Force 76.

Gunn, Will A.
COLONEL—AIR FORCE

Gunn is a 1980 graduate of the United States Air Force Academy (graduating with military honors). He served as an Admissions Advisor for the Academy and later served as a Contract Negotiator. In 1983, he was selected for the Air Force Funded Legal Education Program, attending Harvard Law School and graduating cum laude in 1986.

He attended Squadron Officer School, and received a Bachelor of Science from the United States Air Force Academy at Colorado Springs, Colorado. He also holds a Doctor of Jurisprudence from Harvard Law School, and earned a Master of Laws in Environmental Law, from George Washington University. He is a graduate of the Air War College, and holds a Master of Science from the Industrial College of the Armed Forces in Washington, D.C.

Gunn has served as an Assistant Staff Judge Advocate; as Area Defense Counsel at Mather Air Force Base in

1988; as a Circuit Defense Counsel at Travis Air Force Base in 1989; as a White House Fellow to the Associate Director of Cabinet Affairs in the Executive Office of the President, at the White House in 1990; and as a Trial Attorney in the General Litigation Division of the Military Personnel Branch in Rosslyn, Virginia in 1991. In 1994, he served as an Instructor at the Judge Advocate General School at Maxwell Air Force Base in Alabama. In 1996, he was assigned as Staff Judge Advocate at Pope Air Force Base in Texas. In 1999, he was selected to serve as Chief Circuit Defense Counsel at Randolph Air Force Base in Texas. In 2002, he was assigned as Executive Officer to the Judge Advocate General in Washington, D.C. In February 2003, Gunn was selected to serve as acting Chief Defense Counsel for the Department of Defense, Office of Military Commissions (OMC), in Washington, D.C. In this position, he is responsible for supervising all defense activities and the efforts of Detailed Defense Counsel to ensure zealous representation of all accused referred to trial before a military commission. His duties also include administering the Department of Defense General Counsel on matters relating to military commission defense activities.

Hacker, Benjamin Thurman

REAR ADMIRAL—NAVY

Born in Washington, D.C., Hacker married the former Jeanne House of Springfield, Ohio, and they have three children, Benjamin, Jr., Bruce, and Anne. He attended high school in Daytona Beach, Florida, and Dayton, Ohio. Following completion of Aviation

Officer Candidate School in Pensacola, Florida, he was commissioned an ensign in September 1958.

Hacker's operational assignments have included serving concurrently as Commander of Fleet Air Mediterranean; Commander of Maritime Surveillance and Reconnaissance Forces, United States Sixth Fleet; and Commander of Maritime Air Forces Mediterranean, Naples, Italy, from 1982 to 1984. In 1973 he reported to Patrol Squadron 24, Jacksonville, Florida, where he served as Executive Officer and later Commanding Officer. During this tour, the squadron made highly successful deployments to Keflavik, Iceland, and was heavily tasked in major operational exercises in the northern and central Atlantic.

Hacker reported in 1970 to Patrol Squadron 47 at Moffett Field, California, where the squadron completed numerous deployments in the P3C Orion aircraft to Adak, Alaska, and the western Pacific. His first operational assignment was to Patrol Squadron 21 in Brunswick, Maine, where he flew the P2V Neptune antisubmarine warfare aircraft. His shore assignments have included serving on the staff of the Chief of Naval Operations in 1984 as Director of Total Force Training and Education Division.

In 1972 he established the NROTC unit at Florida A&M University in Tallahassee, Florida, where he served as its first Commanding Officer and Professor of Naval Science. He served as the Commanding Officer of the United States Naval Facility at Argentina, Newfoundland, and Personnel Officer and Instructor in the P-3A Aircraft while attached to Patrol Squadron 31, Naval Air Station, Moffett Field.

In 1975, he was assigned to the Bureau of Naval Personnel as a Division Director and Special Assistant to the Chief of Naval Personnel in Washington, D.C. In 1980, he assumed duties as Commander of United States Military Enlistment Processing Command at Fort Sheridan, Illinois. On March 1, 1981, he was promoted to Rear Admiral. From July 1982 to October 1984, he was assigned as Commander of Fleet Air Mediterranean and Commander of Maritime Surveillance and Reconnaissance Force, SIXTH Fleet/ADDU: COMAREAASWFORSIXTHFLT. From October 1984 to August 1986, he was assigned to the Office of Chief of Naval Operations (Director for Total Force Planning/Training Division) (OP 11). In August 1986, he was selected to serve as Commander of the Naval Training Center/Commander of the Naval Base at San Diego, California.

His military awards and decorations include the Defense Superior Service Medal; the Legion of Merit (with gold star in lieu of second award); the Meritorious Service Medal; the Navy Unit Commendation awarded Task Group 81.1; the National Defense Service Medal; and the Armed Forces Expeditionary Medal (Cuba).

Hackett, Craig D.

MAJOR GENERAL—ARMY

Craig Hackett received a Bachelor of Science degree in Physical Education from Howard University and

January 1986, he served as Commander of C Company, 82nd Combat Aviation Battalion, 82nd Airborne Division, at Fort Bragg. In July 1986, he was selected Aide-de-Camp to the Secretary of the Army in the Office of the Secretary of the Army, Washington, D.C. In August 1987, he was assigned as Executive Officer for the 2nd Battalion, later S-3 (Operations), Aviation Brigade, with the 82nd Airborne Division, at Fort Bragg. He was promoted to Lieutenant Colonel on December 1, 1988.

From August 1989 to April 1991, he served as the Commander of the 1st Battalion, 227th Aviation, with the 1st Cavalry Division at Fort Hood, Texas and he served with the 1st Cavalry Division in Saudi Arabia during Operations Desert Shield/Desert Storm. He returned to the United States in May 1991 Senior Service College Fellowship to report as a student at Harvard University in the JFK School of Government in Cambridge, Massachusetts. In August 1992, he was assigned as Plans Officer, J-5, with the United States Central Command at MacDill Air Force Base, Florida. He was promoted to Colonel on January 1, 1994.

From July 1994 to August 1996, he served as the Commander of the Aviation Brigade, with the 4th Infantry Division (Mechanized), Fort Hood, Texas. In September 1996, he was selected Senior Army Fellow on the Council on Foreign Relations in New York City. In August 1997, he assumed the assignment as Director of Integration in the Office of the Deputy Chief of Staff for Operations and Plans, United States Army, Washington, D.C. In August 1998, he was ordered to serve as Assistant Division Commander (Support), 25th Infantry Division (Light), at Schofield Barracks, Hawaii. He was promoted to Brigadier General on September 1, 1998.

In July 1999, he returned to Washington to serve first as Director of Requirements in the Office of the Deputy Chief of Staff for Operations and Plans, later Director of Materiel, Office of the Deputy Chief of Staff for Programs, United States Army, Washington, D.C. In August 2001, he was selected to serve in Turkey as Deputy Commander with the Joint Sub-Regional Command Southeast. He was promoted to Major General on January 1, 2002.

In September 2003, he was selected to serve as the Commanding General of the United States Army Security Assistance Command at Fort Belvoir, Virginia.

His awards and decorations include the Distinguished Service Medal; the Legion of Merit (with two oak leaf clusters); the Bronze Star Medal; Meritorious Service Medal (with four oak leaf clusters); Joint Service Commendation Medal; Army Commendation Medal (with oak leaf cluster); Army Achievement Medal; Senior Parachutist Badge; Master Army Aviator Badge; Ranger Tab; and Army Staff Identification Badge.

was commissioned a second lieutenant through the ROTC program. He earned a Masters of Science degree in Education Administration from the University of Southern California.

His military education includes the Aviation Officer Basic Course; the Infantry Officer Basic and Advanced Courses; United States Army Command and General Staff College; and Senior Service College Fellowship at Harvard University.

His first assignment was in September 1971, as Platoon Leader and Support Platoon Leader with B Company, 2nd Battalion (Airborne), 505th Infantry, 82nd Airborne Division at Fort Bragg, North Carolina. In October 1972, he was a Student in the Officer Rotary Wing Aviator Course at Fort Rucker, Alabama. In July 1973, he was assigned as Platoon Leader with the 3rd Aviation Detachment, 19th Aviation Battalion, with the Eighth United States Army in South Korea. In July 1974, he was ordered to Fort Myer, Virginia, to serve as Platoon Leader in C Company, 1st Battalion (Reinforcement), later, Assistant Ceremonies Officer, and later Commander, D Company, with the 3rd United States Infantry. In April 1977, he was a student, in the Infantry Officer Advance Course at Fort Benning, Georgia. In June 1978, he was assigned first as Operations Officer, next as Executive Officer with B Company, later S-1 (Personnel), and later Aviation Operations Officer, G-3 (Operations) 3rd Infantry Division (Mechanized), United States Army Europe and Seventh Army, Germany. In August 1982, he was a student at the United States Army Command and General Staff College at Fort Leavenworth, Kansas. In June 1983, he was assigned as the Chief Infantry Advisor, later Chief of Combat Arms Branch, later Chief of Operations and Training Branch in Readiness Group Bragg, Second United States Army, at Fort Bragg. In

Hall, Andrew L.
COMMAND SERGEANT MAJOR—ARMY

Command Sergeant Major Andrew L. Hall was born

in Shreveport, Louisiana. He graduated from Coushatta High School in Coushatta, Louisiana, in May of 1977. He enlisted in the United States Army and attended Basic Combat Training at Fort Jackson, South Carolina in July 1977.

His military education includes the Retention NCO Course; Total Fitness Course; Civilian Employee Personnel Management Course; the First Sergeants Course; Battle Staff Course; and the United States Sergeants Major Academy.

His military assignments include serving with 15th PSC, 1st Cavalry Division, at Fort Hood, Texas; the 257th PSC at Wiesbaden, German; the United States Army Personnel Command at Alexandria, Virginia; Company A, 120th AG Battalion (Reception), and Headquarters & Headquarters Company, Training Center Command, at Fort Jackson, South Carolina; and Headquarters Company, USASMA at Fort Bliss, Texas.

Hall, David M.

BRIGADIER GENERAL—AIR FORCE

Born in Gary, Indiana, Hall married the former Jacqueline Branch of Washington, D.C. They have two sons, Glen and Gary. He was graduated from Roosevelt High School in Gary, Indiana, in 1946. He graduated from Howard University with a bachelor's degree in Business Administration in 1951. He earned a master's in Educational Sociology from Agricultural and Technical State University of North Carolina at Greensboro in 1966. He is a graduate of Squadron Officer School, Air Command and Staff College, and Air War College, all located at Maxwell Air Force Base, Alabama, and the Industrial College of the Armed Forces at Fort Lesley J. McNair in Washington, D.C. In 1976 he attended the advanced management program at Massachusetts Institute of Technology.

He enlisted in the Air Force in August 1951 and received his commission as a second lieutenant in June 1953 through the Air Force Officer Candidate School. Early in his career General Hall served in a variety of career fields, which included supply, accounting and finance, data processing, and as an instructor in the Air Force Reserve Officers Training Corps program. In 1958 General Hall cross-trained into the data processing career field while stationed at Oxnard Air Force Base, California. He was assigned to Clark Air Base in the Philippines in July 1960 as a data processing officer.

He became Assistant Professor of Aerospace Science in the Reserve Officers Training Corps program at the Agricultural and Technical State University of North Carolina in June 1962. In August 1966 he returned to the data processing career field concurrent with his assignment to Ubon Royal Thai Air Force Base, Thailand, where he also served as Comptroller of the 8th Tactical Fighter Wing. General Hall was assigned to the Air Force Accounting and Finance Center, Denver, in September 1967. He was chief, Computer Operations Division, Directorate of Data Automation, until 1969 when he joined a software development division as an analyst programmer.

In March 1971 he was assigned to Scott Air Force Base, Illinois, where he became Chief of the Computer Operations Division for Military Airlift Command, and in March 1972 he became the Assistant for Social Actions in the Office of the Deputy Chief of Staff for Personnel at Scott. He became the Deputy Base Commander for Scott Air Force Base in May 1974 and Base Commander in February 1975. General Hall was assigned to Headquarters of Air Force Logistics Command at Wright-Patterson Air Force Base in June 1976 as Assistant Deputy Chief of Staff, Comptroller (data automation). In August 1977 he was assigned as Deputy Chief of Staff, Comptroller, Air Force Logistics Command, Wright-Patterson Air Force Base.

He was appointed to Brigadier General on August 1, 1980, with date of rank July 23, 1980. He retired from the Air Force on June 1, 1983.

His military decorations and awards include the Legion of Merit, Meritorious Service Medal (with oak leaf cluster), and Air Force Commendation Medal (with oak leaf cluster).

Hall, Gerard W.

COMMANDER—NAVY

Born in New Orleans, Louisiana, Commander Hall graduated from Southern University with a Bachelor of Science degree in Mechanical Engineering. He received his commission through the Aviation Officer Candidate School and was designated a Naval Aviator in March 1988.

Following initial MH-53E training in November 1988, he reported to Helicopter Mine Countermeasures Squadron Fifteen (HM-15) where he served as Aircraft Division Officer and qualified as Airborne Mine Countermeasure Mission Commander and Functional Check Pilot. During this period he deployed in

USS *Tripoli* (LPH 10) to *Westpac* 89 and Bahrain in 1991.

In February 1994, he reported to USS *Shreveport* (LPD 12) as Air Boss and Administration Officer. He deployed to Operation Strong Resolve '95 and completed a Mediterranean cruise. During this period, he qualified as Officer of the Deck Underway (OOD) and earned his Surface Warfare designation.

Upon completion of MH-53E refresher training in 1996, Commander Hall reported to Airborne Mine Countermeasures Weapons Systems Training School as the Executive Officer. During this period, he was temporarily assign to Helicopter Mine Countermeasure Squadron Fourteen (HM-14) as the Training Officer and deployed to Blue Harrier/EURO 97-4.

In September 1998, he reported to HM-14 where he served as Department Head for Safety and Aircraft Maintenance until June 2000. During this tour he deployed off the coast of southern California onboard USS *Bonhomme Richard* (LHD 5) for exercise Kernel Blitz and was Officer-in-Charge responsible for a four aircraft forward deployed AMCM/COD detachment in Bahrain.

In August 200, he attended the Naval War College in Newport, Rhode Island, where he earned a master's degree in National Security and Strategic Studies.

Hall, James Reginald, Jr.
LIEUTENANT GENERAL—ARMY

General Hall was born in Anniston, Alabama, married the former Helen A. Kerr, and they have three children, Sheila, James, and Cheryl. Upon completion of work toward a Bachelor of Arts degree in Political Science at Morehouse College, he enlisted in the Army.

Following basic training at Fort Chaffee, Arkansas, and Advance Individual Training at Fort Carson, Colorado, Hall attended Officer Candidate School, where he was commissioned a Second Lieutenant in 1958. He also holds an advanced degree in Public Administration from Shippensburg State College.

His military schooling includes completion of the Armed Forces Staff College and the United States Army War College. Among his Command and Staff positions, he has served as Commander of Company C, 2nd Battalion (Airborne), 503rd Infantry, 173rd Airborne Brigade, United States Army, Okinawa and Vietnam; 1st Battalion, 9th Infantry Brigade, 2nd Infantry Division, Eighth United States Army, Korea; 4th Regiment, United States Military Academy Corps of Cadets, West Point; 197th Infantry Brigade at Fort Benning, Georgia; Assistant Division Commander of the 4th Infantry Division (Mechanized) at Fort Carson, Colorado; Commanding General of the United States Army Military Personnel Center at Alexandria, Virginia; Commanding General of the 4th Infantry Division (Mechanized) at Fort Carson, Colorado; and Commanding General of the Fourth United States Army, Fort Sheridan, Illinois.

On January 22, 1982, he was promoted to Brigadier General; on June 1, 1986, to Major General; and on May 31, 1989, to Lieutenant General.

General Hall's staff assignments include Sub-sector Adviser on Advisory Team 9l, and Joint Planner on Joint Planning Group II Field Force in United States Military Assistance Command, Vietnam; Personnel Management Officer in the Assignment Section, Infantry Branch, Officer of Personnel Directorate, Office of Personnel Operations, Washington. D.C.; Assistant Executive Officer to the Deputy Chief of Staff for Personnel, Department of the Army, Washington, D.C.; Executive Officer in the Office of the Deputy Chief of

Staff for Training, United States Training and Doctrine Command at Fort Monroe, Virginia; Assistant Deputy Chief of Staff for Personnel and Assistant Deputy Chief of Staff for Operations, United States Forces Command, Fort McPherson, Georgia.

From August 1984 to June 1985, he was assigned as the Director of Enlisted Personnel Management Branch at the United States Army Military Personnel Center at Alexandria, Virginia; From June 1986 to June 1988, he was assigned as the Commanding General of the 4th Infantry Division (Mechanized) at Fort Carson, Colorado. From June 1988 to May 1989, he was selected to serve as the Deputy Inspector General at the Department of the Army in Washington, D.C. In May 1989, he was selected to serve as Commanding General of the Fourth United States Army at Fort Sheridan, in Illinois. He retired from the military on September 30, 1991. His military decorations and awards include the Legion of Merit; Bronze Star; Meritorious Service Medal (with oak leaf cluster); Army Commendation Medal (with oak leaf cluster); Combat Infantryman Badge; Parachutist Badge; and Army Staff Identification Badge.

Hall, Titus C.

Major General—Army

General Hall was born in Pflugerville, Texas, and he married the former Clarissa Douglas of Hastings, Florida. They have three children, Sandra, a graduate of Howard University in Washington, D.C.; Pamela, a 1978 graduate of Ohio State University; and a son, Titus, Jr.

Hall was graduated from I.M. Terrell High School in Fort Worth, Texas, in 1944. He received a Bachelor of Science in Electrical Engineering from Tuskegee Insti-

tute, Alabama, in 1952. He was a distinguished graduate of the Reserve Officers Training Corps program. He also earned a master's degree in Systems Engineering Management from the University of Southern California, Los Angeles, in 1971.

He entered active duty with the United States Air Force in March 1952. After completing communications officers training at Scott Air Force Base, Illinois, in June 1953, he was assigned as a Communications Intelligence Operations officer with the United States Air Force Security Service in Japan, serving at Johnson and Shiroi Air Bases. The general attended Basic Navigator Flying School at Ellington Air Force Base, Texas, and Advanced Bombing and Navigation School at Mather Air Force Base, California, from March 1956 to January 1958.

He spent the next six years flying B-47s with Strategic Air Command units at Davis-Monthan Air Force Base, Arizona, with frequent missions to Guam and Alaska. In June 1964 he was assigned to the Space Systems Division in Los Angeles as the Satellite Range Instrumentation Support Officer. He later served as Commander of the Kodiak Satellite Tracking Station in Alaska and returned to Los Angeles in March 1969 as Executive Officer of the Space and Missile Systems Organization (now the Air Force Space Division).

Following graduation from the University of Southern California, he was assigned to Da Nang Air Base, South Vietnam, in January 1971 and flew EC-47s in Southeast Asia for a year. General Hall became Chief Avionics Engineer for the B-1 strategic manned bomber at the Headquarters of the Aeronautical Systems Division at Wright-Patterson Air Force Base, Ohio, in March 1972. Two years later, after the design and test of the B-1 Avionics Suite, he became Systems Program Director of the Division's Avionics Program Office. He was later designated the Assistant Deputy for the Reconnaissance/Strike/Electronic Warfare System Program Office. In April 1975 he became Vice Commander of the 2750th Air Base Wing at Wright-Patterson Air Force Base, and Assumed Command of the wing in January 1977. He was then appointed Director of Materiel Management for San Antonio Air Logistics Center at Kelly Air Force Base, Texas. He became Deputy for Systems (now Reconnaissance and Electronic Warfare Systems) at Headquarters, Aeronautical Systems Division, Wright-Patterson Air Force Base, in July 1978. In May 1981 he became Commander of Lowry Technical Training Center and Lowry Air Force Base in Colorado.

He was promoted to Major General on July 1, 1981, with date of rank September 1, 1977. He was a master navigator with 4,000 flying hours in FB-111s, EF-111s, F-4G Wild Weasels, and United States Navy A-7Ds.

His military decorations and awards include the Distinguished Service Medal, Legion of Merit, Distinguished Flying Cross, Bronze Star, Meritorious Service Medal (with oak leaf cluster), and Air Medal (with two oak leaf clusters).

Hamilton, West A.

BRIGADIER GENERAL—ARMY

A native of Washington, D.C., West entered the United States Army in 1905 and was commissioned a Captain in 1920. In the years prior to World War II,

he was largely responsible for the training and development of black National Guard and Reserve Officers during summer camps. His military experience included service in the Mexican Border Campaigns as well as in France during both World Wars.

Hamlet, James Frank

MAJOR GENERAL—ARMY

Hamlet was born in Alliance, Ohio, and received a Bachelor of Science degree in Business Administration from St. Benedict's College in Atchison, Kansas. His military education includes Infantry School Basic and Advanced Courses; the United States Army Command and General Staff College; and the United States Army War College.

He has held a wide variety of important command and staff positions. From August 1963 to May 1966, he served as Project Officer, later as Doctrinal Developments Officer, in the United States Army Combat Developments Command Combined Arms Agency at Fort Leavenworth, Kansas. From May 1966 to July 1967, he served first as Operations Officer in the 11th Aviation Group, 1st Cavalry Division; then Commanding Officer of the 227th Aviation Battalion; later Executive Officer in the 11th Aviation Group, 1st Cavalry Division, United States Army, Vietnam.

He returned from overseas and was selected as a student at St. Benedict's College, from August 1967 to February 1968. From February 1968 to June 1969, he was Chief of the Air-Mobility Branch of the Doctrine and Systems Division in the United States Army Combat Developments Command Combat Arms Group at

Fort Leavenworth. From August 1969 to June 1970, he was a student at the United States Army War College at Carlisle Barracks, Pennsylvania.

He returned to Vietnam from July 1970 to August 1972, where he first served as Commanding Officer of the 11th Aviation Group, 1st Cavalry Division (Airmobile); next as Assistant Division Commander of the 101st Airborne Division (Airmobile); and later as Commanding General of the 3rd Brigade, 1st Cavalry Division, United States Army, Vietnam.

In August 1972 he returned to the United States and was assigned as Commanding General of the 4th Infantry Division at Fort Carson, Colorado. In 1974 he was assigned as Inspector General at United States Army Headquarters in Washington, D.C. From December 1974 to September 1977, he served as the Deputy Inspector General (Inspections, Safety, and Survey) for the United States Army in Washington, D.C.

He was appointed to Major General on June 1, 1973, and retired from the Army on February 1, 1981, with over 38 years of service. His military awards and decorations include the Distinguished Service Medal (with oak leaf cluster); Legion of Merit (with two oak leaf clusters); Distinguished Flying Cross; Soldier's Medal; Bronze Star (with oak leaf cluster); Air Medal (49 awards); Army Commendation Medal (with three oak leaf clusters); Combat Infantryman Badge; Parachutist Badge; and Master Army Aviator Badge. He is also a member of the United States Army Aviation Hall of Fame and the United States Infantry Hall of Fame.

Hammond, Douglas

CHIEF WARRANT OFFICER 4—ARMY

Hammond joined the staff of the United States Military Academy Band in May 2004 as Associate Bandmaster and Director of the Jazz Knights. Prior to enlisting in the Army, he attended the University of Miami at Coral Gables, Florida, majoring in Music Theory and Composition with emphasis on Conducting.

He has served in the Army Band program for a total of 27 years, first as a tuba player, pianist and arranger before being accepted into the Warrant Officer program in 1992. He was most recently Commander of the 113th Army Band at Fort Knox, Kentucky. Also known as "The Dragoons," this band has a rich history as the second oldest United States Army Band. He has also commanded the 82nd Airborne Division Band at Fort Bragg and the 10th Mountain Division Band at Fort Drum.

Hansen-Purnell, Isabella M.
COMMAND MASTER CHIEF—NAVY

A native of Baltimore, Maryland, Hansen-Purnell enlisted in the United States Navy in November 1982. She completed Basic Military Training at Recruit Training Center, Orlando, Florida, and graduated from Cryptologic Technician "Communications" "A" school at Naval Technical Training Center, Pensacola, Florida. Her education includes United States Navy Senior Enlisted Academy, Class 111 (Gold) and a Bachelors of Arts degree.

In May 2004, she was assigned as the Command Master Chief for USS *Lassen* (DDG 82).

Harden, Gloria J.
SERGEANT MAJOR—MARINE

Sergeant Major Harden enlisted in the United States Marine Corps during September 1973 and attended recruit training at Parris Island, South Carolina. After graduating, she attended the Basic Personnel Administration School at Parris Island. Upon completion of the school, she transferred to Woman Marine Company, Marine Corps Base, Camp Lejeune, North Carolina, where she served as an administration clerk with G-3, Assistant Chief of Staff for Training. She was meritoriously promoted to Lance Corporal and Corporal.

In 1987, she received orders to Headquarters Marine

Corps where she worked as Operations Chief in the Disbursing Branch, until her selection to the rank of First Sergeant in 1988. She then attended the Staff Non-Commissioned Officer Advanced Course at SNCO Academy, Marine Corps Combat Development Center, at Quantico, Virginia. After completion of school, First Sergeant Harden was transferred to the 3rd FSSG at Okinawa, Japan, as the First Sergeant of Engineer Maintenance Company.

In 1990, she transferred to Marine Corps Base, Camp Lejeune, North Carolina, where she served as the First Sergeant for Military Police and Alpha Companies. In March 1993, she reported to Parris Island, and served as the Fourth Recruit Training Battalion Sergeant Major. In April 1998, she received orders to report to Marine Air Control Group 48, Fourth Marine Air Wing, Marine Forces Reserve, in Highwood, Illinois. She assumed duties as Sergeant Major at Marine Corps Reserve Support Command, Kansas City, Missouri, on June 14, 2000.

Harding, Robert Anthony
MAJOR GENERAL—ARMY

General Harding was born in New York City, New York. He received his commission as a second lieutenant from the Officer Candidate School at Fort Belvoir, Virginia, on April 18, 1969. His assignments included tours in the continental United States, Panama, West Germany, and South Korea.

His military education includes the Intelligence Research Officers Technical Course; the Military Intelligence Officers Advanced Course; the Armed Forces Staff College; and the Naval War College. He holds a Bachelor of Science degree in Business Administration from Bowie State University; a Master of Science degree from Salve Regina University; and a Masters of Arts degree in National Security and Strategy from the United States Naval War College.

His first military assignment in September 1969 was as Intelligence Research Officer with the 108th Military Intelligence Group at Fort Devens, Massachusetts. In April 1971, he served as Commander of the Field Office of the 502nd Military Intelligence Battalion, Eighth United States Army, Korea. He returned to the United States in June 1972, to serve as a Team Leader with the 14th Military Intelligence Battalion, later in December 1972, as Team Leader with the 519th Military Intelligence Battalion, at Fort Bragg, North Carolina. From July 1973 to March 1975 he served as the Commander of Headquarters Company of the 1st Military Intelligence Battalion at Fort Bragg.

He has held a wide variety of command and staff assignments, including service as Director, J-2, Intelligence Directorate, United States Southern Command, where he was responsible for directing and managing daily collection and reporting activities. He planned and executed intelligence support to military operations, including contingency planning and crisis actions. He was promoted to Colonel on October 1, 1991.

He also served in a variety of command and staff positions. He commanded a Military Intelligence Battalion (Collection and Exploitation), and a Military Intelligence Group (Counterintelligence). His staff assignments include service with the United States Forces Command; the United States Army Intelligence and Security Command; the Army Staff; and the United States Southern Command. He was promoted to Brigadier General on July 1, 1996.

From December 1996 to March 2000, he served as Director of Operations with the Defense Intelligence Agency in Arlington, Virginia. With his role as Director for Operations, he served as the Director for Defense Human Intelligence (HUMINT) Service (DHS), Director of Central MASIN Office (CMO), and the Department of Defense Functional Manager for Intelligence Collection. He was promoted to Major General on October 1, 1999.

General Harding was appointed to the position of Assistant Deputy Chief of Staff for Intelligence for the United States Army in April 2000. He retired from military service in September 2001.

The military awards and decorations which he has received include the Defense Superior Service Medal; the Legion of Merit (with three oak leaf clusters); the Defense Meritorious Service Medal; and the Meritorious Service Medal (with two oak leaf clusters); the Army Commendation Medal (with two oak leaf clusters); and the Army Staff Identification Badge.

Hardy, Linton
SERGEANT MAJOR—MARINE

Hardy entered the Delayed Enlistment Program in October of 1979, and upon graduation from high school was shipped to Marine Corps Recruit Depot at Parris Island, South Carolina, in August 1980. Following completion of recruit training, he was designated as a Supply Specialist and underwent military on-the-job training at Camp Lejeune, North Carolina.

His key military assignments include serving as Drill Instructor, Senior Drill Instructor and Series Gunnery Sergeant. He also served as Battalion Warehouse Chief at Marine Corps Security Forces in Norfolk, Virginia; as Marine Detachment Guard Chief on board USS *John F. Kennedy*; as First Sergeant of the 8th Motor Transportation Battalion; as First Sergeant of Headquarters and Service Company; and as First Sergeant of Bravo Company. In January 2005, he was serving as Sergeant Major of Marine Wing Support Squadron 273rd, Marine Wing Support, with the Second Marine Aircraft Wing.

Harewood, Collin C.
COMMAND SERGEANT MAJOR—ARMY

Command Sergeant Major Collin C. Harewood entered the Army in February 1971, and completed Basic and Advanced Individual Training at Fort Jackson, South Carolina.

He has completed three years towards a degree in Business Management from Park College in Parkville, Missouri. His military education includes the Light Weapons Infantryman's Course; Nuclear Weapons Electronics Specialist Course; Ammunition Advance Course; NCO Logistics Program Course; Nuclear Weapons Courier Course; the Logistics Management Development Course; Battle Staff NCO Course; the First Sergeants Course; and the United States Army Sergeants Major Academy. His most recent assignments include serving three years as the First Sergeant of the 24th Ordnance Company at Hunter Army Airfield in Georgia; as the Operations Sergeant, for the 6th Ordnance Battalion at Camp Ames, South Korea; as Chief of Quality Assurance Branch, 583rd Ordnance Company at Muenster-Handorf, Germany; as the Nuclear Surety NCO at the Sierra Army Depot at Herlong, California; and as the Nuclear Surety NCO with the 2nd Infantry Division at Camp Casey, South Korea.

Harleston, Robert Alonzo
BRIGADIER GENERAL—ARMY

Harleston was born in Hempstead, New York, and married the former Bernice Robinson. They have three children, Robert, Bernice, and Paul. He received a Bachelor of Arts degree in Business Administration from Howard University in 1958, a Master of Science in Political Science and Public Safety from Michigan State University in 1965, and a J.D. from Georgetown University Law Center in 1984.

His military career began in 1958 when after graduating from Howard University he was commissioned a second lieutenant in the Military Police Corps. He entered the Military Police Officers Basic Course at Fort Gordon, Georgia, and afterwards became leader of a Military Police security platoon at a nuclear weapons storage facility in Romulus, New York.

From June 1959 to June 1961, he was assigned as a Security Officer in the 823rd Ordnance Company, later as Platoon Leader in the Military Police Company, at North Depot Activity, Romulus. From June 1961 to

September 1961, he was assigned as the Assistant Physical Security Officer at the 4th Logistics Command with the United States Army in Europe. From September 1961 to January 1964, he served as the Administrative and Management Officer, later as Chief of the Investigation and Security Branch, Provost Marshal Division, at the 4th Logistics Command, United States Army in Europe. In January 1964, he served as the Provost Marshal with the 4th Logistics Command at Fort Lee, Virginia. From August 1966 to July 1967, he served as an Operations Officer, later Assistant Division Provost Marshal, for the 1st Infantry Division with the United States Army in Vietnam. In June 1968, he was assigned as Chief of the Physical Security Division at the Provost Marshal Office and later as an Operations Officer in the Plans and Operations Division in Hawaii with the United States Army Pacific. From June 1970 to April 1971, he served as the Commander of Hawaii Armed Forces Police, Armed Forces Police Detachment, at Fort DeRussy, Hawaii. From May 1971 to December 1971, he served as Provost Marshal for the 179th Military Police Detachment with the United States Army in Vietnam. From December 1971 to December 1972, he served as the Personnel Management Officer, later Chief of Personnel Actions Section, with the Military Police Branch at the Office of Personnel Operations in Washington, D.C.

From December 1972 to November 1974, he served as the Commander of Area Confinement Facility, 532nd Military Police Company, at Fort Dix, New Jersey (the Army's largest confinement facility). From November 1974 to July 1975, he was assigned as an Action Officer with the Correction Branch in the Office of the Deputy Chief of Staff for Personnel in Washington, D.C. From June 1976 to June 1978, he served as

Director of Operations in the United States Army Criminal Investigation Command. From June 1978 to February 1980, he was assigned as Provost Marshal (chief of police) at Fort Hood, Texas. At Fort Hood, with 1,500 military police officers and enlisted members under his command, he ensured the safety and well-being of more than 65,000 people on a 339-square-mile post, one of the largest geographical installations and concentrations of troops in the free world.

From August 1985 to July 1986, he served as Chief of the Law Enforcement Division, Human Resources Development Directorate, Office of the Deputy Chief of Staff for Personnel, in Washington, D.C. He was promoted to the rank of Brigadier General on July 2, 1986.

From July 1986 to March 1988, he served as the Assistant Inspector General for Inspections at the Office of the Secretary of Defense in Washington, D.C. In March 1988, he was assigned Director of Human Resources Development at the Office of the Deputy Chief of Staff for Personnel with the United States Army in Washington, D.C. From September 1988 to July 1989, he served as the Deputy Commanding General, United States Army Community and Family Support Center in Alexandria, Virginia.

General Harleston retired from military service on July 31, 1989, but did not retire from criminal justice work. Shortly after leaving the Army, he became warden at the Eastern Correctional Institution, Maryland's newest prison.

His military awards and decorations include the Legion of Merit; Bronze Star (with oak leaf cluster); Meritorious Service Medal; Air Medal; and Army Commendation Medal (with oak leaf cluster).

Harrell, Ernest James
MAJOR GENERAL—ARMY

General Harrell was born in Selma, Alabama. He received a Bachelor of Science degree in civil engineering-construction from Tuskegee Institute and a Master of Science degree in engineering from the University of Arizona. Military schools attended by Harrell include Engineer School, Officer Basic and Advanced Courses, and the United States Army War College.

He joined the United States Army in 1960 as a student in the Engineer Officer Orientation Course in Fort Belvoir, Virginia. In November 1960, he was first assigned as a Platoon Leader with Company A, later Company C, later as Construction Officer with the 94th Engineer Battalion with the United States Army in Europe.

In April 1963 he was appointed Commander of Company B, 94th Engineer Battalion, with the United States Army in Europe. From June 1965 to December 1967, he was a Civil Engineer with the 539th Detachment, 1st Special Forces Group (Airborne), 1st Special Forces, Okinawa. From December 1967 to July 1970, he served as an Instructor, later Assistant Professor, of Military Science at Arizona State University at Tempe, Arizona.

Harrell, M. S.
SERGEANT MAJOR—MARINE

He enlisted in the United States Marine Corps in July 1980, and attended recruit training at Marine Corps Recruit Depot Parris Island, South Carolina. In March 1981, he reported for duty with Detachment A, 3rd Force Service Support Group at Iwakuni, Japan, for duty as a personal financial records clerk. In April 1982, he transferred to Marine Aviation Support Group 90 in Millington, Tennessee, where he was promoted to Sergeant in August 1983.

In September 1983, he attended Financial Management School in Marine Corps Combat Service Support School at Camp Johnson were he earned the 3451 MOS. In April 1991, he reported to Drill Instructor School at Marine Corps Recruit Depot in San Diego, California. Upon successful completion of Drill Instructor School, he was assigned to Lima Company, Third Recruit Training Battalion, where he served as a Drill Instructor and Senior Drill Instructor. In August 1993, after a successful tour on the Drill Field, he was assigned to Headquarters and Support Battalion, at Marine Corps Base, Camp Pendleton, California, where he served as Fund Administrator and Comptroller Chief.

In January 1996, he transferred to Headquarters and Support Battalion at Marine Corps Base, Camp Butler where he served as Alpha Company Gunnery Sergeant. While stationed at Camp Butler, he volunteered as the Commanding Officer of the Camp Foster Young Marines. In March 1997, he was ordered to Headquarters and Service Battalion, 2nd Force Service Support Group at Camp Lejeune, North Carolina, where he served as Comptroller Chief at Headquarters Company Gunnery Sergeant, Service Company First Sergeant and Company Gunnery Sergeant. He was selected for promotion to First Sergeant and transferred to 2nd Maintenance Battalion, 2nd Force Service Support Group for duty as Engineer Maintenance Company First Sergeant. He was reassigned to Forward Maintenance Company Alpha until chosen to serve as the Sergeant Major Combat Service Support Detachment 26 and

From July 1970 to May 1971, he served as Executive Officer of the 809th Engineer Battalion (Construction) Thailand. From June 1974 to June 1976, he was appointed Inspector General, Inspector General Office, Washington, D.C. From October 1977 to July 1979, he served as Commander of the 43rd Engineer Battalion (Combat) (Heavy) at Fort Benning, Georgia. From July 1979 to July 1982, he served as a Personnel Assignments Officer in the Lieutenant Colonels Division and Colonels Division.

He was promoted in September 1981 to Lieutenant Colonel, and in October 1982 to Colonel while serving at the United States Army Military Personnel Center at Alexandria, Virginia.

From June 1984 to July 1986, he served as Commander of the 2nd Engineer Group, Eighth United States Army, in South Korea. From July 1986 to October 1986, he was assigned as the Assistant Director for Civil Works at the Office of the Chief of Engineers, United States Army, in Washington, D.C. From October 1986 to July 1988, he was selected to serve as the Commanding General of the United States Army Engineer Division Ohio River in Cincinnati, Ohio. On March 1, 1988, he was promoted to Brigadier General.

In July 1988, he was assigned as Commanding General of the United States Army Engineer Division in Europe. On March 3, 1991, he was selected to serve as the Commander and Division Engineer for the North Pacific Division of the United States Army Corps of Engineers in Portland, Oregon. He was appointed Major General on February 1, 1991.

His military decorations and awards include the Legion of Merit; Bronze Star; Meritorious Service Medal (with three oak leaf clusters); Air Medal; Army Commendation Medal; National Defense Service Medal; Vietnam Service Medal (with four oak leaf clusters); Combat Infantryman Badge; and the Parachutist Badge.

Sergeant Major Marine Expeditionary Unit, Service Support Group 26 for Landing Force Sixth Fleet 1-03 deployment. Upon return to Conus Sergeant Major Harrell returned to 2nd Maintenance Battalion as First Sergeant at Headquarters and Service Company, where he served until assuming the duties as Sergeant Major of the 2nd Maintenance Battalion. He was next assigned as the Sergeant Major of Assault Amphibious Schools Battalion at Camp Pendleton, California.

Harrigan, Kevin D.
SERGEANT MAJOR—MARINES

He completed recruit training at Marine Corps Recruit Depot, Parris Island, South Carolina in September 1979. After graduating from boot camp, he attended the School of Infantry at Camp Pendleton, California.

His civilian education includes a Bachelor of Arts in National Security, a Bachelor of Arts in History, and a Master of Education, all from the University of Washington in Bothell, Washington.

In January 1992, he left the active force and joined the Select Marine Corps Reserve. He was promoted to Gunnery Sergeant and assigned to Bulk Fuel Company B(-), 6th Engineer Support Battalion in Tacoma, Washington. He was billeted as the Company Gunnery Sergeant and acting Company First Sergeant. In December 1996, he was selected First Sergeant. He was subsequently appointed as the Company First Sergeant, 4th Landing Support Battalion, Fort Lewis, Washington. During this tour he also served as the Director of the Battalion's Corporal's Course, one of only a handful of programs in the Select Marine Corps Reserve. He was selected Sergeant Major in December 1999. In February 2000, he was transferred to 4th Medical Battalion in San Diego, California as the Battalion Sergeant Major. In February 2003, he was assigned as the 4th Landing Support Battalion Sergeant Major.

Harris, Curtis
SERGEANT MAJOR—MARINES

He enlisted into the Marine Corps on June 30, 1975, in Compton, California. He report for Basic Recruit Training at the Marine Corps Recruit Depot in San Diego, California.

In February 1993, First Sergeant Harris was promoted to Sergeant Major, and in July 1993, was assigned to Marine Aerial Refueler Transport Squadron 352. In 2002, he was serving as the Sergeant Major of the 31st Marine Expeditionary Unit.

Harris, Dyfierd A.
COLONEL—ARMY

Colonel Harris is a native of Fayetteville, North Carolina. He attended Duke University where he earned a Bachelor of Science in Zoology and was commissioned as a Chemical Corps Officer in 1980 through the North Carolina A&T State University ROTC program. He earned a Master of Arts in International Relations from the University of Florida.

His military education includes the Chemical Officers Basic Course; Army Aviation Rotary Wing Flight School; Aviation Officers Advanced Course; Command and General Staff College; Joint Professional Military Education Phase II; and the Army War College.

His military assignments include serving as Platoon Leader with the 530th Supply & Services Battalion at Fort Bragg, North Carolina; Platoon Leader and Company Executive Officer in the 501st Combat Aviation Battalion at Illesheim, Germany; Company Commander in the 501st Attack Helicopter Battalion at Katerbach, Germany; Foreign Area Officer at the United States Embassy in Malawi, Africa; Battalion Executive Officer, in the 4/229th Attack Helicopter Battalion, Operations Officer of the 6-6th Cavalry Squadron at

Illesheim; Politico-Military Analyst at the United States Central Command at MacDill Air Force Base Florida; Battalion Commander of the 1/4th Attack Helicopter Battalion at Illesheim; Director for Planning, Training, Mobilization and Security Directorate at the United States Army Aviation Center at Fort Rucker, Alabama; and Chief of Staff for Strategy, Plans and Policy Directorate (DAMO-SSZ), in the Headquarters of the Department of the Army, Deputy Chief of Staff G3, Washington, D.C. In June 2005, he was serving as Commander of the 4th Brigade, 1st Armored Division.

Harris, Gail
CAPTAIN—NAVY

Captain Harris retired from the United States Navy in on December 1, 2001, as the highest-ranking black female in the United States Navy. Her military career highlights include serving as the Navy's first female and first African American Instructor at the Armed Forces Air Intelligence Training Center, being the first female and first African American to head the Intelligence Department for Fleet Air Reconnaissance Squadron Two in support of United States Military Operations during the Gulf War, and serving as the Intelligence Planner at Commander United States Naval Forces Central Command.

Her military decorations include the Defense Superior Service Medal; the Defense Meritorious Service Medal; the Navy Meritorious Service Medal; and the Navy Commendation Medal.

Harris, Leroy
SENIOR EXECUTIVE SERVICE

His federal service began at Robins Air Force Base in 1979 with engineering assignments with the PAV TACK Laser Ranging System, AC-130H Spectre Gunship and Mh-53 (J) PAVE LOW III, F-111, F-15 and the ALR-69 Radar Warning Receiver and Global Positioning System and JSTAR software production.

His education includes a Bachelor of Science in Engineering Technology from Savannah State University in Savannah, Georgia, in 1973; Post-baccalaureate study in Computer Science at the University of Central Florida, in Orlando, Florida in 1975; and a Master of Science in Administration and Management from Georgia College and State University in Milledgeville, Georgia in 1988; Advanced Program Management in Defense Acquisition University at Fort Belvoir, Virginia, in 1998; and Special Operations Command Leadership and Management Course in United States Special Operations Command at MacDill Air Force Base, Florida, in 2001. He also earned a second Master of Science in National Security Strategy from the National War College at the National Defense University at Fort McNair, Washington, D.C., in 2002.

From September 1985 to May 1986, he served as Electronics Engineer, Special Project Assistant to Material Management Directorate, and Chief Engineer in the Materiel Management Directorate at Warner Robins Air Logistics Center at Robins Air Force Base, Georgia. From May 1986 to July 1987, he was Chief Engineer in the Item Management Division of the Materiel Management Directorate at Warner Robins Air Logistics Center. From July 1987 to November 1987, he was Chief of the Special Operations Forces Helicopter and Fixed Wing Aircraft Engineering Section in the System Program Office Division of the Materiel Management Directorate at Warner Robins Engineering Section, System Program Office Division, Materiel Management Directorate, at Warner Robins Air Logistics Center. In November 1987, he became Chief of the Technical Advisor Engineering Branch, Electronic Warfare Management Division, Materiel Management Directorate, Warner Robins Air Logistics Center. In April 1988, he became Chief of the Radar Warning Receiver Branch in the Engineering Division, Electronic Warfare Management Directorate, Warner Robins Air Logistic Center. In June 1992, he became Chief of the F-15, F-11, and ARL-69 Electronic Warfare Tactical Engineering Branch, Electronic Warfare Management Directorate, Warner Robins Air Logistics Center. In April 1995, he became Chief for the Joint Surveillance Target Radar System Software Production Branch, Space and Special Systems Management Directorate, Warner Robins Air Logistics Center. In March 1997, he became Chief of Machinery, Materials and Tools; Weapons; Computers; and Bare Base Systems Division, Space and Special Systems Management Directorate, Warner Robins Air Logistics. In February 2001, he was appointed Deputy Program Executive Officer for Fixed Wing Aircraft Acquisition in the United States

Special Operations Command, at MacDill Air Force Base. From October 2002 to July 2003, he served as Deputy Director for Space and Special Systems Management Directorate at Warner Robins Air Logistics Center. In July 2003, he was selected to serve as the Deputy Director for Intelligence in the Surveillance and Reconnaissance Directorate at Warner Robins Air Logistics Center. Harris was promoted to GA-15 in February 2001.

Harris, Marc D.
LIEUTENANT COLONEL—ARMY

Marc Harris received his commission as a Second Lieutenant from the United States Military Academy at West Point in 1986.

After graduating from the Signal Officer's Advanced Course, he earned a Master's Degree in Computer Science from George Washington University in Washington, D.C. He then applied his craft as an Assistant Professor at the United States Military Academy.

At Fort Huachuca, Arizona, he served as the Assistant Brigade S-3 for Automation, 11th Signal Brigade. Three months later, he was commanding the forward deployed C Company (Separate/Provisional) of the 11th Signal Brigade in Bahrain. He returned to Fort Huachuca to become the Aide-de-Camp to the Deputy Commanding and then Commanding General of the Information Systems Command. In 1991, he deployed to Dhahran, Saudi Arabia to serve as the Assistant Brigade S-4, 11th Signal Brigade. He was assigned to command the 505th Signal Company, 86th Signal Battalion, 11th Signal Brigade in Riyadh, Saudi Arabia. Upon completion of the Command and General Staff College in June of 1998, he served as the Operations Officer and then as the Executive Officer for the 122nd Signal Battalion, 2nd Infantry Division at Camp Red Cloud South Korea. He then served as the Chief of Current Operations Branch for the White House Communication Agency, Washington, D.C. In November 2004, Harris was serving as the Commander of the 16th Signal Battalion.

Harris, Marcelite Jorder
MAJOR GENERAL—AIR FORCE

Born in Houston, Texas, Harris is the daughter of Cecil O'Neal and Marcelite Elizabeth Terrell Jordan. She married Maurice A. Harris of Portsmouth, Virginia. They have a son, Steven, and a daughter, Tenecia. She was graduated from Kashmere Gardens Junior-Senior High School, Houston, in 1960. She earned a Bachelor of Arts degree in Speech and Drama from Spelman College in 1964 and a Bachelor of Science Degree in Business Management from the University of Maryland, Asian Division, in 1989. General Harris completed Squadron Officer School in 1975; Air War College in 1983; Harvard University's Senior Officers National Security Course in 1989; and the CAPSTONE General and Flag Officer Course in 1990.

In September 1965 she entered the United States Air Force through Officer Training School at Lackland Air

Force Base, Texas. Upon graduation in December 1965, she was assigned to the 60th Military Airlift Wing at Travis Air Force Base, California, as Assistant Director for Administration. In January 1967 she became Administrative Officer for the 388th Tactical Missile Squadron at Bitburg Air Base, West Germany, and in May 1969 was reassigned as Maintenance Analysis Officer for the 388th Tactical Fighter Wing in Bitburg.

She completed her tour of duty in West Germany and upon graduation in May 1971 from the Aircraft Maintenance Officer Course at Chanute Air Force Base, Illinois, became the Air Force's first woman to be an Aircraft Maintenance Officer. Three months later she became Maintenance Supervisor with the 49th Tactical Fighter Squadron at Korat Royal Thai Air Force Base, Thailand. On return to the United States, she was assigned as Job Control Officer with the 916th Air Refueling Squadron at Travis Air Force Base, in September 1973 she became the Maintenance Supervisor. In September 1975 General Harris was assigned as a Personnel Staff Officer at the Headquarters of the United States Air Force, Washington, D.C., where she served as a White House aide to President Jimmy Carter.

In May 1978 she became Commander of Cadet Squadron 39 at the United States Air Force Academy at Colorado Springs, Colorado, as assignment that made her one of the first two women to be Air Officers Commanding. The general returned to maintenance when she became Maintenance Control Officer of the 384th Air Refueling Wing at McConnell Air Force Base, Kansas, in July 1980. In July 1981 she became Strategic Air Command's first woman Maintenance Squadron Commander when she assumed command of the 384th Avionics Maintenance Squadron at McConnell. Eight months later, she assumed Command of McConnell's 384th Field Maintenance Squadron.

In November 1982 she was assigned to the Pacific Air Forces Logistic Support Center at Kadena Air Base, Japan. She became the Air Force's first woman Deputy Commander for Maintenance at Keesler Air Force Base, Mississippi, in March 1986 and the first woman Wing Commander in Air Training Command's 3300th Technical Training Wing, Keesler Technical Training Center, in December 1988. In September 1990, she was selected Vice Commander of Oklahoma City Air Logistics Center at Tinker Air Force Base.

On May 1, 1991, she was promoted to Brigadier General, becoming the first black female General in the United States Air Force. From July 1993 to August 1994, she served as the Director of Technical Training at Headquarters Air Education and Training Command at Randolph Air Force Base, Texas. From September 1994 to February 1997, she was the Director of Maintenance at Headquarters United States Air Force in Washington, D.C. She organized, trained, and equipped a work force of more than 125,000 technicians and managers, and maintains the $260 billion plus Global Reach-Global Power aerospace weapons system inventory. She was promoted to Major General on May 25, 1995, and retired on February 22, 1997.

General Harris's military awards and decorations include the Bronze Star, Meritorious Service Medal (with four oak leaf clusters), Air Force Commendation Medal (with oak leaf cluster), Presidential Unit Citation, Air Force Outstanding Unit Award (with "V" device and seven oak leaf clusters), Air Force Organizational Excellence Award (with oak leaf cluster), National Defense Service Medal, Vietnam Service Medal (with three service stars), Air Force Overseas Ribbon-Short, Air Force Overseas Ribbon-Long (with oak leaf cluster), Air Force Longevity Service Award Ribbon (with four oak leaf clusters), Republic of Vietnam Gallantry Cross (with palm), and Republic of Vietnam Campaign Medal.

Harris, Michael M.
COMMAND SERGEANT MAJOR—ARMY

Harris was born in Chillicothe, Ohio. He joined the Army in July 1974, and served in a variety of positions of responsibility the United States Army and the Army Reserve in Germany.

He is a graduate of the United States Army Sergeants Major Academy, the Army Management Staff College Sustaining Base Leadership and Management course, and several Army Reserve Readiness Training Center (ARRTC) courses.

After active duty with the Armored Cavalry Regiment and the 3rd Armored Division, he transitioned from active duty to the reserve component in 1983. His first reserve assignment in 1983 was with the 454th Replacement Detachment at Rhein Main Airport, where he held all Noncommissioned Officer (NCO) leadership positions. He transferred to the 3747th USARF School in Munich, Germany in 1987 as a Senior NCO Education System Instructor. He returned to the 454th and served as the First Sergeant from August 1992 to

April 1994. He then assumed duties as the Senior Operations Sergeant and NCO in Charge of the 330th Rear Tactical Operations Center, Kaiserslautern, Germany. He deployed with the 330th during Operations Joint Endeavor from December 1995 to September 1996.

He was briefly assigned as the Senior NCO, International Affairs Support Division of Headquarters, 7th Army Reserve Command. In July 1997, he returned to the 3747th Training Brigade in Grafenwoehr on a temporary assignment as the Acting Commandant. He was subsequently assigned as the Deputy Commandant of the NCO Academy. He served as the Command Sergeant Major for the 3747th Training Brigade from July 2000 until March 2003. In 2004, Harris was serving as the Command Sergeant Major for the 7th United States Army Reserve Command.

Harris, Octavia D.
SENIOR CHIEF PETTY OFFICER—NAVY

Octavia Harris was born in Long Island, New York, and attended Sidney Lanier High School. In September of 1982, she reported to Recruit Training Command in Orlando, Florida, and then graduated from YN "A" School. She earned a Bachelor of Arts degree in Health Care Administration.

Her initial assignment was in November 1982 onboard Helicopter Training Squadron Eighteen, homeported in Milton, Florida. Her other assignments include Training Squadron Three (Milton, Florida); Patrol Squadron Five Fleet Composite Squadron Ten (Guantanamo Bay, Cuba), Naval Technical Training Center Pensacola, Florida; USS *Nimitz* (CVN 68-Bremerton, Washington); and Space and Naval Warfare System Command in San Diego, California. In October

2002, she reported to the Commander of Amphibious Squadron One as the N1 Department Head and Command Senior Chief Enlisted Advisor.

Harris, Stayce D.

COLONEL—AIR FORCE

Born in Los Angeles, California, Stayce Harris graduated from 71st High School in Fayetteville, North Carolina, in 1977. In 1981, she received a commission in the Air Force as a Second Lieutenant through the University of Southern California's ROTC Program and attended undergraduate Pilot Training at Williams Air Force Base, Arizona.

Her education includes a Bachelor of Science Degree in Industrial Systems Engineering from the University of Southern California and a Master of Aviation Management from Embry-Riddle Aeronautical University in 1987. She completed Squadron Officer School (Residence) in 1988; the Air Command and Staff College; and the Air War College in 2000.

She is a Command Pilot with more than 2500 hours in the C-141B/C aircraft. She separated from active duty in August 1990 and began working for United Airlines where she is a First Officer on the Boeing 747-4000 aircraft.

She joined the Air Force Reserves in April 1991 as a Captain assigned as an Air Operations Officer, C-141B Pilot, with the 44th Airlift Control Flight, 445th Airlift Wing, at March Air Force Base, California. From February 1995 to January 1997, she served as a Mobility Force Planner for DC Staff/Plans and Operations at Headquarters United States Air Force at the Pentagon. From January 1997 to January 2000, she was assigned as Individual Mobilization Augmentee to Deputy Assistant Secretary of the Air Force at the Pentagon. From February 2000 to January 2001, she was as-

signed as the Reserve Deputy Commander of the 452nd Operations Group, 452nd Air Mobility Wing, at March Air Reserve Base. In January 2001, she made history when she was selected to serve as the first black female to command an active Flying Squadron in the United States Air Force. She served as the Commander for the 729th Airlift Squadron at March Air Reserve Base. In May 2002, she was selected to serve as the Vice Commander of the 507th Air Refueling Wing at Tinker Air Force Base, Oklahoma. She was promoted to Colonel on April 1, 2002.

On May 15, 2005, she became the first African American woman in the Air Force Reserve Command, and perhaps the Air Force to Command a Flying Wing. She accepted command of the 459th Air Refueling Wing and its KC-135R Stratotankers in a ceremony on May 15, 2005, at Andrews Air Force Base, in Maryland.

Harris, Vera F.

COMMAND SERGEANT MAJOR—ARMY

A native of Dallas, Texas, Harris enlisted in the United States Army Women Corps in November 1975. She attended Basic Combat Training and Advanced Individual Training at Fort Jackson, South Carolina.

Her military education includes all the Noncommissioned Officer Education System Courses and the United States Army Sergeants Major Academy. She is one of only a few enlisted soldiers who are certified by the International Food Service Executive Association as a Certified Food Service Executive and as a Certified Professional Food Manager. She holds an associate's degree from Pikes Peak College in Colorado; a bachelor's degree from Trinity Southern University in Texas; and a Bachelor of Science from Excelsior College in New York.

She has held a wide variety of leadership positions and assignments to include serving as a Dining Facility Manager; Food Operations Sergeant; Supply and Logistics Noncommissioned Officer in Charge; First Sergeant; and two assignments as Brigade Food Advisor. She was selected to serve as the Senior Noncommissioned Officer in Charge and Program Manager for the Department of the Army Philip A. Connelly program. In October 2004, she was serving as the Command Sergeant Major for the Regimental Support Squadron, 2nd Armored Cavalry Regiment at Fort Polk, Louisiana.

Harrison, Ronnie L.
SERGEANT MAJOR—ARMY

Harrison was born in Charleston, South Carolina in September 1965. He enlisted in the United States Marine Corps in September 1983, and completed Boot Camp at Marine Corps Recruit Depot at Parris Island, South Carolina. He was recognized as the Most Physically Fit Marine of the graduating company. In January 1984, he reported to Camp Lejeune, North Carolina, for MOS School and upon graduation, he attained the MOS of 0481 (Longshoreman Specialist).

He has served in numerous key leadership positions, including Senior Drill Instructor for his last three platoons in which two were designated as the Company Honor Platoon, and spent his third year serving as with the Physical Training Department. He also served as the Combat Service Support Chief for 3rd Surveillance Reconnaissance Intelligence Group (SRIG). In September of 1996, he served as the Senior Enlisted Advisor for 7th Company, 2nd Battalion, at the United States Naval Academy (USNA); and later as First Sergeant for Small Craft Company, 2nd Marine Division; and First Sergeant of Weapons Company, 3rd Battalion, 6th Marines. He deployed with the 26th Marine Expeditionary Unit (MEU) Special Operations during Operation Enduring Freedom. After the deployment, he once again found himself reassigned as Company First Sergeant for Headquarters and Service Company, 3rd Battalion, 6th Marines. During this tour, he was selected and later promoted to Sergeant Major in January 2004. In November 2004, he was serving as the Sergeant Major for Headquarters and Headquarters Squadron at Marine Corps Air Station (MCAS) Futenma.

Hawkins, Alvin C.
CHIEF WARRANT OFFICER—COAST GUARD

Alvin Hawkins entered the Coast Guard in 1972 from Detroit, Michigan. After graduating from Coast Guard Indoctrination School, his first assignment was United States Coast Guard Washington Radio Station, in Alexandria, Virginia.

He has graduated from Electrician's Mate "A" School

at Governor's Island, New York; Aids to Navigation School; Senior Petty Officer's Leadership & Management School in Yorktown, Virginia; Electrician's Mate "17" School; Instructor Basic School at Norfolk, Virginia; and United States Coast Guard Contract Quality Assurance Schools.

His military assignments include serving at Coast Guard Base, Gloucester City, New Jersey; Coast Guard Cutter *Northwind* (WAGB 282); 9th Coast Guard District Civil Engineering Office, Cleveland, Ohio; Coast Guard Cutter *Mariposa* (WLB 396); and United States Coast Guard Contract Quality Assurance Schools. In March 2005, he was serving as a Maritime Science Instructor.

Hawkins, Billy R.
SERGEANT MAJOR—MARINES

A native of Camden, Arkansas, Hawkins enlisted in the United States Marine Corps in August 1976 and attended Recruit Training at Marine Corps Recruit Deport, San Diego, California.

In January 1981, Hawkins became a Platoon Sergeant for Charlie Company, 1st Battalion, 2nd Marine Division. In July 1984, he reported to Field Medical Service School, where he served as the Senior Enlisted Advisor. In 1989, he was assigned as a Drill Instructor, Senior Drill Instructor, Series Gunnery Sergeant and Company Chief Drill Instructor with the Second Recruit Training Battalion. In 1992, he served as Platoon Commander and Company Gunnery Sergeant for Bravo Company. In 1995, he was assigned as First Sergeant for Headquarters and Service Company, Second Surveillance, Reconnaissance, and Intelligence Group. From 1995 to July 1999, he was First Sergeant

for Bravo Company, 2nd Marine Expeditionary Force. In July 1999, he was transferred overseas and reported to Marine Tactical Air Command Squadron–18, later servings as First Sergeant for the 3rd Intelligence Battalion. In June 2002, he was assigned as the Sergeant Major of the 3rd Intelligence Battalion. In November 2002, he was assigned as the Sergeant Major for the 3rd Transportation Support Battalion.

Hawkins, John Russell, III

MAJOR GENERAL—ARMY

General Hawkins received a Bachelor of Arts Degree in Political Science and Marketing from Howard University and earned a Masters of Public Administration in Governmental Management and Public Policy from the American University. He also earned a jurisdiction doctor degree in Law from the Washington College of Law at American University, with international study at University of London Law Faculty. He is also a published Fellow of the John F. Kennedy School of Government at Harvard University. His military education includes the Adjutant General Officer Basic and Advanced Courses; United States Army Command and General Staff College; and the United States Army Senior Service College Fellowship.

He received a commission to second lieutenant after completing the ROTC program at Howard University on July 22, 1971. From October 1986 to October 1987, he was assigned as a Public Affairs Officer (IMA) in the Office of the Chief of Public Affairs in Washington, D.C. While in this assignment, he served as Plans Officer for the Supreme Allied Commander-in-Chief, Atlantic, Joint Control Group Winter Exercise, at Norfolk, Virginia. From October 1990 to October 1994, he was assigned as Field Representative, National Committee for Employer Support of the Guard and Reserve, Washington, D.C.

From October 1994 to July 1996, he served as a Congressional Liaison Officer in the Office of the Assistant Secretary of the Army for Financial Management, in Washington, D.C. In June 1997, he was assigned as Chief of the Office of Programs and Liaison, later as Director of Public Affairs and Liaison Directorate, in the Office of the Chief of Army Reserve in Washington, D.C. From May 2000 to November 2001, he served as Deputy Chief for Public Affairs (IMA) in the Office of the Chief, Public Affairs in Washington, D.C.

From November 2001 to April 2002, he served as the Director of the Coalition Information Service, Operation Enduring Freedom, Combined Joint Public Affairs Center at Islamabad, Pakistan. In April 2002, he was retuned to his assignment as Deputy Chief for Public Affairs (IMA) in Washington, D.C. He was promoted to Brigadier General on May 13, 2001.

His military awards and decorations include the Legion of Merit; the Defense Meritorious Service Medal; Meritorious Service Medal (with oak leaf cluster); the Army Commendation Medal; Army Achievement Medal; National Defense Medal; the Secretary of Defense Identification Badge; and the Army Staff Identification Badge.

Hawkins, Ronnie D., Jr.

BRIGADIER GENERAL—AIR FORCE

General Hawkins was born in Anchorage, Alaska, and received his commission in 1977 as a distinguished graduate of the ROTC Program at Angelo State University, entering active duty in January 1978.

His military and civilian education includes a Bachelor of Business Administration degree in Computer Science from Angelo State University in San Angelo, Texas. He also earned a Master of Science degree in Management and Human Relations from Abilene Christian University in Texas and a Master of Science degree in National Resource Strategy from the Industrial College of the Armed Forces, National Defense University, at Fort Lesley J. McNair, Washington, D.C.

He is a Distinguished Graduate of Squadron Officer School at Maxwell Air Force Base, Alabama, and a Distinguished Graduate of Air Command and Staff College at Maxwell Air Force Base.

Hawkins has held a variety of Communications Leadership positions. From July 1981 to June 1985, he was Chief of the Data Automation Division, 96th Bomb Wing, later Chief of the Operations Division, 1993rd Information Systems Squadron at Dyess AFB, Texas. From June 1985 to June 1988, he was Inspector, later Executive Officer to the Vice Commander, Air Force Communications Command, Scott AFB, Illinois. From June 1988 to July 1992, he was Commander of Cadet Squadron 24, later Executive Officer to the Superintendent, at the United States Air Force Academy, Colorado Springs, Colorado. From July 1993 to July 1996, he served as Support Manager for Command, Control, Communications and Computer Systems, later Action Officer for the Defense Information Systems Network and Integrated Data Systems (J-6), the Joint Staff, Washington, D.C. From July 1997 to June 1998, he was Commander of the Computer Systems Squadron, Air Combat Command, at Langley Air Force Base, Virginia. From July 1998 to March 1999, he was Commander of the Communications Group, ACC, at Langley Air Force Base. From April 1999 to April 2000, he was Director of Command, Control, Communications and Computer Systems, Joint Task Force Southwest Asia, at Riyadh, Saudi Arabia. From May 2000 to April 2003, he was Director of Communications and Information, Headquarters Pacific Air Force, at Hickam Air Force Base, Hawaii. In May 2003, Hawkins was assigned as Director of Communications Operations in the Office of the Deputy Chief of Staff for Installations and Logistics at Headquarters United States Air Force, Washington, D.C.

Hawkins, Tomas R.

COMMAND SERGEANT MAJOR—ARMY

Sergeant Major Hawkins' military education includes the First Sergeant Course; the United States Army Sergeants Major Academy; Equal Opportunity Representative Course; Strategic Deployment School; and the Air Assault Course.

CSM Hawkins hails from The Bronx, New York City. He entered the United States Army in August 1976, attended Basic Training at Fort Leonard Wood, Missouri and Advanced Individual Training at the Military Police School at Fort McClellan, Alabama. After his first enlistment, Command Sergeant Major Hawkins left the military to pursue his education. He re-entered in the United States Army in July 1981 and attended the Motor Transportation Course at Fort Dix, New Jersey. Command Sergeant Major Hawkins has held every NCO leadership position from Team Leader; Squad Leader; Platoon Sergeant; and First Sergeant to Command Sergeant Major.

In 2002, he was serving as the Command Sergeant Major of the 3rd Brigade, 91st Division Training Support (TS) at Travis Air Force Base, California.

Hawkins, Walter L.

COMMAND SERGEANT MAJOR—ARMY (THE AUTHOR)

Hawkins was born in Atlanta, Georgia, and graduated from South Fulton High, in East Point, Georgia (1967), and attended Dekalb College and the University of Georgia. His military education includes: He entered the United States Army in December 1968, and attended Basic Combat Training, at Fort Benning, Georgia; I Advanced Individual Training, Fort Polk, Louisiana, (1969); all the Noncommissioned Officer

Education System Courses; Senior Noncommissioned Officer Course at Camp Edwards, Massachusetts; Senior Supply Management Course; Logistics Management Course, Fort Lee, Virginia; Personnel Management Course; Military Police Course; Battle Staff Course; the EEO Management Course; United States Army Sergeants Major Academy, Fort Bliss, Texas; United States Army Command Sergeants Major (D) Course, Fort Bliss, Texas.

His military assignments include: in 1969, assigned with the Supply Point 39, 8th Army, in Korea; promoted to Sergeant on April 6, 1970; from 1974 to 1978, assigned with the 310th Civil Affairs Unit, Atlanta, Georgia; promoted to Staff Sergeant on October 5, 1974, and to Sergeant First Class on September 14, 1977; from 1978 to 1980, assigned to the 335th Signal Command; was promoted to Master Sergeant on July 9, 1980; from July 1980 to February 1986, served as the Chief Logistics Noncommissioned Officer G-4, at the 81st Army Reserve Command, Atlanta, Georgia; from 1986 to 1989, served with the 335th Signal Command first as Senior Supply Noncommissioned Officer, later from 1989 to 1993, as Sergeant Major of Logistics Noncommissioned Officer (S-4), promoted to Sergeant Major on June 27, 1989; in December 1993, selected to serve in the Command Sergeant Major Program; from December 1993 to December 1997, served as the Command Sergeant Major for the 1st Battalion, 4th Brigade, 87th Division (EX), Fort Gillem, Georgia; in March, 1998, was selected to serve as the Command Sergeant Major for the 75th Combat Support Hospital (HUB), located in Tuscaloosa, Alabama. My military awards and decorations include: Army Meritorious Service Medal; Army Commendation Medal (with oak leaf clusters); Army Reserve Components Achievement Medal (with two oak leaf cluster); National Defense Service Medal (with bronze service star); Good Conduct Medal(with five oak leaf clusters); Armed Forces Expeditionary Medal (Korea); Army Force Reserve Medal (with 2nd 10-year device); Army Service Ribbon; Army Reserve Components Overseas Training Ribbon (with number 2); NCO Professional Development Ribbon (with the numeral 4); Two Unit Citations. His Civilian Occupation: A career as a professional Law Enforcement Officer, and held a wide variety of important command and staff positions, culminating in current position. He served as a Police Officer, Police Narcotic Detective and Internal Investigation Investigator with the Atlanta Police Department, from 1971 to 1975. From 1975 to 1987, first with the Fulton County's new Police Department as one of the first four black police officers with that department in history. He was promoted as the first black police Sergeant with the Fulton County Police Department. Also work with the Fulton County Sheriff's Department. In January 1990, he was appointed Postal Police Officer and in April 1997, he was promoted to Postal Police Sergeant and in August 2000, he was promoted to Captain/Manager for Postal Police in the Southeast Area.

His other books include: *African American Biographies: Profiles of 558 Current Men and Women*; *African American Generals and Flag Officers*; *African American Biographies 2: Profiles of 332 Current Men and Women*.

Hayes, Aaron W.

COLONEL—ARMY

Colonel Hayes was born in Lexington, South Carolina, and was raised and educated in Columbia, South Carolina. He graduated from the United States Military Academy at West Point, New York, in 1976 and was commissioned as a second lieutenant in the Infantry.

Colonel Hayes received his Bachelor of Science degree from the United States Military Academy in 1976, and a Master of Arts in Law and Diplomacy in International Relations from Tufts University at Medford, Massachusetts, in 1986. He earned a Ph.D. in International Relations in 1993 from Tufts, and earned a Master of Science degree in National Resource Strategy from the Industrial College of the Armed Forces at Fort McNair, Washington, D.C.

His assignments include serving as Executive Officer of the 302nd Forward Support Battalion, 2nd Infantry Division at Camp Casey, Korea; as Commander of the 142nd Corps Support Battalion at Fort Polk, Louisiana; as an Army Staff Officer at the Congressional Inquiry Division Office, Office of the Chief of Legislative Liaison at the Pentagon; and as Deputy Commanding Officer with the 19th Theater Support Command.

Hayes, Ethbin E.
SERGEANT MAJOR—MARINES

He is a native of Chicago, Illinois, where he graduated from Westinghouse Vocational High School in 1981. He joined the Delayed Entry Program in 1980 and departed for Recruit Training in San Diego, California, in July 1981. After completion of recruit training in October 1981, he attended his primary MOS school for Aviation Operations Specialists in Meridian, Mississippi.

In 1990, he was transferred to Marine Corps Air Station Kaneohe Bay, Hawaii, where he was assigned to Marine Medium Helicopter Squadron-364 to assume the duties as Operations Chief, where he completed two more successful unit deployments to Okinawa and South Korea. In June 1994, he was transferred to Marine Air Group–36, 1st Marine Air Wing, Okinawa, where he served as the Group Operation Chief until July 1995. He was appointed Operations Chief of Marine Aircraft Group-11, 3rd Marine Aircraft Wing, in Miramar, California. He next served as the Senior Operation Representative during the base closure and realignment of 3rd Marine Aircraft Wing from Marine Corps Air Station El Toro, California, and as First Sergeant, Reconnaissance Company, 1st Marine Division at Camp Pendleton, California. In March 2000, he returned to Hawaii, where he was attached to the Headquarters Company of the 3rd Battalion, 3rd Marine Regiment where he completed another deployment to Okinawa, Japan and Korea. He then served as Sergeant Major at Recruiting Station, Nashville, Tennessee. In April 2004, he was selected as 9th Marine Corps Recruiting District Sergeant Major.

Hayes, Lou V.
COMMAND SERGEANT MAJOR—ARMY

Hayes entered the United States Army in September 1978. She completed Basic Training and Advanced Individual Training at Fort Jackson, South Carolina.

Her military and civilian education includes all the Noncommissioned Officer Education System Courses; Unit Deployment Course; Master Fitness Course; Bat-

tle Staff Course; the Inspector General Course; First Sergeant Administrative Course; the United States Air Force Senior Noncommissioned Officer Course; and the United States Army Sergeants Major Academy (Class 51). She holds Associate and Bachelors of Arts degrees from the University of Tampa and a Master of Arts in Management from Webster University.

Her military assignments include serving in every leadership position from Squad Leader to Command Sergeant Major. She was assigned to Headquarters and Headquarters Company at Fort Huachuca, Arizona; at Headquarters of the Defense Communication Agency (DCA) in Washington, D.C.; Readiness Command at MacDill Air Force Base, Florida; 501st Military Intelligence Group at Camp Humphries, South Korea; Headquarters, Allied Powers, in Belgium; Delta Company, Special Forces Diving School, in Key West, Florida; the Joint Staff (J8), Washington, D.C.; Headquarters United States Central Command, MacDill Air Force Base; Alpha Company, 120th Adjutant General Battalion, Fort Jackson, South Carolina; and Forces Command Inspector General Sergeant Major at Fort McPherson, Georgia. In January 2005, she was serving as the Command Sergeant Major, Unites States Army, NATO, Allied Forces North Battalion.

Haynie, Demetrius J.
LIEUTENANT COMMANDER—NAVY

Demetrius Haynie is a native of Atlanta, Georgia. He attended the United States Naval Academy and was commissioned in May 1991. He is a graduate of the Naval Postgraduate School and holds a Masters of Science in Applied Physics. He also holds a Master of Arts in National Security and Strategic Studies.

His sea assignments have included service as Weapons Officer and Combat Systems Officer onboard USS *Milius* (DDG 69); EDSRA Zone Manager, Link

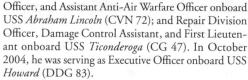

Officer, and Assistant Anti-Air Warfare Officer onboard USS *Abraham Lincoln* (CVN 72); and Repair Division Officer, Damage Control Assistant, and First Lieutenant onboard USS *Ticonderoga* (CG 47). In October 2004, he was serving as Executive Officer onboard USS *Howard* (DDG 83).

Hazzard, Milton B.
COMMAND SERGEANT MAJOR—ARMY

Command Sergeant Major Milton B. Hazzard enlisted the United States Army in 1960. He was one of only seven Command Sergeants Major selected on a world-wide basis for retention for 35 years of active service.

He became a Squad Leader in Basic and Advanced Individual Training in 1960, a Corporal in 1961, a Sergeant in 1965, a Staff Sergeant in 1966, a Sergeant First Class in 1967, a First Sergeant in 1972 and a Command Sergeant Major in 1977.

As Regimental Sergeant Major from October 1989 to March 1994, he worked tirelessly to promote standards of excellence in enlisted training and education, and laid a solid foundation for growth and development of the Quartermaster Noncommissioned Academy. He retired in 1994.

He was inducted as a Distinguished Member of the Quartermaster Regiment in 1994. In June 1999, the Auditorium at the Quartermaster Noncommissioned Officer Academy was dedicated in his honor.

Henderson, Daniel P.
COMMANDER—NAVY

Daniel Henderson enlisted in the United States Navy in June 1979. Following his graduation from Recruit Training at Recruit Training Center and Service School Command Great Lakes, Illinois, he served aboard USS *W.S. Sims* (FF 1059), USS *Preble* (DDG 46) and Ser-

vice School Command at Great Lakes, Illinois. Throughout his enlisted career, he participated in numerous Cold War operations while deployed in the Mediterranean Sea, North Atlantic, Indian Ocean and the Caribbean. He was commissioned as an Ensign under the Engineering Surface Repair Limited Duty Officer (LDO) Program in October 1987. In November 2000, he graduated with an Associate of Arts from Saint Leo University. After successful completion of Limited Duty Officer in Pensacola, Florida, his first commissioned assignment was as the Engineering Maintenance/Main Propulsion Assistant onboard USS *Preble* (DDG 46).

In November 1990, he was assigned to the Commander of Naval Beach Group Two as the Staff Material/Training and Readiness Officer. He deployed to the Persian Gulf and served as the OIC for the Reconstitution of the Maritime Prepositioning Force (MPF) following Operation Desert Storm. After completing six months of Department Head School, he reported in October 1993 to USS *Samuel Eliot Morison* (FFG 13) as the Chief Engineer. During this tour, he participated in Operations "Able Vigil" and "Uphold Democracy."

In October 2002, he was assigned as Maintenance Officer for the Commander of Regional Support Group Mayport, Florida. In October 2004, he was serving as the Commanding Officer at Shore Intermediate Maintenance Activity at Pascagoula, Mississippi.

Henry, Charles A., Sr.
COMMAND SERGEANT MAJOR—ARMY

Henry is a native of Rochester, New York. He entered the United States Army in September 1978, and attended One Stop Unit Training at Fort Gordon, Georgia. His military and civilian education includes all the Noncommissioned Officer Education System Courses;

the First Sergeants Course; the Battalion Motor Officers Course; the Senior Officer Logistics Management Course; and the United States Army Command Sergeant Major Academy. He earned a Bachelor of Science Degree in Education from the University of Louisville and is working on a master's degree.

His assignments include serving as Command Sergeant Major of both the 704th DSB and the 4th FSB. At Fort Knox he served with the 4/16th Cavalry Regiment and the 2/16th Cavalry Regiment. In August 24, 2004, he was serving as the Command Sergeant Major for the 4th Infantry Division Support Command at Fort Hood, Texas.

Henry, Oliver T.
CHIEF WARRANT OFFICER—COAST GUARD

He served in the United States Coast Guard during World War II, and successfully moved from the wardroom as a Steward to the engine room as a Motor Machinist's Mate, one of (if not the first) African Americans to do so.

Herring, Janet L.
COMMAND SERGEANT MAJOR—ARMY

Janet Herring is a native of Clinton, North Carolina. She enlisted in the United States Army in January 1978, and attended Basic Combat Training and Advanced Individual Training at Fort Jackson, South Carolina.

Her military and civilian education includes all the Noncommissioned Officer Education System Courses; Battle Staff Course; the United States Army Pre-com-

missioning Course; Standard Property Book System Redesigned Course; First Sergeant Course; United States Army Sergeants Major Academy; and the Command Sergeant Major Course. She holds an associate's degree in General Studies; and a Bachelor of Science degree in Management.

Her key military assignments include serving as Support Operation Sergeant Major at Headquarters and Headquarters Company, 507th Corps Support Group (Airborne); Interim Sergeant Major for 530th Supply and Service Battalion (Airborne) at Fort Bragg, North Carolina; Operation Sergeant Major for Headquarters and Headquarters Company, 507th Corps Support Group (Airborne) at Fort Bragg, North Carolina; Command Sergeant Major of 225th Forward Support Battalion, 25th Infantry Division.

Hicks, David H.
MAJOR GENERAL—ARMY

David Hicks received a direct commission to Captain on August 16, 1974. He received a Bachelor of Science degree in Religious Theology from United Wesleyan College. He also earned a Master of Divinity degree in Religious Theology from Princeton Theological Seminary and a Master of Theology degree in Religious Theology from Duke University. His military education includes Chaplain Officer Basic and Advanced Course; United States Army Command and General Staff College; and the United States Army War College.

Since entering the Army in August 1974, General Hicks has held a variety of assignments with increasing responsibility throughout his career. He served as Chaplain of the 759th Military Police Battalion at Fort Dix, New Jersey. From July 1976 to May 1978, he served as Assistant Brigade Chaplain for the 3rd Brigade, 3rd Armored Division, United States Army Europe, in West Germany. In May 1978, he served as

Chaplain for the 1st Battalion, 509th Infantry Battalion (Airborne Combat Team), in Vicenza, Italy. After completion of Chaplain Officer Advanced Course, at Fort Monmouth, New Jersey, he was a student in the Divinity School at Duke University, in Durham, North Carolina. From May 1985 to June 1988 he was assigned as Chaplain/Instructor at the United States Infantry Center and School at Fort Benning, Georgia. He was promoted to Lieutenant Colonel on June 1, 1988.

In June 1988, he served as the Post Chaplain for the United States Army Garrison at Fort Richardson, Alaska. From 1989 to May 1990, he was assigned as Chaplain of the 6th Infantry Division (Light) at Fort Richardson, Alaska. In June 1991, he was assigned as a Force Development Action Officer, later Force Structure Plans Officer, in the Office of the Chief of Chaplains, Washington, D.C. From June 1993 to March 1996, he was assigned as the Chief for Chaplain Support Management, later Command Chaplain, for the United States Army Special Operations Command at Fort Bragg, North Carolina. He was promoted to Colonel on November 1, 1993.

In March 1996, he was ordered to Germany to serve as Chaplain for V Corps, later Command Chaplain and next Chaplain of United States Army Europe, and Seventh Army, in Germany. He returned to the United States in July 1999 and was selected Deputy Chief of Chaplains, for the United States Army in Washington, D.C. He was promoted to Brigadier General on July 1, 1999.

From June 1999 to July 2003, he served as Deputy Chief of Chaplains, United States Army, in Washington, D.C. In July 2003, he was selected to serve as the Chief of Chaplains, United States Army, at the Pentagon. He was promoted to Major General on August 1, 2003.

His awards and decorations include the Legion of Merit (with two oak leaf clusters); the Meritorious Service Medal (with five oak leaf clusters); the Master Parachutist Badge; and Army Staff Identification Badge.

Higgins, Vidaurri
SERGEANT MAJOR—MARINES

Higgins enlisted in the United States Marine Corps in September 1980. Upon completion of Recruit Training at the Marine Corps Recruit Depot (MCRD) in San Diego, California, he was assigned to Infantry Training School at Camp Pendleton, California.

In January 1988, he was assigned to Drill Instructor School as a student. Upon graduation, he was assigned to Third Recruit Training Battalion, Lima Company for duty as Drill Instructor and Senior Drill Instructor. In January 1990, he was assigned to Drill Instructor School as an Instructor and served with the Inspector-Instructor Staff at Twenty Third Marine Regiment, Fourth Marine Division, in Los Alamitos, California. He performed duties as Training Chief, NBC Senior Noncommissioned Officer and Career Planner and in July 1997 received orders to the Fifth Marine Regiment for duty with Third Battalion, Fifth Marines Weapons Company as the Combined Anti-Armor Team (CAAT) Platoon Commander. In December 1998, he was assigned to Headquarters and Service Company as the Company Gunnery Sergeant. In October 1999, he was transferred to Kilo Company, Third Battalion, Fifth Marines as the Company First Sergeant. In June 2000, he received orders to Inspector-Instructor Staff in Galveston, Texas, and in July 2003, he was selected as the Sergeant Major for First Battalion, Twelfth Marines at Marine Corps Base Hawaii.

Hill, Mack C.
BRIGADIER GENERAL—ARMY

Mack Hill was born in Tampa, Florida and married the former Dale Wegener of Beverly, Massachusetts. He holds a bachelor's degree from Florida A&M University and a master's degree from Webster University. Upon entering the Army in June 1968, he attended the Army Medical Department (AMEDD) Officer Basic Course and the Medical Supply Course at Fort Sam Houston, Texas.

Upon completion of the Medical Supply Course in November 1968, he was assigned as a Company Commander to Training Detachment 1, Medical Field Service School, at Fort Sam Houston. In March 1969, he was assigned to the 9th Infantry Division in South Vietnam, where he served as Executive Officer for Company A of the 9th Medical Battalion and Medical Supply Officer with the 99th Combat Support Battalion in Tan An. After completing his tour in Vietnam in March 1970, he was assigned as the Chief of Supply Branch at the 33rd Field Hospital in Wurzburg, West Germany.

He returned to Fort Sam Houston in June 1974 for the AMEDD Officer Advance Course and remained for a tour as an Instructor in the Logistics Management

Directorate at the Academy of Health Sciences. He was then assigned in July 1978 to the United States Army Medical Department Activity at Fort Carson, Colorado as the Chief of the Materiel Branch. Following graduation from the Command and General Staff College in 1981, he went to Heidelberg, West Germany, where he was the Chief of Supply Services and Chief of the Logistics Division with the 130th Station Hospital. Subsequently in July 1985, he was assigned to the Headquarters of the 7th Medical Command where he served as the Chief of the Materiel Branch.

In July 1986, he was assigned as Commander for the 47th MEDSOM, 13th Corps Support Command, at Fort Hood, Texas, from 1986 to 1988. Following this command, he served in the Logistics Directorate at the Office of the Surgeon General at Falls Church, Virginia. He was promoted to Colonel on February 1, 1990.

Following attendance at the Industrial College of the Armed Forces in 1990, he served as the Commander of the United States Medical Materiel Agency (USAMMA) at Fort Detrick, Maryland. His next tour in June 1992 was as the Chief of the Logistics Division at Tripler Army Medical Center in Honolulu, Hawaii. He returned to the Office of the Surgeon General in July 1994 and assumed the duties as the Director of Logistics. In addition, he also served as the Health Services Materiel Consultant to the Surgeon General and the Chief of Medical Service Corps. He was promoted to Brigadier General on November 1, 1996.

From October 1996 to September 1998, he served as the Assistant Surgeon General for Force Management/Chief Medical Service Corps in the Office of the Surgeon General. In September 1998, he was selected to serve as the Commanding General of Madigan Army Medical Center/Northwest Health Service Support Activity in Tacoma, Washington. He retired from the military on August 31, 2000.

His awards and decorations include the Legion of Merit (with two oak leaf clusters); the Bronze Star; the Purple Heart; the Meritorious Service Medal (with five oak leaf clusters); Army Commendation Medal (with oak leaf cluster); Army Achievement Medal; Combat Medic Badge; and the Army Staff Identification Badge.

Hill, Marvin

COMMAND SERGEANT MAJOR—ARMY

Marvin Hill received a Bachelor of Science degree in Liberal Arts and Science from St. Thomas Aquinas College at Sparkill, New York. He is a graduate of the Drill Sergeant School; Air Assault School; Rappel Master Course; Master Fitness Trainers Course; Sniper School; and the United States Army Sergeants Major Academy.

CSM Hill entered the United States Army on January 18, 1978. He attended Basic Combat Training at Fort Leonard Wood, Missouri, and Advanced Individual Training (AIT) at Fort Benning, Georgia, graduating as an Infantryman in May 1978. Upon completion of AIT he attended the Dragon Gunners course at Fort Benning, Georgia. He has served in positions ranging from Rifleman to Command Sergeant Major in Infantry Units. Additionally he has served as a Scout Platoon Sergeant, a Battalion Operations Sergeant, and Tactical Noncommissioned Officer at the United States Military Academy at West Point, New York. As a Drill Sergeant, later as a Drill Sergeant Instructor, and as a Faculty Advisor at the United States Army Sergeants Major Academy at Fort Bliss, Texas. He also served as Task Force Command Sergeant Major for TF 1-502 Infantry, Multinational Force and Observers in Sinai, Egypt. He deployed to Kosovo as the Task Force Falcon Command Sergeant Major with serving as the Brigade Command Sergeant Major for 2nd Brigade, 101st Airborne Division (Air Assault).

He serves as the Command Sergeant Major for 101st Airborne Division (Air Assault) and Post Command Sergeant Major at Fort Campbell, Kentucky.

Hill, Weltia K., Sr.

COMMAND SERGEANT MAJOR—ARMY

Hill enlisted in the United States Army Reserves in 1975, and was assigned to the 808th Station Hospital in Hempstead, New York.

His military education includes all the Noncommissioned Officer Education System Courses, the Battle Staff Course and the United States Army Sergeants Major Academy.

He subsequently served in numerous positions of authority including serving as Supply Sergeant, NBC NCO, First Sergeant of Headquarters Company 8th Medical Brigade. In 1996, he was promoted to Sergeant Major and assigned to the 301st Support Group as the Senior Supply Service NCO. His first assignment as a Command Sergeant Major was as Command Sergeant of the 8th Personnel Battalion at Fort Trotten, New York. He then transferred and served as Command Sergeant Major of the 301st Area Support Group at Fort Trotten; Command Sergeant Major of the 310th Military Police Battalion in Uniondale, New York; the Command Sergeant Major of the 411th Engineer Brigade in New Windsor, New York; and Command Sergeant Major for the 77th Regional Readiness Command from January 2004.

Hillman, Lawrence
COMMAND SERGEANT MAJOR—ARMY

Lawrence Hillman is a native of East Hampton, Long Island, New York, and entered the Army in May 1982, after attending the State University of New York at Delhi. He completed One Station Unit Infantry Training and Basic Airborne School at Fort Benning, Georgia, and was immediately assigned to Fort Bragg, North Carolina.

His military education includes all the Noncommissioned Officers Education System Courses; Basic Airborne School; Recondo School; Jumpmaster School; Air Movement Operations Course; Drop Zone Safety Team Leaders Course; M60 Machine Gun Leaders Course; Jungle Warfare Training Course; Northern Warfare Training Course; Battle Staff NCO Course; Drill Sergeant School; the First Sergeant Course; the United States Army Sergeants Major Academy (class 51); and Command Sergeant Major Course. He holds a bachelor's degree from Excelsior College.

His military assignments include serving as Platoon Sergeant; Support Operations NCOIC; Senior Drill Sergeant; Executive Officer; Battalion Operations NCO; First Sergeant; and Operations Sergeant Major for the 1st Cavalry Division's DISCOM. In August 2004, he was serving as the Command Sergeant Major for 215th FSB.

Hines, Charles Alfonso
MAJOR GENERAL—ARMY

Charles Hines was born in Washington, D.C. He and his wife, Veronica, have seven children, Tracy, Charles, Kelley, Christina, Michael, Nicholas, and Timothy.

Upon completion of the Reserve Officers Training Corps curriculum as a distinguished military graduate and the educational course of study at Howard University in 1942, he was commissioned a Second Lieutenant and awarded a Bachelor of Science degree in physical education. He also holds a Master of Science degree in police administration and public safety from Michigan State University. He received a Master of Military Arts and Science from the United States Army Command and General Staff College and a Ph.D. in Sociology from Johns Hopkins University. His military education includes completion of the Infantry Officer Basic Course; the Military Police Officer Advanced Course; the United States Army Command and General Staff College; and the Army War College.

He has held a wide variety of important command

and staff positions, culminating in his last assignment as Commanding General of the United States Army Chemical and Military Police Centers and Fort McClellan, Alabama. From February 1954 to January 1957, he was assigned in the enlisted service, initial active duty training at Fort Jackson, South Carolina, and was later assigned to Battery A, 504th Field Artillery Battalion at Fort Kobbe, Canal Zone, and Company M, 20th Infantry Regiment at Fort Davis, Canal Zone. From March 1962 to February 1964, he was a student in the Infantry Officer Orientation Course (later Airborne Course) at the United States Army Infantry School at Fort Benning, Georgia. From May 1962 to September 1963, he was assigned as a Mortar Section Leader, later Liaison Officer and Assistant S-3 (Training Officer), at Headquarters Company, later as Operations Officer, Office of the Provost Marshal, 2nd Battalion, 9th Infantry, at Fort Benning. From February 1964 to June 1966, he was assigned first as Platoon Leader, next as the Assistant Operations Officer and Operations Officer, in the Office of the Provost Marshal, later as Commander of the 521st Military Police Company (Service), at Fort Belvoir, Virginia.

From July 1966 to June 1967, he was assigned as Operations Officer in the Office of the Provost Marshal with the 90th Military Police Detachment the United States Army in Vietnam. In June 1967, he was assigned first as a student in the Military Police Officer Advance Course, later as an Instructor of Military Police Science and Administration Division, at the United States Army Military Police School, at Fort Gordon, Georgia. He was promoted to Major on September 25, 1968.

From June 1971 to June 1972, he was assigned as Chief of Plans and Operations in the Office of the

Provost Marshal in the Eighth United States Army. From 1972 to July 1979, he was assigned as the Chief of Criminal Intelligence Program, later as Operations Officer, and later as Chief of Criminal Information Division, at the United States Army Criminal Investigation Command in Washington, D.C. From May 1977 to March 1979, he served as Commander of the 519th Military Police Battalion, later as Acting Director of Personnel and Community Activities at Fort Meade, Maryland. From June 1980 to July 1981, he was assigned as a Strategic Research Analyst, later as Director of Evaluation and Organization Effectiveness, at the United States Army War College Staff and Faculty at Carlisle Barracks, Pennsylvania. From July 1983 to July 1985, he served as the Commander of the 14th Military Police Brigade and Provost Marshal for VII Corps with the United States Army in Europe. From August 1985 to December 1987, he served as Director of the Officer Personnel Management Center in Alexandria, Virginia. He was promoted to Brigadier General on September 1, 1985.

From December 1987 to August 1989, he was assigned as Director of Manpower in the Office of the Deputy Chief of Staff for Personnel in Washington, D.C. He was promoted to Major General on September 1, 1988.

In August 1989, he was selected to serve as the Commanding General of the United States Army Chemical and Military Police Centers/Commandant of the United States Army Chemical School at Fort McClellan, Alabama.

General Hines completed the executive Development Course at the University of Maryland; the Executive Development Course at the John F. Kennedy School of Government, Harvard University; the program for Senior Executives in National and International Security at the John F. Kennedy School of Government; and the Federal Bureau of Investigation National Academy. He retired from the military on August 31, 1992.

His awards and decorations include the Legion of Merit (with three oak leaf clusters), Bronze Star, Meritorious Service Medal (with six oak leaf clusters), Army Commendation Medal (with two oak leaf clusters), Parachutist Badge, and Army General Staff Identification Badge.

General Hines appears in *Who's Who in American Colleges and Universities* and was selected to the Outstanding Young Men of America Foundation, and serves as an adviser to the president's Committee on Employment of People with Disabilities.

Hobbs, Johnny J.

MAJOR GENERAL—AIR FORCE

General Hobbs was born in Newark, New Jersey. He was graduated from Barringer High School in Newark in 1960 and Rutgers University in 1964 where he earned a Bachelor of Arts degree in Sociology. He also received a master's in Social Work Administration from Rutgers University in 1972. He later attended law school at Loy-

ola University, New Orleans, and received his law degree (J.D.) in 1983. His military education includes Squadron Officer School, 1981; Air Command and Staff College, 1982; and the National Security Management Course of the Industrial College of the Armed Forces, 1985 (outstanding graduate). He began his military career as an Air Force Reserve Officer Training Corps cadet at Rutgers University in 1960. Upon graduation in June 1964, he was commissioned a second lieutenant. He received his wings in June 1966 upon completion of undergraduate pilot training at Williams Air Force Base, Arizona. His first assignment was George Air Force Base, California, where he became an F-4C Pilot in February 1967. He was then assigned to the 497th Tactical Fighter Squadron (Night Owls) at Ubon Royal Thai Air Base, Thailand, for a combat tour flying F-4C aircraft. From 1968 to 1970, he was assigned to the 35th Tactical Fighter Squadron at Yokota Air Base, Japan.

He was released from active duty in June 1970. In 1974, he joined the Michigan Air National Guard in Battle Creek and served until 1976 as a Squadron Pilot in a forward air controller mission. He then transferred to the Louisiana Air National Guard where he served in numerous positions, ranging from Squadron Pilot to Assistant Operations Officer to Squadron Commander of the 122nd Tactical Fighter Squadron (TFS) until 1985. General Hobbs, as Squadron Commander, led the 122nd TFS through the conversion to the F-15. He transferred to the 113th Tactical Fighter Wing (parent wing of the 122nd Tactical Fighter Squadron) in 1985 and assumed the position of Vice Wing Commander in October 1985.

From June 1988 to February 1993, he was selected to serve as the Deputy Commanding General for Air in the District of Columbia National Guard, with command

and control over all elements of the District of Columbia Air National Guard. He was promoted to Brigadier General on June 22, 1989.

From February 1993 to September 1995, he served as Deputy Chief of Staff at the Headquarters of the New York Air National Guard, Division of Military and Naval Affairs, at Latham, New York. In September 1995, he was selected to serve as Air National Guard Assistant to the Director of the Air National Guard in Washington, D.C. He was promoted to Major General on August 2, 1996, and retired on August 31, 1998.

The General is a Command Pilot with more than 4,000 flying hours in the T-37, O-2, and F-100, F-4C, and F-4 D aircraft. His awards and decorations include the Distinguished Flying Cross, Air Medal, Meritorious Service Medal (with one oak leaf cluster), Presidential Unit Citation, National Defense Service Medal, Armed Forces Expeditionary Medal, Vietnam Service Medal, Air Force Longevity Service (with five devices), Armed Forces Reserve Medal, Small Arms Expert Marksmanship Ribbon, Air Force Training Ribbon, Republic of Vietnam Gallantry Cross, Republic of Vietnam Campaign Medal, and District of Columbia Meritorious Service Medal.

Holling, Richard
COMMAND CHIEF MASTER SERGEANT—AIR FORCE
Command Chief Master Sergeant Richard Holling graduated from Hattiesburg High School in Hattiesburg, Mississippi. He entered in the United States Air Force in December 1976. He hold an associate's degree in Applied Science, Environmental Medicine Technology, and a bachelor's degree in Human Resource Management. He also earned a master's in Business from the University of LaVerne, California. He is a graduate of the United States Air Force Senior Noncommis-

sioned Officer Academy at Maxwell/Gunter Complex, Alabama. Holling has served with the United States Air Force Europe (USAFE) Tactical Evaluation Team, Royal Air Force in Alconbury, United Kingdom. He was handpicked to become the first Air Force Special Operations Command Enlisted Functional Manager for the Public Health Career Field at Hurlburt Field, Florida; during this tour he wrote the doctrine establishing mission unique AFSOC medical terms.

He is currently serving as the Command Chief Master Sergeant of the 311th Human Systems Wing in Brooks City, Texas.

Hollings, Robert C.
SERGEANT MAJOR—MARINES
Robert Hollings joined the Marine Corps in June 1979 and underwent recruit training at Parris Island, South Carolina. Upon graduation from recruit training and MOS school as a Basic Warehouseman, he served his first tour with 3rd Battalion, 4th Marines, 3rd Marine Division, in Okinawa, Japan.

His key military assignments include serving as Warehouse Chief and Logistic Chief at Marine Corps Logistics Base in Albany, Georgia, and as a Drill Instructor, Senior Drill Instructor, and Chief Drill Instructor at Marine Corps Recruit Depot in San Diego, California. He was assigned to the 2nd Force Service Support Group at Camp Lejeune, North Carolina, as the Platoon Sergeant, NCOIC of 904, and as the Company Gunnery Sergeant for Supply Company, 2nd Supply Battalion, in which capacity he deployed with the unit in support of Operations Desert Shield/Desert Storm. In March 1992, he was assigned to Headquarters Marine Corps and served as the Supply Monitor with MMEA. He also served as the First Sergeant with the 3rd Maintenance Battalion, 3rd FSSG, Okinawa,

Japan; as the Company First Sergeant with Headquarters and Service Company, 3rd Maintenance Battalion; as First Sergeant for Marine Expeditionary Unit Service and Support Group-31, 31st Marine Expeditionary Unit; and as Company First Sergeant with the General Support Maintenance Company, 3rd Maintenance Battalion. In March 1998, he was appointed as the Sergeant Major for the 3rd Supply Battalion, 3rd FSSG. In March 1999, he was assigned to Recruiting Station Jacksonville, Florida, and later as Sergeant Major of Marine Helicopter Squadron One at Quantico, Virginia. In January 2005, he was serving as Marine Corps Recruit Depot/Eastern Recruiting Region Sergeant Major.

Hollis, Evelyn
COMMAND SERGEANT MAJOR—ARMY

Evelyn Hollis enlisted in the Army on July 16, 1979. She attended Basic Combat Training at Fort Leonard Wood, Missouri, and Advanced Individual Training at Fort Jackson, South Carolina. Her military and civilian education includes all the Noncommissioned Officers Leadership Courses, the Air Defense Artillery Intelligence Assistant Operator Course, the Army Recruiting Course, the First Sergeant Course, and the Sergeants Major Academy. She holds a Master of Arts degree in Human Resources Development and Management.

Her assignments include serving as the S-3 Sergeant Major for the 108th Air Defense Artillery Brigade. In April 2004, she became the first female Command Sergeant Major of a Combat Arms Unit when she assumed command of the 1st Battalion, 1st Air Defense Artillery Command. The change of command ceremony was held at the Fort Bliss Air Defense Artillery Museum on April 26, 2004.

Holmes, Arthur, Jr.
MAJOR GENERAL—ARMY

General Holmes was born in Decatur, Alabama, and married the former Wilma King. They have three children, Deborah, Sharon, and Arthur O. Holmes. He received a Reserve Officer Training Corps commission as second lieutenant in 1952 and has over 30 years of active commissioned service. General Holmes' civilian education includes a Bachelor of Science degree from Hampton Institute and a Master of Business Administration degree from Kent State University. His military schooling includes the Field Artillery Officer Basic Course, the Ordnance Officer Advanced Course, the Command and General Staff College, and the United States Naval War College.

General Holmes' career was characterized by a succession of demanding assignments in both staff and command positions. He commanded the 724th Maintenance Battalion, 24th Infantry, at Fort Riley, Kansas, from 1968 to 1969. In 1979 he commanded the 62nd Maintenance Battalion, United States Army Qui Nhon Support Command, in South Vietnam. While assigned to the 1st Infantry Division at Fort Riley from 1975 to 1977, General Holmes served first as the Commander of the Division Support Command and then as Assistant Division Commander. He was assigned as Executive to the Secretary of the Army in Washington, D.C., from 1977 to 1979 and immediately thereafter served as Deputy Commanding General of the United States Army Tack-Automotive Materiel Readiness Command in Warren, Michigan. In 1980 General Holmes became Director of Readiness at the United States Army Materiel Development and Readiness Command at Alexandria, Virginia, and in 1982, he moved to the Head-

quarters of the Department of the Army in Washington, D.C., where he was assigned as Deputy Inspector General for Inspections. He served in that capacity until 1983 when he assumed duties as the Assistant Deputy Chief of Staff for Logistics, United States Army, Washington, D.C.

In August 1984, he was named Commanding General of the United States Army Tank-Automotive Command at Warren. General Holmes has earned a number of awards and decorations, including the Legion of Merit, Bronze Star, Meritorious Service Medal (with oak leaf cluster), Joint Service Commendation Medal, and Army Commendation Medal (with oak leaf clusters).

Holmes, Bert W., Jr.
BRIGADIER GENERAL—ARMY

Virginia State University alumnus, Bert W. Holmes, Jr., was promoted to Brigadier General on February 15, 2001. He became the first African American general in the Virginia National Guard.

In a ceremony at the State Capitol, the 37 year career soldier received stars on his uniform. Along with obtaining the rank of Brigadier General, the father of three was appointed by the governor to become the assistant adjutant general in the Virginia Department of Military Affairs, which commands the state's Army and Air National Guard.

General Holmes began his military career at the undergraduate and graduate level at Virginia State University, where he was a member of the University's ROTC program. After leaving Virginia State University, he obtained his medical degree from Howard University.

He has served as commander of the Virginia Guard's medical detachment in Richmond, and as the Guard's Flight Surgeon. In his regular Army career, he served as a company commander with the Fourth Infantry Division.

Holmes, Frankie
SERGEANT MAJOR—MARINES

He is a native of Charleston, South Carolina, and enlisted in the Marine Corps in June 1976. He attended recruit training at Marine Corps Recruit Depot, Parris Island, South Carolina. Upon completion of recruit training, he attended Infantry Training School at Camp Pendleton, California.

In August 1991, he was promoted to Gunnery Sergeant. In October, he received orders to First Battalion, Sixth Marines where he served as Company Gunnery Sergeant and was appointed the Platoon Commander for Dragon Platoon. While there he attended the Advanced Staff Noncommissioned Officers Course and was promoted to First Sergeant. In July 1995, he served as First Sergeant for Charlie Company, First Battalion, Sixth Marines; in August 1995, he received orders to Marine Corps Recruit Depot at Parris Island, South Carolina, for the third time and was assigned as First Sergeant of Golf Company, Second Battalion; in August 1996, he was selected to be the First Sergeant of Drill Instructor School until his selection to Sergeant Major in March 1998; in May 1998, he was promoted to Sergeant Major and assumed the position as Sergeant Major of the Second Recruit Training Battalion; in May 1999, he assumed the duties as the Squadron Sergeant Major of VMFA (AW)-332 in Hungry, Tazar during Operation Enduring Freedom. During this assignment he deployed twice to the West PAC; and in March 2003, he was transferred to 1st Marine Aircraft Wing Okinawa Japan for duty as Sergeant Major Marine Air Group 36. In August 2004, he was reassigned to duty as Sergeant Major Materiel Readiness Battalion, 3rd Force Service Support Group.

Holmes, Ronnie L.
SERGEANT MAJOR—ARMY

Sergeant Major Ronnie L. Holmes was born in Miami, Florida. He entered in the Army in January 1980. He received his Basic Combat Training at Fort Leonard Wood, Missouri, and his Advanced Individual Training at Fort Sam Houston, Texas, as a Dental Specialist.

He received a Bachelor of Business Administration degree from the University of the Incarnate Word in San Antonio, Texas, and a Master of Business degree from Western International University in Phoenix, Arizona. He is currently pursuing a Doctorate in Leadership.

His military education includes the Dental Administration Course; Recruiter Course; Equal Opportunity Advisor Course; Instructor Training Course; Small Group Instructor Training Course; Air Assault Course; NBC Course; Master Fitness Course; Battle Staff Course; First Sergeants Course; and the Sergeants Major Course.

He is currently assigned as the Sergeant Major for the Europe Regional Dental Command in Heidelberg, Germany.

Honor, Edward
LIEUTENANT GENERAL—ARMY

He was born in Melville, Louisiana, and married the former Phyllis Whitehurst. Upon completion of the Reserve Officers Training Corps curriculum and the educational course of study at Southern University A&M College, he was commissioned a second lieutenant and awarded a Bachelor of Arts degree in Education. His military education includes completion of the Basic Armor Officer Course, the Basic and Advanced Courses of the Transportation School, the United States Army Command and General Staff College, and the United States Army War College.

He has held a wide variety of important command and staff positions. He served as Commander of the 36th Transportation Battalion, later Commander of the 24th Transportation Battalion, Cam Ranh Bay Support Command in South Vietnam from 1969 to 1970. His staff assignments includes service as Director for Transportation, Energy, and Troop Support in the Office of the Deputy Chief of Staff for Logistics, United States Army, Washington, D.C.; Director of Plans, Doctrine, and Systems in United States Army Materiel Development and Readiness Command in Alexandria, Virginia; Director of Personal Property, Military Traffic Management and Terminal Service in Washington, D.C.; and Chief of the Transportation Service Branch, Transportation Division, Office of the Chief of Staff for Logistics, United States Continental Army Command at Fort Monroe, Virginia. He also served as Passenger Movements Officer and as Chief of Passenger Service Division with the Military Traffic Management and Terminal Service, Washington, D.C.

Other key assignments held include command assignments as Commander of Military Traffic Management Command for Transportation Terminal Group Europe at Rotterdam, Netherlands. He also served as Commander of the 37th Transportation Group, 4th

Transportation Brigade, United States Army in Europe. In 1979 he was assigned to the Joint Chiefs of Staff at the Pentagon as Deputy Director for Plans and Research.

His military awards and decorations include the Defense Superior Service Medal, four awards of the Legion of Merit, two awards of the Bronze Star, two awards of the Meritorious Service Medal, Joint Service Commendation Medal, and two awards of the Army Commendation Medal.

Honore, Charles E.
MAJOR GENERAL—ARMY

He was born in Baton Rouge, Louisiana, he is married to Jane Auzenne Honore, and they have four children, Charles, Jr., Melinda, Marlene, and Myra. Upon completion of the Reserve Officers Training Corps curriculum and the education course of study at Southern University Agricultural and Mechanical College in 1956, he was commissioned a second lieutenant and awarded a Bachelor of Arts degree in Geography. He also holds a Master of Science in Administration from George Washington University. His military education includes completion of the Armor Basic and Advanced Officer courses; the United States Army Command and General Staff College; and the Industrial College of the Armed Forces.

He has held a wide variety of command and staff positions in Vietnam, Europe, and the United States. He served as Deputy Chief of Staff for Support/Commander of United States Army Element in Central Army Group, Europe, and Chief of the United States Army Readiness Group in Los Angeles, California. In addition to duty with the Department of the Army Office of the Inspector General in the where he served

as an Investigator and later as the Inspector General, Investigations Division, General Honore has had tours of duty as Commander of the 1st Brigade, 5th Infantry Division (Mechanized); Commander of Headquarters Command at Fort Polk, Louisiana; Deputy Commander of the Schweinfurt Military Community, Federal Republic of Germany; Commander of the 2nd Battalion 64th Armor, 3rd Infantry Division; Executive Officer of the 1st Squadron, 7th Cavalry, 1st Cavalry Division; and Assistant Division Commander of the 3rd Infantry Division (Mechanized), United States Army, Europe.

General Honore retired on July 31, 1990. His military awards and decorations include the Legion of Merit, Bronze Star, Meritorious Service Medal (with oak leaf cluster), Air Medal, Army Commendation Medal, and the Combat Infantryman Badge.

Honore, Russel Luke

LIEUTENANT GENERAL—ARMY

He is a distinguished military graduate of Southern University Agriculture and Mechanical College at Baton, Rouge, Louisiana, and was commissioned in January 1971. Following the Infantry Officer's Basic Course at Fort Benning, Georgia, he was assigned to the Combat Development Command at Fort Ord, California. There he served as a training officer and executive officer with E Troop, 9th Cavalry at Fort Hunter Liggett, California.

He served with the 1st Battalion, 23rd Infantry, 2nd Infantry Division in South Korea from February 1974 to June 1976. There he served as an anti-tank platoon leader and as the Company Commander for a Combat Support Company. In June 1976, he was assigned as an Instructor in the Leadership Department at the

United States Army Armor School at Fort Knox, Kentucky. In June 1978, he was assigned as the Commander of C Company, 4th Battalion, 5th Infantry (Mechanized) at Fort Knox, Kentucky. From September 1979 to June 1980, he was selected to serve as the Assistant G-1 (Personnel) for the 1st Infantry Division (Forward), United States Army Europe and Seventh Army, West Germany. In June 1980, he served as the Aide-de-Camp to the Commander, Allied Forces Central Europe, in Brunnsum, Netherlands. In June 1983, after completing the United States Army's Command and General Staff College, he was ordered to serve as the Executive Officer for the 2nd Battalion, 16th Infantry, 1st Infantry Division, at Fort Riley, Kansas. From July 1984 to May 1986, he served as the Chief of Operations, G-3 (Operations), 1st Infantry Division, at Fort Riley. In May 1986, he was assigned as an Instructor in the Tactical Department of the United States Army Command and General Staff College at Fort Leavenworth, Kansas. He was promoted to Lieutenant Colonel on November 1, 1988. From June 1989 to June 1991, he served as the Commander of the 4th Battalion, 16th Infantry, 1st Infantry Division (Forward), United States Army Europe and Seventh Army, Germany and Operations Desert Shield/Desert Storm in Saudi Arabia. He returned to the United States in June 1991, and reported as a student to the Air War College at Maxwell Air Force Base, Alabama. In June 1992, he was assigned as the Senior Mechanized Task Force Trainer with the United States Army National Training Center at Fort Irwin, California. He was promoted to Colonel on September 1, 1993.

From June 1992 to October 1994, he served as the Senior Mechanized Task Force Trainer at the United States Army National Training Center at Fort Irwin, California. In November 1994, he assumed an assignment as Commander of the 1st Brigade, 24th Infantry

Division (Mechanized), later re-flagged 3rd Infantry Division (Mechanized), at Fort Stewart, Georgia. In September 1996, he was ordered to Fort Hood, Texas, to serve as Assistant Division Commander (Maneuver), later (Support), 1st Cavalry Division. He was promoted to Brigadier General on September 1, 1997.

From August 1998 to August 1999, he served as Deputy Commanding General/Assistant Commandant of the United States Army Infantry Center and School at Fort Benning, Georgia. In August 1999, he was selected Vice Director for Operations, J-3, The Joint Staff, Washington, D.C. In October 2000, he was selected as the Commanding General of the 2nd Infantry Division, Eighth United States Army. He was promoted to Major General on November 1, 2000.

From July 2002 to June 2004, he served as Commander of the Joint Force Headquarters for Homeland Security, United States Northern Command, in Norfolk, Virginia. From June 2004 to July 2004, he was assigned Special Assistant to the Commanding General of United States Army Training and Doctrine Command at Fort Monroe, Virginia. In July 2004, he was assigned as the Commanding General of the First United States Army at Fort Gillem, Georgia. He was promoted to Lieutenant General on August 1, 2004.

General Honore's awards and decorations include the Legion of Merit (with four oak leaf clusters); the Bronze Star; the Defense Meritorious Service Medal; the Meritorious Service Medal (with three oak leaf clusters); Army Commendation Medal (with three oak leaf clusters); the Army Achievement Medal; Expert Infantry Medal; Expert Infantry Badge; Parachutist Badge; and the Joint Staff Identification Badge.

When the city of New Orleans suffered massive flooding from Hurricane Katrina in 2005, General Honore was assigned to lead the military response to the disaster. Honore was widely praised for his work.

Hooker, Olivia J.
YEOMAN SECOND CLASS—COAST GUARD

Olivia Hooker first applied to the Navy's WAVES but was rejected. She enlisted in the Coast Guard after

her friend Alex Haley encouraged her to apply. Upon completing Basic Training and Yeoman School, she worked at the Separation Center in Boston. Upon her discharge from the Coast Guard in 1946 as a Yeoman Second Class, she used her GI Bill to continue her education. She earned a master's degree in Psychology from Columbia University and a doctorate in Psychology from the University of Rochester, New York, in 1962.

She retired from the Kennedy Child Study Center and Fordham University, and also served 17 years on the Board of Terence Cardinal Cooke Services, the Visiting Nurse Services of Westchester and the now closed White Plains Early Learning Center. She served on the executive Committee of the White Plains — Greenburgh NAACP.

Hooper, Chauncey M.
BRIGADIER GENERAL—ARMY

Chancey Hooper was born in New Jersey. He entered the Army on July 14, 1916, as a Private in Company B, 15th Infantry Battalion. He was assigned to Headquarters of the 15th Infantry Battalion on April 1, 1917.

He served as Battalion Sergeant Major for Headquarters Company 15th Infantry (369th) from July 15, 1917, to January 4, 1918. On November 1, 1918, he was commissioned as a Second Lieutenant. He was promoted to First Lieutenant on May 29, 1919, while serving as the Adjutant General for the 369th Infantry. He was promoted to Captain on August 20, 1926, while serving with the 369th Infantry. He was promoted Major on February 26, 1931, and assigned to the Headquarters of the 1st Battalion of the 369th Infantry. He received his promotion to Lieutenant Colonel on March 18, 1938, and was promoted to Colonel on December 18, 1940. During World War II, the 369th AAA Group to which he was assigned was transferred to the New York National Guard Headquarters and redesigned as a Supply and Service Battalion.

Hooper served in both World Wars. A former lawyer and politician, he held the rank of Colonel in the army when he retired in 1946. He remained active in the 369th Anti-Aircraft Artillery Group of New York,

which he commanded during World War II. He became the first black to achieve the rank of Brigadier General in the New York National Guard, and was promoted to that rank on June 30, 1954. He retired on June 5, 1958, and died on December 31, 1966.

Hopper, Christina
CAPTAIN—AIR FORCE

Hooper, first black female and only black female F-16 Fighting Falcon Instruction Pilot, was deployed with her squadron in March 2003, when the war in Iraq started. She and the other squadron pilots were bombing targets on the second day of the war. Her husband, Captain Aaron Hopper, is also an F-15 pilot in the 522nd Fighter Squadron.

Hopper, John D., Jr.
LIEUTENANT GENERAL—AIR FORCE

He received his commission in 1969 upon graduating from the United States Air Force Academy. He has flown in combat in Vietnam and as Commander of the 1660th Tactical Airlift Wing (Provisional) in the Middle East during Operation Desert Storm. He also served as the Commandant of Cadets at the United States Air Force Academy and on the Joint Staff at the Pentagon. He is a command pilot with more than 3,500 flying hours in 12 different aircraft.

In 1969, he received a bachelor's degree from the United States Air Force Academy in Colorado Springs, Colorado. In 1974, he was a distinguished graduate from the Squadron Officer School at Maxwell Air Force Base, Alabama. In 1977, he was a distinguished graduate and earned a Master of Science degree in Logistics Management from the Air Force Institute of Technology, at Wright-Patterson Air Force Base, Ohio. In 1982, he was a distinguished graduate from Air Command and Staff College at Maxwell Air Force Base. In 1988, he graduated from the Industrial College of the Armed Forces at Fort Lesley J. McNair, Washington, D.C. In 1997, he completed the National Security Leadership

Course at Maxwell School of Citizenship and Public Affairs at Syracuse University, New York, and the Paul H. Nitze School of Advanced International Studies at Johns Hopkins University, Washington, D.C.

From February 1971 to May 1972, he was a C-130 pilot at Ching Chuan Kang Air Base, Taiwan, and in Vietnam. He returned to the United States in May 1972 to serve as a T-37 Instructor Pilot, Academic Instructor and Class Commander for the 71st Flying Training Wing at Vance Air Force Base, Oklahoma. In June 1977, he was assigned Deputy Director of Cadet Logistics and aide to the superintendent and air officer commanding Cadet Squadron 12 at the United States Air Force Academy in Colorado Springs. In 1982, he was assigned as Chief of Wing Command Post, 438th Military Airlift Wing, later as Commander of the 438th Field Maintenance Squadron, at McGuire Air Force Base, New Jersey. He was promoted to Colonel on July 1, 1988.

In July 1988, he was ordered to serve as Chief for Exercise Division, at Headquarters United States Forces Command at Fort McPherson, Georgia. From July 1990 to August 1991, he served as the Deputy Commander for Operations for the 63rd Military Airlift Wing at Norton Air Force Base, California. From December 1990 to May 1991, he was Commander of the 1660th Tactical Airlift Wing (Provisional) at Thumrait, Oman. In August 1991, he served as Commander of the 89th Operations Group at Andrews Air Force Base, Maryland. In August 1992, he was assigned as Commander of the 63rd Airlift Wing at Norton Air Force Base. In December 1993, he assumed command of the 375th Airlift Wing at Scott Air Base, Illinois. He was promoted to Brigadier General on July 15, 1994.

From November 1994 to July 1996, he served as the Commandant of Cadets and Commander of the 34th

Training Wing at the United States Air Force Academy. In July 1996, he served as Vice Director for Logistics of the Joint Staff at the Pentagon. He was promoted to Major General on January 1, 1997.

In July 1998, he was assigned as Director of Operations for Headquarters Air Mobility Command at Randolph Air Force Academy in Colorado Springs. From July 1999 to October 2000, he was assigned as Commander of the 21st Air Force at McGuire Air Force Base, New Jersey. In October 2000, he was selected for the position of Vice Commander for Air Education and Training Command at Randolph Air Force Base, Texas. He was promoted to Lieutenant General on January 1, 2001.

His awards and decorations include the Defense Distinguished Service Medal; the Defense Superior Service Medal; the Legion of Merit (with two oak leaf clusters); the Distinguished Flying Cross; the Meritorious Service Medal (with three oak leaf clusters); Air Medal (with two oak leaf clusters); Air Force Commendation Medal (with oak leaf cluster); Southwest Asia Service Medal (with two service stars); and Kuwait Liberation Medal (Kingdom of Saudi Arabia).

Howard, Burnadette

SERGEANT MAJOR—MARINES

She was born in Augusta, Georgia. She graduated from T.W. Josey High School at Augusta, Georgia in June 1966. She entered the Marine Corps Recruit Depot at Parris Island, South Carolina, in September 1966. She is a graduate of the Marine Recruiter School and the United States Army Sergeants Major Academy at Fort Bliss, Texas.

She has served in a variety of leadership assignments including as Female Marine Corps Recruiter at the Marine Corps Recruiting Station, Headquarters, 12th Marine Corps District, in Santa Ana, California. She was

assigned as a Staff Sergeant in the Women Marine Company of Headquarters Battalion at Headquarters Marine Corps, Washington, D.C., where she was assigned in the Personnel Section. After completion of this tour, she returned to Recruiting Duties at to the 12th Marine Corps District in Santa Ana, California. She served as First Sergeant with the Marine Corps Administrative Detachment at Fort Bliss, Texas, and as First Sergeant with the 2nd Force Service Support Group at Camp Lejeune, North Carolina. She was frocked to Sergeant Major in February 1988, and assigned as Battalion Sergeant Major of the 2nd Supply Battalion, 2nd Force Service and Supply Group.

Howard, David

FIRST SERGEANT—ARMY

He is a native of New Orleans, Louisiana, and entered the military in August 1987. His military education includes all the Noncommissioned Officer Education System Courses and the First Sergeant Course.

He has served as a Squad Leader; Section Sergeant; Quality Control Supervisor; Platoon Sergeant; and First Sergeant. His assignments include the 1-7th Cavalry at Fort Hood, Texas; 4-7th Cavalry at Camp Stanton, South Korea; 2-101st at Fort Campbell, Kentucky; 2-226th at Fort Rucker, Alabama; 2-229th at Fort Bragg, North Carolina; and 3-227th in Germany.

In March 2005, he was serving as the First Sergeant for the 1st Squadron, 7th Cavalry, at Fort Hood.

Howard, Michelle J.

REAR ADMIRAL—NAVY

Captain Howard is a 1978 graduate of Gateway High School in Aurora, Colorado. She attended the United States Naval Academy, graduating in 1982. She was a Distinguished Graduate from Department Head School in September 1990. She graduated from the

United States Army's Command and General Staff College in June 1998. She completed a master's in Military Arts and Sciences with a focus in History.

Her key military assignments include serving onboard USS *Mount Hood* (AE 29) as Chief Engineer in 1990 and deployment to the Persian Gulf for Operations Desert Shield and Desert Storm. She assumed duties as First Lieutenant onboard the USS *Flint* (AE 32) in July 1992. In December 1993, she rotated to the Bureau of Personnel as the Navy's liaison to the Defense Advisory Committee on Women in the Military Services. She was also the Action Officer for the assignment of women in the Navy policy. In January 1996, she became the Executive Officer of USS *Tortuga* (LSD 46). She was the first woman in the Navy to be assigned duties as XO of a combatant. During her tour, the ship deployed to the Adriatic Sea in support of Operation Joint Endeavor, a peacekeeping effort in the former Republic of Yugoslavia. Sixty days after returning from the Mediterranean deployment, *Tortuga* departed on a West African training cruise where the ship's sailors, with embarked Marines and United States Coast Guard detachment, operated with the naval services of seven African nations.

When she assumed command of USS *Rushmore* (LSD 47) on 12 March 1999, she became the first African American woman to command a ship in the United States Navy. *Rushmore* is the Navy's only Amphibious "Smart Ship." The "Smart Ship" concept integrates and evaluates commercial off the shelf technologies for future fleet application. In December 1999, *Rushmore* became the first Smart Ship to complete a six-month deployment. In November 2000, she was assigned to J-3, Global Operations, and Readiness on the Joint Staff in the Pentagon. In February 2003, she became the Exec-

utive Assistant to the Joint Staff Director of Operations. In May 2004, she assumed duties as Commander of Amphibious Squadron Seven. She was frocked as a Rear Admiral on May 26, 2006.

Howell, Walter L.
SERGEANT MAJOR—MARINES

Howell was born in Washington, DC. He joined the Marine Corps in October 1979, and reported for recruit training in August 1980 at Parris Island, South Carolina. After recruit training he transferred to MWSG 37 at El Toro, California, for duty as a Bulk Fuel Specialist.

In June 1982, he attended Marine Security Guard School at Quantico, Virginia. After school, he was assigned to American Embassies in Malaysia, Burma, and Thailand. In March 1986, he was transferred to 1st Bulk Fuel Company, 7th E'SB at Camp Pendleton, California, for duty as Platoon Sergeant; in July 1989, he was transferred to MCI Company at Marine Barracks in Washington, D.C. and assigned as a Course Developer for the 1300 Occupational Field. Laster, he attended Marine Security Guard School. After school, he was assigned as Detachment Commander at American Embassies in Pakistan and Spain. In May 1996, he was transferred to Marine Air Group 13 MWSS 371 for duty as Bulk Fuel Chief; in September 1997, he transferred to the 3rd Marine Division and was assigned to Communication Company, Headquarters Battalion; and in September 1999, he was assigned to Headquarters Company, 4th Marine Regiment, where he served until May 2002. He served as Sergeant Major Combat Assault Battalion from May 2002 to September 2003. In September 2003, Sergeant Major Howell was transferred to Marine Air Group 24 and assigned as Sergeant Major HMT-301, and was reassigned in June 2004 to HMH-362.

Huff, Edgar R.
SERGEANT MAJOR—MARINES

A native of Gadsden, Alabama, Edgar Hugg enlisted in the Marine Corps on September 24, 1942, and received recruit training with the 51st Composite Defense Battalion, Montford Point Camp, at New River, North Carolina. Following graduation, he joined the 155mm Gun Battery of the 51st Composite Defense Battalion and served with that Unit as a Gun Commander.

In early 1943, he was assigned duty under Instruction at Drill Instructors School, and upon completion of his course, he was assigned duty as a Drill Instructor in March 1943. At that time, Montford Point Camp was the receiving point for all blacks entering the Marine Corps, and by November 1944, Sergeant Major Huff had been assigned duty as Field Sergeant Major of all recruit training at Montford Point Camp.

In November 1944, he was promoted to First Sergeant, and assigned duty with the 5th Depot Company, departing for the Western Pacific Area, serving as First Sergeant with this Unit on Saipan, Okinawa, and in North China.

He was promoted to Sergeant Major on December 31, 1955, becoming the first black Marine to receive this rank. He served two tours in Vietnam, retired September 30, 1972, and died May 2, 1994, at Camp Lejeune Naval Hospital.

Hughes, Kelvin A.
COMMAND SERGEANT MAJOR—ARMY

Hughes was born in Haynesville, Louisiana, and entered the United States Army in August 1979. Upon completion of Basic Combat and Advanced Individual Training he was assigned to Fort Sill, Oklahoma. His military education includes all the Noncommissioned Officer Education System Courses; Battle Staff Course; First Sergeant Course (Honor Graduate); Air Assault School; Rappel Master Course; Air Movement Operations School; Load Planners Course; Equal Opportunity Course; Joint Fire Power Control Course; and the United States Army Sergeants Major Academy (class 53).

He has served in a wide variety of assignments including serving as Fire Support Liaison Specialist with the 2nd Battalion, 36th Field Artillery at Fort Sill, Oklahoma; Forward Observer with the 1st Battalion, 83rd Field Artillery at Baumholder, Germany; Company Fire Support Sergeant in the 2nd Battalion, 13th Infantry Regiment at Mannheim, Germany; Company Fire Support Sergeant in the 1st Battalion, 82nd Field Artillery 1CD at Fort Hood, Texas; Operations/Air Sergeant in the 2nd Battalion 17th Field Artillery at Camp Pelham, South Korea; Battalion Fire Support Sergeant in the 1st Battalion, 9th Infantry Regiment at Camp Greaves, South Korea; Battalion Fire Support Sergeant in the 1st Battalion, 3rd Field Artillery 2AD at Fort Hood; Battalion Fire Support Sergeant in the 7th Battalion, 8th Field Artillery at Schofield Barracks, Hawaii; Chief Enlisted Advisor at Fayetteville, Arkansas; First Sergeant in Bravo Battery, 1st Battalion, 77th Field Artillery Brigade at Fort Sill; First Sergeant of HHB 75th Field Artillery Brigade at Fort Sill; Senior ROTC Instructor at the University of Oklahoma at Norman, Oklahoma; and NCO Journal Special Project Officer at the United States Army Sergeants Major Academy at Fort Bliss, Texas. In October 2004, he was Command Sergeant Major of the 1st Battalion, 21st Field Artillery at Fort Hood.

Humphrey, Tyrone
SERGEANT MAJOR—MARINES

Born in Washington, D.C., Tyrone Humphrey enlisted in the United States Marine Corps in October 1979 and departed for Recruit Training at Marine Corps Recruit Depot at Parris Island, South Carolina, in January 1980.

His key military assignments include serving as Drill Instructor and Senior Drill Instructor at Fox Company, 2nd Battalion, and as Drill Instructor at the Drill Instructor School. In October 1994, he became Operation Chief at Marine Air Group 39 Headquarters. He also served as First Sergeant of the 1st Battalion, 1st Marines, at Camp Pendleton, California. In May 2001, he was First Sergeant for Weapon Company, 1st Marines, at Camp Pendleton. In August 2001, he deployed with BLT 1, 1 on West Pac 2-01 where his unit spear-headed Marine Corps participation in Operation Enduring Freedom. In January 2005, he was serving as Sergeant Major at Marine Corps Recruiting Station in Richmond, Virginia.

Hunter, Milton
MAJOR GENERAL—ARMY

Hunter is a native of Houston, Texas, and married to the former Karina Bechtle of Pforzheim, Germany. They have two sons, Alexander and Patrick. He is a 1967 distinguished military graduate with a Bachelor of Architectural Engineering degree from Washington State University. He also holds a master's degree in Engineering (Construction Management) from the University of Washington. His military schooling includes the Engineer Officer Basic and Advanced Courses; the Command and General Staff College; and the Army War College. Additionally, General Hunter completed the Executive Development Program at the Darden School of Business Administration at the University of Virginia; the Construction Executive Program at Texas A&M University; and the Senior Managers in Government Program at the John F. Kennedy School of Government at Harvard University.

Hunter's assignments with the Corps of Engineers included serving as Deputy District Engineer for the Charleston Engineer District. He also served as Platoon Leader in the 339th Engineer Battalion (Construction) at Fort Lewis, Washington; as Executive Officer and Company Commander with Headquarters and Headquarters Company, 937th Engineer Group (Combat), 18th Engineer Brigade, Vietnam; and as Assistant Division Engineer of the 8th Infantry Division (Mechanized) at Bad Kreuznach, West Germany.

From June 1983 to June 1985, he served as Commander of the 79th Engineer Combat Battalion (Heavy), 18th Engineer Brigade at Karlsruhe, West Germany. From June 1986 to August 1988, he was assigned as an Program Analyst at the Program Analysis and Evaluation Directorate in the Office of the Chief of Staff of the United States Army in Washington, D.C. From September 1988 to August 1989, he served as the Assistant Director for Civil Works (Central Region),

United States Army Corps of Engineers, Washington, D.C. From September 1989 to January 1992, he served as Commander of the Engineer District in Seattle, Washington. In January 1992, he was assigned as the Chief of Staff in the office of the Chief of Engineers, United States Army, in Washington, D.C. From November 1992 to September 1994, he was selected to serve as Commanding General of the United States Army Engineer Division, South Pacific, in San Francisco, California. He was promoted to Brigadier General on June 1, 1993.

From September 1994 to July 1997, he served as the Commanding General of the United States Army Engineer Division, North Atlantic, in New York, New York. He was promoted to Major General on August 1, 1996.

In July 1997, he was selected to serve as the Director of Military Programs for the United States Army Corps of Engineers in Washington, D.C. He retired from the military on August 31, 2001.

General Hunter served as a Military Social Aide to the White House and was selected as one of the "Outstanding Young Men of America" in 1979. He was presented the 1991 Distinguished Alumni Award from his alma mater, Washington State University. In 1997, he was awarded an honorary Doctor of Science degree from the New Jersey Institute of Technology.

His military awards and decorations include the Army Distinguished Service Medal (two awards); Bronze Star; Meritorious Service Medal (two awards); the Army Commendation Medal (two awards); Meritorious Unit Citation; the Army General Staff Identification Badge, and the Parachutist Badge.

Hunton, Benjamin Lacy
BRIGADIER GENERAL—ARMY

Hunton was born in Washington, D.C. He married the former Jean Cooper, and they had a son, Benjamin. He graduated from Dunbar High School in 1936. He is a graduate of Howard University, receiving a Bachelor of Science degree in 1940, and a Master of Arts degree in History in 1942. He earned a Ph.D. degree from American University in 1954.

From 1942 to 1966, he was a teacher and administrator in the Washington, D.C., school system. From 1966 to 1970, he served the Department of Interior and the Department of Health, Education, and Welfare. In 1970, he was appointed Assistant Director of Education and Training for the Bureau of Mines, U.S. Department of Interior, in Washington, D.C. He administered a nationwide health and safety training program for the mineral industries and supervised all education and training efforts assigned to the bureau under the Coal Mine Health and Safety Act of 1969.

Hunton was commissioned during World War II and is a graduate of the Army Command and General Staff College at Fort Leavenworth, Kansas. He has written two studies which were published by the public schools of Washington, D.C.—"Basic Track in Junior High School" in 1962 and "Study of Selected School Drop-

outs, 1963–1966" in 1967. He was promoted to Brigadier General on June 10, 1971, with an effective date of June 4, 1971. He became the first black General in the Army Reserves. He assumed his duties as Commander of the 97th Army Reserve Command in Fort George G. Meade, Maryland, in November 1972.

His awards include the Meritorious Service Award, the World War II Victory Medal, the American Theatre Service Medal and the Armed Forces Reserve Medal (with hourglass). He was a member of the White House Committee on Civil Rights and Minority Affairs and the District of Columbia Commission on Academic Facilities.

Hussey, Robert
COMMAND SERGEANT MAJOR—ARMY

He is a native of Philadelphia, Pennsylvania. He entered the Army in January 1975, and attended Basic Combat Training at Fort Jackson, South Carolina, and Advanced Individual Training at Fort Lee, Virginia. His military and civilian education includes the Personnel and Logistics Course; Battle Staff; First Sergeants Course; and the United States Army Sergeants Major Academy (class 49). He is a graduate of Saint Leo College.

His assignments include serving as Unit Supply Sergeant; S4 (Logistics) Senior Supply NCO; Property Book Team NCO; Property Book NCOIC; Supply Sergeant Management Information Systems Office; First Sergeant for the 3rd Forward Support Battalion; First Sergeant of Alpha Company in Headquarters Command (Garrison); Command Major for 2nd Forward Support Battalion; and Command Sergeant Major for the 27th Main Support Battalion. In August 2004, he was serving as Command Sergeant Major for Division Support Command, 1st Cavalry Division.

Hyde, Mark A.
COMMAND SERGEANT MAJOR—ARMY

He is a native of Chicago, Illinois, and entered the United States Army in September 1979. He attended Basic Combat Training at Fort McClellan, Alabama, and attended Advanced Individual Training (Honor Graduate) at Redstone Arsenal, Alabama. His military education includes all the Noncommissioned Officer Education System Courses; Eagles Logistic Course; Air Assault Course; Rappel Master Course; Equal Opportunity Representative Course; United States Army Recruiting Course; United States Army Station Commander Course; United States Army Bradley Fighting Vehicle Course; and the United States Army Sergeants Major Academy. He holds an Associates of Science Degree in Applied Science from Regents College, New York.

He has served in leadership positions as a Squad Leader; Platoon Sergeant; Maintenance Control Supervisor; Recruiting Station Commander; Battalion Maintenance Sergeant; First Sergeant; and Command Sergeant Major.

His key assignments included serving as the G3 Sergeant Major of the 544th Maintenance Battalion, 64th Corps Support Group, 13th Corps Support Command at Fort Hood, Texas; Command Sergeant Major for the 544th Maintenance Battalion, 64th Corps Support Group, 13th Corps Support Command at Fort Hood; Command Sergeant Major of the 702nd Main Support Battalion, 2nd Infantry Division at Camp Casey, South Korea. In August 2004, he was serving as the Command Sergeant Major, 23rd Area Support Group, 19th TSC, in South Korea.

Ingram, Isaac, Jr.
COMMAND MASTER CHIEF—NAVY

He is a native of Chicago, Illinois. He enlisted into the Navy in August 1968, and attended Recruit Training

at the Great Lakes Training Center in Illinois. After Basic Training, he completed Basic Submarine Training in Groton, Connecticut. He is a graduate of the Navy Senior Enlisted Academy in March 1985.

During his military career, he has served in numerous leadership and other key assignments including serving as a Submarine Machinist Mate on board Submarines; as a Recruiter in charge of his own Recruiting Station; as an Assignment Officer at the Naval Military Personnel Command in Washington, D.C.; as the Overseas Screening Program Manager at Naval Military Personnel Command; and as the Command Master Chief of Naval Military Personnel Command.

Ingram, Jeffery C.
COMMAND SERGEANT MAJOR—ARMY

He was born in Fort Lauderdale, Florida. He completed Basic Combat Training and Advanced Individual Training at Fort Jackson, South Carolina.

His military education includes all the Noncommissioned Officer Education Courses and the Recruiter Course. He has earned a bachelor's degree from Touro International University in San Diego, California.

His military assignments include serving as an Administrative Specialist/Computer Operator for the Army Athletic Association at West Point, New York. In February 1986, he served with the 30th Postal Detachment in Darmstadt, West Germany and was later assigned as a Field Recruiter in the Culver City Recruiting Station in Los Angeles Recruiting Battalion. In August 1992, he was assigned to the Tampa Recruiting Battalion as Station Commander. In August 1997, he was assigned to the 1st Special Forces Operation Detachment Delta at Fort Bragg, North Carolina, and was later selected as the Noncommissioned Officer in Charge

with the Department of Defense Top Special Operation Unit. In July 2000, he was assigned as First Sergeant at the USAREC Office of the Inspector General at Fort Knox, Kentucky. In January 2005, he was serving as the Command Sergeant Major of the United States Army Sacramento Recruiting Battalion, 6th United States Army Recruiting Brigade.

Irby, Elvis
COMMAND SERGEANT MAJOR—ARMY

He was born in Coldwater, Mississippi, and entered the United States Army in November 1977. He attended Basic Training and Advanced Individual Training at Fort Knox, Kentucky.

His military and civilian education includes all the Noncommissioned Officer Education System Courses; Instructor's Course; Maintenance Operations Course; Battle Staff Course; Garrison Sergeants Major Course; the United States Army Sergeants Major Academy (class 49); and numerous other professional courses. He holds an associate's degree in Business Management from Regents College.

He has held a variety of leadership positions including Shop Foreman; Team Chief; Motor Sergeant; Instructor; Senior Instructor, Subject Matter Expert/Senior Writer for Tested Material; Squad Leader; Section Sergeant; Platoon Sergeant; and First Sergeant. He is currently Command Sergeant Major of the United States Army Garrison at Aberdeen Proving Ground, Maryland.

Isaac, Opan V.
COMMAND SERGEANT MAJOR—ARMY

Opan Isaac was born in Manchester, Jamaica, and entered the Army in September 1976 at Fort Jackson, South Carolina. In January 1977, she graduated from Advanced Individual Training at the United States

Army Personnel School at Fort Benjamin Harrison, Indiana.

Her military education includes all the Noncommissioned Officer Education System Courses; the Airborne School, graduating as the #1 female of her class; the United States Army Sergeants Major Academy; and the Command Sergeant Major Course.

She has held numerous key leadership assignments, being one of the first Females assigned to the 82nd Division. She held every supervisory position in finance units including Squad Leader, Platoon Sergeant, Platoon Leader, Cash Control Officer, Disbursing Officer, Operation Noncommissioned Officer, Chief Internal Control, Detachment Commander, First Sergeant, and Battalion Command Sergeant Major.

Her overseas assignments include one tour in Kuwait, at Headquarters and Headquarters Company, ARCENT Kuwait, Camp Doha; Operations Desert Shield and Desert Storm; the Balkans Region in support of Stabilization Force Seven, supporting the 49th Armored Division in Bosnia-Herzeqovina, Croatia, and Hungary in 2000; and in Germany support Reforger 87 (Phantom Saber VII), in support of III Corps, serving as the Finance Liaison Officer. In October 2004, she was serving as the Command Sergeant Major for the 39th Finance Battalion.

Isaac, Rebecca B.

CHIEF WARRANT OFFICER—ARMY

She enlisted in the United States Army on November 11, 1975, through the delay entry program at Fort Jackson, South Carolina. She entered active duty status and graduated from Basic Training at Fort Jackson, South Carolina. Upon qualifying in military occupational specialty (MOS) 35M Avionic Navigation Equipment Repairer, she graduated from Advanced Individual Training (AIT) at Fort Jackson, South Carolina. She obtained the rank of Chief Warrant Officer 4.

Ivory, Lacey

SERGEANT MAJOR—ARMY

He is a native of Kansas City, Missouri, and lost his life in the attack on the Pentagon at the age of 43. He was assigned to the Office of the Assistant Chief of Staff for Personnel, and was attending a meeting in Lieutenant General Timothy J. Maude's Office on September 11, 2001, at the time that the plane struck the Pentagon.

His wife, Deborah, was stationed at an Army Base near the Pentagon and had phoned her husband's office right after the plane struck. His voice mail still worked, and thought that meant his office was intact.

Jackson, Abraham

COMMAND MASTER CHIEF—NAVY

A native of Northwestern Louisiana, Jackson graduated from Allen High School in May 1979 and began his naval career in June of that same year. He attended Recruit Training Command, San Diego, from June to August 1979. He then completed the Submarine Fire Control Technician pipeline including Basic Enlisted Submarine School and Class "A" and "C" schools. Upon completion, he reported to his first operational command, the Gold Crew of the USS *James Monroe* (SSBN-622). Assigned to the command from October 1980 to August 1985, he obtained his Submarine Warfare designation, advanced from E3 to E6, completed nine strategic patrols, and was the first E-6 to qualify and stand Diving Officer of the Watch. His final duties prior to detaching from this command were as First Lieutenant, Torpedo Fire Control Division Leading Petty Officer.

His next assignment was as Company Commander at Recruit Training Command Orlando, Florida, from October 1985 to October 1988, where he led eight companies of approximately 83 recruits per company through the rigorous eight-week training course. He was advanced to Officer in September 1986 and earned the designation of Master Training Specialist. His assignment while attached was as an Instructor for Basic Military Orientation classes and as a Drill Master for the Commander's Drill Division.

In October 1988, he returned to sea as part of the Gold Crew of USS *Lewis and Clark* (SSBN 644), completing six additional deterrent patrols prior to its decommissioning: he also advanced to Senior Chief Petty Officer. While onboard, his duties included Division Officer for Torpedo Fire Control Divisions, First Lieutenant, and as Ship's CMS Custodian.

In September 1991, he transferred to the Gold Crew of USS *Casimir Pulaski* (SSBN 633), where he completed another five deterrent patrols. He held similar duties as on the *Lewis and Clark*, and served as Chief of the Boat for several months. In April 1993, he reported to USS *Billfish* (SSN 676) as Chief of the Boat. While aboard USS *Billfish*, he completed five deployments and participated in operations.

In September 1996, he reported to Naval Air Engineering Station, Lakehurst, New Jersey, as the Command Master Chief. After two years, he reported to the USS *Emory S. Land* (AS 39) in Norfolk, Virginia, and later changed homeport to LaMaddalena, Italy, where he served until May 2001. He reported to his next assignment as Command Master Chief aboard the general-purpose Amphibious Assault Ship USS *Saipan* (LHA 2) in October 2002.

Jackson, Anthony L.

BRIGADIER GENERAL—MARINES

He was born in Fort Lewis, Washington. He graduated from Oakland High School, Oakland, California, in 1967 and San Jose State University in 1971. In 1973, he completed his Master of Arts in History at San Jose State.

In May 1975, he enlisted in the Marine Corps to attend Officer Candidates School. On graduating from the Basic School in June 1976, he was assigned to 1st Battalion, 5th Marines, 1st Marine Division, at Camp Pendleton, California. While there, he served as a Rifle and Weapons Platoon Commander and Battalion Adjutant. In 1978, he left the regular Marine Corps; however, he continued to serve in the reserves as the Weapons Platoon Commander, "L" Company, 3rd Battalion, 25th Marines, in Pittsburgh, Pennsylvania.

Upon returning to the regular Marine Corps in December 1979, he was assigned to 1st Battalion, 5th Marines. During this tour, he served as the Assistance Operations Officer and as a Rifle and Weapons Company Commander. In February 1982, he was transferred to the Marine Corps Recruit Depot at San Diego, California. While there, he served as a Battalion Operations Officer, Company Commander, and Officer-in-Charge of the Recruit Field Training Division. In June 1984, General Jackson was assigned as the Commanding Officer of the Marine Detachment on USS *Long Beach* (CGN-9), which was home ported in San Diego, California. In July 1988, he was transferred to the 1st Marine Expeditionary Brigade at Kaneohe Bay, Hawaii. While in Brigade, he served consecutively as a Company Commander, as a Combat Service Support Plans Officer, and as the Operations Officer and Executive Officer of 3rd Battalion, 3rd Marines.

After completing his tour with 1st Marine Expeditionary Brigade, General Jackson attended the Armed Forces Staff College at Norfolk, Virginia. Upon graduation in June 1990, he then served as a Senior Emer-

gency Action Officer in the National Military Command Center, J-3, Joint Staff, in Washington, D.C., until July 1992. Upon transfer, he served as the Chief of Instructors at the Basic School in Marine Corps Combat Development Command at Quantico, Virginia. From July 1993 to June 1995, he was the Commanding Officer of Marine Security Forces of the Naval Submarine Base at Kings Bay, Georgia. In June 1997, he completed an assignment as the Advisor to the Commandant of the Marine Corps on Equal Opportunity Matters as the Head of the Equal Opportunity Branch at the Headquarters of the Marine Corps.

In June 1998, Jackson graduated from the United States Army War College at Carlisle, Pennsylvania. He served in that billet from June 1998 to June 2000. He then served as the Commanding Officer, 1st Marine Regiment, 1st Marine Division. After that assignment, he was assigned to the 3rd Marine Division at Okinawa, Japan, where he was the Division's Chief of Staff. During that assignment, he served concurrently as the Chief of Staff for Joint Task Force-555 in support of Operation Enduring Freedom-Philippines. In August 2004, he returned from Operation Iraqi Freedom, and assigned as the Assistant Chief of Staff, G-5, I Marine Expeditionary Force at Camp Pendleton, California. He was promoted to Brigadier General in May 2005.

He completed both the Amphibious Warfare School and the Marine Corps Command and Staff College. His personal decorations include the Legion of Merit (with two gold stars in lieu of second and third awards); Bronze Star; the Defense Meritorious Medal; Meritorious Service Medal (with two gold stars in lieu of second and third awards); Navy and Marine Corps Commendation Medal (with gold star in lieu of second award); the Navy and Marine Corps Achievement Medal; the Global War on Terrorism Expeditionary Medal; the Global War on Terrorism Service Medal, and the Korea Defense Service Medal.

Jackson, Bernard R.

CAPTAIN—NAVY

A native of Macon, Georgia, Bernard Jackson received a Bachelor of Science degree in Chemistry, and his commission in December 1976, through the NROTC program at Savannah State University.

His first tour of duty was as Gunnery Officer and Damage Control Assistance on board USS *El Paso* (LKA 117). During his tour, *El Paso* completed an extensive overhaul and conducted a major deployment to the Indian Ocean. In August of 1982, he reported to the Naval POTC Unit at Savannah State College, where in addition to performing duties as Recruiting Officer/Sophomore Instructor he obtained a Bachelor of Science degree in Mathematics.

In November 1985, he reported to USS *Connole* (FF-1052) as Engineering Officer until October 1987. During his tour, *Connole* conducted a major deployment and was awarded the Battle "E." In October 1987, he reported to USS *Josephus Daniels* (CG-27) as Engineering Officer until October 1989. During his tour, *Josephus*

Daniels participated in Operation Earnest Will, was awarded the battle "E" and named the recipient of the Arleigh Burke Award as the most improved surface combatant.

He served on the staff on Comcrudesgru Eight from October 1989 until November 1991. During his tour, CCDG-8 participated in several complex operations, including Operation Desert Shield/Desert Storm while embarked in USS *Saratoga* (CV-60). From March 1992 to October 1993, he served as the Executive Officer for USS *Ticonderoga*. During this tour, *Ticonderoga* participated in several fleet exercises and completed the first AEGIS overhaul.

In November 1993, he attended the Naval War College in Newport Rhode Island where he earned a master's degree in National Security and Strategic Studies. Subsequently, from December 1994 to December 1996, he served as an action officer in the Strategic Plans and Policy Directorate (J-5) of the Joint Staff in Washington, D.C.

Captain Jackson served as Commanding Officer of USS *McFaul* (DDG-74) from June 1997 to November 1999. As the commissioning Commanding Officer, he guided *McFaul* through accelerated work-ups and deployment preparations, deploying September 1999 with the JFK Battle Group as flagship for COMDESRON Two Four. *McFaul* was awarded the Retention Excellence award for FY 1999.

In January 2000, he was assigned to the Office of the Chief of Naval Operations, where he worked for the Director of Theater Air Warfare. In September 2001, he was selected to serve as Commodore and he assumed Command of Destroyer Squadron 14.

His military awards and decorations include the Defense Meritorious Service Medal; Meritorious Service Medal (three awards); the Navy Commendation Medal (three awards); and the Navy Achievement Medal.

Jackson, Blaine H.

SERGEANT MAJOR—MARINES

He entered the Marine Corps Recruit Depot at Parris Island, South Carolina, for Recruit Training in September 1983. His key military assignments include serving in April 1990, with Charlie Battery, 1st Battalion, 10th Marine Regiment, 2nd March Division, at Camp Lejeune, North Carolina, and served as a Section Chief. He was deployed to the Middle East, where he participated in Operations Desert Shield and Desert Storm. In 1991, he was reassigned to 10th Marine Regiment, 10th Marines Field Artillery Training School, as an Artillery Instructor. In July 1993, he received orders to Drill Instructor School at Parris Island, South Carolina. Upon graduating he was assigned to India Company, Third Recruit Training Battalion, where he served as a Drill Instructor. In October 1997, he was reassigned to the Staff Noncommissioned Officer Academy as an Instructor/Advisor. As a First Sergeant, he deployed during Operation Iraqi Freedom, two Combined Arm Exercises, Task Force Betio, with 3rd Battalion, 5th Marine in support. His next assignment was Sergeant

Major for the 2nd Assault Amphibian Battalion. In January 2004, he was assigned as the Sergeant Major at Marine Medium Helicopter Squadron 365, Aircraft Group 29, 2nd Marine Aircraft Wing.

Jackson, Brian K.

SERGEANT MAJOR—MARINES

He entered the United States Marine Corps in August 1980, and attended Basic Training at Marine Corps Recruit Depot, San Diego, California. He graduated with honors, and he was meritoriously promoted to Private First Class.

Upon graduation, he was assigned to the United States Marine Corps Recruiting Substation in Gary, Indiana, as a Recruiter's Assistant. He appreciably enhanced his station's mission attainment by personally referring 16 civilians of which 11 subsequently enlisted in the Marine Corps.

After completing Recruiter's Assistance, he attended Marine Corps Communications Electronic School in 29 Palms, California, in 1981. Initially, he was assigned as a Field Radio Operator, but upon graduating first in his class, he was awarded an upgraded MOS as a High Frequency Communications Central Operator. After graduating from HFCCOC, he was assigned to Communications Support Company, 9th Communications Battalion at 29 Palms. During this time, he served as the Training Noncommissioned Officer and the Assistant Section Leader. He was then assigned the duties as the Naval Warfare Publications Library Clerk. He attended Drill Instructor School at Marine Corps Recruit Depot, San Diego, California. He served as a Drill Instructor with the 3rd Recruit Training Battalion, Lima Company from 1984 to 1986. During this assignment he also served as a Senior Drill Instructor and a Chief Drill Instructor.

His key leadership assignments include serving as the Communications Chief from 1986 to 1987 at Marine Air Control Squadron-4, Marine Corps Air Station Futenma, in Okinawa, Japan. From October 1987 to December 1991, he served as the Radio Chief/Communications Chief with Marine Wing Support Squadron 173 (later redesignated 174), Marine Aircraft Group 24, in Kaneohe Bay, Hawaii. During this Tour he served in Desert Shield/Desert Storm. He served with the Service Company of the 7th Communications Battalion at Camp Hansen, as Radio Chief in the Radio Platoon; Communication Chief in the Satellite Platoon; and Detachment Commander for Detachments in Cobra Gold (Thailand). He also served as Company First Sergeant in the Service Company from July 1992 to 1995. He served as Communications Instructor/Instructor Trainer with the Expeditionary Warfare Training Group. He served as First Sergeant for Headquarters and Service Company, 3rd Assault Amphibian Battalion, and as Sergeant Major for the Marine Medium Helicopter Squadron 165th, Marine Aircraft Group 16. He served as the Sergeant Major for the Aviation Combat Elements with the 13th Marine Expeditionary Unit for Operation Enduring Freedom in support of the War

on Terrorism. He also participated in Operations Ana-
conda and Harpoon in Bagram, Afghanistan. He was
assigned as the Sergeant Major for the 3rd Battalion,
12th Marine Regiment with the 3rd Marine Division.

In November 2004, he was serving as the Sergeant
Major for Headquarters Battalion, 3rd Marine Division, and also doubling as the Camp Sergeant Major
for Camps Courtney and McTureous.

Jackson, Gilda

COLONEL—MARINES

Gilda Jackson is a native of Columbus, Ohio. She is
a 1968 graduate of Bishop Hartley and at the age of 18,
enlisted into the Marine Corps. She completed Marine
Corps Recruit Training and reported to Supply Administration School, and spent three years as an enlisted Marine.

She then graduated from Ohio Dominican College
where she received her Bachelor of Arts in Economics.
She was commissioned a second lieutenant in Decem-
ber 1975. Her assignments have included Supply
Officer, Station Operations, and Engineering Squadron,
Marine Corps Air Station at El Toro, California; Group
Aviation Supply Support Center Officer, Marine Air-
craft Group-12, Marine Corps Air Station at Iwakuni,
Japan; and Fiscal Officer, Marine Aircraft Group 16,
3rd Marine Aircraft Wing, Marine Corps Air Station at
Tustin, California.

After graduating from Amphibious Warfare School
in June 1983, Colonel Jackson reported to Headquarters and Maintenance Squadron, Marine Air Group 13,
Marine Corps Air Station at El Toro. She was selected
to serve with Marine Medium Helicopter Training
Squadron 301, Marine Air Group-16, as the Group
Supply Officer.

She graduated from the Marine Corps Command
and Staff College at Marine Corps Base, Quantico, Virginia, and was assigned as the Executive Officer of
Naval Aviation Depot at Cherry Point, North Carolina.

In 1997, Colonel Jackson became the first African
American woman ever to achieve the position of colonel in the Marine Corps as well as the first female commanding officer in the 56-year history of the Cherry
Point Navel Aviation Depot.

She was honored as one of the most outstanding
alumni of Ohio independent College and universities
for paving the way for women and minorities in the
United States Armed Forces. On April 10, 2002 Colonel Jackson was inducted into the Ohio Foundation of
Independent Colleges Hall of Fame in Columbus.

Jackson, James N.

LIEUTENANT COLONEL—ARMY

He holds a Bachelor of Arts degree in Sociology from
the City College of New York. He earned a Master of
Science degree in Social Work from Columbia University, and a Doctor of Social Work Degree from Catholic
University.

His previous assignments include Chief of Social
Work Service at Fort Belvoir, Virginia; Chief of Social

Work Service in Yongsan, South Korea; Chief of Social
Work Service at the Military Prison at Fort Leaven-
worth, Kansas; a Staff Officer at Headquarters, 7th
Medical Command in Heidelberg, Germany; a Staff
Officer at Walter Reed Army Medical Center in Wash-
ington, D.C.; Instructor in Family Practice Medical
Residency at Fort Bragg, North Carolina; Research Sci-
entist, Walter Reed Army Institute of Research, Wash-
ington, D.C.; and Chief of Army Community Service,
United States Army Community and Family Support
Center at Alexandria, Virginia. In February 2005, he
was serving as a member of the professional staff of the
Defense Task Force on Domestic Violence.

Jackson, Larry D.

COMMAND SERGEANT MAJOR—ARMY

Command Sergeant Major Larry D. Jackson entered
the military in October 1975 with the Georgia National
Guard. On February 22, 1976, he entered active duty
with the regular Army.

He earned an associate's degree in Social General
Science from Central Texas College, and he is a graduate of the United States Army Sergeants Major Academy.

His military assignments include serving as Platoon
Sergeant with the 78th Engineer Battalion and as the
Operation Sergeant with the 19th Support Command
in South Korea. He was assigned as a Drill Sergeant, and
as an Instructor at the Primary Leadership Develop-
ment Course, and was the Senior Instructor for the 12B
Basic Noncommissioned Officer Course at Libby NCO
Academy at For Leonard Wood, Missouri. He served as

First Sergeant with the 24th Infantry Division, 3rd Engineer Battalion, serving one tour each in Somalia and Kuwait. He was assigned to the 54th Engineer Battalion on July 9, 1999, as Battalion Command Sergeant Major.

Jackson, Leonard L.
COLONEL—ARMY

He entered the United States Army during World War II, and was commissioned a Second Lieutenant in the Artillery upon graduating from Officer Candidate School at Fort Sill, Oklahoma, in July 1942. He went to Italy as a Commander in Battery B, 597th Field Artillery Battalion, and participated in the Rome, Arno, Po Valley, and North Apennines campaigns in the last year of the war.

After the war he transferred to the Organized Reserves, but returned to active duty as a Quartermaster officer in 1949. Over the next quarter century he held a variety of troop training and logistic support assignments overseas (USAREUE and USARPAC) and at military installations in CONUS.

His final active duty assignment was as Deputy Commander of United States Army Logistics Doctrine in the Systems and Readiness Agency at New Cumberland Depot, where he conducted far-reaching logistical studies for the Army's Deputy Chief of Staff for Logistics.

Jackson, Patricia A.
CAPTAIN—NAVY

She began her naval career by enlisting in the United States Navy in 1974. After receiving her Bachelor of Science degree in Health Care Administration in 1981, she was commissioned through Officer Candidate

School in Newport, Rhode Island. Her education includes a Master of Arts degree in National Security and Strategic Studies from the Naval War College; a Master of Arts degree in Personnel Management from Central Michigan University; and a Ph.D. in Humanities (International Relations) from Salve Regina University. She completed the Armed Forces Staff College, and in 1997 she completed the six month Italian Language course at the Defense Language Institute.

Her military assignments include serving as the Director of the United States Naval Academy Family Service Center and as an Instructor at the United States Naval Academy. She was assigned to the United States Atlantic Command serving as Military Liaison Officer at the United States Embassy in Haiti; as Commanding Officer of the Personnel Unit at Treasure Island, California; and as the Commanding Officer of United States Naval Support Activity in Gaeta, Italy. In November 1999, she reported to the Office of the Secretary of Defense, International Security Affairs, as Country Director for East Africa. In June 2003, she was assigned as the Commander of Naval Station Ingleside.

Jackson, Paul J.
COMMAND SERGEANT MAJOR—ARMY

Command Sergeant Major Paul L. Jackson enlisted in the Alabama National Guard in 1973, attended Basic Combat Training at Fort Jackson, South Carolina, and Advanced Individual Training at Fort Gordon, Georgia. Upon completion of his training he returned home and served with a National Guard Communications Unit headquartered in Citronelle, Alabama.

His military education includes Noncommissioned Officers Logistical Program; the Senior Supply Sergeant Course; the First Sergeant Course; the United States

Army Sergeant Major Academy (class 41); and the Command Sergeants Major Course.

He joined the Regular Army in March 1974 and was assigned to Fort Monmouth, New Jersey, as a Supply Specialist. In 1975, he was assigned to the island of Okinawa, Japan and served as a Supply Specialist and Supply Sergeant. In 1978, he returned to the United States and was assigned to Fort Gordon. In 1982, he was assigned to the 2nd Infantry Division in Korea as a Supply Sergeant for 3rd Brigade Headquarters and Headquarters Company. In 1983, he was assigned to Fort Jackson. In 1987, he was ordered to serve with the 1st Infantry Division (Forward) in Groppining, West Germany. In 1990, he again returned to the United Stated and was assigned to the 3rd Brigade in the 4th Infantry Division (Mech.) as the Brigade Supply Sergeant (NCOIC S-4), at Fort Carson, Colorado. He was further assigned to the Division Support Command with the 4th Forward Support Battalion, Alpha Company as the First Sergeant. In 1993, he was assigned to Fort Richardson, Arkansas, as the Operations Sergeant for the 306th Forward Support Battalion 6th Infantry Division (Light) and later assumed the duties as the Battalion Command Sergeant Major. In 1999, he was reassigned to the 1st Infantry Division, with duties as the 235th Base Support Battalion Command Sergeant Major for the communities of Ansback and Illesheim, Germany. He served as the Command Sergeant Major for the 23 Area Support Group at Camp Humphrey, later as Area 1 Support Activity Command Sergeant Major in South Korea.

Jackson, Sherry R.

COMMAND SERGEANT MAJOR—ARMY

She entered the active military service in January

1982 as a Petroleum Supply Specialist, Private First Class, at Fort Dix, New Jersey. Upon completion of Basic Combat Training and Advanced Individual Training at Fort Lee, Virginia, and Airborne School at Fort Benning, Georgia, she was assigned to the 229th Supply and Service Company in Augsburg, West Germany, where she served for 18 months.

Her education includes a bachelor's degree in Physical Education from Southern University in Baton Rouge, Louisiana; all the Noncommissioned Officer Education System Courses; the Airborne School; the Defense Equal Opportunity Management Course; and the United States Army Sergeants Major Academy.

Jackson has served in various command, staff and leadership positions including serving as a Section Sergeant with a Petroleum, Oil, and Lubricants Platoon with the 226th Field Service Company in Ludwigsburg, Germany; as a Petroleum Oil Platoon Sergeant, later a Headquarters Platoon Sergeant and Support Operations Non-Commissioned Officer in Charge; as a Platoon Sergeant with the 705th Main Support Battalion, 5th Infantry Division, at Fort Polk, Louisiana; as the Warrior Brigade's Equal Opportunity Advisor; as Noncommissioned Officer-in-Charge of the Defense Fuel Office-Korea; and as Support Operations Non-Commissioned Officer-in-Charge at the 142nd Corps Support Battalion. While at Fort Polk, she served twice as the Command Sergeant Major of the 142nd Corps Support Battalion and First Sergeant of the 229th Field Service Company. She was assigned as Sergeant Major for Petroleum and Water Departments at Fort Lee, Virginia, and was selected to serve as the Command Sergeant Major for the 240th Quartermaster Battalion at Fort Lee. In April 2005, she was serving as Command Sergeant Major for the 505th Quartermaster Battalion in Japan.

Jacobs, Talmadge Jeffries
BRIGADIER GENERAL—ARMY

He was born in Pendleton, North Carolina. He received a Bachelor of Science degree from Morgan State University. He earned a Doctor of Osteopathic Medicine degree from the Philadelphia College of Osteopathic Medicine. He has held a variety of both career building and command staff assignments.

Jacobs served in several capacities at the Headquarters of the 79th Army Reserve Command, being assigned as the Assistant to the Commanding General, as the Deputy Chief of Staff for Personnel and Administration, and as the Chief of Staff for the Commanding General. He later served as the Commander of the 157th Infantry Brigade. In the United States Army Reserves he was appointed to the rank of Brigadier General.

James, Avon C.
BRIGADIER GENERAL—AIR FORCE

He was born in Hampton, Virginia. He married the former Borma M. Upton of Ipswich, England. They have a son, Stephen, and a daughter, Sheryl. He was graduated from Frederick Douglass High School in Baltimore in 1947 and earned a bachelor's degree from Morgan State University in 1951.

He enlisted in the Air Force in 1951, serving as a weather observer with the Air Weather Service prior to entering Officer Candidate School. Following commissioning as a second lieutenant in June 1953, he attended Personnel Officer School and was assigned to the 81st Fighter Wing at Royal Air Force Station, Bentwaters, England, as a personnel officer. In July 1957 he returned to the United States and was assigned to the 1001st Air

Base Wing at Andrews Air Force Base, in Maryland. While serving with the wing, General James was assigned as a Personnel Officer with the Field Maintenance Squadron, Operations Group, Maintenance and Supply Group, and completed his tour of duty as Chief of the Consolidated Base Personnel Office.

In June 1963 he returned to England with the 304th Munitions Maintenance Squadron at Royal Air Force Station, Alconbury, where he served as Chief of Personnel and Administration. In September 1965 he was assigned to the 7232nd Munitions Maintenance Group at Ramstein Air Base, West Germany, as Chief of the Personnel and Administration Division. He returned to the United States in March 1967, assigned to the Analysis and Programming Branch of the Air Force Command Post's Systems Division at the Headquarters of the United States Air Force in Washington, D.C. During this assignment he served in several positions, each involving the development of applications software in support of the United States Air Force command and control system In July 1972 General James was assigned as a Computer Systems Staff Officer with the Automatic Data Processing Equipment Selection Directorate at Hanscom Air Force Base, Massachusetts, until July 1963 when he was assigned as Chief of Staff of the Electronic Systems Division at Air Force Systems Command, Hanscom Air Force Base. In June 1978 he was assigned as the first Deputy Commander for Data Automation at the Headquarters of Air Force Communications Command at Scott Air Force Base, Illinois, responsible for the overall management and direction of eight data automation organizations that provided a broad range of services to the Office of the Secretary of Defense and major commands, bases, and designated government agencies. In February 1980 he was assigned as Director of Computer Resources in the Office of the Comptroller of the Air Force in Washington, D.C. He was promoted to Brigadier General on June 1, 1980, with the same date of rank.

His military decorations and awards include the Legion of Merit (with one oak leaf cluster), Meritorious Service Medal, Air Force Commendation Medal (with one oak leaf cluster), and the Air Force Organizational Excellence Award.

James, Daniel "Chappie," Jr.
GENERAL—AIR FORCE

The youngest of seventeen children, he was born on February 11, 1920, in Pensacola, Florida. His parents were Daniel James, Sr., a lamplighter before electricity reached the black section of Pensacola, and coal-dolly man in a gas plant, and Lillie Anna (Brown) James, who ran an elementary school for black children in her home. Ten of his brothers and sisters died before Daniel Jr. were born because there wasn't any medical care available for blacks in that area.

He graduated from Washington High School in June 1937. From September 1937 to March 1942, he attended Tuskegee Institute, where he received a Bachelor of Science degree in Physical Education and completed civilian pilot training under the government-sponsored Civilian Pilot Training Program. He remained at Tuskegee as a Civilian Instructor Pilot in the Army Air Corps Aviation Cadet Program until January 1943 when he entered the program as a cadet and received his commission as a second lieutenant in July 1943. He next completed fighter pilot combat training at Selfridge Field, Michigan, and was assigned to various units in the United States for the next six years.

In September 1949, James went to the Philippines as Flight Leader for the 12th Fighter-Bomber Squadron, 19th Fighter Wing, at Clark Field. In July 1950, he left for Korea, where he flew 101 combat missions in F-15 and F-80 aircraft. He returned to the United States and in July 1951 went to Otis Air Force Base, Massachusetts, as an all-weather jet fighter pilot with the 58th Fighter-Interceptor Squadron (FIS) and later became Operations Officer.

In April 1953 he became Commander of the 437th FIS, and in August 1955 he assumed Command of the 60th FIS. He graduated from the Air Command and Staff College in June 1957. In December 1966 he went to Ubon Royal Thai Air Force Base, Thailand, and flew 78 combat missions into North Vietnam. He led a flight in the Bolo MiG Sweep in which seven communist MiG-21s were destroyed, the highest total kill of any mission during the Vietnam War. He became Deputy Assistant Secretary of Defense (Public Affairs) in March 1970, and during his tenure at the Pentagon, James was promoted to Brigadier General on July 1, 1970. He was promoted to Major General on August 1, 1972, and promoted to Lieutenant General on June 1, 1973. He assumed duty as Vice Commander of the Military Airlift Command at Scott Air Force Base, Illinois, on September 1, 1975, and was promoted to full General on September 1, 1975. James was the First black American to be a full General in the history of the United States military. He was assigned as Commander in Chief of NORAD/ADCOM, North American Air Defense Command. General James had operational command of all United States and Canadian Strategic Aerospace Defense Forces. He was responsible for the Surveillance and Air Defense of North American Aerospace and for providing warning and assessment of hostile attack on the continent by bombers or missiles.

On February 1, 1978, Gen. Daniel "Chappie" James, Jr., ended a long military career at the top of the heap after beginning as a young black lieutenant who risked court-martial to fight racial segregation. The Air Force arranged full military honors for General James's retirement ceremony, which marked the close of his nearly 35 years of service, spanning three wars. At a farewell Pentagon news conference, he reflected with obvious satisfaction that he had made it to the top of the heap, a dream fulfilled.

The general was widely known for his speeches on Americanism and patriotism for which he was editorialized in numerous national and international publications. Excerpts from some of the speeches have been read into the Congressional Record. He was awarded the George Washington Freedom Foundation Medal in 1967 and again in 1968. He received the Arnold Air Society Eugene M. Zuckert Award in 1970 for outstanding contributions to Air Force professionalism as a "fighter pilot with a magnificent record, public speaker, and eloquent spokesman for the American Dream we so rarely achieve." The F-4C Phantom warplane flown by James sits outside the Aerospace Science and Health Education Center named in his honor at Tuskegee University. General James died on February 25, 1978.

James, Daniel, III

LIEUTENANT GENERAL — AIR FORCE

He was born in Tuskegee, Alabama, and he married the former Dana Marie Williams of San Diego. He is one of three children born to General and Mrs. Daniel "Chappie" James, Jr. General "Chappie" James was the national's first African American to attain four-star rank. As a member of a military family, Daniel James III lived in a variety of states and countries. He graduated from the American High School in Lakenheath, England, in 1963. Following his graduation, he enlisted in the United States Air Force Reserves and spent a year on extended active duty before continuing his education. He was awarded a Bachelor of Arts degree from the University of Arizona in 1968 with a major in Psychology. He was a distinguished graduate of the Air Force Reserve Officer Training Corps program and received his regular commission as a second lieutenant. His military education includes the Air Command and Staff College and the National Security Management Course.

He immediately entered undergraduate pilot training, completing the course a year later. In the first of two active duty tours in Southeast Asia, he served from June 1969 to August 1970, as a Forward Air Controller at Cam Ranh Bay Air Base in South Vietnam. He returned to the United States in August 1970, to serve as a Squadron Instructor Pilot, later as Squadron Flight Training Class Commander, at Williams Air Force Base, Arizona. From February 1973 to December 1973, he was assigned to the Headquarters of the United States Air Force in Washington, D.C., as an Operations Staff Officer. In June 1974, he was ordered to serve as Squadron Assistant Flight Commander at Udorn Republic of Thailand Air Force Base, Thailand. In May 1975, he was assigned as Squadron Pilot, later as Squadron Flight Commander, at Nellis Air Force Base, in Nevada.

In 1978, he separated from active duty to pursue a career as a commercial airline pilot. That year he joined the 182nd Fighter Squadron. He has served in a number of positions within the squadron and group before his assignment as the Vice Commander of the 149th Fighter Wing. He is a command pilot with over 4,000 hours in fighter and trainer aircraft. He is a combat veteran with over 300 missions in Vietnam.

He was promoted to Brigadier General on September 25, 1996. He was promoted to Major General on October 10, 1998, and appointed Adjutant General of the State of Texas with Headquarters at Camp Mabry,

Austin, Texas. He was responsible for formulating, developing, and coordinating all policies, plans and programs affecting the Army National Guard and the Air National Guard members in Texas. He was responsible for execution of both the Federal and State missions.

He was promoted to Lieutenant General on June 3, 2002, and selected to serve as the Director of the Air National Guard in Arlington, Virginia. He is responsible for formulating, developing and coordinating all policies, programs and plans affecting more than 104,000 Guards members, in 1,841 units.

General James' awards and decorations include the Legion of Merit; the Distinguished Flying Cross (with oak leaf cluster); Meritorious Service Medal; Air Medal (with six oak leaf clusters); Air Force Commendation Medal; Air Force Achievement Medal; Air Force Presidential Unit Citation; Air Force Outstanding Unit Award (with valor device); Combat Readiness Medal (with five devices); National Defense Service Medal (with one device); Vietnam Service Medal(with four devices); Air Force Longevity Service Award (with six devices); Armed Forces Reserve Medal; Small Arms Expert Marksmanship Ribbon; Air Forces Reserve Medal; Small Arms Expert Marksmanship Ribbon; Air Force Training Ribbon; Vietnam Gallantry Cross (with one device); Vietnam Campaign Medal; Long Star Distinguished Service Medal; Texas Outstanding Service Medal; Texas Medal of Merit; Governor's Unit Citation; Adjutant General's Individual Award; and Texas Faithful Service Medal (with three devices).

James, Nathaniel
MAJOR GENERAL—ARMY

He was born in Branchville, South Carolina. He married the former Mary Louise Kuykendall of New Orleans, and they have four children and four grandchildren. The children are Roslyn Rever Williams, Nathaniel Jr., Darryl and Eric Michael. The grandchildren are Adrien, Sean James, Amani, and Shana Williams. He graduated from Bronx Vocational High School in 1956, and received a Bachelor of Arts degree from the University of New York.

He was commissioned second lieutenant of artillery in June 1959 and was assigned to the New York Army National Guard. His assignments included Assistant Executive Officer in Field Artillery Batteries "A," "B," & "C" of the 970th Field Artillery Battalion. He served as Ammunition Officer, Executive Officer and Battery Commander/S-4 of Service Battery, 1st Howitzer Battalion 369th Field Artillery Battalion. His command was reorganized as a Transportation Battalion and he was additionally qualified as a Transportation Officer. He was assigned and served as Company Commander of both the 1469th, and 719th Transportation Companies, and the S-4, of the 569th Transportation Battalion. The battalion was reorganized as the 369th Transportation Battalion. He served as the Division Artillery Commander, and Division Support Command Commander, in the 42nd Infantry Division.

On January 5, 1988, he was assigned Assistant Adjutant General for New York and attached to the Headquarters Troop Command as the Deputy. He was promoted to Brigadier General on September 28, 1988. On June 1, 1989, he was assigned as Commander of Troop Command, New York Army National Guard. The General's picture hangs in a position of honor at the United States Field Artillery OCS Hall of Fame at Fort Sill, Oklahoma. General James was promoted to the rank of Major General on March 3, 1992.

The General's military decorations and awards includes the Meritorious Service Medal (with oak leaf cluster), Army Commendation Medal, Good Conduct Medal, Armed Forces Reserve Medal (with three oak leaf clusters), Army Achievement Medal, National Defense Medal (with oak leaf cluster), Reserve Components Medal, New York State's Long and Faithful Medal 35 years, New York State Commendation Medal, New Aid to Civil Authority Medal, New York Humanitarian Service Medal and the Ancient Order of Saint Barbara.

Jefferson, Eddie Lee
COMMAND SERGEANT MAJOR—ARMY

He was born in Holly Springs, Mississippi. He graduated from W.T. Simms High School in Holly Springs, Mississippi. He received an Associate of Art degree from St. Louis Community College and earned a Bachelor of Science degree from Western Kentucky University. He the United States Army at Fort Polk, Louisiana, on May 8, 1963. He attended the United States Army Airborne School at Fort Benning, Georgia, in 1963.

His first assignment was with Company B, 2nd Battalion, 503rd Infantry, 173rd Airborne Brigade on Okinawa, where his duties included ammo bearer, assistant gunner, gunner, and squad leader of a mortar squad, on a tour lasting eighteen months. His rank at this time was SP/4–E–4.

He returned to the United States on April 7, 1965, and was assigned to the 1st Infantry Division at Fort Riley, Kansas, for about three months and then as transferred to Fort Bragg, North Carolina, and assigned to Company A, 2nd Battalion, 3rd Brigade, 82nd Airborne Division, being sent to the Dominican Republic as a mortar squad leader. During this time he was promoted to Sergeant.

In August 1966, he returned to Fort Bragg, and remained with the 82nd Airborne Division unit May 1967, when he was sent to Fort Jackson, North Carolina, to attend the 3rd Army's Drill Instructor School. On June 20, 1968, he separated from active duty and the following year completed his six-year obligation before receiving his discharge. In February 1973, he joined the active Army Reserves, and was assigned to Company A, 1st Battalion, 335th Regiment, 85th Training Division (BCT) in St. Louis, Missouri. While a member of the 85th Division he was promoted to Sergeant First Class (E-7). In 1978, he was assigned to 5038th USARF School, 102nd ARCOM in St. Louis, Missouri, as a senior instructor of NCOES and other types of training. During this assignment he was promoted to Master Sergeant in 1980, and was appointed chief instructor and course manager of all NCOES. He was later promoted to assistant director of NCOES, a post he held until 1990. In 1990, he was promoted to Sergeant Major and was assigned as assistant director of enlisted courses with the 3290th USARF School in Nashville, Tennessee. In 1993, he was selected Command Sergeant Major of the 5010 United States Army Hospital in Louisville, Kentucky. In November 1994, he was assigned as Command Sergeant Major of the 332nd Medical Brigade in Nashville, Tennessee.

Jefferson, Varner
COMMAND SERGEANT MAJOR—ARMY

He entered the United States Army in May 1982. His military and civilian education includes all the Non-Commissioned Officer Education System Courses; the Manager Development Course; Supervisor Development Course; Radiation Safety Course; Military Operations on Urban Terrain Course; Physical Security Course; Instructor Training Course; the Master Fitness Course; Drill Sergeant School; the United States Army First Sergeant Course; and the United States Army Sergeants Major Academy. He earned an associate's degree from Gadsden State Community College; a Bachelor of Science degree from Excelsior College; and a Graduate Certificate in Emergency and Disaster Management from Touro University.

His military assignments include serving as Company NBC Non-Commissioned Officer (NCO), 2nd Maintenance Company in South Korea; as Battalion NBC Non-Commissioned Officer (NCO), 8th Engineer Battalion, 1st Cavalry Division; as Brigade NBC Non-Commissioned Officer, Engineer Brigade, 1st Cavalry Division as Squad Leader, 44th Chemical Company, 2nd Armored Division; as Squad Leader, 4th Chemical Company, 2nd Infantry Division, in

South Korea; as Drill Sergeant, D Company, 82nd Chemical Battalion; as Instructor, Headquarters and Headquarters Company, 84th Chemical Battalion; as First Sergeant, Headquarters and Headquarters Detachment, Engineer Brigade, 1st Cavalry Division; as First Sergeant, Headquarters and Headquarters Detachment, 2nd Chemical Battalion; as First Sergeant, 44th Chemical Company, 2nd Chemical Battalion; as First Sergeant, 31st Chemical Company, 2nd Chemical Battalion; as First Sergeant 7th Chemical Company, 83rd Chemical Battalion; as the Chemical Sergeant Major, 3rd Infantry Division; and as the Command Sergeant Major, 23rd Chemical Battalion.

Jenkins, C.C., Jr.
COMMAND SERGEANT MAJOR—ARMY

He was born in Yazoo City, Mississippi. He completed Basic Combat Training and Advanced Individual Training at Fort Leonard Wood, Missouri, in 1977. His military education includes all the Noncommissioned Officers Education System Courses; NBC Course; Battle Staff Course; Truck Master Curse; the Logistics Management Course; the Noncommissioned Officer Logistics Program; and the United States Army Sergeants Major Academy. He also holds a Masters of Science (Management) and an associate's degree in Applied Science (Transportation). He is the first recipient of the annual C.C. Jenkins' Student Recognition Award presented by City Colleges Chicago.

He has served in a variety of key assignments to include Operation Sergeant and S3 Noncommissioned Officer in Charge for the 330th Corps at Fort Bragg, North Carolina; Division Transportation Noncommissioned Officer in Charge for G4, 2nd Infantry Division at Camp Red Cloud, South Korea; G3 Support Operations Sergeant Major; Command Sergeant Major of the 330th Movement Control Battalion; Command Sergeant Major for Troop Support Battalion; Operation Command Sergeant Major, 1st COSCOM, XVIII Airborne Corps, at Fort Bragg, North Carolina; Command Sergeant Major, 44th Corps Support Battalion, 593rd Corps Support Group, 1st Corps, at Fort Lewis, Washington. In September 2004, he was serving as the Command Sergeant Major at the HQ 2nd Infantry Division DISCOM Command Team at Camp Casey, Dongduchon, South Korea.

Jenkins, Kenneth

COMMAND SERGEANT MAJOR—ARMY

CSM Jenkins is a native of St. Helena Island, South Carolina. He graduated from Beaufort High School in June 1979 and entered the United States Army. He attended Basic Training at Fort Knox, Kentucky, in June 1979 and Advanced Infantry Training at Fort Benning, Georgia.

He has served in a variety of leadership positions including the Senior Noncommissioned Officer Advisor to the 29th Infantry Division Field Training Group; First Sergeant; Platoon Sergeant; Squad Leader and Team Leader.

Jenkins, Samuel Edward

COMMAND SERGEANT MAJOR—ARMY

He entered the United States Army at Fort Jackson, South Carolina, in 1951. He received fourteen weeks of Basic Training and Advanced Individual Training in the 42nd Company, 40th Infantry Battalion, at Schofield Barracks, Hawaii.

His military and civilian education includes the SEA Loading Course, United States Marines; Explosive Ordinance Recognition Course; Air Transportation Ability Course; Non Commissioned Officers Academy 25th Infantry Division; CBR Detection and Decontamination Course; Emergency Medical Care Course; Jungle Operation Course; Senior Non-Commissioned Officer Course; Staff NCO Course; and Racial Awareness Course. He holds an Associates of Arts in Business Administration from Dekalb College; and an Associate of Arts in Business Management from Phillips College. He also attended one year of Law School and Federal Law Enforcement Training Center Course.

His key military assignments include service from 1951 to 1952 with the 24th Infantry Regiment, 25th Infantry Division, in Korea during the war. In 1954, he returned to Korea as a Machine Gun Platoon Section Sergeant, Company H, 7th Infantry Regiment, 3rd Infantry Division. In 1957, he served as a Platoon Sergeant and Mortar Instructor, Company C, 7th Battalion, 2nd Regiment, at Fort Jackson, South Carolina. In 1960, he served as Platoon and Section Sergeant, 13th Infantry and 18th Infantry Battle Group 8th Infantry Division at Mannheim, West Germany. He served as an Instructor for Basic Training Personnel, Basic Signal Personnel (OCS), Basic Military Police Personnel, at Fort Gordon, Georgia. In 1967, he was Platoon and First Sergeant in Company B, 5th Battalion, 3rd Infantry, 6th Infantry Division, at Chu Che, South Vietnam. In 1968, he was First Sergeant for Company B, 5th Battalion, 3rd Infantry, 6th Infantry Division, at Fort Campbell, Kentucky. In 1970, he became First Sergeant of Company B, 2nd Battalion, 1st Basic Combat Training Brigade, at Fort Gordon, Georgia. From 1971 to 1974, he served as First Sergeant for Company A, 14th Battalion, 4th Advanced Individual Training Brigade at Fort Jackson, South Carolina. From 1974 to 1975, he was First Sergeant for the 2nd AG Company, 2nd Infantry Division, at Camp Casey, South Korea. In 1975, he was selected to serve as Sergeant Major at Headquarters Committee Group, 1st Brigade, Fort Gordon, Georgia. In 1978, he was assigned as the Command Sergeant Major, 1st Battalion, 1st Signal Training Brigade, at Fort Gordon, Georgia.

Jiggetts, Charles B.

BRIGADIER GENERAL—AIR FORCE

He was born in Henderson, North Carolina, and married the former Barbara Mosley of Frederica, Delaware. They have one daughter, Victoria Lynn. He was graduated from high school at Henderson Institute in 1943 and received a Bachelor of Arts degree in Political Science from Howard University in 1950. He graduated from Squadron Officer School at Maxwell Air Force Base, Alabama, in 1957 and completed Air Command and Staff College in 1963. He completed the Air War College in 1970 and the Industrial College of the Armed Forces Associates program in 1972.

In 1944 he enlisted in the United States Army Air Forces and was honorably discharged in May 1946. He was commissioned a second lieutenant in August 1950 through the Reserve Officers Training Corps program. His initial assignment was as a group Adjutant and Supply Officer with the Basic Military Training Center at Sampson Air Force Base, New York. He attended flying school at James Connally Air Force Base, Texas, in 1952 and later became an aircraft observer and radar intercept officer. He served in that capacity at Tyndall Air Force Base, Florida; McGuire Air Force Base, New Jersey; and Elmendorf Air Force Base, Alaska.

In July 1957 he joined the 98th Fighter-Interceptor Squadron at Dover Air Force Base, Delaware, as Flight and later Squadron Radar Officer. He attended the Communications Officer Course at Keesler Air Force Base, Mississippi, in 1959. Upon completion of the course in 1960, he was assigned to the 27th Communications Squadron at Anderson Air Force Base, Guam, as Squadron Operations Officer. In June 1963, General Jiggetts was a Maintenance Officer, chief of maintenance, and wing communications-electronics officer with the 92nd Strategic Aerospace Wing at Fairchild Air Force Base, Washington. The wing had operational responsibility for Fairchild-based Atlas E intercontinental ballistic missiles, B-52 bombers, and KC-135tanker planes. Transferring to the Headquarters of the Seventh Air Force at Tan Son Nhut Air Base, South Vietnam, in May 1966, the general served as a Communications-Electronics Requirements Officer. General Jiggetts returned to the United States in May 1967 as a joint Communications Staff Officer with the United Strike Command at MacDill Air Force Base, Florida. In August 1969 he was assigned to the Headquarters of the United States Air Force in Washington, D.C. as Technical Assistant to the Director for Telecommunications Policy in the Office of the Assistant Secretary of Defense (Installations and Logistics). He next served at Headquarters Strategic Air Command at Offutt Air Force Base, Nebraska, as Chief of the Program Management Division for Communications-Electronics.

From September 1971 to July 1974, General Jiggetts served as Military Assistant to the Director of the Office of Telecommunications Policy in the Executive Office of the President of the United States in Washington, D.C. He then became Vice Commander of the Air Force Communications Command's Northern Communications Area at Griffiss Air Force Base, New York. He served as Commander of the Northern Communications Area from July 1976 to June 1979. The general transferred to Pacific Command at Camp H. M. Smith, Hawaii, as Director of Communications and Data Processing (later reorganized as Directorate of Command,

Control, and Communications System), J-6. In February 1981 he was assigned to Scott Air Force Base as Air Force Communications Command's Deputy Commander for Combat Communications and Reserve Force Matters. He assumed his present duties in July 1981.

He was appointed Brigadier General on April 1, 1977, with date of rank March 29, 1977. He retired November 1, 1982.

His military decorations and awards include the Distinguished Service Medal, Defense Superior Service Medal, Legion of Merit (with one oak leaf cluster), Bronze Star, Meritorious Service Medal, Joint Service Commendation Medal, and the Air Force Commendation Medal. He also wears the Air Traffic Controller's Badge.

Johns, Rudolph
COMMAND SERGEANT MAJOR—ARMY

He served as the Command Sergeant Major for the 123 Signal Battalion, 3rd Infantry Division (Mechanized), at Fort Stewart, Georgia. He served with the 3rd Infantry Division during the War with Iraq.

Command Sergeant Major Rudy Johns enlisted in

the Army on the Delayed Entry Program as a Private E-2 on May 31, 1979. He attended Basic Training and AIT at Fort Gordon, Georgia. He was assigned to the 8th Engineer Battalion at Fort Hood, Texas. In 1985, he attended and graduated from Airborne School at Fort Benning, Georgia. In 1993, he attended the Sergeant Major's Academy at Fort Bliss, Texas.

Johnson, Alan Douglas
MAJOR GENERAL—ARMY

Johnson was born in Kakamura, Japan. He and his

wife, Elfriede, have four daughters, Mrs. Kim Adams, Mrs. Noelle Kain, Mrs. Erika Powell, and Nichol Johnson. They have four grandchildren. He graduated from the Field Artillery Officer Candidate School in 1970, and was commissioned as a Second Lieutenant. He has a Bachelor of Science degree in Business, a master's degree in Business Administration, and a master's degree in National Security and Strategic Studies. His military schooling includes the Field Artillery Officer Basic and Advanced Courses; the Command and General Staff College; and the Naval War College.

General Johnson was assigned to Fort Carson, Colorado, in 1970, where he served in various positions. He then joined the 23rd Infantry Division (America) in Vietnam as a Forward Observer and Fire Direction Officer. He was assigned to the 2nd Battalion, 18th Field Artillery at Fort Sill, Oklahoma, in 1972 where he served as S-1 and Battery Commander. From 1976 until 1979, he served as an Area Commander in the Long Island Recruiting District. He then joined the 1st Armored Division in West Germany where he served as Battery Commander and Battalion S-3.

After a tour as the Assistant Professor of Military Sciences at the University of Colorado, he went to Fort Carson where he served as the Executive Officer of the 3rd Battalion, 29th Field Artillery, and Deputy Fire Support Officer and S-3, 4th Infantry Division Artillery, from 1986 to 1988. He returned to the 1st Armored Division and Commanded the 6th Battalion, 1st Field Artillery. He served as an Army Staff Officer in the Office of the Deputy Chief of Staff for Operations and Plans, Force Programs from 1992 to 1993. He was promoted to Colonel on April 1, 1993.

In May 1993, he came back to Fort Carson and commanded the 4th Infantry Division Artillery (Mechanized). From June 1995 to January 1996, he served as Chief of Staff of the 4th Infantry Division (Mechanized) at Fort Carson. In January 1996, he was selected to serve as the Chief of Staff, with the 4th Infantry Division (Mechanized), at Fort Carson. In September 1996, he served as Director of Plans, J-5, at the United States Space Command at Peterson Air Force Base, Colorado. He was promoted to Brigadier General on October 1, 1996. From August 1998 to June 2000, he served as Deputy Commanding General of the First United States Army (North) at Fort George G. Meade, Maryland. In June 2000, he was assigned as the Commanding General of the United States Army in Japan/ 9th Theater Support Command.

On January 1, 2000, he was promoted to Major General. He retired from the military on January 1, 2003.

His military awards and decorations include the Legion of Merit; the Meritorious Service Medal (with five oak leaf clusters); the Air Medal; the Commendation Medal (with one oak leaf cluster); the Army Achievement Medal; the Vietnamese Cross of Gallantry; and the Army Staff Identification Badge.

Johnson, Anthony J.
COMMAND MASTER CHIEF—NAVY

He is a native of Chicago, Illinois, and a graduate of Richard T. Crane High School. He entered the Navy in July 1977 and attended recruit training at Recruit Training Command, San Diego, California. He holds a Bachelor of Science degree in Business Management from Hampton University.

Following completion of recruit training in September 1977, he reported to Naval Technical Training Center in Meridian, Mississippi, to attend Storekeeper "A" School and then to Indian Head, Maryland. During this tour he was assigned to the Naval School Explosive Ordnance Disposal (NAVSCOLEOD) where he was advanced to Storekeeper Third Class.

While assigned to USS *Reuben James* he was the Supply Leading Chief Petty Officer, Section Leader and Helicopter Control Officer, and while assigned to USS *Fisc* in Yokosuka, Japan, he was assigned as Chief Master at Arms. He also served as the Technical Advisor to the Supply Enlisted Community Manager (CNO/N1). In October 2004, he was serving as Command Master Chief, assigned to Yellow Jackets of VAQRON 138 home ported in Whidbey Island, Washington. He deployed onboard USS *Carl Vinson* (CVN70).

Johnson, Anthony R.
COMMAND SERGEANT MAJOR—ARMY

He is a 1977 graduate of Morehead Senior High School in Eden, North Carolina. He enlisted in the United States Army in June 1977, and attended Basic Combat Training and Advanced Individual Training at Fort Knox, Kentucky.

His military and civilian education includes all the Noncommissioned Officer Courses; Support Operations Course Phase I; Battle Staff Course; First Sergeant Course; and the United States Army Sergeants Major Academy. He holds a Bachelor of Arts degree in Business

Administration from Chaminade University in Honolulu, Hawaii.

His key leadership assignments include serving as Platoon Sergeant and Repair Control Sergeant for B Company, 782nd Maintenance, 82nd Airborne Division at Fort Bragg, North Carolina; Mobile Maintenance Team Chief for the 536th Maintenance Company, 17th Corps Support Battalion; Support Operations Maintenance Noncommissioned Officer for Headquarters and Headquarters Detachment, 17th Corps Support Battalion at Schofield Barracks, Hawaii; S-3 Operations Sergeant Major in Headquarters and Headquarters Company DISCOM, 2nd Infantry Division at Camp Casey, South Korea; S-3 Operations Sergeant Major for the 25th Infantry Division (Light), Support Command at Schofield Barracks; and Command Sergeant Major for the 325th Forward Support Battalion, 25th Infantry Division.

Johnson, Arthur J.
REAR ADMIRAL—NAVY

He is a native of Burlington, Vermont. He graduated from the United Naval Academy in May 1979 with a Bachelor of Science degree in International Security Affairs. In June 1994, he graduated with a master's degree in Public Administration from Harvard University's John F. Kennedy School of Government, where his studies focused on U.S. Business and Government Relationships and Third World Politics. He is also a member of the Millennium Class at the National War College in Washington, D.C. and was awarded a master's degree in National Strategic Studies in June 2000.

Rear Admiral Johnson attended flight training in Pensacola, Florida, and earned his Naval Aviator Wings of Gold in February 1981. He served in command and various staff positions in Hawaii; California; Keflavik,

Iceland; and the Pentagon. He deployed extensively throughout the Arabian Gulf, Indian Ocean, and Pacific region. Afloat, he served as Operations Officer, Administrative Assistant, as well as Sea and Anchor Detail Officer of the Deck onboard USS *Carl Vinson* (CVN 70), where he earned Third Fleet's Ship Handler of the Year honors for 1990.

He completed command tours at Naval Air Station Barbers Point, Hawaii, where he commanded the "Golden Swordsmen" of Patrol Squadron 47 and at Naval Air Station Brunswick, Maine, as Commander of Patrol and Reconnaissance Wing Five. He served as the Assistant Deputy Director for Politico-Military Affairs-Asia in the Strategic Plans and Policy Directorate of the Joint Staff.

His awards include the Defense Superior Service Medal; the Legion of Merit; the Meritorious Service Medal (two awards); the Navy Commendation Medal (five awards) and the Navy Achievement Medal.

Johnson, Carolina D.
FIRST SERGEANT—ARMY

She is a native of Marianna, Florida, and entered the United States Army in May 1985. She attended Basic Combat Training and Advanced Individual Training at Fort Jackson, South Carolina. She holds a master's degree in Human Resource Management from Troy State University. Her military education includes all the Noncommissioned Officer Education System Courses; the Battle Staff Course; and the First Sergeant Course.

She has held numerous key military assignments, including serving as FORSCOM Enlisted Strength Manager; Detachment First Sergeant; Senior Personnel

Sergeant; Enlisted Records Team Sergeant; and Squad Leader. In October 2004, she was serving as the First Sergeant for Joint Sub-Regional Command South-Central with the United States Army, NATO.

Johnson, Charles D.
COMMAND SERGEANT MAJOR

He is a native of Birmingham, Alabama. He entered the United States Army in 1979. His military education includes all the Noncommissioned Officer Education System Courses; the First Sergeant Course; Air Assault School; Senior Leaders Course; the United States Army Safety Course; and the United States Army Sergeants Major Academy.

His assignments include serving as Gunner; Section Chief; Gunnery Sergeant; Platoon Sergeant; and First Sergeant. In August 2004, he was serving as the Command Sergeant Major for the 6th Brigade, 1st Region Sergeant Major, with the 3rd Infantry Division (Mechanized) at Fort Stewart, Georgia.

Johnson, Clarence E.
LIEUTENANT COLONEL—ARMY

Lieutenant Colonel Clarence E. Johnson is a distinguished military graduate of Texas College, class of 1983. He earned a Bachelor of Science degree in Business Administration, and a Master of Science degree in Acquisition Management from the Florida Institute of Technology. His military education includes the Air Defense Artillery (ADA) Officer Basic and Advanced Courses; the Army Command and General Staff College; and the Advanced Program Manager's Course.

His troop assignments include serving as Vulcan and Stinger Platoon Leader, Maintenance Officer and Executive Officer with the 3-67 Air Defense Artillery; 3rd Infantry Division in Kitizgen, Germany; Battalion Main-

tenance Officer; Commander of B Battery, Assistant S-3, and Operations Officer 2-44 Air Defense Artillery; 101st Airborne (Air Assault) at Fort Campbell, Kentucky. Lieutenant Colonel Johnson assumed Command of the Ronald Reagan Ballistic Missile Defense Test Site (RTS) at the United States Army Kwajalein Atoll (USAKA) on July 24, 2001. Before arriving at USAKA, Johnson served as a Department of the Army Systems Coordinator (DASC) on the Theater High Altitude Area Defense (THAAD) and the Navy's Cooperative Engagement Capability (CEC) systems.

Johnson, Clifton H.
COMMAND SERGEANT MAJOR—ARMY

He entered the United States Army in August 1983 and attended Basic Combat and Advanced Individual

Training at Fort Jackson, South Carolina. His military and civilian education includes all the Noncommissioned Officer Education System Courses; the Battle Staff Course; Master Fitness Course; the First Sergeant Course; and the United States Army Sergeants Major Academy (class 53). He earned an associate's degree in Business Administration from Northwest Business College and holds a Bachelors of Arts degree in Liberal Arts from Excelsior College.

In August 2004, he was serving as the Battalion Command Sergeant Major, 26th Fire Support Battalion, 3rd Infantry Division, at Fort Stewart, Georgia.

Johnson, Darfus L.
LIEUTENANT COLONEL—ARMY

He was commissioned as a Second Lieutenant of Infantry from Prairie View A&M University in 1984. His military education includes the Infantry Basic and Advanced Courses; the Command and General Staff College; and the School of Advanced Military Studies at Fort Leavenworth, Kansas. He holds a bachelor's degree in Political Science from Prairie View A&M University; and a master's degree in Military Arts and Science from SAMS at Fort Leavenworth, Kansas.

His military assignments include serving as Commander of Headquarters and Headquarters Troops for the Combat Aviation Brigade in the 2nd Armored Division during Operations Desert Shield/Desert Storm. From 1999 to 2000, he was assigned to the 3rd Infantry Division Headquarters at Fort Stewart, Georgia, as the Chief of G-4, during the 3rd Infantry Division train-up and preparation for deployment in support of NATO operations in Bosnia. From 2000 to 2002, he was assigned as the Deputy Commander of the 24th Corps Support Group at Fort Stewart. He was assigned to the 3rd United States Army with duty as the Army Central Command—Saudi Arabia Assistant Chief of Staff G-4 during Operations Desert Shift and Enduring Freedom. In August 2002, he returned to Fort Hood, and was assigned as the III Corps Transportation Officer.

Johnson, Delouris
SERGEANT MAJOR—MARINES

She was born in Gainesville, Florida, and enlisted into the United States Marine Corps in February 1963. She completed Recruit Training at Marine Corps Recruit Depot at Parris Island, South Carolina. She is a graduate of the Marine Corps Recruiter School; the First Sergeants School at Parris Island; and the United States Army Sergeants Major Academy.

She has held numerous leadership positions including serving as a Recruiter in Philadelphia and Washington, D.C.; as the Administration Chief in the Force Supply Office for Fleet Marine Force, Atlantic, at Norfolk Base, Virginia; and as Supply Chief at Marine Corps Air Station at Tustin, California. She made history when she was assigned as the First Female First Sergeant assigned to Bravo Company, Infantry Training School, Marine Corps Base at Camp Pendleton, California. She was then assigned as First Sergeant for Alpha Company, Engineer Support Battalion (REIN), 3rd Force Service Support Group, and later served as First Sergeant of the Engineer Support Company of the First Service Support Group. In 1982, she was selected to serve as Sergeant Major for the Headquarters of the Service Battalion and the 1st Medical Battalion. She was promoted to Sergeant Major in 1983, and in October 1984, she was assigned as Sergeant Major at the Marine Corps Base Camp Lejeune, North Carolina. In 1988, she was selected to serve as Sergeant Major at HMT-301, MAG-16, 3D, Marine Air Wing, Tustin.

Johnson, Frederick B.
COMMAND SERGEANT MAJOR—ARMY

Command Sergeant Major Frederick B. Johnson was born in Jacksonville, Texas. He earned an associate's degree in Business Management from Parks Community College. He entered the Army in November 1974, and received his Basic Training and Advanced Individual Training at Fort Knox, Kentucky. He completed his training and was assigned to the 4th Battalion, 73rd Armor at Bobligen, West Germany as his first Armored Unit. As an Armored Crewman, he has held positions from Loader to Tank Commander.

His most recent assignments include serving as the Command Sergeant Major of the 2nd Battalion, 34th Armor, 1st Brigade, 1st Infantry Division; as the Group Command Sergeant Major of Operations Group at Fort Irwin, California; and as Command Sergeant Major in Bosnia-Herzegovina in support of Operation Joint Endeavor.

Johnson, Gilbert H.
SERGEANT MAJOR—MARINES

Sergeant Major Gilbert Johnson entered Stillman College in Alabama in 1922, aspiring to become a minister. He left college the following year and joined the Army. At the end of his enlistment in October 1929, Johnson was discharged as a corporal. After four years of civilian life, he decided to try the Navy. The Navy accepted Johnson into the Steward's Branch, the only job available to blacks at that time, and he served for nearly 10 years. Johnson was aboard the USS *Wyoming* during the bombing of Pearl Harbor in December 1941.

The following year, when President Franklin D. Roosevelt ordered the integration of the Armed Forces, Johnson requested transfer from the Navy to the Ma-

rine Corps. He went on to serve the last 17 years of his 32 year military career in the Marine Corps. In 1943, he was among the first black men to be trained as Marine Drill Instructors. He also served as Field Sergeant in Charge of all recruit drill training at Montford Point. He served in the Korean War with the 1st Shore Party Battalion then later with the 2nd Battalion, 1st Marines and finally as Administrative Advisor at the Headquarters of the Korean Marine Corps.

He became one of the first black Sergeants Major in the Marine Corps. He transferred to the Fleet Marine Force Reserve in 1957 and retired in 1959. He died of a heart attack on August 5, 1972, in Jacksonville, North Carolina, while addressing an annual meeting of the Montford Point Marine Association.

On April 19, 1974, the Montford Point Facility at Camp Lejeune was dedicated as Camp Gilbert H. Johnson, Montford Point, in honor of the outstanding Marine.

Johnson, James Avery
REAR ADMIRAL—NAVY

He was born in Wilmington, North Carolina, and spent his formative years in Chicago, Illinois, and Washington, D.C. He earned his undergraduate degree at the University of Rochester in Rochester, New York. He served both his internship and residency at the University of California at Los Angeles.

He was commissioned in the Ensign 1915 program in 1966. His early assignments included serving as the Senior Medical Officer aboard the amphibious assault ship USS *New Orleans*, and as a General Medical Officer at Marine Corps Recruit Depot, California. During a subsequent assignment to the Naval Hospital at Camp Pendleton, California, he held a progression of assignments such as Staff Surgeon; Chairman of the Department of Surgery; and finally Director of Surgical Services.

ican Medical Association, National Medical Association, American Medical Association, American College of Physician Executives, Association of Military Surgeons of the United States, and Society of Medical Consultants to the Armed Forces.

His military decorations include the Defense Superior Service Medal; the Legion of Merit; Meritorious Service Medal; the Navy and Marine Corps Commendation Medal; the Joint Meritorious Unit Citation; Navy Meritorious Unit Citation; National Defense Medal; Vietnam Service Medal; Armed Forces Service Medal; Humanitarian Service Medal; Philippine Presidential Unit Citation, United Nations Medal (Yugoslavia); the NATO Medal; and the Vietnam Campaign Medal.

Johnson, James E.
DEPUTY SECRETARY OF THE NAVY

In 1967 James E Johnson became the first black in U.S. Naval History to be appointed to the Secretariat in the Department of the Navy. He had served as Vice Chairman of the U.S. Civil Service Commission. He was born in Madison, Illinois, on March 3, 1926, and holds a Bachelor of Science degree from George Washington University and a Law Degree from the University of Maryland. He served as Legal Officer and Military Instructor for the U.S. Marine Corps and as Public Relations Officer for liaison between foreign countries and U.S. Military Bases in Asia.

Johnson, Janice M.
COLONEL—MARINES

She enlisted in the Marine Corps in 1968 right out of high school, and served three years before enrolling in college. After receiving her degree in 1975, she received a commission in the Marine as a second lieutenant. She

He was next assigned to Naval Hospital, San Diego, as Assistant Chairman of the Department of Surgery. In 1989, he was transferred to Washington, D.C., where he held the position of Deputy Chief of the Medical Corps. Upon transfer to San Diego in July 1991, he was assigned as Medical Director at Naval Hospital San Diego, and was subsequently named Deputy Commander, a position which he held until February 1994. During his next assignment, he assumed Command of Fleet Hospital Six, which deployed on a United Nations mission in Croatia. In October 1994, he became the Commanding Officer of Naval Hospital, Bremerton, Washington, where he served until August 1997. He was then selected as the Principal Director for Clinical and Program Policy in the Office of the Assistant Secretary of Defense for Health Affairs. In August 1998, Admiral Johnson was reassigned as Medical Officer of the Marine Corps Headquarters, in Washington, D.C. In October 2001, he assumed command of Naval Medical Center San Diego and became Lead Agent, TRICARE Region Nine. He assumed duties as the Regional Director of TRICARE Regional Office-West (TROWest) in November 2003, the first of three Regional Directors to be named, overseeing health care contracts and the health care delivery system in twenty states with more than 2,000,000 TRICARE eligible beneficiaries.

He earned certificates from the American Board of Surgery and the American Board of Medical Management. He is an Assistant Clinical Professor of Surgery at the Uniformed Services University of Health Sciences. His affiliation with civilian medical organizations include his status as a Fellow of the American College of Surgeons, and he is a member of the Amer-

became the first black female in the Marine Corps' 223 year history to obtain the grade of Colonel.

Johnson, Jerome

MAJOR GENERAL—ARMY

A native Georgian, he was commissioned a second lieutenant in the Ordnance Corps on July 7, 1973, after graduation from Fort Valley State University, Georgia. While at Fort Valley State University, he received honors as Distinguished Military Graduate and received a bachelor's degree in Business Administration. He also holds a Master of Business Administration from Syra-

cuse University in New York. His military education includes completion of the Ordnance Officer Basic and Advance Courses; the Senior Service College-Advance Operational Studies Fellowship; the Command and General Staff College; and Ordnance Officer Mobilization Advanced Course.

From November 1973 to September 1974, he was assigned as a Maintenance Officer with the 67th Maintenance Battalion, 36th Engineer Group, at the United States Army Infantry Center at Fort Benning, Georgia. From September 1974 to December 1977, he served as a Maintenance Officer, later as Shop Officer, later Supply and Service Officer, later as Company Commander, with the 598th Light Maintenance Company, 67th Maintenance Battalion, 36th Engineer Group, at the United States Army Infantry Center at Fort Benning. He was promoted to Captain on July 7, 1977. From August 1978 to June 1981, he was assigned as a Personnel Distribution Officer at the United States Total Army Personnel Command in Alexandria, Virginia. From June 1983 to January 1988, he was assigned as an Financial Management Officer, later Chief of the Finance Management Office, later Chief of Force Modernization Division, later Executive Officer, with the 21st Support Command, United States Army Europe and Seventh Army, in West Germany. He was promoted to Major on November 1, 1984.

From January 1988 to May 1990, he served as Program Analyst, later Logistics Staff Officer, in the Office of the Deputy Chief of Staff for Logistics, United States Army, in Washington, D.C. From May 1990 to May 1992, he served as the Commander of the 227th Maintenance Battalion, Eighth United States Army, in South Korea. He was promoted to Lieutenant Colonel on April 1, 1990.

His military assignments include serving as Executive Officer to the Deputy Commanding General of the United States Army Materiel Command at Alexandria, and as Group/Brigade Commander with the 29th Support Group in Kaiserslautern, Germany. In May 1993, he was assigned as Director of Campaign Planning at the School of Advanced Military Studies of the United States Army Command and General Staff College at Fort Leavenworth, Kansas. From July 1994 to June 1996, he served as Chief of Staff, later Deputy Commander/Support Operation Officer, 3rd Corps Support Command, United States Army Europe and Seventh Army, in Germany. He was promoted to Colonel on August 1, 1995. In June 1996, he was assigned as Commander of the 29th Support Group, 21st Theater Army Area Command, in Germany. He returned to the United States in July 1998, to assume the assignment of Executive Officer to the Deputy Commanding General of United States Army Materiel Command in Alexandria. In August 1999, he was selected the Commanding General of United States Army Field Support Command at Rock Island Arsenal, Illinois. On July 27, 2001, he was selected as the Director of Plans, Operations, and Readiness, G-4, United States Army at the Pentagon. He was promoted to Brigadier General on October 1, 2000.

In June 2004, he was again assigned as the Commanding General of United States Army Field Support Command at Rock Island Arsenal. He was promoted to Major General in March 17, 2005.

His military awards and decorations include the Legion of Merit (with two oak leaf clusters); the Meritorious Service Medal (with four oak leaf clusters); Army Commendation Medal; National Defense Service Medal; Armed Forces Service Medal; the Armed Forces Reserve Medal; NATO Medal; and the Army Staff Identification Badge.

Johnson, Julius Frank
BRIGADIER GENERAL—ARMY

Born at Fort Leavenworth, Kansas, he received a Bachelor of Science degree in Social Science from Lincoln University and a Doctor of Medicine in Counseling Psychology. He received a ROTC commission to Second Lieutenant in February 1964.

From February 1964 to April 1964, he was a student in the United States Army Infantry Center and School at Fort Benning, Georgia. From June 1964 to July 1965, he served as a rifle Platoon Leader, later Reconnaissance Platoon Leader, later Assistant S-3 Operations Officer, Headquarters, 3rd Battalion, 32nd Infantry, Eighth United States Army, in Korea. From July 1965 to January 1967, he was assigned as a Platoon Leader, later Commander, Company E (Honor Guard), 1st Battalion, 3rd Infantry (Old Guard), at Fort Meyer, Virginia.

He was promoted to 1st Lieutenant on August 1, 1965, and Captain on November 1, 1966. From January 1967 to March 1967, he was a student in the Special Forces Officer Qualification Course of the United States Army Special Warfare School at Fort Bragg, North Carolina. From July 1967 to June 1968, he served as Adjutant, 1st Battalion, 327th Infantry; later Commander, Company A, 1st Battalion, 327th Infantry;

later S-4 Logistics Officer, 1st Battalion, 327th Infantry, 101st Airborne Division, United States Army, Vietnam.

From June 1968 to July 1969, he was a Platoon Adviser in the 2nd Student Battalion, Student Brigade, and was later a student at the United States Army Infantry Center and School at Fort Benning, Georgia. From July 1969 to July 1972, he served as Assistant Professor of Military Science at Lincoln University in Jefferson City, Missouri. From July 1972 to February 1973, he was the Commander of the Mobile Security Training Team, then the S-3 (Operations) Officer for Field Training Command, United States Military Advisory Group, Military Assistance Command, Vietnam.

From April 1973 to June 1974, he was assigned as the Operations Officer in the Department of Non-Resident Instruction, and later a student at the United States Army Command and General Staff College at Fort Leavenworth. From July 1974 to May 1976, he served first as Operations Officer, G-2 (Intelligence), Staff, United States Army Element, I Corps Group, Eighth United States Army, Korea, later as the S-3 (Operations) Officer, 4th Brigade, 2nd Infantry Division, with the United States Army in Korea. From June 1976 to April 1981, he was Personnel Management Officer in the Officer Personnel Management Division at the United States Army Military Personnel Center in Alexandria, Virginia, then Personnel Staff Officer, Officer Division, in the Office of the Deputy Chief of Staff for Personnel, United States Army, in Washington, D.C.

He was promoted to Major on June 9, 1976, and Lieutenant Colonel on July 14, 1979. From June 1981 to June 1983, he was Commander of the 2nd Battalion, 36th Infantry, 3rd Armored Division, United States Army, in Europe. From June 1983 to June 1984, he was a student at the United States Army War College at Carlisle Barracks, Pennsylvania. From June 1984 to March 1985, he was Director of Operations (J-3) for the Armed Forces Inaugural Committee at Fort Lesley J. McNair, in Washington, D.C.

He was promoted to Colonel on November 1, 1984. From February 1988 to July 1989, he served as Director of Joint Staff on the Armed Forces Inaugural Committee in Washington, D.C. From July 1989 to June 1990, he was Assistant Division Commander of the 1st Armored Division, United States Army, Europe, and the Seventh Army. He was promoted to Brigadier General on September 1, 1989.

In June 1990 he was assigned as Commanding General of the First Reserve Officer Training Corps Region at Fort Bragg, North Carolina. He retired from the military on August 31, 1993.

He has received numerous awards and decorations, including the Silver Star, the Bronze Star (with two oak leaf clusters), Defense Meritorious Service Medal, Defense Superior Service Medal, Meritorious Service Medal, Air Medal, Army Commendation Medal (with oak leaf cluster), Combat Infantryman Badge, Parachutist Badge, and Air Assault Badge.

Johnson, Karen
LIEUTENANT COLONEL—AIR FORCE

She was born in Jersey City, New Jersey, and she joined the Air Force as a Nurse. Through an Air Force sponsored education, Johnson received a Bachelor of Science degree in 1977. In 1980, she was selected "Nurse of the Year" at the Air Force's largest Medical Center in San Antonio, Texas.

During her military career, she served a year in Thailand, and on Air Force Bases as the hospital's Equal Opportunity and Treatment Officer. In 1992, she retired from the military.

Johnson, Leon A.
BRIGADIER GENERAL—AIR FORCE

He entered the Air Force in 1971 as a distinguished graduate of the Oregon State University Reserve Officer Training Corps program, earning a Bachelor of Science degree in Political Science. He has commanded an Air Force Reserve Fighter Squadron and a Reserve Fight Group. He joined the Air Force Reserve as a traditional reservist in 1980, entered the Air Reserve Technician program as a full-time civil service employee in April 1982, and returned to the traditional reservist program in 1986. He is a command pilot with more than 3,400 flying hours in the A-10, A-37, and T-37.

In May 1986, as Chief of Wing Training in the 442nd Tactical Fighter Wing at Righards-Gebaur Air Force Base, Missouri. In November 1991, he served as Chief of Weapon and Tactics for the 930th Tactical Fighter Group at Grissom Air Force Base, Indiana. From May 1992 to May 1994, he served as the Commander of the 45th Tactical Fighter Squadron at Grissom Air Force Base. He was promoted to Colonel on June 1, 1994.

In September 1994, he was assigned as a Special Assistance to the Commander of the 434th Air Refueling Wing at Grissom Air Reserve Base. In May 1995, he was assigned as Mobilization Assistance to the Deputy to the Chief of the Air Force Reserve in Washington, D.C. In December 1997, he served as Vice Commander of the 19th Air Force at Naval Air Station Fort Worth Joint Reserve Base, Texas. He was promoted to Brigadier General on September 13, 1999.

From January 2000 and April 2000, he served as the Mobilization Assistant to the Director of Operations at Headquarters Air Education and Training Command at Randolph Air Force Base, Texas. In April 2000, he was selected to serve as Mobilization Assistant to the Assistant Secretary of the Air Force for Manpower and Reserve Affairs at the Pentagon.

His military awards and decorations include the Legion of Merit (with oak leaf cluster); the Meritorious Service Medal; the Air Force Commendation Medal (with one oak leaf cluster); the Air Force Achievement Medal (with one oak leaf cluster); Combat Readiness Medal (with one oak leaf clusters); and the Air Force Reserve Medal (with one oak leaf cluster).

Johnson, Ozell
COMMAND SERGEANT MAJOR—ARMY

He was born in Brownsville, Tennessee, where he graduated from Haywood High School. He enlisted in the United States Army in May 1983, and completed Basic Training and Advanced Individual Training as an Infantryman at Fort Benning, Georgia.

His military education includes all the Noncommissioned Officer Education System Courses; Army Recruiting Course; Army Guidance Counselor Course; First Sergeant Course; the United States Army Sergeants Major Academy (class 53); the Command

Sergeant Major Course; and Command Sergeant Major Course.

He has served in virtually every duty position in the 79 Career Management Field, including as a Field Recruiter from 1989 to 1992; as on-production Station Commander and limited production Station Commander; as a Guidance Counselor from 1992 to 1994; as Assistant Operations Noncommissioned Officer for the Headquarters of United States Army Recruiting Command Recruiting Operations Directorate's Plans, Policies, and Programs Division; as First Sergeant for Vancouver Recruiting Company, United States Army Portland Recruiting Battalion in Oregon from 1997 to 2000; and as Operations Noncommissioned Officer from 2000 to 2002 at the Portland Recruiting Battalion. In January 2005, he was serving as the Command Sergeant Major for the Chicago Recruiting Battalion.

Johnson, Patricia
MAJOR—MARINES

She enlisted in the Marine Corps out of high school, and after graduating with honors from two military schools, the Marine Corps gave her a full scholarship to Memphis State University. She graduated with a degree and a commission to second lieutenant.

Johnson, Ronald L.
MAJOR GENERAL—ARMY

He was commissioned in the Corps of Engineers after receiving a Bachelor of Science degree from the United States Military Academy at West Point in 1976. He earned a Masters of Science degree from the Georgia Institute of Technology, and a Master's of Military Art and Science degree from the United States Army Command and General Staff College. His military education includes the Engineer Officer's Basic Course;

the Armor Officer's Advanced Course; the United States Army Command and General Staff College; the School of Advanced Military Studies; and the Senior Service College Fellowship at the Joint Center for Political and Economic Studies.

His first tour was with the 9th Engineer Battalion at Aschaffenburg, West Germany, where he served as Platoon Leader, Company Executive Officer, Assistant S-4 and Company Commander. From 1985 to 1988, he served at the United States Military Academy as the Course Director for Freshman Calculus, as well as an Instructor and Assistant Professor in the Department of Mathematics. From 1988 to 1990, he attended the Command and General Staff College and the School for the Advanced Military Studies (SAMS) at Fort Leavenworth, Kansas. Upon graduation, he was assigned to the 25th Infantry Division (Light) where he served as the Assistant Division Engineer, then became the Executive Officer of the 65th Combat Engineer Battalion, 25th Infantry Division (Light), at Schofield Barracks, Hawaii. In April 1992, he was assigned as Commander of the 14th Combat Engineer Battalion (Corps), 7th Infantry Division (Light), at Fort Ord, California. From May 1993 to May 1994, he served as the Commander of the 14th Combat Engineer Battalion (Corps), 555th Engineer Group, Fort Lewis, Washington.

In June 1995, he was selected to serve as the Senior Aide-de-Camp to the Secretary of the Army Washington, D.C. From June 1996 to July 1998, he served as the Commander of the 130th Engineer Brigade, V Corps, United States Army Europe and Seventh Army, in Germany, in which capacity he participated in Operation Joint Endeavor in Bosnia and Operation Joint Guard in Croatia. He was promoted to Colonel on September 1, 1996.

He returned to the United States in July 1998, and

was assigned as the Executive Officer to the Secretary of the Army in Washington, D.C. From August 1999 to July 2001, he served as the Assistant Commandant at the United States Army Engineer School and Deputy Commanding General for Initial Entry Training at Fort Leonard Wood, Missouri. He was promoted to Brigadier General on January 1, 2001.

In July 2001, he was selected to serve as the Commanding General of the United States Army Engineer Division, Pacific Ocean, at Fort Shafter, Hawaii. From July 2003 to June 2004, he served as Director of Military Programs in the United States Army Corps of Engineers and the Director of the Program Management Office of the Coalition Provisional Authority during Operation Iraqi Freedom. He was promoted to Major General on January 1, 2004.

In August 2004, he was assigned as the Director for the Installation Management Agency in Arlington, Virginia.

His military awards and decorations include the Legion of Merit (with two oak leaf clusters); the Meritorious Service Medal (with three oak leaf clusters); the Army Commendation Medal (with oak leaf cluster); the Army Achievement Medal; Parachutist Badge; Air Assault Badge; and Army Staff Identification Badge.

Johnson, Roscoe L., Jr.

COMMAND SERGEANT MAJOR—ARMY

Command Sergeant Major Roscoe L. Johnson, Jr. was born in Cleveland, Tennessee. He graduated from Cleveland High School and West Kentucky State Vocational Technical School. He was drafted into the Army in December 1970 and attended Basic Training at Fort Knox, Kentucky, and completed on-the-job training (OJT) at Fort Meade, Maryland. He has completed the Noncommissioned Officer Logistic Course and the United States Army Sergeants Major Academy.

He has served in a variety of positions including Platoon Sergeant; First Sergeant; Sergeant Major; and Command Sergeant Major of the 46th Forward Support Battalion, 548th Corps Support Battalion, 10th Mountain Division Support Command (DISCOM), and the 45th Corps Support Group (Forward), at Schofield Barracks, in Hawaii. He is currently the Command Sergeant Major for the United States Army Aviation and Missile Command at Redstone Arsenal, Alabama.

Johnson, Thomas C.

BRIGADIER GENERAL—ARMY

He was born in Baltimore, Maryland. He graduated from Carver Vocational Technical High School in Baltimore, Maryland. He received a Bachelor of Science degree in Liberal Arts from the University of New York in Albany. His military education includes completion of Artillery and Missile School, Officer Candidate and Officer Basic Course; Airborne Course; Pathfinder Course; Jumpmaster Course; Infantry School Instructor Training Course; Infantry Officer Advanced Course; and Command and General Staff College. He was commissioned a second lieutenant on March 21, 1967.

He entered the United States Army in March 1967, and his first assignments included serving as Executive Officer with Battery A, 3rd Battalion, 21st Artillery, and as Executive Officer for the 5th Battalion, 81st Artillery, 8th Infantry Division. In January 1969, he was assigned as Liaison Officer at Headquarters and Headquarters Battery, 5th Battalion, 27th Artillery.

While still on active duty, he was assigned in March 1970 as Company Commander of Company A, 4th Battalion, 3rd Basic Training Brigade, and later as Executive Officer of the Headquarters of the 4th Battalion, 3rd Basic Training Brigade. In December 1971, he was assigned as an Instructor with the 72nd Company, Infantry School, later as an Instructor, Ranger Department, Infantry School.

In October 1973, he joined the Maryland Army National Guard and was assigned as Instructor at Headquarters and Headquarters Detachment. In September 1974, he served as Commander of the Operational Detachment, later as Executive Officer with Company A, 5th Special Forces Battalion, 20th Special Forces Group. In September 1978, he served as Company Executive Officer, Company C, 1st Special Forces Battalion. In October 1979, he became Battalion S-3 (Operations), Headquarters and Headquarters Company. In April 1982, he was assigned as Communications and Electronics Staff Officer at Headquarters and Headquarters Detachment, 29th Air Traffic Control Group. He was promoted to Lieutenant Colonel on June 19, 1986.

In October 1987, he served as Battalion Commander for the 1st Battalion, 175th Infantry, 29th Infantry Division (Light). In December 1989, he was assigned as the Recruiting and Retention Manager at Headquarters, State Area Command. In December 1990, he served as Division Support Command Commander at Headquarters and Headquarters Material Management

Center, 29th Support Command. He was promoted to Colonel on January 28, 1991.

In September 1992, he was assigned as Director of Plans, Operations and Training at Headquarters, State Area Command. In March 1993, he was selected to serve as Assistant Division Commander, for the 29th Infantry Division (Light). He was promoted to Brigadier General on May 3, 1994.

His military awards and decorations include the Bronze Star (with one oak leaf cluster); the Meritorious Service Medal; the Air Medal; Army Commendation Medal (with one oak leaf cluster); Army Achievement Medal; Good Conduct Medal; Army Reserve Components Achievement Medal (with four oak leaf clusters); National Defense Service Medal (with one bronze service star); Vietnam Service Medal (with three bronze service stars); Armed Forces Reserve medal (with one hourglass device); Army Service Ribbon; Overseas Service Ribbon; Army Reserve Components Overseas Training Ribbon; Republic of Vietnam Campaign Medal (with "60" device); Republic of Vietnam Gallantry Cross Unit Citation (with Palm); Expert Infantry Badge; Senior Parachute Badge; Two Overseas Bars; Ranger Tabs; Pathfinder Badge; Special Forces Badge; and the National Guard Recruiter Badge.

Johnson, Tyrone
COMMAND SERGEANT MAJOR—ARMY

Born in Charleston, South Carolina, Johnson entered the United States Army in July 1983 and attended Basic Combat Training at Fort Jackson, South Carolina, and Advanced Individual Training at Fort Gordon, Georgia.

His military education includes all the Noncommissioned Officers Education System Courses; Airborne Course; Jumpmaster Course; Nodal Operations Man-

agement Course; Mobile Subscriber Equipment Phase II Course; Drill Sergeant School (Leadership Award and Commandants list); Battle Staff NCO Course; First Sergeant Course; and the United States Army Sergeants Major Academy (class 53). He hold an associate's degree in Applied Science from Excelsior College.

He has held the following key leadership positions: Radio Teletype Team Chef; Cable and Wire Systems Section Sergeant; Single Channel Radio Systems Section Sergeant; Transmission and Switching Systems Section Sergeant; Platoon Sergeant of Assault Command Post Platoon (ACP); Platoon Sergeant of Contingency Communication Platoon (CCP); Battalion S-3 Operation Sergeant; Drill Sergeant; and Senior Drill Sergeant. His assignments as First Sergeant include C Company, 3-13th Infantry Regiment at Fort Jackson; B Company, 304th Signal Battalion at Camp Long, South Korea; and HHC 3rd Signal Brigade at Fort Hood, Texas. His previous assignment was Development Division Sergeant Major for III Corps G-6 Force. In August 2004, he was serving as the Command Sergeant Major for the 36th Signal Battalion, 1st Signal Brigade, in South Korea.

Johnson, Vickki
MAJOR—ARMY

She enlisted in the United States Army in 1983 upon completion of high school and was assigned to the 440th Signal Battalion at Darmstadt, West Germany; the 35th Signal Brigade at Fort Bragg, North Carolina; the 122nd Signal Battalion at Camp Casey, South Korea; and the 19th Theater Support Command at Taegu, South Korea.

Her military education includes the Primary Leadership Development course; the Basic Noncommissioned Officer Course; the United States Army Airborne

School; Adjutant General Officer Basic and Advance Courses; and the Combined Arms Senior Staff School. She holds a Master of Science degree in Health Services Administration from Central Michigan University, and is pursuing a Doctorate in Public Health.

Upon her return to the United States, she was commissioned in the Adjutant General Corps as a Distinguished Military Graduate of Officer Candidate School in 1992. After completing the Adjutant General Officer Basic Course, she returned to Fort Bragg and was assigned to XVIII Airborne Corps, where she served as Chief of the Reassignments Division, Executive Officer and Battalion Personnel Officer, 18th Personnel Services Battalion. Upon completion of the Adjutant General Officer Advanced Course, she was assigned to V Corps at Heidelberg, Germany, as Chief of the Enlisted Management Branch and Commander of Headquarters and Headquarters Company, 1st Personnel Command.

Upon returning from Germany, she was assigned to the National Capital Region to serve in several positions including Operations Officer at the Headquarters of United States Army Materiel Command; Distribution/Assignment Officer; Chief of Officer Promotions; and Chief of Officer Evaluation Policy for United States Army Human Resources Command.

Johnson, Walter Frank, III
BRIGADIER GENERAL—ARMY

He was born in Charleston, South Carolina. He earned a Bachelor of Science degree in Zoology from West Virginia State College and a Master of Arts Degree in Political Science from the University of Missouri.

His military career began in July 1961 when he entered the United States Army as a Doctor in the Medical Service Corps, Officer Orientation Course, Medical Field Service School, at Fort Sam Houston, Texas. From September 1961 to July 1963, he was assigned as a Platoon Leader, Headquarters and Headquarters Company, 2nd Airborne Brigade, 504th Infantry, 82nd Airborne Division, at Fort Bragg, North Carolina. From August 1963 to June 1966, he was assigned first as a Platoon Leader, Company D, then Commander, Company D, then Platoon Leader, Company B, later as Commander, Company B and S-1 Adjutant all with the 8th Medical Battalion, 8th Infantry Division, United States Army, Europe.

In June 1966 he returned to the United States, a student in the Medical Service Corps Officer Advanced Course at Fort Sam Houston, Texas. From December 1966 to January 1968, he was assigned as the Assistant Plans and Operations Officer, later Plans Officer, 44th Medical Brigade, United States Army, Vietnam. Returning to the United States in January 1968, he was assigned as an Instructor at the Brooke Army Medical Center at Fort Sam Houston. From July 1970 to June 1971, he was a student at the United States Command and General Staff College at Fort Leavenworth, Kansas.

From June 1972 to May 1977, Johnson was assigned first as a Plans Officer, later Chief of Force Structure

Branch, Plans and Operations Division, Health Care Operations Directorate, Office of the Surgeon General in Washington, D.C. From May 1977 to May 1978, he served as Commander of the 2nd Medical Battalion, 2nd Infantry Division, in South Korea. From May 1978 to June 1980, he was assigned as the Assistant Executive Officer in the Office of the Surgeon General in Washington, D.C. From June 1980 to June 1981, he was a student at the Industrial College of the Armed Forces at Fort Lesley J. McNair in Washington, D.C.

From October 1981 to October 1985, he was assigned to the Surgeon General Office, Washington, D.C., serving first as the Assistant to the Chief of Medical Service Corps, Deputy Director, Personnel; and then as Chief Executive to the Surgeon General.

On November 1, 1985, Johnson was promoted to Brigadier General and assigned as the youngest Chief ever appointed of Medical Service Corps and Director of Health Care Operations, United States Army, at Falls Church, Virginia. Gen. Walter Frank Johnson III retired on October 31, 1988.

His military awards and decorations include the Distinguished Service Medal, Legion of Merit (with oak leaf cluster), Bronze Star, Meritorious Service Medal (with oak leaf cluster), Army Commendation Medal (with oak leaf cluster), Senior Parachutist Badge, and Expert Field Medical Badge.

Johnson, Wendell Norman
REAR ADMIRAL—NAVY

He was born in Boston, Massachusetts, and married the former Helen Underwood of Boston. They have three children, Laura, Lois, and W. Norman, Jr. He graduated from the New England College of Pharmacy and holds a Master of Arts degree in International Communications from American University.

He was commissioned an Ensign in May 1957 and began his Navy career on the auxiliary ship USS *Lookout*.

A graduate of the United States Naval Postgraduate School, Engineering Curriculum, and the Armed Forces Staff College, Johnson also attended the National War College where he was recognized for outstanding scholarship by the college commandant and the Chief of Naval Operations.

Subsequent sea duty included Fire Control and Gunnery Officer on the aircraft carrier USS *Coral Sea* and weapons officer on the destroyer USS *Ingraham*, later serving as Executive Officer on the destroyer USS *Jonas Ingram*. Johnson served as Commander of the Charleston Naval Base in February 1987, and in August 1987 he assumed Command of Mine Warfare Command in an additional duty capacity. Johnson was promoted to Rear Admiral in 1983.

Rear Admiral Johnson retired from the Navy on April 14, 1989. Johnson's outstanding civic contributions were recognized by his mayoral appointment to a Community Relations Commission serving Duval County and the city of Jacksonville, Florida.

Rear Admiral Johnson's decorations and awards include the Legion of Merit; Meritorious Service Medal (with gold star in lieu of second award); Navy Commendation Medal (with gold star in lieu of second award); Navy Achievement Medal; Navy Combat Action Ribbon; Republic of Vietnam Honor Medal First Class; and the Order of Sikatuna from the Philippine Government.

Johnson-Brown, Hazel W.

BRIGADIER GENERAL—ARMY

She was born in West Chester, Pennsylvania, and she is the daughter of Clarence L. and Garnett Johnson. She married David B. Brown. She earned a diploma in nursing from Harlem Hospital in New York City, a bachelor's degree in Nursing from Villanova University, a master's degree in Nursing Education from Teacher's College, Columbia University, and a doctorate in Educational Administration from Catholic University. In addition, she holds Honorary Doctorates from Morgan State University, Villanova University, and the University of Maryland.

From 1950 to 1953, she worked as a Staff Nurse in the Emergency Ward of Harlem Hospital in New York. Her responsibilities included evening and night duty and initial admission work-up for patients in all departments except obstetrics. From 1953 to 1955, she was a Staff Nurse in the Medical Cardiovascular Ward at the Veterans Administrative Hospital in Philadelphia, Pennsylvania. There she became Head Nurse on ward within three months of employment. Entering the Army Nurse Corps in 1955, she served for the next 12 years in a variety of positions at Walter Reed Army Medical Center, the 8169 Hospital in Japan, Madigan General Hospital, Letterman General Hospital, the 45th Surgical Hospital at Fort Sam Houston, and Valley Forge General Hospital.

From 1967 to 1973, she was assigned to the Staff of the United States Army Medical Research and Development Command as a project director in the Army Medical Department field hospital system. Upon completion of her doctoral studies, she was appointed Director of the Walter Reed Army Institute of Nursing. In 1978, she was transferred to South Korea to assume the positions of Assistant for Nursing in the Office of the Surgeon for the Eighth Army Command; Chief of the Department of Nursing at the United States Army Hospital, 121 Evacuation Hospital, in Seoul, South Korea; and Chief of Consultant for Nursing Matters to the Senior Medical Officer with the Eighth Army Command.

In 1979 she was selected to the position of Chief of the Army Nurse Corps, and was promoted to the rank of Brigadier General. General Johnson-Brown became the sixteenth Chief of the Army Nurse Corps, the first Chief holding an earned Doctorate, the fourth Chief to hold the rank of Brigadier General, and the first black woman General in the history of the United States military services.

Among General Johnson-Brown's significant recognitions are Army Nurse of the year awards from Letterman General Hospital and the Daughters of the American Revolution, the Army Commendation Medal (with oak leaf cluster), the Meritorious Service Medal, and the Legion of Merit. Upon retirement from active duty in 1983, General Johnson-Brown received the Distinguished Service Medal.

Prior to joining the faculty at George Mason University, Dr. Johnson-Brown served as assistant professor in the Graduate Nursing Administration program at Georgetown University and Director of Governmental Affairs for the Washington office of the American Nurses' Association.

From 1983 to the present, Dr. Johnson-Brown has endeavored to translate her leadership skill and concern for young people, especially black youth, to work in her civilian position. As director, Division of Governmental Affairs, she worked diligently to increase the minority participation in professional positions with her office and the professional organization. That work continues in her teaching in her present organization, George Mason University. Within the university, she served as chair of the Minority Affairs Committee, consultant to the George Mason University Alumni Association, member of the Cultural Diversity Committee of the School of Nursing, and mentor to three black nursing students — further indication of her interest in furthering the careers of young black men and women. In addition to these activities, she maintains her membership in Black Women United for Action of Northern Virginia and was appointed in 1986 a member of the Board of Military Affairs for the Commonwealth of Virginia by Douglas Wilder, governor of Virginia.

In 1984, she was one of 13 women to receive the Outstanding Women of Color Award and one of 12 women to receive the National Coalition of 100 Black Women's Candace Award. Dr. Hazel Johnson-Brown, professor and member of the graduate faculty at the School of Nursing at George Mason University, was named in August 1989 Director of the Center for Health Policy, a new center in the School of Nursing. Dr. Johnson-Brown currently teaches healthcare public policy and health-care administration.

Jones, Carol A.
COLONEL—ARMY

She hails from Pennsylvania. After completing secondary education in Pittsburgh, she moved to New York, New York, enrolled and completed a diploma program in nursing from Harlem Hospital School of Nursing. She earned a Bachelor of Science in Nursing from Tuskegee University in Alabama; a master's degree in Community Health Nursing from Emory University in Atlanta, Georgia; and a master's degree in Nursing Education from Columbia Teachers' College in New York. She is a Wharton Fellow and recently completed the Program for Nurse Executives at the University of Pennsylvania.

She is a graduate of the Industrial College of the Armed Forces (ICAF) at the National Defense University. Other professional military education includes Command and General Staff College; Officer Basic and Advanced Courses; Combat Casualty Care Course; Principles of Advanced Nursing Practice; Personnel Management for Executives; and the Federal Interagency Institute for Health Care Executives.

She served in several key positions including National Defense University Nurse Consultant at Fort McNair, Washington, D.C.; Chief of Nursing Administration, WRAMC, in Washington, D.C.; Nursing Consultant and Chief Nurse 18th Medical Command at Yongsan, South Korea; Chief of the Medical/Surgical/Psychiatric Nursing Section at the 97th General Hospital at Frankfurt, Germany; Chief Nurse for Joint Task Force Bravo in Honduras; and Deputy Director of the Practical Nurse Course at William Beaumont Army Medical Center in El Paso, Texas.

In September 2004, she was serving as Chief Nurse of North Atlantic Regional Medical Command (NARMC) and Chief Nurse at Walter Reed Army Medical Center (WRAMC) in Washington, D.C.

Jones, Dorian F.
COMMANDER—NAVY

He is a native of Austin, Texas. He attended Austin College in Sherman, Texas, and graduated with a Liberal Arts degree in English and History in 1984. He graduated from Officer Candidate School in Newport, Rhode Island, in February 1985, and after attending Surface Warfare Officers School Basic Course was assigned as Second Division Officer aboard USS *Ranger* in August 1985.

Following completion of Surface Warfare Department Head School, he was assigned as Engineer Officer aboard USS *Fort Fisher* from July 1993 to April 1996, where he completed a third Arabian Gulf Deployment in support of Operations Southern Watch and United Shield. From June 1996 to June 1997, he attended the Army Command and Generals Staff College at Fort Leavenworth, Kansas, where he earned a Master of Military Arts and Science (MMAS). He later attended the Armed Forces Staff College in Norfolk, Virginia, from June 1997 to September 1997. From April 1998 to September 1999, he was assigned to USS *Duluth* as Executive Officer and after completing a fourth deployment to the Arabian Gulf, he was detailed to the forward-deployed Staff of Commander Amphibious Group One as Operations Officer (N3) in Okinawa, Japan, where he directed numerous multinational exercises and operations in support of Operation Enduring Freedom. While serving in Japan, he was selected and given to take command of ACU One.

Jones, Dan F.
COMMAND SERGEANT MAJOR—ARMY

A native of Gulfport, Mississippi, he enlisted in the

Army National Guard on May 28, 1976, and attended Basic Training at Fort Jackson, South Carolina. He attended Advanced Individual Training (AIT) at Fort Eustis, Virginia, as a Helicopter Repairman. On February 7, 1977, he enlisted in the Regular Army as a Redeye Gunner and attended AIT at Fort Bliss, Texas. His first permanent duty station was Fort Polk, Louisiana, where he served as Redeye Gunner and Team Chief in the 3/77 Armor Battalion, 5th Infantry Division. In 1981, he graduated from his third AIT at Fort Huachuca, Arizona, as an Imagery Interpreter.

He has held all the key leadership position from Squad Leader to Group Command Sergeant Major. His military schools include the First Sergeants Course and the Battle Staff Course. He is also a graduate of the Sergeant Major Academy, Class 48 and the Command Sergeants Major Course. He has completed three years of college.

His awards and decorations include the Meritorious Service Medal (4OLC), Joint Service Commendation Medal, Army Commendation Medal (4OLC), Army Achievement Medal (2OLC), Good Conduct Ribbon (8th Award), National Defense Ribbon with Bronze Star, Armed Forces Expeditionary Medal, Southwest Asia Service Medal with Bronze Star, Armed Forces Service Medal, Humanitarian Service Ribbon, NCO Professional Development Ribbon (numeral 4), Army Service Ribbon, Overseas Ribbon (numeral 4), NATO Medal, Kuwait Liberation Medal (from the Government of Kuwait and the Kingdom of Saudi Arabia), Army Superior Unit Award, Meritorious Unit Award and the Aircraft Crewman Badge. He is also the recipient of the Thomas Knowlton Award.

Jones, Donald L., II
SERGEANT MAJOR—MARINES

He was born in Fort Carson, Colorado. He enlisted into the United States Marine Corps in March 1981. Upon completion of recruit training at United States Marine Corps Recruit Depot at San Diego, California. He attended Infantry Training School at Camp Pendleton, California, and was designated 0311 (MOS). He was the assigned to the Marine Barracks of Naval Weapons Station Concord, California.

While a member of Fox Company 2/5, he served as a Fire Team Leader, Squad Leader and as the Platoon Right Guide. During this tour, 2/5 was rotated under the UDP to Camp Hansen, Okinawa. While on Okinawa, Sergeant Major Jones participated in jungle training at the Northern Training Area on Okinawa, then participated Operations Bear Hunt '83 and Silver Spear '83 in Korea.

He was deployed on the USS *Juneau* (LPD-10) to the Philippine Islands for a Battalion live fire exercise with the Philippine Marines in the Zambalas Training Area and attended the Jungle Escape Survival Training (JEST) Beginner and Advanced Courses. Upon his return from Okinawa, he reenlisted, making a lateral move in 1985 to the 3043 MOS. He was transferred

Marine Heavy Helicopter-361, Marine Aircraft Group-16 at Marine Corps Air Station Tustin. His squadron deployed to Marine Corps Air Station. His squadron deployed to Marine Corps Air Station Futenma in 1985 under the UDP and participated in Exercise Team Spirit '85 in Korea. In July 1988, he was promoted to Sergeant and then ordered to report to Marine Detachment. USS *Ranger* (CV-61) based at Naval Station North Island of Coronado, California. While assigned to *Ranger*, he was the Supply NCO and the Commander of the Guard. Deployments aboard the RANGER included Team Spirit 87, Rouge Trade 87 and a scheduled WESTPAC to the Indian Ocean. Reassigned in October 1988, was transferred to MACS-4, MACG-18 in Okinawa. After that tour, Sergeant Major Jones was sent to Drill Instructor School at Marine Corps Recruit Depot Parris Island in August 1989. After completion of Drill Instructor School, he was assigned to Golf Company, 2nd Recruit Training Battalion, as a Drill Instructor and Senior Drill Instructor until February 1992.

Sergeant Major Jones was transferred back to Okinawa, assigned to MASS-2, MACG-18 for duty until March 1993. He was assigned to Inspector-Instructor Staff, 1st Battalion, 14th Marines, 4th Marine Division in Alameda, California. Upon completion of his duties in May 1998, he was promoted to Gunnery Sergeant and reassigned back to the Fleet Marine Force with Supply Battalion, 1st Force Service Supply Group in Camp Pendleton, California. While assigned, he was hand picked by the Battalion Commander and Sergeant Major to assume the responsibilities and billet as First Sergeant for Supply Company, still as a Gunnery Sergeant. Sergeant Major Jones held that billet until July 1997. He was then transferred to Marine Expeditionary Unit Service Support Group-13, 13th Marine Expeditionary (SOC), as the Chief of the Supply Detachment. The 13th MEU (SOC) participated in many

large-scale exercises while deployed on WESTPAC '98–'99 which included Exercises "Eagar Mace" in Kuwait and "Edged Mallet" Humanitarian Assistance Operation (HAO) in Kenya. He was promoted to First Sergeant in September 1999, he was then assigned to 1st Transportation Support Battalion, 1st Force Service Supply Group as the First Sergeant for "General Support Company" and then "Support Company."

He transferred to Marine Corps Security Force Company, London in May 2000, where he served with numerous British Royal Marines in the United Kingdom. Sergeant Major Jones was the last First Sergeant of the Marine Corps Security Force Company in London, England, before its deactivation on June 28th 2002. He was assigned to 1st Battalion, 1st Marine Regiment, 1st Marine Division. His Battalion was assigned to the 13th Marine Expedition Unit (SOC), and the First Battalion Landing Team designated to be a part of the Expeditionary Strike Group-One. The 13th Marine Expedition Unit (SOC) participated in many large-scale exercises while deployed on WESTPAC '03-02 which included Exercises "Eagar Mace" in Kenya; "Edged Mallet" in the United Arab Emirates; and Operation Swenny in Iraq with British Army. Returning to the CONUS in March of 2004, his Battalion was assigned in June to be the Ground Combat Element for the 15th Marine Expedition Unit (SOC), ESG-5. Promoted and reassigned on December 1, 2004, he assumed the billet of the Squadron Sergeant Major for Marine Wing Support Squadron 372 at Camp Pendleton, California.

Jones, Ethan Allen
SERGEANT MAJOR—ARMY

He is a native of Frankfort, Kentucky. He holds a Bachelor of Arts degree in Mass Communication from Pain College in Augusta, Georgia, and one in Public Relations from Clark-Atlanta University in Atlanta, Georgia.

After graduation in 1984, he entered the United States Army and completed Basic Training at Fort Leonard Wood, Missouri, and Advance Individual Training at Fort Lee, Virginia, where he was awarded the Military Occupation Specialty 76P, Material Accounting Specialist, which is now 92A, Automated Logistics Management Specialist. His assignments included being assigned as an Automated Logistics Management

Specialist to the 182nd Maintenance Company, 71st Maintenance Battalion at Nuremberg, Germany, and to Headquarters and Headquarters Company, 54th Engineers Battalion, Fort Belvoir at Virginia.

He serves as the Sergeant Major for United States Army Contracting Command Europe and Sergeant Major to the Principal Assistant Responsible for Contracting USAREUR.

Jones, John L.
BRIGADIER GENERAL—ARMY

He was born in Albany, New York. He is the father of a son, Gary and two daughters, Michelle and Melissa. His son served proudly as an aviator in the United States Coast Guard. He received a Bachelor of Science degree in Liberal Arts from the State University of New York Albany. His military education includes the Fort Dix Chemical, Biological and Radiological, Installation Level Chemical Course; the Armor Officer Basic Course; the Infantry Officer Basic Course; and Command and General Staff College.

He entered the United States Military in 1957 as a Private in the 1st Battalion of the 106th Infantry in Brooklyn, New York, and rose to the rank of Staff Sergeant. In 1965, he was selected to attend Officer Candidate School at Fort Benning, Georgia. After this tasking course of instruction he was commissioned as a Second Lieutenant in the Infantry on May 13, 1965.

He returned to the 106th Infantry where he was assigned as a Platoon Leader and then Company Com-

mander of Company C, 2nd Battalion, 106th Infantry. Concurrent with this assignment and for the following thirteen years he served as an Instructor, Staff Officer, Company Commander, and Battalion Executive Officer at the Empire State Military Academy. He was promoted to First Lieutenant on May 12, 1968, and to Captain on July 9, 1970.

In 1967, he was assigned as the Adjutant of the 101st Cavalry Squadron in Staten Island. In 1971, he was assigned to the 2nd Brigade, 42nd Infantry Division as the Assistant S3 (Operations). He subsequently was promoted to Major on March 7, 1977, and assigned as the S3 of the 1st Battalion, 107th Infantry, and in 1980, and returned to the 2nd Brigade as the S3.

On January 19, 1984, he was promoted to Lieutenant Colonel and reassigned as the G3 (Operations), for the 42nd Infantry Division. In 1986, he returned to the 2nd Brigade as Executive Officer and in the following year returned to the Headquarters of the 42nd Infantry Division as G3 (Operations), and upon his promotion to Colonel on September 5, 1989, was appointed Chief of Staff.

General Jones returned to the 2nd Brigade, 42nd Infantry, as its Commander in 1989. On October 1, 1990, the 2nd Brigade was re-designated the 107th Brigade. On May 1, 1993, he was reassigned as Chief of Staff of the 42nd Infantry Division. In October 1993, he became the Deputy Director of the Challenge Program at Camp Smith, New York. On February 1, 1994, he was selected as the Commander of Camp Smith Training Site. On June 1, 1994, he was assigned as the Assistant Adjutant General of Headquarters and Headquarters Detachment, State Area Command, New York Army National Guard. He was promoted to Brigadier General on June 1, 1994. In October 1997, he was still serving as the Commander of Headquarters 53rd Troop Command at Camp Smith, New York.

His military awards and decorations include the Meritorious Service Medal (with three oak leaf clusters); Army Commendation Medal; Army Reserve Components Achievement Medal; National Defense Service Medal (with one bronze service star); Armed Forces Reserve Medal (with two hourglass devices); and the Army Service Ribbon.

Jones, Kenneth E.
COMMAND MASTER CHIEF—NAVY

He enlisted in the Navy at the MEPS in Montgomery, Alabama, in May 1979, at the age of 17. Following recruit training in Orlando, Florida, he attended Basic Dental Technician "A" School from October to December 1979 at Naval School of Dental Assisting and Technology (NSDAT) in San Diego, California.

His key military assignments include attending the Senior Enlisted Academy in Newport, Rhode Island in 1995. In October 1995, he assumed duty as the Command Senior Chief of the United States Naval Dental Center at Yokosuka, Japan. In October 2004, he was

serving as the Command Master Chief at the Naval Dental Center Mid-Atlantic.

Jones, Larry C.

SERGEANT MAJOR—MARINES

He enlisted into the United States Marine Corps in October 1979 and attended Recruit Training at Marine Corps Recruit Depot, San Diego, California.

His key assignments include serving in September 1985, he was transferred to the 1st Tank Battalion, 1st Marine Division at Camp Pendleton, California, were he served as a Section Leader and Platoon Sergeant. In 1992, he was assigned to Villanova University and University of Pennsylvania for ROTC duty. In April 1996, he was transferred to Marine Forces Unit as a Company First Sergeant. In April 1998, he was assigned to

Headquarters and Service Company, 2nd Marine Division. In October 1998, he transferred to United States Marine Corps Forces, Atlantic, in Norfolk, Virginia, as the First Sergeant. In October 1999, he was assigned as Sergeant Major to MAG-42 Det "B." In October 2004, he was serving as Sergeant Major at Marine Heavy Helicopter Squadron 461, Marine Aircraft Group 26, Second Marine Aircraft Wing.

Jones, Leonard B.

CAPTAIN—NAVY

He is a native of Matthews, Georgia. He is a June 1978 Navy ROTC graduate of Savannah State College with a Bachelor of Science degree in Chemistry. He began Navy career with division officer tours as First Lieutenant in USS *Higbee* (DD 806) homeported in Seattle, Washington, and First Lieutenant and Gunnery Officer in USS *Dahlgren* (DD 43) homeported in Norfolk, Virginia, until January 1982.

After completing two years of Officer Recruiting Duty at Navy Recruiting District, Atlanta, in April 1984, he attended Department Head School in September 1984. He served two years as Operations Officer in USS *Charles F. Adams* (DDG 2) homeported in Mayport, Florida, until October 1986.

He then served two years as Operations Officer on the staff of Destroyer Squadron 31 homeported in San Diego, California, until December 1988. He then attended the Naval Postgraduate School in Monterey, California, where he received a Master of Science degree in Applied Science specializing in Anti-Submarine Warfare in March 1991. Following the Naval Postgraduate School, he served as Executive Officer in USS *Vincennes* (CG 49) homeported in San Diego until February 1993.

His next assignment was Staff Operations and Plans Officer for Commander of Afloat Training Group Western Pacific in Yokosuka, Japan from March 1993 until July 1995, where he led training for all ships in the 7th Fleet and Forward Deployed Naval Forces. He then completed a year at the National War College, National Defense University, in Washington, DC, where he earned a Master of Science degree in National Security Affairs in June 1996.

He then served as Commanding Officer of Navy Recruiting District Atlanta from October 1996 to September 1998, where his area of responsibility included 25 Navy recruiting stations throughout Georgia and South Carolina. He served as the Naval Attache/Liaison Officer to the U.S. Embassy at Nassau, Bahamas from November 1998 until February 2001 which included service as the Senior U.S. Defense Representative for the Bahamas and Turks and Caicos for U.S. Southern Command.

From March 2001 to July 2004, Captain Jones served as Director of the Latin American, Caribbean and Middle East Division at the Navy International Programs Office in Washington, DC, overseeing State Department Security Assistance and Department of the Navy Foreign Military Sales programs. In July 2005, he was serving as Professor of Naval Science and Commanding

Officer of Navy ROTC unit Savannah State University at Savannah, Georgia.

Jones, Michele S.
COMMAND SERGEANT MAJOR—ARMY

She was born in Baltimore, Maryland. CSM Jones has an Associate of Arts degree in General Studies and a Bachelor of Science degree (Cum Laude) in Business Administration from Fayetteville State University. She is currently completing her Master of Arts in Management/International Relations. Her military education includes the Battle Staff Operations Course; First Sergeant's Course; Instructor Training Course; Civil Affairs Operation Course; Master Fitness Course; Retention NCO Basic and Advanced Courses; and the Sergeants Major Academy. She entered the Army in 1982. She attended Basic Training at Fort Jackson, South Carolina, and Advanced Individual Training at Fort Benjamin Harrison, Indiana. She has held every key NCO position, including squad leader, platoon sergeant, and first sergeant and command sergeant. She was the first woman to serve as Class President at the United States Sergeants Major Academy (Class 48). Her overseas assignments include Hanau and Rhineberg, Germany; Honduras and Panama. She was called to active duty for Operations Desert Shield/Desert Storm; Restore Hope; Provide Comfort; Joint Endeavor; and Noble Eagle. Her most resent assignment was that of Command Sergeant Major of the 78th Division (Training Support) at Edison, New Jersey.

On August 28, 2002, she was selected as the ninth Command Sergeant Major of the Army Reserve. She is the first woman in the Army's history to serve as a top Command Sergeant Major for the Army Reserves. She took office on October 28, 2002.

Jones, Michelle K.
COMMAND SERGEANT MAJOR
Michelle K. Jones is a native of Gainesville, Florida

and received a Bachelor of Arts Degree from Excelsior University in New York. Her military education includes Air Load Movement Course, Security Managers Course, Master Fitness Course, Battle Staff Course, First Sergeant Course, the United States Army Sergeants Major Academy and the Command Sergeant Major Course.

She entered the United States Army in January 1982. She attended Basic Combat Training at Fort Jackson, South Carolina and Advanced Individual Training (AIT) at Fort Ben Harrison, Indiana as a Pay Specialist.

Command Sergeant Major Jones has served in a variety of positions of increased responsibility to include: serving as the Command Sergeant Major for the 230th Finance Battalion, at Fort Hood, Texas; as a Staff Sergeant Major, with the United States Army and NATO at Shape in Belgium; as a First Sergeant at Headquarters Company 13th Finance Group, at Fort Hood, Texas. She now serves as the Command Sergeant Major for the 13th Finance Group, at Fort Hood, Texas.

Jones, Richard L.
BRIGADIER GENERAL—ARMY
He was born in Albany, Georgia. He received his Bachelor of Science degree from the University of Cincinnati, Ohio. He served in the all black Infantry National Guard Regiment, the 178th Regimental Combat Team, which was called to duty during World War II.

The name of the regiment was eventually changed to the 369th Coast Artillery (AA) Group. He remained in the Illinois Army National Guard after World War II. In June 1950, he led the 2000 members of the Illinois National Guard's 178th Regimental Combat Team into summer training at Camp McCoy, Wisconsin, from July 1, through July 15, 1950. He held a wide variety of important command and staff positions culminating in an appointment to the rank of brigadier general in the Illinois Army National Guard. Chicago's Richard L. Jones National Guard Center was named in his honor. He died in 1977.

Jones, Synthia
COMMANDER—NAVY

She was born in Daphne, Alabama, where she graduated from Fairhope High School in 1979. She received a Bachelor of Science in Mathematics with a minor in Computer Science from the University of Alabama in Tuscaloosa. Upon receiving her degree, she attended Navy Officer Candidate School in Newport, Rhode Island. She was commissioned Ensign and her first tour of duty was at the Washington Navy Yard.

Jones, Walter I.
BRIGADIER GENERAL—AIR FORCE

He was born in Baltimore, Maryland. He entered the Air Force in 1974 through the ROTC program, after he earned a Bachelor of Science degree in Mathematics from the University of Maryland Eastern Shore in Princess Anne, Maryland. He earned a master's degree in Business Administration in 1977 from Troy State University in Troy, Alabama. In 1985, he earned a master's degree in Computer Science from George Washington University in Washington, D.C. His military

education includes in 1977 Squadron Officer School at Maxwell Air Force Base, Alabama. In 1986, he completed the Air Command and Staff College. In 1992, he graduated from the Air War College at Maxwell Air Force Base. In 1995, he graduated from the Program for Senior Officials in National Security at the John F. Kennedy School of Government at Harvard University. He attended the 2001 Seminar XXI — Foreign Politics, International Relations and National Interests, Center for International Studies, Massachusetts Institute of Technology, in Cambridge, Massachusetts.

He has held a variety of assignments in communications, as well as command positions at the Wing, Air Force Headquarters, Unified Command and Defense Agency levels. In July 1988, he was assigned as Chief of the Telecommunications Management Division, J6, United States Pacific Command, at Camp H.M. Smith, Hawaii. In August 1991, he was a student at the Air War College at Maxwell Air Force Base, Alabama. He was promoted to Colonel on January 1, 1992.

From July 1992 to April 1994, he served as the Commander of the 5th Combat Communications Group at Robins Air Force Base, Georgia. From November 1992 to March 1993, he served as Director of C4 Systems, J6, Operation Southern Watch, Joint Task Force, in the Middle East. In May 1994, he was assigned as Deputy Chief of the Defense Information Systems Agency at Arlington, Virginia. In November 1994, he was assigned as Vice Commander of the Defense Information Systems Agency Western Hemisphere at Fort Ritchie, Maryland. From June 1995 to July 1996, he served as Commander of the 436th Support Group at Dover Air Force Base, Delaware. In July 1996, he was assigned as Director of Communications and Information at Headquarters Air Mobility Command, later as Director of Command, Control, Communications and Computer Systems, and Chief Information Officer at Scott Air Force Base, Illinois. He was promoted to Brigadier General on October 1, 1998.

In July 2000, he was assigned as Vice Commander of the Air Force Communications and Information Center, later Assistant Deputy Chief of Staff for Communications and Information, at the Headquarters of the United States Air Force in Washington, D.C. In August 2001, he was selected to serve as Director for Command, Control, Communication and Computer Systems and Chief Information Officer at the United States Joint Forces Command in Norfolk, Virginia.

His military awards and decorations include the Defense Superior Service Medal (with two oak leaf clusters); the Legion of Merit; the Defense Meritorious Service Medal; the Meritorious Service Medal (with oak leaf cluster); Joint Service Commendation Medal; Air Force Commendation Medal; Southwest Asia Service Medal (with service star); the Humanitarian Service Medal.

Jordan, Kenneth U.
BRIGADIER GENERAL—AIR FORCE

He was born in South Pittsburgh, Tennessee. He

received a Bachelor of Science degree in Public Administration from the University of Tennessee in Knoxville, Tennessee, in 1966, and a J.D. degree from Vanderbilt University School of Law in Nashville, Tennessee, in 1974.

He was commissioned a Second Lieutenant in the United States Air Force through the ROTC program while at the University of Tennessee. From 1966 to 1968, he served as a Squadron Section Commander at Minot Air Force Base, North Dakota. From 1968 to 1969, he was the Executive Support Officer at Ubon Royal Thai Air Force Base, Thailand. From 1969 to 1970, he was Commander of the Headquarters Squadron at MacDill Air Force Base, Florida.

Jordan left active duty in 1970, and accepted a position as an employee relations specialist for General Foods Corporation in White Plains, New York. From 1974 to 1975, he was an Associate Director, Fair Employment Practices Clinic, and Clinical Instructor at Vanderbilt Law School. From 1975 to 1977, he was the Assistant Dean for Administration at Vanderbilt Law School. He joined the Tennessee Air National Guard in 1976. From 1977 to 1981, he was the Director of the Opportunity Development Center at Vanderbilt University. From 1981 to 1983, he served as Executive Assistant to the President, later as Interim Vice President for Development and public Relations, later Vice President for Administration and General Counsel, at Meharry Medical College in Nashville, Tennessee.

From 1983 to 1984, he was a student at the Air Command and Staff College at the Air University at Maxwell Air Force Base in Montgomery, Alabama. From January 1985 to October 1985, he served as an Attorney-Adviser to the Director of Equal Employment Opportunity Staff on the Department of Justice in Washington, D.C. From October 1985 to January 1987, he

served first as Executive Assistant to the Assistant Attorney General for Administration, then as Chief of Staff in the Justice Management Division of the Department of Justice, Washington, D.C. He also served on the board of Directors for the Department of Justice Federal Credit Union.

From January 1987 to August 1988, he served as an Executive Assistant to the Governor (a cabinet-level appointment) of Tennessee in Nashville. He also served as Chairman of the Governor's Task Force on Housing.

In September 1988 he was promoted to Brigadier General, becoming the first black to serve as the Assistant Adjutant General for the Tennessee Air National Guard. He has served on numerous boards, both civic and community: including the Tennessee Task Force on the Supply of Minority Teachers (governor's representative); Statewide Area Health Education Centers (AHEC) Advisory Committee at Meharry Medical College; Boy Scouts' Inner-City Task Force Finance Committee; Chairman of the Project Blueprint Committee for the United Way of Middle Tennessee; National Committee for Employers Support of the Guard and Reserve (Tennessee committee); and United States Department of Defense (term expired January 1994).

Jordan, Larry Reginald

LIEUTENANT GENERAL—ARMY

He was born in Kansas City, Kansas, he married the former Nannette Pippen, and they have two sons, Larry, Jr., and Karl. He received a Bachelor of Science degree from the United States Military Academy in 1968 and a Master of Arts degree from Indiana University in 1975. His military schooling includes the Armor School

Basic Course (1968); United States Marine Corps Amphibious Warfare School (1972); United States Army Command and General Staff College (1979); and the National War College (1987).

He received his commission as a Second Lieutenant in 1968 after he graduated from the United States Military Academy. From August 1968 to October 1968, he was a student at the Ranger Course at the United States Army Infantry School at Fort Benning, Georgia. His initial assignment was with the 2nd Battalion, 66th Armor at Fort Hood, Texas, as a tank Platoon Leader. From July 1969 to March 1970, he was assigned to Vietnam where he served with the 1st Infantry Division as an infantry Platoon Leader with Company B, 2nd Battalion, 2nd Infantry and 1st Infantry Divisions, United States Army, Vietnam. From March 1970 to June 1970, he was Executive Officer for Troop A, 2nd Squadron, 1st Cavalry Division, United States Army, Vietnam.

He returned to the United States in July 1970 and was assigned as Commander of Company C (later Headquarters Company), 1st Battalion, 63rd Armor, 1st Infantry Division (Mechanized) at Fort Riley, Kansas. Subsequent assignments included tours with the Combat Arms Training Board, Headquarters, TRADOC; and the faculty of the United States Military Academy. In 1979 he was reassigned to USAREUR where he served as Executive Officer of the 3rd Battalion, 33rd Armor, 3rd Armored Division, and later as War Plans Officer in the Office of the Deputy Chief of Staff for Logistics, United States Army, Europe; In May 1982 he returned to the United States and was assigned as Staff Action Officer in the Office of the Deputy Chief of Staff for Operations and Plans, United States Army, Washington, D.C.

In November 1983 General Jordan assumed Command of 1st Battalion, 67th Armor, 2nd Armored Division, and remained until May 1986. Following completion of studies at the National War College, he was assigned duties with the Directorate of Operational Plans and Interoperability, J-7, OJCS. Prior to assuming duties as Assistant Division Commander for Support in the 1st Armored Division, General Jordan served as the Assistant Division Commander for Support in the 3rd Armored Division at Hanau, Germany; Chief of Staff for the 1st Armored Division at Ansbach, Germany; and Commander of the 2nd Brigade, 3rd Infantry Division at Kitzingen, Germany. In November 1991 he was assigned as Assistant Division Commander of the 8th Infantry Division (Mechanized), later as Assistant Division Commander of the 1st Armored Division, with the United States Army, Europe, and Seventh Army. He was appointed Brigadier General in November 1991.

In July 1992, he was assigned as the Deputy Commanding General of the United States Army Armor Center, and Fort Knox, at Fort Knox, Kentucky. From October 1993 to June 1995, he served as Commanding General of the United States Armor Center and Fort Knox/Commandant of the United States Army Armor School at Fort Knox, Kentucky. He was promoted to Major General on January 1, 1995.

In June 1995, he was assigned as Assistant Deputy Chief of Staff for Personnel in the Office of the Deputy Chief of Staff for Personnel, United States Army in Washington, D.C. From July 1995 to October 1997, he was selected as Deputy to the Inspector General, later as the Inspector General, in the Office of the Secretary of the Army in Washington, D.C. He was promoted to Lieutenant General on November 1, 1997.

From August 1999 to October 2001, he was assigned as Deputy Commanding General of the United States Army Europe and the Seventh Army in Germany. In October 2001, he was selected to serve as the Deputy Commanding General/Chief of Staff for the United States Army Training and Doctrine Command at Fort Monroe, Virginia. He retired from the military in August 2003.

His military decorations and awards include the Silver Star, Bronze Star Medal (with "V" device and one oak leaf cluster), Bronze Star (with two oak leaf clusters), Defense Meritorious Service Medal, Army Meritorious Service Medal (with two oak leaf clusters), Army Commendation Medal (with "V" device), Army Commendation Medal (with oak leaf cluster), Army Achievement Medal (with oak leaf cluster), Combat Infantryman Badge, Parachutist Badge, Ranger Tab, Joint Chiefs of Staff Identification Badge, and Army Staff Identification Badge.

Jordan, William
SERGEANT MAJOR—MARINES

He born in Talladega, Alabama, and enlisted in the United States Marine Corps in May 1980. He attended Recruit Training at the Marine Corps Recruit Depot San Diego, California. In August 1980, he attended

Engineer Equipment School at Court House Bay, Camp Lejeune, North Carolina. In June 1984, was transferred to I-I Staff Company C, 4th Landing Support Battalion, Naval Base at Charleston, South Carolina, as the Engineer Chief. He was selected to attend Airborne School at Fort Benning, Georgia.

His key assignments include serving as Platoon Sergeant; Engineer Chief; and Drill Instructor. In July 1996, he was assigned to Landing Support Company, Combat Service Support Group 3, Marine Corps Base, Kaneohe, Hawaii, serving as the Engineer Equipment Chief.

In September 1998, he was assigned to the Headquarters and Service Battalion of the III Marine Expeditionary Force at Okinawa, Japan, as the Engineer Section Chief. In August 1999, he was assigned to Headquarters and Service Company United States Marine Corps Forces Atlantic at Norfolk, Virginia as the Company First Sergeant. In October 2004, he was assigned as the Sergeant Major for the 2nd Battalion, 1st Marine Division.

Joseph, Annette
COMMAND SERGEANT MAJOR—ARMY

She is a native of Dallas, Texas, where she graduated from High School in May 1978 and began her career in the United States Army on June 5, 1978. Her military and civilian education includes all the Noncommissioned Officers Leadership Courses; Distinguished Honor Graduate of Class 03-83 of the III Corps Noncommissioned Officer Academy; Battle Staff Course; First Sergeants Course; and the United States Army Sergeants Major Academy. She holds an associate's degree in General Studies from Central Texas College; a Bachelors of Science degree in Management/Human

Resources from Park College; and a Master of Science Degree in Human Resource Management from the University of Central Texas.

Her assignments include Motor Transport Operator; Unit Clerk; Assistant Personnel Staff NCO; Battalion Personnel Staff NCO; Brigade Personnel Staff NCO; Group Personnel Staff NCO; United States Army Pacific Liaison NCO; Senior Analyst; First Sergeant for Headquarters and Headquarters Detachment of the 546th Personnel Service Battalion; First Sergeant for 21st Replacement Company; and Battalion Command Sergeant Major for the 203rd Personnel Services Battalion at Fort Wainwright, Alaska. In August 2004, she was serving as the Command Sergeant Major for 3rd Personnel Group at Fort Hood, Texas.

Joseph, Mark D.
COMMAND SERGEANT MAJOR—ARMY

He is a native of Louisiana, and entered the United States Army on June 4, 1981, in Houston, Texas. He attended Basic Combat Training and Advanced Individual Training at Fort Leonard Wood, Missouri. His military and civilian education includes completing all Noncommissioned Officer Education System Courses; Battle Staff Course; the First Sergeant Course; and the United States Army Sergeants Major Academy (class 53). He earned an associate's degree in Science Transportation from City College of Chicago, and is pursuing a bachelor's degree in Logistics Management.

His military assignments include serving as First Sergeant of Alpha Company, 172nd Support Battalion at Fort Wainwright, Alaska and G4 Sergeant Major of the 1st Cavalry Division at Fort Hood, Texas. In August 2004, he was serving as Command Sergeant Major for the 115th Forward Support Battalion.

Joseph, Phyllis R.

COMMAND SERGEANT MAJOR—ARMY

She is a native of West Palm Beach, Florida. She entered the United States Army in February 1980. She attended Basic Combat Training at Fort Leonard Wood, Missouri, and Advanced Individual Training at Fort Sam Houston, Texas, as a Combat Medic.

She holds a Bachelor of Science degree from Benedict College in Columbia, South Carolina. Her military education includes all the Noncommissioned Officer Education System Courses; Medical NCO Course (91B); Emergency Medical Technician Course; Small Group Leaders Course; Instructor Development Course; Mobilization Officer Course; Movement Course (Ground and Air); Air Operation Movement Course; Master Fitness Course; Battle Staff Course; First Sergeants Course; the United States Army Sergeants Major Academy (class 52); and the Command Sergeants Major Course.

She has served in a variety of positions of increased responsibility, including Command Sergeant Major, Troop Command, BAMC; Chief Operations NCO, VII Corps NCO Academy, Augsburg, Germany; Noncommissioned Officer in Charge of Resource Management, Southwest Asia; Chief of Operations for the NCO Academy (PLDC and BNCOC), Fort Carson, Colorado; Senior Medical Operation NCO, Readiness Group 5th United States Army, Salt Lake City, Utah; First Sergeant, Echo Company, 232nd Medical Battalion, Fort Sam Houston, Texas; Plans and Operations NCO, V CORPS Surgeon's Office, Heidelberg, Germany; and Sergeant Major for the Command Surgeon of the Combined Coalition Component Land Forces, 3rd United States Army, Kuwait. She deployed in support of Operation Desert Shield/Desert Storm, Operation Enduring Freedom; and Operation Iraq Freedom. In January 2005, she was serving as Command Sergeant

Major of Moncrief Army Community Hospital at Fort Jackson South Carolina.

Joseph, Ronald H.

COMMAND SERGEANT MAJOR—ARMY

He was born in Trinidad and Tobago in the West Indies, and is the fourth of seven children. When he was 18, his family moved to Brooklyn, New York. It was there that he was inspired to join the Army in 1978.

He holds a master's degree in Business Administration from Campbell University in North Carolina and is a graduate of all the NCO Courses, including the Sergeants Major Academy and the Army Management Staff College.

His Army career has spanned numerous assignments both in the United States and abroad, including First Sergeant of Special Operations Command in Europe and Assistant Inspector General of the 6th Area Support Group in Stuttgart. He has also deployed to Saudi Arabia in support of Operations Desert Shield and Desert Storm, and to San Vito, Italy, in support of Operation Joint Endeavor. He has served as the Command Sergeant Major for the 80th Area Support Group in Chievres, Belgium. In 2004 he was selected as the Command Sergeant Major of the 26th Area Support Group.

Joyner, Dennis S.

CHIEF WARRANT OFFICER 3—ARMY

He entered the United States Army in August 1976, after graduating from Pine Forest Sr. High School in Fayetteville, North Carolina. After completing his first tour of duty, he decided to pursue a career in computer science, specifically information systems. After successfully completing the Army Computer Programmer/

Analyst Advanced Individual Training, he was assigned to Vint Hill Farm Station (VHFS) at Warrenton, Virginia, as a computer programmer.

His military and civilian education includes a bachelor's degree in Management Information Systems (cum laude) from Park College, Missouri, and an associate's degree in Computer Science and Data Processing. In 1997, he earned a Masters of Science in Management Information Systems from George Washington University. He is also a graduate of the Army Management Staff College; the Advanced Management Program at the National Defense University; and the Federal Executive Institute.

Upon leaving the Army in February 1984, he returned to Vint Hill Farm Station as a civilian employee where he held the positions of Systems Programmer, Chief of the Executive Software Branch; Chief of Operations and Systems Integration Division, and Deputy Director of Information Management. In 1991, he was promoted to Director of Information Management at Vint Hill Farm Station.

In 1994, he joined the staff of the United States Army Military District of Washington as the Assistant Deputy Chief of Staff for Information Management (ADC-SIM). He served as the principal civilian advisor for Information Systems Management providing staff and technical advice to the Commander, staff and tenant activities of six installations. He also served as the Career Program Manager for the Information Management professionals, identifying their developmental and training needs.

In October 2002, Mr. Joyner became the first National Capital Region Director of Information Management (NCR-DOIM), which is a subordinate organization of the Installation Management Agency, Northeast Regional Office.

Mr. Joyner also served as a Chief Warrant Officer 3, Information Systems Technician, in the Virginia Army National Guard. As a reservist, he led a team engaged in providing Information Assurance support to the active component, the National Guard Bureau Headquarters, and the National Guard Directors of Information Management throughout the United States. In 2003, Mr. Joyner retired from the Army National Guard after 27 years of military service.

Joyner, Joel L.
SERGEANT MAJOR—ARMY

He is a native of Newport News, Virginia, and he is the proud father of two sons, Brandon and Keanan, and one daughter, Arleana. He holds a Bachelor of Music Education degree from Shaw University in Raleigh, North Carolina. Before entering the Army he served as a music educator and performing/recording artist in Quebec, Canada.

He entered the Army in December 1977, upon completion of Basic Training, and was assigned to Fort Polk, Louisiana. His military education includes the First Sergeant Course and the United States Army Sergeants Major Academy, where he exceeded course standards and was also the first soldier/musician to earn both the "Iron Person Award" and "John O. Marsh, Jr. Award" for academic excellence and physical fitness. His military assignments include serving with The United States Continental Army Band; on Combat Tour in support of Operations Desert Shield/Desert Storm with the 1st Armored Division Band; with the United States Army in Europe Band and Chorus, 24th Infantry Division Band, where he was the recipient of the Commanding General's "Pot of Gold Award" for volunteered youth service; and the Army Ground Forces Band.

Sergeant Major Joyner is currently assigned as the

Enlisted Bandleader of the United States Army Europe Band and Chorus, and Musical Director "Soldiers of Swing" 18-piece jazz ensemble.

Keasley, Dawn
MAJOR—AIR FORCE

In July, 2004, she was selected as the new Commander of the 375th Mission Support Squadron at Scott Air Force Base, Illinois. On the same day her twin sister Major Shawna O'Brien took command of the 319th MSS at Grand Forks Air Force Base, North Dakota.

Keit, Patricia A.
COMMAND SERGEANT MAJOR—ARMY

She is a Georgia native and entered the United States Army in July 1976. She graduated from Basic Combat Training at Fort Jackson, South Carolina, and Advanced Individual Training as a Radio Operator at Fort Monmouth, New Jersey.

Her military education includes all the Noncommissioned Officer Education System Courses; Communications Security Custodian Course (Honor Graduate); the Instructor Training Course; Systems Approach to Training; Small Group Leadership Course; the First Sergeant Course; the Command Sergeant Major's Designee Course; and the United States Army Sergeants Major Academy (class 50). She earned an associate's degree in Applied Science from Georgia Military College at Milledgeville, Georgia.

Her key military assignments include serving as Instructor at the Regimental Noncommissioned Officer's Academy at Fort Gordon, Georgia; Nodal Platoon Sergeant with the 304th Signal Battalion at Camp Colbern, South Korea; Operations Sergeant of the 15th Regimental Signal Brigade at Fort Gordon; First Ser-

geant of Alpha and Bravo Company, 551st Signal Battalion, at Fort Gordon; Fist Sergeant of Alpha Company, 307th Signal Battalion at Camp Carroll; First Sergeant of Headquarters and Alpha Company, 369th Signal Battalion at Fort Gordon; Special Projects Sergeant Major at the United States Army Sergeant's Major Academy at Fort Bliss, Texas; Command Sergeant Major, 551st Signal Battalion, Fort Gordon; and Command Sergeant Major, 41st Signal Battalion, at Yongsan Garrison, South Korea. In August 2004, she was serving as the Command Sergeant Major, Area IV Support Activity, in South Korea.

Keller, Sherry B.
LIEUTENANT COLONEL—ARMY

She is a native of Virginia, began her military career as an enlisted soldier. She served as a 91B (Medic) in the 18th Field Hospital at Norfolk, Virginia. She is a graduate of Hampton University where she was commissioned as a Second Lieutenant in the Ordnance Corps. She holds a master's degree from Central Michigan University. Her military schooling includes the Ordnance Course, the Nuclear Biological School, the Combined Arms Services Staff School, the Support Operations Course and the Command and General Staff College.

Her assignments includes serving Executive Officer of the Aviation Support Battalion, then as the Division Logistics Planner, followed up as the G4 (Forward) for Task Force Falcon and finally served as the Division Deputy G4 with the 1st Infantry Division in Germany. She served as Commander of the Missile Maintenance Company with the 24th Infantry Division at Fort Stewart, Georgia; and was selected to serve as the Special Assistant to the Commanding General of Army Materiel Command in Alexandria, Virginia. In August 2004, she was serving as the Commander of the 6th Ordnance Battalion.

Kelley, Mildred C.
COMMAND SERGEANT MAJOR—ARMY

She graduated from Knoxville College, Tennessee, with a bachelor's degree in Chemistry in 1949. She briefly taught high school before joining the Army in 1950. She became the first black female Sergeant Major in the Army while serving at the Pentagon in 1972. She achieved another first two years later when she became the first female Command Sergeant Major at a Major Installation.

Retiring in 1976, she remained active by serving on a multitude of boards and commissions such as the Women in Military Service for America Memorial Foundation, the Maryland Veterans Commission and the Veterans Advisory Board. She passed away on January 27, 2004, at the age of 75, after struggling with cancer. She is buried in section 67 of Arlington National Cemetery.

Kellman, Juian A.
COMMAND SERGEANT MAJOR—ARMY

Command Sergeant Major Juian A. Kellman entered the United States Army in July 1976. He completed his Basic Combat Training at Fort Jackson, South Carolina, and Advanced Individual Training at Fort Benning, Georgia. He earned an associate's degree in Business Administration from Troy State University in Alabama. His military education includes the Advanced Airborne Courses; Light Leaders Courses; Pathfinders Course; Ranger Course; Recondo Course; Basic Instructor Course; Bradley Infantry Fighting Vehicle Course; Jungle Warfare Course; Battle Staff Course; First Sergeant Course; and United States Army Sergeants Major Academy. He has served in virtually every enlisted leadership position from Team Leader to Brigade Command Sergeant Major. He has served in every type of unit, including Mechanized Infantry, Ranger Infantry, Light Infantry, and Airborne Infantry. He served as an ROTC Instructor and Ranger Instructor.

He is currently serving as the 3rd Infantry Division (Mechanized) Division Command Sergeant Major at Fort Stewart/Hunter Army Airfield, Georgia.

Kelly, James C., Jr.
CHIEF MASTER SERGEANT—AIR FORCE

He is a native of Richmond, Virginia, and entered the United States Air Force in May 1977 as an aircraft armament systems technician. He has held various assignments in aircraft maintenance including Maintenance Superintendent for two fighter squadrons and two operations groups. His assignments include bases in the Philippines, New Mexico, Idaho, Texas, North Carolina, Italy, and Georgia. He has participated in Operations Southern Watch, Deny Flight, Deliberate Force, Allied Force and Enduring Freedom.

In July 2004, he was assigned as Chief Master Sergeant for the Commander of the 52nd Fighter Wing at Spangdahlem Air Base, Germany. He serves as the

Chief Master Sergeant for the 4,600 enlisted personnel assigned to the wing.

Kelly, Shelton J.
COMMAND SERGEANT MAJOR—ARMY

He enlisted in the United States Army in November 1977. He attended Once Station Unit Training at Fort Sill, Oklahoma, as a Cannoneer/Gunner. His military and civilian education includes completing the Basic Airborne School; Jump Master Course; Air Assault School; Unit Armor Course; 155mm Atomic Projectile Supervisor Course; Academy Small Group Instruction Training Course; Toxic Agent Training at the Chemical Defense Training Facility; and Gennan Head Start. He is also a graduate of the First Sergeants Course and the Advanced and Basic Noncommissioned Officer Leadership Courses. He holds an Associate of Science degree.

His assignments include serving as Section Chief; Platoon Sergeant; Chief Instructor; First Sergeant; FSE Sergeant Major; and Battalion Command Sergeant Major. In August 2004, he was serving as Command Sergeant Major for the 2nd Battalion, 17th Field Artillery.

Kelsey, Edward G. E.
FIRST SERGEANT—ARMY

He was born in Philadelphia, Pennsylvania, and entered the United States Army in August 1989. He completed Basic Combat Training at Fort Knox, Kentucky, and Advanced Individual Training at Fort Sam Houston, Texas, as a Patient Administrative

Specialist and then volunteered to cross train as a as a 91B and was awarded the Combat Medical Specialist MOS.

His military education includes all the Noncommissioned Officer Education System Courses; the Instructor Trainer Course; the Master Fitness Course; the Battle Staff Noncommissioned Officer Course; and the Drill Sergeant School. He earned a Bachelor of Science degree in Nursing with a minor in Management from Thomas Edison State College.

He has held numerous positions of responsibility, including serving as a Small Group Leader/Instructor for the Primary Leadership Development Course; as Chief Wardmaster/Treatment Platoon Sergeant/First Sergeant for C Company, 501st Forward Support Battalion, in Friedberg, Germany; as Wardmaster, Pediatric Ward and Chief Clinical NCO, Maternal Child Health Nursing Section, at Womack Army Medical Center at Fort Bragg, North Carolina; as Platoon Drill Sergeant/Senior Drill Sergeant, A Company, 232nd Medical Battalion; and as the Non-Commissioned Officer in Charge of the IET Training Division in the Department of Combat Medic Training, G Company, 232nd Medical Battalion, at Fort Sam Houston, Texas. In April 2005, he was serving as the First Sergeant for Bravo Company, 232nd Medical Battalion, at Fort Sam Houston.

Kendall, Gene R.
REAR ADMIRAL—NAVY

He was born in Newport News, Virginia. He married the former Sandra A. Olivier of Milwaukee, Wisconsin. They have two sons, Jerome and Christin. He is the son of Mr. and Mrs. Hugh Kendal of Greensboro, North Carolina. His military education includes Surface Warfare Officer School.

He graduated from James B. Dudley High School in Greensboro, North Carolina, in 1963. After attending Duke University for two years, he enlisted in the United States Navy as a seaman apprentice in the Nuclear Field. He completed Nuclear Power training in 1965 and was assigned as a NESEP student at the University of Kansas. After graduating with a Bachelor of Science degree in Engineering Physics in 1972, he was commissioned as an Ensign. He earned a Masters of Science degree in Engineering.

In March 1972, he was assigned as Gunnery and Missile Officer on the USS *Berkeley* (DDG-15). From August 1975 to March 1978, he was the Executive Officer on the USS *Grasp* (ARS-24). From January 1979 to November 1980, he was assigned as Chief Engineer on the USS *McDonnell* (FF-1043). In November 1980, he received an assignment as Readiness, Administration and Training Officer on the reactivated staff of Commander Destroyer Squadron Eight.

From December 1982 to April 1984, he served as the Commissioning Executive Officer on the USS *Williamette* (AO-180). From May 1984 to March 1987, he reported as the First Director of the Engineering Officer of the Watch Courses at the Surface Warfare Officer's School Command in Newport, Rhode Island. In July 1987, he was selected as the Commander of USS *Sphinx* (ARL-24). In January 1991, he was assigned as the Special Assistant to the Chief of Naval Operations (CNO) for Equal Opportunity. On May 8, 1996, Secretary of Defense William J. Perry nominated him to Rear Admiral of the Lower Half. He was assigned as Director of Surface Warfare Manpower and Training Requirements Branch in Washington, D.C. In April 1998, he was assigned as Director of the Commander in Chief Liaison Division in Washington, D.C.

His military awards and decorations include the Meritorious Service medal (with two oak leaf clusters); the Navy Commendation Medal (with two oak leaf clusters); the Good Conduct Medal; and the Navy Achievement Medal.

Kennedy, Deborah A.
CHIEF MASTER SERGEANT—AIR FORCE

She is a 1980 graduate of Effingham County High School in Springfield, Georgia. After high school she entered the Air Force and completed Administrative Apprentice Course at Keesler Air Force Base, Mississippi, in 1981. Her military and civilian education includes Eighth Air Force Noncommissioned Officer Leadership School; Strategic Air Command Noncommissioned Officer Academy; and Senior Noncommissioned Officer Academy. She holds an associate's degree in Administrative Management from the Community College of the Air Force; an associate's degree in Business Administration; and a bachelor's degree in Communications from Louisiana Tech University at Ruston, Louisiana; and a Master of Arts Degree in Human Resources Development from Webster University in St Louis, Missouri.

She has held numerous key leadership positions to include serving as Noncommissioned Officer in Charge of Administration, Deputy Chief of Staff for Plans, Headquarters Eighth Air Force, Barksdale Air Force Base, Louisiana; Chief of Information Management for the Communications-Electronics Logistics Division of the 99th Electronic Combat Range Group at Barksdale Air Force Base; Executive Superintendent of the Contracting Directorate of the Human Systems Center at Brooks Air Force Base, Texas; Superintendent of

the Support Directorate at Armstrong Laboratory, Brooks Air Force Base, Texas; Superintendent of the Command Section of Headquarters Third Air Force at Royal Air Force Mildenhall, England; Career Field Manager at the Headquarters of the United States Air Force in Europe, Ramstein Air Base, Germany; Superintendent of Systems Support Flight, 1st Communications Squadron, and 3A0X1 Functional Manager, 1st Fighter Wing, Langely Air Force Base, Virginia; in October 2004, she was serving as the Superintendent, Network Services and 3A0X1 Functional Manager, 1st Fighter Wing, Langley Air Force Base, Virginia.

Kennedy, Randall D.
SERGEANT MAJOR—MARINES

He enlisted in the United States Marine Corps in September 1978. Upon completion of Recruit Training at Marine Corps Recruit Depot, Parris Island, South Carolina, he attended Infantry Training School at Camp Lejeune, North Carolina, and was assigned to 2nd Battalion, 6th Marines as a rifleman.

In August 1979, he was transferred to 3rd Battalion, 3rd Marines, at Marine Corps Air Station Kaneohe Bay, Hawaii, where he served as a Fire Team Leader and Squad Leader. He completed three West Pac Deployments on board various ships during this assignment.

In June 1983, he graduated from Drill Instructor School at Marine Corps Recruit Depot, Parris Island, South Carolina, and completed a successful tour as a Drill Instructor and Senior Drill Instructor with 3rd Recruit Training Battalion in June 1985.

From July 1985 to August 1988, Sergeant Major Kennedy was assigned to Security Battalion, Marine Corps Combat Development Command, Quantico, Virginia, where he served as S-3 Chief, Guard Chief, and as a Sergeant Instructor at the Officer Candidate School.

In September 1988, he transferred to 2nd Battalion, 7th Marines, where he served as a Platoon Sergeant and Section Leader of an 81mm mortar platoon. During this time he completed a unit deployment to Okinawa, Japan, and participated in Operation Desert Shield/ Desert Storm from August 1990 to March 1991.

In July 1991, Sergeant Major Kennedy was reassigned to Marine Corps Recruit Depot, Parris Island, South Carolina, where he served as a Field Skills Instructor, Section Leader and Company First Sergeant with the Field Training Unit, Support Battalion, Recruit Training Regiment.

In August 1994, he transferred to 1st Battalion, 3rd Marines, Marine Corps Air Station, Kaneohe Bay, Hawaii, where he served as a Platoon Sergeant, Company Gunnery Sergeant and Company First Sergeant. During this time he completed two unit deployments to Okinawa, Japan.

From August 1997 to August 2000, Sergeant Major Kennedy was assigned as the First Sergeant, Inspector Instructor Staff, Company B, 4th Combat Engineer Battalion, 4th Marine Division, Marine Forces Reserve, in Roanoke, Virginia.

During August 2000 until June 2003, Sergeant Major Kennedy was assigned as Sergeant Major, 2nd Recruit Training Battalion, RTR, Marine Corps Recruit Depot, at Parris Island, South Carolina.

In July 2003, he assumed duties as the Sergeant Major, MWCS-28, 2nd Marine Air Wing, Cherry Point, North Carolina.

Kennon, James Lewis
BRIGADIER GENERAL—ARMY

He was born in Kinston, North Carolina. He holds a Bachelor of Science degree in Behavioral Science from Chaminade University of Honolulu, a Master of Science in Management from Central Michigan University, and a Master of Science degree in National Resource Management from the National Defense University. His military education includes completion of the Basic and Advanced courses at the Quartermaster School; the Combined Arms and Services Staff School; the United States Army Command and General Staff College; and the Industrial College of the Armed Forces.

He entered the Army in August 1969 from the Bronx, New York. He completed eight years of service as a Noncommissioned Officer and Chief Warrant Officer and was commissioned a second lieutenant through the Fort Benning Officer Candidate School in February 1978.

He has served in command and various staff positions in Vietnam, Japan, Hawaii, Korea, Fort Bragg, Fort Hood, PERSCOM, and the Pentagon, including service with the 1st Calvary Division, 25th Infantry Division, 82nd Airborne Division, 101st Airborne (Air Assault) Division, 19th Theater Army Area Command, and 1st Corps Support Command.

From August 1979 to April 1979, he was assigned as a Platoon Leader, with B Detachment, 407th Supply

and Service Battalion, 82nd Airborne Division, at Fort Bragg, North Carolina. From April 1979 to February 1980, he was assigned as the S-4 (Logistics), 407th Supply and Service Battalion, 82nd Airborne Division, at Fort Bragg, North Carolina. From February 1980 to July 1981, he served first as the Operations Officer for Company A, later as the Commander of Company C, 407th Supply and Service Battalion, with the 82nd Airborne Division at Fort Bragg. From December 1981 to December 1984, he served as the Assistant G-4 (Supply), later Assistant G-4 (Plans), with the 25th Infantry Division (Light), at Schofield Barracks, Hawaii. From May 1986 to May 1987, he was assigned as a Systems Automation Officer, with the United States Army Information Systems Command in Washington, D.C. From May 1987 to May 1988, he was assigned as a Quartermaster Personnel Assignment Officer with the United States Army Total Army Personnel Agency in Alexandria, Virginia. From June 1989 to May 1991, he served as a Joint Logistics Plans Officer in Korea with the United States Forces Korea/Combined Forces Command. He was promoted to Major on July 1, 1989.

From May 1991 to September 1992, he was assigned as a Support Operations Officer, later Executive Officer, with the 227th Maintenance Battalion, Eighth United States Army, in Korea. From October 1992 to May 1994, he served as a Staff Leader, with the Combined Arms Services Staff School, United States Army Command and General Staff College, at Fort Leavenworth, Kansas. He was promoted to Lieutenant Colonel on July 1, 1993.

From May 1994 to June 1996, he was assigned as Commander of the 264th Support Battalion, XVIII Airborne Corps, at Fort Bragg. From June 1996 to July 1997, he served as Chief of the Quartermaster Branch, Officers Personnel Management Directorate, with the United States Total Army Personnel Command in Alexandria, Virginia. He was promoted to Colonel on June 1, 1998.

In June 1998, he was assigned as Commander of the 45th Corps Support (Forward), United States Army Pacific at Schofield Barracks, Hawaii. From June 2000 to August 2001, he served as the Chief of Staff at the United States Army Combined Arms Support Command at Fort Lee, Virginia. In August 2001, he was assigned as the Deputy Commander of United States Army Soldier and Biological Chemical Command in Natick, Massachusetts. In July 2002, he was selected to serve as the Director of Logistics, Engineering and Security Assistance, J4, for the United States Pacific Command at Camp H.M. Smith, Hawaii. He was promoted to Brigadier General on August 1, 2003.

On April 12, 2005, he was assigned as Deputy Commanding General of the Army and Air Force Exchange Service in Texas.

His military awards and decorations include the Legion of Merit (with oak leak cluster); the Bronze Star; Defense Meritorious Service Medal; the Meritorious Service Medal (with four oak leaf clusters); Army Commendation Medal (with five oak leaf clusters); the Joint Service Achievement Medal; Army Achievement Service Medal; the Humanitarian Service Medal; Armed Forces Expedition Medal; Parachutist Badge; and the British Parachutist Badge.

Kent, Carlton W.

SERGEANT MAJOR—MARINES

Sergeant Major Carlton W. Kent completed recruit training at Marine Corps Recruit Depot at Parris Island, South Carolina, in March 1976 and was assigned to the 1st Marine Brigade. In May 1978, he was trans-

ferred to Marine Security Guard and Parachute Riggers School at Fort Lee, Virginia. In June of 1982, he was assigned as 2nd Air Delivery Platoon Commander, and parachute rigger in billets in various commands aboard Camp Lejeune. In June 1992, he transferred to the 4th Marine Regiment. In June 1993, he transferred to the Army Sergeants Major Academy at Fort Bliss, Texas. After graduation, in February 1994 he was transferred and assigned as First Sergeant, Battery L, 3rd Battalion, 12th Marines. In December 1994, he assumed the duties as Sergeant Major, 3rd Battalion, with 12th Marines. In August 1997, he was transferred to the Marine Corps Recruit Depot at San Diego, California where he was assigned duties as Sergeant Major of the Second Recruit Training Battalion and in September 1999 as Sergeant Major Recruit Training Regiment.

Kindred, Samuel Lee

BRIGADIER GENERAL—ARMY

He was born in Omega, Alabama. He received a Bachelor of Science degree in Business Management from Hampton University. He earned a Masters of Art degree in Business Administration from Central Michigan University. His military education includes the Transportation Officer Basic and Advanced Courses; United States Army Command and General Staff College; Defense Systems Management College; and Industrial College of the Armed Forces.

He entered the United States Army as an enlisted soldier and later a warrant officer, before receiving a direct appointment to Second Lieutenant on February 14, 1969. In September 1969, he was assigned as a Flight Training Analysis Officer, later Instructor, United

States Army Primary Helicopter School, at Fort Wolters, Texas. In December 1970, he joined the 23rd Infantry Division in Vietnam, and was assigned first as a Supply Platoon Leader in Company E, 723rd Maintenance Battalion, later Maintenance Platoon Leader, with Company A, 123rd Aviation Battalion. He was promoted to First Lieutenant on February 13, 1970, and to Captain on February 14, 1971.

In November 1971, he returned to the United States to serve as Special Assistant to the Inspector General at the Headquarters of the United States Army Transportation Center at Fort Eustis, Virginia. From December 1973 to January 1977, he was assigned as the Commander of the United States Army Recruiting Command in Columbus, Ohio. In April 1977, he was assigned as an Aviation Advisor with Readiness Region VI at Fort Knox, Kentucky. He was promoted to Major on July 7, 1977.

In May 1980, he was selected to serve as the Assistant Chief of the Technical Management Division of the Defense Contract Administration Services Region of the Defense Logistics Agency in St. Louis, Missouri. In May 1983, he joined the 45th Support Group at Schofield Barracks, Hawaii, as the first Commander of the 347th Transportation Company (AVIM), then as Logistics Operations Officer and later as Commander of the 124th Transportation Battalion. He was promoted to Lieutenant Colonel on June 1, 1985.

In June 1987, he was assigned as Assignment Officer in the Colonels Division of the Officer Personnel Agency in Alexandra, Virginia. In July 1989, he was assigned as Assistant Deputy Chief of Staff for Production at the United States Army Materiel Command in Alexandria, Virginia. On June 1, 1985, he was promoted to Colonel.

In August 1990, he returned to Schofield Barracks, Hawaii, to serve as the Commander of the 45th Support Group. From August 1992 to January 1994, he was assigned as Chief Aviation Logistics Officer in the Office of the Deputy Chief of Staff for Logistics in Washington, D.C. From January 1994 to January 1995, he served as Executive Officer to the Commanding General of United States Army Materiel Command in Alexandria, Virginia. In January 1995, he was selected Deputy Commanding General of the 21st Theater Army Area Command, United States Army Europe Command, United States Army Europe and Seventh Army, Germany. He was promoted to Brigadier General on July 1, 1995, and then appointed Commanding General of the 3rd Corps Support Command, United States Army Europe and Seventh Army, Germany. In November 1996, he was appointed the Deputy Commanding General of United States Army Recruiting Command at Fort Knox, Kentucky.

His military awards and decoration include the Legion of Merit (with two oak leaf clusters); the Bronze Star (with two oak leaf clusters); the Air Medal; the Army Commendation Medal (with two oak leaf clusters); Senior Army Aviator Badge; and the Army Staff Identification Badge.

King, Celes III
BRIGADIER GENERAL—ARMY

Brigadier General King was born in Chicago, Illinois. He is a former Air Force Pilot with the Tuskegee Airmen, and served as a United States Army Reserve Brigadier General in California. He received a LLB degree in Urban Planning from Pacific Coast University; a Master of Business Management degree from Pepperdine University; and a Doctor of Philosophy from Laurence University.

He is a founding charter member of the National Association of Black Military Officers and member of the Los Angeles Chapter of 100 Black Men.

King, Dennis M.
COMMAND SERGEANT MAJOR—ARMY

Command Sergeant Major Dennis M. King is a native of Haines City, Florida. He entered the United States Army on July 28, 1976, and attended Basic and Advanced Individual Training at Fort Sill, Oklahoma. He holds an associate's degree from Central Texas College and is pursuing a Bachelor of Science degree from the University of Phoenix. His military education include the Field Artillery TACFIRE/Fire Support Course; the First Sergeants Course; Nuclear, Biological, and Chemical School; the Drill Sergeant School; the Air Assault School; Airborne School; the All American 82nd Airborne Division Jumpmaster School; and the United States Army Sergeants Major Academy.

During the military career, he has served three tours in West Germany; five tours at Fort Bragg, North Carolina; two tours at Fort Sill, Oklahoma; a tour at Fort Stewart, Georgia; and a tour at Camp Pelham, South Korea. His most recent assignments include serving as

Command Sergeant Major of the 1st Battalion, 319th Airborne Field Artillery Regiment. In June of 1996, he was assigned to Babenhausen, Germany, where he served as the Command Sergeant Major of the 1st Battalion, 27th Field Artillery; and was then assigned as Command Sergeant Major of the 41st Field Artillery Brigade in Germany. In April of 2000, he returned to Fort Bragg to serve as the Command Sergeant Major of the 3rd Battalion, 27th Field Artillery; then as the Command Sergeant Major for the 18th Field Artillery Brigade (Airborne). In May of 2002, Command Sergeant Major King was selected to serve as the Command Sergeant Major of the Field Artillery Training Command and the United States Army Field Artillery School at Fort Sill, Oklahoma.

King, Elijah, Jr.
COMMAND SERGEANT MAJOR—ARMY

He is a native of Tuskegee, Alabama, where he attended Lewis Adams Elementary School and Tuskegee Institute High School. Upon graduation he attended Florida A&M University, where he majored in Instrumental Music Education.

His military career began in 1977, when he enlisted in the Regular Army as a Field Artillery Cannon Crewman. He attended Basic Combat and Advanced Training (OSBUT) at Fort Sill, Oklahoma, and was selected as a course Honor Graduate. His military education includes all the Noncommissioned Officer Education System Courses; the Field Artillery Weapons Mechanic Course at Fort Sill (Distinguished Graduate); the Nuclear Weapons Supervisor Pre-Fire Course; United States Army Recruiters and Retention Course at Fort

Benjamin Harrison, Indiana; Battle Staff Course; First Sergeant Course; and the United States Army Sergeants Major Academy. He holds a Bachelor of Science degree in Liberal Arts from Regents College and the State University of New York at Albany.

His key assignments include serving in 1997 as First Sergeant for C Battery, 3-82nd Field Artillery, 1st Cavalry Division, at Fort Hood, Texas. During Operations Desert Shield and Desert Storm, he served as the Platoon Sergeant for 1st Platoon, B Battery, 3-82nd Field Artillery, 1st Cavalry Division; his Platoon is credited with firing the most rounds of any United States Army Artillery Platoon in this campaign including 8 Copperhead target hits. Since the war he returned to Kuwait three times for Operation Intrinsic Action, Operation Iris Gold, and Operation Vigilant Warrior. During Vigilant Warrior he was the First Sergeant for C Battery 4-41 Field Artillery, 24th Infantry Division. He has participated in National Training Center rotations, serving in position from Cannoneer to Battalion Command Sergeant Major for 3-82nd Field Artillery in June 1998. He currently serves as the Command Sergeant Major for 3rd Battalion, 16th Field Artillery, 4th Infantry Division (Mechanized) at Fort Hood, Texas.

King, J. B.

CAPTAIN—ARMY

He was drafted into the United States Army in April 1963. He served on active duty for over 23 years and retired July 31, 1986. He served two combat tours in Vietnam from 1966–67 and 1971–73. He served as First Sergeant (E-8) and later as Captain, Commander of Headquarters and Headquarters Company at Fort McPherson, Georgia.

He earned a Bachelor of Arts degree in Business/Administration.

His awards include the Good Conduct Medal (7th award); Army Commendation Medal (3rd award); the Joint Service Commendation Medal; Meritorious Service Medal; Bronze Star; and the Combat Infantry Badge.

King, John Q. Taylor, Sr.

LIEUTENANT GENERAL—ARMY

He was born in Memphis, Tennessee, and married the former Marcet Alice Hines of Chicago, Illinois. They have three sons, one daughter, and nine grandchildren. He was graduated from Anderson High School in Austin, Texas. He received a Bachelor of Arts degree from Fisk University in Nashville, Tennessee, in 1941; a Bachelor of Science degree from Huston-Tillotson College in Austin, Texas; a Master of Science from DePaul University in Chicago, Illinois; and a Ph.D. from the University of Texas at Austin. He received an honorary Doctor of Law from Southwestern University in Georgetown, Texas, and St. Edward's University in Austin, Texas; an honorary Doctor of Humane Letters from Austin College in Sherman, Texas, and Fisk University; and an honorary Doctor of Science from Huston-Tillotson College.

He entered World War II as a Private, served as a Captain in the Pacific theater, and retired from the Army as a Major General on August 22, 1983. Since World War II, he has served in Alaska, Japan, Korea, Okinawa, Germany, Hawaii, and many other United States Army and United States Air Force installations. He has completed courses at several senior service schools, including the Command and General Staff College, the Air War College, the Industrial College of the Armed Forces, the Logistics Executive Development

King, Kevin
MAJOR—AIR FORCE

Major King is a T-38 Instructor Pilot in the 5th Flying Training Squadron at Vance Air Force Base, Oklahoma. He is a graduate of the United States Air Force Academy, and a Vance Air Force Base graduate of Class 88-05.

King, Teresa V.
COMMAND SERGEANT MAJOR—ARMY

She was born in Fernandina Beach, Florida. She entered the United States Army in August 1974 as a clerk typist completing three years of active duty before leaving the Army in 1977. After a brief departure, she returned to active duty as a Motor Transport Operator in 1978.

Her military education includes all the Non-Commissioned Officer Education System Courses; Drill Sergeant School; the First Sergeant School; and the

Course, and the SROG at the Army War College. He has received many military awards and decorations.

Former Texas Governor Mark White appointed him Lieutenant General in the Texas State Guard in 1985. He joined the faculty of Huston-Tillotson College in 1947, was Professor of Mathematics for several years and Dean of the college for five years, and was appointed president in 1965 and Chancellor in 1987. He retired on June 30, 1988, and served as Director and Chair of the Center for the Advancement of Science, Engineering, and Technology (CASET), a research component of the college.

Well known as a writer, collaborating with others on four textbooks in mathematics and contributing many articles to professional and religious journals, Dr. King is a coauthor with his wife of two books, *Stories of Twenty-Three Famous Negro Americans* and *Famous Black Americans,* and a booklet on the life of Mrs. Mary McLeod Bethune. General King served as a member of the board of directors of several organizations including Texas Commerce Bank-Austin, Austin Chapter National Conference of Christians and Jews, the Capitol Area Council, and Boy Scouts of America, and as former chair of the Lone Star District. A former chairman of the Austin Civil Service Commission, he is a trustee of Austin College, a former trustee of Fisk University, and a member of the Philosophical Society of Texas. A licensed mortician, he served as president of King-Tears Mortuary, Inc.

He has received many awards and honors, including the Roy Wilkins Meritorious Award from the NAACP; the Arthur B. DeWitt Award; the Martin Luther King, Jr., Humanitarian Award; the Military/ Education Award: the Whitney M. Young, Jr., Award; and the Minority Advocate of the Year Award from the Austin Chamber of Commerce.

United States Army Sergeants Major Academy (class 49).

Her key military assignments include serving as a Drill Sergeant, in Charlie, Delta and Alpha Companies at Fort Dix, New Jersey; as a PLDC Instructor in the 64th Support Battalion in Wiesbaden, Germany; as a Squad Leader with the 15th Supply and Transport Battalion; as a Drill Sergeant Leader at the Drill Sergeant School at Fort Knox, Kentucky; as a Transportation Coordinator, 227th Maintenance Battalion at Yongson, South Korea; as a Platoon Sergeant, Bravo Company, 724th Main Support Battalion, at Fort Stewart; as First Sergeant, 24th Forward Support Battalion at Fort Stewart; as an Active Duty Advisor with the National Guard, 1454th Transportation Battalion at Concord, North Carolina; as the Non-Commissioned Officer in Charge of the Division Transportation Office, 2nd Infantry Division, Camp Red Cloud, South Korea; as both First Sergeant and Command Sergeant Major at Fort Story, Virginia; as Command Sergeant Major, Advanced Individual Training Battalion, 58th Transportation Battalion at Fort Leonard Wood, Missouri. From May 2001 to June 2003, she was the Brigade Command Sergeant Major, 1st Transportation Movement Control Agency, in Kaiserslautern, Germany. In July 2005, she was serving as the Command Sergeant Major for the Installation Management Agency-European Region in Heidelberg, Germany.

Kirk-McAlpine, Patricia
SENIOR EXECUTIVE SERVICE

She began her Federal Service as a member of the three-year United States Army Career Intern Program. Following graduation from the intern program, she was immediately assigned as lead negotiator with the United States Army Missile Command's Hawk Missile System

Program Office. As an Air Force civilian, her first assignment with the Air Force Plant Representative Office at Northrop Corporation was followed by a position as negotiator for the Space and Missile Systems organizations Advanced Ballistic Reentry System. Shortly thereafter, she became a contracting officer for the Secretary of the Air Force Office of Special Projects. In January 2005, she was serving as Director of Contracting at the Space and Missile Systems Center in the Air Force Space Command at Los Angeles Air Force Base, California.

Her education includes a Bachelor of Arts degree from Stillman College at Tuscaloosa, Alabama, and a Master of Business Administration degree from Alabama A&M University. She has also completed the Executive Development Course at the University of Southern California; Defense Systems Management Course at Fort Belvoir, Virginia; Senior Executive Fellows Program at Harvard University in Cambridge, Massachusetts; Leadership for a Democratic Society at the Federal Executive Institute; National Security Leadership Course at Johns Hopkins University; and the Defense Systems Management College at Fort Belvoir.

Kirkland, William Charles
BRIGADIER GENERAL—ARMY

He is a Distinguished Military Graduate of the ROTC program at North Carolina State University. He was commissioned a Second Lieutenant and received a Bachelor of Science degree in Industrial Operations Educations. He has also received a Master of Science degree in Physiology and a Doctor of Medicine degree from the University of Illinois. His military education includes the Ordnance Officer Basic

Course; the Armor Officer Advanced Course; the United States Army Command and General Staff College; and the United States Army War College.

He entered the Army in May 1976, as a student in the Ordnance Basic Course at Aberdeen Proving Ground, Maryland. His first assignment was as a Magazine Platoon Leader, later as a Control Officer with the 664th Ordnance Company, at Fort Hood, Texas. In April 1978, he was assigned as a Branch Chief with the Munitions Supply Branch of the 4th Support Center at Fort Hood, Texas. From July 1978 to January 1979, he served as the Protocol Officer/Escort Officer with the III Corps at Fort Hood. In January 1979, he served as a Maintenance Platoon Leader with the 70th Ordnance Company (General Support) in Turkey. From March 1980 to December 1980, he was a student in the Armor Officer Advanced Course at Fort Knox, Kentucky. From December 1980 to May 1982, he served as the Assistance S4 (Logistics) with the 1st Brigade, 1st Infantry Division, at Fort Riley, Kansas.

In October, he received his first Army Reserve assignment, as Commander of A Troop, 3rd Squadron, 337th Cavalry Regiment, in Rockford, Illinois. From October 1986 to September 1989, he was assigned as Operations Officer of the 3rd Squadron, 337th Calvary Regiment, in Rockford. In October 1989, he was assigned as the Executive Officer with the 3rd Battalion, 85th Infantry Regiment at Arlington Heights Illinois. From June 1991 to February 1993, he served as the Commander of the 2nd Battalion, 377th Infantry Regiment, in Chicago, Illinois. In March 1993, he was selected to serve as the Commander of the 1st Battalion of the 84th Infantry Regiment, 1st Brigade, 84th Division (Training), in Chicago.

From September 1994 to January 1998, he was assigned as the Assistant Deputy Chief of Staff for Operations, Schools, 84th Division (Institutional Training), in Milwaukee, Wisconsin. He was assigned as Commander of the 1st Brigade, Infantry One Station Unit Training, 84th Division (Institutional Training) in Livonia, Michigan. From June 2001 to April 2002, he was assigned as the Assistant Division Commander for the 84th Division (Institutional Training) in Milwaukee, Wisconsin. In April 2002, he was selected as the Command of the 88th Regional Support Group in Indianapolis, Indiana.

His military awards and decorations include the Legion of Merit; the Meritorious Service Medal (with oak leaf cluster); the Army Commendation Medal (with two oak leaf clusters); the Army Achievement Medal; and the Parachutist Badge.

Kirkman, Allen, Jr.
COLONEL—AIR FORCE

He entered the Air Force in 1980, after completion of the Air Force Reserve Officers Training Corps as a distinguished graduate.

His military and civilian education includes a bachelor's degree in Biology and Chemistry from North Carolina Central University in Durham, North Car-

olina; a master's degree in Human Resources Management and Development from Chapman University in Orange, California; and a master's degree in National Security & Strategic Studies, from the Naval War College, at New Port, Rhode Island; Squadron Officer School, at Maxwell Air Force Base, Alabama; Marine Corps Command & Staff College; Academic Instructor School, Maxwell Air Force Base, Alabama; Air Command and Staff College; Air War College; Armed Forces Staff College, Norfolk, Virginia; National Defense Fellow, at Massachusetts Institute of Technology, Cambridge, Massachusetts; College of Naval Command & Staff, at Newport, Rhode Island.

His key military assignments include serving from April 1991 to April 1992, as Executive Support Officer, Command Protocol, Headquarters Strategic Air Command, at Offutt Air Force Base, in Nebraska; In June 1994, he was assigned as Operations Officer NCA SIOP adviser), Operations Officer (military readiness) and Executive Officer, Directorate for Operations (J-3), Joint Staff, at Pentagon, Washington, D.C.; in March 1998, he was assigned as Commander, 4th Space Operations Squadron, at Schriever Air Force Base, in Colorado; in March 2001, as Commander, 341st Operations Group, Malmstrom Air Force Base, Montana; in January 2005, he was serving as Commander, 460th Space Wing, Buckley Air Force Base, Colorado. As base host, the wing services 43 associates and approximately 88,000 people in the Front Range.

While assigned to the Pentagon, he built and maintained the Chairman of the Joint Chiefs of Staffs critical decision-making document, the Nuclear Decision Handbook for the President of the United States, to assist with executing United States Strategic and Theater Nuclear Forces.

This black pilot-scientist with a Ph.D. in nuclear

chemistry was killed in an aircraft crash. In 1997, 30 years later, the Air Force officially recognized Maj. Lawrence as an astronaut, thus clearing the way for the Astronaut Memorial Foundation to etch his name in the Space Mirror.

Klugh, James Richard
MAJOR GENERAL—ARMY

He was born in Greenwood, South Carolina, he married the former Theresa Minnis, and they have three children, Jerome, James, and Denise. He received an Army Reserve commission as a second lieutenant through the Reserve Officer Training Corps Program at South Carolina State University, where he also received a Bachelor of Science degree in Public Administration. His military education includes the Infantry School, the Chemical School, the United States Army Command and General Staff College, the Logistics Executive Development Course, and the United States War Army College.

He has held a wide variety of command and staff assignments, including a tour in Germany and staff assignment with the 101st Airborne Division in Vietnam. His significant assignments include: Commander, 502nd Supply and Transportation Battalion, 2nd Armored Division, Fort Hood, Texas; Chief of Staff, United States Army Tank-Automotive Command, Warren, Michigan; Commander, Dugway Proving Ground, Utah; Deputy Director, Officer Personnel Management Division, United States Army Military personnel Center, Alexandria, Virginia; and Deputy Commander for Training Development, United States Army Logistics Center, Fort Lee, Virginia. He was promoted to Brigadier General October 1, 1983.

He was assigned at Aberdeen Proving Ground, Maryland, in February 1984 as Deputy Commanding General, Chemical Materiel, United States Army Armament, Munitions and Chemical Command, Commanding General, United States Army Chemical Research and Development Center. From June 1986 to July 1987, he was assigned as the Deputy Chief of Staff for Personnel, at the United States Army Materiel Command, in Alexandria, Virginia. He was promoted to Major General on March 1, 1987.

From July 1987 to March 1990, he served as the Assistant Deputy Chief of Staff for Logistics, in the Office of the Deputy Chief of Staff for Logistics, in Washington, D.C.

His military awards and decorations include: Distinguished Service Medal; the Legion of Merit (with two oak leaf clusters); Meritorious Service Medal (with oak leaf cluster); several Air Medals; Army Commendation Medal (with two oak leaf clusters); and the Parachutist Badge.

In 1982 General Klugh was inducted into the South Carolina College Army Reserve Officer Training Corps Hall of Fame for outstanding contributions to the United States of America. He retired on March 31, 1990.

Knight, Anthony E.
COMMAND MASTER CHIEF—NAVY

He enlisted in the United States Navy in June 1976. He reported to Recruit Training Command in Orlando, Florida on 23 June 1976. After completing Basic Recruit Training he reported to Fleet Training Center, at Norfolk, Virginia, and on to his first duty station, USS *Howard W. Gilmore* (AS 16). He attended Electrician's Mate "A" School and return to USS *Howard W. Gilmore* (AS 16) and USS *Holland* (AS 32), before

reporting to Commander, Naval Support Antarctica, Port Hueneme, California, and Christ Church, New Zealand. Following completion of Electrician's Mate "C" School, he served a Naval Support Activity, Naples, Italy and USS *Mount Whitney* (LCC 20) as Leading Chief Petty Officer of Electrical Division.

He transferred to Recruit Training Command, Orlando, Florida, as a Company Commander; he served onboard the USS *Mississippi* (CGN 40) as Electrical Division Officer; and onboard USS *George Washington* (CVN 73) as Senior Enlisted Advisor to the Chief Engineer; during this tour of duty, he was promoted to Master Chief Petty Officer at Naval Computer and Telecommunications area Master Station Europe Central. He is a graduate of the Senior Enlisted Academy. In October 2004, he was serving as Command Master Chief, Surface Warfare.

Knightner, Larry
MAJOR GENERAL — ARMY

He is a native of Columbia, South Carolina, and graduated from C.A. Johnson High School in 1968. He and his wife Tonja, have two grown children, Joielle and Jason. He was a distinguished military graduate fro South Carolina State University, where he earned a Bachelor of Science degree in Business Administration in 1972. He earned his Master of Science in Business Administration, from Atlanta University in 1974. His military education include: the adjutant General Officer Basic and Advanced Courses; the United States Army Command and General Staff College; United State Army War College.

He was commissioned into the United States Army Reserves as a second lieutenant on May 14, 1972, after completing the ROTC program at South Carolina State College. His senior staff and command assignments include: In April 1987, serving as Chief, Officer Person-

nel Management Branch, later as Chief, Personnel Actions Branch, with the 120th Army Reserve Command, at Fort Jackson, South Carolina. In September 1989, he was assigned as the Commander of the 815th Personnel Services Company, in Orangeburg, South Carolina.

In September 1990, his Company was deployed to Saudi Arabia. The 815th Personnel Company, returned to Orangeburg, South Carolina in May 1991. From April 1992 to September 1993, he was assigned as Director, Enlisted Courses, 3287th United States Army Reserve Forces School, in Columbia, South Carolina. In September 1993, he was assigned as Chief, Personnel, Plans, and Management Division, with the 120th Army Reserve Command, at Fort Jackson, South Carolina. From September 1994 to June 1997, he was assigned as the Commander, 360th Personnel Replacement Battalion (Continental United States Replacement Center), at Myrtle Beach, South Carolina. In June 1997, he assigned as Deputy Chief of Staff, Operations; later Chief of Staff; later Deputy Commander, of the 81st Regional Support Group, at Fort Jackson, South Carolina. In December 2001, he was selected to serve as the Commander of the 81st Regional Support Group, at Fort Jackson, South Carolina. He was promoted to Brigadier General on August 5, 2002. He was promoted to Major General in May 2005.

His military awards and decorations include: the Bronze Star Medal; the Meritorious Service Medal (with four oak leaf clusters); Army Commendation Medal; National Defense Medal.

Knox, Frank J.
SERGEANT MAJOR — MARINE

He enlisted in the United States Marine Corps in June 1977 and graduated from Recruit Training in September 1977.

He has held numerous leadership position to include serving as Drill Instructor; Senior Drill Instructor with First Recruit Training Battalion; Instructor at Drill

Instructor School; Platoon Sergeant, 81mm Mortar Platoon; First Sergeant Weapons Company, 1st Battalion, 8th Marines; Inspector-Instructor Staff, Military Police Company — B; Sergeant Major, Marine Heavy Helicopter Squadron 461, Marine Aircraft Group 26, 2nd Marine Aircraft Wing; Sergeant Major, 26th Marine Expeditionary Unit, the 26th Marine Expeditionary Unit returned from participating in combat operations in Iraqi Freedom and Humanitarian Operations in support of Joint Task Force Liberia, in October 2003.

Knox, Ricky
COMMAND SERGEANT MAJOR—ARMY

He is a native of Frankford, Delaware and enlisted in the military in 1979 as a 64C Motor Transport Operator and attended OSUT at Fort Dix, New Jersey. During his career he has obtained an Associates Degree in General Studies, from Central Texas College; he also holds a Bachelors Degree in Human Resources Management. His military education includes all the Noncommissioned Officers Education System Courses; the First Sergeant Course; the United States Army Sergeants Major Academy.

His key leadership assignments include serving as Squad leader; Platoon Sergeant/Platoon Leader; Section Chief; First Sergeant; Health Promotion NCOIC at the Sergeants Major Academy. He was promoted to Command Sergeant Major on March 1, 2003. He is currently being assigned as the Battalion Command Sergeant Major of the 49th Movement Control Battalion at Fort Hood, Texas.

Lacy, Lewis, Jr.
SERGEANT MAJOR—ARMY

Sergeant Major Lewis Lacy, Jr. is a native of West Virginia. He married the former Roxanne Powell from Philadelphia, Pennsylvania, and they have three Children, Lewis III, Clarence; and Gabrielle. His military

education include: the United States Army Sergeants Major Academy (#46).

He entered the Army on February 20, 1975, at Fort Knox, Kentucky. Upon completion of his Basic Training and Advanced Individual Training as an Armor Crewman, he was assigned to A Company, 1/33rd Armor Battalion, Gelenhausen, in German. After Germany, he was assigned to the Test Evaluation Command at Aberdeen Proving Ground, in Maryland. He has held leadership positions from Squad Leader to First Sergeant and Sergeant Major. As a Company First Sergeant, B Company, 4/67th Armor Battalion, he deployed to Saudi Arabia in support of Operations Desert Shield/Desert Storm. While assigned to the 1st Armored Division in Germany, he also deployed to Bosnia-Herzegovina in support of Operations Joint Endeavor/Joint Guard. He also served as an Assistant Inspector General, for the 1st Calvary Division, Fort Hood, Texas.

He is currently serving as the Sergeant Major for the 5th Brigade, Fourth Region, United States Army Cadet Command, in Fort Sam Houston, Texas

Lane, Ray D.
COMMAND SERGEANT MAJOR—ARMY

He is a native of West Palm Beach, Florida where he attended Palm Beach Gardens High School. He entered the Army under the Delayed Entry Program in October of 1976 and completed both Basic and Advanced Individual Training at Fort Sill, Oklahoma. Command Sergeant Major Lane

ended his term of service in 1980 and returned to his hometown. He reenlisted in 1981, after attending school with The National Association of Home Builders, graduating number one in his class.

His military education includes: he was an Honor Graduate of Advanced Individual Training; all levels of the Noncommissioned Officers Education System Courses; the Master Fitness Course; the United States Army Sergeants Major Academy (class 48); the Command Sergeants Major (D) Course. He holds an Associates of Arts Degree from the University of Maryland; a Bachelor of Business Administration from McKendree College; in 2004, he was enrolled in Boston University, pursuing a Master's Degree.

He has served in numerous leadership positions from Squad Leader, Senior Drill Sergeant, First Sergeant, Battalion Communication Chief, Battalion Signal Officer, Division G6 Sergeant Major, and Battalion Sergeant Major.

He was inducted into the prestigious USAREUR Sergeant Morales Club in 1986. He was selected as both the 160th Signal Brigade and 52nd Signal Battalion Noncommissioned Officer of the Year. He was also selected as the 46th Infantry Drill Sergeant of the Year. He was also selected as the 46th Infantry Drill Sergeant of the Year.

Langford, Victor C., III
BRIGADIER GENERAL—AIR FORCE

He was born in Detroit, Michigan. He married the former Luana Calvert and they have four children, Tanya; Natalie; Kineta; and Victor IV.

He received a Bachelor of Arts degree from Seattle Pacific College. He earned a BD degree and a MD degree from Concordia Seminary.

He began his military career with the Washington State National Guard, as a Chaplin in 1972. He retired as a Brigadier General, the Washington National Guard State Chaplin.

Langston, William E.
COMMAND SERGEANT MAJOR—ARMY

CSM Langston is a native of Suffolk, Virginia. He earned a Bachelor of Science degree in Human Resource Management from Troy State University and a Associate of Science Degree in Management from Park College. His military education includes: the United States Army Sergeant Major Academy, the First Sergeant Course; the TRADOC IET Pre-Command Course.

He entered the United States Army in June 1976. He completed Basic Combat Training at Fort Knox, Kentucky, and Advanced Individual Training for Medical Specialist at Fort Sam Houston, Texas.

Leardo, Eduardo E.
SERGEANT MAJOR—MARINE

He was born in Brooklyn, New York. He enlisted into the Marines Corps in August 1976 and reported to Recruit Depot, Parris Island in October the same year. Upon graduating from Camp Pendleton Infantry Training School, he received the MOS 0311, and subsequently reported to Marine Barracks, Subic Bay, Philippines for duty.

His key leadership assignments include serving as Sergeant of the Guard; Squad Leader; Patrol Leader; Mortar Section Leader; Battalion Career Planner; Weapons Platoon Commander; Platoon Sergeant; Platoon Commander; Drill Instructor; Chief Drill Instructor; Company Gunnery Sergeant; First Sergeant; Squadron Sergeant Major; ACE Sergeant Major.

In March 2002, he received orders to Brigade Support Service Group-1 (BSSG-1), 1st FSSG. Assigned to Headquarters & Service Battalion in February 2003, he deployed with Combat Service Support Battalion (CSSB-18) for Operation Enduring Freedom and Operation Iraqi Freedom. In August 2004, he was serving as Sergeant Major, of Headquarters and Service Battalion, 1st FSSG, the most diverse battalion in the Marines Corps.

Lee, Cheryl A.
MAJOR—AIR FORCE

She earned her Bachelor of Science Degree in Health, Physical Education and Recreation from North Carolina Agricultural and Technical State University (N.C.A. & T.S.U.) in 1981 and was commissioned through their United States Air Force Reserve officer Training Corps Program. She later graduated with her Master's Degree in Administrative Management from Central Michigan University in 1992. She earned a Master from the Air Command and Staff College. She entered the Air Force in December 1981.

Her initial assignment at 443rd Tactical Training Squadron, Altus Air Force Base, Oklahoma, was as Instructor, Unit Chief and finally standardization Officer, Military Airlift Command Classroom Instructor Course. She was the Morale, Welfare, and Recreation (MWR) Operations Officer, Tinker Air Force Base, in Oklahoma. She held the position of Chief, Military Resource Management Division, Foreign Technology Division, at Wright-Patterson Air Force Base, in Ohio. She was assigned as Flight Commander, Military Personnel Flight (MPF), 305th Mission Support Squadron, McGuire Air Force Base, in New Jersey. She returned to Wright-Patterson Air Force Base as Associate Registrar, Air Force Institute of Technology (AFIT) in 1997.

She was selected to serve as the Executive Officer to the Director of Personnel, Headquarters AFMC in 1998. During this time she also completed Air Command and Staff College. She was selected and served as Commander of the AFMC Headquarters Squadron from 1998 to 2000. She served as the Commander of the Fort Dix Military Entrance Processing Station. She was assigned as the Chief, of Military Equal Opportunity (MEO), for the 88th Air Base Wing, AFMC, at Wright-Patterson Air Force Base. As the Chief, she coordinated one to the largest United Stated Air Force Human Relations Education and MEO programs supporting over 54,000 DoD personnel. In November 2004, she was serving as the Commander, of the Fort Dix, New Jersey Military Entrance Processing Station (MEPS).

Lee, Irvin B.
COLONEL—AIR FORCE

He was born in Richmond, Virginia. He earned a Bachelor of Science Degree (with honors) in Industrial Engineering from Georgia Tech in 1981 and a Masters of Science Degree in Industrial Engineering from Georgia Tech in 1985. He was commissioned through the Reserve Officers Training Corps as a distinguished graduate in 1981.

His military education include Squadron Officer School, Maxwell Air Force Base, Alabama; Air Command and Staff; Air War College, Maxwell Air Force Base, Alabama.

His key military assignments include serving as Chief, Environmental Management Flight, 1st Civil Engineer Squadron, Langley Air Force Base, Virginia; Facility Requirements Officer, Air Combat Command, at Langley Air Force Base, Virginia; in May 1996, Commander, 510th Civil Engineer Squadron, United States Air Force Academy, in Colorado; in July 1997,

Commander, 10th Civil Engineer Squadron, United States Air Force Academy, in Colorado; in June 1999, Commander, 2nd Civil Engineer Squadron, Barksdale Air Force Base, Louisiana; in July 2001, as a Member of the Joint Staff Engineer Officer, Logistics Directorate, at the Pentagon, Washington, D.C.; in January 2005, he was serving as the Commander, 6th Mission Support Group, MacDill Air Force Base, Florida.

Leeper, Michael A.
COLONEL—ARMY

He was born in Richmond, Virginia. In 1973, he graduated from Virginia State University with a Bachelor's Degree in Electronics Technology, and was commissioned as an Air Defense Artillery Officer.

His military education includes: the Air Defense Officer Basic and Advanced Courses; the Army Command and General Staff College; the Armed Forces Staff College; the Logistic Executive Development Course; and the Army War College.

His military assignments include: serving as RED-EYE Platoon Leader, Combat Support Company, 1st Battalion 506th Infantry, Fort Campbell, Kentucky; Fire Control Platoon Leader and Executive Officer, 2nd Battalion 44th Air Defense Artillery (Nike Hercules), Republic of Korea; Battery Commander and the Battalion Adjutant (S-1), 2nd Battalion, 55th Air Defense Artillery (HAWK), Fort Bliss, Texas; Chief, Supply and Services Division, G-4, and Assistant Inspector General, 32nd Army Air Defense Command, in Darmstadt, Germany; Forward Area Support Coordinating Officer, Division Support Command, 7th Infantry (Light), Fort Ord, California; Operation Officer (S-3), 7th Battalion, 7th Air Defense Artillery Regiment (CHAPARRAL), Fort Ord, California; Commander, 4th Battalion, 7th Air Defense Artillery Regiment (PATRIOT), Fort Lewis, Washington; Joint Staff Officer for the Joint Doctrine Center, J-7, Joint Staff, Naval Air Station, Norfolk, Virginia; Deputy Brigade Commander, 35th Air Defense Artillery Brigade, Fort Lewis, Washington; Deputy Brigade Commander, 35th Air Defense Artillery Brigade, Fort Lewis, Washington; as Missile Defense Policy Planner to the Joint Staff at the Pentagon, in Washington, D.C.; as Deputy Director for the U.S. Army Evaluation Center, in August 1999. In March 2005, he was serving as Senior Army Instructor, at Huguenot High School JROTC.

Leflore, Adrian
SERGEANT MAJOR—MARINE

He enlisted into the United States Marine Corps in November 1982. He completed Recruit Training at Marine Corps Recruit Depot, San Diego, California in January 1983. After completing A-4 maintenance schools at Naval Air Station (Millington). Memphis, Tennessee and Marine Corps Air Station Cherry Point, North Carolina, then he were assigned to VMA-211, at Marine Corps Air Station El Toro, Santa Ana, California.

His key military assignments include serving as Drill Instructor, 1st Recruit Training Battalion, Delta Company, at Marine Corps Recruit Depot, San Diego, California; Drill Master, 3rd Recruit Training Battalion, San Diego, California; as Senior Noncommissioned Officer in Charge of Life Support Systems, VMA-231, Marine Corps Air Station, Cherry Point, North Carolina; Wing Drill Master and Personnel Inspection Coordinator, Marine Corps Air Station, Cherry Point, North Carolina; as First Sergeant, Alpha Company, 1st Battalion, 1st Marines; as First Sergeant, with 11th and 15th Marine Expeditionary Unit in support of Operation Enduring Freedom at Camp Rhino, Afghanistan; First Sergeant, Supply Company, Supply Battalion, 1st FSSG; as the Sergeant Major, 3rd Low Altitude Air Defense Battalion.

Legette, Jessie, Jr.
COMMAND SERGEANT MAJOR—ARMY

Command Sergeant Major Jessie Legette, Jr. entered the United States Army in March 1974. Upon completion of Basic Training at Fort Jackson, South Carolina, and Advanced Individual Training at Fort Knox, Kentucky, he was assigned to Fort Hood, Texas in A Company, 1-67 Armor, from July 1974 to November 1975. In December 1975, he was assigned to USAREUR, joining the 3rd ID assigned to 3rd Battalion 64th Armor in Schweinfurt, Germany until 1978. In April 1979, he was assigned to Company A, 1st Squadron 2nd Armored Cavalry Regiment in Bayreuth. While assigned in the 2nd Armor Cavalry he worked on the Regimental Staff as the Border NCOIC responsible for the surveillance along the East/West German and Czechoslovakian borders during the Cold War from September 1983 until April 1986.

His most recent assignments include: served as the Command Sergeant Major for the 2nd Battalion, 64th

Armor, 3rd Infantry Division, later with the 1st Battalion, with the 77th Armor, 1st Infantry Division. While serving as the Task Force 1-77th Armor Command Sergeant Major in Bosnia, he was very instrumental in organizing Infantry and Military Police Squads to assist in United States Civilians and the International Police. He was also the Command Sergeant Major of 1-77th Armor, the first Tank Battalion to enter Kosovo in the Balkans immediately following the bombing campaign. CSM Legette has held every key leadership position from Section sergeant to Command Sergeant Major. He was also the Command Sergeant Major of the 2nd Battalion, 69th Armor Regiment at Fort Benning, Georgia. He is currently assigned to the 280th Base Support Battalion Schweinfurt, Germany.

His military education include: M1 Master Gunner Course; Equal Opportunity Instructors Course; First Sergeant Course, at Ford Bliss, Texas; the United States Sergeant Major Academy.

Leigh, Fredric Homer

MAJOR GENERAL—ARMY

He was born in Ohio. He received a Bachelor of Arts degree in history from Central State University, a Master of Science degree in Public Relations from Syracuse University. He earned a Master of Military Science from the United States Army Command and General Staff College.

He entered the United Stated Army in 1963 with an ROTC commission as second lieutenant. From September 1963 to November 1963, he was a student in the Infantry officer Basic Course at the United States Army Infantry Center and School, Fort Benning, Georgia. From December 1963 to February 1964, he was a student in the Ranger Course at the United States Army Infantry Center and School. From February 1964 to May 1964, he was a Platoon Leader in Company B, 1st Battalion, 2nd Infantry Brigade, at Fort Devens, Massachusetts. From May 1964 to September 1964, he served as a member of the Infantry Committee, First United States Army Demonstration and Instruction Team, Camp Drum, New York.

He was promoted to First Lieutenant on February 4, 1965, and in March 1965 assigned as an Assistant Operations Officer in the 2nd Brigade, 5th Infantry Division (Mechanized), Fort Devens, Massachusetts. He was promoted to Captain on August 225, 1966.

In July 1966 he was the Commander of Company B, the 2nd Infantry Brigade, 1st Infantry Division, with the United States Army, in Vietnam. From September 1966 to November 1968, he served as an Assistant Professor of military science at Tuskegee Institute, Tuskegee, Alabama. From December 1968 to December 1969, he served first as an Assistant S-3 (Operations), then as Assistant G-3, Plans Officer, Headquarters and Headquarters Company, 101st Airborne Division (Air Assault), United States Army, Vietnam. From January 1970 to September 1970, he a was a student in the Infantry Officer Advanced Course at the United States Army Infantry Center and School, Fort Benning, Georgia.

He was promoted to Major on January 20, 1970. From August 1972 to June 1973, he was a student at the United States Army Command and General Staff College, Fort Leavenworth, Kansas. From June 1973 to January 1976, he served as a plans, program, and budget officer in the Command Information Division, Office of the Chief of Information, United States Army, Washington, D.C. From January 1976 to May 1978, he served first as the Executive Officer of the 2nd Battalion, 503rd Infantry, then as Executive Officer of the 2nd Brigade, 101st Airborne Division (Air Assault) Fort Campbell, Kentucky.

He was promoted to Lieutenant Colonel on August 4, 1977. From July 1978 to July 1979, he was Commander, 1st Battalion, 38th Infantry, 2nd Infantry Division, United States Army, Korea. From August 1979 to August 1981, he was a Military Assistant with the Assistant Secretary of the Army (Manpower and Reserve Affairs), United States Army, in Washington, D.C. From August 1981 to June 1982, he was a student at the National War College, Fort McNair, in Washington, D.C. From June 1982 to June 1983, he served as the Senior Military Assistant, Office of the Secretary of the Army, United States Army, Washington, D.C.

From June 1983 to June 1985, he served as Deputy Director, Army Staff, Office of the Chief of Staff, United States Army, Washington, D.C. He was promoted to Colonel on September 1, 1983. From July 1985 to May 1987, he was Chief of Staff, 19th Support Command, Eighth United States Army, in Korea. From August 1987 to August 1989, he served as Commander, 1st Brigade, 101st Airborne Division (Air Assault) Fort Campbell, Kentucky. From August 1989 to March 1990, he served as Director, Senior Leadership Research, United States Army War College, Carlisle Barracks, in Pennsylvania. In March 1990 he was assigned as Assistant Division Commander, 7th Infantry Division (Light), Fort Ord, California. He was promoted to Brigadier General on August 1, 1990.

From August 1991 to May 1993, he was assigned as the Deputy Director, National Military Command Center, J-3, The Joint Staff, in Washington, D.C. From June 1993 to December 1993, he served as Director of Management, Office of the Chief of Staff, United States Army, Washington, D.C. He was promoted to Major General on August 1, 1993, and retired from the military on December 31, 1993.

He has received numerous awards and decorations including the Legion of Merit (with two oak leaf clusters), Bronze Star Medal (with four oak leaf clusters), Bronze Star Medal (with "V" device), Meritorious Service Medal (with two oak leaf clusters), Air Medal, Army Commendation Medal (with oak leaf cluster), Combat Infantryman Badge, Parachutist Badge, Air Assault Badge, and Ranger Tab.

Lenhardt, Alfonso Emanual

MAJOR GENERAL—ARMY

He was born in New York, New York. He received a Bachelor of Science degree in Criminal Justice from

the University of Nebraska at Omaha. He received a Master's Law Administration from Central Michigan University.

He enlisted in the United States Army in November 1965. In October 1966 he entered the Tactical Officer, Infantry Officer Candidate School, 60th Company, of the 6th Student Battalion, Student Brigade, United States Army Infantry School, at Fort Benning, Georgia. From October 1967 to September 1968, he was a Platoon Leader in Company C, 4th Battalion, 12th Infantry, 199th Infantry Brigade, in Vietnam. From October 1968 to June 1969, he served as Commander; Company A, 10th Battalion, 4th Advanced Individual Training Brigade (Military Police), United States Army Training Center, Fort Gordon, Georgia.

He was promoted to Captain on October 19, 1968. From June 1969 to December 1969, he served as Chief, Military Police Subjects Committee, 4th Advanced Individual Training Center, Fort Gordon. From December 1969 to August 1970, he served as Assistant S-2 (Intelligence), S-3 (Operations) Officer, 4th Advanced Individual Training Brigade (Military Police), Fort Gordon.

From August 1970 to May 1971, he was a student at the Military Police Officer Advanced Course at Fort Gordon. From May 1972 to August 1972, he served as an action officer in the Special Activity Division, Operations Directorate, United States Army Criminal Investigation Command, in Washington, D.C. From August 1972 to February 1973, he served as Chief, Operations Center, United States Army Criminal Investigation Command, Washington, D.C. From February 1973 to June 1973, he was chief of the Region Coordination Division, United States Army Criminal Investigation Command, Washington, D.C. From June

1973 to September 1973, he was a student at the Federal Bureau of Investigation National Academy, Quantico, Virginia. From September 1973 to August 1975, he was Commander, Fort Eustis Field Office, 1st Regional United States Army Criminal Investigations Division Command, Fort Eustis, Virginia. From August 1975 to June 1976, he was a student at the United States Army Command and General Staff College, Fort Leavenworth, Kansas.

He was promoted to Major on June 5, 1976. From June 1976 to December 1976, he was a student at Wichita State University, Wichita, Kansas. From December 1976 to June 1977, he served as Operations Officer in the Provost Marshal Office, Fort Dix, New Jersey. From June 1977 to June 1978, he was executive officer, 759th Military Police Battalion, Fort Dix, New Jersey. From June 1978 to June 1980, he served as company tactical Officer, Staff and Faculty, United States Army Military Academy. From June 1980 to May 1981, Lenhardt served as Chief, Policy Branch, Office of the Provost Marshal, United States Army, Europe, and Seventh Army. He was promoted to Lieutenant Colonel on July 13, 1980.

From June 1981 to May 1983, he served as 385th Military Battalion, VII Corps, United States Army, in Europe. From May 1983 to June 1984, he was a student at the National War College, Fort Lesley J. McNair, in Washington, D.C. From June 1984 to March 1985, he was Deputy Director, Research, and Assistant to Director, Strategic Defense Initiative Organization, Office of the Secretary of Defense, Washington, D.C. He was promoted to Colonel on November 1, 1984. From March 1985 to June 1986, he was Executive Officer and Assistant to the Director, Strategic Defense Initiative Organization, Office of the Secretary of Defense, Washington, D.C. From June 1986 to June 1988, he was the Commander of the 18th Military Police Brigade, V Corps, United States Army, in Europe. From July 1988 to August 1989, he served as Deputy Provost Marshal, Office of the Provost Marshal, United States Army, Europe, and Seventh Army. On July 1, 1990, he was promoted to Brigadier General.

From September 1989 to July 1992, he was assigned as Deputy Commanding General, East, United States Army Recruiting Command, in Fort Sheridan, Illinois. From July 1992 to July 1994, he served as Deputy Chief of Staff for Personnel and Installation Management, with Forces Command, at Fort McPherson, in Georgia. He was promoted to Major General on February 1, 1994.

From July 1994 to February 1996, he was assigned as the Commanding General, of the United States Chemical and military Police Centers/Commandant, United States Military Police School, at Fort McClellan, in Alabama. In February 1996, he was selected to serve as the Commanding General, United States Army Recruiting Command, at Fort Knox, in Kentucky. He retired from the military on August 31, 1997.

He has received numerous awards and decorations: the Distinguished Service Medal; the Defense Superior

Service Medal, Bronze Star Medal, Purple Heart, Meritorious Service Medal (with two oak leaf clusters), Air Medal, Joint Service Commendation Medal, Army Commendation Medal (with two oak leaf clusters), Army Achievement Medal, Humanitarian Service Medal, Combat Infantryman Badge, and Parachutist Badge.

Letcher, Maj.

MAJOR—ARMY

He was commissioned at Emporia State University in May 1989 as a Lieutenant in Armor. He is a graduate of the Armor Officers Basic and Advanced Courses; the Combined Arms Service Staff Course; the Command and General Staff Course; the Command and General Staff Officers Course; and the School of Advanced Military Studies. He holds a Bachelor of Science Degree from the Emporia State University; a Master Degree from Kansas University; and a Masters Degree from the School of Advanced Military Studies.

His assignments include: serving as Tank Platoon Leader during Operation Desert Shield/Desert Storm; as a Support Platoon Leader and the Battalion Adjutant; Commander, D Company, 2nd Battalion, 70th Armor Regiment; as the Executive Officer for the Digital Force Coordination Cell; Commander, Headquarters and Headquarters Company, 1st Battalion, 66th Armor Regiment in the 4th Infantry Division in April of 1997; he served as the lead Project Officer for Information Operations with the TRADOC Program Integration Office for Army Battle Command Systems at Fort Leavenworth, Kansas; as the Aide-de-Camp for the Deputy Commandant of the Command and General Staff College; in 1999, he was selected to attend the Command and General Staff College; in 2004, he was serving as the Operations Officer for 1-37th Armor, 1st Armor Division.

Lewis, Alfred M.

COLONEL—AIR FORCE

He entered Basic Training in October 1975 and completed Technical Training as a Law Enforcement Specialist. He completed Officer Training School in April 1982 as a Security Police Officer.

His civilian and military education includes: Squadron Officer School, at Maxwell Air Force Base, Alabama; a Bachelor of Arts in Administration of Justice, from Golden Gate University, San Francisco; he holds a Master of Public Administration in Justice Administration, Golden Gate University, in San Francisco; he earned a Master of Strategic Studies, from the United States Army War College, Carlisle Barracks; Air Command and Staff College; and the Air War College.

He has served in numerous key assignments to include: in June 1984, as Executive Officer, in the Office of Inspector General, Air force System Command, at Andrews Air Force Base; in October 1985, as Air Base Ground Defense/Antiterrorism Program Manager, Air Force Systems Command, at Andrews Air Force Base; in July 1987, as Chief, of Operations, 375th Security Police Squadron, at Scott Air Force Base; in January 1990, as Chief, Security Police, 690th Electronic Security Wing, at Tempelhoff Central Air Port, Berlin, Germany; in July 1991, as Operations Security Analyst, Air Force Cryptologic Support Center, at Kelly Air Force Base, Texas; in December 1992, he was assigned as Chief, Mission Support Branch, Inspector General, Air Intelligence Agency, at Kelly Air Force Base, Texas; in August 1994, as Commander, Headquarters Squadron Section, Air Intelligence Agency, Kelly Air Force Base, Texas; in July 1995, as Commander, 66th Security Police Squadron, Hanscom Air Force Base; in July 1998, as Commander, 341st Training Squadron, Lackland Air Force Base, Texas; in July 2001, as Chief, Force Protection, 9th Air Force/United States Central Air Force, at Shaw Air Force Base, in South Carolina; in July 2003, he served as Director, Force Protection, United States Central Air Force Al Udeid Air Base, Qatar; in August 2004, he was selected to serve as Commander, 28th Mission Support Group, at Ellsworth Air Force Base, in San Diego.

Lewis, Doarin R.

COLONEL—MARINE

He is a native of Sheffield, Alabama. He enlisted in the Marine Corps in February 1979, and obtained the rank of corporal (meritoriously), while serving as an administrative clerk at Marine Corps Recruit Depot Parris Island, South Carolina. He was commissioned a second lieutenant in December 1980 through the Enlisted Commissioning Program. After completing The Basic School in June 1981, he attended both the United States Army's NBC Defense School at Fort McClellan, Alabama and the Field Artillery School at Fort Sill, Oklahoma.

He is a graduate of the University of Alabama with a Bachelor of Arts in History (1978), the Naval War College with a Master of Arts in National Security and Strategic Studies (1995), and the Marine Corps War College with a Masters of Arts in Strategic Studies (2001). He is also a graduate of the Joint Forces Staff College (1996). He is a graduate of the Amphibious Warfare School, in Quantico, Virginia.

His key leadership assignments include: He was assigned in July 1995 to joint duty with the United States Central Command, MacDill Air Force Base, Tampa, Florida, as a Logistics Staff Officer. During this time he deployed to Saudi Arabia in support of Operations Desert Focus and Southern Watch; In July 1997, he was selected to serve as the Executive Officer to the Director, J-4 Logistics Directorate. In June 1998, he returned to Iwakuni and assumed command of Marine Wing Support Squadron 171; In June 2001, he was assigned as a Faculty Advisor and the Joint Professional Military Education Coordinator at the Marine Corps Command and Staff College; he reported Okinawa in July 2003 for duty as the Assistant Chief of Staff, G-4/Inspector, 3rd Force Service Support Group; he assumed command of 3rd Transportation Support Battalion on 22 January 2004.

Lewis, Doris L.

COMMAND SERGEANT MAJOR—ARMY

She joined the United States Army Women's Army Corps in September 1965. Her military career included serving three tours in South Vietnam. After leaving active duty, she joined the United Army Reserve in December 1971. While serving in the Army Reserve, became the first black female promoted to the rank of Command Sergeant Major in the 89th Regional Support Command, in Wichita, Kansas.

She served as the Command Sergeant Major for the 139th Medical Group; Command Sergeant Major, at the 146th Aviation Group; Command Sergeant Major for the 410th Evacuation Hospital; as the Command Sergeant Major for the 135th Military Intelligence Battalion; and her final assignment in the United States Army Reserve, as Command Sergeant Major for the 917th Corps Support Group. She retired in September 2002, after 37 years of meritorious service.

Lewis, James A.

LIEUTENANT COMMANDER—NAVY

He was commissioned after graduating from the United States Naval Academy in Annapolis, Maryland with the class of 1990. His military education includes the Surface Warfare Department Head School; the Defense Language Institute in Monterey, California; the German Armed Forces Staff College in Hamburg, Germany, from August 2000 to August 2002.

His initial assignment was aboard USS *Kinkaid* (DD 965) in San Diego, California from January 1990 to January 1994. While onboard *Kinkaid*, he served as

Communications Officer, Navigator, and C3 Officer. His next assignment was Maintenance Support Center Officer onboard USS *Carl Vinson* (CVN 70) in Alameda, California from January 1994 until August 1995. After completing Surface Warfare Department Head School in March 1996. He served as Operations Officer onboard USS *Reuben James* (FFG 57) in Pearl Harbor, Hawaii until August 1997. He was assigned as Operations Officer onboard USS *Chosin* (CG 65) in Pearl Harbor, Hawaii until November 1999. In October 2004, he was serving as Executive Officer in Surface Warfare/Aviation Warfare.

Lewis, Neville

COMMAND SERGEANT MAJOR

He entered the Army on July 5, 1977, from the Bronx, in New York. He completed Basic Combat Training at Fort Knox, Kentucky and his first Advance Individual Training as a Personnel Administration Specialist at Fort Benjamin Harrison, Indiana. In February 1981, he returned to his second Advance Individual Training at Fort Leonard Wood, Missouri, where he completed the 51R (Electrician) Course.

His military education includes: all the Noncommissioned Officer Education System Courses; the Master Fitness Course; the First Sergeant Course; Operational and Intelligence Course; Battle Staff Course; the United States Army Sergeants Major Academy (class 48), at Fort Bliss, Texas.

His key military assignments include: in 1990, he served as a Platoon Sergeant and later First Sergeant with the 46th Engineer Battalion as a Platoon Sergeant, and deployed in support of Desert Shield/Desert Storm; as First Sergeant for both Bravo Company and Headquarters Support Company, with the 864th Engineer Battalion; as the Directorate Plan, Training,

Security and Mobilization Sergeant Major for the United States Army in Alaska; in July 2000, he returned to Fort Lewis as 864th Engineer Battalion Command Sergeant Major; in March 2003, he deployed with the 864th Engineer Battalion to Iraq in support of Operation Iraqi Freedom.

Lewis, Todd A.
COMMANDER—NAVY

He was commissioned through the Naval Reserve Officer Training Corps (ROTC) program at Norfolk State University, where he graduated with honors and received a Bachelor of Science Degree in Electronic Technology. After graduating from Surface Warfare Division Officer School, he reported to USS *Mississippi* (CGN-40) IN January 1991 and served as OT, OI and First Division Officer. While on USS *Mississippi*, he deployed to the Red sea in support of Operations Desert Shield/Desert Storm.

In June 1994, he received orders to the Naval Postgraduate School in Monterey, California. While at Naval Postgraduate School, he received a Master of Science Degree in Mechanical Engineering, with a thesis specialization in Robotics and Controls Systems.

After graduating from Surface Warfare Officer Department Head School, he reported to USS *Portland* (LSD-37) in May 1997 as First Lieutenant. While on *Portland* he completed a six month deployment to the Mediterranean Sea.

In October 1998, he reported to USS *Kearsarge* (LHD-3) AS First Lieutenant. While on *Kearsarge*, he deployed to the Mediterranean for six months as part of a NATO Task Force in support of Operation Noble Anvil. In August 2000, he reported to the United States Marine Corps Command and Staff College in Quan-

tico, Virginia. While there, he completed Joint Professional Military Education Phase I and received a Master of Arts Degree in Military Studies, with thesis study in Littoral Warfare. In June 2001, he reported to the United States Southern Command in Miami, Florida and was assigned to the J3 Directorate. While there, he served as the UNITAS Naval Exercise Planner for the Commander United States Southern Command and was the Naval Liaison Officer to 13 nations throughout South America, Central America and the Caribbean. He assumed the position as USS *Juneau*'s (LPD 10) Executive Officer on the 13th of September 2003.

Lightner, Rosetta A. Armour
COLONEL—AIR FORCE

She received a Bachelor of Arts degree in Psychology, from Talladega College, in Alabama. She earned a Master of Arts degree in Counseling from Springfield College, in Massachusetts. She is a graduate of the Air War College.

She was commissioned in March 1963. She was the first woman instructor at any Air Force ROTC unit (Ohio State University) as well as the first black woman line colonel in the Air Force. She also served as Professor of Aerospace Studies and Commander, Air Force ROTC Detachment at Grambling State University.

Lindsay, Timika B.
LIEUTENANT COMMANDER—NAVY

She is a 1992 graduate from the United States Naval Academy, with a Bachelor of Science Degree in General Science. In 1998, she was selected to attend Naval

Postgraduate School in Monterey, California. She graduated in December 1999 with a Masters of Science Degree in Information Technology Management.

In January 2000, she returned to the United States Naval Academy and served her first year as Protocol Officer for the Superintendent (Vice Admiral John Ryan, USN [Ret]). She moved to the Office of Admissions where she served as Senior Admissions Counselor and Senior Minority Admissions Counselor until September 2002. She contributed to the department's achievement for processing and admitting the most diverse class (at that time) in United States Naval Academy history with the Class of 2004, and again in 2005.

In October 2002, she transferred to Arlington, Virginia, where she served on the Assistant for Administration, Undersecretary of the Navy (AAUSN), Office of Process, Technology and Information (OPTI). She was team co-lead and Legacy Applications Coordinator, responsible for the Secretary of the Navy claimancy's transition to the Navy-Marine Corps Intranet (NMCI). In August 2003, she was handpicked from a group of volunteers to serve in Iraq in support of Operation Iraqi Freedom. There she simultaneously held the roles of Deputy Director and Executive Officer of the Communications Support Office for the Coalition Provisional Authority. She retuned to Office of Process, Technology and Information in March 2004, and soon after began her transition to her assignment as Executive Officer, United States Naval Computer and Telecommunications Station Bahrain.

Littlejohn, Harold
COMMAND SERGEANT MAJOR—ARMY

He is a native of Shelby, North Carolina. He entered the United States Army in August 1978 and attended Basic Combat Training and Advanced Individual Training at Fort Sill, Oklahoma as a Radio Mechanic. He later attended Basic Airborne Training at Fort Benning, Georgia.

His military education includes: all the Noncommissioned Officer Education System Courses; the First Sergeant Course; Air Assault Course; Basic Airborne School; Advanced Airborne School; the United States Army Sergeants Major Academy.

He served in various leadership and staff positions to include: serving as Squad Leader; Section Chief; Platoon Sergeant; Company Communication's Chief; Battalion Communication Chief; First Sergeant; Battalion Operation Sergeant Major; and Battalion Command Sergeant Major. In January 2005, he was serving as the Command Sergeant Major for the 233rd Base Support Battalion, in Darmstadt, Germany.

Lockett, Lewis C.
COMMAND SERGEANT MAJOR—ARMY

Command Sergeant Major Lewis C. Lockett was born in Reform, Alabama. He entered the Army in August 1975 and completed Basic Training at Fort Jackson, South Carolina and Advanced Individual Training at Redstone Arsenal, in Alabama.

His civilian and military education includes: he earned a Liberal Arts degree from Western Illinois University, in Macomb, Illinois; he is a graduate of the NCO Logistics Program Course; the III Corps First Sergeants Course; the United States Army First Sergeants Course; the Garrison Sergeant Major Course; and the United States Army Sergeants Major Academy.

His most recent assignments includes: assigned as Senior Instructor Missile Division, at Redstone Arsenal, Alabama; as Senior Maintenance NCO and First Sergeant, 4th Ordnance Company, in Miesau, Germany; he served as a Hawk Missile Repairman, 1-44th ADA, Camp Howard, Korea; Radar Repairman, 2-55 ADA at Fort Bliss, Texas; He also served as the Command Sergeant Major for the 6th Ord Battalion, with the 19th TAACOM, in Korea.

Lofton, Samuel, III
COLONEL—UNITED STATES AIR FORCE

He was born in Goldsboro, North Carolina and graduated from East Carolina University in 1981. He earned his commission through the Reserve Officers Training Corps in 1981, and earned a Bachelor of Science, Business Administration, at East Carolina University, in Greenville, N.C. In 1985, he completed the Squadron Officer School; in 1989, he earned a Master of Science (with Honors) in Public Administration, from Troy State University; in 1994, he was an Honor Graduate of the Air Command and Staff College, at Maxwell Air Force Base, Alabama; in 1998, he completed the Air War College; in 1999, he earned a Master of Science, from the National Resources Strategy, Industrial College of the Armed Forces, National Defense University, at Fort McNair, Washington, D.C.; in 2002, he completed the LOGTECH Advanced Program in Logistics and Technology, University of North Carolina, Chapel Hill, N.C.

In 2005, he was serving as the director of the F-15 Aircraft/System Support Management Directorate, Warner Robins Air Logistics Center, Robins Air Force Base, Georgia. The directorate manages engineering and manufacturing development, production, of more than 1,190 F-15 fighter aircraft for units of the F-15 single manager for F-15 supply chain management, development, and oversight of combat support, sustainment, and engineering for fielded systems and technical order management.

Loggins, Stacy B.
PETTY OFFICER FIRST CLASS—NAVY

He holds a Bachelor of Science in Music, Cameron University; and a Master's of Music from East Carolina University. He has preformed with the Lawton Philharmonic Orchestra, the McLean Orchestra and Georgetown Symphony. He is a member of the United States Navy Band.

Lomax, Stanley A., Jr.
COMMAND MASTER CHIEF—NAVY

He entered the United States Navy Basic Training at Naval Recruit Training Command, Great Lakes, Illinois.

He is a graduate of George of George Westington House High School, Brooklyn, New York; Food Service Administration School, Norfolk, Virginia; Food Service Records and Return School, Charleston, South, Carolina; Bachelor Enlisted Quarters School, San Diego, California; Euro Barber School, Jacksonville, Florida; Senior Enlisted Academy, (class 103), Gold Group, Newport, Rhode Island.

In October 2004, he was serving as the Command Master Chief onboard the USS *Samuel B. Roberts* (FFG-58), Mayport, Florida.

Lovall, Harry L.
COMMAND SERGEANT MAJOR—ARMY

Command Sergeant Major Harry L. Lovall, Jr. enlisted in the Army on January 14, 1972. He earned an Associate degree in Criminal Justice, from Temple University. He has held many leadership positions some of which include: assignments as Infantry Squad Leader; Military Police Squad Leader; Military Police Platoon Sergeant; Mechanized Infantry Company First Sergeant; Command Sergeant Major of the 455th Chemical Brigade, of the 77th Regional Support Command; assigned as Command Sergeant Major of the 2nd Brigade (FE) 78th Division. He is currently serving as the Command Sergeant Major of the 77th Regional Support Command, in Fort Totten, New York

Lowry, Michael A.
COMMAND MASTER CHIEF—NAVY

He is a native of Baltimore, Maryland. He enlisted into the United States Navy in January 1978. After completing Boot Camp and Hospital Corps School in Great Lakes, Illinois, he was assigned to Naval Hospital Beaufort, South Carolina.

He is a graduate of the Navy's Senior Enlisted Academy. He has earned a dual Master's Degree in Health Service Management and Public Administration from Webster University; a Bachelor of Science Degree from Norfolk States University in Medical Technology; and an Associates Degree in Science from George Washington University.

His military assignments include: serving as Command Master Chief, U.S. Navy Hospital Guantanamo Bay, Cuba; Senior Enlisted Leader, Nursing Services

Directorate, Nava Medical Center, Portsmouth Virginia; Senior Enlisted Leader for the Directorate of Ancillary Services and Blood Bank Officer, U.S. Naval Hospital, Sigonella, Italy; Senior Laboratory Instructor, Naval School of Health Sciences, Fort San Houston, Texas; Marine Wing Service Support 273, Cherry Point, North Carolina; the Third Medical Battalion, Combat Service Support Detachment 31, Okinawa, Japan; USS *Sperry* (AS12); and USS *Ajax* (AR8). In June 2005, he was serving as the Master Chief and Senior Enlisted Leader for the Academic Directorate at the Naval School of Health Sciences, (Aviation Warfare/Fleet Marine Force) United States Navy, in Portsmouth, Virginia.

Lucas, Ruth
COLONEL—AIR FORCE
She received her undergraduate degree from Tuskegee Institute and earned a Master of Arts degree from Colombia University. She was commissioned into the

United Air Force in 1942. She was the First black Woman to attend the traditionally all-male Armed Forces Staff College at Norfolk, Virginia. She served for over 28 years in the United States Air Force. Her assignments were both staff and command positions to include an assignment at the Pentagon in Washington, D.C. While

on this assignment she helped organize programs designed to raise educational level of Air Force Personnel. She was the First black Woman to be promoted to the rank of Full Colonel in the United States Air Force. She retired in 1970, the highest ranking black woman to ever serve in the Air Force up to that time.

Lyle, Phillip L.
COMMAND SERGEANT MAJOR—ARMY
Command Sergeant Major Lyle is a native of Meherrin, Virginia. He entered the service in 1979 at Fort Dix, New Jersey, where he attended Basic Training. He graduated from Advance Initial Training at Aberdeen Proving Grounds and awarded 63W, Wheel Vehicle Mechanic as his primary MOS.

His first assignment was at Fort Ord, California where he served as a Squad Leader. Other assignments include: two tours in Germany; one at Fort Campbell, Kentucky; Fort Jackson, South Carolina; Camp Humphrey's, Korea; and Fort Bragg, North Carolina. During his tours he served as Team Chief, Third Shop Maintenance NCOIC; Platoon Sergeant in Maintenance Company; Senior Drill Sergeant Leader at Fort Jackson United States Army Drill Sergeants School and two tours as First Sergeant. While assigned to the Sergeants Major academy he attained an Associates Degree, in Applied Science Technical Studies.

Lyles, Lester L.
GENERAL—AIR FORCE
He was born in Washington, D.C., he married the former Mina McGraw of Washington, D.C. They have four children, Renee, Phillip, Leslie, and Lauren. He was graduated from McKinley Technical High School in 1963. He earned a Bachelor of Science Degree in

Mechanical Engineering from Howard University in 1968 and a Master of Science Degree in Mechanical and Nuclear Engineering, through the Air Force Institute of Technology program, from New Mexico State University in 1969. He completed the Defense Systems Management College in 1980, Armed Forces Staff College in 1981, and National War College in 1985. He attended the National and International Security Management Course at the John F. Kennedy School of Government, Harvard University, in 1991.

A distinguished graduate of the Air Force Reserve Officer Training Corps program he was commissioned as a second lieutenant in 1968. Upon completion of graduate school in February 1969, General Lyles was assigned as a Propulsion and Structures Engineer in the Standard Space Launch Vehicles Program Office, Headquarters, Space and Missiles Systems Organization, Los Angeles Air Force Station, in California. In November 1971 he became a Propulsion Engineer in the Headquarters, Aeronautical Systems Division, Wright-Patterson AFB, in Ohio, located in the Short-Range Attack Missile Program Office. In July 1974 the general was assigned to Headquarters, United States Air Force, Washington, D.C., as program element monitor for the SRAM Strategic Missile and was subsequently reassigned as Executive Officer to the Deputy Chief of Staff for Research and Development.

In March 1978 General Lyles was selected as Aide-de-Camp and Special Assistant to the Commander of Air Force Systems Command. He later attended the Defense Systems Management College from January to June 1980. Upon graduation from the Armed Forces Staff College in January 1981, the general returned to Wright-Patterson AFB as Avionics Division Chief in the F-16 System Program Office. He later became the Deputy Director for Special and Advanced Projects. He completed National War College in June 1985; he served as Director of Tactical Aircraft Systems under the Deputy Chief of Staff for Systems, AFSC Headquarters. The general was reassigned to Los Angeles AFS in June 1987 as Director, Medium Launch Vehicles Program Office. In April 1988 he became Assistant Deputy Commander for Launch Systems at Headquarters, Space Systems Division, in Los Angeles. He was reassigned as the Assistant Deputy Chief of Staff for requirements, AFSC Headquarters, in August 1989. He was appointed Brigadier General on May 1, 1991, with same date of rank.

From July 1992 to November 1994, he served as Vice Commander, later Commander, of Ogden Air Logistics Center, at Hill Air Force Base, Utah. He was promoted to Major General on August 6, 1993. He was promoted to Lieutenant General on November 16, 1994.

From November 1994 to August 1996, he served as Commander, Space and Missile Systems Center, Los Angeles Air Force Base, in California. From August 1996 to May 1999, he was assigned as Director, of the Ballistic Missile Defense Organization, Department of Defense, in Washington, D.C. In May 1999, he was assigned as Vice Chief of Staff, at Headquarters United States Air Force, in Washington, D.C. He was promoted to General on July 1, 1999.

In April 2000, he was selected as Commander of the Air Force Materiel Command, at Wright-Patterson Air Force Base, Ohio. The command conducts research, development, test and evaluation, and provides acquisition management services and logistics support necessary to keep Air Force weapons systems ready for war.

His military awards and decorations include: Defense Distinguished Service Medal; Distinguished Service Medal; Defense Superior Service Medal; the Legion of Merit; Meritorious Service Medal (three oak leaf clusters); Air Force Commendation Medal; Senior Missileman Badge; Space Badge.

Lyons, Lucinda
CAPTAIN—ARMY

She was commissioned through the Reserve Officer Training Corps (ROTC) in 1999. She earned a Bachelor of Science Degree in Psychology from North Carolina Agricultural and Technical State University. Her military education includes: the Basic Combat Training; Advanced Individual Training as a Personnel Management Specialist; the Army Medical Department Officer Basic Course; Officer Advanced Course; and the Human Resource Managers Course.

She is assigned as the Commander, 568th Medical Company.

Lyons, Samuel I.
COMMAND SERGEANT MAJOR—ARMY

CSM Lyons was born in Murfreesboro, Tennessee on 5 November 1956. He entered the United States Army in April 1975, and begins Basic Training at Fort Jackson, South Carolina and Advanced Individual Training at Fort Polk, LA. His Military education includes: graduation from the First Sergeant Course at Fort Bliss, Texas; and the Sergeant Major Academy.

His assignments include: serving as Squad Leader, Platoon Sergeant, First Sergeant, Operations Sergeant at all levels.

Manley, Audrey Forbes
REAR ADMIRAL—HEALTH AND HUMAN SERVICES

She was born in Jacksonville, Mississippi. She is married Albert Manley, former president emeritus of Spelman College. She received a Bachelor of Arts degree from Spelman College in Atlanta, Georgia in 1955; an M.D. degree from Meharry Medical College in Nashville, Tennessee, in 1959; an M.P.H. degree from John Hopkins University, School of Hygiene and Public Health, Baltimore, Maryland, in 1987. She took residency in the pediatrics department at Cook County Children's Hospital and received additional training in neonatology at the Abraham Lincoln School of Medicine, University of Illinois. She was appointed Deputy Assistant Secretary, Department of Health and Human Services, on May 5, 1989, by Health and Human Services Secretary Louis W. Sullivan, M.D.

As Deputy Assistant Secretary for Health, Manley

was the principal advisor and assistant to the assistant secretary for Health, and shared responsibility of directing the United States Public Health Service includes: the Alcohol, Drug Abuse and Mental Health Administration (ADAMHA); the Centers for Disease Control (CDC); the Food and Drug Administration (FDA); the Health Resources and Services Administration (HRSA); the Indian Health Service (IHS); the National Institutes of Health (NIH); the Agency for Toxic Substances and Disease Registry (ATSDR).

Before assuming this position, she was Director of the National Health Service Corps; she served as Health Resources and Services Chief Medical Officer and Deputy Associate Administrator for planning, evaluation and legislations; she joined the public health service in 1976;in 1962, she was the First African American Woman to be named Chief resident of Cook County's 500-bed Children's Hospital; in 1980, was the First to Achieve the rank of Assistant Surgeon General in the United States Public Health Service; she is the First Woman to be name to the post she of Deputy Assistant Secretary for Health; she had held adjunct or associate positions at the University of California at San Francisco, Howard University in Washington, D.C., and the Uniformed Services University of Health Services in Bethesda, Maryland.

Mann, Marion
BRIGADIER GENERAL—ARMY

He was born in Atlanta, Georgia. He and his wife, Ruth, have two children — Marion, Jr., and Judith R. He received a Bachelor of Science degree from Tuskegee Institute in 1940 and a MD degree from Howard University College of Medicine in 1954. In 1961, he earned a PhD. from Georgetown University. General Mann

began his military career in 1942 during World War II. He remained in the Army until 1950, when he transferred to the United States Army Reserves. He has held a wide variety of important command and staff positions, culminating in his final assignment, from 1975 to 1980, as a Brigadier General in the United States Army Reserves. He retired from the United States Army Reserves in 1980. He also served as dean of the College of Medicine of Howard University from 1970 to 1979. He served in positions from assistant to full professor in the Department of Pathology, and in 1988 he was appointed associate vice president for research at Howard University. He holds membership in numerous organizations, including the National Medical Association, and the National Academy of Sciences. He has received numerous honors and awards, civic and military.

Marable, Renard

COLONEL—ARMY

He received a Bachelor of Arts degree in political Science from Fayetteville State University and Masters Degrees from the University of Missouri-Columbia and the Industrial College of the Armed Forces. He is a graduate of the Industrial College of the Armed Forces, United States Army Command and General Staff College, Infantry Officers Advance Course, Special Forces Qualification Course and the Range Course.

He was commissioned in 1969 as an Infantry Officer, at the Infantry Officer Candidate School at Fort Benning, Georgia. His initial assignments included a tour with the 3rd Special Forces Group at Fort Bragg, North Carolina and in the Republic of Vietnam with the 5th Special Forces Group.

After Vietnam, he was assigned to the 6th Special Forces Group at Fort Bragg. In 1971, he was reassigned and spent four years with the 82nd Airborne Division

where he served as an Assistant Brigade Operations Officer with the 2nd Brigade and Battalion Operations Officer Air; Battalion Adjutant; and Company Commander in the 3rd Battalion (Airborne), 325th Airborne Infantry Regiment.

After finishing the Infantry Officer Advanced Course, he was assigned as an Assistant Professor of Military Science at Lincoln University in Jefferson City, Missouri. In 1979, he returned to Fort Bragg where he served as an Assistant Personnel Officer on the XVIII Airborne Corps Staff. In 1982, he began a five-year tour in Germany, initially serving as a Battalion Executive Officer for the USAREUR Support Battalion in Heidelberg. Subsequent assignments included a tour with the 8th Infantry Division (Mechanized) as the Operations Officer and Executive Officer for the 1st Brigade.

In 1987, he returned to the 82nd Airborne Division as the Executive Officer for the 2nd Brigade and later commanded the 1st Battalion (Airborne), 325th Airborne Infantry Regiment. Shortly after taking command, he was injured in a parachute accident and had to be taken out of command. While recuperating, he worked as the Deputy Corps Personnel, XVIII Airborne Corps and as the 2nd Brigade Executive Officer.

In October 1989, he assumed command of the 1st Battalion, 504th Parachute Infantry Regiment. During his tenure as the Battalion Commander, he worked as the Chief, Division Exercise Cell, where he established an external evaluation program for the division. In June 1992, he became the Inspector General for the Military District of Washington stationed at Fort McNair, in Washington, D.C.

Marchbanks, Vance

COLONEL—AIR FORCE

Colonel Marchbanks, a former Tuskegee Airman,

had served as group surgeon with the 332d Fighter Group in Italy during World War II. He played an important role at NASA in the 1960s. When John Glenn circled the earth in the Friendship 7 capsule, Marchbanks monitored Glenn's respiration, pulse, temperature, and heartbeat from a base in Kano, Nigeria.

Marin, Hector G.
COMMAND SERGEANT MAJOR—ARMY

He is a native of Honduras (Central America). He entered the United States Army in September 1981 and attended Basic Combat Training at Fort Leonardwood, Missouri. He attended Advanced Individual Training at Fort Eustis, Virginia.

His civilian and military education includes: a Bachelors and Associates Degrees in Professional Aeronautical Science from Embry Riddle University. He attended numerous military schools to include: all the Noncommissioned Officer Education System Courses; the Army Master Fitness Course; Army Aviation Safety Course; the First Sergeants Course; and the United States Army Sergeants Major Academy.

His key leadership assignments include: from 1993 to 1995, serving as First Sergeant at D Troop, 6/6th Cavalry, 11th Aviation Regiment, in Illesheim, Germany; from 1998 to 1999, he served as First Sergeant at B Company, (AVIM), 7-159th Aviation Regiment, in Giebelstadt, Germany; from 1999 to 2000, he served as the First Sergeant for the 7-159th Aviation Regiment, in Illesheim, Germany; from 2000–2001, as First Sergeant for the 11th Aviation Regiment, in Illesheim, Germany; from 2001 to 2003, he was assigned as the Division Aviation Fleet Manager Sergeant Major, at Headquarters and Headquarters Company DISCOM, 1st Infantry Division, in Germany; from 2003 to 2005, he was selected to serve as the Command Sergeant Major for the 4th Squadron, 2D ACR, Fort Polk, Louisiana; in March 2005, he was assigned as the Command Sergeant Major for the 12th Aviation Brigade, in Giebelstadt, Germany.

Marks, Andrea R.
COMMAND SERGEANT MAJOR—ARMY

She was born in Kingston, Jamaica. She moved to the United States from London, England in 1980. In October 1981, she enlisted into the United States Army.

Her civilian and military education includes: a Bachelor of Science Degree, from Regents College; a Masters Degree in Public Administration, from Troy State University; she is a distinguished graduate of the United States Army Sergeants Major Academy; the Command Sergeant Major Course; the Garrison Command Sergeant Major Course; First Sergeant Course; Battle Staff Course; Army Force Management School; the Defense Equal Opportunity School; all the Noncommissioned Officer Education System Courses; Drill Sergeant School; Airborne School; Master Fitness Trainer Course; and the Personnel administrative Specialist Course.

She has served in a variety of assignments both in

the Continental United States and overseas. She completed Basic Training at Fort Dix, New Jersey, and Advanced Individual Training at Fort Jackson, South Carolina. Her assignments include Fort McClellan, Alabama; Bremerhaven, Germany; Fort McPherson, Georgia; Fort Benjamin Harrison, Indiana; K-16 Airbase, Korea; Staff Action Control Office, Deputy Chief of Staff for Operations and Plans, Pentagon; Office of the Chief of Staff, Army, Pentagon; Fort Meade, Maryland; Eighth United States Army, Korea; Joint Action Control Office, Deputy Chief of Staff for Operations and Plans, Pentagon; Fort Bliss, Texas and the Defense Threat Reduction Agency, Fort Belvoir, Virginia. She served as the Command Sergeant Major for the Headquarters Command Battalion, Fort George G. Meade, in Maryland. In January 2005, she was serving as the Command Sergeant Major for the 1st Personnel Command, in Germany.

Marsh, W. Clyde
REAR ADMIRAL—NAVY

He is a native of Wedowee, Alabama, was raised in Alabama and Georgia. He received his commission following graduation from Alabama A&M University in 1973. He later earned a Master of Science Degree in International Relations from Tray State University in 1988 and is a graduate of the Armed Forces Staff College. He is also a graduate of the National Defense University Capstone Course and the Regional Security Senior Executive Program at Harvard University's John F. Kennedy School of Government.

His operational sea tours includes: duty as Gunnery Officer in USS *Ozbourn* (DD846); Missile Officer in USS *Parsons* (DDG33) forward deployed to Yokosuka, Japan; Operations Officer and Navigator in USS *Prairie* *(AD 15)*; Weapons Officer in USS *Manley* (DD940; First Lieutenant in USS *Pensacola* (LSD 38) in support of the amphibious landing at Beirut, Lebanon; Exec-

utive Officer in USS *St. Louis* (LKA116) (3 Battle "E" Awards) forward deployed to Sasebo, Japan; and as Executive Officer of USS *Essex* (LHD 2) in support of Operation United Shield, the amphibious assault and withdrawal of United National Forces from Somalia.

He command tours includes: tow Mediterranean deployments in support of Operation Sharp Edge and Operation Silver Pines as Commanding Officer, USS *Sumter* (LST1181) (3Battle "E" Awards); an Arabian Gulf deployment in support of Operation Southern Watch as Commanding Officer, USS *Cleveland* (LPD7) (3 Battle "E" Awards); Commander, Amphibious Squadron Five and Commander, USS *Essex* Amphibious Ready Group. He earned Battle Efficiency "E" Awards on every ship he was assigned since joining the Amphibious Expeditionary Force in 1981.

His shore assignments include: duty as Simulation Support Officer at Fleet Combat Training Center Atlantic; Surface Engineering Branch Head at Chief of Naval Education and Training; Conventional War Plans and Japan Desk Officer, Strategic Planning and Policy Directorate (J5), United States Pacific Command. In July 1995, he was selected by Admiral J.M. Boorda, Chief of Naval Operations (CNO) as Special Assistant for Equal Opportunity (NOOE). In this capacity he was the advisor to the Navy's top leadership and the Chief of Naval Operations personal representative at military as well as civilian equal opportunity forums nation wide. He was promoted to Rear Admiral (Lower Half) on September 1, 2000, and his most recent assignment was as Deputy Director, Expeditionary Warfare Division (N75) in the Office of the Chief of Naval Operations.

Rear Admiral Marsh's personal awards and decorations include: the Legion of Merit (with three oak leaf clusters); the Defense Meritorious Service Medal; the Meritorious Service Medal (with three oak leaf clusters); the Navy and Marine Corps Commendation Medal; Joint Service Achievement Medal; Navy and Marine Corps Achievement Medal and various campaign and unit awards.

Marshall, Berlin L.
LIEUTENANT COLONEL—ARMY

He received his commissioned as a Second Lieutenant and a Distinguished Military Graduate from the University of Arkansas Pine Bluff and entered the United States Army in December 1982. After his initial Officer Basic Training at Fort Lee, Virginia, he was assigned to the 7th Infantry Division at Fort Ord in Monterey, California.

His education includes: a Bachelor of Science Degree; a Masters Degree in Management/Human Resources Development at Webster University, St Louis, Missouri; the Quartermaster Officer Basic and Advanced Courses; the Combined Arms and Service School; the Logistic Management Development Course; the Petroleum Officers Course and the Command and General Staff College.

His military assignments include: serving in Palmerola, Honduras, Central America; two tours in the Republic of Korea; Fort Bliss, Texas; Saudi Arabia & Kuwait (During Operation Desert Shield/Desert Storm); the United States Army Aviation and Troop Command in St. Louis, Missouri; at Fort Lee, Virginia; the Republic of Croatia; Fort Sam Houston in San Antonio, Texas; and the 75th Division (Training Support) in Houston, Texas.

He retired from the active army after 22 years service. He joined the Houston Independent School District team of JROTC instructors at Jones High School as the Senior Instructor in November 2004.

Martain, Rosvelt
COMMAND SERGEANT MAJOR—ARMY

Command Sergeant Major Roosevelt Martain enlisted

in the Army in 1952, and attended Basic Training at Fort Jackson, South Carolina and completed his Advanced Individual Training, at the Telephone and Instrument Repair School, Fort Gordon, Georgia. He has earned a Bachelors of Arts in Social Science. His military assignments included: assigned to the 2nd Infantry Division, in Korea; Fort Campbell, Kentucky; 2nd Armored Division, Fort Hood, Texas; Fort Benning, Georgia; 1st Cavalry Division, in Korea; 3rd Armored Division, in Germany; 2nd Field Force, Republic of Vietnam; 4th AIT Brigade, at Fort Jackson, South Carolina; Eighth Army/United States Forces Korea/United Nations Command/Combined Forces Command, Korea; United States Army Quartermaster Center and School, at Fort Lee, Virginia. He was the first Quartermaster Corps Regimental Command Sergeant Major in 1986. He also served as the Deputy Commandant/School Command Sergeant Major at Camden Military Academy. He retired with more than 35 years of military service.

Martin, Michael

LIEUTENANT COLONEL—ARMY

He is a native of Falls Church, Virginia and was commissioned in the Army as a Field Artillery Officer following his graduation from Hampton University in 1985. After initially serving in various field artillery duty positions in the 8th Infantry Division, Baumholder, Germany, he was transferred into the transportation corps.

His military and civilian education includes: a Bachelors Degree in Mass Communications from Hampton University; a Masters Degree in Business Administration from Central Michigan University, Mount Pleasant, Michigan; the Field Artillery Officer Basic Course; the Transportation Officer Advance Course; Combine

Arms Staff and Service School; and the Command and General Staff College.

His military assignments include: serving as Commander, 8th Transportation Company (air cushioned vehicle), 11th Transportation Battalion, 7th Transportation Group, at Fort Story, Virginia; served as Assignments Officer, United States Army Personnel Command, in Alexandria, Virginia; selected to serve as the Aide-de-Camp to the Vice Chairman of the Joint Chiefs of Staff, at the Pentagon, in Washington, D.C.; assigned as a Division Transportation Officer, 3rd Infantry Division and as Support Operations Officer, 87th Corps Support Battalion, 24th Corps Support Group, Fort Stewart, Georgia; as Chief, Transportation Plans Branch, Combined Forces Command, Yongsong, South Korea; as Executive Officer to the Commanding General, Fort Eustis, Virginia; in July 2005, was serving as the Deputy Commanding Officer, 7th Transportation Group, at Fort Eustis.

Martinez, Laura A.

COMMAND MASTER CHIEF—NAVY

She joined the United States Navy under the Delayed Entry Program. She reported to Boot Camp at Recruit Training Center, Orlando, Florida on April 16, 1979. She attended Hospital Corps "A" School at Great Lakes, Illinois.

She is qualified as an Enlisted Fleet Marine Warfare Specialist. She is a graduate of the Navy Senior Enlisted Academy and the Air Force Senior Non-Commissioned Academy.

In February 1981, she was assigned to Naval Hospital, Guam, in the Staff Medical Record Section, Manpower Department and Officer in Charge, Inpatient Medical Records Department, she was selected Naval Hospital Guam, "Sailor of the Year."

In March 1984, she transferred to Naval Hospital, Jacksonville, Florida for duty as the Administrative Assistant to the Director, Branch Medical Clinics. She was subsequently reassigned as the Command's Career Counselor. She was selected as Naval Hospital, Jacksonville "Sailor of the Year" and Jacksonville, Florida's Military "Woman of the Year." Her next assignment started her sea duty with the Fleet Marine Force.

In March 1988, she attended Field Medical Service School, Camp Johnson, Reporting to 2nd Force Service Support Group, Headquarters & Service Battalion, she was assigned to the Navy Personnel Office as the Group Education Service Officer and Career Counselor. After her promotion to Chief Petty Officer, she was reassigned to Medical Logistics Company, 2nd Supply Battalion serving as Leading Chief Petty Officer of the Battalion Medical Administration Team (BMAT) and Administrative Chief.

In November 1991, she was selected to fill a hot fill billet on the staff of the Surgeon General, Bureau of Medicine and Surgery (BUMED), in Washington, D.C. She served as the Administrative Assistant to the Chief of Staff for the Bureau and Administrative Chief for the Officers and Enlisted Staff assigned. In September 1993, she requested termination of shore duty for overseas sea duty for rotational purposes to Naval Hospital, Okinawa, Japan. Her assignments during this tour included: Medical Board Coordinator and Assistant Head, Patient Administration Department. During this tour she was promoted to Senior Chief Petty Officer.

In January 1996, Senior Chief Martinez was transferred to 3rd Medical Battalion, 3rd Force Service Support Group. During this tour of duty, she as the Executive Officer, Bravo Surgical Company where she deployed to Korea for Ulch Focus Lens and Thailand for Operation Cobra Gold. She was promoted to Mas-

ter Chief Petty Officer. In July 2000, she returned back to the Naval Hospital, Okinawa, Japan as the Command Master Chief.

In August 2002, Chief Martinez reported as the Command Master Chief, 2nd Force Service Support. She deployed to Southwest Asia as Command Master Chief of the Marine Logistics Command, Kuwait.

Matlock-Williams, Saundra A.
COMMAND SERGEANT MAJOR—ARMY

She retired from the United States Army in 2004, after 26 years of service. Her last assignment was that of Installation Command Sergeant Major at Fort Meade, MD.

McBride, Alexander
SERGEANT MAJOR—MARINE

He was born in Greenwood, Mississippi. He later moved to Columbus, Mississippi where he joined the Marine Corps at the age of 17, after graduating from S.D. Lee High School in June 1976. Upon completion of basic training at Marine Corps Recruit Depot San Diego, California, he then attended the Anti-Tank Warfare School at Camp Pendleton, California.

He holds a Bachelor of Science Degree in Management from the Wayland Baptist University and earned a Masters Degree in Elementary Education from the Wheelock University of Boston, MA.

His key military assignments include participating in Operations Desert Shield/Desert Storm; as an Instructor for the F-18 Hornet; as the Combat Service Support Group-3, Motor Transport First Sergeant; served as Sergeant Major of HMH-366; as the Sergeant Major, Marine Fighter Attack Squadron (VMFA)-312; assigned to Marine Corps Recruit Depot, at Parris Island, South Carolina, where he served as the 1st

Battalion Sergeant Major; in December 2004, he was serving as the Sergeant Major of Headquarters and Headquarters Squadron Marine Corps Air Station, at Beaufort, South Carolina.

McBride, Evins

SERGEANT MAJOR—MARINE

He entered the Marine Corps on November 2, 1977. Upon completion of recruit training at Marine Corps Recruit Depot, San Diego, California and Infantry Training School at Camp Pendleton, he was assigned to Marine Barracks, Bermuda, for duty as a Security Guard.

Has served in numerous key leadership positions to include in April 1984, he reported to Parris Island, in South Carolina for duty as a Drill Instructor. There, he was promoted Staff Sergeant and had a successful tour on the drill field with the 3rd Recruit Training Battalion. Upon completion of Drill Instructor duty, he received orders in August 1986 to Inspector-Instructor Staff at Raleigh, North Carolina for duty as an Assistant Marine Officer Instructor. During his tour, he trained many officer candidates at Officer Candidate School in Quantico, Virginia. His next assignment was at 1st Battalion, 8th Marines, as a Platoon Sergeant, Weapons Platoon. During this assignment he received temporary additional duty orders to platoon sergeant school, where he was promoted to Gunnery Sergeant. He deployed to Saudi Arabia in December 1990 and in February of 1991 he participated in Operation Desert Shield/Desert Storm. Upon completion of this operation, he returned in September 1993 and participated in Operation "Continue Hope/Deny Flight" as part of Combine Task Force 62 and Joint Task Force Provide promise, aboard the USS *Shreveport* in the Adriatic Sea to train Kuwait soldiers in close combat tactics, offensive and defensive operations. During November 1993

the USS *Shreveport* participated in Operation "Continue Hope/UNOSOM II" as part of COMMARFORSOMALIA (CT 158) and Joint Task Force Somalia while deployed in the Indian Ocean. In August 1994, he reported to Chesapeake, Virginia for training as a Marine Security Guard Chief. Upon completion of training, he received orders to Kings Bay, Georgia, for duty. During this tour, he was promoted to the rank of First Sergeant with approximately one year on station and reported to Headquarters Battalion, 2nd Marine Division for duty as Company First Sergeant for Truck Company, Headquarters Battalion, with the 2nd Marine Division. During this tour, he was selected for Sergeant Major. Upon being frocked, he reported to the Marine Corps Activity, Kansas City, Missouri for duty as the Command Sergeant Major on February 2, 1999.

He joined the 24th Marine Regiment, in Kansas City, Missouri for duty as the Inspector-Instructor Sergeant Major on July 1, 2003.

McCall, James Franklin

LIEUTENANT GENERAL—ARMY

He was born in Philadelphia, Pennsylvania. He received a Bachelor of Science degree in Economics from the University of Pennsylvania and a Master's of Business Administration in Comptrollership from Syracuse University. He entered the United States Army in March 1958 and became a Platoon Leader in Company A, 12th Battalion, 4th Training Regiment, United States Army Training Center, Fort Knox, Kentucky. From December 1958 to August 1959, he was the Commander of Company A, 12th Battalion, 4th Training Regiment, United States Army Training Center. From August 1959 to March 1960, he was an Instructor in the 12th Battalion, 4th Training Regiment. On September 4, 1959, he was promoted to First Lieutenant. From

March 1960 to June 1961, he was a Platoon Leader, Combat Support Company, 1st Battle Group, 7th Cavalry, United States Army, in Europe. From June 1962 to January 1963, he served as Assistant S-4 with the 1st Battle Group, 3rd Infantry, Fort Myer, and Virginia. He was promoted to Captain on September 4, 1962. From January 1963 to June 1963, he was Commander, Company C, 1st Battle Group, 3rd Infantry, Fort Myer, Virginia. From August 1963 to July 1964, to October 1965, he served as the S-2, From November 1965 to April 1966; he was Secretary of the General Staff, Headquarters, Berlin Brigade, United States Army, in Europe. From June 1966 to November 1966, he was the Commander of Company M, 34th Battalion, 2nd Basic Training Brigade, Fort Dix, New Jersey. He was promoted to the rank of Major on November 23, 1966. From April 1967 to May 1968, he served as an Adviser on Advisory Team 96, United States Military Assistance Command, in Vietnam. From May 1968 to May 1969, he was a student at the United States Command and General Staff College, Fort Leavenworth, Kansas. From June 1969 to July 1970, he was a student at Syracuse University. From August 1970 to July 1973, he served as a Military Assistant, Office of the Assistant Secretary of the Army (Financial Management), in Washington, D.C. He was promoted to Lieutenant Colonel on November 9, 1971. From August 1973 to August 1973 to August 1974, he was Commander, 1st Battalion, 31st Infantry, and 2nd Infantry Division, in Korea. From September 1974 to August 1975, he served as a Staff Officer with the Army Materiel Acquisition Review Committee-Armament, United States Materiel Command, in Alexandria, Virginia. From August 1975 to June 1976, he was a student at the Industrial College of the Armed Forces, Fort Lesley J. McNair, in Washington, D.C. On February 1, 1976, he was promoted to Colonel. From June 1976 to June 1977, he served as Executive Officer, Office of the Director of the Army Budget, Comptroller of the Army, Washington, D.C. From July 1977 to April 1979, he was the Commander of the 4th Training Brigade, United States Army Armor School, Fort Knox, Kentucky; from June 1979 to July 1980, Chief, Procurement Programs and Budget Division, Materiel Plans and Programs Directorate, Office of the Deputy Chief of Staff for Research, Development, and Acquisition, United States Army, Washington, D.C. He was promoted to Brigadier General on March 1, 1980. From July 1980 to June 1984, he served as Comptroller, United States Army Materiel Development and Readiness Command, Alexandria, Virginia. He was promoted to major general on September 1, 1983. From June 1984 to July 1988, he served as the Director of the Army Budget, Office of the Comptroller, United States Army, in Washington, D.C. On July 1, 1988, he was promoted to lieutenant general. In July 1988, he was assigned as Comptroller of the Army, in the Office of the Secretary of the Army, in Washington, D.C. He retired from the military on June 30, 1991. He has received numerous awards, decorations and badges including: the Parachutist Badge; Distin-guished Service Medal; Legion of Merit (with oak leaf cluster); Meritorious Service Medal; Air Medal, Army Commendation Medal (with oak leaf cluster); Combat infantryman Badge.

McCoy, Gary T.
BRIGADIER GENERAL—AIR FORCE

He is a native of South Carolina. General McCoy was commissioned through the Officer Training School in July 1976. He received a Bachelor of Science Degree in Sociology, from Culver-Stockton College, in Missouri. He holds a Master of Arts Degree in Human Resources Management, University of Redlands, California. His military education includes: Squadron Officer School, at Maxwell Air Force Base, in Alabama; the Marine Corps Command and Staff College; Air Command and Staff College, at Maxwell Air Force Base, in Alabama; the National Security Management Program; Armed Forces Staff College, Joint and Combined Staff Officer School, in Norfolk, Virginia; Air War College, at Maxwell Air Force Base.

He has served in a variety of command and staff assignments. He began his career as a logistics officer with the Air Force Communications Service and was then assigned as a senior management consultant with the Leadership and Management Development Center, Air University. A career logistics officer, he has commanded a supply squadron and a logistics group, deputy program manager, a joint duty officer with the Defense Logistics Agency and an air logistics center product director. Prior to his current assignment, he served as Deputy Director of Maintenance, Deputy Chief of Staff for Installations and Logistics, Headquarters U.S. Air Force. He was promoted to Brigadier General on April 1, 2003.

In November 2003, he was assigned as the Director

of Logistics, at Headquarters Air Force Materiel Command, at Wright-Patterson Air Force Base, in Ohio.

McCoy, Herbert
COMMAND SERGEANT MAJOR—ARMY

He is a native of Arkansas, and entered the United States Army in July 1976. He attended Basic Combat Training and Advanced Individual Training at Fort Bliss, Texas, where he was a Distinguished Honor Graduate of his class and awarded the MOS 16R short-Range Air Defense Artillery Crewman. He was also trained as a Aircraft Armament Fire Control Repairman. In 1982, he reclassified to MOS 67T Tactical Transportation Helicopter Repairman as an Honor Graduate.

His military education include all the Noncommissioned Officer System Courses; Aviation Life Support Equipment Course; Aviation Safety Course; SERE C High Risk Course; 160th SOAR Selection and Training Course; Airborne School; Air Assault School; First Sergeant Course; United States Army Sergeants Major Academy; Command Sergeant Major Course. He holds an Associate Degree in Aviation Technology, from North Central Institute, Clarksville, Tennessee.

He has served in various positions of leadership to include serving as Senior Gunner; Squad Leader; Section Sergeant; Aircraft Technical Inspector; Crew Chief; Flight/Maintenance Platoon Sergeant; First Sergeant; Battalion Sergeant Major; Command Sergeant Major, 12th Aviation Battalion, Fort Belvoir, Virginia. .

McCoy, Leslie J.
COMMANDER—NAVY

He graduated from the United States Naval Academy in 1979 with a Bachelor of Science Degree in Physical Science. He earned a Master's of Art Degree, in Na-

tional Security and Strategic Affairs, from the Naval War College in Newport, Rhode Island.

He was designated a Naval Aviator in June 1981 and reported to Naval Air Station Lemoore, California in October 1981, where he flew the UH-1N Helicopter in addition to the fixed-wing UC-12B, providing logistics support. In October 1983, he transitioned to the SH-2F LAMPS MK-I Helicopter a HSL-31, Naval Air Station North Island, California.

He transferred to the "Easy Riders" of HSL-37, Naval Air Station Barbers Point, Hawaii, serving as Detachment Officer in Charge (OIC). He deployed onboard: USS *Badger* (FF1071); USS Robert E. Peary (FF 1073), USS *Harold E. Holt* (FF 1074), and USS *Brewton* (FF 1086).

In January 1987, he returned to Naval Air Station North Island as a Fleet Replacement Squadron Instructor Pilot with HSL-31 and was later designated the West Coast NATOPS Evaluator (SH-2F) for Commander, Naval Air Force Pacific (COMNAVAIRPAC). He transferred to the HSL-33 "Sea Snakes" in August 1989 and deployed as Detachment Office in Charge of USS *Mahlon S. Tisdale* (FFG 27) and USS *Reid* (FFG 30). In October 1993, he was assigned as Executive Officer of the HSL-41 "Seahawk." In May 1995, he transferred to HSL-47, as Executive Officer and served as the "Saberhawk" Commanding Officer from September 1996 through November 1997. In 1998, he reported to the Pre-commissioning Unit (PCU) of the USS *Bonhomme Richard* (LHD 7) as the ship's "Air Boss" in Pascagoula, Mississippi. He also served as the ship's Commissioning Coordinator, planning and directing her Pensacola, Florida, commissioning in August 1998.

He transferred to CINCPACFLT, Pearl Harbor, Hawaii, in January 2000, serving as the Deputy Director of Fleet Warfare Requirements until October 2002. In March 2003, he assumed Command of Naval Base Guantanamo Bay, Cuba.

McCray, Russell

COMMAND SERGEANT MAJOR—ARMY

He is a native of Bishopville, Carolina, where he attended Mount Pleasant High School. After graduating in 1981, he entered the United States Army in January 1982. He completed the One Station Unit Training at Fort Benning, Georgia.

His military and civilian education includes: all the Non-Commissioned Officer Education System Courses; Light Leader Course; Battle Staff Course; Jungle Operation Training Course; Instructor Trainer Course; Air Assault School; Air Borne School Master Fitness School; First Sergeant Course (AUSA Leadership Recipient); Drill Sergeant Course (Honor Graduate, Leadership Award); the United States Army Sergeants Major Academy (class 54); the Command Sergeant Major Course. He earned a Degree in Business Management from Excelsior College of New York.

His military assignments include: serving as Squad Leader, B Company, 1st/2nd Regiment, 4th Infantry, in Neu Ulm, Germany; Scout Section Leader, Headquarters and Headquarters Company, 1st Regiment, 4th Infantry, Hohenfels, Germany; Drill Sergeant and Senior Drill Sergeant, at Fort Benning, Georgia; Chief Drill Instructor, Fort Benning, Georgia; Platoon Sergeant, A Company, 1/21st Infantry, Schofield Barracks, Hawaii; First Sergeant, C Company, 1/21st Infantry, Schofield Barracks, Hawaii; First Sergeant, Headquarters and Headquarters Company, 25th Infantry Division (Light), Schofield Barracks, Hawaii; as the G-5 Non-Commissioned Officer in Charge, 25th Infantry Division; as Operations Sergeant Major, 1/3rd Infantry Battalion (TOG); as Command Sergeant Major, 3rd United States Infantry Regiment (the Old Guard), in Washington, D.C.

McCutchen, Braley E., III

COMMAND SERGEANT MAJOR—ARMY

He was born in Sumter, South Carolina. He enlisted into the United States Army in May 1978. He completed Basic Combat Training and Advanced Individual Training (AIT) at Fort Gordon, Georgia as a 36k Field Wiring Specialist.

His military and civilian education include: All the Noncommissioned Officers Education Systems Courses; Drill Sergeant Course; Master Fitness Course; the United States Army Sergeants Major Academy Class 50. He has earned an Associate Degree in General Studies from Central Texas College.

His military assignments include serving Installation Section Chief, Headquarters and Headquarters Battery, 2/21st Field Artillery, Fort Polk, Louisiana; Communications Chief, Company F, 40th Armor, Berlin, Germany; Platoon Sergeant and First Sergeant, 408th Military Intelligence Company, Fort Davis, Panama; Communications Developer, Engineer School, Fort

Leonard Wood, Missouri; First Sergeant, Company C, 29th Signal; Communications Chief and First Sergeant, Headquarters and Headquarters Battery, 2/17th Field Artillery, Camp Hovey, Korea; Command Sergeant Major of the 1110th Signal Battalion, Fort Detrick, Maryland; Command Sergeant Major of 307th Signal Battalion, Camp Carroll, Korea; in January 2005, he was serving as the Command Sergeant Major, 1st Signal Brigade, Yongsan, Korea.

McDew, Darren W.

COLONEL—AIR FORCE

He received his commission in 1982, and after completing Pilot Training at Williams Air Force Base, in Arizona, he began his career military career flying in the K/KC-135 at Loring Air Force Base, in Arizona.

In 1992, he was assigned as Directorate of Personnel Plans and served as a member of the Chief of Staff of the Air Force Operations Group at the Pentagon. In 1994, he was assigned as an Air Force Aide to President Bill Clinton. In 1997, he became Commander of the 14th Airlift Squadron, at Charleston Air Force Base, South Carolina. In 2001, he deployed as Commander of the 60th Air Expeditionary Group. In 2002, he became the Commander of the 375ht Air lift Wing and Installation Commander at Scott Air Force Base, in Illinois. In 2003, he was assigned as Chief, Air Force Senate Liaison Division, in Washington, D.C. In 2005, he was serving as the Commander of the 43rd Airlift Wing, at Pope Air Force Base.

He is a Command Pilot with more than 3,000 hours. He was promoted to Colonel in April 2000.

McDowell, Billy D.
FIRST SERGEANT—MARINE

He was born in Snow Hill, North Carolina. He enlisted into the United States Marine Corps in August 1982 and completed Recruit Training at Marine Corps Recruit Depot at Parris Island, North Carolina and upon completion Recruit Training he attended Infantry Training School located at Camp Geiger, North Carolina and upon completion, he was assigned the MOS 0311 Infantryman.

In May 1983, he reported to 2nd Battalion, 6th Marines located at Camp Lejeune, North Carolina, where he served as a Rifleman in Golf Company. In February of 1985, he was assigned to Marine Corps Security Forces Atlantic, located at Camp Lejeune, North

Carolina, where he served as a member of the Service Storage Facility (SSF). In June 1987, he executed Permanent Change of Station (PCS) orders to 3rd Battalion, 2nd Marines located at Camp Lejeune, North Carolina. During this tour, he fulfilled duties as Fire Team and Squad Leader. While deployed as a member of the 4th Marine Expeditionary Brigade, he participated in Operation Desert Shield/Desert Storm.

In August 1991, he reported to Drill Instructor School at Marine Corps Recruit Depot at Parris Island, South Carolina. Upon completion he was assigned as both Drill Instructor and Senior Drill Instructor, with the 3rd Recruit Training Battalion, at Parris Island, South Carolina. In February 1994, he reported to 3rd Battalion, 8th Marines where he served as Platoon Sergeant and Platoon Commander. In March 1997, he was reassigned to 2nd Battalion, 8th Marines where he served as a Platoon Sergeant. In April 1999, he reported to the Staff Non Commissioned Officer Academy (SNCOA), located at Camp Geiger, North Carolina, where he served as a Squad Advisor for both the Sergeant's Course, and the Career Course.

In April 2001, 1st Sergeant McDowell was assigned to the 2nd Force Service Support Group, where he served as TRT PME/School Chief Coordinator. While serving with the 2nd Force Service Support Group, he deployed to Kuwait in February 2003, to participate in Operation Iraqi Freedom. He was selected to 1st Sergeant on the in March 2003. He then transferred to Military Police Battalion. In November 2003, he was assigned as Company 1st Sergeant at Headquarters and Service Company, 2nd Supply Battalion. In September 2004, he was selected to serve as the Sergeant Major for the 2nd Supply Battalion.

McFadden, Jackie
COMMAND SERGEANT MAJOR—ARMY

He entered the military service in March 1977. His military education includes Basic Combat Training, at Fort Dix, New Jersey; all the Noncommissioned Officer Education System Courses; Advance Individual Training (AIT) as a Combat Medic, 91B (91W) and Behavioral Science Specialist 91G (91X), Test and Evaluation Officer Course; Drill Sergeant School; First Sergeants Course; the United States Army Sergeants Major Academy (class 53). He also holds an Associate of Arts Degree from St. Thomas Aquinas College; a Bachelor of Social Work Degree, from Tarleton State University; and earned a Masters Degree in Human Resource Management, at Webster University.

His key assignments include serving as a Drill Sergeant, C, 187th Medical Battalion, at Fort Sam Houston, Texas; Research Development Test and Experimentation Noncommissioned Officer, Test and Experimentation Command, at Fort Hood, Texas; Fist Sergeant, C, Company, 204th Field Support Battalion, 4th Infantry Division, Fort Hood, Texas; First Sergeant, E, Company, 204th Field Support Battalion, Fort Hood, Texas; Future Operations NCO, III Corps HQ., Fort Hood, Texas; in September 2004, he was serving

as Command Sergeant Major 187th Medical Battalion, Fort Sam Houston, Texas.

McFadden, Willie
LIEUTENANT COLONEL—ARMY

Lieutenant Colonel McFadden joined the Department of Systems Engineering at the United States Military Academy, at West Point, New York, in June 2000. He graduated from the United States Military Academy in 1983, and was commissioned in the Field Artillery. His research interests are engineering of organizational Systems, computer-based knowledge systems, and program management.

McKinney, Gene C.
SERGEANT MAJOR OF THE ARMY

He was born in Monticello, Florida. He married the former Wilhelmina Hall of Tallahassee, Florida and they had a son, Zuberi. He entered the United States Army in August 1968. During his more than 26 years of Service, Sergeant Major of the Army (SMA) Gene C. McKinney has served in every enlisted leadership position from scout leader to command sergeant major. He holds an Associate of Applied Science Degree in General Management with El Paso Community College, and a Bachelor of Science degree in Management/ Human Resources with Park College. SMA McKinney's military education includes Airborne Training, Parachute Pack, Maintenance and Airdrop course (Honor Graduate), 11D NCO Basic Course, Dragon Weapon Systems Course, M60A1/A3 Master Gunner Course, Armor Advanced Course, (Honor Graduate), the United States Army First Sergeant Course and a graduate of Class 31, the United States Army Sergeant Major Academy. His assignments include on combat infantry tour in Vietnam, from 1969–1970, and has been an armored cavalryman for more than two decades. Before becoming the tenth Sergeant Major of the Army, he was Command Sergeant Major of the United States Army Europe. His other assignments include: Command Sergeant Major, 1st Armored Division; Command Sergeant Major 8th Infantry Division (Mechanized), Bad Kreuznach, Germany; 1st Brigade, 1st Armored Division, Vilseck, Germany; 173rd Airborne Brigade, Vietnam; 612th Quartermaster, Fort Bragg, North Carolina; 1st Battalion, 58th Mechanized Infantry, 197th Brigade, Fort Benning, Georgia; 3rd Squadron, 12th Cavalry Regiment, Budingen, Germany; and 2nd Armored Cavalry Regiment, Bamberg Germany. SMA McKinney's awards and decorations include: Legion of Merit; Bronze Star Medal (with one oak leaf cluster); Meritorious Service Medal (with three oak leaf clusters); Army Commendation Medal; Army Achievement Medal; Good Conduct Medal (8th award); National Defense Service Medal; Vietnam Service Medal; NCO Professional Development Ribbon, with a Four; Army Service Ribbon; Overseas Service Ribbon; Republic of Vietnam Campaign Medal; Combat Infantrymen Badge; and Parachutist Badge.

McKinnon, Joseph J.
COMMAND SERGEANT MAJOR—ARMY

He is a native of Fayetteville, North Carolina and entered the United States Army in July 1981. He completed Basic Combat Training (BCT) at Fort Leonard, Missouri and also completed his Advanced Individual Training (AIT) at Fort Gordon, Georgia as a Multichannel Communications Radio Operator.

His civilian and military education includes: he earned an Associate Degree from Central Texas College; he completed all the Noncommissioned Officer Education Systems Courses; Multi-channel Communications Equipment Operator Primary Technical Course (PTC), (Honor Graduate); Drill Sergeant School; Master Fitness Trainer Course (MFT); the Joint Tactical Automated Switching Network Supervisor Course; the Nodal Manager Integration Training Course; Defense Equal Opportunity Management Institute (DEOMI); the First Sergeant Course; the United States Army Sergeants Major Academy (class 51); and the Command Sergeant Major Course.

His key assignment includes: serving as a Multichannel Communication Radio Team Chief and Section Sergeant, 269th Signal Company, Karlsruhe, Germany; as a Drill Sergeant, later as Senior Drill Sergeant Alpha Company, 1st Battalion, 26th Infantry, 3rd Brigade, at Fort Dix, New Jersey; as a Platoon Sergeant and Physical Fitness Instructor, with Delta Company 42nd AG Battalion, at Fort Dix, New Jersey; as a Multi-channel Communication System NCO and Platoon Sergeant for Cable with the Alpha Company 307th Signal Battalion, at Camp Carroll, Korea; as Platoon Sergeant and later First Sergeant, of 167th Signal Company, Vicenza, Italy; as a Platoon Sergeant, with 58th Signal Company, in Manheim, Germany; as a Platoon Sergeant, Camp Pleso, Croatia, Bosnia; as the First Sergeant, Charlie Company, 123rd Signal Battalion, at Fort Stewart, Georgia; served as Tritac Plans NCO in Headquarters and Headquarters Company, 5th Signal Command, in Heidelberg, Germany; as the Deputy G-6, Sergeant Major, at Headquarters and Headquarters, Company, 125th Signal Battalion, Schofield Barracks, in Hawaii; as the Command Sergeant Major, 30th Signal Battalion, 516th Signal Brigade at Fort Shafter Hawaii; in March 2005, as the Command Sergeant Major for the 307th Signal Battalion, 1st Signal Brigade at Camp Carroll in Waegwan, Korea.

McKnight, William, Jr.
SERGEANT MAJOR—MARINE CORPS

Sergeant Major William McKnight, Jr. enlisted in

the United States Marine Corps in August 1975. After completing recruit training at Marine Corps Recruit Depot, Parris Island, South Carolina, he was assigned to 2nd supply Battalion, Marine Corps Base Camp Lejeune, North Carolina, where he served as a Warehouseman. He then served at Camp Foster, Okinawa, Japan with Supply Company, 3rd Supply Battalion.

He was promoted to First Sergeant in 1989, while serving with Headquarters and Service Battalion, 1st FSSG, at Camp Pendleton, California. On April 1, 1995, he was promoted to Sergeant Major and assigned as the Sergeant Major for the 2nd Medical Battalion, 2nd FSSG. He also served as Sergeant Major for 2nd FSSG Forward. In April 1996, he was assigned to 8th Engineer Support Battalion, 2nd FSSG, (Forward). In April 1997, he was assigned to the Expeditionary Warfare Training Group in Norfolk, Virginia. He was selected as the Sergeant Major of the 26th Marine Expeditionary Unit at Camp Lejeune, in November 1999. He has completed two LF6f Mediterranean Deployments and most recently participated in Operations Swift Freedom and Enduring Freedom in Pakistan and Afghanistan.

McLarin, Benita A.
LIEUTENANT COLONEL—ARMY

She is a native of Memphis, Tennessee. She enlisted into the United States Reserve and completed Basic Training in 1980, while still in high school. After graduating from Central High School in 1981, she went on to complete her Advanced Individual Training (AIT) as a Medic and Pharmacy Technician. She received her commission as a Second Lieutenant in the Adjutant General Corps through the Reserve Officer Training Corps (ROTC) at Washington University in 1984. She continued to serve actively in the United States Army Reserve until she entered active duty service in the Medical Service Corps in 1986.

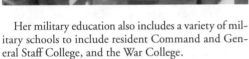

Her military education also includes a variety of military schools to include resident Command and General Staff College, and the War College.

She received a Bachelor of Arts Degree in Psychology from Washington University, in St. Louis, Missouri in 1985. She received a Master of Health Administration Degree from Chapman University in 1990; and a Master of Science Degree from Harvard University School of Public Health, Boston, Massachusetts in 1995.

Her military assignments include: deployments with the Joint Task Force Bravo Medical Element in Honduras as a Medical Planner; Company Commander in Saudi Arabia during Operations Desert Shield and Desert Storm; Operation Joint Forge in Bosnia while assigned to the 3rd Infantry Division (Mechanized) at Fort Stewart, Georgia as the Division Medical Operations Officer. Her career culminated with her assignment to the TRICARE office of the Lead Agent, Travis Air Force Base, California, as Director of the Health Plan Management Division. In February 2005, she was serving as the Commander of the 168th Medical Battalion in Seoul, South Korea.

McMichael, Alford L.
SERGEANT MAJOR OF THE MARINE CORPS

Sergeant Major Alford L. McMichael was born in Hot Springs, Arkansas. He enlisted in the Marine Corps on August 27, 1970, and attended boot camp at Marine Corps Recruit Depot at San Diego, California. In June 1971, after completing Infantry Training School and Basic Infantry Training at Camp Pendleton, California, he was assigned to Marine Barracks, Pearl Harbor, Hawaii. In May 1973, he was transferred to 2nd Battalion, 5th Marines, 1st Marine Division, at Camp Pendleton, California.

In December 1973, Sergeant Major McMichael returned to Marine Corps Recruit Depot at San Diego, California, where he served as a Drill Instructor, Series Gunnery Sergeant, and Battalion Drill Master. In December 1975, he was transferred to 1st Battalion, 7th Marines, 1st Marine Division, at Camp Pendleton, California. In January 1978, he transferred to the 3rd Marine Division where he served as a shore party chief with the 3rd Division Support Group. In January 1979, he received orders to Marine Security Guard School and, upon completion of the school, was assigned to the American Embassy in Copenhagen, Denmark. In May 1981, he returned to Quantico, Virginia, to serve as an Instructor for the Marine Security Guard School. In May 1983, Sergeant Major McMichael was assigned to the University of Minnesota where he served as the Assistant Marine Officer Instructor for the NROTC program. In December 1984, after completing the Staff Noncommissioned Officers Academy Advanced Course, he was transferred to Okinawa, Japan, to serve as the First Sergeant of Company C, 3rd Reconnaissance Battalion. In January 1986, he was ordered to Marine Barracks, Roosevelt Roads, Puerto Rico, to serve as the Barracks' First Sergeant.

He served as the director of the Staff Noncommissioned Officers Academy at Marine Corps Air Station El Toro, California, from May 1989 to May 1991 after having served as the school's Deputy Director since August 1988. In May 1991, he was transferred to Quantico, where he served as the Sergeant Major of Officer Candidates School. In June 1994, he returned to Okinawa, Japan, where he served as the Sergeant Major of the 31st Marine Expeditionary Unit until July 1995, when he was reassigned as the Sergeant Major of the 1st Marine Aircraft Wing. From January 1997 to June 1999, he served as the Sergeant Major for Manpower and Reserve Affairs Division at the Headquarters of the United States Marine Corps.

Sergeant Major McMichael assumed his current post as the 14th Sergeant Major of the Marine Corps on July

1, 1999. He is the first African American in the History of the Marine Corps to be selected as the Senior Non-commissioned Officer in the Corps.

McMillan, Raymond V.

BRIGADIER GENERAL—AIR FORCE

He was born in Fairmont, North Carolina, and married the former Maxine Tyler of Hillside, New Jersey. They have two children, Raymond and Debra. He earned a Bachelor and Master of Science degrees in Electrical Engineering from the University of Wyoming in 1970 and 1971, respectively. The general graduated from Squadron Officer School at Maxwell Air Force Base, Alabama, in 1962 and from the Armed Forces Staff College at Fort Lesley J. McNair, Washington, D.C., in 1977. He completed the Senior Executive Course at the Massachusetts Institute of Technology in 1983. After enlisting in the United States Air Force in August 1950 and completing Basic Training at Lackland Air Force Base, Texas, he was assigned to Highland Air Force Station in New Jersey as a Radar Maintenance Technician. Upon attaining the rank of Technical Sergeant, McMillan attended Officer Candidate School at Lackland Air Force Base and was commissioned a Second Lieutenant in December 1958. He was then assigned as a student in the Armament Officers Course at Lowry Air Force Base, Colorado, and remained there as a Technical Instructor in the Avionics Officer Course. During this period he attended Squadron Officer School at Maxwell Air Force Base. In June 1964, the general was assigned to Francis E. Warren Air Force Base, Wyoming, as a Minuteman Missile Launch Officer. After completing this assignment in 1968, he attended the University of Wyoming under the Air Force Institute of Technology Program. He was assigned to

Hanscom Air Force Base, Massachusetts, in January 1971 as a Radar Engineer in the Airborne Warning and Control System Program Office for E-3As. General McMillan was a radar engineer on the first flight of one of the radar test aircraft and had more than 200 flying hours as a Test Engineer in the Airborne Warning and Control System Program. He attended the Armed Forces Staff College from January 1973 to July 1973. He was then assigned to Andrews Air Force Base, Maryland, and served as Chief of the Airborne Warning and Control System Division, Air Force Systems Command, later as Executive Officer for the Deputy Chief of Staff for Systems. He then attended the Industrial College of the Armed Forces. Returning to Hanscom Air Force Base in June 1977, the general served as Program Director of the SEEK IGLOO Program, the program to replace all Surveillance Radars in Alaska. While at Hanscom, he also served as program Director of the Joint Surveillance System, the replacement program for the Semi-Automatic Ground Environment System, and as Assistant Deputy Chief of Staff for Surveillance and Control system. In March 1980, General McMillan was given the task of forming an Air Force Systems Command detachment in Colorado Springs, Colorado. The detachment assists the Commander of Space Command in resolving system acquisition problems. When the Space Command System Integration Office was formed in 1981, he became the Deputy Chief of the organization and served in both positions until May 1983. The general then returned to Andrews Air Force Systems Command. He returned to the Headquarters of the North American Aerospace Defense Command and Space Command in April 1984 as Deputy Chief of Staff for Systems Integration, and Chief of the Systems Integration Office in Space Command. In September 1985 Brigadier General McMillan served as Chief of the System Integration Office, and Assistant Deputy Chief of Staff for Systems Integration, Logistics and Support at the United States Air Force Space Command at Peterson Air Force Base, Colorado. He was appointed Brigadier General on September 1, 1984, with the same date of rank. He retired from the military on September 1, 1987. He died on April 8, 2002. His military decorations and awards include the Defense Superior Service Medal; Legion of Merit; Meritorious Service Medal (with oak leaf cluster); Air Force Commendation Medal; Air Force Outstanding Unit Award; Air Force Organizational Excellence Award; and Army Good Conduct Medal (with two bronze loops). He wears the Space Badge and the Senior Missile Badge.

McMillon, Brye

CHIEF MASTER SERGEANT—AIR FORCE

He was born and grew up in Orrville, Alabama. He entered the Air Force in April 1981 and completed Basic Military Training at Lackland Air Force Base, Texas. His military education includes the 15th Air Force NCO Leadership School; Strategic Air Command NCO Academy; Community College of the Air Force

(where he was awarded the Aerospace Management Certificate); Federal Bureau of Investigation National Academy at Quantico, Virginia; and Senior Noncommissioned Officer Academy. He holds a Bachelor of Arts degree in General Studies from Hampton University.

He has held a myriad of positions during his career, serving as the Operations Superintendent for the 305th Security Forces Squadron at McGuire Air Force Base, New Jersey. The Chief also performed duties as the Superintendent of Nuclear Security Policy at the Air Combat Command Directorate of Security Forces, where he was involved in coordinating initiatives affecting both long and short range nuclear plans. As Superintendent for Manpower and Resources, he managed over 500 active and 5,000 reserve security force positions assigned to some 19 units. In this capacity he coordinated closely with ACC Manpower Office to ensure units supporting the command's most critical resources maintained the necessary personnel and equipment to perform their mission. During his tenure as the Security Forces Manager of the 89th Security Forces Squadron, he led a unit of over 680 Air Force Active, Guard and Reserve Force Protectors in providing topnotch security for resources supporting our nation's leaders. In August 2004, he was serving as the Command Chief Master Sergeant for the 89th Airlift Wing, at Andrews AFB, Maryland.

McMullen, Keith A.
COMMAND SERGEANT MAJOR—ARMY

He entered the United States Army under the "One Stop Unit Training" at Fort Leonard Wood, Missouri. His military education includes the Battle Staff Course; Sapper Leader's Course; First Sergeants Course; Drill Sergeant School; Advanced NBC Course; and the United States Army Sergeants Major Academy.

He has held every key leadership position including

Team Leader; Squad Leader; Drill Sergeant; Platoon Sergeant; Senior Instructor; Operations Sergeant; ACRC Advisor; Observer Controller; First Sergeant; and Operation Sergeant Major of the 21D Engineer Brigade. In August 2004, he was serving as the Command Sergeant Major for the 91st Engineer Battalion, Engineer Brigade, 1st Cavalry Division.

McNeil, Joseph
MAJOR GENERAL—AIR FORCE

He is from Wilmington, North Carolina, and now lives in Hempstead, New York. While attending North Carolina A&T as a 17-year-old freshman and member

of the ROTC, he and three other freshmen — the late David Richmond, Franklin McCain, and Jibreel Khazan-entered the Woolworth's in downtown Greensboro on February 1, 1960. They were refused service of coffee and pie, which sparked a protest at the Woolworth's lunch counter and other protests and sit-ins at lunch counters all over the south. A piece of the Woolworth lunch counter recently was put on display at the Smithsonian Institution's National Museum of American History in Washington, D.C. McNeil graduated from Agricultural &Technical State University in 1963 and was commissioned a Second Lieutenant in the United States Air Force. He served as a navigator on tankers refueling other planes off the Vietnamese coast during the Vietnam War. He left the Active Air Force in 1969 and became an investment banker before joining the Federal Aviation Administration, for which he still works out of the New York area. He remained in the Air Force Reserve and began a steady rise through the command structure. He earned his first star as a brigadier general in 1994 and his second star in 1996.

McNeil, Robert J.
COLONEL—ARMY

He was born in Rowland, North Carolina. He is a graduate of North Carolina A&T State University in Greensboro, North Carolina, where he received a Bachelor of Science degree in Political Science, and his commission as a Second Lieutenant in the United States Army. In addition, he holds a master's degree in Logistics Management from the Florida Institute of Technology.

His military education includes the Basic and Advanced Courses; Command and General Staff College; Logistics Executive Development Course; and the United States Army War College.

He entered active duty in August 1975. Over the past 29 years, he has held a number of command and staff positions. His duty experiences include Platoon Leader in Korea; Battalion S-4 (Logistic) and Company Commander at Fort Lewis, Washington; Battalion Executive Officer, Battalion Commander, and Division G-4 (Logistic), at Fort Carson, Colorado; Brigade Commander in Okinawa, Japan; and most recently, Chief of Plans and Operations for the C-4, Combined Forces Command, in South Korea. He is the Commandant of the Army Logistics Management College at Fort Lee, Virginia.

McNeirney, Violet C.
COMMAND SERGEANT MAJOR—ARMY

She is a native of New York and enlisted into the United States Army in December 1982. She completed Basic Combat Training and Advanced Individual Training at Fort Jackson, South Carolina.

Her military education includes the Leadership Team Awareness Course (DEOMI 04V); First Sergeant Course; all the Non-Commissioned Officer Education System Courses; Publications Managers Course; Equal Opportunity Representative Course; Combat Lifesavers Course; Instructor Training Course; Cadre Training Course; Airborne School; the United States Army Sergeants Major Academy (class 53); the Command Sergeants Major Course; and Garrison Command Sergeant Major Course.

Her military assignments include Battalion Administrative NCO at Fort Bragg, North Carolina; Administrative Supervisor, G-1, VII Corps, in Germany; Secretary of the General Staff, Administrative Non-Commissioned Officer in Charge, VII Corps — in Germany; Administrative Non-Commissioned Officer in Charge to the Commanding General, VII Corps,

during this assignment, she deployed to the Middle East in support of Operations Desert Shield/Desert Storm and Operation Provide Comfort; Executive Administrative Assistant to the Commanding General, Training and Doctrine Command, at Fort Monroe, Virginia; Senior Drill Sergeant, 1st Battalion, 26th Infantry Regiment (BCT); Operations Non-Commissioned Officer in Charge, S3, 1/34th Infantry Regiment, at Fort Jackson, South Carolina; Protocol Non-Commissioned Officer-in-Charge, United States Forces Korea (USFK) and Eighth United States Army (EUSA), in Korea; First Sergeant of Headquarters and Headquarters Company, 43rd AG Battalion; First Sergeant of the Fitness Training Company at Fort Leonard Wood, Missouri; Sergeant Major, SGS/SACO, Headquarters Military District of Washington (MDW), Washington, D.C.; and Command Sergeant Major, Headquarters Command Battalion, at Fort Myer, Virginia.

McPherson, Carl B., Sr.
COMMAND SERGEANT MAJOR—ARMY

Command Sergeant Major Carl B. McPherson, Sr. was born in Fort Jackson, South Carolina. He enlisted in the Army in June 1974. He earned an associate's degree in General Studies from Central Texas College, and over three years of college credits towards a bachelor's degree in Criminal Justice.

His military education includes the Battle Staff Course; the First Sergeants Course; the Master Fitness Trainer Course; and the United States Army Sergeants Major Academy at Fort Bliss, Texas. His most recent assignments include service as a Drill Sergeant at Fort Sill, Oklahoma; Gun Chief; Firing Battery Platoon Sergeant; Ammo Platoon Sergeant; Physical Security NCO; Operations Sergeant; First Sergeant; and Battalion Command Sergeant Major. He has served as the Command Sergeant Major for the 1-7th Field Artillery Battalion from July 1997 to June of 2000. His battalion was the first battalion to fire the Paladin Howitzers

in the Balkans. The Battalion fired in support of recon elements of the 1-26th Infantry Battalion while deployed to Camp Monteith, Kosovo. He is currently the Commandant for the United States Army Noncommissioned Officer Academy at Fort Sill.

McQueen, Adolph, Jr.
BRIGADIER GENERAL—ARMY

He was commissioned a First Lieutenant on April 21, 1982. His education includes a Bachelor of Science degree in Criminal Justice from Wayne State University; a Master of Science degree in Strategic Studies from the United States Army War College; the Quartermaster Officer Basic and Advanced Courses; Adjutant General Officer Advanced Course; Military Police Officer Advanced Course; United States Army Command and General Staff College; and Associate Logistics Executive Development Course.

He has held numerous key leadership assignments to including serving as Commander of the Headquarters and Headquarters Company, 5064th United States Army Garrison, 123rd United States Army Reserve Command at Romulus, Michigan; Assistant Inspector General, 506th United States Army Garrison, 123rd United States Army Reserve Command at Inkster, Michigan; Acting Inspector General, 5064th United States Army Garrison, 123rd United States Army Reserve Command at Inkster; Executive Officer of the 3rd Battalion, 333rd Regiment, 2nd Brigade (Infantry), 70th Division (Training) at Flint, Michigan; Executive Officer of the 5089th United States Army Reception Battalion, 70th Division (Institutional Training) at Saginaw, Michigan; Commander of the 5089th United States Army Reception Battalion, 70th Division (Institutional Training) at Saginaw; Commander of the 3rd Battalion (Military Police), 3rd Brigade (Combat

Support), 84th Division (Institutional Training) at Inkster; and Law and Order Operations Officer of the Eighth United States Army Continental United States Detachment 2, 88th Regional Support Command at Southfield, Michigan. He was promoted to Colonel on March 30, 2001, while serving as Provost Marshal, Eighth United States Army, Detachment 2, 88th Regional Support Command at Southfield. He also served as Deputy Commander of the 300th Military Police Brigade, 88th Regional Support Command at Inkster; Commander of the Joint Detention Operations Group, United States Southern Command, Joint Task Force Guantanamo, Guantanamo Bay, Cuba; and Commander of the 645th Area Support Group, 88th Regional Readiness Command (Provisional) at Southfield. In April 2005, he was serving as the Commander of the 11th Military Police Brigade, 99th Regional Readiness Command (Provisional) at Ashley, Pennsylvania.

Adolph McQueen was promoted to Brigadier General on October 20, 2004.

McRae, Claude
COMMAND SERGEANT MAJOR—ARMY

Claude McRae was born in North Carolina and began his military career in September 1977. His initial assignment was B Company 1/509th Airborne Battalion Combat Team, Italy from 1977 to 1979. His next assignment was with the 82nd Airborne Division, 1/325th Parachute Infantry Regiment. From this assignment he changed into the Career Management Field of Transportation MOS 88N, Traffic Management Coordinator. He then moved to Frankfurt, West Germany, where he was assigned to the 5th Corps MCC from 1982 to

1985. He has served in a variety of positions in the Transportation Corps, including Movement Specialist in a Forward Support Battalion and Staff Movement Supervisor DISCOM, 82nd Airborne Division, at Fort Bragg, North Carolina. He then served as Staff Movement NCO in the Special Operation G-4 at Fort Bragg. He was then assigned to the 3rd Infantry Division DISCOM Staff Movement NCO at Kissigen, Germany. He was assigned as Operations Sergeant, 507th Corps Support Group, at Fort Bragg, North Carolina and as the Transportation Sergeant of the 96th Civil Affairs at Fort Bragg. He served during Operation Restore Hope in Somalia from 1993 to 1995; as First Sergeant of the 110th Medium Truck Company and 1097th Boat Company; as Operations Sergeant Major of the 8th Transportation Battalion at Shreveport, Louisiana; and as Command Sergeant Major of the 106th Transportation Battalion at Fort Campbell, Kentucky. In January 2005, he was serving as the Command Sergeant Major of Fort Eustis and the United States Army Transportation Center.

McShan, Angela Marie
MASTER CHIEF PETTY OFFICER—COAST GUARD

Master Chief Petty Officer Angela Marie McShan was born on May 4, 1961, in Newport, Rhode Island. She joined the Coast Guard in July 1979, and was serving as an Instructor at the Chief Petty Officers Academy which she helped establish in New London, Connecticut, in June 1998. She was the first female African American in the Coast Guard to be advanced to Master Chief.

At age 39, she passed away on December 29, 2000, due to heart failure and complications from cancer. Normally junior enlisted people act as pallbearers at a Coast Guard funeral, but when Master Chief Petty

Officer McShan's body arrived in Northport, Alabama, for burial, four Chief Petty Officers volunteered to make the four hour trip from the district office in Mobile to render honors, three of them graduates of the Chief Petty Officer Academy she helped establish. Funeral services were held January 6, 2001, at the Porter St. Paul SME Church in Northport, Alabama. Her Interment was at the Cedar Oak Cemetery in Tuscaloosa, Alabama, with full military honors.

More senior enlisted people turned out for a drill team and a rifle squad. Dozen of people who had worked with her during her 21-year career, officers and enlisted persons made the trip from all around the country. Even the service's most senior enlisted person, Master Chief Petty Officer of the Coast Guard Vince Patton, attended her funeral.

McWilliams, Terrance D.

COMMAND SERGEANT MAJOR—ARMY

He enlisted into the United States Army in March 1977 under the Delayed Entry Program for Combat Arms and attended Basic Combat Training at Fort Knox, Kentucky, under the One Unit Station Training.

His military education includes all the Noncommissioned Officer Education System Courses; the Equal Opportunity Course; Dragon Instructor and Master Gunner Course; French Commando School; Battle Staff Course and the Small Group Instructor Course; Mobile Reenlistment Course; 3rd Infantry Division NCO Academy; United States Army First Sergeant Course; and the United States Army Sergeants Major Academy. He also earned an Associate of Science degree in Supervisory Leadership from Hawaii Pacific University.

His key leadership assignments include serving as First Sergeant for C Troop, 1st Squadron, 3rd Armored Cavalry Regiment and E Troop, 2nd Squadron, 3rd Armored Cavalry Regiment; Instructor for the First Sergeants Course, Fort Bliss, Texas; Command Sergeant Major of 1st Battalion, 68th Armor Regiment, 4th Infantry Division (Mech.) at Fort Carson, Colorado; Command Sergeant Major for the United States Army Armor School and Fort Knox, Kentucky; and Post Command Sergeant Major for the United States Army National Training Center and Fort Irwin, California. In June 2005, he was serving as the Command Sergeant Major of the 7th Infantry Division and Fort Carson.

Meeks, Cordell D.

COLONEL—ARMY

He was born in Kansas City, Kansas. He graduated from Sumner High School in Kansas City as class valedictorian in 1960. He received a Bachelor of Arts degree in Political Science, from the University of Kansas, in Lawrence, Kansas in 1964. He earned a Juris Doctor from the University of Kansas Law School, and was elected class President in 1967. He is a 1968 graduate of the University of Pennsylvania Law School.

His military education includes Basic Combat Training at Fort Leonard Wood; Advanced Individual Training, Combat Medic (Honor Graduate), at Fort Sam Houston, Texas; The JAG School, JAG Officer Basic and Advanced Courses; the Command and General Staff College; and the United States Army War College.

He entered the military on February 9, 1968, as a Private E-1, and served as an enlisted soldier until June 1970. He as a Staff Sergeant E-6 was commissioned as a First Lieutenant in the Kansas Army National Guard on June 8, 1971. He was assigned as Assistant Staff Judge Advocate with Company A, Administration, 169th the

Support Battalion, 69th Infantry Brigade (Mech). From December 1, 1976, to October 1977, he served as the Race Relations/Equal Opportunity Officer with Headquarters and Headquarters Company, 69th Infantry Brigade (Mech). On October 15, 1977, he was assigned Assistant Staff Judge Advocate with Company A, 169th Support Battalion, 69th Infantry Brigade (Mech). From September 1, 1979, to April 30, 1984, he served as Staff Judge Advocate for Headquarters and Headquarters Detachment, STARC (-), with the Kansas National Guard. He was promoted to Lieutenant Colonel on March 1, 1984.

From March 1, 1984, to August 13, 1989, he served as Staff Judge Advocate at Headquarters and Headquarters Company with the 35th Infantry Division (Mech), Kansas National Guard. In August 1989, he was assigned as State Judge Advocate General, Headquarters, STARC (-), Kansas National Guard. On June 29, 1990, he was assigned as Senior Military Judge at Headquarters, STARC (-), Kansas Army National Guard. He was promoted to Colonel on March 4, 1991.

On July 21, 1992, he was selected by the National Guard Bureau to serve on the Department of the Army Selection Board for promotions worldwide from Lieutenant Colonel to Colonel at the United States Total Army Personnel Command in Washington, D.C.

He currently serves as District Judge for the 29th District of Kansas, Division 6, Kansas City, in Wyandotte County, Kansas. He is a former Presiding Judge of the Municipal Court of Kansas City, Kansas; and Senior Partner, in the Law firm of Meeks, Sutherland and McIntosh.

He was elected as the 99th National President of the American Lung Association in May 2001; and serves as President of the American Lung Association of Kansas; President of the local Chapter of the American Red Cross; Legal Aid Society; and Mental Health Association.

Mercer, Roosevelt, Jr.

MAJOR GENERAL—AIR FORCE

He graduated from the University of Puget Sound at Tacoma, Washington, where he was commissioned as a distinguished graduate through the Reserve Officer Training Corps program in 1975. He earned a Master of Science/Art degree in Counseling from the University of Oklahoma at Norman, Oklahoma.

In 1975 he served on the Titan II Missile Combat Crew at Sheppard Air Force Base and underwent Titan II Initial Qualification Training at Vandenberg Air Force Base, California. In 1982, he was a Distinguished Graduate of Squadron Officer School at Maxwell Air Force Base, Alabama; and in 1986, he was the top third graduate in the Air Command and Staff College at Maxwell Air Force Base. In 1995, he graduated from the Air War College at Maxwell Air Force Base. He also completed the National Security Senior Executive Course at Syracuse University, New York.

From April 1976 to January 1980, he was assigned as a Combat Missile Crewmember with the 381st

Strategic Missile Wing at McConnell Air Force Base, Kansas. His next assignment was as an Instructor with the 4315th Combat Crew Training Squadron at Vandenberg Air Force Base, California. In October 1981, he served as Assistant Chief of Protocol with the 1st Strategic Aerospace Division at Vandenberg Air Force Base. From June 1983 to July 1985, he served as Chief of Missile Career Development in the Directorate of Assignments at Headquarters Strategic Air Command at Offutt Air Force Base, Nebraska. In June 1986, he was selected as Chief of Congressional Affairs, Executive Officer, Directorate of Personnel Plans, Deputy Chief of Staff Personnel, Headquarters United States Air Force, at the Pentagon, Washington, D.C. In July 1989, he was assigned as Commander of the 447th Strategic Missile Squadron, 321st Strategic Missile Wing, later as Deputy Commander of the 321st Maintenance Group at Grand Forks Air Force Base, North Dakota. From February 1992 to June 1994, he served as Chief of the Nuclear Division of the Plans and Policy Directorate at the Headquarters of United States European Command in Stuttgart, Germany. He was promoted to Colonel on January 1, 1993.

After completing Air War College in June 1995, he was assigned as Commander of the 45th Logistics Group at Patrick Air Force Base, Florida. In July 1996, he was assigned first as Commander of the 91st Operations Group, later as Vice Commander of the 91st Space Wing, at Minot Air Force Base, North Dakota. From June 1998 to June 1999, he served as Commander of the 30th Space Wing at Vandenberg Air Force Base. From July 1999 to April 2000, he was assigned as Vice Director of Plans in the Directorate of Plans at the Headquarters of United States Space Command at Peterson Air Force Base, Colorado. In May 2000, he served as Deputy Director of Operations at the Headquarters of Air Force Space Command at Peterson Air Force Base. In September 2000, he was selected to serve as Commander of the 81st Training Wing at Keesler Air Force Base, Mississippi. He was promoted to Brigadier General on October 1, 2000. In January 2003, he was assigned as Director of Plans and Programs at the Headquarters of Air Force Space Command at Peterson Air Force Base. He was promoted to Major General on January 1, 2005.

His military awards and decorations include the Defense Superior Service Medal; the Legion of Merit; Defense Meritorious Service Medal; Meritorious Service Medal (with four oak leaf clusters); Air Force Commendation Medal; Combat Readiness Medal; Air Force Achievement Medal (with one oak leaf cluster); National Defense Service Medal; and the Roy Wilkins Renown Service Award.

Middleton, Ray

COMMAND SERGEANT MAJOR—ARMY

He was born in Brooklyn, New York, and entered the United States Army in December 1977.

His military education includes all the Noncommissioned Officer Education System Courses; Airborne School; Drill Sergeant School; Nuclear Biological Chemical School; Defense Equal Opportunity Management Institute; the First Sergeant Course; Battle Staff Course; the Garrison Sergeant Major Course; the Defense Equal Opportunity Management Institute; the United States Army Sergeants Major Academy; and the Command Sergeant Major Course.

His leadership assignments include serving as Drill Sergeant of Alpha Company, 4th Battalion, 26th Infantry Brigade at Fort Dix, New Jersey; Platoon Sergeant, Truck Master and First Sergeant with the 78th Transportation Company at Russellheim, Germany; Equal Opportunity Advisor, First Sergeant, Headquarters and Headquarters Company at Aberdeen Proving Grounds, Maryland; First Sergeant at the 25th Transportation Movement Control Agency in Seoul, South Korea; First Sergeant of the 119th Transportation Company at Fort Story, Virginia; Command Sergeant Major of the 3rd Forward Support Battalion, 3rd Infantry Division (Mech) at Fort Stewart, Georgia; Command Sergeant Major of the 25th Transportation Movement Control Battalion in Seoul; Command Sergeant Major of the 34th Area Support Group in Seoul; Command Sergeant Major, 53rd Transportation Battalion, Fort McPherson, Georgia; in January 2005, he was serving as Command Sergeant Major for ARCENT-Kuwait.

Mike, Marion L.

COMMAND SERGEANT MAJOR—ARMY

He is a native of Charleston, South Carolina. He graduated from Baptist High School in 1982. He entered the Army in February 1983 and received One Unit Station Training (OUST) at Fort Bliss, Texas.

His military education includes all the Noncommissioned Officer Education System Courses; the Winter Warfare Course; Ski Instructor (Norway); Air Assault School; Total Army Instructor Trainer Course; First Sergeant Course; and the United States Army Sergeants Major Academy (class 53). He holds an associate's degree in Applied Science from Excelsior College.

He served in a variety of leadership positions and duty stations, including Redeye Gunner with the 1st Battalion, 55th Air Defense Artillery at Fort Polk, Louisiana; Stinger Team Chief with the 2-61st Air

Defense Artillery at Camp Stanton, South Korea; Section Sergeant of the 1st Battalion, 3rd and 2nd Battalion, 44th Air Defense Artillery at Fort Campbell, Kentucky; Field Recruiter and Station Commander at the New Orleans Recruiting Battalion; Platoon Sergeant (Bradley and Stinger) 5-3rd Air Defense Artillery at Mainz, Germany; Operation Sergeant at Montgomery, Alabama (TRADOC); First Sergeant of the 5-5th Air Defense Artillery at Camp Casey, South Korea; 6th Battalion, 52nd Air Defense Artillery in Katterbach, Germany; and Operation Sergeant Major of the 2nd Battalion, 44th Air Defense Artillery at Fort Campbell. In January 2004, he was assigned as the Command Sergeant Major of the 6th Battalion, 52nd Air Defense Artillery, in Ansbach, Germany.

Milburn, Dwayne S.
MAJOR—ARMY

Captain Dwayne S. Milburn entered the service in 1992, after receiving his commission from the United States Army Officer Candidate School at Fort Benning, Georgia. He went on to receive the President Benjamin Harrison Award for highest overall achievement in the Adjutant General Officer Basic Course at Fort Benjamin Harrison, Indiana. He received a Bachelor of Music Education degree from the University of California, Los Angeles, in 1986 and earned a Master of Music degree in Orchestral Conducting from the Cleveland Institute of Music in 1992.

Prior to graduate studies, he was the Director of Cadet Music at the United States Military Academy at West Point, New York. During his tenure as Director of the West Point Cadet Glee Club, the group performed with nationally and internationally acclaimed musical organizations such as the Dallas Symphony Orchestra, the Houston Pops Orchestra, the United States

Military Academy Band and the United States Army Band ("Pershing's Own"). Additionally, the Glee Club and Cadet Band made their first European performances under Captain Milburn's stewardship, appearing in Ireland in 1998.

In addition to his conducting duties, he is in great demand as a composer and arranger. During his undergraduate and graduate careers he was a Staff Arranger for the ABC-TV Special Project Division and the Cleveland Orchestra, respectively. His arrangements and compositions can be found in the band, orchestra and choral libraries of UCLA, the United States Military Academy Band, Marist College, the Cleveland Institute of Music, the United States Continental Army Band, and the United States Army Band.

Prior to his arrival at the Army Ground Forces Band, he served as FORSCOM Staff Bands Officer at Fort McPherson, Georgia. He has also served as the Executive Officer for the United States Army Europe Band and Chorus and the United States Continental Army Band, and as the Associate Bandmaster with the United States Army Band, where he directed the United States Army Chorus and the United States Army Chorale, two of the Army's premiere vocal ensembles. In June 2002, he was selected as Commander of the United States Army Ground Forces Band.

Miller, Cynthia
CAPTAIN—NAVY

She is a native of Morven, Georgia. She graduated from Savannah State University in 1977 with a Bachelor of Science degree in Business Administration. She earned a Master of Arts degree in Business Management from Central Michigan University. She was selected for the Navy's Advanced Education Program and earned additional graduate credits from the University

of North Florida in 1986. Following graduation from the NROTC Program at Savannah State College, she was commissioned an Ensign in the United States Navy.

From 1977 to 1980, she was assigned to the Naval Air Station in Atlanta, Georgia, as the Legal Officer/Traffic Court Judge/BEQ Officer. From 1980 to 1984, she was a Navy Recruiting Program Manager. From 1984 to 1986, she was assigned to the Naval Air Station at Jacksonville, Florida. In 1986, she was selected to serve in the Office of the Chief of Naval Operations (OP-12) as the European Troop Strength Manager.

From 1989 to 1991, she was assigned to the Navy Recruiting District in New Jersey as the Executive Officer. In 1991, she was selected as a Student at the United States Marine Corps Command and Staff College. From 1992 to 1994, she was assigned to the Bureau of Naval Personnel (BUPERS) as Branch Head for Special Shore Programs Enlisted Detailing (PERS 4010). In June 1994, she was selected as a Student at the Armed Forces Command and Staff College. From 1994 to 1996, she was selected to serve as the Commanding Officer of the Military Entrance Processing Station in New York.

From 1996 to 1999, he served as Head of the Chaplain/Religious Program Specialist Manpower Branch (NO97). In 1999, she was selected as Deputy Director of Navy Staff in the Office of the Chief of Naval Operations (NO9B) in Washington, D.C. She was promoted to the rank of Captain on October 1, 1998. She has served as Manpower, Personnel, Training and Analysis Proven Specialist, Graduate of Joint Professional Military Education I & II and a Joint Services Officer (Nominee).

On May 1, 2001, she was selected to serve as Commodore of Navy Recruiting Region South.

Her military awards and decorations include the Defense Meritorious Service Medal; Meritorious Service Medal (two awards); the Navy Achievement Medal; National Defense Medal; Meritorious Unit Commendation (tree awards); Navy Recruiting Ribbon (two awards); and 13 Gold Wreath Recruiting awards.

Miller, Dorie

One of the first American heroes of the Second World War, Miller was a mess attendant on the battleship USS *West Virginia* during the Japanese attack at Pearl Harbor on December 7, 1941. Though he had no gunnery training, Miller took charge of an anti-aircraft machine gun when its crew was disabled. Popular legend has it that he shot down several of the 29 enemy planes claimed that day. Ship's officers also cited him for his part in rescuing sailors who had jumped or been thrown overboard.

For his heroism, Miller was awarded the Navy Cross by Admiral Chester W. Nimitz, commander of the Pacific fleet. The citation extolled the young man's distinguished devotion to duty, extreme courage and disregard for his own personal safety during attack.

Miller, Frank Lee, Jr.

MAJOR GENERAL—ARMY

He was born in Atchison, Kansas; and married the former Paulette C. Duncan of Tacoma, Washington. They have three children, Frank III, Michael, and Toni. He received a Bachelor of Arts degree in business administration from the University of Washington in 1973 and a Master of Science degree from Troy State University in 1979. He entered the Army in October 1965 as a private and attended the Field Artillery Officer Candidate School immediately after basic training. He was commissioned on September 13, 1966, and assigned to Fort Lewis, Washington, as a basic training company-training officer. From June 1967 to September 1968, he served as a forward observer with Battery B, 1st Battalion, 5th Artillery, 1st Infantry Division, United States Army, Vietnam. He returned to the United States in September 1986, and then attended Field Artillery Officer Advanced Course, United States Army Field Artillery School at Fort Still, Oklahoma. Upon graduation, he returned to Fort Lewis and was assigned to the 212th Field Artillery Group where he commanded A Battery, 2nd Battalion, 34th Field Artillery. After Fort Lewis, General Miller served a tour in Korea at battalion and division levels. Returning from Korea in 1971, he attended the University of Washington at Seattle. In August 1973 he was assigned as Motor Officer in the 1st Infantry Division at Fort Riley, Kansas. While assigned to the 1st Division Artillery, General Miller Commanded his second battery, served as a battalion S-3, participated in four REFORGER exercise. In June 1977, after he graduated from the United States Army Command and General Staff College at Fort Leavenworth, Kansas, he was assigned as operations and intelligence officer, with Silk Purse Control Group, United

States European Command at Mildenhall, England. Returning to the United States in July 1980, he was promoted to Lieutenant Colonel and selected to Command the 1st Battalion, 35th Field Artillery at Fort Stewart, Georgia. After 30 months of that Command, he was selected for promotion to Colonel and attended the Naval War College in Newport, Rhode Island, where he graduated with distinction in June 1984.

General Miller served as Chief of Staff of the United States Army National Training Center from July 1984 to July 1986. He was promoted to Colonel on November 1, 1984. In August 1986, he was assigned to Athens, Greece, where he assumed Command of the 558th United States Army Artillery Group. He returned to Fort Sill, Oklahoma, as Chief of Staff. From June 1992 to October 1993, he served as Director of Operations, J-3, at the United States Forces Command at Fort McPherson, Georgia. He was promoted to Major General on July 1, 1993. In October 1993, he was assigned as the Deputy Commanding General of III Corps and Fort Hood, Texas. In July 1995, he was selected to serve as Assistant Chief of Staff for Installation Management in the Office of the Chief of Staff of the Army in Washington, D.C. He retired from the military on December 31, 1996. His decorations and awards include the Legion of Merit (with three oak leaf clusters); Distinguished Flying Cross; Bronze Star (with "V" and two oak leaf clusters); Joint Service Commendation Medal; Army Commendation Medal (with four oak leaf clusters); State of Georgia Meritorious Service Medal; Vietnamese Cross of Gallantry (with Silver Star); and Aircraft Crewmember Badge.

Miller, Ruby
COMMANDER—NAVY

She is a native of Colorado Springs, Colorado. She received a Bachelor of Science in Journalism from the University of Colorado in 1975. She also earned a master's degree in National Security and Strategic Studies and International Relations from Salve Regina College. She is a graduate of the Naval Officer Candidate School in Newport, Rhode Island; and the Junior Course of the Naval War College.

She enlisted into the United States Navy in May 1976. She held numerous leadership, operational and management positions on senior Navy staffs, and was selected twice to Command. She was among the select few nominated as a Navy Federal Executive Fellow to study Post-Soviet military strategy and Central Asian politics at Boston University and Harvard University.

Her military assignments include serving as a Journalist at Naval Postgraduate School in Monterey, California. In 1978, she was commissioned an Ensign into the United States Navy Reserves and served as a Computer System Analyst at the Naval Regional Data Automation Command and the Defense Intelligence Agency in Washington, D.C. she served as Flag Secretary and Flag Lieutenant to the Commander of Naval Forces, Caribbean and as Officer in Charge of Personnel Support Activity for Detachment Willow Grove,

Pennsylvania. She was selected to serve as a Company Commander of the United States Naval Academy. She retired in September 1999 from the Navy.

In August 2002, she was selected as the Deputy Director of the Department of Veterans Affairs (VACO) Center for Minority Veterans. In this position she advises the Director of the Center for Minority Veterans in the management, development progress and the coordination of programs and activities.

Milton-Stewart, Clifford L.
SERGEANT MAJOR—MARINES

He was born in Green Pond, South Carolina. He enlisted in the United States Marine Corps in August 1975. He graduated from Marine Corps Recruit Depot Parris Island, South Carolina.

His key military assignments include serving as a Drill Sergeant and Senior Drill Instructor with F Company, 2nd Recruit Training Battalion and as Testing NCO at the School of Infantry in the Marine Corps Base at Camp Pendleton, California. From June 1981 to March 1982, he was Section Chief in the Supply Company, 1st Supply Battalion, 1st Forces Service and Supply Group at Camp Pendleton. From June 1982 to June 1984, he was Senior Drill Instructor and Series Chief Drill Instructor, H Company, 3rd Recruit Training Battalion, Marine Corps Recruit Depot Parris Island. From June 1984 to May 1985, he was Warehouse Chief in Marine Aircraft Group 31, Marine Corps Air Station, at Beaufort, South Carolina. From May 1985 to April 1988, he was Officer in Charge and Noncommissioned Officer in Charge of the Supply Company, 3rd Supply Battalion, 3rd Forces Service and Supply Group in Okinawa, Japan. In January 1990, he served as Detachment First Sergeant, CSSD-35, Republic of the

Philippines. From April 1990 to May 1991, he was First Sergeant of the Engineer Maintenance Company, 3rd Marine Maintenance Battalion in Okinawa. From May 1991 to April 1994, he served as Inspector Instructor and First Sergeant, G Company, 2nd Battalion, 23rd Marines, 4th Marine Division at Los Alamitos, California. In April 1994, he was assigned as First Sergeant of C Company, 1st Battalion, 4th Marine Division at Los Alamitos. From April 1995 to December 1996, he was Battalion First Sergeant, 1st Battalion, 4th Marine Corps Division at Los Alamitos. From January 1997 to June 1999, he served as Recruiting Station Sergeant Major at Recruiting Station New York, Garden City, New York. In June 1999, he was assigned as District Sergeant Major of the 1st Marine Corps District at Garden City. From September 2000 to August 2003, he was Sergeant Major at Marine Corps Recruiting Command in Quantico, Virginia. In January 2005, he was serving as Sergeant Major for the United States Marine Corps Forces, Atlantic.

Mines, Janie
LIEUTENANT COMMANDER—NAVY

The first black Female to graduate from the U.S. Naval Academy, she entered Annapolis as part of the first class of women and received a Bachelor of Science in Engineering. A Sloan Fellow, she holds a master's degree from Alfred P. Sloan School of Business Management at the Massachusetts Institute of Technology.

During her military career she served as a Supply Corps Officer holding several logistics positions, including a tour at the Navy Annex to the Pentagon and aboard the USS *Emory S. Land* (39). She holds several certifications including ASQ Six Sigma Black Belt.

Minnigan, Anthony F.
COMMAND SERGEANT MAJOR—ARMY

He was born in Newark, New Jersey. He enlisted into the United States Army in April 1980. He attended Basic Combat Training at Fort Jackson, South Carolina, and Advanced Individual Training at Fort McClellan, Alabama.

His military and civilian education includes all the Noncommissioned Officer Education System Courses; the Basic Recruiter Course; Station Commander Course; Guidance Counselor Course; the First Sergeants Course; and the United States Army Sergeants Major Academy (class 53). He earned a Bachelor of Arts degree in Human Resource from Touro University in Los Alamitos, California.

He joined the Recruiting Command in May 1991 as a Detailed Recruiter with the Tampa Recruiting Battalion. He was later assigned as a Station Commander within the battalion. Upon selection to master sergeant he assumed duties as the Senior Counselor in the Columbia Recruiting Battalion and later becoming the First Sergeant within the Columbia Recruiting Company. His subsequent assignment was as the Operations Sergeant of the Jacksonville Recruiting Battalion. In January 2005, he was serving as the Command

Sergeant Major, United States Army Mid-Atlantic Recruiting Battalion, 1st Recruiting Brigade, at Fort Meade, Maryland.

Mitchell, Clayton O.
COMMANDER—NAVY

He was born at Fort Bragg, North Carolina, and raised in San Mateo, California. He graduated from California Polytechnic State University at San Luis Obispo with a Bachelor of Science in Industrial Engineering. He was employed as an industrial engineer in the aerospace industry prior to being commissioned as a Civil Engineer Corps Officer thought the Officer Candidate School in Newport, Rhode Island. He earned a Master of Science in Civil Engineering from the University of California, Berkeley.

His military assignments include serving as Assistant Resident Officer in Charge of Construction at Andrews Air Force Base, Maryland; as Assistant Officer in Charge with the Naval Mobile Construction Battalion FORTY at Detail Sigonella, Italy; as Officer in Charge at Detail Diego Garcia for British Indian Ocean Territories; as Shops Engineer, Director of Utilities, and Customer Liaison Officer in the Public Works Department at the United States Naval Academy; as Planning Director for Public Works Center Yokosuka; and concurrently as Staff Civil Engineer to the Commander Naval Forces, Japan, for nine months of this tour. His second assignment with the Seabees was as Operations Officer of Naval Mobile Construction Battalion Seventy Four; he also led task-oriented details to Honduras and Guantanamo Bay, Cuba, during the Puerto Rico deployment. He then served as Navy Legislative Fellow on the staff of Senator Trent Lott of Mississippi and as the Base Realignment and Closure/Installations Planning Officer with the Ashore Readiness Division (OPNAV N46), Deputy Chief of Naval Operations, Fleet Readiness and Logistics. In March 2005, he was serving as Executive Assistant to the Deputy Assistant Secretary of the Navy (Installation and Facilities) and Special Civil Engineer Corps Assistant to the Assistant Secretary of the Navy (Installations and Environment).

Mitchell, Darphaus L.
COLONEL—AIR FORCE

He entered the Air Force in 1978 through the Reserve Officer Training Corps program at the University

of South Carolina. He received a Bachelor of Science degree in Political Science from Newberry College, South Carolina, and a Master of Science degree in Systems Management from the University of Southern California.

He was a distinguished graduate of the Squadron Officer School and the Air Command and Staff College at Maxwell Air Force Base, Alabama. He earned his second master's degree in National Security Strategy from the National War College at Fort McNair in Washington, D.C. He attended Seminar XXI at the Center for International Studies at the Massachusetts Institute of Technology.

From March 1978 to July 1978, he was in Missile Combat Crew Training at Vandenberg Air Force Base, California. From July 1978 to July 1982, he was assigned as a Minuteman III Missile Combat Crewmember, Wing Instructor, and Wing Evaluator with the 321st Strategic Missile Wing at Grand Forks Air Force Base, North Dakota. He was promoted to Captain on November 1, 1981.

From July 1982 August 1985, he was Missile Procedures Trainer-Operator, Emergency War Order Training Officer, and Emergency War Order Plan Officer with the 341st Strategic Missile Wing at Malmstrom Air Force Base, Montana. From August 1985 to September 1988, he served as the Chief of Inter-Continental Ballistic Missile (ICBM) C3 Modernization with the 1st Strategic Aerospace Division at Vandenberg Air Force Base, California. From September 1988 to August 1991, he was assigned as Future Concepts Plans Officer with the Policy and Doctrine Analyst in the Directorate of Plans at the Headquarters of Strategic Air Command at Offutt Air Force Base, Nebraska. He was promoted to Major on November 1, 1988.

From July 1992 to August 1994, he served as Arms Control Policy Analyst and Deputy Chief of Counter-Proliferation Policy with the Headquarters of the United States Air Force at the Pentagon. He was promoted to Lieutenant Colonel on February 1, 1994.

From August 1994 to July 1996, he was assigned as Commander of the 740th Missile Squadron at Minot Air Force Base, North Dakota. From June 1977 to May 1999, he was assigned as Chief of the Nuclear Operations Division of the Headquarters of the United States Air Force at the Pentagon. He was promoted to Colonel on September 1, 1998.

From May 1999 to July 2001, he served as Commander of the 45th Operations Group, Cape Canaveral Air Station, Florida. In July 2001, he was selected to serve as Vice Commander of the 341st Space Wing at Malmstrom Air Force Base, Montana. The wing is responsible for the operation, maintenance and security of the intercontinental ballistic missile force in central Montana. The wing provides deterrence for the United States through the operation of Minuteman III missiles located throughout a 23,500 square mile complex comprising 200 launch facilities.

Mitchell, Edith P.

BRIGADIER GENERAL—AIR FORCE

She entered the Air Force in 1973, while attending medical school at the Medical College of Virginia at Richmond, and began her military career by receiving a commission through the Health Professions Scholarship Program. She graduated in 1974 in the Accelerated Graduation Program and entered active duty in 1978 after completion of her residency in Internal Medicine at Meharry Medical College at Nashville, Tennessee. She completed a fellowship in Medical Oncology

at Georgetown University. She is board-certified in Internal Medicine and Medical Oncology and is a Flight Surgeon. Prior to assuming her current position, she served as the State Air Surgeon of Missouri and Director of Diversity at the Headquarters of the Missouri Air National Guard.

Her education includes a Bachelor of Science degree in Biochemistry from Tennessee State University in Nashville in 1969. She earned a Doctor of Medicine degree, from the Medical College of Virginia in 1974. She also completed the Air War College in 1995.

In February 1987, she served as a Physician, later as Commander with the 131st Medical Squadron at Lambert-St. Louis International Airport, Missouri. From October 1995 to December 2000, she served as the State Air Surgeon at the Headquarters Missouri Air National Guard in Jefferson City, Missouri. In December 2000, she was selected as the Air National Guard Assistant to the Command Surgeon at the United States Transportation Command and the Headquarters of the Air Mobility Command at Scott Air Force Base, Illinois. In this assignment she served as the senior medical Air National Advisor to the Command Surgeon and was the medical liaison between the active Air Force and the Air National Guard. In March 2004, she was assigned as the Assistant Adjutant General — Air, also serving as the Deputy Commander for Missouri, Joint Force Headquarters, at Jefferson City, Missouri.

Her awards and decorations include the Meritorious Service Medal (with one oak leaf cluster); the Air Force Commendation Medal; Air Force Achievement Medal; Air Force Outstanding Unit Award (with one oak leaf cluster); Air Force Organizational Excellence Award; National Defense Service Medal; Humanitarian Service Medal; Air Force Longevity Service Award (with four oak leaf clusters); Armed Forces Reserve Medal (with hourglass device); Small Arms Expert Marksmanship Ribbons; Air Force Training Ribbon; Missouri National Guard Conspicuous Service Medal; Missouri National Guard Commendation Ribbon; Missouri National Guard Long Service Ribbon for 10 years; and Missouri National Guard Recruiting and Retention Ribbon.

Mitchell, Harold L.

BRIGADIER GENERAL—AIR FORCE

He attended Robert Smalls High School at Beaufort, South Carolina, and graduated from Carolina State University with a Bachelor of Science degree in Business Administration in 1972. His military education includes Naval Air Training at Naval Air Station, Kingsville, Texas; Air War College; Squadron Commander's Course; and National Security Decision Making Seminar.

He served on active duty from 1972 to 1978 with the United States Marine Corps flying the KC-130. The general joined the Air Force Reserve in 1983 as a traditional reservist assigned to the 728th Airlift Squadron at Norton Air Force Base. From September 1995 to September 1997, he served as Commander of the 728th

Airlift Squadron at McChord Air Force Base, Washington. He was promoted to Colonel on April 1, 1997.

In September 1997, he was assigned as Chief of Transportation at the Headquarters of the Fourth Air Force at McClellan Air Force Base and March Air Force Base, California. In April 1999, he was assigned as Vice Commander of the Fourth Air Force at March Air Reserve Base, California. On May 20, 2002, he was promoted to Brigadier General.

In September 2002, he was selected to serve as Mobilization Assistant to the Fifteenth Air Force Commander at Travis Air Force Base, California. He has more than 3,500 fight hours and has flown the T-34, T-2, TA-4J, KC130, C-141B, and C-17.

His awards and decorations include the Legion of Merit; Meritorious Service Medal (with three oak leaf clusters); the Air Force Commendation Medal; Air Force Achievement Medal; Air Force Outstanding Unit Award (with three oak leaf clusters); Navy Meritorious Unit Commendation; Combat Readiness Medal (with three oak leaf clusters); National Defense Service Medal (with one bronze service star); Southwest Asia Service Medal (with two bronze service stars); Armed Forces Reserve Medal (with bronze hourglass); and the Kuwait Liberation Medal.

Mitchell, Ronald

SERGEANT MAJOR—ARMY

Sergeant Major Ronald Mitchell entered the United States Army in July 1972, and completed Basic Training and Advanced Individual Training at Fort Jackson, South Carolina. He graduated from the United States Army's Sergeants Major Academy in 1994.

His military assignments include serving in July 1983 as NCOIC Warehouse Section Property Disposal Noncommissioned Officer for the United States Regional Support Element at Camp Zama, Japan. In July 1994,

puter and Telecommunication Station Kelfavik, Iceland, in October 2004.

Mixon, Laurence M.
LIEUTENANT COLONEL—ARMY

He is a graduated from the United States Military Academy at West Point and was commissioned as a

he was assigned as First Sergeant of B Company, 24th FSB, at Fort Stewart, Georgia. In 1994, he was promoted to Sergeant Major and assigned as Sergeant of S-3 (Operation) with the 24th Corps Support Group at Fort Stewart. From July 1996 to June 1997, he was assigned as Sergeant Major at the 6th Support Center at Camp Henry Taegue, South Korea. In July 1997, he was ordered to serve as Sergeant Major of G-4 (Logistics) NCO for the 3rd Army at Fort McPherson, Georgia.

Mitchell, Terrence R.
SENIOR CHIEF—NAVY

He was born in Birmingham, Alabama, where he graduated from Fairfield High School May 31, 1984. He enlisted into the United States Navy in February 1985, and attended Basic Training at Recruit Training Command in San Diego, California. Upon completion of Basic Training in April 1985, he proceeded to Raidoman "A" School and follow-on International Morse Code School (IMCO). After graduating Morse Code School in December 1985, he was assigned onboard USS *Fahrion* (FFG-220), home ported at Mayport, Florida.

In April 2001, he reported to Dam Neck for Information System Administrator School. Upon completing school in August 2001, he reported to AFLOATRAGRU MAYPORT as the Communications/C41 LCPO where he was advanced to Senior Chief Petty Officer. Following attending the Air Force Senior Non-Commissioned Officer Academy, he reported to Naval Com-

Second Lieutenant on May 28, 1968. He holds a Bachelor of Science degree in Engineering Management (Mechanical) from West Point and a Masters of Engineering in Systems Engineering from the University of Virginia.

His military education includes the Military Intelligence Officer Basic Course; the Military Intelligence Advanced Course; and the United States Army Command and General Staff College.

His military assignments include serving as Force Integration Officer, Department of the Army G-3; Brigade S-3, Military Intelligence Brigade; Battalion S-3, 202nd Military Intelligence Battalion; Chief Battle Technology Lab, Battle Command Battle Lab at Huachuca; Instructor at the Military Intelligence Transition Course; Commander of Alpha Company, 204th Military Battalion, 66th Military Brigade; Collection Requirements Manger at the Foreign Science and Technology Center; Division Collection Manager with the 9th Infantry Division; Battalion S-2, 2-23rd Infantry Battalion (M); Platoon Leader, 109th Military Intelligence Battalion; Assistant S2 in the 1-31st Infantry Battalion, 2nd Infantry Division in South Korea.

Monroe, James W.
MAJOR GENERAL—ARMY

He was born in Laurinburg, North Carolina. He married the former Charlyne Williams, and they have a daughter and son. Donya, their daughter, is a graduate of the University of Nevada at Las Vegas. Bryan, their son, is a journalist graduate of the University of Washington in Seattle. He received a Bachelor of Science degree in electrical engineering from West Virginia State College in 1963 and a Master of Arts degree in Political Science from the University of Cincinnati in 1973. He received an ROTC Commission to second

lieutenant on October 5, 1963. From October 1963 to December 1963, he was a student in the Ordnance Officer Basic Course at the United States Army Ordnance Center and School at Aberdeen Proving Ground, Maryland. From February 1964 to April 1964, he was a student in the Armor Officer Basic Course at the United States Army Armor School at Fort Knox, Kentucky. From August 1964 to February 1966, he served as platoon leader, Armored Cavalry, B Troop; later platoon leader, Troop A, 2nd Squadron, 9th Cavalry, 24th Infantry Division, United States Army in Europe. He was promoted to First Lieutenant on April 5, 1965. From February 1966 to June 1967, he was Commander of the 621st General Supply Company, United States Army in Europe. Promoted to Captain on September 20, 1966, from June 1967 to June 1968, he was a student in the Defense Language Institute, East Coast Branch, United States Naval Station, Anacostia, in Washington, D.C. From June 1968 to June 1969, he was assigned as Ordnance Adviser at the United States Military Training Mission in Saudi Arabia. From July 1969 to June 1970, he was a student in the Ordnance Officer Advanced Course at the United States Army Ordnance Center and School at Aberdeen Proving Ground, Maryland. From June 1970 to June 1972, he served as Assistant Professor of Military Science with the First United States Army at Fort Meade, Maryland, with duty at the University of Cincinnati, Ohio. From August 1973 to July 1976, he served as Chief of Staff for Intelligence, United States Army, in Washington, D.C. From August 1976 to June 1977, he was a student in the United States Army General and Command Staff College at Fort Leavenworth, Kansas. From June 1977 to July 1978, he was Commander of the 61st Maintenance Company, Eighth United States Army, in South Korea. From July 1978 to October 1979, he was assigned as Executive Officer of the 709th Maintenance Battalion, 9th Infantry Division, at Fort Lewis, Washington. From November 1979 to June 1982, he was Deputy Commander, later Commander, of the Division Materiel and Management Center, and Executive Officer of Division Support Command of the 9th Infantry Division at Fort Lewis, Washington. He was promoted to Lieutenant Colonel on November 7, 1979. From June 1982 to March 1985, he was the Commander of the 71st Maintenance Battalion, VII Corps, United States Army, Europe. From June 1985 to June 1986, he was a student in the Industrial College of the Armed Forces, Fort Lesley J. McNair, in Washington, D.C. He was promoted to Colonel on February 1, 1986. From June 1986 to June 1987, he served as a Member of the Faculty of the Senior Service College at the National Defense University at Fort Lesley J. McNair. From July 1987 to July 1989, he was the Commander of the Division Support Command, 24th Infantry Division (Mechanized) at Fort Stewart, Georgia. From July 1989 to July 1990, he was assigned as Assistant Chief of Staff, G-4 (Logistics), Third United States Army at Fort McPherson, Georgia. From August 1990 to April 1991, he served in Saudi Arabia, where he was assigned the duties of Logistics Officer on the Third Army staff and designated the Deputy Chief for logistics and host nation support at ARCENT (Army Central Command). In this position, he was a close Logistics Planner and Adviser to the in-country United States Army Commander. General Monroe initiated the logistics planning and arrangements to support United States Army forces and certain Marine and Air Force units in Desert Shield and Desert Storm. He coordinated host-nation support requirements and acquisition from Saudi Arabia, which aided the United States ground forces in prosecuting a quick victory over enormous distances and against a larger enemy force. In this position, he was a close Logistics Planner and adviser to the in country U.S. Army Commander, Lt. Gen. John Yeosock, as well as the Commander-in-Chief of U.S. Central Command, General H. Norman Schwarzkopf. He was promoted to Brigadier General on July 1, 1991. From June 1991 to June 1994, he served as Deputy Commanding General for Systems and Logistics with the United States Army Tank-Automotive Command at Warren, Michigan. On April 1, 1994, he was promoted to Major General. In June 1994, he was assigned as Commanding General of the United States Army Ordnance School at Aberdeen Proving Ground. In September 1995, he was assigned as the Commanding General of the United States Army Industrial Operations Command in Rock Island, Illinois. He retired from the military in October 1998. His decoration and awards include the Legion of Merit (with three oak leaf clusters), Bronze Star, Defense Meritorious Service Medal, Meritorious Service Medal (with four oak leaf clusters), and Army Commendation Medal.

Monroe, Lewis E., III
COMMAND CHIEF MASTER SERGEANT—AIR FORCE

Chief Monroe graduated from Rancho High School in Las Vegas, Nevada, in 1979. He entered the Air Force in 1979, and has held a variety of positions in the Security Forces career field including Security Forces Manager at Squadron Level.

From June 1991 to April 1996, he was assigned as Flight Sergeant with the 341st Missile Security Group at Malmstrom Air Force Base, Montana. From April 1996 to April 2000, he was assigned as Operations Superintendent/Security Forces Manager with the 6th Security Forces Squadron at MacDill Air Force Base, Florida. He was promoted to Chief Master Sergeant on November 1, 1999.

In April 2000, he was selected as the Command Chief Master Sergeant of the 6th Air Mobility Wing at MacDill Air Force Base.

Monroe, Paul D., Jr.
MAJOR GENERAL—ARMY

Born in Berkeley, California, he graduated from Castlemont High School in Oakland, California. He received a Bachelor of Arts Degree in Public Administration from the University of San Francisco in San Francisco, California. He received a commission from Officer's Candidate School as a Second Lieutenant on May 1, 1962. From May 1962 to October 1963, he was assigned as a Platoon Leader in Company A, 49th Signal Battalion. In 1963, Gen. Monroe graduated from Signal Officer Basic Course at Signal School. From October 1963 to January 1968, he was assigned first in the S-1 section at the Headquarters of the 49th Signal Battalion, and then as Telephone and Teletype Officer at the Headquarters of the 49th Signal Battalion; Commander of Company A, 49th Signal Battalion; and S-1 at the Headquarters of the 49th Signal Battalion. On April 30, 1965, he was promoted to First Lieutenant and on August 25, 1966, promoted to Captain. From

January 1968 to March 1970, he served first as the S-3/Air at Headquarters, and as 1st Battalion, 159th Infantry Communications Electronic Officer, Headquarters. From March 1970 to February 1973, he served as Adjutant officer with the Headquarters of the 49th Support Battalion. In 1971, the General graduated from Infantry School, Signal Officer Basic Course. On December 19, 1973, he was promoted to Major. From February 1973 to January 1974, he served as Plans and Operations Officer with the 49th Support Battalion. From January 1974 to June 1974, he was assigned as Operations Officer with the 49th Military Police Battalion. In 1974, he graduated from the Military Police Officer Orientation Course at Military Police School. From January 1975 to June 1976, he served as the Executive Officer at the Headquarters of the 49th Military Police Battalion. From July 1976 to April 1978, he was assigned as the Executive Officer at Headquarters, 49th Military Police Battalion. He graduated from Command and General Staff College in 1977. In 1978, he graduated from the National Defense University's National Security Management Course. From April 1978 to September 1980, he served as the Executive Officer with the 143rd Military Police Battalion. From October 1980 to November 1981, Monroe was assigned as Plans and Operations Officer at the Headquarters of the 49th Police Brigade. On November 9, 1981, he was promoted to Lieutenant Colonel. From November 1981 to February 1985, he was the Commander of the 49th Military Police Battalion. From February 1985 to July 1987, he served as the S-3 Operation Officer with the 49th Military Police Brigade. From July 1987 to July 1989, he was a student at the United States Army War College. On April 2, 1989, he was promoted to Colonel and also in 1989, he graduated from the Army War College. From July 1989 to May 1990, he served as Director of Facilities at the Headquarters of the State Area Command of the California Army National Guard. From June 1990 to June 1991, he was assigned as Public Affairs Officer at the Headquarters of the State Area Command of the California Army National Guard. From June 1991 to February 1993, he served as the Deputy Commander of the 49th Military Police Brigade. From February 1993 to September 1993, he was assigned as Assistant Chief of Staff at the Headquarters of the State Area Command of the California Army National Guard. From September 1993 to March 1994, he was assigned Special Assistant to the Adjutant General at the Headquarters of the State Area Command of the California Army National Guard. On April 1, 1994, he was assigned as Assistant Adjutant General for Plans and Mobilization at the Headquarters of the State Area Command of the California Army National Guard. On July 28, 1995, he was promoted to Brigadier General. On April 28, 1999, California Governor Gray Davis appointed General Monroe as Adjutant General for the State of California. As Adjutant General, he commanded the largest National Guard Force in the United States, with more than 18,000 Army and 4,900 Air National Guard members. His

military awards and decorations include the Legion of Merit; the Army Meritorious Service Medal (with two oak leaf clusters); the Army Commendation Medal (with oak leaf cluster); the Army Achievement Medal; Army Good Conduct Medal; the Army Reserve Components Achievement Medal (with silver oak leaf cluster); the National Defense Service Medal; Armed Forces Reserve Medal (with three hourglass devices); the Army Service Ribbon; the Army Reserve Components Overseas Training Ribbon (with numeral 4); Order of California Merit (with two oak leaf clusters); California Commendation Medal (with two oak leaf clusters); the California Medal, and State Service Ribbon.

Montgomery, Jerry G.
COMMAND SERGEANT MAJOR—ARMY

He is a native of Baldwyn, Mississippi. Upon graduating from Tupelo High School, he enlisted in the United States Army. After completing Basic Combat Training and Advanced Individual Training as a Cannon Crewman (13B), he was assigned to the 2nd Battalion, 34th Field Artillery at Fort Sill, Oklahoma.

His military education includes all the Noncommissioned Officer Education System Courses; Drill Sergeant School; Master Fitness Trainer Course; First Sergeant Course; the United States Army Sergeants Major Academy; and the Command Sergeant Major Course. He holds an associate's degree in Science Management from Pikes Peak Community College, the University of Maryland and Park College.

He has served in numerous leadership positions including Howitzer Driver; Gunner; Special Weapon Section Chief; Howitzer Section Chief; Gunnery Sergeant; Platoon Sergeant; Senior Drill Sergeant; Assistant Fire Support Sergeant; and First Sergeant. He

served as the Command Sergeant Major of the 3rd Battalion, 18th Artillery.

Moody, John E., Jr.
COMMAND SERGEANT MAJOR—ARMY

He is a native of Fort Lauderdale, Florida. He entered the military in June 1979 as a 19E M60A1 Armor Crewman at Fort Knox, Kentucky.

His military education includes all levels of the Noncommissioned Officers Education System Courses; the Drill Sergeant School; the 7th ATC Mini Master Gunner Course, and NBC School.

His military assignments include tours in Germany at Baumholder, Buedingen, and two assignments in Friedberg, Germany. His stateside assignments include Fort Hood, Texas; Fort Stewart, Georgia; and Fort Knox, Kentucky. His deployments include Operation Desert Storm in 1991; Guantanamo Bay in 1994; Bosnia in 1998; and in support of Operation Iraqi Freedom in 2003. He was the Operations Sergeant Major in 2nd Battalion, 37th Armor in Friedberg, Germany; as well as the Command Sergeant Major of the 1st Battalion, 66th Armor. He has also served as a Drill Sergeant.

In February 2005, he was serving as Command Sergeant Major of the 4th Brigade, 4th Infantry Division at Fort Hood.

Moore, Clarence H., Jr.
CHIEF MASTER SERGEANT—AIR FORCE

He completed Basic Military Training and Security Police Technical School at Lackland Air Force Base, Texas, in July 1980.

His military education includes Noncommissioned Officer Professional Military Education at Phase I & II Noncommissioned Officer Leadership School in 1983; Tidewater Policy Academy associate's degree in Instructional Methodology from the Community Col-

lege of the Air Force in 1986; and Technical Training Instructor Course in 1989. In 1991, he earned an associate's degree in Criminal Justice from the Community College of the Air Force; in 1995, he attended the United States Navy's Senior Enlisted Academy at Newport, Rhode Island; in 2000, he attended the University of Maryland United States Air Force Inspector General Course at Hickam Air Force Base, Hawaii.

He have served in numerous key leadership positions including as Security Police Academy Instructor at Lackland Air Force Base, Texas; Noncommissioned Officer in Charge of the United States Air Force Drill Team/NCOIC Ceremonial Flight of the United States Air Force Presidential Honor Guard at Bolling Air Force Base in Washington, D.C.; Support Group Superintendent at Bolling Air Force Base; Training and Resources Superintendent for the Security Force Squadron at Vandenberg Air Force Base, California; Security Forces Squadron Operations Superintendent at Misawa Air Base, Japan; Support Group Chief Enlisted Manager at Misawa Air Base; and Security Forces Manager for the Security Force Squadron Hick Air Force Base. In 2002, he was selected as the 374th Airlift Wing Command Chief Master Sergeant at Yokota Air Base, Japan; and in June 2003, he was selected as the Command Chief Master Sergeant for the United States Forces, Japan and the Fifth Air Force. As senior enlisted advisor, he advises the commander on matters relating to readiness, welfare and effective utilization of over 14,000 enlisted members assigned to the Fifth Air Force and the joint service enlisted members assigned to United States Forces in Japan.

Moore, Dale E.
COMMAND SERGEANT MAJOR—ARMY

Command Sergeant Major Dale E. Moore was born September 3, 1952, in Mobile Alabama. He married the former Luree R. Price. They have four children, Anthony; Felicia; Clara; and Lorneshia. He and his wife have three grandchildren.

He entered the Army in July 1970. He earned an associate's degree in General Studies from Central Texas College. He is a graduate of the United States Army Sergeants Major Academy. He has served in numerous assignments including as Command Sergeant Major for 2nd Battalion, 7th Infantry Regiment, 24th Infantry Division (Mechanized), at Fort Stewart, Georgia; as Command Sergeant Major of the 4th Battalion, 8th Regiment (Mechanized), in Mannheim, Germany; as Command

Sergeant Major of the 1st Battalion, 2nd Infantry Division, later as Command Sergeant Major of the 3rd Brigade, 2nd Infantry Division, at Fort Lewis, Washington. . He is currently serving as the Command Sergeant Major of the United States Army Cadet Command at Fort Monroe, Virginia.

Moore, Edward, Jr.
VICE ADMIRAL—NAVY

He was born in New York City, New York. He is the eldest son of Mrs. Freddie Moore of Little Rock, Arkansas. He is married to the former Deborah Marcia Cooper of Champaign, Illinois. They have three daughters, Kimberly, Erica and Stacey, and a son, Edward III (Tony). Admiral Moore holds a Bachelor of Arts degree in Psychology and a Master of Science degree in Business Administration. He enlisted in the United States Naval Reserve in April 1963, and was commissioned an Ensign after graduation from Southern Illinois University in June 1968. He reported for active duty in July 1968 aboard USS *Severn* (AO 61) where he served as Gunnery Officer, Communications Officer and Navigator. Assigned to the *Precomunit,* he reported as communications officer in USS *Lang* (DE 1060) upon the ship's commissioning in March 1970, and subsequently served as operations officer. From September 1972 to June 1974, he was a student at the Naval Post-Graduate School. He was then assigned to the Bureau of Naval Personnel as a Junior Officer Assignment Officer (Detailer) and Shore Assignments Coordinator. He then attended the Department Head Course at the Surface Warfare Officers School Command; the Fleet Combat Training Center, Atlantic; and the Naval Guided Missile School. Assignment as the weapons officer on USS *Sterett* (CG 31) followed. He re-

ported to USS *Buchanan* (DOG 14) as executive officer in March 1979. In December 1980, he was assigned as an Operations Analyst on the Staff of Commander in Chief, U.S. Navy, Pacific Command. Upon completion of Prospective Commanding Officer training from March 1984 to July 1984, he then commanded the San Diego-based Guided Missile Frigate USS *Lewis B. Puller* (FFG 23) from July 1984 to October 1986. He followed that tour as the Assistant Chief of Staff for Manpower and personnel on the staff of the Commander in Chief of the U.S. Pacific Fleet until June 1989. Admiral Moore returned to sea as the first Commanding Officer in Chief of USS *Cowpens (CG 63)* in October 1989 and led the successful *Tomahawk* strike against a sensitive target in Iraq in January 1993. After completion of Capstone at the National Defense University, he reported to assignment as Commandant of Naval District Washington in July 1993. He served next as Commander of Cruiser-Destroyer Group THREE. On July 7, 1993, he was designated Rear Admiral (Lower Half) while serving in billets commensurate with that grade. On April 1, 1994, he was promoted to Rear Admiral (Lower Half). On October 1, 1996, he was promoted to Rear Admiral, and served as the Commander of Cruiser-Destroyer Group THREE. Vice Admiral Moore assumed duties as Commander of Naval Surface Force, United States Pacific Fleet on August 7, 1998. His military awards and decorations include the Legion of Merit (with four gold stars); the Defense Meritorious Service Medal; Meritorious Service Medals (with two oak leaf clusters); the Navy Achievement Medal; and other service and campaign ribbons including the Coast Guard Special Operations Service Ribbon. He is a life member of KAPPA ALPHA PSI Fraternity, Inc. and the National Naval Officer Association.

Moore, John J.
COMMAND SERGEANT MAJOR—ARMY

He was born and raised in Michigan. He enlisted into the United States Army and attended Basic Combat Training at Fort Jackson, South Carolina, and Advanced Individual Training for the UH-60 helicopter at Fort Eustis, Virginia. His military educations include all the Noncommissioned Officer Education System Courses; the Airborne Course; Jumpmaster Course; Air Movement Officers Course; the Air Force Hazardous Cargo Course; Aviation Maintenance Management Course; Aviation Operations Specialist Course; Aviation Accident Prevention Course; Combat Lifesavers Course; Pre-Commissioned Officer Course; Battle Staff Noncommissioned Officer Course; First Sergeant Course; the United States Army Sergeants Major Academy; and the Command Sergeants Major Course. He holds an associate's degree from Pierce College in Tacoma, Washington.

Moore, Johnnie P.
COMMAND SERGEANT MAJOR—ARMY

He enlisted in the military on November 14, 1979,

and attended Basic Training and Advanced Individual Training at Fort Knox, Kentucky. He has attended all levels within the NCO Education System and is a graduate of the United States Army Sergeants Major Academy at Fort Bliss, Texas. He holds an associate's degree in Applied Science and Administrative/Management Studies from Excelsior College.

He has held numerous leadership positions including Tank Commander, Platoon Sergeant, Basic Training Drill Sergeant, first Sergeant of a Divisional Cavalry Squadron (1-10 Cav.), First Sergeant of HHC 1-72 AR (Korea), and Operations Sergeant Major for the 1st Battalion 66th Armor of 1st BDE 4th ID Fort Hood, TX. In August 2004, he was serving as the Command Sergeant Major for the 69th Armor Battalion, 3rd Infantry Division (Mechanized).

Moore, Tony E.
COMMAND SERGEANT MAJOR—ARMY

Command Sergeant Major Tony E. Moore earned a Bachelor of Science degree in Liberal Studies from Excelsior College. He entered the United States Army on August 2, 1977, and attended Basic Training and Advanced Individual Training at Fort Dix, New Jersey.

His military education includes the Senior Supply Sergeant Course at Fort Lee, Virginia; the Defense Equal Opportunity Management Institute; the First Sergeant Course; Garrison Command Sergeants Major Course; and the United States Army Sergeants Major Academy.

He was assigned as the Command Sergeant Major, for the 25th Brigade Support Battalion, 25th Infantry Division (Light), at Fort Lewis, Washington, before assuming the assignment on June 2, 2002, as Command Sergeant Major for the 20th Support Group and Area IV at Camp Henry, South Korea.

Moorman, Holsey A.
BRIGADIER GENERAL—ARMY

He was born in Roanoke, Virginia. He and his wife Carrie have one son, Gary. He graduated from Thomas A. Edison College in Trenton, and received an Associate of Arts degree, and he received his Bachelor of Science degree in Business Management/Human Resources from Park College in Parkville, Missouri. During the period  of 1964 to 1982, he served in positions ranging from Training Officer to Command Administrative Officer to State Equal Employment Opportunity Officer in the New Jersey Army National Guard. In June 1984, he was assigned as Chief of Human Relations Field Operating Activity in the Office of Human Resources at the National Guard Bureau. From June 1986 to June 1987, he was assigned to the Office of the Deputy Chief of Staff for Personnel as a Personnel Policy Integrator. He was responsible for Reserve Component Readiness. Additional duties required coordinating all Army policies and procedures related to the Defense Advisory Committee for Women in the Services (DACOWITS). From June 1987 to June 1991, he served as Military Assistant in the Office of the Assistant Secretary of the Army (Manpower and Reserve Affairs). He was promoted to Colonel on March 28, 1990. From June 1991 to January 1992, he was assigned as the Assistant Deputy to the Assistant Secretary of the Army for Reserve Forces and Mobilization. From January 1992 to March 1994, Gen. Moorman served as Military Executive in the Office of the Secretary of the Army (Army Reserve Forces Policy Committee). In this capacity, he functioned as the principal Military Executive Officer to the ARFPC with responsibility for performing a myriad of functions as the full-time representative of the committee chairman. General Moorman was appointed by Governor Christine Todd Whitman to his current position of Deputy Adjutant General in March 1994. He was promoted to the rank of Brigadier General on July 28, 1995. He has served more than thirty years in the Army National Guard beginning with the rank of

Private and ascending to the rank of Brigadier General. He is a graduate of both the Command and General Staff College and US Army War College Senior Reserve Component Officer Course. His military awards and decorations include the Legion of Merit (1 OLC), Meritorious Service Medal, Army Commendation Medal, Army Reserve Component Achievement Medal (4 OLC), National Defense Service Medal, Armed Forces Reserve Medal (2 Hourglasses), Army Service Ribbon, Army Superior Unit Award, the Department of the Army Staff Identification Badge, New Jersey Medal of Merit, the New Jersey Medal of Honor, New Jersey Good Conduct Award, Desert Storm Ribbon, the New Mexico Medal of Merit, the Governor's Unit Award, and the Unit Strength Award. In 1993 he was presented the NAACP Roy Wilkens Renown Service Award in recognition of his service to the military and community, and in 1994 received the National Guard Bureau Eagle Award.

Morgan, Betty L. G.
COMMAND CHIEF MASTER SERGEANT—AIR FORCE

She was born in May 1950 in Savannah, Georgia, and graduated from Sol C. Johnson High School in 1968. She enlisted into the Georgia Air National Guard in March 1978, and after Recruit Training was assigned to the 165th Airlift Wing in Savannah, Georgia.

Her military education include Personnel Technical School; Combat Aircrew Training; Personnel Intelligence Course; Senior Noncommissioned Officer Academy; Noncommissioned Officer Academy Instructors Course; Chief Executive Course; and the Human Relations Course in 2002. Her civilian education includes a Bachelor of Arts in Elementary Education from Savannah State University in 1972; she earned a Master of Education in Elementary and Middle School concentrating in Reading from Armstrong and Savannah State University.

In January 2003, was selected as the first African American and first female to serve in the top enlisted position as the Command Chief Master Sergeant for the Georgia Air National Guard. As the Georgia Air National Guard's Command Chief Master Sergeant, Morgan is a member of the Senior Staff of the Georgia Air National Guard and represents the issues and concerns of the 2,500-member enlisted force.

Prior to her selection to this top enlisted position, she was the Human Resources Advisor for the Georgia Air National Guard assigned to State Headquarters in Atlanta. A thirty-five year veteran of the Georgia Air National Guard, she was also the first African American female selected as Wing Command Chief for Savannah's 165th Airlift Wing. She competed against twelve other senior enlisted officers for the command position.

She has been employed for 24 years with the Savannah — Chatham County Public School System. She is a sixth grade Language Arts Teacher at John W. Hubert Middle School where she was twice selected Teacher of the Year including the year 2002. She was recently named WTOC-TV "Top Teacher" for 2002. She has also been named the New Future's Initiative Teacher of the Year on two occasions. In 1988, she was selected for Who's Who Among American's Best Teachers and is the recipient of the prestigious Woman of Achievement Award 2000 for the Port City's Business and Professional Women's Organization, Inc.

Morgan, Ernest R.
MAJOR GENERAL—ARMY

He was born in Petersburg, Virginia. General Morgan is a graduate of Virginia State College and the University of Maryland. He has held a wide variety of

important command and staff positions. He was the staff officer in the Officer of the Chief of Staff for Force Development at the Pentagon in Washington, D.C. He served as the Director of the National Security Seminars at United States Army War College. He also served as Professor of Military Science at Prairie View A&M College. He was appointed to the rank of Brigadier General and assigned as the Adjutant General for the District of Columbia National Guard. He was appointed to the two star rank of Major General and assigned as the Adjutant General of the Virgin Islands.

Morgan, John W., III

MAJOR GENERAL—ARMY

He holds a Bachelor of Science degree in Criminology from the University of Delaware. He earned a Masters of Science degree in National Security and Strategic Studies from the National Defense University. His military education includes the Field Artillery Officer Basic and Advanced Courses; the United States Army Command and General Staff College; the National War College; and the Language Course at the Defense Language Institute at the Presidio of Monterey, California.

He was commissioned a Second Lieutenant on June 6, 1979, after graduating from the ROTC program at the University of Delaware. His first military assignment was in October 1979, as the Executive Officer/Training Officer, E Battery, later Operations Officer, with A Battery, 5th Training Battalion, United States Army Field Artillery Training Center, at Fort Sill, Oklahoma. From May 1995 to June 1997, he served as the Commander of the 1st Battalion, 41st Field Artillery, 24th Infantry Division (Mechanized), later redesignated 3rd Infantry Division (Mechanized), at Fort Stewart, Georgia. In June 1998, he was assigned as the Special Assistant to the Chief of Staff of the Army in

Washington, D.C. He was promoted to Colonel on June 1, 1998.

From June 1999 to July 2001, he was assigned as the Commander of Division Artillery, 1st Infantry Division, United States Army Europe and Seventh Army, Germany and Kosovo. From July 2001 to July 2002, he was assigned as the Assistant Deputy Director for International Negotiations and Middle East/Africa, J-5, at the Joint Staff in Washington, D.C. In July 2002, he was selected to serve as the Deputy Director for Politico-Military Affairs (Africa) and International Negotiations, J-5, at the Joint Staff in Washington, D.C. He was promoted to Brigadier General on November 1, 2003.

From July 2003 to February 2004, he served as Assistant Division Commander (Maneuver) for the 1st Infantry Division, United States Army Europe and Seventh Army in Germany. In February 2004, he was deployed with the 1st Infantry Division in support of Operation Iraqi Freedom, Iraq. He was frocked Major General in April 2006.

His military awards and decorations include the Legion of Merit; Meritorious Service Medal (with five oak leaf clusters); Army Commendation Medal (with oak leaf cluster); Army Achievement Medal; and Arm Staff Identification Badge.

Morgan, Joseph M.

SERGEANT MAJOR—MARINES

Sergeant Major Joseph M. Morgan enlisted in the Marine Corps on December 27, 1973, in the 180 day delay program. He graduated from Recruit Training on September 9, 1974. He attended Infantry Training at Camp Lejeune, North Carolina, where he was assigned the MOS of 0311. Upon graduation from

Infantry Training School, he was assigned with the 8th Marines.

He was promoted to First Sergeant on August 1, 1989, and was transferred to Marine Corps Base Camp Lejeune to serve as First Sergeant for an Infantry Training Battalion. He was promoted to Sergeant Major in April 1993, and was assigned as the Sergeant Major for Marine Combat Training Battalion. On January 18, 1994, he reported for duty with Headquarters at Futenma in Okinawa, Japan, to serve as Squadron Sergeant Major. On May 15, 1995, he received orders to report to the Staff Noncommissioned Officers Academy at Marine Corps Base Camp Butler and served as the Director until he was transferred to the School of Infantry. On June 27, 1997, he was assigned as the Sergeant Major of the School of Infantry. On January 26, 2001, he assumed duties as the Sergeant Major of the 2nd Marine Division at Camp Lejeune.

Morris, Larry W.

SERGEANT MAJOR—MARINES

He graduated from Coffee High School in Douglas, Georgia in 1981. He enlisted into the United States Marine Corps and completed Recruit Training at Parris Island, South Carolina.

His key military assignments include serving as Unit Diary Chief for Headquarters and Service Battalion at Marine Corps Recruit Depot, Parris Island, South Carolina; Drill Instructor of the Third Recruit Training Battalion at Parris Island; Drill Instructor, Physical Training Instructor and Platoon Sergeant at Officer Candidate School, Quantico, Virginia; Administration Chief of Marine Light Attack Helicopter Squadron (HMLA) 169, at Camp Pendleton, California; Administrative Chief of Depot Consolidated Administrative Center at Marine Corps Recruit Depot, Parris Island; First Sergeant of Company L, Third Recruit Training Battalion at Parris Island; First Sergeant of Drill Instructor School at Parris Island; First Sergeant of Heavy Maintenance Company, Second Force Service Support Group at Camp Lejeune, North Carolina; First Sergeant of Heavy Maintenance Company at Camp Lejeune; Senior Enlisted, Second Maintenance Battalion Rear, later assigned as the Battalion's assignment to operations in Kuwait; and Sergeant Major at Marine Aviation Logistic Squadron (MALS) 31, Marine Aircraft Group (MAG) 31, Marine Aircraft Wing (2nd MAW). In January 2005, he was serving as the Sergeant Major of Marine Fighter Attack Squadron 122, Marine Aircraft Group, Beaufort, South Carolina.

Moseley, Alphronzo

COLONEL—AIR FORCE

Colonel Alphronzo Moseley is a native of Albany, Georgia. He enlisted in the Air Force in 1977. He received a four-year Air Force ROTC scholarship and commissioning program and enrolled in Tuskegee University in 1975. In December 1978, he received a Bachelor of Science degree in Electrical Engineering (summa cum laude), and he was commissioned a Second Lieu-

tenant and recognized as a distinguished graduate of Tuskegee's Air ROTC program. He earned a Master of Science degree in Electrical Engineering (digital flight control) from the Air Force Institute of Technology (AFIT) at Wright-Patterson Air Force Base, Ohio. He graduated from Squadron Officer School at Maxwell Air Force Base, Alabama; Air Command and Staff College; the Program Managers Course at the Defense Systems Management College at Fort Belvoir, Virginia; and the Air War College at Maxwell Air Force Base. In 2002, he graduated from the New Case Based Program Manager's Course at the Defense Acquisition University at Fort Belvoir.

In June 1997, he served as Chief of Command Section Internal Operations at the Space and Missile Systems Center at Los Angeles Air Force Base, California; in November 1998, he was assigned as the Deputy Program Manager, later Program Manager of Global Broadcast Service, MILSATCOM, Joint Program Office, Space and Missile Systems Center Los Angeles Air Force Base, California; in August 2000, he was assigned as Director of the Air Force Satellite Control Network Satellite and Launch Control Systems Program Office at the Space and Missile Systems Center at Los Angeles Air Force Base; in June 2002, he was selected to serve as System Program Director of Global Air Traffic Operations/Mobility Command and Control Systems Program Office at the Electronic Systems Center in Hanscom Air Force Base, Massachusetts.

Moten, Alphonso

COMMAND SERGEANT MAJOR—ARMY

Command Sergeant Major Moten was born in Columbia, South Carolina. He and his wife Vickie have two children, Kennisha and Alphonso Jr. He enlisted in Army in February 1976, completed Basic Training at

Fort Jackson, South Carolina, and Advanced Individual Training (AIT) and Airborne School at Fort Benning, Georgia. He was assigned as First Sergeant of B-Troop, 5/9 Cavalry, at Wheeler Army Air Field, Hawaii; as First Sergeant of D Company, 1-82nd Aviation Regiment., at Fort Bragg, North Carolina; and as the Sergeant Major of S-3 (Operations NCO), 82nd Aviation Brigade, later assigned as the Sergeant Major for the 82nd Airborne Division G-5, at Fort Bragg. He is currently serving as the Command Sergeant Major for the 11th Aviation Regiment, V Corps, United States Army.

Moton, Melvin V.
COMMAND SERGEANT MAJOR—ARMY

He enlisted in the United States Army in October 1976 as an Armor Crewman. After completing Basic Combat Training and Advanced Individual Training under the One Station Unit Training (OSUT) program, he was assigned to 2/33 Armor in Kirch Goens, Germany. He has served in Armor positions as loader, driver, gunner and Tank Commander for the M60A1 and M1 Abrams Tanks. He served as a Squad Leader, Section Sergeant, Platoon Sergeant, First Sergeant and Command Sergeant Major for Aviation units in the past 25 years.

His military education includes all the Noncommissioned Officer Education System Courses; Drill Sergeant Course; First Sergeant Course; the United States Army Sergeants Major Academy (class 51); and Command Sergeant Major Course.

Muhammad, Randoph
COMMAND SERGEANT MAJOR—ARMY

He is a native of Cleveland, Ohio, and entered the United States Army in September 1982. He attended basic training at Fort Sill, Okalahoma, and Advanced Individual Training at Fort Jackson, South Carolina.

His military education includes all the Noncommissioned Officer Education System Courses; the First Sergeants Course; and the United States Army Sergeants Major Academy. Civilian education degrees obtained are associate's and bachelor's, with a master's degree in International Relations.

He has held every leadership position including Section Noncommissioned Officer in Charge; Squad Leader; Platoon Sergeant; Operations Sergeant; and First Sergeant. He has also served in two Special Duty assignments, Assistant Inspector General and Active Component/Reserve Component. In September 2004, he was serving as Command Sergeant Major for the 546th Personnel Services Battalion (PSB), COSCOM at Fort Hood, Texas.

Mulzac, Hugh
CAPTAIN—MERCHANT MARINE

He was born March 26, 1886, on Union Island, St. Vincent Group, British West Indies. In his youth, he entered the Swansea Nautical College in South Wales to prepare for a seaman's career. He became an American citizen in 1918, and continued his training at the Ship-

ping Board in New York. He earned his Captain's rating in the Merchant Marine in 1918, but racial prejudice denied him the right to command a ship.

He was offered the command of a ship with an all-black crew, but refused. Twenty-two years would pass before he would get another offer to command a ship. During World War II, he becomes the first black Captain to command a ship, the *SS Booker T. Washington*.

He died in 1971, at age 84, without achieving veteran status for service to his country. Mariners only received veteran status in 1988 after a long court battle.

Murakata, Linda A.
CAPTAIN—NAVY

She was born in Manhattan and grew up in Long Branch, New Jersey, and finished Monmouth Regional High School in Shrewsbury, New Jersey.

In August 1972, she joining the Air Force, and completed her Basic Training at Lackland Air Force Base, Texas. She completed ground radio operator schooling at Keesler Air Force Base, Mississippi.

In 1978, after her four year commitment in the Air Force was up, she got out of the Air Force to go to college full time. In 1979, she joined the United States Coast Guard. She earned a bachelor's degree in Biology and a minor in Chemistry from Montclair University, New Jersey, in 1981. She started medical school in 1981, and graduated in 1985 with a degree in Medicine from the University of Medicine and Dentistry at the New Jersey Medical School in Newark, New Jersey.

She finished four years of Anatomical and Clinical Pathology and a year of Internal Medicine in 1990. She was commissioned in the United States Navy, and held several staff positions at the Institute of Pathology in

Washington, D.C., include officer in charge of the POW registry in the Department of Environmental and Toxicological Pathology, and Associate Editor for the Institute's Center for Scientific Publications. She serves as a Medical Doctor and Navy Commander at the Armed Forces Walter Reed Army Medical Center in Washington.

Murphy, Herman F.
COMMAND MASTER CHIEF—NAVY

He enlisted in the Navy in March 1985, and completed Basic Training at Great Lakes, Illinois. His first assignment was in USS *Connole* (FF 1066) as a Deck Seaman. He completed two Mediterranean deployments, two Law Enforcement Operations and advanced to Petty Officer Second Class.

In June 1991, he was assigned to Naval Air Station Oceana Security Detachment as a Patrol Supervisor enforcing state and federal law and the UCMJ. He was advanced to Petty Officer First Class.

After a successful tour of law enforcement he reported in May 1994 to USS *Mitcher* (DDG 57) as the Leading Petty Officer. He was advanced to Chief Petty Officer, and subsequently assumed the Leading Chief Petty Officer position. He completed two Mediterranean deployments.

In October 1998, he reported to PCU *Oscar Austin* (DDG 79) and commissioned her USS *Oscar Austin* (DDG 79), as the Leading Chief Petty Officer and advanced to Senior Chief Petty Officer in April 1999.

In September 2001, he was hand picked by CINCLANTFT for CNO project and reported to JOINT VENTURE (HSV X1) and advanced to Master Chief Petty Officer in May 2002.

He reported to USS *Stout* (DDG 55) in October 2003 and departed for assignment to the PCU *Forrest Sherman* (DDG 98) in September 2004.

He is a graduate of the United States Navy Senior Enlisted Academy, Class of 95 (Gold).

Murray, Aurilia "Vicki"
CHIEF WARRANT OFFICER—ARMY

In June 1973, her father Air Force Senior Master Sergeant Thomas Murray recruited her into the Air National Guard in Ohio. In August 1974, she transferred to the Army National Guard. In October 1977, she assumed the full-time position of Battalion Command Administrative Specialist. In Mach 1978, she was promoted to Warrant Officer (WO1), becoming the first African American female Warrant Officer in the Ohio National Guard.

Her education includes graduating Magna Cum Laude from Park College with a bachelor's degree in Social Psychology. In August 1999, she graduated from the Warrant Officer Senior Staff Course.

From May 1983 to June 1987, she entered the Title 10 program on active duty with the National Guard. She once again became the first female to serve as an Instructor and Training Support Writer at the Ohio National Guard Professional Education Center in Arkan-

sas. From June 1987 to June 1988, she was assigned to the National Guard's Financial Services Office at Fort Benjamin Harrison, Indiana. In June 1988, she served as a State Recruiting and Retention Specialist in the Title 32 program. In March 1993, she was assigned to the National Guard Bureau as a Military Personnel Technician in the Personnel Division, and then became the "First Female" to be assigned to the position of Program Manager of the Warrant Program.

On November 4, 1999, she became the first African American female promoted to Chief Warrant Officer 5 in the Army National Guard.

Murray, William E., Jr.
MASTER SERGEANT—AIR FORCE

He received his Bachelor of Music degree from Howard University in Washington, D.C. He has also worked toward his Master of Music degree in Composition from the University of Denver. He is one project away from completing his Master of Science degree in Computer Information Systems. While still in college, he was frequently called on by Lionel Hampton to display his alto and other woodwind talents. After graduation, he auditioned for the Louie Bellson Big Band and landed the job of splitting the lead alto chair. Before leaving the band, he had the opportunity to record the *Live in London* album with Mr. Bellson.

In 1985, he joined the United States Air Force Academy Band. He is the non-commissioned officer in charge of the Concert Band and performs with the Marching Band and Falconaires.

He is the recipient of the Silver Medal from the Royal Society of Arts of London for musical and academic excellence, and a certificate of appreciation for Outstanding Service to Jazz Education from the International Association of Jazz Educators. He has played lead alto with Pearl Bailey, Tony Bennett, Sarah Vaughn, and Diane Schuur. He has also performed with other notable artists such as Jon Hendricks, Bob Hope, Lou Rawls, Sammy Davis, Nancy Wilson, Ella Fitzgerald, and Dizzy Gillespie. He has also been a faculty member of the Clark Terry Great Plains Jazz Camp, and recorded with other Philadelphia International recording artists. He can be heard on Leslie Drayton's CD, *Until Further Notice*, which is on the New Perspective Jazz Ltd. label. Along with mastering all the woodwinds, he is also a very accomplished percussionist and set drummer. In 1994, he was the first runner-up in the Hennesy Jazz Search.

Murrell, Edmond O.
COMMAND SERGEANT MAJOR—ARMY

He is a native of Sunnyside, Texas. He entered the United States Army in 1977 and attended Basic Combat Training and Advanced Individual Training at Fort Sill, Oklahoma.

His military education includes all the Noncommissioned Officer Education System Courses; Master Fitness Course; Military Instruction Course; Sergeants Major Academy; First Sergeants Course; and Battle

Staff Course. He holds a Bachelor of Science degree in Political Science and Physical Education from Prairie View A & M University, Texas.

He enlisted in the United States Army in 1977. His military assignments include the Field Artillery Basic Course for Cannon Fire Directions at Fort Sill, Oklahoma. He was assigned as a Chart Operator for an 8-inch Howitzer Battery in Bamberg, Germany; Section Sergeant in a 155MM Howitzer Battery at Fort Carson, Colorado; Fire Control NCO with the 2nd Infantry Division at Camp Stanley, South Korea; First Sergeant in Korea; Fort Bragg; and Fort Lewis, Washington; Sergeant Major for the 3rd Brigade, Fourth Region (ROTC), at Presidio of Monterey, California; and Command Sergeant Major of Division Artillery with the 25th Infantry Division in Hawaii.

Murriel, Jeffery S.
COMMAND SERGEANT MAJOR—ARMY

He is a native of Trenton, Tennessee. In 1982 he attended One Unit Station Training at Fort Still, Oklahoma. Upon completion of Basic Training, and advanced Individual Training, he was awarded the MOS of 13F10 and assigned to the 2nd Battalion, 12th Field Artillery (8-inch), at Fort Still, Oklahoma.

His military education includes all the Noncommissioned Officer Education System Courses; the Drill Sergeants School; Master Fitness Trainers Course; Fire Support TACFIRE Course; the United States Air Force Air/Ground Observers School (AGOS); the United States Army Battle Staff Course; the United States Army First Sergeant's Course; the United States Army Staff Management College; the United States Army Sergeants Major Academy (class #53); and the Garrison Command Sergeant Major Course.

His civilian education includes a Bachelor's Degree in Management from Excelsior College of Albany, New

York, and a master's degree in Human Relations from the University of Oklahoma.

He has served in many leadership positions including Liaison Specialist; Liaison Sergeant; Company Fire Support NCO; Battalion Fire Support NCO; Brigade Fire Support NCO; Drill Sergeant; Operations Sergeant; First Sergeant; Operations Sergeant Major; and Garrison Command Sergeant Major for the United States Army Garrison at West Point from April 2005.

Nabors, Robert Lee
MAJOR GENERAL—ARMY

He was born in Boston, Massachusetts and grew up in Lackawanna, New York. He and his wife, Valerie, have three children, Robert, Richard, and Jonathan. He holds a Bachelor of Science degree in Systems Engineering from the University of Arizona; a Master of Science degree in Systems Management from the University of Southern California; and a Certificate from Harvard University as a graduate of the Senior Officials in National Security Program. His military schooling includes the Signal Officer Candidate School, Signal Officer Basic and Advanced Courses, and the Armed Force Staff College. His first duty assignment in November 1967 was with the 67th Signal Battalion at Fort Riley. After a tour in Vietnam (1969), he served from October 1969 to May 1970, as Commander of Company D, 1st Battalion, 5th Combat Support Training Brigade at Fort Dix, New Jersey. He was promoted to Captain on November 2, 1969. From June 1970 to September 1971, he was assigned as Assistant S-2/3 (Intelligence/Operations); later S-2/S/3, at the Headquarters of the 5th Combat Support Training Brigade at Fort Dix. From September 1971 to August 1972, he was a student in the Signal Officer Advanced Course at the United States Army Signal Center and School at Fort

Monmouth, New Jersey. From August 1974 to May 1977, he was assigned as Chief of the Military Skills Branch; later as an Instructor of Combat Arms Branch; then as Chief of the Allied Liaison School at Aberdeen Proving Ground, Maryland. From May 1977 to October 1979, he served as a Radio Officer, later Chief of the Transmission Systems Branch in the Telecommunications Division. Next he served as Deputy Chief of Staff for Operations and Plans, 5th Signal Command, United States Information Systems Command, and concurrently as a Staff Action Officer, Deputy Chief of Staff for Information Management, United States Army Europe and Seventh Army. He was promoted to Major on October 6, 1978. In November 1979, Gen. Nabors was selected as Aide-de-Camp for the Commanding General, VII Corps. He was attached to the J-6 Staff of the Combined Forces Command/United States Forces Korea and subsequently served as the S-2/3 of the 41st Signal Battalion. He was assigned in December 1983 to the Office of the Director of Plans, Programs and Policy at the United States Readiness Command and was then selected to Command the 509th Signal Battalion, 5th Signal Command, United States Army Information Systems Command in Italy. He was promoted to Lieutenant Colonel on September 1, 1984. From August 1986 to June 1987, he was a Fellow at the United States Army War College, Harvard University National Security Fellowship, and Cambridge, Massachusetts. In July 1987, he served as an Executive Assistant for the United States Army Director of Information Systems for Command, Control, Communications and Computers. He was also Chief of the Integration Division in the Office of the Director for Information Systems for Command, Control, Communications, and Computers, Office of the Secretary of

the Army, in Washington, D.C. From February 1989 to December 1990, he was assigned as Deputy Commander of the White House Communications Agency, Defense Communications Agency. He was promoted to Colonel on June 1, 1990. Prior to assuming Command of the 2nd Signal Brigade in December 1990, he served as Deputy Commander of the White House Communications Agency. Before his assignment as Director, Single Agency Manager for Pentagon Information Technology Services, he served as the Executive Officer for the Director of Information Systems for Command, Control, Communications and Computers, United States Army. In July 1995, he was selected Commanding General of the 5th Signal Command, United States Army in Europe and Seventh Army (Germany). He was promoted to Brigadier General on July 1, 1995. From November 1996 to July 1998, he served as the Commanding General/Deputy Chief of Staff for Information Management, 5th Signal Command, United States Army Europe and Seventh Army, Germany. He was promoted to Major General August 1, 1998. He was selected to serve as Commanding General for the United States Army Communications-Electronics Command and Fort Monmouth, New Jersey, in July 1998. He retired from the military in October 2001. His military awards and decorations include the Defense Superior Service Medal; Legion of Merit (with four oak leaf clusters); the Bronze Star; Meritorious Service Medal (with three oak leaf clusters); the Joint Service Commendation Medal; the Army Commendation Medal (with three oak leaf clusters); the Department of the Army Staff Identification Badge; the Joint Meritorious Unit Award; and the Presidential Support Badge. He is a member of the American Mensa Society.

Nelson, Aloysius Ali

COMMAND MASTER CHIEF—NAVY

He enlisted under the delayed entry program in December 1981. He completed Basic Training in June 1982 in Orlando, Florida. He attended Storekeeper "A" School in Meridian, Mississippi, where he graduated with honors.

He served aboard the USS *Tattnall* (DDG 19) as DLR Storekeeper and Work center Supervisor; USS *Mobile Bay* (CG 53) as S1 Division LCPO and Supply Dept. Leading Chief Petty Officer (LCPO); USS *Robert G. Bradley* (FFG 49) as Command Senior Chief and Supply Department LCPO; and USS *Enterprise* as Supply Dept LCPO. During his career he completed a total of eight deployments and where he operated in the Arabian Gulf, Western Pacific, North Atlantic, and Mediterranean.

His overseas assignments include service at Naval Communication Station, Keflavik Iceland, and a forward deployment in Yokosuka, Japan, onboard USS *Mobile Bay* (CG 53).

Ashore, he served as an Independent Duty Storekeeper at Naval Air Station, Jacksonville, Florida; Naval Aviation School Command, Pensacola, Florida; as Supply Department LCPO at Recruit Training Command,

Great Lakes, Illinois; and as a Recruit Division Commander and Military Training Director LCPO, where he earned his designation as a Master Training Specialist. He served as the Command Master Chief for Transient Personnel Unit, Great Lakes.

Master Chief Nelson graduated from the United States Navy Senior Enlisted Academy in Newport, Rhode Island, in 2002. He earned his Bachelor of Science degree from Southern Illinois University in August 2003. He was selected for the Command Master Chief Program in June 2003. He serves as the Command Master Chief for USS *Austin* (LPD-4).

Nelson, Jerry
COMMAND SERGEANT MAJOR—ARMY

Command Sergeant Major Jerry Nelson is a native of Summerton, South Carolina, and enlisted in the

United States Army in 1974. During his career, he has served in every enlisted leadership position in his Career Management Field from Section Chief to Division Artillery Command Sergeant Major. He served as Operations Sergeant Major for the 24th Infantry Division Artillery; Command Sergeant Major of the 3rd Battalion, 41st Field Artillery

(PALADIN); Command Sergeant Major of the 1st Battalion, 9th Field Artillery; and Command Sergeant Major of the 3rd Infantry Division Artillery at Fort Stewart, Georgia. He is currently serving as the Command Sergeant Major of ARCENT in Saudi Arabia.

His military education includes the 155mm Atomic Projectile Supervisor Course; Lance Missile Electronic Course; Lance Missile Mechanic Course; NBC Course; the Master Fitness Course; Instructor Training Course; the First Sergeant Course; and the United States Sergeants Major Academy. He has also earned an associate's degree in Liberal Arts from the City College of Chicago.

Nelson, Lynn
CHIEF WARRANT OFFICER—MARINES

Chief Warrant Officer 3 Nelson served as the Traffic Management Officer at Marine Corps Logistics Base in Albany, Georgia.

He was honored for teaching educators, chief executive officers, health care professionals and college and high school students how to establish, manage and market community outreach and cross-culture programs.

He led the first all–African American paramissionary and medical mission teams to South Africa to live and work among the people in black townships. Using social problems common in Albany as a model, the team helped the South Africans face and seek solutions to such problems as unemployment, crime, pornography, alcoholism, teen-age pregnancy, child abuse, spouse abuse, drugs, sexually transmitted diseases, illiteracy and gangs.

He established and directs the Albany-South Africa exchange program, which trains South Africans in Albany. He also serves on the Albany Gang Task Force and developed educational programs to help the community keep kids out of gangs.

Nero, Carrie Lee
BRIGADIER GENERAL—ARMY

She received a Bachelor of Science degree in Social and Behavioral Science from the University of South Florida. She earned a Master of Arts degree in Guidance and Counseling and a Masters of Science degree in Nursing from the University of South Florida. She has also earned an Ed.D Degree in Higher Education from Nova University. Her military education includes the Army Medical Department Officer Advanced Course; the United States Army Command and General Staff College; and the United States War College.

She received a direct commission to First Lieutenant on March 11, 1975. She was first assigned as a Medical Surgical Nurse, later as Head Nurse, Operating Room, with the 349th Combat Support Hospital in St. Petersburg, Florida. From December 1986 to January 1991, she was assigned as the Chief of Nursing Services at the 349th Combat Support Hospital at St. Petersburg. In January 1991, she served as Casualty Assistance Officer at the 3388th United States Army Reserve Forces School in Tampa, Florida. From July 1991 to August 1992, she was assigned as Staff Nurse Advisor and Chief of the Drug Abuse Prevention program at the 349th Combat Support Hospital in St. Petersburg. In August 1992, she was selected to serve as Army Medical Department Advisor, Task Force, Future Army School-2-1, Operation Division Office, Chief Army Reserves, in Washington, D.C. From February 1993 to January 1995, she was assigned as Chief of Drug Team and Chief of Nursing Service at the 349th Combat Support Hospital in St. Petersburg.

From February 1995 to January 1996, she was assigned as Chief of Drug Team and Chief of Nursing Service at the 73rd Field Hospital in St. Petersburg. From February 1996 to May 2001, she was assigned as Chief of Nursing Service at the 345th Combat Support Hospital in Jacksonville, Florida. In May 2001, she was selected to serve as the Chief Nurse, for the 3rd Medical Command in Decatur, Georgia.

General Nero's military awards and decorations include the Army Commendation Medal; Army Achievement Medal; and National Defense Medal.

Nesby, Charles W.
SENIOR EXECUTIVE SERVICE

He is a former United States Navy Captain and Air Wing Commander who retired from the Navy in 1997. He is a second-generation fighter pilot named after his father, Charles Nesby, Sr., one of the original Tuskegee Airmen of World War II.

He reported to Aviation Officer Candidate School in Pensacola, Florida, in June of 1973 and received his wings as a Naval Aviator in January 1975. Following deployment to the Western Pacific and Mediterranean, he completed pilot training for the Navy F-14A Tomcat fighter. From August 1978 to September 1981, he completed two deployments onboard the USS *America* (CV-66). During this tour, he graduated from the United States Navy Fighter Weapons School (Topgun) and was a distinguished graduate in the Maritime Air Superiority syllabus (Topscope). He served as an Instructor Pilot, Operations Officer and Readiness Officer from 1981 to 1989. A distinguished graduated from the Industrial College of the Armed Forces at Fort McNair in Washington, D.C., he assumed Command of Strike Training Squadron Twenty Two at Naval Air Station Kingsville, Texas, in 1992. Under his command, the Squadron flew more than 114,000 mishap-free flight hours and was named best Training Squadron in the

Naval Air Training Command. In September 1993, he assumed dual duties as Director of Air Force and Navy Requirements, Joint Primary Aircraft Training System, and Director of the Joint Cockpit Officer/Wright Laboratories at Wright-Patterson Air Force Base, Ohio. He served as Commander of Strike Training Air Wing Two in Kingsville from September 1995 until his retirement in 1997.

In November 2001, he was appointed Director of the Department of Veterans Affairs Center for Minority Veterans. As Director, he is the principal advisor to the Secretary of Veterans Affairs on policies and programs affecting minority veterans. Prior to his appointment, he managed a computer-based training project for D.P. Associates of San Diego, California. He was responsible for developing software and hardware components to support a flight training program for Navy and Marine Corps Combat Aircrews.

Newsome, Gary M.
COMMAND SERGEANT MAJOR—ARMY

He is a native of Fremont, North Carolina, and graduated from Charles B. Aycock High School in 1975. He entered the United States Army in March 1980 and attended Basic Combat Training and Advanced Individual Training at Fort Sill, Oklahoma.

His military education includes all the Noncommissioned Officer Education System Courses; the Air Assault School; MLRS Cadre Course; Drill Sergeant School; First Sergeant Course; and the United States Army Sergeant Major Academy (class 50). He earned an Associate of Arts degree in Business Management from Regents College.

In November 2004, he was serving as Command Sergeant Major for the Field Artillery Training Center at Fort Sill, Oklahoma.

Newton, Lloyd W. "Fig"
GENERAL—AIR FORCE

He was born in Ridgeland, South Carolina, and graduated from Jasper High School in 1961. General Newton is married to the former Elouise M. Morning of St. Petersburg, Florida. They have five children, Bernard, Lloyd Jr., Cheryl, James and Lori. He earned a Bachelor of Science degree in aviation education from Tennessee State University, Nashville, where he was commissioned as a distinguished graduate through the Reserve Officer Training Corps Program in 1966. After completing pilot training at William's Air Force Base, Arizona, in June 1967, he was assigned to George Air Force Base, California, where he received combat training in the F-4 Phantom. He was transferred to Da Nang Air Base, South Vietnam, in April 1968 and flew 269 combat missions, including 79 over North Vietnam. In November 1969 he was assigned to 523rd Tactical Fighter Squadron of the 405th Tactical Fighter Wing at Clark Air Base in the Philippines. Returning to the United States in 1974, he became an F-4 Phantom fight instructor at Luke Air Force Base, Arizona. The general joined the United States Air Force Aerial

Demonstration Squadron (The Thunderbirds), in November 1974; he became the first black pilot to become a member of the Thunderbirds. He held several positions with them, including narrator and advance coordinator in 1975, slot in 1976–77, and right wingman in 1978. In December 1978, he became a congressional liaison officer with the United States House of Representatives, Air Force Office of Legislative Liaison, Office of the Secretary of the Air Force, Washington, D.C. In February 1982, General Newton was assigned to MacDill Air Force Base, Florida, where he transitioned to the F-16. He then was assigned to the 8th Tactical Fighter Wing at Kunsan Air Base, South Korea, as assistant deputy commander for operations, then to the 388th Tactical Fighter Wing at Hill Air Force Base, Utah. Upon completion of the Industrial College of the Armed Forces in June 1985, he was assigned to the Headquarters of the United States Air Force in Washington, D.C., as assistant deputy director for operations and training in the Directorate of Operations. In November 1986, he was named assistant director of special projects in the Directorate of Plans at Air Force Headquarters. He assumed command of the 71st Air Base Group at Vance Air Force Base, Oklahoma, in July 1988, and was assigned as commander of the 71st Flying Training Wing, also at Vance Air Force Base, in May 1989. He then became commander of the 833rd Air Division at Holloman Air Force Base, New Mexico, in August 1991, and then commander of the 49th Fighter Wing at Holloman following deactivation of the 833rd Air Division in November 1991. He was promoted to Brigadier General on August 3, 1991. From July 1993 to May 1995, he was director of operations, J-3, United States Special Operations Command. He was promoted to Major General on August 10, 1993. From June 1995 to March 1997, he served as assistant vice Chief of Staff at the Headquarters of the United States Air Force, Washington, D.C. He was promoted to Lieutenant General on May 25, 1995. On April 1, 1997, he was promoted to the rank of General and he assumed command of the Air Force's Air Education and Training Command located at Randolph Air Force Base in Texas. The general is a command pilot with more than 4,000 flying hours. He retired effective August 1, 2000. His military awards and decorations include the Defense Distinguished Service Medal; Distinguished Service Medal (with oak leaf cluster); the Legion of Merit (with oak leaf clusters); the Distinguished Flying Cross (with oak leaf cluster); Meritorious Service Medal (with oak leaf cluster); Air Medal (with 16 oak leaf clusters); Air Force Commendation Medal, Air Force Outstanding Unit Award, Philippines Presidential Unit Citation, Vietnam Service Medal and Republic of Vietnam Campaign Medal.

Nicholas, Javier A.
SERGEANT MAJOR—MARINES

He enlisted in the Marine Corps in October 1976, and attended Boot Camp at the Marine Corps Recruit Depot in Parris Island, South Carolina. After completing boot camp in January 1977, he attended the Field Artillery Fire Direction Control Man Course in Fort Sill, Oklahoma. After graduating his Artillery School, he was assigned as a Surveyor to Headquarters Battery, 2nd Battalion, 11th Marines in Camp Pendleton, California. He also attended the Career Course in El Toro, California, and the Field Artillery Operations Chief School at Fort Sill, Oklahoma.

He has held numerous leadership positions including service as Sergeant of the Guard; Special Services Noncommissioned Officer in Charge; Battery Operations Chief; Battalion Survey Chief; Inspector-Instructor; Operations Chief on the Inspector-Instructor Staff; First Sergeant; and Senior Noncommissioned Officer in Charge of the Marine Corps Cadre Detachment at Submarine Base Bangor, Washington. In August 2004, he was serving as Sergeant Major of the CSSG-11, 1st Force Service Support Group.

Nichols, Marvin
COMMAND MASTER CHIEF—NAVY

He is a native of Little Rock, Arkansas. He enlisted into the United States Navy in February 1989, under the delayed Entry Program. He graduated from Recruit Training Center at Great Lakes, Illinois, in June 1989. He attended Air Traffic Control "A" School from June to October 1989.

He holds an Associates of Arts degree from East Mississippi Community College in 1998; a Bachelor of Science degree from Mississippi State University (Meridian Campus in 1999); and a Master of Business Administration degree from Touro University International in August 2003.

In January 2001, he reported to Atlantic Fleet Weapons Training Facility, Puerto Rico, as the Air Traffic Control Leading Chief Petty Officer. He was

responsible for the safe operation and execution of five JTFEX's, Five Comptuex's and several of the Joint Services Exercises. He reported to tactical Air Control Squadron TWELVE in June 2003 as the Training Chief. He was later promoted to the Command Chief position.

Nicholson, Emiel
COMMAND MASTER CHIEF—NAVY

Nicholson is a native of Kingston, Jamaica. He enlisted into the United States Navy in August 1983 and came on active duty in January 1984. After completing Basic Training in Orlando, Florida, he attended Aviation Storekeeper "A" School at Naval Training Center Meridian, Mississippi.

His sea duty assignments include serving aboard USS *Constellation* (CV 63) home-ported in North Island, California; USS *Saratoga* (CV 60) home-ported in Mayport, Florida; USS *Kitty Hawk* (CV 63) and USS *Independence* (CV 62) both home-ported in Yokosuka, Japan; HS-5 in Jacksonville, Florida deploying aboard USS *Eisenhower* (CVN 69) and USS *George Washington* (CVN 73); and HC-4 at Naval Air Station Sigonella, Italy. His shore tours were at HSL-36 Mayport, Florida, and Naval Air Station Cecil Field in Jacksonville, Florida.

He was selected for Master Chief in April 2002, and for Command Master Chief in January 2004. He reported to the EASY RIDERS of HSL-37 as Command Master Chief in August 2004.

Nicholson, Tracey E.
COLONEL—ARMY

She was born in Philadelphia, Pennsylvania. She was

commissioned into the United States Army in 1982, following graduation from Rutgers University, New Brunswick, New Jersey. She began her military career in the Adjutant General Corps, assigned to Fort Sam Houston, Texas.

Her military education includes a Bachelor of Arts degree in Journalism and Communications from Rutgers University; a Master of Science degree in Administration, Human Resource Management, from Central Michigan University; and a Master of Arts degree in Strategic Studies from the United States Army War College in Carlisle, Pennsylvania. She is a graduate of the United States Army Command and General Staff College; the Adjutant General Basic and Advanced Courses; and the Defense Equal Opportunity Course (distinguished graduate).

Her key military assignments include Installation Postal Officer at Fort Sam Houston, Texas; Army Emergency Relief Officer; Chief of the Operations Division and Assistant Adjutant for the Deputy Chief of Staff for Information Management; Installation Equal Opportunity Officer at Fort McClellan, Alabama; Chief Administrative Officer in the J-6, Joint Communications Directorate, South Korea; Liaison Officer in the United States Total Army Personnel Command (PERSCOM) for the Commander 8th Personnel Command; Deputy Chief of the Prisoner of War/Missing in Action (POW/MIA) Division and the Military Secretariat for the Director of Operations (J-3), the Joint Staff; Chief of the Casualty Operations Division during the Global War on Terrorism and the Chief of the Personnel Services Support Division in the Adjutant General Directorate, United States Army Human Resources Command. Her previous commands include serving as Commander of Headquarters Company at the

United States Army Chemical and Military Police Center at Fort McClellan; Commander of the 516th Personnel Services Company in South Korea; Commander of St. Louis Military Entrance and Processing Station; and Garrison Commander of the United States Army Garrison at Selfridge, Michigan. In March 2005, she was serving as the Garrison Commander at Fort Hamilton, Brooklyn, New York.

Noble, James M.
COMMAND SERGEANT MAJOR—ARMY

He enlisted in the United States Army in September 1976. He attended Basic Combat Training and Advanced Individual Training at Fort Knox, Kentucky.

His military education includes all the Noncommissioned Officer Education System Courses; M1 Abrams Course; Armor Noncommissioned Officer Course; Drill Sergeant School; Instructor's Training Course; Tank Commander Certification Course; Senior Noncommissioned Officer Equal Opportunity Course; First Sergeant Course; Battle Staff Course; the United States Army Sergeants Major Academy (class 49) at Fort Bliss, Texas; and the Command Sergeant Major Course at Fort Bliss.

His key military assignments include serving as a Drill Sergeant, Senior Drill Sergeant, and Operations Sergeant at Fort Knox, Kentucky. He was assigned as a Platoon Sergeant during Operation Desert Shield/Desert Storm with the 2nd Armored Cavalry Regiment at Bindlach, Germany. He served as Platoon Sergeant, First Sergeant, Armor Platoon Observer Controller, and Cobra Team Senior Non-Commissioned Officer Trainer for the Armor Task Force/Cavalry Squadron at the National Training Center at Fort Irwin, California. He served as Command Sergeant Major for the 1st Squadron, 11th Armored Cavalry Regiment at Fort Irwin; and as Command Sergeant Major of the 1st Battalion, 34th Armor at Fort Riley, Kansas, while serving as Task Force Centurion Command Sergeant Major during Intrinsic Action 01-03. In March 2005, he was serving as the Garrison Command Sergeant Major, 24th Infantry Division (Mechanized) and Fort Riley.

Norman, James P., III
COMMAND SERGEANT MAJOR—ARMY

He enlisted into the United States Army on July 14, 1981, and entered Basic Training at Fort Jackson, South Carolina. He completed his Advanced Individual Training at Fort Huachuca, Arizona.

He has attended numerous training programs including all the U.S. Army's Noncommissioned Officer Edu-

cation Systems training; Drill Sergeant School; the First Sergeant Course; Ground Surveillance Course; the Sergeants Major Academy; Military Mountaineering Course; Surveillance Radar Course; Rappel Master Course; and Battle Staff NCO Course.

In August 2004, he was serving as Command Sergeant Major for the 4-7th Cavalry Squadron in South Korea.

Nowlin, Lennie
COMMAND MASTER CHIEF—NAVY

He is a native of Marianna, Pennsylvania. He enlisted in the United States Navy in February 1975, and completed Basic Recruit Training in April 1975. He reported to Naval Training Center in Orlando, Florida, for Basic Electricity, Electronic and Torpedoman "A" and "C" schools.

He graduated with honors and was inducted into Phi Theta Kappa national honor fraternity for junior colleges, and earned a Bachelor of Science degree from Southern Illinois University. From August to October 1992, he attended the Senior Enlisted Academy in Newport, Rhode Island.

In October 1992, he reported to Recruit Training Center Orlando and served as a Battalion Commander and Drill Division Officer. He also trained three gender-integrated Companies, one earning the coveted "Hall of Fame" award. He served as the Command Master Chief of VFA-105 and Naval Hospital, Jacksonville.

O'Brien, Shawna
MAJOR—AIR FORCE

In August 2004, she was serving as the Commander of the 319th Mission Support Squadron at Grand Forks

Air Force Base, North Dakota. Her twin sister, Major Dawn Keasley, took command of the 375th Mission Support Squadron at Scott Air Force Base, Illinois, on the same day.

Odom, Curtis B.
CAPTAIN—COAST GUARD

He is the Commanding Officer of the Coast Guard Training Center at Cape May, New Jersey. It is the home of the Coast Guard's enlisted corps and our nation's oldest Coast Guard enlisted accession point and recruit training center. In addition to "Boot Camp," it hosts four other training programs. These include Recruiter School, Company Commander School, Reserve Enlisted Basic Indoctrination and the Maritime Academy Reserve Training Program.

Oggs, Dennis I.
COMMAND SERGEANT MAJOR—ARMY

He entered the United States Army at Fort Knox under the One-Stop Unit Training as an Armor Crewman 11E10. His military education includes completing all levels of the Noncommissioned Officers Education System; First Sergeant Course; Battle Staff Course; Drill School Sergeant School; Master Fitness School; Instructor Trainer Course

for Cadet Command; and the Command Sergeant Major Academy. He holds a Bachelor of Business Administration degree from Mckendree College. He holds a Master of Business Administration degree in Aviation from Embry Riddle Aeronautical University.

He has served in virtually every leadership position from Squad Leader to Command Sergeant Major.

Ousley, Allie R.

COMMAND SERGEANT MAJOR—ARMY

He is a native of Albany, Georgia. He attended Basic Combat Training at Fort Jackson, South Carolina, and Advanced Individual Training at Fort Sill, Oklahoma. His military education includes all levels of the Non-commissioned Officers Education System (NCOES); Recruiting and Retention NCO Course; Basic Airborne School; Air Assault School; Pershing II Transition Course; School of Cadet Command; First Sergeants Course; Battle Staff NCO Course; the United States Sergeants Major Academy; and the Command Sergeant Major Course.

His key leadership assignments include serving as Section Chief; Gunnery Sergeant; Operations Sergeant; Platoon Sergeant; Chief of Firing Battery; Drill Sergeant; Senior Drill Sergeant Instructor; Senior Enlisted O/C; Battalion Regimental Noncommissioned Officer in Charge; First Sergeant; Brigade Operations Sergeant Major (ROTC), Battalion Command Sergeant Major; and Brigade Command Sergeant Major at Fort Sill, Oklahoma. In August 2004, he was serving as the Commandant of the United States Army Noncommissioned Officer Academy at Fort Sill, Oklahoma.

Overton, Norris W.

BRIGADIER GENERAL—AIR FORCE

He was born in Clarksville, Tennessee, and married the former Patricia Cole of Waukegan, Illinois. He was graduated from Crispus Attucks High School in Indianapolis in 1946. He received a Bachelor of Science degree in Accounting in 1951 from Indiana University and was designated as a distinguished military graduate of the Air Force Reserve Officers Training Corps program and commissioned a Second Lieutenant. He received a master's in Business Administration from the Air Force Institute of Technology in 1959 and was graduated from the Advanced Management Program at the Harvard University School of Business Administration in 1972. General Overton completed the Air Command and Staff College and the Industrial College of the Armed Forces by correspondence and the Air War College by seminar. After completing the Accounting and Disbursing Officer Course at Fort Benjamin Harrison, Indiana, he was assigned as Finance Officer with the 18th Fighter-Bomber Wing at Chinhai, Korea, in February 1952. Assignments followed as Deputy Finance Officer at Forbes Air Force Base, Kansas; Finance Officer at Grenier Air Force Base, New Hampshire; Finance Officer at Bordeaux Air Base, France; and Deputy Accounting and Finance Officer at Lindsey Air Base, West Germany. In 1959, he became Chief of the

Comptroller Services Division at the Air Force Plant Representative Office, Curtis-Wright Corporation at Woodridge, New Jersey. A similar assignment followed in 1960 to the Milwaukee Contract Management District, Milwaukee. In January 1963, General Overton assumed duties as the Staff Accounting and Finance Officer at Karamursel Common Defense Installation, Turkey. He was an associate Professor of Aerospace Studies at the University of Iowa from 1964 to September 1968, then reassigned as Base Comptroller at Tan Son Nhut Air Base, South Vietnam. He was transferred to the Headquarters of the United States Air Forces Washington, D.C., in October 1969, as Executive Officer to the Deputy Assistant Comptroller for Accounting and Finance. In November 1972, he became Deputy Chief of Staff, Comptroller, United States Air Force Academy. He was assigned as Deputy Chief of Staff, Comptroller, Headquarters of Pacific Air Forces, in February 1976. In June 1979, he became assigned Vice Commander of Army and Air Force Exchange Services in Dallas. He was appointed Brigadier General on May 1, 1979, with date or rank April 24, 1979. His military decorations and awards include the Legion of Merit (with oak leaf cluster); Bronze Star (with oak leaf cluster); Air Force Commendation Medal; Air Force Outstanding Unit Award Ribbon; Republic of Korea Presidential Unit Citation; and Republic of Vietnam Gallantry Cross (with palm).

Page, Felton

SENIOR EXECUTIVE SERVICE

He is a native of Buffalo, New York. He received a Bachelor of Science degree from Central State University in Wilberforce, Ohio. He was honored as a ROTC distinguished military graduate, and commissioned as a Second Lieutenant.

He was Airborne and Ranger qualified, which afforded

him numerous challenging assignments. Those assignments included serving as Company Commander; Intelligence Officer (S-2) of Special Forces battalion; and Operations Officer (S-3). He pursued an advanced degree in criminal justice from Wichita State University in Wichita, Kansas.

He began his equal opportunity career while on active duty as a Race Relations Officer. He is a graduate of the Defense Equal Opportunity Management Institute, the premier Department of Defense school for Race Relations.

In July 1987, he joined the National Guard Bureau Headquarters as an EEO Specialist. In 1991, he was selected as the Special Emphasis Programs Manager. He has successfully had the National Guard recognized and included as a member of the Department of Defense, Joint Services, Diversity Education/Special Emphasis Program Planning Group. He successfully planned, coordinated and supervised the National Guard's hosting of all military events as DOD's lead service during the 83rd and 90th NAACP Conventions, and the 21st and 28th National IMAGE Conventions.

He serves as the Director of the Office of Equal Opportunity and Civil Rights for the National Guard bureau, with responsibility for Equal Opportunity and Equal Employment Opportunity Policy and Regulatory guidance affecting all Army and Air National Guard, Military and Civilian personnel in the 54 states and territories.

Paige, Emmett, Jr.
LIEUTENANT GENERAL—ARMY

He was born in Jacksonville, Florida, the son of Emmett and Elizabeth Core Paige. He married the former Gloria McClary and the have three children, Michael, Sandra and Anthony. General Paige dropped out of

high school at age 16, not to hang out in the streets but to fulfill his lifelong dreams of a military career. After leaving Stanton High School at that early age, he enlisted as a private in the United States Army. He began his army career in August 1947. He held a host of important assignments in the United States and abroad, including Japan, Germany, Korea, the Philippines, and Vietnam. Earlier in his 39-year military career, the general was with the 25th Infantry Division in Nara, Japan, as a Morse code radio operator in the late 1940s. A short while after enlisting in the Army, Paige had earned his GED high school diploma and later received a bachelor's degree in General Arts from the University of Maryland before receiving a master's in Public Administration from Penn State University. He entered Officer Candidate School at Fort Monmouth, New Jersey, graduating in July 1952. When asked why he chose the Army, he said, "The Army and Air Force were all one and the same back then, and they sent me down to MacDill Airbase in Tampa, Florida. I took a battery of tests and the Sergeant said, 'Well, you qualified for the ground forces or the Air Corps,' and I said, 'Where does the Air Corps give basic training?' He said, 'Sheppard Field in Texas.' When I found out the temperature there was 110 degrees, I told him I'd go with the ground forces — they trained at Fort Dix in New Jersey." Asked if race made a difference in his career, he said, "Officer Candidate School comes to mind. I've never forgotten whom I am, having been born and raised in the South. When I went to Officer Candidate School in Fort Gordon, Georgia, I was the first and only black in the leadership course you had to finish to get into OCS. The commandant of the school, a West Pointer, said at the end of the course, 'Student Paige, I guess you think that we've been very unfair and given you a harder time than necessary,' and I said, with a smile on my face, 'As a matter of fact, sir, I do.' Then he said,

'You're right. You have set the standard for the blacks that are going to have to be just as good as your white contemporaries. You're going to have to be twice as good. I'm not saying that that's fair or that's right, but those are the facts.' As he went on talking, I could see he was about to come to tears. Inside, the tears were there, but I didn't let them come out because I was pissed that I had to go through this. But I knew he was right. I had seen it as an enlisted man — black lieutenants sitting at a separate table in the officers' mess, in a black field artillery battalion where the bulk of the officer corps was white. And then, at OCS in Fort Monmouth, it was the same thing. But I was determined not to let the bastards kick me out. So yes, race has made a difference, but if anything, I think it's made me a better person." After OCS, tours followed at Fort Bliss, Texas (1952–1953), Karlsruhe, West Germany (1954–1956), and still later at Fort Devens, Massachusetts, and Fort Carson, Colorado. He was in Korea from 1959–60 and in the Philippines with the Defense Communications Agency at Clark Air Force Base from 1962–65. From May 1965 to August 1968, he served as project officer and later Deputy Project Manager for the Integrated Wide Band Communications System in the Procurement and Production Division of the Office of the Project Manager at the United States Army Communications Systems Agency at Fort Monmouth. In 1969, he commanded the 361st Signal Battalion in Vietnam as a Lieutenant Colonel with the famed 1st Signal Brigade, returning to the Defense Communications Agency at Arlington, Virginia, in 1970. From August 1973 to June 1974, he was a student in the United States Army War College at Carlisle Barracks, Pennsylvania. He was assigned as Deputy Chief of Staff in the United States Army Communications Command at Fort Huachuca, Arizona. In January 1975, he was selected Commander of the 11th Signal Group, United States Communications Command at Fort Huachuca. On June 1, 1976, he was promoted to Brigadier General. From April 1976 to June 1979, he was assigned as the Commander of both the United States Communications-Electronics Engineering and Installation Agency at Fort Huachuca and the United States Army Communications Systems Agency at Fort Monmouth, New Jersey. He was promoted on April 3, 1978. From June 1979 to May 1981, he was assigned as Commander of the United States Army Communications Research and Development Command at Fort Monmouth. In 1981, he took command of the United States Army Electronics Research and Development Command headquartered in Adelphi, Maryland. General Paige was promoted to Lieutenant General on July 1, 1984. From June 1984 to June 1988, he served as the Commander of the United States Army Information Systems Command, a worldwide organization headquartered at Fort Huachuca. He remained in this assignment until his retirement in 1988. One of General Paige's most challenging military jobs was as the Project Manager of the Integrated Wide Band Communications System installed in Southeast Asia; it was the largest communications system ever installed in a combat environment. His military awards and decorations include the Distinguished Service Medal (with oak leaf cluster); the Legion of Merit (with two oak leaf clusters); the Bronze Star for Meritorious Service; the Meritorious Service Medal; the Army Commendation Medal; and the Army Good Conduct Medal. Following his retirement from the Army in 1988, General Paige became the President and Chief Operating Officer of OAO Corporation, an Aerospace and Information Systems Company in Greenbelt, Maryland. Following his retirement from the Army in 1988, General Paige became the President and Chief Operation Officer of OAO Corporation, and Aerospace and Information Systems Company in Greenbelt, Maryland. General Paige was and appointed by President Bill Clinton and confirmed by Congress as the Assistant Secretary of Defense for Command, Control, Communications and Intelligence in May 1993. General Paige has an undergraduate degree from the University of Maryland, University College and received his advanced degree from Pennsylvania State University. He has been awarded an honorary Doctor of Law degree from Tougaloo College at Tougaloo, Mississippi, and an honorary doctorate from the University of Maryland, Baltimore County and an honorary Doctorate of Science degree, Honoris Causa from Clarkson University in May 1995. Both the University of Maryland and Penn State have honored General Paige as a Distinguished Alumnus. Penn State also selected him as an Alumni Fellow in 1993. General Paige has received numerous awards from the civil sector. Information Week Magazine selected him as the Chief Information Officer of the Year in 1987; the Data Processing Management Association selected him for the coveted Distinguished Information Sciences Award for outstanding service and contributions internationally to advancements in the field of Information Sciences; University of Maryland, Baltimore County, selected him as Engineer of the Year in February 1995; and he was given the Black Engineers Lifetime Achievement Award in February 1995.

Parker, Julius, Jr.
MAJOR GENERAL—ARMY

He was born in New Braunfels, Texas. He married the former Dorothy June Henry, and they have three children, Julian R., Jules G., and Dorvita J. He was commissioned into the United States Army upon completion of the Reserve Officers Training Corps curriculum, and graduating from Prairie View A&M University with a Bachelor of Science degree in Biology and Chemistry. He also received a master's degree in Public Administration from Shippensburg State College. His military education includes completion of the Infantry Officer Basic and Advanced Courses, the United States Army Command and General Staff College, and the United States Army War College. From May 1956 to February 1957, he was assigned as a Platoon Leader with Company I, 10th Infantry, at Fort Ord, in California. From February 1957 to June 1957, he was assigned

as Weapons Umpire with Battery B, 1st Howitzer Battalion (105mm), 19th Artillery, United States Army Combat Development Experimental Center, at Fort Ord. He was promoted to First Lieutenant on May 13, 1957. From December 1957 to January 1959, he was assigned as a Motor Officer, later Platoon Leader, at Headquarters and Headquarters Company, 2nd Battle Group, 12 Cavalry, 1st Cavalry Division, United States Army, in South Korea. From January 1960 to June 1960, he was assigned as the Commander of Company D, 1st Battle Group, 22nd Infantry Brigade, with the 4th Infantry Division, at Fort Lewis, Washington. From June 1960 to July 1962, he was assigned first as Executive Officer, later as Commander, at Headquarters Company, 1st Battle Group, 22nd Infantry Brigade, next as Liaison Officer, with the 4th Infantry Division, at Fort Lewis, Washington. He was promoted to Captain on May 10, 1961. He has held a wide variety of important command and staff positions. He was assigned as Executive to the Assistant Chief of Staff for Intelligence, United States Army, Washington, D.C.; Deputy Chief of Staff for Intelligence, United States Army Forces Command at Fort McPherson, Georgia; Deputy Chief of Staff for Intelligence, United States Army, Europe, and the Seventh Army; and Deputy Director for Management and Operations, Intelligence Agency, Washington, D.C. He was promoted to Major on February 7, 1966. General Parker served in Vietnam as a Senior District Adviser. Returning to the United States, he performed duties as Combat Intelligence Staff Officer, Ground Surveillance Officer, and Branch Chief, Office of the Assistant Chief for Intelligence, United States Army, Washington, and D.C. From 1969 to 1972, he commanded the Military Intelligence Battalion, 66th Military Intelligence Group, United States

Army, and Europe. He was promoted to Lieutenant Colonel on January 14, 1970. From July 1972 to December 1973, he served as the Assistant Chief of Staff, G-2 (intelligence), 3rd Armored Division, Europe, followed by attendance at the United States Army War College at Carlisle Barracks, Pennsylvania. Upon graduation, General Parker was retained at Carlisle Barracks as a Faculty Member and Strategic Analyst in the Strategic Studies Institute until May 1977. He was promoted to Colonel on February 1, 1976. Assigned to Colonel-level Command in South Korea from July 1977 to July 1979, he successfully organized and integrated four independent Intelligence Units to form the Army's first Multidiscipline Brigade-level Intelligence Organization, the 501st Military Intelligence Group. He remained in this position until he was assigned as Commanding General of the United States Army Intelligence Center/Commandant of the United States Army Intelligence School. While serving as the Chief of Intelligence for FORCOM, at Fort McPherson, he was promoted to Brigadier General on October 1, 1980. From August 1984 to July 1985, he served as the Deputy Director for Management and Operations at the Defense Intelligence Agency in Washington, D.C. He was promoted to Major General on May 1, 1984. His military awards and decoration includes the Distinguished Service Medal; the Defense Superior Service Medal; the Legion on Merit, the Bronze Star (with "V" device and oak leaf cluster); Purple Heart; Meritorious Service Medal (with three oak leaf clusters); Combat Infantryman's Badge; Parachutist Badge; the Air Medal; and the Army Commendation Medal (with oak leak cluster).

Parker, Lionel H.
COMMAND SERGEANT MAJOR—ARMY

He entered the United States Army on June 18, 1965. He completed Basic Training at Fort Polk, Louisiana, and Advanced Individual Training as an Administrative Specialist at Fort Ord, California. He has completed all Noncommissioned Officer Courses, including First Sergeant Course; Battle Focus Instructor Training Course (BFITC); and the Command Sergeant Major Designee Course. CSM Parker served as the Command Sergeant Major of the 311th Theater Signal Command. His prior assignments include serving as the Command Sergeant Major of 4th INF OSUT Brigade, at Fort Story, 80th Division; Drill Sergeant School Commandant at the 80th Division; Comptroller Sergeant Major for the Special Operations Command Central (SOCCENT) at MacDill AFB in Tampa, Florida.

Patin, Jude Wilmot Paul
BRIGADIER GENERAL—ARMY

He was born in Baton Rouge, Louisiana. He received a Bachelor of Science degree in Architectural Engineering from Southern University in 1962 and a Master of Science in Industrial Engineering from Arizona State University in 1971. He received a ROTC commission to Second Lieutenant in 1962, and from September 1962, he was a student in the Field Artillery Officer Basic Course at the United States Army Field Artillery School at Fort Sill, Oklahoma. From December 1962 to October 1963, he was a Reconnaissance Survey Officer, Service Battery, 1st Missile Battalion, 42nd Artillery, United States Army, Europe. From October 1963 to January 1964, he was a Survey Officer with the 3rd Missile Battalion, 32nd Artillery, 214th Artillery Group at Fort Sill. On March 4, 1964, he was promoted to the rank of First Lieutenant. From January 1964 to February 1965, he was the Commander of Headquarters Battery, 3rd Missile Battalion, 32nd Artillery, 214th Artillery Group at Fort Sill. From March 1965 to June 1966, he served as an Architectural Engineer in the Installation Section, 593rd Engineer Company at Fort Sill. He was promoted to Captain on April 16, 1966. From July 1966 to May 1967, he served as Commander of the 697th Engineer Company (Pipeline); then Commander of the 561st Engineer Company (Construction), 44th Engineer Group (Construction), United States Army, Thailand. From June 1967 to March 1968, he was a student in the Army Engineer Officer Advanced Course at the United States Army Engineer School at Fort Belvoir, Virginia. From January 1969 to March 1969, he served as Assistant Division Engineer for the 65th Engineer Battalion, 25th Infantry Division, United States Army, Vietnam. From April 1969 to December 1969, he was the Operations Officer of the Operations Division of the United States Army Engineer Construction Agency in Vietnam. He was promoted to the rank of Major on July 11, 1969. From January 1970 to June 1971, he was a student at Arizona State University in Tempe, Arizona. From June 1971 to June 1974, he served as Technical Operations Officer, then Chief of the Plan and Program Branch of the Management Analysis Office, United States Army Logistics Doctrine, Systems and Readiness Agency, then as the Program Analysis Officer for the Administration and Management Office, United States Army Logistics Evaluation Agency, Deputy Chief of Staff for Logistics, United States Army at New Cumberland, Pennsylvania. From June 1974 to May 1976, he served as the S-3 (operations officer) then as Executive Officer of the 84th Engineer Battalion, 25th Infantry Division at Schofield Barracks, Hawaii. From June 1976 to June 1977, he was a student at the United States Army Command and General Staff College at Fort Leavenworth, Kansas. From June 1977 to May 1980, he served as an advisor to the 1138th Engineer Brigade, United States Army in Europe. He was promoted to Lieutenant Colonel on December 9, 1978. From May 1983 to April 1985, he was a student, later Director, of Insurgency Operations at the United States Army War College at Carlisle Barracks. He was promoted to Colonel on October 1, 1984. From May 1985 to July 1987, he was Commander of the 1st Training Support Brigade; later Commander of the 136th Engineer Brigade at the United States Army Training and Engineer Center at Fort Leonard Wood, Missouri. From August 1987 to September 1989, he served as the Assistant Chief of Staff for Engineering and Housing, 21st Support Command, United States Army, Europe, and the Seventh Army. He was promoted to Brigadier General on November 1, 1989. In October 1989, he was appointed Commanding General of the United States Army Engineer Division, North Central, Chicago, Illinois. He has received numerous awards and decorations, including the Legion of Merit, the Bronze Star, Meritorious Service Medal (with two oak leaf clusters), Air Medal, Army Commendation Medal (with oak leaf cluster), and Parachutist Badge.

Patrick, Dwayne

COMMAND MASTER CHIEF—NAVY

Command Master Chief Dwayne Patrick enlisted in the Navy in September 1978 in Flint, Michigan. After attending recruit training in Great Lakes, Illinois, he attended Mess Management Specialist "A" school in San Diego, California. As a Mess Management Specialist his first tour of duty was at the Headquarters of Commander of Submarine Force, United States Atlantic Fleet, at Norfolk, Virginia. In July 1981, he reported to his first sea command, USS *Arkansas* (CGN 41), followed by a tour on USS *Waddell* (DDG 24) in August 1983 where he advanced up through the ranks to Mess Management Specialist second class.

He then went on to a shore tour at Administrative Command, Naval Training Center, San Diego, California, where he attended the Command Career Counselor Course in March 1987 and became a Navy Counselor. This led him to USS *Alamo* (LSD 33) in July 1987 where he was selected as Senior Sailor of the Year for *Alamo* and Amphibious Squadron Seven. In September 1990 he was promoted to Chief Petty Officer and decommissioned the *Alamo* and reported to the USS *Juneau* (lpd-10) in December 1990, participating in Operation Desert Shield/Desert Storm. His next tour of duty took him to Naval Command Control and Ocean Research Center, Research Development, Test and Evaluation Center, San Diego. In October 1992, he was advanced to Senior Chief Petty Officer in April 1993. That tour was followed by a tour a Shore Intermediate Maintenance Activity in San Diego in December 1993. He then reported to the Senior Enlisted Academy at Newport, Rhode Island. He reported to the USS *Boxer* (LHD 4) in January 1996 and reported to USS *Cleveland* (LPD 7) in January 1997. He reported

to Fleet Logistic Support Squadron 30 (VRC 30) in May 2000. He was then selected as a Fleet Command Master Chief and reported to the Third Fleet in September, 2001.

Patterson, George Travis

SERGEANT MAJOR—ARMY

He is a native of Darlington Heights, Virginia. He graduated from Winston-Salem State University in 1975 and enlisted in the United States Army in April 1978. After Basic Combat Training and Advanced Individual Training at Fort Jackson, South Carolina, he attended the Army International Postal School at Fort Benjamin Harrison, Indiana, and was assigned to the 502nd Adjutant General Company, 2nd Armored Division at Fort Hood, Texas, as an Administrative Specialist.

His military schools include all the Noncommissioned Officer Education System Courses; the International Postal School; Allergy/Immunization Course; Administrative Specialist Course; Combat Medical Specialist Course; Emergency Medical Technician Course; Alcohol and Drug Coordinator Course; Hearing Conservation Course; Personnel Actions Specialist Course; Supervisor Development Course; Senior Enlisted Equal Opportunity Workshop; the Northern Warfare Cold Weather Orientation Course; the United States Air Force Senior Non Commissioned Officer Academy (Class 05-A); and the United States Military Police School Anti-Terrorism Officer's Course. He holds an Associate of Applied Science degree in Paralegalism. He also holds a Bachelor of Arts degree from Winston-Salem State University.

He served in a variety of duty positions and assignments. They include service as Postal Inspector at Fort Hood, Texas; Administrative Specialist for the Headquarters and Headquarters Company, 2nd Infantry Division at Camp Casey, South Korea; Administrative Specialist at Patterson Army Community Hospital at Fort Monmouth, New Jersey; and Senior Personnel Actions Specialist for the Headquarters and Headquarters Company, 108th Division (Training) at Charlotte, North Carolina.

After a short break in service to continue his education, he attended the Combat Medical Specialist Course at Fort Sam Houston, Texas, in 1983. Upon completion of training he was further assigned to Moncrief Army Community Hospital at Fort Jackson as a Medical Specialist. He then served as Medical Evacuation Sergeant with the 2nd Battalion, 32nd Armor, and 2nd Battalion, 67th Armor, in Friedberg, Germany, where he completed a tour of duty along the Iron Curtain dividing East and West Germany at the furthest outpost of freedom with the 3rd Recon Squadron, 11th Calvary. He has also served as NCOIC of the Outpatient Clinic at Dunham United States Army Health Clinic at Carlisle Barracks, Pennsylvania; Senior Medical Treatment NCO with the 1st Battalion, 7th Infantry, 3rd Infantry Division at Aschaffenburg, Germany, where he was deployed on Operations Desert Shield Desert

Storm and Desert Calm; Non-Commissioned Officer in Charge of the Emergency Room and the Department of Family Practice and Community Medicine; Non-Commissioned Officer in Charge of the Directorate of Primary Care and Community Medicine at Fort Belvoir, Virginia; Non-Commissioned Officer in Charge of the Troop Medical Clinic at the First Sergeant Medical Detachment at Fort Richardson, Alaska; and First Sergeant of the Medical Holding Company and Garrison Sergeant Major at Walter Reed Army Medical Center in Washington, D.C.

Patterson, La Warren V.
COLONEL—ARMY

He is a native of Portsmouth, Virginia. He graduated from Norfolk State University in 1982 with a Bachelor of Science degree in Mass Communications and was commissioned as a Second Lieutenant in the Signal Corps. He is a graduate of the Command and General Staff College at Fort Leavenworth, Kansas, and holds a Master of Science degree in General Administration from Central Michigan University and a master's in Strategic Studies from the United States Army War College. He has also completed the Communications-Electronics Staff Officer's Course; the Communications-Electronics Warfare Course; and the Combined Arms Services Staff School.

He has held numerous key leadership assignments including service as the Battalion Signal Officer of the 2nd Signal Battalion, 5th Cavalry (Armor), and later as a Platoon Leader in the 13th Signal Battalion. In 1985, he was assigned to West Germany and the 87th Maintenance Battalion where he served as the Communications-Electronics Maintenance Officer in Battalion S-2/3 and Commander of the 85th Light Equipment Maintenance Company (LEMCO). Following com-

pany command, he was assigned to the 3rd Infantry Division's staff as the Division Radio Officer. Returning from Germany in 1990, he was assigned to the Pentagon and the Joint Chief of Staff's (JCS) Intern Program. While in Washington, D.C., he was assigned to PERSCOM and performed duties as the Signal Branch Lieutenant's and Captain's Assignment Officer. In 1995, he was assigned to the 304th Signal Battalion 1st Signal Brigade in South Korea as the Battalion S-3 and later Executive Officer. After completion of a two year tour in Korea, he was reassigned to the Pentagon where he served as an Action Officer and Branch Chief with the Joint Staff's Year 2000 Task Force. In 1999, he returned to Germany to assume Command of the 440th Signal Battalion. His next assignment was at the G-6 Staff in the Headquarters Department of the Army as the C4 Systems, Space and Networks Division Chief. In August 2004, he was assigned as the Brigade Commander of the 1st Signal Brigade, Eighth United States Army Regional Chief Information Officer and the G6 for the Eighth United States Army at Yongsan, South Korea.

Patterson, Leonard Eric
BRIGADIER GENERAL—AIR FORCE

General Patterson received a Bachelor of Science degree in Business Administration from Howard University in Washington, D.C., and earned a Master of Science degree in Business Administration from Webster University in St. Louis, Missouri. He began his career as a missile Launch Officer in September 1975, prior to joining the Office of Special Investigations, where he served as the Director of Operations at OSI Headquarters. Throughout his career, he has held a variety of leadership positions, including Detachment Commander, Field Investigation Squadron Commander and Region Commander. On May 11, 2002, he was assigned

as the 14th Commander of the Office of Special Investigations.

Patterson, Michael L.

COMMAND SERGEANT MAJOR—ARMY

A native of Cumberland, Virginia, he entered the United States Army in September 1982 and attended Basic Combat Training at Fort Jackson, South Carolina, and Advanced Individual Training at Aberdeen Proving Ground, Maryland.

His military education includes all the Noncommissioned Officer Education System Courses; Master Fitness Course; First Sergeant Course; and the United States Army Sergeants Major Academy. He also holds an Associate in Applied Science degree from Austin Peay State University and a Bachelor of Liberal Arts from the Parks University.

His assignments include serving with the 17th Corps Support Battalion, where he served as the First Sergeant of the 536th Maintenance Company; the 225th FSB at Schofield Barracks, Hawaii; the 725th MSB at Schofield Barracks, Hawaii; 5th Army West at Fort Lewis, Washington; the 101st Airborne Division (Air Assault); and the 1st Armor Division in Ansbuch, Germany. In September 2004, he was serving as Command Sergeant Major for the Special Troops Battalion, 13th COSCOM.

Patton, Marquis A.

LIEUTENANT COMMANDER—NAVY

He is a native of Sylacauga, Alabama. He entered

the United States Navy in 1979, advanced to Torpedoman Mate Chief Petty Officer in 1989 and earned his commission in August 1992 through the Limited Duty Officer (LDO) Program. He graduated from Recruit Training in July 1979.

His sea duty assignments include the USS *Dixie* (AD 14); the USS *Prairie* (AD 15); the USS *Jarrett* (FFG 33); and the USS *John Paul Jones* (DDG 53). His shore and staff assignments include Naval Training Center, Great Lakes, Illinois, from July 1979 to September 1979; Naval Training Center, Orlando, Florida, from September 1979 to December 1979; Naval Air Station, Cubi Point, Republic of the Philippines, from June 1983 to July 1985; Naval Weapons Station, Seal Beach, California, from April 1989 to August 1992; and Fleet Training Center, San Diego, California, from December 1992 to January 1994. He has also served as Commander of Afloat Training Group Pacific at San Diego, California, from September 1997 to September 1999 and again from February 2002 to February 2004. In October 2004, he was serving as Commanding Officer of Mobile Mine Assembly Unit (MOMAU) Eleven at Naval Weapon Station Charleston in Goose Creek, South Carolina.

Patton, Oscar R.

COMMAND SERGEANT MAJOR—ARMY

He enlisted into the U.S. Army in 1965 and attended Basic Training at Fort Polk, Louisiana, and Advanced Individual training at Fort Ord, California. His other schools and training completed include Airborne Training, Instructor Training, the First Sergeant Course, and the United States Army Sergeants Major Course.

During his 30-year career, he held a variety of critical command and staff positions. Some of his assignments were Command Sergeant Major of the 23rd

Quartermaster Brigade at Fort Lee, Virginia; Command Sergeant Major for the 142nd Supply and Service Battalion in Wiesbaden, Germany; Command Sergeant Major for the 16th Corps Support Group in Hanau, Germany; DCSLOG Sergeant Major for the 6th United States Army at the Presidio of San Francisco, California; and Sergeant Major for the Directorate of Installation Support at White Sands Missile Range, New Mexico.

He served as the Honorary Sergeant Major of the Quartermaster Regiment from October 1996 until June 2000.

Patton, Vincent, III
MASTER CHIEF OF THE COAST GUARD

A native of Detroit, Michigan, Master Chief Patton enlisted in the United States Coast Guard in June 1972. His first assignment after graduating from Radioman School in 1973 was aboard the USCGC *Dallas*, Governors Island, New York. Other duty stations as a radioman include Coast Guard Group and Air Station Detroit, Michigan, and Recruiting Office Chicago, Illinois.

All of Master Chief Patton's college education was earned while on active duty. He received his Doctor of Education degree in 1984 from American University in Washington, D.C. He also earned a master's degree in Counseling Psychology from Loyola University of Chicago, Illinois; a Bachelor of Science degree in Social Work from Shaw College in Detroit, Michigan, and a Bachelor of Arts degree in Communications from Pacific College at Angwin, California. He is a graduate of the United States Coast Guard Chief Petty Officer Academy, United States Army Sergeants Major Academy (with distinction), and the Department of Defense Equal Opportunity Management Institute.

He became the Eighth Master Chief Petty Officer

of the Coast Guard on May 22, 1998. He is the first African American in the History of the United States Coast Guard to be selected to the position of Master Chief Petty Officer of the United States Coast Guard. He is the principal advisor to the Commandant of the Coast Guard on matters affecting over 36,000 active duty and reserve enlisted personnel.

Payne, Foster P., II
COLONEL—ARMY

A distinguished Military Graduate of Virginia State University, Colonel Payne also holds a Master of Arts degree in Public Administration and Management from Webster University in St. Louis, Missouri. His military schools include the Officers Basic and Advanced Courses; the Combined Arms Services and Staff School; the United States Army Command and General Staff College; and the Senior Service College.

He has served in a variety of command and staff positions at the Company, Battalion, Brigade and Division Levels. His key assignments include serving as Commander of Headquarters Company, 4th Brigade at Fort Leonard Wood, Missouri; S-2, Division Artillery and Commander Company C, 522nd Military Intelligence Battalion, 2nd Armored Division at Fort Hood, Texas; S-3 and Executive Officer of the 532nd Military Intelligence Battalion, 501st Military Intelligence Brigade at Seoul, South Korea; Congressional Liaison Officer to the House of Representatives in the Office of the Chief of Legislative Liaison; Assistant Chief of Staff, G-2, 2nd Infantry Division at Camp Red Cloud, South Korea; Commander of the 125th Military Intelligence Battalion (Light), 25th Infantry Division at Schofield Barracks, Hawaii; and Chief of J2X (Counter Terrorism, Human Intelligence, Counter Intelligence) at United States Central Command at MacDill Air Force Base, Tampa, Florida. He took Command of the 504th Military Intelligence Brigade on June 26, 2002.

Pearce, Bennie O.
COMMAND MASTER CHIEF—NAVY

He enlisted in the United States Navy in November 1983 and attended Basic Recruit Training at the Recruit Training Command in Orlando, Florida. Following Basic Training he attended Yeoman "A" School in Meridian, Mississippi. He is a graduate of the United States Navy Senior Enlisted Academy (class 094) (Khaki Group). He holds a Bachelor of Science degree in Management from Park University and is currently pursuing a master's degree in Public Administration at Troy State University.

His assignments include serving as Ship's Secretary onboard USS *Reuben James* (FFG 57) at NAVSTA Pearl

Harbor, Hawaii; as Deputy Director and then Director of the Military Manpower and Personnel Division in the Office of the Chief of Naval Research at Arlington, Virginia; as Administrative Department Leading Chief Petty Officer with Strike Fighter Squadron 105 at NAS Oceana, Virginia; as Command Master Chief on USS *Normandy* (CG 60) at NAVSTA Norfolk; and as Command Master Chief at the Naval Surface Warfare Center, Indian Head Division . He was selected as Naval District Washington Regional Command Master Chief in June 2004.

Pearson, Clint
COMMAND SERGEANT MAJOR—ARMY

Command Sergeant Major Clint Pearson entered the United States Army on May 2, 1977, and completed Basic Combat Training at Fort Jackson, South Carolina. He attended Advanced Individual Training and Airborne School at Fort Benning, Georgia.

His military education also includes the Battle Staff Course; the Air Assault School; Air Borne School; Jump Master Course; Ranger School; the French Commando School; the Honduran Airborne Course; and the United States Army Sergeants Major Academy.

His most recent assignments include serving as a First Sergeant in the 44th Engineer Battalion, 2nd Infantry Division, in South Korea until October 1996 and as a First Sergeant with the 249th Prime Power Battalion at Fort Belvoir, Virginia, until July 1997. In July 1997, he attended the Sergeants Major Academy at Fort Bliss, Texas, and was then assigned as the S-3 (Operations) Sergeant Major with the 1st Cavalry Division Engineer Brigade at Fort Hood, Texas. He was selected to serve in his first Command Sergeant Major position as the Command Sergeant Major of the 20th Engineer Battalion in January 1999. In August 2001 he was selected

as the Command Sergeant Major for the 1st Cavalry Engineer Brigade.

Pearson, Ervin
COLONEL—ARMY

He received a Bachelor of Science degree in Accounting Auditing from South Carolina State University. He earned a Master of Engineering degree in Communications and a Master of Science degree in Accounting from Southern University and A&M College. His military education includes completion of the Finance Officer Basic and Advanced Courses; the United States Army Command and General Staff College; and the United States Army War College.

He received a commission as Second Lieutenant on July 5, 1975, after graduating from the ROTC program. His first assignment in October 1975 was a Disbursing Officer, later Commander of the 12th Finance Section, at Fort Knox, Kentucky. In February 1978, he was assigned as Chief of the Central Accounting Division, late Chief, Pay and Examination Division, later Deputy Finance Officer/Executive Officer, for the 39th Finance Section, Hanau Military Community, V Corps, United States Army Europe and Seventh Army, Germany. From June 1987 to August 1989, he was assigned as Commander of the 107th Finance Support Unit, XVIII Airborne Corps, at Fort Bragg, North Carolina. In August 1989, he was assigned as the S-2 (Intelligence Officer)/S-3 (Operations Officer), with the 18th Corps Finance Corps at Fort Bragg. From January 1990 to May 1992, he served as Program Budget Officer in the Office of the Assistant Secretary of the Army for Financial Management in Washington, D.C. He was promoted to July 1, 1992.

From March 1993 to June 1994, he was assigned as Chief of the Program and Budget Team in the Office of the Deputy Chief of Staff for Operations in Wash-

ington, D.C. In March 1993, he served as Commander of the 177th Finance Battalion, 2nd Infantry Division, Eighth United States Army in South Korea. In June 1994, he returned to Washington, to serve as Comptroller Proponency Officer, in the Office of the Assistant Secretary of the Army (Financial Management and Comptroller) in Washington, D.C. In June 1996, he was selected to serve as the Military Assistant, later Executive Officer/Senior Military Assistant to the Assistant Secretary of the Army (Financial Management and Comptroller), in Washington, D.C. He was promoted to Colonel on February 1, 1998.

In June 1999, he was assigned as the Commander of the 13th Finance Group, III Corps, at Fort Hood, Texas. In September 2001, he returned to Washington to serve as the Chief of Operating Forces in the Office of the Assistant Secretary of the Army for Financial Management and Comptroller, Washington, D.C.

His military awards and decorations include the Defense Superior Service Medal; the Legion of Merit (with oak leaf cluster); Meritorious Service Medal (with four oak leaf clusters); Army Commendation Medal (with oak leaf cluster); Army Achievement Medal; Parachutist Badge; and Army Staff Identification Badge.

Peete, Arthur F.
COMMAND SERGEANT MAJOR—ARMY

His military assignments include serving as a Drill Sergeant at Fort Leonard Wood, Missouri; as First Sergeant of the 11th Heavy Equipment Transportation Company with the 4th Transportation Battalion during Operation Desert Shield/Desert Storm; as Command Sergeant Major for the 14th Transportation Battalion in Vicenza, Italy; as Command Sergeant Major for the 71st Transportation Battalion at Fort Eustis, Virginia; as Commandant for the Fort Eustis Noncommissioned Officer Academy; as Command Sergeant Major of the 28th Transportation Battalion in Mannheim, Germany; and as Command Sergeant Major for

the 37th Transportation Command in Kaiserslautern, Germany. He currently leads the 21st Theater Support Command.

Peggins, Terry X.
FIRST SERGEANT—ARMY

He is a native of Fort Wayne, Indiana. He began his career in the United States Army in June 1987. He completed Basic Combat Training and Advanced Individual Training at Fort Sill, Oklahoma, and Fort Benjamin Harrison, Indiana.

His military and civilian education includes all the Noncommissioned Officer Education System Courses; the Tropic Lighting Fighters Course; Combat Lifesavers Course; MAC Airlift Planners Course; Drivers Training Course; Unit Alcohol and Drug Coordinators Course; NBC Officer/NCO Course; the Army Recruiter Course; Master Driver Course; and Commanders' Total Fitness Course. He earned an associate's degree in Liberal Arts from Chaminade University of Honolulu and a bachelor's degree in Liberal Studies from Excelsior College.

In November 2004, he was serving as First Sergeant for Bravo Company, III Corps NCO Academy and Fort Hood, Texas.

Pegues, John E.
COMMAND SERGEANT MAJOR—ARMY

He is native of Oxford, Mississippi. He entered the military on September 1, 1976. Upon completion of Basic Combat Training and Advanced Individual Training, he was awarded MOS 17K, Ground Surveillance Radar Crewman. His military education includes all the Noncommissioned Officer Education System Courses; Intelligence Advanced Noncommissioned Officers Course; the First Sergeants Course; and the United States Army Sergeants Major Academy (class 50).

His key military assignments include serving as First Sergeant of the 6th Infantry Division at Fort Wainwright, Alaska; First Sergeant of D Company, 110th Military Intelligence Battalion, at Fort Drum, New York; First Sergeant of C Company, 102nd Military In-

telligence Battalion, 2nd Infantry Division, South Korea.

Penn, Buddie J.
ASSISTANT SECRETARY OF THE NAVY

He is a native of Peru, Indiana. He received his Bachelor of Science from Purdue University in West Lafayette, Indiana, and his Master of Science from George Washington University in Washington, D.C. He has also received certificates in Aerospace Safety from the University of Southern California and in National Security for Senior Officials from the Kennedy School at Harvard University.

He began his career as a Naval Aviator. He amassed over 6500 flight hours in sixteen different types of aircraft. He was EA-6B Pilot of the Year in 1972. Significant leadership assignments include service as Executive Officer/Commanding Officer VAQ 33; Battalion Officer at the United States Naval Academy (including Officer-in-Charge of the Plebe Detail for the class of 1983); Air Officer in USS *America*; Special Assistant to the Chief of Naval Operations; Commanding Officer of Naval Air Station, North Island, California; and Deputy Director of the Navy Office of Technology Transfer and Security Assistance.

Prior to becoming the Assistant Secretary of the Navy (I&E), he was the Director of Industrial Base Assessments from October 2001 to March 2005. In the position, he was responsible for the overall health of the United States Defense Industrial Base; the Department's policies and plans to ensure existing and future industrial capabilities can meet the Defense missions; guidelines and procedures for maintaining and enhancing and transformation of the Defense industrial base, industrial base impact assessments of acquisition strategies of key programs, supplier base considerations, and offshore production.

On March 1, 2005, he was appointed Assistant Secretary of the Navy (Installations and Environment). Mr. Penn is responsible for formulating policy and procedures for the effective management of Navy and Marine Corps real property, housing, and other facilities; environmental protection ashore and afloat; occupational health for both military and civilian personnel; and timely completion of closures and realignments of installations under base closure laws.

Penn, Damon C.
COLONEL—ARMY

His military career began in June of 1978, when he enlisted into the North Carolina Army National Guard as an Artillery Crewman. He was commissioned a Second Lieutenant in Armor in May of 1981, after graduating from the University of North Carolina in Charlotte with a bachelor's degree in Criminal Justice.

He earned master's degrees from Central Michigan University and the United States Naval War College. He is also a graduate of the United States Army's Command and General Staff College.

His military assignments include serving as Platoon Leader, Squadron Adjutant, and Cavalry Troop XO with the 2nd Squadron, 2nd Armored Cavalry Regiment in Bamberg, Germany; Senior Controller for the Battle Command Training Program at Fort Leavenworth, Kansas; Regimental Plans Officer and Operations for the 2nd Squadron, 2nd Armored Cavalry Regiment; Senior Operations Officer in the National Military Command Center at the Office of the Chairman of the Joint Chiefs of Staff in Washington, D.C.; as a Career Manager for Armor Majors and Lieutenant Colonels at the United States Army Personnel Command; Commander of the 1st Battalion, 67th Armor, 4th Infantry Division and later Division Inspector Gen-

eral; as Armor Branch Chief at the United States Army Human Resources Command at Alexandria, Virginia; and as DENCOM Commander at Fort Knox, Kentucky.

Penton, Chris L.
COMMAND MASTER CHIEF—NAVY

He was born in Bogalusa, Louisiana, in December 1960. He entered the Navy at Los Angeles, California, in September 1981. After Recruit Training and Apprentice Training in San Diego, California, he reported to the USS *Fearless* (MSO 442) at Charleston, South Carolina, in January 1982. After three years on the *Fearless* he transferred to the Staff Commander Iceland Defense Force at Keflavik, Iceland.

In October 1988, he transferred to Recruit Training Command, San Diego, California, as a Recruit Company Commander. While assigned to the Recruit Training Command, San Diego, he was designated Master Training Specialist. In January 1991, he reported to USS *Spruance* (DD 963) as Deck Division LCPO and later served as Operations Department LCPO until April 1995. In May 1995, he attended the Senior Enlisted Academy in Newport, Rhode Island, and then reported to USS *Belleau Wood* (LHA-3) at Sasebo, Japan, as Deck Department LCPO.

In October 1997, he transferred to USS *Bunker Hill* (CG-52) at Yokosuka, Japan, as Command Master Chief. Following an emergency, unscheduled deployment to the Arabian Gulf from January to June 1998, *Bunker Hill* changed homeport to San Diego, California, in August 1998. In May 1999, he was selected to be the Command Master Chief of Naval District Washington, a CNO-Directed Command Master Chief billet. In February 2001, he reported to USS *Belleau Wood* (LHA-3) at San Diego, California, as Command Master Chief. In January 2004, he reported to the USS

Nimitz (CVN-68) at San Diego, California, as Command Master Chief.

Peoples, Willie C., Jr.

COMMAND SERGEANT MAJOR—ARMY

He is a native of Slocomb, Alabama. He enlisted in the United States Army in June 1978 and completed Basic Combat Training, Advanced Individual Training and the Airborne Course at Fort Benning, Georgia. He holds a Bachelor of Science degree in Management from Park University.

mand Sergeant Major of the 54th Signal Battalion in Saudi Arabia, as well as Command Sergeant of the 86th Signal Battalion at Fort Huachuca, Arizona. In 2003, he was serving as the Command Sergeant Major of the 15th Regimental Signal Brigade at Fort Gordon.

Peters, Michael

COMMAND SERGEANT MAJOR—ARMY

He entered the United States Army in October 1977, attended Basic Training at Fort Jackson, South Carolina, and Advanced Individual Training at Fort Knox, Kentucky. His military education includes all the Noncommissioned Officer Education System Courses; the

In his rise from Private to Command Sergeant Major, he served with distinction in a wide variety of important career building positions. In August 2004, he was serving as the Commandant of the JRTC & Fort Polk Noncommissioned Officer Academy at Fort Polk, Louisiana.

Peppers, Reuben L.

COMMAND SERGEANT MAJOR—ARMY

Entered the United States Army in June 1975 and completed Basic Training at Fort Jackson, South Carolina, and Advanced Individual Training at Fort Gordon, Georgia. Command Sergeant Major Peppers' military education includes the Instructional Training Course, Drill Sergeant School, Primary Leadership Course, Communications-Electronics Operations Advance Course (Honor Graduate), and the Sergeants Major Academy (Class July 1995).

During his more than 26 years of service, he has served in every leader position from Team Leader to Command Sergeant Major. His assignments include one tour in the Middle East with the 35th Signal Brigade. His most recent assignments were as Com-

Bradley Master Gunner Course; Drill Sergeant School; First Sergeants Course; and the United States Army Sergeants Major Academy. He holds an associate's degree in General Studies from Central Texas College.

He has served in every enlisted leadership position in Armor and Cavalry organizations from Scout Squad Leader to Brigade Command Sergeant Major. He served as the TF 1-63 AR Command Sergeant Major during Operation Iraqi Freedom.

Petersen, Frank E., Jr.
LIEUTENANT GENERAL—MARINES

He was born in Topeka, Kansas. He earned both a bachelor's degree and a master's degree from George Washington University in Washington, D.C. Virginia Union University awarded him an Honorary Doctor of Law degree. In June 1950, he joined the United States Navy as an apprentice seaman, serving as an electronic technician. On October 1, 1952, Frank E. Petersen was commissioned Second Lieutenant in the Marine Corps after completing the Naval Aviation Cadet Program. He had considerable flight activity in Korea where he served as the Commander of a Marine Fighter Squadron, a Marine Aircraft Group, a Marine Amphibious Brigade, and a Marine Aircraft Wing. During his two tours of duty in Korea and Vietnam, General Petersen flew 350 combat missions with over 4,000 hours in various fighter and attack aircraft, and he earned the Distinguished Flying Cross, America's highest aviation medal, and six Air Medals. General Petersen was the first black in the naval services to command a tactical air squadron. In 1968, he commanded Marine Fighter Attack Squadron 314 in Vietnam. Under his command, this squadron received the Hanson Award for Aviation as the best fighter squadron in the Marine Corps. In 1979, while General Petersen was serving as Chief of Staff of the 9th Marine Amphibious Brigade on Okinawa, President Jimmy Carter nominated him for advancement to Brigadier General. With the Senate confirmation, Petersen, the Marine Corps's first black Aviator, became the first black Marine to attain General rank. When he retired from the Marine Corps on August 1, 1988, he was serving as Commanding General of Marine Corps Development and Education at Quantico, Virginia. When he left the service, he was the Senior Ranking Aviator in the United States Marine Corps and the United States Navy, with respective titles of "Silver Hawk" and "Grey Eagle." In this regard, the date of his designation as an aviator preceded all other aviators in the United States Air Force and the United States Army. His numerous decorations include the Defense Superior Service Medal, Legion of Merit (with combat "V"), Distinguished Flying Cross, Purple Heart, Meritorious Service Medal, Air Medal, Navy Commendation Medal (with combat "V"), and Air Force Commendation Medal. Gen. Petersen relinquished duties as the Commanding General of Marine Corps Combat Development Command at Quantico on July 8, 1988. He served as the Special Assistant to the Chief of Staff from July 8, 1988, until July 31, 1988, and retired from the Marine Corps on August 1, 1988.

Phillips, John F.
MAJOR GENERAL—AIR FORCE

He was born in Neches, Texas. He and his wife, Blanche, have three children. After graduating from Climons High School in Neches in 1959, he received a Bachelor of Science degree in Biology and Chemistry (with honors) from Jarvis Christian College in 1963 and a Master of Science degree in Logistics Management from the Air Force Institute of Technology in 1975.

He pursued additional studies at North Texas State University and Texas Southern University. He is an honor graduate of the Institute of Aerospace Safety Engineering (graduate and under-graduate school) at the University of Southern California. He completed Squadron Officer School in 1971, Industrial College of the Armed Forces in 1976, and the National War College in 1983. He was commissioned as a Second Lieutenant through Officer Training School at Lackland Air Force Base, Texas, in December 1963 and earned his navigator wings at James Connally Air Force Base, California, where he flew as an Instructor Navigator. During this time he flew regular combat missions in Vietnam, accumulating more than 300 combat flying hours. He entered pilot training at Williams Air Force Base, Arizona, and graduated with top honors in July 1970. He was then assigned to the 1st German Air Force Squadron, Sheppard Air Force Base, Texas, as a T-37 Instructor Pilot and was awarded German Pilot's Wings. From December 1973 to August 1975, he served as an inspector and flight examiner with the Air Training Command Inspector General's staff at Randolph Air Force Base, Texas. He then attended the Air Force Institute of Technology at Wright-Patterson Air Force Base. Upon graduation in September 1976, he became system manager for the F-100 and J-85 engines at Kelly Air Force Base, Texas. In December 1978, he was assigned as a Logistics Systems Analyst at Doshan Tappeh Air Base, Iran, until the fall of the Shah. Phillips remained in Iran under the Khomeini regime until his expulsion in February 1979. He transferred to Wright-Patterson and served as Deputy Program Manager for Logistics in the KC-10 Joint Program Office. In January 1982, he was appointed System Program Director for the TR-1 and later become Director of all airlift and trainer systems. Phillips attended the National War College from August 1982 to September 1983 and distinguished himself in both academics and athletics. He was then assigned to the Weapons System Program Division in the Directorate of Logistic Plans and Programs at the Headquarters of the United States Air Force in Washington, D.C. He first served as Deputy Division Chief, then Chief, and later as Deputy Director of Logistics Plans and Programs. From July 1985 to July 1986, he was Military Assistant to the Assistant Secretary of the Air Force for research development and logistics. After this assignment, he served as Vice Commander of the Logistics Management Systems Center at Wright-Patterson Air Force Base, Ohio. He was promoted to Brigadier General on October 1, 1988. From October 1988 to December 1992, he was assigned as the Deputy Chief of Staff for Communications-Computer Systems at the Headquarters of Air Force Logistics Command at Wright-Patterson Air Force Base. He was promoted to Major General on August 1, 1991. From January 1992 to June 1992, he served as Assistant to the Commander, later Commander of Joint Logistics Systems Center, at Wright-Patterson Air Force Base. In May 1993, he was selected to serve as the Commander of Sacramento Air Logistic Center at McClel-

lan Air Force Base, California. He retired from the Air Force on October 1, 1995. General Phillips was appointed by President Bill Clinton as Under Secretary of Defense for Logistics in October 1995. He is a senior pilot with more than 3,000 flying hours. His military awards and decorations include the Legion of Merit, Meritorious Service Medal (with two oak leaf clusters), Air Medal, Air Force Commendation Medal (with oak leaf), Combat Readiness Medal, and Republic of Vietnam Gallantry Cross (with palm).

Pinckney, CSM
COMMAND SERGEANT MAJOR—ARMY

He enlisted in the United States Army in January 1977. He completed Basic Combat Training at Fort Jackson, South Carolina, and Advanced Individual Training at Fort McClellan, Alabama. His military education includes all the Noncommissioned Officer Education System Courses, the Sergeants Major Academy and the Command Sergeant Major (D) Course.

His military assignments include serving as First Sergeant for B Battery, 6th Battalion, 32nd Field Artillery at Fort Sill, Oklahoma; Chief Enlisted Advisor of Readiness Group Lee at Fort Lee, Virginia; Battalion Command Sergeant Major with the 2nd Battalion (TS) Field Artillery, 306th Regiment, at Fort Stewart, Georgia; and Fire Support Sergeant Major with V Corps Artillery in Germany. In August 2004, he was serving as Command Sergeant Major for the 41st Field Artillery Brigade in Babenhausen, Germany.

Pinckney, Alma
COMMAND SERGEANT MAJOR—ARMY

She entered the United States Army on November 17, 1981 and completed both Basic Combat Training and

Advanced Individual Training at Fort Jackson, South Carolina. Her military education includes all the Noncommissioned Officer Education System Courses; the First Sergeants Course; the Command Sergeants Major Course; and the United States Army Sergeants Major Academy. She holds a Bachelors of Arts in Political Science from the University of Mississippi and is pursing her master's degree in Human Resource Development.

Her first duty assignment was with the 1st Infantry Division at Fort Riley, Kentucky. She has served in a myriad of duty positions including Squad Leader; Platoon Sergeant; Personnel Sergeant, SIDPERS-3; Writer/Developer and 75 Series Chief; First Sergeant of Headquarters and Headquarters Detachment, 55th Personnel Services Battalion; and Sergeant Major for the Directorate of Human Resource and Adjutant General Division at Fort Jackson. In October 2004, she was serving as the Command Sergeant Major of Regional Command South, Allied Forces Southern Europe at Naples, Italy.

Pinckney, Belinda

BRIGADIER GENERAL—ARMY

She was commissioned into the United States Army on February 22, 1979, as a second Lieutenant. She holds a Bachelor of Science degree in Business Administration from the University of Maryland; a master's in Public Accounting-Finance from Golden Gate University; and a Master of Science degree in National Resources Strategy from the National Defense University. Her military education include the Finance Officer Basic and Advanced Course; United States Army Command and General Staff College; and the Industrial College of the Armed Forces.

She has served in numerous key military positions to include serving as Chief of Commercial Operations Division, later Commander of Headquarters and Headquarters Company, 266th Theater Finance Command, United States Army Europe and Seventh Army, Germany, and Program Budget Officer in the Office of the Chief of Staff Army, Washington, D.C. In June 1995, she served as Military Assistant Secretary of the Army (Financial Management and Comptroller), in Washington, D.C. In September 1996, she served as Commander of Training Support Battalion, later Director of Financial Management and Operation Department of the United States Army Soldier Support Institute of the United States Training Center at Fort Jackson, South Carolina. In June 2000, she was assigned as Commander of the 266th Finance Command, United States Army Europe and Seventh Army, Germany.

She was selected the first African American woman to be inducted in the Officer Candidate School's Hall of Fame in 2003. She begins her military career as an enlisted soldier. She entered the Army as a Private, and after two years in the Army at the rank of Specialist, she was accepted into Officer Candidate School at Fort Benning, Georgia, and was subsequently promoted to lieutenant.

She is assigned as a Congressional Appropriations Liaison Officer for the Undersecretary of Defense Comptroller, Plans and Systems Office at the Pentagon in Washington, D.C. In September 2004, the Secretary of Defense nominated her for promotion to the rank of Brigadier General. On July 3, 2005, she was selected Brigadier General and assigned as the Deputy Director of the Defense Finance and Accounting Service in Washington, D.C.

Pinson, L. Tracey

SENIOR EXECUTIVE SERVICE

Born in Washington, D.C., Pinson received a Bachelor of Science degree in Political Science from Howard University and a Law Degree from Georgetown University Law Center. She is a member in good standing of the Maryland Bar Association and the National Contract Management Association.

She participated in the Lyndon Baines Johnson Internship with the United States House of Representatives. She worked in the Congressional Office of Representative Augustus Hawkins and was responsible for constituent affairs and legislative analysis. From November 1982 to June 1986, she served as Counsel to the Committee on Small Business in the United States House of Representatives and Special Counsel to the late Representative Joseph P. Addabbo. From 1986 to 1995, she served as Assistant to the Director of the Office of Small and Disadvantaged Business Utilization in the Office of the Secretary of Defense. During this time frame she served as the program manager of the DOD Small Disadvantaged Business Program and the HBCU/MI Program. She also developed the implementation strategy for the DOD Mentor-Protégé Program resulting in over 250 participants with a budget allocation as high as $120 million.

She became the Director for Small and Disadvantaged Business Utilization in the Office of the Secretary of the Army in May 1995. Ms. Pinson advises the Secretary of the Army and the Army Staff on all small business procurement issues and is responsible for the implementation of the Federal acquisition programs designed to assist small businesses, including small disadvantaged businesses and women-owned businesses. She is responsible for the management of the Historically Black Colleges and Universities and Minority Institutions Program, and develops policies and initiatives to enhance their participation in Army-funded programs.

Piper, Terry W.

COMMAND MASTER CHIEF—NAVY

He was born in Lake Charles, Louisiana, and is a 1982 graduate of Deridder High School, in Deridder, Louisiana. After briefly attending Northwestern State University on a track scholarship, he enlisted in the United States Navy in March 1984. He attended Basic Training in Great Lakes, Illinois, where he completed Gunner's Mate Class "A" School. He has a certification as an Electronic Mechanic through the United States Department of Labor and an associate's degree in General Studies from Central Texas College.

His key military assignments include serving as a member of the caretaker crew for USS *Cole* (DDG 67) after the terrorist attack in Aden, Yemen; as a Navy Recruiter at Navy Recruiting District, Miami, Florida; and as a Vertical Launching System Advanced Technician (VAT) at Naval Sea Systems Command at Port Hueneme, California. In October 2004, he was assigned as the Command Master Chief onboard USS *Howard* (DDG 83).

Pittard, Dana J.H.

BRIGADIER GENERAL—ARMY

Colonel Dana J.H. Pittard graduated from the United States Army Military Academy at West Point, New York, and received his commission as an Armor Officer in May 1981. He holds a master's degree in Military Arts and Sciences from the School of Advanced Military Studies (SAMS) at Fort Leavenworth, Kansas, and was a National Security Fellow at the John F. Kennedy School of Government at Howard University.

His military education includes the Basic Armor Officer Course and the Advanced Infantry Officers Course; the Service Staff School; Combined Arms Course; and Command and General Staff College.

In April 1990, he was assigned as Commander of Delta Company, 1-37th Armor, United States Army in Europe's Canadian Army Trophy (CAT) competition unit. Prior to the competition, the Company deployed to the Middle East, where he led his unit in combat operations against Iraq during Operations Desert Shield/Desert Storm. From November 1996 to January 1999, he served as a Military Aide to President Bill Clinton, who promoted him to Lieutenant Colonel in the Oval Office. In June 1999, he assumed Command of the 1-32nd Armor 11-14th Cavalry at Fort Lewis, Washington. In July 2001, he was selected to serve as the Commander of the 3rd Brigade, 1st Infantry Division. In 2003, he was serving as the Deputy Commander for Maneuvers for Multi-National Brigade (East) in Kosovo. He was frocked Brigadier General in June 2006.

Plummer, Henry V.

CAPTAIN—ARMY

He was born a slave in Prince George's County, Maryland, in 1844. He joined the United States Navy in 1864, during the Civil War, serving as a sailor aboard the USS *Coeur de Lion*.

Upon leaving the Navy at the end of the War, he taught himself to read and write, and attended the Wayland Seminary, where he became a Baptist Minister. He served as Pastor of several churches in the District of Columbia before accepting a commission as an Army Chaplain in 1884.

He served with the 9th Cavalry Regiment, the famous Buffalo Soldiers, as a Chaplin for 10 years before he was dismissed from the service in 1894 after facing a court-martial on the grounds of conduct unbecoming an officer. A dismissal for an officer is the equivalent of a dishonorable discharge for an enlisted soldier.

Plummer had joined the Regiment's Sergeant Major and two other Noncommissioned Officers to celebrate a sergeant's promotion. The Noncommissioned Officers toasted the promotion with alcohol and Plummer had an altercation with a Noncommissioned Officer.

In the resulting court-martial, all witnesses agreed that Plummer had consumed alcohol with enlisted troopers and had provided enlisted troopers with alcohol, and had cursed in front of one man's children and wife. All activities were considered offenses as conduct unbecoming an Officer under the Articles of War in use at the time, and President Grover Cleveland approved his dismissal in November 1894.

On February 10, 2005, the Army Board for the Correction of Military Records reviewed the case. While it did not overturn the court martial, it concluded that racism extant at the time contributed to his treatment and the characterization of his service that led to the dismissal. The Board determined Plummer deserved an Honorable Discharge to restore equity. The Army redressed a wrong and issued an Honorable Discharge to the first African American to be commissioned a Chaplin in the Army. Major General David H. Hicks, United States Army Chief of Chaplains, said it was time the Army corrected its errors.

Poe, Larry L.

REAR ADMIRAL—NAVY

He was born in Rowan County, North Carolina. He and his wife Barbara have two children, a daughter Kristin and a son, Larry Jr. He received a bachelor's degree in Zoology from the University of North Carolina at Chapel Hill and a master's degree in Public Administration from the University of Southern California. He is a 1989 graduate of the United States Naval

War College (College of Naval Warfare) where he received a master's degree in National Security and Strategic Studies. He was commissioned as an Intelligence Officer (1635) in 1967 after completion of Aviation Officer Candidate School at Pensacola, Florida. From August 1967 to May 1968, he served as Air Intelligence Office (AIO). From May 1968 to May 1970, he was assigned as a Photo Interpretation Officer (PIO) for Heavy Photographic Squadron 61 (VAP-61) while deployed to Southeast Asia (Vietnam, South Korea, and Thailand). His last active duty assignment from June 1970 to June 1972 was with the Defense Intelligence Agency's National Photographic Interpretation Center as a Soviet Naval Analyst. Following his release from active duty in 1972, Rear Admiral (Sel) Poe was assigned to Light Photographic Squadron 306 (VFP-306) as the AIO/PIO. During his twenty-three year affiliation with the Naval Reserve Intelligence Program, Rear Admiral (Sel) Poe served in many leadership positions. From October 1, 1987, to September 30, 1989, he was Naval Reserve OSD Technology Transfer O166 at the Naval Air Facility in Washington, D.C.; from October 1, 1989, to September 30, 1990, he served as the Deputy Reserve Intelligence Area Commander (DRIAC) for Training and Readiness, Naval Reserve Volunteer Training, Intelligence Unit 0106, Washington, D.C.; from October 1, 1990, to September 30, 1991, he was assigned as Commanding Officer at Naval Reserve Operational Intelligence Center 0566, Naval Air Facility, Washington, D.C.; from October 1, 1991, to September 1, 1993, he served as Deputy Chief of Staff for Intelligence and Mutual Support for COMNAVRESINTCOM at the Naval Reserve Intelligence Command at Dallas, Texas. In October, 1993, Rear Admiral Poe served as the Reserve Intelligence Area Commander at Area Nineteen, a command of over nine hundred drilling reservists who support national-level Navy and Joint Commands in the Washington area. In 1996, he assumed command of the Naval Reserve Intelligence Command in Washington, D.C., with over 4,000 reservists national-wide. In his civilian occupation, Rear Admiral (Sel) Poe is a member of the Central Intelligence Agency (Senior Intelligence Service) and currently serves as CIA's Senior Representative to the Office of the Secretary of Defense. His military awards and decorations include the Meritorious Service Medal; Joint Service Commendation Medal; Navy Commendation Medal; the Armed Forces Expeditionary Medal; and the Armed Forces Reserve Medal.

Pope-Dixon, Tracy A.
MASTER SERGEANT—ARMY

She is a native of Pennsylvania and entered the United States Army in February 1983. She completed her Advanced Individual Training as a Material Control and Accounting Specialist at Fort Lee, Virginia.

Her military and civilian education includes all the Noncommissioned Officers Education System Courses; the Standard Army Retail Supply System Objective Course; Hazardous Materials and Waste Management Course; Military Operations in Urbanized Terrain Course; Standard Army Intermediate Level Supply Course; and the Support Operations Phases I & II. She graduated from the University of Maryland with an associate's degree and earned a Bachelor of Science degree in Business Administration from the same University.

She has held a variety of military leadership positions including serving as Squad Leader in the 263rd Maintenance Company at Stuttgart, Germany/Fort Hood, Texas; Section Sergeant in the 4th CORPS Materiel Management Center at Fort Hood; Platoon Sergeant and Class III (P) Warehouse Non-Commissioned Officer in Charge of the 123rd Main Support Battalion at Anderson Barracks, Dexheim, Germany; Sergeant of the Guard, Theater Troop Issue Subsistence Activity Non-Commissioned Officer in Charge, and Clothing Exchange Supervisor of the 123rd Main Support Battalion (Forward); Detachment Non-Commissioned Officer in Charge of the 123rd Main Support Battalion (Rear); Senior Enlisted Authorized Stockage List Manager for the 10th Division Support Division (Forward) at Fort Drum, New York; Logistics Manager for the Headquarters of the 10th Mountain Division (Forward) at Fort Drum; Platoon Sergeant and Interim First Sergeant of Alpha Company, 710th Main Support Battalion at Fort Drum; Support Operations Non-Commissioned Officer in Charge of the 20th Area Support Group at Camp Hialeah in Busan, Korea.

Porter, Terry J.
COMMAND SERGEANT MAJOR—ARMY

Command Sergeant Major Terry J. Porter entered the military service on June 7, 1973, and attended Basic Training at Fort Jackson, South Carolina, and Advanced Individual Training at Fort Sam Houston, Texas. His military education includes the Master Fitness Course; Battle Staff Course; the First Sergeant Course; and the United States Army Sergeants Major Academy.

He was assigned as the First Sergeant with Head-quarters and Headquarters Company, 2nd Battalion, 41st Infantry Regiment, 2nd Armored Division at Fort Hood, Texas; as First Sergeant of Foxtrot Company, 27th Main Support Company, Division Support Command, with the 1st Cavalry Division at Fort Hood; as First Sergeant of Headquarters and Support Company, 61st Area Support Medical Battalion, 1st Medical Group, 13th COSCOM at Fort Hood; as Command Sergeant Major of the 52nd Medical Evacuation Battalion, 18th Medical Command, in South Korea; as Command Sergeant Major for the 21st Combat Support Hospital, 1st Medical Brigade, 13th COSCOM, at Fort Hood; and as the Command Sergeant Major, Task Force MED Eagle SFOR 6, Operation Joint Forge in Bosnia and Herzegovina. He is currently assigned as the Command Sergeant Major of the William Beaumont Army Medical Center at Fort Bliss, Texas.

Powell, Clive A.

MASTER CHIEF PETTY OFFICER—NAVY

He was born in Hanover, Jamaica. At age 13, his family moved to America, settling in the South Bronx of New York City. He graduated from high school and attended a technical college while working part-time at a grocery store. In November 1976, he enlisted in the United States Navy, and in January 1977 headed off to Boot Camp.

While serving as the Master Chief in charge of the Aircraft Carrier *Essex*'s Food Services, the ship won two Captain Edward F. Ney Memorial Awards for food-service excellence and the distinction of being named "Best Mess in the Pacific" three years in a row.

He was selected to serve as the Master Chief at the White House, providing worldwide food service, security and personal support to the President and first family. Under his command, the White House Mess won the prestigious Five-Star Diamond Award from the American Academy of Hospitality Sciences. The White House Mess has won the award for the second time under Chief Powell's command, the first time being in 2003. The White House Mess is the only military-run mess to ever win the award.

Powell, Colin Luther

GENERAL—ARMY

Born in New York City, he married the former Alma Vivian Johnson, and they have three children, Michael, Linda and Annemarie. Around 1940 the family, which Powell recalls as having been "strong and close," moved to the South Bronx, where he was graduated from Morris High School in 1954. At the City College of New York he majored in Geology and got his first taste of military life as a cadet in the ROTC. He has explained that he enrolled in ROTC because as an ambitious young black man in the 1950s, he had learned to take advantage of what few attractive opportunities existed and found his temperament well suited to military discipline. Former classmates remember that he displayed rare leadership ability on campus, motivating many other students to succeed. General Powell was appointed Commander of the Pershing Rifles, the ROTC class of 1958, with the rank of Cadet Colonel. As one of the more than 16,000 American military advisers sent to South Vietnam by President John F. Kennedy, Powell was assigned from October 1962 to January 1963 as South Vietnam Self Defense Corps Training Center Advisor, 2nd Infantry Division, I Corps, Military Assistance Advisory Group. From January 1963 to November 1963, he served a Senior Battalion Advisor, Unit

Advisory Branch, and later Assistant G-3 (Operations) Advisor, 1st Infantry Division, Army of the Republic of Viet Nam Military Assistance Advisory Group. While marching through a rice paddy one day in 1963, he stepped into a punji-stick trap, impaling his foot on one of the sharpened stakes concealed just below the water's surface. He was given a Purple Heart, and in that same year he was awarded the Bronze Star. In 1968, Powell returned for a second Vietnam tour of duty with Infantry as a Battalion Executive Officer and Division Operation Officer. He was injured a second time in a helicopter crash landing. In 1971, he earned a Master of Business Administration degree from George Washington University. In 1972, he was selected to be a White House Fellow and served his fellowship year as Special Assistant to the Deputy Director in the Office of the President. In 1973, he assumed Command of the 1st Battalion, 32nd Infantry, in South Korea. Upon completion of the National War College in 1976, he assumed Command of the 2nd Brigade, 101st Airborne Division (Air Assault) at Fort Campbell, Kentucky. In 1977, General Powell went to Washington to serve in the Office of the Secretary of Defense. Over the next three years, he served as Senior Military Assistant to the Secretary of Energy. In 1981, he became the Assistant Division Commander for Operations and Training of the 4th Infantry Division (Mechanized) at Fort Carson, Colorado. In 1983, he returned to Washington to serve as Senior Military Assistant to Secretary of Defense Caspar Weinberger. In July 1986, he assumed Command of the V United States Army Corps in Frankfurt, Germany. In January 1987, Powell returned to the White House to serve as Deputy Assistant to National Security Adviser Frank Carlucci. A military man at heart, he had to be persuaded to accept the job by his Commander in Chief, President Reagan. After the Iran-Contra scandal, Powell distinguished himself by reorganizing the National Security Council according to the recommendations of the Tower Commission. He also proved invaluable as the Chairman of the interagency review group that coordinated the activities of the CIA, the State Department, the Defense Department, and other agencies. When Carlucci took over as Secretary of Defense in 1989, Powell became Assistant to President Reagan on National Affairs (Military Matters), the first black to hold this position. In April 1989, General Powell assumed command of the United States Army Forces Command (FORSCOM), which directs operations and training for all Active and Reserve troop units in the continental United States as well as all Army National Guard units in the 48 continental states, Alaska, Puerto Rico, and the Virgin Islands. Powell became the first black general to command FORCOM, his first four-star assignment. (The FORSCOM functions as the Army component of the Atlantic Command, responsible for command and control of assigned forces in the Atlantic-Caribbean area.) In August 1989, he was nominated as Chairman of the Joint Chiefs, the first black general nominated for the top post in the armed forces, passing over 30 other four star generals,

most of them more senior. In October 1989, General Powell was confirmed by the United States Senate as Chairman of the Joint Chiefs of Staff. The Chairman of the Joint Chiefs serves as the principal military adviser to the President; the National Security Council; and the Secretary of Defense, and as a member of the Pentagon Executive Committee established by Defense Secretary Dick Cheney. Since taking over this post, he has been more willing to use military force than any of his predecessors since the 1960s. Other Joint Chiefs chairmen, fearing another Vietnam-type disaster, have been reluctant to commit United States troops. But General Powell tells the President: "if you want to use force, we can do it." His military career was impressive by its content and the unprecedented rise he made to the Chairman of the Joint Chiefs of Staff. Being the nation's senior military leader was an accomplishment distinguished by its very importance and influence. General Powell was selected as the recipient of the NAACP's 1991 Spingarn Award, the highest honor bestowed by the nation's oldest and largest civil rights organization. The announcement of his selection was made by Dr. Benjamin L. Hooks, the NAACP executive director. His military awards and decorations include the Defense Distinguished Service Medal, Legion of Merit (with oak leaf cluster), Soldier's Medal, Bronze Star, Air Medal, Joint Service Commendation Medal, Army Commendation Medal, Expert Infantryman Badge, Combat Infantryman Badge, Parachutist Badge, Pathfinder Badge, Ranger Tab, Presidential Service Badge, Secretary of Defense Identification Badge, Army Staff Identification Badge, and Joint Chiefs of Staff Identification Badge.

Powell, Elliott, Jr.
CAPTAIN—NAVY

He was born in February 1956 in Wiesbaden, Germany. A 1974 graduate of General H.H. Arnold High School, he was commissioned an Ensign through North Carolina Central's Naval ROTC program in 1978. He holds a Bachelor of Arts degree in Political Science from North Carolina Central University and a Master of Arts degree in National Security Affairs from the Naval Postgraduate School, and is a 1993 graduate of the National War College.

He has held numerous key assignments including serving in May 1991 as the Commander of the USS Leader (MSO 490) and participated in mine clearance operations in the Persian Gulf. Following his return to the United States, he took Command of the USS Exultant (MSO 441) in September 1991. He was assigned to OPNAV Staff as the Tomahawk Requirements Officer, prior to taking Command of USS Robert G. Bradley (FFG 49) in August 1994. During this tour, USS Robert G. Bradley participated in Operation Sharpguard, the United Nations embargo of the former Yugoslavia, and was selected to be the First American Warship to visit the nation of Slovenia. At the conclusion of his tour, he was assigned to the Commander of the Second Fleet as the Operations Officer in May 1996. Following his tour with Second Fleet, he was assigned to the Joint Staff, Deputy Director International Negotiations, J5, as an Action Officer in the Conventional Arms Control Division from April 1998 until May 1999. In May 1999, he served on the Staff of the National Security Council as the Director of the White House Situation Room, Systems and Technical Planning Directorate until June 2001. In November 2004, he was assigned to the Navy International Programs Office as the Director of the Security Assistance Directorate.

Powell, William E., Jr.
REAR ADMIRAL—NAVY

He was born in Indianapolis, Indiana, and married Loretta Braxton Mitchell of Norfolk, Virginia. They have two sons, William Clinton Powell III and David Anthony Powell. He received a Bachelor of Science (naval science) degree from the United States Naval Academy in 1959 and a Master of Business Administration from George Washington University in 1969. Powell's first duty after Supply Corps School in Athens, Georgia, was as the Supply Officer aboard the USS *Nicholas* (DDE 449). In 1962, he was assigned as the Planning Officer at the Naval Air Station at Point Mugu, California. This assignment was followed by two years at the Naval Supply Depot at Subic Bay, Philippines, where he obtained experience in inventory management and assisted in special support projects in Vietnam. From July 1966 until 1968, Powell served as Ship Design and Fleet Support Coordinator for the Naval Supply Systems Command in Washington, D.C. In May 1969, he was assigned as the Financial Management and Planning Officer for the Staff Commander of Cruiser-Destroyer Force Atlantic. Reporting to USS *Intrepid* CV 11 in August 1971, Powell assumed

duties as the Supply Officer and participated in deployments to northern Europe and the Mediterranean. In April 1974, he reported to the Aviation Supply Office and was initially assigned as Industrial Support Officer, later as Stock Control Branch head for power plants. Powell attended the Industrial College of the Armed Forces in 1977, and upon completion in 1978 he reported to the Naval Supply Center at Oakland, California, as Director of the Planning Department. In July 1980, he returned to Washington, D.C., and served as the Assistant for Supply Policy to the Director of the Aviation Programs Division in the Office of the Chief of Naval Operations. From 1982 through 1984, he served as Commanding Officer of Naval Supply Depot, Subic. He was then assigned to Naval Supply Systems Command as Director of Supply Corps Personnel, until May 24, 1985, when he assumed command of the Naval Supply Center at Norfolk, Virginia.

Rear Admiral Powell was promoted to Rear Admiral on October 17, 1985. He retired on November 1, 1988.

His military awards and decorations include the Legion of Merit, Meritorious Service Medal with Gold Star, Navy Commendation Medal with Gold Star, the Armed Forces Expeditionary Medal, and National Defense Service Medal with one Bronze Star.

Powell-Mims, Janie Mae
COMMANDER—NAVY

She earned a Master of Arts degree in Business Administration from Webster University in Corpus Christi, Texas, in 1992. She earned a Bachelor of Science in Business Administration from Mississippi Valley State University in Itta Bena, Mississippi, in 1990. Her professional military education includes the Command and General Staff College at Fort Leavenworth,

Kansas, graduating in 2003, and the Joint Forces Staff College in Norfolk, Virginia, graduating also in 2003.

She entered the United States Navy in November 1990 through Officer Candidate School in Newport, Rhode Island. Her first duty assignment took her to Naval Air Station Corpus Christi, Texas, where she served as Public Affairs Officer/Administrative Officer from December 1990 through December 1993. In January 1994, she became the Administrative, Military Standards, Training Support and Administration Schools Officer at the Naval Technical Training Center in Meridian, Mississippi. She served in that position until January 1998 when she became Officer-in-Charge of the Naval Air Facility at Misawa, Japan, until January 2000. She then moved on to Pensacola, Florida, where she served as Aviation Machinist Mate Schools and Statistical Officer at the Naval Air Technical Training Center from January 2000 through June 2002. In November 2004 she was serving as the Commander of the Amarillo Military Entrance Processing Station in Amarillo, Texas.

Powers, Winston Donald
LIEUTENANT GENERAL—AIR FORCE

He was born in New York City and married the former Jeanette Wyche. They have two children, Diane and David. He received a Bachelor of Arts degree from McKendree College in Lebanon, Illinois, in 1961. He also attended graduate school at the George Washington University in Washington, D.C., and completed the Industrial College of the Armed Forces at Fort Lesley J. McNair in Washington, D.C. He began his military career by enlisting in the United States Air Force in November 1950. After basic training he was assigned to the Air Defense Command at Hancock Field Base,

Texas, in September 1952 and graduated the following year. He then had combat crew training at Randolph Air Force Base in Texas and upon completion was assigned as a navigator instructor at Ellington Air Force Base in August 1953. In May 1957 he entered the Tactical Communications Officer Training School at Scott Air Force Base, Illinois. After graduation in June 1958, he was assigned as Commander of Detachment 2, 6123rd Air Control and Warning Squadron at Cheju-Do Auxiliary Airfield, South Korea. He returned to Scott Air Force Base in June 1959 for duty with the 1918th Communication Squadron. From August 1961 to July 1963, Powers was assigned to the Air Force Command Post at the Pentagon as a Communications Officer. He was then selected to attend the communications system-engineering program of American Telephone and Telegraph Company in New York. In August 1964, he completed the education-with-industry program and became a communications engineer for the Defense Communications Agency— United Kingdom at Royal Air Force Station Croughton, England. Powers transferred to the Tactical Communications Area at Langley Air Force Base, Virginia, in August 1967 as Director of Tactical Communications Operations and then as Director of Fixed Communications Operations. He returned to a flying assignment in July 1970, with the 460th Reconnaissance Wing at Tan Son Nhut Air Base, South Vietnam, flying 75 combat missions in EC-47s. From July 1971 to October 1973, he was assigned to the Organization of the Joint Chiefs of Staff as the Air Force member of the Plans and Policy Division, J-6. General Powers then moved to the Headquarters of the United States Air Force, Washington, D.C., as Special Assistant for joint matters in the Directorate of Command, Control, and Communications in the Office of the Deputy Chief of Staff for Programs and Resources. When he returned to South Korea in February 1974, he served as Commander of the 2146th Communications Group and Director of Communications-Electronics for the 314th Air Division at Osan Air Base. Upon his return to the United States in November 1974, he was again assigned to Air Force headquarters as Chief of the Plans and Programs Division in the Directorate of Command, Control, and Communications, where he also served as Chairman, Command, Control, and Communications Panel, and later as a member of the Program Review Committee of the Air Staff Board. The general became Deputy Director of Telecommunications and Command and Control Resources in the Office of the Assistant Chief of Staff for Communications and Computer Resources at Air Force Headquarters in September 1975; he became Director in June 1978. In July 1978, he was appointed Deputy Director of Command, Control, and Communications at the Headquarters of the United States Air Force. He transferred to Peterson Air Force Base, Colorado, in October 1978 and served initially as the Deputy Chief of Staff for Communications, Electronics, and Computer Resources of North American Aerospace Defense Command. He became Chief of the

Systems Integration Office at the Headquarters of the Aerospace Defense Center in January 1981, and took command of the Space Communications Division at Peterson Air Force Base in January 1983. He was assigned as Director of the Defense Communications Agency in Washington, D.C., in September 1983. He was appointed Lieutenant General on October 1, 1983. General Powers is a Master Navigator with more than 4,000 flying hours. His military decorations and awards include the Distinguished Service Medal; Legion of Merit; Meritorious Service Medal (with two oak leaf clusters); Air Medal (with oak leaf cluster); Air Force Commendation Medal; Presidential Unit Citation Emblem; and Air Force Outstanding Unit Award Ribbon (with "V" device).

Prado, John J.

SERGEANT MAJOR—MARINES

He enlisted in the Marine Corps in December 1976. After completion of Basic Training and receiving MOS 2512, Private First Class Prado was transferred to A Company, 1/10th at Camp Lejeune, North Carolina. He graduated fro Marine Security Guard School at Quantico, Virginia.

He has served in a variety of key leadership positions to include serving as a Drill Instructor; Senior Drill Instructor; Communications Chief; Company Gunnery Sergeant; and First Sergeant. In April 1996, he was promoted to Sergeant Major assigned to VMFA-212 at Miramar in San Diego, California; in May 2000, he reported for duty as Sergeant Major of MALS-12, MCAS, in Iwakuni, Japan; in November 2000, he was transferred to Marine Air Control Group-18 in Okinawa, Japan; and in June 2003, he assumed the duties as the Sergeant Major of the 1st Marine Aircraft Wing in Okinawa, Japan.

Prather, Thomas Levi, Jr.

MAJOR GENERAL—ARMY

He was born in Washington, D.C. He married the former Beulah Sullivan. They have three children, Delia, Marcia and Thomas III. He is a native of Gaithersburg, Maryland; and received his commission and a Bachelor of Science degree upon graduation from Morgan State University in Baltimore, Maryland, in 1962. He also holds a Master of Science degree in Contracting and Procurement from the Florida Institute of Technology. His military education includes completion of the Ordnance Officer Basic Course, the Armor Officer Basic Course, the Ordnance Officer Advanced Course, the United States Army Command and General Staff College, and the Army War College. He received an ROTC commission as Second Lieutenant on July 19, 1962. From October 1962 to May 1964, he was assigned as a Platoon Leader in the Service, Supply, and Recovery Platoon of the 546th Ordnance Company, and later as Ordnance Supply Officer of the 84th Ordnance Battalion, United States Army, Europe. He was promoted to First Lieutenant on January 19, 1964. From May 1964 to August 1965, he was assigned as an Ordnance Supply Officer with the 66th Ordnance Battalion in Europe. From August 1965 to October 1965, he was a student in the Armor Officer Basic Course at the United States Army Armor School at Fort Knox, Kentucky. From October 1965 to April 1966, he served as the Executive Officer of Headquarters Company, 1st Battalion, 66th Armor, 2nd Armored Division at Fort Hood, Texas. He was promoted to Captain on April 1, 1966. From April 1966 to May 1967, he served as the Commander, Battalion Maintenance Officer, S-4 (Logistics), Headquarters Company, 1st Battalion, 66th

Armor, 2nd Armored Division at Fort Hood. From June 1967 to September 1968, he was a student in the Ordnance Officer Advanced Course at the United States Ordnance School at Aberdeen Proving Ground, Maryland. He was promoted to Major on May 23, 1969. From September 1969 to July 1970, he was assigned as Chief of the Consolidated Equipment Maintenance Division in the Mobility Training Department of the School Brigade at the United States Army Ordnance School at Aberdeen Proving Ground. From July 1970 to June 1971, he was a student in the United States Army Command and General Staff College at Fort Leavenworth, Kansas. From June 1971 to August 1973, he served as a Personnel Management Officer in the Assignment Section of the Ordnance Branch of the Officer Personnel Management Directorate at the United States Army Military Personnel Center in Alexandria, Virginia. From September 1973 to September 1974, he was a student at the Florida Institute of Technology at Melbourne, Florida. From September 1974 to June 1975, he served as a Project Officer in the Industrial Planning Branch of the Industrial Management Division of United States Army Materiel Command in Alexandria. From June 1975 to June 1977, Prather was assigned as a Military Assistant to the Office of the Assistant Secretary of the Army (Installations and Logistics) in Washington, D.C. From June 1977 to January 1979, he was Commander of the Division Materiel Management Center, 8th Infantry Division, United States Army, Europe. He was promoted to Lieutenant Colonel on July 11, 1977. From August 1981 to June 1982, he was a student at the United States Army War College in Carlisle Barracks, Pennsylvania. From July 1982 to December 1984, he was assigned as Director of the Materiel Management Directorate in the United States Army Communications-Electronics Command at Fort Monmouth, New Jersey. He was promoted to Colonel on August 1, 1983. From December 1984 to July 1987, he was Commander of Tobyhanna Army Depot, Depot Systems Command, United States Army Materiel Command in Tobyhanna, Pennsylvania. From July 1987 to July 1989, he served as Deputy Commander of the 2nd Support Command, VII Corps, United States Army, Europe, and Seventh Army. From July 1989 to August 1990, he was assigned as Deputy Commanding General of the United States Army Armament, Munitions and Chemical Command at Rock Island, Illinois. He was promoted to Brigadier General on September 2, 1989. In August 1990 he was selected Commanding General of United States Army Troop Support Command at St. Louis, Missouri. On August 1, 1992, he was promoted to Major General and he served as the Military Assistant to the Assistant Secretary of the Army (Installations and Logistics) in Washington, D.C. He retired from the military on July 31, 1995. His military awards and decorations include the Defense Superior Service Medal; the Legion of Merit; the Bronze Star; the Meritorious Service Medal (with three oak leaf clusters); the Army Commendation Medal (with two oak leaf clusters); and the Army Staff Identification Badge.

Praymous, Vernon R.
COMMAND SERGEANT MAJOR—ARMY

A native of Melbourne, Florida, he enlisted in the Army in December 1983 and attended Basic Combat Training at Fort Jackson, South Carolina, and Advanced Individual Training at Fort Gordon, Georgia.

His military education includes all the Noncommissioned Officer Education System Courses; Battle Staff Course; First Sergeants Course; and the United States Army Sergeants Major Academy (class 52). He also holds a bachelor's degree in Data Communications.

His military assignments include serving with the 67th Signal Battalion; 304th Signal Battalion; 16th ATC; 59th Ordinance; 97th Signal Battalion; 2/46th Infantry; 1114th Signal Battalion; 57th Signal Battalion; HHC 50th Signal Battalion; and 82nd Signal Battalion. In August 2004, he was serving as the Command Sergeant Major for the 57th Signal Battalion, 3rd Signal Brigade.

Prescod, Wayne
COMMAND MASTER CHIEF—NAVY

He was born and raised in Bridgetown, Barbados. He is a graduate of St. Leonard's Boys School. In December 1976, he enlisted into the United States Navy and in November 1977 he attended Recruit Training at Recruit Training Center Great Lakes, Illinois. He attended Fundamental Familiarization Course at Naval Training Center Great Lakes. After completion of school, he reported to Naval Air Facility Sigonella, Sicily.

His leadership assignments include serving with Helicopter Anti-Submarine Squadron Light Four Two in November 1990, where he was assigned duties as Quality Assurance Supervisor and Maintenance Control Chief. In December 1993, he transferred to Sea Duty

with Helicopter Anti-Submarine Light Four Two and deployed on board USS *Klakring* (FF 42), and in January 1996, he was assigned as Commander of Senior Helicopter Anti-Submarine Light Four Two. He reported for duty on the Staff of the Commander of Helicopter Wing Atlantic Fleet in July 1997. In April 1998, he was promoted to Master Chief Petty Officer and assumed the duties of CHSLWL Maintenance Master Chief. In 2000, he was selected for the Command Master Chief Program and attended the Senior Enlisted Academy in Newport, Rhode Island, in May 2001. He reported to Helicopter Anti-Submarine Naval Air Station Jacksonville, Florida, in July 2001, deploying on board USS *Kennedy* (CV 67) and USS *George Washington* (CVN 73). In February 2005, he was serving as the Command Master Chief at Naval Air Station Oceana.

Pretlow, Norman, Jr.

COMMAND MASTER CHIEF—NAVY

He was born in Baltimore, Maryland. He entered the Navy in June 1982 and completed Recruit Training in Great Lakes, Illinois.

He attended Instructor Training, Recruit Company Commander and Recruit Division Commander "C" Schools. He is a graduate of the Navy Senior Enlisted Academy (class of 1990).

His assignments include serving aboard USS *Durham* (LKA 114); USS *Cape Cod* (AD 43); USS *Cleveland* (LPD 7); USS *Kinkaid* (DD 965) and USS *Decatur* (DDG 73) where he assumed his first Command Master Chief assignment. He has also served at Recruit Training Command San Diego, California, as a Recruit Company Commander; and Recruit Training Command, at Great Lakes, Illinois where he served the Recruit Division Commander "C" School Director and subsequently became the Recruit Training Command,

Great Lakes Seventh Fleet Master Chief where he was responsible for over 5000 recruit and 180 Recruit Division Commanders. He also served as the Command Master Chief for the Commander of Helicopter Anti-Submarine Wing, United States Pacific Fleet. In March 2005, he was serving as Command Master Chief for USS *Pearl Harbor* (LSD 52).

Prettyman-Beck, Yvonne J.

COLONEL—ARMY

She was commissioned upon graduation from New Mexico Military Institute in 1979 and is a 1981 graduate of Angelo State University at San Angelo, Texas. She holds a Bachelor of Science degree in Biology; a Master of Science degree in Management Science, and a Master of Science degree in National Security and Strategic Studies. Her military education includes the Engineer Basic and Advanced Courses; the Combined Arms School; Services Staff School; the Command and General Staff College; and the National War College.

Her assignments include serving as Commander of the 84th Engineer Combat Battalion (Heavy) at Schofield Barracks, Hawaii; at the Headquarters of the Department of the Army Secretary for Joint Affairs at the Pentagon; as Secretary of the General Staff and Facilities Engineer for 13th Corps Support Command, and Battalion Operations Officer of the 62nd Engineer Combat Battalion (Heavy) at Fort Hood, Texas; as Executive Officer of the Office Distribution Division at the United States Army Personnel Command at Alexandria, Virginia; as Plans and Operations Officer at the Defense Nuclear Agency at Alexandria; as Company Commander and Battalion Adjutant, 249th Engineer Combat Battalion (Heavy), and Brigade Intelligence Officer, 18th Engineer Brigade at Karlsruhe, Germany; as Executive Officer and Platoon Leader, HHC, 30th

Engineer Topographic Battalion at Fort Belvoir, Virginia; and as Test Officer for Training and Doctrine Combined Arms Test Activity at Fort Hood. Her most recent assignment was Operations Officer in the Joint Operations Directorate of the Joint Staff at the Pentagon.

Since August 4, 2003, she has served as the Commander of the Norfolk District Engineers, overseeing the Corps water resources development and the operation of navigable waterways for four river basins in the Commonwealth of Virginia. She is also responsible for the Corps military design and construction projects for Army, Army Reserve and Air Force Installations throughout Virginia.

Price, George Baker
BRIGADIER GENERAL—ARMY

Born in Laurel, Mississippi, he married the former Georgianna Hunter, and they have two children, Katherine James and William Robert. He received a Bachelor of Science degree in Physical Education from South Carolina State College in 1951, and a Master of Science degree in College Counseling from Shippensburg State College. He was commissioned a Second Lieutenant on June 16, 1951, and served as a platoon leader. He was promoted to First Lieutenant on March 18, 1953, and to Captain on December 17, 1956. He has held a wide variety of important command and staff positions including serving as Operations Officer from 1957 to 1961; Personnel Manager from 1961 to 1962, and Adviser with the 1st Vietnamese Infantry Division from 1964 to 1965. He was promoted to Major on November 14, 1962, and to Lieutenant Colonel on September 14, 1966. He returned to the United States and was assigned as a Staff Officer with the Department of the Army in Washington, D.C., from February 1966

to June 1968. From June 1968 to January 1970, he served as Commander of the 4th Battalion (Mechanized), 20th Infantry, 193rd Infantry Brigade at Fort Clayton in the Panama Canal Zone. From January 1970 to June 1970, he was assigned as Deputy Chief of Staff of United States Southern Command at Fort Amador, Canal Zone. From July 1970 to June 1971, he was a student at the United States Army War College at Carlisle Barracks, Pennsylvania. From July 1971 to November 1971, he was a student at Shippensburg State College, Pennsylvania. He was promoted to Colonel on March 8, 1972. From December 1971 to June 1973, he served as the Commander of the 3rd Brigade, 3rd Infantry Division with the United States Army in Europe and Community Commander at Aschaffenburg, West Germany. From June 1973 to June 1974, he was assigned as Chief of Staff of the 8th Infantry Division (Mechanized), United States Army, Europe. From July 1974 to July 1976, General Price served as Assistant Division Commander with the 1st Armored Division, United States Army in Europe. He was promoted to Brigadier General on September 1, 1974. From August 1976 to October 1, 1978, he was assigned as Chief of Staff of the First United States Army at Fort George G. Meade, Maryland. The General retired October 1, 1978. His military awards and decorations included the Legion of Merit; Bronze Star; Purple Heart; Meritorious Service Medal; Army Commendation Medal; Infantryman Badge; Airborne Ranger Tab; and Parachutist Badge.

Pringle, Cedric E.
COMMANDER—NAVY

He earned his Bachelor of Science degree from the University of South Carolina in December 1986, which was followed by his commissioning in January 1987. He attended Naval Postgraduate School in Monterey, California, graduating in December 1998 with a Master of Science degree in Financial Management. While at Naval Postgraduate School, he completed an advanced study of the Smart Gator Concept that is currently in use on USS *Rushmore* (LSD 47) and published *Smart Gator, an Analysis of Reduced Manning on the Mission Readiness of United States Naval Amphibious Ships*. He earned a Master of Arts degree in National Security Strategy and Decision Making from the Naval War College in Newport, Rhode Island, in November 2002.

He began his Navy career at Surface Warfare Officers School in Coronado, California, after which he reported to USS *Ranger* (CV 61) where he earned qualification as Engineering Officer of the Watch and Surface Warfare Officer. After completing his initial sea tour, he was assigned to Navy Recruiting Area Three in Macon, Georgia, as Area Minority Recruiting Officer and Officer Programs Manager; he also served as the Executive Officer of USS *Fort McHenry* (LSD 43) which was home ported in Sasebo, Japan, followed by a tour as Chief Staff Officer for the Commander of Amphibious Squadron Four embarked on USS *Wasp*

(LHD-1). He assumed command of USS *Whidbey Island* (LSD 41) on July 19, 2004, while the ship was deployed in support of Operation Iraqi Freedom.

Pringle, Randy A.
MASTER CHIEF PETTY OFFICER—NAVY

He is a native of Charleston, South Carolina. He attended recruit training at Recruit Training Center, Orlando, Florida, from August to October 1983. After boot camp, he attended Hospital Corps "A" School at the Naval School of Health Sciences in San Diego, California.

Upon completion of Navy Hospital Corps School in San Diego, he reported to Naval Hospital Portsmouth, Virginia, where he served in a number of roles until his transfer in December of 1984 to Physical Therapy Technician "C" at Fort Sam Houston, Texas. In June of 1985 after graduation, he reported to Naval Hospital Patuxent River, Maryland, for independent duty where he remained until September 1986.

In October 1989, he reported to Field Medical Service School at Camp Johnson, North Carolina. After successful completion of FMSS in January of 1990, he reported as LPO to 1st Battalion, 6th Marines, 2nd Marine Division where he made multiple deployments that included participation in Operations Desert Shield/ Desert Storm and Cease Fire. Upon his selection to Chief Petty Officer in 1991 he was assigned as LCPO Headquarters Battalion, 2nd Marine Division at San Diego. Prior to graduation he was selected to Senior Chief and reported to USS *Constellation* (CV 64) in February 1995 as medical department LCPO.

In April 1998, he was promoted to his present rank and since has served as Senior Enlisted Leader and Directorate for Primary Care at Naval Medical Center San Diego. He reported as Command Master Chief to the 3rd Medical Battalion, 3rd Force Service Support Group in Okinawa, Japan, in January 2003.

Proctor, Hawthorne L.
MAJOR GENERAL—ARMY

He was born in North Carolina. He received a Bachelor of Science degree in Agricultural Economics from North Carolina Agricultural and Technical State University. He also received a Master of Art degree in Public Administration from Central Michigan University. His military education includes graduation from Quartermaster Officer Basic and Advanced Courses; United States Army Command and General Staff College; and the United States Army War College. He was commissioned as a Second Lieutenant on January 2, 1969, and after graduation from Quartermaster Officer Basic Course. From March 1969 to July 1969, he was assigned first as Training Officer, and next as Assistant S-4 (logistics), Company E, 1st Battalion, Second Training Brigade, at Fort Ord, California. From October 1969 to December 1970, he was assigned as Billeting Officer at the United States Army Garrison at Carlisle Barracks, Pennsylvania. From December 1970 to March 1971, he was as assigned as Contract Team Leader with II Corps, United States Military Assistance Command Vietnam. On January 2, 1971, he was promoted to Captain. From March 1971 to December 1971, he served as Logistics Support Officer for Military Region 2, United States Military Assistance Command Vietnam. From March 1972 to December 1973, he was Budget Officer, later Commissary Officer, United States Army Support Activity, in Thailand. In January 1974, he was a student at the Quartermaster Advanced Course at the United

States Army Quartermaster School at Fort Lee, Virginia. From October 1974 to April 1975, he served as the S-4 (Logistic Officer) for the 25th Supply and Transport Battalion, 25th Infantry Division at Schofield Barracks, Hawaii. From April 1975 to September 1976, he was Commander of Company A, 25th Supply and Transport Battalion, 25th Infantry Division at Schofield Barracks, Hawaii. From September 1976 to November 1977, he was assigned as a Technical Supply Officer to Headquarters and Light Maintenance Company, 725th Maintenance Battalion, 25th Infantry Division at Schofield Barracks. From November 1977 to May 1978, he was a Supply Officer, Class II, IV, and VII, Division Materiel Management Center, 25th Infantry Division, Schofield Barrack. In May 1978, he was selected Chief of the Production Management Branch at the Defense Industrial Supply Center, Defense Logistics Agency, Philadelphia, Pennsylvania. He was promoted to Major on November 10, 1979. From August 1980 to June 1981, General Proctor was a student at the United States Army Command and General Staff College at Fort Leavenworth, Kansas. From June 1981 to September 1982, he served as Materiel Management Officer at Combined Field Army for United States Forces in Korea. From September 1982 to May 1985, he served as a Logistics Staff Officer in the Office of the Deputy Chief of Staff for Logistics, United States Army, in Washington, D.C. From May 1985 to July 1987, he served as Battalion Commander of the 25th Supply and Transport Battalion, 25th Infantry Division (Light) at Schofield Barracks. He was promoted to Lieutenant Colonel on August 1, 1985. In August 1987, he was a student at the United States Army War College at Carlisle Barracks. In June 1988, he first served as Director of the Logistics Career Department, then in June 1989, as Director of Supply and Professional Development Department at the United States Army Quartermaster Center and School at Fort Lee. From May 1990 to May 1992, General Proctor served as Chief of the Combat Service Support Career Division of the Enlisted Personnel Management Directorate at the United States Total Army Personnel Command in Alexandria, Virginia. On May 1, 1991, he was promoted to Colonel. From May 1992 to August 1994, he was assigned as Group Commander of the 45th Corps Support Group (Forward) at Schofield Barracks. In August 1994, he returned to Washington, D.C., to serve as Executive Officer, later Director of Plans and Operations, in the Office of the Deputy Chief of Staff for Logistics, United States Army. On July 1, 1996, he was promoted to Brigadier General. In July 1996 he was assigned as Commander of the Defense Support Center Philadelphia, Defense Logistics Agency, in Philadelphia, Pennsylvania. From August 1998 to July 1999, he served as Deputy Chief of Staff for Operations and Logistics at the United States Materiel Command in Alexandria. In July 1999, he was selected to serve as Commanding General/Commandant for the United States Army Quartermaster Center and School at Fort Lee. He was promoted to Major General on September 1, 1999. In

July 2001, he was selected to serve as Director of Logistic Operations (J-3) for the Defense Logistics Agency at Fort Belvoir, Virginia. He retired from the military on January 1, 2004. His military awards and decorations include the Defense Superior Service Medal; Distinguished Service Medal; the Legion of Merit (with three oak leaf clusters); Bronze Star; Meritorious Service Medal (with three oak leaf clusters); Joint Service Commendation Medal; Army Commendation Medal (with two oak leaf clusters); Air Assault Badge; and Army Staff Identification Badge.

Pugh, William R.
SERGEANT MAJOR—ARMY

Sergeant Major William R. Pugh enlisted in the United States Army in January 1980. He completed Basic Training at Fort Jackson, South Carolina, and Advanced Individual Training at Fort Lee, Virginia, for Subsistence Supply Specialist.

Pugh holds an associate's degree from Regents University and is working on a bachelor's degree in Business Administration at Touro University International. He is also a graduate of the Commissary Officer Course; Combat Lifesaver Course; Logistic Management Course; the First Sergeant Course; Battle Staff Course; Garrison Sergeant Major Course; and the United States Army Sergeants Major Academy.

He recently served as Support Operations Sergeant Major with the 46th Corps Support Group, 1st Corps Support Command at Fort Bragg, North Carolina, and as Support Operations Sergeant Major with Headquarters and Headquarters Company of the 501st Corps Support Group at Camp Red Cloud, South Korea.

He is currently serving as the United States Army

Garrison Sergeant Major Area 1 Support Activity at Camp Red Cloud.

Purdy, Tony H.
COMMAND SERGEANT MAJOR—ARMY

He was born in Gainesville, Florida, and raised in St. Petersburg, Florida. He enlisted in the Army in January 1979. He attended the Basic Combat Training (BCT) and Advanced Individual Training (AIT) at Fort Bliss, Texas. His military education includes the Air Defense Academy, all the Noncommissioned Officer Leadership Courses, Drill Sergeants School, the First Sergeants Course, and the United States Army Sergeants Major Academy (class 53).

His assignments include Light Vehicle Driver; Senior Gunner; Squad Leader; Drill Sergeant; Platoon Sergeant; First Sergeant; Defense Artillery Observer Controller at National Training Center; and Operations Sergeant Major. In August 2004, he was serving as Command Sergeant Major for the 1st Battalion, 56th Air Defense Artillery Regiment.

Rainey, Della H.
MAJOR—ARMY

The first black nurse to report for duty at Fort Bragg was Lieutenant Della H. Rainey of Suffolk, Virginia. She was later transferred to the hospital at Tuskegee Air Field as Chief Nurse. She also served as Chief Nurse at the station hospital at Fort Huachuca, Arizona, and at Camp Beale, California. Officer Rainey was promoted in 1945 to the rank of Captain and in 1946 to Major. Before she retired from the Army Nursing Corps, Officer Rainey was its highest-ranking black officer.

Ramble, Pamela M.
COMMAND SERGEANT MAJOR—ARMY

She was born in Monterrey, California, and her military career began in February 1981. Her military education includes the completion of all the Noncommissioned Officer Education System Courses; Instructor Trainer Course; Small Group Instructor Training; Battle Staff Course; First Sergeants Course; and the United States Army Sergeants Major Academy. Her civilian education includes a bachelor's degree in Business and she is currently pursuing a master's in Applied Arts in Organization Development through the University of Incarnate Word.

Her assignments include three tours with the 267th Finance Battalion at Fort Richardson, Alaska; support of Desert Storm; ARCENT Kuwait; 201st Finance Support Unit at Frankfurt, Germany; Readiness Group at Fort Jackson, South Carolina; and Headquarters and Headquarters Company at Fort Sam Houston, Texas. In September 2004, she was serving as the Command Sergeant Major of the 106th Finance Battalion at Wurzburg, Germany.

Randolph, Bernard P.
GENERAL—AIR FORCE

He was born in New Orleans to Phillip J. Randolph and Claudia Randolph, he married the former Lucille Robinson in 1956, and they have six children, Michelle, Julie, Michael, John, Liane and Mark. General Randolph received a Bachelor of Science degree in Chemistry (magna cum laude) at Xavier University of Louisiana in New Orleans and a Master of Science degree in Electrical Engineering from the University of North Dakota at Grand Forks through the Air Force Institute of Technology in 1964 and 1965, respectively. He completed Squadron Officer School in 1959, Air Command and Staff College as a distinguished graduate, concurrently earning a master's in Business Administration from Auburn University in 1969, and was a distinguished graduate of the Air War College in 1974, all at Maxwell Air Force Base, Alabama. He was commissioned a Second Lieutenant on November 9, 1955, and promoted to First Lieutenant on May 9, 1957. His first assignment after completing aviation cadet training at Ellington Air Force Base, Texas, and Mather Air Force Base, California, was with the Strategic Air Command at Lincoln Air Force Base, Nebraska, from June 1956 to June 1962. He was promoted to Captain on February 5, 1960. He instructed and evaluated KC-97 and B-47 flight crews. While there, he was a member of a select crew. General Randolph attended the University of North Dakota until July 1965 and was then assigned to Los Angeles Air Force Station as Chief of On-Orbit Operations with the Space Systems Division. He was next assigned as Assistant Deputy Program Director for Launch and Orbital Operations and was responsible for all payload operations. He was promoted to Major on January 20, 1967. From August 1968 to October 1969, Randolph attended Air Command and Staff College at Auburn University. He was then assigned to

South Vietnam as an airlift operations officer at Chu Lai and airlift coordinator at Tan Son Nhut Air Base. He was responsible for the total operation of about 50 C-7 and C-123 airlift sorties daily from Chu Lai and later coordinated the operations of all airlift control elements throughout South Vietnam. Upon his return to the United States in November 1970, General Randolph was assigned to Air Force Systems Command Headquarters as Chief of Command Plans in Test Evaluation and Executive Officer to the Deputy Chief of staff for Operations at Andrews Air Force Base, Maryland. He was promoted to Lieutenant Colonel on April 1, 1971. From August 1973 to June 1974, he was a student at the Air War College at Maxwell Air Force Base, Alabama. From June 1974 to June 1980, General Randolph received sequential assignments at Los Angeles Air Force Station, California. First he served as Director of Space Systems Planning, Space and Missile Systems, then as Deputy System Program Director of the Air Force Satellite Communications Systems; then as System Program Director of the Air Force Satellite Communications System; and later as Program Director for Space Defense Systems in the Space Division. He was promoted to Colonel July 1, 1975. From July 1980 to September 1981, he served as Vice Commander of the Warner Robins Air Logistics Center at Robins Air Force Base, Georgia. He was promoted to Brigadier General on September 8, 1980. From September 1981 to May 1983, he was Director of Space Systems and Command, Control and Communications in Office of the Deputy Chief of Staff for Research, Development, and Acquisition at the Headquarters of the United States Air Force in Washington, D.C. He was promoted to Major General on November 1, 1982. From May 1983 to June 1984, he was Vice Commander and Deputy Commander for Space Systems Acquisition in the Space Division at Los Angeles Air Force Station. From June 1984 to May 1985, he served as Vice Commander of Air Force Systems Command at Andrews Air Force Base, Maryland. He was promoted to Lieutenant General on June 28, 1984. From May 1985 to July 1987, he was Deputy Chief of Staff, Research, Development, and Acquisition at the Headquarters of the United States Air Force in Washington, D.C. From July 1987 to April 1990, he served as Commander of Air Force Systems Command at Andrews Air Force Base. During this assignment, he directed the research, development, testing, evaluation, and acquisition of aerospace systems for Air Force Operational and Support Commands. As the Commanding General, he was responsible for over 60,000 men and women, and a $32 billion annual budget, one-third of that of the entire Air Force. He managed some 24,000 active contracts worth some $151 billion. He was also responsible for developing and directing the development and purchasing of all new weapons systems for the Air Force, including the F-15-E Fighter, the MX Missile, the B-1 Bomber, and the C-17 Transport Aircraft. He was promoted to the rank of General on August 1, 1987, the second African American to obtain this grade. General Randolph's military awards and decorations include the Distinguished Service Medal, Legion of Merit (with one oak leaf cluster), Bronze Star, Meritorious Service Medal, Air Force Commendation Medal, Presidential Unit Citation, Air Force Organizational Excellence Award, Vietnam Service Medal (with four service stars), Republic of Vietnam Gallantry Cross (with palm), and Vietnam Campaign Medal.

Randolph, Leonard M., Jr.
MAJOR GENERAL—AIR FORCE

He was born in Washington, D.C. He and his wife Linda have five children, Nathaniel, Holly, Brion, Chad, and Judd. He received a Bachelor of Science degree in Biology from Marietta College in Marietta, Ohio. He received a Master of Science degree in Microbiology from Howard University in Washington, D.C., before earning a Doctor of Medicine degree from Meharry Medical College in Nashville, Tennessee. His military education includes Aerospace Medicine Primary Course at the USAF School of Aerospace Medicine at Brooks Air Force Base, Texas, in 1978; Air Command and Staff College at Maxwell Air Force Base, Alabama, in 1980; and the Air War College at Maxwell Air Force Base in 1984. In 1989, he was a student in the Physician in Management I/II at the American College of Physician Executives in Tampa, Florida, and also attended the Advanced Health Care Administration Interagency Institute for Federal Health Care Executives in Washington, D.C. in 1990. He entered the Air Force in 1970 while attending medical school at Meharry Medical College. On March 4, 1970, he was commissioned a Second Lieutenant. On May 28, 1971, he was promoted to First Lieutenant. He graduated in 1972 as a distinguished graduate and a member of the Alpha Omega Alpha National Honor Medical Society. He served as general surgery resident at Kessler Air Force Base, Mississippi, from July 1972 to June 1977. On May 28, 1972, he was promoted to Captain and on May 28, 1975, he was promoted to Major. From July 1977 to June 1983, he served as Chief of Surgery at Bergstrom Air Force Base, Texas. On May 28, 1980, he was promoted to Lieutenant Colonel. From July 1983 to June 1984, he was assigned as a Staff Surgeon at Wright-Patterson Medical Center in Ohio. From July 1984 to September 1985, he served as Director of Medical Education at Wright-Patterson Medical Center. From October 1985 to August 1986, he was assigned as Chief of Hospital Services at Minot Air Force Base, North Dakota. On May 28, 1986, he was promoted to Colonel. From August 1988 to April 1990, he was assigned as Commander of the 831st Medical Group at George Air Force Base, California. From May 1990 to August 1991, he was assigned as the Deputy Command Surgeon at the Headquarters of Tactical Air Command at Langley Air Force Base, Virginia. In August 1990, during Operation Desert Shield and Desert Storm he served as the Forward Command Surgeon for the United States Central Command Air Force in Riyadh, Saudi Arabia. From August 1991 to January 1994, he was assigned as the Command Surgeon of the United

States Central Command at MacDill Air Force Base, Florida. On May 25, 1995, Dr. Randolph was promoted to Brigadier General. From January 1994 to August 1997 he served as the Commander of the 60th Medical Group at David Grant Medical Center, the Lead Agent of Department of Defense Health Service Region 10 since January 1994. Based at Travis Air Force Base, California, the center is a premier United States Air Force Medical Center and Tri-Service Regional lead agent for 440,000 beneficiaries. The 60th Medical Group provides or arranges education, research, aeromedical staging and DOD and Veterans Administration Joint Ventures. David Grant Medical Center annually has more than 400,000 outpatient visits, 10,000 admissions, 50,000 dental visits, and 200 research protocols, with a staff of 2,100 members, 148 residents and a budget of $92 million. The lead agent directs the provision of health care for the DOD Health Service Region 10, assuring optimum access to care and quality healthcare services at the most reasonable cost for Army, Navy and Air Force beneficiaries in the region. Dr. Randolph was promoted to Major General on November 1, 1998. From November 1999 to July 2001, he served as Deputy Surgeon General at the Headquarters of the United States Air Force at Bolling Air Force Base in Washington, D.C. In July 2001, he was selected to serve as Deputy Executive Director and Program Executive Officer for TRICARE Management Activity at the Office of the Undersecretary of Defense for Personnel and Readiness in Washington, D.C. In May 2003, he was assigned as the acting Deputy Assistant Secretary of Defense for Health Plan Administration, Health Affairs and Chief Operating Officer, TRICARE Management Activity, Washington, D.C. He retired from the military on September 1, 2003. His military awards and decorations include the Defense Superior Service Medal (with oak leaf cluster); Legion of Merit (with oak leak cluster); Meritorious Service Medal (with two oak leaf clusters); Air Force Commendation Medal; National Defense Service Medal (with bronze star); Armed Forces Expeditionary Medal; Southwest Asia Service Medal (with three bronze stars); Humanitarian Service Medal; and the Kuwait Liberation Medal.

Raybon, Herman, Jr.
SERGEANT MAJOR—MARINES

Sergeant Major Herman Raybon, Jr., attended Recruit Training at Marine Corps Recruit Depot, Parris Island, South Carolina. He was promoted to Private First Class upon graduation from recruit training and preceded to Marine Corps Communication and Electronics School in San Diego, California, where he underwent training to become a Field Radio Operator. In March 1975, he was ordered to Okinawa, Japan, for duty with Communication Company, Headquarters Battalion, with the 3rd Marine Division.

During his sixteen month tour with the Division, he was assigned as a Section Leader and Platoon Sergeant and participated in Operation Frequent Wind,

the evacuation of refugees from South Vietnam. He competed successfully for meritorious promotion on several occasions, attaining the rank of Sergeant in February 1976.

In August 1996, he was assigned as Battalion Sergeant Major for the 1st Combat Engineer Battalion, 1st Marine Division, at Camp Pendleton, California; in June 1999, he reported to the Commanding General at Marine Corps Base Camp S.D. Butler for duty as the Sergeant Major of Headquarters and Service Battalion; and in March 2001, he was selected to serve as the Sergeant Major for the 12th Marine Regiment, 3rd Marine Division.

Reason, Joseph Paul
ADMIRAL—NAVY

Born in Washington, D.C., he married the former Dianne Lillian Fowler of Washington, D.C., and they have two children, Rebecca L. and Joseph P., Jr. He graduated from the United State Naval Academy in 1965 with a Bachelor of Science (Naval Science). He received a Master of Science degree in Computer Systems Management from Naval Postgraduate School in Monterey in 1970. He completed the CAPSTONE, National Defense University, 1988. The Admiral completed Naval Nuclear Power School at NTC Bainbridge, Maryland (*DUINS*); and Naval Destroyer School at Monterey. Prior to being trained in nuclear propulsion engineering, he served as Operations Officer on the USS *J.D. Blackwood* (DE 219). Upon completion of training, he was assigned duties on the USS *Truxtun* (DLGN 35) and participated in her first deployment to Southeast Asia in 1968. Joining the USS *Enterprise* (CVN 65) as Electrical Officer in 1971, he deployed twice to Southeast Asia and the Indian Ocean. After service as Combat Systems Officer, again on USS *Truxtun,* Admiral Reason began a tour as Surface Nuclear Assignment Officer at the Bureau of Naval Personnel. In late 1976, he was assigned as Naval Aide to the President to the United States. He served as aide to President Carter from December 1976 to June 1979. From June 1979 to May 1981, he served as the Executive Officer of the USS *Mississippi* (CGN 40). From September 1981 to December 1982, he served as the Commander of the USS *Coontz* (DDG 40). From April 1983 to July 1986, he served as Commander of the USS *Bainbridge* (CGN 25). Prior to assuming his duties as Commander of Naval Surface Force, Atlantic Fleet in January 1991, Admiral Reason commanded Cruiser-Destroyer Group One. He led Battle Group *ROMEDO* through operations in the northern and western Pacific and Indian Ocean regions and the Persian Gulf. As Commander of Naval Base Seattle from 1986 through 1988, he was responsible for all naval activities in Washington, Oregon, and Alaska. On November 15, 1996, he was designated Admiral while serving in billets commensurate with that grade. In December 1996, he was assigned as the Commander in Chief of the United States Atlantic Fleet. On February 1, 1997, he was selected Admiral with the same date of rank. He is the first black American four-star Admiral. His military awards and decorations include the Distinguished Service Medal, Legion of Merit (with two gold stars), Navy Unit Commendation awarded USS *Enterprise* (CVN 65), Meritorious Unit Commendation awarded USS *Mississippi* (CGN 40), Armed Forces Expeditionary Medal (with one bronze star), Vietnam Service Medal (with two bronze stars and one silver star), Sea Service Deployment Ribbon (with bronze star), Republic of Vietnam Armed Forces Honor Medal (First Class), Republic of Vietnam Gallantry Cross Unit Citation, Republic of Vietnam Campaign Medal, Navy "E" Ribbon (four awards), and El Commandant General de la Armada.

Reaves, Joel C.
COMMANDER—NAVY

He was born in Plant City, Florida. He graduated from Tampa Bay Technical High School in June 1973, and enlisted into the United States Navy in September 1973. Upon completion of Basic Training at Recruit Training Command in Orlando, Florida, he attended Electronics Technician Class "A" School at Treasure Island, California, and the Precision Electronics Maintenance course at Lowry Air Force Base in Denver, Colorado. A commissioning crewmember in USS *Nimitz* (CVN 68), Commander Reaves worked as a Communications Technician and precision test equipment Repair Technician. In 1976, he was selected for the Broadened Opportunity for Officer Selection and Training program (BOOST), and upon completion was appointed to the United States Naval Academy, where he graduated as a member of the Class of 1981.

After commissioning, he completed Surface Warfare

School, Division Officer Course at Newport, Rhode Island. His first assignment as a Commissioned Officer was in USS *Biddle* (CG 34) where he served as a Gunnery Assistant and Communications Officer. A second sea tour followed, and as a participant in the Carrier Readiness Improvement Program (CVRIP), he served as a Boilers Officer and Auxiliaries Officer in USS *America* (CV 66). In 1987, he was assigned to the Naval Post Graduate School Monterey, California, where he earned his master's degree in Electrical Engineering. He then attended the Department Head Course at Surface Warfare Officer's School in Newport, Rhode Island, after which it was back to sea in 1990 as the Combat Systems Officer in USS *Nicholson* (DD 982). A Second Department Head tour followed where he served as Operation Officer in USS *Leyte Gulf* (CG 55). He left *Leyte Gulf* in February of 1994 and served as Executive Officer in USS *Philipine Sea* (CG 58) from June 1994 to October 1995. More sea duty followed where he served as Training and Readiness Officer on the then-newly formed Western Hemisphere Group Staff from October 1995 to September 1997. Joint duty followed where he served as Chief of Operations Planning Group and Chief of the Maritime Operations Branch at the United States Southern Command in Miami, Florida, from September 1997 to July 2000. He was assigned as Executive Officer and Associate Professor of Naval Science at Morehouse College NROTC from July 2000 to July 2004. In March 2005, he was serving as the Executive Officer of the Navy ROTC Unit at Savannah State University in Savannah, Georgia.

Reese, Andrea D.
CHIEF MASTER SERGEANT—AIR FORCE

She was born in San Juan, Trinidad. She entered the Air Force in November 1977, receiving Basic Military Training at Lackland Air Force Base, Texas.

Her military education includes Inventory Management Specialist School at Lowry Air Force Base, Colorado; Noncommissioned Orientation Course at Clark Air Base; United States Air Force Supervisory Development Course, Clark Air Base, Philippines; Noncommissioned Officer Academy at Keesler Air Force Base, Mississippi; and United States Air Force Senior Noncommissioned Officer Academy at Maxwell Air Force Base, Gunter Annex, Alabama. She also holds an Associate of Applied Sciences degree in Logistics Management from the Community College of the Air Force and a Bachelor of Science degree in Business Technology from Peru State College in Peru, Nebraska.

Her key military assignments include serving from September 1979 to September 1983 as Funds Management Specialist at Clark Air Base; from November 1983 to August 1987 as Noncommissioned Officer-in-Charge of Requirements, (NCOIC) Stock Control, and NCOIC Procedures Element at Moody Air Force Base, Georgia; from September 1987 to September 1990 as Noncommissioned Officer in Charge of Stock Control, 43rd Supply Squadron at Anderson Air Base, Guam; from

October 1990 to May 1997 as Supply Procedures Superintendent in the Directorate of Logistics at the Headquarters of Strategic Air Command; as Resource Manager of the Command Section of United States Strategic Air Command; Superintendent of Materiel Management Flight; and Chief of Materiel Storage and Distribution Flight of the 55th Supply Squadron at Offutt Air Force Base, Nebraska; from June 1997 to June 2000 as Chief of Management and Systems Flight of the 31st Supply Squadron at Aviano Air Base, Italy; and from June 2000 to May 2004 as Chief of Supply Systems Management Branch at Maxwell Air Force Base, Gunter Annex, Alabama. In January 2005, she was serving as Chief Master Sergeant, Superintendent for the Headquarters Standard Systems Group. She is responsible for advising the Executive Director on matters affecting the 750 enlisted members, 250 officers and 600 civilian personnel.

Reese, Fenton

SERGEANT MAJOR—MARINES

He enlisted in the Marine Corps on August 25, 1980, and attended recruit training at Marine Corps Recruit Depot Parris Island, South Carolina. In November 1980, he reported for duty with Headquarters Battery, Naval Gunfire Section, 1st Battalion, 10th Marines, 2nd Marine Division, at Camp Lejeune, North Carolina, and served as a Field Radio Operator/Forward Observer. In January 1982, his section was attached to Battalion Landing Team 2/2 and deployed aboard the USS *Shreveport*. In Aug of 1982, his section was attached to Battalion Landing Team 2/4 and deployed aboard the USS *Guadalcanal*.

In December 1983, he was meritoriously promoted to Corporal and served as a section leader. In April 1984, Corporal Reese was ordered to Marine Corps Air

Ground Combat Center at 29 Palms, California, for duty as an instructor with the Radio Operator Training Section of the Marine Corps Communications Electronics School. In May 1985, he was meritoriously promoted to Sergeant and served as a senior instructor.

In Dec 1985, Sergeant Reese reported to Drill Instructor School at Marine Corps Recruit Depot, Parris Island. Upon successful completion of Drill Instructor School, he was assigned to "H" Company, Third Recruit Training Battalion, where he served as a Drill Instructor/Senior Drill instructor. In March 1988, after a successful tour on the drill field, he was assigned to the Light Anti-Aircraft Missile Battalion, 1st Marine Air Wing, for duty as the Battalion Radio Chief. He also served as the Communications Platoon Sergeant, Battalion Color Sergeant, and Battalion Training Noncommissioned Officer. He competed for and was subsequently selected for Marine of the Year, Okinawa, Japan, in December 1989.

In April 1990, Staff Sergeant Reese reported to Recruiter School, MCRD, San Diego. Upon successful completion of recruiter school, he was assigned to Recruiting Station New York for duty as a canvassing recruiter at Recruiting Substation Brooklyn. In December 1990, he became the Noncommissioned Officer in Charge of RSS Brooklyn, and was meritoriously promoted to Gunnery Sergeant on 2 July 1992.

While serving on recruiting duty he was the recipient of numerous awards and accolades. Most notably he was selected as the NCOIC of the year for three consecutive years and the Marine of the Year at Recruiting Station New York for two of his three and a half year tenure. In addition, he led his recruiting substation to become RSS of the year for three consecutive years. In April 1992 he attended the SNCOA Career Course and the Advance Course in August 1993 and was selected as the distinguished graduate for Leadership and Motivation during both occasions. Gunnery Sergeant Reese was featured in the May 1993 issue of *Marine Magazine* for his exemplary performance on recruiting duty. In December 1993, after completing a successful tour of recruiting duty, he was reassigned to the 3rd Combat Engineer Battalion, 3rd Marine Division, for duty as the Battalion Communications Chief. He also served as the Headquarters and Service Company Gunnery Sergeant and Battalion Equal Opportunity Officer.

In 1995, Gunnery Sergeant Reese was again ordered to Recruiting Station New York, this time for duty as the NCOIC Recruiting Substation Nassau County. In May 1997, he was promoted to First Sergeant, and was transferred to Communications Company, Headquarters and Service Battalion, 2nd Force Service Support Group at Camp Lejeune. First Sergeant Reese was transferred to Headquarters Company, Headquarters and Support Battalion in June 1998 for duty as the Company First Sergeant where he served until his selection to Sergeant Major and subsequent reassignment as the Sergeant Major Marine Expeditionary Unit, Service Support Group 22, 22nd Marine Expeditionary

Unit. Upon his return to CONUS he was reassigned as the Sergeant Major of the 2nd Maintenance Battalion. In June 2002 he received orders to become the Sergeant Major of Recruiting Station New York. He currently is the Sergeant Major of the 1st Marine Corps District.

Reeves, William C., Jr.
SENIOR EXECUTIVE SERVICE

He received a Bachelor of Science degree in Physics and a Masters in Business Administration from Alabama A&M University in Normal, Alabama.

He has been a member of the Senior Executive Service since May 1996, and has over 35 years of government experience in science, engineering, test and evaluations, systems engineering and integration, personnel and resource management. His government experience covers a broad spectrum of areas including electro-optical guided weapon systems; directed energy weapon systems; focal plane arrays; signal and data processing; booster and kill vehicle propulsion; aero-optics; aero-thermodynamics; missile structures and materials; kill vehicle lethality; aerodynamics; aero-ballistic controls; fusing; electrical power; nuclear effects; information technology; and battle management/command, control, communications, computers, intelligence, surveillance, and reconnaissance.

In January 2005, he was serving as the Assistant to the Deputy Commanding General for Research, Development and Acquisition and the Director of the Technical Interoperability and Matrix Center, United States Army Space and Missile Defense Command/United States Army Forces Strategic Command. As the Assistant to the Deputy Commanding General for Research, Development and Acquisition, he performs the organization's functional and operational executive oversight and directs its staff. He also manages the research, development, and test and evaluation of advanced technology supporting integration and interoperability for space and missile defense. He ensures that efforts are coordinated and linked to the needs of the Army, Joint Armed Forces, and Allies.

Reid, Carlton B., Jr.
COLONEL—ARMY

He was commissioned in the Field Artillery in 1981 at the United States Military Academy at West Point, New York.

His military education includes a Bachelor of Sci-

ence degree with concentrations in Arabic and Spanish from West Point; a Master of Science degree in Nuclear Physics from the Naval Postgraduate School; and a master's in Strategic Studies from the United States Army War College. He is also a graduate of the United States Army's Command and General Staff College and the Advanced Strategic Arts Program.

He has served in numerous leadership positions including serving as an Instructor and Assistant Professor of Physics on the staff and faculty of the United States Military Academy from 1990 to 1993. He was assigned to the 4th Infantry Division (Mechanized) at Fort Carson, Colorado, and served as Executive Officer for the 3rd Battalion, 29th Field Artillery from June 1994 until his reassignment to the On-Site Inspection Agency in July 1996. Following that, he served as a Mission Commander and Inspection Team Chief with the On-Site Inspection Agency (OSIA) from 1996–1999. While assigned to the START-Nuclear Division, he assumed leadership of the Nuclear and Cooperative Threat Reduction Branch Responsible Program. He returned to Fort Hood to command the 1st Battalion, 21st Field Artillery, 1st Cavalry Division from 1999 to 2001. Subsequently, he served as the Deputy G-3 Operations, Eighth United States Army in Yongsan, South Korea. Next, he joined the Army staff in the Office of the Deputy Chief of Staff, G-3 Strategy, Plans and Policy serving as Chief of Army International Affairs Plans, Programs and Resource Integration Division in Washington, D.C. In January 2005, he was serving as the Commander of the 17th Field Artillery Brigade.

Reid, Jerry L.
COMMAND SERGEANT MAJOR—ARMY

He was born in Fitzgerald, Georgia, and entered the United States Army in August 1977. He completed Basic Combat Training and Advanced Individual Training at Fort Dix, New Jersey.

His military education includes all the Noncommissioned Officers Education System Courses; the First Sergeant Course; Master Fitness Course; NBC School; Strategic Mobility Planner Course; Battle Staff Course; Logistics Program Course; the United States Army Sergeants Major Academy.

He has held numerous leadership positions including serving as Squad Leader; Platoon Sergeant; Truck Master; Drill Instructor at Fort Dix; Platoon Sergeant of the 416th Transportation Company at Hunter Army Airfield in Savannah, Georgia; First Sergeant at Fort Stewart, Georgia; First Sergeant for the Air Terminal Movement Control Team for the 39th Transportation

Battalion; First Sergean t for the 66th and 89th Transportation Company; First Sergeant for 89th Transportation Company, 6th Transportation Battalion, 7th
Group; Command Sergeant Major of the 6th Transportation Battalion, 7th Trans Group, at Fort Eustis,
Virginia; Command Sergeant Major of the 39th Transportation Battalion; and Brigade Command Sergeant
Major of the TRANSCOM. In August 2004, he was
serving as the Command Sergeant Major for the 21st
Theater Support Command.

Rice, Edward A., Jr.
MAJOR GENERAL—AIR FORCE

He is a 1978 distinguished graduate of the United
States Air Force Academy, and received a Bachelor of
Science degree in Engineering Sciences. He was commissioned a second lieutenant on May 31, 1978. He
earned a Master of Science degree in Aeronautical Science and Technology from Embry-Riddle University in
1986. He is also a distinguished graduate from Squadron Officer School at Maxwell Air Force Base, Alabama;
a 1984 graduate of the Air Command and Staff College at Maxwell Air Force Base; a 1989 distinguished
graduate, earning a master's degree in National Security and Strategic Studies of the Naval War College in
Newport, Rhode Island; and a 1984 National Security
Fellow at Harvard University in Cambridge, Massachusetts.

From July 1978 to February 1980, he was a distinguished graduate of undergraduate pilot training at
Williams Air Force Base, Arizona. From February 1980
to January 1984, he was assigned as a B-52G Co-Pilot
and Aircraft Commander with the 69th Bombardment
Squadron at Loring Air Force Base, Maine. He was promoted to Captain on May 31, 1982. From January 1984
to February 1985, he served as the Air Staff Training

Program Assistant Deputy Chief with the Executive
Services Division, Directorate of Administration, at
the Headquarters of the United States Air Force in
Washington, D.C. From February 1985 to July 1988, he
was assigned as a B-52G Instructor Pilot, later as Chief
of the Standardization and Evaluation Branch, and later
as Flight Commander, with the 441st Bombardment
Squadron at Mather Air Force Base, California. He was
promoted to Major on April 1, 1986.

In July 1989, he was assigned as Programmer for the
Air Crew Management Branch in the Office of the
Deputy Chief of Staff for Air and Space Operations at
the Headquarters of the United States Air Forces in
Washington, D.C. He was promoted to Lieutenant
Colonel on April 1, 1990. From November 1991 to July
1992, he served as Chief of the Standardization and
Evaluation Division of the 410th Operations Group at
K.I. Sawyer Air Force Base, Mich. He was promoted
to Colonel on February 1, 1994. In July 1995, he was as-
signed as the Deputy Commander for the 509th Op-
erations Group at Whiteman Air Force Base, Missouri.
In July 1996, he was assigned as Commander of the
552nd Operations Group at Tinker Air Force Base,
Oklahoma. From June 1997 to June 1999, he served as
Deputy Executive Secretary for the National Security
Council at the White House in Washington, D.C. In
June 1999, he was selected to serve as the Deputy Di-
rector for Expeditionary Aerospace Force Implemen-
tation in the Office of the Deputy Chief of Staff for Air
and Space Operations at the Headquarters of the
United States Air Force in Washington, D.C. From
May 2000 to May 2002, he was assigned as Comman-
der of the 28th Bomb Wing at Ellsworth Air Force
Base, South Dakota. In May 2002, he was selected as
Commander of the Air Force Recruiting Service at the
Headquarters of Air Education and Training Command
at Randolph Air Force Base, Texas. He is a command
pilot with more than 3,800 flying hours in the B-1B, B-
52G/H, E-3, B-2, T-37 and T-38. He was promoted
to Brigadier General on February 1, 2002.

In January 2004, he was selected to serve as Chief
of Staff for the Office of the Representative and Executive Director for the Coalition Provisional Authority
in the Office of the Secretary of Defense in Washington, D.C. Next he was selected for promotion to Major
General and reassignment as the Commander of the
13th Air Force at Andersen Air Force Base, Guam.

His military awards and decorations include the Defense Superior Service Medal (with oak leaf cluster);
the Legion of Merit (with oak leaf cluster); Meritorious
Service Medal (with three oak leaf clusters); and the
Air Force Commendation Medal.

Richardson, Clarence W.
SERGEANT MAJOR—MARINES

He enlisted in the United States Marine Corps in
February 1980, and attended Recruit Training at Marine Corps Recruit Depot, Parris Island, South Carolina. His key military assignments include serving as
a Platoon Sergeant; Senior Drill Instructor; Company

Gunnery Sergeant; Maintenance Chief; Quality Control Staff Noncommissioned Officer; and First Sergeant of Headquarters Service Company. In October 2004, he was serving as Sergeant Major of Marine Wing Support Squadron 272, Marine Wing Support, Second Marine Aircraft Wing.

Richardson, Cornell, Jr.
COMMAND SERGEANT MAJOR—ARMY

He is a native of Gainesville, Florida, and he enlisted into the United States Army in December 1979. He completed Basic Combat Training at Fort Jackson, South Carolina, and Advance Individual Training at Fort Sam Houston, Texas, as a Combat Medic.

His military and civilian education includes all the Non-Commissioned Officer Education System Courses; Air Assault School; Drill Sergeant School; Faculty Development Course; Master Fitness School; Department of Defense Intelligence Analyst Course; Foreign Weapons Course; First Sergeant Course; and Sergeant Major Academy (class 53). He holds a Masters of Science in Business Administration from Lexington University.

His key military assignments include serving as Evacuation Sergeant/Aid Station Non-Commissioned Officer in Charge; Medical Platoon Sergeant; Operation Just Cause/Promote Liberty; Drill Sergeant; SR SDT Writer/EFMB Test Control Officer; Senior Technical Intelligence Analyst; First Sergeant for C Company, 302nd FSB; B Company, 187th Medical Battalion; Deputy Commandant AMEDD Non-Commissioned Officer in Charge Academy; III Corps Surgeons Sergeant Major and MNC-I Surgeons Sergeant Major for Operation Iraq Freedom II; and Command Sergeant Major with AMEDD.

Richardson, Sandra V.
COLONEL—ARMY

She is a native of Beatrice, Alabama and was commissioned a Second Lieutenant in the Finance Corps in 1978.

Her military and civilian education includes the Finance Officer Basic and Advanced Courses; Joint Professional Military Education Course; Professional Military Comptroller School; United States Army Command and General Staff College; and the Army War College. She earned a Bachelor of Science degree in Accountancy from Tuskegee University and a Master of Accounting from the University of Alabama.

She has held a variety of command and staff positions to include Commander of the 176th Finance Battalion at Yongsan, South Korea; Commander of the 45th Finance Support Unit and Deputy Finance and Accounting Officer at Kaiserslautern, Germany; Training/Executive Officer and Chief of the Military Pay Branch at the United States Army Military Police School and Training Center at Fort McClellan, Alabama; and Central Accounting Officer of the Second Infantry Division at Camp Casey, South Korea.

She also served as Military Assistant for the Assistant Secretary of the Army (Financial Management and Comptroller); Chief of Financial Management in the Office of the Comptroller and the Joint Staff, and Program/Budget Officer in the Office of the Assistant Secretary of the Army (Financial Management and Comptroller) in Washington, D.C.; and Staff Finance Officer and Assistant Executive Officer in the United States Finance and Accounting Center at Indianapolis, Indiana. In September 2004, she was assigned as the Senior Military Assistant to the Director of the Defense Finance and Accounting Service.

Richardson, Velma L.
BRIGADIER GENERAL—ARMY

Born and educated in South Carolina, she received a Bachelor of Science Degree in Mathematics from Livingstone College in Salisbury, North Carolina, in May 1973. Upon graduation from college, she received a direct commission as a second lieutenant in the United States Army Reserve. She earned a Master of Arts degree in Human Resources Management from Pepperdine University. Her military education includes graduating from the Air Defense Artillery Officer Basic Course; Signal Officer Advanced Course; United States Army Command and General Staff College; and the United States Army War College.

In August 1973, she entered active duty at Fort McClellan, Alabama, as a member of the Women's Army Corps. Following her initial orientation, she attended

the Air Defense Officer Basic Course and the Communications-Electronics Staff Officer Course. She was assigned as the Signal Officer for the 1st Battalion, 55th Air Defense Artillery, at Fort Bliss, Texas. An assignment to South Korea ensued, where she served as Platoon Leader and Company Commander in the 51st Signal Battalion. After attending the Signal Officer Advanced Course, new challenges and horizons awaited her with schooling and a subsequent assignment in November 1978 as an Organizational Effectiveness Staff Officer at Fort Gordon, Georgia. From June 1984 to November 1986, she was assigned as a Personnel Assignment Officer at the United States Army Military Personnel Center at Alexandria, Virginia. In December 1986, she was assigned as a Plans Officer with the 35th Signal Brigade, XVIII Airborne Corps, at Fort Bragg, North Carolina. In May 1987, she served as the Executive Officer, with the 426th Signal Battalion, 35th Signal Brigade, XVIII Airborne Corps at Fort Bragg. From June 1988, he served as a Company Grade Management Officer, G-1 (Personnel), XVIII Airborne Corps at Fort Bragg.

Following a 19-month tour of duty in Europe as the United States Army Signal Center Liaison Officer for Mobile Subscriber Equipment, she assumed Command in September 1991 of the 426th Signal Battalion, later reflagged the 51st Signal Battalion at Fort Bragg. In July 1994, she was assigned as a Staff Analyst in the Office of the Assistant Secretary of Defense for Command, Control, Communications and Intelligence. She was promoted to Colonel on June 1, 1996.

In June 1996, she assumed Command of the 1108th United States Army Signal Brigade at Fort Ritchie, Maryland. On July 7, 1998, she was assigned as the Deputy Commander of the United States Signal Center and Fort Gordon. She was the first woman to hold either title at Fort Gordon and was responsible for over-

seeing the communications training of nearly 20,000 service members and foreign students each year. On February 1, 2000, she was promoted to Brigadier General.

In September, 2000, she assigned as the Deputy Commanding General for the Army and Air Force Exchange Service in Dallas, Texas. In July 2002, she was selected to serve as Deputy Commanding General for the Network Enterprise Technology Command at the 9th United States Army Signal Command at Arlington, Virginia. She retired from the military in October 2003.

Her awards and decorations include the Legion of Merit (with oak leaf cluster); the Army Commendation Medal; the Army Achievement Medal; the National Defense Service Medal (2nd award); and the Department of Defense Identification Badge.

Richie, Sharon Ivey
COLONEL—ARMY

She was born in Philadelphia, Pennsylvania. The second eldest of seven children raised in a Philadelphia government-housing project, she is married to Mr. Paul A. Henri. She earned her Bachelor of Science degree in Nursing at Wagner College, New York, in 1971. Subsequently she received a Master of Science degree in Psychiatric Nursing as a Clinical Nurse Specialist from the University of Texas, San Antonio. She was a doctoral student at George Washington University, majoring in Organizational Behavior and Spirituality in Organizations. Her military education includes graduation from the United States Army War College, as well as completion of Command and General Staff College; the Field Combat Nursing Course at Fort Sam Houston, Texas; Combat Psychiatry at Baumholder, Germany;

AMEDD Officer's Advanced Course at Fort Sam Houston; United States Navy Alcoholism Orientation Course at Long Beach, California; Clinical Head Nurse Course at Fort Sam Houston; Psychiatric Mental Health Clinician Course at Walter Reed Army Medical Center in Washington, D.C.; and AMEDD Officer's Basic Course at Fort Sam Houston. From November 1971 to July 1972, she was a staff nurse in the Orthopedic Ward, and later in Medical Intensive Care Unit, at Walter Reed Army Medical Center in Washington, D.C. From December 1972 to July 1974, she was the Assistant Head Nurse at the Behavior Modification Ward at Walter Reed Army Medical Center. From August 1974 to August 1975, she was the Assistant Head Nurse in the Psychiatric Ward at Brooke Army Medical Center at Fort Sam Houston. From August 1976 to September 1977, she was assigned as Hospital Psychiatric Nurse consultant and Head Nurse of the 2nd General Hospital in Landstuhl, Germany. From October 1977 to June 1979, she served as a Psychiatric Clinical Nurse specialist at the Alcoholism Treatment Facility in Stuttgart, Germany. From January 1980 to August 1980, she served as a Nursing Consultant and Clinical Liaison Officer for the United States Surgeon General for Drug and Alcohol Abuse at the Pentagon. From September 1982 to September 1983, she served as a White House Fellow in the Office of Intergovernmental Affairs at the White House. From October 1983 to February 1984, she was the Assistant Chief Nurse for Evenings/Nights at Letterman Army Medical Center in the Presidio of San Francisco, California. In January 1984, she was Profis Chief Nurse at the 8th Evacuation Hospital at Fort Ord, California. In February 1984, she was assigned as Chief of Ambulatory Nursing Service at Letterman Army Medical Center. From August 1985 to May 1986, she was assigned as Director of Quality Assurance for the Department of Nursing at Letterman Army Medical Center. From May 1986 to June 1987, she served as both Chief and Assistant Chief of the Department of Nursing at Kimbrough Army Community Hospital at Fort Meade, Maryland. In June 1988, she was assigned as Chief of Clinical Nursing Service at Walter Reed Army Medical Center. In May 1990, she was assigned Chief of the Department of Nursing at Letterman Army Medical Center. In October 1991, she was assigned Director of the Health Services Directorate, United States Army Recruiting Command at Fort Knox, Kentucky. In August 1993, she was selected as the new Chief Nurse Southeast Health Service Support Area/DOD Region III and Chief of the Department of Nursing at Dwight D. Eisenhower Army Medical Center at Fort Gordon, Georgia.

Colonel Richie is a member of the American Nurses Association (ANA); Sigma Theta Tau, the national nursing honor society; and the Association of Military Surgeons. She served as a San Francisco and St. Louis WHF Regional Commissioner, as the Second Vice President of the White House Fellow Association and most recently as the Minority Recruitment Chair for this White House program. She has been a consultant to the United Army Surgeon General, an Assistant Director of Drug and Alcohol Abuse Prevention for the Department of Defense and has published articles in several professional nursing and military journals. Selected for early promotion to the ranks of Major, Lieutenant Colonel and Colonel, Colonel Richie has been awarded the Surgeon General's "A" Prefix for excellence in nursing administration and in 1993, certified in advanced administration by the ANA. She has been listed in *Who's Who Among Black Americans*; *Who's Who of American Women*; and *Who's Who in American Nursing*. Colonel Richie was honored as one of America's Best and Brightest Business and Professional Women in 1992 was inducted into the African American Biographies Hall of Fame in 1994; and is the recipient of several military awards including the Legion of Merit and the Secretary of Defense Meritorious Service Medal. In December 1993, President Bill Clinton awarded Colonel Richie the Presidential Service Badge.

Riddick, Thelma L.
COMMAND SERGEANT MAJOR—ARMY

She was selected to serve as the Command Sergeant Major and Commandant for the Department of the Army's Non-Commissioned Officer Academy at Fort Eustis, Virginia.

Rivera, Sonya L.
SENIOR CHIEF PETTY OFFICER—NAVY

She was born in Queens, New York, and graduated from high school in Brooklyn New York. She enlisted into the United States Navy in January 1985 and attended Recruit Training in Orlando, Florida, followed by Radioman "A" School at Service School Command, San Diego, California.

Her key military assignments include serving at Naval Telecommunications Center in Mayport, Florida; NAVCOMMDET Guantanamo Bay, Cuba, as Leading

Petty Officer; NAVCOMTELESTA, Jacksonville, Florida, as Leading Petty Officer; USS *John Hancock* (DD 981) as Division Leading Chief; USS *John F. Kennedy* (CV 67) as Division Leading Chief; USS *Barry* (DDG 52) as Division Leading Chief. In October 2004, she was serving as the Senior Enlisted Advisor to the Commander of Carrier Strike Group Twelve.

Robbins, Rodney D.
SERGEANT MAJOR—MARINES

He is a native of Philadelphia, Pennsylvania. He enlisted into the United States Marine Corps in June 1979 and attended Basic Recruit Training at the 3rd Recruit Training Battalion, Recruit Training Regiment at Marine Corps Depot, Parris Island, South Carolina.

Upon graduating from Fort Belvoir, Virginia, in March 1980, he was assigned to 2nd Marine Aircraft Wing at Cherry Point, North Carolina, and served with the Marine Air Support Squadron 1, Air Support Radar Team, Marine Air Command Group 28 for duty as a Surveyor. In October of 1982, he returned to the Marine Corps Recruit Deport, Parris Island, for duty as a Drill Instructor. While with Support Battalion and Fox Company, 2nd Recruit Training Battalion, he served as a Drill Instructor, Senior Drill Instructor, and Series Chief Drill Instructor, and was meritoriously promoted to Staff Sergeant. In January 1986, he was assigned to First Marine Aircraft Wing at Okinawa, Japan, as the Noncommissioned Officer in Charge of Engineer Operations Section with Marine Wing Support Squadron 174, and also as Squadron Gunnery Sergeant with Headquarters and Headquarters Squadron 17. In January 1987, he transferred to the Second Marine Aircraft Wing, Marine Air Support Squadron 1, Air Support Radar Team, Marine Air Command Group 28 for duty as the Noncommissioned Officer in Charge of the Survey Sections. In January 1989, he was assigned as a Drill Instructor and the Noncommissioned Officer in

Charge of Battalion 1, Aviation Officer Candidate School. In October 1991, he earned the distinction as the Drill Instructor of the Year. In January 1992, he was assigned as Platoon Chief for the 3rd Surveillance and Reconnaissance Group, Intelligence Company, 3rd Topographic Platoon at Camp Lejeune, North Carolina. In June 1994, he returned to Marine Corps Recruit Depot, Parris Island, where he served as the Company First Sergeant for Lima and Kilo Companies, 3rd Recruit Training Battalion. In January 1997, he was selected for Sergeant Major. In May 1997, he was assigned as the Sergeant Major for the 1st Recruit Training Battalion. In March 1998, he assumed the duties as Squadron Sergeant Major for Marine Aerial Refueler Transport Squadron 152, Marine Aircraft Group 36, 1st Marine Aircraft Wing. In March 1999, he was assigned as Group Sergeant Major for Marine Aviation Training Support Group 33 at Naval Air Station Oceana, Virginia. In October 2001, he returned to Marine Corps Recruit Depot to assume duties as the Battalion Sergeant Major for Headquarters and Service Battalion. In August 2004, Sergeant Major Robbins was assigned as the Sergeant Major for the 12th Marine Regiment, 3rd Marine Division at Okinawa.

Roberts, Bruce
COMMAND SERGEANT MAJOR—ARMY

He is a native of Georgia. He entered the Army in September 1977 and completed Basic and Advanced Individual Training at Fort Sill, Oklahoma. He is a graduate of all the Noncommissioned Officer Courses, Army Recruiting Course, Station Commander Course, Battle Staff Course, the First Sergeant Course, and the Sergeants Major Academy. He holds an associate's degree from the University of Maryland, and is pursuing his Bachelor of Arts.

He has held numerous positions in the Field Artillery, to include serving as Command Sergeant Major for the 8th Field Artillery, at Fort Lewis, Washington. In August 2004, he was serving as Command Sergeant Major for the 3rd Battalion, 7th Field Artillery, at Schofield Barracks, Hawaii.

Roberts, James
SERGEANT MAJOR—MARINES

He enlisted through the delayed entry program in October 1979 at the MEPS in Columbia, South Carolina. He arrived at Marine Corps Recruit Depot at Parris Island, South Carolina, on August 11, 1980, for basic training.

Upon completion of recruit training, he was assigned to Communication and Electronic School, at Camp Geiger, North Carolina. After graduation in December 1980, he was transferred to 4th Battalion, 10th Marines at Camp Lejeune, North Carolina, for duty with Headquarters and Service Company Communication Platoon as a field wireman.

He completed the Basic Electrician School at Court House Bay, and was ordered to Marine Corps Logistics Base at Albany, Georgia, where he was assigned to Base Maintenance. Upon completion of the Utility Chief course in 1989 at Court House Bay he was given orders to Marine Corps Air Station in Iwakuni, Japan.

In 1994, he was promoted to Gunnery Sergeant and transferred to Marine Corps Air Station Cherry Point, North Carolina, for duty with MWSS-274 Utility Platoon from 1994 to 1998.

In February 1998, Gunnery Sergeant Roberts received orders back to Marine Corps Air Station Iwakuni, Japan, for a one year tour with MWSS-171, serving as the Squadron Gunnery Sergeant. He was promoted to First Sergeant in September 1998 and transferred to MAG-12, serving as the PSD First Sergeant. In February 1999, First Sergeant Roberts received orders to Marine Corps Base, Camp Lejeune, North Carolina for duty with Headquarters and Service Company, MCCSSS Camp Johnson.

In 2000, he was transferred back to Marine Corps Air Station Cherry Point for duty with Headquarters and Service Battery, 2nd LAAD Battalion. He was promoted to Sergeant Major on January 1, 2004, and received orders to Marine Corps Air Station, Beaufort, South Carolina for duty as the Sergeant Major for VMFA 115.

Roberts, Perry L.
COMMAND SERGEANT MAJOR—ARMY

Command Sergeant Major Roberts was born in Speed, North Carolina. He enlisted in the United States Army in March 1973. Upon completion of Basic Combat Training at Fort Jackson, South Carolina and Advanced Individual Training at Fort Sill, Oklahoma, he was assigned to C battery, 1st Battalion, 38th Field Artillery, at Camp Stanley, South Korea.

His assignments include Assistant Gunner; Howitzer Chief; Gunner Howitzer; Gunnery Sergeant; Pla-

toon Sergeant; Senior Drill Sergeant; Director of Reserves Component; Command Sergeant Major of the Field Artillery Training Center; Command Sergeant Major of Field Artillery Training Command; and Command Sergeant Major of the 4th Brigade; 78 Division, (Training Support). He is currently serving as the Command Sergeant Major of the United States Accessions Command.

Roberts, Robert E., Jr.
SERGEANT MAJOR—MARINES

He is a native of Pennsylvania. In June 1978, he arrived at Parris Island, South Carolina, for Marine Corps Recruit Training. After graduation from Recruit Training in September 1978, he reported to the Basic

Artillery School at Fort Sill, Oklahoma. After finishing school, he reported to his first duty station December 1978 and was assigned to 1st Field Artillery Group at 29 Palms, in California.

His key military leadership assignments include service as Assistant Battalion Operation Chief of the 2nd Battalion, 12th Marines, 3rd Marine Division; Battery Operations Chief of the 5th Battalion, 11th Marines, 1st Marine Division at 29 Palms; as a Drill Instructor and Senior Drill Instructor in the 1st Recruit Training Battalion; as the Battery Operations Chief for the 1st Battalion, 10th Marines; deploying on Operations Desert Shield and Desert Storm; and as Platoon Sergeant with the 3rd Battalion, 2nd Marines, 2nd Marine Division in the 81st mm Mortar Platoon. In October 1993, he received orders to the 3rd Battalion, 14th Marines, 4th Marine Division for Inspector and Instructor Duty as the Training and Operations Chief in Reading, Pennsylvania. He also served as First Sergeant for the Marine Corps Security Force Company in Naples, Italy; and as the Squadron Sergeant Major for Marine Wing Support Squadron 271 at Cherry Point, North Carolina. He deployed to Kuwait in support of Operation Enduring Freedom and then into Iraq during Operation Iraqi Freedom. In August 2003, Sergeant Major Roberts reported to the 3rd Radio Battalion at Marine Corps Base Hawaii to assume the duties as the Battalion Sergeant Major; since his arrival, he has returned to Iraq on two separate occasions to continue supporting the Global War On Terrorism. Sergeant Major Roberts currently serves as Regimental Sergeant Major of the 3rd Marine Regiment.

Robertson, Craig H.

COMMAND SERGEANT MAJOR—ARMY

He entered the United States Army in January 1981, and attended Basic Combat Training at Fort Benning, Georgia. His career has taken him to assignments in Hawaii; Jackson, Tennessee; Fort Bragg, North Carolina; Fort Jackson, South Carolina; Fort Myer, Virginia; and South Korea.

His military and civilian education includes all the Noncommissioned Officer Education System Courses; Air Assault School; Ranger School; Drill Sergeant School; Recruiter Course; Path Finder School; Jumpmaster School; First Sergeant Course; and the United States Army Sergeants Major Academy. He holds a Bachelor of Science degree.

He has held numerous leadership positions to include serving as Command Sergeant Major 1-506th Infantry (Air Assault); Battalion Operations Sergeant Major for the 3rd United States Infantry (TOG); First Sergeant of Delta and Hotel Company, 3rd United States Infantry (TOG); First Sergeant and Senior Drill Sergeant of the 1/61st Infantry Basic Training Battalion; Platoon Sergeant of the 2/505th Airborne Infantry Battalion; Recruiter at the Jackson, Mississippi, Recruiting Battalion; and Platoon Sergeant, Section Sergeant and Squad Leader, with the 1/27th Infantry Battalion.

Robertson, Samuel

COMMAND SERGEANT MAJOR—ARMY

Command Sergeant Major Samuel Robertson is a native of Ridgeway, South Carolina. He enlisted in the Army in 1974, and attended Basic Combat Training at Fort Jackson, South Carolina. He completed his Advanced Individual Training at Fort Bliss, Texas.

He has held a wide variety of noncommissioned leadership positions including Squad Leader in a Battery 2-60 ADAFRG (32nd AADCOM); Team Chief and Section Sergeant at HHB 2-31 FA, Fort Campbell, Kentucky; Shorad Instructor at HHB Group, Fort Bliss, Texas; Recruiter at Long Island Recruiting Battalion; Platoon Sergeant and Operation Sergeant of the HHC 194th Armor Brigade at Fort Knox, Kentucky; Operation HHB 1-5 ADA, Fort Stewart, Georgia; First Sergeant for D Battery 4-3 ADAFRG; ROTC Instructor at Syracuse, New York; Support Troop Sergeant Major at White Sands Missile Range, New Mexico; and Command Sergeant Major for 3-43 ADA. He participated in Operation Desert Shield/Desert Storm, and as a Command Sergeant Major deployed twice to the Middle East.

He holds a bachelor's degree and has completed the First Sergeants School and the United States Army Sergeant Major Academy.

Robinson, Bruce

MAJOR GENERAL—ARMY

He was born in Abington, Pennsylvania. After high school he attended the United States Military Academy at West Point, where he graduated with a Bachelor of Science degree in General Engineering and received his commission as a Second Lieutenant in June 1970. He holds a master's degree in Business Management from Central Michigan University and a Juris Doctorate degree for the University of Richmond. He graduated from the Infantry Officer Basic and Advance Courses; Airborne and Ranger Schools; Command and General Staff College; and the Army War College.

He served as a Weapons Platoon Leader and the Battalion S-3, Air with 1-48 Infantry Battalion, 2nd Brigade, 3rd Armored Division, at Gelnhausen, Germany; and as a Racial Relations Instructor for the 2nd Brigade, 3rd Armored Division, in Gelnhausen. He was then assigned to Headquarters at Fort Dix, New Jersey, as the Assistant Billeting Officer.

In June 1976, he began his career with the United States Army Reserves and 80th Division (Institutional Training), at Richmond, Virginia, as an Equal Opportunity Officer. He has held a progression of staff and command positions in the 80th Division (Institutional Training) culminating as the Assistant Division Commander of the 80th Division (Institutional Training). He was selected Commander of the 98th Division (Institutional Training) in New Jersey on July 2, 2002. As commander, he controls all of the Institutional Training Army Reserve Force assigned in eight Brigades spread throughout the six New England states, New York and New Jersey.

His military awards and decorations include the Meritorious Service Medal (with two oak leaf clusters); the Army Commendation Medal (with oak leaf cluster); Army Achievement Medal; Army Reserve Components Achievements Medal (with five oak leaf clusters); National Defense Service Medal (with bronze star); Armed Forces Reserve Medal (with bronze hourglass device); Overseas Ribbon; the Parachutist Badge; and the Ranger Tab.

Robinson, Harry L.
SERGEANT MAJOR—ARMY

He received a bachelor's degree in Occupational Education with a specialization in Health Care Administration from Wayland Baptist University and a mas-

ter's degree in Educational Leadership from Troy State University. He is a graduate of the Sergeants Major Academy; the First Sergeants Course; and Basic and Advanced NCO Courses.

Sergeant Major Robinson was born in Indianapolis, Indiana, and entered the Army in August 1976, attending Basic and Advance Individual training at Fort Still, Oklahoma, as an Artillery Canon Crewman. He later attended the Combat Medic and Practical Nurse Course at the AMEDD Center and School at Fort Sam Houston, Texas.

He has served in a wide variety of leadership assignments including Sergeant Major of the 248th General Hospital; Senior Clinical Non-commissioned Officer; Chief Wardmaster; First Sergeant; Senior Medical Advisor to the Army Reserve and National Guard; and Operations NCO; and Wardmaster.

He is currently serving as the Senior Enlisted Advisor for the Executive Director of the TRICARE Management Activity. He serves as a resource, liaison, and advocate for enlisted members of the armed forces and their family members and represents their interests to the senior leadership of the Military Health System.

Robinson, Hugh Granville
MAJOR GENERAL—ARMY

Born in Washington, D.C., he is the son of Colonel and Mrs. James H. Robinson. He married the former Matilda Turner. They have three children, Hugh G. Robinson, Jr.; Susan Robinson; and Mia Turner Robinson. He was commissioned in the United States Army Corps of Engineers in June 1954 after graduation from West Point. He earned a Master of Science degree (Civil Engineering) from Massachusetts Institute of Technology. He received an honorary Doctor of Laws from Williams College in 1983. His military education includes the Armed Forces Staff College and the National War College. He served as a Platoon Leader and Company Commander in South Korea from April 1955 to July 1956. He was promoted to First Lieutenant on December 4, 1955, and to Captain on August 11, 1960. He has held a wide variety of important command and staff positions. From 1963 to 1965, he served as Chief of the Combat Branch of the Engineer Strategic Studies Group in Washington, D.C. He was promoted to Major on August 5, 1964, and to Lieutenant Colonel on December 13, 1967. From May 1965 to January 1969, he was Army aide to President Lyndon Johnson on the White House Detachment in Washington, D.C. From May 1967 and January 1969, he was assigned as the Army Assistant to the Armed Forces Aide to the President in the Office of the President at the White House. In August 1969, he subsequently served as Executive Officer of the 45th Engineer Group, then as Battalion Commander of the 39th Engineer Battalion (Combat) in Vietnam. General Robinson served in a variety of important career-building assignments preparatory to his most recent duties. In Vietnam he served from 1970 to 1972 as Chief of the Regional Capabilities Branch of the Office of Deputy Chief of Staff for Operations,

War Plans Divisions, at the Pentagon. From June 1972 to June 1974, he served subsequently as Executive Officer of the 3rd Regiment, USCC at West Point, New York, then as Commanding Officer at the 3rd Regiment, USCC, at West Point. He was promoted to Colonel on June 14, 1973. From June 1974 to June 1976, he was Commanding Officer of the United States Army Engineer School Brigade at Fort Belvoir, Virginia. From June 1976 to July 1978, he served as district engineer, United States Army. Robinson served as Deputy Director of Civil Works in the Office of the Chief of Engineers, United States Army, Washington, D.C. He was promoted to Brigadier General on July 1, 1978, and to Major General on February 1, 1981. From August 1980 to July 1983, he was assigned as the Division Engineer for the United States Army Engineer Division Southwestern, Dallas in Texas. In 1983, General Robinson retired, joining the Southland Corporation as vice president after election by the board of directors. City Place Development Corporation, a wholly owned subsidiary of Southland Corporation, was formed in January 1984, and General Robinson was appointed its president. His awards and decorations include the Distinguished Service Medal, Legion of Merit (with oak leaf cluster), Bronze Star (with oak leaf cluster), Meritorious Service Medal, Air Medal (with two oak leaf clusters), Joint Service Commendation Medal, Army Commendation Medal (with oak leak cluster), Vietnamese Cross of Gallantry (gold star), Vietnamese Service Medal, Vietnam Campaign Medal, American Defense (with oak leaf cluster), Presidential Service Badge, Army Service Ribbon, Overseas Service Ribbon, Meritorious Unit Citation, Henry O. Flipper Award (1985), and Vietnam Veteran of the Year Award (1985).

Robinson, Kenneth B.
BRIGADIER GENERAL—ARMY

He received a Bachelor of Science degree in Business Economics from the Pennsylvania Military College/ Widener University in 1972. He earned a Masters of Art degree in Personnel Management from Central Michigan University in 1980. His military education includes completion of the Officer Rotary Wing Aviator Course; Armor Officer Advance Course; and the United States Army War College.

His military career began in the United States Army Reserve in 1971. He was appointed a Second Lieutenant in the United State Army in 1973. From May 1973 to December 1974, he was assigned as a Training Officer with Company B, later as Operations Officer with Company E, 15th Battalion, 4th Basic Combat Training Brigade, at Fort Knox, Kentucky. From December 1974 to June 1976, he served first as a Motor Officer with Headquarters and Headquarters Company, later as Platoon Leader with Company B, next as the S-3 Air with Headquarters and Headquarters Company, 1st Battalion 72nd Armor, with the 2nd Infantry Division in South Korea. He was promoted to First Lieutenant on June 6, 1976. He was promoted to Captain on June 6, 1977. From March 1978 to July 1979, he was

assigned as Aeroscout Platoon Commander, of Troop C, 3rd Squadron, 4th Cavalry, 25th Infantry Division at Schofield Barracks, Hawaii. From July 1979 to November 1980, he was assigned as Liaison Officer, later as Squadron Training Officer, next as Assistant S-3, with Headquarters and Headquarters Troop, 3rd Squadron, 4th Cavalry, 25th Infantry Division, at Schofield Barracks in Hawaii. From December 1980 to January 1982, he was assigned as Flight Instructor at the United States Aviation Center at Fort Rucker, Alabama.

He was appointed a Chief Warrant Officer 2 in the Ohio Army National Guard in 1985, and as a Captain of Aviation in 1986. From October 1986 to February 1987, he was assigned as Platoon Leader of Troop F Attack Helicopter Troop (Combat Aviation Squadron), 107th Armored Cavalry Regiment, at Worthington, Ohio. In February 1987, he was assigned as the Commander of Troop E, Attack Helicopter Troop (Combat Aviation Squadron), at Worthington. From November 1987 to December 1988, he served as an Aviation Safety Officer at Headquarters State Area Command in Columbus, Ohio. In December 1988, he was assigned as Executive Officer, later as Commander of the Headquarters Detachment of the 1st Battalion, 137th Aviation (Aviation Intermediate Maintenance), in Columbus. From October 1994 to April 1995, he was assigned as the State Aviation Officer at Headquarters State Area Command in Columbus. In April 1995, he served as Commander of the 371st Support Group at Kettering, Ohio. He was promoted to Colonel on May 19, 1995.

From January to June 1999, he was assigned as the Evaluation Team Chief at Headquarters State Area Command in Columbus. In June 1999, he was selected as the Commander of the 16th Engineer Brigade in Columbus. He was promoted to Brigadier General on June 16, 1999. He retired from the military on October 30, 2002.

His military awards and decorations include the Meritorious Service Medal (with three oak leaf clusters); Army Commendation Medal (with three oak leaf clusters); Army Reserve Component Achievement Medal (with three oak leaf clusters); National Defense Service Medal; Armed Forces Reserve Medal; Army Service Ribbon; Overseas Service Ribbon; Army Reserve Component Overseas Training Ribbon; Master Army Aviator Badge; Senior Army Aviator Badge; and Army Aviator Badge.

Robinson, Neal T.
BRIGADIER GENERAL—AIR FORCE

He received a Bachelor of Science degree in International Relations from the United States Air Force Academy in Colorado Springs, Colorado. He earned a Master of Arts degree in National Security Affairs from the Naval Post Graduate School in Monterey, California. His military education includes Squadron Officer School at Maxwell Air Force Base, Alabama; the Army Command and General Staff College at Fort Leavenworth, Kansas; Inter-American Defense College at Fort Lesley J. McNair, Washington, D.C.; the Intelligence and Policy Seminar at the John F. Kennedy School of Government at Harvard University in Cambridge, Massachusetts; and the Senior Executive Program at Columbia University Graduate School of Business in Harrison, New York.

He entered the Air Force after graduating from the United States Air Force Academy in 1974. After Signals Intelligence School at Goodfellow Air Force Base, Texas, he served as the Flight Commander and Chief of Operations Management with the 6903rd Electronic Security Squadron at Osan Air Base, South Korea. He subsequently was assigned to the National Security Agency as an intern and later at both the Defense Intelligence Agency and the Air Force Intelligence Agency as a Middle East analyst. In 1990, he went to United States Southern Command at Quarry Heights, Panama, and served in the Directorate of Operations as Chief of Intelligence for the Deployable Joint Task Force. He retuned to South Korea from June 1993 to February 1995, to serve as the Director of Intelligence for 7th Air Force; later as Commander of the 607th Air Intelligence Group, and Assistant Chief of Staff of Intelligence, A2, Air Component Command at Osan Air Base. He was promoted to Colonel on February 1, 1994.

In March 1995, he was assigned to the Air Intelligence Agency at Kelly Air Force Base, Texas, as Director of Operations. The general has served as the Director of Intelligence, C2, of NATO Combined Air Operations Center at Vicenza, Italy, and as Director of Intelligence for United States Air Forces in Europe. He later served as the Associate Director of Operations for Command, Control Intelligence, Surveillance and Reconnaissance with the Directorate of Air and Space Operations at Headquarters Air Combat Command at Langley Air Force Base, Virginia. From March 1999 to September 2001, he was assigned as the Director of Intelligence for United States European Command in Stuttgart, Germany. He was promoted to Brigadier General on July 1, 2000.

In September 2001, he was assigned as Vice Commander of the Air Intelligence Agency at Lackland Air Force Base, Texas. In October 2001, he was selected as Director and Vice Commander of the Headquarters of the Air Force Cryptologic Office at Fort George G. Meade, Maryland.

His military awards and decorations include the Defense Superior Service Medal; the Legion of Merit; the Defense Meritorious Service Medal (with two oak leaf clusters); the Meritorious Service Medal; the Joint Service Commendation Medal (with oak leaf cluster); the Air Force Commendation Medal; Humanitarian Service Medal; and NATO Medal.

Robinson, Roscoe, Jr.

GENERAL—ARMY

He was born in St. Louis, Missouri, where he received his elementary and secondary education. After graduation from Charles Sumner High School, he was appointed to the United States Military Academy at West Point. He was graduated in 1951, with a Bachelor of Science degree in Military Engineering and commissioned a Second Lieutenant. After graduation, Robinson attended the Associate Infantry Officer Course and the Basic Airborne Course at Fort Benning, Georgia. He then joined the 11th Airborne Division at Fort Campbell, Kentucky, where he served as a platoon leader in the 188th Airborne Infantry Regiment until he went to Korea in October 1952. On January 30, 1953, he was promoted to First Lieutenant. In Korea, he served in the 31st Infantry Regiment, 7th Infantry Division, as a rifle company commander and battalion S-2. He was awarded the Bronze Star for his service in Korea. He was promoted to Captain on December 7, 1956. Upon returning to the United States, he served in a variety of school and airborne unit assignments, highlighted by a tour with the United States Military Mission to Liberia in the late 1950s and the receipt of a master's in International affairs from the University of Pittsburgh in the early 1960s. On October 26, 1962, he was promoted to Major. From June 1963 to September 1963, he was an Author-Instructor in the Department of Command, United States Army Command, and General Staff College at Fort Leavenworth, Kansas. From September 1963 to January 1965, he was a student at the University of Pittsburgh, Pennsylvania. From January 1965 to July 1967, he served as Personnel Management, Officer, Infantry Branch, Officer Directorate, Office of Personnel Operations, United States Army, in Washington, D.C. He was promoted to Lieutenant Colonel on September 6, 1966. From July 1967 to January 1968, he was assigned as the G-4, on the staff of the 1st Air Cavalry Division, then as the first black to Command the 2nd Battalion, 7th Cavalry Division (Airmobile), United States Army, Pacific-Vietnam. For his Vietnam service, he was decorated with the Silver Star for valor. From August 1968 to July 1969, he was a student in the National War College, Washington, D.C. Upon completion to the National War College, he served from July 1969 to May 1971, as first Plans Officer, and later Southeast Asia Special Actions Officer, J-5, United States Special Actions in Hawaii, until his promotion to Colonel on February 22, 1972. He assumed Command of the 2nd Brigade, 82nd Airborne Division at Fort Bragg, North Carolina, from May 1972 to July 1972. On July 1, 1973, he was promoted to Brigadier General. Since that time, he has been assigned as the Commanding General of the United States Garrison at Okinawa; Commanding General of the 82nd Airborne Division; and Commanding General of the United States Army in Japan/IX Corps. He was promoted to Major General on July 1, 1976, and promoted to Lieutenant General on June 1, 1980. In August 1982 he became the first black to become a four-star general in the Army (the second black in the armed forces, after General Daniel "Chappie" James). He also served as the United States representative to the North Atlantic Treaty Organization (NATO) Military Committee. In his over 31 years of active duty service, General Robinson has been awarded the Silver Star (with oak leaf cluster), the Legion of Merit (with two oak leaf clusters), the Star Medal, ten Air Medals, the Army commendation Medal, the Combat Infantryman Badge (second award), and the Master Parachutist Badge.

Rochelle, Michael D.

LIEUTENANT GENERAL—ARMY

He is a native of Norfolk, Virginia, and married the former Grace Hickman, also of Norfolk, Virginia. He and Mrs. Rochelle have three children, Shernita Rochelle-Parker; First Lieutenant Shawnette Rochelle, a 1999 graduate of the United States Military Academy; and Michael, Jr. He received a Bachelor of Arts degree in Foreign Language Education from Norfolk State University and a Masters of Arts degree in Public Administration from Shippensburg University. His military education includes the Field Artillery Officer Basic Course; the Adjutant General Officer Advanced Course; the United States Army Command and General Staff College; and the United States Army War College.

He was commissioned as a Regular Army Officer in 1972. He first served a combat arms detail as a lieutenant of field artillery with the 101st Airborne Division (Air Assault), located at Fort Campbell, Kentucky. He was then assigned as a Forward Observer and Fire Directions Officer with the 321st Field Artillery, 101st Airborne Division (Air Assault) at Fort Campbell. In March 1980, he was assigned as the Assistant Secretary to the General Staff/Protocol Officer at the United States Military Academy at West Point, New York.

Commanding both at the grade of captain and major, he commanded first the 226th Adjutant General Company (Postal) in Munich, Germany, and later, in June 1983, the United States Military Entrance Processing Station at Portland, Maine. In November 1988, he served as the Commander of the United States Army

Recruiting Battalion, 1st Recruiting Brigade (Northeast), in Brunswick, Maine. In May 1991, he was assigned as the G-1/Adjutant General (Personnel), with the 101st Airborne Division (Air Assault), at Fort Campbell. In June 1994, he was assigned as Assistant Deputy Chief of Staff for Base Operations Support at the United States Army Training and Doctrine Command at Fort Monroe, Virginia. He was promoted to on February 1, 1995.

From April 1995 to June 1997, he served as the Installation Commander for Fort Monroe, Virginia. From July 1997 to June 1999, he was assigned as Special Assistant for General/Flag Officer Matters for the Joint Staff in Washington, D.C. In June 1999, he was selected to serve as Senior Military Assistant to the Deputy Secretary of Defense in Washington, D.C. He was promoted to Brigadier General on September 1, 1999.

From August 2000 to January 2002, he served as Commanding General of the United States Army Soldier Support Institute at Fort Jackson, South Carolina. He was promoted to Major General on December 1, 2002. In January 2002, he was assigned as the Commanding General of the United States Army Recruiting Command at Fort Knox, Kentucky. He was promoted to Lieutenant General on June 7, 2006.

His military awards and decorations include the Defense Distinguished Service Medal; the Distinguished Service Medal; Defense Superior Service Medal; Legion of Merit (with two oak leaf clusters); Defense Meritorious Service Medal; Meritorious Service Medal (with two oak leaf clusters); Joint Service Achievement Medal; Secretary of Defense Badge; Army Staff Identification Badge; and Recruiter Badge.

Rodriguez, Carl H.

SERGEANT MAJOR—MARINES

He enlisted in the United States Marine Corps in May 1978. He completed Recruit Training in August 1978 at Marine Corps Recruit Depot, Parris Island, South Carolina.

His key military assignments include serving in Operations Desert Shield/Desert Storm, and deployment with BSSG-6 Interrogator/Translator Unit Guantanamo Bay Cuba during Operation Sea Signal in November 1991, as advisor to the Refugee Camp Commander, attached to the United States Army 82nd Airborne Special Operation Unit. He also served as Training Operations Chief with the 6th ESB Bulk Fuels Company; First Sergeant for Company B, 3rd Recon Company, 3rd Marine Division, Okinawa, Japan; First Sergeant of Headquarters Company, Weapons and Field Training Battalion Marine Corps Recruit Depot, Parris Island, South Carolina; and Sergeant Major of Marine Light/Attack Helicopter Squadron 269th, Marine Air Group 29.

Rogers, Charles Calvin

MAJOR GENERAL—ARMY

He was born in Claremont, West Virginia, he married

the former Margarete Schaefer, and they have two children, Jackie Linda and Barbara. He received a Bachelor of Science degree in Mathematics from West Virginia State College, a Master of Science degree in Vocational Education from Shippensburg State College, and a Master of Science degree in Theology from the University of Munich, West Germany. His military education includes the Field Artillery School Basic Course; the United States Army Artillery and Missile School Advanced Course; the United States Army Command and General Staff College; and the United States Army War College. He was commissioned a Second Lieutenant on June 15, 1951, and was next promoted to First Lieutenant on December 27, 1952. He was promoted to Captain on December 17, 1956, and to Major on November 9, 1961. From June 1966 to November 1967, he was the Commanding Officer of the 1st Battalion, 2nd Brigade, at Fort Lewis, Washington; from November 1967 to February 1968, he served as Commander of the 1st Infantry Division Artillery, United States Army, Pacific-Vietnam; and from February 1968 to November 1968, he was Commanding Officer of the 1st Battalion, 5th Artillery, 1st Infantry Division, United States Army, Pacific-Vietnam. He was promoted to Lieutenant Colonel on September 13, 1966, and distinguished himself in action while serving as Commanding Officer with the 1st Battalion during the defense of forward fire support base Fishhook near the Cambodian border in Vietnam. In the early morning, the fire support base was subjected to a concentrated bombardment of heavy mortar, rocket, and rocket-propelled grenade fire. Simultaneously the position was struck by a human ground assault wave led by sappers who breached the defensive barriers with bangalore torpedoes and penetrated the defensive perimeter. Lieutenant Colonel Rogers, with complete disregard for his safety, moved to the embattled area through the hail of fragments from bursting enemy rounds. He aggressively rallied the dazed artillery crewmen to man their howitzers, and he directed their fire on the assaulting enemy. Although knocked to the ground and wounded by an exploding round, General Rogers sprang to his feet and led a small counterattack force against an enemy element that had penetrated the howitzer positions. Although painfully wounded a second time during the assault, General Rogers pressed the attack, killing several of the enemy and driving the remainder from the positions. Refusing medical treatment, General Rogers reestablished and reinforced the defensive positions. As a second human wave attack was launched against another sector of the perimeter, he directed artillery fire on the enemy and led a second counterattack against the charging forces. His valorous example rallied the beleaguered defenders to repulse and defeat the enemy onslaught. Rogers moved from position to position through the heavy enemy fire, giving encouragement and direction to his men. At dawn the determined enemy launched a third assault against the firebase in an attempt to overrun the position. Rogers moved to the threatened area and directed lethal fire on the enemy

forces. Seeing a howitzer inoperative due to casualties, Rogers joined the surviving members of the crew to return the howitzer to action and was seriously wounded by fragments from a heavy mortar round which exploded on the parapet of the gun position. Although too severely wounded to lead the defenders, General Rogers continued to give encouragement and direction to his men in defeating and repelling the enemy attack. General Rogers's dauntless courage and heroism inspired the defenders of the fire support base to the heights of valor to defeat a determined and numerically superior enemy force. His relentless spirit of aggressiveness in action was in the highest traditions of the military service and reflected great credit upon himself, his unit, and the United States Army. For his bravery, he received the Congressional Medal of Honor, the highest award for bravery that can be given to any individual in the United States military. From January 1969 to July 1969, he served as Operations Chief, J-3, United States Military Assistance Command, in Vietnam. From August 1969 to May 1970, he served as a Staff Officer with the Readiness Division (later redesignated Troop Operations and Readiness Division) in the Operations Directorate of the Office of Deputy Chief of Staff for Military Operations in Washington, D.C. In June 1970, he was selected to attend the United States Army War College at Carlisle Barracks, Pennsylvania. After completion of the War College, his assignment from September 1971 to January 1972 was Assistant Deputy Commander, later Deputy Commander, V Corps Artillery, United States Army, in Europe. On March 8, 1972, he was promoted to Colonel, and on July 1, 1973, he was promoted to Brigadier General. From January 1972 to June 1973, he served as Commanding General of the VII Corps Artillery, United States Army, in Europe. On September 1, 1975, he was appointed Major General. From 1975 to 1978, he served as Deputy Chief of Staff of ROTC Headquarters Training and Doctrine Command at Fort Monroe, Virginia. He returned to Europe in 1978, where he served first as Deputy Commanding General, V Corps, and from 1980 to 1983 Commanding General of VII Corps Artillery. He retired in October 1983. General Rogers's military awards and decorations include the Congressional Medal of Honor; Legion of Merit (with oak leaf cluster); Distinguished Flying Cross; Bronze Star (with "V" device and three oak leaf clusters); Air Medal (10 awards); Joint Service Commendation Medal; Army Commendation Medal (with three oak leaf clusters); Purple Heart; and Parachutist Badge.

Rogers, Dennis E.
BRIGADIER GENERAL—ARMY

He is a graduated from the University of South Alabama in May 1980, with a Bachelor of Arts degree in History and a commission as Second Lieutenant in the United States Army. His first assignment was as A Platoon Leader, later Executive Officer, B Troop, 2nd Squadron, 9th Cavalry, 24th Infantry Division (Mechanized) at Fort Stewart, Georgia.

He received a Master of Science degree in National Security Strategy from the United States Army War College and earned a master's in Public Administration (MPA) at Shippensburg University. He is also a graduate of the Armor Officer Basic Course; Air Assault School; Ranger School; Armor Officer Advanced Course; Combined Arms and Services Staff School and the United States Army Command and General Staff College.

His military assignments include serving as Executive Officer of the 2nd Battalion, 37th Armor, 3rd Infantry Division (Mechanized), United States Army Europe and Seventh Army in Germany; as Chief, G-3 (Operations), 3rd Infantry Division (Mechanized), United States Army in Europe and Seventh Army in Germany; as Pacific War Planner in the Conventional War Plans Division, J-7, The Joint Staff, in Washington, D.C.; as Commander of the 4th Battalion (TUSKERS), 64th Armor Regiment, 3rd Infantry Division at Fort Stewart; as the Senior Armor Task Force Observer/Controller, Operations Group, at the National Training Center at Fort Irwin, California; and as the 2nd Brigade Commander with the 4th Infantry Division (Mechanized) at Fort Hood, Texas, during Operation Iraqi Freedom. In July 2003, he was assigned as Assistant Chief of Staff, G-3, III Corps, with duty as Deputy Chief of Staff for Operations, G-3, Multi-National Corps-Iraq at Fort Hood during Operation Iraqi Freedom.

On March 18, 2005, he was confirmed by the U.S. Senate for appointment to Brigadier General.

Rogers, Lawrence C.
COMMAND SERGEANT MAJOR—ARMY

Command Sergeant Major Lawrence C. Rogers joined the Army on June 19, 1974, completed Basic Combat Training at Fort Knox, Kentucky, and Advanced Individual Training at Redstone Arsenal, Alabama. His military education includes the United States Army First Sergeants Course and the United States Army Sergeants Major Academy at Fort Bliss, Texas.

His military assignments includes serving with the 144th Ordnance Company in Wildflecken, Germany; with the 5th Infantry Division Material Management Center (DAO) at Fort Polk, Louisiana; with the 267th Ordnance Company at Fort Riley, Kansas; with the 5th Quartermaster Detachment, Headquarters and Headquarters Company 66th Maintenance Battalion, in Kaiserslautern, Germany; with the 2nd Armored Division Material Management Center (DAO); with Surveillance Accountability and Control Team Two at Camp Humphrey, South Korea; and with the 6th Ordnance Battalion, 19th TAACOM, in South Korea.

Rogers, Lunslee L.
COMMAND MASTER CHIEF—NAVY

He was born and raised in Anguilla in the British West Indies. He enlisted in the United States Navy under the Delayed Entry Program in July of 1979. Upon graduation from Basic Recruit Training Command in Orlando, Florida, he reported to Machinist's Mate "A" School in Great Lakes, Illinois.

He attended the Senior Enlisted Academy in October of 1996, then was assigned to the USS *Theodore Roosevelt* (CVN 71), where he served as Auxiliaries Division Leading Senior Chief and also as Engineering Department Master Chief. In November of 2000, he reported to VF 211 as Command Master Chief. Following a successful tour he reported to PSA Atlantic as Command Master Chief. In October 2004, he was serving as the Command Master Chief PERSUPPACT Atlantic.

Roundtree, Melvin
SERGEANT MAJOR—MARINES

He is a native of Chicago, Illinois, where he graduated from Englewood High School in 1976. He enlisted into the United States Marine Corps in October 1977, and attended Recruit Training at the Marine Corps Recruit Depot in San Diego, California. Upon completion of recruit training, he attended Infantry Training School (ITS) at Camp Pendleton, California.

His key military assignments include serving as Sergeant Instructor for the Platoon Leaders Course at Officer Candidate School in 1981; Drill Instructor and Senior Drill Instructor of the 1st Recruit Training Battalion at Marine Corps Recruit Depot, San Diego, California; Battalion Operation Chief (S-3); Platoon Sergeant and Company Gunnery Sergeant at the Officer Candidate School at Quantico; Company First Sergeant of Bravo Company at Officer Candidate School at Quantico; First Sergeant of Golf Company and Weapons Company, 2nd Battalion, 4th Marines, 1st Marine Division; Sergeant Major, 2nd Battalion, 5th Marines; Sergeant Major, Infantry Training Battalion; and Sergeant Major of the Weapons and Field Training Battalion. In January 2005, he was serving as the Sergeant Major of the 5th Marine Regiment.

Rountree, Gregory A.
MAJOR GENERAL—ARMY

Born in Jonesville, Louisiana, Rountree received a Bachelor of Science in Psychology from Southern University of Agriculture and Mining. He also received a Master of Arts degree in Management and Human Relations from Webster University. His military education includes the Air Defense Artillery Officer Basic and Advanced Courses; the United States Army Command and Staff College; Defense Systems Management College Program Management Course; and the United States Army War College. He received his commission to Second Lieutenant on July 7, 1970. From November 1970 to January 1974, he was assigned as Assistant Team Commander, later Team Commander, 31st Artillery Detachment, 559th Artillery Group, United States Army Southern European Task Force, in Italy. He was promoted to First Lieutenant on July 7, 1973. From February 1974 to January 1976, He served as the Commander of Battery B, 1st Battalion, 65th Air Defense Artillery, United States Naval Air Station, in Key West, Florida. From May 1976 to December 1976, he was a student at the Air Defense Artillery Officer Advanced Course at Fort Bliss, Texas. From January 1977 to January 1978, he served as Chief of the Management Control Unit, C-3/J-3/G-3, United Nations Command/United States Forces in Korea. He was promoted to Captain on July 7, 1977. He returned to the United States in January 1978, to serve as Assistant S-3 (Operations), later Project Officer, in the Weapons System Development Branch of the United States Army Air Defense Artillery School at Fort Bliss. In March 1980, he was assigned as the S-4 (Supply) with the 108th Air Defense Artillery Group in West Germany. He was promoted to Major on October 1, 1981. In June 1983, General Rountree returned to Fort Leavenworth, Kansas, as a student at the United States Army Command and General Staff College. From June 1984 to August 1984, he was a student in the Materiel Acquisition Management Course at the United States Army Logistics Management Center at Fort Lee, Virginia. From August 1984 to May 1986, he was assigned as a Staff Officer with the Missiles and Air Defense Systems Division Systems Management College at Fort Belvoir, Virginia. From May 1986 to December 1986, he attended the Program Management Course of the Defense Systems Management College at Fort Belvoir. In March 1987, he served as Commander of the 6th Battalion, 43rd Air Defense Artillery at Fort Bliss, later under 69th Air Defense Artillery Brigade, 32nd Army Air Defense Command in West Germany. From June 1989 to June 1990, he was a student at the United States Army War College at Carlisle Barracks, Pennsylvania. He returned to Germany in January 1991, to serve as Commander of the 69th Air Defense Artillery Brigade in West Germany. He was promoted to Colonel on June 1, 1991. From July 1993 to February 1994, he was assigned as Deputy Commander of the United States Army Space and Strategic Defense Command at Peterson Air Force Base, Colorado. From February 1994 to August 1995, he served as the Commanding General of the 2nd Reserve Officer Training Corps Region at Fort Knox, Kentucky. He was promoted to Brigadier General on January 1, 1995. In August 1995, he was assigned as Deputy Commanding General of the United States Army Air Defense Artillery Center and Fort Bliss. He was promoted to Major General on October 1, 1997. In August 1998, he was assigned as Assistant Chief of

Staff for Operation (J-3/J-7), Regional Command North, in the Netherlands. From August 2000 to November 2000, he was assigned as Special Assistant to the Deputy Chief of Staff for Operations and Plans, United States Army, in Washington, D.C. In October 2000, he was selected to serve as the Principal Director to the Deputy Assistant Secretary of Defense for European and NATO Policy, in the Office of the Assistant Secretary of Defense for International Security Affairs, in Washington, D.C. He retired from the military in May 2003. His military awards and decorations include the Legion of Merit (with oak leaf cluster), Meritorious Service Medal (with two oak leaf clusters), Army Commendation Medal (with two oak leaf clusters), Army Achievement Medal, Ranger Tab, and Army General Staff Identification Badge.

Royal, Nathaniel

SERGEANT MAJOR—MARINES

He was born in Cordele, Georgia, and entered into the Marine Corps and in July 1974. He attended Recruit Training at the Marine Corps Recruit Depot at Parris Island, South Carolina. He attended Infantry Training School in October 1974 at Camp Pendleton, California.

His key assignments include serving as a Drill Instructor with Company A, 1st Recruit Training Battalion; as Platoon Sergeant for Rifle Company, 81mm Mortar and Dragon Platoons; and as Instructor for Ceremonial Drill, Color and a 24-hour Guard Security Force. In this post, he performed honor ceremonies for the Supreme Allied Commander Atlantic and the Commander in Chief Atlantic. In 1988, he was transferred to Naval Reserve Officer Training Corps at Prairie View A&M University as the Assistant Marine Officer Instructor; in 1991, he was transferred to 2nd Battalion, 2nd Company as Gunny and First Sergeant; in 1994, he

served on the Inspector-Instructor Staff at Lynchburg, Virginia; and in 1997, he served as the Sergeant Major at the Recruiting Station Atlanta. He is now Sergeant Major of Marine Aircraft Group 42, 4th Marine Air Wing, Marine Forces Reserve.

Royster, Gary A.

COLONEL—ARMY

He was born in Oxford, North Carolina, and began his career as an enlisted soldier in 1973. After completing Basic Combat Training at Fort Jackson, South Carolina, and Advanced Individual Training at Fort Devens, Massachusetts, he was assigned to United States Army Field Station San Antonio, Texas as a Morse Intercept Operator. He attended Officer Candidate School and Airborne School at Fort Benning, Georgia. After receiving his commission, he was assigned to the 313th Army Security Agency Battalion, 82nd Airborne Division at Fort Bragg, North Carolina, with duty at the 101st Air Assault Division.

His military education includes the Military Intelligence Officers Basic and Advanced Courses; Armed Forces Staff College; United States Army War College; and Airborne and Air Assault School. He holds a Bachelor of Business Administration degree in Economics and Finances from Austin Peay State University in Clarksville, Tennessee. He earned a Master of Science degree in Management Science from the University of Tennessee in Knoxville.

He has served in a variety of leadership positions including as Chief of Automation and Data Processing Plans and Management Division; Brigade Operations Officer S3, with the 703rd Military Intelligence Brigade at the Kunia Regional Signals Intelligence Operations Center; and Chief of Military Intelligence Branch at PERCOM. He served as the Executive Assistant to the

Director of the National Security Agency at Fort Meade, Maryland. From July 1998 to August 2000, he served as the Brigade Commander of the 704th Military Intelligence Brigade, and then served as Director of Intelligence Policy in the Office of the Deputy Chief of Staff for Intelligence, Department of the Army, in Washington, D.C. He next assumed duties as G2, Deputy Chief of Staff for Intelligence, United States Army, Pacific, in August 2001.

Rozier, Jackson Evander

MAJOR GENERAL—ARMY

Born in Richmond, Virginia, Rozier received a Bachelor of Science in Educational Administration from Morgan State University and a Master of Arts in Educational Administration from Howard University. He entered the United States Army on January 11, 1960, as a Second Lieutenant. From January 1960 to May 1960, he was a student in the Signal Officer Basic Course at Fort Monmouth, New Jersey. From May 1960 to July 1962, he was assigned first as Executive Officer, later Commander of the Headquarters Company in the Combat Surveillance and Target Acquisition Training Command at Fort Huachuca, Arizona. His first overseas assignment was from July 1962 to November 1962, when he served as a Radio Officer for the 51st Signal Battalion in Europe. From December 1962 to October 1963, he was then assigned as a Special Services Officer with I Corps, Special Troops, in South Korea. He returned to the United States as a student in the Air Defense Career Course at Fort Bliss, Texas. From March 1964 to December 1965, he was assigned as an Electronic Warfare Officer with the 24th Artillery Group in Coventry, Rhode Island. From December 1965 to December 1967, he was assigned first as a Materiel Officer, later Executive Officer, with the 71st Maintenance Battalion, and next as Secretary to the General Staff of the 3rd Support Brigade, in Europe. He was promoted to Major on October 11, 1967. He left Europe in December 1967 for Vietnam, where he served first as a supply officer with the United States Army Support Command. In June 1968, he was assigned as the Deputy Director General for Supply. Returning to the United States in January 1969, Rozier was a student in the Army Logistics Management Course at Fort Lee, Virginia. From June 1969 to October 1970, he was a student at the Armed Forces Staff College in Norfolk, Virginia. From August 1972 to March 1975, he was Personnel Management Officer in the United States Army Military Personnel Center in Alexandria, Virginia. He was promoted to Lieutenant Colonel on June 1, 1974. From March 1975 to October 1976, General Rozier served as Commander of the 801st Maintenance Battalion, 101st Airborne Division (Air Assault) at Fort Campbell, Kentucky. From November 1976 to July 1977, he was Executive Officer with Division Support Command, 101st Airborne Division (Air Assault) at Fort Campbell, Kentucky. From August 1977 to June 1978, he was a student in the Industrial College of the Armed Forces at Fort Lesley J. McNair in Washington,

D.C. From September 1978 to December 1978, he was a student in the Defense Language Institute at the Presidio of Monterey, California. From December 1978 to March 1981, he was Commander of Division Support Command, 8th Infantry Division (Mechanized), United States Army, Europe. He was promoted to Colonel on January 1, 1979. From March 1981 to October 1983, he served as Commanding General of the United States Army Ordnance Center and School at Aberdeen Proving Ground, Maryland. Rozier was promoted to Brigadier General on November 1, 1981. From November 1983 to June 1986, General Rozier served as the Director of Plans and Operations in the Office of the Deputy Chief of Staff for Logistics in Washington, D.C. In June 1986, he returned to Europe as Deputy Chief of Staff for Logistics of United States Seventh Army. On July 1, 1987, he was promoted to Major General. He returned to the United States in October 1989 to his last assignment, Director of Supply and Maintenance in the Office of the Deputy Chief of Staff for Logistics, United States Army, Washington, D.C. Major General Rozier retired from the Army on June 30, 1990. His military decorations and awards include the Legion of Merit, Bronze Star, Meritorious Service Medal (with two oak leaf clusters), Parachutist Badge, and Army Staff Identification Badge.

Rush, Richard H.

SERGEANT MAJOR—MARINES

He enlisted in the Marine Corps in June 1978 and completed Recruit Training at Marine Corps Recruit Depot, Parris Island, South Carolina. He graduated from Military Occupational Specialty Training at Marine Aviation Training Support Group in Meridian, Mississippi.

His military leadership positions include serving as Drill Instructor of Company E, Second Recruit Train-

ing Battalion at Marine Corps Recruit Depot, Parris Island. In May 1993, he was transferred to Marine Corps Air Station Beaufort, South Carolina, and assigned to Marine Air Logistics Squadron–31 Supply. He deployed with Marine Fighter Attack Squadron (All Weather) 533 to Aviano, Italy, as part of Operation Deny Flight. In 1996, he was selected First Sergeant and assigned to the 1st Marine Division at Camp Pendleton, California. He also served as First Sergeant for Company E, 2nd Battalion, 5th Marines, and Sergeant Major of Recruiting Station San Francisco, 12th Marine Corps District, San Diego. In March 2005, he was serving as Sergeant Major for the Marine Corps Logistics Base at Barstow, California.

Russ, William Henry
MAJOR GENERAL—ARMY

Born in Caryville, Florida, he received a Bachelor of Technology degree in Electronics from Florida A&M University and a Master of Science degree in Public Administration from Shippensburg University. His military education includes completion of the Signal School Basic and Advanced Courses; Armed Forces Staff College; and the United States Army War College. He was commissioned a Second Lieutenant on June 7, 1972. From October 1972 to January 1973, he was a student in the Signal Officer Basic Course at Fort Gordon, Georgia. From February 1973 to January 1977, he served as a Communications Officer with the 1st Battalion, 32nd Armor Division, United States Army Europe and Seventh Army, Germany. He was promoted to First Lieutenant on June 7, 1974, and promoted to Captain on June 7, 1976. From January 1977 to August 1977, he was a student in the Signal Officer Advanced Course at Fort Gordon. From August 1977 to Novem-

ber 1977, he served as Assistant S-3 of the 67th Signal Battalion (Combat) at Fort Gordon. From November 1977 to February 1979, he was assigned as the Commander of Company A, 67th Signal Battalion (Combat) at Fort Gordon, Georgia. From February 1979 to May 1980, he was assigned as a Communications and Electronics Officer with the United States Army Joint Support Group-Joint Support Area, United States Forces Korea. From May 1980 to January 1983, he first served as an Instructor, later Branch Chief of the Officer Advanced Division, Officer Training Directorate, United States Army Signal Center and School at Fort Gordon. He was promoted to Major on December 1, 1981. From January 1983 to July 1983, he was a student at the Armed Forces Staff College in Norfolk, Virginia. From July 1983 to April 1986, he was assigned as a Personnel Assignment Officer with the Signal Branch of Total Army Personnel Center in Alexandria, Virginia. From April 1986 to April 1987, he served as Associate Director (Information Mission Area Steering Group) of the 5th Signal Command, United States Army Europe and Seventh Army, Germany. He was promoted to Lieutenant Colonel on April 1, 1987. From April 1987 to June 1988, he was assigned as Executive Officer for the Deputy Chief of Staff for Information Management, 5th Signal Command, United States Army Europe and Seventh Army, Germany. From June 1988 to July 1990, he served as Commander of the 43rd Signal Battalion, 5th Signal Command, United States Army Europe and Seventh Army, Germany. From July 1990 to June 1991, he was a student at the United States War College at Carlisle Barracks, Pennsylvania. From June 1991 to April 1992, General Russ was assigned as a Staff Officer in the Office of the Director for Information Systems, Command, Control, Communications and Computers, United States Army, Washington, D.C. From April 1992 to May 1994, he served as Commander of the 1st Signal Battalion, United States Forces, in Korea. He was promoted to Colonel on May 1, 1992. From May 1994 to April 1995, he was assigned to the Secretariat for Military Communications Electronics Board for the Joint Staff, Washington, D.C. From April 1995 to December 1996, he was assigned as Executive Assistant, J-6, for the Joint Staff at the Pentagon. In December 1996, he was selected as Deputy Commanding General/Director of Information Systems Command/Command, Control, Communications and Computers, G-6, United States Army Forces Command at Fort McPherson, Georgia. He was promoted to Brigadier General on July 1, 1997. From July 1998 to August 1999, he served as Director of Programs and Architecture in the Office of the Director of Information Systems for Command, Control, Communications and Computers in Washington, D.C. From August 1999 to July 2001, he served as the Commanding General of the United States Army Signal Command at Fort Huachuca, Arizona. He was promoted to Major General on September 1, 2000. In July 2001, he was assigned as Commanding General of the United States Army Communications-Electronics Command and

Fort Monmouth, New Jersey. He retired from the military on September 1, 2004. His military awards and decorations include the Defense Superior Service Medal, the Legion of Merit, Meritorious Service Medal (with four oak leaf clusters), Army Commendation Medal (with oak leaf cluster), Parachutist Badge, Ranger Tab, Joint Chief Identification Badge and the Army Staff Identification Badge.

Russell, Horace Laverne
BRIGADIER GENERAL—ARMY

Born in Jamaica, New York, he married the former Catherine Allen of Oxford, North Carolina, and they have two children, Horace Jr. and Patricia Alice. He was graduated from Highland High School in Gastonia, North Carolina, in 1954. He received a Bachelor of Science degree in Mechanical Engineering from Bradley University in 1958, a Master of Science degree in Aerospace Engineering from the Air Force Institute of Technology in 1965, and a Ph.D. in Engineering from Purdue University in 1971. As a 1976 Air Force research associate, he attended the National Security Program at Mershon Center, Ohio State University, and was recognized as a Mershon Fellow. He completed Squadron Officer School in 1963, Air Command and Staff College in 1972, and the Industrial College of the Armed Forces in 1979. After completing the Air Force Reserve Officer Training Corps program as a distinguished graduate, he was commissioned a Second Lieutenant in June 1958 and assigned to the University of Wisconsin for training in Meteorology. In July 1959, he was assigned to Seymour Johnson Air Force Base, North Carolina, as base operations Weather Officer. He was promoted to First Lieutenant December 28, 1959. In June 1960, he became a Weather Officer at the Head-

quarters of the 19th Air Force at Seymour Johnson Air Force Base. From July 1962 to December 1965, he was assigned to the 341st Strategic Missile Wing at Malmstrom Air Force Base, serving as an Instructor and Deputy Minuteman Combat Crew Commander, then as Crew Commander. He was promoted to Captain on December 28, 1962. He transferred to the Air Force Aero-Propulsion Laboratory at Wright-Patterson Air Force Base, Ohio, as a Project Engineer for advanced development of aircraft jet engines in December 1965. From September 1967 to June 1970, he attended Purdue University and then returned to Wright-Patterson as Chief of the Aerospace Dynamics Branch at the Air Force Flight Dynamics Laboratory. He was promoted to Major on February 1, 1969. In June 1973, he was assigned to the Headquarters of Air Force Systems Command at Andrews Air Force Base, Maryland, as Program Manager for Energy Conversion and Mechanics, then as Chief of the Physical and Engineering Sciences Division. He was promoted to Lieutenant Colonel on October 1, 1974. He was assigned to the Air Force Office of Scientific Research at Bolling Air Force Base, Washington, D.C., as Deputy Director for Plans and Operations from July 1975 to September 1976. In June 1977, he was assigned as Study Director for Tactical Command, Control, and Communications in the Office of the Assistant to the Chief of Staff for Studies and Analyses at the Headquarters of the United States Air Force in Washington, D.C., as a Faculty Member and student. He was promoted to Colonel on May 1, 1979. He served as Chief of the Programming Division in the Office of the Deputy Chief of Staff for Research, Development, and Acquisition at Air Force Headquarters from June 1979 until July 1980. He then became Director of Defense Programs at the National Security Council Staff in the White House. In August 1984, he became Director for the Joint Chiefs of Staff in Washington, D.C. In September 1986, he was assigned as Deputy Director for the National Strategic Target List on the Joint Strategic Target Planning Staff at Offutt Air Force Base, Nebraska. He was appointed Brigadier General on June 1, 1984, with date of rank October 1, 1983. His military decorations and awards include the Defense Superior Service Medal (with one oak leaf cluster), Meritorious Service Medal (with three oak leaf clusters), Air Force Commendation Medal, Air Force Outstanding Unit Award (with one oak leaf cluster), and Combat Readiness Medal.

Sadler, Russell W.
COMMAND SERGEANT MAJOR—ARMY

Command Sergeant Major Russell W. Sadler was born January 29, 1957, in Saint Thomas, United States Virgin Islands. He graduated from Charlotte Amile High School in St. Thomas. He entered the United States Army on November 1, 1977, at Fort Jackson, South Carolina, and Completed Advanced Individual Training at Fort Eustis, Virginia, as an AH-1 Attack Helicopter Repairman.

He earned an associate's degree in Professional Aero-

nautics from Embry Riddle University. His military education includes the Attack Helicopter Repairman Course; Airborne School; Air Assault School; Nuclear, Biological and Chemical School; Anti-Armor Leadership Course; Air Movement Operations Course; Equal Opportunity Leader Course; First Sergeant Course; Battle Staff Course; and the United States Army Sergeants Major Academy.

His most recent assignments includes serving as the First Sergeant for Headquarters and Headquarters Company, 2/227th Aviation Battalion at Hanau, Germany; as the First Sergeant of D Company, 3/227th Aviation Battalion at Hanau, Germany; as the Command Sergeant Major of 3-101st Aviation Regiment, later 7-101st Aviation Regiment, at Fort Campbell, Kentucky; and most recently, as Command Sergeant Major of 2-501st Aviation Regiment at Hanau.

Salter, Ned W.
COLONEL—ARMY

He was born in Luverne, Alabama. He is married to the former Eula M. Provitt. They have three children, Alfreda; Adolphus; and Adrian. He enlisted in the Army in January 1960, completed the Officer Candidate School at Aberdeen Proving Ground, Maryland, as a distinguished graduate and was commissioned a Second Lieutenant of Ordnance in April 1967. He holds a Bachelor of Science degree in Business Administration and a master's in Procurement. His military education includes the Ordnance Officer Basic and Advanced Course; the Program Managers Course; the Army Command and General Staff College; and the Army Senior Service College. He has held a wide variety of key command and staff positions. Key assignments held are Program Manager of Maintenance, Waste Management and Cleaning for the Olympic Committee; Commander of the 61st Ordnance Brigade at the United States Army Ordnance Center and School at Aberdeen Proving Ground, Maryland; Director of Training and

Doctrine for the United States Army Ordnance Center and School at Aberdeen Proving Ground; Chief of Maintenance, J4, United States Forces Korea; Assistant Chief of Staff, G-4, 2nd Infantry Division, Korea; and Commander of the 27th Maintenance Battalion, 1st Cavalry Division at Fort Hood, Texas. While enlisted, he served at Fort Hood; Fort Bliss, Texas; Camp Ames, South Korea; Fort Jackson, South Carolina; Fort Lewis, Washington; Nuremberg, Germany; and APG; and attended the United States Army Repair Parts Course at APG and the 7th Army NCO Academy at Bad Tols, Germany. After being commissioned, his initial assignment was to USAEUR, where he was the Technical Supply Officer/Platoon Leader, Company C, 703rd Maintenance Battalion 3rd Infantry Division and later the S-4 Officer of this battalion. His Vietnam service includes serving as Commander of Headquarters and Main Support Company, and S-2/3 Officer with the 63rd Maintenance Battalion at Quang Tri. Other key assignments include Contracting Officer for Procurement and Production Directive at Fort Manmouth, New Jersey; Commander of the 659th Maintenance Company at Fort Bragg, North Carolina; Procurement/Production Officer for the M1 Tank Program at Warren, Michigan; and Program Manager of the Subsystem Integrating Program at the NATO Integrating Communication System Management Agency in Brussels, Belgium. His military awards and decorations include the Legion of Merit; the Bronze Star; the Meritorious Service Medal (with four oak leaf clusters); Army Commendation Medal (with three oak leaf clusters); Army Achievement Medal; Good Conduct Medal and numerous campaign ribbons and awards.

Sanders, James
MAJOR GENERAL—AIR FORCE

He received a Bachelor of Science degree in Electrical Engineering from the University of Maryland in

From September 1996 to February 1998, he was assigned as the Commander of the 349th Air Mobility Wing at Travis Air Force Base, California. From February 1998 to April 1999, he was assigned as the Mobilization Assistant to the Commander of the 15th Air Force at Travis Air Force Base. In April 1999, he was selected to serve as the Mobilization Assistant to the Commander of the Pacific Air Forces (PACAF) at Hickam Air Force Base Hawaii. He was promoted to Major General on February 29, 2000.

His military awards and decorations include the Legion of Merit; Meritorious Service Medal (with two oak leaf clusters); Air Medal; Air Force Commendation Medal (with one oak leaf cluster); Air Force Outstanding Unit Award (with Valor device and six oak leaf clusters); Air Good Conduct Medal; National Defense Service Medal (with bronze service star); Vietnam Service Medal; Southwest Asia Service Medal (with two campaign stars); Republic of Vietnam Gallantry Cross (with Palm); Republic of Vietnam Campaign Medal; Kuwait Liberation Medal (Kingdom of Saudi Arabia); and Kuwait Liberation Medal (Emirate of Kuwait).

College Park, Maryland, in 1972. His military education includes Pilot Training; Air Command and Staff College; and the Air War College.

He entered the Air Force after graduating from Mackenzie High School in Detroit, Michigan, in 1963. He served as a Crew Chief on the B-58 Hustler at Bunker Hill Air Force Base and the F-105 "Thunderchief" at Takhli Royal Thai Air Force Base, Thailand, before earning his commission through Officer Training School in June 1972. After completing pilot training he was assigned in December 1974 as a KC-135 Pilot with the 904th Air Refueling Squadron at Mather Air Force Base, California.

From July 1975 to February 1978, he was assigned as a T-39 Pilot with Detachment 1, 1400 Military Airlift Squadron, at McClellan Air Force Base, California. From February 1978 to June 1983, he was assigned as a KC-135 Pilot, later KC-135A Pilot/Aircraft Commander, with the 336th Air Refueling Squadron at March Air Force Base, California. In June 1983, he served as Flight Commander, later as Flight Commander/KC-135 Pilot-Examiner, then as Commander, of the 336th Air Refueling Squadron at March Air Force Base. In August 1993, he was assigned as Special Assistant to the Commander, later as Vice Commander, of the 452nd Air Refueling Wing at March Air Force Base. He was promoted to Colonel on August 1, 1993.

From January 1994 to April 1994, he was assigned as the Commander of the 445th Airlift Wing at March Air Force Base. From April 1994 to March 1995, he served as Vice Commander of the 452nd Air Refueling Wing, later as Vice Commander of the 452nd Air Mobility Wing, at March Air Force Base. In Mach 1995, he served as Vice Commander of the 4th Air Force at McClellan Air Force Base. He was promoted to Brigadier General on August 2, 1996.

Santiful, Luther L.
SENIOR EXECUTIVE SERVICE

He is a native of Waverly, Virginia. After completing his apprenticeship, he received a certificate in Industrial Management from the University of Virginia and later a Bachelor of General Studies from George Washington University.

He served as Deputy for EEO Policy and Director of the United States Army Equal Employment Opportunity Agency following his tour as Director of EEO for the United States Army in Europe, headquartered in Heidelberg, Germany. Prior to that, he served as Equal

Employment Opportunity Officer for United States Army V Corps, headquartered in Frankfurt, Germany. Before his assignment with the United States Army, he held several positions in EEO, Public Affairs and Production Department with the United States Naval Air Rework Facility in Norfolk, Virginia.

In January 2005, he was serving as Director of Equal Employment Opportunity and Civil Rights for the Department of the Army. As a member of the Senior Executive Service, he is responsible for policy, guidance, direction, and oversight of all plans and programs affecting equal employment opportunity for Army civilian personnel. In addition to directing the EEO staff, he has oversight of accessibility issues that affect the Army workplace and public use of Army facilities.

Sass, Arthur H.

COLONEL—MARINES

He is a native of Charleston, South Carolina, was commissioned as a Second Lieutenant in May 1976. Upon completion of the Basic School and Supply Officer's Course, he was given his first assignment as the Battalion Supply Officer for the 1st Battalion, 9th Marines, 3rd Marine Division on Okinawa, Japan, in May 1977.

In August 2000, he was assigned duties as the Assistant Chief of Staff, G-4, 3rd Force Service Support Group, 3rd Marine Expeditionary Force in Okinawa; in July 2001, he assumed the duties of Chief of Staff of Marine Corps Logistics Command in Albany, Georgia; and in August 2004, he was assigned as Commander of the Maintenance Center in Barstow, Carolina.

Satcher, David

VICE ADMIRAL—SURGEON GENERAL

He was born in Anniston, Alabama. He and his wife Nola have four children. He graduated from Morehouse College in Atlanta, Georgia, in 1963. He received his M.D. and Ph.D. from Case Western Reserve University in 1970. He did his residency training at Memorial Hospital, University of Rochester, UCLA, and King-Drew, in Los Angeles, California.

He served as professor and Chairman of the Department of Community Medicine and Family Practice at Morehouse School of Medicine from 1979 to 1982. He is a former Faculty Member of the UCLA School of Medicine and Public Health and the King-Drew Medical Center in Los Angeles, where he developed and chaired the King-Drew Department of Family Medicine. From 1977 to 1979, he served as the Interim Dean of the Charles R. Drew Postgraduate Medical School, during which time he negotiated the agreement with UCLA School of Medicine and the Board of Regents that led to a Medical Education program at King-Drew. He also served as Directed the King-Drew Sickle Cell Research Center for six years.

In 1993, President Bill Clinton appointed him Director of the Centers for Disease Control and Prevention and Administrator of the Agency for Toxic Substances and Disease Registry, where he served until 1998.

President Bill Clinton selected him to serve as the Surgeon General for the United States. On February 13, 1998, Dr. David Satcher was sworn in as the 16th Surgeon General of the United States. He was also named Assistant Secretary for Health. He became the only second person in history to hold simultaneously the positions of Surgeon General and Assistant Secretary for Health. In these roles, he serves as the Secretary's senior advisor on public health matters and as director of the Office of Public Health and Science. The Surgeon General holds the military rank of Vice Admiral.

He the recipient of numerous distinguished awards and honors, including 18 Honorary degrees; the Jimmy and Roslyn Carter Award for Humanitarian Contributions to the Health of Humankind from the National Foundation for Infectious Diseases; and the Bennie Mays Trailblazer Award.

Saunders, Mary L.

MAJOR GENERAL—AIR FORCE

She was born in Nacogdoches, Texas, and grew up in Houston. She began her military career through the Officer Training School at Lackland Air Force Base, Texas. Her education includes receiving a Bachelor of Science Degree in Social Work in 1970 from Texas Woman's University in Denton a Master of Arts degree in Guidance and Counseling in 1978 from Rider College in Lawrenceville, New Jersey. In 1973, she graduated from Squadron Officer School at Maxwell Air Force Base, Alabama; in 1993, she graduated from the Air War College at Maxwell Air Force Base; and in 1997, she completed the National Security Leadership Course at Johns Hopkins University in Baltimore, Maryland. She was commissioned a Second Lieutenant and entered active duty in 1971. She has held various assignments in transportation and logistics plans, in the squadron, wing, numbered air force, headquarters and joint arenas. In August 1971, she was assigned as Protocol Officer of the 437th Aerial Port Squadron at Charleston Air Force Base, South Carolina. From November 1971 to February 1973, she was assigned as Traffic Duty Officer with the 610th Military Airlift Support Squadron at Yokota Air Base, Japan. From No-

vember 1973 to July 1975, she was assigned as Air Terminal Operations Officer, then in July 1975, she was assigned as Assistant Airfreight Officer, with the 610th Military Airlift Support Squadron at Yokota Air Base. In January 1976, she returned to the United States to serve as Deputy Commander, and later Commander of the Military Air Traffic Coordinating Office in Military Traffic Management Command at McGuire Air Force Base, New Jersey. From July 1979 to April 1982, she was Transportation Staff Officer at the Headquarters of the 10th Air Force at Bergstrom Air Force Base, Texas. In April 1982, she became Chief of Transportation with the 6168th Combat Support Squadron at Teague Air Base, South Korea. From May 1983 to November 1984, she served as Deputy Director for Transportation with the 5th Air Force at Yokota Air Base. She was promoted to major on March 1, 1983. In November 1984, she was selected Commander of the 475th Transportation Squadron at Yokota Air Base. In July 1986, she became Transportation Staff Officer in the Joint Deployment Agency at MacDill Air Force Base, Florida. She was promoted to Lieutenant Colonel on October 1, 1987. From September 1988 to October 1990, she was Transportation Staff Officer, J5 in the United States Transportation Command at Scott Air Force Base, Illinois. From October 1990 to August 1992, she served as Chief of the Contingency Plans Division, J5, in the United States Southern Command in Quarry Heights, Panama. She was promoted to Colonel on November 1, 1992. From July 1993 to August 1996, she was assigned as Chief for Logistics Plans at the Headquarters of the Air Force Reserve at Robins Air Force Base, Georgia. In August 1996, she was selected as the Director of Transportation in the Office of the Deputy Chief of Staff for Installations and Logistics at the Headquarters United States Air Force in Washington, D.C. Mary L. Saunders was promoted to Brigadier General on August 1, 1997, making her the only black female General on active duty in the Air Force at that time. As Director of Transportation, she is responsible for developing policies, plans and programs to move passengers, personal property and cargo, by all modes, commercial and military. The guidance she provides pertains to approximately 32,000 active-duty and Reserve personnel, their training, and the entire 115,000-vehicle fleet valued at $3.8 billion. She supports overall readiness through coordination with other services, the Joint Staff, the Department of Defense, and other government agencies. From August 1998 to September 2001, she served as the Commander of the Defense Supply Center Columbus at the Defense Logistics Agency in Columbus, Ohio. She was promoted to Major General on May 24, 2001. In September 2001, she was selected as Director of Supply in the Office of Deputy Chief of Staff for Installations and Logistics at the Headquarters of the United States Air Force in Washington, D.C. In late 2002, she was selected to serve as the Vice Director for the Defense Logistics Agency at Fort Belvoir, Virginia. Her military awards and decorations include the Legion of Merit; Defense

Meritorious Service Medal (with oak leaf cluster); Meritorious Service Medal (with two oak leaf clusters); Joint Service Commendation Medal (with oak leaf cluster); Air Force Commendation Medal (with oak leaf cluster); Joint Service Achievement Medal; Air Force Achievement Medal; and the National Defense Service Medal (with service star).

Saunders, William R.
COLONEL—AIR FORCE

Colonel William R. Saunders graduated from Tuskegee University in Alabama in 1977 with a Bachelor of Science degree in Mechanical Engineering and was an Air Force ROTC distinguished graduate. He holds a Master of Business Administration from Golden Gate University in San Francisco, California.

His military education includes Squadron Officer School at Maxwell Air Force Base, Alabama; Marine Corps Command and Staff College; Air Command and Staff College (correspondence); in 1990, Air Command and Staff College at Maxwell Air Force Base; and Air War College. He earned a master's degree in National Resource Strategy from the National Defense University at Fort McNair, Washington, D.C.; and also attended the Industrial College of the Armed Forces at the National Defense University at Fort McNair.

From August 1993 to February 1994, he served as Chief of the Operations Watch Branch at the Headquarters of the United States Air Force Combat Operations Center, Air Staff, Pentagon, Washington, D.C. In March 1994, he was assigned as Military Assistant for the Total Force Policy and Counterdrug Operation in the Officer of the Assistant Secretary of the Air Force for Manpower, Reserve Affairs, Installation and Environment, at the Pentagon. From June 1997 to August 1999,

he served as Senior Exercise Planner/Regional Exercise Program Manager at the Directorate for Operational Plans and Interoperability, J-7, Joint Staff at the Pentagon. From September 1999 to August 2000, he was assigned as the Deputy Commander of the 22nd Operations Group at McConnell Air Force Base, Kansas. In August 2000, he was assigned as the Special Assistant to the Commander, later as Director of Staff, with 319th Air Refueling Wing at Grand Forks Air Force Base, North Dakota. In July 2002, he was selected as the Inspector General at Warner Robins Air Logistics Center at Robins Air Force Base, Georgia.

Saxton, Richard
BRIGADIER GENERAL—ARMY

Saxton served for over 30 years in both active service and in the Army National Guard. The source for this fact was both the Nations Guard and the *Black Americans in Defense of Our Nation (1985)* published by the Department of Defense, Office of Deputy Assistant Secretary of Defense for Equal Opportunity and Safety Policy. No other information could be obtained.

Sayles, Martin L.
COLONEL—AIR FORCE

He attended Alabama State University in Montgomery, Alabama. In 1980, he earned a Bachelor of Science degree in Business Administration and was commissioned into the Air Force through the Air Force Reserve Officer Training Corps. His career has encompassed a wide range of administration, personnel and command assignments. He has served at Base, Air Staff and Joint Unified Command levels.

He earned a Master of Arts degree in Human Resource Management from Golden Gate University in San Francisco, California. His military education includes

Squadron Officer School at Maxwell Air Force Base, Alabama; the Air Command and Staff College at Maxwell Air Force Base; Armed Forces Staff College at Norfolk, Virginia; and, in 2000, the Air War College at Maxwell Air Force Base.

In 1989, Sayles was assigned as the Commander of Detachment 1, 6005th Air Postal Squadron at Osan Air Base, South Korea; in October 1992, he was assigned as Commander of Detachment 2 at Pacific Air Forces Air Postal Squadron at Yokota Air Base, Japan; in June 1995, he was assigned as Commander of the 47th Mission Support Squadron at Laughlin Air Force Base, Texas; in July 1997, he served as Commander of the United States Strategic Command Headquarters Section at Offutt Air Force Base, Nebraska; in July 2000, he was selected to serve as the Director of Headquarters Air Force Education and Training in the Office of the Assistant Vice Chief of Staff, Headquarters United States Air Force, at the Pentagon; in August 2002, he was assigned as Chief of the Manpower and Readiness Division of the United States Pacific Command at Camp Smith, Hawaii; and in May 2003, he was selected to serve as Commander of the 325th Mission Support Group at Tyndall Air Force Base, Florida. He was promoted to Colonel on May 1, 2002.

Scott, Darryl A.

MAJOR GENERAL—AIR FORCE

He graduated from the United States Air Force Academy in 1974, receiving a Bachelor of Science degree in Economics. He earned a master's degree in Logistics Management with distinction from the Air Force Institute of Technology Graduate School of Systems and Logistics at Wright-Patterson Air Force Base, Ohio. His military education includes the Air Command and

Staff College at Maxwell Air Force Base, Alabama; Industrial College of the Armed Forces at Fort Lesley J. McNair in Washington, D.C., as a distinguished graduate; and Squadron Officer School at Maxwell Air Force Base as a distinguished graduate.

He received a commission as a Second Lieutenant in 1974 from the United States Air Force Academy. His military career began in 1974 as a Computer Operations Officer with Headquarters Command at Bolling Air Force Base in Washington, D.C. In early assignments, he served as a Principal Contracting Officer and supported command, control and intelligence systems valued at more than $500 million. He also developed the first Contracting for Computers and Information Systems class in the Department of Defense. In 1991, he served as Commander of General Dynamics' Defense Plant Representative Office where he was responsible for contract management, program and technical support and quality assurance for programs such as the Tomahawk cruise missile, Atlas space launch vehicles and the Centaur upper stage. He was promoted to Colonel on January 1, 1993.

As Division Chief at the Electronic System Center at Hanscom Air Force Base, Massachusetts, he was responsible of all contracting for $2.8 billion of advanced radar programs for the United States Airborne Warning and Control System fleet; $5.2 billion in foreign military sales support of NATO and Japan; and sustainment for all AWACS aircraft across multiple international theaters. He became the center's Director of Contracting in 1995, contracting for more than 212 state-of-the-art command, control, communication and intelligence combat systems valued at more than $59.7 billion. From March 1999 to August 2000, he served as Director of Contracting at Air Force Materiel Command at Wright-Patterson Air Force Base. In August 2000, he was selected to serve as Deputy Assistant Secretary for Contracting in the Office of the Assistant Secretary of the Air Force for Acquisition at the Headquarters of the United States Air Force in Washington, D.C. He was promoted to Brigadier General on October 1, 2000.

From March 2003 to December 2003, he was assigned as Vice Commander of Warner-Robins ALC at Robin Air Force Base, in Georgia. In December 2003, he was selected as Director of the Defense Contract Management Agency in Alexandria, Virginia. As the Director, he is responsible for leading and managing over 12,500 civilian and military leaders, managers and technical experts to perform worldwide acquisition life cycle contract management for Department of Defense weapon system programs, spares, supplies and services. He was promoted to Major General on July 1, 2004.

His military awards and decorations include the Legion of Merit (with oak leaf cluster); Defense Meritorious Service Medal; Meritorious Service Medal (with two oak leaf clusters); and the Air Force Commendation Medal.

Scott, Donald Laverne
BRIGADIER GENERAL—ARMY

He was born in Hunnewell, Missouri. He received a Bachelor of Science in Art from Lincoln University and earned a Master of Science in Human Relations from Troy State University. He received an ROTC commission as a Second Lieutenant on September 24, 1960. From September 1960 to November 1960, he was a student in the Infantry Officer Orientation Course at the United States Army Infantry School at Fort Benning, Georgia. From November 1960 to December 1961, he was a Platoon Leader for Company E, 2nd Battalion, 2nd Training Regiment at the United States Army Training Center at Fort Leonard Wood, Missouri. He was promoted to First Lieutenant on March 24, 1962, and from December 1961 to July 1962, he was the Commander of Company E, 2nd Battalion, 2nd Training Regiment at Fort Leonard Wood. From July 1962 to November 1962, he was a student in the Intelligence Research Course in the United States Army Intelligence School at Fort Holabird in Baltimore. From November 1962 to December 1964, he was assigned as a Intelligence Research Officer for Region I, 113th Intelligence Corps Group at duty station Chicago, Illinois. He was promoted to Captain on July 9, 1964. From December 1964 to December 1965, he was a student in the Vietnamese language at the Defense Language Institute West Coast Branch at the Presidio of Monterey, California. From December 1965 to September 1967, he served as an Intelligence Research Officer, later Chief of Counterintelligence Section, for the 441st Military Intelligence Detachment, 1st Special Forces Group (Airborne), 1st Special Forces, United States Army, Okinawa. From September 1967 to May 1968, he served as a Staff Officer with the 97th Civil Affairs Group, 1st

Special Forces, United States Army, in Okinawa. He was promoted to Major on March 28, 1968. From May 1968 to June 1969, he was a student in the Infantry Officer Advanced Course of the United States Army Infantry School at Fort Benning, Georgia. From June 1969 to November 1969, he served as Psychological Operations Officer in the Office of the Assistant Chief of Staff, G-5, 4th Infantry Division, United States Army, Vietnam. From November 1969 to March 1970, he served as Executive Officer, 1st Battalion, 35th Infantry, with the 4th Infantry Division in Vietnam. From March 1970 to June 1970, he served as S-3 of the 1st Battalion, 14th Infantry, 4th Infantry Division, with the United States Army, Vietnam. From June 1970 to May 1972, he was an Assistant Professor of Military Science at Tuskegee Institute at Tuskegee, Alabama. From August 1972 to February 1973, he was the Senior Adviser in the Office of the Territorial Forces, United States Military Assistance Command, Vietnam. From February 1973 to July 1974, he served as Project Officer in the Threats Branch, War Games Division, Combat Operations Analysis Directorate; later Project Officer (combat developments), Program Management Integration Office, United States Army Combined Arms Development Activity at Fort Leavenworth, Kansas. From August 1974 to June 1975, he was a student at the United States Army Command and General Staff College, Fort Leavenworth, Kansas. From June 1975 to May 1977, he served as Chief of the Training Division of the United States Army Garrison at Fort Lewis, Washington. He was promoted to Lieutenant Colonel on September 9, 1976. From May 1977 to October 1978, he served as Executive Officer of the 1st Infantry Brigade, 9th Infantry Division, at Fort Lewis. From October 1978 to June 1980, he was Commander of the 3rd Battalion, 47th Infantry, with the 9th Infantry Division at Fort Lewis. From June 1980 to June 1981, he served as Professor of Military Science at Tuskegee Institute. From June 1981 to May 1982, he was a student at the War College at Maxwell Air Force Base, Alabama. From May 1982 to May 1983, he served as Deputy Inspector General in the Office of the Inspector General for United States Army, Europe, and the Seventh Army. He was promoted to Colonel on October 1, 1982. From March 1985 to October 1986, he was the Inspector General of VII Corps, United States Army, Europe. From October 1986 to August 1988, he served as Assistant Division Commander of the 1st Cavalry Division at Fort Hood, Texas. On March 1, 1988, he was promoted to Brigadier General. In September 1988, he was appointed Chief of Staff of the Second United States Army at Fort Gillem, Georgia. In April, 1991, General Scott retired from the Army to join the staff Mayor Maynard H. Jackson of Atlanta as the city's Chief Operating officer. He left Atlanta in December 1992 for a new job in Washington, D.C. His military awards and decorations include the Legion of Merit; the Bronze Star (with five oak leaf clusters); Meritorious Service Medal; Air Medal; Army Commendation Medal; Combat Infantryman Badge; and the Parachutist Badge.

Scott, Frank

SERGEANT MAJOR—MARINES

He is a native of Kingstree, South Carolina. He entered the Marine Corps in July 1979 at Florence, South Carolina, and attended Recruit Training at the Marine Corps Recruit Depot at Parris Island, South Carolina.

His key assignments include serving as a Drill Instructor at the 3rd Recruit Training Battalion at the Marine Corps Recruit Depot in San Diego, California. While at the Marine Corps Recruit Depot, he served as Instructor for two Platoons and as a Senior Drill Sergeant. In 1991, he was assigned to Marine Helicopter Squadron One at Quantico, Virginia, as Maintenance Administrative Chief and Aircraft Maintenance Data Analyst Technician; in 1998, he was posted as the First Sergeant of the 3rd Intelligence Company in Okinawa, Japan; in July 1999, he served as First Sergeant for the 3rd Battalion, 12th Marines; in November 2000, he was assigned as the First Sergeant for Marine Aviation Training Support Squadron One; and in February 2002, he was selected Sergeant Major, and assigned to MAG-42 Detachment "C" in Belle Chase, Louisiana.

Scott, Winston E.

CAPTAIN—NAVY

Born in Miami, Florida, he married the former Marilyn K. Robinson and they have two children. He graduated from Coral Gables High School in Coral Gables, Florida, in 1968. He received a Bachelor of Arts degree in Music from Florida State University in 1972 and a Master of Science degree in Aeronautical Engineering from the United States Naval Postgraduate School in 1980.

He entered Naval Aviation Officer Candidate School after graduation from Florida State University in December 1972. He completed flight training in fixed-wing and rotary-wing aircraft and was designated a Naval Aviator in August 1974. He then served a 4-year tour of duty with Helicopter Anti-Submarine Squadron Light Thirty Three (HSL-33) at the Naval Air Station (NAS) North Island, California, flying the SH-2F Light Airborne Multi-Purpose System (LAMPS) helicopter. In 1978, he was selected to attend the Naval Postgraduate School at Monterey, California, where he earned his Master of Science degree.

He served as a production Test Pilot at the Naval Aviation Depot at Naval Air Station Jacksonville, Florida, flying the F/A-18 Hornet and the A-7 Corsair aircraft. He was also assigned as Director of the Product Support (engineering) Department. He was next assigned as the Deputy Director of the Tactical Aircraft Systems Department at the Naval Air Development Center at Warminster, Pennsylvania. As a Research and Development Project Pilot, he flew the F-14, F/A-18 and A-7 aircraft. Scott has accumulated more than 4,000 hours of flight time in 20 different military and civilian aircraft, and more than 200 shipboard landings. Additionally, he was an Associate Instructor of Electrical Engineering at Florida A&M University and Florida Community College at Jacksonville.

Scott was selected by NASA in March 1992, and reported to the Johnson Space Center in August 1992. He served as a Mission Specialist on STS-72 in 1996 and STS-87 in 1997, and has logged a total of 24 days, 14 hours and 34 minutes in space, including 3 space walks totaling 19 hours and 26 minutes.

STS-72 (January 11–20, 1996) was a 9-day flight during which the crew retrieved the Space Flyer satellite, and conducted two space walks to demonstrate and evaluate techniques to be used in the assembly of the International Space Station. The mission was accomplished in 142 orbits of the Earth, traveling 3.7 million miles, and logged him a total of 214 hours and 41 seconds in space, including his first EVA of 6 hours and 53 minutes.

STS-87 (November 19 to December 5, 1997) was the fourth United States Microgravity Payload flight, and focused on experiments designed to study how the weightless environment of space affects various physical processes, and on observations of the Sun's outer atmospheric layers. Scott performed two space walks. The first, a 7 hour 43 minute EVA featured the manual capture of a Spartan satellite, in addition to testing EVA tools and procedures for future Space Station assembly. The second space walk lasted 5 hours and also featured space station assembly tests. The mission was accomplished in 232 Earth orbits, traveling 6.5 million miles in 376 hours and 34 minutes.

Captain Scott retired from the NASA and the United States Navy at the end of July 1999, to accept a position at his alma mater, Florida State University, as Vice President for Student Affairs.

Seals, McGregory

COMMAND SERGEANT MAJOR—ARMY

He is a native of Lakeland, Florida, where he graduated from Mulberry High School. He attended Basic and Advanced Individual Training at Fort Leonard Wood, Missouri.

His military and civilian education includes all the Noncommissioned Officer Education System Courses; First Sergeant Course; Battle Staff NCO Course; Nuclear Biological and Chemical Course; Support Operations Course; Logistics Operation Management Course; Combat Lifesaver Course; Master Fitness Trainer's Course; Hazardous Cargo Transportation Course; and the United States Army Sergeants Major Academy (class 52).

His key leadership assignments include serving as First Sergeant of Headquarters and Headquarters Company, 7th Transportation Group at Fort Eustis, Virginia; First Sergeant of the 497th Port Construction Engineer Company at Fort Eustis, Virginia; First Sergeant of Headquarters and Headquarters Detachment, 6th Transportation Battalion at Fort Eustis; Noncommissioned Officer in Charge of the Director at Logistics at Camp Doha, Kuwait; First Sergeant of Headquarters and Headquarters Company, 10th Transportation Battalion, at Fort Eustis; First Sergeant of the 24th Transportation Battalion at Fort Eustis; First Sergeant of the 567th Cargo Transportation Company at Fort Eustis; Sergeant Major of the 24th Transportation Battalion at Fort Eustis; G-4 Sergeant Major at Camp Red Cloud, South Korea; and Command Sergeant Major of the 17th Corps Support Battalion at Schofield Barracks, Hawaii.

Shanks, Mary Joe

COLONEL—ARMY

Col. Shanks enlisted in the United States Army as a Private First Class in 1977. In 1980, she was commissioned through the Officer Candidate School Program as a Second Lieutenant in the Ordnance Corps and joined the 124th Maintenance Battalion, 2nd Armored Division at Fort Hood, Texas.

She holds a Bachelor of Science degree in Business Administration and master's degrees in both Education and Public Administration.

Her assignments include serving as Commander of the 201st Materiel Management Center in Livorno, Italy; Executive Officer of the 16th Ordnance Battalion, 61st Ordnance Brigade; Executive Officer of the 61st Ordnance Brigade at Aberdeen Proving Ground, Maryland; Special Assistant to the Secretary for Defense for Reform, OSD; and in 2003, Headquarters Commandant of United States European Command at Patch Barracks, Germany.

Shannon, John W.

UNDER SECRETARY OF THE ARMY

He was born in Louisville, Kentucky. He and his wife Jean are the parents of a son John, Jr. He attended public school in Louisville and in 1955 graduated from Central State University in Wilberforce, Ohio, with a Bachelor of Science degree. He earned a Master of Science degree in 1975 from Shippensburg State College in Shippensburg, Pennsylvania, pursued additional postgraduate studies at Catholic University, and was a graduate of the United States Army War College. Upon graduation from college, he was commissioned into the Regular Army as a Second Lieutenant of Infantry. He served on active duty for over 23 years from 1955 to

1978. During that time, he served in various capacities as a commander and staff officer. His active duty service included two tours in South Vietnam as an advisor and as an infantry battalion commander. He retired in the grade of Colonel. Shannon's experience in the areas of military force development, force structure, personnel policy and administration, and congressional affairs activities includes working as a congressional liaison officer in the Office of the Secretary of the Army and serving as special assistant for Manpower, Reserve Affairs and Logistics to the Assistant Secretary of Defense for Legislative Affairs. He was sworn in as the Under Secretary of the Army August 14, 1989. Prior to this appointment, Shannon had served as Assistant Secretary of the Army (installations and logistics) since December 7, 1984. In this position, he was the principal advisor and assistant to the Secretary of the Army for Department of the Army policy and activities in the areas of logistics installation operations and construction, environmental preservation and restoration, and safety. He also directed commercial activities and accompanying contract administration throughout the Department of the Army and managed the Army's Chemical Stockpile Disposal Program. Additionally, from June 1981 to December 1984, he served as the Deputy Under Secretary of the Army. His military awards and decorations include the Department of the Army Distinguished Civilian Service Award; the Defense Superior Service Medal; Bronze Star; Meritorious Service Medal (with oak leaf cluster); Legion of Merit; Combat Infantry Badge; Secretary of Defense Award for Outstanding Public Service; Defense Meritorious Civilian Service Award; Air Medal; Vietnamese Cross of Gallantry (with palm); Roy Wilkins Meritorious Service Award; and the Korean Gugseon Medal; Parachutist Wings; and the Ranger Tab.

Sharpe, Carolyn R.
LIEUTENANT COLONEL—ARMY

She is a native of Nashville, Tennessee. She entered the Army in February 1983 as an Administrative Specialist. Upon completion of Basic Combat and Advanced Individual Training, she was assigned to the 124th Military Intelligence Battalion (Communications Electronic Warfare Intelligence (CEWI) at Fort Stewart, Georgia. She attended Officer Candidate School in April 1985 and was commissioned into the Finance Corps on July 25, 1985.

Her military and civilian education includes the Primary Leadership Development Course; Finance Officer Basic and Advanced Courses; Nuclear, Biological and Chemical Course; Resource Management Course; Combined Arms and Service Staff School; United States Army Training with Industry Program-National City Bank in Indianapolis, Indiana; Command and General Staff College; and the TRADOC Training Development Middle Managers' Course. She holds a Bachelor of Business Administration degree in Finance from Middle Tennessee State University.

From July 2001 to July 2002, she served as the Deputy Brigade Commander of the 175th Finance Command in Yongsan, South Korea. Other key assignments include Disbursing Officer and later Plans and Operations Officer of the 501st Finance Support Unit at Nuernberg, West Germany (January 1986 to June 1989); Accounting Officer for 13th Corps Support Command (December 1989 to August 1990), Commander of Headquarters and Headquarters Detachment, 3rd (Corps) Finance Support Unit (August 1990 to August 1991), Deputy Finance Officer, 502nd Finance Support Unit (August 1991 to February 1992),

Comptroller of 13th Corps Support Command (December 1992 to July 1993), all at Fort Hood, Texas; Budget Officer of Joint Task Force Bravo in Honduras (February 1992 to December 1992); Department of the Army Banking Officer, United States Army Finance Command, in Indianapolis, Indiana (October 1994 to June 1997); Finance and Accounting Officer for Europe Regional Medical Command in Landstuhl, Germany (July 1997 to June 1999); Executive Officer of 106th Finance Battalion in Wuerzburg, Germany (June 1999 to July 2001); and Director of the Finance Training Department of the United States Army Finance School at Fort Jackson, South Carolina (July 2001 to 2002).

Sheffey, Fred Clifton
MAJOR GENERAL—ARMY

Born in McKeesport, Pennsylvania, he is married to the former Jane Hughes of Providence, Kentucky, and they have two sons, Alan and Steven, and a daughter, Patricia. He was graduated from the ROTC program at Central State College in Wilberforce, Ohio, in June 1950, and received a Bachelor of Science degree in Economics. As a distinguished military graduate, he was commissioned a second lieutenant in the United States Army. In October 1950, he joined the 25th Infantry Division, fighting in Korea, as an infantry Platoon Leader. He was wounded and medically evacuated to the United States in April 1951, and several weeks later was promoted to First Lieutenant on April 20. After hospitalization, he was assigned as a Weapons Instructor with the 5th Infantry Division Faculty at Indiantown Gap Military Reservation, Pennsylvania. He was detailed to the Quartermaster Corps in 1953, and attended the Quartermaster Officer Basic and Ad-

vanced Courses at Fort Lee, Virginia. From August 1953 to June 1962, in addition to attending these schools, he had a series of logistical assignments in inventory management, supply, and maintenance at the Nahbollenback Depot in Europe and the Columbus General Depot in Columbus, Ohio. He was promoted to Captain on July 9, 1954, and to Major on November 28, 1961. While at Columbus General Depot, he engaged in business studies at Ohio State University and received a Master of Business Administration degree in June 1962. From June 1962 to December 1964, he served on the Staff of the United States Army Communications Zone, Europe. Following this assignment, he attended the Command and General Staff College, graduating in May 1965. He was then assigned to the 4th Infantry Division at Fort Lewis, Washington, where he served as Division Supply Officer, later Executive Officer of the 4th Division Supply and Transport Battalion. On January 11, 1966, he was promoted to Lieutenant Colonel and assigned as Commander of the 266th Quartermaster Battalion at Fort Lewis. He deployed with this unit to Vietnam in June 1966. On his return to the United States, he was assigned to the Office of the Deputy Chief of Staff for Logistics in the Department of the Army as Chief of Base Operations Branch in Financial Management. He graduated from the National War College in June 1969, and continued studies in International Affairs at George Washington University. For the latter, he was awarded a Master of Science degree in September 1969. He was promoted to Colonel on November 20, 1970. In May 1971, he took Command of the 54th General Support Group in Vietnam. In July 1972, he was again assigned to the Office of the Deputy Chief of Staff for Logistics in the Department of the Army, where he served as the Director of Financial Resources in the Pentagon until his promotion to Brigadier General on July 1, 1973. On July 2, 1973, he became Director of Operation and Maintenance Resources (Provisional), and served in this capacity until May 20, 1974, when he was assigned as Deputy Director of Supply and Maintenance. He joined the United States Army Materiel Development and Readiness Command in Alexandria, Virginia, in August 1975 as the Director of Materiel Management. In March 1976, he was nominated by the president for promotion to Major General and was promoted on August 2, 1976. On September 29, 1977, he became the first black General to serve as Commander of Fort Lee, Virginia. The appointment created controversy even before General Sheffey began his duties. He was named Commanding General of Fort Lee and the Quartermaster Center and Commandant of the Quartermaster School in Mid-August 1977. Ten days later, the Army announced that his orders had been amended to state he was assigned only as the Commandant of the Quartermaster School, blaming the original orders on an "administrative error." After protests by several predominantly black political organizations, and a request for an investigation by the Secretary of the Army, the Army reassigned Sheffey to command Fort Lee in its entirety. His military awards and decorations include the Purple Heart; Legion of Merit (with two oak leaf clusters); Bronze Star; Meritorious Service Medal; Army Commendation Medal (with two oak leaf clusters); Army of Occupation Medal (Germany); United Nations Service Medal; National Defense Service Medal (with one oak leaf cluster); Korean Service Medal (with three Battle Stars); Vietnamese Service Medal (with six stars); Republic of Vietnam Campaign Medal (with 60 devices); Vietnam Gallantry Cross (with Palm); Combat Infantryman Badge; and General Staff Identification Badge.

Shepard, Melvin L.

SERGEANT MAJOR—MARINES

He enlisted into the Marine Corps Delayed Entry Program on March 14, 1977, and entered boot camp on July 13, 1977. He attended recruit training with Company D, 2nd Recruit Training Battalion, Marine Corps Recruit Depot, at Parris Island, South Carolina.

After boot camp, he attended the Personnel Administration School at Parris Island and graduated in December 1977 with the MOS of 0151.

He has held numerous military assignments including serving at the Movement Center at Camp Pendleton; the 3rd Marine Division at Okinawa, Japan; the Marine Corps Depot at San Diego, California; the Military Entrance Processing Station at San Diego, California; the 3rd Marine Aircraft Wing at El Toro, California; Wing Transportation Squadron 37, (redesignated as Marine Wing Support Squadron 373), MWSG 37; Headquarters and Maintenance Squadron 13; Marine Aircraft Group 13; and Marine Air Traffic Control Squadron 38, Marine Air Control Group 38. In 1988, he was transferred to the Marine Detachment on USS

Nimitz (CVN-68) for a two year tour of duty at sea. Upon completion of a Western Pacific deployment with the MARDET in 1990, he was promoted to the rank of Gunnery Sergeant and transferred to Marine Corps Recruit Depot at San Diego to attend Drill Instructor School.

Upon completion of Drill Instructor School, in September 1991, he was assigned to Company "D" as the Series Chief Drill Instructor. In February 1992, he was assigned to the staff of the Drill Instructor School. In May of 1993, he was transferred to the Military Entrance Processing Command serving as the Non-Commissioned Officer in Charge of Operations, MEPS, in Jacksonville, Florida. In May of 1995, he was promoted to the rank of First Sergeant and was transferred to the First Marine Division. He was assigned to Battery "C," 1st Battalion, 11th Marines, as the Battery First Sergeant. After completing a deployment with the 11th MEU in 1997, he was promoted to Sergeant Major in 1998. In April of 1998, Sergeant Major Shepard was transferred to Marine Heavy Helicopter squadron 465, Marine Aircraft Group 16, 3rd Marine Aircraft Wing. He completed two deployments under the Unit Deployment Program to Okinawa, Japan, while serving as the Squadron Sergeant Major. He was then assigned to the Marine Corps Recruit Depot in San Diego as the Support Battalion Sergeant Major in January of 2002. He was assigned as the Recruit Training Regiment Sergeant Major on October 31, 2003.

Shephard, Nathaniel, III

COMMAND SERGEANT MAJOR—ARMY

He is a native of Georgetown, South Carolina. He entered the United States Army in June 1977. His military and civilian education includes all the Noncommissioned Officers Education System Courses; Air

Assault School; Master Fitness Trainer Course; Trainer Development Course; Drill Sergeant School; First Sergeant Course; Garrison Sergeant Major Course; Senior Enlisted Equal Opportunity Course; and the United States Army Sergeants Major Academy. He holds a Bachelor of Arts in Human Resource Development from Hawaii Pacific University and a Masters of Science in Administration Concentration in Human Resource from Central Michigan University.

His key leadership assignments include serving as Section Leader of Troop C, 21st Cavalry, 2nd Armored Division, FWD, Germany; Platoon Sergeant of the 52nd Personnel Service Company in Fula, Germany; Drill Sergeant, 4th/14th Combat Soldier Support Training Brigade at Fort Jackson, South Carolina; First Sergeant of Company C, 120th Adjutant General Battalion at Fort Jackson, South Carolina, and Command Sergeant Major of the 556th Personnel Service Battalion.

Shepherd, Edward L.
COMMAND SERGEANT MAJOR—AIR FORCE

CSM Shepherd entered military service at Fort Jackson, South Carolina, in April 1960, and attended Advanced Individual Training at Fort Knox, Kentucky. His subsequent military education included graduating from the Primary Leadership Development Course and the Sergeants Major Academy.

He has held a wide variety of key logistical command and staff positions during his distinguished career, including Command Sergeant Major of the 260th Quartermaster Battalion, 24th Infantry Division, Hunter Army Airfield and in support of Operation Desert Storm; Command Sergeant Major of the 262nd Quartermaster Battalion at Fort Lee, Virginia; and Sergeant Major of Area 2 and 25th Transportation in South Korea; Sergeant Major at the Aviation/Transportation School at Fort Eustis, Virginia.

Sherfield, Michael Bruce
MAJOR GENERAL—ARMY

He was born in Brooklyn, New York. He graduated from the University of Tampa with a Bachelor of Science degree in History. He also earned a Master of Public Administration from Pennsylvania State University. He entered the United States Army in January 1967 as an enlisted soldier and was commissioned a Second Lieutenant December 11, 1967. After his commission to second lieutenant he was assigned as Training Officer of Company E, 1st Battalion, 2nd Basic Combat Training Brigade at the United States Army Training Center at Fort Dix, New Jersey, in January 1968. He was promoted to First Lieutenant on December 11, 1968. From November 1968 to March 1969, he was assigned as Platoon Leader of Company C, 1st Battalion, 506th Infantry, 101st Airborne Division, United States Army, Vietnam. In March 1969, he served as Assistant Adjutant for the 1st Battalion, 506th Infantry, and next in July 1969, he was assigned as Assistant Adjutant with the 3rd Brigade, 101st Airborne Division, United States Army, Vietnam. He was promoted to Captain on December 10, 1969. In January 1970, he was assigned first as Operations Officer at the United States Atlantic Area Installation Command at Fort Sherman, Panama. Next he was assigned in June 1970 as Commander of Company C, later as S-4 (logistics) officer, 3rd Battalion, 5th Infantry, 193rd Infantry Brigade, at Fort Kobbe, Panama. He returned to the United States in December 1972 as a student in the Infantry Officer Advanced Course in the United States Army Infantry School at Fort Benning, Georgia. In November 1973, he was a student in the Special Forces Officer Course of the United States Army Institute for Military Assistance at Fort Bragg, North Carolina. From April 1974 to April 1975, he served as Operations and Training Officer with

the United States Military Assistance Command, Thailand. He returned to the United States in May 1975 as a student at the University of Tampa in Tampa, Florida. From May 1976 to May 1977, he served as the Assistant S-3 Officer (Operations) with the 1st Brigade, 101st Airborne Division (Air Assault) at Fort Campbell, Kentucky. From May 1977 to August 1978, he was assigned as the S-3 Officer (Operations) with the 2nd Battalion, 327th Infantry, 101st Airborne Division (Air Assault), at Fort Campbell. Then in August 1978, he served as the S-3 Officer (Operations), with the 1st Brigade, 101st Airborne Division (Air Assault), at Fort Campbell. He was promoted to Major on May 9, 1978. From July 1979 to June 1980, he was a student at the Command and General Staff College at Fort Leavenworth, Kansas. After graduating, from June 1980 to January 1982, he was assigned as Plans Officer in the Office of the Deputy Chief of Staff for Operations, United States Army Europe, in Germany. From January 1982 to April 1983, he served as the Deputy Inspector General for the 8th Infantry Division (mechanized), United States Army Europe, in Germany. In June 1983, he returned to the United States to serve as Commander of the 1st Battalion, 502nd Infantry, 101st Airborne Division (air assault), at Fort Campbell. He was promoted to Lieutenant Colonel on April 1, 1984. In June 1985, he served as an Infantry Assignment Officer in the Colonel's Division of the United States Army Military Personnel Center at Alexandria, Virginia. From June 1986 to June 1987, he was assigned as the G-3 Officer (Operations) with the 2nd Infantry Division, Eighth United States Army, in Korea. From July 1987 to June 1988, he was a student in the United States Army War College at Carlisle Barracks, Pennsylvania. From June 1988 to August 1989, he served as a Staff Officer, later Division Chief, Combat Maneuver Division, Office of the Deputy Chief of Staff for Operations and Plans, United States Army, Washington, D.C. In September 1989, he returned to Korea to serve as Commander of the 3rd Brigade, 2nd Infantry Division, Eighth United States Army. Later he was assigned as Chief of Staff of the 2nd Infantry Division, Eighth United States Army, Korea, from October 1991 to August 1992. In September 1992, he was selected as Executive Secretary to the Department of Defense, Office of the Secretary of Defense, Washington, D.C. On July 1, 1993, he was promoted to Brigadier General. In September 1993, he became Assistant Division Commander of the 101st Airborne Division (Air Assault) at Fort Campbell. In February 1995, he was selected Commanding General of the Joint Readiness Training Center and Fort Polk, Louisiana. He was promoted to Major General on August 1, 1996. From May 1997 to September 1998, he served as the Commanding General of the 2nd Infantry Division, Eighth United States Army, in Korea. In October 1998, he was selected to serve as Deputy Chief of Staff for Education at the United States Army Training and Doctrine Command at Fort Monroe, Virginia. He died on May 22, 2000. His military awards and decorations include the

Defense Distinguished Service Medal; the Silver Star; the Legion of Merit (with oak leaf cluster); the Bronze Star; Purple Heart; Meritorious Service Medal (with three oak leaf clusters); the Air Medal; the Joint Service Commendation Medal; Army Commendation Medal (with oak leaf cluster); the Army Achievement Medal; Combat Infantryman Badge; Parachutist Badge; Air Assault Badge; Office of the Secretary of Defense Identification Badge; and the Army Staff Identification Badge.

Sherman, Jerald
SERGEANT MAJOR—ARMY

He was born December 18, 1942, in Los Angeles, California. He is the youngest of three children. He and his wife Diane, have one child, Chiyedo. He entered the Army on January 4, 1966.

His college education consists of studies in Criminal Justice and Computer Science. His military schooling includes the First Sergeant Course; Terrorism Course; Counter Terrorist Plan Course; Physical Security and Traffic Accident Investigation Courses; Dynamics of International Terrorism Course; Battalion Training Management System Courses; and Basic Training. His first duty assignment was at Fort Leavenworth, Kansas. As a Military Policeman in the 205th MP Company from July 1966 to January 1968, he was promoted to the rank of Sergeant E-5. From February 1968 to July 1971, he was assigned to USARPAC—Japan where he served in Traffic Investigation, AWOL Apprehension Team, and Military Police Investigation. In December 1969, he was promoted to Staff Sergeant. His next assignment was in Thailand, where he was assigned to the 13th Military Police Company until February 1973. His duties were special investigation in conjunction

with the host Nation Law Enforcement Activity, along with Japanese criminal investigations. In May 1984, he was transferred to Atlanta, Georgia, and assigned to USAG, Law Enforcement Activity at Fort McPherson, Georgia. He had a short assignment with B Company, LEA and then was assigned to Headquarters 3rd United States Army as the Physical Security NCO. On January 1, 1989, he was promoted to Sergeant Major and served the remaining of his tour as the Provost Marshal Sergeant Major. In September 1990, he was deployed to the Middle East. He was responsible for coordinating and supervising all security matters involving mobilization to the Middle East. He has extensive expertise in Middle Eastern affairs as well as having worked with Middle Eastern government and law enforcement officials.

Short, Alonzo Earl, Jr.
LIEUTENANT GENERAL—ARMY

He was born in Greenville, North Carolina, and married the former Rosalin Reid of Orange, New Jersey. He holds a Bachelor of Science in Education from Virginia State College and a master's in Business Management from the New York Institute of Technology on Long Island, New York. His military education includes the United States Army Signal School Officer Basic and Advanced Courses, the Military Advisor and Technical Assistance School, the Armed Forces Staff College, the Communications/Electronics Systems Engineer Course, and the Army War College. Since entering the Army in June 1962, General Short has held a variety of assignments with increasing responsibility throughout his career. He was promoted to First Lieu-

tenant on November 28, 1963. He was a Platoon Leader and Staff Officer at Fort Riley, Kansas. From December 1964 to April 1965, he was assigned as a Division Telephone and Teletype Officer with the 121st Signal Battalion, 1st Infantry Division, at Fort Riley, Kansas. He was promoted to Captain on October 8, 1965. From April 1965 to September 1967, he first served as Commander of Headquarters Detachment, 102nd Signal Battalion, next as Commander of the 510th Signal Company, with the 22nd Signal Group, next as the S-4 officer (logistics), later Executive Officer with the 102nd Signal Battalion, United States Army Europe. He was promoted to Major on November 27, 1966. In 1967, he was assigned as a Staff Planning and Engineering Officer in Vietnam, followed by an assignment to Okinawa, first as Battalion S-3 (operations), then Executive Officer, and finally, Battalion Commander in the Strategic Communications Command-Okinawa Signal Group. He served his second tour in Vietnam, from January 1972 to March 1973, as a Deputy G-6 Advisor with the First Regional Assistance Command, United States Military Assistance Command, in Vietnam. In May 1973, he returned to the United States and was a student at the Armed Forces Staff College at Norfolk, Virginia. After graduating in January 1974, he remained as the Academic Plans Officer at the Armed Forces Staff College in Norfolk, Virginia. From June 1974 to July 1975, he was a student in systems engineering at Fort Monmouth, New Jersey. From July 1975 to November 1975, he was a student at the New York Institute of Technology in Old Westbury, New York. In 1975, Short was assigned as a Staff Officer in the Defense Communications Agency. His next assignment was as Battalion Commander in the 101st Airborne (Air Assault) Division at Fort Campbell, Kentucky. He was promoted to Lieutenant Colonel. In February 1978, he served as Special Assistant to the Chief of Staff for Reforger Operations Planning with the 101st Airborne (air assault) at Fort Campbell. From June 1978 to June 1979, he was a student at United States War College at Carlisle Barracks, Pennsylvania. From June 1979 to May 1981, he was assigned as Chief of the Plans Branch of the Operations Division, later as Chief of the Plans and Requirements Branch, Plan Division, Office of States Army Communications Command, at Fort Huachuca, Arizona. He was promoted to Colonel on August 1, 1981. In June 1981, he was assigned at Fort Hood, Texas, first as Assistant Corps Communications and Electronics Officer with III Corps, later as Commander of the 3rd Signal Brigade. From July to September 1984, he served as Chief of Staff with the 7th Signal Command at Fort Ritchie, Maryland. From September 1984 to October 1986, he was the Commander of the United States Army Information Systems Management Agency/United States Army Electronics Systems Engineering Installation Activity/ Project Manager of Defense Communications Systems at Fort Monmouth, New Jersey. On June 1, 1986, he was promoted to Brigadier General. In October 1986, he was assigned as Deputy Commanding General/

Deputy Program Manager at Army Information Systems in the United States Army Information Systems Engineering Command at Fort Belvoir, Virginia. In October 1987, General Short was assigned as the Commanding General of the United States Army Information Systems Engineering Command/Program Manager of Army Information Systems at Fort Huachuca. In September 1988, he served as the Deputy Commanding General of the United States Army Information Systems Command at Fort Huachuca. He was promoted to Major General on August 1, 1989. In June 1990, he was selected the Commanding General of the United States Army Information Systems Command at Fort Huachuca. He was promoted to Lieutenant General on July 1, 1990. In August 1991, he was selected as the Director of the Defense Communications Agency in Washington, D.C. His military awards and decorations include the Distinguished Service Medal, the Legion of Merit, the Bronze Star (with oak leaf cluster), Meritorious Service Medal (with oak leaf cluster), Parachutist Badge, and Air Assault Badge.

Short, James E.
SENIOR EXECUTIVE SERVICE

He began his federal career in 1967 with the Federal Bureau of Investigation as a fingerprint examiner. He joined the United States Marine Corps infantry in 1968 and was honorably discharged in 1970, after completing a 13-month tour of duty in Vietnam. He has more than 19 years experience in federal financial management.

His education includes a bachelor's degree in Ac-

counting with honors from Strayer University in Washington, D.C.; the Executive Leadership Development Program of the Department of Defense; and the Federal Executive Institute in Charlottesville, Virginia.

Prior to coming to the Air Force, he served as Senior Advisor to the Deputy Controller at the Office of Management and Budget. In this position, he led government-wide efforts to implement the Chief Financial Officers Act and produce auditable financial statements for executive branch departments and agencies. As a member of the Senior Executive Service, he serves as the Deputy Assistant Secretary for Financial Operation in the Office of the Assistant Secretary for Financial Management and Comptroller at the Headquarters United States Air Force in Washington, D.C.

Shorts, Vincient F.
CAPTAIN—NAVY

He grew up in Oakland, California, where he graduated from Castlemont High in 1976. He received his commission in 1980 from the United States Naval Academy in Annapolis, Maryland, earning a degree in Aerospace Engineering.

Entering flight training in August 1980, he earned his Naval Aviator wings in April 1982 from Training Squadron Seven in Meridian, Mississippi. His initial assignment was as a student in Attack Squadron One Two Two for training in the A-Corsair II. In 1983, he reported to his first operational assignment with the "Blue Diamonds" of Attack Squadron One Four Six Corsair II. While a member of the Blue Diamonds he made two deployments to the Indian Ocean on board USS *Kittyhawk* (CV-63). He left the Blue Diamonds of Attack Squadron One Four Six in June 1986 and joined the Eagles of Training Squadron Seven, Flying the TA-4J Skyhawk as an Advanced Strike flight instructor in Meridian. After only a year in Training Squadron Seven, he was selected to join the Chief of Naval Air Training (CNATRA) staff in Corpus Christi, Texas, as the Advanced Strike Standardization Officer. He was responsible for standardizing training received by all new tactical aviators. While attached to the Chief of Naval Air Training, he earned his Naval War College degree through the Naval War College.

Ha left CNATRA in June of 1989 and joined the Sharpshooters of Marine Fighter Attack Training Squadron One Zero One for training in the FA-18 Hornet. Following Hornet training, he reported to Strike Fighter Squadron Two Five, Fist of the Fleet, for his Department Head tour. He was the squadron's operations officer during operation Desert Shield/Desert Storm while deployed to the Persian Gulf onboard USS *Independence* (CV-62).

He left the Fist of the Fleet in May of 1992 and reported to the Naval Postgraduate School in Monterey, California, a student in the Applied Mathematics curriculum. He graduated in September 1994 with a master's degree in Applied Mathematics. While attending Postgraduate School he was selected for operational command of a Hornet Squadron. He joined the Rough

Raiders Strike Fighter Squadron One Two Five for Hornet refresher training in October 1994. He assumed duties of Executive Officer of Strike Fighter Squadron Two Seven, The Royal Maces, in May 1995. As Executive Officer he prepared the squadron for transition to Carrier Air Wing Five in Atsugi, Japan. In June 1996, the squadron left Lemoore, California, and moved all personnel and equipment to Japan. Captain Shorts assumed command of the Royal Maces in July 1996.

In October 1997, he completed his Command tour and joined the staff of the Commander-in-Chief of the United States Pacific Fleet as the Fleet Readiness Officer and Flying Hour Program Manager. In December 2000, he was assigned to the Aviation Distribution Branch of Naval Personnel Command. Captain Shorts served as the Deputy J3 for Joint Task Force Southwest Asia in Saudi Arabia and as the Director of Combat Operations during Operation Enduring Freedom in Iraq. He left the Bureau of Personnel in April 2003. In March 2005, he was serving as the Commander of the Strike Fighter Wing of the United States Pacific Fleet. During his aviation career, he has logged more than 4,000 tactical jet hours and logged over 600 carrier landings.

Shuffer, George Macon, Jr.
BRIGADIER GENERAL—ARMY

He was born in Palestine, Texas, and married the former Maria Cecilia Rose. They have 11 children and 12 grandchildren. He received an Associate of Arts degree from Monterey Peninsula College and a Bachelor of Science degree from the University of Maryland. In 1959, he completed requirements for a Master of Arts in History at the University of Maryland. He enlisted

in the Army on August 16, 1940, at Fort Huachuca, Arizona. After basic training, he was promoted to corporal and assigned as a Training Instructor at Camp Wolters, Texas. He attained the rank of Sergeant before selection for the Infantry Officer Candidate School at Fort Benning, Georgia, in October 1942. In World War II, he served as an intelligence and reconnaissance Platoon Leader with the 93rd Infantry Division in the Pacific theater. He participated in campaigns in the northern Solomon Island the Bismarck Archipelago, New Guinea, and the southern Philippines. Near the war's end he was appointed regimental Intelligence Officer and assisted in the interrogation, processing and repatriation of over 8,000 Japanese prisoners of war. He served as an Infantry Company Commander in the 25th Infantry Division during the Korean War, participating in the first United Nations offensive, the Communist Chinese intervention, the United Nations counteroffensive, and the Communist Chinese spring offensive. On April 16, 1951, he suffered a serious head wound while making an assault crossing of the Han-Tan River. He recovered fully after 15 months of hospitalization at Walter Reed Army Medical Center in Washington, D.C. After recovery from his wound, he was determined to complete his formal education. While serving as a Regimental Operations Staff Officer at Fort Ord, California, he graduated with an Associate of Art degree, from Monterey Peninsula College in Monterey, California, in 1953. Three years later while on a duty tour in Europe, he graduated from the University of Maryland with scholastic honors in Military Science. While assigned as a Military Advisor to the Army of the Republic of China in Taiwan from 1962 to 1964, he taught five semesters of evening courses in American History and Western Civilization for the University of Maryland. Students completing each course received three units of resident college credit. In 1964, he returned to the United States and took Command of the 2nd Battalion, 2nd Infantry, at Fort Devens, Massachusetts. When the United States military forces were committed to combat in South Vietnam a year later, Shuffer took his Battalion into battle. He returned to the United States in 1966 at the United States War College at Carlisle Barracks, Pennsylvania. Upon graduation from the War College in 1967, he was assigned to Staff Duty in the Office of the Deputy Chief of Staff for Military Operations at the Pentagon. He became a Military Assistant in the Office of the Secretary of Defense in 1968. He conducted research and developed plans for managing and organizing the Department of Defense to improve the performance of its functions. He also prepared presentations or organizational and management problems to be used within the Department of Defense and for the Executive Office of the President and the Congress. From April 1970 to October 1971, he served as Commander of the 193rd Infantry Brigade in the Panama Canal Zone. Returning to the Pentagon in October 1971, he served as Assistant Director of Individual Training in the Office of the Deputy Chief of Staff for Personnel. He became Assistant

Division Commander of the 3rd Infantry Division in West Germany in 1973, and served in that position until 1974, when he was hospitalized at Walter Reed Army Hospital. On July 1, 1975, he was medically retired from the Army in the rank of Brigadier General, having completed 35 years of active service. His military awards and decorations include the Distinguished Service Medal, three Silver Stars, the Purple Heart, three Bronze Stars, six Air Medals, the Parachutist Badge, three Combat Infantryman Badges, Army Commendation Medal, the Legion of Merit (three oak leaf clusters), Secretary of Defense Identification Badge, Presidential Unit Citation, General Staff Identification Badge, and the Meritorious Service Medal.

Simmons, Anthony L.

LIEUTENANT COMMANDER—NAVY

He is a native of Alabama and attended Austin Peay State University in Clarksville, Tennessee, on a football scholarship and graduated with a Bachelor of Science degree in Industrial Engineering (Robotics) in August 1989. He was commissioned through Officer Candidate School (OCS) at Newport, Rhode Island, in June 1990. He is a graduate of the Air Command and Staff College Air University at Maxwell Air Force Base in Montgomery, Alabama. He graduated from the Naval Postgraduate School in Monterey, California, with a Master of Science degree in Mechanical Engineering in March 1997.

His sea duty assignments include tours in USS *Hurricane* (PC 3) as the Commanding Officer; USS *Caron* (DD 970) as Engineer Officer; USS *Gettysburg* (CG 64) as Damage Control Assistant and USS *Manitowoc* (LST 1180) as Auxiliaries Officer and Combat Information Center Officer. In October 2004, he was serv-ing as the Executive Officer onboard the USS *Chafee* (DDG 90).

Simmons, Bettye Hill

BRIGADIER GENERAL—ARMY

Born in San Antonio, Texas, General Simmons received a Bachelor of Science degree in Nursing from Incarnate Word College and Master of Science degree in Nursing (Medical Surgery) from the University of Texas School of Nursing. Her military schooling includes the United States Army Medical Officer Basic and Advanced Courses; the United States Army Command and General Staff College; and the United States Army War College. She was commissioned a Second Lieutenant on November 9, 1970. From September 1971 to November 1971, she was a student at the United States Army Medical Field Service School at Brooke Army Medical Center at Fort Sam Houston, Texas. She was promoted to First Lieutenant on May 23, 1971. In November 1971, she was assigned first as a Clinical Staff Nurse, next as a Nurse Instructor, later as the Deputy Director of the Clinical Specialist Course at Brooke Army Medical Center. She was promoted to Captain on May 23, 1974. From July 1975 to July 1977, she served as Army Nurse Corps Counselor for the Midwestern Region of the United States Army Recruiting Command at Fort Sheridan, Illinois. In July 1977, she was assigned as a Medical Surgical Nurse/Clinical Head Nurse at the 121st Evacuation Hospital with the 8th United States Army in Korea. In August 1978, she returned to the United States to serve as Clinical Coordinator at Walter Reed Army Medical Center in Washington, D.C. She was promoted to Major on September 4, 1980. In November 1980, she was a student at the Army Medical Officer Advanced Course in the Academy

of Health Sciences at Fort Sam Houston. From June 1981 to June 1982, she was assigned as the director of Patient Care Specialist Course at Fitzsimmons Army Medical Center in Aurora, Colorado. From July 1982 to June 1983, she was a student at the United States Army Command and General Staff College at Fort Leavenworth, Kansas. From June 1983 to June 1991, she was assigned first as the Assistant Inspector General for the United States Army Health Services Command, next as Chief of the Officer Instructional Branch, later Deputy Chief of the Nursing Science Division in the Academy of Health Sciences at Fort Sam Houston. She was promoted to Lieutenant Colonel on September 1, 1986. From 1991 to March 1994, she was assigned as the Chief of the Department of Nursing at the United States Army Medical Department Activity at Fort Polk, Louisiana. She was promoted to Colonel on November 1, 1992. From March 1994 to December 1995, she was assigned Chief Nurse of the United States Army Medical Command at Fort Sam Houston. In January 1996, she was selected Deputy Commandant of the United States Army Medical Department Center and School at Fort Sam Houston. She was promoted to Brigadier General on December 1, 1996. In April 1999, she was assigned as the Commanding General of the United States Army Center for Health Promotion and Preventive Medicine at Aberdeen Proving Ground, Maryland. She retired in January 2000. Her military awards and decorations include the Legion of Merit, the Meritorious Service Medal (with four oak leaf clusters), Army Commendation Medal (with two oak leaf clusters), and the Army Achievement Medal.

Simmons, Harry E.

COMMAND SERGEANT MAJOR—ARMY

He is a native of Chicago, Illinois, and the entered the United States Army in November 1979 and completed Basic Combat Training and Advanced Individual Training at Fort Sill, Oklahoma, in May 1980.

His military education includes all the Noncommissioned Officer Education System Courses; NBC Defense Course; CONSEC Custodian Course; Drill Sergeant School; First Sergeant Course; and the United States Army Sergeants Major (class 53). He earned an associate's degree in General Studies from Central Texas College at Killeen, Texas, and a Bachelor of Science degree in Liberal Arts from Excelsior College at Albany, New York.

His key military assignments include service as the S3 Sergeant Major for the 3rd Signal Brigade and Combined Joint Task Force, 7th Signal in Baghdad, Iraq; First Sergeant of Bravo Company, 123rd Signal Battalion, at Fort Stewart, Georgia; Brigade Communication Chief of the 1st Brigade Combat Team at Fort Stewart; Communication Chief of the 503rd Infantry Battalion (Air Assault) Camp Casey, South Korea; Section Sergeant of the 163rd Military Intelligence Battalion at Fort Hood, Texas; Communication Chief of the 16th Medical Logistics Battalion at Camp Carroll, South Korea; Communications Chief of A Company, 3rd

United States Infantry Regiment; Battery Communications Chief of Bravo Battery, 1st 27th Field Artillery Battalion; and Drill Sergeant Leader, at Fort Sill, Oklahoma. In August 2004, he was serving as the Command Sergeant Major of the 304th Signal Battalion in South Korea.

Simmons, Janet A.

LIEUTENANT COLONEL—ARMY

She is a Distinguished Military and magna cum laude graduate of South Carolina University, where she received a Bachelor of Science Degree in Criminal Justice and a commission as a Second Lieutenant in the United States Army in 1987. She also earned a Master of Science degree in Administration from Central Michigan University in July 2000.

After completion of the Military Intelligence Officer Basic Course, she was assigned to the 533rd Military Intelligence Battalion, 3rd Armored Division, in Frankfurt, Germany, where she served as a Collection and Jamming Platoon Leader. She then served as Electronic Warfare Liaison Officer of the 2nd and 3rd Brigades, 3rd Armored Division; Company Executive Officer (XO); and Commander of the 533rd Military Intelligence Battalion (rear). After her overseas tour, she attended the Military Intelligence

Officer Advanced Course and the Imagery Intelligence Tactical Exploitation Course at Fort Huachuca, Arizona. After graduation, she received assignment to Fort Eustis, Virginia, as the S2 of the 7th Transportation Group and later as Commander of the Headquarters Company at the United States Army Transportation Center and Fort Eustis. From Fort Eustis, she moved to the Chicago Recruiting Battalion, United States Army Recruiting Command, where she commanded the Libertyville Recruiting Company. Following command in United States Army Recruiting Command, she was assigned to the Defense HUMINT Service (DHS), Defense Intelligence Agency (DIA), in Arlington, Virginia, where she served as a Reports Officer in the Latin America Division; Chief of Defense HUMINT Service Situation Room; and Assistant Executive Officer to the Director of Operations. Following this assignment, she attended the Command and General Staff College (CGSC) in Fort Leavenworth, Kansas, before reporting to the Signals Intelligence (SIGINT) Directorate of the National Security Agency (NSA) at Fort George G. Meade, Maryland, as the Chief of the Military Exercises Branch and Deputy Chief of the Exercises Division. While at Fort Meade, she transferred to the 704th Military Intelligence Brigade, Intelligence and Security Command (INSCOM), where she served as the Executive Officer of the 741st Military Intelligence Battalion. Her successful tour at Fort Meade was followed by her most recent assignment to the White House Drug Policy Office, where she served as a Senior Intelligence Officer. In June 2005, Lieutenant Colonel Simmons was serving as Commander of the Headquarters Battalion at Fort Belvoir.

Simms, Darren V.
SERGEANT MAJOR—MARINES

He is a native of Brooklyn, New York. He graduated from Recruit Training at the Marine Corps Recruit Depot Parris Island, South Carolina, in Septem-

ber 1980. Upon graduation he was sent to Headquarters and Service Company Infantry Training School at Camp Geiger, North Carolina. After completing Infantry Training School, he was assigned the MOS 0341 of Mortarman and attached to Kilo Company, 3rd Battalion, 8th Marines, 2nd Marine Division.

His key leadership positions include serving as Drill Instructor; Mortar Instructor; Unit Leader; Weapons Platoon Commander; Noncommissioned Officer in Charge of Naval Gunfire School; 3rd Marine Expeditionary Force Operations Chief in Subic Bay, Republic of the Philippines; Instructor at (FTU) Field Training Unit and Noncommissioned Officer in Charge of Marine Liaison at Charleston International Airport, processing Recruits for training at Parris Island; Training Chief in S-3; Platoon Sergeant and Leadership Instructor, training Officer Candidates and Midshipmen from the U.S. Naval Academy; Company Gunnery Sergeant; and Company First Sergeant. In April 2003, he was promoted to the rank of Sergeant Major and transferred to Marine Corps Air Station New River, Headquarters & Headquarters Squadron for Duty.

Simms, Earl Myers
BRIGADIER GENERAL—ARMY

He was born in Maryland. He holds a Bachelor of Arts degree from West Virginia State College and earned a master's degree in Public Administration from Shippensburg University. His military education includes completion of the Adjutant General Officer Basic and Advanced Courses, the United States Command and General Staff College and the United States Army War College. He was commissioned a Second Lieutenant on February 19, 1968. From June 1968 to January 1969, he served as Chief of the Trainee Personnel Division at the United States Army Training

Center at Fort Campbell, Kentucky. He was promoted to First Lieutenant on February 14, 1969. From February 1969 to February 1970, he was the Administrative Officer with the 2nd Civil Affairs Company, United States Army, in Vietnam. He was promoted to Captain on February 16, 1970. In March 1970, he was assigned as the Adjutant at the Armed Forces Entrance and Evaluation Station in Newark, New Jersey. He was promoted to Captain on February 16, 1970. From March 1972 to August 1972, he was a student at the Adjutant General Officer Advanced Course at Fort Harrison, Indiana. From September 1972 to July 1976, he was assigned as the Adjutant, later Executive Officer, with the United States Army Garrison at Fort Buchanan, Puerto Rico. From August 1976 to June 1978, he was assigned first as Officer in Charge of Team 3, next he served as Deputy Chief, later as Chief of the Personnel Services Division, 4th Adjutant General Company, 4th Infantry Division, at Fort Carson, Colorado. He was promoted to Major on June 8, 1977. From June 1978 to May 1979, he was a student at the United States Army Command and General Staff College at Fort Leavenworth, Kansas. From June 1979 to June 1982, he served as the Admissions Officer at the United States Military Academy at West Point, New York. From July 1982 to May 1986, he was assigned Chief of the Personnel Actions Division, 1st Personnel Command, next as Adjutant General, later as the G-1/Adjutant General, 3rd Infantry Division, United States Army Europe, in Germany. He was promoted to Lieutenant Colonel on October 1, 1989. In June 1986, he returned to the United States to serve as Adjutant General Corps colonel's assignment officer, United States Army Military Personnel Center at Alexandria, Virginia. From July 1987 to July 1989, he served as the Commander of the Military Entrance Processing Station at Baltimore, Maryland. In August 1989, he return to Germany to serve as Director of the Theater Personnel Plans Office with the 1st Personnel Command, United States Army, Germany. He was promoted to Colonel October 1, 1989. In June 1990, he returned to the United States and was assigned as a student at the United States Army War College at Carlisle Barracks, Pennsylvania. From June 1991 to February 1992, he was assigned as the Commandant of the Adjutant General School at Fort Benjamin Harrison, Indiana. From March 1992 to August 1994, he served as the Commander of Military Entrance and Processing Command at Great Lakes, Illinois. From September 1994 to November 1995, he served as the Commandant of the Adjutant General School at Fort Jackson, South Carolina. In November 1995, he was selected as the Adjutant General/Commanding General of the Physical Disability Agency in Alexandria, Virginia. He was promoted to Brigadier General on May 1, 1996. In November 1998, he was assigned as Commanding General of the Soldier Support Institute at Fort Jackson. He retired from the military on August 31, 2000. His military awards and decorations include the Defense Superior Service Medal, the Legion of Merit, the Bronze Star, Defense Meritorious Service Medal

(with three oak leaf clusters), Joint Service Commendation Medal, Army Commendation Medal (with two oak leaf clusters), and Army Achievement Medal.

Simon, Larry E.
COMMAND SERGEANT MAJOR—ARMY

He is a native of Baker, Florida, and entered the United States Army in April 1976. He attended Basic Combat Training at Fort Jackson, South Carolina, and attended his Advanced Individual Training as an Attack Helicopter Repairman at Fort Eustis, Virginia.

His military education includes all the Noncommissioned Officers Education System Courses; First Sergeant Course; the United States Army Sergeants Academy (class 49); Attack Helicopter Inspector Course (66Y); Aviation Life Support Course; and Aviation Research and Development Course. He also holds an associate's degree in Applied Science from Excelsior University.

His key military assignments include serving as Command Sergeant Major of the 2nd Aviation Brigade, at Camp Stanley, South Korea; Command Sergeant Major of the 2nd Battalion, 2nd Brigade at Camp Stanley; and First Sergeant of Headquarters and Headquarters Company, 1-25th ATK Battalion. In August 2004, he was serving as the Command Sergeant Major of the 17th Aviation Brigade.

Simpson, Arthur J.
SERGEANT MAJOR—MARINES

He enlisted in the Marine Corps in April 1983, and reported to the Recruit Training, 1st Recruit Training Battalion, Recruit Training Regiment, Marine Corps Recruit Depot, at Parris Island, South Carolina. His military education includes Transportation Management School; the Army Jump School at Fort Benning, Georgia; and the Drill Instructor School.

Electronic Fighting Vehicle System, the M993 Multiple-Launched Rocket System Carrier, the Armored Medical Treatment Vehicle, and the Armored Medical Evacuation Vehicle. In March 2005, he had been serving as Project Manager for Combat Ammunition Systems for Artillery Munitions Systems since October 2001.

Small, Julius, Jr.
COMMAND SERGEANT MAJOR—ARMY

He was born May 3, 1938, in Savannah, Georgia. He married the former Dorothy Green, and they have five children, Calvin, Terry, Lucinda, Kenneth, and Shirley. He was raised in Beaufort, South Carolina, graduated from St. Helena High School, and holds an Associate of arts degree from St. Leo College in St. Leo, Florida.

In July 1958, Julius Small enlisted in the United States Army and completed his basic training at Fort Jackson, South Carolina. In October 1958, he was assigned as a unit supply specialist at Fort Benning, Georgia, and in October 1959, he was assigned to the Headquarters of the 1st Cavalry Division in South Korea. In December 1960 he returned to Fort Jackson, South Carolina, where he was assigned as a supply clerk in the G-4 at Division. In August 1961, he re-enlisted and was assigned as the unit supply sergeant, providing logistical support to the Military Policy School and to the 42nd Civilian Affairs Group. He was assigned in August 1966, to the 2nd Armored Cavalry Regiment at Bamberg, West Germany, as the Squadron Supply sergeant. In August 1969, he was assigned to Headquarters, USARV, Vietnam, as AGI/CMMI inspector with the G-4, at Division. In November 1970, he was assigned to Fort Lee, Virginia, as an instructor with the General Subject Branch, and in January 1976, he was

His key military assignments include serving as Embark Chief; Sergeant/Logistics Specialist; Drill Instructor; Logistics Chief; and First Sergeant. In July 2002, he was transferred to the 3rd FSSG at Okinawa, Japan, where he served as First Sergeant for the Electronics Maintenance Company. In August 2004, he was serving as the Sergeant Major, MSSG-31, 3rd Marine Division.

Sledge, Nathaniel H., Jr.
COLONEL—ARMY

He was born at Fort Hood, Texas, and was commissioned a Second Lieutenant of Armor in June 1979. He was awarded a Bachelor of Science degree in Engineering from the United States Military Academy at West Point in 1979 and a Master of Science in Engineering and Doctor of Philosophy in Mechanical Engineering from the University of Texas at Austin in 1986 and 1997, respectively. Additionally, he is a 1997 graduate of the Advanced Program Manager's Course at the Defense Systems Management College at Fort Belvoir. He is a graduate of the Army's Command and General Staff College and the United States Army War College.

His military assignments include serving as Commander of Company A, 1st Battalion, 72nd Armor at Tongduchon, South Korea, and as Tank Company Executive Officer and Tank Platoon leader in Company B, 2nd Battalion, 8th Cavalry (Armor) at Fort Hood, Texas. From July 1986 to July 1990, he served as Test Officer, Mechanical Engineering Project Manager, and Research and Development Coordinator in the Project Management Office for the Abrams Tank. From June 1991 to July 1994, he served as Operational Evaluator for all variants of the Abrams tank and the Armored Gun System, managing the development, testing, and production of the Command and Control Vehicle, the

assigned to Headquarters, NATO, Shape Support Group (NSSG), Shape, Belgium, where he was supervisor for the stock record accounting (RA) in the Supply and Maintenance Division.

In January 1977, he was assigned to Fort Bliss, Texas, where he attended the Sergeant Academy and upon graduation was assigned to the United States Army Quartermaster School at Fort Lee, Virginia, as first sergeant for an AIT Unit and later as the Command Sergeant Major of the 4th Battalion, United States Army Quartermaster Brigade. In August 1981, CSM Small was assigned to Headquarters, 12th Combat Aviation Group at Lindsey Air Station in Wiesbaden, West Germany. From October 1983 to April 1985, he was assigned to the United States Army Quartermaster School in Fort Lee, Virginia, this time as the Command Sergeant Major of the Quartermaster School. He established the noncommissioned officers school, and with 45 trainers ran the academy that trained 6,000 students annually. CSM Small was selected as the first commandant of the Noncommissioned Officers Academy at Fort Lee. In October 1987, he was assigned to the Headquarters of the 20th Area Support Group, in Taiga, South Korea, as the installation and Area V Command Sergeant Major. In May 1988, he was assigned to the Headquarters of the 19th Support Command in Taiga as the Command Sergeant Major for the Support Command. He assumed the duties of Command Sergeant Major of the United States Army Garrison at Fort McPherson, Georgia, on June 18, 1990. He was the first African American Army Command Sergeant Major to serve in this capacity in the history of Fort McPherson. On March 26, 1993, retired Command Sergeant Major Julius Small, Jr., became the first Noncommissioned Officer and the first African American NCO to be named to the Quartermaster Regiment Hall of Fame at Fort Lee.

Small, Stanley
COMMAND SERGEANT MAJOR—ARMY

He is a native of Huntsville, Alabama, and joined the army under the Delayed Entry Program in June 1977. After graduating from Lee High School in June 1978, he entered One Stop Unit Training (OSUT) as an Armor Crewman at Fort Knox, Kentucky.

His military and civilian education includes all courses in the Noncommissioned Officer Education System; Master Gunner Courses; First Sergeants Course; and the United State Army Sergeants Major Academy (class 50). He hold an associate's degree in Science from Saint Thomas Aquinas College and holds a Bachelor of Science (Cum Laude) from Regents College at the University of the State of New York.

He has served in numerous positions in armor and cavalry units including as a Tank Gunnery Instructor; Drill Sergeant at the United States Army Armor Center at Fort Knox; Tank Commander, Platoon Sergeant and Battalion Master Gunner with 1st Battalion, 10th Cavalry, at Fort Knox; Platoon Sergeant and Troop Master Gunner, 2nd Squad, 3rd Armored Cavalry Reg-

iment at Fort Bliss; Small Group Leader; Company and Regimental Tactical Noncommissioned Officer at the United States Corps of Cadets at West Point, New York; First Sergeant and Operation Sergeant Major, 1st Battalion, 12th Cavalry Regiment; and Command Sergeant Major, 3rd Battalion, 8th Cavalry, both at Fort Hood, Texas. In August 2004, he was serving as the Command Sergeant Major for the 1st Brigade, 1st Cavalry Division.

Smith, Barbara S.
COMMAND SERGEANT MAJOR—ARMY

She holds a Bachelor of Science degree from the University of the State of New York, and earned a Master of Business Administration degree from Tarleston State University. Her military education includes Drill Sergeant Course; the First Sergeant Course; the Sergeants Major Course; and the Command Sergeant Major Course.

CSM Barbara S. Smith entered the United States Army in May 1977 from Greensboro, North Carolina. She attended Basic Training at Fort McCellan, Alabama. In July, she was awarded the MOS 75C, after graduation from Advanced Individual Training at Fort Benjamin Harrison, Indiana. Her first duty assignment was Personnel Actions Clerk with VII Corps Headquarters in Stuttgart, West Germany.

In 1987, she volunteered for Drill Sergeant Duty. After completion of the Drill Sergeant Instructor Course at Fort Knox, Kentucky, she was assigned to Fort Dix, New Jersey, first as a Drill Sergeant and

then as Senior Drill Sergeant, with Company B, 4th Battalion, 26th Infantry Brigade. After completion of her Drill Sergeant tour, she was selected to become First Sergeant of the same Basic Training Company.

In July 1999, she was reassigned as the Senior Enlisted Advisor to the Commander in Chief of Pacific Command at Camp Smith, Hawaii. After two years she was selected to become Battalion Command Sergeant Major of Headquarters Command Battalion at Fort George G. Meade, Maryland. One year later she was selected as the Post Command Sergeant Major at Fort Belvoir, Virginia.

Smith, Danny
SERGEANT MAJOR—MARINES

He was born in Charleston, South Carolina. He graduated from Baptist Hill High School in June 1980. He enlisted into the Marine Corps in November 1979 and after seven months in the Delayed Entry Program, attended Recruit Training at Marine Corps Recruit Depot, Parris Island, South Carolina.

Smith, Issac Dixon
MAJOR GENERAL—ARMY

Born in Wakefield, Louisiana, he married the former Mildred L. Pierre, and they have two children, Debra J. and Ronald L. Upon completion of the Reserve Officer Training Corps curriculum and the educational course of study at Southern University A&M College, he was commissioned a Second Lieutenant and received a Bachelor of Science degree in Agriculture. He also holds a master's in Public Administration from Shippensburg State College. His military education includes completion of the Field Artillery School Basic and Advanced Courses; United States Army Command and General Staff College; and the United States Army War College. From August 1955 to August 1957, he was as-

signed as the Assistant Executive Officer with Battery B, later Executive Officer with Battery C, later Liaison Officer at the Headquarters Battery of the 65th Area Field Artillery Battalion, 3rd Armor Division, United States Army in Europe. He was promoted to First Lieutenant on August 13, 1956. From August 1957 to May 1959, he was assigned as the Executive Officer with Battery B, later Communication Officer at the Headquarters Battery of the 2nd Howitzer Battalion, 6th Artillery, 3rd Armor Division, United States Army in Europe. He returned to the United States in June 1959 and was assigned to Fort Lewis, Washington, first as Commander of Headquarters Battery, next in November 1959, as Communications Officer with Headquarters Battery, later in December 1960, as Commander of Battery A, 6th Howitzer Battalion, 29th Artillery, at Fort Lewis. He was promoted to Captain on January 13, 1961. In June 1961, he returned to Europe as the Commander of the Headquarters Detachment of the 528th United States Army Artillery Group, United States Army. From July 1962 to November 1962, he was a student in the Field Artillery Officer Advanced Course at the United States Army Artillery and Missile School at Fort Still, Oklahoma. From December 1962 to December 1963, he was assigned as the S-3 (operations) officer with the 5th Howitzer Battalion, 16th Artillery, at Fort Lewis. From December 1963 to August 1964, he served as the assistant S-3 officer (operations) of the 4th Infantry Division Artillery at Fort Lewis. From August 1964 to November 1965, he served as the commander of Battery A, 5th Battalion, 83rd Artillery, with the Infantry Division, United Army, Europe. He was promoted to Major on October 27, 1965. He has held a wide variety of important command and staff positions, including service as Chief of the Doctrine and Systems Integration Division in the Requirements Directorate of the Office of the Deputy Chief of Staff for Operations and Plans in Washington, D.C.; Commanding General of the United States Second Reserve Officer Training Corps Region at Fort Knox, Kentucky; and Assistant Division Commander of the 1st Armored Division, United States Army, in Europe. General Smith served as Deputy Chief of Staff for Operations and Intelligence with Allied Forces Central Europe. In Vietnam, he was Commander of the 8th Battalion, 4th Artillery, XXIV Corps Artillery, United States Army, Vietnam, and later served as Operations Officer with the 23rd Army of the Republic of Vietnam Infantry Division, United States Military Assistance Command, in Vietnam. He followed this assignment with a tour in Europe as Commander of the 2nd Battalion, 75th Field Artillery, 36th Field Artillery Group, V Corps Artillery, United States Army, in Europe. He returned to the United States as a Staff Officer in the Unit Training and Readiness Division of the Office of the Assistant Chief of Staff for Force Development, later Office of the Deputy Chief of Staff for Military Operations in Washington, D.C. He served as the Deputy Director of the Army Equal Opportunity Programs in the Human Resources Directorate of the Office of the Deputy Chief of Staff for Personnel, in Washington, D.C. He was assigned as Commander of Division Artillery for the 1st Infantry Division (Mechanized) at Fort Riley, Kansas, and later became Special Assistant to the Commander of the Third Reserve Officer Training Corps Region at Fort Riley. He also served as Chief of Staff of the 1st Infantry Division (Mechanized) at Fort Riley. He was promoted to Major General on September 1, 1985. He retired on September 30, 1989. His military awards and decorations include the Distinguished Service Medal; the Silver Star; the Legion of Merit (with oak leaf cluster); Bronze Star; Meritorious Service Medal (with oak leaf cluster); and Army Commendation Medal (with two oak leaf clusters); Army General Staff Identification Badge.

Smith, Melody D.

LIEUTENANT COLONEL—ARMY

She is a native of Jacksonville, Florida, and graduated from the United States Military Academy at West Point in 1989 with a Bachelor of Science degree in Mathematics and was commissioned in the United States Army Corps of Engineers.

She attended the Officer Basic Course at Fort Belvoir, Virginia. She is a graduate of the Command and General Staff College; the Combined Armed Staff Service School; the Mapping, Charting, and Geodesy Officer's Course; the Engineer Officer's Advanced Course; and the Engineer Officer's Basic Course.

While serving with the 34th Engineer Combat Battalion (Heavy) at Fort Riley, Kansas. As a Vertical Construction Platoon Leader, she deployed with her platoon to Bolivia to conduct humanitarian civil-action projects and also served in Saudi Arabia and Kuwait for Operation Desert Storm as Bravo Company's Executive Officer.

In January 2005, she was serving as the Deputy Commander of the United States Army Corps of Engineers, Rock Island District.

Smith, Mitte A.

COMMAND SERGEANT MAJOR—ARMY

She joined the United States Army in November 1981. She completed Basic and Advanced Individual Training (AIT) at Fort Jackson, South Carolina, as an Administrative Specialist.

Her military education includes Training Course (Honor Graduate), NBC Course (Distinguished Honor Graduate), Basic Noncommissioned Officer Course (Honor Graduate), Drill Sergeant School (Distinguished Honor Graduate and Leadership Award), Master Trainers Course, Advanced Noncommissioned Officer Course (Leadership Award), First Sergeants Course (Commandant's List), Cadre Training Course, Graduate of the Sergeants Major Academy, and the Garrison Sergeants Major Course. She holds a Bachelor of Science degree in Business and Management from the University of Maryland and a master's degree in Computer Resources and Information Management from Webster University at St. Louis, Missouri.

She has held numerous leadership positions, including Squad Leader, Personnel Management NCOIC, Primary Leadership Development Course Instructor, Senior Drill Sergeant, Platoon Sergeant, Operations Sergeant, Chief/Adjutant of the Personnel and Administration Division, Detachment Sergeant, and First Sergeant. In 2004, she was serving as the Garrison Command Sergeant Major at Hunter Army Airfield, 3rd Infantry Division, in Savannah, Georgia.

Smith, Nathaniel

COLONEL—ARMY

In 1995, Colonel Smith was assigned to the White House Communications Agency in Washington, D.C., where he served as a Director for Presidential Travel Support. From June 1998 to July 2000, he commanded the 141st Signal Battalion, 1st Armored Division in Bad Kreuznach, Germany.

He also served as the Chief of Signals with the United States Army Total Personnel Command Center in Alexandria, Virginia.

Smith, Otis

COMMAND SERGEANT MAJOR—ARMY

He entered the United States Army on March 1975, attending Basic Training at Fort Jackson, South Carolina, and Advanced Individual Training at Fort Knox, Kentucky. Command Sergeant Major Smith has served in virtually every leadership position available, from squad leader to his present position as Command Sergeant Major of the 2nd Brigade in Kuwait, part of the 3rd Infantry Division (Mechanized). He and his Brigade and his 3rd Infantry Division lead the attack on Iraq in March 2003.

Smith, Vicki A.R.

LIEUTENANT COLONEL—ARMY

She assumed command of the 53rd Transportation Battalion, Third United States Army. Her other previous assignments include platoon leader and executive officer of the 24th Transportation Battalion, commander of Headquarters and Headquarters Detachment, MTMC Bremerhaven Terminal, commander of 1301st Major Port Command, Baltimore Detachment and commander of 272nd Movement Control Team: Support Operation Officer, ARCENT in Kuwait.

Smith, Vinson E.

REAR ADMIRAL—NAVY

Born in Carthage, Tennessee, he is a 1969 graduate

of Gordonsville High School and a 1974 graduate of Tennessee Technological University. After commissioning, he reported to the Precommissioning Unit for USS *Nimitz* (CVN 68). Following Surface Warfare Qualifications, three division officer tours, and three deployments in *Nimitz*, he completed two years at the Naval Amphibious School in Little Creek, Virginia, as an Instructor. He completed department head tours as Operations Officer in USS *Charles F. Adams* (DDG 2) and Weapons Officer in USS *Luce* (DDG 38). As a department head, he deployed to the North Atlantic with the Standing Naval Force Atlantic and to the Arabian Gulf during the Iran/Iraq tanker war.

In October 1985, he reported to the Staff of the Commander of Naval Surface Force and United States Atlantic Fleet as the N3 Cruiser/Destroyer Scheduler. In July 1987, he reported to USS *Tattnall* (DDG 19) as Executive Officer. This tour was highlighted by Mediterranean and Black Sea deployments. He earned two Master of Arts degrees, one in Strategic Studies and National Defense from the Naval War College and one in International Relations from Salve Regina University. He reported to United States Central Command at MacDill Air Force Base in Florida in July 1990 serving in a joint billet as Navy Branch Chief for Current Operations in the J3 directorate. During this tour, he deployed to Riyadh, Saudi Arabia, in support of Operation Desert Shield/Desert Storm from August 1990 until April 1991.

Following his joint duty assignment, he assumed command of USS *Robert G. Bradley* (FFG 49) on October 21, 1992. During his tenure, the ship was awarded the COMNAVSURFLANT Safety Award and three consecutive Battle Efficiency Awards. In August 1994, he retuned to the Staff of the Commander of Naval

Surface Force, with the United States Atlantic Fleet as the Combat Systems/C41 Officer. In February 1996, he assumed command of Naval Station San Diego, home port for 50 Navy ships and 50 other tenant commands. While under his command, the Naval Station assumed responsibility for Port Operations as part of the Southwest regionalization effort. In this post, he also served as Assistant Chief of Staff for Port Operations on the Staff of the Commander of Navy Region Southwest. In August 1999, he reported to the Staff of Deputy Chief of Naval Operations, serving as Director of Personal Readiness and Community Support with the Washington Liaison Detachment (Pers-6/N15B) and as Branch Head for Plans and Policy (N461) for the Shore Installation Management Division (N46). His most recent assignment was as Commander of Navy Region Northwest and Naval Surface Group, Pacific Northwest.

His military awards and decorations include the Legion of Merit; Bronze Star; Defense Meritorious Service Medal; Meritorious Service Medal (with two Gold Stars); the Navy Commendation Medal; Meritorious Unit Award; Commendation Medal (with Bronze Star); Battle Efficiency Award with four "E's"; National Defense Service Medal (with Bronze Star); Sea Service Deployment Ribbon (with four Bronze Stars); Southwest Asia Service Medal (with two Bronze Stars); and Kuwait Liberation Medal (Kuwait).

Solomon, Billy King
LIEUTENANT GENERAL—ARMY

Born in Oakwood, Texas, Solomon received a Bachelor of Science degree in Agriculture from Prairie View A&M University in 1966 and a Masters of Science degree in Procurement/Contract Management from the Florida Institute of Technology in 1982. He began his military career on October 10, 1966, as a Second Lieutenant in the Quartermaster Officer Basic Course at Fort Lee, Virginia. In December 1966, he was first assigned as Officer in Charge, later as Platoon Leader of Company A, 502nd Supply and Transpiration Battalion with the 2nd Armored Division at Fort Hood, Texas. He was promoted to First Lieutenant on October 10, 1967, and was assigned as the Stock Control Officer of the 624th Supply and Service Company, 226th Supply and Service Battalion, with the United States Army in Vietnam. In January 1968, he served as a Platoon Leader with the 506th Supply and Service Company, and later as

S-3 (Operations) Officer with the 266th Supply and Service Battalion. He was promoted to Captain on October 10, 1968. In October 1968, he returned to the United States and was assigned G-4 (Logistics) Officer with the 2nd Armored Division at Fort Hood, Texas. He became a student in the Quartermaster Officer Advanced Course from October 1970 to August 1971. From August 1971 to March 1972, he served as Commander of Headquarters Company with the 88th Supply and Service Battalion in Vietnam. From March 1972 to September 1972, he was assigned as the S-3 Officer (Operations) for Logistical Support Activity in Vietnam. In the fall of 1972, he was assigned as a Supply and Logistics Officer with the 109th Military Intelligence Group in Fort Meade. Beginning in May 1974, he served for a year as a Civil Affairs Officer for the 902nd Military Intelligence Group at Fort Meade, Maryland. From May 1975 to December 1977, he served as the Chief Logistics Officer with the United States Army Communications Command Agency in the Canal Zone at Fort Clayton, Panama. He was promoted to Major on June 5, 1976. From December 1977 to July 1978, he was a student at the Armed Forces Staff College at Norfolk, Virginia. From July 1978 to June 1982, he was assigned as a Personnel Management Officer with the Military Personnel Center at Alexandria, Virginia. He was promoted to Lieutenant Colonel on March 1, 1982. From June 1982 to June 1983, he served as Protocol Officer in the Office of the Chief of Staff of the Army in Washington, D.C. From June 1983 to June 1985, he served as the Commander of the 498th Support Battalion with the 2nd Armored Division, United States Army in Europe and Seventh Army. From June 1985 to June 1986, he was a student in the Industrial College of the Armed Forces. From June 1986 to May 1989, he served as Chief of Quartermaster/ Chemical Branch, later as Chief of the Combat Service Support Division of the Enlisted Personnel Management Directorate at the United States Army Personnel Command in Alexandria. He was promoted to Colonel on January 1, 1989. In May 1989, he was assigned as the Commander of the Division Support Command with the 5th Infantry Division (Mechanized) at Fort Polk, Louisiana. In January 1992, he was assigned as the Commander of the 13th Corps Support Command, III Corps at Fort Hood, Texas. He was promoted to Brigadier General on October 1, 1992. From January 1993 to May 1993, General Solomon served as the Commander of the Joint Logistics Task Force for the United Nations Operations in Somalia. In May 1993, he returned to Fort Hood, Texas, to as the Commander of the 13th Corps Support Command, III Corps. From July 1993 to June 1995, he served as the Assistant Chief of Staff, J4/C4/G4 with United States Forces in Korea/United Nations Command/Combined Forces Command/Eighth United States Army, Korea. In June 1995, he was assigned as the Chief of Staff for the United States Army Materiel Command in Alexandria. He was promoted to Major General on October 1, 1995. From August 1997 to September 1999, he served as the

Director for Logistics and Security Assistance, J-4/J-7, with the United States Central Command, at MacDill Air Force Base, Florida. In September 1999, he was selected to serve as the Commanding General of the United States Army Combined Arms Support Command and Fort Lee, Virginia. He was promoted to Lieutenant General on September 15, 1999. He retired on September 30, 2002. His military awards and decorations include the Defense Distinguished Service Medal (with oak leaf cluster); Defense Superior Service Medal, Legion of Merit (with twice oak leaf clusters), Bronze Star Medal (with oak leaf cluster), Meritorious Service Medal (with three oak leaf clusters), Army Commendation Medal (with oak leaf cluster), and the Army Achievement Medal.

Sparrock, Robert C.
COMMANDER—NAVY

He is a native of Brooklyn, New York. He graduated from the United States Naval Academy in May 1988 with a Bachelor of Science degree in Oceanography. He was selected for the Immediate Graduate Education Program (IGEP) and attended the Scripps Institution of Oceanography at the University of California, San Diego (SlO-UCSD) in La Jolla, California.

Upon graduation, he reported to the Atmospheric Sciences Department Los Alamos National Laboratory in New Mexico for a summer internship. In 1990, he earned a Master of Science in Physical Oceanography and completed published thesis work in ocean acoustics in support of global warming research. He completed Navy Nuclear Power and Surface Warfare Officer Training in route to USS *Virginia* (CGN 38) in July 1992 and completed Surface Warfare and Engineering qualifications.

He completed two deployments and served as in Engineering Department as Damage Control Assistant, Reactor Electrical Division Officer, and Chemical/Radiological Controls Assistant. In December 1994, he reported onboard USS *Ticonderoga* (CG 47), as the Ship's Navigation, Administrative and Legal Officer. He completed a Mediterranean Sea deployment on USS *Conolly* (DD 979) as Combat Systems Officer and deployed to the Caribbean Sea for Counter Narcotic Operations prior to the ship's decommissioning. In September 1998, he volunteered for overseas duty at Joint Task Force, South West Asia (JTF-SWA) in Riyadh, Saudi Arabia, as Chief Long Range Plans, where he collaborated with Joint and Multinational Forces for Combat Strikes during Operations Desert Fox in Southern Iraq.

In January 1999, he reported to USS *Theodore Roosevelt* (CVN 71) as the Reactor Training Officer. In March 2001, he reported to PCU *Ronald Reagan* (CVN 76) as the Damage Control Assistant and served as acting Chief Engineer. In October 2004, he was serving as the Executive Officer onboard USS *Mount Whitney* (LCC/JCC 20)

Spaulding, Vernon Charles
BRIGADIER GENERAL—ARMY

He was born in Los Angeles, California. He married the former Paula Rae Cady of Berkeley, California. They have two children: Raymond and Rebecca. He attended public school in Los Angeles and graduated with a Bachelor of Science degree in Public Health from the University of California, Berkley, in 1965. His military education includes completion of Army Medical Officer Basic and Advanced Courses, the United States Army Command and General Staff College, and the United States Army War College. He entered the United States Army on June 12, 1968, when he was commissioned a Second Lieutenant through the Senior Medical Student Program and graduated with a Medical Degree from Howard University in 1969. He was promoted to First Lieutenant on 6 June 1969. He completed a Rotating Internship and Internal Medicine Residency at Walter Reed Army Medical Center from 1969 to 1973. He was promoted to Captain on June 5, 1972. He was promoted to Major on June 6, 1972. He completed a Gastroenterology Fellowship at Letterman Army Hospital from 1975 to 1977. He was promoted to Lieutenant Colonel on June 6, 1977. From July 1973 to June 1975, he served as Chief of the Department of Medi-

cine, United States Army Medical Activity, at Fort Huachuca, Arizona. From June 1977 to June 1978, he was assigned as the Assistant Chief of Gastroenterology Service at Madigan Army Medical Center in Tacoma, Washington. He was promoted to Colonel on August 1, 1983. From June 1983 to June 1986, he served first as Chief of Ambulatory Medicine, next as Chief of the Ambulatory Care Department/Assistant Deputy Commander of Clinic Services, later as the Deputy Commander of Clinical Service with the 2nd General Hospital, Seventh Medical Command, United States Army Europe, Germany. From June 1987 to July 1989, he served as the Commander of the United States Army Medical Activity at Fort Lee, Virginia. In June 1990, he was assigned as the Commander of the United States Army Medical Activity at Fort Benning, Georgia. From March 1993 to December 1993, he served as a member of President Clinton's Health Care Services Task Force at Fort Benning. In November 1993 he was promoted to Brigadier General, and assigned in December 1993, as the Commanding General of Eisenhower Medical Center at Fort Gordon, Georgia. He retired from the military on December 31, 1996. His military awards and decorations include the Legion of Merit (with two oak leaf clusters); the Meritorious Service Medal; the Army Commendation Medal; Expert Field Medical Badge; Parachutist Badge; and the Air Assault Badge. He is Board Certified in Internal Medicine, Gastroenterology, and Medical Management. He is a member of the American College of Physicians, the American Society of Gastrointestinal Endoscopy, and the American College of Physician Executives.

Spencer, Chery E.
CHIEF WARRANT OFFICER-MARINE

Chief Spencer enlisted in the United States Marine Corps in October 1978. She attended Basic Training at the Marine Corps Recruit Depot, Parris Island, South Carolina in January 1979. She is a graduate of the Drill Sergeant School; the Advanced Administration Chief School; Marine Corps Automotive Mechanic Course; and the Officer Basic School at Marine Corps Combat Development Command at Quantico, Virginia.

Her assignments include serving as a Unit Diary Clerk at Headquarters and Service Battalion, Second Force Service Support Group, at Camp Lejeune, North Carolina; as Unit Diary Clerk at Marine Corps Inspector-Instruction Staff, at Waukegan, Illinois; and as a Drill Instructor at the 4th Battalion Marine Corps Recruit Depot at Parris Island. She was commissioned a Warrant Officer on December 14, 1990.

She was promoted to Chief Warrant Officer 5, effective February 1, 2005, and is now the Director of the Consolidated Personnel Administration Center at Parris Island.

Spencer, Kathleen M.

COLONEL—AIR FORCE

She is originally from Pittsfield, Massachusetts, and entered the Air Force through the Officer Training School in March 1977, receiving her commission in June 1977.

Her military and civilian education includes a Bachelor of Science in Geology (cum laude) from the University of Massachusetts at Amherst, Massachusetts, in 1976; Squadron Officer School (distinguished graduate) at Maxwell Air Force Base, in Alabama; Air Command and Staff College; Air War College; and the Industrial College of the Armed Forces at Fort McNair in Washington, D.C. She earned a Master of Science degree in International Relations at Troy State University–Europe and a Master of Science degree in National Resource Strategy from the National Defense University at Fort McNair.

She has held a variety of munitions and aircraft maintenance positions in several major commands and at Air Staff, and also served as an instructor at the Air University and military assistant to the Executive Secretary in the Office of the Secretary of Defense.

Her key command assignments include serving from July 1990 as Commander of the 6519th Component Repair Squadron at Edwards Air Force Base, California, and from July 1992 as Commander of the 412th Logistics Test Squadron at Edwards Air Force Base. In November 1996, she was selected to serve as Chief of Logistics at Battlelab Integration Division at the Pentagon; in January 1999, she was selected to serve as the Senior Logistics Representative for the Quadrennial Defense Review at the Pentagon; in August 1999, she was assigned as the Deputy Director at the Logistics Information System Program Office at Maxwell Air Force Base, Alabama; in July 2000, she was assigned as the Commander of the 355th Logistics Group at Davis-Monthan Air Force Base, Arizona; and in August 2002, she was selected to serve as the Deputy Director of the Logistics Management Directorate at Warner Robins Air Logistics Center at Robins Air Force Base, Georgia. She was promoted to Colonel on March 1, 1999.

Spencer, Larry O.

BRIGADIER GENERAL—AIR FORCE

He was born in Washington, D.C. He received his Bachelor of Science degree in Industrial Engineering Technology from Southern Illinois University in Carbondale, Illinois, in 1979. He was accepted in the Officer Training School that same year. He graduated for Officer Training School in February 1980 as a distinguished graduate. He earned a Master of Science degree in Business Management from Webster College in St. Louis, Missouri. His military education includes completion of Squadron Officer School at Maxwell Air

Force Base in 1983; Marine Corps Command and Staff College at Quantico, Virginia, in 1990; and the National Defense University, Industrial College of the Armed Forces at Fort McNair in Washington, D.C., in 1994, as a distinguished graduate.

He was the first Comptroller Officer and most junior officer in the Air Force to Command a Support Group and Wing. He was also the first Air Force Officer to serve as Assistant Chief of Staff in the White House Military Office. In February 1980 he was assigned as Chief of the Cost Analysis Branch at the Headquarters of the Air Force Reserves at Robins Air Force Base, Georgia. From July 1982 to August 1986, he was assigned as a Cost/Budget Officer at the Headquarters of the United States Air Force at the Pentagon. In August 1986, he served as Budget Officer and Executive Officer at the Headquarters Military Airlift Command at Scott Air Force Base, Illinois.

In June 1990, he was assigned as Comptroller Squadron Commander of the 4th Wing at Seymour Johnson Air Force Base, North Carolina. From June 1994 to August 1996, he served as Assistant Chief of Staff at the White House Military Office in the White House, Washington, D.C. In August 1996, he was assigned as the Commander of the 72nd Support Group at Tinker Air Force Base, Oklahoma. He was promoted to Colonel on January 1, 1998.

From February 1998 to July 1999, he served as the Commander of the 75th Air Base Wing at Hill Air Force Base, Utah. In September 1999, he was selected to serve as the Command Comptroller at the Headquarters of Air Combat Command at Langley Air Force Base, Virginia.

His military awards and decorations include the Defense Superior Service Medal; the Legion of Merit; Meritorious Service Award (with four oak leaf clusters); the Air Force Commendation Medal; Air Force Achievement Medal; and Air Force Special Recognition Ribbon (with one oak leaf cluster).

Spencer, Tangela
MAJOR—AIR FORCE

She earned a Bachelor of Science degree in Business Administration from Grambling State University and was commissioned a Second Lieutenant through the Air Force Reserve Officer Training Corps program in 1987.

She entered active duty in October of 1988 and was stationed at Laughlin Air Force Base, Texas, as a Squadron Section Commander in the 47th Supply Squadron. In 1990, she was reassigned to Kunsan Air Base, South Korea, as a Squadron Section Commander in the 8th Security Police Squadron. Upon completion of her remote tour in 1991, she was assigned to Barksdale Air Force Base, Louisiana, as Executive Officer for the 2nd Consolidated Aircraft Maintenance Squadron. Upon the squadron's deactivation in 1992, she was reassigned as Squadron Section Commander for the 2nd Security Police Squadron at Barksdale.

In 1993, she was selected to be an Officer Training

School Instructor at Maxwell Air Force Base, Alabama. After training at Academic Instructor School, she held positions as Flight Training Officer and Flight Commander until her reassignment in May 1997. After completing training at the Defense Equal Opportunity Management Institute at Patrick Air Force Base, Florida, she assumed duties as the Chief of Social Actions at Keesler Air Force Base, Mississippi. She assumed an assignment as Military Personnel Flight Commander until March 2000, when she was reassigned to the Air Force Personnel Center at Randolph Air Force Base, Texas, where she was Chief of Personnel Officer Assignments and Chief of the United States Air Force Academy and Joint Professional Military Education Faculty Assignments. In November 2004, she was serving as the Commander of the Raleigh Military Entrance Processing Station.

Spivey, Willie G.
FIRST SERGEANT—ARMY

He is a native of Byromville, Georgia. He enlisted into the United States Army in June 1981, and completed Basic Combat Training at Fort Jackson, South Carolina. He attended Advanced Individual Training at Fort Benjamin Harrison, Indiana.

His military and civilian education include Primary Leader-

ship Course; Basic and Advanced Noncommissioned Officer Courses; Personnel and Logistic Courses; Battle Staff NCO Course; Master Fitness Trainer Course; and Jumpmaster Course. He holds a Bachelor of Science degree from Troy State University of Montgomery.

In January 2005, he was serving as the First Sergeant of United States Army NATO, SHAPE Headquarters Company.

Spooner, Richard E.
MAJOR GENERAL—AIR FORCE

General Spooner was born in Dayton, Ohio, and married the former Cora Marie Waugh of Denver, Colorado. He graduated from Germantown High School in May 1964. Having completed the United States Air Force Preparatory School in 1965, he graduated from the United States Air Force Academy at Colorado Springs, Colorado, in 1969 where he earned a Bachelor of Science degree in Engineering. He was commissioned a Second Lieutenant in June 1969. He received his navigator wings in May 1971 upon completion of undergraduate navigator training at Mather Air Force Base, California. He earned a Master of Science degree in human resource management from the University of Utah at Salt Lake City in 1977. His military schools include Squadron Officer's School (1976); Air Command and Staff College (1980); and National Security Management (1989). His next assignment was Barksdale Air Force Base, Louisiana, where he served as a Squadron Navigator flying KC-135s with the 71st Air Refueling Squadron, 2nd Bombardment Wing, at Strategic Air Command. During the two years he was assigned to the 71st and 913th Air Refueling squadrons,

Spooner deployed to Southeast Asia during the Vietnam conflict, where he flew on 41 combat missions in the tactical and strategic air effort. In 1973, the General was assigned to George Air Force Base, California, where he became qualified as a Weapon Systems Officer in the F-4D and was then assigned to the 435th Tactical Flying Squadron at Ubon Royal Thai Air Base, Thailand. Upon its closure, he went on to serve as Chief of Squadron Training with 13th Tactical Fighter Squadron, 432nd Tactical Fighter Wing, at Udorn Royal Thai Air Base. In March 1975, he was assigned to a consecutive tour at Royal Air Force, Lakenheath, United Kingdom, and joined the 48th Tactical Fighter Wing as an F-4D Weapons Systems Officer; he also served as Chief of Squadron Training for the 492nd Tactical Fighter Squadron and the Chief of Flying Training for the 48th TFW. General Spooner's next assignment was at Luke Air Force Base, Arizona, in June 1977 as an F-4D Instructor Weapon Systems Officer with the 311th Tactical Training Squadron, and Squadron Assistant Operations Officer with the 58th Tactical Training Squadron. In August 1979, General Spooner was released from active duty and joined the 121st Tactical Fighter Squadron, 113th Tactical Fighter Wing, District of Columbia Air National Guard, where he served as an Electronic Warfare Officer, Squadron and Instructor Weapons Systems Officer, Flight Commander and Assistant Operations Officer, until 1989. General Spooner then was appointed Deputy Commander for Support, 113th TFW, until January 1993, when he assumed his present position of Deputy Commanding General, Air, District of Columbia National Guard. He was promoted to Brigadier General and federally recognized on September 23, 1994. He was assigned as the Deputy Commanding General (Air) of the District of Columbia National Guard, responsible for command and control of two District of Columbia Air National Guard flying units, a combat communications squadron and a weather flight. He also supervised and coordinated the activities of the headquarters staff. In August 2000, he was selected to serve as Air National Guard Assistant to the Chief of the National Guard Bureau, for technology integration, intelligence oversight, and information operations, in Arlington, Virginia. He was promoted to Major General on August 15, 2000. In June 2003, he was selected to serve as Director of the Command, Control, Communications, and Computer Systems Division (J6) in National Guard Bureau at Arlington. General Spooner is a master navigator. His awards and decorations include the Meritorious Service Medal (with two oak leaf clusters), the Air Medal, Air Force Commendation Medal (with oak leaf cluster), the Combat Readiness Medal (with silver oak leaf cluster), Air Force Good Conduct Medal, National Defense Service Medal (with one bronze star), Vietnam Service Medal, Air Force Overseas Short and Long Tour Ribbons, Air Force Longevity Service Award Ribbon (with one silver and one bronze oak leaf cluster), Armed Forces Reserve Medal, Small Arms Expert Marksmanship Ribbon, Air Force Training Ribbon,

Republic of Vietnam Gallantry Cross with Palm, the Republic of Vietnam Campaign Medal and the District of Columbia Meritorious Service Medal. The general is a full-time program director for Martin Marietta Corporation in Springfield, Virginia. His civic affiliations include the National Guard Associations of the United States and District of Columbia; the Air Force Association; the Association of Graduates of the United States Air Force Academy and the East Coast Chapter of the Tuskegee Airmen, Inc.

Stanford, John Henry
MAJOR GENERAL—ARMY

He was born in Darby, Pennsylvania. He is married to the former Patricia Corley. They have two sons, Steven and Scott. He received a Bachelor of Arts in Political Science from Pennsylvania State University and a master's in Personnel Management/Administration from Central Michigan University. He received an ROTC commission to Second Lieutenant on June 10, 1961. His military education includes the Infantry School Basic Course; the Transportation School Advanced Course; the United States Army Command and General Staff College; and the Industrial College of the Armed Forces. He was promoted to First Lieutenant on December 10, 1962. From January 1962 to June 1964, he was first assigned as a Platoon Leader with Company D, next as S-3 Operation officer (Air), later Liaison Officer at Headquarters, 2nd Air Reconnaissance Battalion, 36th Infantry, 3rd Armored Division; then as Commander of the 40th Transportation Company, 15th Quartermaster Battalion, 6th Quartermaster Group, United States Army, Europe. From November 1964 to August 1965, he was a student in the Officer

Fixed Wing Aviator Course, at the United States Army Aviator School in Fort Rucker, Alabama. He was promoted to Captain on January 6, 1965. From August 1965 to October 1965, he served as the Assistant S-1 (Personnel), at the Headquarters of the Troop Brigade at Fort Rucker. From January 1966 to April 1966, he served as a Fixed Wing Army Aviator with the 55th Aviation Company, Eighth United States Army, in South Korea. From August 1966 to July 1967, he was assigned as a Fixed Wing Aviator with the 73rd Aviation Company (Aerial Surveillance), 222nd Aviation Battalion, United Army in Vietnam. From July 1967 to February 1968, he was a student in the Aircraft Maintenance Officer Course of the United States Army Transportation School at Fort Eustis, Virginia. From February 1968 to June 1968, he was assigned as Chief of the Electrical Section at the United States Army Transpiration School at Fort Eustis, Virginia. He was promoted to Major on June 20, 1968. From June 1968 to February 1969, he was a student in the Transportation Officer Advanced Course, United States Army Transportation School, Fort Eustis. From February 1969 to September 1969, he was a Platoon Commander with the 73rd Aviation Company, 210th Aviation Battalion (Combat), United States Army, in Vietnam. From September 1969 to May 1970, he was Commander of the 56th Transportation Company, 765th Transportation Battalion, 34th General Support Group, United States Army, in Vietnam. From May 1970 to July 1971, he served as Personnel Staff Officer in the Directorate of Personnel and Community Activities of the United States Army Transportation Center at Fort Eustis. From July 1971 to June 1972, he was a student in the United States Army Command and General Staff College at Fort Leavenworth, Kansas. From June 1972 to November 1972, he was a Personnel Management Officer in the Office of Personnel Operations in Washington, D.C. From November 1972 to September 1975, he served as Aviation Assignments Officer, later Personnel Management Officer, in the Transportation Branch Office of the Personnel Directorate at the United States Army Military Personnel Center in Alexandria, Virginia. He was promoted to Lieutenant Colonel on June 1, 1975. From June 1975 to May 1977, he was the Commander of the 34th Support Battalion, 6th Cavalry Bridge (Air Combat), III Corps at Fort Hood, Texas. From June 1977 to May 1979, he served as a Military Assistant to the Under Secretary of the Army in the Office of the Secretary of the Army in Washington, D.C. From June 1979 to June 1980, he was a student at the Industrial College of Armed Forces at Fort Lesley J. McNair in Washington, D.C. He was promoted to Colonel on August 1, 1980. From July 1980 to June 1981, he was Commander of Division Support Command, 2nd Infantry Division, United States Army, in Korea. From June 1981 to June 1984, he was First Executive Assistant to the Special Assistant to the Secretary of Defense, later serving as Executive Secretary for the Department of Defense in Washington, D.C. From June 1984 to September 1986, he was Commander of Military Traffic Management Command, Western Area, at Oakland Army Base in Oakland, California. He was promoted to Brigadier General on September 1, 1984. From September 1986 to June 1987, he was the Deputy Commander for Research and Development at the United States Army Aviation Systems Command in St. Louis, Missouri. From June 1987 to August 1989, he was Commanding General of the Military Traffic Management Command in Washington, D.C. He was promoted to Major General on May 1, 1988. In September 1989, he was appointed Director of Plans, J-5, United States Transportation Command at Scott Air Force Base, Illinois. His military awards and decorations include the Distinguished Service Medal, Defense Distinguished Service Medal, Defense Superior Service Medal, Legion of Merit (with oak leaf cluster), Distinguished Flying Cross, the Bronze Star with "V" Device (with four oak leaf clusters), the Meritorious Service Medal (with oak leaf cluster), the Air Medal, Army Commendation Medal (with three oak leaf clusters), the Expert Infantryman Badge, the Parachutist Badge, Master Army Aviator Badge, and Ranger Tab. He retired from the Army on August 1, 1991, to accept the job of Fulton County Manger in Atlanta, Georgia. As the Fulton County Manager, he managed an employee force of more than 4,800 and oversaw a budget of approximately a half-billion dollars. He was the first black in history to serve as Manager Fulton County, which includes most of the city of Atlanta. In 1995, he was selected Superintendent of Schools of the Seattle, Washington, School District, which served more than 47,000 students. His philosophy is "to love them and lead them." General Stanford died on November 28, 1998.

Stanley, Clifford L.
MAJOR GENERAL—MARINES

General Stanley is married to the former Rosalyn Hill of Charleston, South Carolina. They reside in Alexandria, Virginia and have a daughter, Angela. He was commissioned in October 1969 after graduating from South Carolina State University. He received his Master of Science from Johns Hopkins University in 1977. His formal military education includes Amphibious Warfare School (1978); the Naval War College (1983); United States Marine Corps Command and Staff College (1984); and National War College (1988). After completing the Basic School at Quantico, Virginia, Stanley served as a Supply and Fiscal Officer both in overseas and continental United States commands. Upon being redesignated an infantry officer, he completed tours of duty as a Platoon Commander and later Commanding Officer of Company M, 3rd Battalion, 8th Marines; Commanding Officer, Headquarters Company, 4th Marines; Executive Officer of the 1st Battalion, 6th Marines; and Commanding Officer of the 1st Marine Regiment. General Stanley maintains the secondary military occupational specialty of parachutist, and his assignments outside of the Fleet Marine Forces include Psychology and Leadership Instructor

at the United States Naval Academy; Executive Officer at the Marine Corps Institute; Parade Commander at Marine Barracks, Washington, D.C.; Special Assistant and Marine Corps Aide for the Assistant Secretary of the Navy; and Desk Officer in Officer of the Assistant Secretary Of Defense, East Asia and Pacific Region, the Pentagon. Other assignments include Depot Inspector and Commander of the First Recruit Training Battalion at Parris Island in July 1986, and the White House Fellowship Program in June 1988, where he served as Special Assistant to the Director of the FBI. General Stanley previously served as the Fleet Marine Officer, 2nd Fleet, USS *Mt. Whitney*, LCC-20, in Norfolk, Virginia. He was assigned on July 15, 1994, as the Assistant Deputy Chief of Staff for Manpower and Reserve Affairs (Manpower Plans and Policy) at the Headquarters of the Marine Corps in Washington, D.C. He was promoted to Brigadier General on August 1, 1994. He was assigned as Director of Public Affairs at the Headquarters of the Marine Corps in Washington, D.C. On June 10, 1998, he was selected as Commanding General of the Marine Corps Air Ground Combat Center at Twenty Nine Palms, California, and later as Commanding General of the Marine Corps Base in Quantico, Virginia. He was selected for promotion to Major General on December 22, 1998, and was then selected to serve as Deputy Commanding General of Marine Corps Combat Development Command. His military awards and decorations include the Legion of Merit; Defense Meritorious Service Medal; Meritorious Service Medal with Gold Star; Navy Commendation Medal; and Navy Achievement Medal.

Starghill, Renee
COMMAND CHIEF MASTER SERGEANT—AIR FORCE

She was born in Detroit, Michigan, and entered the United States Air Force in October 1983. She attended Basic Military Training at Lackland Air Force Base, Texas, and Advanced Individual Training (Basic Personnel Course) at Keesler Air Force Base, Mississippi.

Her military and civilian education includes all the Noncommissioned Officer Education System Courses; Noncommissioned Officer Academy at Royal Air Force Upwood, England; and the Senior Noncommissioned Officer Academy at Gunter Air Force Base, Alabama. She earned an associate's degree in Human Resource Management and Personnel Administration from Community College Air Force; a Bachelor of Science in Business Administration and Management from the University of Maryland; and a Master of Business Administration degree from Webster University.

Her key military assignments include serving as Noncommissioned Officer in Charge of the Personnel Orderly Room at Galena Airport, Alaska; from May 1990 to May 1992 as Noncommissioned Officer in Charge of Classification and Training at Rhein-Main Air Base, Germany; from May 1992 to May 1994 as Noncommissioned Officer in Charge of Logistics Officer Assignments at the Headquarters of United States Air Force Europe at Ramstein Air Base; from 1994 to June 1995 as Noncommissioned Officer in Charge of Evaluations and Career Enhancements at Osan Air Base, South Korea; from July 1995 to March 1997 as Superintendent, Military Personnel Flight at Bolling Air Force Base in Washington, D.C.; from March 1997 to May 2000 as Air Force Enlisted Aide Manager and Superintendent for the Air Force Gen-

eral Officer Matters Office at the Headquarters of the United States Air Force in Washington, D.C.; from June 2000 to November 2001 as Superintendent of the Secretary of the Air Force Military Personnel Division at the Headquarters United States Air Force in Washington, D.C.; from November 2001 to July 2003 as Executive Assistant to the Vice Chief of Staff at the Headquarters United States Air Force in Washington, D.C.; and from August 2003 to January 2004 as Superintendent of the 86th Contingency Response Group at Ramstein Air Base.

In October 2004, she was serving as the Command Chief Master Sergeant of the 86th Airlift Wing at Ramstein Air Base.

Starling, Bridgette Y.
COMMAND SERGEANT MAJOR—ARMY

She is a native of Warren, Arkansas. She entered the United States Army in November 1984 and attended Basic Combat Training at Fort Dix, New Jersey. Upon graduation, she attended the Chaplain Assistant Advanced Individual Training Course at Fort Monmouth, New Jersey.

Her education includes: all the Noncommissioned Officer Education System Courses; Fund Clerk Course; Fund Manager Course; Training Manager Course; Instructor Training Course; Drill Sergeant Course; Airborne Training Course; First Sergeant Course; and the United States Army Sergeants Major Academy. She holds an Associates Degree in General Studies; a Bachelor of Science in Human Resource Management with Troy State University. She is currently pursuing a Masters Degree from Touro University International.

Her assignments include: serving as serving as Senior Drill Sergeant, Headquarters Company, USA Chaplain Center and School, at Fort Jackson, South Carolina;

Non-Commissioned Officer in Charge, 26th Area Support Group, Heidelberg, Germany; Non-Commissioned Officer in Charge, Installation Chaplain Office, at Fort Benning, Georgia; Non-Commissioned Officer in Charge, Military District of Washington, Fort Leslie McNair, Washington, D.C.; 3rd United States Army, Coalition Forces Land Component Command (CFLCC) Chaplain Sergeant Major, Fort McPherson, Georgia and Camp Arfijan, Kuwait; Command Sergeant Major, United States Army Chaplain Center and School, at Fort Jackson, in South Carolina.

Steele, Toreaser A.

BRIGADIER GENERAL—AIR FORCE

She received a Bachelor of Science degree in Home Economics Education from Tennessee State University in Nashville, Tennessee. She earned a Master of Science degree in Guidance and Counseling from Central Michigan University at Mount Pleasant. Her military education includes Squadron Officer School at Maxwell Air Force Base, Alabama; Air Command and Staff College; Armed Forces Staff College; the Industrial College of the Armed Forces at Fort Lesley J. McNair; and the Senior Executive Program at Columbia University in New York.

She was commissioned through the Air Force ROTC program at Tennessee State University and began her career as a Personnel Officer. She has served at the major Command and Air Force Headquarters levels. She has commanded at the squadron group and wing levels. In January 1986, she was assigned as Squadron Commander, Division Chief and Group Commander at United States Air Force Academy in Colorado Springs, Colorado. From June 1990 to June 1992, she was assigned as Command Division Chief and Special Assistant to the Commander in Chief of Strategic Air Command at

Offutt Air Force Base, Nebraska. From June 1993 to January 1995, she was assigned as the Assistant Director for Officer Plans and Programs in the Office of the Secretary of Defense in Washington, D.C. She was promoted to Colonel on January 1, 1995.

In January 1995, she was selected to serve as the Military Assistant to the Principal Deputy Assistant Secretary of Defense for Force Management Policy in the Office of the Secretary of Defense in Washington, D.C. From July 1996 to September 1998, she was assigned as Commander of the 737th Training Group at Lackland Air Force Base, Texas. From September 1998 to August 2000, she served as the Commander of the 17th Training Wing at Goodfellow Air Force Base, Texas. From August 2000 to July 2002, she served as the Director of Personnel Resources and Director of the Air Force Personnel Operations Agency in the Office of the Deputy Chief of Staff for Personnel at the Headquarters of the United States Air Force in Washington, D.C. She was promoted to Brigadier General on April 1, 2001.

In July 2002, she was selected to serve as the Vice Commander of the Army and Air Force Exchange Service in Dallas, Texas. AAFES is a $7.5 billion retail, food and services business that operates nearly 10,000 facilities in 29 countries and 50 states. AAFES employs more than 52,000 associates, many of them military family members. In July 2002, she was selected to serve as Vice Commander of the Army and Air Force Exchange Service in Dallas, Texas.

Her military awards and decorations include the Defense Superior Service Medal; the Legion of Merit (with oak leaf cluster); Meritorious Service Medal (with four oak leaf clusters); Air Force Commendation Medal; Air Force Outstanding Unit Award (with two oak leaf clusters); National Defense Service Medal (with service star); and Air Force Overseas Ribbon-Long.

Stephens, Robert L., Jr.

BRIGADIER GENERAL—ARMY

Born in Welch, West Virginia, he married the former Delores O. Bennett of Bishop, Virginia and they have a son and two daughters. He received a Bachelor of Science degree in Education from West Virginia State College and a Master of Science degree in Vocational Education Guidance from Alfred University in New York. His military schools attended include the Infantry School, Basic and Advanced Courses; United States Army Command and General Staff College; and the National War College. He received an ROTC commission and entered the Army as a Second Lieutenant on August 10, 1962. From November 1962 to April 1964, he served as a Platoon Leader for Company C, later S-4 (Logistics), 1st Airborne Battle Group, 327th Infantry, 101st Airborne Division at Fort Campbell, Kentucky. From June 1964 to December 1964, he was a student at the Defense Language Institute at the Presidio of Monterey, California. From January 1965 to April 1965, he was a student in the Special Forces Officer Course of the United States Army Special Warfare School at Fort Bragg, North Carolina. From April 1965 to June 1967,

he served as Executive Officer, later Commander, of Company B, 8th Special Forces Group (Airborne), 1st Special Forces at Fort Gulick, Panama. He was promoted to Captain on April 11, 1966. From June 1967 to July 1968, he was Assistant G-5 (Civil Affairs, Civic Action), later Commander of Company B, 1st Battalion, 7th Cavalry, and was later Commander of Headquarters Company, 3rd Brigade, 1st Cavalry Division (Airmobile), United States Army, Vietnam. From July 1968 to July 1969, he served as Senior Platoon Advisor. Later he was a student in the Infantry Officer Advanced Course of the United States Army Infantry School at Fort Benning, Georgia. On June 27, 1969, he was promoted to Major. From July 1969 to May 1971, he served as Assistant Professor of Military Science at Alfred University. From August 1971 to June 1972, he was a student at the United States Army Command and Staff College at Fort Leavenworth, Kansas. From June 1972 to March 1973, he was assigned as the S-3 (Operations) Adviser for Delta Region Assistance Command, United States Military Assistance Command, in Vietnam. From March 1973 to June 1976, he served as Division Race Relations Officer, later Headquarters Commandant, later Executive Officer, of the 3rd Battalion, 187th Infantry, later Adjutant of the 3rd Brigade, and then as Assistant G-1 (Personnel) of the 101st Airborne Division (Airmobile) at Fort Campbell, Kentucky. From June 1976 to April 1978, he served as Personnel Staff Officer on the Alcohol and Drug Policy Branch of the Leadership Division of the Office of Deputy Chief of Staff for Personnel in Washington, D.C. From April 1978 to April 1979, he served as Military Secretary, J-3 (Operations), Organization of the Joint Chiefs of Staff, in Washington, D.C. He was promoted to Lieutenant Colonel on September 12, 1978. From May 1979 to June 1981, he was Commander of the 2nd Battal-

ion, 39th Infantry, 9th Infantry Division, at Fort Lewis, Washington. From June 1981 to June 1982, he served as Personnel Staff Officer in the Leadership Division of the Office of the Deputy Chief for Personnel in Washington, D.C. From June 1982 to June 1983, he was a student at the National War College at Fort McNair in Washington, D.C. From June 1983 to April 1985, he was assigned as Inspector General of the Military District of Washington at Fort McNair. He was promoted to Colonel on October 1, 1983. From April 1985 to June 1987, he was Commander of Task Force Bayonet (later designated 193rd Infantry Brigade), United States Army South, Panama. From June 1987 to September 1988, he was assigned as Deputy Director for Readiness, Mobilization, and Exercises in the Office of the Deputy Chief of Staff for Operations and Plans in Washington, D.C. From September 1988 to February 1990, he was Assigned as assistant Division Commander of the 9th Infantry Division (Motorized) at Fort Lewis. He was promoted to Brigadier General on July 1, 1989. In February 1990 he was appointed Chief of Joint United States Military Assistance Group, Thailand. He retired from the military on May 31, 1993. He has received numerous awards and decorations, including the Legion of Merit, Bronze Star (with "V" device and two oak leaf clusters), Purple Heart, Meritorious Service Medal (with five oak leaf clusters), Air Medal (with "V" device and three oak leaf clusters), Joint Service Commendation Medal (with oak leaf cluster), Combat Infantryman Badge, Air Assault Badge, Master Parachutist Badge, Joint Chiefs of Staff Identification Badge and the Army General Staff Identification Badge.

Stevens, William E.

BRIGADIER GENERAL—AIR FORCE

He was born in Wilson, North Carolina. He and his wife Carolyn, have four children, William III, Saundrell, Kayle and Camille. He received a Bachelor of Science degree in Business Administration from North Carolina Agricultural and Technical State University in Greensboro, N.C., and a Master of Arts degree in National Security Affairs and Africa Studies from Naval Postgraduate School in Monterey, California. Other schools attended include Squadron Officer School at Maxwell Air Force Base, Alabama; the Armed Forces Staff College at Norfolk, Virginia; Department of State Senior Seminar in Washington, D.C.; and the Massachusetts Institute of Technology's Seminar XXI program. He was commissioned a Second Lieutenant on May 21, 1970. The general entered the Air Force in 1970 as a distinguished graduate of North Carolina A&T State University's Reserve Officer Training Corps program. From June 1970 to June 1971, he was a student in under-graduate pilot training at Laughlin Air Force Base, Texas. He was promoted to First Lieutenant on December 27, 1971. From July 1971 to July 1975, he was assigned as a C-130E Aircraft Commander and a T-37th and T-38 Test Pilot with the 83rd Flying Training Squadron at Webb Air Force Base, Texas. He was promoted to Captain on December 27, 1973. From

June 1977 to December 1978, he was a graduate student at the Naval Postgraduate School and Defense Language Institute in Monterey, California. From January 1979 to June 1979, he was Attaché to Liberia, Sierra Leone, Ghana, Niger, Upper Volta and Ivory Coast. From August 1981 to January 1985, he was assigned as an Action Officer Middle East, Africa and South Asia Plans, Executive Officer to the Deputy Director of Plans at the Headquarters of the United States Air Force in Washington, D.C. He was promoted to Major on June 1, 1982. From January 1985 to July 1985, he was a student at the Armed Forces Staff College in Norfolk, Virginia. From August 1985 to November 1985, he was assigned to C-130E Qualification Training at Little Rock Air Force Base, Arkansas. From December 1985 to December 1989, he was a C-130E Instructor Pilot; Assistant Operations Officer, Chief Pilot; Operations Officer; and Commander of the 37th Tactical Airlift Squadron, 435th Tactical Airlift Wing at Rhein-Main Air Base, West Germany. He was promoted to Lieutenant Colonel on March 1, 1986. From January 1990 to July 1991, he served as a Division Chief for Middle East, Africa and South Asia Plans in the Directorate of Plans under the Deputy Chief of Staff for Plans and Operations at the Headquarters of the United States Air Force. From August 1991 to July 1992, he was a student at the Department of State Senior Seminar in Washington, D.C. He was promoted to Colonel on November 1, 1991. From August 1992 to August 1993, General Stevens served as the Commander of the 89th Air Wing at Andrews Air Base, Maryland; and Commander of the 1610th Airlift Support Group at Cairo West Air Base, Egypt. In September 1993, he was selected as Assistant to the Under Secretary and Principal Deputy Under Secretary of Defense for Policy at

the Pentagon. From June 1995 to May 1996, he served as Commander of 86th Airlift Wing and the Kaiserslautern Military Community at Ramstein Air Base, Germany. He was promoted to Brigadier General on April 1, 1996. In June 1996, he was selected to serve as the Assistant Deputy Under Secretary of the Air Force for International Affairs at the Headquarters of the United States Air Force. He retired from the military on September 1, 1998. He died January 6, 2003. His military awards and decorations include the Defense Superior Service Medal; the Legion of Merit; the Defense Meritorious Service Medal; the Meritorious Service Medal (with two bronze oak leaf clusters); the Air Medal; Air Force Commendation Medal; Presidential Unit Citation (with bronze oak leaf cluster); Air Force Outstanding Unit Award (with four bronze oak leaf clusters); the Combat Readiness Medal (with bronze oak leaf cluster); the National Defense Service Medal (with bronze service star); the Vietnam Service Medal; the Republic of Vietnam Gallantry Cross (with Palm); and the Republic of Vietnam Campaign Medal.

Stinson, Lonnie T.
COMMAND SERGEANT MAJOR—ARMY

He entered the Army in April 1975. His civilian and military education includes a bachelor's degree in Business Administration; all the Noncommissioned Officer Education System Courses; the Master Fitness Trainers Course; the First Sergeants Course; and the United States Army Sergeants Major Academy.

His key military leadership assignments include serving as Noncommissioned Officer in Charge of the Strength Management Branch at the Headquarters of the United States Army Recruiting Command at Fort Sheridan, Illinois; Noncommissioned Officer in Charge of the Accession Management Branch at the Headquar-

ters of the Department of the Army where he served as the key manager of the Recruit Quota System; First Sergeant of the 258th Personnel Services Company in Wurzburg, Germany; Battalion Sergeant Major for the 38th Personnel Services Battalion in Giebelstadt, Germany; Command Sergeant Major of the United States Military Entrance Processing Command at Great Lakes, Illinois; Command Sergeant Major for Allied Forces North, United States Army, NATO, Brunssum, Netherlands; Command Sergeant Major of Joint Task Force North during Operation Iraqi Freedom; and Command Sergeant Major of the United States Army Garrison at Fort Myer, Virginia.

Stove, Charles E.

FIRST SERGEANT—MARINES

He enlisted into the United States Marine Corps in January 1985, and completed Basic Combat Training at the Marine Corps Recruit Depot at San Diego, California.

After a four-year tour in Okinawa, Japan, Staff Sergeant Stove received orders to Navy Air Station Pensacola for Instructor duty at NATTC in July 1997. Training over 800 military students while serving his tour of 4 years at Pensacola, he received orders to return to Okinawa with MALS-36 for a 1-year tour in July 2001. In July 2002, he was ordered to North Carolina at MALS-26, MCAS New River. In January 2003, he took over duties as First Sergeant of Headquarters Squadron 26, Marine Aircraft Group 26, Second Marine Aircraft Wing.

Strand, Eloise A. Brown

COLONEL—ARMY

She was born in Stamford, Connecticut, and received her primary and secondary education in Bedford, Vir-

ginia, and Philadelphia. She enrolled in Virginia State College in 1946 and graduated with a Bachelor of Science degree in home economics in 1950. After college she taught in the Bedford public school system from 1950 to 1955. In 1955, she began postgraduate training at the University of Pennsylvania, receiving a certificate in occupational therapy in 1956. In 1956, she was commissioned in the United States Army. For the next six years, she was a student and staff therapist at Valley Forge and Walter Reed Army Hospitals. In 1963, she became the supervisor of a general clinic, and the following year she began working as the occupational therapy clinical affiliation coordinator at Letterman General Hospital in San Francisco. She enrolled in New York University in 1965, and after receiving a Master of Arts degree in Occupational Therapy in 1966 served as educational coordinator for the occupational therapy section and occupational therapy clinical affiliation coordinator at Walter Reed Army Medical Center until 1969. In 1969, she became chief of the occupational therapy section at the 97th General Hospital in Frankfurt, Germany, moving later to the same position at Letterman Army Medical Center. In 1972, she began working toward her second master's degree at the United States Army Academy of Health and Baylor University. She received a master's degree in health care administration in 1973. After serving as a health care administrative resident from 1973 to 1974, Strand became Chief of the Occupational Therapy Section at Walter Reed Army Medical Center and served in this capacity until 1978, meanwhile becoming Chief of the Occupational Therapy Section in the Office of the Surgeon General (1976 to 1982). In 1978, Strand was made chief of the Army Medical Specialist Corps; she was the first black to hold such a position. A full Colonel, Strand held the second highest rank of all women in the Army Medical Corps. In 1982, she became special assistant to the United States Surgeon General. In the same year she became recruitment coordinator for the occupational therapy department of Howard University's College of Allied Health Sciences. After her retirement she served as the international liaison of the national office of the American Occupational Therapy Association. Her military awards and decorations include the "A" Professional Designator; the Surgeon General's Award for Professional Excellence; the Legion of Merit; the Army Meritorious Service Medal; the Army Commendation Medal (with oak leaf cluster); and the United States Army Service Army.

Strayhorn, Earl E.
LIEUTENANT COLONEL—ARMY

Born in Columbus, Mississippi, he married Lyndia E. Jackson and the couple has two children, Donald and Earlene. He graduated from Edmund Burke high school in Chicago, Illinois. He received a Bachelor of Arts degree from the University of Illinois at Urbana in 1941 and earned a Doctor of Jurisprudence degree from DePaul University College of Law in 1948. He enlisted in the United States Army as a Private on October 15, 1941, and was sent to Fort Custer, Michigan, for basic training. In November 1941, he was assigned to Tuskegee Air Force Base where he assisted in the establishment of the Military Police Section as sergeant-in-charge. He was admitted to the Artillery School Officer Candidate School in April 1942, and was awarded a commission as a Second Lieutenant of artillery in June 1942. He was assigned to 184th Field Artillery Regiment at Fort Custer and saw Foreign Service with the 600th Field Artillery Battalion of the 92nd Division Artillery in Italy where he served as executive officer of a 155mm-howitzer battery. He separated from service as a First Lieutenant and served as a member of the 184th Field Artillery Battalion of the Illinois Army National Guard in 1948. He was assigned successively as Commander of B Battery, Battalion Intelligence Officer as a Captain, and then in the rank of Lieutenant Colonel as Commander of the 2nd Battalion, 178th Infantry, Illinois National Guard. He is currently sitting on the Criminal Court of Cook County.

Stuart, Deborah S.
LIEUTENANT COLONEL—ARMY

She received a ROTC (DMG) commission from the University of Texas at El Paso in 1986, after serving three and a half years of enlisted service as an Intelligence Analyst.

Her military education includes the Adjutant General Basic and Advanced Courses; Systems Automation Course; and Command and General Staff College.

Her military assignments include serving as Chief Personnel Actions and Executive Officer of the 400th Personnel Service Company in Ansbach, West Germany (1986 to 1990); Chief of Resource Management and Force Development Officer for United States Army

Personnel Command in Alexandria, Virginia (1990 to 1993); Company Commander, Executive Officer and Battalion Operations Officer of the 120th Adjutant General Reception Battalion at Fort Jackson, South Carolina; Systems Engineer Project Manager and Chief Operation Officer of the 1st Signal Brigade in Seoul, South Korea (1997 to 1998); Chief of the Policy and Programs Division in Seoul (1998 to 1999); Executive Officer of the 1/61st Infantry Battalion at Fort Jackson (1999 to 2000); and Military Secretary at the Directorate for Force Structure Resource Assessment at the Pentagon (2001 to 2004). In October 2004, she was serving as the Commander of Regional South Allied Forces Southern Europe at NATO in Naples, Italy.

Stubbs, Laura
CAPTAIN—NAVY

She is a native of Philadelphia, Pennsylvania. She began her naval career in July 1980, when she was commissioned a Lieutenant. Her first assignment was as a Naval Nuclear Power School Instructor. She was the First African American to become a Nuclear Power School Instructor, at the United States Naval Academy.

Her education includes a Bachelor of Science degree in Engineering from the University of Pennsylvania in 1979 and a master's degree in Mechanical Engineering and Applied Mechanics from the University of Pennsylvania in 1980. She has also earned a Ph.D. in Mechanical Engineering from the University of Maryland at College Park, Maryland.

In 1983, she was assigned to the United States Naval Academy as an Assistant Professor in the Mechanical and Naval Systems Engineering Departments. She left active duty in 1986 and joined the Naval Reserve as a Line Officer. She served in a numerous leadership assignments to include, serving as Chief Learning Officer

for the Naval Surface Warfare Center, and as a qualified Engineering Duty Officer in the Naval Reserves.

Stuppard, Charles L.

COMMANDER—NAVY

He graduated from Cornell University in 1982 with a degree in Mechanical and Aerospace Engineering. He worked for three years as a Design and Test Engineer for Fairchild Republic Corporation in the A-10a, T-46 and SF-340 Aircraft programs. He subsequently joined the Navy in 1985 as an Aviation Officer Candidate.

After commissioning and flight training he switched to Surface Warfare. He reported to USS *Biddle* (CG 34) in Norfolk where he served as Boiler Officer and Advanced Combat Direction System/Computer Officer (September 1987 to July 1990). After NTU School, he reported to USS *Reeves* (CG 24) in Pearl Harbor serving as Electronics Readiness Officer, then as Fleeted-up Combat System Officer (November 1990 to May 1992).

After Department Head School, he assumed duties as Commissioning Combat Systems Officer of USS *Gonzalez* (DDG 66) until September 1997. From September 1997 to November 1998, he attended the Naval War College in Newport and earned a master's in National Security and Strategic Studies, followed by PXO and Leadership School. He then obtained his Joint Professional Military Education Phase II at the Armed Forces Staff College. He served as Executive Officer of USS *Nicholas* (FFG 47) stationed in Norfolk, Virginia, from June 1999 to September 2000.

He reported to the Pentagon in September 2000. He served on The Joint Staff Directorate of Strategic Plans and Policy, J-5, as an Action Officer for the Western European and NATO Policy. From February 2002 to July 2003, he served as the Executive Assistant to the Deputy Director for Politico-Military Affairs Europe, J-5. He assumed Command of the USS *Arleigh Burke* (DDG 51) on March 5, 2004.

Sturdivant, Lash L.

COMMAND SERGEANT MAJOR—ARMY

He entered the United States Army in 1972 from Memphis, Tennessee. His assignments include serving with the 1st Battalion, 75th Field Artillery in Bamberg,

West Germany. In 1974 was assigned to Alpha Battery, 4th/4th Field Artillery at Fort Sill, Oklahoma; in 1977, he was assigned to Bravo Company, 2nd/33rd Field Artillery in New-Ulm, West Germany; in 1980, he was assigned Fort Sill, Drill Sergeant; in 1982, he was Chief of Firing Battery and First Sergeant of Charlie/2nd/41st Field Artillery in Bad Kissingen, West Germany; in 1984, he returned to the United States and was assigned as a First Sergeant, Bravo 1st/21stArtillery, 1st Cavalry Division at Fort Hood, Texas; and in 1986, he was First Sergeant to B/1st/7th Field Artillery, 10th Mountain Division at Fort Drum. He then served in the 75th Field Artillery Brigade at Fort Sill during Desert Shield/Desert Storm; 6/29th, 2/29th, 1st Armor Division in Germany; 1/37th Field Artillery at Fort Lewis; and 1/8th Field Artillery, 25th Infantry Division. He is now Command Sergeant Major of the 3rd Armored Corps.

Sullivan, Lynell
COMMAND SERGEANT MAJOR—ARMY

Command Sergeant Major Lynell Sullivan made United States Army history when she assumed her duties as the First Female Command Sergeant Major selected to serve a Major General. She was selected to serve as Major General James Monroe's enlisted advisor and Command Sergeant Major of the Industrial Operations Command at Rock Island, Illinois.

Sumlin, CSM
COMMAND SERGEANT MAJOR—ARMY

He is a native of Rocky Mount, North Carolina. He enlisted in the United States Army in September 1976.

He attended Basic Combat Training at Fort Knox, Kentucky, and Advanced Individual Training at Fort Benjamin Harrison, Indiana.

He has held numerous leadership positions throughout his career, including serving as 73rd Ordnance Battalion Command Sergeant Major and Corps Ammunition Management Office Noncommissioned Officer in Charge, 4th CMMC at Fort Hood, Texas; First Sergeant of the 608th Ordnance Company at Fort Benning, Georgia; First Sergeant of the 65th Ordnance Company at Camp Page, South Korea; Training Developer/Functional Analyst SAAS-MOD, CASCOM at Fort Lee, Virginia; NCOIC/Senior Instructor, Stock Control and Accounting Division, OMMCS at Redstone Arsenal, Alabama; Platoon Sergeant of the 70th Ordnance Company at Cakmakli, Turkey; Single Manager for Conventional Ammunition at Rock Island Arsenal, Illinois; Basic Load/GMLR Section Chief, 800th CMMC at Nellingen Barracks, Germany; Ammunition Operations Sergeant and Platoon Sergeant of the 501st Ordnance Company at Crailsheim, Germany; PAC Supervisor, STB 2nd SUPCOM at Nelligen Barracks, Germany; and PSNCO, 7th S&T Battalion at Fort Ord, California. In October 2004, he was serving as the Command Sergeant Major for the 83rd Ordnance Battalion at Kure, Japan.

Summerville, Lewis L.
SERGEANT MAJOR—MARINES

He entered the United States Marine Corps in June 1974, and attended Recruit Training at Parris Island, South Carolina. His military education includes the Drill Instructor School; Senior Noncommissioned Officer Enhancement Course; and Staff Noncommissioned Officer Academy. He has held numerous key positions to include serving as Drill Instructor; Motor Transport Detachment Platoon Sergeant; Senior Drill

First Sergeant; Brigade S-3 Sergeant Major; Sergeants Major Academy Non-Resident Course Facilitator; and Battalion Command Sergeant Major of the 1st Space Battalion, Air Defense Artillery Regiment, at Fort Bliss, Texas. In October 2004, he was serving as Command Sergeant Major for the 1st Space Brigade, Space and Ballistic Missile Defense Forces.

Swinnie, Kenneth B.

COMMAND SERGEANT MAJOR—ARMY

Born in Pinehurst, North Carolina, he entered the United States Army in September 1982 and completed his Basic Combat Training and Advanced Individual Training (AIT) at Fort Sill, Oklahoma.

Instructor; Assistant Marine Officer Instructor (AMOI) at Virginia Tech; First Sergeant of the Truck Company at Camp Hansen; and Inspector-Instructor of Delta Company, 8th Tank Battalion, in Columbia, South Carolina. As Squadron Sergeant Major for HMM 166 at Marine Corps Station El Toro, California, he participated in numerous unit deployments with the Squadron, including WestPac 2000 as the Air Combat Element Sergeant Major. In November 2001, he was transferred to Marine Corps Air Station New River in Jacksonville, North Carolina, for duty as the Headquarters and Headquarters Squadron Sergeant Major.

Sumpter, Daryall

COMMAND SERGEANT MAJOR—ARMY

He enlisted in the United States Army in August 1976. He attended Basic Combat Training at Fort Bliss, Texas. His military education includes all the Noncommissioned Officers Education System Courses; Chaparral Crewman/Redeye-Stinger Gunner Course; Patriot Transition Course; Instructor Training Course; Drill Sergeant School; Defense Equal Opportunity Management Institution; First Sergeants Course; and the United States Army Sergeants Major Academy (class 50). He holds an Associate of Arts degree from El Paso Community College and a Bachelor of Science degree from Regents University.

He has served two tours in Korea; one tour in Panama; and one tour in Germany. He has been on one rotation to the Middle East; and one rotation to South Korea as a First Sergeant. His stateside assignments include four tours at Fort Bliss, Texas.

His duty positions have included serving as Redeye Gunner; Stinger Team Chief; Squad Leader; Drill Sergeant; Stinger Section Chief; Writer/Instructor; Brigade Equal Opportunity Advisor; Platoon Sergeant;

His military education includes all levels of the Non-commissioned Officers Education System Courses; Equal Opportunity Advisor Course; the First Sergeant Course; the United States Army Sergeants Major Academy; Drill Sergeant School; Air Assault School; Airborne Course; Master Fitness Trainers Course; and the Field Artillery Weapons Maintenance Course. His civilian education includes an associate's degree in General Studies from Pikes Peak Community College and a bachelor's degree in Interdisciplinary Studies from Cameron, University.

He has served in numerous duty and leadership positions including Section Chief; Platoon Sergeant; Operations Sergeant; Equal Opportunity Advisor; and First Sergeant. In February 2005, he was serving as the Command Sergeant Major for the 1st Battalion, 82nd Field Artillery.

Tate, Willie C.

COMMAND SERGEANT MAJOR—ARMY

Command Sergeant Major Willie C. Tate entered active duty service in December 1975, and he received Basic Training at Fort Knox, Kentucky, and Advanced Individual Training at Fort Jackson, South Carolina.

He is a graduate of the Drill Sergeant Course; the Support Operations Course; the Senior Supply Sergeant Course; Noncommissioned Officer Logistics Program; the Special Operations Course; Force Integration/Development Course; Basic Airborne Course; the United States Army Sergeants Major Academy; and the Command Sergeants Major Designee Course.

He has held such responsible positions as Squad Leader; Drill Sergeant; Section Sergeant; Platoon Sergeant; Chief Logistics Operations Sergeant; First Sergeant; Support Operations Sergeant Major; and Command Sergeant Major.

His most recent assignment include the Special Operations Support Command, United States Army Special Operations Command, at Fort Bragg, North Carolina, and Troop Support Battalion, 1st COSCOM, at Fort Bragg. He is currently serving as the Command Sergeant Major with Area 1 Support Activity, 19th TSC, in South Korea.

Taylor, Christopher

COMMAND SERGEANT MAJOR—ARMY

He enlisted into the United States Army in September 1975, from Starkville, Mississippi. His military education include all the Noncommissioned Officer Education System Courses; Instructor Training Course; Drill Sergeant School; Master Fitness Training Course; First Sergeant Course; and the United States Army Sergeants Major Academy (class 47).

His key military assignments include serving as an Instructor at the NCO Academy; Drill Sergeant with the 2nd Battalion, 46th Infantry; First Sergeant of the 5th Squadron, 15th Cavalry Regiment; and Command Sergeant Major of the 3rd Squadron, 4th Cavalry Regiment.

Taylor, Clarence E., Jr.

COLONEL—AIR FORCE

He is a native of Kansas City, Kansas, and a 1974 graduate of J.C. Harmon High School. He received his commission and a bachelor's degree in Public Administration from Golden Gate University in San Francisco, California, and in 1999 he earned a master's degree in National Resource Management from the Industrial College of the Armed Forces at Fort McNair in Washington, D.C.

He is a Master Navigator with 2,458 hours in B-1 and B-52 bomber aircraft. He assumed command of the 2nd Support Group at Barksdale Air Force Base, Louisiana. He directs and manages all communications,

He has had numerous assignments, from Guam to Colorado and now Washington, D.C., and has performed duties as First Sergeant and Superintendent and in Military/Civilian Training. He was the lead architect in the development of the National Capitol Region's Enlisted Mentor Program, currently is President of the National Capital Region's Chiefs Group and is the Senior Enlisted Representative for the East Coast Chapter of Tuskegee Airmen International.

Taylor, Francis X.
BRIGADIER GENERAL—AIR FORCE

He is married to the former Constance Oates of Columbus, Georgia. They have three children: Jacquis, Justin and Shari. Upon graduation from the University of Notre Dame in South Bond, Indiana, as a distinguished graduate of the Reserve Officer Training Corps program, he was commissioned a second lieutenant on June 6, 1970, and entered active duty. His education includes a Bachelor of Arts degree in Government and International Studies from Notre Dame; a Master of Arts degree in Government and International Studies from Notre Dame; Squadron Officer School at Maxwell Air Force Base, Alabama; Air Command and Staff College; the Armed Forces Staff College in Norfolk, Virginia; and the Air War College at Maxwell Air Force Base. From July 1970 to September 1970, he was Agent Trainee on the Base Investigative detachment, Air Force Office of Special Investigations District 11, Tinker Air Force Base, Oklahoma. From September 1970 to November 1970, he was a student in the United States Air Force Special Investigations School in Washington, D.C. From November 1970 to August 1972, he was assigned as an Analyst in the Middle East, Africa

computer systems, engineering, fire protection, environmental programs, personnel programs, community services, law enforcement and security support provided to the 2nd Bomb Wing and 34 associate units, including the Headquarters of the Eighth Air Force and the 917th Air Force Reserve Center.

Taylor, Earl, III
CHIEF MASTER SERGEANT—AIR FORCE

He is a 28-year Air Force member, has completed all phases of Professional Military Education and holds a Bachelor of Science degree in Management and Business.

and South Asia Division of the Analysis and Dissemination Branch in the Counterintelligence Division of the Headquarters Air Force Office of Special Investigations in Washington, D.C. He was promoted to First Lieutenant on January 15, 1972. From August 1972 to August 1974, he was a student Africa Area Specialist in the Air Force Institute of Technology at Notre Dame. He was promoted to Captain on February 15, 1974. From August 1974 to April 1976, he was assigned as an Area Supervisor in the Acquisition and Analysis Division of the Directorate of Counterintelligence at the Headquarters of the Air Force Office of Special Investigations in Washington, D.C. From April 1976 to September 1977, he served as Chief of the Counterintelligence Acquisition and Analysis Branch in Air Force Office of Special Investigations District 69 in Ankara, Turkey. From September 1977 to June 1979, he was the Commander of Air Force Office of Special Investigations Detachment 411 at Bolling Air Force Base in Washington, D.C. From June 1979 to October 1980, he served as Chief of the Resource Career Management Division in the Directorate of Personnel at the Headquarters of the Air Force Office of Special Investigations at Bolling Air Force Base. From June 1979 to October 1980, he was assigned Chief of the Resource Career Management Division of the Directorate of Personnel at the Headquarters of the Air Force Office of Special Investigations at Bolling Air Force Base. From October 1980 to August 1983, he was assigned as Commander of Headquarters Squadron Section and Assistant Executive to the Commander in the Headquarters of the Air Force Office of Special Investigations at Bolling Air Force Base. From August 1983 to January 1984, he was a student at the Armed Forces Staff College in Norfolk, Virginia. From January 1984 to July 1987, he served as Deputy Director for Operations in the Directorate of Counterintelligence and Investigative Programs in the Office of the Deputy Under Secretary of Defense for Policy at the Pentagon. He was promoted to Lieutenant Colonel on March 1, 1985. From July 1987 to July 1988, he was a student at the Air War College at Maxwell Air Force Base, Alabama. From July 1988 to July 1990, he was the Deputy Commander of the 487th Combat Support Group at Comiso Air Station, Italy. He was promoted to Colonel on February 1, 1991. From July 1990 to July 1992, he served as the Commander of the Air Force Office of Special Investigations District 45 at Osan Air Base, South Korea. From July 1992 to July 1994, he served the Commander of the Air Force Office of Special Investigation Region 2 at Langley Air Force Base, Virginia. From August 1994 to August 1995, he was assigned as Director of Mission Guidance at the Headquarters of the Air Force Office of Special Investigations at Bolling Air Force Base. From August 1995 to July 1996, he was Director of Special Investigations in the Office of the Inspector General the Air Force at the Pentagon. In July 1996, he was selected as the 13th Commander of Headquarters of the Air Force Office of Special Investigations, a Field Operating Agency of the Air Force, at

Bolling Air Force Base. He was promoted to Brigadier General on September 1, 1996. General Taylor is responsible for providing commanders of all Air Force activities independent professional investigative services regarding fraud, counterintelligence and major criminal matters by using a worldwide network of military and civilian agents stationed at all major Air Force installations and a variety of special operating locations. After 31 years of military service, he retired on July 1, 2001. His military awards and decorations include the Defense Superior Service Medal; the Legion of Merit; the Meritorious Service Medal (with three oak leaf clusters); the Air Force Commendation Medal (with two oak leaf clusters); and the Air Force Achievement Medal (with oak leaf cluster).

Taylor, Henry "Hank" L.
BRIGADIER GENERAL—AIR FORCE

He began his military career in 1968 as a communications specialist in the United States Navy. He concluded his naval career in 1972 as an adviser to the South Vietnamese Navy, and in 1973, enrolled in a two-year ROTC program he completed as a distinguished graduate. He holds a Bachelor of Arts degree in Psychology (cum laude) from Coe College in Cedar Rapids, Iowa. He earned a master's degree in Human Relations from the University of Oklahoma. He is a distinguished graduate from both Squadron Officer School and the Air Command and Staff College. He has also attended the National War College; and he earned a Master of Science degree in National Security Strategy from the National Defense University.

From 1968 to March 1972, he served as a Radioman

in the United States Navy, and from February 1975 to May 1977, he was assigned as a Flightline Maintenance Supervisor with the 19th Organizational Maintenance Squadron at Robins Air Force Base, Georgia. In May 1977, he was assigned as a Maintenance Supervisor with the 19th Organizational Maintenance Squadron. From October 1978 to April 1979, he was assigned as the Officer-in-Charge of Wing Control with the 19th Bombardment Wing at Robins Air Force Base. In April 1979, he served as Chief of the Field Maintenance Evaluation Section of the Maintenance Standardization and Evaluation Team at the Headquarters of Strategic Air Command at Offutt Air Force Base, Nebraska. In June 1987, he was assigned as a Faculty Instructor, at the Air Command and Staff College at Maxwell Air Force Base, Alabama. From June 1988 to June 1989, he served as Chief of Programs at the Air Command and Staff College. In June 1989, he was assigned as the Commander of the 509th Organizational Maintenance Squadron at Pease Air Force Base, New Hampshire. From April 1990 to September 1991, he was assigned as the Assistant Deputy Commander for Maintenance with the 416th Bombardment Wing at Griffiss Air Force Base, New York, and from August 1990 to April 1991, he was assigned as the Deputy Commander for Maintenance with the 1702nd Air Refueling Wing Provisional during Operations Desert Shield/Desert Storm in Saudi Arabia. In September 1991, he was assigned as Deputy Commander, later Commander, of the 416th Logistics Group at Griffiss Air Force Base. From May 1993 to July 1995, he served as the Commander for the 509th Logistics Group at Whiteman Air Force Base, Missouri. In July 1996, he was assigned as the Deputy Director of Technology and Industrial Support Directorate at Warner-Robins Air Logistics Center at Robins Air Force Base, Georgia; in February 1997, he served as the Director of the Aircraft Directorate, later as Director of Commodities, with Ogden Air Logistics Center at Hill Air Force Base, Utah; and in September 2000, he was selected to serve as the Deputy Director of Logistics Operations at the Headquarters of Air Force Materiel Command at Wright-Patterson Air Force Base, Ohio. He was promoted to Brigadier General on January 1, 2002.

In July 2002, he was assigned as Vice Director for Logistics at the Joint Staff in Washington, D.C. He retired from the military on January 1, 2005.

His military awards include the Legion of Merit; Bronze Star; Meritorious Service Medal (with five oak leaf clusters); Air Force Commendation Medal (with oak leaf cluster); Air Force Outstanding Unit Award (with "V" device and three oak leaf clusters); the Air Force Organizational Excellence Award; National Defense Service Medal (with service star); Vietnam Service Medal (with two service stars); Southwest Asia Service Medal (with two service stars); the Air Force Overseas Ribbon-Short; the Air Force Overseas Ribbon-Long; the Air Force Longevity Service Award Ribbon (with six oak leaf clusters); Republic of Vietnam Gallantry Cross with Palm; Republic of Vietnam Campaign Medal; and

Kuwait Liberation Medal (Government of Saudi Arabia); Kuwait Liberation Medal (Government of Kuwait). In 1983, he received the Lew Allen, Jr., Trophy from Strategic Air Command. In 1991, he received a second Lew Allen, Jr. Trophy for excellence in sortie production.

Taylor, Jerry L.
COMMAND SERGEANT MAJOR—ARMY

He entered the United States Army on 29 August 1979. His military and civilian education includes Jungle Expert School; Air Assault; Airborne; Master Fitness; Battle Staff; First Sergeants Course; Joint Fire Power Control Course; all the Noncommissioned Officer Education System Courses; and the United States Army Sergeants Major Academy. He holds an associate's degree in General Studies from Central Texas College.

He has served with distinction in all enlisted leadership positions from Section Chief to Command Sergeant Major. His positions of increased responsibility include serving as a Howitzer Section Chief with C Battery 1/21 Field Artillery, B Battery 3/16 Field Artillery, Ammunition Platoon Sergeant, Gunnery Sergeant, Firing Battery Platoon Sergeant, Senior Artillery Advisor for the Saudi Arabian National Guard, Intelligence NCOIC, First Sergeant for Headquarters and Headquarters Service Battery, First Sergeant for Fox Battery and Fire Support Operations Sergeant Major. In 2004 he was serving as Command Sergeant Major for the 1st Battalion, 6th Field Artillery.

Taylor, Preston M., Jr.
BRIGADIER GENERAL—AIR FORCE

He was born in Mobile, Alabama. He and his wife, Audrey, have a son, Christopher, and a daughter, Cinthia. He attended LaSalle University in Philadelphia,

Pennsylvania, and earned a Bachelor of Arts degree in Personnel Management from Pepperdine University, California, and a Master of Arts in Personnel Management from Central Michigan University. His military education includes completion of numerous aircraft communication and avionics courses and graduation from the Industrial College of the Armed Forces, Air Command and Staff College, and the Air Force Squadron Officer's School. While at Lakehurst, he completed the Naval Air Systems Command five-year Senior Executive Management Development Program and the Naval Air Engineering Center's six-month Executive Development Courses. His military assignments include an active duty tour with the Air Force from 1954 to 1960, service as a Communications Electronics Staff Officer, State Inspector General, and Chairman of the Minority Officer Recruiting committee for the New Jersey Air National Guard. He was the Director of Aircraft Maintenance for the New Jersey Air National Guard Headquartered at McGuire Air Force Base. He was employed as the Senior Planner in the Office of Policy and Planning for the New Jersey Department of Military and Veterans' Affairs. In 1993, he was serving as the Deputy Adjutant General of New Jersey as a Brigadier General. He is retired from Civilian Federal Employment having served as a supervisor in the Naval Aircraft Engine and Avionics Logistics Section at the Naval Air Engineering Center at Lakehurst, New Jersey. General Taylor's military awards and decorations include the Meritorious Service Medal, the Air Force Commendation Medal, Air Force Organizational Excellence Award, the Good Conduct Medal (second award), National Defense Service Medal (with one bronze oak leaf cluster), the Air Force Longevity Service Award Ribbon (with one silver and two bronze oak

leaf clusters), Armed Forces Reserve Medal (with one hourglass device), Small Arms Expert Marksmanship Ribbon, and the Air Force Training Ribbon. His State military awards include the New Jersey Distinguished Service Medal, the New Jersey Medal of Honor (with one bronze oak leaf cluster), New Jersey Merit Award (with silver star and two silver oak leaf clusters), Desert Storm Support Ribbon, the New Jersey State Service Award, Recruiting Medal, Governor's Unit Award (with one bronze oak leaf cluster), and the New Jersey Strength Award. The General is active in both the National Guard Association of the United States and the National Guard Association of New Jersey. Within his community he served as a member of Waterford Township's Planning Board and as a Trustee of the Township's Library.

Terrell, Francis D'Arey

MAJOR GENERAL—ARMY

He was born in Caledonia, New York. He and his wife Mary Jane have two sons, Derek and Randall. He is a graduate of the University of Toledo, where he earned a Bachelor of Science Degree in Chemical Engineering (1962). He also graduated from Columbia Law School, receiving a J.D. degree in 1973. His military schools include the Air Defense Artillery Officers Basic and Advance Courses; the United States Army Infantry Airborne School; Special Warfare School; Defense Language Institute (Vietnamese); Judge Advocate Officers Basic and Advanced School; Air Defense Artillery Officers Advance School; Civil Affairs Officers Advanced School; Command and General Staff College; and the United States Army War College. He was commissioned as a Second Lieutenant in 1963, after completing ROTC training as a Distinguished Military Student. Some of his military assignments include his first assignment overseas was an Assistant Team

Commander and Team Commander of the 52nd Artillery Detachment (Nike-Hercules) USAREUR; he then served on active duty in successive assignments as an Infantry Regimental Staff Advisor on the 3rd Battalion, 31st ARVN Infantry Division; IV Corps, Military Assistance Command Vietnam (MACV); Tactical Operations Officer with the IV Corps, MACV; and Senior Advisor to the 35th Field Artillery Battalion (155-mm howitzer), 21st ARVN Infantry Division. After joining the Reserves in 1977 he served consecutively as Defense Counsel in the 63rd JAG Court Martial Defense Detachment; Military Justice Officer 4th JAG Military Law Center; Chief International Law/Claims, 4th JAG Military Law Center; Commander of the 64th Court Martial Defense Detachment; Deputy Staff Judge Advocate with the 77th ARCOM; Staff Judge Advocate 77th ARCOM; and Commanding General of the 77th ARCOM. The 77th ARCOM reorganized into the 77th Regional Support Command in April 1995. General Terrell has been decorated with the Bronze Star, three Meritorious Service Medals, the Air Medal; Army Commendation Medal (with 2 oak leaf clusters); the Army Achievement Medal; the Army Reserve Components Achievement Medal; the National Defense Service Medal (with Bronze Service Star); Vietnam Service Medal; the Army Service Ribbon; two Republic of Vietnam Staff Medals; the Republic of Vietnam Honor Medal; the Republic of Vietnam Gallantry Cross (with Bronze Star); the Republic of Vietnam Campaign Medal (with four stars); the Parachute Badge; and the Combat Infantryman Badge. He has been the Director of the Greenberg Center for Legal Education and Urban Policy for the City College of New York since October 1988. In 1991, General Terrell received the prestigious Roy Wilkins NAACP Meritorious Service Award for significant contributions to the military and community. In 1995, General Terrell received the Whitney M. Young National Boy Scout Award. In March 1995, the Secretary of the Army, the Honorable Togo West, selected General Terrell to serve on the Army Reserve Forces Policy Committee at the Pentagon.

Thanars, Don M.
MAJOR—MARINES
He was assigned to Marine Corps Base Parris Island

in August 1997 and became a valuable asset to the local military and civilian community. His actions in coordinating the Coming of Age Program, which is designed to better equip and prepare the fifth grade male students at St. Helena Elementary School in making good decisions as they move in to middle school.

Because of his com-

mitment to the community, the National Association for the Advancement of Colored People is recognized him with the NAACP's Roy Wilkins Renown Service Award. The Award was presented to him at the Armed Services and Veterans Affairs Dinner in Baltimore on July 11, 2000.

Theus, Lucia
MAJOR GENERAL—AIR FORCE
He was born in Madison County, Tennessee, and married the former Gladys Marie Davis of Chicago, Illinois. He graduated from Community High School in Blue Island, Illinois. He earned a Bachelor of Science degree from the University of Maryland in 1956 and a Master of Business Administration from George Washington University in 1957, and is a 1969 graduate of the Harvard Advanced Management Program of the Harvard University Graduate School of Business Administration. During his Air Force career, General Theus attended the Statistical Control Officers School at Lowry Air Force Base, Colorado, in 1948, and in 1966 he was graduated with distinction from the Air War College at Maxwell Air Force Base, Alabama. During World War II, he entered the Army Air Corps as a private in December 1942. After basic training, he attended the Army Administration School at Atlanta University. For the remainder of World War II, he served as an Administrative Clerk, Chief Clerk, and First Sergeant of Preaviation Cadet and Basic Training Squadrons at Keesler Field, Mississippi. He entered Officer Candidate School, graduating second in his class with a commission as Second Lieutenant in January 1946. He was promoted to First Lieutenant on August 25, 1947. Following a one-year tour of duty as Squadron Adjutant at Tuskegee Army Airfield, Alabama, Theus went to Lockbourne Air Force Base, Ohio, as Base Statistical Control Officer. In August 1949, he was transferred to Erding Air Depot, Germany,

455   Thomas • Thomas

where he served as the Analysis and Presentation Officer, and later as Commander of the Statistical Control Flight and Depot Statistical Control Officer. Theus was assigned to the Headquarters of Central Air Materiel Forces Europe at Chateauroux Air Base, France. He was promoted to Major on April 24, 1956. In January 1959, Theus was assigned as Chief of the Management Service Office of the Eastern Air Logistics Office in Athens, Greece. In February 1961, he was appointed Chief of Management Analysis in the Headquarters of Spokane Air Defense Sector at Larson Air Force Base, Washington. He was promoted to Lieutenant Colonel on July 15, 1962. In December 1962, Theus was assigned as Base Comptroller at Kingsley Field, Oregon. His next assignment was Base Comptroller at Cam Ranh Bay Air Base, South Vietnam. For more than five months of this assignment, he also was acting Deputy Base Commander at Cam Ranh Bay. Upon his return to the United States in July 1967, Theus was reassigned to the Office of the Comptroller of the Air Force as a Data Automation Staff Office in the Directorate of Data Automation. He served initially as Chief of the Technology and Standards Branch; then as Chief of the Plans, Policy, and Technology Division; and later as Chief of the Program Management Division. During that assignment, he also performed additional duty as Chairman of the Inter-Service Task Force on Education in Race Relations in the Office of the Secretary of Defense. The recommendations of the task force led to establishment of the Defense Race Relations Institute and the Department of Defense Education Program in Race Relations. He was promoted to Colonel on July 20, 1967. In 1968, he attended the Department of Defense Computer Institute. In July 1971, he was assigned as Director of Management Analysis in the Office of the Comptroller of the Air Force. In June 1972, he was appointed Special Assistant for Social Actions, Directorate of Personnel Plans, Deputy Chief of Staff of Personnel at the Headquarters of the United States Air Force. He was promoted to Brigadier General on August 1, 1972. On June 10, 1974, he was appointed Director of Accounting and Finance in the Office of the Comptroller of the Air Force and Commander of the Air Force Accounting and Finance Center at Denver, Colorado. General Theus was promoted to Major General effective May 1, 1975, with date of rank of July 1, 1972. His military decorations and awards include the Distinguished Service Medal; the Legion of Merit; Bronze Star Medal; the Air Force Commendation Medal (with one oak leaf cluster); Air Force Outstanding Unit Award Ribbon; Good Conduct Medal; the American Campaign Medal; World War II Victory Medal; Army of Occupation Medal (Germany); National Defense Service Medal (with one Bronze Service Star); Vietnam Service Medal; Air Force Longevity Service Award (with one Silver and one Bronze Oak leaf cluster); Small Arms Expert Marksmanship Ribbon; and Republic of Vietnam Campaign Medal.

Thomas, Buford
COMMAND SERGEANT MAJOR—ARMY

He has an exemplary military record in both conventional and special operations aviation. He served as the 160th Special Operations Aviation Regiment Command Sergeant Major. In January 2005, he became the new Command Sergeant Major for the Army Aviation and Industry Team.

Thomas, Donald E.
COMMAND SERGEANT MAJOR—ARMY

He is a native of Fairfax, Virginia, and was drafted into the United States Army in January 1971. After completion to Basic Combat and Military Police Advanced Individual Training, he was assigned to numerous installations both stateside and overseas.

His military education includes all the Noncommissioned Officer Education System Courses; Military Police Investigation Course; the First Sergeant Course; and the United States Army Sergeants Major Academy (class 31). He also holds an Associate in Arts degree from the University of Maryland and a Bachelor of Science degree from the University of the States of New York.

His key leadership assignments include serving as Platoon Sergeant/Internal Security NCO at the Supreme Headquarters of Allied Powers Europe at Mons, Belgium; Training NCO in the 437th Military Police Company at Fort Belvoir, Virginia; Military Security Force, Office of the Chairman of the Joint Chiefs of Staff at the Pentagon; First Sergeant of Military Police Company, United States Chemical Activity, Johnston Island; First Sergeant of the 259th Military Police Company at White Sands Missile Range, New Mexico; Provost Sergeant Major at the Air Defense Center and Fort Bliss; Command Sergeant Major of the 720th Military Police Battalion at Fort Hood, Texas; Command Sergeant Major of the 92nd Military Police

Battalion, Panama; and Command Sergeant Major of the 8th Military Police Brigade at Yongsan, South Korea.

Thomas, Gerald Eustis

REAR ADMIRAL—NAVY

Born in Natick, Massachusetts, he is the son of Walter W. and Leila L. (Jacobs) Thomas. He married the former Rhonda Holmes Henderson and they have three children, Kenneth A., Steven E., and Lisa D. Admiral Thomas received his Bachelor of Arts degree from Harvard in 1951, a Master of Science degree from George Washington University in 1966, and a Ph.D. in Diplomatic History from Yale in 1973. He began his Navy career in 1951, and for over thirty years he held a wide variety of important command and staff positions. From 1962 to 1963, he was the Commanding Officer of the USS *Impervious*. From 1963 to 1965, he served as the Commander of the College Training Programs of the Bureau of Naval Personnel. From 1966 to 1968 he served as the Commanding Officer of the USS *Bausell*. From 1968 to 1970 he served as the Commanding Officer and Professor of Naval Science at Prairie View A&M College Naval ROTC Unit. After his promotion to the flag rank of Admiral, he was assigned as the U.S. Navy, Commander of Destroyer Squadron 5, from 1973 to 1975. He was assigned as the acting Deputy Assistant Secretary of Defense for International Security Affairs and Director of the Near East, South Asia and Africa Region at the United States Department of Defense from 1976 to 1978. From 1978 to 1981, he served as the Senior Rear Admiral on the United States Pacific Fleet. He retired in 1981. Until 1983, he was United States Ambassador to Guyana, and from 1983 to 1986 was United States Ambassador to Kenya from 1983 to 1986. From 1986 to 1991, he served as a Yale University lec-

turer in the African American studies program and history department. In May 1991, Dr. Thomas was named the new Master of Davenport College in Grand Rapids, Michigan. For a man who has commanded squadrons of ships as an admiral in the United States Navy and who has supervised hundreds of diplomats as ambassador, becoming master of a residential college might seem insignificant. But Dr. Thomas took the role very seriously. His experience as teacher, scholar and leader in the highest echelons of government brought knowledge that proved to be invaluable to Davenport and the entire Yale community. Davenport College President Benno Schmidt, Jr., appointed Dr. Thomas to a five-year term, selecting him from a list of candidates compiled by a student and faculty search committee.

Thomas, John R.

BRIGADIER GENERAL—MARINES

He graduated from Appalachian State University with a Bachelor of Science degree. He earned a master's degree in Business Administration from Prairie View A&M University. His military education includes the Naval War College, where he received a Master of Science in National Security and Strategic Studies; Advanced Communications Officer School; the United States Marine Corps Command and Staff College; and the College of Naval Warfare.

His previous command assignments include serving as the Commanding Officer of the 1st Surveillance, Reconnaissance, and Intelligence Group, I Marine Expeditionary Force; Commanding Officer of the 7th Communication Battalion, III Marine Expeditionary Force; Commanding Officer of Communications Company, 3rd Force Service Support Group; and Platoon Commander.

He has served as Deputy Director of Command, Control, Communications and Computers at the Headquarters of the Marine Corps; as Director of Programs Division, Programs and Resources Department at the Headquarters of the United States Marine Corps; as Assistant Chief of Staff G-6, Marine Forces Pacific; as the Assistant Chief of Staff G-6, First Marine Expeditionary Force; as Chief of the Command Centers Support Division, Command, Control, Communication and Computers Directorate (J6), with the Joint Staff in Washington, DC; as Communication Support Officer at the National Military Command Center; as the Program Coordinator with the Space, Command and Control Directorate, Chief of Naval Operations; and as Marine Officer Instructor at Prairie View A&M University.

In 2002 and 2003, he was assigned as Director for Command, Control, Communications and Computers (C4) for the United States Marine Corps, becoming the Chief Information Officer (CIO) of the Marine Corps component to the Joint Task Force for Computer Network Operations.

His military awards and decorations include the Legion of Merit; Defense Superior Service Medal; Meritorious Service Medal (with gold star); Navy and Marine Corps Commendation Medal (with gold star); National Defense Service Medal (with bronze star); and the Humanitarian Service Medal.

Thomas, Joseph, Jr.
COMMAND SERGEANT MAJOR—ARMY

He entered the United States Army in July of 1976. He attended Basic Combat Training and Advanced Individual Training at Fort Gordon, Georgia, as a Radio-Teletype Operator. His military and civilian education

includes completion of all the Noncommissioned Officers Leadership Courses, Master Fitness Course, Nuclear Biological Chemical Course, Drill Sergeant Course, Battle Staff Course and the United States Army Sergeants Major Academy. He earned an associate's degree in Liberal Arts, a bachelor's degree in Business Administration, and a master's degree in Business Administration.

His duty positions include serving as Team Chief for Headquarters and Headquarters Company, 1st Battalion, 15th Infantry Regiment at Kitzingen, Germany; Section Chief of Headquarters and Headquarters Company, 17th Combat Engineer Battalion at Fort Hood, Texas; Section Chief of Headquarters and Headquarters Company, 304th Signal Battalion at Camp Colbern, South Korea; Section Chief of Headquarters and Headquarters Company, 2nd Battalion, 70th Armor at Fort Stewart, Georgia; Drill Sergeant of Company B, 3rd Battalion, 5th Training Brigade at Fort Dix, New Jersey; Drill Sergeant Instructor at the United States Army Noncommissioned Officer Academy/Drill Sergeant School at Fort Dix; First Sergeant of Company D, 369th Signal Battalion at Fort Gordon; S-1 (Personnel) Sergeant Major with the 93rd Signal Brigade at Fort Gordon; Command Sergeant Major of the 41st Signal Battalion at Yongsan, South Korea; and Command Sergeant Major of the 551st Signal Battalion at Fort Gordon.

Thomas, Michael
COMMANDER—NAVY

A native of Brooklyn, New York, he enlisted in the United States Navy through the Broaden Opportunity for Officer Selection and Training (BOOST) program and was subsequently awarded a Naval ROTC scholarship. He is a 1989 graduate of Florida Agricultural and Mechanical University (FAMU). He was commissioned an Ensign in 1989. He received a Masters of Arts in Business from Webster University in 1995.

His key assignments include serving as Disbursing and Sales Officer in USS *Underwood* (FFG 36), Staff of the Commander of Destroyer Squadron EIGHT, Sales and Assistant Material Officer in USS *John F. Kennedy* (CV 67), and Supply Officer in USS *John Hancock* (DD 981). He has also served as Logistics and Senior Assessment Officer at Shore Naval Air Station, Jacksonville, Florida; Commander of Afloat Training Group Middle Pacific at Pearl Harbor, Hawaii; Deputy Program Manager for Business and Financial Management for Cruise Missiles Weapons Systems and Navy Unmanned Aerial Vehicles Programs; and Program Executive Officer for Strike Weapons and Unmanned Aviation at Patuxent River, Maryland. In October 2004, he was serving as the Executive Officer of the Navy Supply Corps School in Athens, Georgia.

Thomas, Nello A.
LIEUTENANT COLONEL—ARMY

A native of Richmond, Virginia, he is a graduate of Virginia Polytechnic Institute and State University

(Virginia Tech), where he earned a Bachelor of Science degree in Mathematics. He also holds a Masters of Public Administration from Auburn University Montgomery and a Master of Military Operational Art and Science from Air University. He was commissioned August 6, 1985, into the Signal Corps.

His military education includes the Signal Officers Basic Course, Signal Officers Advance Course, the Combined Arms and Services Staff School, the Command and General Staff College, the Air Command and Staff College, and the Joint Forces Staff College.

His assignments include serving as Platoon Leader of the 332nd Military Intelligence Company at Uijongbu, South Korea; Area Node Platoon Leader and Executive Officer of the 505th Signal Company, 11th Signal Brigade at Fort Huachuca, Arizona; Engineer for Communication-Electronic Command at Vint Hill Farms Station in Warrenton, Virginia; Plans Officer for the Southern European Task Force at Vicenza, Italy; Brigade Scholarship Officer with the 5th Brigade, 2nd ROTC Region at Redstone Arsenal, Alabama; Chief of the Requirements Branch, Program and Policy Division Officer with the 63rd Signal Battalion, 93rd Signal Brigade at Fort Gordon, Georgia; and Inspector General of the 1st Signal Brigade at Youngsan, South Korea. In August 2004, he was serving as Commander of the 369th Signal Battalion, 15th Signal Brigade, at Fort Gordon.

Thomas, Robert N., III
SERGEANT MAJOR—MARINES

He was born in St. Louis, Missouri, where he enlisted into the United States Marine Corps in September 1976. He attended Recruit Training at Marine Corps Recruit Depot, at San Diego, California, and meritoriously promoted to Private First Class. In De-

cember 1976, he was ordered to the 1st Marine Brigade at Marine Corps Air Station, Kaneohe Bay, Hawaii, for duty with Kilo Company, 3rd Battalion, 3rd Marines, with the Weapons Platoon as a mortar man, scout sniper, assault section leader, and Correctional Custody Unit Instructor. He transferred to Marine Corps Development Education Command in April 1981 for duty as Sergeant Instructor and Physical Training Instructor at Officer Candidate School in Quantico, Virginia, for Charlie and Golf Companies.

In August 1983, he was transferred back to the 1st Battalion, 3rd Marines, 1st Marine Brigade at Marine Corps Air Station, Kaneohe Bay, for duty with Weapons Company as a 81mm Mortar Section Leader and Brigade Human Affairs Senior Non-Commissioned Officer in Charge until September 1986. Sergeant Major Thomas attended Drill Instructor School in October 1986, where he put through two platoons as a Junior Drill Instructor and six platoons as a Senior Drill Instructor.

In March 1989, he was transferred to Marine Corps Base, Camp Pendleton, California, for duty with the Marine Combat Training Battalion at the School of Infantry as a Platoon Commander and Company Gunnery Sergeant.

In January 1992, then Sergeant Major Thomas was transferred to the 3rd Battalion, 1st Marine Corps Base, at Camp Pendleton, where he served as the Company Gunnery Sergeant. In April 1996, he served as the First Sergeant for Delta Company, Student Administration Company and Advanced Infantry Training Company at the School of Infantry at Camp Pendleton.

Upon being promoted to Sergeant Major in January 2000, he was transferred to Inspector, 1st Battalion, 14th Marines, 4th Marine Division, in Alameda, California, to assume duties as the Inspector-Instructor Sergeant Major. During June 2000, Sergeant Major Thomas served as the Sergeant Major for Inspector-Instructor of 5th Battalion, 14th Marines Headquartered at the Naval Weapons Station at Seal Beach, California.

In May 2005, he was serving as the Sergeant Major for the 11th Marine Regiment, 1st Marine Division. In September 2005, he was assigned as the Sergeant Major for the 1st Marine Division.

Thomas, Ronald
CAPTAIN—NAVY

He is a native of Memphis, Tennessee, and graduated in 1976 from Wabash College in Crawfordsville, Indiana, where he obtained a Bachelor of Arts Degree in History. He is also a 2000 graduate of the National War College in Washington, D.C., where he received a Master of Science Degree in National Security Strategy. Commissioned an Ensign in September 1978 at the Officer Candidate School in Newport, Rhode Island, his initial assignment was in USS *Bradley* (FF 1041) where he served as the First Lieutenant and the Main Propulsion Assistant.

He completed his initial tour in 1982 and was assigned

to the Surface Warfare Division Officer School in Coronado, California, as a Steam Engineering Instructor. After completion of this first shore assignment and the Department Head Course in Newport, Rhode Island, he was assigned as Engineering Officer in USS *Fresno* (LST 1182) in March 1986. As his second Department Head tour, he served as an Examiner on the Pacific Fleet Propulsion Examining Board in 1988. He completed that tour and in March 1990 he reported to USS *Bristol County* (LST 1198) as Executive Officer. He then served on the staff of Commander of Amphibious Squadron Nine in San Diego from January 1992 to February 1994 as Maintenance and Readiness Officer. As a Commander, he first served in the Pentagon on the staff of the Chief of Naval Operations, Expeditionary Warfare Division as the Amphibious Ships Platform Sponsor. He returned to sea as the Commanding Officer of USS *Anchorage* (LSD 36), home ported in San Diego, California. After commanding *Anchorage*, he served as the Naval Advisor to the Officer of International Security Operations in the State Department's Bureau of Political-Military Affairs. He served as the Commanding Officer of Amphibious Squadron Seven, which is home ported in San Diego, California. In October 2004, he was serving as the Chief of Staff of Amphibious Force Seventh Fleet Amphibious Group One Task Force 76.

Thompson, Arthur J.

SERGEANT MAJOR—MARINES

He graduated from Bethune Cookman College in 1974. After two years in the Public School System, he enlisted into the United States Marine Corps in August 1976. He completed Recruit Training at Marine Corps Recruit Depot, and Administrative Clerk Course at Parris Island, South Carolina.

His key leadership assignments include serving as a Drill Instructor and Senior Drill Instructor at Marine Corps Recruit Depot, Parris Island, South Carolina; Administrative Chief for the Commanding General of United States Marine Reserve Force Headquarters at New Orleans, Louisiana; and Senior Administrative Inspector for the Marine Reserve Forces . In September 1992, he became Battalion Adjutant and Legal Officer for the 91st Motor Transport Battalion, 3rd Force Support Service Group, in Okinawa, Japan. He later served as Squadron Administrative Chief for Marine Training Squadron 203, 2nd Marine Aircraft Wing at Cherry Point, North Carolina; and as First Sergeant for B Company, later A Company, at the Marine Logistics Base in Albany, Georgia. In December 1998, he was assigned as First Sergeant for I Battery, 11th Battalion, 11th Marines, 1st Marine Division; in April 2000, he was promoted to Sergeant Major and assigned to the 151st Tank Battalion, where he participated in Bright Star 2000 in Egypt and Operations Enduring Freedom in 2003; and in March 2005, he was serving as Sergeant Major for the United States Marine Wing Support Group 27.

Thompson, Hayward

COMMAND SERGEANT MAJOR—ARMY

Command Sergeant Major Thompson was born in Orangeburg, South Carolina. In 1976, he enlisted in the United States Army and attended Basic Training and Advanced Individual Training at Fort Polk, Louisiana, where he was awarded the MOS 11B.

His military education includes the Bradley Fighting Vehicle Course; First Sergeants Course; Observer Controller Course; Command Sergeant Major Designee Course; Master Fitness Training; Air Assault Course; Basic Combat Lifesavers Course; the Airborne School; and the United States Army Sergeants Major Academy.

He was assigned as the First Sergeant for Headquarters Company, 1-52nd Infantry (Mechanized); as a Platoon Sergeant with the 3rd United States Infantry (The Old Guard); as a Noncommissioned Officer Escort in the Office of Congressional Legislative Liaison at the Pentagon; as a Senior Mechanized Observer at the National Training Center (NTC) in the Operations Group at Fort Irwin, California; as First Sergeant with Company A, 1st Battalion, 3rd United States Infantry in Washington, D.C.; and as the G-3 Operations Sergeant Major with the 2nd Infantry Division in South Korea, CRC. He is currently serving as the Command Sergeant Major for the 1-503rd Infantry Regiment (AASLT).

Thompson, James A.
FIRST SERGEANT—MARINES

He enlisted into the United States Marine Corps in March 1983 and graduated from recruit training in May 1983. After recruit training, he reported to the infantry training school where he underwent training to become an infantry rifleman 0311.

After completion of Infantry Training School, he reported to Roosevelt Roads, Puerto Rico, where he was meritoriously promoted to Private First class. He also held the billet of Corporal of the Guard until he was transferred in April 1985. He reported to 2nd Marine Division, 3rd Battalion, 4th Marines where he was meritoriously promoted to Corporal. While deployed on MAU SOC BLT 3/4, he conducted operations off the coast of Libya. He then transferred to Sea School at Marines Corps Recruit Depot in San Diego. Upon completion of Sea School, he reported to USS *Hollard* where he attended NCO school.

In May 1989, he transferred to 3rd Marine Division, 3rd Recon Battalion, where he participated in Team Spirit in Korea and was a recon Platoon Sergeant. In June 1990, he was transferred to 1st Battalion, 8th Marines where he was rapidly deployed and participated in Operations Desert Shield/Desert Storm.

Upon his return from Desert Storm in March 1991, he was again deployed to Kuwait in May 1991 in support of training the Kuwaiti Marine Corps and military personnel. In July 1992, he attended the Infantry Platoon Sergeant's Course. In August 1993, he deployed and conducted operations in Somalia.

In 1994 he was transferred to Parris Island as a Basic Warrior Training Instructor, and promoted to the rank of Staff Sergeant. In January 1997, he attended Drill Instructor School, where he served with 2nd Recruit Training Battalion. He held the billets of Senior Drill Instructor and Series Gunnery Sergeant.

After a successful tour on the drill field, he was transferred to the 1st Battalion, 2nd Marines where he held the billets of Platoon Commander Weapons Platoon Bravo Company, Charlie Company Gunnery and Company First Sergeant Thompson deployed to Okinawa, Japan, in June 2001. In September 2001, he deployed from Okinawa to Guam in support of September 11, 2001, for security operations. After returning to the United States in December 2001, he was selected to First Sergeant in March 2002, and transferred to Alpha Company, 1st Battalion, 2nd Mariens. Once in Alpha Company, he was deployed to Iraqi Freedom, where he served as Sergeant Major of Troops aboard USS *Portland* until arriving in Kuwait City and joining the rest of his Battalion.

He returned from Iraqi Freedom in June 2003 and was transferred to Marine Corps Detachment at Aberdeen Proving Grounds in July 2003, where he serves as the Marine Corps Detachment First Sergeant.

Thompson, John R.
COLONEL—ARMY

He was born in Sanford, North Carolina. He married the former Wynndolyn L. Barge of Selma, Alabama, and they have one son, John Warren. Upon graduation from North Carolina A&T State University as a Distinguished Military Graduate, he was commissioned as a Second Lieutenant in the United States Army's Signal Corps and received a Bachelor of Science degree in Education. He also has a Master of Science degree in Business Administration from North Carolina A&T State University. His military education includes Airborne School; the Signal Officer Basic and Advanced Courses; the Telecommunications Officer Course; the Armed Forces Staff College; and the United States War College. His first field assignment was with the 26th Signal Battalion, 7th Signal Brigade, in Heilbronn, West Germany, in 1973. He served as a Communications Center Officer, Signal Center Platoon Leader and Company Commander. In 1978, Colonel Thompson was selected for assignment to the Joint Communications Support Element (JCSE), United States Readiness Command at MacDill Air Force Base, Florida, where he served as the Operations Officer and Commander of the Joint Task Force Detachment. In 1981, he was selected to attend the United States Army Command and General Staff College, and was assigned to the Army Communicative Technology Officer in the Army Training Support Center at Fort Eustis, Virginia, where he served as an Operations Officer and as a Communications Electronic Systems Engineer. In 1985, he was selected for assignment to the White House Communications Agency, in Washington, D.C., where he served as executive officer of the Transmission Systems Unit and as commander of the Staff Support Unit in support of the President of the United States. In 1990, Colonel Thompson took command of the 102nd Signal Battalion in Frankfurt, West Germany. In 1993, he

was selected as Chief of the Command and Control Signal Division in the Office of the Deputy Chief of Staff for Operations and Plans at the Pentagon. On August 10, 1994, he assumed command of the 15th Signal Brigade at the United States Army Signal Center and School at Fort Gordon, Georgia. His military awards and decorations include the Defense Meritorious Service Medal (with two oak leaf clusters); Meritorious Service Medal (with two oak leaf clusters); Joint Service Commendation Medal; National Defense Service Medal; Humanitarian Service Medal; Joint Meritorious Unit Citation (with two oak leaf clusters); Parachutist Badge; Aircraft Crewman Badge; Presidential Service Badge; and the Army Staff Identification Badge.

Thompson, Lawrence E.
SERGEANT MAJOR—MARINES

Sergeant Major Lawrence E. Thompson enlisted in the Marine Corps Reserve in March 1976. After Recruit Training at Marine Corps Recruit Depot Parris Island, South Carolina, he was assigned to the 1st Battalion, 10th Marines to attend the Basic Field Artillery Cannoner's Course.

In May 1992, he was assigned as the First Sergeant for Company A, 3rd Light Anti-Aircraft Missile Battalion. In August 1994, he was assigned as the First Sergeant for the General Support Maintenance Company, 2nd Force Service Support Group, Combat Service Support Detachment 66 and several other small deployments while at the 2nd Maintenance Battalion and was promoted to Sergeant Major. In March 1996, he was assigned as the Sergeant Major of the 3rd Battalion, 10th Marines at Fort Bragg, North Carolina, and also deployed to 29 Palms, California, with the 3/10th Marines. In January 1998, he was assigned to the 4th Supply Battalion for Inspector-Instructor duty. In June 2000, he was assigned

as Sergeant Major for the Marine Air Support Squadron 1 in June of 2000. He selected and assigned as the Group Sergeant Major from February 2001 to March 2002, for the Marine Wing Support Group 27, 2nd Marine Aircraft Wing Cherry Point, North Carolina. He is currently serving as the Sergeant Major for the 3rd Marine Corps Division.

Thompson, Wilbert R.
COMMAND SERGEANT MAJOR—ARMY

He entered the United States Army Reserves in 1980, completing Basic Combat Training at Fort Dix, New Jersey, and Advanced Individual Training at Fort Benjamin Harrison, Indiana.

His military and civilian education includes an associate's degree from Columbia College; a bachelor's degree from Saint Leo University; a master's degree from Central Michigan University; and a master's certificate from George Washington University. He has completed all the Noncommissioned Officer Education System Courses and graduated from the United States Army Sergeants Major Academy in May 2000.

In March 1990, he was assigned as Programmer Analyst at the 87th Maneuver Area Command (MAC) at Birmingham, Alabama. In April 1994, he reported to the Headquarters of the United States Army Reserve Command in Atlanta, Georgia, as a Senior Analyst; during this time he was selected for promotion to Sergeant Major in March 2001. In March 2005, he was serving as the Command Sergeant Major at the United States Army Human Resources Command in St. Louis.

Thornton, Leon S.
SERGEANT MAJOR—MARINES

He graduated from John Graham Senior High School in June 1979, enlisted in the United States Marine Corps in April 1980 and reported to Marine Corps Recruit Depot (MCRD), Parris Island, South Carolina, in August 1980.

In March 1987, he was assigned to Drill Instructor School at Marine Corps Recruit Depot, Parris Island, South Carolina, and assigned as Drill Instructor and Senior Drill Instructor; in March 1990, he served as Senior Drill Instructor with Charlie Company, 1st Recruit Training Battalion; in July 1990, he was assigned as the Regimental Wire Chief at the Headquarters Company of the 2nd Marine Regiment, 2nd Marine Division, Communication Platoon; in August 1990, he deployed to Southwest Asia in support of Operation Desert Shield/Desert Storm; in January 1992, he attended the Wire Chief Course in 29 Palms, California; and in June 1993, he was transferred to Champaign, Illinois, for duty with the Naval Reserve Officer Training Corps at the University of Illinois as the Assistant Marine Officer Instructor. While assigned to the University of Illinois, he was in charge of the Marine Option Program, Battalion Physical Training, Exhibition Drill Team and all Marine field training. During the summer months, he was temporarily assigned to duty at Officer Candidate School in Quantico, Virginia, as a Sergeant Instructor and Platoon Sergeant. In July 1996, he was assigned as the Classified Material Control Custodian (CMCC) for Marine Forces Atlantic (MARFORLANT) at Camp Lejeune, North Carolina. In September 1997, he became the Company Wire Chief for Alpha Company, 8th Communications Battalion. In January 1998, he assumed the duties as Alpha Company First Sergeant; in August 1998, he was reassigned to Headquarters Company as the Battalion S-3 Training Officer where he was responsible for the tracking and monitoring of all annual and fiscal year training for over 1200 Marines assigned to the battalion;

in May 2000, he was assigned as the First Sergeant at Marine Barracks, 8th & I, Washington, D.C., for duty as the Company First Sergeant of Marine Corps Institute Company; in February 2002, he was reassigned as Company First Sergeant of Bravo Company, Marine Barracks; and in April 2004, he transferred to 1st Marine Aircraft Wing in Okinawa, Japan, for duty as the Squadron Sergeant Major for HMM-262.

Tigs, Dwayne A.
FIRST SERGEANT—ARMY

He is a native of Annapolis, Maryland. He entered military service and attended military service and attended Basic Combat Training at Fort Dix, New Jersey, in August 1981. He attended Advanced Individual Training at the United States Army Transportation Schools at Fort Eustis, Virginia.

His education includes all the Noncommissioned Officer Education System Courses; Instructor Training Course; and the First Sergeant Course.

He has served in a variety of leadership positions ranging from Section Sergeant, Platoon Sergeant, and First Sergeant. Some of his other positions include instructor for the Powertrain and Propulsion Branch and Division Chief for the Aircraft Armament Division, and presently the Sergeant Major of the 78th Aviation Battalion (Provisional).

Tillman, Johnie S.
COLONEL—ARMY

He was born in Richmond, Virginia. He was commissioned as a Second Lieutenant in the Medical Service Corps (Reserves) while a sophomore medical student at the Medical College of Virginia. He entered

active duty status upon graduating from medical school in May 1978.

He earned his bachelor's degree in Physics from Dartmouth College in 1974 and was awarded a Doctorate of Medicine from the Medical College of Virginia in 1978. He completed his internship and residency at Madigan Army Medical Center at Fort Lewis, Washington, in 1981. His military education includes the Medical Officers' Basic Course; Medical Officers Advanced Course; Combat Casualty Care Management Course; Health Professionals' Management Course for Alcohol and Drug Abusers; Combined Arms Staff Service School; the United States Army Command and General Staff College; and the United States Army War College.

He has held numerous assignments including serving as Commander of Defense for Pacific Regional Medical Command; Deputy Commander for Readiness at Tripler Army Medical Center in Honolulu, Hawaii; and as Brigade Surgeon for the 3rd Brigade, 9th Infantry Division, at Fort Lewis. In June 1982, he was assigned as a staff physician at Reynolds Army Community Hospital at Fort Still, Oklahoma; in July 1985, he served as the Clinic Director of the Family Practice Residency Program at Dwight D. Eisenhower Army Medical Center at Fort Gordon, Georgia; and later as the Division Surgeon, 5th Infantry Division (Mechanized); and in July 1991 to July 1993, he served as the Chief of Primary Care and Community Medicine at Bayne-Jones Army Community Hospital at Fort Polk, Louisiana. He next served as Professor and Vice Chair of the Department of Military and Emergency Medicine in the Uniformed Services University of the Health Sciences at Bethesda, Maryland, from 1993 to June 1997. He was selected to serve as Commander of McDonald Army Community Hospital at Fort Eustis, Virginia, from July 1997 to July 1999. Colonel Tillman currently serves as the Deputy Commander for the Pacific Regional Medical Command and Deputy Commander for Readiness at Tripler Army Medical Center.

Titus, Barbara J.
SERGEANT MAJOR—MARINES

She enlisted in the United States Marine Corps Reserves in March 1978 and reported to Women Recruit Training Command, Company "L" at Parris Island, South Carolina. Upon graduating from Recruit Training, she was assigned as an Administrative Clerk to the 3rd Battalion 24th Marine Division, United States Marine Corps Reserves at Springfield, Missouri.

In March 1979, she augmented into the Marine Corps and reported on active duty to Headquarters and Headquarters Squadron 90, Marine Air Traffic Support Group 90 at Naval Air Station, Millington, Tennessee, to attend Aviation Electronics and Air Traffic Control Maintenance Schools, to become an Air Traffic Control Navigational Aids Repairman.

Her tours of duty as a Repairman/Technician include two tours at Marine Air Traffic Control Squadron 28, Marine Air Control Group 28, 2nd Marine Air Wing at New River, North Carolina; Station Operations and Maintenance Squadron, Ground Electronic Maintenance Squadron, Ground Electronic Maintenance Branch at Marine Corps Air Station, Kaneohe Bay, Hawaii; and Marine Air Traffic Control Squadron 18, Marine Control Group 18, Marine Corps Air Station Futenma in Okinawa, Japan. She participated in Solid Shield and supported Naval Air Landing Field Norfolk, Virginia, and the airfield on the island of Iwo Jima as the Senior Non-Commissioned Officer in Charge with Field Carrier Landing systems.

In February 1989, she graduated from Drill Instructor School at Marine Corps Recruit Training, Parris Island, South Carolina. She was assigned as a Drill Instructor and later a Senior Drill Instructor and Chief Drill Instructor. She returned to Headquarters and Headquarters Service 90, MATSG 90 at Naval Air Station, Millington, Tennessee, in August 1991 for duty as an Instructor at the Air Traffic Control Maintenance School.

In May 1995, she assumed the duties as First Sergeant and served tours with Headquarters Company, 7th Communications Battalion, III Marine Expeditionary Force, in Okinawa, Japan; the Electronics Maintenance Company, 3rd Maintenance Battalion, 3rd Force Service Support Group; and Company "O" and Company "P," with the 4th Recruit Training Battalion, Recruit Training Regiment, at Parris Island, South Carolina.

In July 1998, Sergeant Major Titus reported for duty as the Battalion Sergeant Major for the Support Battalion, RTR, Marine Corps Recruit Depot, in San Diego, California. In December 2000, she was assigned to Marine Tactical Air Command Squadron 38, 3rd Marine Air Wing, Miramar, where she served in Operation Enduring Freedom and Operation Iraqi Freedom. In July 2003, Sergeant Major Titus assumed the duties of the Marine Corps Detachment Sergeant Major, at Fort Leonard Wood, Missouri. In March 2005, she was assigned as the Marine Corps Systems Command Sergeant Major.

Tolbert, Jim
CHIEF WARRANT OFFICER 5—ARMY

After enlisting into the United States Army, he attended Basic Combat Training at Fort Knox, Kentucky. He completed Advanced Individual Training in MOS 76Y at Fort Lee, Virginia.

He was appointed as a Warrant Officer on March 31, 1984, after completing the Warrant Officer Candidate Course at Fort Rucker, Alabama. Since then, he has served in a variety of career enhancing assignments that include service as Battalion Supply Technician of the 223rd Aviation Battalion at Heilbrunn, Germany. During this assignment, in December 1990, he deployed to Saudi Arabia in support of Operation Desert Shield/Desert Storm. He also served as Property Book Team Chief and later Chief of the Asset Visibility Section Division at the Materiel Management Center of the 4th Infantry Division; Property Book Officer in the United States Army Central Command at Camp Doha Kuwait; Instructor/Writer at the United States Army Quartermaster Center and School; and Personnel Career Management Officer at the United States Total Army Personnel Command in Alexandria, Virginia.

CW5 Tolbert has completed every level of the Warrant Officer Education System. His military schooling includes the Warrant Officer Candidate Course; Supply and Service Management Officer Course; Standard Property Book System Course; Corps Supply Staff Officer Course; Warrant Officer Advance Course; Contracting Officer Representative Course; and the Warrant

Officer Senior Staff Course. He holds a bachelor's degree in Logistics Systems Management from Colorado
Technical University at Colorado Springs, Colorado.

On September 1, 2002, he assumed the position of
Regimental Warrant Officer at the United States Army
Quartermaster Center and School at Fort Lee.

Toney, Ian A.

COMMAND SERGEANT MAJOR—ARMY

He was born in the Republic of Trinidad and To-
bago and graduated from Bushwick High School in
Brooklyn, New York. He entered the United States
Army in February 1977 and attended Basic Training at
Fort Knox, Kentucky, and Advanced Individual Train-
ing at Fort Benjamin Harrison, Indiana.

Throughout his more than 27-year career, he has
held every key NCO leadership position from Squad
Leader to Platoon Group Command Sergeant Major,
culminating in his position as Command Sergeant
Major of the United States Army Finance Command.

Toney, Robert Lee

REAR ADMIRAL—NAVY

He was born in Monroe, Louisiana, and married the
former Flora J. Wallace of San Diego, California. They
have two daughters and one son. Admiral Toney attended Youngstown University in Youngstown, Ohio,
from 1952 to 1954, and in 1957 was graduated from
California State University, Chico, with a Bachelor of
Arts degree. Admiral Toney was commissioned an Ensign in the United States Navy Reserve on October 21,
1957. He completed the NATO Defense College in
1977. Admiral Toney's early Navy tours included duty
as the Assistant Communications Officer aboard the

USS *Bennington* (CVA-20); Staff Officer to the Com-
mander of Training Command, United States Pacific
Fleet; Operations Officer on USS *Guadalupe* (A-32);
Combat Information Officer on USS *Topeka* (CLG-8);
Senior Projects Officer for the Destroyer Development
Group, Pacific Fleet; Special Projects Officer for the
Commander of Cruiser-Destroyer Group, Pacific;
Executive Officer, Officer on USS *Cowell* (DD-547);
Special Assistant to the Chief of Naval Personnel in
Washington, D.C.; Commander of Navy Recruiting
Command for Minority Affairs (Recruiting); Execu-
tive Officer on USS *Wichita* (AOR-1); and command
of USS *Kiska* (AE-35). Admiral Toney also served on
the Staff of the Commander of Allied Forces, Southern
Europe, from August 1977 to April 1979, and as Chief
of Staff for the Commander of Service Group One from
April 1979 to March 1983. In August 1983, he became
Commanding Officer of the USS *Roanoke* (AOR-1).
Upon promotion to flag rank in August 1984, Admiral
Toney assumed duties as Deputy Commander of Naval
Surface Forces Pacific, in September 1984. In October
1985, he also assumed the additional duties as Com-
mander of Naval Surface Group, Long Beach. He as-
sumed command of Naval Base, San Francisco, and
Combat Logistic Group one in January 1986. In May
1988, Rear Admiral Toney was selected for promotion
to Rear Admiral (upper half). He was assigned as the
Director for Logistics and Security Assistance for
United States Pacific Command at Camp H.M. Smith,
Hawaii, in February 1989. He advises the Commander in Chief, United States Pacific Command, on all
matters dealing with the defense of the United States
through bilateral logistics agreements, cooperative
funds, logistic planning, transportation, civil engineering, and security assistance. His military awards and
decorations include the Legion of Merit; Defense

Meritorious Service Medal; Navy Meritorious Service Medal (second award), Navy Commendation Medal; Meritorious Unit Commendation; Armed Forces Expeditionary Meal; the Vietnam Service Medal (fifth award); Republic of Vietnam Campaign Medal; and the National Defense Service Medal.

Toomer, Daryll J.
SERGEANT MAJOR—MARINES

He enlisted in the United States Marine Corps in April 1980, and attended recruit training at Marine Corps Recruit Depot at Parris Island, South Carolina. In July 1980, he completed recruit training and was assigned to the Personnel Administration School at Parris Island.

In September 1988, he transferred to the 3rd Marine Aircraft Wing at Marine Corps Air Station, El Toro, California, where he served as the 3rd Marine Air Wing Personnel Chief; in October 1991, he transferred to Headquarters Marine Corps M&RA, MMEA, where he served as the Enlisted Orders Manager, the Enlisted Assignment Module Manager, the Recruit Distribution Module Manager and the Headquarters Recruiter Screening Team Module Manager in January 1993; in May 1997, he was transferred to Marine Corps Institute Company, Marine Barracks 8th & I, and assumed duties as the Company First Sergeant; in April 1999, he received orders to Marine Corps Security Forces Battalion; in May 1999, upon completion of Marine Corps Security Force Supervisor Course, he was transferred to Marine Corps Security Force Company, Bahrain, as a Company First Sergeant; in July 2000, he transferred to Headquarters and Service Company, Instructor Battalion, the Basic School, and assumed duties as the Company First Sergeant; in November 2001, he was transferred to Marine Corps Air Station Cherry Point, North Carolina, where he assumed duties as the First Sergeant Major of Naval Air Maintenance Training Marine Unit Cherry Point; and in July 2003, he received orders to MAG-14, 2nd Marine Aircraft Wing, and assumed duties as the Sergeant Major for Marine Tactical Electronic Warfare Squadron 2, Marine Aircraft Wing.

Toro, Herman
COMMAND SERGEANT MAJOR—ARMY

He was born in Brooklyn, New York. He entered the United States Army in 1976 as an Infantryman. His military and civilian education includes all the Non-commissioned Officer Education System Courses; Air Assault Course; Generator Operator Course; Jungle Warfare School; Organizational Supply Management Course; Joint Hazardous Material Packing Course; Strategic Mobility Course; Battle Staff Course; Instructor Training; Naval Senior Enlisted Academy; the United States Army Sergeants Major Academy; the Command Sergeants Major (D) Course; and the Garrison Command Sergeant Major Course. He earned an associate's degree in General Studies with Central Texas College and a bachelor's degree in Management/Health Care from Park University, Missouri.

His military assignments include serving as Platoon Sergeant of the 382nd Personnel Records Service Company at Fort Devens; Detachment Sergeant of the Personnel Service Company in Boeblingen, Germany; NCOIC VII Corps Non-divisional (IS) Data Base 7th Personnel Group, Germany; VII Corps Data Base Manager and Casualty Operations NCOIC during Operation Desert Shield/Storm; Personnel Sergeant of Law Enforcement Command at Fort Leonard Wood; First Sergeant of the United States Army Element at Brunnsum, Netherlands; and Command Sergeant Major of the 516th Personnel Service Battalion in Seoul, South Korea.

Trowell-Harris, Irene
MAJOR GENERAL—AIR FORCE

She received a Bachelor of Arts degree in Health Education (Cum Laude) from Jersey City State in New Jersey and a Master of Science degree in Public Health from Yale University in New Haven, Connecticut. She earned a Doctorate of Health Education, distinguished alumni, Columbia University, in New York, New York. She graduated from Columbia Hospital School of Nursing. Her military education includes the Air Command and Staff College; National Security Management Course, where she was a distinguished graduate; and the Air War College.

She was commissioned in the New York Air National Guard in April 1963, where she held the positions of Chief Nurse, Nurse, Administrator, Flight Nurse Instructor and Flight Nurse Examiner. She was appointed Commander of the 105th United States Air Force Clinic in Newburgh, New York, in March 1986, becoming the first Nurse in Air National Guard History to

command a Medical Clinic. She subsequently served on active duty, from July 1987 to February 1993, as Air National Guard Advisor to the Chief of the Air Force Nurse Corps. She was promoted to Colonel on June 16, 1988.

In February 1993, she served as Air National Guard Assistant to the Director of Medical Readiness and Nursing Services in the Office of the Surgeon General at the Headquarters of the United States Air Force in Washington, D.C. She was promoted to Brigadier General on October 25, 1993, becoming the first African American Female in the National Guard and Air National Guard to receive the General rank.

From September 1998 to September 2001, she served as the Air National Guard Assistant to the Director of the Air National Guard for Human Resources Readiness in Washington, D.C. She was promoted to Major General on September 1, 1998. She retired from the Air National Guard on September 29, 2001.

General Trowell-Harris became the first female in history to have a Tuskegee Airmen, Inc., Chapter named in her honor, the Major General Trowell-Harris Chapter, in Newburgh, New York. Her military awards and decorations include the Legion of Merit; Meritorious Service Medal; Air Force Outstanding Unit Award; Air Force Organizational Excellence Award (with one oak leaf cluster); National Defense Service Medal (with service star); Armed Forces Expeditionary Medal; Air Force Expeditionary Medal; Air Force Longevity Service Award Ribbon (with seven oak leaf clusters); Armed Forces Reserve Medal (with hourglass); Small Arms Expert Marksmanship Ribbon; and Air Force Training Ribbon.

Trower, Peter J., Jr.
SERGEANT MAJOR—MARINES

Sergeant Major Peter J. Trower, Jr., enlisted in the

United States Marine Corps on July 25, 1975. After completion of Recruit Training and Infantry Training School he was assigned to Company G, 2nd Battalion, 8th Marines, 2nd Marine Division at Camp Geiger in Jacksonville, North Carolina. In September 1976, he transferred to 1st Marine Brigade in Kaneohe Bay, Hawaii, where he was assigned to Company I, 3rd Battalion, 3rd Marines as an M-60 Machine Gun Team Leader. One year later, he was assigned as Machine Gun Section Leader and meritoriously promoted to the rank of Sergeant.

In May 1998, he was ordered to the 3rd Marine Aircraft Wing where he was assigned as the Sergeant Major of Marine Medium Helicopter Squadron 364. In May 2001, he was assigned to Marine Light Attack Helicopter Squadron 369 (Marine Aircraft Group II) and served as the Squadron Sergeant Major during the unit's deployment to Okinawa, Japan, in January 2002.

Tsikouris, Michael
COMMAND MASTER CHIEF—NAVY

Born in New York City, he enlisted in the Navy in 1975 and attended Recruit Training in Orlando, Florida. He went on to Great Lakes, Illinois, to complete Machinist's Mate "A" school and reported aboard the destroyer USS *Harold J. Ellison* (DD 864) in 1976 for his first sea tour.

His duty assignments include USS *Guam* (LPH 9); USS *Fulton* (AS 11); and USS *Coontz* (DDG 40), where he qualified as an Enlisted Surface Warfare Specialist. He was advanced to Chief Petty Officer in 1984, and began his first shore tour at Service School Command, Great Lakes, Illinois, as a Company Commander in the Integrated Training Brigade of Service School Command. In 1987, he was selected as Senior Chief Petty Officer, and in 1988, after graduating from the Senior Enlisted Academy in Newport, Rhode Island (Class 31); he reported aboard USS *America* (CV 66) where he was assigned to the Engineering Department. He advanced to Master Chief Petty Officer in 1991 and reported as Staff Engineer/Collateral Duty Command Master Chief for the Commander of Carrier Group Eight aboard USS *Theodore Roosevelt* (CVN 71). In July 2001, he assumed the duties of Command Master Chief on USS *Bataan* (LHD 5), and participated in Operation Enduring Freedom in Iraq. In January 2003, he was selected to assume the duties of Command Master Chief of Recruit Training Command at Great Lakes, Illinois. He assumed the duty of Command Master Chief in August 2003.

Tuck, Frank O.
SENIOR EXECUTIVE SERVICE

He entered the Air Force in 1970 after completing his Bachelor of Science degree in Mechanical Engineering at Tuskegee Institute, Alabama. While in the Air Force, he earned a master's degree in Business Administration from the University of Rochester, and then was assigned to Wright-Patterson Air Force Base as a Systems Acquisition Officer.

His education includes the Program Management Course of the Defense Systems Management College at Fort Belvoir, Virginia; Program for Senior Officials in National Security in the John F. Kennedy School of Government at Harvard University in Cambridge, Massachusetts; the Federal Executive Institute in Charlottesville, Virginia; Program Management Level III Certification; Senior Managers in Government, John F. Kennedy School of Government, Harvard University; and National Security Leadership Course at Johns Hopkins University in Baltimore, Maryland.

After leaving the Air Force, he entered federal civil service. He has managed and directed a variety of Air Force acquisitions programs including engine support equipment projects, numerous common and standard avionics programs, electronic warfare systems and major aircraft programs. He also has served as Director of Technology and Industrial Support at the Sacramento Air Logistics Center.

He served as the Director of the Air Combat System Program Office, Aeronautical Systems Center, Air Force Materiel Command at Wright-Patterson Air Force Base, Ohio. As director, his responsibilities include planning, acquisition and sustainment activities related to Air Combat Command.

Tucker, Hinton T.

SERGEANT MAJOR—MARINES

He enlisted into the United States Marine Corps in July 1962. He attended Recruit Training at Marine Corps Recruit Depot, Parris Island, South Carolina, and he completed Infantry Training School at Camp Geiger, North Carolina.

He has held every leadership position in the enlisted ranks, including serving as a Drill Instructor with the 3rd Recruit Training Battalion at Marine Corps Recruit Depot, San Diego, California; Chief Drill Instructor of the 1st Recruit Training Battalion at Marine Corps Recruit Depot, San Diego; First Sergeant for the Marine Detachment onboard USS *Kitty Hawk*; First Sergeant of C Company, Marine Corps Barracks, the Philippines; and First Sergeant for the Sea School and Staff Noncommissioned Officer at the Officer Schools at San Diego; He was selected to serve his first assignment as Sergeant Major at Marine Air Base Squadron–4 in Futema, Japan. In August 1990, he was assigned as the Sergeant Major of Marine Aircraft Group-16 which deployed in support of Operations Desert Shield/ Desert Storm.

Tull, Garry

COMMAND SERGEANT MAJOR—ARMY

He is a native of New Church, Virginia. He enlisted into the United States Army in 1978, and attended Basic Combat Training at Fort Gordon, Georgia. His military education includes all the Noncommissioned Officer Education System Courses; Master Fitness Course; Assignment Management PDNCO Course; Airborne School; COMSEC Custodian Course; MSE Nodal Management Course; Instructor Training Course; First Sergeant Course; the United States Army Sergeants Major Academy (class 51); and the Command Sergeants Major Course. He holds a bachelor's degree in Sociology from Paine College in Augusta, Georgia.

His key assignments include serving as a Platoon Sergeant; Instructor; Battalion Communications Chief; First Sergeant of Headquarters and Headquarters Com-

pany, 10th Transportation Battalion, at Fort Eustis, Virginia; and S-3 Sergeant Major of the 304th Signal Battalion at Camp Colbern, South Korea. During this assignment he was selected Command Sergeant Major.

Tunstall, Stanley Q.
COLONEL—ARMY

He is a native of Fayetteville, North Carolina. He attended Officer Candidate School at Fort Benning, Georgia, in 1981 and was commissioned as a Second Lieutenant in the Chemical Corps.

He holds a Bachelor of Science degree in Zoology from the University of Georgia and has earned a master's degree from the University of Southern California,

the Florida Institute of Technology, and the Naval War College.

His military education includes Chemical Officer Basic and Advanced Courses; Naval Command and Staff College; and a Senior Service College Fellowship at the United States Institute of Peace in Washington, D.C.

His first four was in Germany where he served as a Platoon Leader, Company Executive Officer, and Group Staff Officer. In 1986, he was assigned to the 75th Ranger Regiment and went on to command the Headquarters and Headquarters Company of the 4th Ranger Training Battalion, at Ranger Training Brigade. He was reassigned in 1990 to the Army Personnel Command in Alexandria, Virginia. After completing the Navy Command and Staff College in 1993, he went to Fort Bragg, North Carolina, where he was the Operations Officer (S3) in the 83rd Chemical Battalion and later served as the Assistant Division Chemical Officer of the 82nd Airborne Division. This assignment was followed by a two-year tour on the Combined and Joint Staff of United States Forces, Korea. From 1997 to 1999, he commanded the 83rd Chemical Battalion at Fort Bragg. Following battalion command, he returned to the Army Personnel Directorate. Most recently, he served in the Pentagon in the Office of the Deputy Under Secretary of Defense for Technology Security Policy and Counterproliferation. In October 2004, he was serving as the Commander of the 45th Corps Support Group.

Turner, Abraham J.
MAJOR GENERAL—ARMY

He received a Bachelor of Science degree in Music from South Carolina State University, and a Master of Public Administration from Shippensburg University. His military education includes Infantry Officer Basic and Advanced Courses; the United States Army Command and General Staff College; and the United States Army War College.

His military career began on June 2, 1976, when he received a commission as a Second Lieutenant from the ROTC program at South Carolina State University. His first military assignment was in November 1976, as Executive Officer, later as Commander, of Company B of the 1st Battalion, 1st Advanced Individual Training Brigade, at the United States Army Infantry Center at Fort Benning, Georgia. In August 1978, he was assigned as an Instructor with the 3rd Ranger Company at Fort Benning Ranger Division, Ranger Department, United States Army Infantry School at Fort Benning. In June 1980, he was assigned as the S-4 (Supply Officer), later as Commander, with the 2nd Battalion, 505th Infantry, 82nd Airborne Division, at Fort Bragg, North Carolina. In April 1982, he was selected to serve as Schools Commandant, G-3, with the 82nd Airborne Division at Fort Bragg. From September 1983, he served as Assistant Professor of Military Science in the 1st Reserve Officer Training Corps Region, with duty at South Carolina State College at Orangeburg, South

bat Infantryman Badge; Expert Infantryman Badge; Master Parachutist Badge (with combat star); Pathfinder Badge; and Ranger Tab.

Turner, Archie L.
COMMAND SERGEANT MAJOR—ARMY

Command Sergeant Archie L. Turner is a native of Miami, Florida. He earned an associate's degree in Liberal Arts from the University of Maryland. He is currently pursuing a bachelor's degree in Business Administration.

He entered the United States Army in January 1973. He attended Basic Training at Fort Knox, Kentucky, and Advanced Individual Training at Fort Ord, California.

His military education includes Air Assault School; Garrison Sergeants Major Course; CGSC Force Integration/Development Course; Noncommissioned Officer Logistics Program (LP); First Sergeants Course; Battle Staff Course; the United States Army Sergeants Major Academy; and the Command Sergeants Major Designee Course.

He was assigned as Sergeant Major of the J-3, Equipment Authorization/Force Development, at Forces Command at Fort McPherson, Georgia, and United States Army Central Command at Fort Force, Kuwait; as Command Sergeant Major with the 3rd United States Army Central Command at Fort McPherson, Georgia; as the Command Sergeant Major for the 129th Corps Support Battalion, 101st Corps Support Group, at Fort Campbell, Kentucky; as the Command Sergeant Major for the 34th Area Support Group and Area II at Yongsan, South Korea; and as the Command Sergeant Major at the 19th Theater Army Area Command in Taegu, South Korea. In February 2000, he departed

Carolina. In June 1987, he was assigned as the S-4 (Supply Officer), 1st Battalion (Mechanized), 5th Infantry, 2nd Infantry Division, in South Korea. He returned to the 82nd Airborne Division to serve as S-4 (Supply); Executive Officer; Deputy G-3 (Operation); and Commander. In June 1995, he was assigned as Regimental Tactical Officer at the United States Military Academy at West Point, New York. From December 1996 to December 1998, he served as the Commander of the Infantry Training Brigade of the United States Army Infantry School at Fort Benning. On September 1, 1996, he was promoted to Colonel.

In December 1998, he served as Chief for the Joint Exercise and Training Division, J-7, of the Joint Staff in Washington, D.C. From February 2000 to April 2001, he served as a Special Assistant to the Assistant to the Chairman of the Joint Chiefs of Staff at the Pentagon. From April 2001 to June 2002, he served as Chief of the House Legislative Liaison Division in the Office of the Chief of Legislative Liaison for the United States Army in Washington, D.C. In June 2002, he was selected to serve as the Assistant Division Commander (Operations) of the 82nd Airborne Division at Fort Bragg. He was promoted to Brigadier General on October 1, 2002. On March 28, 2005, he was selected to serve as Deputy Chief of Staff for Operations and Training in the United States Army Training and Doctrine Command at Fort Monroe, Virginia.

From June 2003 to January 2004, he served as Assistant Chief of Staff, C-3, Coalition Forces Land Component Command at Camp Doha, Kuwait. In January 2004, he was selected to serve as Commanding General of the United States Army Training Center and Fort Jackson, South Carolina.

His military awards and decorations include the Defense Superior Service Medal; the Legion of Merit; Bronze Star; Meritorious Service Medal; Army Commendation Medal; Army Achievement Medal; Com-the 19th TAACOM to take the Senior Enlisted position at the Defense Logistics Agency.

Turner, Guthrie L.
BRIGADIER GENERAL—ARMY

He was born in Chicago, Illinois. He received a Bachelor of Science degree in Biology from Shaw University in 1949, Doctor of Medicine degree from Howard University in 1953, and a master's degree in Public Health from Harvard University in 1966. Military schools attended include the Medical Service School Advanced Course; the United States Army Command and General Staff College; and the United States Army War College. He was promoted to First Lieutenant on June 23, 1953. He was promoted to Captain on February 10, 1956, and was promoted to Major on March 20, 1962. He has held a wide variety of important command and staff positions, including the following key assignments. From January 1965 to August 1965, he served as assistant Chief of the Department of Aviation Medicine at Lyster Army Hospital at Fort Rucker, Alabama. From September 1965 to June 1966, he was a student at Harvard School of Public Health in Boston, Massachusetts. On April 18, 1966, he was promoted to Lieutenant Colonel. From July 1966 to June 1968, he was a Resident in Aerospace Medicine at the United States Air Force School of Aerospace Medicine at Brooks Air Force Base, Texas. From June 1968 to June 1969, he served as the Commander of the 15th Medical Battalion and Surgeon, 1st Cavalry Division (Airmobile) in Vietnam. From August 1969 to July 1972, he served as the Commander of Beach Army Hospital and Surgeon (later Chief), Medical Activities Division, United States Army Primary Helicopter Center and School, at Fort Wolters, Texas. From August 1972 to July 1974, he was assigned as a Surgeon with the

VII Corps in Europe. From July 1974 to July 1976, he was assigned as the Commander of the 130th General Hospital in Europe. He served as a consultant for aviation medicine in the Office of the Surgeon General in Washington, D.C., from 1976 to March 1978. He was then assigned as the Commander of the United States Army Medical Command in Korea; and Surgeon for the United Nations Command, the United States Forces Korea and the Eighth United States Army. On May 9, 1980, he was promoted to the rank of Brigadier General, becoming the Commanding General of the Madigan Army Medical Center in Tacoma, Washington. He retired on July 31, 1983. His numerous military awards and decorations include the Distinguished Service Medal; the Legion of Merit; the Air Medal; Army Commendation Medal; Master Parachutist Badge; and the Senior Flight Surgeon Badge.

Turner, Hershel L.
COMMAND SERGEANT MAJOR—ARMY

He entered the United States Army in July 1979. He completed Basic Combat Training and Advanced Individual Training at Fort Sill, Oklahoma.

His military and civilian education includes all the Noncommissioned Officer Education Systems Courses; Drill Sergeant School; Air Assault School; Master Fitness School; First Sergeant Course; and the United States Army Sergeants Major Academy. He holds an associate's degree in General Studies from Pikes Peak Community College.

He has served in numerous leadership positions from Howitzer Section Chief to Command Sergeant Major. His assignments include Gunner and Howitzer Section Chief of B Battery, 2nd Battalion, 18th Field Artillery; Howitzer Section Chief of A Battery, 1st Battalion, 10th Field Artillery; Drill Sergeant of B Battery, 1st Battalion,

19th Field Artillery; Gunnery Sergeant of B Battery, 2nd Battalion, 11th Field Artillery; Chief of Firing Battery for A Battery, 2nd Battalion, 11th Field Artillery; First Sergeant of 4th Battalion, 82nd Field Artillery; First Sergeant of Headquarters and Headquarters Service Battery, 2nd Battalion, 2nd Field Artillery; Senior Enlisted Instructor of Reserves Officer Training Corps (ROTC) at Kent State University; Command Sergeant Major of 3rd Battalion, 30th Field Artillery; Command Sergeant Major of 2nd Battalion, 15th Field Artillery; Command Sergeant Major for the Division Artillery at Schofield Barracks, Hawaii; and Command Sergeant Major for White Sands Missile Range, New Mexico.

Turner, Joseph Ellis
MAJOR GENERAL—ARMY

He was born in Charleston, West Virginia. He is the son of Joseph Turner and Annetta Frances Malone. He and his wife, Norma Jean, have three children, Dr. Alan T., Brian D., and Joseph E., Jr. Upon completion of high school, Turner attended West Virginia State College where he graduated and received his ROTC commission as a Second Lieutenant in 1961. Upon entering the Army, he attended the Signal Officer's Basic Course. Later he graduated from the Aviation Fixed and Rotary Wing courses, the Command and General Staff College, the Industrial College of the Armed Forces (National Security Management Course), and the Air War College of the Armed Forces (National Security Management Course). He has completed the Federal Aviation Administration's Air Traffic Indoctrination Course, the University of Southern California's Aviation Safety and Management at the University of Utah. His active duty assignments include two tours of duty in Vietnam, where he served as a Fixed Wing Aviator in the 17th Aviation Company, 1st Air Cavalry Division; Signal Officer with the 17th Aviation Group; and Commander of Headquarters Company, 210th Combat Aviation Battalion. He also served as a Fixed Wing Aviator for the Third United States Army, Aviator and Communications Officer with the 187th Airplane Company, and Signal Platoon Leader, 1st Battle Group, 29th Infantry. As an Army Aviator, he compiled more

than 3000 hours of military flight time. He began his military career as a Reserve Officer in January 1961, and was appointed a Regular Army Officer in April 1966. His principal Reserve assignments have included Commander of the 335th Signal Group and the 3283rd United States Army Reserve Forces School. In the 81st United States Army Reserve Command, he served as Deputy Chief of Staff for Logistics, Deputy Chief of Staff for Resources Management, Operations/Training Officer, Aviation Safety Officer, and Communication/Electronics Officer. In March 1988 he was promoted to Brigadier General. In March 1988, he was assigned as Deputy Commander of the 335th Signal Command in East Point, Georgia. He became the first black Georgia reservist and the first black in the 81st United States Army Reserve Command to be promoted to general officer rank. In 1988, he was inducted into the Georgia Hall of Fame. In September 1991, he was assigned as the Commander of the 335th Signal Command. On May 21, 1992, General Turner was promoted to Major General. He is employed by Delta Airlines, where he serves as captain on L1011 aircraft. He is a member of the Reserve Officer Association, the Signal Corps Association, the Armed Forces Communications/Electronics Association, the Airline Pilot's Association, and the organization of black Airline Pilots. His military awards and decorations include the Bronze Star (with oak leaf cluster); Meritorious Service Medal (with oak leaf cluster); the Air Medal (with ten oak leaf clusters); Army Commendation Medal (with oak leaf clusters); the Army Achievement Medal; Presidential Unit Citation (1st Air Cavalry Division); Army Reserve Components Achievement Medal (with three oak leaf clusters); National Defense Service Medal; Vietnam Service Medal (with eight bronze service stars); Armed Forces Reserve Medal; Army Service Ribbon; Vietnam Gallantry Cross with Palm Unit Citation Badge; and Vietnam Campaign Medal (with Device and Master Army Aviator Badge).

Tutt, Veronica
COMMAND MASTER CHIEF—NAVY

She was born in Augusta, Georgia, and entered the

United States Navy TAR program in 1978 as a Store-keeper Seaman and attended Storekeeper "A" School at the Naval Air Technical Training Center in Meridian, Mississippi.

Her key military assignments include in 1990 she transferred to Inshore Undersea Warfare Group One in San Diego as the Logistics Supervisor Chief Petty Officer. In 1993, she was selected to attend the United States Army Sergeants Major Academy at Fort Bliss, Texas. After completion of the academy, she transferred to Readiness Command Region Nineteen where she received her master's degree in Human Resource Management and selected for Master Chief Petty Officer. In 1995, she requested sea duty onboard USS *John F. Kennedy* (CV 67). There she served in various divisions within the Supply Department, including being the Supply Department Leading Chief. During her tour at sea, she earned both her Surface Warfare and Air Warfare qualifications. In 1998, she was selected to the Command Master Chief program and attended the Senior Enlisted Academy in Newport, Rhode Island. She reported to Naval and Marine Corps Reserve Center Jacksonville, Florida, after completion of the academy as the Command Master Chief.

She moved to New Orleans in February 2000, to serve as the Senior Enlisted Advisor and Assistant Department Director at the Naval Reserve Personnel Center. She assumed duties as Naval Reserve Readiness Command Southeast's Command Master Chief in September 2003.

Tyree-Hyche, Ida
CHIEF WARRANT OFFICER—ARMY

Chief Tyree-Hyche is a native of Tuscaloosa, Alabama, where she graduated Magna Cum Laude from Stillman College. She has also earned a Juris Doctorate degree in General Law from Birmingham School of Law in Birmingham, Alabama.

She has served over twenty-seven years in Federal Civilian employment and 30 years in the United States Army Reserves. Her military education includes the

Leadership and Development Course; Personnel Managers Course; the Warrant Officer Advanced Course; Staff Judge Advocate's Course for Federal Labor Advocate's; Staff Officer Action Course; the Organizational Leadership Course for Executives.

She has served in numerous leadership assignments including serving as a Family Readiness Branch and Replacement Operations Personnel Warrant for the 3rd Personnel Command in Jackson, Mississippi; and positions within the Office of the Deputy Chief of Staff for Personnel (DCSPER) (G-1), at the 81st RSC.

Tyson, Lynda K.
SERGEANT FIRST CLASS—ARMY

She is the recipient of the NAACP's Roy Wilkins Meritorious Service Award, given to the United States Military members who distinguish themselves by contributing to military equal opportunity policies and programs.

"While assigned at the 704th Military Intelligence Brigade at Fort George G. Meade, Maryland, she consistently strived for better understanding between people through educational and service programs," her award citation noted.

She is a founding member of the Joint Services Black Heritage Committee, a nonprofit organization at Fort Meade that raises money to feed the homeless in local shelters and to provide scholarships for local high school students.

She also helped organize Fort Meade's first Juneteenth celebration (June 19 is celebrated in Texas and parts of the South in observance of the day in 1865 when slaves in Texas were proclaimed free). She directed her unit's first Women's Equality Day observance and participated in the Black History Month outreach programs of various Maryland district schools and the "Adopt-A-School" program.

She initiated a "Pact for Life" program that provides a free ride home for soldiers who have had too much to drink.

Tzomes, C. A. Pete
CAPTAIN—NAVY

He is a native of Williamsport, Pennsylvania. He attended the State University of New York before graduating from the United States Naval Academy and receiving a commission as an Ensign in June 1967, one of only two blacks to graduate that year. He is a graduate of the Navy's one year Nuclear Power Training program at Vallejo, California; Submarine Training at the Naval Submarine School in Groton, Connecticut; and Engineer Officer School.

He has served as a trailblazer for black Americans in his naval career. His assignments include the history-making assignment as the first black American to serve as the Commander of a Nuclear Submarine, commanding the USS *Houston* (SSN-713) until May 1986. In June 1986, he became Force Operations Officer on the Staff of the Commander for Submarine Forces, United States Pacific Fleet, and in June 1990, he was selected

to serve as the Director of the Equal Opportunity Division of the Naval Military Personnel Command and the Personnel Advisor to the Chief of Training Command at Great Lakes.

Valentin, Eleanor V.
CAPTAIN—NAVY

She is a native of Seattle, Washington. After receiving a Bachelor of Science degree in Zoology and Psychology from the University of Washington, she completed a master's degree in Public Health (Health Policy and Planning) and a Master of Science degree in Public Health (Biostatistics) at the University of Hawaii.

Following graduation she became a health planner with the Santa Clara County Health Systems Agency in California.

In 1982, she was commissioned as a Lieutenant Junior Grade in the Medical Service Corps of the United States Navy, and for the next decade she managed a variety of administrative officer positions. Those assignments included Assistant Head of the Outpatient Administrative Department and Assistant to the Director for Administration at the Naval Hospital in San Diego, California; Administrative Officer for the Admiral J.T. Boone Branch Medical Clinic in Norfolk, Virginia; as Department Head of Operating Management and Facilities at the Naval Medical Clinic in

Norfolk, Virginia; as Department Head of the Manpower Management Department at the United States Naval Hospital in Guam; as the Administrative Officer of the Armed Forces Institute of Pathology in Washington, DC; and as the Department Head of the Quality Management Department at the United States Naval Hospital in Yokosuka, Japan. She supervised the Naval Medical Clinic Administration Department in Pearl Harbor, Hawaii, as the Director from 1994 until 1997. She then reported to the Bureau of Medicine and Surgery and became the Branch Head for TRICARE Marketing and Communications. In October 2000, Captain Valentin took over as the director for Regional Operations in the Office of the Secretary of Defense (Health Affairs) TRICARE Management Activity. There she led staff and joint service teams in developing plans and strategies to implement statutory and policy guidance for the delivery of healthcare services to eligible beneficiaries worldwide. She was the TRICARE Management Activity's primary liaison and advisor to 11 CONUS and three OCONUS TRICARE Regional Offices. Her responsibilities included initiating actions to enhance the Military Health System's operational efficiency, through integration of several multi-billion dollar purchased healthcare care contracts with healthcare provided in DoD military treatment facilities. In June 2005, Captain Valentin was serving as the Executive Officer of the Naval Hospital at Corpus Christi, Texas.

Varnado, Frederick E.
LIEUTENANT COLONEL—ARMY

He was born in Magnolia, Mississippi. He graduated from Alcorn State University, receiving a Bachelor of Arts degree in Political Science and earned a Master of Arts degree in Personnel Management and

Administration from Central Michigan University. His military education includes the Infantry Officer's Basic and Advanced Schools; the Airborne School; Jungle Warfare School; Military Intelligence School; Combined Arms Service and Staff School; and the Command and General Staff College.

He has held numerous staff and command assignments including serving as Squad Leader; Platoon Leader; Company Commander; Battalion Commander; Chief of Intelligence Analysis and Production Section with the 179th Military Intelligence; G-2 Officer with the 1st Armored Division in Ansbach, Germany; Executive Officer of the Foreign Intelligence Directorate of the Office of the Deputy Chief of Staff for Intelligence (ODCSINT); and Assistant Executive Officer at ODCSINT Headquarters in the Department of the Army at the Pentagon.

Varnado, Sheila
COLONEL—ARMY

She is a native of Cleveland, Ohio, and was commissioned into the United States Women's Army Corps at Fort McClellan, Alabama, after receiving her master's degree from Syracuse University. After completing her Basic Military Training, she was branched into the Adjutant General's Corps, where she has served the full spectrum of command and staff assignments during her career.

In July 1997, she became the first African American and first female to serve as a Professor of Military Science and Commander of the University of Southern Mississippi Army Reserve Officer Training Corps Battalion. In July 1999, she was reassigned to the 3rd United States Army stationed at Fort Stewart, Georgia. She and her daughter deployed in support of Operations Iraqi Freedom, working just a building apart at Camp Doha, Kuwait. Colonel Varnado was assigned to the Headquarters of Combined Forces Land Component Command in Camp Doha.

She is married to retired Lieutenant Colonel Fred Varnado.

Vaught, Ralph J.
SERGEANT MAJOR—MARINES

He enlisted in the United States Marine Corps in April 1979. In September 1979, he attended Recruit Training with the 2nd Recruit Training Battalion at Marine Corps Recruit Depot, Parris Island, South Carolina.

His key military assignments include serving as a Drill Instructor; Senior Drill Instructor; and Regimental Drill Master. In September 1996, he was reassigned to Inspector and Instructor Staff on the Fourth Supply

Battalion, Fourth Force Service Support Group, Marine Forces Reserve in Albany, Georgia, as the First Sergeant; in November 1997, he was transferred to Marine Aerial Refueler Squadron 252, where he was assigned as Squadron Sergeant Major, until his reassignment to Marine Wing headquarters; and in November 1998, he was reassigned to Marine Tactical Air Command Squadron 28 until he departed in April 2001. He reported to Marine Wing Headquarters Squadron during May 2001, and in April 2002 was reassigned to the 12th Marines Regiment as its Sergeant Major.

Via, Dennis L.
BRIGADIER GENERAL—ARMY

On September 15, 1980, he received an ROTC commission to Second Lieutenant in the United States

Army. His military and civilian education includes Signal Officer Basic and Advanced Courses; the United States Army Command and General Staff College; and the United States Army War College. He holds a Bachelor of Science degree in Industrial Arts from Virginia State University and a Master of Engineering degree in Human Resources from Boston University.

He has held a variety of command and staff assignments, including S-3 (Operations), later Executive Officer, of the 82nd Signal Battalion, 82nd Airborne Division at Fort Bragg, North Carolina; Commander of the 82nd Signal Battalion, 82nd Airborne Division at Fort Bragg; Deputy Assistant Chief of Staff, G-6, III Corps at Fort Hood, Texas; Chief of the Joint Requirements Oversight Council Management Division in the Office of the Deputy Chief of Staff, G-8, United States Army, Washington, D.C.; and Deputy Director for Operation (D3) in the Defense Information Systems Agency at Arlington, Virginia. On March 28, 2005, he was selected to serve as Commanding General of the 5th Signal Command/Deputy Chief of Staff, G-6, United States Army, in Germany.

His military awards and decorations include the Legion of Merit; the Defense Meritorious Service Medal (with oak leaf cluster); Meritorious Service Medal (with four oak leaf clusters); Army Commendation Medal (with oak leaf cluster); Joint Service Achievement Medal; Master Parachutist Badge; and the Army Staff Identification Badge.

Vines, Joe L.
SERGEANT MAJOR—MARINES

He is a native of Spring Hope, North Carolina, and enlisted in the Marine Corps in June 1980. After completing Boot Camp at Parris Island, South Carolina, he attended Infantry Training School at Camp Pendleton, California. Upon graduating, he was selected for sea duty. He was the Honor Graduate at Sea School

and he was meritoriously promoted to Private First Class. He was then assigned to the Marine detachment aboard the USS *Midway*, where he served as a Sentry, Corporal, Sergeant of the Guard, Squad Leader, Section Leader and Non-Commissioned Officer in Charge of the ship's Color Guard.

He attended the Drill Instructor School and served as Sea School Instructor; Drill Instructor; Regimental Drill Master; Marine Corps Recruit Depot Drill Instructor with Company C of the 1st Battalion, 1st Marines with Company C; First Sergeant of the Drill Instructor School; and Sergeant Major of 3rd Battalion, 5th Marines.

Voorhees, John H.
MAJOR GENERAL—AIR FORCE

He was born in New Brunswick, New Jersey, he married the former Jeanine Carter, and they have two children, Melanie Shemyne and John Carter. He was graduated from New Brunswick High School in 1954. He received a Bachelor of Science degree in Chemistry from Rutgers University in 1958 and a master's degree in Management from the University of Southern California in 1967. He was designated a senior executive fellow of Harvard University in 1981. The general completed Squadron Officer School in 1962 and the National War College in 1983. He received his commission in 1958 as a distinguished military graduate of the Air Force Reserve Officer Training Corps program at Rutgers. He then completed navigator training at James Connally Air Force Base, Texas, and Mather Air Force Base, California. From April 1960 to June 1966, he was a B-52 Navigator with the 668th Bombardment Squadron at Griffiss Air Force Base, New York. He then entered the Air Force Institute of Technology program and completed his master's degree at the University of

Southern California. In June 1968 the general joined the 14th Tactical Fighter Squadron at Ubon Royal Thai Air Force Base, Thailand, as an F-4 Navigator systems operator. During this assignment, he flew 176 combat missions, including 100 over North Vietnam. Upon returning to the United States in May 1969, he was assigned to the Space and Missile Systems Organization headquarters at Los Angeles Air Force Station as Chief of the Systems Effectiveness Branch and later as Chief of the Test Support Division. After graduation from the National War College in June 1973, he remained in Washington, D.C., as a research and development planner in the Organization of the Joint Chiefs of Staff. Moving to Wright-Patterson Air Force Base in July 1976, Voorhees was initially assigned as Chief of the Strategic Plans Division, then as Director of Plans at the Air Force Logistic Command Headquarters. From July 1979 to May 1981, he was Chief of the B-52 and Missile Systems Management Division of Oklahoma City Air Logistic Center at Tinker Air Force Base, Oklahoma. He then became Director of Materiel Management for the Sacramento Air Logistics Center at Mc-Clellan Air Force Base, California. In August 1982, he took command of the Defense Contract Administration Services Region in Los Angeles. He was assigned as Deputy Director of Logistic and Security Assistance, J4/7, at the Headquarters of European Command at Vaihingen, West Germany, in June 1984. In August 1986, he assumed command of the Defense Personnel Support Center of the Defense Logistics Agency in Philadelphia. He was promoted to Major General on June 1, 1986. In January 1990, he became Deputy Chief of Staff for Contracting and Manufacturing in the Headquarters of Air Force Logistics Command at Wright-Patterson Air Force Base, Ohio. His duties include management of an $11 billion contracting program in support of the command's logistics mission. Air Force Logistics Command annually completes almost 450,000 contracting actions that support the United States Air Force as well as more than 70 friendly foreign air forces under the foreign military sale program. He is a master navigator with 3,000 flying hours in the B-52 and F-4C.

Walker, Larry D.
COMMAND SERGEANT MAJOR—ARMY

He is a native of Sparta, Georgia, and has over 25 years of active military service in the Army. His military education includes all the Noncommissioned Officer Education System Courses; the First Sergeant Course; and the United States Army Sergeants Major Academy (class 50). He holds an Associate of Arts degree in General Studies from Central Texas College and a Bachelor of Science degree from Excelsior College.

His military assignments include serving as a Maintenance Support Team Supervisor, Maintenance Control Supervisor, Inspector, Platoon Sergeant, Instructor, Small Group Leader, Support Operation NCOIC and First Sergeant. He was assigned to Aberdeen Proving Ground, Maryland, with the 143rd Ordnance Bat-

talion from September 1989 to October 1992, as Instructor and Small Group Leader. He served in 3rd COSCOM, 71st Corps Support Battalion from December 1992 to June 1999, as Platoon Sergeant, Maintenance Control Supervisor, Support Operations NCOIC and First Sergeant. He was assigned to the 21st Theater Support Command, 51st Maintenance Battalion from July 2001 to August 2004, as the Battalion Command Sergeant Major. In January 2005, he was serving as the Command Sergeant Major for the 29th Support Group.

Walker, Ted
COMMAND SERGEANT MAJOR—ARMY

He entered the Army's Delayed Entry program in January 1973, with a reporting date of June 21, 1973, to Basic Training at Fort Knox, Kentucky, and Advanced Individual Training at Fort Ord, California.

His military education includes Airborne and Jumpmaster School; Ranger School; Jungle Warfare Training Course; the Master Fitness Course; Drill Sergeant School; First Sergeants Course; the United States Army Sergeants Major Course (class 46); and all the U.S. Army Noncommissioned Officer Education System Courses. He holds a Bachelor of Science degree from Troy State University in Resource Management.

His military assignments include serving at Banderhauf Kaserne, Germany, as a Motor Transport Operator and Repair Parts Section Leader and on several tours at Fort Benning, Georgia, in various duty positions ranging from Platoon Sergeant and Senior Drill Sergeant for Infantry One Station Unit Training to Ranger Instructor, Light Leader Instructor, First Sergeant and acting Command Sergeant Major for the 4th Ranger Training Battalion. In 2004, he was serving at Fort Drum, New York, where he served as Battalion Command Sergeant Major and the 1st Brigade's Command Sergeant Major.

Walker, Tyler, II
COMMAND SERGEANT MAJOR—ARMY

Command Sergeant Major Tyler Walker II is a native of Pensacola, Florida. He graduated from Washington High School in June 1971 and attended Central Texas College. He entered the United States Marine Corps in December 1972 and attended Basic and Advanced Infantry training at Parris Island, South Carolina. In October 1974, he joined the United States Army.

His military education includes completing all the Noncommissioned Officer Education System Courses; Drill Sergeant School; the First Sergeant Course; and the United States Army Sergeant Major Academy.

He has served in a variety of positions including Installation Command Sergeant Major, Section Sergeant, Platoon Sergeant, Drill Sergeant, Correctional Custody NCOIC, and First Sergeant.

He served as the Command Sergeant Major for the United States Army Material Command Installation.

Walker-Kimbro, Carolyn
SENIOR EXECUTIVE SERVICE

She entered the federal civil service in 1984. She has held a variety of positions in several Comptroller disciplines, including disbursement accounting, budget and cost analysis, and financial management.

Her education includes receiving a Bachelor of Arts in Languages/Political Science from Tougaloo College, Mississippi, in 1973 and a master's in Public Administration from Tennessee State University in Nashville, Tennessee. Her military schools include the Disbursement Accounting Specialist Technical Training at Sheppard Air Force Base, Texas, in 1975; Officer Training School at Lackland Air Force Base, Texas, in 1979; and Professional Military Comptroller School at Maxwell Air Force Base, Alabama, in 1990.

In June 1992, she served as Supervisory Budget Analyst Chief in the Operations and Maintenance Division Directorate of Financial Management at the Headquarters Air Force Materiel Command at Wright-Patterson Air Force Base, Ohio. In February 1993, she became Supervisory Budget Analyst, Chief of the Defense Business Operations/Cost Policy Branch, and Chief of the Materiel Support Division Financial Management Branch of the Air Force Working Capital Fund in the Directorate of Financial Management Headquarters Air Force Materiel Command at Wright-Patterson Air Force Base. In August 2000, she was Chief, Special Project Division in the Directorate of Financial Management Headquarters Air Force Materiel Command at Wright-Patterson Air Force Base. In January 2003, she was selected to serve as the Director of the Comptroller Directorate at Warner Robins Air Logistics Center at Robins Air Force Base, Georgia.

As Director, she is responsible for the management and oversight of all appropriated and working capital funds. She oversees and assures budgets, financial analysis, cost analysis/studies and fund distributions are accomplished in a timely manner and that financial execution is in accordance with public law. She is responsible for the commitment accounting and reporting of financial transactions. She serves as a focal point for de-

termining funding propriety and directs the training assignments and career broadening/development for the financial management career field.

Wallace, Johnny A.
COMMAND SENIOR CHIEF—NAVY

He was born and raised in Birmingham, Alabama, and enlisted into the United States Navy under the delayed entry program in January 1983. He completed Basic Recruit Training with honors at Recruit Training Command, Orlando, Florida, in August 1983 and graduated from Ship's Serviceman "A" School at Meridian, Mississippi, in September 1983.

He served aboard USS *Blue Ridge* (LCC 19), forward deployed Flag Ship to COMSEVENTHFLT as Assistant Sales Officer and interim Supply Department Leading Chief Petty Officer. He was Sales and Services Supervisor aboard USS *Dwight D. Eisenhower* (CVN 69), and served in USS *Raleigh* (LPD-1), and USS *John F. Kennedy* (CV 67). During his career he completed a total of ten deployments to the Arabian Gulf, Western Pacific, North Atlantic, Mediterranean and Middle East.

Ashore, he served as Basic Qualification Course Instructor at the Navy Supply Corps School at Athens, Georgia, and Course Supervisor Ship's Serviceman "A" NTTC at Meridian, where he earned his designation as Master Training Specialist. He was also assigned to NRD Richmond, Virginia, as a Production Recruiter.

Waller, Calvin Agustine Hoffman
LIEUTENANT GENERAL—ARMY

He was born in Baton Rouge, Louisiana. He received a Bachelor of Science in Agriculture from Prairie View A&M University and a Master of Science in Public

Administration from Shippensburg State University. He entered the United States Army in August 1959 as a student in the Infantry Officer Base Course at the United States Infantry School at Fort Benning, Georgia. In June 1961, he was assigned as Commander of the 247th Chemical Platoon at Fort Lewis, Washington. On July 30, 1962, he was promoted to First Lieutenant. From June 1963 to August 1963, he was a student at the United States Army Chemical Center and School at Fort McClellan, Alabama. He was promoted to Captain on July 29, 1963. From December 1963, to June 1964, he served as the Chief of the Chemical, Biological, and Radiological Center at the Office of the Assistant Chief of G-2/G-3, 7th Logistics Command, Eighth United States Army, in Korea. From February 1965 to April 1967, he served as a Chemical Officer of the Headquarters and Headquarters Company; and later as Brigade Chemical Officer, of the 2nd Brigade, 82nd Airborne Division at Fort Bragg, North Carolina. He was promoted to Major on September 5, 1967. From July 1968 to May 1969, he was a student at the United States Army Command and General Staff College at Fort Leavenworth, Kansas. From May 1969 to May 1970, he was assigned as a Chemical Operations Officer in the Chemical Operations Division in the Office of the Assistant Chief of Staff, J-3, United States Military Assistance Command in Vietnam. From May 1970 to April 1971, he was Personnel Management Officer in the Schools Division of the Personnel Actions Section, Chemical Branch Officer Personnel. From April 1971 to July 1972, he served as a Training Staff Officer in the Policy and Programs Branch of the Office of the Deputy Chief of Staff for Personnel, United States Army, in Washington, D.C. On June 1, 1975, he was promoted to Lieutenant Colonel. From August 1975 to May 1977, he was Commander of the 1st Battalion, 77th Armor, 4th Infantry Division (Mechanized) at Fort Carson, Colorado. From August 1977 to June 1978, he was a student at the United States Army War College, Carlisle Barracks, Pennsylvania. From July 1980 to June 1981, he was Senior Military Assistant in the Office of Assistant Secretary of Defense (Manpower, Reserve Affairs and Logistics) in Washington, D.C. On August 1, 1980, he was promoted to Colonel. From August 1983 to December 1983, he served as Chief of Staff for the 24th Infantry Division (Mechanized) at Fort Stewart, Georgia. From December 1983 to June 1984, he was Chief of Staff of the XVIII Airborne Corps at Fort Bragg. He was promoted to Brigadier General on November 1, 1984. From July 1986 to July 1987, he served as Deputy Commanding General of I Corps and the Commanding General of the 8th Infantry Division (Mechanized), V Corps, United States Army, Europe, and Seventh Army. On November 1, 1987, he was promoted to Major General. From August 1989 to November 1990, he was the Commanding General of Fort Lewis, and I Corps. He was promoted to Lieutenant General on August 3, 1989. In November 1990, he was named Deputy Commander-in-Chief of Central Command (Forward) during Op-

eration Desert Storm in Saudi Arabia. From March 1991 to November 1991, he returned as the Commanding General of Fort Lewis. His military awards and decorations include the Distinguished Service Medal (with oak leaf cluster); Defense Superior Service Medal; the Bronze Star (with oak leaf cluster); Meritorious Service Medal (with three oak leaf clusters); the Air Medal; Army Commendation Medal; Master Parachutist Badge; Secretary of Defense Identification Badge; Army Staff Identification Badge.

Walls, George H., Jr.
BRIGADIER GENERAL—MARINES

He was born in Parkesburg, Pennsylvania. He married the former Portia Diane Hall of Ahoskie, North Carolina. They have three sons, George III, Steven, and Kevin. He was graduated from West Chester State College in 1964 with a Bachelor of Science in Education and was commissioned in 1965 upon completion of Officer Candidate School at Quantico, Virginia. He earned a master's in Education from North Carolina Central University at Durham in 1975. In 1966, following completion of the Basic School at Quantico and the Combat Engineer Officer Course at Camp Lejeune, North Carolina, he reported to the 3rd Engineer Battalion, 3rd Marine Division in Vietnam. His assignments included Platoon Commander and Assistant Operations Officer for the Battalion. He was promoted to First Lieutenant in October 1966. Returning to the United States in 1967, he served as a Platoon Commander and Company Executive Officer with the 2nd Engineer Battalion, 2nd Marine Division, at Camp Lejeune. During this assignment, he was promoted to

Captain in July 1967. He was later assigned to duty as Senior Instructor with the Combat Engineer Instruction Unit of the Marine Corps Engineer School. He was transferred to the Headquarters of the 4th Marine Corps District in Philadelphia, Pennsylvania, where he served as an Officer Selection Officer and Assistant Head of the Personnel Procurement Branch. He next served aboard the USS *Franklin D. Roosevelt* (CVA 42) as Commanding Officer of a Marine detachment. In 1972, General Walls was assigned duty as Marine Officer Instructor of the NROTC Unit at the North Carolina Central University. He also served for two years as the unit's Executive Officer. He was promoted to Major in August 1974, and while in this assignment completed his requirements for a Master of Arts degree. From 1975 to 1976, he was a student at the Command and Staff College at Quantico. Upon completion of the school, he reported to the Marine Corps Engineer School at Camp Lejeune where his assignments included. Assistant School Director, Director of Instruction, and Commanding Officer of the Engineer Equipment Instruction Company. He was assigned as the Marine Corps representative at the United States Army Engineer School at Fort Belvoir from 1980 to 1982, and was promoted to Lieutenant Colonel in August 1980.

Walton, Michael L.
LIEUTENANT COLONEL—ARMY
Lieutenant Colonel Michael L. Walton is a graduate

and completed the ROTC program at Eastern Kentucky University. He was commissioned as a Signal Corps Second Lieutenant and earned his Bachelor of Arts degree in Speech Communications and Human Relations and in Public Relations in 1982. He returned to Eastern Kentucky and in 1992 earned his Master of Science degree in Recreation and Parks Administration with emphasis in Outdoor Recreation.

His military educations includes Command and General Staff College; the Combined Arms Service School; the Signal Officers Basic and Advanced Courses; the Adjutant General Officer Advanced Course; Combat Signal Officer Course; the Information Officer Course; and the NATO Nuclear—Biological Staff Officer Course. In 2001, he became one of a few selected by the Army to participate in the Department of Defense (DOD) Course in Communications at the University of Oklahoma. He was also selected to attend the Army's Management Staff College and the Senior Public Affairs Officer Course.

His most recent assignments include serving as the First Emerging Media Team Chief in the Army Reserves, with the 88th Regional Support Command at Fort Snelling, Minnesota. He is currently serving as the Commander of the 318th Public Affairs Operations Center (PAOC) at Forest Parks, Illinois, and is part of the 88th Regional Support Command.

Ward, William Edward
GENERAL—ARMY
He was born in Baltimore, Maryland. He earned a Bachelor of Arts degree in Political Science from Morgan State University and a Master of Arts degree in Political Science from Pennsylvania State University. His military education includes the Infantry Officer Basic and Advanced Courses; the United States Army Command and General Staff College; and the United States

Army War College. He was commissioned a Second Lieutenant on June 6, 1971. In September 1971, he was assigned as a Rifle Platoon Leader, and later an Executive Officer, with Company A, 3rd Battalion, 325th Infantry, 82nd Airborne Division, at Fort Bragg, North Carolina. He was promoted to First Lieutenant on October 9, 1972. From December 1972 to May 1974, he served as an Anti-Tank Platoon Leader, later as Motor Officer, with the 3rd Battalion, 325th Infantry, 82nd Airborne Division, at Fort Bragg; from May 1974 to October 1974 he was the Liaison Officer with the 2nd Brigade, 82nd Airborne Division, at Fort Bragg, North Carolina; in October 1974, he was assigned as a Rifle Platoon Leader with Company B, 1st Battalion (Mechanized), 17th Infantry, 2nd Infantry Division, Eighth United States Army, South Korea; and in April 1975, he was selected Commander of Company C, 1st Battalion (Mechanized), 17th Infantry, 2nd Infantry Division, Eighth United States Army, South Korea. He was promoted to Captain on June 9, 1975. From April 1976 to December 1976, he was a student in the Infantry Officer Advanced Course at the United States Army Infantry School at Fort Benning, Georgia. From December 1976 to November 1978, he was a student at Pennsylvania State University at University Park, Pennsylvania. From November 1978 to April 1982, he was an Instructor of Social Sciences, later Assistant Professor, in the Department of Social Sciences at the United States Military Academy at West Point, New York. From April 1982 to June 1983, he was a student at the United States Army Command and General Staff College in Fort Leavenworth, Kansas. He was promoted to Major on January 1, 1983. In August 1983, General Ward was assigned as the S-4 (Logistics) for the 210th Field Artillery Brigade, VII Corps, United States Army Europe and Seventh Army, Germany. In May 1985, he served as Executive Officer of the United States Army Military Community Activity-Aschaffensberg, United States Army Europe and Seventh Army, Germany. From June 1986 to June 1987 he was assigned as Executive Officer with the 1st Battalion (Mechanized), 7th Infantry, 3rd Infantry Division, United States Army Europe and the Seventh Army, Germany. From July 1987 to October 1988, he was assigned as a Staff Officer (Logistics), in the Office of the Deputy Chief of Staff for Logistics, United States Army, in Washington, D.C. From October 1988 to September 1990, he served as the Commander of the 5th Battalion, 9th Infantry, 2nd Brigade, 6th Infantry Division (Light), at Fort Wainwright, Alaska. He was promoted to Lieutenant Colonel on February 1, 1989. His next assignment was also at Fort Wainwright, as the G-4 Staff Officer (Logistics) of the 6th Infantry Division (Light Infantry). From August 1991 to June 1992, he was a student at the United States Army War College at Carlisle Barracks, Pennsylvania; and from June 1992 to June 1994, he was Commander of the 2nd Brigade, 10th Mountain Division (Light Infantry) at Fort Drum, New York, later Mogadishu, Somalia, later Fort Drum, New York. He was promoted to Colonel on June 1, 1992. From July

1994 to July 1995, he served as Executive Officer to the Vice Chief of Staff for the United States Army in Washington, D.C., and from July to September 1996, he served as Deputy Director for Operations at the National Military Command Center, J-3, The Joint Staff, at Pentagon. He was promoted to Brigadier General on April 1, 1996. General Ward was assigned as the Assistant Division Commander for the 82nd Airborne Division at Fort Bragg in September 1996. In February 1998, he was assigned as Chief in the Office of Military Cooperation at the American Embassy in Egypt. He was promoted to Major General on February 1, 1999. From July 1999 to November 2000, he served as the Commanding General of the 25th Infantry Division (Light) and United States Army, Hawaii at Schofield Barracks, Hawaii. From November 2000 to October 2002, he served as the Vice Director for Operations, J-3, The Joint Staff, in Washington, D.C. In October 2002, he was selected to serve as the Commander of the Stabilization Force for Operation Joint Forge. He was promoted to Lieutenant General on October 8, 2002. In November 2003, he was assigned as the Deputy Commanding General/Chief of Staff of the United States Army Europe and Seventh Army. He was promoted to General in May 3rd 2006.

His military awards and decorations include the Distinguished Service Medal: the Defense Superior Service Medal (with oak leaf cluster); the Legion of Merit (with two oak leaf clusters); the Defense Meritorious Service Medal; Meritorious Service Medal (with six oak leaf clusters); Joint Service Commendation Medal; Joint Service Commendation Medal; Army Commendation Medal (with three oak leaf clusters); Army Achievement Medal (with oak leaf cluster); the Combat Infantryman Badge; Expert Infantryman Badge; Master Parachutist Badge; the Joint Chiefs of Staff Identification Badge; and the Army Staff Identification Badge.

Ware, Earl L.

COMMAND SERGEANT MAJOR—ARMY

Command Sergeant Major Earl L. Ware was born on April 23, 1952, in Leland, Mississippi. He joined the Army on November 27, 1974, and attended Basic Training at Fort Jackson, South Carolina, and Advanced Individual Training at Fort Benjamin Harrison, Indiana. His military education includes, all NCOES level courses, including the Sergeants Major Academy, the Battle Staff Noncommissioned Officer Course, the Command Sergeants Major Designee Course and the Garrison Sergeant Major Course. He is currently pursuing his Bachelor of Science degree in Business Administration.

He has served in a variety of leadership positions including First Sergeant of Special Activities at Fort Myers, Virginia; First Sergeant of Headquarters and Headquarters Company, 8th PERSCOM, at Camp Coiner, South Korea; G-1 (Personnel NOCIC) Sergeant Major with the 101st Infantry Division (Air Assault) at Fort Campbell, Kentucky; and Command Sergeant Major of the 38th Personnel Services Battal-

ion at Bamburg, Germany. He is currently serving as the Installation Command Sergeant Major at Fort Meade, Maryland.

Ware, Ezell, Jr.
BRIGADIER GENERAL—ARMY

He was born Critchin, Alabama. He graduated from Magee High School in Mississippi in 1959. He received a Bachelor of Arts degree in Government from California State University in Sacramento, California. He

earned a master's degree in Human Resources Management from Troy State University in Montgomery, Alabama. His military schools attended include Aviation School, Warrant Officer Rotary Wing Aviation Course (1967); Infantry School, Infantry Officer Basic Course (1969) and Advanced Course (1974); Aviation School, OH-58 Instructor Pilot Course (1970); Naval Air Station, Combined Service Support School (1970); Fort MacArthur, Combat Intelligence Staff Officers Course (1973); Defense Race Relations Institute, Race Relations/Equal Opportunity Development Courses (1974) and (1975); Command and General Staff College; and the National Defense University, Reserve Components National Security Course. His military service began in October 1959, when he enlisted as a Private in the United States Marine Corps. He transferred to the United States Army in 1966, and attended the United States Army Aviation School as a Warrant Officer Candidate. Upon completion of Warrant Flight Training in 1967, he was assigned to the 61st Assault Helicopter Company as a Helicopter Gunship Pilot and served in South Vietnam. Upon returning from the combat tour, he was assigned to the Air troop, 2nd Armored Cavalry Regiment, 2nd Armored Division in West Germany. Upon his return from Germany, Colonel Ware was commissioned in October 1969 as a First Lieutenant in the Infantry Branch and assigned to the 291sr Aviation Company at Fort Sill, Oklahoma. In July 1970, he was assigned to the 2nd Infantry Division, where he served as Standardization Instructor Pilot (SIP) with the 2nd Aviation Battalion in South Korea. In 1972, Colonel Ware was assigned to the 101st Airborne Division, where he served as the Assistant Division Aviation Officer. He joined the California Army National Guard in November 1973, and was assigned as a Command Helicopter Pilot with the 49th Aviation Battalion in Stockton, California. He was transferred to the Office of the Adjutant General in Sacramento in 1974, where he held the positions of Equal Opportunity Officer, Personnel Officer, Comptroller, Selective Services Officer, Movement Officer and Chief Operations Officer. Between March 1985 and April 1987, he served as Battalion Commander with 49th Military Police Battalion. In May 1987, he was again assigned to the Office of the Adjutant General where he served as Logistics Officer. In September 1989, he was assigned as Executive Officer with 49th Military Police Brigade, and in January 1990, he was assigned as Deputy Brigade Commander. In June 1990, Colonel Ware was selected to attend the Air War College at Maxwell Air Force Base, Alabama, and graduated in July 1991. After a brief tour as Assistant Chief of Staff Army Division, he resumed his position of Deputy Commander of the 49th Military Police Brigade. On October 1, 1994, he assumed the position of Commander of the 49th Military Police Brigade. On April 28, 1999, he was selected to serve as Chief Assistant Adjutant General for the California National Guard. He was also promoted to the rank of Brigadier General. His military awards and decorations include: Meritorious

Service Medal (with two oak leak clusters); Air Medal (with twelve oak leaf clusters); Army Commendation Medal (with two oak leaf clusters and a V Device for Valor); National Defense Service Ribbon; Vietnam Service Medal; Vietnam Campaign Medal; Overseas Service Bar; Vietnamese Cross of Gallantry with Palm; Armed Forces Expeditionary Medal (Korea); and Army Campaign Achievement Medal (3rd Award).

Ware, Larry
BRIGADIER GENERAL—ARMY

He received an Associate of Arts degree in Business Administration from Northwood Institute and a Bachelor of Arts degree in Business Administration, also from Northwood Institute. His military education includes Air Defense Artillery Officer Basic Course at Air Defense School; Chemical, Biological and Radiological Course at the Armor Center; Military Police Officer Advance Course at Military Police School; Command and General Staff College; Senior Officer's Preventive Logistics Course at Armor School; and Military Police Doctrine Refresher Course at the Military Police School.

His military career began in November 1, 1972, when he received an OCS commission to Second Lieutenant. In November 1972, he was assigned as Assistant S3 at the Headquarters and Headquarters Battery of the 1st Battalion, 177th Air Defense Artillery, in the Michigan Army National Guard. In June 1973, he was assigned as Fire Control Platoon Leader with Battery C, 1st Battalion, 177th Air Defense Artillery, Michigan Army National Guard. In August 1974, he as Assistant S3, at the Headquarters at Headquarters Detachment of the 146th Military Police Battalion, Michigan Army National Guard. From May 1977 to July 1979, he was assigned as the S-4 (Supply Officer), later S-1 (Personnel Officer), at the Headquarters and Headquarters Detachment of the 147th Military Police Battalion, Michigan Army National Guard. In July 1979, he was assigned as the Race Relations and Equal Opportunity Officer, later Prisoner of War/Confinement Officer, later Prisoner of War Officer and later Maintenance Staff Officer, at the Headquarters and Headquarters Company of the 177th Military Police Brigade, Michigan Army National Guard. From April 1987 to September 1990, he was assigned as Battalion Commander of the 146th Military Police Battalion, Michigan Army National Guard. In September 1990, he served as Provost Marshal at the Area Command Headquarters for the Michigan Army National Guard. He was promoted to Colonel on January 1, 1991. From August 1992 to September 1995, he served as Deputy Commander at Headquarters and Headquarters Company for the 177th Military Police Brigade, Michigan Army National Guard. From September 1995 to September 1998, he served as the Commander of Headquarters and Headquarters Company of the 177th Military Police Brigade, Michigan Army National Guard. He was promoted to Brigadier General on July 2, 1996. He retired from the Army National Guard on September 28, 1998.

His military awards and decorations include the Meritorious Service Medal; Army Commendation Medal (with two bronze oak leaf clusters); Army Achievement Medal (with one bronze oak leaf cluster); Army Reserve Component Achievement Medal (with three bronze oak leaf clusters); National Defense Service Medal (with one bronze service star); Armed Forces Reserve Medal (with one hourglass device); Army Service Ribbon; and Army Reserve Components Overseas Training Ribbons (with numeral one).

Washington, Arthur L.
COMMAND SERGEANT MAJOR—ARMY

Command Sergeant Major Arthur L. Washington is a native of Philadelphia, Pennsylvania, and enlisted the Army in 1980. He earned an associate's degree and is pursuing a bachelor's degree in Management. His military education includes the Drill Sergeant Course; the First Sergeant Course; and the United States Army Sergeants Major Academy.

His most recent assignments include serving as Drill Sergeant/Senior Drill Sergeant with the 1/31st Field Artillery; as a Radio Teletype Section Chief and Signal Center Platoon Sergeant with the 11th Air Defense Battalion in Darmstadt, Germany; as a Wire Team Chief with the 2/7th Cavalry Mechanized Infantry at Fort Hood, Texas; and as a Tactical Wire Operations Specialist with the 6/14th Field Artillery in Nuremburg, Germany. He is currently serving as the Command Sergeant Major for the 141st Signal Battalion in Germany.

Washington, Bette R.
COLONEL—ARMY

She served as Group Commander of the 501st Corps Support Group in 2002. She entered the Army Quartermaster Corps in 1980 after receiving a degree in Economics from Alcorn State University at Lorman, Mississippi. She received her graduate degree in Food Marketing and Distribution (Agricultural Economics) from Cornell University in Ithaca, New York, in 1989.

Her military education includes the Quartermaster Officer Basic and Advanced Courses, the Combined Arms Service and Staff School, the Support Operations Course, the Command and General Staff College and the United States Army War College.

Washington, George K.
COLONEL—ARMY

He was commissioned in the Transportation Corps in 1979, upon graduation from Virginia State University with a Bachelor of Science degree in Business Administration. He also earned a master's degree in Business Administration from Saint Martin's College. In addition to the Transportation Basic and Advanced Courses, Colonel Washington's military education includes the Strategic Mobility Planning Course; Airborne Supply and Service Course; United States Army Command and General Staff College; and the Industrial College of the Armed Forces, where he earned a master's degree in National Resource Strategy.

His key military assignments include serving as Chief of the Transportation Team with Readiness Group at Fort Lewis, Washington; Commander of the 2nd Combat Service Support Battalion, 191st Infantry Brigade at Fort Lewis; Commander of the 6th Transportation Battalion at Fort Eustis, Virginia; Chief of Army Directorate and Chief of Agreements and Operations Directorate with the Office of Defense Cooperation Turkey in Ankara, Turkey; Director of Combat Developments Transportation and with the United States Army CASCOM at Fort Lee, Virginia. In October 2004, he was serving as Commander of the 20th Support Group.

Washington, Major
COMMAND SERGEANT MAJOR—ARMY

He enlisted into the United States Army on October 13, 1976. He attended Basic Combat Training at Fort Knox, Kentucky.

His military and civilian education includes the Air Assault Course, Basic Airborne Course, all the Noncommissioned Officer Courses, Drill Sergeant Course, First Sergeant Course, and the United States Army Sergeant Major Academy (class 49). He holds an Associate of Arts degree in Criminal Justice from Pikes Peak College.

He has held every noncommissioned leadership position in the Army, including Squad Leader, Section Sergeant, Platoon Sergeant, First Sergeant, and Operation Sergeant Major. His assignments include A Troop, 2nd Squadron, 9th Calvary at Fort Stewart, Georgia; 24th Infantry Division Noncommissioned Officer Academy at Fort Stewart; and 1st Battalion, 39th Infantry Division (Mechanized) at Baumholder, Germany. He has also served as Command Sergeant Major of the 1st Battalion, 81st Armor ("Red Lions") at Fort Knox, Kentucky, and Command Sergeant Major with the Cadet Command Eastern Region Headquarters at Fort Knox.

Washington, Perry K.
COMMAND SERGEANT MAJOR—ARMY

He is a native of Foley, Alabama. His military education includes completion of all the Noncommissioned Officer Education System Courses, the Unit Supply Course, Communication Language Program, Senior Leadership Course, and the United States Army Sergeants Major Academy.

His military assignments include Fort Jackson, South Carolina; Fort Lee, Virginia; Fort Knox, Kentucky; Fort Leavenworth, Kansas; Fort Hood, Texas; and Fort Carson, Colorado. His overseas tours include Germany, Japan, Alaska and South Korea.

He serves as the Command Sergeant Major of the United States Army Operations Support Command.

Watkins, Gregory
COMMAND SERGEANT MAJOR—ARMY

He was born in Danville, Georgia, on June 23, 1960. He entered the United States Army in November, 1978, and attended Basic Combat Training and Advanced Individual Training at Fort Leonard Wood, Missouri.

His military education include completing Noncommissioned Officers Leadership Courses; First Sergeant Course; Drill Sergeant School; Pathfinder School; Master Fitness Course; and the United States Army Sergeants Major Academy.

He has held every key leadership position including Team Leader; Squad Leader; Drill Sergeant; Platoon Sergeant; Operations Sergeant; and First Sergeant. In August 2004, he was serving as Command Sergeant Major for the 2nd Brigade, 3rd Troops Battalion, 3rd Infantry Division (Mechanized), at Fort Stewart/ Hunter Army Airfield.

Watkins, John Marcella, Jr.
BRIGADIER GENERAL—ARMY

He was born in Evergreen, Alabama, and married the former Doris Bryant. They have two children, Monica and Daphne. He received a Bachelor of Science degree in Industrial Management from Tuskegee University in 1966 and a Master of Business Administration from the New York Institute of Technology in 1976. His military schooling include the Signal School Basic (1966) and Advanced Course (1969); the United States Army Command and General Staff College (1975); the Defense Systems Management College (1979); and the Industrial College of the Armed Forces (1984). From June 1966 to August 1966, he was a student at the Signal Officer Basic Course of the United States Army Signal Center and School at Fort Gordon, Georgia. From December 1966 to September 1967, he was assigned as a Radio Platoon Leader, Company B, 50th Signal Battalion (Airborne) at Fort Bragg, North Carolina. He was promoted to First Lieutenant on 30 May 1967. From September 1967 to April 1968, he was assigned as a Communications Platoon Leader, later Signal Officer, Headquarters and Headquarters Company, 11th Infantry Brigade, United States Army in Vietnam. From April 1968 to November 1968, he served as the Commander of Company C, 523rd Signal Battalion, United States Army in Vietnam. He was promoted to Captain on 30 May 1968. From February 1969 to November 1969, he was a student in the Signal Officer Advanced Course at the United States Army Signal Center and School at Fort Gordon. From January to December 1970, he was a student in the Communications Systems Engineer Course at the United States Army Signal School at Fort Monmouth, New Jersey. From January 1971 to June 1973, he was assigned as Project Officer of the Tactical Data Systems Branch, Communications Support Branch, United States Army Combat Developments Command Communications Electronics Agency at Fort Monmouth. From July 1973 to June 1974, he was assigned as a Radio Officer at Headquarters of the Eighth United States Army in South Korea. He returned to the United States in August 1974, as a student in the United States Army Command and General Staff College at Fort Leavenworth, Kansas. In June 1975, he was assigned as Personnel Management Officer at the United States Army Military Personnel Center at Alexandria, Virginia. He was promoted to Major on June 10, 1975. From April 1978 to April 1979, he served as Executive Officer for the 122nd Signal Battalion, 2nd Infantry Division, United States Army, in South Korea. From July 1979 to December 1979, he was a student in the Program Management Course at the Defense Systems Management College at Fort Belvoir, Virginia. He moved to Fort Hood, Texas, in December 1979, where he was assigned as the Assistant Corps Communications-Electronics Officer with the 3rd Signal Brigade, III United States Corps. He was promoted to Lieutenant Colonel on August 13, 1979. From July 1980 to November 1982, he served as the Commander of the 16th Signal Battalion, and later in November 1982, he became the Deputy Commander of the 3rd Signal Brigade, at Fort Hood. In June 1984, he was a Student in the Industrial College of the Armed Forces at Fort McNair in Washington, D.C. From June 1984 to February 1985, he was assigned as Deputy Director (J-6) for Communications on the Armed Forces Presidential Inaugural Committee at Fort McNair. In February 1985, he moved to the Pentagon where he was assigned as Chief of the Plans Division, Office of the Assistant Chief of Staff for Information Management. He was promoted to Colonel on October 1, 1985. From July 1986 to November 1988, he was the Commander of the 11th Signal Brigade, United States Army Information Systems Command, at Fort Huachuca, Arizona. From November 1988 to November 1990, he served as Secretary for the Military Communications Electronics Board, J-6 the Joint Staff in Washington, D.C. From November 1990 to September 1992, he served as Commanding General of the United States Army Information Systems Engineering Command/Program Manager for Army Information Systems at Fort Huachuca. He was promoted to Brigadier General on February 1, 1991. From September 1992 to July 1993, he served as Deputy Commanding General of the United States Army Information Systems Command at Fort Huachuca. In July 1993, he was assigned as the Director for Defense Information Services Organization, Defense Information Systems Agency, in Arlington, Virginia. He retired from the military on August 31, 1995. His military awards and decorations include the Defense Superior Service Medal; Legion of Merit (with oak leaf cluster); the Bronze Star; Defense Meritorious Service Medal; Meritorious Service Medal (with four oak leaf clusters); Army Commendation Medal; Parachutist Badge; the Joint Chiefs of Staff Identification Badge; and the Army Staff Identification Badge.

Watkins, Michael J.
SERGEANT MAJOR—MARINES

He was born in Quitman, Georgia. He entered the Marine Corps in July of 1978 at Parris Island, South Carolina, and was assigned as a Rifleman. After completing Recruit Training and the School of Infantry, he was assigned to Marine Barracks 8th & I in Washington, D.C., as a member of the Marine Corps Color Guard. In May 1981, he was meritoriously promoted to the rank of Sergeant and became the first black Color Sergeant of the Marine Corps.

In May of 1983, he went into the Aircraft Training Operation Program and became a 6018 and Engine Mechanic for the OV10 Bronco Aircraft and was transferred to VMO-2, Camp Pendleton, California. There, he deployed several times to Marine Aircraft Group–36 in Okinawa, Japan. He was then reassigned to Marine Aircraft Group–46 at Naval Air Station Atlanta (Marietta) Georgia. There he served as the flight line supervisor and a quality assurance representative for the OV10 aircraft.

In August of 1989, he was assigned to VMO-1 Marine Corps Air Station New River at Jacksonville, North Carolina. There his squadron deployed to Saudi Arabia for duty. During the Gulf War he received a Meritorious Combat Promotion to the rank of Gunnery Sergeant for his superior performance. After returning from the Gulf War he was reassigned to the Marine Corps Recruit Depot, Parris Island South Carolina for duty as a Drill Instructor. There he held the billets of Drill Instructor, Senior Drill Instructor, Series Gunnery Sergeant and Squad Instructor at the Drill Instructor School.

After his tour on the drill field he was transferred to Marine Corps Security Forces where he was assigned to the Marine Detachment USS *Carl Vinson* as the Guard Chief. In October of 1995 he was promoted to the rank of First Sergeant and was assigned back to Marine Corps Recruit Depot at Parris Island South Carolina. There he served as the First Sergeant for Headquarters Company; Headquarters and Support Battalion; Company First Sergeant for Hotel Company Second Recruit Training Battalion; and as the Chief Instructor for Drill Instructor School. On April 30, 1999, Sergeant Major Watkins was frocked to his present rank of Sergeant Major and was transferred to the 3rd FSSG, 3rd Medical Battalion at Okinawa for duty as the Battalion Sergeant Major.

In July of 2000 Sergeant Major Watkins was reassigned to the 3rd Reconnaissance Battalion, 3rd Marine Division, in Okinawa as the Battalion Sergeant Major.

During June of 2002 Sergeant Major Watkins was transferred to the Marine Corps Recruiting Command, where he served as the Recruiting Station Sergeant Major for Recruiting Station New Orleans, Louisiana.

Watson, Anthony John

REAR ADMIRAL—NAVY

He was born in Chicago, Illinois. He married the former Sharon Shires Waddell of Chicago, and they have two daughters, Erica Elena and Lindsay Ruth. He earned a Bachelor of Science degree in Naval Science from the United States Naval Academy. His military schools include Naval Recruit Training Command; Naval Nuclear Power School; and Naval Submarine School. He was commissioned an Ensign in the United States Navy on June 3, 1970. From July 1970 to October 1970, he was at Naval Recruit Training Command Chicago, Illinois. From October 1970 to April 1971, he was a student at the Naval Nuclear Power School, NTC, at Bainbridge, Maryland (DUINS). From April 1971 to November 1971, he was assigned as an AEC Schenectady Naval Reactors Officer and Nuclear Power Training Unit at Windsor, Connecticut (DUINS). He was promoted to Lieutenant (junior grade) on September 3, 1971. From November 1971 to December 1971, he was a student at the Naval Submarine School at Groton, Connecticut. From December 1971 to March 1974, he served with USS *Snook* (SSN 592) as Damage Control Assistant. From March 1974 to April 1975, he served with USS *Robert E. Lee* (SSBN 601) (Blue) as

Electrical Division Officer. He was promoted to Lieutenant on July 1, 1974. From April 1975 to December 1976, he served as Commander of Submarine Squadron One as Material Officer. From December 1976 to June 1977, he was a student in the Naval Submarine Squadron School in Groton, Connecticut (DUINS). From June 1977 to October 1980, he served with the USS *Archerfish* (SSN 678) as the Engineering Officer. He was promoted to Lieutenant Commander on September 1, 1978. From October 1980 and March 1982, he was assigned as an Instructor at the Naval Submarine School in Groton. He was released from active duty on March 22, 1982. On October 17, 1983, he reported for active duty in the United States Naval Reserve. From October 1983 to January 1984, he served on the USS *Birmingham* (SSN 695) as a Combat Systems Officer. From January 1984 to February 1984, he was a student at the Naval Submarine School at Groton. From March 1984 to December 1986, he was assigned as the Deputy Commander of USS *Hammerhead* (SSN 663). He was promoted Commander on May 1, 1984. From December 1986 to April 1987, he served in the Department of Energy with the United States Naval Reactors. From April 1987 to June 1987, he served as the Commander with Submarine Force of the United States Atlantic Fleet (DUINS). From September 1987 to November 1987, he served as the Deputy Commander for Training with Comsubron Eight. From November 1987 to November 1989, he was assigned to USS *Jacksonville* (SSN 699). From November 1989 to March 1992, he served as the Deputy Commander of the United States Naval Academy at Annapolis, Maryland. He was promoted to Captain on September 1, 1990. From March 1992 to August 1993, he served as the Commander of

Submarine Squadron Seven. On August 1, 1993, he was designated Rear Admiral (lower half) while serving in billets commensurate with that grade. In Aug 1993, he was selected as the Deputy Director for Operations at the National Military Command Center, J-3, (NMCC-5), Joint Staff. On October 1, 1994, he was promoted to Rear Admiral (lower half). In July 1995, he was assigned as Commander of the Navy Recruiting Command. His military awards and decorations include the Legion of Merit; Meritorious Service Medal (with three gold stars); Navy Commendation Medal (with two gold stars); Navy Achievement Medal; Navy Unit Commendation (with one bronze star); Navy "E" Ribbon; the Navy Expeditionary Medal; the National Defense Medal (with one bronze star); the Vietnam Service Medal (with two bronze stars); Sea Service Deployment Ribbon; the Navy Arctic Service Ribbon; Expert Rifleman Medal; and Expert Pistol Shot Medal.

Watson, Larry James

CAPTAIN—NAVY

He is the second of ten children born to Alonzo and Pearline Watson. He graduated from the United States Naval Academy, class 1975. His postgraduate education includes Master of Science degrees in Management (Material Logistics) from Naval Postgraduate School (1987) and National Security Strategy from the National War College (1997).

His sea duty assignments include Main Propulsion Assistant in USS *Manltowoc* (LST 1180), 1976–1979; Flag Lieutenant for the Commander of Cruiser-Destroyer Group Twelve, 1979–1981; Engineer Officer in USS *John L. Hall* (FFG 32), 1982–1985; Executive Officer in USS *Aubrey Fitch* (FFG 34), 1987–1989; Commanding Officer in USS *Flatley* (FFG 21), 1992–1994; and Commanding Officer of USS *Pelellu* (LHA 5), 1999–2001.

His shore assignments include serving as Director for the Chief of Naval Operations and APOS's Broadened Opportunity for Officer Selection and Training (BOOST) Program in San Diego, California, 1989–1991; as Deputy Assistant Chief of Staff for Operations on the Staff of the Commander of United States Naval Forces and Central Command/Commander of the United States Fifth Fleet at Manama, Bahrain, 1994–1996; as Assistant Chief of Staff for the Readiness and Training on the Staff of the Commander of Amphibious Group Two at Little Creek, Virginia; as Head Officer for Plans and Policy (N131) on the staff of the Chief of Naval Operations at Navy Annex, Washington, D.C.; and as Commanding Officer of Naval Reserve Officer Training Corps (NROTC) Consortium at Houston and Professor of Naval Science at Rice University and Prairie View A&M University.

Weary, Joey A.

CHIEF MASTER SERGEANT—AIR FORCE

Weary serves as the Marketing Superintendent at the Headquarters of the Air Force Recruiting Service. He develops, formulates, and implements national-level

policies, programs and procedures. He provides marketing guidance in support of the Enlisted Accessions, Officer Accessions and Air Force Reserve Officer Training Corps.

He also monitors and coordinates day-to-day marketing activities of four recruiting groups and 28 recruiting squadrons nationwide. He has direct oversight of marketing training programs used to prepare squadron commanders, superintendents, and front line recruiters. He prepares briefings, staff documents, and critical background material for senior Air Education and Training Command and Department of the Air Force Staff.

He provides Senior Noncommissioned Officer Leadership over all functional and operational marking activities within Air Force Recruiting Service.

He holds a Bachelor of Science degree in Occupational Education from Wayland Baptist University and an associate's degree in Personnel Administration and Education and Instructional Technology from the Community College of the Air Force. He is also a graduate of the Air Force Senior Noncommissioned Officer Academy.

Weatherington, Lisa D.

COLONEL—ARMY

She is a native of Petersburg, Virginia, and in 1978 earned a Bachelor of Arts degree from Saint Augustine's College. She received a Master of Science degree in Personnel Management in 1983 from Troy State University.

Her military education includes the Army Medical Department Basic and Advanced Courses; the Military Personnel Officer's Course; the Personnel Management Officer Course; the Staff Service School; the Army Command and General Staff College; Personnel Management for Executive Course; and Fundamentals of Systems Acquisition Management.

She entered the Army as a Medical Service Corps

Office in 1978. She graduated Magna Cum Laude from St. Augustine's and was designated a Distinguished Military Graduate upon graduation from ROTC. She has enjoyed a variety of assignments as Battalion Personnel Officer at Fort Polk, Louisiana; Hospital Adjutant and Company Commander at Fort Rucker, Alabama; Clinic Administrator in Germany; Medical Department Recruiter Administrative Officer in Washington, D.C.; Personnel Management Officer and Executive Officer in South Korea; Deputy Division Chief, PERSCOM, at Alexandria, Virginia; Health Policy Analyst and Force Management Officer at Falls Church, Virginia; Chief Operating Officer at the Rader Health Clinic at Fort Myers, Virginia; Assistant Chief of Staff for Personnel for the North Atlantic Regional Medical Command at Walter Reed Medical Center, the Deputy Chief of Staff for Personnel, G-1 and Troop Commander, United States Army Medical Research and Material Command at Fort Detrick, Maryland. In May 2004 she was assigned as the Deputy Chief of the Medical Service Corps at Fort Detrick, Maryland.

Weathers, Richard B.
COLONEL—AIR FORCE

He is a 1976 graduate of the four-year ROTC program and entered active duty into the United States Air Force that same year.

His education includes a bachelor's degree in Economics from North Carolina A&T State University at Greensboro, North Carolina; a master's degree in Business Administration and Finance at Webster University in St. Louis, Missouri; Squadron Officer School; Air Command and Staff College; and Air War College.

He has served at all management levels including Wing, Major Command, at Headquarters Air Force. His assignments include serving as Chief of the Head-

quarters Management Branch at the Headquarters of Tactical Air Command at Langley Air Force Base, Virginia. In October 1987, he served as Wing Comptroller at Comiso Air Station in Italy. From October 1988 to December 1992, he was an Air Staff Budget Analyst in the Budget Operations Directorate in the Officer of the Assistant Secretary of the Air Force (Financial Management and Comptroller) at the Pentagon. In February 1992, he was assigned as Comptroller Squadron Commander at MacDill Air Force Base, Florida; from June 1994 to July 1996, he served as Chief of the Budget Integration Division in the Office of the Assistant Secretary of the Air Force (Financial Management and Comptroller) in the Pentagon. In July 1996, he was selected to serve as Military Assistant to the Assistant Secretary of the Air Force (Financial Management and Comptroller) at the Pentagon; from August 1997, he was assigned as Chief of the Programs and Analysis Division in the Directorate of Comptroller at the Headquarters of Air Mobility Command at Scott Air Force Base, Illinois; from March 1999 to July 2000, he served as Command Budget Director in the Directorate of Comptroller at the Headquarters of Air Mobility Command at Scott Air Force Base; in July 2000, he was assigned as Chief of the Aircraft and Technology Division in the Office of the Assistant Secretary of Air Force (Financial Management and Comptroller) at the Pentagon; and from March 2002 to May 2004, he served as the Comptroller, at Headquarters for the United States Air Forces in Europe at Ramstein Air Base, Germany. In May 2004, he was selected to serve as the Commander of the 38th Combat Support Wing at the Headquarters of the United States Air Force in Europe at Ramstein Air Base. He was promoted to Colonel in January 1999.

Wells, Larry G.
LIEUTENANT COMMANDER—NAVY

He enlisted into the United States Navy in February 1980. After completion of Boot Camp at Recruit Training Center, Orlando, Florida and graduation from EW "A" School at Naval Telecommunications Training Center Corry Station (NTTC), in Pensacola, Florida, he was assigned to USS *Duluth* (LPD 6), at San Diego, California, from May 1981 to March 1984 where he earned his Enlisted Surface Warfare Specialist (ESWS) pin. From March to November 1984, he received Advanced Electronic Warfare maintenance training at the NTTC Corry Station in Pensacola. He served on USS *Belleau Wood* (LHA 3), San Diego from December 1984 to December 1986. In January 1987, he returned to Pensacola, Florida, as an Electronic Warfare "A" School Instructor and was advanced to Electronic Warfare Commander in September 1988, earned the Master Training Specialist designation and selected as NTTC Instructor of the Year.

After instructor duty, he transferred to USS *La Salle* (AGD 3) in Bahrain in April 1990 to April 1991. He served as LCPO for Electronic Warfare Division and qualified as CIC Watch Officer. In July 2003, he transferred to Naval Computers and Telecommunications Station, Puerto Rico as the Electronics Material Officer and designated as the Executive Officer. In June 2005, he was serving as the Officer in Charge of Naval Computer and Telecommunications Area Master Station, Pacific Detachment Diego Garcia.

Wells, Marvin

COMMAND MASTER CHIEF—COAST GUARD

He enlisted into the United States Coast Guard in September 1978. Upon graduation from recruit training, he was assigned to Coast Guard Base Miami Beach, where he was immediately reassigned to Coast Guard Center Cape Gull. In 1979, he reported to Coast Guard Air Station Kodiak, Alpat Section as an AT#, where he served as a crewmember and trainee on HC-130 and HH-52 aircraft. In 1981, he reported to Coast Guard Air

Station Clearwater for the first of three tours, where he served as a Navigator Examiner/Instructor ensuring standardization among their navigators. In 1987, he arrived at Coast Guard Air Station Sacramento, where he served as Avionics Training Petty Officer and later as Shop Supervisor. He returned to Clearwater in January 1991, performing the Shop Maintenance and Avionics Night Maintenance and later the Engineering Administration Chief duties. Returning to Air Station Sacramento in 1995, he once again served as the Avionics Chief and upon advancement to Senior Chief assumed the Engineering Leading Chief duties where he coordinated personnel transfers, evaluations and work area assignments.

In 2000, he reported to Coast Guard Air Station Miami, where he served as the Avionics Leading Chief. Upon advancement to Master Chief, he transferred to Air Station Clearwater and assumed the duties as the Silver Badge Command Master Chief. Master Chief Wells was selected in 2003, as the Command Master Chief for the Seventh District East and assumed that duty on July 15, 2003.

West, Togo Dennis, Jr.

SECRETARY OF THE ARMY

He was born in Winston-Salem, North Carolina. He married the former Gail Estelle Berry and they have two children, Tiffany Berry and Hilary Carter. He received a Bachelor of Science degree in Education from Howard University in 1965, and then earned a Doctor of Jurisdiction degree from Howard University in 1968. He entered on active military service in 1969, and served in the United States Army's Judge Advocate General Corps. He left the Army in 1973, with the rank of Captain. From 1977 to 1979, he served as General

Counsel for the Department of the Navy. At the age of 34, he served to overseen the work of some 200 Navy Lawyers Worldwide. In 1979, he was appointed Special Assistant to the Secretary and Deputy Secretary of the Department of Defense and in 1980, he was appointed General Counsel. In 1990, he became the chief Washington lobbyist at the defense contractor Northrop Corporation. In 1993, he was selected Secretary of the Army and in 1998 President Clinton nominated him to head the Veterans Affairs Department. He became acting VA Secretary on January 2, 1998.

West-Waddy, Harriet M.
LIEUTENANT COLONEL—ARMY

She joined the United States Women's Army Auxiliary Corps (WAAC) in 1942, and completed training at Fort Des Moines, Iowa. She was the first black woman commissioned as an Officer, and the first black woman to attend Officer Candidate Class. She was of only two black females to obtain the rank of Major during World War II.

She was assigned in Washington, D.C., where previously had worked for Mary McLeod Bethune, Director of the Administration's Division of Negro Affairs in the 1930s. Upon her return to Washington in 1942, she went to work for Oveta Culp Hobby, Director of the Women's Army Auxiliary Corps.

After the Women's Army Auxiliary Corps became the Women's Army Corps in July 1943 and made part of the regular Army, she graduated from Adjutant General's School and was given responsibility for 50 civil-

ian typists in the Casualty Branch. After that assignment, she went on to serve in many locations, both in the Continental United States and overseas and became known for her independence, drive, patriotism and love of country.

Lieutenant Colonel West-Waddy served 25 years, a period that included World War II; the Korean War; and Vietnam War. She died at the age of 94. At the time of her death, the U.S. Army stated they couldn't locate the records showing she was promoted to Lieutenant Colonel in 1948. Therefore, when she died, the veterans' cemetery where she was buried refused to allow her rank to be placed on the grave marker until records were produced.

The United States Army Women's Museum at Fort Lee, Virginia, has a collection of artifacts of Lieutenant Colonel Harriet M. West-Waddy. Her military ID shows her correct rank.

Whitehead, James T.
LIEUTENANT GENERAL—AIR FORCE

He was born in Jersey City, New Jersey; and married the former Saunder L. Beard. They have six children, Janet, Sara, Rebecca, Marie, Joel, and Kenneth. He graduated from Dwight Morrow High School at Englewood, New Jersey, in 1952. He then received a Bachelor of Science degree in Education from the University of Illinois in 1957, and he attended Monmouth College at Long Branch, New Jersey, completing 18 graduate credits in counseling. He completed the Squadron Officer Course in 1961, the Air Command and Staff Course in 1978, and the Air War College in 1981. General Whitehead has attended many senior seminars and management courses, including the Reserve Component National Security Course. He began his military career by enlisting in the New Jersey Army National Guard in May 1952. He served until May 1955, when

he was placed in the Army Standby Reserve with the rank of private. He received his commission as a Second Lieutenant upon his graduation from Air Force ROTC in June 1957. In November 1957, he entered pilot training at Malden Air Base, Missouri, and later at Vance Air Force Base, Oklahoma. He was awarded his pilot wings in November 1958, and completed combat crew training in the KC-135 at Castle Air Force Base, California, and Barksdale Air Force Base, Louisiana. Upon completion, he was assigned as a KC-135 Combat Crew Copilot in the 913th Air Refueling Squadron at Barksdale AFB from May 1959 to April 1962. During this period he served as Squadron Assistant Air Operations officer, Squadron Ground Training officer, and copilot on the Wing Standardization Evaluation Crew. In April 1962, he received a regular officer appointment in the United States Air Force, was transferred to the 68th Air Refueling Squadron at Bunker Hill Air Force Base, Indiana, and was upgraded to Aircraft Commander. His crew flew special air missions from England, Turkey, Vietnam and Laos. In 1965, he was selected to be the first black U-2 pilot. After completing his upgrade to a combat-ready U-2 pilot, he flew many JCS and higher HQ-directed missions. He then completed short tours of duty as a guard member with the Nebraska and New Jersey Air National Guard, flying RF-84s and C-121s from October 1967 to September 1969. General Whitehead joined the 103rd Tactical Air Support Squadron, Willow Grove NAS at Willow Grove, Pennsylvania, in September 1969. He served as flight commander and during this time was promoted to Major. In March 1977, he was appointed as Squadron Commander of the 103rd and promoted to Lieutenant Colonel in April 1977. During his years of command, the unit transitioned from the O-2 to the OA-37 aircraft. In June 1983, he was assigned to Headquarters, PAANG, as Director of Operations. During this period he was responsible for establishing a highly successful and now annual joint Army and Air Guard training exercise name Keystone Vigilant. He served in that capacity until April 15, 1987, when he was assigned duty as Deputy Commander. As Deputy Commander, he was responsible to advise the Commander, Pennsylvania Air National Guard (PaANG). He served as Deputy Commander from April 15, 1987, until his selection as Air National Guard Assistant to the Director, Air National Guard, as Air National Guard assistant to the Director of the Air National Guard in Washington, D.C., General Whitehead's duties were to advise the Director on all force management issues relating to Air National Guard units, including minority policy matters. This input had a major impact on force preparedness and meeting the defense challenge of tomorrow. In civilian life, he is an Accident Prevention Program manager with the FAA. He also performed duties as an air carrier operations specialist. Previously he was a pilot and flight engineer with Trans World Airlines at John F. Kennedy Airport in New York City from 1967 until his retirement in July 1986. During that period, he accumulated over 15,000 hours on the Boeing 727, 707, and 747. In addition to training TWA personnel, he instructed and checked crewmembers from Olympic, Sandia, and Alia airlines and USAF E-4 crewmember. After his retirement from TWA in 1986, he was hired as manager and was later promoted to senior director of Flight Operations, for Orion Air, a major contractor of pilots for UPS, Emery, and Purolator Cargo. His military awards and decorations include the Legion of Merit, the Meritorious Service Medal, Air Force Commendation Medal (with oak leaf cluster), Air Force Outstanding Unit Award (with seven oak leaf clusters), Air Force Organizational Excellence Award, Combat Readiness Medal (with two oak leaf clusters), National Defense Service Medal, Vietnam Service Medal, Armed Forces Reserve Medal (with hourglass device), the Pennsylvania Meritorious Service Medal, Pennsylvania Twenty Year and General Thomas J. Steward Award. He is a command pilot with over 5,000 hours of military flying time. He has had experience flying numerous aircraft in a wide variety of scenarios. He was appointed Major General on May 15, 1991.

Whitfield, Walter John
BRIGADIER GENERAL—ARMY

He was born November 5, 1948, in Jackson, Mississippi. He received a Bachelor of Arts degree in Liberal Arts from the University of New York in Albany. He received his commission to Second Lieutenant on February 6, 1968. His military schools include Field Artillery Officers Candidate School at Field Artillery School; a Nuclear, Biological, Chemical Officers Course at Chemical School; Field Artillery Officers Advanced Course at Field Artillery School; Command

and General Staff College; and Infantry Officer Advanced Course at the Infantry School. From March 1968 to July 1968, he was assigned as a forward observer/fire direction officer with Battery C, 5th Battalion, 3rd Field Artillery, 6th Infantry Division. From July 1968 to December 1968, he was assigned as Training Officer of Company E, 10th Battalion, 2nd Training Brigade. From January 1969 to June 1969, he served as the Executive Officer of Battery B, 4th Battalion, 76th Field Artillery, 7th Infantry Division. From July 1969 to January 1970, he was assigned as a Forward Observer/Battalion Fire Support Officer attached to the 2nd Infantry Division. From February 1970 to September 1970, he was assigned first as the Battalion Fire Direction Officer at Headquarters and Headquarters Battery, next as Commander/S4, for the Service Battery, with the 3rd Battalion, 19th Field Artillery, 1st Armored Division. He also served as TDY-Assistant G3 Operations, Project Master, Master Test Division, from June 1970 to September 1970. He then served until October 1970 as Battalion Communication Electronics officer at Headquarters and Headquarters Battery, 3rd Battalion, 19th Field Artillery, 1st Armored Division. From October 1970 to January 1971, he served as the Commander of Battery B, 3rd Battalion, 19th Field Artillery, 1st Armored Division. From February 1971 to June 1973, he was not on active duty, being assigned to the United States Army Reserves Control Group. In July 1973, he was promoted to Captain and entered the active Illinois Army National Guard. His first assignment was as Motor Officer with the Headquarters and Headquarters Battery, next as Battery Commander of the Headquarters and Headquarters Battery, 2nd Battalion, 122nd Field Artillery, 33rd Infantry Brigade, from February 1974 November 1974. From November 1974 to October 1978, he was assigned as Battery Commander, Battery C, 2nd Battalion, next as Battalion S2 Officer, later as S3 Officer 2nd Battalion, 122 Field Artillery, 33rd Infantry Brigade. He was promoted to Major on May 6, 1977. From November 1978 to March 1985, he was assigned as Battalion Executive Officer, later as Battalion Commander, with the 2nd Battalion, 122nd Field Artillery, 33rd Infantry Brigade. He was promoted to Lieutenant Colonel on July 21, 1981. From April 1985 to September 1985, he served as Brigade Civil Affairs Officer (G5), 33rd Infantry Brigade. From October 1985 to September 1986, he was assigned as Training Officer for the Directorate of Plans, Operations and Training States Area Command with the Illinois Army National Guard. From October 1986 to September 1988, General Whitfield was assigned the Commander of the 44th Support Center, Rear Area Operations, Illinois Army National Guard. He was promoted to Colonel on October 11, 1988. From October 1988 to January 1990, he served as Director of Personnel and Administration, State Area Command, Illinois Army National Guard. From February 1990 to January 1992, he served as the Deputy Commander of the 22nd Infantry Brigade. In January 1992, he was selected Commander of the 33rd Infantry Brigade, Illinois Army Na-

tional Guard. He was promoted to Brigadier General on October 27, 1992. His civilian occupation is Senior Field Sales Engineer for the Furnas Electric Company in Oak Brook, Illinois. His military awards and decorations include the Meritorious Service Medal; the Army Commendation Medal; Army Achievement Medal; Army Reserve Components Achievement Medal (with three oak leaf clusters); National Defense Service Medal; Armed Forces Expeditionary Medal; Armed Forces Reserve Medal (with one hourglass device); Army Service Ribbon; and Army Reserve Components Overseas Training Ribbon (with Numeral 2).

Whitley, Regina
COMMAND SERGEANT MAJOR—ARMY

CSM Whitley has proven herself to be one of the AMEDD's premier NCO leaders. Her elevation through the Noncommissioned Officers ranks in the United States Veterinary Services began in 1985, where she served as the NCOIC of the 167th Medical Detachment (VS), in Stuttgart, Germany, during the height of the Cold War providing technical guidance for the procurement and storage of subsistence in the logistical supply system covering eight United States Army Communities.

In 1997, she was selected as a Faculty Advisor for the Non-Resident Course at the United States Sergeants Major Academy. She also served a one year tour as the Command Sergeant Major of the 168th Medical Battalion (Area Support). She arrived at Fort Bragg in June of 2000, where she has held the Troop Command Sergeant Major position at Womack Army Medical Center.

Wiggins, Clyde

SERGEANT MAJOR—ARMY

Sergeant Major Clyde Wiggins is married to the former Christiane E. Weidner, and they have two children, Christopher and Charmaine. He entered the United States Army on August 29, 1974. He attended basic Combat Training at Fort Knox, Kentucky, and Advanced Individual Training at Fort Sill, Oklahoma. He graduated from the Sergeants Major Academy at Fort Bliss, Texas in 1995.

He has served overseas in Italy, Germany and Bosnia-Herzegovina. His assignments include a tour as a Sergeant Missile Crewman in Bravo Battery, 2nd Battalion, 30th Field Artillery in Vicenza, Italy; as Section Chief with the 1st United States Army Field Artillery Detachment at Wesel, Germany; as Platoon Sergeant in Service Battery, 3rd Battalion, 79th Field Artillery in Giessen, Germany; as First Sergeant in A Battery, 2nd Battalion, 12th Field Artillery at Herzo Base, Germany; as First Sergeant with B Battery, 2nd Battalion, 14th Field Artillery, in Bamberg, Germany; as Operations Sergeant Major of the 1st Armored Division Artillery in Baumholder, Germany; and Operations Sergeant Major with the 1st Armored Division Artillery in Bosnia-Herzegovina.

He is currently serving as the Sergeant Major for the Second Brigade, First Region (ROT).

Wilcox, Steven

COMMAND SERGEANT MAJOR—ARMY

He began his military career in October 1975, after taking the oath of enlistment in Philadelphia, Pennsylvania. He attended Basic Combat Training at Fort Dix, New Jersey, and completed Advance Individual Training at Fort Bragg, North Carolina.

His military education includes all the Noncommissioned Officer Education System Courses; Basic Airborne Course; the Jumpmaster Course; the Northern Warfare Training Center (NWTC) Summer and Winter Instructor Qualification Courses at Fort Greely, Alaska; the Support Operations Course (SOC); the Noncommissioned Officer Logistics Program (NCOLP) at Fort Lee, Virginia; the Security and Training Courses at the Defense Institute for Security Assistance Management (DISAM) located at Wright Patterson Air Force Base, Ohio; the First Sergeants Course; the Battle Staff NCO Course; and the United States Army Sergeants Major Academy (class 49).

Wilkerson, Philip L.

COLONEL—ARMY

He was born in Newport News, Virginia, and married the former Carol E. James. They have two children, a son, Philip L. III, and a daughter, Lois. He graduated from Hampton High School in Hampton, Virginia in June 1968, and from the Virginia Military Institute on May 21, 1972, where he was a Distinguished Military Student and a Distinguished Military Graduate. He was commissioned a Second Lieutenant in Armor on July 28, 1972, after attending Army

ROTC summer camp at Fort Indiantown Gap, Pennsylvania. His military schooling includes Airborne School (Pathfinder and Rotary Wing Qualification); Jungle Expert Courses; the Armor Basic and Advanced Courses; the Army Command and General Staff College; and the National War College. He was initially assigned to the 1st Squadron, 4th Cavalry, at Fort Riley, Kansas, where he served as an Armored Cavalry Platoon Leader. Reassigned to South Korea in August 1974, he served as an Armored Cavalry Platoon Leader, then a Troop Executive Officer, and finally as Commander of Troop B, 4th Squadron, 7th Cavalry (later redesignated the 4th Squadron, 4th Cavalry). In November 1975, he was assigned to Fort Rucker, Alabama, as a rotary wing flight student and received his wings in October 1976. In January 1977, he was once again assigned to South Korea, this time to Troop D, 4th Squadron, 7th Cavalry, as an Aero-weapon Section Commander and then as the Aero-reconnaissance Platoons Commander. In October 1978, he was assigned to Troop B, 1st Squadron (AIR), 17th Cavalry (AIRBONE), 82nd Airborne Division at Fort Bragg, North Carolina, where he served as the Aero-weapons Platoon Commander, troop Operations Officer and then as the Troop's Executive Officer. Subsequently, he was assigned to Company D (ATK), 82nd AVN Battalion as the Company's Executive Officer. In July 1983, Colonel Wilkerson was assigned to the headquarters of United States Army, Europe (USAREUR), in the office of the Deputy Chief of Staff for Operations as the Berlin Planner. In July 1985, he was reassigned to the 3rd Infantry Division, where he served as the Executive Officer for the 3rd Squadron, 7th Cavalry (later redesignated the 4th Squadron, 4th Cavalry).

In August 1987, he was assigned to the Pentagon in the Office of the Chief of the Army Reserve as a Mobilization Planner/Staff Officer. His next assignment was that of Commander of the 4th Battalion, 1st Aviation

Regiment on May 10, 1990. He deployed with the Diamondback battalion during Operation Desert Shield and Operation Desert Storm. From 10 May 1990 to 15 May 1992, the battalion grew from 320 to over 500 soldiers for combat and then returned to strength of 356 soldiers upon the battalion's return to CONUS.

After completion of Battalion Command on May 15, 1992, he served as the 4th Brigade's Deputy Commander while awaiting his reporting date to the National War College (NWC). Upon graduating from the National War College, he was assigned to the Department of Defense in the Office of the Inspector General (IG), where he served as a Joint Operations analyst in the Program Evaluation Directorate until June of 1994. Currently, he serves as the Chief of the Force Integration Division in the Program Evaluation Directorate of the Office of the Inspector General, at the Department of Defense.

His military awards and decorations include the Bronze Star; Meritorious Service Medal (with five oak leaf clusters); Air Medal; Army Commendation Medal (with 1 oak leaf cluster); Army Achievement Medal; the National Defense Ribbon; the Southwest Asia Service Medal with two Bronze Stars; the Army Service Ribbon; the Overseas Ribbon (with the number 3); the Senior Aviator Badge; Master Parachutist Badge; the Pathfinder Badge; the Army Staff Identification Badge; and the Joint Staff Identification Badge.

Williams, Alexander

SERGEANT MAJOR—MARINES

He was born in Leland, Mississippi, and entered the Marine Corps on June 3, 1980. He graduated recruit training from Marine Corps Recruit Depot San Diego on September 12, 1980. Upon graduation from recruit training, he reported to El Toro, California, where he completed the Commanding General's Course in Culinary Arts and was assigned the MOS 3381.

He was then assigned to 1st Recruit Training Battalion, Permanent Personnel, at Parris Island, South Carolina. After receiving a promotion to Lance Corporal, he received orders to Drill Instructor School in March 1983.

Upon graduation from Drill Instructor School at Parris Island in May 1983, he was assigned to Company D, 2nd Recruit Training Battalion and Support Battalion, Recruit Training Regiment as a Drill Instructor. He was promoted to the rank of Sergeant.

In May 1985, he received orders to the 3rd Light Anti-aircraft Battalion, Marine Air Command Group 28, 2nd Marine Aircraft Wing, Marine Corps Air Station, Cherry Point, North Carolina, where he served as the NCOIC of the battalion supply field mess.

In July 1986, he received orders to Marine Wing Support Squadron-172, Marine Wing Support Group-17, 1st Marine Aircraft Wing, in Okinawa, Japan, where he was assigned as a food service specialist and served on Operation Team Spirit 87. He was selected to the rank of staff sergeant.

During July 1987, he reported to Drill Instructor School at Parris Island. Upon graduation, he was assigned to Company E and Company F, 2nd Recruit Training Battalion, where he served as a Drill Instructor, Senior Drill Instructor and Series Chief Drill Instructor. During May 1989, he was assigned to the Drill Instructor School Staff as an Instructor where he taught the subject Standing Operating Procedures for Recruit Training and was promoted to the rank of Gunnery Sergeant.

In October 1990, he received orders to Marine Corps Base, Camp Lejeune, North Carolina, where he was assigned as an Instructor with Marine Corps Culinary Arts/Specialist School, Marine Corps Service Support School.

During August 1993, he reported to Drill Instructor School at Parris Island. Upon graduation, he was assigned to Company H, 2nd Recruit Training Battalion, where he served as a Series Chief Drill Instructor until his promotion to First Sergeant.

In May 1994, he was frocked to First Sergeant and reassigned to Company G, 2nd Recruit Training Battalion, at Parris Island.

In July 1995, he received orders to Amityville, New York, where he served as the Inspector-Inspector Staff First Sergeant of Company A, 6th Communication Battalion. He participated in Operation Battle Griffin 96 in Norway.

After his selection to Sergeant Major, he was frocked and assigned as the Sergeant Major for 3rd Maintenance Battalion, 3rd Force Service Support Group, in Okinawa in May 1998.

During April 1999, after the merger of Supply and Maintenance Battalion into Materiel Readiness Battalion, Sergeant Major Williams was assigned to Materiel Readiness Battalion, 3rd Force Service Support Group, in Okinawa.

In July 1999, he transferred to 3rd Battalion, 12th Marines, 3rd Marine Division, in Okinawa. During

March 2000, he transferred to Combat Assault Battalion, 3rd Marine Division, in Okinawa. He served as the Battalion Sergeant Major until March 2001.

During April 2001, Sergeant Major Williams transferred to Marine Tactical Air Command Squadron, Marine Air Control Group 28, Marine Aircraft Win, at Cherry Point, North Carolina. He served as the Squadron Sergeant Major until October 2003.

In November 2003, he reported to the 2nd Battalion, 14th Marines, Grand Prairie, Texas, where he served as the Battalion Sergeant Major and the Inspector-Instructor Sergeant Major until May 2005.

Williams, Anthony J.
COMMAND SERGEANT MAJOR—ARMY

A native of Canton, Mississippi, he married the former Corinne Jones of Richmond, California, and they

have on daughter, Tanika. He graduated from Rosa Fort High School in Tunica, Mississippi, and joined the Army on October 1972. He attended Basic Training at Fort Leonard Wood, Missouri, and completed Sergeant Missile Advanced Individual Training at Fort Sill, Oklahoma.

His military education includes the Basic Airborne Course, the 25th Division Air Assault School, the Drill Sergeant School, the Field Artillery Advanced Noncommissioned Officers Course, the First Sergeants Course, the Sergeant's Major Course and the Command Sergeants Major Course.

Command Sergeant Major Williams assumed duties as Command Sergeant Major of the United States Army Training and Doctrine Command at Fort Monroe, Virginia, on December 1, 2001.

Williams, Anthony L.
COLONEL—ARMY

He is a native of McComb, Mississippi. He holds a Bachelor of Arts degree from Arkansas State University and a master's degree from Central Michigan University. His military education includes the United States Army War College; the Quartermasters Officer Basic and Advanced Courses; Combined Arms Services Staff School; Command and General Staff College; and the Army War College.

He has served in a variety of command and staff positions including Company Commander of the 259th Field Service Company; Logistics Operations Officer of the 530th Supply and Service Battalion; Quartermaster Team Chief and Reserve Component Advisor of the

Readiness Group at Fort Indiantown Gap; Plans and Programs Officer (J4) for United States Forces, Korea; Executive Officer of the 215th Forward Support Battalion; DISCOM Support Operations Officer, Deputy (G4); Support Operations Officer of Main Support Battalion; Operations Officer and Deputy Commander of the 29th Area Support Group, 21st Theater Support Command at Kaiserslatern, Germany; Commander of the 530th Supply and Service Battalion at Fort Bragg, North Carolina; and Director of Special Operations Command in Joint Forces Command at Norfolk, Virginia. In February 2005, he was serving as the Commander of the 10th ASG Support Group in Japan.

Williams, Bennie E.
MAJOR GENERAL—ARMY

He received a Bachelor of Science degree in Education Administration from Morgan State University and a Master of Science degree in Transportation Management from the Florida Institute of Technology. His military education includes the Infantry Officer Basic Course; the Transportation Officer Advanced Course; United States Army Command and General Staff College; and the United States Army War College.

After completing the ROTC program at Morgan State University, he was commissioned a Second Lieutenant on June 7, 1972. In December 1972, he was assigned as a Platoon Leader with A Company, 2nd Battalion, 50th Infantry, 2nd Armored Division, at Fort Hood, Texas. From December 1973 to April 1975, he was assigned as Motor Officer with the 2nd Battalion, 50th Infantry, 2nd Armored Division, at Fort Hood. In September 1975, he was assigned as Assistant S-2 (Intelligence/Security)/S-3 (Operations) and Comman-

der of Headquarters and Headquarters Detachment, 69th Transportation Battalion, in South Korea. He was promoted to Captain on June 7, 1976.

In April 1977, he was assigned as a Transportation Staff Officer, later Project Officer, with the 1st Staff and Faculty Company, 2nd Battalion, Troop Support Brigade at the United States Army Transportation School at Fort Eustis, Virginia. In September 1979, he was assigned as Commander of A Company, 3rd Battalion, 5th Training Brigade, at Fort Dix, New Jersey. From August 1982 to July 1985, he was assigned as Installation Transportation Officer with the 54th Area Support Group, 21st Support Command, United States Army Europe and Seventh Army, Germany. He was promoted to Major on October 1, 1983.

In October 1989, he was assigned as the Executive Officer with the 507th Corps Support Group (Airborne), 1st Corps Support Command, at Fort Bragg and Operations Desert Shield/Storm in Saudi Arabia. In August 1991, he was assigned as the Deputy Commander of the 330th Transportation Center (Movement Control Center), 1st Corps Support Command, at Fort Bragg. From July 1992 to June 1994, he served as the Commander of the 169th Maintain Battalion, 13th Corps Support Command, at Fort Hood, Texas, and Operation Restore Hope in Somalia. He was promoted to Colonel on February 1, 1995.

From June 1995 to July 1997, he was Commander of the 16th Corps Support Group, 3rd Corps Support Command, V Corps, United States Army Europe and Seventh Army, Germany, and Operation Joint Endeavor in Bosnia. In July 1997, he was assigned as Chief of Staff of 3rd Corps Support Command, V Corps, United States Army Europe and Seventh Army in Germany. From July 1998 to July 1999, he was assigned as

Chief of Transportation (Policy) in the Defense Logistics Agency at Fort Belvoir, Virginia. From July 1999 to August 2000, he was assigned as Chief of Staff for the Defense Logistics Support Command in the Defense Logistics Agency at Fort Belvoir. In August 2000, he was selected to serve as the Deputy Commanding General for the 21st Theater Support Command, with the United States Army Europe and Seventh Army in Germany. He was promoted to Brigadier General on September 1, 2000.

In June 2003, he was selected to serve as the Commanding General of the 21st Theater Support Command, United States Army Europe and Seventh Army in Germany. He was promoted to Major General on October 1, 2003.

His military awards and decorations include the Defense Superior Service Medal; the Legion of Merit; the Bronze Star; Meritorious Service Medal (with four oak leaf clusters); Army Commendation Medal (with oak leaf cluster); Army Achievement Medal; and Parachutist Badge.

Williams, Bryant D.
COMMAND SERGEANT MAJOR—ARMY

He enlisted into the United States Army from Benton Harbor, Michigan, in October 1978. He completed his Basic Combat Training and Advanced Individual Training at Fort Jackson, South Carolina.

His military education includes all the Non-Commissioned Officer Education System Courses; Air Assault Courses; the First Sergeant School; and the United States Army Sergeants Major Academy (class 53).

His key military assignments include serving as Battalion Motor Supervisor of the 29th Engineer Battalion at Fort Shafter, Hawaii; as Brigade and Battalion Maintenance Supervisor for the 17th Field Artillery

Brigade at Fort Still, Oklahoma and 2/11 Field Artillery Battalion, at Schofield Barracks, Hawaii; as First Sergeant of Headquarters and Headquarters Company, 29th Engineer Battalion; as First Sergeant of the Service Battery, 3rd Battalion, 18th Field Artillery Brigade; as First Sergeant of Headquarters and Headquarters Battery, 17th Field Artillery Brigade; and as First Sergeant, HHS, 2-11 Field Artillery Battalion. He was selected to serve as Command Sergeant Major for the 2-11th Field Artillery Battalion; and as Command Sergeant Major of the 194th Maintenance Battalion at Camp Humphreys, South Korea.

Williams, Cathay
PRIVATE—ARMY

During the first two years of the Buffalo Soldiers, there was a black female who passed herself off as a man and enlisted with the 38th Infantry, which later became the 25th Infantry.

Cathay Williams was born to Martha Williams outside Independence, Missouri, in 1842. Although her father was a free man, she was born into slavery. She grew up in Jefferson City, Missouri, and was a house girl for William Johnson, a wealthy farmer. After her master died in Jefferson City and the Civil War broke out, Union soldiers under Colonel Benton of the 13th army corps pressed Cathay and a number of others into service. They took her and the other servants to Little Rock, Arkansas. The officers wanted her to cook, something with which she was not familiar. She did not want to go. However, she did not have much of a say and she went to Arkansas, and in Little Rock she learned to cook. She traveled with the army and was at the Battle of Pea Ridge in Arkansas. She moved with them around Arkansas and Louisiana watching as they burned cotton, and she saw captured rebel gunboats burn on the Red River at Shreveport. From there she went to New Orleans, then by way of the Gulf went to Savannah and then to Macon as well as other places around the South.

She was sent to Washington to be a cook and laundress for Gen. Phil Sheridan made his raids in the Shenandoah Valley. From Virginia she went to Iowa and afterwards to Jefferson Barracks, ten miles south of St. Louis, where she stayed for some time. All of this exposure to the military must have given her an understanding of its workings and expectations.

Cathay Williams participated in military life during the Civil War to the greatest extent a woman could. The Union Army, however, only enlisted black men to fight. After the Civil War, these soldiers, many of who had served honorably, deserved a chance to continue their career, limited as it was. And slaves now freed from Southern plantations needed employment. Some Congressmen felt a certain dose of retaliation was due the South, so arming former slaves seemed just. After Congress passed an act on July 28, 1866, to enlist black troops, Cathay joined Company A of the Thirty-Eighth United States Infantry, commanded by Captain Charles E. Clarke. On November 15 in St. Louis, Mis-

souri, she enlisted as William Cathay. At that time medical examinations were not required to enlist and, as Cathay Williams intimated to a newspaperman, the uniforms worn by her regiment were not flattering to a woman's figure. According to her discharge papers, she was five feet nine inches tall, in addition to the notation of skin, eye and hair color that was the extent of her examination. There were only two people in her regiment who knew her true identity, a cousin and a "particular friend." Cathay apparently returned the favor and let her friend remain anonymous.

When Section 3 of an Act of Congress authorized the formation of six all-black regiments, two cavalry and four infantry, it initially designated the 38th, 39th, 40th and 41st Infantries. The 9th Cavalry was established in Greenville, Louisiana, and the 10th Cavalry at Fort Leavenworth, Kansas. These cavalry regiments conducted campaigns against American Indian tribes on a Western Frontier that extended from Montana in the North to Texas, New Mexico, and Arizona in the South. The Infantry regiments initially designated as the 38th, 39th, 40th and 41st Infantries were merged in 1869 into the 24th and 25th Infantries.

After her enlistment by Major Merricum in St. Louis, she contracted small pox, and was sick at a hospital in what is now East St. Louis. Her unit, Company A of the 38th Infantry, went to Fort Cummings to relieve Company D of the 25th Colored Troop who immediately left for Fort Union. 101 black enlisted men and their white commanding officers, Captain Charles Clarke, Regimental Adjutant First Lieutenant William E. Sweet, and Second Lieutenant Henry F. Leggett, arrived for duty at Fort Cummings on October 1, 1867.

As soon as Cathay recovered, she joined her company in New Mexico at Fort Cummings, located between Fort Seldon and Fort Bayard in Southwest New Mexico. Today, Fort Cummings' adobe walls have melted back into the earth, and its location is on private property. Fort Seldon is forty-five minutes north of Las Cruces, and Fort Bayard is on the outskirts of Silver City. Fort Cummings was active between the years of 1863 and 1873. The fort protected immigrants traveling westward through Cooke's Canyon pass, the most dangerous point of the southern route to California. The soldiers also protected the nearby miners.

At some point in late 1889 or early 1890, Cathay Williams was hospitalized in Trinidad for nearly a year and a half. Again, no record has surfaced detailing when she left the hospital. She filed in June 1891 for an invalid's pension based upon her military service. Her application brought to light the fact that an African American woman served in the Regular Army. The original application for the pension, sworn before the local County Clerk (as was the procedure for all pension applications), gave her age as 41. She stated that she was one and the same as William Cathey.

Williams, Charles E.
COMMAND SERGEANT MAJOR—ARMY

A native of Lyon, Mississippi, reenlisted in the United

States Army in October 1976 as a Chaparral Missile Crewmember.

His military education includes all the Noncommissioned Officer Education System Courses; Drill Sergeant School; Small Group Instructor Course; and the United States Army Sergeants Major Academy. He holds an associate's degree in Administration and Management from Central Texas College.

He has served in a variety of leadership positions including serving as Task Force Sergeant Major in the Forward 1st Battalion, 1st Air Defense Artillery in Kuwait; Sergeant Major of the 1st Battalion, 1st Air Defense Artillery S-3 Operations at Fort Bliss, Texas; First Sergeant of Charlie Battery, 1st Battalion, 3rd Air Defense Artillery at Fort Stewart, Georgia; and First Sergeant of Bravo Battery, 1st Battalion, 7th Air Defense Artillery at Kaiserslautein, Germany. In January 2005, he was serving as the Command Sergeant Major for Headquarters and Headquarters Battery, 4th Battalion, 5th Air Defense Artillery, 1st Cavalry Division, at Fort Hood, Texas.

Williams, Charles E.
MAJOR GENERAL—ARMY

He was born in Greensboro, Alabama. He married the former Marjorie Seymour and they have three children, Patty, Charles, Jr., and Calvin. Upon completion of the Reserve Officers Training Corps curriculum and the educational course of study at Tuskegee Institute in 1960, he was commissioned a Second Lieutenant and awarded a Bachelor of Science degree in Biology. He also earned a Master of Business Administration from Atlanta University. His military education includes: completion of the Engineer Officer Advanced Course; the United States Army Command and General Staff College; and the United States War College. General Williams has held a wide variety of important command and staff positions. His early command and staff assignments were with the 70th Engineer Battalion at Fort Campbell, Kentucky; the 37th Engineer Group in Germany; the First Aviation Brigade and the 18th Engineer Brigade, both in South Vietnam. His mid-level assignments include a two-year tour in the Office of the Comptroller of the United States Army Materiel Command in Alexandria, Virginia, where he served as Management Analyst; a three-year tour in Washington, D.C., in the Officer of the Comptroller of the Army, where he served as Staff Assistant to the Comptroller of the Army; Senior Budget Analyst for Training; and Executive Officer to the Director of Operations and Maintenance of the Army. His later assignments included serving as Commander of the 3rd Engineer Training Battalion at Fort Belvoir, Virginia; as Deputy Brigade Commander of the Engineer Training Brigade at Fort Belvoir; as Chief of the Installations Planning Division in the Office of the Assistant Chief of Engineers Washington, D.C.; as Commander of the 18th Engineer Brigade and Karlsruhe Military Community in Germany; and as Director of Operations and Maintenance in the Office of the Comptroller of the Army.

General Williams' military awards and decorations include the Legion of Merit (with oak leaf cluster); the Distinguished Flying Cross; the Bronze Star (with oak leaf cluster); the Meritorious Service Medal (with oak leaf cluster); several Air Medal with "V" Device; and the Army General Staff Identification Badge.

Williams, Charlie E., Jr.
SENIOR EXECUTIVE SERVICE

He was born in Nashville, Tennessee. He holds a Bachelor of Science degree from Middle Tennessee State University in Murfreesboro and a master's degree from Tennessee State University in Nashville. He is also a 1996 graduate of the Industrial College of the Armed

Forces, where he earned a master's degree in National Resource Management.

He entered federal service in 1982 as a member of the Air Force Logistics Command Mid-Level Management Training Program at Kelly Air Force Base, Texas. He has served in a variety of positions including Deputy for Contractions Operations Division, Deputy Assistant Secretary for Contracting, and Assistant Secretary of the Air Force for Acquisition all at the Headquarters United States Air Force in Washington, D.C. He is currently Associate Deputy Assistant Secretary for Contracting in the Office of the Assistant Secretary of the Air Force for Acquisition at the Headquarters United State Air Force in Washington, D.C.

Williams, Daryl L.
COMMAND SERGEANT MAJOR—ARMY

He is a native of St. Petersburg, Florida. He enlisted in the United States Army in December 1977, and completed Basic Combat Training at Fort Jackson, South Carolina, and Advanced Individual Training at Fort Benning, Georgia.

His civilian and military education includes an associate's degree in Applied Science (Administrative Management Studies) from Excelsior College; all the Noncommissioned Officer Education System Courses; the First Sergeant Course; the United States Army Sergeants Major Academy; and the Command Sergeant Major Course.

His key military leadership assignments include serving as First Sergeant for Company C and Headquarters/A Company, 305th Quartermaster Company, in Yongsan, South Korea; as First Sergeant 190th GS Maintenance Company, at Fort Hood, Texas; and as Command Sergeant Major, 210th Forward Support Battalion at Fort Drum, New York. In January 2005, he was serving as the Command Sergeant Major for 553rd Corps Support Battalion, 64th Corps Support Group.

Williams, David E.
COMMAND SERGEANT MAJOR—ARMY

He is a native of Fayetteville, North Carolina, entered the Army on June 9, 1975. He attended OUST at Fort Polk, Louisiana, and upon completion of the OUST, his MOS was 11B (Infantry).

He then attended Airborne School at Fort Benning, Georgia. Upon completion of Airborne School in October 1975, he was assigned to A Troop, 1/17th CAV, 82nd Airborne Division at Fort Bragg, North Carolina. While assigned to the 1/17th CAV, he served as a Rifleman, Automatic Rifleman, and Machine Gunner.

In January 1990, he was assigned as the First Sergeant for B Company, 1/41 MECH INFANTRY. While assigned there, he deployed on Operation Desert Shield/Desert Storm. He later redeployed to Germany and remained until the installation closed in June 1992. He was then assigned to B Company, 1/505th, 82nd ABN Division as First Sergeant, until December 1993. In January 1994, he attended the Sergeants Major Acad-

emy. Upon graduation in July 1994, he was assigned to 1st Region ROTC, where he served at Georgia Military College as the Chief Instructor of Military Science.

Upon appointment as Command Sergeant Major, on February 7, 1997, he was assigned to the 3rd Battalion, 505th Parachute Infantry Regiment as the Battalion Command Sergeant Major. He later served as the Brigade Command Sergeant Major of the 1st Combat Basic Training Brigade at Fort Jackson, South Carolina. In 2004, he was serving as Post Command Sergeant Major at Fort Monroe.

Williams, David L.
COMMAND SERGEANT MAJOR—ARMY

Williams is a native of Beaufort, South Carolina, and graduated from Beaufort High School in May 1976. He entered the United States Army in May 1978 and attended Basic Combat Training at Fort Sill, Oklahoma. His military and civilian education includes Basic Noncommissioned Officer Course; Drill Sergeant School; Master Fitness Trainer Course; First Sergeant Course; and the United States Army Sergeants Major Academy. He holds an associate's degree in General Studies from Saint Leo College in Florida.

He has served in a variety of assignments including serving as a Forward Observer; Assistant Gunner; Section Chief; Gunnery Sergeant; Drill Sergeant; Chief of Firing Battery; First Sergeant; and Command Sergeant Major for the 2nd Battalion, 305th Field Artillery, 3rd Brigade, 87th Division at Camp Shelby, Mississippi. In August 2004, he was serving as the Command Sergeant Major for the 1st Battalion, 38th Field Artillery ("Steel Behind the Rock"), 2nd Infantry Division is South Korea.

Williams, Dwight

COMMAND SERGEANT MAJOR—ARMY

He was born in Baltimore, Maryland, and enlisted in the United States Army in January 1979, and attended Basic Combat Training and Advance Individual Training at Fort Jackson, South Carolina.

His military education includes all the Noncommissioned Officer Education System Courses; Drill Sergeants School; Master Fitness Course; Instructor Training Course; SPBS-R, ADPCP, RIP (Ranger In-

doctrination Program); ROP (Ranger Orientation Program); Battle Staff; Hazardous Cargo; Air Assault; Airborne; First Sergeants School; and the United States Army Sergeants Major Academy (class 51). He also holds an associate's degree.

His assignments include serving two tours of duty as a Drill Sergeant at Fort Dix, New Jersey and Fort Lee, Virginia; Supply Sergeant 4-27 Field Artillery at Wertheem, Germany; Senior Logistician, 1-75th Ranger Battalion; Senior Logistician JSA at Camp Bonifas, South Korea; First Sergeant of Bravo Company, 526th Field Support Battalion; First Sergeant of Headquarters/Alpha Company at Fort Campbell, Kentucky; First Sergeant of the 602nd ASB at Camp Stanley, South Korea; and Command Sergeant Major of the 266th Quartermaster Battalion at Fort Lee, Virginia

Williams, Eric

LIEUTENANT COLONEL—ARMY

He is a native of Shreveport, Louisiana. After graduating from Southern University and A&M College at Baton Rouge, Louisiana, he was commissioned as a Second Lieutenant of Infantry, entering active duty in 1985.

His military education includes the Infantry Basic and Advanced Courses; the Combined Arms Services Staff School; and the Inspector General School at Fort Belvoir, Virginia.

His military assignments include serving as an Anti-Armor Platoon Leader, Executive Officer and Company Commander consecutively in the same company, Echo Company, 1st Battalion, 39th Infantry (Mechanized), in Germany. He was later assigned as an Instructor/Tactical Officer (TAC) at the United States Army Signal Center and School at Fort Gordon, Georgia, during which he was selected as the Instructor of the Year and served as TAC Officer for ten Signal Officer Basic Courses. In 1994, he was assigned to the Regional Training Detachment (RTD) as a Company Trainer and eventually Team Chief in support of the 256th Separate Infantry Brigade (SIB) of the Louisiana Army National Guard in Lake Charles and Lafayette, Louisiana, where he assisted the 3rd Battalion, 256th Infantry prepare for a National Training Center rotation during Bradley Gunnery at Annual Training. In October 1997, he was reassigned to the 4th Infantry Division (Mechanized) at Fort Hood, Texas, serving as the Chief of G-3 Operations and Active Component/Reserve Component advisor to the Commanding General. In June 1999, he was reassigned as the Battalion Operations Officer (S3), 2nd Battalion, 8th Infantry (Mechanized). In November 1999, he assumed duties as the Brigade Operations Officer (S3), 2nd Brigade, 4th Infantry Division (Mechanized). Lieutenant Colonel Williams was assigned to the United States Army Europe and 7th Army in the Office of the Inspector General, Investigations Branch. In June 2003, he was selected to serve as the Commander of the 3rd Training Support Battalion, 196th Infantry Brigade in Guam.

Williams, Gail M.

COMMAND SERGEANT MAJOR—NATIONAL GUARD

She is from Lugoff, South Carolina, and in 1976 joined the South Carolina National Guard. In 1995, she became the first black female to be promoted to the rank of First Sergeant in the South Carolina Army National Guard.

In October 2003, she was promoted to Command Sergeant Major, becoming the first black female to receive this rank in the history of the South Carolina National Guard. Her promotion ceremony took place at the Office of the Adjutant General of South Carolina Major General Stanhope S. Spears in Columbia, South Carolina.

She is assigned as the Command Sergeant Major for the 218th Regiment based in Columbia, South Carolina. In her civilian life, she is the Floor Supervisor for the Radiology Department at Moncrief Army Hospital at Fort Jackson, South Carolina.

Williams, Gerald W.

COMMAND SERGEANT MAJOR—ARMY

He is a native of Arkansas, who upon graduating from high school enlisted into the United States Army. He completed Basic Combat Training in February 1985, at Fort Dix, New Jersey.

His military assignments include serving as Team Chief and Section Sergeant of Charlie Company, 8th Signal Battalion, 8th Infantry Division; Section Sergeant of Delta Company, 426th Signal Battalion, 35th Signal Brigade (Airborne); Assistant S-3 Non-Commissioned Officer in Charge of the 426th Signal Battalion, 35th Signal Brigade (Airborne); MSE Network Controller of the 35th Signal Brigade, 18th Airborne Corps; Node Center Supervisor and Platoon Sergeant of Charlie Company, 123rd Signal Battalion; Platoon

Sergeant of Bravo Company, 123rd Signal Battalion; First Sergeant of Bravo Company, 123rd Signal Battalion, 3rd Infantry Division; First Sergeant of Bravo Company, 121st Signal Battalion, 1st Infantry Division; First Sergeant of Delta Company, 16th Signal Brigade, III Mobile Armored Corps; Command and Control, Communication, Computers and Information Systems (C4IS) Division Sergeant Major at the Headquarters of the United States Army in Europe and 7th Army; and Deputy Chief of Staff for Operations, Sergeant Major, 5th Signal Command. He was then selected to serve as the Command Sergeant Major of the 29th Signal Battalion at Fort Lewis, Washington.

Williams, Harvey Dean

MAJOR GENERAL—ARMY

He was born in Whiteville, North Carolina. He received a bachelor's degree in Political Science from West Virginia State College and a master's in International Relations from George Washington University in Washington, D.C. His military schooling includes the Armed Forces Staff College, the Naval War College, and the Artillery School. He was commissioned a Second Lieutenant on January 16, 1951.

He was promoted to First Lieutenant on August 4, 1952, promoted to Captain on August 14, 1956, promoted to major on August 20, 1962, and promoted to Lieutenant Colonel on August 2, 1966.

From August 1966 to January 1968, he served as Assistant Chief of Staff, G-2, 2nd Region, United States Army Air Defense Command at Richards-Gebaur Air Force Base, Missouri. From February 1968 to June 1968, he was a student at the Armed Forces Staff College at Norfolk, Virginia. From July 1968 to June 1969, he was assigned as Commanding Officer of the 2nd

Battalion, 3rd Basic Combat Training Brigade, United States Army Training Center, Engineer, at Fort Leonard Wood, Missouri. From August 1969 to July 1970, he served as the Assistant G-4; next Deputy G-4, I Field Force; later Commanding Officer of the 1st Battalion, 92nd Artillery, I Field Force, United States Army, Vietnam. From September 1970 to July 1971, he was assigned as Chief of the Security Division in the Office of the Assistant Chief of Staff for Intelligence, United States Army, in Washington, D.C. From August 1971 to June 1972, he was a student at the Naval War College Newport, Rhode Island. He was promoted to Colonel on October 14, 1971. From July 1972 to April 1973, he served as a Military Advisor to the United States Arms Control and Disarmament Agency in Washington, D.C. From May 1973 to December 1974, he served as Commanding Officer of the 75th Field Artillery Group, III Corps Artillery, at Fort Sill, Oklahoma. From January 1975 to June 1975, he served as member of the Special Review Board in the Office of the Deputy Chief of Staff for Personnel, United States Army, Washington, D.C. From June 1975 to February 1977, he served as the commander of the United States Army Military District for Washington, D.C. at Fort Myer, Virginia. He was promoted to Brigadier General on September 1, 1977. He then was selected to serve as the Deputy Commanding General of VII Corps Artillery, United States Army Europe. His next assignment was as Deputy Inspector General (Inspections and Compliance) of the United States Army in Washington, D.C. He was promoted to Major General on March 1, 1980.

He was then selected Commanding General at United States Army Readiness and Mobilization Region III and Deputy Commanding General of the First United States Army at Fort George G. Mead, Maryland. He retired in 1982.

His military awards and decorations include the Legion of Merit; Bronze Star (with oak leaf cluster); Air Medals; and Army Commendation Medal (with three oak leaf clusters).

Williams, Hattie
COMMAND SERGEANT MAJOR—ARMY

She is a native of Norfolk, Virginia. She enlisted into the United States Army in December 1979 and attended Basic Combat Training and Advanced Individual Training at Fort Gordon, Georgia, under the One Stop Unit Program as an OSB Radio Operator.

Her military and civilian education includes all the Noncommissioned Officer Education System Courses; Drill Sergeant School; Instructor Training Courses; Legal Clerk Course; First Sergeant Course; United States Army Sergeants Major Academy; and Command Sergeants Major Course. She also holds a Bachelor of Science degree in Liberal Arts from Regents College.

Her key leadership assignments include serving as First Sergeant and Commo Chief for the 1st Armor Brigade, 2nd Infantry Division at Camp Casey, South Korea; Noncommissioned Officer in Charge, Net

CECOM at Fort Monmouth, New Jersey; First Sergeant in the Joint Logistic Support Command (JLSC) for Operation Uphold Democracy in Haiti; First Sergeant of D Company, 122nd Signal Battalion, 2nd Infantry Division at Camp Casey; First Sergeant/Senior Drill Sergeant at Fort Dix, New Jersey; Platoon Sergeant/Commo Chief, 3/52nd ADA at Fulda, Germany; Platoon Sergeant/Com Section Custodian/Commo Chief of the 24th Aviation Brigade at Hunter Army Airfield, Georgia; and Command Sergeant Major of the 125th Signal Battalion, 25th Infantry Division at Schofield Barracks, Hawaii.

Williams, Hayward
SERGEANT MAJOR—MARINES

He enlisted into the United States Marine Corps in January 1977, and attended Recruit Training at the Marine Corps Recruit Depot at Parris Island, South Carolina. Next he completed training as an Artillery Batteryman.

His key leadership assignments include serving in April 1997 as the First Sergeant for Charlie Company, 2nd Tank Battalion. In April 1998, he transferred to Inspector-Instructor Staff at Frederick, Maryland, where he served as the First Sergeant. In April 2001, he was transferred to Marine Corps Air Station New River, North Carolina. He currently serves as Sergeant Major for Marine Medium Helicopter Squadron-264 (REIN), Marine Aircraft Group–26.

Williams, Herman "Tracy," III
COLONEL—ARMY

Born and raised in Virginia, he graduated from Virginia Commonwealth University with a Bachelor of Science degree in Administration of Justice. He received a Regular Army commission as a Second Lieutenant of Infantry from the University of Richmond in May 1981. He earned a Master of Science degree in Administration of Justice from Webster University and a Master of Strategic Studies from the United States Army War College.

His military education includes Airborne School; the Infantry Officer Basic Course; the Infantry Mortar Platoon Officer Course; the Military Police Officer Basic Course; the Infantry Mortar Platoon Officer Course; the Military Police Officer Advanced Course; the Battalion S1 Course; the Combined Arms Services Staff School; the Conventional Physical Security Course; Advanced Airborne School; Air Assault School; Air Movements Operations Course; the United States College; the Armed Forces Staff College; the United States Army Command and General Staff College; the

United States Marine Corps Command and Staff College; and the United States Army War College.

His military leadership assignments include serving as a Rifle Platoon Leader, 81mm Mortar; Executive Officer and 107th MM Mortar Platoon Leader, 2nd Battalion (Airborne) 508th Infantry, 82nd Airborne Division, at Fort Bragg, North Carolina; Commander of the 552nd Military Police Company at Camp Hialeah in Pusan, South Korea; Assistant S3 Plans, Dragon Brigade, Headquarters XVIII Airborne Corps at Fort Bragg; S3, (Air) 503rd Military Police Battalion at Fort Bragg; Deputy Provost Marshal of the XVIII Airborne Corps at Fort Bragg; Aide de Camp to the Under Secretary of the Army in the Office of the Secretary of the Army in Washington, D.C.; Chief of Operations Division in the Office of the Provost Marshal for United States Forces in Korea; S3, 8th Military Police Brigade in Yongsan, South Korea; Joint Exercise Planner of the Joint Interoperability Division, Joint Training Directorate, United States Atlantic Command; Executive Officer to the Director of Joint Training and Commander of the Joint Warfighting Center, United States Atlantic Command; Special Assistant to the Commanding General of United States Army Training and Doctrine Command; and Commander of the 787th Military Police Battalion and Deputy Commander of the 14th Military Police Brigade. In January 2005, he was serving as the Commander of the 104th Area Support Group.

Williams, James L.
BRIGADIER GENERAL—MARINES

He was born in Bethlehem, Pennsylvania, and raised in Reading and Philadelphia. He received a Bachelor of

Science degree from Slippery Rock University in 1975. He reported to Officer Candidate School in January 1976, and received his commission in March 1976. He received master's degrees from Georgetown University in Government and National Security Affairs in 1981, from Yale University in Hospital Management/Public Health in 1984, and from the United States Army War College in International Security Studies in 2000. He is working on a master's degree in Computer Engineering and Computer Science.

Upon completion of the Basic School at Quantico, Virginia, in 1976, he did a short tour with the Officer Selection Office in Pittsburgh, Pennsylvania. He was subsequently assigned in December 1976 to the 3rd Marine Division to serve with 3rd Battalion, 9th Marines, serving as a Rifle Platoon Leader and Super Squad Platoon Leader.

Returning from overseas in January 1978, he reported to 2nd Force Troops (now 2nd Force Service Support Group) as the Assistant Command Inspector. In March 1978, he was assigned to 2nd Force Reconnaissance Company as a Force Recon Platoon Leader and deployed several times for NATO exercises. During this period he attended reconnaissance training schools.

In January 1979, he was transferred to Marine Barracks at Washington, D.C. He was promoted to Captain in September 1980. During this tour he served as Ceremonial Platoon Leader; White House Presidential Military Social Aide to President Carter and Reagan; Coach of the Barracks boxing team; and Head of the Basic School Correspondence Course at the Marine Corps Institute. He attended graduate school at Georgetown University from 1979 to 1981 and completed the Amphibious Warfare Non-Resident Course in 1980.

In August 1981, he was assigned to the Reserve component of the Marine Corps and was assigned to duty with the 14th Marines where he served with 2nd Battalion, 14th Marines, as a Forward Observer, Battery Executive Officer, Battery Commanding Officer, and Battalion Logistics Officer. While with the 14th Marines, in 1986, he was the recipient of the Outstanding Junior Marine Corps Reserve Officer Award presented by the Reserve Officers Association. He was promoted to Major in October 1987. He also completed graduated school at Yale University during this period in 1984.

He was then assigned to the 4th Reconnaissance Battalion in October 1988, where he served as the Battalion Operations and Training Officer, Battalion Diving Officer, and Executive Officer. During 1990 and 1991, the Battalion was called to duty for Operation Desert Shield/Storm. One reconnaissance company was assigned to lead the reconnaissance efforts for both the 1st and 2nd Divisions in their attacks on Iraq. The remainder of the Battalion was assigned to conduct counter-narcotics operations in CONUS and OCONUS. In 1991, he attended the Marine Corps Reserve Command and Staff College Course as a student.

In 1992, he completed school and was assigned to the 4th Marine Division as Assistant Operations Officer. In July 1993, he completed the Air Command and Staff College Reserve Component Course. In October 1993, he was assigned as the Assistant G-6. He was promoted to Lieutenant Colonel in October 1994. In September 1995, he was assigned as Commanding Officer of the 1st Battalion, 23rd Marines. In 1997, the battalion was assigned to the 1st Marine Regiment, 1st Marine Division, to be the lead battalion in the Kernal Blitz exercise. He was selected in July 1997 to attend the U.S. Army War College Distant Education Program. He was promoted to Colonel in October 1998.

He was then selected and assigned to be the Deputy Commander of the 1st Marine Expeditionary Force Augmentation Command Element (I MACE) in April 2000; he graduated from the U.S. Army War College. In 2002, while in this assignment he was assigned as the Deputy Director of Operations CJTF-180, conducting combat operations in Afghanistan for Operation Enduring Freedom. He was selected for promotion to Brigadier General in February 2003.

In 2003, he also served as the Assistant Chief of Staff, G-9, for Innovation Technology, with the 1st Marine Expeditionary Force. This was a new experimental billet for I MET and the Marine Corps. This billet was established in January 2003, and provides the beginnings of a collaborative technical relationship with all the historical Marine Corps technology organizations, joint service organizations, the I MEF battle-staff, and I MEF MSCs. In November 2003, he became the Commanding General of the 1st Marine Expeditionary Force Augmentation Command Element based at Camp Pendleton, California.

In January 2005, he was serving as the Acting Commanding General of the I Marine Expeditionary Force Augmentation Command Element (I MACE) at Camp Pendleton, California.

Brigadier General Williams' personal military decorations include the Legion of Merit; Bronze Star; Meritorious Service Medal; the Navy Achievement Medal; and the Outstanding Volunteer Medal.

Williams, James T.
COMMAND SERGEANT MAJOR—ARMY

He entered the United States Army in June of 1979, and received his Basic Combat Training and Advanced Individual Training at Fort Knox, Kentucky. His military education includes the NCO Leadership Courses; Tank Commander Certification

Course; Drill Sergeant School; the United States Sergeants Major Course (class 52); and the Command Sergeants Major Course. He holds a Bachelor of Science degree in Administrative Management from Excelsior University of Albany, New York.

His assignments includes serving as Tank Commander, Drill Sergeant; Senior Drill Sergeant; Platoon Sergeant; First Sergeant; and Observer. In August 2004 he was serving as the Command Sergeant Major for the 1st (Iron) Brigade, 2nd Infantry Division, in South Korea.

Williams, Jerry
COMMAND MASTER CHIEF—NAVY

He is a native of Aiken, South Carolina, and a graduate of Aiken High School. He enlisted in the United States Navy in November 1975. Upon graduation from Basic Recruit Training in Orlando, Florida, he transferred to Millington, Tennessee for Aviation Ordnanceman "A" School. After completion of Aircrew Candidate School, he earned his Naval Aircrew Wings in November of 1982. He later transferred to the "Batmen" of Patrol Squadron Twenty-Four as an in-flight ordnanceman. While there he was selected as a Squadron Ordnance NATOPS Evaluator. His next assignment was as a Recruit Company Commander at Great Lakes, Illinois, from July 1985 to January 1989. He successfully trained five Rifle Companies, four Ceremonial Units, and 15 Ceremonial Drill Team Units (three earning the coveted "Hall of Fame" Award). He was twice selected as the distinguished leader of the graduating companies, and subsequently selected as the Recruit Training Command and Naval Training Center 1987 Sailor of the Year.

In January 1989, he received orders to the "Pelicans" of Patrol Squadron Forty-Five as the Ordnance Branch Chief Petty Officer. After a successful sea tour with the "Pelicans" he reported to Commander of Patrol Wing Eleven as Assistant Weapons Officer and Training Department Leading Chief Petty Officer. He received orders in May 1995 to the Pre-commissioning Unit for USS *John C. Stennis* (CVN 74), serving as the Weapons Department Leading Chief Petty Officer. In November 1996, he assumed duties as Command Master Chief of the World Famous "Bulls" of VFA-37 and deployed to the Mediterranean aboard the USS *Theodore Roosevelt* (CVN 71). In November 1998, he reported as the Command Master Chief of Commander Helicopter Anti-Submarine Light Wing, United States Atlantic Fleet. In July 2001, he was selected as the Command Master Chief for the "Mad Foxes" of Patrol Squadron Five.

He has earned the Enlisted Aviation Warfare Specialist, Naval Aircrew Wings, Master Training Specialist Badge and is a Graduate of the Senior Enlisted Academy (class 87).

Williams, Juan D.
SERGEANT MAJOR—MARINES

He enlisted in the United States Marine Corps in October of 1976. After completion of recruit training at Parris Island, South Carolina, and Military Police School at Fort McClellan, Alabama, he was assigned to the 1st Marine Aircraft Wing, Marine Corps Air Station at El Toro, California.

In 1981, he was assigned to Marine Corps Air Station at New River, North Carolina, as the Noncommissioned Officer-in-Charge of the Traffic Accident Investigation and Management Division; in June 1986, he was assigned as an Instructor at the 2nd Marine Division Noncommissioned Officer Academy, and then as the Noncommissioned Officer in Charge of the newly developed Sniper and Combat Marksmanship;

in 1988 he served as a Drill Instructor at the Marine Corps Recruit Depot at Parris Island, South Carolina, during this tour serving as a Drill Instructor, Senior Drill Instructor, and Series Chief Drill Instructor; and in May of 1990, he served as Battery Field Artillery Chief for Battery "F," 2nd Battalion, 12th Marines, 1st Marine Expeditionary Force; deploying with this unit to the Persian Gulf for Operations Desert Shield and Desert Storm. After the Gulf War he was assigned as the Staff Noncommissioned Officer in Charge of the newly developed Sergeant's Course, at Marine Corps Air Station Kaneohe Bay, Hawaii. In 1994, he was assigned to the 12th Marine Regiment, where he was the Field Artillery Chief for Headquarters Battery, 2nd Battalion, 12th Marines. He served as First Sergeant of Headquarters Battery, 12th Marines. In May of 1996, he was assigned to Lima Battery, 3rd Battalion, 12th Marines, 3rd Marine Division; in June 1997, he was transferred to the Inspector-Instructor Staff, 4th SCAMP, 4th Marine Division in Mobile, Alabama; in August 2003, he was assigned to the 3rd Battalion, 3rd Marine Regiment based in Kaneohe Bay, Hawaii, during this tour serving as Sergeant Major for five separate Battalion Landing Teams and three Special Purpose MAGTF's; and in October 2002, he transferred to 1st Rad Battalion FMF PAC., where he deployed to the Persian Gulf to participate in support Operations Enduring Freedom and Iraqi Freedom. In August 2003, he was assigned as the Sergeant Major of the Headquarters Service Battalion of United States Marine Forces Pacific.

Williams, Keith L.
SERGEANT MAJOR—MARINES

He was born in Los Angeles, California, where he graduated from La Puente High School and entered the Marine Corps in the summer of 1976. He attended Recruit Training at the Marine Corps Recruit Depot in San Diego, California. After recruit training, he next completed the Basic Administrative School at Marine Corps Base Camp Pendleton, California.

His key military assignments include serving as Administrative Chief Marine Corps Air Station, El Toro, California, during which post he was selected to the All-Marine Football Team; as a Drill Instructor for Echo Company, 2nd Battalion; and as Administrative Chief at Marine Corps Barracks, North Island. In October 1990, he was assigned as Drill Instructor Monitor in the Special Assignments Branch at Marine Corps Headquarters, Washington, D.C.; in August 1992, he was hand picked for the Commandant's core values briefing team, where he helped author, edit, and deliver presentations associated with today's "Core Value"; in April 1994, he became Personnel Chief MWSS-171 and Radio Broadcaster for the Far-East Network (FEN) in Iwakuni, Japan; in May 1995, he served as First Sergeant with the 3rd Assault Amphibious Battalion, 7th Marines at 29 Palms, California; and in May 1997 he was First Sergeant of the Marine Corps Security Force Company at Naval Air Station, North Island. He subsequently served as First Sergeant of Company G,

2nd Recruit Training Battalion at Marine Corps Recruit Depot, San Diego. In August 1999, he became Sergeant Major of the 1st Recruit Training Battalion, Marine Corps Recruit Depot, San Diego; and in January 2005, he was serving as the Sergeant Major for Marine Aviation Logistics Squadron 11.

Williams, Kewyn L.
COLONEL—ARMY

Colonel Kewyn L. Williams entered the United States Army on September 5, 1979, later earning an ROTC commission from Marshall University. He

received a Bachelor of Science degree in Criminal Justice from Marshall University; a Master of Science in Administrative Studies from Central Michigan University; and a Master of Strategic Studies from the United States Army War College. He is also a graduate of the Command and General Staff College.

Upon completion of the Engineer Officer Basic Course he served as a Platoon Leader, Company Executive Officer, and Battalion Staff Officer in the 46th Engineer Battalion, 1st Aviation Brigade, at Fort Rucker, Alabama. He then served as Company Commander and Battalion Staff Officer in the 9th Engineer Battalion, 7th Engineer Brigade, in Aschaffenburg, Germany. He was assigned to Fort Knox, Kentucky, with duty in Columbus, Ohio, as Director of Engineering and Housing for the Columbus Support Detachment. He served as a Staff Officer and Chief of the Military Engineering and Topographic Division, OD-CSENGR, on the USAREUR Staff. He then joined the 130th Engineer Brigade, 94th Engineer Battalion, as the Executive Officer. Upon his return to the United States, he served as Engineer Team Chief and Combat Support Division Chief at Readiness Group Redstone in Huntsville, Alabama. He then served as Commander of the 2nd Engineer Battalion, 2nd Infantry Division, at Camp Castle, South Korea. His follow on assignment was to the Joint Forces Staff College in Norfolk, Virginia, as an Instructor. On August 1, 2002, he assumed Command of the United States Garrison and Fort Hamilton in Brooklyn, New York.

Williams, Leo V., III

MAJOR GENERAL—MARINES

He received a Bachelor of Science degree from the United States Naval Academy in 1970 and later earned a Master of Business Administration degree from Southern Illinois University in 1978.

He served on active duty from June 1970 to September 1978. His assignments included Staff Platoon Commander at the Basic School; Executive Officer for Battery I, 3rd Battalion, 11th Marines, 1st Marine Division; Headquarters Commandant of the 1st Battalion, 11th Marines; Commanding Officer of Battery F, 2nd Battalion, 3rd Marine Division; Assistant Operations Officer of the 2nd Battalion, 12th Marines, 3rd Marine Division; and Officer Assignments Officer of the Manpower Personnel Branch at the Headquarters of the Marine Corps.

He transferred to the Marine Corps Reserve in October 1978. His assignments included serving as Headquarters Commandant of the 1st Battalion, 24th Regiment, 4th Marine Division; Assistant Operations Officer of the Amphibious Brigade Support Staff; Detachment Commanding Officer at Wing Headquarters Squadron, 4th Marine Aircraft Wing; and Site Executive Officer of the 472nd Wing Support Squadron Detachment B, 4th Marine Aircraft Wing.

Other assignments included Commanding Officer of the 472nd Wing Support Squadron, Detachment B, 4th Marine Aircraft; Squadron Executive Officer dur-

ing Operation Desert Storm with the 5th Marine Expeditionary Force; Group Logistics Officer of the 47th Marine Wing Support Group, 4th Marine Aircraft Wing; Commanding Officer of Marine Training Unit Michigan 1, Marine Training Unit, IRR; Deputy Director for Plans with Headquarters Marine Corps, Policy, Plans and Operations IMA Detachment; Commanding General, 4th Force Service Support Group Marine Forces Reserve in New Orleans, Louisiana; and Commanding General of the Marine Corps Reserve Support Command in Kansas City, Missouri. He was promoted to Major General in January 2001.

Williams, Leroy, Jr.

SERGEANT MAJOR—MARINES

He enlisted in the Marine Corps and attended Recruit Training at Marine Corps Recruit Depot, Parris Island, South Carolina, in December 1979. After graduation, he reported to Communication Electronics School at 29 Palms, California, for military occupational specialty training as a Field Radio Operator. In March 1985, he completed Drill Instructor School at Parris Island, South Carolina.

In November 1990, he reported to Communication Company Headquarters and Service Battalion, 2nd Force Service Support Group at Camp Lejeune, North Carolina, where he served in numerous billets, including Company Gunnery Sergeant, Platoon Commander, Communication Chief, and Operations Chief. During this assignment, he was deployed to Saudi Arabia and participated in Operations Desert Shield and Desert Storm and deployed to the Mediterranean while assigned with Marine Expeditionary Unit Service Support Group 24.

In July 2000, he was promoted to Sergeant Major

and assigned as the Battalion Sergeant Major at the Infantry Training Battalion School of Infantry, Training Command, at Camp Lejeune, North Carolina. After completing his tour at the School of Infantry in February 2003, he was assigned to his current billet as Sergeant Major of Marine Aviation Squadron 26.

Williams, Louis A.

REAR ADMIRAL—NAVY

Born in Ypsilanti, Mississippi, he married the former Faye Ursula and they had two children, Ivan and Kirk. He attended Mississippi State Normal College in Ypsilanti from 1950 to 1951. He attended San Francisco City College from 1951 to 1952. He received a Bachelor of Science degree in business administration from the Naval Postgraduate School in 1975. Some of his major duty assignments were: USS *Hancock* (CVA 19); Air Anti-Submarine Squadron 23 (Aviation Maintenance Officer); Operations Officer for Carrier Airborne Early Warning Squadron 114; Executive Officer of Carrier Airborne Early Warning Squadron 114; Commanding Officer of Carrier Early Warning Squadron 110; Commanding Officer of Naval Air Station, Agana, Guam; Deputy Director of the Aviation Programs Division in the Office of Chief of Naval Operations; Commander of the Training Command, Atlantic at Norfolk, Virginia; Commander of the Anti-Submarine Warfare Wing of the United States Pacific Fleet; and Deputy Commander in Chief for the Iberian-Atlantic Area. He enlisted in the United States Naval Reserve in 1949. After several tours of duty and an honorable discharge, he was appointed an Ensign in the United States Naval Reserve on March 1, 1954. He was promoted to Lieutenant (junior grade) on September 1, 1955, Lieutenant on February 1, 1958, Lieutenant Commander

on August 1, 1963, Commander on February 1, 1968, Captain on July 1, 1973 and Rear Admiral (lower half) in August 1978. His military awards and decorations include the Air Medal (with numerical 2); Joint Service Commendation Medal; Navy Commendation Medal (with one gold star in lieu of second award); Navy Unit Commendation Medal (award USS *Kitty Hawk* CVA 63 and Attack Carrier Air Wing Eleven); National Defense Service Medal (with one bronze star in lieu of second award); Armed Forces Expeditionary Medal; Vietnam Service Medal (with three bronze stars); Republic of Vietnam Meritorious Unit Citation Gallantry Cross Color; and the Republic of Vietnam Campaign Medal (with device).

Williams, Marshall

SERGEANT MAJOR—ARMY

He served as the Senior Enlisted Advisor to three Secretaries of Defense. In 2002, he retired from the Army after 23 years of service. His education includes a Bachelor of Science degree in Management; a Master of Science in Management; and a Master of Science in Human Resource Management and Development from National-Louis University. He also holds an Executive Master of Business Administration from the University of Maryland and a Ph.D. in Organizational Behavior from Northwestern University.

During his military career he held a variety of leadership positions and earned numerous honors, including "Soldier of the Year" on two separate occasions. He also served as a White House Fellow.

Williams, Melvin Gene, Jr.

REAR ADMIRAL—NAVY

A native of San Diego, California, he received a Bachelor of Science degree in Mathematics from the

attack submarines. A Squadron Four submarine was selected as the best all around ship in the United States Atlantic Fleet for 1999 (Battenberg Cup). This was the first time in the 96-year history of the Battenberg Cup competition that a submarine has won this prestigious award for excellence.

He served as Chief of Staff for the Commander of Carrier Group Five, in the Navy's only permanently forward deployed Battle Group (*Kitty Hawk* Battle Group); homeported in Yokosuka, Japan, from October 2000 to August 2002. Carrier Group Five is compromised of 10 ships, approximately 8,000 people, and 72 aircraft. During this sea intensive period the *Kitty Hawk* Battle Group participated in Operation Enduring Freedom, Operation Noble Eagle, post EP-3 incident contingency operations, as well as several joint and coalition exercises. Commander, Carrier Group Five earned the Meritorious Unit Commendation for operations in 2001. In September 2002, he was selected to serve in the Office of the Chief of Naval Operations as Director of the Submarine Warfare Division (N77). He was selected for the Admiral rank in 2002.

Admiral Williams' awards include the Legion of Merit (four awards); the Defense Meritorious Service Medal; the Bronze Star; Meritorious Service Medal; the Joint Meritorious Unit Award; Navy and Marine Corps Commendation Medal (with gold star); the Navy and Marine Corps Achievement Medal (with gold star); Navy "E" Ribbon; Sea Service Deployment Ribbon; Southwest Asia Service Medal (with one bronze star); and the Kuwait Liberation Medal.

Williams, Mitchell L.
COMMAND SERGEANT MAJOR—ARMY

A native of Aberdeen, Mississippi, he entered the

United States Naval Academy in 1978. He earned a Master of Science degree from the Catholic University of America in 1984. He completed the United States Naval Nuclear Power School, NTC, in Orlando, Florida, in February 1979; and Naval Submarine School at Groton, Connecticut, in December 1979.

He entered military service on June 7, 1978, after receiving a commission as Ensign from the United States Naval Academy. His first Submarine assignment onboard USS *Jack* (SSN 650), from January 1980 to November 1982, followed by a shore assignment as a Joint Service Cruise Missile (Tomahawk) project officer at the Headquarters of the Defense Mapping Agency (DMA) Washington, D.C., from December 1982 to June 1984. His next submarine assignment was as Engineer Officer onboard USS *Woodrow Wilson* (SSBN 624) (GOLD), later becoming Commanding Officer.

During his five strategic deterrent patrols in command, USS *Nebraska* was selected as the top Navy and Air Force Strategic Missile Unit (Omaha Trophy). This was the first time a *Trident* submarine was selected for this prestigious award for excellence. *Nebraska* also earned the Meritorious Unit Commendation, Battle Efficiency Award, the Atlantic Fleet Outstanding Ballistic Missile Submarine Award, the Strategic Mission Excellence "S," the Tactical Readiness Top Performer distinction, the Engineering Excellence Partnership awards, and the CINCLANTFLT Silver Anchor Award for retention and taking care of people.

He also served as Executive Assistant to the Director of the Submarine Warfare Division on the Chief of Naval Operations (CNO) Staff in Washington, D.C., from July 1997 to January 1999, before reporting as Commander of Submarine Squadron Four in April 1999. He was promoted to Captain on September 1, 1997.

As Commander of Submarine Squadron Four, safety, readiness, and esprit de corps improved for his six fast

United States Army in June 1982. He attended Basic Combat Training at Fort Knox, Kentucky, followed by Advanced Individual Training (AIT) at Fort Sill, Oklahoma. His military and civilian education include all the Noncommissioned Officer Education System Courses; First Sergeant Course; Master Fitness Course; Battle Staff Course; Senior Officers Logistic Maintenance Course; the United States Army Sergeants Major Academy; and the Command Sergeants Major (D) Course. He holds a Bachelor of Science degree from Regents College and also received an Associate of Science degree from the University of Kentucky.

His military assignments include serving as Radar Section Chief; Platoon Sergeant; Army Advisor; First Sergeant of a Service Battery; Battalion Sergeant Major of a Training Support Battalion; and Battalion Command Sergeant Major of a Light Artillery Battalion. In August 2004, he was serving the Command Sergeant Major for the 2nd Battalion, 4th Field Artillery "Attack-Seven."

Williams, Pat L.
LIEUTENANT COMMANDER—NAVY

She graduated Cum Laude from Mississippi State University in December 1982, earning a Bachelor of Arts degree in Communications. She enlisted in the Navy in August 1984 and was commissioned an Ensign in July 1989 through the Officer Candidate Program.

She graduated with honors from Communication Officer Ashore School in Newport, Rhode Island. She graduated from the Naval Postgraduate School in Monterey, California, in December 1995 with a master's degree in National Security Affairs — Area Studies (Western Hemisphere). She earned a master's degree in National Security and Strategic Studies from the Command and Staff College at the Naval War College in Newport, Rhode Island.

She has served in numerous key military assignments including serving from August 1989 to October 1991 as Administrative Officer and later Budget and Supply Officer at Personnel Support Activity at New London, Connecticut. In December 1991, she reported to Naval Computer and Telecommunications Station Diego Garcia as Head of the Message Center. In December 1992, she reported as Officer in Charge of the Personnel Support Detachment at the Naval Hospital Long Beach. From January 1996 to January 1997, she served as Head of the Benefits and Eligibility Branch, as well as Personnel Program Manager of the Defense Enrollment Eligibility Reporting System/Real-Time Automated Personnel Identification System (D'EERS/RAPIDS) at the Bureau of Naval Personnel in Washington, D.C. From February 1997 to July 1998, she served as Flag Aide to Rear Admiral Barbara McGann, the Commander of Navy Recruiting Command. During this time, she made invaluable ceremonial contributions as a White House Social Aide. In August 1998, she moved with the Bureau of Naval Personnel from Washington, D.C. to Millington, Tennessee, as a Fleet Sup-

port Officer Detailer. After two years as an assignments officer, she attended the Naval War College prior to assuming command of the San Antonio Military Entrance Processing Station in January 2002.

Williams, Reginald J.
COMMAND SERGEANT MAJOR—ARMY

He enlisted in the United States Army in October 1977 under the Delayed Enlistment Program. He attended Basic Combat Training and Advanced Individual Training at Fort Gordon, Georgia.

His military education includes all the Noncommissioned Officer Education System Courses; Battle Staff Course; Air Assault Course; the United States Navy Water Survival Course; Airborne Jumpmaster School; Australian Airborne Exchange; Army Survival Evasion Resistance and Escape (SERE) Level C Training; the First Sergeants School, and the United States Army Sergeants Major Academy (class 53). He also holds a Bachelor of Art in Criminal Justice from Campbell University and a Bachelor of Science in Liberal Arts/Studies from Excelsior University.

Throughout his years of military service he has served in virtually every leadership position. His assignments include serving as Senior Enlisted Advisor; Joint Operations Center Task Force Six (JTF-6) at El Paso, Texas; Unit Sergeant Major; Unit First Sergeant Operating Detachment (1SGTFOD); Operations Noncommissioned Officer in Charge of the Joint Special Command of the Joint Communications Unit at Fort Bragg, North Carolina; Battalion Communication Chief, Operations Noncommissioned Officer in Charge, and Team Leader for the 1st Battalion, 160th Special Operations Aviation Regiment (SOAR) "Nightstalker" Airborne, at Fort Campbell, Kentucky. In August 2004,

he was serving as Command Sergeant Major for the 1st Satellite Control Battalion, United States Army Space and Missile Defense, in Colorado Springs, Colorado.

Williams, Reginald L.
CHIEF MASTER SERGEANT—AIR FORCE

He entered the Air Force under the delayed entry program. After completion of Basic Training, he was assigned in February 1982 for Technical Training at Sheppard Air Force Base, Texas. His military and civilian education includes Noncommissioned Officer Preparatory Course; Pacific Air Forces Noncommissioned Officer Leadership School; and Air Education and Training Command Noncommissioned Officer Academy. He holds an associate's degree in Health Care Management/Administration from the Community College of the Air Force and a Bachelor of Science degree in Business Administration from the University of Phoenix.

He is a career Health Services Administration specialist and has been assigned to a variety of positions at the Wing, Major Command and Air Force Headquarters levels. His key military assignments include serving as Deputy Air Force Surgeon General Enlisted Executive Assistant and Superintendent in the Air Force Biomedical, Research & Development at the Headquarters Air Force of the Medical Operations Agency of the Office of the Air Force Surgeon General; Directorate Superintendent and Command Superintendent for Managed Care in the TRICARE and Patient Administration Division of the Texas Headquarters Air Education and Training Command Office of the Command Surgeon at Randolph Air Force Base, Texas; Group Superintendent and Chief Enlisted Manager of the 36th Medical Group at Anderson Air Base, Guam; Group Superintendent and Chief Enlisted Manager of the 2nd Medical Group at Barksdale Air Force Base, Louisiana; Group Superintendent and Chief Enlisted Manager of

the 31st Medical Group at Aviano Air Base, Italy; and Acting Command Chief Master Sergeant of the 31st Fighter Wing at Aviano Air Base. In July 2004, he was assigned as the Command Chief Master Sergeant of the 311th Human System Wing at Brooks City-Base, Texas.

Williams, Ronald
SERGEANT MAJOR—MARINES

He enlisted in the Marine Corps in September 1977 and attended Recruit Training at Marine Corps Recruit Depot, Parris Island, South Carolina.

He has held a variety of important positions including Drill Instructor; Senior Drill Instructor; Chief Drill Instructor; Operations Section Radio Chief; and Communications Chief. In 1977 he was selected Sergeant Major. In August 2004, he was serving as Sergeant Major for the 3rd Force Service Support Group.

Williams, Sarah J.
COLONEL—AIR FORCE

She served in the Air Force Medical Branch and Nursing Education Department. In 1984, she developed the first curriculum for its Basic Nursing Staff Development Course, which is still in use today. She was selected as military consultant in nursing education to the Air Force Surgeon General in 1989 and was named senior military consultant for nursing staff development to the Air Force Europe Command Surgeon during Operation Desert Shield/Desert Storm.

In 2004, she was assigned at Randolph Air Force Base, Texas, and is the Chapter President of the San Antonio Chapter of the Tuskegee Airmen, Inc.

Williams, Scarlett V.
SERGEANT MAJOR—ARMY

In August 2004, she was serving as the G-1 Sergeant Major at Forces Command (FORSCOM) at Fort Mc-Pherson, Georgia. She serves as the personnel Sergeant Major and enlisted advisor to the G-1. She interfaces with division chiefs and advises the AG-1 on G-1 programs directly or indirectly affecting enlisted soldiers across FORSCOM; including employee reception, training and status; HQ FORSCOM enlisted manning; office climate and physical environment. She also serves as the G-1 POC for Garrison and subordinate Command Sergeants.

Williams, Theodore J.
SENIOR EXECUTIVE SERVICE

He served in the Air Force more than 26 years retiring in rank of Colonel in 1999. While on active duty, he worked for the AFAA more than 11 years as an Acquisition Auditor, Audit Manager, Branch Chief, acting Office Chief, Program Manager and Executive Officer to the Air Forces Auditor General. He was also an AC-130, KC-135, and EC-135 Navigator, Instructor and Evaluator for more than 10 years. He was assigned to the Defense Finance and Accounting Service Headquarters as the Assistant Deputy Director for Customer Service and the first Director of Program Control in the services accounting systems program office.

His education includes a Bachelor of Science degree in Business Administration from Northwestern State University of Louisiana, Natchitoches; a Master of Business Administration degree in Management and Accounting from Rensselaer Polytechnic Institute in Troy, New York; and a Master of Science degree in Management and Accounting from Rensselaer Polytechnic Institute. He has also completed the Professional Military Comptroller Course; Program Management Course at Fort Belvoir, Virginia; and Senior Managers in Government Program at the John F.

Kennedy School of Government at Harvard University in Cambridge, Massachusetts.

His assignments in the Senior Executive Service have included serving as Assistant Auditor General for Field Activities (AFAA) at Arlington, Virginia, and as Assistant Auditor General for Acquisition and Logistics Audits (AFAA) at Wright-Patterson Air Force Base, Ohio.

Williams, Thomas W.
COLONEL—ARMY

Colonel Thomas W. Williams graduated from the United States Military Academy at West Point in 1979. He earned a Bachelor of Science degree in Engineering and was commissioned a Second Lieutenant in the Air Defense Artillery. His military education includes the National War College, where he earned a Master of Science degree in National Security Strategy; the United States Army Ranger Course; Airborne School; Jumpmaster School; Jungle Warfare School; the Combined Arms Services Staff School; the Army Command and General Staff College; the Force Integration and Management Course; and the National War College. From 1995 to 1997, he was assigned as Commander of the 2nd Battalion, 43rd Air Defense Artillery (Patriot), Airborne Corps. He then west to the Pentagon to serve with the Policy Division as a Missile Defense Policy Planner for the Theater Missile Defense and Space Policy Branch from 1997 to 1999. His next assignment was Executive Officer for the Assistant Chief of Staff for Installation Management (ACSIM) from 2000 to 2002. On July 11, 2002, he was selected to serve as the Garrison Commander for Fort Belvoir, Virginia.

Williams, Willie J.
MAJOR GENERAL—MARINES

He was born in Livingston, Alabama. He received a Bachelor of Arts in Business Administration from Still-

man College in Tuscaloosa, Alabama. He earned a Master of Arts degree in Business Administration from National University at San Diego, California, and a Master of Science Degree in Strategic Resources Management from the Industrial College of the Armed Forces National Defense University.

He was commissioned in the Marine Corps in May 1974, via the PLC program. He has held a variety of Command and Staff billets since starting his career with the 11th Marine Artillery Regiment in May 1975, serving first as the Battalion Supply Officer for the 3rd Battalion, and later as the Regimental Supply Officer/Assistant S4 (supply officer). In October 1977, he was ordered to the 3rd Force Service Support Group as the Officer-In-Charge of Inventory Control Point Iwakuni, Japan. Returning from Japan in 1978, he served in San Diego, California, as the Ship's Detachment Supply Officer, Pacific Ocean Area/Marine Barracks Supply Officer and Barracks Executive Officer. He reported to Quantico, Virginia, in June 1982, as a Platoon Commander at Officer Candidate School and later attended the Amphibious Warfare School.

In May 1983, he became the Supply Officer at the Mountain Warfare Training Center in Bridgeport, California. From August 1985 to June 1989, he served as the Assistant Division Supply Officer of the 3rd Marine Division at Okinawa, Japan, prior to attending the Armed Forces Staff College. While serving with the 3rd Marine Division, he stood duty as the Logistics Officer for Contingency Marine Air Ground Task Force 3-88 during its Persian Gulf Deployment from May to December 1988.

After completing Armed Forces Staff College, he was assigned to joint duty with the Department of Defense Inspector General's Office in January 1990, and subsequently, attended the Industrial College of the Armed Forces in 1993. Upon graduating from ICAF, he reported to the 31st Marine Expeditionary Unit (Special Operations Capable).

He was assigned as the Commanding Officer of the MEU Service Support Group from September 1994 to September 1996, after which he served as the Assistant Chief of Staff G-4 for the 3rd Force Service Support Group. He was then transferred to the 1st Force Service Support Group in June 1997 for duty as the Assistant Chief of Staff for G3 (operations), and in 1998 as the Commanding Officer of Brigade Service Support Group I. In June 2001, he was selected to serve as the Commanding General for the 3rd Force Service Support Group at Camp Elbert L. Kinser on Okinawa. He was promoted to Brigadier General on September 1, 2002.

In October 2003, he was selected to serve as Assistant Deputy Commandant of Installations and Logistics (Facilities) at the Headquarters of the United States Marine Corps. In February 2005, he was nominated by the President of the United States to be promoted to Major General.

His awards and decorations include the Legion of Merit with gold star in lieu of second award, the Defense Meritorious Service Medal, the Navy and Marine Corps Commendation Medal, the Navy and Marine Corps Achievement Medal, the Armed Forces Expeditionary Medal, the Humanitarian Service Medal, the National Defense Service Medal and the Department of Defense Service Badge.

Williamson, Arthur J.

COMMAND SERGEANT MAJOR—ARMY

He was born in Washington, D.C., in February 1952. He attended school in the District of Columbia Public Schools System. He received a Bachelor of Science degree in Managerial Science from National-Louis University. His military education includes all phases of the Noncommissioned Officers Education System, including the United States Army Sergeants Major Academy.

He has consistently distinguished himself through various assignments and duties. He deployed with the 547thth Transportation Company to Saudi Arabia as the First Sergeant in support of Desert Shield/Desert Storm during the period September 1990 to April 1991. He was promoted to Sergeant Major in 1998 and appointed as Command Sergeant Major in October 1999. In November 2004, he was serving as Command Sergeant Major for the Washington, D.C., National Guard.

Williamson, Carl

COLONEL—AIR FORCE

He was commissioned in 1980. His education includes a Bachelor of Science in Chemistry from Hampton Institute, in Hampton, Virginia; Advanced Research Techniques (Distinguished Graduate) at the Smith Corona Corporation in Cleveland, Ohio; Communications Electronics Officer Course at Keesler Air Force Base, Mississippi; the Missile Launch Officer Course; Squadron Officer School at Maxwell Air Force Base, Alabama; the Marines Command and Staff College; and the Air War College at Maxwell Air Force

Base. He earned a Master of Arts Degree in Business Administration and Management (dual degree) from Webster University in St Louis, Missouri, and a master's degree in National Security Affairs from the Industrial College of the Armed Forces at Fort McNair in Washington, D.C.

He has held numerous assignments in the former Strategic and Tactical Air Commands, Air Force Space Command, Air Combat Command, and the United States Central Command, including his first assignment in April 1980, as a Student in Communication Systems Officer School at Keesler Training Center at Keesler Air Force Base. In December 1980, he was assigned as Officer-in-Charge of Voice and Command Post Communications Operations in the 1913th Communication Group at Langley Air Force Base, Virginia; in May 1983, he was assigned as Deputy Crew Commander for ACP Titan ICBM, 533rd Strategic Missile Squadron, at McConnell Air Force Base, Kansas; in January 1984, he was Crew Commander of ACP Titan ICBM, 533rd Strategic Missile Squadron at McConnell Air Force Base; in November 1984, he was assigned as an Instructor Crew Commander for the Titan 381st Strategic Missile Squadron at McConnell Air Force Base; from July 1985 to July 1986, he served as Missile EWO Instructor for the Titan at the 381st Strategic Missile Wing at McConnell Air Force Base; in July 1986, he was assigned as Chief of the Voice Operations Branch in the Space Communications Division at Colorado Springs, Colorado; in November 1988, he was Commander of Detachment 1, 1930th Communications Squadron at King Salmon Airport, Alaska; in December 1989, he was assigned as Chief Integration Division at the Headquarters of the Tactical Communications Division at Langley Air Force Base; from July 1990 to February 1991, he served as Executive Officer of the Tactical Communications Division at

Langley Air Force Base; in February 1991, he was assigned as the Communication-Computer Operations Inspector on the Inspector General Team at the Headquarters of Tactical Air Command at Langley Air Force Base; and in February 1992, he was assigned as MAJ-COM Quality Course Director at the Headquarters of Tactical Air Command at Langley Air Force Base. In July 1993, Colonel Williamson was assigned as Deputy Director of ACC Quality Education and Training at Langley Air Force Base; from July 1996 to July 1998, he served as Commander of the 838th Engineering Installation Squadron at Kelly Air Force Base, Texas; in June 1999, he was Chief of the Exercise and Engineering Branch in United States Central Command at MacDill Air Force Base, Florida; in January 2000, he was assigned as Deputy Political Advisor with United States Central Command at MacDill Air Force Base; and from January 2002 to May 2003, he served as Chief of the Program Management Division of the Communications and Information Directorate of United States Pacific Command at Hickam Air Force Base, Hawaii. In May 2003, he was selected to serve as the Commander of the 3rd Combat Communications Group at Tinker Air Force Base, Oklahoma. He was promoted to Colonel in April 2002.

Williamson, Shannon
COMMAND MASTER CHIEF—NAVY

He enlisted in the Navy on October 24, 1986. He holds an associate's and Bachelor of Science degree in Business Administration from San Diego Mesa College and Strayer University.

In August 1997, he reported to the Joint Personal Property Shipping Office at Fort Belvoir, Virginia. In July 2000, he reported to San Diego, California, to

serve on board the USS *Bunker Hill* (CG 52). He transferred to Naval Medical Center San Diego Mercy Detachment in July 2003 and currently serves as the Senior Enlisted Leader at Marine Corps Air Station Miramar Branch Medical Clinic and as the Command Master Chief on board USNS MTF Mercy.

Willis, Eric Leonard
COMMAND SERGEANT MAJOR—ARMY

A native of Atlanta, Georgia, He graduated from Henry Grady High School in 1980 and entered the United States Army in January 1981. He attended Basic Combat Training at Fort Leonard Wood, Missouri, and Advanced Individual Training at Fort Gordon, Georgia.

His military education includes all the Noncommissioned Officer Education System Courses; the First Sergeant Course; Basic Airborne School; NATO LRRP Leader Course; Master Fitness Trainer Course; Battle Staff-Noncommissioned Officer Course; Drill Sergeant School; Unit Equal Opportunity Advisor Course; Tactical Communication Chief/Officer Course; and the United States Army Sergeants Major Academy.

His leadership assignments include serving as Communication Section Chief with the 1/325th Infantry (Airborne), 82nd Airborne Division. In 1988, he was selected to serve as Communication Chief/Platoon Sergeant for the newly activated Long Range Surveillance Detachment (LRSD), 1st Armored Division, in Ansbach, Germany, and later deployed with the unit for Operation Desert Storm. He served as Drill Sergeant/Senior Drill Sergeant at Fort Sill, Oklahoma, and became Drill Sergeant of the Cycle in 1993. He later served as the Signal Senior Enlisted Advisor for the United States Army Readiness Group Pacific at Fort Shafter, Hawaii; as First Sergeant for the 390th Signal Company and later as the Battalion Operations Sergeant for the 30th Signal Battalion; and as the G-6 Sergeant Major for the XVIII Airborne Corps. He was in charge of forming the Combined Joint Task Force–180, J6 operations cell in Afghanistan supporting Operation Enduring Freedom. He was selected for appointment to Command Sergeant Major and reassigned as the Command Sergeant Major for the 504th Signal Battalion at Fort Huachuca, Arizona and deployed with the unit in support of Operation Iraqi Freedom.

Willis, Melvin D.
CHIEF MASTER SERGEANT—AIR FORCE

He was born in Chicago, Illinois, but spent most of his formative years in Haiti, Missouri. He graduated from Haiti High School in 1977. He entered the United States Air Force in December 1978 as a Security Specialist and later retrained into the Cost Analysis career field while assigned to Minot Air Force Base, North Dakota.

His military and civilian education includes an associate's degree of Applied Science from the Criminal Justice Community College of the Air Force; an associ-

ate's degree of Applied Science from the Financial Management Community College of the Air Force; a Bachelor of Science in Business Administration from Hawaii Pacific University; and a master's degree in Business Administration from Webster University. He also attended Air Force NCO Leadership School at England Air Force Base, Louisiana; the Strategic Air Command NCO Academy at Barksdale Air Force Base, Louisiana; and Senior NCO Academy, Maxwell Air Force Base-Gunter Annex, Alabama.

His key military assignments include serving as Chief of Cost Analysis with the 834th Airlift Division at Hickam Air Force Base, Hawaii; Noncommissioned Officer in Charge of the Financial Analysis Branch for the 23rd Comptroller Squadron at Pope Air Force Base, North Carolina; Superintendent of the 92nd Comptroller Squadron, 92nd Air Refueling Wing at Fairchild Air Force Base, Washington; Superintendent of the 437th Comptroller Squadron, 437th Airlift Wing at Charleston Air Force Base, South Carolina; and Superintendent of the 51st Comptroller Squadron, 51st Fighter Wing at Osan Air Base, South Korea. In January 2005, he was serving as Command Chief Master Sergeant of the 437th Airlift Wing at Charleston Air Force Base, South Carolina.

Wilson, Charles E.
MAJOR GENERAL—ARMY

He received a Bachelor of Science degree in Criminal Justice from Wayne State University and a Master of Science in Administration from Central Michigan University. His military career began in July 1966, when he completed Basic Training at Fort Knox, Kentucky, and Advanced Individual Training at Fort Leonard Wood, Missouri, as a Combat Engineer (12B). After completing Transportation Officer Candidate School (OCS) at Fort Eustis, Virginia, he was commissioned as a Second Lieutenant in October 1967. His initial assignment was as a Basic Combat Training Officer with 1st Brigade (BCT) at Ford Ord, California. In July 1969, he attended and completed the Aviation Maintenance Officer Course at Fort Eustis. In October 1969, he was deployed to South Vietnam where he served as a Logistics Officer with the Aviation Materiel Management Command, 34th General Support Group. He was promoted to Captain on October 11, 1969.

Upon release from active duty in October 1970, he returned to civilian life to pursue studies at Wayne State University in Detroit, Michigan. In May 1975, he joined the United States Army Reserves and served as a Company Commander of the BCT Company with the 2nd/330th Regt. 1st Brigade, 70th Division (Tng). In April 1978, he transferred to the Battalion Staff and served as Battalion Supply Officer and then as Brigade S-4. He was promoted to Major on October 10, 1979.

In July 1981, he transferred to the 70th Division Headquarters as the Transportation Officer and later as the Assistant Division G-4. In June 1983, he took command of the 406th Maintenance Battalion in Ann Arbor, Michigan. In September 1985, he returned to the 70th Division (TNG) as the Assistant Chief of Staff G-4. In December 1987, he transferred to the 5032nd United States Army Reserve Forces (USARF) School in Romulus, Michigan, and served as a CAS3 Staff Group Leader (Instructor). In May 1988, he was assigned as Commander of the 5032nd United States Reserve Forces School (USRFS), 123rd United States Army Reserve Command, in Inkster, Michigan. He was promoted to Colonel on August 15, 1988.

In May 1991, he was assigned as the Commander of the 5064th United States Army Garrison, 123rd United States Army Reserve Command in Inkster. In November 1993, he took command of the 3rd Brigade (FE), 85th Division (Exercise) at Selfridge Army National Guard Base, Michigan. From August 1996 to May 1997, he served as Commander/Project Officer with the 3rd Brigade, 85th Division (Exercise), at Selfridge Army National Guard Base. In May 1997, he was assigned as the Deputy Commanding General of the 80th Division (Institutional Training) in Richmond, Virginia. He was promoted to Brigadier General on November 10, 1997.

From March 2000 to August 2002, he served as the Commander of the 98th Division (Institutional Training) at Rochester, New York. He was promoted to Major General on October 7, 2000. In March 2000, he was selected to serve as the Commander of the 98th Division (Institutional Training) at Rochester. In August 2002, he was appointed Deputy Commanding General of the United States Army Reserve Command at Fort McPherson, Georgia.

His military awards and decorations include the Bronze Star, Meritorious Service Medal (with two oak leaf clusters); Good Conduct Medal; Reserve Components Achievement Medal; National Defense Service Medal; Vietnam Service Medal; Armed Forces Reserve Medal; Republic of Vietnam Campaign Medal; Army Meritorious Unit Award; Republic of Vietnam Presi-

dential Unit Citation; and the Republic of Vietnam Gallantry Cross Unit citation.

Wilson, Cornell A., Jr.
MAJOR GENERAL—MARINES

He attended the University of South Carolina on an NROTC Scholarship and graduated with a Bachelor of Science degree in Chemistry in 1972. Upon graduation he was commissioned a Second Lieutenant and assigned to the Basic School at Quantico, Virginia.

His military education includes the Senior Information Warfare Application Course; Logtech Course; Revolution in Business Practices; National Defense University's Capstone Course; and the Naval War College's Strategy and Policy Course.

After graduation from the Basic School and Armor Officer Basic in 1973, he reported to the 1st Marine Division, where he served as a Tank Platoon Commander, Company Executive Officer, Battalion Assistant Operations Officer and Tank Company Commander in the 1st Tank Battalion.

In 1976, he was assigned to the USS *Inchon* as the Combat Cargo Officer at NOB Norfolk, Virginia and to Quantico, Virginia in 1978, where he served as an Advanced Tactics Instructor at the Basic School. He was selected to attend Amphibious Warfare School in 1979 and, following its completion in 1980, reported to the 2nd Marine Division. He was assigned to the 2nd Tank Battalion, commanded H&S Company and served on the Battalion S-4 staff as Maintenance Management Officer before leaving the active component in 1982.

He served on the Maintenance Battalion staff in Charlotte, North Carolina, before taking Command of the Communications Company in Greensboro, North Carolina, in 1985. In 1987, he was assigned to the H&S Battalion staff in Marietta, Georgia, and served as the Battalion's Operations Officer and Executive Officer before assuming Command of the Battalion in

1990. In 1993, he was assigned as the Executive Officer for the 25th Marine Regiment in Worchester, Massachusetts.

Upon completing his tour with the 25th Marines, he served as the Depot Inspector for MCRD Parris Island in 1995, and served as the II MACE G-4 before taking command of the 4th Supply Battalion in Newport News, Virginia in 1997. During this tour, he was selected for Brigadier General in 1999.

From 1999 to 2000, General Wilson's first assignment as a General Officer was as the Deputy Commander for MARCENT at the United States Central Command in Tampa, Florida. Following this tour, he became the Commanding General for the 4th FSSG in New Orleans, Louisiana. In July 2002, he assumed command of the Augmentation Command Element of the Second Marine Expeditionary Force and was subsequently activated in support of Operation Enduring Freedom.

On January 13, 2003, Secretary of Defense Donald H. Rumsfeld announced that the president had nominated Brigadier General Cornell A. Wilson, Jr., for appointment to the rank of Major General. From February 2003 to May 2003, he commanded the Combined Joint Task Force Consequence Management (C/JTF-CM), headquartered in Camp Doha, Kuwait, and supported Operations Enduring and Iraqi Freedom. On July 9, 2004, he assumed command of the 2nd Marine Expeditionary Brigade at Camp Lejeune, North Carolina, where he serves as the Marine Expeditionary Brigade Commander and the Deputy Commander for II Marine Expeditionary Force.

His military awards and decorations include the Legion of Merit; the Meritorious Service Medal; and the Navy Commendation Medal.

Wilson, Danyell E.

SERGEANT—ARMY

She was born in 1974 in Montgomery, Alabama, and she joined the Army in February 1993. She became the first black female in history to earn the prestigious Tomb Guard Badge and become a sentinel at the Tomb of the Unknowns on January 22, 1997.

Before earning the tomb badge, she was a military police officer assigned to the Military Police Company, 3rd United States Infantry Regiment (The Old Guard). She completed testing and a rigorous eight-month trial period and became part of the Honor Guard Company of the Old Guard, the oldest and one of the most elite units in the United States Army.

Wilson, Jerry Lee

COMMAND SERGEANT MAJOR—ARMY

He was born in Thomson, Georgia, on June 28, 1958. He graduated from Thomson High School in 1976 and entered the United States Army in June of that year. He attended Basic Training at Fort Jackson, South Carolina, and completed his Advanced Individual Training at Fort Benning, Georgia, as an Infantryman.

His first assignment was Fort Ord, California, where he served as an M60 Gunner and later as a 90mm Recoilless Rifleman with B Company, 6th Battalion, 31st Infantry Regiment. He was then reassigned to Fort Wainwright, Alaska, in 1978 as a Scout Observer with E Company, 4th Battalion, 9th Infantry Regiment (MANCHU) and held the positions of Senior Scout Observer and Assistant Squad Leader.

In 1980, he was assigned to Fort Benning, Georgia, with B Company, 1st Battalion, 29th Infantry Regiment as a Team Leader and later as a Squad and Section Leader. His next assignment was Dahlonega, Georgia, where he served as a Drill Sergeant Instructor. In late 1983, he volunteered for Drill Sergeant with D Company, 4th Battalion, 2nd Infantry Training Brigade. In 1986 he was reassigned to Fort Kobbe, Panama. He served as a Platoon Sergeant with C Company, 2nd Battalion, 187th Infantry (Airborne), and as the Battalion S3 Operations Sergeant with the 1st Battalion, 508th Infantry (Airborne).

In 1989, he was assigned to Fort Benning, Georgia, for the third time as a Senior Ranger Instructor with the 4th Ranger Training Brigade. In 1990, he volunteered for ROTC duty at Central State University in Dayton, Ohio, where he served as the chief instructor. He was then reassigned once again to Fort Wainwright, Alaska, where he served as the First Sergeant for A Company, 4th Battalion, 9th Infantry Regiment (MANCHU), and as the Brigade S3 Operations Sergeant Major of the 1st Brigade, 6th Infantry Division (Light).

His next assignment was to the Sergeants Major Academy (class of 47). After the Academy, he served his third tour in Alaska as the Battalion Command Sergeant Major of 2nd Battalion, 1st Infantry Regiment at Fort Wainwright. Following this assignment, he served as the 1st Battalion, 502nd Infantry Regiment Battalion Command Sergeant Major at the 101st Airborne Division (Air Assault) at Fort Campbell, Kentucky.

His last assignment was as 2nd Brigade, 502nd Infantry Regiment Command Sergeant Major at Fort Campbell and as part of Operation Iraqi Freedom in Mosul, Iraq.

He lost his life during this last assignment, and was survived by his two sons, Mantrell and Sidney, and a granddaughter, Jeklya Jackson Wilson.

Wilson, Jesse A.
COMMANDER—NAVY

He was born in Norfolk, Virginia, and was raised in California and Maryland. He received a Bachelor of Science degree in Mathematics from the United States Naval Academy in May 1986.

In 1991, he earned a Master of Science degree in Operations Research from the United States Naval Postgraduate School at Monterey, California; and a Master of Arts degree in National Security and Strategic Studies in June 2001 from the Naval War College at Newport, Rhode Island.

During his initial sea tour in USS *Reasoner* (FF 1063), he served as Main Propulsion Assistant and Combat Information Officer from January 1987 to August 1989. As a Department Head, he served as Engineer Officer in USS *Antrim* (FFG 20) from June 1992 to November 1993. As a second tour Department Head assignment, he served as Space Examiner in the Gas Turbine Branch, CINCLANTFLT Propulsion Examining Board from November 1993 to November 1995. From April 1999 to July 2000, he served with the USS *Fitzgerald* (DDG 62) as Executive Officer.

Ashore, he was assigned to the United States Naval Academy from December 1995 to November 1998, where he served as the Twenty-Seventh Company Officer. He also served at the Pentagon on the Joint Staff, J8-Force Structure, Resources, and Assessment where he served as a Joint Warfighting Analyst from June 2001 to June 2004.

Wilson, Johnnie E.
GENERAL—ARMY

He was born in Baton Rouge, Louisiana. He married the former Helen McGhee, and they have three children, Johnnie, Jr.; Charlene; and Scott. They also have five grandchildren. His father was a steel mill worker, and his mother worked part-time in a movie theater. He grew up in an economically deprived family, the second oldest of 12 children. At one point in high school, he held down three part-time jobs to contribute to the family income. He received a Bachelor of Science degree in Business Administration from University of Nebraska at Omaha and a Master of Science degree in Logistics Management from Florida Institute of Technology. His military schools attended include the Ordnance School Advanced Course; United States Army Command and General Staff College; and the Industrial College of the Armed Forces. He entered the service in August 1961 as an enlisted soldier and attained the rank of Staff Sergeant before attending Officer Candidate School. He was commissioned a Second Lieutenant on May 31, 1967, at Aberdeen Proving Ground, Maryland. From May 1967 to September 1969, he served as Mechanical Maintenance Officer, and later Commander, of Company A, 782nd Maintenance Battalion, 82nd Airborne Division, at Fort Bragg, North Carolina. On May 31, 1968, he was promoted to First Lieutenant, and on May 31, 1969, he was promoted to Captain. From October 1969 to November 1970, he was Assistant Brigade Supply Officer, and later Commander of Company C, 173rd Support Battalion (Airborne), 173rd Airborne Brigade, United States Army, Vietnam. From January 1971 to September 1971, he was

a student in the Ordnance Officer Advanced Course of the United States Army Ordnance School at Aberdeen Proving Ground. From December 1971 to December 1973, he was a student at the University of Nebraska at Omaha. From January 1974 to June 1976, he was the Commander of Company B, later Technical Supply Officer, 123rd Maintenance Battalion, 1st Armored Division, United States Army, Europe. He was promoted to Major on June 9, 1976. From August 1976 to June 1977, he was a student at the United States Army Command and General Staff College at Fort Leavenworth, Kansas. From June 1977 to November 1977, he was a student at the Florida Institute of Technology at Melbourne, Florida. From November 1977 to November 1980, he served as Professional Development Officer, later Personnel Management Officer, then Chief of the Ordnance Assignment Branch, Combat Service Support Division, United States Army Military Personnel Center at Alexandria, Virginia. From December 1980 to May 1983, he was he was Commander of the 706th Maintenance Battalion, 9th Infantry Division, at Fort Lewis, Washington. He was promoted to Lieutenant Colonel on July 13, 1980. From May 1983 to June 1984, he was a student at the Industrial College of the Armed Forces at Fort McNair in Washington, D.C. From August 1984 to December 1986, he served as the Commander of Division Support Command, 1st Armored Division, United States Army, in Europe. After being promoted to Colonel on November 1, 1984, he served as Commander of the 13th Support Command at Fort Hood, Texas. From July 1988 to July 1990, he was assigned as Deputy Commanding General of the 21st Theater Army Area Command, United States Army, Europe, and Seventh Army. On September 1, 1989, he was promoted to Brigadier General. In July 1990, he was selected Commanding General of the United States Ordnance Center/Commandant of the United States Army Ordnance School at Aberdeen Proving Ground. From July 1992 to February 1994, he served as Chief of Staff of the United States Army Material Command at Alexandria. He was promoted to Major General on July 1, 1992, and promoted to Lieutenant General on February 9, 1994. From February 1994 to March 1996, he was Deputy Chief of Staff for Logistics, United States Army, in Washington, D.C. He was promoted to the rank of four star General on May 1, 1996. He was assigned as the Commanding General of the United States Army Materiel Command in Alexandria. As head of the Army Materiel Command, General Wilson ran one of the Army's larger commands. Army Materiel Command (AMC) is allotted $20 billion a year, a third of the Army's annual budget. The General was in charge of 68,000 people, most of them civilians, who were based at 350 locations in 40 states and six foreign countries. He retired from the military on May 31, 1999. His military awards and decorations include the Distinguished Service Medal (with oak leaf cluster); Legion of Merit (with oak leaf clusters); Bronze Star (with two oak clusters); the Meritorious Service Medal (with two oak leaf clusters); Army Commendation

Medal; Master Parachutist Badge; and Special Forces Tab.

Wilson, Kevin D.
SERGEANT MAJOR—MARINES

Sergeant Major Kevin D. Wilson was born in Chicago, Illinois, on April 10, 1961. He joined the delayed entry program on October 28, 1978, and after completing high school, he entered the Marine Corps on July 16, 1979. In October 1985 he reported to Parris Island for Drill Instructor School. Upon graduation from Drill Instructor School in January 1986, he was assigned to the Third Recruit Training Battalion, H Company. He filled the billets of Drill Instructor and Senior Drill Instructor, and was promoted to Staff Sergeant in January 1988.

In October 1998, he was transferred to Weapons and Field Training Battalion Edson range area at Camp Pendleton, California. He was the first Sergeant for Range Company from October 1998 until June 1999 when he transferred to Headquarters Company. He was promoted to Sergeant Major in April 2001 and transferred to Headquarters and Headquarters Squadron at Marine Corps Air Station, Okinawa, Japan.

Wilson, Randy D.
COMMAND SERGEANT MAJOR—ARMY

Command Sergeant Major Randy D. Wilson first entered the military service as a Marine Corps Infantryman in 1974. As a marine, he completed a WESTPAC tour and was honorably discharged in 1977. He then reentered the military service in the United States Army in August 1980 to attend Advanced Individual Training and qualified for the Military Intelligence Specialty, MOS 98 Kilo. His military education includes the Sergeants Major Academy and the Command Sergeants Major Course.

In 1995, he reported to Germany to serve as First Sergeant of Headquarters and Headquarters Company

of the 103rd Military Intelligence Battalion (later rede-signated as HHC, 101st Military Intelligence Battalion) until 1996. From 1996 to 1998, he was assigned to the 742nd Military Intelligence Battalion, 704th Intelligence Brigade. He was then assigned as Sergeant Major of the Requirements and Analysis Group at the National Security Agency. From 1998 to 2000, he was assigned as the Command Sergeant Major of the 311th Military Intelligence Battalion at Fort Campbell, Kentucky.

He is currently serving as the Command Sergeant Major of the 704th Military Intelligence Brigade.

Wilson, Robert D., Jr.

CAPTAIN—NAVY

Born in Columbus, Ohio, he graduated from California State University at Fresno and received his commission from Aviation Officer Candidate School at Pensacola, Florida, in 1981. He was designated a Naval Flight Officer in April 1982.

In July of 1982, he reported to his first operational assignment flying the ERA-3B Skywarrior with the "Firebirds" of Tactial Electronic Warfare Squadron Thirty Three (VAQ 33). While assigned to the "Firebirds," he made numerous detachments while conducting operational and electronic warfare missions in support of fleet operations for Second and Third Fleet air and surface units. His next assignment was with Fleet Air Reconnaissance Squadron One (VQ-1) at Navy Air Station Agana, Guam, flying Skywarriors. During his tour, he made multiple deployments in USS *Enterprise* (CV 65), USS *Kitty Hawk* (CV 63) and USS *Midway* (CV 41) to the Indian Ocean, South China Sea and Mediterranean Sea. He next reported to the Commander of the Operational Test and Evaluation Force at Norfolk, Virginia, in October 1988. In July of 1991, he transitioned to the ES-3A Shadow and reported to Fleet Air Recon-

naissance Squadron Five (VQ-5) at Naval Air Station Agana in March 1992. He served as the Training Officer, Operations Officer and Detachment ALFA Officer-in-Charge, where he led the first operational deployment of the ES-3A to the Persian Gulf in November 1993 embarked in the USS *Independence* (CV 62). His next assignment was with the Program Executive Officer Air, ASW, Assault and Special Mission Program Office (PMA-290), in Arlington, Virginia, in April. During this tour, he served as Deputy Program Manager for the ES-3A.

In April 1996, he reported to Fleet Air Reconnaissance Squadron Six (VQ-6) as Executive Officer and in June 1997 became the Commanding Officer. In July 1998, he reported to the Industrial College of the Armed Forces at Fort McNair, Washington, D.C., where he received a Master of Science degree in Strategic Resource Strategy and in July 1999 reported to the National Reconnaissance Office in Chantilly, Virginia, for his Joint tour. In May 2002, he reported to CO-MUSNAVCENT/Fifth Fleet located in Bahrain where he was the Assistant Chief of Staff for Communications (N6) during Operation Iraqi Freedom and in October 2003, he became the Commanding Officer of Naval Station Roosevelt Roads in Puerto Rico, where he led the congressionally mandated closure of Naval Station. In February 2005, he was serving as the Commander of Fleet Activities in Okinawa.

Wilson, Rosa L.

COMMAND MASTER CHIEF—NAVY

In October 2004, she was serving as the Command Master Chief for the Legendary Black Knights of Helicopter Anti-Submarine Squadron Four at Naval Air Station North Island, San Diego, California.

The Black Knights spent 2002–2003 on a world-record western Pacific deployment aboard the USS

Abraham Lincoln (CVN 72). Their accomplishments included military engagement with Pakistan, detachments in Kuwait and CSAR training in Australia, all in support of Operation Southern Watch and Operation Enduring Freedom. During Operation Iraqi Freedom, HS-4 supported Navy SEAL, British Commando and Polish GROM forces in Kuwait and Iraq and were the primary force protection for the USS *Abraham Lincoln* Battle Group. The nine and one half month deployment (a record since WWII) included 1283 Sorties and 3228 flight hours' flown, setting post–Vietnam War records. With its current compliment of six helicopters, 27 officers and 162 enlisted personnel, the Black Knights are the most decorated helicopter anti-submarine squadron in history.

Wilson, Samuel

COMMAND SERGEANT MAJOR—ARMY

He enlisted in the United States Army on July 11, 1978, and completed his Basic and Advanced Individual Training at Fort Knox, Kentucky.

His military and civilian education includes all the Non-Commissioned Officer courses, including the First Sergeant Course, Master Gunner School, Drill Sergeant School, Master Fitness School, Instructor Trainer Course and the Sergeants Major Academy (class 49). He has earned an associate's degree in Administrative/Management Studies with Regents College.

He has served as Tank Loader, Tank Gunner, Tank Commander, Section Sergeant, Platoon Sergeant, Company Master Gunner, Tank Gunnery Instructor, Senior Drill Sergeant, First Sergeant, Operations Sergeant Major, and Chief Enlisted Army Adviser. In August 2004, he was serving as the Command Sergeant Major for the 2nd Battalion, 81st Armor Division.

Wilson, Samuel F.

COMMAND SERGEANT MAJOR—ARMY

He is a native of Fort Wayne, Indiana. He entered the United States Army in 1984, after graduating from Indiana University and completed OSUT training at Fort Benning, Georgia. His military education includes Air Assault School, Rappel Master Course; Drill Sergeant School; Master Fitness Trainer Course; Battle Staff NCO Course; the Inspector General's Course; Equal Opportunity Staff Advisor Course; Instructor Development Course; First Sergeant Course; the United States Army Sergeants Major Academy (class #53); and the United States Army Command Sergeant Major Course. He holds a Master of Business Administration degree in International Business from Indiana University; a Master of Science degree in General Administration from Central Michigan University; and a Master of Arts degree in Human Resources Development from Webster University.

His assignments includes serving as Drill Sergeant; Detachment Sergeant; Inspector General NCO; First Sergeant; Senior Equal Opportunity Advisor; 71L

Career Management NCO; Operation Sergeant; Command Sergeant Major for the 1/34th Infantry Regiment at Fort Jackson, South Carolina; and Command Sergeant Major of Allied Forces North, USANATO.

Wilson, Willy
COMMAND SERGEANT MAJOR—ARMY

He served as Director of Enlisted Maintenance Training, a position previously held by either a Colonel or Lieutenant Colonel. He first served in Army Aviation as an aircraft mechanic. On his first combat tour in Vietnam he served as mechanic and door gunner in both Army and Navy helicopter gunships.

Wilson-Burke, Iva
COLONEL—ARMY

Georgia Army National Guard Colonel Iva Wilson-Burke was pinned to the rank of Colonel by her father, retired Chief Warrant Officer Ivory Wilson, and Brigadier General Terry Nesbitt of the Georgia Army National Guard on January 11, 2003. She is the first African American female to be promoted to Colonel in the Georgia National Guard. She is the former commander of Georgia's Headquarters Detachment, State

Area Command. Her new assignment was as the Military Personnel Officer and the Distance-Learning Manager.

Winfield, W. Montague
MAJOR GENERAL—ARMY

He received a Bachelor of Science degree in Health and Physical Education in Virginia State University. He earned a Master of Education degree from Virginia State University and a Masters of Science degree in Industrial Management from the University of Pennsylvania. His military education includes the Armor Officer Basic Course; the Infantry Officer Advanced Course; the United States Marine Corps Command and General Staff College; and the United States Army War College.

He was commissioned a Second Lieutenant in the United States Army on July 7, 1977, after completing the ROTC program at Virginia State University. Beginning in October 1977, he was assigned to the United States Army Europe and Seventh Army, Germany as Platoon Leader of I Troop, Executive Officer of K Troop, and Commander of the Headquarters and Headquarters Troop, all in the 3rd Squadron; and Commander of B Troop, 1st Squadron, 2nd Armored Cavalry Regiment.

From July 1990 to July 1992, he was a Staff Officer in the Army Initiatives Group, later Strategic Analyst/Speech Writer in the Office of the Deputy Chief of Staff for Operations and Plans, United States Army, Washington, D.C. From November 1992 to October 1994, he served as the Commander of the 1st Squadron, 10th Cavalry (later redesignated 1st Battalion, 70th Armor), Combined Arms Task Force, 194th Separate Armored Brigade at Fort Knox, Kentucky, and Oper-

ation Uphold Democracy in Haiti. In October 1994, he was assigned as the Deputy Commander of the 16th Cavalry Regiment at the United States Army Armor Center at Fort Knox, Kentucky. From July 1996 to July 1998, he served as Commander of the 3rd Brigade, 1st Infantry Division (Forward), United States Army Europe and Seventh Army, Germany and Operation Joint Guard in Bosnia-Herzegovina. He was promoted to Colonel on September 1, 1996.

In July 1998, he was selected a Fellow on the Council on Foreign Relations in New York City. In July 1999, he was assigned as Executive Officer/Military Assistant to the Commander of Stabilization Force (COMSFOR) in Bosnia-Herzegovina. From October 1999 to June 2000, he was assigned as the Executive Officer to the Commanding General of the United States Army Europe and Seventh Army in Germany. From June 2000 to October 2000, he served as the Special Assistant to the Deputy Chief of Staff for Operations and Plans for the United States Army in Washington, D.C. In October 2000, he was selected to serve as the Deputy Director for Operations at the National Military Command Center, J-3, with the Joint Staff in Washington, D.C. He was promoted to Brigadier General on October 1, 2001.

From August 2002 to September 2002, he served as Deputy Commanding General of Multinational Division (North), Stabilization Force-11 and Operation Joint Forge in Bosnia-Herzegovina. From September 2002 to October 2003, he served as the Assistant Division Commander (Support) of the 25th Infantry Division (Light) at Schofield Barracks, Hawaii. In October 2003, he was selected to serve as Commander of Joint Prisoner of War/Missing in Action Accounting Command for United States Pacific Command at Hickham Air Force Base, Hawaii. He was promoted to Major General on October 1, 2004.

His military awards and decorations include the Legion of Merit (with oak leaf cluster); Meritorious Service Medal (with five oak leaf clusters); Joint Service Commendation Medal; Army Commendation Medal (with two oak leaf clusters); the Army Staff Identification Badge; the Expert Infantryman Badge; Ranger Tab; and the Parachutist Badge.

Wingate, Cedric F.
COLONEL—ARMY

He is a graduated from Florida A&M University in 1980 with a Bachelor of Science degree in Sociology and a ROTC commission. He holds a master's in Management from Webster University in St. Louis.

His military education includes the Officer Basic Course at the Infantry School; Mortar Platoon Course at the Infantry School; Chemical, Biological and Radiological Officer Course; Unit and Organization Supply Procedures Course; Armor Officer Advanced Course at the Armor School; Defense Equal Opportunity Management Course; Command and General Staff College; and Civil Affairs Advanced Course.

Early in his career, he was a Weapons Platoon Leader,

a Rifle Platoon Leader and a 4-2 Mortar Platoon Leader with the Infantry in Kansas and South Korea.

In 1995, he was assigned as the Equal Opportunity Officer for St. Louis until 1998, when he transferred to Fort Jackson and Atlanta as the Chief of the United States Army Readiness Command. His next assignment was at Fort Buchanan, Puerto Rico, where he performed as Chief of Operations and Readiness Officer; Assistant Deputy Chief of Staff; and Deputy Mobilization Commander. In June 2005, he was serving as Deputy Commander for Readiness at the 94th Regional Readiness Command, United States Army Reserves.

Winns, Anthony L.
REAR ADMIRAL—NAVY

He is a native of Jacksonville, Florida. He graduated with distinction from the United States Naval Academy earning a Bachelor of Science degree in June 1978. He completed initial flight training at NAS Pensacola, Florida, and advanced navigator training at Mather AFB, California, where he was designated a Naval Flight Officer in January 1980.

Following initial P-3 training at Patrol Squadron Thirty-One (VP-31), he was assigned to Patrol Squadron Six (VP-6) at NAS Barbers Point, Hawaii, in July 1980. Flying the P-3B MOD aircraft, he served as Legal Officer and Aircraft Division Officer. He completed two deployments to NAS Cubi Point, Philippines, and detachments throughout the Pacific and Indian Oceans.

In January 1984, he was assigned to the Naval Military Personnel Command in Washington, D.C. During his tour, he served in the Aviation Junior Officer Assignment Branch as Fixed Wing Initial Assignment Officer and VP Community Shore Duty Detailer. In April 1986, he reported aboard USS Forrestal (CV 59), homeported in Mayport, Florida, as Operations

Commanding Officer, *Essex* was awarded the Battle "E" and deployed to the Persian Gulf for Operation Southern Watch.

He was assigned as the Policy Division Chief of the Strategic Plans and Policy Directorate (J-5) on the Joint Chiefs of Staff in Washington, D.C. In May 2000, he became the first officer in his Naval Academy class selected for Flag rank. He assumed duties as Commander of Patrol and Reconnaissance Force, Pacific, and Commander of Task Force 32 on June 22, 2001. In September 2003, he was selected to serve as the Deputy Director of the Air Warfare (N78F) Staff of the Chief of Naval Operations.

His military awards and decorations include the Defense Superior Service Medal; the Legion of Merit; Meritorious Service Medal (with three oak leaf clusters); Navy Commendation Medal (with three oak leaf clusters); the Navy Achievement Medal; and various unit, campaign and service awards.

Winsett, Jackson A.
COMMAND CHIEF MASTER SERGEANT—AIR FORCE

He entered the United States Air Force Reserve in 1981 after serving initially on active duty in the United States Army from 1966 to 1969, with tours in Berlin, Germany, and in South Vietnam. He holds a Bachelor of Arts degree in Psychology and Business and a Master of Arts degree in Business and Counseling.

His military assignments in the Air Force Reserve included serving as an Administrative Specialist, Military Personnel Flight Specialist, Group Career Advisor, First Sergeant and Command Chief Master Sergeant. He served as the Senior Enlisted Advisor for the 442nd Fighter Wing at Whiteman Air Force Base, Missouri, before serving as the Command Chief Master Sergeant for the 10th Air Force at Naval Air Station Joint Reserve Base at Fort Worth, Texas. In 2004, he was selected

Administration Officer. He qualified as Fleet Officer of the Deck Underway and Tactical Action Officer, and deployed to the Mediterranean and Caribbean Seas and the North Atlantic Ocean. Following this tour, he attended the Naval Post Graduate School in Monterey, California. He graduated with distinction in December 1989, earning a Master of Science degree in Financial Management.

After refresher training in Patrol Squadron Thirty (VP-30), he reported to Patrol Squadron Fifty-Six (VP-56) at NAS Jacksonville in June 1990. During this assignment, he served as Special Projects Officer and administrative Officer, and deployed to Keflavik, Iceland. He then reported to the Commander of Patrol Wing Eleven as CNO Special Projects Officer.

He served as Executive Officer and Commanding Officer of Patrol Squadron Eleven (VP-11) from August 1992 to July 1994. During his tour as Commanding Officer, Patrol Squadron Eleven deployed to Sigonella, Sicily, and Roosevelt Roads, Puerto Rico, and participated in Operation Sharp Guard/Sharp Edge in Bosnia and Caribbean Drug operations. During the Sigonella deployment, the squadron became the first patrol squadron to employ the Maverick Missile System. During his command tour, Patrol Squadron Eleven was awarded the coveted Battle "E," Golden Wrench Award for aircraft maintenance (4th consecutive), and numerous unit awards.

From August 1994 to March 1995, he was assigned to the Roles and Missions Staff of the Chief of Naval Operations in Washington, D.C. He became Executive Officer aboard USS *Guam* (LPH 9) in August 1995 and deployed to the Mediterranean Sea. He reported aboard USS *Essex* (LHD 2) in December 1996 as the ship's Executive Officer and assumed command as Commanding Officer in May 1997. During his tour as for the top enlisted position in the United States Air Force Reserve Command.

Wise, Ronald D.
SERGEANT MAJOR—MARINES

He is a native of Baltimore, Maryland, and enlisted in the United States Marine Corps on the delayed entry program in September 1974 in Stamford, Connecticut. He attended Recruit Training at Marine Corps Recruit Depot Parris Island, South Carolina, in December 1974, where he was the Platoon Honor man and received a meritorious promotion to Private First Class.

In August 1976, he was transferred to Marine Corps Recruit Depot Parris Island, for Drill Instructor School. After successful completion of Drill Instructor School, he was assigned as a Drill Instructor and Senior Drill Instructor with Company I, 3rd Recruit Training Battalion. Upon completion of Drill Instructor duty, he was transferred to MCCDC at Quantico, Virginia in 1978 where he was assigned as Training NCO at the Basic School and was later transferred to Officer Candidate School as a Physical Training Instructor and a Platoon Sergeant for Company C. In March 1987, he was transferred to the College of the Holy Cross in Worcester, Massachusetts, where he was assigned as the Assistant Marine Officer Instructor for the NROTC Program, and during the summer months worked at the Naval Science Institute in Newport, Rhode Island as a Company Gunnery Sergeant for Company A. In September 1990, he transferred to 3rd Battalion, 5th Marines, deploying to the Middle East in support of Operation Desert Storm and Desert Shield. Upon his return from the Gulf War, he was selected to First Sergeant and was transferred to Company I, 3rd Battalion, 5th Marines as the Company First Sergeant. After numerous assignments as First Sergeant, he was selected as Sergeant

Major in April 1996 and assigned to Marine Corps Air Station El Toro, California, as the Sergeant Major of Headquarters Squadron. In July 1999, he was assigned as Sergeant Major for the First Combat Engineer Battalion at Camp Pendleton, California. In April 2000, he was assigned as Group Sergeant Major, MACG-38, MCAS Miramar, at San Diego, California. In June 2002, he was assigned as Group Sergeant Major for the MATSG-21 in Pensacola, Florida.

Witherspoon, J. P., Jr.
SERGEANT MAJOR—MARINES

Sergeant Major Witherspoon entered the Marine Corps in February 1977 and was sent to Marine Corps Base Parris Island, South Carolina, for recruit training. He completed Infantry Training School at the Marine Corps Base at Camp Pendleton, California.

In March 1990, he received orders to Tustin, California. He served as Operations Chief with MATCS-38, deploying to the Persian Gulf for Operation Desert Storm/Desert Shield. On October 19, 2000, he was selected as the Sergeant Major of Marine Heavy Helicopter Squadron 462, Marine Aircraft Group 16, 3rd Marine Aircraft Wing.

Witherspoon, John Gordon
CAPTAIN—COAST GUARD

He first served in the United States Army, before enlisting into the United States Coast Guard in 1963. He rose to Quartermaster First Class, was selected for Officer Candidate School and was commissioned an Ensign in 1971. He became the Coast Guard's first African American to Command a Coast Guard Cutter and Shore Unit, during his distinguished career.

He served as the Commander of the *Mallow, De-*

pendable and *Valiant*. He was also selected to serve as the Chief of the Eighth Coast Guard District Search and Rescue Branch in New Orleans.

The Coast Guard named its highest leadership award, the Captain John G. Witherspoon Leadership Award, for Captain Witherspoon. This award is an annual presentation given to the Coast Guard Officer who exemplifies the Coast Guard core values of Honor, Respect, and Devotion to Duty.

Wolfolk, Sharon Bingham
MASTER SERGEANT—AIR FORCE

She is a native of Washington, D.C. She began her

military career in 1983. She holds a Bachelor of Music degree from the Catholic University of Virginia. She is a past winner of the Friday Morning Music Club Student Concerto Competition, and as the winner performed as a soloist with the McLean (Virginia) Symphony Orchestra.

An active freelance musician in the Washington, D.C., area, she has performed regularly as a violist with the Fairfax and Prince George's Symphonies, Landon, and the Beethoven ensemble Strings for Christ.

In 1985, she was awarded a scholarship to the renowned Aspen Music Festival in Colorado. She is a violist with the United States Air Force Band at Bolling Air Force Base in Washington, D.C.

Wood, Eddie
COMMAND SERGEANT MAJOR—ARMY

He was born in Valdosta, Georgia. He enlisted in the Army in June 1977 and attended One Station Unit Training at Fort Sill, Oklahoma. His military and civilian education includes all the Noncommissioned Officer Education System Courses; Recruiter Course; Station Commander's Course; First Sergeant Course; the United States Army Sergeants Major Academy (class 48); and the Command Sergeant Major (D) Course. He holds an Associate of Arts degree from Mount Wachusett Community College in Gardner, Massachusetts.

His military assignments include a variety of leadership positions including Chief of Section; Gunnery Sergeant; Platoon Sergeant; Chief of Firing Battery; Recruiter, Senior Enlisted Advisor; First Sergeant; and Battalion Command Sergeant Major. In August 2004, he was serving as the Command Sergeant Major for the 212th Field Artillery Brigade at Fort Sill.

Woodcock, Terry A.
COMMAND MASTER CHIEF—NAVY

He enlisted in the Navy in June 1979, and attended Recruit Training in Orlando, Florida. Following recruit training, he attended Hospital Corpsman "A" school in Great Lakes, IL.

He reported to Naval Hospital Guantanamo Bay, Cuba, in February 1980. After successful first tour, he attended Basic Laboratory Technician "C" school in San Antonio, Texas and earned the 8501 NEC. Upon completion of "C," school, he reported to the Military Entrance Processing Station at Sioux Falls, South Dakota.

His additional assignments as a Laboratory Technician include Naval Hospital Great Lakes, where he served in every division of the Laboratory Department. His next shore assignment was in October 1987, at the Naval School of Health Sciences in San Diego, California, as a student at Independent Duty Corpsman School. Upon graduation in September of 1988, he was assigned as the Senior Medical Department Representative onboard the USS *Hewitt* (DD 966). There he earned his ESWS pin and was selected for Chief Petty Officer.

Following his Independent duty tour, he was assigned as Medical Inspector for Commander Logistics Group WESTPAC Detachment at Yokosuka, Japan. His next assignment was Medical Inspector and Specialty Advisor to the Commander of Naval Surface Force. In 1998, he reported to the USS *Essex* (LHD 2) as Laboratory Chief Petty Officer in the Medical Department. He completed the largest amphibious ship hull swap with the USS *Belleau Wood* (LHA 3). Leaving the Belleau Wood, he reported to the Enlisted Placement Management Center (EPMAC) where he

was assigned as Division Officer for Medical and Dental Placement. He terminated shore duty and accepted orders to the USS *John S. McCain* (DDG 56) as Command Master Chief.

Woods, Joseph E.
COMMAND SERGEANT MAJOR—ARMY

CSM Joseph E. Woods is a native of Alabama. He attended Sulligent High School and holds a bachelor's degree in Political Science from Columbia College. He is currently working on a Master of Science in Management.

Upon entering the Army in July 1981, CSM Woods received Basic Training and Advanced Individual Training (AIT) as an 88M at Fort Dix, New Jersey. Following his initial training, he was assigned to the 471st Transportation Company, Fort Sill, Oklahoma, as a Heavy Transport Operator. In 1982, he was reassigned to the 233rd Engineer Bn, Baumholder, West Germany, as a Heavy Vehicle Driver and Squad Leader. Subsequently assigned to the 28th Trans Bn in Mannheim, West Germany, CSM Woods served as a Squad Leader and Platoon Sergeant. From 1988 through 1991 his duties included Platoon Sergeant, Drill Sergeant and Senior Drill Sergeant with both the 58th Trans Bn and the 577th Engineer Bn at Fort Leonard Wood, Missouri. While assigned to both HQ 58th Trans Bn at Ft. Leonard Wood, CSM Woods served as Operations Sergeant and Instructor Writer. He later served as Unit Trainer and Truck Master in the 1221st Transportation Company, 5th US Army Readiness Group. In 1997 CSM Woods served as the First Sergeant of the 46th Transportation Company in Camp Humphries, South Korea, followed in 1998 by an assignment as First Sergeant of the 96th Transportation Company at Fort Hood, Texas. During this assignment, he was selected as Sergeant Major (SGM) and assigned as the Plans and Operations Sergeant Major, G-4 III Corps at Fort Hood. In 2001 he was selected to become a Command Sergeant Major (CSM) and assigned to 765th Transportation Battalion at Fort Eustis, Virginia. He is currently the Command Sergeant Major, 8th Transportation Brigade, Fort Eustis.

His military education includes the Junior Leadership Course, Primary Leadership Development Course, Basic and Advanced Noncommissioned Officers Course, Air Assault School, Drill Sergeant School, Battle Staff Course, Equal Opportunity Advisor Course, the 1SG Course, NCO Logistics Course, Signal Leadership Course, Hazardous Materials Handling Course, Safety Officer Risk Management Course, Command Retention Course, TRADOC Pre-Command Course, The Command Sergeants Major Course and the United States Army Sergeant Major Academy Class 28.

CSM Woods has received numerous awards and decorations including Meritorious Service Medal (3rd Award); Army Commendation Medal (2nd Award); Army Achievement Medal (10th Award); Overseas Service Ribbon #3; NCO Development Ribbon #4; Army Service Ribbon, Air Assault Badge; Driver and Mechanic

Badge; Drill Sergeant Badge; Korea Defense Service Medal; Global War on Terrorism Service Medal; Good Conduct Medal (7th Award); and the National Defense Service Medal with Bronze Star.

Woods, Robert
COMMAND SERGEANT MAJOR—ARMY

He entered the United States Army in November 1973 at Fort Jackson, South Carolina. After Basic Combat Training at Fort Jackson and Field Artilleryman Advanced Individual Training at Fort Sill, Oklahoma, he was assigned to B Battery, 2-10 Field Artillery, 197th Infantry Brigade at Fort Benning, Georgia. His military education include all the Noncommissioned Officer Education System Courses; Army Recruiter Course; Recruiting Station Commander Course; Guidance Counselor and Recruiting Operations Course; Recruiting First Sergeant Course; and the United States Army Sergeants Major Academy in 1995.

He began his recruiting career in the Baltimore-Washington District Recruiting Command from 1981 to 1984 in Washington Recruiting Company. His next assignment was a return to Field Artillery in West Germany. He served as a Section Chief, Platoon Sergeant, First Sergeant and re-enlistment NCO, and he returned to recruiting duty in 1987, serving the Philadelphia Recruiting Battalion as a Field Recruiter, Limited Production Station Commander (CPSC), Guidance Counselor and Senior Operation NCO. His next assignment was at the Jackson, Mississippi, MEPS as Senior Guidance Counselor, and at New Haven Recruiting Company. He also served as the First Sergeant in Albany, New York, and as Chicago Recruiting Battalion Sergeant Major, followed by assignment to ESD, RO Division at Fort Knox, Kentucky. In October 2004, he was serving as the Command Sergeant Major of the United States Army Recruiting Command Mission Support Battalion.

Woods, Spencer R.
COMMAND SERGEANT MAJOR—ARMY

He earned a Bachelor of Science in Sociology from the University of Southern Mississippi and a Master of Arts in Human Resource Development. In his civilian occupation he is a deputy sheriff, holding the rank of captain.

He is the senior enlisted soldier in the reserve component element of the 9th Theater Support Command. CSM Woods enlisted in the United States Army in 1975 and served four years on active duty as an armored crewman. He was assigned to the 1st Cavalry Division's Company C, 1st Battalion, 8th Cavalry Regiment. He also served in West Germany with the 4th Infantry Division's Company C, 1st Battalion, 70th Armored Regiment. He left active duty at the rank of Sergeant. He enlisted in the Army Reserves in 1982, and he has since been a leader in a variety of positions and units.

Wooten, Ralph G.
MAJOR GENERAL—ARMY

He was born in LaGrange, North Carolina. He married the former Becky Chavis of Henderson, North Carolina. They have two sons, Kevin and Kenneth. He holds a Bachelor of Science degree, in Biology from North Carolina University. He earned a Master of Arts degree in Logistic Management and a Master of Arts degree in Business Administration from Michigan University. Military schools attended include the Infantry Officer Basic Course; the Chemical Officer Advanced Course; United States Army Command and General Staff College; Industrial College of the Armed Forces; Defense Systems Management College. From October 1967 to July 1968, he served as an enlisted soldier. He

was commissioned a Second Lieutenant on July 29, 1968. From July 1968 to December 1968, he was assigned as the Executive Officer of the 72nd Company, 7th Student Battalion, the Candidate Brigade, United States Army Infantry School at Fort Benning, Georgia. From December 1968 to August 1969, he was assigned Platoon Leader in Company C, 1st Battalion, 18th Infantry, 1st Infantry Division, United States Army, Vietnam. He was promoted to First Lieutenant on July 29, 1969. From August 1969 to March 1970, he was assigned as a Staff Personnel Officer (S-1) to the 1st Battalion, 18th Infantry, 1st Infantry Division, United States Army, Vietnam. From March 1970 to December 1971, he was assigned as the Assistant Operations Officer (S-3) with the 3rd Basic Combat Training Brigade, later Special Project and Chief of Scheduling Section in the United States Army Training Center at Fort Dix, New Jersey. He was promoted to Captain on July 29, 1970. From December 1971 to September 1972, he was a student in the Chemical Officer Advanced Course at the United States Army Chemical School at Fort McClellan, Alabama. From September 1972 to June 1973, he was a Chemical Officer, later a Supply Officer (S-4), with the Division Artillery of the 82nd Airborne Division at Fort Bragg, North Carolina. From June 1973 to November 1973, he was assigned Special Projects Officer of the 82nd Airborne Division at Fort Bragg. From November 1973 to May 1974, he served as Commander of the 14th Chemical Detachment, 82nd Airborne Division, at Fort Bragg. From May 1974 to August 1975, he was assigned as Chemical Officer of the 82nd Airborne Division at Fort Bragg. From August 1975 to January 1976, he was assigned as a Mechanical Maintenance Officer of the 782nd Maintenance Battalion, 82nd Airborne Division, at Fort Bragg. From January 1976 to February 1977, he served as the Commander of Company B, 782nd Maintenance Battalion, 82nd Airborne Division, at Fort Bragg. From February

1977 to July 1979, he served as Chief of the Combined Arms Branch, Chemical Directorate, later Assistant Director of the Training Department of the United States Army Chemical School at Aberdeen Proving Ground, Maryland. He was promoted to Major on May 8, 1979. From July 1979 to June 1980, he was a student at the United States Army Command and General Staff College at Fort Leavenworth, Kansas. From July 1980 to November 1981, he was assigned as a Maintenance Management Officer at the 3rd Armored Division Materiel Management Center, 3rd Armored Division, United States Army, in Germany. From July 1982 to June 1983, he served as the Commander of the Materiel Management Center of the 3rd Armored Division, in Germany. From June 1983 to June 1985, he served as an Advisor, later Team Chief, with the Combat Support Branch of the United States Army Reserve Readiness Group at Redstone Arsenal in Huntsville, Alabama. He was promoted to Lieutenant Colonel on April 1, 1985. From June 1985 to January 1987, he served as Deputy Director for Research, Development and Engineering Support at the United States Army Chemical, Research, Development and Engineering Center at Aberdeen Proving Ground. From January 1987 to December 1987, he served as Chief of Staff, at the United States Army Chemical, Research Development and Engineering Center at Aberdeen Proving Ground. From December 1987 to January 1990, he was assigned as Commander of the 2nd Chemical Battalion, 13th Support Command (Corps) at Fort Hood, Texas. From January 1990 to July 1990, he was assigned Logistics Staff Officer (G-4) of III Corps at Fort Hood. From July 1990 to June 1991, he was a student at the Industrial College of the Armed Forces at Fort McNair in Washington, D.C. He was promoted to Colonel on February 1, 1991. From June 1991 to January 1994, he was assigned commander of the United States Army Environmental Center at Aberdeen Proving Ground. From January 1994 to December 1994, he served as Joint Program Manager for Biological Defense in the Office of the Joint Program Manager for Biological Defense at Falls Church, Virginia. He was promoted to Brigadier General on December 1, 1994. From December 1994 to February 1996, he served as Deputy Commanding General of the United States Army Chemical and Military Police Centers/Commandant of the United States Army Chemical School at Fort McClellan, Alabama. In February 1996, he was frocked Major General and assigned as Commanding General of the United States Army Chemical and Military Police Centers at Fort McClellan. He was promoted to Major General on September 1, 1997. He retired from military service on December 31, 1999. His military awards and decorations include the Defense Superior Service Medal; Legion of Merit; Bronze Star (with two oak leaf clusters); Meritorious Service Medal (with three oak leaf clusters); Air Medal; Army Commendation Medal (with oak leaf cluster); Army Achievement Medal; Combat Infantryman Badge; and Senior Parachutist Badge.

Wortham, Tia F.

PETTY OFFICER FIRST CLASS—NAVY

She earned a Bachelor of Science in Music from Florida State University and a Master of Music from Catholic University. She serves as a member of the United States Navy Band. She is the Principal Bassoon with the band and also a Soloist with the band.

Wrenn, Curtis L., Jr.

COLONEL—ARMY

He and his wife Sheila have one daughter, Carmen. He holds a master's degree in Industrial Technology from Alabama A&M University. He was commissioned in the Air Defense Artillery from Virginia State University (ROTC) in 1979. Following the Air Defense Basic Course, he served as a Vulcan Platoon Leader, 4th Battalion, 1st Air Defense Artillery at Fort Bliss and as a battery executive officer and maintenance officer B Battery, 6th Battalion, 56th Air Defense Artillery in Bitburg, Germany. He served as Commander of A Battery, 6th Battalion, 56th Air Defense Artillery at Spangdahlem, Germany. After completion of the Armor Officer Advance Course, he was assigned as the S-4 (logistics), 2nd Battalion, 3rd Air Defense Artillery at Fort Bliss. He was next assigned as the S-4 (logistics), with the 4th Battalion, 7th Air Defense Artillery (Patriot). Following completion of Command and General Staff College, he was assigned as the Assistant Division Air Defense Officer, G-3, of the 5th Infantry Division (M) at Fort Polk, Louisiana. He later served as the S-3 (operations) Officer of the 3rd Battalion, 3rd Air Defense Artillery, 5th Infantry Division (M). His military awards include the Meritorious Service Medal (with two oak leaf clusters); Army Commendation Medal; the Army Achievement Medal; and the Parachutist Badge.

Wright, Lewin C.

COMMANDER—NAVY

He graduated from Brandeis University and was commissioned through Officer Candidate School in September 1985.

His first assignment was in USS *Vancouver* (LPD 2) homeported in San Diego, California, where he served as Electrical Officer and Electronic Warfare Officer from June 1986 to May 1989. His next assignment was in USS *Buchanan* (DDG 14) also in San Diego where he served as Navigator from July 1989 to March 1991.

Following duty in *Buchanan*, Commander Wright reported ashore to the Navy Recruiting District San Francisco, California, serving as an Officer Recruiter from May 1991 to October 1992. After completing the Surface Warfare Officers Department Head Course, he reported to USS *Lewis B. Puller* (FFG 23) in Long Beach, California, serving as Operations Officer from June 1993 to January 1995. Commander Wright then reported to the Pre-Commissioning unit for USS *Robin* (MHC 54) at the builder's yard in New Orleans, Louisiana. Upon the ship's delivery in January 1996, he served as Executive Officer until May 1998. From

June 1998 to June 1999, he was a student at the Army Command and General Staff College in Fort Leavenworth, Kansas, where he completed Joint Professional Military Education Phase One. Additionally, he earned a master's degree in Business Administration from Benedictine College in Atchison, Kansas. In September 1999, he reported to USS *Samuel Eliot Morison* (FFG 13) homeported in Mayport, Florida, serving as Executive Officer until December 2000. He then reported to the staff of the Chief of Naval Operations at Washington, D.C. in February 2001, serving as the Section Head for strategy for the Director of the Surface Warfare Division (N76). In July 2003, he was selected the first African American to command the USS *Constitution*, America's oldest warship.

Wright, Reginald M.

SERGEANT MAJOR—MARINES

Sergeant Major Reginald M. Wright entered the Marine Corps in May 1977 at Parris Island, South Carolina. After Recruit Training, he reported to Detachment A of the 2nd Force Service Support Group at Cherry Point, North Carolina.

In August 1995, he was transferred to Headquarters of the 2nd Force Service Support Group, 2nd Maintenance Battalion where he was assigned in the S-4 (Logistics) office. On May 1, 1998, he was assigned as the First Sergeant for Inspector-Instructor Staff at the Direct Support Motor Transport Company Alpha, 6th Motor Transport Battalion, with the 4th Force Service Support Group in Orlando, Florida. He was promoted to Sergeant Major and assigned as the Sergeant Major for Marine Air Support Squadron One, Marine Air Command Group 28.

Wright, Sherry L.

COMMAND SERGEANT MAJOR—ARMY

A native of Miami, Florida, she graduated from Basic Training at Fort Dix, New Jersey, in 1981, and Advanced Individual Training at Fort Gordon, Georgia. She has completed the United States Sergeants Major Academy (class 53). She attended Chaminade University and earned an associate's degree in Liberal Studies. She holds a Bachelor of Science degree in Business Administration from Excelsior College. She is pursuing a master's degree in Human Resource Development and a minor in Management. She is a graduate of the Master Fitness Training Course and the Small Group Instructor Training Course.

Some of her military assignments include serving three tours in the Federal Republic of Germany, first at 143rd Signal Battalion; then 101st Military Intelligence; and next with the 17th Signal Battalion. She served a short tour in 1991 in Saudi Arabia during Operation Desert Shield/Desert Storm and served as First Sergeant for five consecutive years. In August 2004, she was serving as the Command Sergeant Major for the 141st Battalion in Wiesbaden, Germany.

She is a member of the prestigious Sergeant Audie Murphy and Sergeant Morales Clubs.

Wyatt, James R.

COMMANDER—NAVY

He enlisted into the United States Navy from his hometown of Atlanta, Georgia, in 1978. He graduated from Florida A&M University with a Bachelors of Science degree in Economics through the Enlisted Commissioning Program in 1988 and was winged as an NFO in 1989.

He reported to VP-56 in Jacksonville, Florida, in 1990 and completed a Keflavik, Iceland, deployment while attaining qualifications as a Patrol Plane NAVCOM and BT NAVCOM. He held positions as Avionics Branch Officer and Legal Officer. Upon the decom-

missioning of VP-56 in 1991, he reported to VP-49 and attained qualification as Patrol Plane TACCO, Primary NATOPS Instructor TACCO, BT TACCO and Patrol Plane Mission Commander. During this tour, he completed a split deployment to Rota, Spain, and Lajes, Portugal, and another full deployment to Keflavik, Iceland, while serving in positions of First Lieutenant Division Officer, Legal Officer, and Safety/NATOPS Division Officer.

His first shore tour was as an Admissions Officer at USNA SE Detachment from 1993 to 1996. He served as Flag Secretary of CARGRU Five aboard USS *Independence* from 1996 to 1998 and attended Air Command and Staff College in Montgomery, Alabama, from 1998 to 1999.

In 2000, Commander Wyatt reported to VP-9 and served as the Administration Officer, Ammunition, and Maintenance Officer while deploying to Seventh and Fifth Fleets.

He served as the Assistant Commanding Officer of Supply for Manpower and Personnel and ACOS for Plans and Operations at COMPATRECONFORPAC from 2001 to 2003, and served as the Deputy Executive Assistant to COMPACFLT in 2003 until reporting to VP-9 as the Executive Officer in May 2005.

Wyche, Larry

COLONEL—ARMY

He was commissioned on Active Duty as a Quartermaster Officer in 1983. His military and civilian education includes a Bachelor of Science degree in Business Management from Texas A&M University in Corpus Christi, Texas; a master's degree in Logistics Management from the Florida Institute of Technology; and a master's degree in National Resource Strategy from the Industrial College of the Armed Forces. He attended the

Industrial College of the Armed Forces; the Joint Professional Military Education Course; the Armed Forces Staff College; the Command and General Staff College; the Logistics Executive Development Course; and the Airborne and Air Assault Schools.

His military assignments include serving as Chief of the Focus Logistics Division at Force Development for the Deputy Chief of Staff Programs (G8); as Chief of Initiative Group for the Deputy Chief of Staff Programs (G8); as the Commander of the 4th Forward Support Battalion, 4th Infantry Division, at Fort Hood, Texas; as a Logistics Planner (G4) Combined Forces Command in South Korea; as Operations Officer (S-3) for the 46th Support Group(Airborne); as the Executive Officer with the 189th Corps Support Battalion (Airborne); as Chief of Readiness for the Assistant Chief of Staff (Assistant Chief of Staff) G-4, XVIII Airborne Corps, at Fort Bragg, North Carolina; as Operations Officer (S-3) for the 502nd Forward Support Battalion, 2nd Armored Division, at Fort Hood; as a Logistics Planner and Chief of Maintenance and Supply, Assistant Chief of Staff G-4, 5th Infantry Division (Mechanized), at Fort Polk, Louisiana; as the Commander of the 114th Quartermaster Company, 2nd Quartermaster Group, in South Korea; and as the Personnel (S-1), 240th Quartermaster Battalion and Platoon Leader of the 267th Quartermaster Company at Fort Lee, Virginia. He also served in the enlisted ranks as a Cavalry Scout, Squad and Section Leader in the 2nd Armored Division at Fort Hood. In July 2005, he was serving as the Commander of the 10th Support Brigade, 10th Mountain Division (LI), at Fort Drum, New York.

Wylie, Ernest J.
SERGEANT MAJOR—MARINES

He was born in Rock Hill, South Carolina. He graduated from Rock Hill High School in 1977 and enlisted into the Marine Corps in the Delayed Entry Program on December 31, 1976. He began recruit training at Parris Island on July 1, 1977. After recruit training, he transferred to Camp Lejeune, North Carolina, and was assigned to Golf Company, 2nd Battalion, with the 8th Marines for on-the-job training as an Antitank Assault Man.

While assigned to Golf Company, 2nd Battalion, 8th Marines, he served as Team Leader and Gunner and deployed on a African and South American Goodwill Cruise aboard the USS *Inchon* which participated in a Presidential Support Mission off Lagos, Nigeria. During this tour he also made three Marine Amphibious Unit deployments to the Mediterranean Sea.

He served as Drill Instructor and Senior Drill Instructor at Marine Corps Recruit Depot, Parris Island, and, in April 1984, as Guard Chief/Platoon Sergeant for 3rd Platoon Guard Company. He also sound as an 81mm Mortar Section Leader with the Weapons Company of the 2nd Battalion, 4th Marines, at Camp Lejeune. In October 1986, he was assigned as Platoon Sergeant in Fox Company, 3rd Platoon. He later served as an Assistant Marine Officer Instructor at Naval Reserve Officer Training Corps Unit at Hampton University at Hampton Roads, Virginia, and as Platoon Sergeant at Officer Candidates School at Quantico, Virginia. In August 1992, he served as Gunnery Sergeant in Kilo Company, 3rd Battalion, 6th Marines at Camp Lejeune, and in October 1992, he assumed the duties as Weapons Platoon Sergeant, later Gunnery Sergeant, and deployed to Marine Mountain Warfare Training Center at Bridgeport, California, for cold weather training and then participated in Exercise Battle

Griffin in Norway. He also deployed to the Mediterranean Sea and participated in Operation Continued Hope with the United Nations in Mogadishu, Somalia. In March 1994, he was assigned to Headquarters and Service Company and assumed the duties as the S-4 Chief; during this deployment, he also participated in Operations Provide Promise/Deny Flight in the Adriatic Sea. After returning from the Mediterranean Sea in June 1994, he and his unit were suddenly recalled and in seven days were again deployed, this time to participate in Operation Support Democracy in Haiti. He then redeployed in January 1995, and participated in Operation Sea Signal and Safe Passage in Guantanamo Bay, Cuba, while a member of Joint Task Force-160. He was promoted to First Sergeant in April 1995 and transferred to B Company, 2nd Combat Engineer Battalion, at Camp Lejeune. In July 1996 Sergeant Major Wylie was again transferred, this time to the Inspector Instructor Staff of the 1st Battalion, 25th Marines at Air Station Cape Cod, Massachusetts.

He was promoted to Sergeant Major in November 1998 and transferred to VMA-311, Marine Air Group-13, 3rd Marine Air Craft Wing, at Yuma, Arizona.

In January 2002, Sergeant Major Wylie was transferred to the Weapons and Field Training Battalion at Marine Corps Recruit Depot Parris Island. On March 22, 2004, he was reassigned to the Recruit Training Regiment as the Regimental Sergeant Major.

Yarn, Doneil C.
SERGEANT MAJOR—MARINES

He enlisted in the Marine Corps on June 3, 1979, and graduated from the Marine Corps Recruit Depot at Parris Island, South Carolina, in August 1979. Completed training at the Basic Helicopter Course at Naval Air Station Millington, Tennessee, in November 1979.

From November 1979 to April 1982, he performed the duties as H-46E Crew Chief/Plane Captain/Aerial Gunner/Mechanic/Collateral Duty Inspector with the Golden Eagles of HMM-162, 2nd Marine Air Wing, MAG-2 at New River, North Carolina.

In 1992, he assumed duties as the Chief Aircrew Instructor/MAG-26 NATOPS Evaluator/Flightline Division Chief/H-46-E Crewchief/Plane Captain with the White Knights of HMT-204 Fleet Replacement Enlisted Skills Training Squadron, (FREST) MAG-26 at MCAS New River. He assumed duties as the Line Division Chief/H-46E Crewchief/Aerial Gunner/Full Systems Collateral Duty Quality Assurance Representative with the ACE of the 22nd Marine Expeditionary Unit. In June 1998, he was promoted to First Sergeant and assumed duties as Alpha Company First Sergeant MCAGCC at Twenty-Nine Palms, California. He then served as First Sergeant of Delta Company at the Computer Science School at Twenty Nine Palms. He was promoted to Sergeant Major in July 2002, and assumed the duties of Squadron Sergeant Major of Marine Medium Helicopter Squadron 163.

Young, Charles
COLONEL—ARMY

One of the most famous of the black graduates from West Point was Charles Young. He was born in 1861 in Mayslick, Kentucky, but educated in Ohio. Upon graduation from high school, he attended Wilberforce University where he was employed as an instructor after graduation. He entered the U.S. Military Academy at West Point on June 15, 1884. During his first year he was found deficient in mathematics and dismissed. He was readmitted in 1885 after passing a reexamination in math. He graduated in 1889, and was commissioned a Second Lieutenant in the Tenth Cavalry. In rapid succession he moved to assignments in the 25th Infantry and 9th Cavalry, each an all-black unit. In 1894, he was assigned to Wilberforce University as Professor of Military Science and Tactics.

When war broke out with Spain in 1898, he left the Army and took a commission as a Major in the Ninth Ohio Volunteer (Colored) Infantry. The unit, however, was never shipped to Cuba and he saw no combat.

In 1899, Young was released from volunteer service and rejoined his old regiment in the Regular Army. Soon thereafter he was promoted to Captain and, despite a kidney ailment, went to the Philippines where he engaged in anti-guerrilla operations for almost two years. Upon his return to the United States, he was named Superintendent of Sequoia and General Grant National Parks in California.

In May of 1904, Captain Young was appointed as U.S. Military attaché to Haiti, the first black officer to hold such a position. In 1911, he served in the Office of the Army Chief of Staff, but was soon named military attaché to Liberia, where he remained until 1915.

When American forces were mobilized in 1917, it was suggested in the black press that Lieutenant Colonel

Young should be named to command a regiment or larger unit in the forthcoming conflict.

He was sixth on the promotion list of colonels. With the rapid wartime expansion of the military, it was certain that he would come up for promotion to brigadier general that year and thus be eligible for a high post such as assistant divisional commander in a black division.

Young's Selection Board recommended him for promotion, and he went on May 23, 1917, to the military hospital at San Francisco for his physical examination. The doctors there reported he was suffering from high blood pressure, and he was retired from active service the day before many colonels were advanced to brigadier. Young protested that he was not sick; his physician certified that his blood pressure was normal for a man of middle age.

Young objected to his forced retirement. In protest, he mounted his favorite horse and rode from Chillicothe, Ohio, to Washington, D.C., to attest to his stamina and to personally appeal for reinstatement to active duty. Many people argued that he had been retired to prevent his being named to General officer status and commanding white troops. Neither their protestations nor his were successful.

The papers of then–Secretary of War Nexton Baker throw further light on the story of Colonel Young. While Young was having his physical in San Francisco, Senator Williams of Mississippi, one of President Wilson's strongest supporters and an outspoken racist, forwarded to the President a complaint from a young white lieutenant in the 10th Cavalry. Wilson passed the message on in a letter to Baker, informing him that the lieutenant wanted to be transferred because he found it "not only distasteful but practically impossible to serve under a black commander," and asking Baker what could be done about it. Although Baker had small patience with such complaints, he consulted with Chief of Staff General Tasker Bliss and wrote the President that Young would be in a hospital under observation "for the next two or three weeks to determine whether his physical condition is sufficiently good to justify his return to active service." Baker added, "There does not seem to be any present likelihood of his early return to which you refer." Three days later, Wilson wrote to Senator Williams that Young "will not in fact have command because he is in ill health and likely when he gets better himself to be transferred to some other service."

The Colonel Young affair indicates that decisions about black officers in the armed forces were political rather than military and casts doubt on the reliability of criticism of the ability of black officers in World War I. It is perhaps the clinching evidence that the military did not want black officers who might succeed. If Colonel Young had been promoted the army would have had to assign him as second in command in a black division, the morale and performance of junior black officers would almost certainly have been better under Young's firm leadership, and Young would probably have won acclaim. But the political decision to oust Young had already been made, quite possibly before Senator Williams' letter to Wilson.

In 1918, Young was recalled to active duty with the Ohio National Guard and promoted to Colonel, but he was given no command. Finally, in 1919 he was returned to Liberia as military attaché where he died in January 1922 from chronic nephritis. He was buried in Arlington National Cemetery.

Young, Eric Coy
COMMANDER—NAVY

He received a Bachelor of Science degree in Chemistry from Angelo State University in 1984. In February 1985, he received his commission from Officer Candidate School in Newport, Rhode Island. After his first Division Officer tour, he was designated a Training and Administration of Reserves (TAR) Officer.

His sea duty assignments include tours of duty in USS *Reid* (FFG 30) as the Ordnance Officer, USS *San Jose* (AFS 7) as the Navigation Officer, USS *Wadsworth* (FFG 9) as the Operations Officer, Destroyer Squadron Thirty-One as the Combat Systems Officer and USS *Ford* (FFG 54) as the Executive Officer.

His shore assignments include serving as Commanding Officer of the Naval Reserve Center at Terre Haute, Indiana; Commanding Officer of the Naval Reserve Center at Danville, Illinois; Manpower Analyst in the Surface Warfare Directorate, Chief of Naval Operations (N76); and Manpower and Personnel Director in Naval Reserve Readiness Command South. In December 1997, he graduated from the Naval Postgraduate School with a Master of Science degree in Financial Management and in June 2002, he was awarded a Master of Arts degree in National Security and Strategic

Studies from the Naval War College. Commander Young assumed command of USS *John L. Hall* on September 8, 2003.

Young, Samuel
CAPTAIN—NAVY

He was born in Ennis, Texas, and raised in San Joaquin Valley of California. His College education began at Occidental College in Los Angeles, California, where he graduated in 1976 with a Bachelor of Arts degree in Mathematics and Chemistry. He then attended Harvard School of Dental Medicine where, in June 1977, he was commissioned an Ensign in the United States Navy as a Health Professions Scholarship recipient. Upon receiving his Doctor of Dental Medicine degree in June 1980, he was promoted to the rank of Lieutenant.

His first active duty assignments were at the 13th Dental Company, MCAS at El Toro, California, from 1980 to 1982, the 11th Dental Company, MCAS in Iwakuni, Japan from June 1983 to June 1984 and then a second assignment with the 13th Dental Company, MCAS, in El Toro through June 1984. He was next assigned to the USS *Prairie* (AD 15) for two years as an assistant dental officer and was selected for an oral surgery residency.

In June 1986, he began a three-year residency in Oral and Maxillofacial Surgery at U.S. Naval Hospital Oakland, California, and was promoted to Lieutenant Commander in June 1987. Upon completing his residency in June 1989, he was indoctrinated into the Oral Surgery specialty with a tour aboard USS *Carl Vinson* (CVN 70). In September 1990, he was transferred to Naval Dental Center, San Francisco, and served as Oral Surgery Department Head at Branch Dental Clinic, Alameda.

In 1991, he was transferred to USS *Ranger* (CV 61)

where he served as Dental Officer and Oral Surgeon through June 1992. Upon the completion of duty aboard the USS *Ranger*, LCDR he was transferred to Naval Dental Center San Diego, where he served as Department Head of Oral and Maxillofacial Surgery and Command Consultant. He was promoted to Commander in June 1993. In July 1996, he reported to Yokosuka, Japan, where he served as Command Consultant and Head of Oral and Maxillofacial Surgery. He was promoted to Captain on February 1, 1999, and was assigned as Director of Branch Dental Clinic in Yokosuka, Japan, through July 2000. He then transferred to NDCSE where served as the Command Consultant Oral and Maxillofacial Surgery. In July 2003, he reported as Executive Officer to the 1st Dental Battalion at Camp Pendleton, California.

Younger, Collin Lester
COMMAND SERGEANT MAJOR—ARMY

He was born in Ayden, North Carolina. His military education includes Ayden North Carolina Senior High School and American University in Washington, D.C., where he earned both AA and BS degrees. He's a graduate of the FBI National Academy at Quantico, Virginia, and attended postgraduate seminars at the University of Virginia in Charlottesville, Virginia. His military education include Basic Combat Training, all the Noncommissioned Officer Education System Courses; Artillery School; Drill Sergeant School; Senior NCO Course; Instructor Training Course; BTMS (TSW) Course; and the Sergeant Major Academy. CSM Younger has held every leadership position in the enlisted corps, including serving in June 1962 as Artillery Section Chief and Drill Sergeant; in August 1966 as Drill Sergeant; in September 1970 as Drill Instructor Leader/Academy; in December 1976 as MOS Instructor; in October 1977 as Chief Instructor; in August 1979 as First Sergeant; in January 1983 as Staff Sergeant Major Brigade S-3; in September 1984 as Battalion Command Sergeant Major; and in August 1987 as Command Sergeant Major of the 80th Division (Tng) in Richmond, Virginia. CSM Younger assumed the duties as the sixth Senior Enlisted Advisor to the Chief of the Army Reserve on August 5, 1991. This was a dual status position that requires CSM Younger to serve as both the Senior Enlisted Advisor to the Office of the Chief Army Reserve (OCAR) and as the first Command Sergeant Major for the United States Army Reserve Command (USARC). He also serves as the Senior Enlisted Advisor to the Office of the Assistant Secretary of Defense (Reserve Affairs). His military decorations include the Meritorious Service Medal; Army Achievement Medal (with two oak leaf clusters); Good Conduct Medal; Army Reserve Components Achievement Medal (with four oak leaf clusters); National Defense Service Medal; Armed Forces Reserve Medal (with Hour Glass device); NCO Professional Development Ribbon; Overseas Service Ribbon; Sergeant Medal; Department of Defense Staff Badge; and Drill Sergeant Medal.

Zanders, Joe K.
COMMAND SERGEANT MAJOR—ARMY

A native of McRae, Georgia, he entered the United States Army in October 1981. He completed One Unit Station Training at Fort Sill, Oklahoma. His military and civilian education includes all the Noncommissioned Officer Education System Courses; Army Recruiting Course; Army Recruiting Station Commander Course; Battle Staff Course; First Sergeant Course; MANPRINT Action Officer Course; and the United States Army Sergeants Major Academy (class 53). He also holds an associate's degree in Business Management from Excelsior College in Albany, New York.

He has held numerous leadership positions in the Field Artillery. His previous assignments include serving as Gunner in B Battery, 6th Battalion, 9th Field Artillery in Germany; as Special Weapons Chief of A Battery, 3rd Battalion, 34th Field Artillery at Fort Lewis, Washington; as Howitzer Section Chief of A Battery, 6th Battalion, 1st Field Artillery in Germany; as Gunnery Sergeant of B Battery, 5th Battalion at Fort Carson, Colorado; with the New Orleans Recruiting Battalion, with duty at Hammond, Louisiana; as Platoon Sergeant of B Battery, 4th Battalion, 42nd Field Artillery at Fort Hood, Texas; as First Sergeant of B Battery, 1st Battalion, 16th Field Artillery, at Fort Hood; as Senior Field Artillery NCO, PEO-GCS at Picatinny Arsenal, New Jersey; and as Command Sergeant Major, 2nd Battalion, 11th Field Artillery, 25th Infantry Division in Hawaii.

Zimmerman, Matthew A.
MAJOR GENERAL—ARMY

He was born in South Carolina. He received a Bachelor of Science degree in Biology and Chemistry from Benedict College in 1962, an Master of Divinity in Pas-

toral Counseling from Duke University in 1965, and a master's in Education from Long Island University in 1975. His military education includes the Chaplain School Basic and Advanced Courses; the United States Army Command and Staff College; and the United States Army War College. He received a commission by direct appointment to the rank of First Lieutenant on March 21, 1967. From April 1967 to August 1967, he was a student at the Chaplain Officer Basic Course at the United States Army Chaplain School at Fort Hamilton, New York. On April 3, 1967, he was promoted to Captain. From August 1967 to January 1968, he served as Chaplain in the Headquarters Detachment of the 3rd Advanced Individual Training Brigade at the United States Army Training Center (Infantry) at Fort Gordon, Georgia. From January 1968 to February 1969, he served as Assistant Chaplain for the IV Corps Tactical Zone, Advisory Team 51, United States Military Assistance Command, in Vietnam. From February 1969 to September 1970, he was an Assistant Chaplain with the Headquarters and Headquarters Company and Band, Support Command, 1st Armored Division at Fort Hood, Texas. From March 1971 to August 1973, he served as Staff Chaplain of the 3rd Armored Division, United States Army in Europe and Seventh Army. From August 1974 to June 1975, he was a student at the Chaplain Officer Advanced Course in the United States Army Chaplain Center and School at Fort Wadsworth, New Jersey. On October 3, 1974, he was promoted to Major. From June 1975 to June 1976, he served as the Operation Training Staff Officer in the Office of Chief of Chaplains in Washington, D.C. From June 1976 to June 1978, he served as the Staff Parish Development Officer in the Office of the Chief of Chaplains in

Washington, D.C. From June 1978 to June 1979, he was assigned as student at the United States Army Command and General Staff College at Fort Leavenworth, Kansas. From June 1979 to July 1980, he served as the Deputy Corps Chaplain (Administrative) to VII Corps, United States Army in Europe and Seventh Army. He was promoted to Lieutenant Colonel on August 6, 1979. From July 1980 to June 1982, he served as the Division Staff Chaplain for the 3rd Infantry Division, United States Army in Europe and Seventh Army. From June 1982 to June 1983, he was a student at the United States Army War College at Carlisle Barracks, Pennsylvania. From June 1983 to June 1984, he was Assistant Command Chaplain for the United States Army

Training and Doctrine Command at Fort Monroe, Virginia. He was promoted to Colonel on July 1, 1984. From December 1985 to August 1989, he served as a Command Staff Chaplain at Forces Command at Fort McPherson in Atlanta, Georgia. From August 1989 to August 1990, he was Deputy Chief of Chaplains in the Office of the Chief of Chaplains for the United States in Washington, D.C. He was promoted to Brigadier General on October 1, 1989, and to Major General on August 1, 1990. In August 1990, he was assigned as Chief of Chaplains for the United States Army in Washington, D.C. His awards includes the Legion of Merit; Bronze Star; and the Meritorious Service Medal (with two oak leaf clusters).

APPENDIX I:
MEDAL OF HONOR WINNERS

The Medal of Honor is presented in the name of Congress to members of the American armed forces who perform acts of valor considered "beyond the call of duty." *Beyond the call of duty* generally means that the individual who performs such an act would not have been ordered to do so. It also means that this voluntary action places that person's life at risk during an outstanding act of bravery. It frequently involves risking one's own life to save the life or lives of a comrade or comrades.

Initially only the Navy awarded a Medal of Honor. The Army Medal of Honor followed shortly. The Navy Medal of Honor was also awarded to members of the Marine Corps, and the Army Medal of Honor was also awarded to individuals of the Army Air Corps. Following World War II, however, the Air Corps became the United States Air Force, an independent military branch. A separate Medal of Honor was struck for this branch of service. Medals of Honor are currently awarded for service in the Army, Navy, and Air Force.

No black American has received the Air Force Medal of Honor. Only one female, Dr. Mary Walker of the Civil War, has been awarded the Medal. The youngest recipient of the Medal of Honor was 14 years old.

After all my research for this book, I can safely say that for the most part black soldiers have not been recognized for outstanding performance that would have qualified them for the Medal of Honor. Nevertheless, some black soldiers' heroic deeds have become so widely known that the Medal of Honor was awarded, if only in response to public outcry.

The following are those black soldiers who have received the Medal of Honor. The listing is in order by date of the action that inspired the award.

William H. Carney, Sergeant, Company C, 54th Massachusetts Infantry, United States Colored Troops, for action at Fort Wagner, South Carolina, July 18, 1863.

Robert Blake, Powder Boy on USS *Marblehead*, for action on the Stone River, December 25, 1863.

Thomas R. Hawkins, Sergeant Major, 6th United States Colored Troops, for action at Deep Bottom, Virginia, July 21, 1864.

Decatur Dorsey, Sergeant, Company B, 39th United States Colored Troops, for action at Petersburg, Virginia, July 30, 1864.

Wilson Brown, USS *Hartford*; John Lawson, USS *Hartford*; and William H. Brown, USS *Brooklyn*; for action at Mobile Bay, August 5, 1864.

Powhatan Beaty, First Sergeant, Company G; **James H. Bronson**, First Sergeant, Company D, 5th United States Colored Troops; **Christian A. Fleetwood**, Sergeant Major, 4th United States Colored Troops; **James Gardiner**, Private, Company I, 36th United States Colored Troops; **Alfred B. Hilton**, Sergeant, Company H, 4th United States Colored Troops; **Milton M. Holland**, Sergeant, 5th United States Colored Troops; **Miles James**, Corporal, Company B, 36th U.S.

Colored Troops; **Alexander Kelly**, First Sergeant, Company F, 6th United States Colored Troops; **Robert Pinn**, First Sergeant, Company I, 5th U.S. Colored Troops; **Edward Ratcliff**, First Sergeant, Company C, 38th U.S. Colored Troops; and **Charles Veal**, Private, Company D, 4th U.S. Colored Troops, for action at Chapins Farm, Virginia, September 29, 1864; and **James H. Harris**, Sergeant, Company B, 38th United States Colored Troops, for action at New Market, Virginia, September 29, 1864.

William H. Barnes, Private, Company C, 38th United States Colored Troops, and **Aaron Anderson**, Landsman, USS *Wyandank*, for action at Mattox Creek, on March 17, 1865.

Emanuel Stance, Sergeant, Company F, 9th United States Cavalry, for action at Kickapoo Springs, New Mexico, July 24, 1870.

John Johnson, Seaman, USS *Kansas*, for action near Graytown, Nicaragua, April 12, 1872.

Joseph B. Noil, Seaman, USS *Powhatan*, for action at Norfolk, Virginia, December 26, 1872.

Adam Paine, Private, Seminole Negro Indian Scouts, for action at Canyon Blanco, Staked Plains, Texas, September 26–27, 1874.

Issac Payne, Private (Trumpeter), Seminole Negro Indian Scouts, for action at Pecos River, Texas, April 22, 1875.

Pompey Factor, Seminole Negro Indian Scouts, for action at Pecos River, Texas, April 25, 1875.

Clinton Greaves, Corporal, Troop C, 9th United States Cavalry, for action at Florida Mountains, New Mexico, June 26, 1879.

John Denny, Sergeant, Troop C, 9th United States Cavalry, for action at Las Animas Canyon, New Mexico, September 18, 1879.

Thomas Boyne, Sergeant, Troop C, 9th United States Cavalry, for action at Chichillo Negro River, New Mexico, September 27, 1879.

Henry Johnson, Sergeant, Troop D, 9th United States Cavalry, for action at Milk River, Colorado, October 2–5.

William Johnson, Cooper, USS *Adams*, for action at Mare Island, California, November 14, 1879.

John Smith, Seaman, USS *Shenandoah*, for action at Rio De Janeiro, Brazil, September 19, 1880.

John Davis, Ordinary Seaman, USS *Trenton*, for action at Toulon, France, February 1881.

Thomas Shaw, Sergeant Troop K, 9th United States Cavalry, for action at Carizzo Canyon, New Mexico, August 12, 1881.

Augustus Walley, Private, Troop I, 9th United States Cavalry, for action at Chichillo Negro Mountains, New Mexico; **John Ward**, Sergeant, Seminole Negro Indian Scouts, for action at Pecos River, Texas; **Moses Williams**, First Sergeant, Troop I, 9th United States Cavalry, for action at Chichillo Negro Mountains, New Mexico; all on August 16, 1881.

Brent Woods, Sergeant, Troop B, 9th United States Cavalry, for action near McEvers Ranch, New Mexico, August 19, 1881.

Robert Sweeney, Ordinary Seaman, for action aboard USS *Kearsage* at Hampton Roads, Virginia, October 26, 1881.

Robert Sweeney, Ordinary Seaman (*Second Award*), for action aboard the USS *Jamestown*, December 20, 1883.

William McBryar, Sergeant, Troop K, 10th United States Cavalry, for action at Elizabethtown, North Carolina, March 7, 1889.

Isaiah Mays, Corporal, Company B, 24th United States Infantry, and **Thomas Boyne**, Sergeant, Company C, 24th United States Infantry, for action at Cedar Springs and Fort Thomas, Arizona, May 11, 1889.

William O. Wilson, Corporal, Troop I, 9th United States Cavalry, for action during the Sioux Campaign, December 30, 1890.

George Jordan, Sergeant, Troop K, 9th United States Cavalry, for action at Carizzo Canyon, New Mexico, May 7, 1890.

Dennis Bell, Private, Troop H; **Fitz Lee**, Private, Troop M; **William H. Thompkins**, Private, Troop G; and **George H. Wanton**, Sergeant, Troop M, 10th United States Cavalry, for action at Tayabacoa, Cuba, June 30, 1898.

Edward L. Baker, Jr., Sergeant Major, 10th United States Cavalry, for action at Santiago, Cuba, July 1, 1898.

Robert Penn, Fireman, First Class, USS *Iowa*, for action off Santiago, Cuba, July 20, 1898.

Alphonse Girandy, Seaman, USS *Tetrel*, for action onboard ship, March 31, 1901.

Freddie Stowers, Corporal, Company C, 371st Infantry Regiment, 93rd Infantry Division, for action during the Champagne Marne Sector, France, September 28, 1918.

George Watson, Private, 2nd Battalion, 29th Quartermaster Regiment, for action near Porlock Harbor, New Guinea, March 8, 1943.

Ruben Rivers, Staff Sergeant, A Company, 761st Tank Battalion, for action near Guebling, France, November 16–19, 1944.

Charles L. Thomas, Major, C Company, 614th Tank Destroyer Battalion, for action near Climbach, France, December 14, 1944.

John Robert Fox, First Lieutenant, Cannon Company, 366th Infantry Regiment, 92nd Infantry Division, for action at Sommocolinia, Italy, December 26, 1944.

Edward Allen Carter, Jr., Staff Sergeant, Seventh Army Infantry, Number 1 Company (Provisional), 56th Armored Infantry Battalion, 12th Armored Division, for action at Speyer, Germany, March 23, 1945.

Vernon James Baker, First Lieutenant, C Company, 370th Infantry Regiment, 92nd Infantry Division, for action near Viareggio, Italy, April 5–6, 1945.

Wily F. James, Jr., G Company, 413th Infantry Regiment, 104th Division, for action near Lippoldsberg, Germany, April 7, 1945.

Cornelius H. Charlton, Sergeant, 24th Infantry Regiment, 25th Division, for action near Chipo-Ri, Korea, June 2, 1951.

William Thompson, Private, 24th Infantry Regiment, 25th Division, for action near Haman, Korea, August 6, 1950.

Milton L. Olive, III, Private First Class, Company B, 2nd Battalion 503rd Infantry, 173rd Airborne Brigade, for action at Phu Cuong, Vietnam, October 22, 1965.

Lawrence Joel, Specialist Sixth Class, Headquarters and Headquarters Company, 1st Battalion, 173rd Airborne Brigade, for action in Vietnam, November 8, 1965.

Donald Russell Long, Sergeant, Troop C, 1st Squadron, 4th Cavalry, 1st Infantry Division, for action in Vietnam, June 30, 1966.

Matthew Leonard, Platoon Sergeant, Company B, 1st Battalion, 16th Infantry, 1st Infantry Division, for action at Suoi Da, Vietnam, February 28, 1967.

James A. Anderson, Private First Class, 2nd Platoon, Company F, 2nd Battalion, 3rd Marine Division, for action at Cam Lo, Vietnam, February 28, 1967.

Ruppert L. Sargent, First Lieutenant, Company B, 4th Battalion, 9th Infantry Division, for action at Hau Nghia Province, Vietnam, March 15, 1967.

Rodney M. Davis, Sergeant, Company B, 1st Battalion, 5th Marines, 1st Marine Division, for action at Quang Nam Province, Vietnam, September 6, 1967.

Webster Anderson, Sergeant, Battery A, 2nd Battalion, 320th Artillery, 101st Airborne Division, for action at Tem Ky, Vietnam, October 15, 1967.

Riley L. Pitts, Captain, Company C, 2nd Battalion, 27th Infantry, 25th Infantry Division, for action at Ap Dong, Vietnam, October 31, 1967.

Clarence E. Sasser, Specialist 5th Class, Headquarters Company, 3rd Battalion, 60th Infantry, 90th Infantry Division, for action at Ding Tuong Province, Vietnam, January 10, 1968.

Dwight H. Johnson, Specialist 5th Class, Company B, 1st Battalion, 69th Armor, 4th Infantry Division, for action at Dak To Kontum Province, Vietnam, January 15, 1968.

Eugene Ashley, Jr., Sergeant, Company C, 5th Special Forces Group (Airborne), 1st Special Forces, for action at Lang Vei, Vietnam, February 7, 1968.

Clifford Chester Sims, Staff Sergeant, Company D, 2nd Battalion, 501st Infantry, 101st Airborne Division, for action at Hue, Vietnam, on February 21, 1968.

Ralph H. Johnson, Private First Class, Company A, 1st Recon Battalion, 1st Marine Division, for action at Quan Duc Valley, Vietnam, March 5, 1968.

Charles C. Rogers, Lieutenant Colonel, 1st Battalion, 5th Infantry, 1st Infantry Division, for action at Fishhook, Republic of Vietnam, November 1, 1968.

John E. Warren, Jr., First Lieutenant, Company C, 2nd Battalion, 22nd Infantry, 25th Infantry Division, for action at Tay Ninh Province, Vietnam, January 14, 1969.

Garfield M. Langhorn, Private First Class, Troop C, 7th Squadron, 17th Cavalry, 1st Aviation Brigade for action at Pleiku Province, Vietnam, January 15, 1969.

Oscar P. Austin, Private First Class, Company E, 7th Marines, 1st Marine Division, for action at Da Nang, Vietnam, February 23, 1969.

Robert H. Jenkins, Jr., Private First Class, 3rd Reconnaissance Battalion, 3rd Marine Division, for action at Base Argonne, March 5, 1969.

William Maud Bryant, Sergeant First Class, Company A, 5th Special Forces Group, 1st Special Forces, for action at Long Khanh Province, Vietnam, March 24, 1969.

APPENDIX II: LEADERS LISTED BY MILITARY BRANCH AND RANK

Air Force

GENERALS

Anderson, Frank J., Jr.
Banton, William C.
Billups, Rufus L.
Bolton, Claude M., Jr.
Brooks, Elmer T.
Brown, William E., Jr.
Clifford, Thomas E.
Coleman, Gary G.
Davis, Benjamin O., Jr.
Davis, Jackson L., III
Davis, Russell C.
Durham, Archer L.
Edmonds, Albert J.
Epps, Mary A.
Ferguson, Alonzo L.
Flowers, Alfred K.
Hall, David M.
Harris, Marcelite Jorder
Hawkins, Ronnie D., Jr.
Hobbs, Johnny J.
Hopper, John D., Jr.
James, Avon C.
James, Daniel "Chappie," Jr.
James, Daniel, III
Jiggetts, Charles B.
Johnson, Leon A.
Jones, Walter I.
Jordan, Kenneth U.
Langford, Victor C., III
Lyles, Lester L.
McCoy, Gary T.
McMillan, Raymond V.
McNeil, Joseph
Mercer, Roosevelt, Jr.
Mitchell, Edith P.
Mitchell, Harold L.
Newton, Lloyd W. "Fig"

Overton, Norris W.
Patterson, Leonard Eric
Phillips, John F.
Powers, Winston Donald
Randolph, Bernard P.
Randolph, Leonard M.
Robinson, Neal T.
Rice, Edward A., Jr.
Russell, Horace Laverne
Sanders, James
Saunders, Mary L
Scott, Darryl A.
Spencer, Larry O.
Spooner, Richard E.
Steele, Toreaser A.
Stevens, William E.
Taylor, Francis X.
Taylor, Henry "Hank" L.
Taylor, Preston M., Jr.
Theus, Lucius
Trowell-Harris, Irene
Voorhees, John H.
Whitehead, James T.

OTHER OFFICERS

Adams, Daniel S., Jr.
Anderson, Charles Alfred "Chief"
Anderson, Michael P.
Anderson, Silvia Signars
Bayless, Harvey
Beckles, Benita Harris
Bluford, Guion S.
Bridges, Timothy K.
Brundidge, Gregory L.
Cagle, Yvonne Darlene
Cherry, Fred
Deloney, Thurmon L.
Drew, Benjamin Alvin
Dryden, Charles
Eichelberger, Claude J.
Forrest, Delores G.
Foster, Mack D.

Green, Phyllis
Gregory, Frederick D.
Gunn, Will
Harris, Stayce D.
Hill, Robin
Hopper, Christina
Johnson, Karen
Keasley, Dawn
King, Kevin
Kirkman, Allen, Jr.
Lawrence, Robert H.
Lee, Chery A.
Lee, Irvin B.
Lewis, Alfred M.
Lightner, Rosetta A. Armour
Lofton, Samuel, III
Lucas, Ruth
Marchbanks, Vance
McDew, Darren W.
Mitchell, Darphaus L.
Moten, Alphonso
O'Brien, Shawna
Patterson, Leonard E.
Saunders, William R.
Sayles, Martin L.
Spencer, Kathleen M.
Spencer, Tangela
Taylor, Clarence E., Jr.
Weathers, Richard B.
Williams, Sarah J.
Williamson, Carl

ENLISTED

Abernathy, Karl, II
Adams, Cheryl
Anderson, Cassandra L.
Archer, Fred
Barnes, Thomas N.
Barnette, Robert
Bentley, Lynn, Jr.
Benton, Valerie D.
Boykin, Louis

Brown, Carl L.
Carter, Normia E.
Ceaser, Deritha
Chandler, Cleveland, Jr.
Coleman, Gary G.
Davis, Anthony
Dickens, Timmothy
Evans, Darlin
Fritz, Dennis L.
Garner, William C.
Holling, Richard
Kelly, James C.
Kennedy, Deborah A.
McMillon, Brye
Monroe, Lewis E., III
Moore, Clarence H., Jr.
Morgan, Betty L.G.
Murray, William E., Jr.
Reese, Andrea D.
Starghill, Renee
Weary, Joey A.
Williams, Reginald L.
Willis, Melvin D.
Winsett, Jackson A.
Wolfolk, Sharon Bingham

Army

GENERALS

Adams, Robert B.
Adams-Ender, Clara L
Alexander, George A.
Alexander, Richard C.
Alexander, Willie Abner
Anderson, Dorian T.
Anderson, Rodney O.
Arnold, Wallace C.
Austin, Lloyd J., III
Bagby, Byron S.
Baker, Cornelius O.
Ballard, Joe Nathan
Becton, Julius W.
Bell, Leroy Crawford.
Bivens, Nolen V.
Blunt, Roger Reckling
Bostick, Thomas P.
Bowman, George Fletcher
Brailsford, Marvin D.
Brisco, Carl E.
Brooks, George M.
Brooks, Harry W.
Brooks, Leo Austin
Brooks, Leo Austin, Jr.
Brooks, Vincent K.
Brown, Dallas C., Jr.
Brown, George J.
Brown, John M., Sr.
Bryant, Albert
Bryant, Albert, Jr.

Bryant, Alvin
Burch, Harold E.
Burke, Rosetta Y.
Bussey, Charles David
Butler, Remo
Byrd, Melvin Leon
Cade, Alfred Jackal
Cadoria, Sherian G.
Cain, Eddie
Cartwright, Roscoe C.
Chambers, Andrew P., Jr.
Chandler, Allen E.
Cheathan, James Arthur
Cleckley, Julia J.
Clemmons, Reginal Graham
Cofer, Jonathan H.
Cooper, Billy Roy
Cowings, John Sherman
Crear, Robert
Cromartie, Eugene Rufus
Curry, Jerry Ralph
Davis, Benjamin O., Sr.
Davison, Frederic Ellis
Dean, Arthur T.
Delandro, Donald J.
Deloatch, Voneree (Von)
DePriest, Oscar S., IV
Dillard, Oliver W.
Doctor, Henry, Jr.
Donald, James Edward
Dougherty, Alonzo
Duckett, Louis
Ebbesen, Samuel Emanuel
Ellis, Larry Rudell
Ferguson, Alonzo L.
Ferguson, Edward A., Jr.
Flowers, Michael C.
Forte, Johnnie, Jr.
Franklin, Calvin G.
Freeman, Warren L.
Frye, William S.
Gaskill, Robert Clarence
Gaskin, Walter E.
Gillespie, Lawrence E., Sr.
Gilley, Alfonsa
Gilliam, Haywood S.
Gorden, Fred Augustus
Gourdin, Edward Orval (Ned)
Granger, Elder
Gray, Kenneth D.
Gray, Robert Earl
Greer, Edward
Gregg, Arthur James
Hackett, Craig D.
Hall, David M.
Hall, James Reginald, Jr.
Hall, Titus C.
Hamilton, West A.
Hamlet, James Frank
Harding, Robert Anthony

Harleston, Robert Alonzo
Harrell, Ernest James
Hawkins, John Russell, III
Hicks, David H.
Hill, Mack C.
Hines, Charles Alfonso
Holmes, Arthur, Jr.
Holmes, Bert W., Jr.
Honor, Edward
Honore, Charles E.
Honore, Russel Luke
Hooper, Chauncey M.
Hunter, Milton
Hunton, Benjamin Lacy
Jacobs, Talmadge Jeffries
James, Nathaniel
Johnson, Alan Douglas
Johnson, Jerome
Johnson, Julius Frank
Johnson, Ronald L.
Johnson, Thomas C.
Johnson, Walter Frank, III
Johnson-Brown, Hazel Winifred
Jones, John L.
Jones, Richard L.
Jones, Walter I.
Jordan, Larry R.
Kennon, James Lewis
Kindred, Samuel Lee
King, Celes, III
King, John Q. Taylor
Kirkland, William Charles
Klugh, James R.
Knightner, Larry
Leigh, Fredic Homer
Lenhardt, Alfonso Emanual
Mann, Marion
McCall, James Franklin
McQueen, Adolph, Jr.
Miller, Frank Lee, Jr.
Monroe, James W.
Monroe, Paul D., Jr.
Moorman, Holsey A
Morgan, Ernest R.
Morgan, John W., III
Nabors, Roberts L.
Nero, Carrie Lee
Paige, Emmett, Jr.
Parker, Julius, Jr.
Patin, Jude Wilmot Paul
Powell, Colin Luther
Prather, Thomas Levi, Jr.
Price, George Baker
Proctor, Hawthorne L.
Richardson, Velma L.
Robinson, Bruce E.
Robinson, Hugh Granville
Robinson, Kenneth B.
Robinson, Roscoe, Jr.
Rochelle, Michael D.

Rogers, Charles Calvin
Rogers, Dennis E.
Rountree, Gregory A.
Rozier, Jackson Evander
Russ, William Henry
Saxton, Richard
Scott, Donald Laverne
Sheffey, Fred Clifton
Sherfield, Michael Bruce
Short, Alonzo Earl, Jr.
Shuffer, George Macon., Jr.
Simmons, Bettye Hill
Simms, Earl Myers
Solomon, Billy King
Spaulding, Vernon Charles
Stephens, Robert L., Jr.
Smith, Issac Dixon
Stanford, John Henry
Terrell, Francis D.
Theus, Lucius
Turner, Abraham J.
Turner, Guthrie L.
Turner, Joseph Ellis
Via, Dennis L.
Waller, Calvin A.H.
Ward, William Edward
Ware, Ezell, Jr.
Ware, Larry
Watkins, John Marcella, Jr.
Whitfield, Walter J.
Williams, Bennie E.
Williams, Charles E.
Williams, Harvey Dean
Wilson, Charles E.
Wilson, Johnnie Edward
Winfield, W. Montague
Wooten, Rallph G.
Zimmerman, Matthew A.

OTHER OFFICERS
Abney, J.C.
Adams-Early, Charity
Allen, Doris
Allen, Reginald E.
Allen, Ulysses
Allensworth, Allen
Anderson, Curtis
Armstead, Michael A.
Armstrong, Ernest W., Sr.
Atkinson, William Earl
Augustine, Carla J.
Bailey, Margarete
Bolton, Larry S.
Boney-Harris, Gwendolyn
Bowen, Clotilde Dent
Brown, Fredrick
Brown, Jerry P.
Bryant, Thomas Milton
Carter, Reginald C.
Caulk, Charles Colton

Chance, Lennox A.
Chiles, Farrell J.
Clay, Patricia
Cleveland, Martha D.
Coffey, Vernon C.
Cole, Eddie L.
Cooper, Irma H.
Cooper, James S
Corley, Harry L.
Cummings, Angela M.
DeBerry, Harold L.
Diego-Allard, Victoria H.
Dix, Richard
Elam, Otis J.
Ellis, Ronnie T.
English, Mark A.
Europe, James Reese
Flipper, Henry O.
Gordon, Robert L., III
Hammond, Douglas
Harris, Marc
Hayes, Aaron W.
Isaac, Rebecca B.
Jackson, James N.
Jackson, Leonard L.
Johnson, Clarence E.
Johnson, Darfus L.
Johnson, Vickki
Jones, Carol A.
Keller, Sherry B.
King, J.B.
Kirkman, Allen, Jr.
Leeper, Michael A.
Letcher, Maj.
Lyons, Luncinda
Marable, Renard
Marhall, Berlin L.
Martin, Michael
McFadden, Willie
McLarin, Benita A.
McNeil, Robert J.
Meeks, Cordell D., Jr.
Milburn, Dwayne S.
Mixon, Laurence M.
Murray, Aurilia "Vicki"
Nickolson, Tracey E.
Patterson, LaWarren V.
Payne, Foster P., II
Pearson, Ervin
Penn, Damon C.
Plummer, Henry V.
Prettyman-Beck, Yvonne J.
Rainey, Della H.
Reid, Carlton B., Jr.
Richardson, Sandra V.
Richie, Sharon Ivey
Royster, Gary A.
Salter, Ned W.
Shanks, Mary Joe
Sharpe, Carolyn R.

Sledge, Nathaniel H., Jr.
Smith, Melody D.
Smith, Nathaniel
Smith, Vicki A.R.
Strand, Eloise Brown
Strayhorn, Earl E.
Stuart, Deborah S.
Thomas, Nello A.
Thompson John R.
Tillman, Johnie S.
Tolbert, James
Tunstall, Stanley Q.
Tyree-Hyche, Ida
Varnado, Frederick E.
Varnado, Sheila
Walton, Micheal L.
Washington, Bette R.
Washington, George K.
Weatherington, Lisa D.
West-Waddy, Harriet M.
Wilkerson, Philip L., Jr.
Williams, Anthony L.
Williams, Eric
Williams, Herman "Tracy," III
Williams, Kewyn L.
Williams, Thomas W.
Wilson-Burke, Iva
Wingate, Cedric F.
Wrenn, Curtis L., Jr.
Wyche, Larry
Young, Charles

ENLISTED
Aarons, Clifton G.
Adams, Richard, Jr.
Adams, Robert L.
Adams, Rodney
Adams, Wilbur V., Jr.
Alcendor, Ralph
Alexander, Alfred
Alford, Gregory H.
Allen, Joseph R.
Alston, Patrick Z.
Anbiya, Tracey
Ash, CSM
Bailem, Lester
Baker, Mark
Baker, Tony L.
Bakker, Esmond
Ballard, Anthony L.
Barr, Caleb, III
Bartelle, Michael
Battle, Reginald C.
Battle, Timothy
Beason, Stanley H.
Bishop, Robert
Blackwell, William S.
Blanks, Charles O'Neal
Blount, Harold
Booker, Robert L.

Boone, Antonio Frenail
Bowers, Timothy O.
Brame, Sherwood A.
Branch, Carlton J.
Bridgewater, Tony
Brinson, Sammy J., Jr.
Brock, Donna A.
Bronson, Gary J.
Brooks, Denise
Brown, Bruce
Brown, Dwight J.
Brown, Edward L.
Burton, William
Butler, George
Byrd, Willie
Cabey, Jihad
Cadet, Eusebius P.
Caffie, Leon
Caldwell, John R.
Campbell, James F.
Carr, Gary
Christopher, Dale A.
Clark, David M.
Clark, William
Clarke, Jerry
Coley, Lloyd
Collins, Harry L.
Collins, Joseph
Covington, Johnny W.
Covington, Ricky
Crutcher, Lucille
Cunningham, Oscar
Cunningham, Pauline W.
Dailey, Charlie L.
Dale, James E.
Daniels, Ira L., Sr.
Darnell, Larry
Davis, Jesse B., Jr.
Davis, Lee A.
Davis, Michael E
Day, Delton D.
Dean, Marvell R.
Denson, Antoine
Dent, Kennis J.
Dickerson, Ira L.
Dimery, Clark, Sr.
Dixon, Althea Green
Dixon, McArthur
Dorsey, Johnny L., Sr.
Douglas, André
Douglas, Phillip D.
Duncan, Elmer H.
Edmonds, Ralph
Ellis, Trent O.
English, Norman
Etienne, Luis
Eubanks, Daniel A.
Evans, William T.
Evy, Lacy
Felder, Robert J.

Ficklin, Reginald
Fleetwood, Christian A.
Floyd, Harold F.
Font, Johnnie M.
Forster, Diane M.
Fountain, Terry
Francis, Keith E.
Friday, Ronald D.
Fuller, Sherman L.
Fullford, Eric W.
Gabriel, Berhane
Gaines, John M., Jr.
Garrett, Ronnie
Gathers, John F.
Gholson, James L.
Gibson, Eddie L.
Gill, Harold L.
Gilliam, Michael
Gilmore, Cornell W.
Godbolt, Enoch L.
Gosha, Lucius G., Jr.
Graham, Frank L.
Grant, Timothy W.
Grant, William M.
Green, Clement D.
Green, Leon J., Jr.
Griffin, Gregory M.
Hall, Andrew L.
Harewood, Collin C.
Harris, Michael M.
Harris, Vera F
Hawkins, Tomas R.
Hawkins, Walter L.
Hayes, Lou V.
Hazzard, Milton B.
Henry, Charles A., Sr.
Herring, Janet L.
Hill, Marvin L.
Hill, Weltia K.
Hillman, Lawrence
Hollis, Evelyn
Holmes, Ronnie L.
Howard, David, Jr.
Hughes, Kelvin A.
Hussey, Robert
Hyde, Mark A.
Ingram, Jeffery C.
Irby, Elvis
Isaac, Opan V.
Ivory, Lacey
Jackson, Larry D.
Jackson, Paul J.
Jackson, Paul L.
Jackson, Sherry R.
Jacobs, Chrysanthamus J.
Jefferson, Eddie Lee
Jefferson, Varner
Jenkins, C.C., Jr.
Jenkins, Kenneth
Jenkins, Samuel Edward

Johns, Rudolph
Johnson, Anthony R.
Johnson, Carolina D.
Johnson, Charles D.
Johnson, Clifton H.
Johnson, Frederick B.
Johnson, Ozell
Johnson, Roscoe L., Jr.
Johnson, Tyrone
Jones, Dan F.
Jones, Ethan A.
Jones, Michele S.
Jones, Michelle K.
Joseph, Annette
Joseph, Mark D.
Joseph, Phyllis R.
Joseph, Ronald H.
Joyner, Joel L.
Keeler, Willie E.
Keit, Patricia A.
Kelley, Mildred C.
Kellman, Julian A.
Kelly, Shelton J.
Kelsey, Edward G.E.
King, Dennis M.
King, Elijah, Jr.
King, Teresa V.
Knox, Ricky
Lacy, Lewis, Jr.
Lane, Ray D.
Langston, William E.
Legette, Jessie
Lewis, Doris L.
Lewis, Neville
Littlejohn, Harold
Lockett, Lewis C.
Lovell, Harry L., Jr.
Lyle, Phillip L.
Lyons, Samuel I.
Marin, Hector G.
Marks, Andrea R.
Marks, Michael O.
Martain, Rosvelt
Matlock-Williams, Saundra A.
McCoy, Herbert W.
McCray, Russell
McCutchen, Braley E., III
McFadden, Jackie
McKinney, Gene C.
Mckinnon, Joseph J.
McMullen, Keith A.
McPherson, Carl B., Sr.
McRae, Claude
McWilliams, Terrance D.
Middleton, Ray
Mike, Marion L.
Minnigan, Anthony F.
Mitchell, Ronald
Montgomery, Jerry G.
Moody, John E., Jr.

Moore, Dale E.
Moore, John J.
Moore, Johnnie P.
Moore, Tony E.
Moten, Alphonso
Moton, Melvin V.
Muhammad, Randoph
Murrell, Edmond O.
Murriel, Jeffery S.
Nelson, Jerry
Newsome, Gary M.
Noble, James M.
Norman, James P., III
Oggs, Dennis I.
Ousley, Allie R.
Parker, Lionel H.
Patterson, Michael L.
Patton, Oscar R.
Pearson, Clint
Peete, Arthur F.
Peggins, Terry X.
Pegues, John E.
Peoples, Willie C., Jr.
Peppers, Reuben
Peters, Michael
Pinckney, CSM
Pinkney, Alma
Pope-Dixon, Tracy A.
Porter, Terry J.
Praymous, Vernon R.
Pugh, William R.
Purdy, Tony H.
Ramble, Pamela M.
Raybon, Herman, Jr.
Reid, Jerry L.
Richardson, Cornell, Jr.
Riddick, Thelma L.
Roberts, Bruce
Roberts, Perry L.
Robertson, Craig H.
Robertson, Samuel
Robinson, Harry L.
Rogers, Lawrence
Sadler, Russell W.
Seals, McGregory
Shephard, Nathaniel, III
Shepherd, Edward L.
Sherman, Jerald
Simmons, Harry E.
Simon, Larry E.
Small, Julius, Jr.
Small, Stanley
Smith, Barbara S.
Smith, Mitte A.
Smith, Otis, Jr.
Spivey, Willie G.
Starling, Bridgette Y.
Stinson, Lonnie T.
Sturdivant, Lash L.
Sullivan, Lynell

Sumlin, CSM
Sumpter, Daryall
Swinnie, Kenneth B.
Tate, Willie C.
Taylor, Christopher
Taylor, Jerry L.
Thomas, Buford
Thomas, Donald E.
Thomas, Joseph, Jr.
Thompson, Hayward
Thompson, Wilbert R.
Tigs, Dwayne A.
Toney, Ian A.
Toro, Herman
Tull, Gary
Turner, Archie L.
Turner, Hershel L.
Walker, Larry
Walker, Ted
Walker, Tyler, II
Ware, Earl L.
Washington, Arthur L.
Washington, Major
Washington, Perry K.
Watkins, Gregory
Whitley, Regina
Wiggins, Clyde
Wilcox, Steven
Williams, Anthony J.
Williams, Cathay
Williams, Charles E.
Williams, CSM
Williams, Daryl L.
Williams, David E.
Williams, David L.
Williams, Dwight
Williams, Gail M.
Williams, Gerald W.
Williams, Hattie
Williams, James T.
Williams, Marshall
Williams, Mitchell L.
Williams, Reginald J.
Williams, Scarlett V.
Williamson, Arthur J.
Willis, Eric Leonard
Wilson, Danyell E.
Wilson, Jerry Lee
Wilson, Randy D.
Wilson, Samuel
Wilson, Samuel F.
Wilson, Willy
Witherspoon, J.P., Jr.
Wood, Eddie
Woods, Joseph E.
Woods, Robert
Woods, Spencer R.
Wright, Sherry L.
Younger, Collin Lester
Zanders, Joe K.

Coast Guard

ADMIRAL
Brown, Erroll M.

OTHER OFFICERS
Brown, Raymond C.
Edwards, Kirk
Hawkins, Alvin C.
Henry, Oliver
Makell, Rhonda Fleming
Odom, Curtis B.
Witherspoon, John Gordon

ENLISTED
McShan, Angela M.
Patton, Vincent W.
Wells, Marvin

CIVILIANS
Alexander, Clifford L., Jr.
Anderson, Charles Alfred "Chief"
Ballard, Tina
Campbell, Phyllis C.
Clark, Patrina
Curtis, Chandra
Davis, Audrey Y.
Duncan, Linda
Fields, Shirley J.
Harris, Leroy
Kirk-McAlpine, Patricia
Johnson, James E.
Johnson, Karen
Luther L. Santiful
Nesby, Charles W.
Penn, Buddie J.
Pinson, L. Tracey
Reeves, William, Jr.
Santiful, Luther L.
Shannon, John W.
Short, James E.
Tuck, Frank O.
Walker-Kimbro, Carolyn
West, Togo Dennis, Jr.
Williams, Charlie E., Jr.
Williams, Theodore J.

Marine Corps

GENERALS
Bolden, Charles F.
Coleman, Ronald S.
Cooper, Jerome Gary
Fields, Arnold
Gaskin, Walter E.
Jackson, Anthony L.
Petersen, Frank E., Jr.

Stanley, Clifford L.
Thomas, John R.
Walls, George H., Jr.
Williams, James L.
Williams, Leo V., III
Williams, Willie J.
Wilson, Cornell A., Jr.

OTHER OFFICERS

Berthoud, Kenneth M., Jr.
Branch, Fred C.
Brewer, Herbert L.
Cole, Carmen E.
Daniels, Doris
Dyer, Michael A.
Grimes, Annie L.
Hodges, Adele E.
Jackson, Gilda
Johnson, Janice M.
Johnson, Patricia
Lewis, Doarin R.
Nelson, Lynn
Sass, Arthur H.
Spencer, Chery E.
Thanuars, Don D.

ENLISTED

Anderson, Curtis
Armstrong, Larona
Ballard, John R.
Bell, Wayne R.
Bellamy, Jefferson
Bennett, Kevin S.
Blair, Jimmie A.
Bly, William H., Jr.
Bradley, R.
Bristol, James A.
Brooks, Janice M.
Brown, Jimmie
Burs, (first name unknown)
Burton, William
Bush, Kenneth D.
Bush, Richard H.
Butts, Robert J.
Campbell, Michael B.
Carter, Clinton
Carter, Randall
Claxton, Vincent
Clay, Aaron
Coaxum, Velva D.
Coaxum, Victor J.
Cordes, Jessie
Cotterell, Collin A.
Crawford, Robert L.
Cunningham, Lorne C.
Daniel, Roland
Daniels, Sylvester D.
Deas, Ruby A.
Diggs, Michael
Dimery, Clark, Sr.

Dingle, Generett
Dubose, William, Jr.
Estrada, John L.
Evans, William T.
Fetherson, Parisa Y.
Fetherson, Ronald E.
Francis, Andre
Franks, Anthony E.
Frye, D. Scott
Futrell, James R.
George, D.R.
Golder, Steven M.
Gray, Kenneth E.
Green, Carl R.
Grell, Theodore
Guerrero, Valentin
Harden, Gloria J.
Hardy, Linton
Harrell, M.S.
Harrigan, Kevin D.
Harris, Curtis
Harrison, Ronnie L.
Hawkins, Billy
Hayes, Ethbin E.
Higgins, Vidaurri
Hollings, Robert C.
Holmes, Frankie
Howard, Burnadette
Huff, Edgar
Humphrey, Tyrone
Johnson, Delouris
Johnson, Gilbert
Jones, Donald L., II
Jones, Larry C.
Jordan, William
Joseph, T.G.
Kennedy, Randall D.
Kent, Carlton W.
Knox, Frank J.
Leardo, Eduardo E.
Leflore, Adrian
McBride, Alexander
McBride, Evins
McKnight, William, Jr.
McMichael, Alford L.
Milton-Stewart, Clifford L.
Morgan, Joseph M.
Morris, Larry W.
Nicholas, Javier A.
Prado, John J.
Raybon, Herman, Jr.
Reese, Fenton
Richardson, Clarence W.
Robbins, Rodney D.
Roberts, James
Roberts, Robert E., Jr.
Robinson, Harry L.
Rodriguez, Carl H.
Roundtree, Melvin
Royal, Nathaniel

Rush, Richard H.
Scott, Frank
Simms, Darren V.
Simpson, Arthur J.
Smith, Danny
Stove, Charles E.
Summerville, Lewis L.
Thomas, Robert N., III
Thompson, Arthur J.
Thornton, Leon S.
Titus, Barbara J.
Toomer, Daryll J.
Trower, Peter J., Jr.
Tucker, Hinton T.
Vaught, Ralph J.
Vines, Joe
Watkins, Michael J.
Williams, Alexander
Williams, Hayward
Williams, Juan D.
Williams, Keith L.
Williams, Leroy, Jr.
Williams, Ronald
Wilson, Kevin Derrick
Wise, Ronald D.
Wright, Reginald M.
Wylie, Ernest J.
Yarn, Doneil C.

Navy

ADMIRALS

Bookert, Reubin B.
Brewer, David Lawrence, III
Chambers, Lawrence C.
Combs, Osie "V," Jr.
Curtis, Derwood C
Davis, Walter Jackson
Elders, M. Joycelyn
Fields, Evelyn J.
Fishburne, Lillian
Fussell, Macea E.
Gaston, Mack Charles
Gravely, Samuel Lee, Jr.
Groom, Bruce E.
Guillory, Victor G.
Hacker, Benjamin Thurman
Howard, Michelle J.
Johnson, Arthur J.
Johnson, James A.
Johnson, Wendell Norman
Kendall, Gene R.
Manley, Audrey Forbes
Marsh, W. Clyde
Moore, Edward, Jr.
Poe, Larry L.
Powell, William E., Jr.
Satcher, David

Smith, Vinson E.
Thomas, Gerald Eustis
Toney, Robert Lee
Watson, Anthony John
Williams, Louis Alvin
Williams, Melvin Gene, Jr.
Winns, Anthony L.

OTHER OFFICERS

Abernethy, R. Sydney, III
Andrews, Annie B.
Barfield, Capt.
Blakely, Shirley A.
Boone, Layne R.
Brault, Laurell A.
Brinkley, Ronald W.
Brown, Jesse LeRoy
Cannon, Louis T., Jr.
Cochran, Donnie L.
Cole, Leon A.
Curbeam, Robert L., Jr.
Curry, Bruce H.
Davis, Robert Edward
Evans, Stephen
Evans, Willie
Figuerres, John M.
Ford, Robert L.
Gained, George L.
Gay, Earl L.
Goodly, Baxter A.
Graham, Christopher
Green, Everett L.
Hall, Gerard W.
Harris, Bernard A.
Harris, Gail
Hawkins, Anita
Hayes, Demetrius J.
Henderson, Daniel P.
Jackson, Bernard R.
Jackson, Patricia A.
Jones, Dorian F.
Jones, Leonard B.
Jones, Synthia
Lewis, James A.

Lewis, Todd A.
Lindsay, Timika B.
McCoy, Leslie J.
Miller, Cynthia
Miller, Ruby
Mines, Janie
Murakata, Linda A.
Patton, Marquis A.
Powell, Elliott, Jr.
Powell-Mims, Janie Mae
Pringle, Cedric E.
Reaves, Joel C.
Scott, Winston E.
Simmons, Anthony
Shorts, Vincient F.
Sparrock, Robert C.
Stubbs, Laura
Stuppard, Charles L.
Thomas, Michael
Thomas, Ronald
Tzomes, C.A. Pete
Valentin, Eleanor V.
Watson, Larry James
Wells, Larry G.
Williams, Pat L.
Wilson, Jesse A.
Wilson, Robert D., Jr.
Wright, Lewin C.
Wyatt, James R.
Young, Eric Coy
Young, Samuel

ENLISTED

Baker, Mark
Banks, Evelyn P.
Beason, Stanley H.
Beldo, April D.
Bernard, Victor E.
Blakely, Shirley A.
Blanks, Charles O'Neal
Brashear, Carl M.
Brault, Laurell A.
Brinkley, Ronald W.
Burton, William W., Jr.

Cook, Odie J
Craddock, Terry
Cullom, Marion
Darnell, Larry
Driver, Anthony R.
Dublin, Marvin D.
Etienne, R.M.
Evans, Renall L.
Gardley, Carl A.
Goosby, Keith
Hansen-Purnell, Isabella M.
Harris, Octavia D.
Hooker, Olivia J.
Ingram, Isaac, Jr.
Jackson, Abraham
Johnson, Anthony J.
Knight, Anthony e.
Loggins, Stacy B.
Lomax, Stanley A., Jr.
Martinez, Laura A.
Mitchell, Terrence R.
Murphy, Herman F.
Nelson, Aloysius Ali
Nichols, Marvin
Nowlin, Lennie
Patrick, Dwayne
Pearce, Bennie O.
Penton, Chris L.
Piper, Terry W.
Powell, Clive A.
Prescod, Wayne
Pretlow, Norman, Jr.
Pringle, Randy A.
Rivera, Sonya L.
Rogers, Lunslee L.
Tsikouris, Michael
Tutt, Veronica
Wallace, Johnny A.
Williams, Jerry
Williamson, Shannon
Wilson, Rosa L.
Woodcock, Robert
Wortham, Tia F.